"Tired of traveling cross-country on boring, endless Interstates? Take the next exit and get yourself onto a two-lane highway. You will have an unforgettable experience. A stylish retro experience. An American experience. And the book to guide you down these soulful and charismatic routes is **Road Trip USA**."

—*Roadside*

"A fantastic guide, easily the best book of its type. The lively text celebrates the pleasures of the open road without ever getting too preachy about it, and vintage WPA photography provides a gorgeous finishing touch."

—*Money*

"Graphically handsome, the book adroitly weaves together sightseeing advice with history and restaurant and lodging recommendations. For budding myth collectors, I can't think of a better textbook."

—*Los Angeles Times*

"A diamond mine for the Harley-Davidson rider, this might just be the perfect book about hitting the summoning highway . . . It's impossible not to find something enticing in **Road Trip USA** to add to your next cycling expedition."

—*Harley-Davidson Enthusiast*

"Although over a dozen writers contributed to **Road Trip USA**, it speaks with a singular, consistent voice that celebrates the pleasures of the open road and small-town America without delving into kitsch or condescension . . . Extensive cross-referencing makes it easy to switch from one section of the book to another, and smartly placed margin notes provide useful nuggets of information on things like the best radio stations and where to watch out for speed traps."

—Condé Nast *Epicurious*

"Jamie Jensen and the 12 intrepid contributors to **Road Trip USA** have been everywhere and seen everything in the course of compiling this exhaustive, delightful, destination-anywhere guide to American road-tripping. As attuned to middle-lowbrow discoveries as it is to the usual roadside kitsch and the possibility of an even finer slice of pie along the next mile, **Road Trip USA** offers any possible traveler his brand of a good time."

—*Washington D.C. Citybooks*

ROAD TRIP USA

Cross-Country Adventures on America's Two-Lane Highways

ROAD TRIP USA

Cross-Country Adventures on America's Two-Lane Highways

SECOND EDITION

JAMIE JENSEN

CONTRIBUTING WRITERS:
Deke Castleman
Andrew Coe
Joe Cummings
Andrew Hempstead
Tom Huhti
Marjorie Jensen
Dave Johnson
Jeffrey Perk
Kevin Roe
Julian Smith
Kap Stann
Stuart Warren

MOON
TRAVEL
HANDBOOKS

ROAD TRIP USA
CROSS-COUNTRY ADVENTURES
ON AMERICA'S TWO-LANE HIGHWAYS
SECOND EDITION

Published by
Avalon Travel Publishing, Inc.
5855 Beaudry St.
Emeryville, CA 94608, USA

Printed by
Colorcraft, Ltd.

Please send all comments,
corrections, additions,
amendments, and critiques to:

ROAD TRIP USA
AVALON TRAVEL PUBLISHING
5855 BEAUDRY STREET
EMERYVILLE, CA 94608, USA
e-mail: info@travelmatters.com
www.travelmatters.com

PRINTING HISTORY
1st edition—1996
2nd edition—May 1999
5   4   3   2

Stephen Dunn's poem "The Sacred," from the volume *Between Angels* and the anthology *Drive, They Said,* is reprinted on page 858 with kind permission of W. W. Norton & Co., Inc.

ISBN: 1-56691-149-4
ISSN: 1085-7036

Editors: Emily Kendrick and Jeannie Trizzino
Map Editor: Jeannie Trizzino
Production & Design: David Hurst
Cartographers: Chris Folks, Allen Leech, and Mike Morgenfeld
Index: Sondra Nation

Cover Photo: Eric Meola Studio, Inc./The Image Bank © 1999

Distributed in the United States and Canada by Publishers Group West
Printed in China

When you come to a fork in the road, take it.

—Yogi Berra

ON THE ROAD

The journeys in this book are as wild and varied as the landscapes they traverse. All celebrate the notion that freedom and discovery await us on the open road. Poets and artists from Walt Whitman to Muddy Waters have long sung the praises of rolling down the highway, and no matter how times have changed we still believe there's nothing more essentially American than hitting the road and seeing the country.

America has always been a nation on the move. From colonial times onwards, each generation pushed relentlessly westward, until the outward frontier finally closed around the turn of the twentieth century. Taking advantage of the internal combustion engine, and inspired by the slogan "See America First," Americans began to explore a new frontier, the system of highways that developed between the Atlantic and Pacific coasts. The first transcontinental route, the Lincoln Highway from New York to San Francisco, was completed in 1915, and motor courts, diners, and other new businesses soon sprang up along the roadside to serve the passing trade.

The half-century from the 1920s until the arrival of the interstate highway system was the golden age of American motor travel, but this book is not especially motivated by nostalgia. Almost all the places described in *Road Trip USA*—soda fountains and town squares, neon-signed motels and minor-league baseball teams—are happily thriving in the modern world, and better yet, they are close at hand. The simple act of avoiding the soulless interstates, with their soggy franchises and identikit chains, opens up a vast, and much friendlier, two-lane world. You'll chance upon monuments marking the actual sites of things you last thought about in high school history classes, or kitschy little souvenir stands flaunting giant dinosaurs outside their doors, and inside still selling the same postcards as they have for decades.

After traveling well over 100,000 miles in search of the perfect stretches of two-lane blacktop, this is the book I wish I'd had with me all along. So, whether you're a biker, RVer, a road warrior, or a Sunday driver, get in, turn the key—and hit the highway.

CONTENTS

US-83: THE ROAD TO NOWHERE

Don't let the nickname fool you: US-83 may not lead to many places you've heard of before, but it's a route you'll never forget. Cutting across the heart of the Great Plains, this arrow-straight highway passes through hundreds of all-American small towns and endless expanses of agriculture, all the way from Canada to the mouth of the Rio Grande.

INCLUDING: Lawrence Welk Birthplace 181-182 • Sitting Bull Memorial 184 • Buffalo Bill Scouts Rest Ranch 191 • Dancing Leaf Earth Lodge 192 • Monument Rocks 195 • The Rio Grande Valley 214-215 • Sabal Palm Grove Sanctuary 216 • Padre Island National Seashore 217

THE GREAT RIVER ROAD

The mighty Mississippi River cuts a scenic swathe from its headwaters in Minnesota to its terminus at the Gulf of Mexico, taking in upland meadows, cypress swamps, urban centers, and plenty of local color—including a growing number of riverfront casinos. The Great River Road hugs the legendary waterway from stem to stern, offering a magical, musical tour of mythic Big Muddy.

INCLUDING: Lake Itasca—Headwaters of the Mississippi 222-224 • Judy Garland's Hometown 227 • The World's Biggest Six-Pack 236 • Mormons and Nauvoo, IL 248-249 • Hannibal, MO: Mark Twain's hometown 251-253 • In Search of Elvis 265 • Delta Blues 272 • Oxford, Mississippi: William Faulkner 274-275 • Birthplace of the Teddy Bear 278 • Natchez Trace Parkway 283 • Plantation Alley 289

THE APPALACHIAN TRAIL . . . . 296~374

Running alongside the nation's longest and most famous hiking trail for over 2,100 miles, this route follows a series of scenic backroads all the way from the rugged terrain of New England to the Great Smoky Mountains and the heart of Dixie. Winding along the Appalachian crest, through quaint villages, historic mill towns, and a series of astoundingly beautiful national parks, the Appalachian Trail shows off the wild side of the East Coast.

INCLUDING: Mount Washington 298-299 • Franconia Notch 303-304 • Delaware Water Gap National Recreational Area 334-335 • Martin Guitar Company 336 • The Shoe House 339 • Gettysburg 343 • Dinosaur Land 348 • Shenandoah National Park 349-350 • Blue Ridge Parkway 352-353 • Mount Airy—Mayberry RFD 357

COASTAL EAST COAST . . . . 376~443

Alternating between roller coaster-rich beach resort areas and long stretches of untouched coastal wilderness, this route follows nearly 2,000 miles of two-lane country roads, within earshot if not eyesight of the Atlantic Ocean almost the entire way. From Atlantic City to the tip of Key West, this road trip passes through offbeat seaside towns and timeless old fishing villages, with surprisingly huge swathes of beaches, wetlands, and woodlands in between.

INCLUDING: Atlantic City 378-380 • Lucy the Elephant 380 • Ocean City, MD 384-385 • Chincoteague National Wildlife Refuge 388 • Virginia Beach 390 • Cape Hatteras National Seashore 395-97 • South of the Border 403 • Myrtle Beach 404-405 • Savannah 411-414 • The Fountain of Youth 420 • The Space Coast: Cape Canaveral 426-427 • Palm Beach 429-430 • Everglades National Park 437 • Key West 442

US-2: THE GREAT NORTHERN . . . . 446~524

Dubbed the Great Northern in memory of the pioneer railroad that parallels the western half of the route, US-2 must be the most stunning and unforgettable of all the great transcontinental road trips. Its international passage is punctuated by towering mountain ranges and the vast horizontal expanses of the Great Plains, and bookended by two great cities, Seattle and Montreal. Even a short stretch of driving the Great Northern is guaranteed to bring new meaning to the expression "getting away from it all."*

INCLUDING: Grand Coulee Dam 456-457 • Glacier National Park 466-467 • Chief Joseph and the Nez Percé 472 • Joe, Montana 476 • Rugby: Center of North America 479 • North Dakota's Roadside Giants 480 • The "Big Nickel" 499 • Ben & Jerry's Ice Cream Factory 512-513 • World's Largest Wooden Indian 520 • Acadia National Park 524

US-20: THE OREGON TRAIL . . . . 526~651

From the wide-open spaces of the West to the dense urban jungles of the East, this is our longest and most involved road trip. Totaling over 3,200 miles—many more if you count all the potential detours, side trips, and parallel roads—this route takes in a little of every- thing during its two-lane trek from Oregon's rugged coast to the glorious sea and sand of Cape Cod. Odd museums, classic diners, idyllic towns, and a chance to follow in the footsteps (and wagon tracks) of early Americans—you'll find it all along this great cross-country highway.*

INCLUDING: Columbia Gorge 533-35 • Craters of the Moon National Monument 546 • Yellowstone National Park 549-551 • Grand Teton National Park 554-555 • Mount Rushmore 562 • The Lincoln Highway 568 • Field of Dreams 568 • Rock and Roll Hall of Fame 586 • Niagara Falls 594 • Cooperstown 600-601 • The Mohawk Trail 608 • Jack Kerouac Birthplace 611 • Holy Land 632 • Cape Cod National Seashore 647-648

US-50: THE LONELIEST ROAD . . . . 654~735

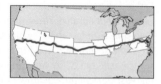

Running across the heart of America, US-50 moves through a dozen different states and four state capitals, as well as the nation's capital, Washington, D.C. Magnificent landscapes line the route: the Appalachian, Rocky, and Sierra Nevada Mountains, the endless farmlands of the Great Plains, and the desiccated deserts of Utah and Nevada. It follows the hoofsteps of riders of the Pony Express and Santa Fe Trail, and the dozens of historic sites and small towns along the way present a living timeline of national development.

INCLUDING: Lake Tahoe 662 • Oldest City in Nevada—Genoa 664 • Great Basin National Park 673 • Arches National Park 679-681 • Cañon City 687-688 • Santa Fe Trail 690-691 • Tallgrass Prairie National Preserve 699-700 • Louisville 714 • Patsy Cline Birthplace 737 • Manassas National Battlefield Park 728 • Arlington National Cemetery 728

US-80: SOUTHERN PACIFIC . . . . 738~791

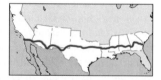

This historic route across America's southern tier presents more varied cultural and physical landscapes per mile than you'll find along any other cross-country route. A few hours from the sands of San Diego, you come upon the incomparable desert Southwest, with its trademark saguaro cacti and unforgettable vistas. Continuing east, US-80 crosses the oil-rich plains of central Texas, easing into the sultry bayous and blues of Louisiana and Mississippi, before ending with a tour of Civil War and Civil Rights sites that winds up at the gorgeous sea islands around beautiful Savannah, Georgia.

INCLUDING: Desert View Tower 742 • "The Center of the World" Pyramid 743-744 • Saguaro National Park 747 • The Thing! 749 • El Paso 756-758 • Ciudad Juárez 759 • Carlsbad Caverns National Park 760-761 • Bonnie & Clyde 770-771 • Jimmie Rodgers 776 • Selma-to-Montgomery 778-780 • Carson McCullers Birthplace 783-784 • Plains, Georgia: Jimmy Carter's Hometown 786

ROUTE 66: THE MOTHER ROAD . . . . 794~849

The mystique of Route 66 draws people from around the world. This legendary old road blazes through the heart of the U.S. on a diagonal trip that takes in some of the country's most archetypal roadside scenes, from the sand and sun of L.A., past the Grand Canyon and the Native American communities of the Southwest, to  *the gritty streets of St. Louis and Chicago. Drive any or all of the 2,000-odd miles that still remain, past the array of neon-signed motels, funky roadside attractions, and homespun diners that give it life, and get your kicks on Route 66.*

INCLUDING: Santa Monica 796 • Roy Rogers and Dale Evans Museum 799 • Grand Canyon National Park 810-811 • Flagstaff 811-812 • Sleep in a Teepee: Wigwam Village 814 • Petrified Forest National Park 815-816 • Cadillac Ranch 823 • Meramec Caverns: Birthplace of the Bumper Sticker 841-842 • The World's Largest Catsup Bottle 843 • The Spindle 848

SPECIAL TOPICS

HOW TO USE THIS BOOK

Road Trip USA describes driving tours of 11 different cross-country highways, giving complete details for over 35,000 miles of two-lane roads. The book was conceived to establish a network of alternatives to the efficient but bland Interstate Highway System, which, to paraphrase the late Charles Kuralt, has made it possible to drive all the way across the country without seeing anything. Driving along these roads may be slower than on the high-speed interstates, not so much because the speed limits are lower, but because you're likely to want to stop that much more often to pull over to the side and enjoy the great variety of roadside attractions. This book works both as an entertaining armchair read, and as a helpful mile-by-mile guide when you're out on the road.

Out of the millions of miles of American road, we have selected these routes because they offer consistent peaks of driving pleasure. We don't always follow a single numbered route slavishly, preferring to suggest more scenic or interesting alternatives, or detours to visit significant sights—veering off US-80 in Texas to tour the Guadalupe Mountains and Carlsbad Caverns region, for example.

Each of the routes has a distinctive character, so each is described in a separate **chapter**. The book begins with six north-to-south routes, followed by four cross-country routes, described from the west to the east—going against historical events, perhaps, but making it easier to follow on the maps. Last, but certainly not least, we guide you along the most famous "old road" of them all, legendary Route 66.

A detailed map highlighting all the routes is printed on the inside front and back covers of this book, and the table of contents on the previous pages lists some of the highlights from each chapter and gives page references, so you can jump in at any point along the way. Places where two routes intersect are clearly cross-referenced throughout the book, so you can organize an itinerary to suit yourself, following US-50 along the Santa Fe Trail, for example, then heading south along US-83, which splits the Great Plains, before getting your kicks on Route 66.

Each chapter begins with a **keynote essay** giving a brief overview of the road, and the chapters themselves are organized in geographical order, so that the words track the changing scene. Each chapter is subdivided into small enough stretches that, with a little practice, it's easy to use even if you're traveling in the opposite direction to the flow of the text. All along the way we've listed the best **places to eat and sleep**, with a definite focus on unique regional specialties, such as lobster pounds in Maine and great ribs joints in Missouri, or historic New England B&Bs and neon-signed motels in the Southwest. All of this background and practical information is woven together in each segment of text, so there's no need to flip through the pages to find a key piece of information.

Throughout each chapter you'll find a series of detailed **maps**, over 100 altogether, which show that chapter's route in a blue tint—useful for keeping track even when wandering the back roads of Appalachia. In between each chapter is a special treat, a fine **old photograph** that captures the feeling of that route; most of these date to the New Deal 1930s, and include work by such talented photographers as Walker Evans, John Vachon, Arthur Rothstein, and Marion Post Wolcott.

Odds and ends of trivia, history, and car culture memorabilia are given in the margins of the text; this is also where we've listed selected radio stations, scenic detours, and other details of passing interest. Longer **sidebars** (in gray boxes) are sprinkled throughout the main text, covering in greater detail some of the many fascinating aspects of the U.S., including tracing Elvis Presley's legacy around Memphis, describing the surviving sites seen by Lewis and Clark in their epic cross-continental exploration, and looking into the mania for extraterrestrials that has swept the "Area 51" section of the Nevada desert.

As part of our effort to devote as much space as possible to guiding you along the "roads less traveled," we have limited coverage of big cities to short **Survival Guides** (in blue boxes). These mini-guides provide essential tips on what to see and where to eat and sleep in some of the nation's biggest cities, so you can make the most of a passing visit.

In the back, you'll find **Road Trip Resources**, an extensive selection of Recommended Reading, describing dozens of great books to take with you on your travels, or to whet your travel appetite in between trips. There's also a **Road Trip Timeline**, which marks historic milestones in the development of the Great American Roadside.

Finally, the extensive index is organized alphabetically by individual locations and state-by-state, so you can quickly find what we have to say about a given place. Interspersed throughout are thematic boxes, some of which detail information such as state tourism office contact numbers as well as contacts for major hotels, motels, and car rental companies.

DID WE MISS SOMETHING?

If you notice something in this book that needs to be fixed, or think we ought to add something to future editions, please drop us a note. We love to hear from readers, and are particularly fond of funny postcards; all correspondence will be answered, sometimes with highly collectible Road Trip USA bumper stickers. Proprietors of hotels, restaurants, and roadside attractions are also invited to tell us what we got wrong—or right. Please address comments and suggestions to:

Road Trip USA
5855 Beaudry Street
Emeryville, CA 94608, USA
e-mail: info@travelmatters.com

ACROSS OREGON

Each chapter breaks down into smaller state-by-state segments as the route travels through the state. A heading, such as "Across Oregon," is followed by a short paragraph or two describing the drive.

Starting at one of the state's most enjoyable small towns, the arts-and-craftsy Pacific Ocean resort community of Cannon Beach, this route traverses the heart of Oregon. From the salty cow pastures along the Pacific Ocean, over the evergreen mantle of the Coast Range to culturally vibrant Portland and the lush Willamette Valley, the route starts where history says we should end up—amid the bountiful land at the west end of the Oregon Trail. From Portland, the state's largest city, you'll climb into the Cascade Mountains, through the amazing Columbia Gorge alongside its signature peak, Mount Hood. East of the Cascades the route drops down into the suddenly dry and desert-like landscape of the otherworldly Columbia Plateau, across which the highway rolls and rocks for 300 miles through old mining camps, fossil beds, and wide open rolling ranch lands before crossing the Snake River into Idaho.

Cannon Beach marks the farthest point reached by the Lewis and Clark expedition to the West Coast. From here, they retreated back to their outpost at Fort Clatsop, near the mouth of the Columbia River, where they spent the winter of 1805-06.

At points in the text where two (or more) of the *Road Trip USA* routes intersect, a bold banner cross-references the other route, so you can easily switch from one route to another.

Scenic US-101's winding route along the Oregon coast is covered more fully on the Coastal West Coast route; for more, see page 39.

Cannon Beach

Unlike most Oregon coast towns, Cannon Beach (pop. 1,221) is hidden from the highway, but it's one place you won't want to miss. Though it has long been known as an artist's colony, and has grown considerably in recent years thanks to its popularity as a weekend escape from Portland, Cannon Beach retains a rustic quality, a walkably small size, and a coastline that rates second to no other in the state.

For further information on Cannon Beach and the Oregon coast, see pages 39-52.

To make it easy to find where you are, throughout *Road Trip USA* the prose is broken up into blocks of text, describing a certain town, or state park, or section of highway. Each of these segments tells you all you need to know: some history, something of the layout of the town, the main attractions, and practical information such as where to eat, sleep, and find further information.

Klootchy Creek and Saddle Mountain State Park

Climbing the edge of the coastal plain, our first stop is the old-growth spruce and fir forest preserved in Klootchy Creek Park, two miles east of US-101. Among the many huge firs and spruce trees is the "World's Largest Sitka Spruce." More than 215 feet high, almost 16 feet in diameter, and thought to be over 700 years old, the tree is pointed out by a sign along the north side of the highway.

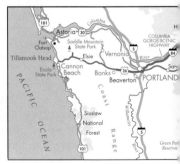

About 10 miles east of US-101, an eight-mile sidetrip to the northeast, along well-signed (but unpaved) Saddle Mountain Road, will lift you quickly above the frequent coastal clouds and fog. Named for a geographical saddle that sits high above the surrounding forests, Saddle Mountain State Park (800/551-6949) has a very steep 2.5-mile hiking trail to the summit, with opportunities to view bleeding heart, Indian paintbrush, monkey flowers, and other rare plants and wildflowers. From the 3,283-foot top of the trail, you can often see the mouth of the Columbia River and the spine of the Coast Range; on a clear day, the panorama may include 50 miles of Pacific coastline and Mounts Hood, St. Helens, and Rainier (with more than a few ugly acres of clear cuts in between). Primitive campsites are open mid-April to October; RVs and other wide bodies should avoid this narrow road.

North of Cannon Beach and Ecola State Park, at the junction where US-26 cuts inland from US-101, the **Crab Broiler** roadside diner (503/738-5313) serves crab and cheese dishes.

Running over the coastal mountains between Cannon Beach and Portland, US-26 is known as the **Sunset Highway**

Short tidbits of text in the margins point out odd facts and interesting pieces of information about that area of the route. Marginal comments may recommend a local radio station, a nearby restaurant, or a scenic detour, or relate a piece of roadside trivia.

Camp 18

Continuing east on US-26, about 20 miles from the coast and a mile west of the hamlet of Elsie, the remarkable **Camp 18 Restaurant** (Sun.-Thurs. 7 AM-9 PM, Friday and Saturday till 10 PM; 503/755-1818 or 800/874-1810) draws travelers for a variety of reasons. Some people come for the absolutely massive portions of very good food, from the gigantic fresh-baked cinnamon rolls and liter jugs of coffee at breakfast, to the steaks, chicken and seafood served up at lunch and dinner. Others are drawn by the playful, Paul Bunyanesque scale of the place: the front door handle is a hefty old ax, the spacious dining room roof is held up by a single log—85-feet-long and probably 8-feet-thick—and many of the tables are made from foot-thick planks of planed and polished wood.

The whole room is packed with an amazing collection of old logging gear, but best of all is the setting, overlooking a babbling brook, with dozens of birdfeeders attracting flocks of finches and other colorful songbirds. Outside, an extensive museum in the parking lot lets visitors examine more old logging equipment to get a feel for a bygone era of misery whips, 20-foot handsaws, and steam donkeys. (Surprise, surprise: there's also a good gift shop.)

For every hundred to two hundred miles of highway, we have included a detailed map. On these maps, which appear every few pages throughout the book, we have highlighted the route in a blue tint, to make it easy to follow. Every element on the map follows the route in the same order as the text. All the towns mentioned in a heading (such as Cannon Beach above) are printed in blue on the map. Other points of interest described in the text are on the map in black.

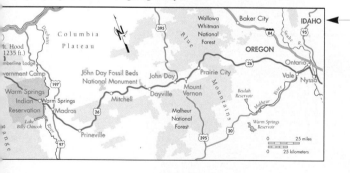

COASTAL
WEST
COAST

COASTAL
WEST COAST

For some reason, when people elsewhere in the country refer to the West Coast, particularly California, they seem to think it's a land of kooks and crazies, an overbuilt suburban desert supporting only shopping malls, freeways, and body-obsessed airheads. All of which may be true in small pockets, but the amazing thing about the West Coast—from the dense green forests of western Washington, to the gorgeous beaches of Southern California—is that it is still mostly wild, open, and astoundingly beautiful country, where you can drive for miles and miles and have the scenery all to yourself.

Starting at the northwest tip of the United States at Olympic National Park, and remaining within sight of the Pacific Ocean almost all the way south to the Mexican border, this 1,500-mile, mostly two-lane route takes in everything from temperate rainforest to near-desert. Most of it is in the public domain, freely if not always easily accessible, and protected from development within national, state, and local parks, which provide habitat for such rare creatures as mountain lions, condors, and gray whales.

Heading south, after the rough-and-tumble logging and fishing communities of Washington state, you cross the mouth of the Columbia River and follow the comparatively peaceful and quiet Oregon coastline, where recreation has by and large replaced industry, and where dozens of quaint and not-so-quaint communities line the ever-changing shoreline. At the midway point you pass through the great redwood forests of Northern California, where the tallest and most majestic living things on earth line the "Avenue of the Giants," home also to some of the best (meaning gloriously kitsch) remnants of the golden age of car-borne tourism: drive-through trees, drive-on trees, houses carved out of trees, and much more. The phenomenally beautiful coastline of Northern California is rivaled only by the incredible coast of Big Sur farther south, beyond which stretch the beachfronts of

Southern California. The land of palm trees, beach boys, and surfer girls of popular lore really does exist, though only in the southernmost quarter of the state.

Along with the overwhelming scale of its natural beauty, the West Coast is remarkable for the abundance of well-preserved historic sites—most of which haven't been torn down, built on, or even built around—that stand as vivid evocations of life on what was once the most distant frontier of the New World. While rarely as old as places on the East Coast, or as impressive as those in Europe, West Coast sites are quite diverse and include the Spanish colonial missions of California, Russian and English fur-trading outposts, and the place where Lewis and Clark first sighted the Pacific after their long slog across the continent.

Last but certainly not least are the energizing cities—Seattle in the north, San Francisco in the middle, and Los Angeles and San Diego to the south—which serve as gateways to (or refuges from) the landscapes in between them. Add to these the dozens of small and not-so-small towns along the coast, with alternating blue-collar ports and upscale vacation retreats, and you have a great range of food, drink, and accommodation options. Local cafes, seafood grills, and bijou restaurants abound, as do places to stay—from youth hostels in old lighthouses to roadside motels (including the world's first, which still stands in lovely San Luis Obispo, California) to homespun B&B inns in old farmhouses.

ALONG THE WASHINGTON COAST

The coast of Washington is a virtual microcosm of the Pacific Northwest, containing everything from extensive wilderness areas to Native American fishing villages and heavily industrialized lumber towns. Starting at splendid **Port Townsend**, US-101 loops west around the rugged Olympic Peninsula, passing near the northwesternmost point of the continental United States while allowing access to the unforgettable natural attractions—sandy, driftwood-strewn beaches, primeval old-growth forests, and pristine mountain lakes and glaciated alpine peaks, to name just a few—of **Olympic National Park**. The roadside landscape varies from dense woods to clearcut tracts of recently harvested timber, with innumerable rivers and streams perhaps the most obvious signs of the immense amount of rainfall (up to 12 feet) the region receives every year. Scattered towns, from **Port Angeles** in the north to the twin cities of **Grays Harbor** on the coast, are staunchly blue-collar communities almost wholly dependent upon natural resources—not only trees, but also salmon, oysters, and other seafood. Though the tourism trade has been increasing steadily, visitor services are still few and far between, so plan ahead.

Though it's not on the coast, the Puget Sound port city of Seattle makes a good starting or finishing point to this coastal road trip. For details, see the Survival Guide to Seattle on pages 450-452.

Port Townsend
Few places in the world can match the concentration of natural beauty or the wealth of architecture found in tiny Port Townsend (pop. 8,727). One of the oldest towns in Washington, Port Townsend was laid out in 1852 and reached a peak of

Fort Worden, on the north side of Port Townsend, is a retired military base that served as a location for the Richard Gere movie *An Officer and a Gentleman*. It now hosts an excellent series of annual music and arts festivals; contact the Centrum Foundation (360/385-3102) for schedules and more information.

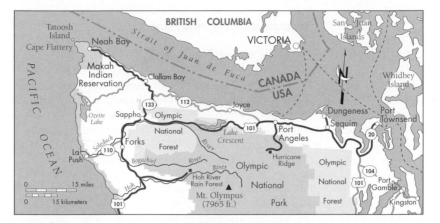

activity in the 1880s. But after the railroads focused on Seattle and Puget Sound as their western terminus, the town sat quietly for most of the next century until the 1960s, when an influx of arts-oriented refugees took over the waterfront warehouses and cliff-top mansions, converting them to galleries, restaurants, and comfy B&Bs while preserving the town's turn-of-the-century character.

Port Townsend is neatly divided into two halves: multistory brick warehouses and commercial buildings line Water Street and the wharves along the bay, while lovely old Victorian houses cover the bluffs above. It's basically a great place to wander, but there are a couple of sights worth seeing, particularly the landmark **City Hall** along the east end of Water Street at 210 Madison Street. Half of this eclectic gothic pile now houses a local historical **museum** (Mon.-Sat. 11 AM-4 PM, Sunday 1-4 PM; donations accepted), with three floors of odds and ends tracing Port Townsend history, including the old city jail where Jack London spent a night on his way to the Klondike goldfields in 1897. The City Hall is also a starting point for Joyce Webb's expertly guided **walking tours** (usually daily 10 AM and 2 PM; $5; 360/385-1967) of the waterfront district.

Not surprisingly, considering the extensive tourist trade, Port Townsend has a number of good restaurants. You'll find many of the best places at the east end of town near the corner of Water and Quincy Streets: for breakfast or lunch, try the **Salal Cafe**, 634 Water Street, or **Bread and Roses**, 230 Quincy Street; for dinner, one of the best seafood places is the **Silverwater Cafe**, near the Quincy Street dock. The same historic building holds the amiable **Town Tavern** bar, and upstairs the **Waterstreet Hotel**, 635 Water Street (360/385-5467 or 800/735-9810), has rooms from $50 a night. The most comfortable accommodations in Port Townsend are the many Victorian B&Bs dotting the bluffs above the port area, including the ever-popular **Old Consulate Inn**, 313 Walker Street (360/385-6753), where a room with a view of Mount Olympus, and a hearty multi-course breakfast, will set you back about $100 a night. For less pricey lodging, there's a **campground** and the **HI Olympic Hostel** (360/385-0655) in the old

The Waterstreet Hotel

TOWARD SEATTLE: PORT GAMBLE

You have a number of options if traveling to or from Port Townsend. You can follow US-101 around the western Olympic Peninsula, or take a ferry via **Whidbey Island** and explore it and the even prettier **San Juan Islands** to the north. Last, but not least, you can take a middle route across the Kitsap Peninsula, then catch a ferry to Seattle, which is covered on pages 450-452.

This last route, which includes a trip on the very frequent (and frequently crowded) Washington State Ferry ($10; 360/842-2345 or 800/843-3779) between Kingston and Edmonds, has the great advantage of taking you through the lovely old logging town of **Port Gamble**, a slice of New England on the shores of Puget Sound. The entire town is a historic district, with dozens of immaculate Victorian buildings standing along maple tree-lined streets; it's also owned lock, stock, and barrel by Pope & Talbot Lumber, which built the town in the 1850s and still operates the large mill. After wandering past the saltbox houses, have a look inside the large **General Store**, which includes a barber shop, a seashell museum, and a small cafe; or visit the photo-filled historical **museum** (daily 10 AM-4 PM in summer only; $1) across the street.

The natural cut of the Hood Canal on the east side of the Olympic Peninsula is one of the West Coast's prime oyster-growing estuaries, source of the gourmet Quilcenes, Hama Hamas, and other varieties available at roadside stands, shops, and restaurants throughout the region.

Army barracks at Fort Worden, on the coast two miles north of town, with dorm beds and a pancake breakfast for $12 members, $15 non-members.

Sequim and Dungeness

A half-hour southwest of Port Townsend via Hwy-20 and US-101, Sequim (pop. 3,616, pronounced Skwim) sits in the rain shadow of the Olympic Mountains, and so tends to be much drier and sunnier than spots even a few miles west. Though it retains its rural feel, Sequim's historic farming-and-fishing economy is quickly switching over to tourism, with tracts of vacation and retirement homes filling up the rolling, waterfront landscape, and a new freeway bypassing the center of town. It's ideal cycling country, for the moment at least, but things are definitely changing, and fast.

Coming in from the east on two-lane US-101, the first thing you pass is the large, modern **John Wayne Marina**, built on land donated by the Duke himself, who spent a lot of time in Sequim cruising around on his converted U.S. Navy minesweeper, the *Wild Goose*. The US-101 frontage through town is lined by the usual franchised fast-food outlets and some unique variations: the ersatz but enjoyable **Hi-Way 101 Diner**, at the heart of town, and **El Cazador**, a standard Mexican restaurant housed inside a minimally converted grain elevator. El Cazador fills the old storage shed but does nothing with the tower—the rooms would be too small, despite the very high ceilings.

Just north of US-101 at 175 W. Cedar Street, the **Sequim-Dungeness Museum** (Wed.-Sun. noon-4 PM; donation) houses everything from 12,000-year-old mastodon bones discovered on a nearby farm, to exhibits of Native American cultures and pioneer farm implements. From the museum, a well-marked road winds

FERRIES TO VICTORIA, BRITISH COLUMBIA

From Port Angeles, a pair of ferries, the MV *Coho* carrying cars and passengers ($27.25 per car one-way, plus $6.75 per person; 360/457-4491) and a faster one, the summer-only *Victoria Express,* carrying passengers only ($12.50 per person one-way; 360/452-8088 or 800/633-1589), shuttle across the water to and from pretty Victoria, the provincial capital of British Columbia, one of Canada's most popular visitor destinations. Both ships leave Port Angeles at the middle of the attractively landscaped waterfront, and arrive very near the center of Victoria, making for a great day-trip from either place. At the Port Angeles dock there's a very helpful information center packed with maps and brochures on Victoria and the rest of B.C., or you can call Tourism Victoria (800/663-3883).

north for 10 miles before reaching the waterfront again at Dungeness, where a seven-mile-long sand spit, the country's longest, protects a shellfish-rich wildlife refuge. All that remains of the abandoned fishing community that existed here through the 1890s is an old schoolhouse, though the excellent **Three Crabs Restaurant** (360/683-4264), overlooking Dungeness Harbor, has been serving up fresh fish and local Dungeness crab for over 25 years.

Stay in Sequim at **Groveland Cottage**, a quaint B&B just a half-mile from the harbor at 4861 Sequim-Dungeness Way (360/683-3565), or at the popular waterfront **Juan de Fuca Cottages**, 182 Marine Drive (360/683-4433), two miles to the west.

Port Angeles

A busy, industrial city at the center of the northern Olympic Peninsula, Port Angeles (pop. 19,000) makes a handy base for visiting the nearby wilderness of Olympic National Park. The town is slowly but surely recovering from its traditional dependence on logging, and the waterfront, which once hummed to the sound of lumber and pulp mills, is now bustling with tourists wandering along a six-mile walking trail and enjoying the sealife (sea slugs, eels, starfish and octopii) on display at the small but enjoyable **Marine Laboratory** (daily 10 AM-8 PM; $2), on the centrally located City Pier.

Malls, gas stations, and fast-food franchises line the US-101 frontage through town, but life in Port Angeles, for locals and visitors alike, centers on the attractive downtown area, two blocks inland from the waterfront around Lincoln Avenue and 1st Street. Here cafes like **First Street Haven**, 107 E. 1st Street,

The Indian-owned **7 Cedars Casino** (800/778-4295) stands above US-101 at the foot of Sequim Bay, fronted by totem poles.

Sequim's annual Irrigation Festival, held every May, is Washington's oldest community celebration.

The well-signed **Olympic Game Farm** (daily 9 AM-4 PM in summer; $6; 360/683-4295), five miles northwest of Sequim, is a 90-acre retirement home for former animal actors and other creatures, great and small. Visitors are very welcome.

offer good, inexpensive soup-and-salad lunches and dinners, and amiable bars and pubs like **Peaks**, around the corner on Lincoln Avenue, draw bikers, hikers and loggers with their pub-grub and good beers. Across from Peaks, occupying a terra-cotta former fire station, **Bonny's Bakery** at 215 S. Lincoln Avenue serves coffees and pastries on a (sometimes) sunny front patio. If you're waiting for a ferry, or are

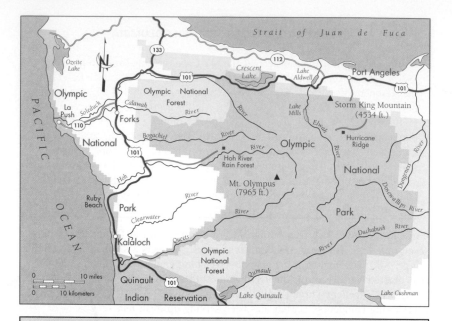

OLYMPIC NATIONAL PARK

Olympic National Park, in the heart of the Olympic Peninsula, is a diversely beautiful corner of the country, combining features of Maine's rocky coast and the snowcapped peaks of the Rocky Mountains with the unique rainforests covering the park's Pacific coastal valleys. The rugged landscape, from rocky shores to impassably dense forests, resisted exploitation and development until the turn of the century, when local conservationists persuaded Teddy Roosevelt to declare most of the peninsula a nature preserve, a movement that eventually resulted in the establishment of Olympic National Park in 1939.

There are no roads and few trails across the peninsula, so you have to choose your points of entry depending upon what you want to see. The most popular part of the park is Hurricane Ridge, which rises high above Port Angeles and offers great views of the silvery peaks and the many glaciers that flank them. On the western slopes, the temperate rainforests of the usually wet and rainy river valleys hold some of the world's largest trees, all draped with a thick fabric of mosses, while the undeveloped coastline, added to the park in 1953, offers miles of sandy beaches and rocky headlands, littered only with driftwood logs and vibrant tidepools.

fresh off of one, a number of places to eat and drink surround the ferry terminal, including the attractive **Landings Restaurant**, great for fish and chips, and the 24-hour **Pete's Pancake House**, across the street at 115 E. Railroad Avenue, which features dozens of omelettes as well as the namesake griddle cakes.

Places to stay in Port Angeles vary from highway motels including the **Uptown**, 101 E. 2nd Street (360/457-9434), to the plusher likes of the **Doubletree** (360/452-9215), on the water at the foot of Lincoln Street. There are also many characterful B&Bs; for details of these, and for more general information, phone the **North Olympic Peninsula Convention and Visitors' Bureau** (800/942-4042), or stop by the Port Angeles tourist office at the ferry terminal, 121 E. Railroad Avenue (360/452-2363).

Information on road conditions and other aspects of visiting Olympic National Park is broadcast continuously on **530 AM.**

Hurricane Ridge

High above Port Angeles, Hurricane Ridge provides the most popular access to Olympic National Park. A paved road, open year-round during daylight hours, twists and turns 17 miles up a steep seven percent grade to the mile-high summit, where, on a clear day, you can gape at the breathtaking 360-degree views of mountain, valley, and sea. A summer-only lodge at the crest provides food and drink, and a concession offers ski and snowshoe rentals on winter weekends. Trails lead down into the backcountry, where you're likely to spot marmots, deer, and bald eagles—and if you're lucky, maybe an elk or a mountain lion. Thrill-seeking drivers and mountain bikers may get a kick out of the Obstruction Point Road, a twisting gravel road that continues (without guardrails!) for another eight miles along the crest from the Hurricane Ridge parking lot. Obstruction Point Road ends at a trailhead; drivers will have to turn around. In winter, the snowed-in road becomes a popular cross-country skiing trail.

Apart from the area right around Hurricane Ridge, most of the Olympic National Park backcountry is fairly wet and rugged, and if you plan to camp overnight, be prepared, and be sure to get a **permit** from the Olympic National Park **ranger station** (360/452-0330) in Port Angeles, two blocks south of US-101 on the road up to Hurricane Ridge. This is also the best place to pick up general information on the rest of the park, which extends all the way west to the rainforest areas along the coastal valleys (see below for more).

Weather on the Olympic Peninsula varies widely from place to place. The peaks and coastal valleys of Olympic National Park receive as much as 200 inches of rainfall each year, while the town of Sequim, a mere 30 miles away, garners an average of just 17 inches annually.

Lake Crescent

One of the most idyllic spots in the entire Pacific Northwest, the fjord-like Lake Crescent, over eight miles long and some 625 feet deep, lies right alongside two-lane US-101, just 20 miles west of Port Angeles. Powerboats are banned, and the placid surface reflects the clouds and surrounding peaks, including 4,534-foot Storm King Mountain; you can rent **rowboats** ($5 an hour) from the Lake Crescent Lodge and float around under your own steam. Also from the lodge, a popular mile-long hike follows a well-maintained nature trail up to the delicate cascade of 90-foot **Marymere Falls**, while along the north shore an abandoned railroad grade is open to hikers and mountain bikers.

Incomparably situated along US-101 on the lake's southeast shore, **Lake Crescent Lodge** (open April-Oct. only; 360/928-3211) was originally built in 1916 and has been hosting visitors ever since. Fairly rustic rooms are available in the old lodge, which also has a cozy dining room; more modern accommodations are available in the adjacent cabins and motel, though the whole place is booked solid on summer weekends, so reserve as soon as you can. Room rates range $75-150 a night. Another nice place to stay is the **Log Cabin Resort** (360/928-3325), three miles north of US-101 on the northeast shore, with motel rooms and waterfront A-frame cabins for around $100 a night in summer.

In the forested hills above US-101, **Sol Duc Hot Springs Resort** (360/327-3583) has cabins, campsites, a restaurant, and relaxing natural hot springs.

Hwy-112: Strait of Juan de Fuca

The Strait of Juan de Fuca, the narrow inlet that links the open Pacific with Puget Sound and divides the U.S. from Canada, was named for the Greek sailor (real name: Apostolos Valerianus) who first mapped it while working for the Spanish Crown in 1610. On a clear day you can get some great views across the strait from Hwy-112, which runs along the shore from US-101 all the way to the tip of the Olympic Peninsula at Neah Bay. Though it looks like a great drive on the map, Hwy-112 is a very narrow and winding road with some surprisingly steep hills and thick woods that block much of the view, all of which (in addition to the plentiful logging trucks) can make it less than ideal for bicycling or even a scenic drive.

That said, there's at least one great reason to make the trip. North of Lake Crescent in the crossroads town of Joyce, the **Family Kitchen**, at 50800 Hwy-112 (360/928-3320), serves the Northwest's biggest hamburgers: eight-inch diameter "Logger Burgers," piled high with cheese and onions atop a freshly baked bun. They're open daily 6 AM-10 PM, and in summer they have great blackberry pies, too.

Neah Bay and Cape Flattery

From the crossroads **Sappho** on US-101, Hwy-113 leads north, linking up with Hwy-112 on a long and winding 40-mile detour through Clallam Bay (home of the nearly-world-famous "Running Fish" statue) to Cape Flattery, the northwestern-most tip of the continental United States. The highway is paved as far as the town of Neah Bay, a tiny and somewhat bedraggled community that's the center of the Makah Indian Reservation. Salmon fishing, both by Makah and by visitors, is about the only activity here, though the tribe does have the impressive and modern **Makah Museum** (daily 10 AM-5 PM in summer, closed Monday and Tuesday the rest of the year; $4), one of the best anthropological museums in the state. Most of the displays are of artifacts uncovered in 1970, when a mudslide revealed the pristine remains of a 500-year-old coastal village—the Pompeii of the Pacific Northwest. Other galleries display finely crafted baskets, a full-scale longhouse complete with recorded chants, and a whaling canoe from which fearless Makah harpooners would jump into the surf and sew up the jaws of dying whales, to keep them from drowning and sinking.

The Hwy-112/113 route twists along the rocky and wooded shore of the Strait of Juan de Fuca, but reaching the actual cape itself isn't difficult. From Neah Bay, the well-maintained western half of the Cape Loop Road winds along the Pacific to a parking area which gives access to a trail that brings you to the top of a 65-foot-high cliff overlooking the crashing surf and offshore **Tatoosh Island**. On a sunny day it's a gorgeous vista, but if the weather's less than perfect (which it often is) your time would be much better spent inside the Makah Museum (360/645-2711).

Forks

Bending southwest along the banks of the Sol Duc River, US-101 passes through miles of green forests under ever-gray skies to reach Forks (pop. 3,460), the commercial center of the northwestern Olympic Peninsula. Named for its location astride the Sol Duc and Bogachiel Rivers, Forks is a die-hard lumber town grappling with the inevitable change to more ecologically sustainable alternatives, mainly tourism. Visitors come to fish for steelhead during the late-summer runs, to beachcomb along the rugged coast, or to visit the remarkable rainforests of Olympic National Park to the southeast. The main attraction in Forks proper is the quirky **Timber Museum** (Tues.-Sat. 10 AM-5 PM; donations), on US-101 on the south edge of town, packed with handsaws, chainsaws, and other logging gear as well as antique cooking stoves and displays telling the town's characterful history. There's also a forest fire lookout tower perched outside the upper floor gallery.

With four gas stations, four motels, and a single stoplight, Forks is not a metropolis by any stretch of the imagination, but it does offer the best range of services between Port Angeles and Aberdeen. Two good burger stands (**Sully's** and the **Caboose**) face each other across US-101 at the north end of town, and there are also two Chinese and two Mexican places, plus the all-American **Rain Drop Cafe**, on US-101 at 111 S. Forks Avenue (next to the local library). Stay at the **Forks Motel**, 351 S. Forks Avenue (360/374-6243), or a more peaceful B&B, the **Miller Tree Inn** (360/374-6806), which sits on 30 acres at 654 E. Division Street, five blocks east of Forks's solitary stoplight. South of Forks along US-101, **Bogachiel State Park** has over 100 forested acres of very nice campsites (with showers!) along the Bogachiel River. Sites are first-come, first-served, and cost $10 for tents, $15 for RV hookups (360/374-6356).

The fish-headed, human-legged, sneaker-wearing statue that stands outside the Clallam Bay General Store is known alternately as "Gill," "The Fishman," and "The Running Fish," for obvious reasons.

As part of an effort to preserve tribal traditions and instill pride in younger Makah, in 1998 the Makah tribe announced plans to resume small-scale hunting of migratory gray whales, which they voluntarily ceased when the whales became endangered a century ago. Though the hunting would be largely ceremonial, the news has raised the hackles of wildlife organizations, who have staged loud protests and promised to prevent any whales from being killed.

The temperate rainforests of the Olympic Peninsula receive an average of 140 inches (nearly 12 feet) of annual rainfall, most of it in winter, though regular downpours drench the region year-round.

For more complete information, contact the Forks **visitor center** (800/44-FORKS or 800/443-6757), next to the Timber Museum.

Hoh River Rainforest

If you have time to visit only one of the lush rainforest areas of Washington's northwest coast, head for the Hoh River Rainforest, 12 miles south of Forks then 18 miles east along a well-signed and well-paved road. Not only is this the most easily accessible of these incredibly lush, old-growth areas, the Hoh River forest is also among the least disturbed, with a thick wet blanket of vibrant green ferns, mosses, and lichens covering every inch of the earth at the foot of massive hemlocks, cedars, and towering Sitka spruce. Displays inside the **visitor center** (daily 9 AM-4 PM, 9 AM-6:30 PM in summer; 360/374-6925) tell all about the forest's flora and fauna. There's also a wheelchair-accessible nature trail and a wide range of hiking trails, including the quickest access to the icy summit of 7,965-foot Mount Olympus, 22 miles away in the glacier-packed alpine highlands at the heart of the park.

If you're very lucky, you might spy one of the rare Roosevelt elk, for whose protection Olympic National Park was established; if you're unlucky, you might also come face to face with a mountain lion, which can be dangerous but generally avoids contact with humans.

The closest services to the Hoh River Rainforest are in Forks, but budget travelers may want to take advantage of the $14-a-night bunks at the amiable **Rain Forest Hostel** (360/374-2270), 23 miles south of Forks along US-101 (between mile markers 169 and 170), midway between the Hoh River Rainforest and the coast at Ruby Beach.

Kalaloch and the Pacific Beaches

Looping around the northern Olympic Peninsula, US-101 finally reaches the coast 27 miles south of Forks at Ruby Beach, where a series of wave-sculpted sea stacks frame a photogenic, driftwood-strewn cove. From Ruby Cove, US-101 runs south through the wild coastal section of Olympic National Park, which is almost always foggy and cool, even when the weather's sunny and hot just a mile inland. While almost the entire coast south from Cape Flattery is protected with the national park, this is the only easily accessible stretch. Parking areas along the highway, numbered from "Beach 6" to "Beach 1" north to south, give access to 20 miles of generally deserted beach, backed by rocky bluffs and packed with tidepools and an incredible variety of flotsam and jetsam.

The old-growth forests of Olympic National Park provide prime habitat for the northern spotted owl, an endangered species whose preservation has sparked heated debate throughout the Pacific Northwest.

At the southern end of this short but sweet stretch of coastline, between "Beach 2" and "Beach 3," 25 miles north of Lake Quinault, **Kalaloch Lodge** (360/962-2271) is a modern resort, with a coffee shop and a nice restaurant overlooking a picturesque cove. There's also a gas station, a summer-only **ranger station** across US-101, and an oceanside **campground** just north.

There are a number of small **Native American communities** on reservation lands along the coast, usually at the mouths of rivers. Most of these are fairly uninspired, haphazard collections of prefab houses and mobile homes; only La Push, 15 miles west of Forks on the Quileute reservation, has tourist services or facilities.

South of Kalaloch, US-101 turns inland along the northern border of the massive Quinault Indian Reservation, not reaching the Pacific again until the mouth of the Columbia River.

Lake Quinault

Spreading in a broad valley at the southwest corner of Olympic National Park, Lake Quinault offers lush rainforest groves within a short walk or drive of most creature comforts. The lake has served for decades as a popular resort destination—cabins, lodges, and stores dating from the 1920s line the southern shore, just outside the park boundary—and the old-growth forests here have survived intact, though the naked tracts of clearcut timber along US-101 north and south of the lake look like Dennis Rodman on a bad hair day, and give a good sense of what the area might have looked like had Teddy Roosevelt and friends not stepped in to protect it around the turn of the 20th century.

The best first stop is the **ranger station** (360/956-2400) on the south shore, where you can get details of the many excellent hikes in the Lake Quinault area, and pick up a map of the guided driving tour around the lake, including the location of the many record-size trees. The roughly four-mile-long **Quinault Loop Trail**, winds on a paved path from the ranger station along crashing Cascade Creek up through an old-growth rainforest of alders and bigleaf maples, whose leaves grow upwards of 12 inches across. Midway along, the trail crosses a raised wooden boardwalk through a fecund cedar swamp, then drops down again along another creek before returning by way of the lakeshore.

The nicest place to stay, right next to the ranger station, is historic **Lake Quinault Lodge** (360/288-2571), with a rustic but spacious lobby opening onto lakefront lawns; peak summer season room rates hover in the $100-150 range. Besides offering comfortable and reasonably priced accommodations and very good food, the nearby **Rain Forest Village** (360/288-2535 or 800/562-0948), at the east end of the lake, also holds the **World's Largest Spruce**, a 191-foot giant.

From US-101 at Hoquiam **Hwy-109** runs west and north along the Pacific Ocean through a series of fishing ports and beach resorts to the heavily-logged lands of the Quinault Indian Reservation.

Grays Harbor: Hoquiam and Aberdeen

The Olympic Peninsula is cut off from the southern Washington coast by the spade-shaped bay of Grays Harbor, named for the early American sea captain and explorer, Robert Gray. Long the state's prime lumber port, Grays Harbor still processes huge piles of trees, but in many ways what's most interesting is the contrast between the two towns here, Hoquiam and Aberdeen.

The **Seventh Street Theater,** 313 7th Street in downtown Hoquiam, was the first purpose-built movie theater in Washington, erected in 1927.

At the western end of Grays Harbor, tidy Hoquiam (kinda rhymes with "requiem," pop. 8,972) celebrates its lumber-based history with an annual Logger's Playday bash, complete with ax-throwing and tree-climbing competitions, the second weekend in September. The rest of the year, get a feel for the bygone days of the lumber industry at red-shingled **Hoquiam's Castle** (daily 11 AM-5 PM; $4), on a hillside three blocks off US-101 at 515 Chenault Avenue, a 20-room mansion built in 1897 by a local lumber baron. Another good place to get a feel for Hoquiam's history is the **Polson Museum**, on US-101 at 1611 Riverside Drive (Wed.-Sun 11 AM-4 PM; $2). Good places to eat in Hoquiam include the family-oriented and inexpensive **River Haven**, at the foot of the US-101 bridge over the Hoquiam River, and the popular **Hum-Dinger** burger stand next door. Hoquiam has one very nice B&B, the $75-a-night **Lytle House** (360/533-2320 or 800/677-2320), next to Hoquiam's Castle at 509 Chenault Avenue; otherwise there are a half dozen motels.

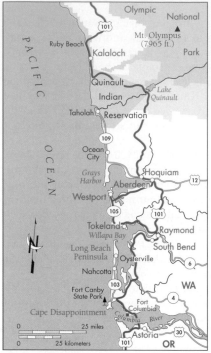

East of Hoquiam along the Chehalis River at the head of Grays Harbor, Aberdeen (pop. 16,600), is much more heavily industrialized and thus has been even harder hit by the continuing downturn in the Northwest timber industry. The downtown area has more than a few rough edges, but it also holds one of the more high-profile of the state-sponsored efforts to move from timber to tourism: **Grays Harbor Historical Seaport** (daily 9 AM-5 PM; $3), a half-mile east of US-101, where a reconstruction of American explorer (and Gray's Harbor namesake) Capt. Robert Gray's ship, the *Columbia Rediviva*, can be toured—when she's not off on one of her regular "goodwill" cruises. The original ship was the first American vessel to visit the area, way back in 1788, and the replica was completed here in 1989, to celebrate the Washington State centennial.

Across the river from Aberdeen, the region's largest employer, a Weyerhaeuser pulp mill, looms alongside US-101 through the inappropriately named town of Cosmopolis, before the road cuts inland toward Raymond and Willapa Bay.

Hwy-105: Westport and Tokeland

Between Hoquiam and Raymond, US-101 cuts inland from the coast, while an alternative route, Hwy-105, loops to the west past miles of cranberry bogs (and occasional wild elk) through the salmon-fishing town of Westport. Once called "The Salmon Capital of the World," and still a prime place for watching migrating gray whales, Westport is a very busy port—and one of Washington's few good surfing and surf-kayaking beaches; the whole place really comes to life during the Labor Day seafood festival. For details on Westport or anywhere along Hwy-105, contact the very helpful **visitors center** (360/268-9422 or 800/345-6223).

One of coastal Washington best-loved destinations, the red cedar, seaside Dunes Restaurant south of Westport in Grayland, burned to the ground in 1997—with no insurance, and so no chance of rebuilding. Now, the only real place nearby with anywhere near comparable character is the 100-year-old **Tokeland Hotel** (360/267-7006), off Hwy-105 on the north shore of Willapa Bay, with $60 rooms and a very nice dining room.

Grunge rock hero and Nirvana lead singer **Kurt Cobain**, who killed himself at age 28, grew up in and around Aberdeen.

From Aberdeen, US-12 cuts inland to the east, passing the Satsop nuclear power plant and one of the most heavily logged areas in Washington before joining the I-5 freeway at the state capital of Olympia. Midway along, the **Grays Harbor HI Hostel** in Elma (360/482-3119) has $10-a-night beds (and a small golf course!).

Willapa Bay: Raymond and South Bend

One of the country's prime oystering grounds, Willapa Bay is sheltered from the Pacific by the Long Beach Peninsula and fed by the Nasalle, Willapa, and North Fall Rivers. There are very few towns or even villages on this stretch of US-101, which winds past tidal marshes, cattle ranches, and some engaging roadside sculptures of people canoeing, birdwatching, cycling, fishing and generally enjoying the Great Outdoors. The landscape is also marked by extensively clearcut forests—which billboards proclaim to be "America's first industrial tree farm," giving dates of harvest, planting, and re-harvest, on a roughly 40-year cycle.

At the northeast corner of Willapa Bay, on the south bank of the Willapa River, stand two towns that jointly embody the natural resource-based history and economy of the Pacific Northwest. Raymond (pop. 2,901) has the lumber mills, while South Bend (pop. 1,551) calls itself the "Oyster Capital of the World"—a claim supported by the piles of oyster shells flanking the road outside packing houses like **Bendickson's Seafood**, on the north side of town. South Bend's other claim to fame is its landmark **Pacific County Courthouse** (Mon.-Fri. 8 AM-5 PM), which since 1910 has loomed like a mini-Taj Mahal on a hill just east of US-101. Step inside for a look at the 30-foot stained glass dome above the rotunda, and wander through the lushly landscaped park next door.

If the weather's right for a picnic, fresh shellfish can be had at bargain prices—by the bite or by the half-gallon—from the area's many producers, wholesalers, and roadside stands; look for them all along US-101. Willapa Bay produces nearly one-sixth of all the oysters consumed in the US.

Long Beach Peninsula

On the western side of Willapa Bay, the Long Beach Peninsula stretches for 28 miles of hard-packed sandy beaches along the roiling Pacific Ocean. Away from the few small towns, beaches and breakers abound along here, and you won't have any problem finding peace and solitude. The center of activity on the

Toll-free hiking and camping information for Washington's state parks is available by calling 800/233-0321.

Long Beach Peninsula is the town of **Long Beach**, two miles west of US-101, with a wanderable collection of crafts galleries and souvenir shops, and one of the coast's best B&Bs, the historic **Shelburne Inn** (360/642-2442), in the Seaview neighborhood at Pacific Way (a.k.a. Hwy-103, the main road) and 45th Street. Rooms start at $70 a night. The Shelburne also houses a friendly pub and a very good restaurant, **The Shoalwater**, rated by many as the best on the Washington coast. At the other end of the taste range, Long Beach is also the home of the "World's Largest Frying Pan," which hangs on a rack in front of the one-of-a-kind **Marsh's Free Museum**, a totally tacky (and wonderfully kitsch) collection of postcards, peep shows and old-time arcade games on Pacific Way near 10th Street.

The rest of the peninsula is quite quiet, dotted with cranberry bogs and historic fishing and oystering towns. In **Nahcotta**, a dozen miles north of Long Beach, **The Ark** (360/665-4133) is another of Washington's most highly regarded restaurants; farther north, **Oysterville** is the peninsula's oldest community, with some nifty historic homes dating back to the 1850s. The peninsula comes to an end in the north at **Leadbetter Point State Park**, a great place for watching gulls, hawks and eagles, and migratory seabirds passing through on the Great Pacific Flyway.

For further information on the Long Beach Peninsula, contact the **visitors bureau** (360/642-2400 or 800/451-2542), at the US-101/Hwy-103 junction.

Cape Disappointment

The high headland marking the place where the Columbia River finally merges into the Pacific Ocean, Cape Disappointment was named by the early explorer Capt. John Meares, who in 1788 incorrectly interpreted the treacherous sandbars offshore to mean that, despite reports to the contrary, there was no major river nor any mythical Northwest Passage here.

Besides the grand view of the raging ocean, the best reason to visit the cape is to tour the small but worthwhile **Lewis and Clark Interpretive Center** (daily 10 AM-5 PM; free), incongruously built atop a WW II-era artillery emplacement a short walk from the end of the road. On November 7, 1805, after five months and more than 4,000 miles, the explorers finally laid eyes on the Pacific from this point; they sat through nine days of continuous rain before fleeing south to Oregon (see pages

Cape Disappointment

176-177 for more on Lewis and Clark). Displays inside the museum give the overall context for their journey of discovery, walking you through the different stages of their two-year roundtrip. The small "Cape D" **lighthouse** stands atop the 60-foot-high cliff, a half-mile walk from the museum.

A pair of statues sculpted by chain saws in a small state park, three miles west of the US-101 bridge across the Columbia River, marks the site where **Lewis and Clark** camped in December 1805 before heading south in search of better weather—which is about the only thing they never found on their epic trip.

The entire area around the cape is protected from development within **Fort Canby State Park**, and the nearest services—gas stations and a couple of cafes—are in nearby **Ilwaco**, a small rough-and-tumble fishing port two miles west of US-101.

Chinook and Fort Columbia

Southeast of Cape Disappointment, toward the Oregon border, US-101 winds along the north bank of the Columbia River. Along with good views of the river's five-mile-wide mouth, the road passes through the quaint town of Chinook, home of "Washington's First Salmon Hatchery," which started here way back in 1893. Also in Chinook is Fort Columbia, where the region's one and only **HI Youth Hostel** (360/777-8755) offers bunk beds in a converted hospital for $10 a night, and pancake breakfasts for 50 cents.

ALONG THE OREGON COAST

Rarely losing sight of the Pacific Ocean during its 365-mile jaunt along the Oregon coast, US-101 winds past rockbound coast, ancient forests, and innumerable towns and villages. While the region also has its share of strip towns and places where the timber boom went bust, the beach loops, historic restorations, and more state parks per mile than any place in the country soften its few hard edges. Every 20 or so miles you'll pass through attractive if moderately touristy towns populated by at most a couple thousand people, but as a general rule it's the mileage between these hamlets that explains why most people visit—to take in one of the most dramatic meetings of rock and tide in the world.

Starting in the north along the Columbia River at historic **Astoria**, one of the oldest settlements in the western U.S., the route winds along the ocean past the very different beachfront hamlets of **Seaside** and **Cannon Beach** before edging slightly inland through the rich dairy lands of **Tillamook County**. Midway along, the popular vacation spots of **Lincoln City**, **Newport**, and **Florence** form the most developed corridor along the coast, but it's still easy to reach unpeopled stretches, especially at the remarkable **Oregon Dunes** stretching to the south. The dunes end abruptly at the heavily industrial port of **Coos Bay**, beyond which the natural beauty returns with a string of state parks and the diverse coastal towns of **Bandon**, **Port Orford**, **Gold Beach**, and **Brookings**.

By state law, there is no self-service gasoline in Oregon; all stations have attendants who pump the gas for you. There's no sales tax, either.

To find out about local issues and current events on the northern Oregon coast, pick up a copy of the excellent *Daily Astorian* newspaper (50 cents), or tune to commercial-free **KMUN 91.5 FM** for NPR news and diverse programming.

Astoria

The oldest American city west of the Missouri River, Astoria (pop. 10,069) is an upbeat mix of lovingly preserved past and busy contemporary commerce. Houses perched atop high hills overlook the Columbia River, creating a favorite backdrop for Hollywood movies, but despite its picturesque appearance, Astoria supports an active commercial fishing fleet and dozens of tugboats guiding tankers and container ships across the treacherous sandbars. As more than a few Astoria bumper stickers proclaim, "We Ain't Quaint." Founded by and named after fur-trade magnate John Jacob Astor in 1811, Astoria protected the tenuous American claim to the Pacific coast until the opening of the Oregon Trail brought substantial settlement. By the turn of the century Astoria was still Oregon's second-largest city, but the downturn in both salmon fishing and logging since the end of WW II has caused an economic decline which, as always, town officials look to tourism to overcome.

US-101 crosses across the Columbia River on the toll-free, high-level Astoria Bridge, completed in 1966, which drops you at the west end of the downtown waterfront. To get a sense of the lay of the land, follow the signs along 16th Street up Coxcomb Hill to the **Astoria Column** (daily 8 AM-dusk; free) for a view of the Columbia meeting the ocean, the coastal plain south to Tillamook Head, and the snowcapped Cascade Range (including, on a clear day, Mount St. Helens) on the eastern horizon. A mosaic chronicling local history is wrapped like a ribbon around the column, tracing the many significant events in the town's past. A spiral staircase climbs to the top.

Back downtown, **Flavel House,** 441 8th Street (daily 10 AM-5 PM in summer; $4) is a red-roofed Queen Anne-style Victorian showplace restored as an elegantly furnished museum of Astoria's first millionaire, Columbia River pilot George Flavel. A half-mile east, near the foot of 17th Street on the north side of waterfront Marine Drive, the **Columbia River Maritime Museum** (daily 9:30 AM-5 PM; $4) displays a large and very impressive collection that tells the story of the lifeblood of this community: the Columbia River.

Fortify yourself at one of the many good seafood places along the water, starting at the ever-popular **Columbian Cafe,** 1114 Marine Drive (503/325-CAFE or 503/325-2233), where chef Uriah Hulsey prepares all sorts of ultra-fresh food in an impossibly cramped galley kitchen, just a countertop away from his legions of foodie fans. Meals are massive yet reasonably priced, so be sure to arrive with an appetite; breakfast and lunch are served Mon.-Sat., dinner Wed.-Saturday. Other Astoria eating options include the bare-bones **Cafe Uniontown** or the pub-like **Ship Inn,** both under the bridge at Marine Drive and 2nd Street. Gourmets might want to visit adjacent **Josephson's Smokehouse,** 106 Marine Drive (503/325-2190), to sample the delicious array of smoked salmon, prepared on the premises and sold all over the country.

Columbian Cafe
1114 Marine Drive
Astoria, OR 97103
503-325-CAFE (2233)

Hours: Mon - Fri 8am - 2pm
Sat 10am - 2pm
Dinners: Wed - Sat. Open 5pm

URIAH HULSEY

To absorb a full portion of Astoria's addictive ambience, stay the night at the riverview **Crest Motel**, three miles east of town along US-30 at 5366 Leif Erickson Drive (503/325-3141), at the comfy HI youth hostel across the river at Fort Columbia (see above), or at one of Astoria's handful of nice B&Bs. For detailed listings or further information, contact the **Astoria Chamber of Commerce**, 111 W. Marine Drive (503/325-6311).

Fort Clatsop

In the conifer forests six miles south of Astoria and three miles east of US-101, Fort Clatsop (daily 9 AM-5 PM; $2) is a credible reconstruction of the site where Lewis and Clark and company camped during winter 1805-06. A range of exhibits in the visitor center, a full-scale replica of the 50- by 50-foot log fort, and summertime "living history" reenactments help conjure the travails of that time. The expedition spent three miserable months here, mingling occasionally with the native Clatsop and Chinook tribes but mostly growing moldy in the incessant rain and damp while being bitten by fleas, sewing new moccasins, and making salt in preparation for the return journey back across the continent.

Gearhart

Just north of boisterous Seaside, but a world away in character and ambience, the tiny town of Gearhart (pop. 1,027) was the home of influential chef and cookbook author James Beard. Beard's culinary legacy lives on in the **Pacific Way Bakery and Cafe**, a half-mile west of US-101 at 601 Pacific Way (503/738-0245), which offers the coast's best coffees and croissants, along with four-star lunches and dinners.

Fort Stevens, off US-101 on the way to Fort Clatsop, was "the only continental U.S. fortification bombed during WW II," sustaining a shelling from a Japanese submarine on June 21, 1942.

Seaside waterfront

Seaside

Nothing else along the Oregon coast prepares you for the carnival ambience of downtown Seaside (pop. 5,359), Oregon's oldest seafront resort. Ben Holladay, who built the place in 1873, included a racetrack, zoo, and plush hotel to lure Portlanders to ride his rail line to the beach. Come during Spring Break, or on a weekend during July or August, and join the hordes wandering among the saltwater taffy stands and video-game arcades along Broadway, or cruising the concrete boardwalk (called "The Prom") along the beach.

Where Broadway meets the beach, a small traffic circle known locally as "The Turnaround" is marked by a statue and a sign proclaiming Seaside as "The End of the Lewis and Clark Trail." South of here, between Beach Drive and The Prom, is a replica of the Lewis and Clark **salt cairn,** where the explorers boiled sea water nonstop for seven weeks to produce enough salt to preserve meat for their return trip east.

For food, enjoy Necanicum River views over breakfast at **Cafe Espresso**, 600 Broadway; brave the franchise-style facade of **Pig n' Pancake**, 323 Broadway, for waffles; or sample the clam chowder at **Dooger's**, 505 Broadway.

A half-mile north of downtown, housed in a wood-shingled old motor court on the banks of the Necanicum River, the **HI Seaside Hostel**, at 930 Holladay Drive (503/738-7911), has $14-a-night dorms, $28 private rooms, canoes and kayaks, an espresso bar—and nightly movies. There are dozens of inexpensive motels and a handful of B&Bs; for listings and other information, contact the **Seaside Chamber of Commerce**, on US-101 at Broadway (503/738-6391 or 800/444-6740).

This part of the Pacific coast marks the beginning of our Oregon Trail route, which runs east across the country along a combination of US-6, US-20 and US-26. Coverage of the route begins on page 526; Portland, just over an hour or so inland from Seaside and Cannon Beach, is covered on pages 530-532.

Ecola State Park

Just north of Cannon Beach, a mile south of the junction between US-101 and US-26 from Portland, the rain-forested access road through Ecola State Park (day use only, $3 per car; 800/551-6949) leads you to one of the most photographed views on the coast: looking south you can see Haystack Rock and Cannon Beach with Neahkahnie Mountain looming above them. Out to sea, the sight of **Tillamook Rock Lighthouse** to the northwest is also striking; operational from 1881 to 1957, the lighthouse is now used as a repository for the ashes of people who've been cremated.

The rest of Ecola State Park protects a series of rugged headlands stretching for nine miles along the coast, with many forested hiking trails including some of the most scenic portions of the Oregon Coast Trail System. The park also marks the southernmost extent of Lewis and Clark's cross-country expedition. Clark and a few other members of the Corps of Discovery expedition traversed the area in search of supplements to their diet of hardtack and dried salmon. They happily bought 300 pounds of tangy whale blubber from local Indians, but these days you'd better bring your own lunch to picnic atop bluffs with sweeping views of the rock-strewn Pacific.

The view from the top of **Tillamook Head,** which rises 1,200 feet above the sea between Seaside and Cannon Beach, was memorialized by explorer William Clark as "the grandest and most pleasing prospect" he had ever beheld. The headland marks the northern border of Ecola State Park, and a number of trails lead to the top.

The word *ecola* means whale in the Chinookan tongue and was affixed to this region by the Lewis and Clark expedition, who found one of these leviathans washed up on a beach.

Cannon Beach

Unlike most Oregon coast towns, Cannon Beach (pop. 1,221) is hidden from the highway, but it's one place you won't want to miss. Though it's little more than a stone's throw south of boisterous Seaside, Cannon Beach has long been known as an artist's colony, and while it has grown considerably in recent years thanks to its popularity as a weekend escape from Portland, it retains a rustic atmosphere.

In terms of traditional "tourist attractions" there's not a lot to do, but Cannon Beach is an unbeatable place in which to stop and unwind, or to take long walks along the seven-mile strand and then retreat indoors to the many good galleries, cafes, and restaurants. For breakfast, fill up on eggs Benedict at the **Lazy Susan Cafe** (closed Tuesday and Wednesday in winter), across from the Mariner Market at 126 N. Hemlock. For vegetarian food tasty enough to satisfy even the most artery-hardened carnivore, head to **Homegrown**, 3301 S. Hemlock (503/435-1803). Reasonably priced rooms near the beach and town can be found at the **McBee Motel**, 888 S. Hemlock (503/436-2569), and the **Hidden Villa**, 188 E. Van Buren (503/436-2237).

At the start of summer, Cannon Beach hosts the largest and most enjoyable sand castle competition on the West Coast, with some 10,000 spectators and as many as 1,000 participants turning out with their buckets and spades.

South of Cannon Beach, the Beach Loop, an extension of Hemlock, runs along a spectacular grouping of volcanic plugs, notably 235-foot-high **Haystack Rock.**

For further information, or details on the annual events and festivals, contact the Cannon Beach **visitor bureau**, 201 E. 2nd Street (503/436-2623).

Manzanita and Neahkahnie Mountain

South of Cannon Beach, US-101 rises 700 feet above the Pacific. Nowhere else along the Oregon coast does the roadbed sit so high above an ocean view. Soaring another thousand feet above you on the other side of this WPA-built stretch of highway is Neahkahnie Mountain; of the dozen marked scenic overlooks and hiking trails in the next 20 miles, your itinerary should include Neahkahnie Wayside, which looks southward at the Nehalem Valley and the ocean between Manzanita and Cape Meares. South of the mountain, and thus spared much of the stormy coastal weather (annual rainfall hereabouts averages 80 inches) is the upscale resort town of Manzanita, where you'll find two of the coast's best restaurants, the **Blue Sky Cafe** at 154 Laneda Avenue (503/368-5712), and

South of Cannon Beach at Oswald West State Park, a half-mile trail winds beneath the highway through an ancient forest to driftwood-laden Short Sands Beach and Smuggler's Cove.

Jarboe's (503/368-5113) across the street. Both are very expensive, but worth it for celebrating special occasions—like a road trip along the Oregon coast.

South of Manzanita, **Nehalem Bay State Park** has a large campground with hundreds of sites (and hot showers). US-101 continues through a series of small towns before winding inland past the sloughs and dairy country along Tillamook Bay.

Tillamook

This town, where cows outnumber people by more than two to one, sprawls over lush grasslands at the southern end of Tillamook Bay. Its motto, "Cheese, trees, and ocean breeze," conjures a clear sense of the place. Tillamook, which translates from the Salish tongue as "land of many waters," is dominated by the **Tillamook Cheese Factory** at the north end of town, one of the busiest tourist draws in the state. Inside, a self-guided tour with informational placards traces Tillamook cheese making from the last century to the present, and a glassed-in observation area lets you watch the stuff being made and packaged.

Tillamook's other odd attraction is east of US-101 and south of town. One of the world's largest wooden structures—300 feet wide, 1,100 feet long, and nearly 200 feet tall—has been preserved as the **Tillamook Air Museum** (daily 10 AM-4 PM, 9 AM-5 PM in summer; $7 adults, under 7s free; 503/842-1130), wherein the story of the WW II surveillance blimps built and maintained here by the US Navy is recounted. There are also displays about these dirigible craft as well as other vintage airplanes, a theater, and a restaurant, all making for a fascinating and unusual stop. There used to be a pair of hangars, but the other one burned down.

Seven miles south of Tillamook, a turnoff east follows a bumpy, one-mile access road leading to the highest waterfall in Oregon's Coast Range, 266-foot Munson Creek Falls. From the parking area at the end of the road, a short trail leads to this year-round cascade.

Three Capes Loop

US-101 veers inland for 50 miles between Tillamook and Lincoln City, the next sizeable town south. If time and weather are on your side, head west along the coast via the well-signed, 35-mile-long Three Capes Loop. Running northwest from Tillamook, the loop reaches the mouth of the Tillamook Bay at **Cape Meares State Park**, which has a restored 1890 lighthouse and an oddly contorted Sitka spruce known as the Octopus Tree.

Heading south through the coastal villages of Oceanside and Netarts, the loop proceeds through dairy country until it climbs onto the shoulder of **Cape Lookout**, where a small sign proclaiming "Wildlife Viewing Area" marks the beginning of a 2.5-mile trail that leads through an ancient forest to the tip of the cape, 100-plus feet above the water. Beside the coastal panorama, in winter and spring this is a prime place to view passing gray whales. From the trailhead, the middle path leads to the cape, while others to the left and right lead down to the water. Cape Lookout State Park (800/ 551-6949) has the area's most popular campground, with hot showers and other creature comforts costing around $18 a night per campsite, less in winter.

The Oregon coast's most famous promontory, **Cape Kiwanda**, sees some of the state's wildest surf battering the sandstone headland. Across from the

45TH PARALLEL HALFWAY BETWEEN THE EQUATOR AND NORTH POLE

cape is **Haystack Rock**, a 327-foot sea stack a half-mile offshore. Along the beach south of the cape, surfers ride waves while dory fisherfolk skid their small craft along the sands every afternoon: a sight worth hanging around to see. The southernmost settlement on this scenic alternative to US-101 is neighboring **Pacific City**, where two fine restaurants, **Grateful Bread Bakery** and **The Riverhouse**, sit beachside on Brooten Road.

Lincoln City

The most overdeveloped section of the Oregon coast stretches for miles along US-101 through Lincoln City (pop. 5,892), seven miles of strip malls, outlet stores, motels, and fast-food franchises. With over 1,000 oceanside rooms, Lincoln City does offer some of the coast's cheapest lodging, especially in the off-season when sign after sign advertises rooms for as low as $25 a night. Apart from cheap rooms, with so much scenic splendor nearby there's no great reason to stop—unless you're a cheeseburger fanatic, in which case you ought to stop by the **Dory Cove** (541/994-5180), a marshland shack off US-101 at 5819 Logan Road, near Road's End State Park. They also make great pies, as many as a dozen different kinds every day, so bring an appetite.

Seven miles south of Lincoln City a sign announces the **Salishan Lodge** (541/764-3600 or 800/452-2300), a beautifully landscaped rustic resort with good off-season value packages (three nights for $239), a five-star dining room, and a surprisingly affordable coffee shop, **The Sun Room**. Down the hill across US-101, **Siletz Bay** is a birdwatcher's paradise.

Depoe Bay

Depoe Bay has an appeal, but so much of its natural beauty is obscured from the highway by gift shops or intruded upon by traffic that you've got to know where to look. In his book *Blue Highways,* William Least Heat Moon wrote, "Depoe Bay used

Five miles northeast of Lincoln City, just east of US-101 on Hwy-18, the **Otis Cafe** (541/994-2813) immortalizes American roadfood, offering excellent waffles and other breakfast treats along with epicurean lunches and berry pies for dessert. It's open for breakfast and lunch daily, plus dinner Thurs.-Sunday.

South of Lincoln City, 2.5 miles east of US-101, the **Drift Creek Covered Bridge** is the oldest of some 50 such structures in the state.

Depoe Bay was originally known as Depot Bay, named after a local Siletz Indian who worked at the local U.S. Army depot and called himself **Charlie Depot.**

Depoe Bay

to be a picturesque fishing village; now it was just picturesque." While it's true that most of the commercial fishing is long gone, you can still park your car along the highway and walk out on the bridge to watch sportfishing boats move through the narrow channel to what the *Guinness Book of World Records* rates as the world's smallest navigable harbor. South of the bridge is another record-setter, the Oregon coast's largest secondhand bookstore, the **Channel Bookstore** (541/765-2352).

The **Sea Hag** restaurant, on US-101 in downtown Depoe Bay, is a time-tested seafood place, as is **Whale Cove Inn**, two miles south of town overlooking a picturesque inlet formerly used by bootleggers during Prohibition.

Cape Foulweather and the Devil's Punchbowl

Between Depoe Bay and Newport, the roadside scenery along US-101 and the parallel "old road," now signed as the Otter Crest Loop, is dominated by miles of broad beaches and sandstone bluffs, including the 453-foot headland of Cape Foulweather, named by Capt. James Cook and offering a 360-degree coastal panorama. (The Otter Crest Loop has frequently been closed by slides and reconstruction efforts, but you can reach it from many access roads.)

Farther south, midway between Depoe Bay and Newport, the aptly named Devil's Punchbowl gives a ringside seat on a frothy confrontation between rock and tide. In the parking area you'll find a small lunch cafe, a branch of Newport's **Mo's**, graced by a chair where "The Boss" (singer Bruce Springsteen) sat on June 11, 1987.

The coast and inland forests along the Siletz River near Newport were the primary location of the Ken Kesey novel (and Paul Newman film) *Sometimes a Great Notion.*

Newport

Another old fishing community turned tourist nexus, Newport (pop. 8,437) started in the 1860s on the strength of sweet-tasting Yaquina Bay oysters, which were in demand from San Francisco to New York City and are still available at local restaurants. Oysters, crabs, and clams, along with sea otters, sharks, and seabirds, are the stars of the show at the large and modern **Oregon Coast Aquarium** (daily 10 AM-6 PM in summer, 10 AM-4:30 PM rest of the year; $8.50; 541/867-3474), south of Newport across the Yaquina Bay Bridge. The aquarium includes an aquatic aviary where sea lions, tufted puffins, and other shorebirds cavort in a simulated rockbound coastal habitat, and over 40,000 square feet of similarly eco-friendly exhibits.

On the north side of the US-101 bridge over Yaquina Bay, turn onto Hubert Street and head for the bayfront, where boatyards and fish-packing plants service a working harbor. Though it's still the state's second-largest fishing port, much of Newport's bay front has been consumed by souvenir shops, a wax museum, a **Ripley's Believe It or Not**, and other tourist traps. But you'll find the original **Mo's**, a locally famous seafood restaurant, at 622 Bay Boulevard; it and its annex across the street are the area's best dining values.

Dining options can also be found at **Nye Beach**, a mélange of old-fashioned beach houses and destination resorts north of the harbor; just look for signs on the western side of US-101. **Don Petrie's**, 613 N.W. 3rd Street (541/265-3663), serves excellent Italian food. Nye Beach is also home to the bohemian **Sylvia Beach Hotel**, 267 N.W. Cliff (541/265-5428), *the* place to stay in Newport for anyone of literary bent. If you can't afford the $75-150 per night rooms—with decor evocative of different authors, including a scary Edgar Allan Poe room based on "The Pit and the Pendulum"—there are dormitory bunk beds for under $25 a night. All rates include breakfast. Also on the west side of US-101 is the **Brown Squirrel Hostel**, a block from the beach at 44 S.W. Brook Street (541/265-3729). You'll find many other cut-rate lodging options along US-101.

The very helpful **Newport Information Center** (800/262-7844) has complete accommodations listings and other useful information.

Waldport

If you want to avoid lines and general tourist bustle, Waldport is a nice alternative to the resort towns surrounding it. Tourism is low-key here, and you can still sense the vestiges of the resource-based economy, byproduct of the town's proximity to rich timber stands and superlative fishing. Stop along US-101 at the **Alsea River Bridge Museum** (Wed.-Sun. 9 AM-4 PM; free) for interesting exhibits on coastal transportation and the local Alsea tribe, as well as a telescope trained on waterfowl and seals in the bay. From the north end of the bridge, you can follow Hwy-34 seven miles upstream to the **Kozy Kove Kafe**, a floating restaurant with good food and bucolic riverside ambience.

Four miles south of Waldport, **Beachside State Park** (800/551-6949) has a very popular campground, with hot showers, RV hook-ups, even a laundromat.

Yachats

The old-growth forests of the **Drift Creek Wilderness** east of Waldport are prime nesting areas for the endangered northern spotted owl.

On the way into Yachats (pronounced YA-hots), beach loops on either side of the Yachats River give a sense of why the area is called "the gem of the Oregon coast." It's a great place to wander and get lost and found again, but one place to catch up on life hereabouts is on US-101 at 4th Street, where the **New Morning Coffeehouse and Bookstore** has good espresso and a (sometimes) sunny outdoor deck-cum-sculpture garden. In the evenings, **Leroy's Blue Whale** (541/547-3399) is a dependable, no-frills seafood restaurant.

The word "cottage" is a popular lodging label here, usually referring to a moderately-priced self-contained cabin or duplex with kitchen. On US-101 between Waldport and Yachats are a half-dozen different "cottage" complexes, each fronting the beach; **Cape Cod Cottages**, two-plus miles south of Waldport at 4150 US-101 (541/563-2106), is a good choice for location and comfort. If you want more than a simple place to spend the night, the **Oregon House** (541/547-3329) on US-101 nine miles south of Yachats has spacious apartment-like rooms, some with fireplaces and ocean views, and all with access to the well-tended grounds and trails leading down the bluffs to a gem of a sandy cove. Its room rates (all of them non-smoking) vary with the seasons, but range $65-125 a night.

Cape Perpetua

For nearly 400 miles along the Oregon coast, US-101 abounds with national forests, state parks and viewpoints, but Cape Perpetua deserves most of your attention. Stop first at the Siuslaw National Forest **visitor center** (541/547-3289), just east of US-101, for seacoast views, exhibits on forestry, and area history. From the visitor center, trails lead across the highway past wind-bent trees, piles of seashells and other artifacts left behind by native peoples, excellent tidepools, and two rock formations, "Spouting Horn" and the "Devil's Churn." During stormy seas both shoot huge spouts of foam into the air. The friendly folks at the visitor center can also point you toward Cape Perpetua's small, summer-only campground ($12), which has bathrooms but no showers or hook-ups.

You can reach the top of 800-foot-high Cape Perpetua itself by following a two-mile-long road, marked by Cape Perpetua Viewpoint signs and leaving US-101 100 yards or so north of the visitor center. Once atop the cape, walk the **Trail of the Whispering Spruce**, a half-mile loop around the rim of the promontory yielding, on a clear day, 150-mile views of the Oregon coast from a rustic, WPA-built stone observation point.

Heceta Head and the Sea Lion Caves

Halfway between Cape Perpetua and Florence, a small bridge just south of Carl Washburne State Park marks the turnoff to **Heceta Head Lighthouse**, perhaps the most photographed beacon in the United States. Built in 1893, it was named for the Spanish mariner who is credited with being the first European to set foot in the region, but you'll have to be content with gazing at it across the cove from a small but rarely crowded beach.

Farther along US-101, 10 miles north of Florence, traffic slows to a stop at the gift shop that serves as the entrance to Sea Lion Caves (daily 8 AM-7 PM in summer, 9 AM-4 PM in winter; $6.50). You can ride an elevator down to America's largest sea cave and the only mainland rookery for the Steller sea lion. Fall and winter offer the best times to see (and smell!) these animals. They are visible for free from a viewpoint a hundreds yards up US-101.

Florence

If first and last impressions are enduring, Florence is truly blessed. As you enter the city from the north, US-101 climbs high above the ocean; from the south, travelers are greeted by the graceful **Siuslaw River Bridge**, perhaps the most impressive of a half-dozen WPA-built spans designed by Conde McCullough and decorated with his trademark Egyptian obelisks and art deco stylings. Unfortunately, the rest of town, visible from US-101, is a bland highway sprawl of motels, gas stations, and franchised restaurants.

To catch your daily dose of Rush Limbaugh and "modern country" hits, tune to **KWRO 630 AM.** The best part of Florence, **Old Town**, is just upstream from the bridge along the north bank of the river. Here, among Bay Street's three blocks of interesting boutiques and galleries, you'll find a number of excellent seafood restaurants. Starting from a nicely landscaped waterfront park at the foot of Laurel Street, choose from the upscale **Bridgewater**, the 24-hour **Fisherman's Wharf**, a riverfront **Mo's**, and the **International C-Food Market**. Back on US-101, across from the A&W, the **Blue Hen** is a popular local cafe.

As far as places to stay, Old Town really lives up to its name at the antique-filled **Johnson House**, 216 Maple Street (541/997-8000), an affordable, century-old, Victorian B&B. Back on US-101 sit a half-dozen garden-variety motels with the **Money Saver**, 170 US-101 (541/997-7131), closest to Old Town.

"Dune Country": Oregon's Sahara

For nearly 50 miles south of Florence, US-101 has an extensive panorama of oceanfront dunes. Though often obscured from view by forests, roadside signs indicate access roads to numerous dunescapes on both sides of the highway. Coming from the north, the first of these access points is **Honeyman State Park,** 10 miles south of Florence, where rhododendrons line a half-mile trail leading to a 150-foot-high dune overlooking a mirage-like lake. A longer trek, leaving from the very pleasant Tahkenitch Lake campground (reservations essential; 800/452-5687), gives a more in-depth look at the dunes' diverse flora and fauna, including swans and occasional black bears. Perhaps the best introduction is at **Umpqua Dunes,** nine miles south of the visitor center in Reedsport. From **Eel Creek Campground,** a 1.5-mile trail leads across small marshes and conifer groves en route to the sea, negotiating lunar-like dunes soaring 300-500 feet, some of the tallest in the world.

Before setting out on any extended exploration, your first stop should be the USFS-run **Oregon Dunes visitor center** (541/271-3611) at the junction of US-101 and Hwy-38 in Reedsport, along the Umpqua River midway between Florence and Coos Bay at the heart of the dunes. The helpful rangers can provide detailed information on hiking and camping throughout the park. Reedsport itself has a line of motels and burger joints —**Don's Old Fashioned** has legions of fans—and you'll find one more interesting option in the **Gardiner Guest House,** 401 Front Street (541/271-4005), which offers comfortable B&B rooms in a restored Victorian home.

Giant rhododendrons, and tumble-down shacks that rent out dune buggies and ATVs, line US-101 between Florence and Coos Bay. One of the best of these rental places is **Sandland Adventures** (541/997-8087), a mile south of Florence's Siuslaw River bridge, which also offers thrilling, sand-in-your-mouth guided dune buggy tours.

While stands of myrtle trees abound along Oregon's coast, the **Oregon Connection,** at 1125 S. 1st Street (800/255-5318) along US-101 on the southwest side of Coos Bay, has the most extensive collection of myrtlewood souvenirs, and is the only place where you can watch objects being made.

Behind the Coos Bay visitors bureau, a monument remembers the region's favorite son, middle-distance runner **Steve Prefontaine,** who electrified the athletic world before his sudden death at age 24 in 1974. There's also an annual 10K memorial run, every September.

Coos Bay

Even if you race right through, it's quite apparent that Coos Bay, once the world's largest lumber port, retains a core of heavy industry. Though many of the big mills have closed, you can still watch huge piles of wood chips, the harbor's number-one export, being loaded onto factory ships in the harbor east of US-101. The chips are sent to Asia where they're turned into low-grade paper. You can also get a sense of Coos Bay's seagoing heritage by visiting the tiny, church-run **Seamen's Center,** a block west of US-101 at 171 N. Broadway, where most every evening old salts mingle with foreign sailors and make model ships. Across the street, the handy Coos Bay **visitors bureau** (541/269-0215 or 800/824-8486) has maps and information on the entire "Bay Area" region.

Big breakfasts, eclectic but inexpensive lunches and dinners, great pies, and a good range of microbrewed beers are served at **The Blue Heron** across from the visitors bureau at 100 Commercial Avenue. There's no shortage of easy-to-find lodging, including **Motel 6** on US-101 at 1445 N. Bayshore (541/267-7171).

On the way to Shore Acres from Coos Bay is **Sunset Bay State Park,** Oregon's best swimming beach. Beyond Shore Acres is **Cape Arago State Park,** complete with tidepools and seals on offshore rocks.

The inland marshes around Bandon are prime cranberry-growing lands; the harvest is celebrated with a festival every September.

Shore Acres State Park

The historical antecedents for Coos Bay port development were laid a century ago by the Simpson lumber company, whose ships transported Oregon logs around the world. The ships returned with seeds that were planted in the Simpson estate's garden, 12 miles west of Coos Bay via the Cape Arago Highway, three miles beyond the busy commercial and sportfishing port of Charleston. Though the Simpson house burned to the ground in 1923, the 750-acre gardens are still a floral fantasia, now open to the public as Shore Acres State Park (daily 9 AM-dusk; $3 per car). Besides the formal gardens, which are illuminated during the Christmas holiday season, there's an observation tower above wave-battered bluffs and a trail down to a delightful beach.

Bandon

There's no sharper contrast on the Oregon coast than the difference between industrial Coos Bay and earthy Bandon, 23 miles to the south. Here, in the **Old Town** section along the banks of the Coquille River, are several blocks of galleries, crafts shops, and fine restaurants, marked by a gateway arch off US-101. Start a tour of Old Town at the corner of 1st and Baltimore, where Big Wheel Farm Supply houses the **Bandon Driftwood Museum** (daily 9 AM-5:30 PM; free). The combination of sculpted tree roots and fertilizer displays gives a good sense of Bandon's back-to-the-land, hippie ethos. A more academic introduction to the town and region can be had at new and improved **Coquille River Museum** (Mon.-Sat. 10 AM-4 PM, plus Sunday in summer; $1; 541/347-2164). Its exhibits on area history, cranberries and local color are artfully done, and the building, on US-101 at 270 Fillmore Street, is easy to find, so be sure to stop. South of town from 1st Street, a **Beach Loop** runs along a ridge overlooking a fantastic assemblage of coastal monoliths.

Bandon Lighthouse

For fish and chips along the waterfront, the **Bandon Fish Market** at 249 1st Street is cheap and cheerful, but for more sit-down fare and a view of the lighthouse, head to **Bandon Boatworks**, on South Jetty Road (541/347-2111). For a place to stay, try the warm and woodsy **Sea Star Guesthouse**, 375 2nd Street (541/347-9632), offering B&B rooms for $40-85 and HI-approved hostel bunks for $16, $13 for members. Private hostel rooms are also available, for around $30.

Port Orford and Humbug Mountain

Pastoral sheep ranches, cranberry bogs, berry fields, and Christmas tree farms dominate the 25-mile stretch south of Bandon, but as you pull into Port Orford (pop. 1,025), you'll notice a huge volcanic plug abutting the crescent-shaped shoreline. Known as **Battle Rock**, it's where early settlers fought off a party of hostile Indians; the rock is most impressive from the harbor below. Due to the southwest orientation, which subjects the harbor to turbulent winds and constant waves, fishing boats have to be lowered into the water by crane.

A nice place to stay in Port Orford is the **Home by the Sea B&B**, 444 Jackson Street (541/332-2855), walking distance to town along a stunning stretch of coastline.

Six miles south of Port Orford you'll come to Humbug Mountain, whose 1,756-foot elevation flanks the west side of the highway. It's the coast's highest peak rising directly off the beach, and its steep contours and tree-covered slopes impart an eerily beautiful quality to the light on this section of US-101. The mountain's name was bestowed by prospectors who found that tales of gold deposits here were just "humbug."

Prehistoric Gardens

On the west side of the highway, midway between Port Orford and Gold Beach, you'll come across one of the Oregon coast's tackiest but most enduring and enjoyable tourist traps, the Prehistoric Gardens (daily 8 AM-dusk; $6 adults, under 3 free). Standing out like a sore thumb on this otherwise unspoiled stretch of US-101, a collection of brightly colored, more or less life-sized dinosaur sculptures inhabits the evocatively lush green forest. Since 1953, when amateur paleontologist E.V. Nelson sculpted his first concrete T. Rex, two dozen more have been added to the forest menagerie.

Gold Beach

Gold Beach was named for the nuggets mined from area black sands during the mid-19th century, but despite its name this is

South of Bandon and 11 miles north of Port Orford, **Cape Blanco** is considered —by Oregonians, at least— the westernmost point of land in the contiguous U.S. Named by early Spanish explorers for the white shells encrusting the 245-foot cliff face, the cape is also the site of Oregon's oldest (circa 1870) and highest lighthouse.

People who keep track of these things say that tiny Port Orford is the **"Most Westerly Incorporated City in the Continental U.S.,"** as well as the rainiest place on the Oregon coast.

Oregon myrtle, a lollipop-shaped laurel tree whose swirling blond grain spawned scores of roadside shops purveying clocks, bowls, and other souvenirs, can be seen overhanging the road around Humbug Mountain.

Southern Oregon coastal forests yield the increasingly rare **Port Orford cedar,** a fragrant, lightweight but strong wood valued at $10,000 a tree, thanks to a high demand for its use in Japanese home construction.

one coastal town where the action is definitely *away* from the beach. The **Rogue River** defines the northern city limits and is the town's economic raison d'être. During salmon season, Gold Beach hotels and restaurants fill up with anglers, while **jet boat tours** of the wild river are also a draw. Along with many other operators hawking their services with billboards next to the highway, **Jerry's Jetboats** ($30; 541/247-4571 or 800/451-3645), by the bridge at the north end of town, takes passengers upstream to the isolated hamlet of **Agness,** where a homespun mountain lodge serves family-style fried chicken lunches and dinners (though the food is not included in the price of the jet boat ride). Other trips head farther upstream to the Rogue River rapids and the roadless wilderness areas of the Siskiyou National Forest; these cost $50-$75.

In town, good seafood can be had across the bridge at **The Rod n' Reel**; save room for the great pie here. Above-average, ocean-view rooms are available at **Ireland's Rustic Lodges,** on US-101 at 1120 S. Ellensburg Avenue (541/247-7718).

Mount Emily, just east of Brookings, was bombed by a submarine-launched Japanese seaplane in September 1942. Though the Japanese plans to ignite the entire coastline in a massive forest fire fizzled, the attack weakened a secession movement by southern Oregonians and Northern Californians to establish a new state, called Jefferson.

The warm mean annual temperature on these parts of the Oregon and Northern California coast is conducive to beautiful flowers ranging from 20-foot high azaleas to acres of Easter lilies, of which the coastal southern Oregon region produces 90% of the world's crop.

Northbound visitors may want to stop to pick up maps and brochures at the **Oregon Welcome Center** (daily 9 AM-5 PM, April-Oct. only), across US-101 from Harris Beach State Park.

Samuel Boardman State Park

Between Gold Beach and Brookings, US-101's windy, hilly roadbed is studded with the cliffside ocean vistas, giant conifers, and boomerang-shaped offshore rock formations of Samuel Boardman State Park. The park covers most of the "Fabulous 50" miles between the two towns, and all of the above-mentioned features come together at **Natural Bridges Cove,** just north of the Thomas Creek Bridge, the highest bridge on the coast north of San Francisco's Golden Gate. Despite a sign, this turnout is easy to miss because, from the highway, it appears to be simply a parking lot fronting some trees; from the south end of the lot, however, a short trail through an old-growth forest leads to a viewpoint several hundred feet above three natural rock archways standing out from an azure cove.

South of the bridge, just north of suburban Brookings, one final piece of nature has been preserved at **Harris Beach State Park,** across US-101 from the Oregon Welcome Center. Here you can walk down to a driftwood-laden beach and look out at numerous bird-infested islands.

Brookings

The drive through Brookings's malled-over main drag offers only fleeting glimpses of the Pacific, and the town itself offers no real reason to stop. Still, if you're hungry, quality food at budget prices can be found at **Mama's Italian Restaurant,** along US-101 at 703 Chetco Avenue, where there really is a five-foot-tall Italian mama to heap your plate with pasta. For Mexican food, try **Rubie's** at the north end of town.

After the last 350-plus miles of scenic splendor, the final few miles along the coast south to California are somewhat anticlimactic, though just over the border is Redwood National Park, truly one of the West Coast's great places.

ALONG THE CALIFORNIA COAST

Stretching along the Pacific Ocean for roughly a thousand miles from top to tail, the California coast includes virgin wilderness as well as the cutting edge of cosmopolitan culture, and covers the full spectrum in between. And for almost the entire way, coastal roads give quick and easy access to all the best parts, with panoramic views appearing so often you'll either run out of film, or simply give up trying to capture it all.

Starting in the north, the green forests of the Pacific Northwest continue well beyond the state border, forming a mountainous seaside landscape that lasts until the edge of metropolitan San Francisco. Along this stretch you'll find a number of old logging and fishing towns, varying from the burly blue-collar likes of Eureka and Crescent City to the upscale ambience of Mendocino, in and amongst endless acres of redwood forest.

At the approximate midpoint of the California coast sits San Francisco, deservedly ranked among the world's favorite cities. The hundred miles of coast stretching south from San Francisco hold numerous remnants of the Spanish and Mexican eras, exemplified by the town of Monterey and the beautiful mission at Carmel. Beyond here is another stretch of wild coastline, the rugged country of Big Sur.

Beyond the southern edge of Big Sur, opulent Hearst Castle marks the start of what most people consider Southern California, the rivers and trees of the north giving way to golden beaches, grassy bluffs, and considerably denser populations. A pair of very pleasant small cities, Midwestern-feeling San Luis Obispo and ritzy Santa Barbara, make excellent stops in themselves, smoothing the transition into the environs of Los Angeles, the unwieldy megalopolis that, seen from the I-5 freeway that links Los Angeles and San Diego, seems like one monstrous, 100-mile-long suburb. While it's true that the natural beauty that brought so many people to Southern California in the first place is increasingly endangered, some lovely, almost untouched places remain, hidden away but within easy access of the fast lane. We've pointed them out; enjoy them while they last.

Jedediah Smith Redwoods State Park

The northernmost of the great redwood groves, Jedediah Smith Redwoods State Park covers nearly 10,000 acres of virgin forest along the banks of the Smith River. Stretching east of US-101, and most easily accessible from US-199, the

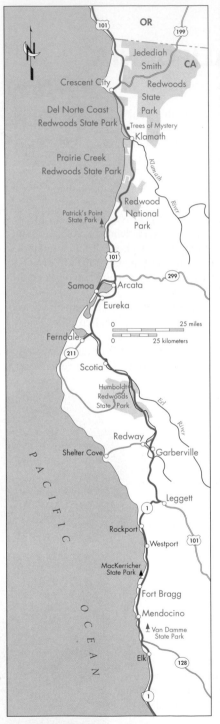

park offers over 30 miles of usually un-crowded hiking trails through the pristine wilderness, and is considered by many to be the most perfect of all the redwood forests. One of the most enjoyable trails leads through **Stout Grove** past the park's tallest tree and a number of summertime swimming holes along the Smith River.

The park is jointly managed by the state and federal governments, which is why there are two **ranger stations** (707/ 464-9533 or 707/458-3134) across from each other along US-199 at the main entrance to the park, four miles east of US-101. There's also a good **campground** with hot showers.

Crescent City

The county seat and largest city in Del Norte County, Crescent City (pop. 4,380) is best treated as a base from which to explore the surrounding wilderness. The foggy weather that helps the redwoods thrive makes the city fairly depressing and gray, and what character it developed since its founding in 1853 has been further eroded by storms; a giant tidal wave, caused by the 1964 earthquake off Alaska, destroyed nearly the entire city.

Crescent City includes the usual motels (including a **Travelodge** and a **Best Western**) and restaurants, as well as one unique spot: the **Ship Ashore**, a gift shop, restaurant, and motel along US-101 about 10 miles north of town, marked by a grounded ship.

Crescent City does have the headquarters for **Redwood National Park**; a block east of US-101 at 1111 2nd Street (707/464-6101), this is the best source of information for southbound travelers.

Del Norte Coast Redwoods State Park

Spreading south from the Jedediah Smith redwoods, Del Norte Coast Redwoods State Park runs along the Pacific Ocean (and US-101) for about 10 miles, containing more than 6,000 acres of first- and second-growth redwoods as well as brilliant blooms of rhododendrons, azaleas, and spring wildflowers. Del Norte also protects miles of untouched coastline, the best stretch of which is accessible from the end of **Enderts Beach Road**, which cuts west from US-101 just north of the park entrance. From here, a 30-mile trail follows the coast to Prairie Creek.

The Smith River and Jedediah Smith redwood park were named in memory of the legendary mountain man, **Jedediah Strong Smith,** who in 1826 at the age of 27 led the first party of Americans overland to California.

The state park area is bounded on the south by an undeveloped section of Redwood National Park. Amongst the trees, the HI Redwood Hostel (707/482-8265), 14480 US-101, 12 miles south of Crescent City and two miles north of the Trees of Mystery, is housed in a historic farmhouse and offers cozy dormitory accommodations and a few private rooms for about $12 per person for members, $15 nonmembers.

Outside Crescent City, California's most violent, long-term criminals are kept behind bars in the state-of-the-art **Pelican Bay State Prison,** built in 1990.

Trees of Mystery and Klamath

Hard to miss along US-101, thanks to the massive statues of Paul Bunyan and Babe the Blue Ox looming over the highway, the Trees of Mystery (daily 8 AM-dusk; $6.50) are literally and figuratively the biggest tourist draws on the Northern California coast. Along the "Tall Tales Trail," chainsaw-cut figures, backed by audio-taped stories, stand in tableaux at the foot of towering redwoods; there's also a huge gift shop and a small free museum of Native American art and artifacts. Across the highway, **Motel Trees** (707/482-3152) has standard rooms from $40 and a coffee shop.

All the land along the Klamath River is part of the extensive **Hoopa Valley Indian Reservation,** which stretches for over 30 miles upstream from the Pacific Ocean.

Along the banks of the mighty Klamath River, four miles south of the Trees of Mystery, the town of Klamath is a brief burst of highway sprawl, supported by anglers who flock here for the annual salmon runs. At the south end of town, drive through the **Tour-Thru Tree** ($2), then cross the Klamath River on a bridge graced by a pair of gilded cement grizzly bears.

Though the Jedediah Smith, Del Norte Coast, and Prairie Creek redwoods are on state-owned land, they are managed jointly under the auspices of Redwood National Park.

Prairie Creek Redwoods State Park

The largest of the trio of north coast redwood parks, Prairie Creek Redwoods State Park is best known for its large herd of endangered **Roosevelt elk**, which you can usually see grazing in the meadows along US-101 at the center of the park, next to the main **ranger station** (707/488-2171). A new freeway carries US-101 traffic around, rather than through, the Prairie Creek redwoods; to reach the best sights, detour along the well-signed "Elk Prairie Parkway," which follows Prairie Creek through the heart of the park.

Another elk herd can be spotted among the coastal dunes at **Gold Bluffs Beach**, which stretches for 11 miles through untouched wilderness; there's a primitive **campground** and trails leading from US-101, or you can follow Davison Road northwest from US-101, three miles south of the ranger station. Apart from the elk, Prairie Creek offers the usual mix of old-growth redwood trees, which here more than in the other parks mingle with dense growths of Sitka spruce and Douglas firs to form a near rainforest of greenery.

Redwood National Park

Established in 1968, and later enlarged at a total cost of over $500 million, Redwood National Park protects some 100,000 acres of redwood forest, including the 30,000 acres previously preserved in the adjacent Smith, Del Norte and Prairie Creek State Parks. To be honest, apart from the adjacent state parks, the trees preserved here aren't by any means the oldest, largest, or most beautiful; in fact, much of the federal parkland is second- or third-growth timber, clearcut as recently as the 1960s. Though redwoods are the fastest-growing softwoods on earth—growing three to five feet a year when young—the groves here are rather disappointing compared to those in nearby areas, and serve more as an environmental buffer zone than a tree-lover's pilgrimage site.

The groves of giant trees in Redwood National Park were used as a location for the *Star Wars* film *Return of the Jedi*. The characters cruised through the forest on airborne cycles. More recently, Patrick's Point played a starring role in *Jurassic Park*.

The author **Bret Harte** was run out of Arcata by angry townspeople in 1860, after writing an editorial in the local paper criticizing a massacre of a local Wiyot tribe.

That said, Redwood National Park does hold two special sights: the **Lady Bird Johnson Grove**, on a logging road a mile east of US-101, dedicated in 1968; and the **Tall Trees Grove**, which holds the world's tallest tree, the 368-foot Libbey Tree, reachable via an all-day hike and by summer-only shuttle buses (see below).

At the south end of the park, enjoy Teutonic breakfasts at the German-run **Rolf's Park Cafe**, attached to the fairly basic, $40-a-night **Prairie Creek Motel** (707/488-3841); for over 15 years, the pair have made a good budget base for exploring Redwood National Park and environs. The roadside strip town of **Orick** stretches south toward the coast, where the main Redwood National Park **visitor center** (707/488-3461) stands at the mouth of Redwood Creek; catch the Tall Trees Grove shuttle bus here.

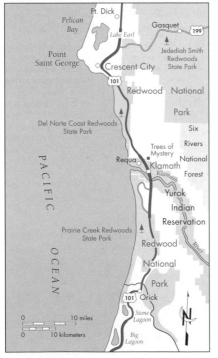

Patrick's Point State Park

If your idea of heaven is sitting on a rocky headland listening to the roar of the Pacific while watching the sunset or looking for passing gray whales, you won't want to pass by Patrick's Point State Park. Three different 200-foot-high promontories at the heart of the park provide panoramic views, while the surrounding acres hold cedar and spruce forests—no redwoods—open pastures bright with wildflowers, great tide-pools, a wide dark sand beach, and two **campgrounds** with hot showers. There's also preserved and restored remnants of a Yurok village; obtain further information and camping reservations from the **visitor center** (707/677-3570).

Continuing south, US-101 becomes a four-lane freeway along the ocean to Arcata and Eureka, but the old US-101 alignment winds along the cliff tops between Patrick's Point and the small town of Trinidad. Along this road you'll find some nice older motels, like the **Patrick's Point Inn** at 3602 Patrick's Point Drive (707/677-3483 or 800/354-7006), which is just a half-mile from the park entrance, and has oceanside rooms from around $60 a night. Also here is the excellent **Larrupin Cafe**, 1658 Patrick's Point Drive (707/677-0230), which serves up bountiful portions of very fresh all-American food in a friendly, homey ambience—California Cuisine without the snooty pretense you sometimes find farther south. It's open for dinner only, every day but Tuesday, and is cash-only; two can dine well for around $50.

Arcata

The most attractive and enjoyable town on the far north coast of California, Arcata (pop. 15,197) makes the best first (or last, depending upon your direction) overnight stop south of the Oregon border. The presence of Humboldt State University campus on the hills above US-101 accounts for the town's youthful, non-conformist energy, especially in the cafes, bookstores, and clubs that surround the lively **Town Plaza**, two blocks west of US-101 at 9th and G Streets, incongruously graced by palm trees and a statue of President McKinley. The *Utne Reader* recently rated Arcata as "the most enlightened small town in California," and spending even a little time here in this vibrant, cooperative Ecotopia may make you wonder whether or not you really do have to race back to the big city 9-to-5 grind.

You can admire the town's many elaborate Victorian-era cottages, hunt wild mushrooms, clamber over sand dunes or hike in the redwoods; afterwards relax with a cup of tea or, better yet, a soak in a hot tub at homey **Cafe Mokka**, the coast's only combo sauna and espresso bar at 5th and J Streets (707/822-2228). Good cheap Mexican health food—try the tofu burritos —can be had from the popular **Casa de Que Pasa**, 854 9th Street a block from the plaza, while micro-

*"Just for the Halibut"
sculpture racing along
Samoa Peninsula*

brewed beers flow from the taps of Arcata's amiable bars, many of which feature live music; try **Jambalaya** at 915 H Street, or the **Humboldt Brewery**, 856 10th Street. For a complete selection of foodstuffs and supplies, and more insight into the local community, head to the large and stylish **Arcata Co-op**, at 8th and I street uphill from the plaza.

KINETIC SCULPTURE RACE

Arcata's creative community comes alive every Memorial Day weekend for the world-famous Kinetic Sculpture Race, in which participants pedal, paddle, and otherwise move themselves and their handmade vehicles across land and sea. Part art, part engineering and part athletic competition, the kinetic sculpture race is like nothing you've seen before. Beginning midday Saturday and running around the clock until Monday afternoon, a mind-boggling array of mobile contraptions—past winners have included everything from dragons and floating flying saucers to Egyptian Pyramids (named "Queen of Denial") and a Cadillac Coupe de Ville—make their way over land, sand and sea from the town square of Arcata to the main street of Ferndale, twice crossing chilly Humboldt Bay.

Rule Number One of the Kinetic Sculpture Race is that all of the "sculptures" must be people-powered; beyond that, imagination is the primary guide. Many "rules" have developed over the years since the race was first run in 1969, including such pearls as: "In the Event of Rain, the Race Is Run in the Rain," but most of these emphasize the idea that maintaining style and a sense of humor are at least as important as finishing the fastest. Since the Grand Prizes are valued at somewhere around $14.98, racers take part solely "for the glory," but prizes are awarded in many categories: first- and last-place finishers are winners, and the racer who finishes in the exact middle of the pack gets the coveted Medio-Car Award—a broken-down old banger.

Spectators are expected to be active participants, too, so be prepared to shout and scream and applaud the competitors, or even jog or bike or kayak alongside them. There are many great vantage points along the route, but you have to be in the right place on the right day. The Kinetic Sculpture Race begins at noon on Saturday with a pre-race line-up around Arcata's Town Square, from where racers wind along country roads to the sandy Samoa Peninsula before spending the first night in downtown Eureka. Sunday morning the racers head across Humboldt Bay from Field's Landing, then camp out overnight along the ocean. Monday's trials include another water crossing and the muddy mess of the Slimey Slope, culminating in a mad dash down the Main Street of Ferndale surrounded by cheering multitudes. It's all good fun, and a great focus for a visit to this remarkable corner of the world.

For further information, call the race organizers (707/786-9259) or the Eureka! visitors bureau (800/346-3482).

For a place to stay, the centrally located **Hotel Arcata** (707/ 826-0217 or 800/344-1221), on the plaza at 708 9th Street, has rooms from $60, or you can take your pick of the usual motels along US-101.

Eureka

Evolving into a lively artists' colony from its roots as a fairly gritty and industrial port, Eureka was well known to fur trappers and traders long before it became a booming lumber and whaling port in the 1850s. Thanks to the lumber trade, Victorian Eureka grew prosperous, building elaborate homes including the oft-photographed but closed-to-the-public *the Carson Mansion*

Carson Mansion along the waterfront at 2nd and M Streets, two blocks west of US-101.

Along with dozens of well-preserved Victorian houses, Eureka has done a fine job of finding new uses for its many ornate commercial buildings, most of which have been preserved to house cafes and restaurants in what's now called Old Town, a half dozen blocks between the waterfront and US-101. This historic downtown quarter has a number of good places to eat and drink, including the pub-like **Cafe Waterfront** at 1st and F Streets, and the popular **Sea Grill**, a block from US-101 at 316 E Street. Another good place is the no-frills **Seafood Grotto** ("We Ketch 'em, Cook 'em, Serve 'em"), south of Old Town along US-101 at 6th and Broadway. Old Town Eureka also has many very nice art galleries, bookshops, and some much-appreciated cafes like **Ramone's Bakery**, 209 E Street.

Inland from Arcata along scenic US-299, the town of Willow Creek claims to be the heart of "Bigfoot Country," boasting a large statue of the furry beast to prove it. US-299 continues east over the coast range through the beautiful Trinity Alps to **Weaverville**, well-preserved site of a mid-1850s gold rush, before linking up with I-5 at Redding.

Accommodation options range from roadside motels—including a handy **Travelodge** on US-101 downtown—to upscale places like the **Carter House Inn**, 1033 3rd Street (707/445-1390), a re-created Victorian manor with spacious rooms and a big breakfast for $125 and up. For a more authentic Victorian experience, stay at one of California's most delightful B&Bs, the **Elegant Victorian Mansion** at 1406 C Street (707/444-3144). A real treasure in a land of nice B&Bs, this magnificently restored 1888 Eastlake-style home has been opulently decorated with real antiques and Bradbury & Bradbury wallpapers by the hospitable Belgian-born innkeeper Lily Vieyra, and offers four nonsmoking rooms, ranging from $85 to $225 a night.

For further information, contact the **Eureka! Humboldt County Convention and Visitors' Bureau** at 1034 2nd Street (707/443-5097 or 800/338-7352).

Samoa

Even if you're just passing through, don't miss the chance to visit the busy mill town of Samoa, across the bay from Eureka but easily reachable via the Hwy-255 bridge. Follow the signs past the piles of logs and belching mill chimneys to the

One unique thing to see in Eureka are the Romano Gabriel Wooden Sculptures, displayed in a plate-glass showcase at 315 2nd Street. This brilliantly colorful folk art extravaganza of faces and flowers originally stood in the front yard of local gardener Romano Gabriel, who made them out of discarded packing crates and other recycled materials over a period of some 30 years before his death in 1977.

The area around Ferndale has been hit by numerous earthquakes, including a destructive tremor in April 1992 that registered 6.9 on the Richter scale.

West of Ferndale, the narrow, winding Mattole Road loops around Cape Mendocino through the northern reaches of the so-called **"Lost Coast,"** a stretch of shoreline justly famous for its isolated beauty. This area was also the site of the first oil wells in California, which were drilled in the 1860s near the town of Petrolia but are long gone.

unique **Samoa Cookhouse** (707/442-1659), built at the turn of the century by the Louisiana Pacific lumber company, which still owns most of the peninsula. Inside the cookhouse, which is packed with logging memorabilia, take a seat at one of the 20-foot-long tables (redwood, of course, covered in checkered oilcloth) and dig into the family-style feast. There are no menus, just huge platters of food at ridiculously low prices—$5.95 for breakfast (from 6 AM, with great hash browns!) and $6.65 for lunch (served till 3 PM), $11.45 for a two-meat, four-course dinner (served 5-9 PM, 5-10 PM in summer).

Ferndale

Well worth the 10-mile detour west of US-101, the historic town of Ferndale (pop. 1,331) is an odd fish along the woodsy Northern California coast, a century-old dairy town that would look more at home in middle America. The three-block-long, franchise-free Main Street includes a fully stocked general store and the Golden Gait/Gate Mercantile, and whitewashed farmhouses dot the pastoral valleys nearby. Ferndale's diverse history is well documented inside the **Ferndale Museum**, off Main Street at Shaw and 3rd Streets (hours vary; 707/786-4466), and the wacky racers that take part in the annual Kinetic Sculpture Race are displayed in the center of town at 393 Main Street.

The fine food at **Curley's Grill**, 460 Main Street, have made it a popular place to eat, while *the* place to stay (or at least to see) in Ferndale is the lushly landscaped late-Victorian **Gingerbread Mansion**, 400 Berding Street (707/786-4000), with deluxe rooms from around $100 a night. Also nice is the **Shaw House**, an 1854 American Gothic masterpiece with B&B rooms and bikes for rent at 703 Main Street (707/786-9958).

Pick up free walking-tour maps and other visitor information at the **chamber of commerce** on Main Street (707/786-4477).

Scotia

Back along US-101, on the banks of the Eel River midway between the coast and the Humboldt Redwoods, Scotia is the only true company town left in California. The Pacific Lumber Company (a.k.a. "PALCO") built it and still owns everything, from the two huge mills to the 10 blocks of white-painted houses, church, and schools that constitute this little community of about 1,000 people.

Stop first at the small **museum**, housed in the redwood-built Greek Revival former bank at the center of town, to pick up passes for self-guided **tours** (Mon.-Fri. 7:30 AM-2 PM; free) of the world's largest redwood mill. Following a yellow painted line through the mill at your own pace, you can gawk at (and listen to—it's a noisy business) every stage of the milling process. First, cut logs get de-barked by a powerful jet of water, then laser-guided band saws slice the logs into rough boards, which are turned into finished lumber. A raised catwalk runs through the center of the mill, and signs explain what's happening at each stage.

The one place to stay in town is the rustic **Scotia Inn** (707/764-5683), which has B&B rooms ($60-160 a night) and a very good restaurant; it's on Main Street, a block from the Scotia museum.

Humboldt Redwoods State Park

Sheltering the biggest and best collection of giant coastal redwoods anywhere in the world, Humboldt Redwoods State Park is an exceptionally breathtaking corner of an exceptionally beautiful region. Covering 50,000 acres along the Eel River, this is the true heart of redwood country, containing the largest and most pristine expanses of virgin forest as well as some of the largest, tallest, and most remarkable trees.

Even if you're just passing through, be sure to turn onto the amazing **Avenue of the Giants**, 31 miles of old highway frontage between Jordan Creek and Phillipsville running parallel to the faster and busier US-101 freeway through the park. At the north end of the park you'll find an impressive collection of trees in the well-marked **Founders Grove**, where a half-mile nature trail leads past the 362-foot-tall, 1,600-year-old **Dyerville Giant**, lauded as the world's tallest tree before it fell during the winter of 1991. West of Founder's Grove, across US-101, the 13,000-acre **Rockefeller Forest** is one of the largest old-growth forests in the world, and includes two of the park's champion trees, each over 360 feet tall and some 17 feet in diameter.

The protection of the mighty redwood forests of Northern California was made possible not by the state or federal governments but primarily by the efforts of the **Save the Redwoods League,** a private organization that has raised, since its founding in 1918, millions of dollars to buy or preserve over 160,000 acres of redwood forest. To support these efforts, write to 114 Sansome Street, Room 605, San Francisco, CA 94104, or call 415/362-2352.

The well-graded fire roads through the Rockefeller Forest make excellent mountain bike routes.

At the south end of Leggett, the "original" Drive-Thru Tree

REDWOOD COUNTRY ROADSIDE ATTRACTIONS

The stretch of US-101 through the redwood country of Humboldt County is lined by pristine groves of massive trees and provides boundless opportunities to come face-to-face with your own insignificance in nature's greater scheme of things.

If you tire of this display of natural majesty, or simply want to keep it in context with the modern "civilized" world, you're in luck: every few miles, amongst the stately trees, you'll come upon shameless souvenir stands selling redwood burl furniture and chainsaw sculptures—including one featuring Biblical figures, called "Carving for Christ"—as well as tacky tourist traps like the "**World of Bigfoot**" or "**Hobbittown USA**," in Phillipsville. None of these is big or bold enough to detract from the main event—the big trees—but since they've been in operation since the early days of car-borne tourism, they're as much a part of the redwood experience as the trees themselves. Most charge only a few dollars' admission, so there's not a lot to lose.

While you're encouraged to stop at any and all of them—at least long enough to buy a postcard or two—some of the more tried-and-true attractions are the **Trees of Mystery**, marked by huge statues of Paul Bunyan and Babe the Blue Ox along US-101 in Klamath (see page 55); the **One-Log House** in Phillipsville, a mobile home carved from a single, 32-foot redwood log; and the **Shrine Drive-Thru Tree**, 13078 Avenue of the Giants (old US-101) in Myers Flat, which wagon-borne travelers drove through more than a century ago. In the south, near the town of Leggett, are two more. **Confusion Hill** is one of those places where water runs uphill and the rules of physics seem not to apply. There's also a little railway train here that chugs uphill to a very nice grove of trees. **Chandelier Drive-Thru Tree**, south of Leggett off old US-101 on Drive-Thru Tree Road, allows you to drive your car through a 315-foot redwood tree.

Most of the old towns along the Eel River were destroyed by a terrible flood in 1964, when the river rose as high as 35 feet above the Avenue of the Giants.

The best source of information on the park is the **visitor center** (707/946-2263) in **Weott**, which also has a pleasant **campground** ($14) with showers, right next door. You may have to drive a ways north (to Ferndale, Eureka, or Arcata) or south (to Garberville) from the park to find a good meal, though there are two nice places to stay at the southern end of the park: the **Country Inn** (707/943-3259) in Myers Flat has B&B rooms from $60, while the hamlet of Miranda holds the pleasant **Miranda Gardens Resort** (707/943-3011), with motel rooms and rustic cabins at $50-140 a night.

Garberville and Redway

Since its recurring presence in the national media during the U.S. government's high-profile, late 1980s raids on local marijuana plantations, Garberville has returned to its previous sleepy self. The US-101 freeway bypasses the town, which stretches for a half-dozen blocks along Redwood Drive, the well-signed business loop off the highway.

Enjoy an early morning breakfast with the old-time locals at the **Eel River Cafe**, 801 Redwood Avenue, or enjoy an espresso and healthy food at the **Woodrose Cafe**, a block south at 911 Redwood Avenue. Garberville also has all the motels you could want, including the **Motel Garberville**, 948 Redwood Drive (707/923-2422).

Just west of Garberville on the old highway, Redway is a small and usually quiet enclave that's best known for organizing the annual **Reggae on the River** festival (707/923-3368), which attracts top performers and thousands of fans to French's Campground near Piercy every August. Redway is worth the short sidetrip during the rest of the year, if only for breakfast, lunch, or dinner at the **Mateel Cafe**, a health-conscious gourmet haunt along Redwood Avenue at the center of town.

Along US-101, four miles south of Garberville, one of the region's most characterful places is the **Benbow Inn** (707/923-2124), a circa 1926 mock Tudor hotel with fairly pricey rooms and a nice restaurant offering afternoon tea and scones on a sunny terrace overlooking Lake Benbow.

Leggett

No longer even a proverbial wide spot in the road since the US-101 freeway was diverted around it, Leggett marks the southern end of the Humboldt redwoods. One exceptional reason to stop here is the **Bell Glen** (707/925-6425), which spreads between the highway and the Eel River and offers a number of comfortable, romantic cottages (from $95) as well as clean but basic dorm beds ($15) in the **Eel River Redwoods Hostel**. A small but worthwhile restaurant on site specializes in local fish and seasonally varying entrees using fresh local produce.

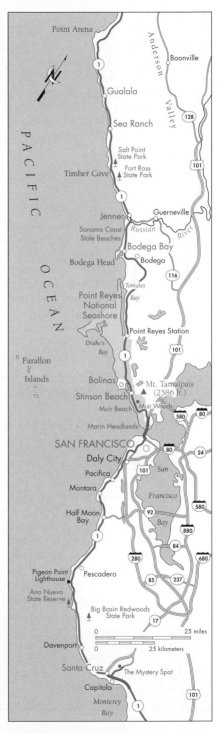

From Redway, a well-maintained road heads over the coast range to **Shelter Cove**, at the center of the wild "Lost Coast."

At the south end of Leggett, a mile from the US-101/Hwy-1 junction along the old highway, stands one of the redwood region's most venerable and worthwhile roadside attractions, the "original" **Drive-Thru Tree** (daily 8 AM-dusk; $3). In addition to the famous tree, which had the hole cut through it in the 1930s, there's an above-average gift shop with a broad range of books, postcards, and schlocky souvenirs.

South of Leggett, US-101 runs inland, while scenic Hwy-1 cuts west over the coastal mountains to Mendocino, winding along the Pacific south to San Francisco.

Fort Bragg

From US-101 at Leggett, Hwy-1 twists over the rugged coastal mountains before hugging the coast through the weatherbeaten logging and fishing communities of **Rockport** and **Westport**. The small and informal **Howard Creek Ranch** (707/964-6725) in Westport offers comfortable B&B rooms, an outdoor hot tub, and easy access to the driftwood-laden beach. Farther south, **MacKerricher State Park** protects seven miles of rocky coast and waterfront pine forest; the campground, as in all California state parks, is reservable through the private concessionaire ParkNet (800/444-PARK or 800/444-7275).

It takes more than an hour to cover the 44 miles between US-101 and the first real town, Fort Bragg (pop. 6,100), whose burly, blue-collar edge comes as something of a shock on the otherwise undeveloped, touristy Mendocino coast. Home to a large Georgia Pacific lumber mill and the region's largest commercial fishing fleet, Fort Bragg takes a mostly no-frills approach to the tourist trade, leaving the

---

US-101 THROUGH THE WINE COUNTRY

If you don't have enough time to follow the gorgeous coastal route along Hwy-1, don't despair: the faster inland route is plenty pretty. US-101 runs through the heart of the wine country of Sonoma and Mendocino Counties, where vineyards and tasting rooms line the roadside, and extensive forests cover the surrounding hills and mountains. Amidst the scenery are a few diverse towns, ranging from the fairly industrial environs of **Ukiah**, midway along, to quiet communities like **Cloverdale**, **Geyserville**, and **Willits**, where the "Skunk Train" runs over the coast to Fort Bragg.

If you only have time for one stop, make it **Hopland**, halfway between Leggett and San Francisco. As the name suggests, this is an old hop-growing district now home to the excellent Mendocino Brewing Company, makers of Red Tail Ale and other fine brews, which you can sample at the brewpub along US-101. Next door to the brewery, the **Cheesecake Lady** bakes excellent desserts and snacks; across the highway, the **Bluebird Cafe** serves up delectable and plentiful meals.

Mendocino

dainty B&B scene to its upscale neighbor, Mendocino. However, there are a few down-to-earth places to eat: very good omelettes and other eggy dishes are available at the appropriately named **Egghead Restaurant**, 326 N. Main Street, while **The Wharf**, along the Noyo River at 780 N. Harbor Drive, serves good value seafood dinners. Fort Bragg's many motels, including the **Fort Bragg Motel**, 763 N. Main Street (707/964-4787), are the coast's only cheap accommodation options, after camping.

For more complete information on the Fort Bragg/Mendocino area, contact the **North Coast Chamber of Commerce**, 332 N. Main Street (707/961-6300 or 800/726-2780).

From Fort Bragg, the California & Western Railroad runs a number of historic steam- and diesel-powered **"Skunk Trains"** over the mountains to Willits and back. Half-day and full-day trips ($25-35; 707/964-6372) run year-round.

Mendocino

One of the prettiest towns on the California coast (as seen in TV shows like *Murder, She Wrote* and numerous movies), Mendocino (pop. 1,100) is an artists-and-writers community par excellence, and an upscale escape for wage-slaving visitors from San Francisco. Originally established as a logging port in the 1850s, Mendocino successfully preserved both its sandstone coastline—great for wintertime whale-watching—and its New England-style clapboard houses, many of which have been converted into $100-a-night inns. The lovely **MacCallum House**, 45020 Albion Street (707/937-0289), includes a beautiful garden, good breakfasts, and a cozy nighttime bar and restaurant. Another place to stay is the circa 1858 **Mendocino Hotel**, on the downtown waterfront at 45080 Main Street (707/937-0511).

Along with its many fine art galleries, bakeries, cafes and bookshops, Mendocino has one of California's best restaurants, **Cafe Beaujolais**, two blocks from the waterfront at 961 Ukiah Street (707/937-5614), which serves a world famous prix fixe gourmet feast of California cuisine delicacies for dinner, nightly 6-9 PM.

Van Damme State Park

South of Mendocino at the mouth of the Little River, Van Damme State Park stretches for five miles along the coastal bluffs and beaches and includes some 1,800 acres of pine and redwood forest. The park's unique attribute is the oddly contorted **Pygmy Forest**, a natural bonsai-like grove of miniature pines, cypress, and manzanita, with a wheelchair-accessible nature trail explaining the unique ecology; the trailhead is four miles east of Hwy-1. There's also a small, very popular campground, and a **visitor center** (707/937-0851) housed in a New Deal-era recreation hall.

One place worth keeping an eye out for is the tiny roadside community of **Elk,** 15 miles south of Mendocino along Hwy-1, which has a good cafe, a general store, and a trail leading down to the Pacific at Greenwood Cove.

Detour: Anderson Valley

From Hwy-1 south of Mendocino, Hwy-128 cuts diagonally across to US-101 through the lovely Anderson Valley, home to numerous fine wineries (including Husch, Navarro, and Kendall-Jackson) and the *Anderson Valley Advertiser*, one of California's most outspoken local newspapers. Anderson Valley also has its own regional dialect, called "Boontling," combining English, Scots-Irish, Spanish, and Native American words into a lighthearted lingo created, some say, simply to befuddle outsiders—to "shark the bright-lighters."

To find out more, stop in the valley's tiny main town, **Boonville**, at the bookshop alongside the Horn of Zeese coffee shop. Another place to check out is next door's Anderson Valley Brewing Company, a pub-like restaurant and saloon that's the birthplace of delicious Boont Amber, the state's finest microbrew.

Gualala

The southernmost 40 miles of Mendocino coastline are almost totally undeveloped and virtually uninhabited, with green forests and coastal coves as far as the eye can see. Situated at the very southern edge of the county, the old logging port of Gualala (pop. 950) has one truly remarkable feature: the Russian Orthodox domes of **St. Orres** (707/884-3303), now a B&B inn and very expensive Francophile gourmet restaurant glowing with polished wood and stained glass, above Hwy-1 on the north side of town. You'll also find inexpensive lodging (rooms for less than $50 a night, a real rarity in these parts) and a locally popular restaurant right in town at the **Gualala Hotel** (707/884-3441).

At the north end of Gualala, be sure to stop at **The Food Company** deli and sample some of the world's finest ginger cookies, baked fresh daily and truly delicious. The deli also offers a full range of picnic foods—salads, dips, breads, beers, wines—and did we mention the ginger cookies?

Sea Ranch

Midway between Mendocino and the San Francisco Bay Area, the vacation home community of Sea Ranch was laid out in the mid-1960s by an enthusiastic group of then-young architects and planners, including Lawrence Halprin and the late Charles Moore, who hoped to show that development need not destroy or negatively impact the natural beauty of the California coast. Strict design guidelines, preserving over half the 5,000 acres as open space and requiring the use of muted natural wood cladding and other barn-like features, made it an aesthetic success, which you can appreciate for yourself at the **Sea Ranch Lodge** (707/785-2371). The lodge offers good meals and rooms from around $100 a night.

The rest of Sea Ranch, however, is strictly private, which has raised the hackles of area activists, who after years of lawsuits finally forced through a few coastal access trails in the mid-1980s; these are marked by turnouts (parking $2) along Hwy-1.

Salt Point State Park

The many sheltered rocky coves of Salt Point State Park make it ideal for undersea divers, who come to hunt the abundant abalone. Along the five miles of jagged shoreline, pines and redwoods clutch the water's edge, covering some 6,000 acres on both sides of Hwy-1. Though parts of the park were badly burned in a 1994 fire, Salt Point is still a prime place for hiking or camping. For more information, or for a guide to the many remnants of the Pomo tribal village that stood here until the 1850s, contact the **visitor center** (707/847-3221).

One of the few positive effects of cutting down the native redwood forests that once covered the Northern California coast has been the emergence of giant-sized rhododendrons in their place. You'll find the most impressive display at the **Kruse Rhododendron Preserve**, high above Hwy-1 at the center of Salt Point State Park, where some 350 acres of azaleas and rhododendrons, some reaching 15 feet in height, burst forth in late spring, usually peaking around the first week of May.

In between Salt Point and Fort Ross, Beniamo Bufano's 72-foot *Peace* statue looms alongside Hwy-1 above craggy **Timber Cove.**

Fort Ross State Historic Park

If you're captivated by California's lively history, one of the most evocative spots in the state is Fort Ross State Historic Park (daily 10 AM-4:30 PM; $5 per car; 707/847-3286), the well-restored remains of a Russian fur-trapping outpost built here in 1812. During a 30-year residency, the Russians farmed wheat and potatoes, traded with native tribes, and trapped local seals and sea otters for their furs, which commanded huge sums on the European market. The near destruction of the sea otter population by 1840 caused the company to shut down operations, and sell the fort to Sacramento's John Sutter, who went bankrupt to finance the purchase. Later, the abandoned fort was badly damaged by the 1906 San Francisco earthquake and later fires, but the state has completed a high-quality restoration and reconstruction project, using hand-hewn lumber and historically accurate building methods to replicate the original barracks and other buildings, including a luminous redwood chapel.

Outside the fort's walls, a modern **visitor center** traces the site's natural, native, and Russian history, and offers information on the park's many fine hiking trails.

Russian Orthodox chapel at Fort Ross

the closing of the Russian River ferry, c. 1931

Jenner and the Russian River

South of Fort Ross, Hwy-1 climbs high above the rugged coastline, offering breathtaking vistas of the Pacific Ocean hundreds of feet below. Twelve miles south of Fort Ross, Hwy-1 reaches the resort community of Jenner (pop. 300), which stretches along the broad mouth of the Russian River.

From Jenner, Hwy-116 runs east along the river, passing through forests, vineyards, and popular summertime resort towns, the largest of which is Guerneville, 12 miles away, with a number of worthwhile cafes and an alternative-minded population. After 35-odd miles, Hwy-116 eventually links up with the US-101 freeway to and from San Francisco, providing a faster alternative to coastal Hwy-1.

The **Russian River** has breached its banks many times in recent years, exceeding its usual level by some 25 feet or more. These floods have destroyed many riverfront businesses and houses, evident in the many abandoned buildings lining the Hwy-116 roadside.

Bohemian Grove, the world's most exclusive men's club, covers 2,500 acres of redwood forest just south of the Russian River outside the village of Monte Rio.

While hiking along the Sonoma Coast, be careful: over 75 people have been drowned by sleeper waves, which rise unannounced and sweep people off the rocky shore.

Sonoma Coast State Beaches

South of Jenner and the Russian River, Hwy-1 hugs the coast along 10 miles of rocky coves and sandy beaches, collectively protected as the Sonoma Coast State Beaches. Starting with Goat Rock at the southern lip of the Russian River mouth, a bluff-top trail leads past intriguingly named and usually unpopulated pocket strands like Blind Beach, Schoolhouse Beach, Shell Beach, and Salmon Creek Beach.

At the southernmost end, the park broadens to include the wildflower-covered granite promontory of **Bodega Head**, which juts into the Pacific and provides a great vantage point during the winter gray whale migrations.

Bodega Bay and Valley Ford

Protected by the massive bulk of Bodega Head, the fishing harbor of Bodega Bay has grown into an upscale vacation destination, with Sea Ranch-style vacation homes lining the fairways of golf resorts, and $120-a-night hotels overlooking the still busy commercial wharves. On the waterfront at 595 Hwy-1, the **Lucas Wharf Deli** dishes up fish and chips and clam chowder.

South of Bodega Bay, Hwy-1 cuts inland around the marshy coastal estuaries, passing by the small town of **Bodega**, which Alfred Hitchcock used for many of the scariest scenes in his 1960 movie, *The Birds*. The next town you pass through, **Valley Ford**, is a photogenic little spot that holds a great old family-run roadhouse, **Dinucci's** (707/876-3260), serving huge portions of unreconstructed Italian food—minestrone, fresh bread, salad, and pasta—for around $10 per person.

Point Reyes

Between Bodega Bay and the Golden Gate Bridge, Hwy-1 slices through one of the country's most scenically and economically wealthy areas, **Marin County**. Though less than an hour from San Francisco, the northwestern reaches of the county are

surprisingly rural, consisting of rolling dairylands and a few untouched small towns; Hwy-1 follows a slow and curving route
along the usually uncrowded two-lane blacktop.

After looping inland south of Bodega Bay, Hwy-1 reaches the
shore again at oyster-rich Tomales Bay, around which it winds
for 20 miles before reaching the earthy but erudite town of
Point Reyes Station. Here the excellent **Station House Cafe** at
3rd and Main Streets serves incredibly good breakfasts and delicious lunches that include great-tasting local oysters, on the
half-shell or barbecued.

West from town, the 74,000-acre Point Reyes National
Seashore offers an entire guidebook's worth of hiking and cycling
trails, broad beaches, dense forests, and more; stop at the Bear Valley **visitor center**
(daily 9 AM-5 PM; free; 415/663-9020) for more information. Eight miles from the
visitor center, the **HI Point Reyes Hostel**, 1380 Limantour Road (415/663-8811),
has $12-15 dorm beds in an old farmhouse on the road to Drake's Bay. The photo-
genic lighthouse at the tip of Point Reyes gives great views over the coast, and in
winter and spring (Dec-June) the steep headland makes an ideal spot for watching
migrating gray whales.

Dozens of delightful inns and restaurants operate in and around Point Reyes; contact the West Marin Chamber of Commerce (415/663-9232) for complete listings.

Tomales Bay marks the rift zone formed by the **San Andreas Fault,** which runs parallel to Hwy-1 and divides Point Reyes from the rest of Northern California.

A sign outside the small white garage on Main Street in Point Reyes Station claims that it is the oldest Chevrolet dealer in California.

Bolinas and Stinson Beach
Sitting at the southern end of the Point Reyes peninsula, Bolinas is a small town
with a well-earned reputation for discouraging tourists; the signs leading you here
from Hwy-1 are regularly torn down by locals bent on keeping the place—little
more than a general store, a bakery, and a bar—for themselves.

In contrast, the broad strands of Stinson Beach, four miles south along Hwy-1,
are the Bay Area's most popular summertime suntanning spots. A grocery store and
deli, the Livewater Surf Shop (which rents boards and the essential wetsuits), and a
couple of outdoor bar-and-grills along Hwy-1 form a short parade at the entrance
to the beach; if you want to stay overnight, try the **Stinson Beach Motel**, 3416
Hwy-1 (415/868-1712).

If you have the chance to plan ahead, try to book a night at
the **Steep Ravine Cabins,** just over a mile south of Stinson
Beach on the ocean side of Hwy-1. Now part of Mount Tamalpais State Park, these 10 rustic redwood cabins are very basic
roofs-over-the-head (bring sleeping bags and food; water faucets
are just outside the door) in an absolutely beautiful coastal
chasm. The cabins cost $30 a night, and reservations are han-
dled by ParkNet (800/444-PARK).

The all-terrain mountain bike, which now accounts for half of all bikes on (and off) the roads, was invented in the late 1970s by a group of daredevil Marin cyclists intent on cruising down the fire roads of Mount Tamalpais at the highest possible speed.

Mount Tamalpais, Muir Woods, and Muir Beach
From the coast, a pair of roads, Panoramic Highway and the Shoreline Highway
(Hwy-1), twist up and over the slopes of Mount Tamalpais (elev. 2,586), the signature peak of the San Francisco Bay Area. Known usually as "Mount Tam," the whole
mountain has been protected in semi-natural state within a series of state and
national parks, and its voluptuous slopes offer incredible views of the urbanized Bay

John Muir

Area and the untouched coastline; drive to within 100 yards of the top for a 360-degree panorama, or stop at the Pan Toll **ranger station** (415/388-2070) for a map of Mount Tam's hiking routes and fire roads.

A deep, dark valley between the coast and Mount Tamalpais holds the last surviving stand of Marin County redwoods, preserved for future generations as the Muir Woods National Monument (daily 8 AM-dusk; free), and named in honor of turn-of-the-century naturalist John Muir. A paved, mile-long trail takes in the biggest trees, but since the park is often crowded with busloads of sightseeing hordes making the tour from San Francisco, you may want to explore the farther-flung areas, climbing up Mount Tamalpais or following Muir Creek two miles downstream to the crescent-shaped cove of Muir Beach, along Hwy-1.

At the junction of Hwy-1 and the US-101 freeway, a historic roadside restaurant has been resurrected as the **Buckeye Roadhouse,** 15 Shoreline Highway (415/331-2600), where you can feast on fine BBQ, great steaks and burgers, and delicious desserts in a lively, retro-Route 66 atmosphere.

Every August since 1904, one of the country's wildest foot races, the Dipsea, has followed a rugged trail from the town of Mill Valley over Mount Tamalpais to Stinson Beach.

Marin Headlands

If you can avoid the magnetic pull of the Golden Gate Bridge and San Francisco, take the very last turnoff from US-101 (northbound drivers take the second turnoff after crossing the bridge) and head west to the Marin Headlands, a former military base that's been turned back into coastal semi-wilderness. A tortuous road twists along the face of 300-foot cliffs, giving incredible views of the bridge and the city behind it. The road continues west and north to the **visitor center** (415/331-1450), housed in an old chapel, with a reconstructed Miwok shelter and details on hiking and biking routes. On certain Sundays you can tour an intact but no longer functioning Nike missile silo.

Nearby, the barracks of old Fort Barry have been converted into the very peaceful **HI Marin Headlands Hostel** (415/331-2777), which has dorm beds and private rooms for $12-15 per person.

Across San Francisco

From the north, Hwy-1 enters San Francisco across the glorious Golden Gate Bridge, where parking areas at both ends let you ditch the car and walk across the elegant two-mile-long span. South from the bridge, Hwy-1 follows 19th Avenue across Golden Gate Park, then runs due south through the outer reaches of San Francisco, finally reaching the coast again at the often foggy town of Pacifica. The most scenic alternate is the "49 Mile Drive," the best part of which heads west from the bridge through Presidio National Park, along Lincoln Boulevard and Camino del Mar, following the rugged coastline to Lands End, where you can hike around and explore the remains of Sutro Baths, play the old-time arcade games at the Musee Mechanique, or experience the wonders of the Camera Obscura. (See the "Survival Guide" below for details.) From Land's End, this scenic route runs south along the oceanfront Great Highway, which eventually links back up with Hwy-1.

For a memorable first or last look at San Francisco, from Pacifica follow the signs to **Sweeney Ridge,** the grass and wildflower-covered coastal summit from which, on November 4, 1769, the Portola expedition first laid European eyes on the great bay.

the opening of the Golden Gate Bridge

Since driving and parking in San Francisco can be frustrating and expensive (Steve McQueen could never make *Bullitt* in today's traffic!), consider parking out here in the 'burbs and taking public transportation into the center of town. Two of the main Muni trolley lines (the N-Judah, along Judah Street, and the L-Taraval, along Taraval Street; fare $1) run between downtown and the coast south of Golden Gate Park, where parking is plentiful.

(continues on page 74)

San Francisco is the start of our cross-country road trip along US-50, beginning on page 654.

SAN FRANCISCO SURVIVAL GUIDE

SAN FRANCISCO IS EASILY THE MOST ENJOYABLE CITY IN THE U.S. Its undulating topography turns every other corner into a scenic vista, while its many engaging neighborhoods are perfect for aimless wandering. Check out the exotic shops of Chinatown, the corridors of power in the Financial District, the Italian cafes of North Beach, the hippie holdouts of Haight-Ashbury, or the brilliant murals of the latino Mission District. Museums document everything from Gold Rush history to cutting edge modern art, while stellar restaurants offer the chance to sample gourmet food from around the world—all in an easily manageable, densely compact small city.

If there's one place in the city you should stop to get your bearings, it's Fort Point, a massive, photogenic Civil War fort standing *(continues on next page)*

along the bay, directly beneath the Golden Gate Bridge. You can wander at will through the honeycomb of corridors, staircases, and gun ports, watch the fearless surfers and windsurfers offshore, and take in a panoramic view of the City by the Bay. From here you can walk up to and across the Golden Gate Bridge, or east along the bay to the heart of the city (about two miles one-way), or follow the numerous walking and cycling trails that wind through the surrounding **Presidio National Park.**

If there's one other place that ought to be on your S.F. itinerary, it's **Alcatraz.** Aptly known as The Rock, from 1934 until 1963 this was America's most notorious prison. Now preserved as a historical park, the island is worth a visit as much for the views of the city and the bay as for its grim past. In the cell house, audio-guided walking tours, narrated by former prisoners and prison guards, recount what it was like to be locked up with the likes of Al Capone, George "Machine Gun" Kelley, and the psychopathic "Birdman" Robert Stroud, who spent 17 years here. To reach Alcatraz, take one of the **Red & White Fleet** ferries which leave throughout the day from Pier 41 at Fisherman's Wharf. Alcatraz is one of the city's prime tourist destinations, so buy your tickets as far in advance as possible (800/229-2784).

Speaking of tickets, pending construction of their new downtown stadium, Barry Bonds and the rest of the **San Francisco Giants** (415/467-8000) play at Candlestick "3Com" Park, south of the city off US-101. The **Oakland A's** (510/638-5100) play across the bay at Oakland-Alameda County Stadium, off I-880 near the Oakland Airport.

Practicalities
San Francisco International Airport (SFO) lies 15 miles south of the city, and handles the great majority of domestic and almost all international flights. It's an easy airport to navigate and offers a wide range of car rental and shuttle bus services. There's also an airport at **Oakland** across the bay, which handles a few domestic flights, mostly cheap Southwest Airlines from the western U.S.; it too has shuttles and rental car places. The main routes into San Francisco by road are **US-101**, which runs from San Jose in the south and across the Golden Gate Bridge from the north, and **I-80**, which heads in from the east via the Bay Bridge.

San Francisco is one of the few American cities on the West Coast where you really don't need a car, since distances are short and public transportation quite extensive; the gridded street plan makes it easy to find your way around. San Francisco's Municipal Railway ("Muni"; 415/673-6864) network of public transit buses, trams, and cable cars will take you all over the city. Park at the west end of one of the transit lines and ride into town.

Given San Francisco's popularity, it's no surprise that room rates are pretty high—around $150 a night is about average. The best budget options are the two HI hostels, one on the bay at Fort Mason (415/771-7277), another downtown at 312 Mason Street (415/788-5604); both cost about $18 a night. There are some nice motels, like the **Holiday Lodge**, 1901 Van Ness Avenue (415/776-4469 or 800/367-8504), a 1950s classic at the west end of the California Street cable car line, with doubles from around $95. Most of the older downtown hotels have been gussied up for expense-account visitors, but one friendly, family-owned survivor is the **San Remo Hotel**, 2337 Mason Street (415/776-8688), in between North Beach and Fisherman's Wharf, where nice rooms with shared bathrooms cost around $60. And if you're lucky enough to have someone else paying your hotel bills, consider a stay at the landmark **Westin St. Francis**, 335 Powell Street (415/397-7000 or 800/228-3000), one of the city's grandest and most centrally located hotels, overlooking the west side of Union Square; rooms run $150 and up.

The only problem for visitors eating out in San Francisco is deciding where to go—there are so many great places that choosing among them can be a painful process. For breakfast, **Sears Fine Foods**, 439 Powell Street on Union Square, and **The Grubstake**, an old trolley car diner at 1525 Pine Street, are both local institutions. **Mel's Drive-In**, 3355 Geary Boulevard, is another institution—no longer a drive-in, alas, but still very popular, serving your basic burger-and-fries in a 1950s vintage chrome-and-lino space. (Another branch of Mel's, now destroyed, was seen in the movie *American Graffiti*.) Two more S.F. culinary landmarks are the **Swan Oyster Depot**, near City Hall at 1517 Polk Street, a simple oyster bar, serving the city's freshest shellfish (Mon.-Fri. till 6 PM only), and **Sam's Grill**, downtown at 374 Bush Street, with incredible grilled meat and fish dishes, melt-in-your-mouth shoestring fries, and ancient-looking wooden booths that seem like set pieces from a Sam Spade mystery.

For other-than-American food, San Francisco has what might be the country's best cheap Chinese place: the **House of Nan King** at 919 Kearny Street, between Chinatown and North Beach. In North Beach proper, Italian food is the order of the day, served up at family-style places like **Capp's Corner**, 1600 Powell Street, or any of the many lined up along Green Street.

The **San Francisco Convention and Visitors Bureau** (415/974-6900) publishes a good free street map and offers extensive listings of attractions, accommodations and restaurants, available from the **visitor center** at Hallidie Plaza, next to the Muni station and cable car turntable at Powell and Market Streets downtown. San Francisco's daily **newspapers**, the morning *Chronicle* and the afternoon *Examiner*, both run events listings. Pick up free papers, like the *Bay Guardian* and the *SF Weekly*, at cafes and bookstores throughout the Bay Area.

The San Mateo Coast

From the San Francisco city limits, Hwy-1 runs along the Pacific Ocean through the rural and almost totally undeveloped coastline of San Mateo County. The first eight miles or so are high-speed freeway, but after passing through the suburban communities of Daly City and Pacifica, the pace abruptly slows to a scenic cruise. The highway hugs the decomposing cliff tops for the next few miles before reaching **Montara**, where the old but still functioning lighthouse has been partly converted into the **HI Point Montara Hostel** (650/728-7177).

Looking for the world's biggest waves? Head down to **Maverick's,** an offshore reef area a half-mile off Pillar Point, three miles north of Half Moon Bay. In winter, when conditions are right, 35-foot mega-waves draw expert surfers from all over the world. For a report, call Maverick's Surf Shop, 530 Main Street in Half Moon Bay (650/726-0469).

The first sizeable coastal town is **Half Moon Bay**, 25 miles south of San Francisco, but seemingly much more distant. A quiet farming community that's slowly but surely changing into a Silicon Valley suburb, Half Moon Bay still has an all-American Main Street, a block east of the Hwy-1 bypass, lined by hardware stores, cafes, bakeries, and the inevitable art galleries and B&Bs housed in 100-year-old farmhouses—like **Zaballa House**, at the north end of town at 324 Main Street (650/726-9123), which has comfortable, $75-a-night B&B rooms in the town's oldest building. The main event here is the annual **Pumpkin Festival**, held mid-October, which celebrates the coming of Halloween with a competition to determine the world's largest pumpkin—winning gourds weigh as much as a half-ton!

For further information, call the Half Moon Bay visitor center (650/726-5202).

Pigeon Point Light Station

Though the San Mateo coastline is quite beautiful, the waters are very cold— and home to a hungry population of **great white sharks,** which have been known to attack surfers as well as seals.

Pescadero and Pigeon Point Lighthouse

The 50 miles of coastline between Half Moon Bay and Santa Cruz are one of the great surprises of the California coast: the virtually unspoiled miles offer rocky tidepools and driftwood-strewn beaches beneath sculpted bluffs topped by rolling green fields of Brussels sprouts, pumpkins, cabbages, and artichokes. The biggest town hereabouts, Pescadero (pop. 500), is a mile or so inland from Hwy-1, well worth the short detour for a chance to sample the fresh fish, great pies, and other home-cooked treats at **Duarte's Tavern**, 202 Stage Road, open daily for breakfast, lunch, and dinner at the center of the block-long downtown.

Ten miles south of Pescadero, the photogenic beacon of Pigeon Point Lighthouse has appeared in innumerable TV and print commercials; the graceful, 115-foot-tall brick tower is open for **tours** (Sunday 10 AM-3 PM; $2 donation), and the adjacent lighthouse quarters function as the very popular **HI Pigeon Point Hostel** (650/879-0633), with a hot tub perched above the crashing surf.

Año Nuevo State Reserve

One of nature's more bizarre spectacles takes place annually at Año Nuevo State Reserve (8 AM-dusk daily; $5 per car), where each winter hundreds of humongous northern elephant seals come ashore to give birth and mate. The males reach up to

20 feet head-to-tail, weigh as much as three tons, and have dangling proboscises that inspired their name. These blubbery creatures were hunted almost to extinction for their oil-rich flesh. In 1920, fewer than 100 were left in the world; their resurgence to a current population estimated at 80,000 has proved that protection does work.

northern elephant seals

Every December hordes of male elephant seals arrive at Año Nuevo, the seals' primary onshore rookery, after spending the summer at sea, ready to do battle with each other for the right to procreate. It's an incredible show, the bulls bellowing, barking, and biting at each other to establish dominance; the "alpha male" mates with most of the females, and the rest must wait till next year. Pups conceived the previous year are born in January, and mating goes on through March. During the mating season, ranger-led **tours** ($4; 800/444-4445) are the only way to see the seals; these tours are very popular, so plan ahead and try to come midweek.

Midway between Año Nuevo and Santa Cruz, the **Davenport Cash Store,** on the east side of Hwy-1 in the village of Davenport, serves hearty breakfasts and lunches. Tiny Davenport is also the birthplace of the Odwalla fresh fruit juice company.

Natural Bridges State Park, two miles north of Santa Cruz via West Cliff Drive, has a natural wave-carved archway and, in winter, swarms of monarch butterflies.

Big Basin Redwoods State Park

The oldest and largest of the California state parks, Big Basin Redwoods State Park protects some 16,000 acres of giant coastal redwoods. Established in 1902, the park has many miles of hiking and cycling trails, high up in the mountains. The heart of the park is most easily accessible from Santa Cruz, but a popular trail winds up from the coast to the crest, starting from Hwy-1 at Waddell Creek Beach, a popular haunt for sailboarders, who sometimes do flips and loops in the wind-whipped waves.

the roller coaster at Santa Cruz

Santa Cruz

The popular beach resort and college town of Santa Cruz (pop. 51,500) sits at the north end of Monterey Bay, an hour's drive from San Francisco, at the foot of a 3,000-foot-high ridge of mountains. Best known for its Boardwalk amusement park, which holds the only surviving wooden roller coaster on the West Coast, and for the large University of California campus in the redwoods above, Santa Cruz takes its name from the ill-fated mission settlement begun here in 1777 but wiped out by an earthquake and tidal wave in 1840. Modern Santa Cruz was all but leveled by another earthquake in 1989, but has since recovered its stature as one of the most diverting stops on the California coast.

The downtown area lies a mile inland, so from Hwy-1 follow the many signs pointing visitors toward the wharf and the beach, where plentiful parking is

Board design has come a long way.

available. Walk, rent a bike, or drive along the coastal Cliff Drive to the world's first **Surfing Museum** (Wed.-Mon. noon-4 PM; donations), which is packed with giant old redwood boards and newer high-tech cutters, as well as odds and ends tracing the development of West Coast surfing. Housed in an old lighthouse, it overlooks one of the state's prime surfing spots, Steamer Lane, named for the steamships that once brought day-tripping San Franciscans to the wharf.

A large part of the Santa Cruz economy still depends upon visitors, and there are plenty of cafes, restaurants, and accommodations options to choose from. Eating and drinking places congregate west of Hwy-1 along Front Street and Pacific Avenue in downtown Santa Cruz, which has a number of engaging, somewhat countercultural book and record shops along with cafes like **Zoccoli's**, 1534 Pacific Avenue, which has great soups and sandwiches. Another place to consider is the **Santa Cruz Brewing Company**, an above-average brewpub at 516 Front Street near the San Lorenzo River, which flows along the south edge of downtown. Vegetarians will enjoy the lively **Saturn Cafe**, open all day at 1230 Mission Street (831/429-8505), along Hwy-1 on the north side of town.

Motels line Hwy-1, and cheaper ones congregate around the waterfront area, with rates ranging $30-100 a night depending upon location and time of year; older, funkier ones stand atop Beach Hill, between the Boardwalk and downtown, where you can also avail yourself of the **HI Santa Cruz Hostel**, 321 Main Street (831/423-8304), with dorm beds in an immaculate 1870s cottage for just $13-15 per person. Another characterful old place is the **Capitola Venetian Hotel** (831/476-6471), a 1920s mission-style complex right on the beach at 1500 Wharf Road in Capitola, three miles east of Santa Cruz. Among the many nice B&Bs is the rustic **Babbling Brook**, 1025 Laurel Street (831/427-2437 or 800/866-1131).

For more complete listings or other information, contact the **Santa Cruz Visitors Council**, 701 Front Street (831/425-1234 or 800/833-3494).

Santa Cruz Boardwalk
The bayfront Santa Cruz Boardwalk should really be your main stop; besides the dozens of thrill rides and midway games, it boasts the art deco Cocoanut Grove ballroom, where throughout the summer swing bands still play the sounds of the

1930s and 1940s, and two rides that are such classics of the genre they've been listed as National Historic Landmarks. The biggest thrill is the **Giant Dipper** roller coaster, open since 1924, a senior citizen compared to modern rides but still one of the Top 10 coasters in the country—the clattering, half-mile-long tracks make it seem far faster than the 40 mph maximum it reaches. Near the roller coaster is the beautiful Charles Looff **carousel**, one of only six left in the country, with 70 hand-carved wooden horses doing the same circuit they've followed since 1911; grab for the brass rings while listening to music pumped out by the 342-pipe organ, imported from Germany and over 100 years old.

Along with these and many other vintage arcade attractions, the amusement park also features a log flume ride, a sky ride, a two-story miniature golf course installed inside the old bath-house, plus a bowling alley and all the shooting galleries, laser tag, and virtual reality machines you could want. The Boardwalk, which has been paved but retains a great deal of charm and character, is open daily in summer, and weekends only during the rest of the year. Admission is free and individual rides vary in cost, with the Giant Dipper costing $3 a trip and all-day passes priced about $15. For more information, call 831/423-5590.

The Mystery Spot

In the hills above Santa Cruz, east of Hwy-1 at 1953 Branciforte Drive, the Mystery Spot (daily 9:30 AM-5 PM; $4) is one of those fortunate few tourist traps that actually gets people to come back again. Like similar places along the Pacific coast, the Mystery Spot is a section of redwood forest where the usual laws of physics seem not to apply (trees grow in oddly contorted corkscrew shapes, and balls roll uphill). Among those who study vortexes and other odd geomantic places, the Mystery Spot is considered to be the real thing, but you don't have to take it seriously to enjoy yourself.

Santa Cruz has just about fully recovered from the 1989 Loma Prieta earthquake, which had its epicenter in the hills southeast of the city.

Watsonville, Castroville, and Moss Landing

Between Santa Cruz and Monterey, Hwy-1 loops inland through the farmlands fronting Monterey Bay. Part freeway, part winding two-lane, Hwy-1 races through, and to be honest there's not a lot worth stopping for: the beaches can be dreary, and the two main towns, Watsonville and Castroville, are little more than service centers for the local fruit and vegetable packers. Watsonville is still reeling from the 1989 earthquake, which destroyed half of the downtown area, though Castroville—where in 1947, then-unknown **Marilyn Monroe** reigned as "Miss Artichoke" during Castroville's Artichoke Festival, still celebrated each September—does have one odd sight: the "World's Largest Artichoke," a concrete statue outside a very large fruit stand at the center of town.

Coastal farms along the Monterey Bay grow nearly 85% of the nation's artichokes, which you can sample along with other produce at stands along Hwy-1.

Back on the coast, midway along Monterey Bay, the port community of Moss Landing is a busy commercial fishery, with lots of trawlers and packing plants—not to mention pelicans aplenty. Moss Landing is also home to the research arm of the Monterey Bay Aquarium, to an obtrusively huge electricity generating plant, and to a handful of oyster bars and restaurants like **The Whole Enchilada** (right on Hwy-1 just south of the power plant), which has spicy seafood and a popular Sunday jazz brunch.

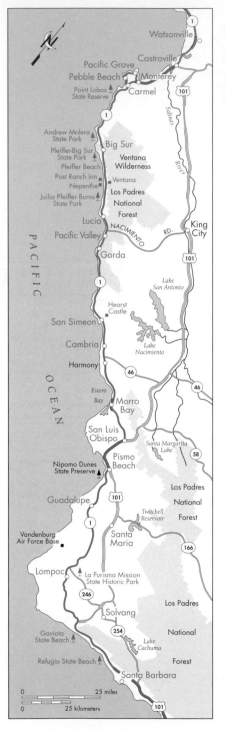

Much of the bayfront north of Monterey formerly belonged to the U.S. Marine Corps base at Fort Ord. Almost the entire parcel was turned over to the state of California to house the **California State University at Monterey Bay**, which opened its doors in 1995.

Detour: San Juan Bautista

Away from the coast, 15 miles inland from Monterey Bay via Hwy-129 or Hwy-156, stands one of California's most idyllic small towns, San Juan Bautista. It centers upon a grassy town square bordered by a well-preserved mission complex, complete with a large church and monastery standing since 1812. Two other sides of the square are lined by hotels, stables, and houses dating from the 1840s through 1860s, preserved in their entirety within a state historic park (daily 10 AM-4:30 PM; $2; 831/623-4881).

Completing the living history lesson, the east edge of the square is formed by one of the state's few preserved stretches of El Camino Real, the 200-year-old Spanish colonial trail that linked all the California missions with Mexico. Adding to the interest, the trail runs right along the rift zone of the San Andreas Fault, and a small seismograph registers tectonic activity. (Incidentally, San Juan Bautista was where the climactic final scenes of Hitchcock's *Vertigo* were filmed—though in the movie, they added a much more prominent bell tower with a seemingly endless staircase.)

The town's Main Street is a block from the mission, and is lined by a handful of antique shops, Mexican restaurants, and cafes like the **Mission Cafe**, 300 3rd Street.

Monterey

The historic capital of California under the Spanish and Mexican regimes,

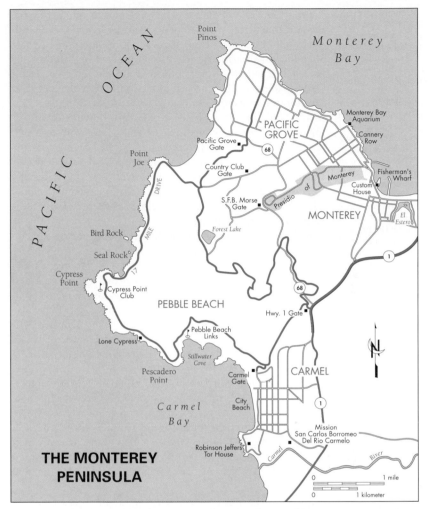

THE MONTEREY
PENINSULA

Monterey (pop. 31,954), along with its peninsular neighbors Carmel and Pacific Grove, is one of the most satisfying stops in California. Dozens of significant historical sites have been well preserved, most of them concentrated within a mile-long walk called the "Path of History" that loops through the compact downtown area. Park in the lots at the foot of Alvarado Street, Monterey's main drag, and start your tour at **Fisherman's Wharf**, where bellowing sea lions wallow in the water, begging for popcorn from tourists. Next stop should be the adjacent **Custom House**, the oldest governmental building in the state, recently restored as the **Monterey State Historic Park visitor center** (10 AM-5 PM; 831/649-2836); here you can pick up maps or join walking tours of old town Monterey.

Along Hwy-1 on the northwest edge of town, the elegant **Hotel Del Monte,** a grand resort that attracted the first wealthy tourists to Monterey beginning in 1880, is now surrounded by the large U.S. Navy Postgraduate School.

The internationally famous **Monterey Jazz Festival** is held every year at the end of summer. For performers, dates, and other information, phone 800/307-3378.

One of Monterey's many intriguing historical sites is the whalebone pavement inlaid into the sidewalk in front of California's First Theater, near the waterfront at the foot of Pacific Street.

The writer John Steinbeck lived in and around the Monterey Peninsula for many years, and set many of his stories here, though things have changed so much in recent years that his beloved Cannery Row is hard to recognize. Steinbeck was born and is buried in Salinas, east of Monterey on US-101, and after spurning him for most of his lifetime Salinas recently opened the **National Steinbeck Center**, 1 Main Street (daily 10 AM-5 PM; $7; 831/753-6411) as a memorial to its literary son.

From the Custom House, which is now surrounded by the modern Doubletree Hotel complex, you can follow the old railroad right-of-way west along the water to **Cannery Row**, where abandoned fish canneries have been gussied up into upscale bars and restaurants—most of them capitalizing on ersatz Steinbeckian themes. The one real attraction here is the excellent **Monterey Bay Aquarium** (daily 10 AM-6 PM; $16; 800/756-3737), 886 Cannery Row, housed in a spacious modern building and loaded with state-of-the-art tanks filled with over 500 species of local sealife. The aquarium is rated by many as the best in the world; displays let visitors touch tidepool denizens, watch playful sea otters, gaze into the gently swaying stalks of a three-story-tall kelp forest, be hypnotized by brilliantly colored jellyfish, or face truly weird creatures that live thousands of feet below the surface of the bay.

Because Monterey gets a considerable tourist trade, there's no shortage of restaurants, though good food at reasonable prices can be hard to find. One good bet is the **Old Monterey Cafe**, 489 Alvarado Street, serving large portions at breakfast and lunch. For seafood, catch an early-bird special (before 6 PM) at one of the dozen restaurants on the wharf—**Cafe Fina** does good pizzas as well. Top of the scale is flashy **Montrio**, 414 Calle Principal (831/648-8880), which serves San Francisco-style grilled chicken and fish in a converted fire station; reservations are essential, ever since *Esquire* magazine rated it "restaurant of the year" for 1995.

Places to stay vary widely, starting with a slew of budget motels like the **Motel 6** at 2124 Fremont Street (831/646-8585) in Seaside near old Fort Ord, which is now Cal-State University at Monterey Bay. Other moderate motels line Munras Street along the old US-101 highway frontage south toward Carmel, while prices in downtown Monterey hover in the $120 range. One exception to the generally high prices is the refurbished and centrally located **Monterey Hotel**, 406 Alvarado (831/375-3184 or 800/727-0960), which offers exceptionally good deals, from $50 a night for two people.

Until 1969, Pacific Grove's Methodist antecedents prevailed, and drinking alcoholic beverages was banned—as was reading Sunday newspapers—within the city limits.

Pacific Grove

Perched at the tip of the Monterey Peninsula, Pacific Grove (pop. 16,117) is a quiet throwback to old-time tourism, dating from the late 1880s when the area was used for summertime Methodist revival meetings. The revivalists' tents and camps later grew into the West Coast headquarters of the populist Chautauqua educational movement, based in upstate New York. The town still has a curiously Midwestern feel, from its many small churches to the rows of well-maintained Victorian cottages lining its quiet streets. Besides the many fine old buildings, the best reason to come here is the beautiful, fully accessible shoreline, which boasts some of the coast's best tidepools, sunset views, and endless opportunities for winter whalewatching.

Pacific Grove's main street, Lighthouse Avenue, runs through the 15-mph commercial district of galleries, movie theaters, and cafes like **Toastie's**, a comfy breakfast and lunch place at 702 Lighthouse Avenue. Nearby **Pepper's**, 170 Forest Avenue, serves very good, fresh Mexican food, while a range of fairly priced fish dishes are on the menu at **The Fishwife**, on Sunset Drive at the north end of the Seventeen Mile Drive.

Places to stay in Pacific Grove are more reasonably priced than in Monterey or Carmel: the **Bide-a-Wee Motel**, 221 Asilomar Boulevard (831/372-2330), is a reliable, old-fashioned motor court two blocks from the ocean. Rustic **Asilomar Conference Center**, 800 Asilomar Boulevard (831/372-8016), has woodsy, Julia Morgan-designed cabins but is often filled with church groups or convention-goers. Of the many luxurious B&Bs, the **Pacific Grove Inn**, 581 Pine Street (831/375-2825), offers the best value.

Pacific Grove is the best known of about 20 places in California where millions of monarch butterflies spend the winter months. From October until March, the butterflies congregate on the "Butterfly Trees," a grove of pines on Ridge Road off Lighthouse Avenue, well signed from downtown.

The Seventeen Mile Drive and Pebble Beach

Spanning the coast between Pacific Grove and Carmel, the Seventeen Mile Drive is one of the most famous toll roads in the nation. Opened in the 1880s, the route initially took guests at Monterey's posh Hotel Del Monte on a scenic carriage ride along the coast through the newly planted Del Monte Forest between Carmel and Pacific Grove. Guided by Samuel F. B. Morse, son of the inventor, the formerly wild area underwent development beginning in the 1920s, first with golf courses like Pebble Beach and Cypress Point, and since then with resort hotels and posh homes.

Enter the drive at any of the gates, where you'll pay the toll ($7.25 at time of writing) and be given a map and guide to the route, pointing out all the scenic highlights, especially the trussed-up old **Lone Cypress**, subject of so many Carmel postcards. It's definitely worth doing, if only to say you have; to be honest, the views from the drive are no more or less splendid than they are from the toll-free drives, like Ocean View Boulevard in Pacific Grove, Scenic Drive in Carmel, or Hwy-1 through Big Sur. You do, however, get to stop at the Lodge, where your toll will be deducted from the price of lunch or dinner. If you're in the mood to splurge on wanton luxury, you can also stay overnight at either of two extremely plush golf and tennis resorts: the modern, suburban-style country club of the **Inn at Spanish Bay**, which is also home to an Ansel Adams photography gallery; or the stately, old-money **Lodge at Pebble Beach**. Both resorts charge upwards of $300 a day; for details on accommodations (or golfing fees and tee times), call 831/ 647-7500.

One event that brought Pebble Beach to national attention was the annual golf tournament hosted by **Bing Crosby.** Originally an informal celebrity get-together, it grew into one of the main events of the professional circuit and is now the ATT-Pebble Beach Pro-Am, held each winter.

Every August for nearly 50 years, classic car collectors from around the world have flocked to Pebble Beach for the annual **Concours d' Elegance,** showing off their immaculately restored luxury automobiles.

Carmel

The exclusive enclave of Carmel-by-the-Sea (to give its complete name) began life in the early years of the 20th century as a small but lively bohemian colony inhabited by the literary likes

Lone Cypress

of Sinclair Lewis, Mary Austin, and Upton Sinclair. However, with a few arts-and-craftsy exceptions, by the 1950s Carmel had turned into the archly conservative and contrivedly quaint community it is today—a place where Marie Antoinette would no doubt feel at home, dressing down as a peasant, albeit in Chaps by Ralph Lauren. Preserving its rural feel by banning street addresses (and skateboards, and home mail delivery), Carmel simultaneously loves and abhors the many thousands of tourists who descend on it every weekend to window-shop its many designer boutiques and galleries that fill the few blocks off Ocean Avenue, the main drag through town.

Though it's easy to be put off by the surface glitz, Carmel does have a lot going for it. The water is too cold and treacherous for swimming, but broad **City Beach** at the foot of Ocean Avenue gleams white against a truly azure cove. To the south, aptly named **Scenic Drive** winds along the rocky coast, past Robinson Jeffers's dramatic Tor House and a seafront Frank Lloyd Wright house (the latter now owned by rock star Sammy Hagar) to another broad beach at the usually unpopulated Carmel River State Park, a favorite spot for scuba divers exploring the deep undersea canyon.

Above the beach, just west of Hwy-1 a mile south of central Carmel, **Carmel Mission** (daily 9:30 AM-4:30 PM; donations) was the most important of all the California missions, serving as home, headquarters, and final resting place of Father Junipero Serra, the Franciscan priest who established Carmel and many of the 20 other California missions, and who is entombed under the chapel floor. The gardens—where on weekends wedding parties alight from limos to take family photos—are beautiful, as is the facade with its photogenic bell tower; this is the mission to visit if you visit only one.

Dozens of good and usually expensive restaurants thrive in Carmel, but one place to see, even if you don't eat there, is the tiny, mock-Tudoresque **Tuck Box Tea Room** on Dolores Street near 7th Avenue. Rebuilt after a fire but still dolls'-house cute, it serves up bacon-and-eggs breakfasts and dainty plates of shepherd's pie and Welsh rarebit for lunch; closed Monday and Tuesday. At the other end of the aesthetic spectrum is the **Hog's Breath Inn**, on San Carlos between 5th and 6th Avenues, owned by Clint Eastwood and specializing in "Dirty Harry" burgers and "Sudden Impact" sausages served to patrons seated on an outdoor patio. If you'd rather join locals than mingle with your fellow tourists, head to **Katy's Place**, on Mission Street between 5th and 6th, serving some of the world's best eggs Benedict.

Carmel has only one place approximating a budget option, the very pleasant **Carmel River Inn** (831/624-1575 or 800/882-8142) just west of Hwy-1 near the Carmel Mission, but even here rates average $100 a night. However, if you want to splurge

Though most of Carmel's many art galleries seem directed at interior decorators, a few are worth searching out, including the **Photography West Gallery** on the southeast corner of Dolores and Ocean Streets, and the **Weston Gallery** on Sixth Avenue near Dolores Street, featuring the works of Edward Weston, Ansel Adams, and other Carmel-based photographers.

on a bit of luxury, Carmel is a good place to do it. Besides the golf course resorts of nearby Pebble Beach, Carmel also has the commodious, 1920s-era, mission-style **Cypress Inn** at Lincoln and 7th (831/624-3871 or 800/443-7443), partly owned by dog-loving Doris Day (and featuring posters of her movies in the small bar off the lobby), with rooms from under $150. A relaxing spot away from downtown is the **Carmel Mission Ranch**, 26270 Dolores Street (831/624-6436 or 800/538-8221), within walking distance of the beach and mission and offering resort-level facilities at room rates that run close to $250 a

Carmel's leading light, **Clint Eastwood,** seems ever-present: besides serving as mayor for many years, he owns the Hog's Breath Inn restaurant and the Mission Ranch resort. As a filmmaker, he used Carmel as the location for one of his most disturbing movies, the psychopathic 1970s film *Play Misty for Me.*

night. At all of these places rates quoted here are peak-season; off-season rates will be much lower, so be sure to ask about any special deals that might be on offer.

Point Lobos State Reserve

The sculpted headland south of Carmel Bay, now protected as Point Lobos State Reserve (daily 9 AM-5 PM, till 6:30 PM in summer; $7 per car), holds one of the few remaining groves of native Monterey cypress, gnarled and bent by the often stormy coastal weather. The name comes from the barking sea lions (*lobos del mar*) found here by early Spanish explorers; sea lions, otters, and—in winter— whales are seen offshore or in the many picturesque coves.

The photogenic **Bixby Creek Bridge,** 15 miles south of Carmel, was the largest concrete bridge in the world when built in 1932. The old coast road runs along the north bank of the creek, linking up again with Hwy-1 near Andrew Molera State Park.

The entrance to the reserve is along Hwy-1, three miles south of Carmel Mission, but in summer the park is so popular that visitors sometimes have to wait in line outside the gates. If possible, plan to come early or during the week.

Andrew Molera State Park

Spreading along the coast at the mouth of the Big Sur River, 21 miles south of Carmel, Andrew Molera State Park is a grassy former cattle ranch on the site of one of Big Sur's oldest homesteads. In the 1850s, immigrant John "Juan Bautista" Roger Cooper bought the land and built a cabin, which still stands along Hwy-1 near the park entrance. Well-blazed trails wind along both banks of the river down to the small beach, horses are available for hire, and there are quite a few nice places to **camp** (walk-in only, $3 per person).

Big Sur Village

South of Andrew Molera, Hwy-1 cuts inland toward the heart of Big Sur, the deep and densely forested valley carved by the Big Sur River. Consisting of little more than three gas stations, a couple of roadside markets, and a number of lodges and restaurants, the mile-long village of Big Sur (pop. 950) represents the only real settlement between Carmel and Hearst Castle.

The northern extent of Big Sur is marked by the volcanic hump of **Point Sur,** 19 miles south of Carmel, a symmetrical dome capped by a 100-year-old lighthouse.

BIG SUR

Big Sur, the 90 miles of coastline south of Carmel from Point Sur Lighthouse all the way to Hearst Castle, is one of the most memorable stretches of coastline on the planet, with 5,000-foot-tall mountains rising straight up from the Pacific Ocean. Early Spanish missionaries dubbed it *El País Grande del Sur,* the "Big Country" to the south of Carmel, and the rugged land has resisted development or even much of a population—the current total of around 1,500 is roughly the same as it was in 1900, and for the 3,000 years before that.

Highway 1, the breathtaking drive through Big Sur, was finally cut across the very steep cliffs in 1937, after 20 years of convict labor and several fatalities. Named the state's first scenic route, so dedicated by Lady Bird Johnson in 1966, it's an incredible trip. Like the Grand Canyon and other larger-than-life natural wonders, Big Sur boggles the mind and, in an odd way, can be hard to handle; you have to content yourself with staring in awestruck appreciation, taking pictures, or maybe toasting the natural handiwork with a cold beer or glass of wine at one of the few but unforgettable cafes and restaurants along the way.

However beautiful the drive along Hwy-1, it's also narrow, twisting, packed with sluggish RVers on holiday weekends, and often closed by mud slides and washouts during torrential winter storms. In 1983, the biggest storm in recent memory closed the road for over a year, and in 1998 70 miles of it were blocked for over four months; sections of it are closed almost every year.

There are also very few services, and most of the overnight accommodations are booked solidly during the peak summer season. Spring brings wildflowers, while fall gets the most reliably good weather. No matter when you come, even if you just drive through in an afternoon, be sure to stop whenever possible and get out of the car; scenic viewpoints line the roadside, and dozens of trails lead off into the wilds.

At the north end of "town," the **Big Sur River Inn** (831/625-5255 or 800/548-3610) has moderately priced, rustic rooms in the lodge and in the motel across the highway; it's also a woodsy, warm, and unpretentious restaurant overlooking the river. A half-mile south, on the river side of the highway, is a small complex that includes crafts galleries, a grocery store, and the homey **Big Sur Village Pub**, which features good beers, pizzas, and pub grub. Continuing south, the next mile of Hwy-1 holds Big Sur's main family-oriented resorts, all offering rustic cabins and campgrounds along the river: **Riverside** (831/667-2414); **Ripplewood** (831/667-2242); and **Fernwood** (831/667-2422).

Pfeiffer–Big Sur State Park
Roughly a half-mile south of Big Sur village, Pfeiffer–Big Sur State Park is the region's main event, an 810-acre riverside forest that's one of the most pleasant (and popular) parks in the state. Besides offering a full range of visitor services—restaurant,

lodge, campground, and grocery store—the park includes one of the Big Sur's best short hikes, a two-mile loop on the Valley View trail that takes in stately redwoods as well as oak and madrone groves, a 40-foot waterfall, and a grand vista down the Big Sur valley to the coast. Campsites cost $15-20 (800/444-7275); for cabins or rooms at the lodge, call 800/4BIG-SUR or 800/424-4787.

The park also has the main **ranger station** (831/667-2315) for all the state parks in the Big Sur area. Just south of the park entrance, a U.S. Forest Service **ranger station** (831/667-2423) on the east side of Hwy-1 has information on hiking and camping opportunities in the mountains above Big Sur, including the isolated (but poison-oak-ridden) Ventana Wilderness.

The best basic guide to Big Sur is an annual free newspaper, *El Sur Grande,* published by Monterey County and available at ranger stations and many other locations in and around Big Sur.

Pfeiffer Beach

South of Pfeiffer-Big Sur park, halfway up a long, steep incline, a small road turns west and leads down through dark and heavily overgrown Sycamore Canyon, eventually winding up at Big Sur's best beach, Pfeiffer Beach. From the lot at the end of the road, a short trail runs through a grove of trees before opening onto the broad white sands, loomed over by a pair of hulking offshore rocks. The water's way too cold for swimming, but the half-mile strand is one of the few places in Big Sur where you can enjoy extended beachcombing strolls. The beach's northern half attracts a clothing-optional crew, even on cool gray days.

Ventana and the Post Ranch Inn

South of Sycamore Canyon, roughly three miles from the heart of Big Sur village, Hwy-1 passes between two of California's most deluxe small resorts. The larger of the two, Ventana (831/667-2331 or 800/628-6500), covers 1,000 acres of Big Sur foothill and offers saunas, swimming pools, and four-star accommodations in 1970s-style cedar-paneled rooms and cabins. Rates range $200-800 a night, and there's also a very fine restaurant with incredible views and reasonable prices, to which guests are ferried in a fleet of golf carts.

The landmark red **farmhouse** along Hwy-1 at the entrance to Ventana was built in 1877 by pioneer rancher W.B. Post, whose descendants developed the Post Ranch Inn.

Completed in 1992 and directly across Hwy-1 from Ventana, the Post Ranch Inn (831/667-2200 or 800/527-2200) is at the forefront of eco-tourism, a low-impact but ultra-high-style luxury resort hanging high above the Big Sur coast. In order to preserve Big Sur's untarnished natural beauty, the Post Ranch Inn is designed to be virtually invisible from land or sea: the 24 accommodations—all featuring a king-sized bedroom and a jacuzzi bath with built-in massage table— blend in with the landscape, disguised either as playful tree houses raised up in the branches of the oaks and pines, or as underground cabins carved into the cliff top. Rates start at $300 a night, but if you want to have a look and plan for a future escape, tours of the resort are given Mon.-Fri. at 2 PM.

VENTANA
BIG SUR

Post Ranch Inn
AT BIG SUR

Nepenthe

One of the most popular and long-lived stopping points along the Big Sur coast, Nepenthe is a rustic bar and restaurant offering

The hilltop where Nepenthe now stands was previously the site of a rustic cabin that **Orson Welles** bought for his wife **Rita Hayworth** in 1944.

good food and great views from atop a rocky headland, a thousand feet above the Pacific. Named for the mythical drug that causes one to forget all sorrows, Nepenthe looks like something out of 1960s James Bond movie, built of huge boulders and walls of plate glass. The menu too is somewhat dated; burgers, steaks, and fried fish predominate.

Sharing a parking lot, and taking advantage of similar views, the neighboring **Cafe Kevah** serves a veggie-friendly range of soups, salads, and quesadillas, plus good teas and coffees and microbrewed beers on a rooftop deck; you'll find a gift shop downstairs selling top-quality arts and crafts and knitwear by Kaffe Fassett, who grew up here and whose family owns the place.

Right along Hwy-1, at a sharp bend in the road just south of Nepenthe, the **Henry Miller Memorial Library** (irregular hours, usually daily 11 AM-5 PM in summer; 831/667-2574) carries an erratic but engaging collection of books by and about the author, who lived in Big Sur for many years in the 1950s.

A half-mile south of Nepenthe on the east side of the highway, one of the oldest and most atmospheric places to stay is **Deetjen's Big Sur Inn** (831/667-2377), a rambling and rustic redwood lodge built by a Norwegian immigrant in the 1930s and now a non-profit operation offering comfortable rooms for $75-150 a night. Deetjen's also serves Big Sur's best breakfasts (8 AM-11 AM) and hearty dinners.

About six miles south of Nepenthe, or a mile from the parking area at Julia Pfeiffer Burns State Park, a steep trail drops down to **Partington Cove,** where ships used to moor in the protected anchorage. The last stretch of the trail passes through a 100-foot-long tunnel hewn out of solid rock.

Julia Pfeiffer Burns State Park

If for some untenable reason you only have time to stop once along the Big Sur coast, Julia Pfeiffer Burns State Park (dawn-dusk daily) should be the place. Spreading along both sides of Hwy-1, about 14 miles south of Big Sur village, the park includes one truly beautiful sight, a slender waterfall that drops crisply down into a nearly circular turquoise-blue cove. This is the only waterfall in California that plunges directly into the Pacific.

From the parking area, east of the highway, a short trail leads under the road to a fine view of the waterfall, while another leads to the remnants of a pioneer mill, complete with a preserved Pelton wheel. Other routes climb through redwood groves up to the chaparral-covered slopes of the Santa Lucia Mountains.

Three miles south of Julia Pfeiffer Burns State Park, the New Age **Esalen Institute** offers a variety of "Human Potential" workshops; they also have an incredible set of natural hot springs, right above the ocean and sometimes open to the public midnight-5 AM. For information or reservations, phone 831/667-3000.

Lucia, Pacific Valley, and Gorda

The southern reaches of the Big Sur coast are drier and more rugged, offering bigger vistas but fewer stopping places than the northern half. The road winds along the cliffs, slowing down every 10 miles or so for each of three gas station/cafe/motel complexes, which pass for towns on the otherwise uninhabited coast. The first of these, 25 miles south of Big Sur village, is Lucia, which has a very good restaurant and lantern-lit cabins. High on a hill just south of Lucia, marked by a slender black cross, is the Benedictine **New Camaldoli Hermitage**, open to interested outsiders as a silent retreat. For details, phone 831/667-2456.

Kirk Creek Campground (831/667-2423), operated by the U.S. Forest Service at the foot of scenic Nacimiento-Ferguson Road, has the most accessible oceanside campsites in Big Sur.

Continuing south, Hwy-1 runs through Pacific Valley, the hills above which are a popular hang-gliding spot, then passes by a number of small but pretty beaches and coves before reaching Gorda, the southernmost stop on the Big Sur coast. Beyond here, a series of small state parks lines the highway, but the next services are 25 miles farther south in San Simeon, at the entrance to Hearst Castle.

San Simeon: Hearst Castle

At the south end of Big Sur, the mountains flatten out and turn inland, and the coastline becomes rolling, open range ranch land. High on a hill above Hwy-1 stands the coast's one totally unique attraction, Hearst Castle. Located 65 miles south of Big Sur village and 43 miles northwest of San Luis Obispo, Hearst Castle is the sort of place that you really have to see to believe, though simple numbers—144 rooms, including 36 bedrooms—do give a sense of its scale.

Even if Hearst's taste in interior design (or his megalomania, which by all accounts was understated by his fictional portrayal in Orson Welles's *Citizen Kane*) doesn't appeal, Hearst Castle cries out to be seen, if only as a revealing landmark to one of this century's most powerful and influential Americans. Hearst inherited the land, and most of his fortune, from his father George Hearst, a mining mogul, and began work on his castle following the death of his mother in 1919. With the help of the great California architect Julia Morgan, who designed the complex to look like a Mediterranean hill town with Hearst's house as the cathedral at its center, Hearst spent 25 years working on his "castle," building, rebuilding, and filling room after room

with furniture, all the while entertaining the great and powerful of the era, from Charlie Chaplin to Winston Churchill.

A small **museum** (daily 9 AM-5 PM; free) in the visitor center, next to where you board the trams that carry you up to the house; details Hearst's life and times. If you want to go on a **tour,** the Introductory Tour gives the best first-time overview, taking in the main house and the two swimming pools. Other tours specialize in different aspects of the house and gardens; each one costs $14 and takes around two hours. Advance reservations (800/444-4445) are all but essential, especially in summer.

Hearst Castle

From Hwy-1 at Kirk Creek, five miles south of Lucia, the narrow **Nacimiento Road** makes an unforgettable climb over the coastal mountains past Mission San Antonio de Padua to the Salinas Valley, linking up with US-101 at King City. Because the road passes through sections of Hunter-Ligget Army Base, you may need to show valid car registration and proof of insurance.

In order to help prevent erosion and mud slides, the roadside along Hwy-1 in the southern half of Big Sur has been planted with odd-looking bunches of pampas grass, which help keep the hills from washing away but have become a intrusive pest, crowding out local flora. The most extreme example of this is at Kirk Creek campground, where the formerly open pastures have changed into a veritable pampas forest.

William Randolph Hearst

The coastal coves just north of San Simeon have become a favored rookery of California's ever-expanding population of northern elephant seals. No Parking signs have been posted along Hwy-1 to protect the animals' privacy, but during mating season people still park and walk down to the shore to see them up close and personal. The only officially sanctioned place to see the elephant seals is at Año Nuevo State Reserve, north of Santa Cruz.

The **James Dean** memorial, 27 miles east of Paso Robles near the junction of Highways 46 and 41, is the site where the talented and rebellious actor crashed his silver Porsche and died on Sept. 30, 1955.

Five miles south of Cambria, **Harmony** (pop. 18) is a former dairy town turned arts and crafts colony, with a range of galleries and a small wedding chapel. The region's other flyspeck town, **Cayucos**, sits along the coast 10 miles farther south.

Every Thursday evening, the main drag of San Luis Obispo, **Higuera Street**, is closed to cars and converted into a very lively farmer's market and block party—with stands selling fresh food and good live bands providing entertainment.

Cambria

Without Hearst Castle, Cambria would be just another farming town, but being next to the state's number-two tourist attraction (after Disneyland) has turned Cambria into quite a busy little hive. Apart from a few hokey, tourist-trapping souvenir shops at the north end of town, it's a casual, walkable, and franchise-free community of arts and crafts galleries, boutiques, and good restaurants; from Hwy-1, Main Street makes a three-mile loop around to the east, running through the heart of town.

Hearty breakfasts are available at the **Redwood Cafe**, 2094 Main Street. Well-prepared multiethnic and vegetarian food is on the menu at **Robin's**, a half-block off Main Street at 4095 Burton Drive. Places to stay range from standard motels like the **Bluebird Motel**, 1880 Main Street (805/927-4634), to the rustic **Cambria Pines Lodge** (805/927-4200), on a hill above Hwy-1 at 2905 Burton Drive.

Morro Bay

Marked by the Gibraltar-like monolith of Morro Rock, which was noted by Juan Cabrillo in 1542 and now serves as a peregrine falcon preserve and nesting site, the busy commercial fishing harbor of Morro Bay (pop. 9,950) is lined by seafood restaurants like **The Galley**, 899 Embarcadero, a half-mile west of Hwy-1. A thin, six-mile-long strip of sand protects the bay from the Pacific Ocean, forming a seabird-rich lagoon that's included within Morro Bay State Park, a mile southeast of the harbor. There's an informative museum with displays on local wildlife, and just down Hwy-1 at the edge of the park the friendly **Bayside Cafe** (805/772-1465) serves lunch daily and dinner Thurs.-Sat. Next door, when the weather's nice, you can rent kayaks ($6 an hour) and paddle around the estuary.

The rest of Morro Bay is pretty quiet; one unusual sight is the giant **outdoor chessboard** on the waterfront in City Park, along the Embarcadero at the foot of Morro Bay Boulevard. For details, or to reserve the waist-high playing pieces, call 805/772-6278.

San Luis Obispo

Located midway between San Francisco and Los Angeles at the junction of Hwy-1 and US-101, San Luis Obispo (pop. 43,000) makes a good stopping-off point, at least for lunch if not for a lengthier stay. Like most of the towns along this route, San Luis, as it's almost always called, revolves around an 18th-century mission, here named **Mission San Luis Obispo de Tolosa**, which is said to be the place where Franciscan missionaries first developed California's traditional red-tiled roofs. Standing at the heart of town, at Chorro and Monterey Streets, the mission overlooks one of the state's liveliest downtown districts, with dozens of shops and restaurants backing onto Mission Plaza, a two-block park on the banks of Mission Creek.

Besides the mission and the lively downtown commercial district that surrounds it, San Luis holds a singular roadside attraction, the **Madonna Inn**, which stands just west of US-101 at the foot of town. One of California's most noteworthy pop culture landmarks, the Madonna Inn is a remarkable example of what architecturally minded academic types like to call vernacular kitsch, decorated in a wild barrage of fantasy motifs: the bright pink honeymoon suites, known as "Just Heaven" and "Love Nest"; the "Safari Room" covered in fake zebra skins with a jungle-green shag carpet; the cavelike "Cave Man Room"; or over 100 others, of which no two are alike. *Roadside America* rated the Madonna Inn as "the best place to spend a vacation night in America," but if you can't stay the night, at least stop for a look at the gift shop, which sells postcards of the different rooms. Guys should head down to the men's room, where the urinal trough is flushed by a waterfall. Room rates run $80-150 a night; for reservations or more information, call 805/543-3000 or 800/543-9666.

Madonna Inn

A pedestrian walkway in downtown San Luis Obispo, off Higuera Street between Garden and Broad Streets, has become known around the world as **Bubble Gum Alley.** Since the 1950s, local kids have written their names and allegiances on the brick walls, using chewing gum rather than the more contemporary spray paint.

Though the Madonna Inn has a huge, banquet-ready restaurant—done up in white lace and varying hues of pink—the best places to eat are located downtown, near the mission. For healthy food in a friendly, sunny space, try the **Rhythm Cafe** overlooking Mission Creek at 1040 Broad Street. For an outstanding Italian meal, head to **Buona Tavola**, 1037 Monterey Street. **Linnaea's Cafe**, 1110 Garden Street off Higuera, serves coffee and tea and sundry snack items all day and night; there's also the lively, multi-culti **Big Sky Cafe**, 1121 Broad Street, and the usual range of beer-and-burger bars you'd expect from a college town.

Along with the Madonna Inn, San Luis has a number of good places to stay, with reasonable rates that drop considerably after the summertime peak season. Besides the national chains—**Embassy Suites, Howard Johnson's, Super 8**, two **Travelodges** and three **Best Westerns**—try the **Adobe Inn**, 1473 Monterey Street (805/549-0321), or **La Cuesta Motor Inn**, 2074 Monterey Street (805/543-2777 or 800/543-2777). There's also the **HI San Luis Obispo Hostel**, 1617 Santa Rosa Street (805/544-4678) near downtown and the Amtrak station.

For more information, contact the San Luis Obispo Chamber of Commerce (805/781-2777), or pick up a copy of the free weekly *New Times*.

Pismo Beach

South of San Luis Obispo, Hwy-1 and US-101 run along the ocean past Pismo Beach (pop. 7,800), a family-oriented beach resort where the main attraction is driving or dune-buggying along the sands. Pismo was once famous for its clams, now overharvested to the point of oblivion, but you may still see people pitchforking a few small ones out of the surf. The area has grown significantly in the past decade,

Another San Luis landmark, the **world's first motel,** opened at 2223 Monterey Street in 1925. Originally called the Milestone Motel, the Spanish revival structure was later renamed the Motel Inn but went out of business long ago and now stands, forlorn but not forgotten, next to US-101 on the grounds of the Apple Farm restaurant and motel.

thanks mainly to an influx of retired people housed in red-roofed townhouses, but Price Street, the old road frontage, offers a wide range of motels and fast-food restaurants—nothing very special, but handy.

At the south end of Pismo Beach, **Nipomo Dunes State Preserve** holds endless acres of sand dunes and marshlands, as well as the buried remains of a movie set used in C.B. DeMille's *The Ten Commandments.*

In the late 1930s, Nipomo was the place where **Dorothea Lange** took that famous photograph of a migrant mother huddling with her children in a farmworkers camp. It's also home to **Jacko's** popular steakhouse and cocktail bar, right off US-101 on Thompson Road, the old highway.

Guadalupe and Santa Maria

South of Pismo Beach, the highways diverge. Hwy-1 cuts off west through the still agricultural areas around sleepy Guadalupe (pop. 5,479), where produce stands sell cabbages, broccoli, and leafy green vegetables fresh from the fields. The town itself feels miles away from modern California, with a four-block Main Street lined by Mexican cafes, bars, banks, and grocery stores. A great place to get a feel for Guadalupe is at the **Far Western Tavern,** open daily for lunch and dinner at 899 Guadalupe Street (805/343-2211). Try the steaks, which are awesome.

If you opt to follow US-101, shopping malls and tract-house suburbs fill the inland valleys through Santa Maria, a town best known for its thick cuts of barbecued beef, which can be sampled at the large and historic **Santa Maria Inn,** a half-mile west of US-101 at 801 S. Broadway (805/928-7777).

Lompoc and La Purisima Mission State Historic Park

The rolling valleys around Lompoc are famed for their production of flower seeds, and consequently the fields along Hwy-1 are often ablaze in brilliant colors. Apart from colorful murals adorning downtown buildings, Lompoc as a town is not up to much, despite the unusual nature of the area's two main nonagricultural employers: a minimum-security federal prison and the Vandenburg Air Force Base, site of numerous missile tests and the aborted West Coast space shuttle port.

With its long arcade reaching across the floor of a shallow, grassy valley, Mission La Purisima (daily 10 AM-5 PM; $5 per car) gives a strong first impression of what the missions may have looked like in their prime. Four miles northeast of Lompoc, between Hwy-1 and US-101 on Hwy-246, the mission here was originally built in 1812 but fell to ruin before being totally reconstructed as part of a WPA make-work scheme in the New Deal 1930s. During the restoration, workers used period techniques wherever possible, hewing logs with hand tools and stomping mud and straw with their bare feet to mix it for adobe bricks. Workers also built most of the mission-style furniture that fills the chapel and the other rooms in the complex. Also here: a functioning aqueduct, many miles of hiking trails, and a small museum.

Solvang

America's most famous mock-European tourist trap, the Danish-style town of Solvang was founded in 1911. Set up by a group of Danish immigrants as a cooperative agricultural community, Solvang found its calling catering to passing travelers, and the compact blocks of cobblestoned streets and Olde Worlde architecture, highlighted by a few windmills and signs advertising the Hamlet Motel among many more suspicious claims to Danishness, now attract tourists by the busload. Many other U.S. towns (Leavenworth, Washington, and Helen, Georgia, to name two) have been inspired by Solvang's success, but to be honest there's nothing much to do here apart from walking, gawking, and shopping for pastries.

Just east of Solvang's windmills and gables, the brooding hulk of **Mission Santa Ynez** stands as a sober reminder of the region's Spanish colonial past. Built in 1804, it was once among the more prosperous of the California missions, but now is worth a visit mainly for the gift shop selling all manner of devotional ornaments.

Gaviota and Refugio State Beaches

Between Solvang and Santa Barbara, US-101 follows the coast past some of California's most beautiful beaches. Dropping through a steep-sided canyon, US-101 reaches the coast at Gaviota State Beach, where a small fishing pier and campground are overwhelmed by the massive train trestle that runs overhead. Continuing south, US-101 runs atop coastal bluffs past prime surfing beaches, usually marked by a few VWs pulled out along the west side of the highway. Midway along this stretch of coast, some 22 miles north of Santa Barbara, Refugio State Beach has groves of palm tress backing a clear white strand. There's also a small, summer-only store, and a number of attractive campsites with hot showers.

Reservations for camping at Gaviota or Refugio, or at any California state beach, must be made through ParkNet (800/444-7275).

Between San Luis Obispo and Santa Barbara, US-101 turns inland from the coast around Point Conception, the traditional dividing line between central and Southern California. Nearly roadless and generally hard to reach, this untouched stretch of California coast is best seen from Amtrak's *Coast Starlight* train, which runs once daily in each direction (800/USA-RAIL for details). Whales, dolphins, and other wildlife, along with the launching pads of the aborted space shuttle port of Vandenburg Air Force Base, are just a few of the attractions of this lovely coastal cruise. To do it in a day, you have to return by Amtrak bus.

The town of Buellton, a block west of US-101 at the Solvang exit, holds one of California's classic roadside landmarks, Andersen's **Pea Soup Restaurant,** advertised up and down the coast.

Pop singer Michael Jackson's **Neverland Ranch** lies in the foothills of the Santa Ynez Valley, southeast of Solvang via the truly scenic Hwy-254, which loops inland south to Santa Barbara.

EL CAMINO REAL AND THE CALIFORNIA MISSIONS

While the American colonies were busy rebelling against the English Crown, a handful of Spaniards and Mexicans were establishing outposts and blazing an overland route up the California coast, along the New World's most distant frontier. Beginning in 1769 with the founding of a fortress and a Franciscan mission at San Diego, and culminating in 1776 with the founding of another outpost at what is now San Francisco, a series of small but self-reliant religious colonies was established, each a day's travel apart and linked by El Camino Real, "The King's Highway," a route followed roughly by today's US-101.

Many of the colonies grew to become the state's largest cities; others were abandoned and all but disappeared. Some of the missions have been preserved, others restored in varying degrees of authenticity and apocryphal romance, and the route itself is in the process of being declared a national historic trail. Some of the most interesting missions are listed below, north to south, followed by the dates of founding.

San Francisco Solano de Sonoma (1823). The only mission built under Mexican rule stands at the heart of this history-rich Wine Country town.

San Juan Bautista (1797). This lovely church forms the heart of an extensive historic park, in the town of the same name. See page 78.

San Carlos Borromeo (1770). Also known as Carmel Mission, this was the most important of the California missions. See page 82.

San Antonio de Padua (1771). This reconstructed church, still in use as a monastery, stands in an undeveloped valley inland from Big Sur in the middle of Hunter-Leggett Army base. Monks still live, work and pray here, making for a marvelously evocative visit.

San Miguel Arcangel (1797). The only mission not to have undergone extensive renovations and restorations—almost everything, notably the vibrantly colorful interior murals, is as it was.

San Luis Obispo de Tolosa (1772). It's the centerpiece of this small central coast city. See page 88.

La Purisima Concepcion (1787). A quiet coastal valley is home to this church, which was restored in the 1930s using traditional methods as part of a New Deal employment and training project. See pages 90-91.

Santa Barbara (1782). Called the "Queen of the Missions," this lovely church stands in lush gardens above the upscale coastal city. See page 94.

San Gabriel Arcangel (1771). Once the most prosperous of the California missions, it now stands quietly and all but forgotten along a remnant of Route 66 east of Los Angeles.

San Juan Capistrano (1776). Known for the swallows that return here each year, this mission has lovely gardens but the buildings have been badly damaged by earthquakes and the elements, meaning they've been under scaffolding for years. See page 105.

CALIFORNIA MISSIONS (1769 - 1823)

San Francisco Solano de Sonoma (1823)
San Rafael (1817)
San Francisco de Asis (1776)
Santa Clara (1777)
San Jose (1797)
Santa Cruz (1791)
San Juan Bautista (1797)
San Carlos Borromeo (1770)
Soledad (1791)
San Antonio de Padua (1771)
San Miguel (1797)
San Luis Obispo de Tolosa (1772)
La Purisima Concepcion (1787)
Santa Ynez (1804)
Santa Barbara (1782)
San Buenaventura (1782)
San Fernando Rey (1797)
San Gabriel Arcangel (1771)
San Juan Capistrano (1776)
San Luis Rey (1798)
San Diego (1769)

OCEAN
PACIFIC

UNITED STATES
MEXICO

El Camino Real

0 — 100 miles
0 — 100 kilometers

Santa Barbara

The geographical midpoint of California may well be somewhere near San Francisco, but the Southern California of popular imagination—golden beaches washed by waves and peopled by blond-haired surfer gods—has its start, and perhaps best expression, in Santa Barbara. Just over 100 miles north of Los Angeles, Santa Barbara has grown threefold in the last 50 years, but for the moment at least it manages to retain its sleepy seaside charm. Much of its character comes from the fact that, following a sizeable earthquake in 1929, the town fathers—caught up in the contemporary craze for anything Spanish revival —required that all buildings in the downtown area exude a mission-era feel, mandating red-tile roofs, adobe-colored stucco, and rounded arcades wherever practicable. The resulting architectural consistency gives Santa Barbara an un-American charm; it looks more like a Mediterranean village than the modern city that, beneath the surface, it really is.

For a good first look at the city head down to the water, where **Stearns Wharf** sticks out into the bay, bordered by palm tree-lined beaches populated by joggers, roller bladers, and volleyball players. From the wharf area, follow State Street away from the sands to the downtown district, where Santa Barbarans parade among the numerous cafes, bars, and boutiques. At the north end of downtown, the coast's best bookshop, Earthling Books, stands across from the excellent **Museum of Art** (Tues.-Sat. 11 AM-5 PM, Sunday noon-5 PM; $3), at 1130 State Street. A block east on Anacapa Street, the **County Courthouse** is one of the finest public buildings in the state, a

*Local sybarites love to soak in the naturally hot waters of **Las Cruces hot spring,** tucked away up a canyon just south of the US-101/Hwy-1 junction.*

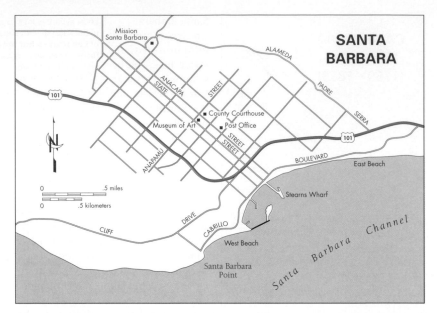

"Rancho del Cielo," the ranch of former President **Ronald Reagan** spreads along the crest of the coastal hills above Refugio State Beach.

Santa Barbara is one of many great places along the coast to go on a whalewatching cruise, on the *Condor* or other boats. Trips take a half-day or full day, and some head out to the Channel Islands. Call for details or reservations (805/963-3564 or 888/77-WHALE or 888/779-4253).

handcrafted Spanish revival monument set in lush semitropical gardens, with an observation tower (daily 9 AM-5 PM; free) giving a fine view over the red-tiled cityscape.

Santa Barbara's reigning attraction, **Mission Santa Barbara** (daily 9 AM-5 PM; $2) stands atop a shallow hill a well-posted mile up from State Street, looking out over the city and shoreline below. Called the "Queen of the Missions" by the local tourist scribes, Mission Santa Barbara is undeniably lovely to look at, its rose-hued stone facade perfectly complemented by the roses and bougainvillea that frame the well-maintained gardens and lawns.

Santa Barbara has perhaps the coast's best variety of places to eat. Early risers can enjoy the greasy spoon breakfasts (daily 6 AM-1 PM, Sunday from 7 AM) at **Esau's Coffee Shop**, 403 State Street, a block north of US-101. State Street holds most of the lunch and dinner places, ranging from the old-fashioned burgers and beers on tap in the dark wood dining room of **Joe's Cafe**, 536 State Street, to the healthy salads and sandwiches at the lively **World Cafe**, 1208 State Street near the art museum. Finally, some of the world's best hole-in-the-wall Mexican food is served a half-mile east of State Street at **La Super-Rica**, 622 N. Milpas Street (805/963-4940), where such distinguished foodies as Julia Child come to chow down on freshly made soft tacos and delicious seafood tamales—all at bargain basement prices.

The city's accommodations, however, are among the central coast's most expensive, especially in summer when even the most basic motel can charge as much as $100 a night. One of the nicest of many motels is the **Franciscan Inn**, 10 Bath Street (805/963-8845), just a short walk from the beach and wharf. At the top of the scale, the **Simpson House**, 121 E. Arrellaga Street (805/963-7067 or 800/676-

1280), offers comfortable, centrally located B&B rooms; money's-no-object visitors can enjoy the deluxe facilities of the **San Ysidro Ranch** (805/969-5046), in the hills above neighboring Montecito, where Jackie and JFK spent some of their honeymoon. A budget

CAUSEWAY, COAST HIGHWAY, BETWEEN VENTURA AND SANTA BARBARA

traveler's only real option is the **Banana Bungalow**, 210 E. Ortega Street (805/963-0154).

For further details on Santa Barbara, stop into the **Visitor Information Center** near Stearns Wharf at 1 Santa Barbara Street (805/966-9222 or 800/676-1266). For current events and nightlife listings, pick up a free copy of the weekly *SB Independent* newspaper at the excellent **Earthling Bookshop**, 1137 State Street, which also operates a late-night cafe.

The national budget chain Motel 6 got its start in Santa Barbara, where they now have five properties, including one near the beach at 443 Corona Del Mar (805/564-1392).

The Channel Islands National Park
South of Santa Barbara, US-101 widens into an eight-lane freeway along the coast. Looking out beyond the partially disguised offshore oil wells, on a clear day you can't miss the outlines of the Channel Islands, whose rocky shores are protected as a national park. Consisting of eight islands altogether, they sit from 12 to nearly 50 miles off the mainland, but only the smallest and closest, Anacapa Island, is easily accessible to the public; daily charters from Ventura Harbor are offered by **Island Packers** (805/642-1393).

Former congressman (and wannabe U.S. senator) **Michael Huffington** *lives in the wealthy enclave of Montecito, just south of Santa Barbara.*

Ventura
Midway between Malibu and Santa Barbara, Ventura (pop. 95,000) is an off-beat little place, its three-block Main Street lined by enough thrift shops (seven at last count) to clothe a destitute retro-minded army. Apart from searching out vintage couture, the main reason to stop is the small and much-reconstructed **Mission San Buenaventura** (Mon.-Sat. 10 AM-5 PM, Sunday 10 AM-4 PM; $1), standing at the center of Ventura at 225 E. Main Street, just east of the US-101 freeway. This was the ninth in the California mission chain, and the last one founded by Father Serra, in 1782. A block from the mission at 113 E. Main Street, the **Albinger Archaeological Museum** (Tues.-Sun. 10 AM-4 PM; free) collects a wide range of artifacts—the oldest

In the beach resort of **Summerland,** *the Nugget Restaurant along the old US-101 highway at 2318 Lillie Avenue (805/969-6135) has a saxophone that President Clinton plays whenever he's vacationing here. The next exit to the south takes you to Santa Claus Lane, a seasonal shopping street with a giant-sized statue of St. Nick.*

Ventura is the birthplace and headquarters of the outdoor equipment and fashion company **Patagonia,** started and still owned by legendary rock climber Yvon Chouinard.

from 1500 B.C, the most recent from early American settlers—all excavated from a single city-block-sized site alongside the mission.

Ventura doesn't get anything like the tourist trade that Santa Barbara draws, but it does have the very pleasant **Bella Magiore Inn,** offering good-value B&B rooms in a nicely restored 1920s courtyard house at 67 S. California Street (805/652-0277 or 800523-8479), between downtown and US-101.

South of Ventura, US-101 heads inland through the San Fernando Valley to Hollywood and downtown Los Angeles, while Hwy-1 heads south through the 10 miles of stop-and-go sprawl that make up the farming community of **Oxnard** (pop. 149,457), then continues right along the coast through Malibu and West L.A.

Detour: Simi Valley

If you opt to follow US-101 rather than coastal Hwy-1 into Los Angeles, be sure to check out the somnolent suburb of Simi Valley, 20 miles east of Ventura. Home to the jury that acquitted the LAPD officers who beat Rodney King, it's also where the hilltop **Ronald Reagan Presidential Library** (daily 10 AM-5 PM; $4; 805/522-8444) fills 150,000 square feet of Spanish-style stucco; to get there, take US-101 to Hwy-23 North, exit at Olsen Road, and follow the signs.

The main route inland from the coast, Malibu Canyon Road, was the setting of the key murder scene in James M. Cain's thriller *The Postman Always Rings Twice.*

The other Simi Valley sight to see is Bottle Village, a complex of small buildings and sculptures built out of glass bottles, TV sets, hubcaps and assorted other recycled refuse in the 1940s and 1950s by the late Tressa Prisbey. Badly damaged in the 1992 Northridge earthquake, and subject of a heated battle between preservationists and those who think it's a pile of junk, the village can be viewed from the road or by occasional guided tours; it's at 4595 Cochrane Street (donations; 805/583-1627), a mile south of the Hwy-118/210 freeway, between the Tapo Canyon and Sterns Road exits.

Pacific Coast Highway Beaches

Running right along the beach, the Pacific Coast Highway (Hwy-1) heads south from Oxnard around the rocky headland of Point Mugu (ma-GOO), where the U.S. Navy operates a missile testing center and the Santa Monica Mountains rise steeply out of the Pacific Ocean. Most of these chaparral-covered granite mountains have been protected as parkland, with hiking, cycling, and riding trails offering grand views and a surprising amount of solitude. A series of state-owned beaches mark your progress along the coastal road, but this stretch is basically natural wilderness —apart from the highway, of course. Biggest and best of the beaches hereabouts is the lovely **Leo Carrillo State Beach**, which has a sandy strand, some great tidepools, and a sycamore-shaded campground (310/457-6589 or 800-444-7275).

South of Leo Carrillo, which marks the Los Angeles County line, there are many more public beach areas, including (in roughly north-to-south order) Nicholas Canyon County Beach, El Pescador, El Matador (where episodes of TV's *Baywatch* are said to be filmed), and big brash Zuma Beach, where the highway bends inland.

Malibu

South of Zuma Beach houses begin popping up along Hwy-1 to block the oceanfront views, and more elaborate multi-million-dollar homes dot the canyons above as well, forming the sprawling exurbia and movie star playground of Malibu, which stretches along Hwy-1 for the next 27 miles into Santa Monica and metropolitan L.A. It's hard to get more than a glimpse of

At the north end of Malibu, the ramshackle **Neptune's Net** restaurant at 42505 Pacific Coast Highway is a great place to hang out and star-gaze while enjoying fresh seafood, served up on paper plates for that down-home Hollywood feel.

the garage doors or wrought iron gates of these palaces, but this is the address of choice for the movers and shakers of the entertainment world: if you can name them, they probably own property here. Most of the truly huge estates are hidden away on ranches high up in the mountains. One of the few accessible hideaways has been evolving since 1993, when Barbra Streisand donated her 22-acre ranch for use as a botanical preserve. It's managed by the Santa Monica Mountains Conservancy and is open to visitors by reservation only; call for current details (310/589-3200).

From Hwy-1, the most prominent sight is the **Pepperdine University** campus, which was described by the late great architect Charles Moore as "an overscaled motel set in obscenely vivid emerald lawns." Better known for its volleyball teams than its academic rigor, Pepperdine is the place Clinton-chasing Special Prosecutor Kenneth Starr agreed to be Dean of the Law School, only to quit in continuing pursuit of Monica Lewinsky a few days later. Below the bluff-top campus, the legendary **Malibu Colony** stretches along the coast in high-security splendor.

About the only place in Malibu where it's fun (and legal) to explore is the area around the landmark **Malibu Pier**, which juts into the ocean at the heart of Malibu's short and rather scruffy commercial strip. North of the pier, which was used most famously in TV's *The Rockford Files*, stretches Surfrider Beach, site of most of those Frankie Avalon and Annette Funicello beach blanket movies made during the 1950s. The pier and the beach are part of **Malibu Lagoon State Park**, which also protects the historic **Adamson House**, 23200 Pacific Coast Highway (Wed.-Sat. 11 AM-2 PM; $2; 310/456-8432), a lovely old circa 1929 Spanish revival courtyard home, right on the beach and full of gorgeous tile work and other architectural features. Tours of the house are given throughout the day, and fascinating exhibits portray Malibu history and the Rindge family who once owned the entire region.

Between Malibu and Santa Monica, Topanga Canyon is home to an alternative community of hippies and New Agers; nearby, but closed until 2001, is the original **J. Paul Getty Museum**, which displayed the oil magnate's art collection prior to the opening of the massive Getty Center above Brentwood. To reach the new Getty Center from the shore, follow winding Sunset Boulevard 10 miles east to the San

Diego freeway, but call first for parking reservations (310/440-7300), which are essential. From Sunset Boulevard south to Santa Monica, the Pacific Coast Highway (Hwy-1) runs along the wide-open sands of Will Rogers State Beach, gifted to the public by the Depression-era humorist.

Santa Monica marks the western start of legendary Route 66, which is described beginning on page 794.

Crossing Los Angeles

From Malibu and Topanga Canyon, the Hwy-1 swoops along the shore, running along the beach as far as the landmark Santa Monica Pier before bending inland through a tunnel and metamorphosing quite unexpectedly into the I-10 Santa Monica Freeway. The second exit off this freeway (which has been officially dubbed the "Christopher Columbus Transcontinental Highway," running all the way east to Jacksonville FL) lets you off at Lincoln Boulevard, which carries the Hwy-1 moniker south through Venice and Marina Del Rey to Los Angeles International Airport (LAX), where it runs into Sepulveda Boulevard.

After passing through a tunnel under the airport runways—worth the drive just for the experience of seeing 747s taxiing over your head—Sepulveda emerges in the Tarantino-esque communities of LA's "South Bay," which utterly lack the glamour of chichi Santa Monica and Malibu. At Hermosa Beach, one of a trio of pleasant if surprisingly blue-collar beach towns, Sepulveda Boulevard changes its name to Pacific Coast Highway, then bends inland to bypass the ritzy communities of the Palos Verdes Peninsula, passing instead through the industrial precincts of San Pedro that border the Los Angeles/Long Beach harbor, one of the busiest on the West Coast.

A half-mile north of the LAX airport, a block west of the I-405 San Diego Freeway at 805 W. Manchester Boulevard, there is one must-see road trip stop: **Randy's Donuts,** a round-the-clock doughnut shop topped by a photogenic, three-story-tall doughnut.

Since Hwy-1 follows slow-moving Lincoln Boulevard and other surface streets across L.A., if you are in any sort of hurry stay on the Santa Monica Freeway (I-10) east to the San Diego Freeway (I-405), and follow that south as far as you're going. Coming from the south, follow the freeways in reverse order—or risk the time-consuming consequences.

Long Beach

Directly south of downtown Los Angeles, the city of Long Beach (pop. 429,433) is the second-largest of LA's constituent cities, but it feels more like the Midwest than the cutting-edge West Coast. Long Beach is probably best known as the home of the cruise ship RMS *Queen Mary,* one of the largest and most luxurious liners ever to set sail. Impossible to miss as it looms over Long Beach harbor, the stately ship is open for self-guided tours (daily 10 AM-6 PM; $10; 562/435-3511).

In place of Howard Hughes's famous "Spruce Goose" airplane, which used to stand next door, there's now a Cold War-era submarine, and across the bay on the main downtown Long Beach waterfront, the new **Aquarium of the Pacific** (daily 10 AM-6 PM; $13.95; 562/590-3100) explores the diverse ecosystems of the Pacific Ocean, from tropical coral reefs (shown off in an amazing, 360,000-gallon display) to the frigid waters of the Bering Sea.

Along with the annual Toyota Long Beach Grand Prix, an Indy Car race held on the city streets every April, other Long Beach attractions include the **world's largest mural,** a 115,000-square-foot painting of whales on the outside of the

LOS ANGELES SURVIVAL GUIDE

LOVE IT OR HATE IT, ONE THING YOU CAN'T DO about L.A. is ignore it. Thanks to Hollywood in all its many guises (movies, television, the music industry), and a recent spate of natural and unnatural disasters, beginning with Rodney King, and continuing through earthquakes, fires, floods, and high-profile murder trials—O.J. and the Menendez Brothers to name the most notorious two—the city is always rearing its head.

Without falling too deeply under the spell of its hyperbole-fueled image-making machinery, it's safe to say that L.A. definitely has something for everyone, though a guide as brief as this can only help to point you in the right direction through its multicultural myriad of attractions. In keeping with its car-centered culture, however, our suggested tour ignores the many individual attractions and focuses instead on three different recommended drives.

The Los Angeles Dodgers (213/224-1448) play at beautiful Dodger Stadium, on a hill above downtown.

Cruising L.A.

Mulholland Drive: Winding along the crest of the Hollywood Hills, Mulholland Drive is the classic L.A. cruise. Starting in the east within sight of the Hollywood Sign and the Hollywood Bowl, this ribbon of two-lane blacktop passes by the city's most valuable real estate, giving great views on both sides, both by day and after dark, ending up eventually at the north end of Malibu on Pacific Coast Highway (PCH).

Sunset Boulevard: Another classic L.A. cruise, running from the scruffy fringes of downtown all the way west to the coast, Sunset Boulevard gives glimpses into almost every conceivable aspect of Los Angeles life. Starting at Olvera Street, the historic core of colonial Los Angeles, Sunset Boulevard's 27-mile course then winds west past Gower Gulch, site of the first Hollywood movie studios. In West Hollywood it gets re-named the "Sunset Strip," still the liveliest nightclub district in town. Farther along, through Beverly Hills, Brentwood, and Bel-Air, Sunset is lined by the largest mansions you're likely to see. After

The Anaheim Angels (714/940-2000) can be seen at Edison International Field.

Los Angeles has been fodder for more essayists and authors than any other American city, but two books stand out from the crowd: the late Charles Moore's *Los Angeles, A City Observed* is the most eye-opening and easy- to-use guide to city's architecture and history, while Mike Davis's thought-provoking collection of essays *City of Quartz* treats the city as postmodern disaster-in-progress.

(continues on next page)

passing beneath the new **Getty Center** (free, but parking reservations are required, call 310/440-7300), it continues by the well-preserved ranch house of Will Rogers, then finally hits the beach.

Wilshire Boulevard: Wilshire is L.A.'s main commercial artery, starting at the heart of downtown. After cutting through MacArthur Park, where someone really ought to sculpt a giant cake and leave it out in the rain, it runs west to the "Miracle Mile," a bustling business district of the art deco 1930s that is now home to a trio of diverse museums: the mastodons and saber-toothed tigers of the La Brea Tar Pits and the George C. Page Natural History Musem, the huge L.A. County Museum of Art, and the not-to-be-missed **Petersen Automotive Museum**, 6060 Wilshire Boulevard (daily 10 AM-6 PM; $7; 213/930-CARS or 213/930-2277). Wilshire then races west through Beverly Hills past the foot of Rodeo Drive before winding up at the bluffs above Santa Monica Bay.

Practicalities

Most flights into Los Angeles arrive at LAX, on the coast southwest of downtown, where you'll find all the usual shuttles and rental car agencies. Other airports, served primarily by short-haul airlines from other West Coast cities, include Hollywood/Burbank, Long Beach, Ontario, and John Wayne, in Orange County.

Arriving by land, the outskirts of Los Angeles stretch for so many miles in all directions that it is truly impossible to tell where it begins or ends. The sprawl sprawls much farther than the eye can see (even on the rare clear days): south as far as San Diego, north nearly to Santa Barbara, and east across the desert toward Palm Springs. However, considering it has a population of nearly 10 million people, and at least as many cars as humans, getting around the 1,000-plus square miles of Los Angeles is not always the nightmare it may at first seem to be. So long as you can avoid "rush hour" traffic (i.e., stay off 7 AM-10 AM, and again 3-8 PM), the freeways are very handy, but visitors see a lot more by following the surface streets to get places.

Before choosing a place to stay, think about where you want to spend your time, and settle near there. Beachfront accommodations range from the handy and cheap **Santa Monica HI Hostel**, 1436 2nd Street, Santa Monica (310/392-0325), to the **Hotel Queen Mary**, Pier J, Long Beach (800/437-2934), offering somewhat cramped quarters in this minimally

Long Beach Arena, and the self-proclaimed **Skinniest House in the USA**, at 708 Gladys Avenue.

Long Beach also marks southern end of L.A.'s reborn streetcar and subway system, and you can ride the Blue Line north to downtown. It's an inexpensive base for exploring the Los Angeles area, especially if you avail yourself of the $15-a-night **HI South Bay Hostel**, 3601 S. Gaffey Street (310/831-8109), on a hill overlooking the harbor area. There's also a **Best Western** at 1725 Long Beach Boulevard (562/599-5555), directly across from a Blue Line train stop, with rooms for $60 a night.

converted old luxury liner; rooms $120-250. High-end places abound, but few are more comfortable, atmospheric or conveniently located than the legendary **Beverly Hills Hotel**, 9641 Sunset Boulevard, Beverly Hills (310/276-2251 or 800/283-8885). Recently re-opened after undergoing over two years of complete renovations, this is the grande dame of L.A. hotels, and one of the classiest in the world. Stop in for breakfast or a late-night drink at the legendary Polo Lounge if you can't manage the $350-a-night (and up) room rates.

For food, one place I always try to stop is the **Apple Pan**, 10801 W. Pico Boulevard (310/475-3585), an ancient (circa 1937?) landmark on the West L.A. landscape, serving the best hamburgers on the planet— though I'll admit to being biased, since I grew up eating them. Take a seat at the counter and dive into a pile of chunky fresh-fried french fries, but be sure to save room for a slice of their wonderful fruit pies. On old Route 66, in the heart of trendy West Hollywood, **Barney's Beanery**, 8447 W. Santa Monica Boulevard (213/654-2287), is a crusty old roadhouse with famous chili and lots of good, inexpensive food, plus a great selection of beers, and plenty of pool tables. Late at night, the huge sandwiches and heart-warming soups at **Canter's Deli**, 419 N. Fairfax Avenue (213/651-2030), draws all kinds of night owls to a lively New York-style deli in the heart of the predominantly Jewish Fairfax District, open 24 hours every day. Downtown, tucked away between Union Station and Olvera Street in the old heart of L.A., **Philippe's French Dip Sandwiches**, 1001 Alameda (213/628-3781) is a classic workingman's cafeteria, offering good food at impossibly low prices, with character to spare.

The usual array of information about hotels, restaurants, and attractions is available through the **Los Angeles Convention and Visitors Bureau**, 695 S. Figueroa Street (213/689-8822 or 800/228-2452). To find out about current events and issues, read the mammoth *Los Angeles Times*, the biggest and best daily newspaper in the state. For articles with attitude and the best listings of events and activities, pick up a copy of the free *L.A. Weekly*, available (along with dozens of similar publications) at cafes, bars, and bookstores all over Southern California.

Los Angeles has a half-dozen different **area codes** to cover its metropolitan area, so to minimize confusion we have included the appropriate prefix in all the phone numbers we've given in this book.

For more information, contact the Long Beach **visitors bureau** (562/436-3645 or 800/452-7829).

Huntington Beach

Winding south and east from Long Beach, Hwy-1 continues along the coast past a series of natural marshlands and small-craft marinas. The first real point of interest is the town of Huntington Beach (pop. 181,519), one of the largest communities in Orange County. Founded in 1909 by Henry Huntington as a stop along his legendary Pacific Electric "Red Car" interurban railway network, Huntington Beach is best known as the place where **surfing** was first introduced to the U.S. mainland. To attract Angelenos down to his new town, Huntington hired Hawaiians to demonstrate the sport, which at the time made use of huge solid wooden boards, 15 feet long and weighing around 150 pounds. Huntington Beach, especially around the pier, is still a very popular surfing spot—though contemporary surfers slice through the waves on high-tech foam-core boards, a third the size of the original Hawaiian long boards and weighing under 10 pounds. The history and culture of West Coast surfing, with examples of boards then and now, is recounted in the small but enthusiastic **International Surfing Museum**, two blocks from the pier at 411 Olive Avenue (daily noon-5 PM) in the heart of the pleasantly ramshackle beachfront business district.

Nearby, within a few blocks of the pier, is a handful of cafes, plus the handy **Colonial Inn Youth Hostel**, 421 8th Street (714/536-3315), with dorm beds for $13 and double rooms for $30.

Disneyland and the Richard Nixon Presidential Library

Like a little bit of Middle America grafted onto the southern edge of Los Angeles, inland Orange County is a totally different world. In contrast to L.A.'s fast-paced, edgily creative multiethnic stew, Orange County is suburban America writ large—mostly white, mostly well-off, and absolutely, totally bland. In short, a perfect place to build the ultimate escapist fantasy, the self-proclaimed "Happiest Place on Earth," Disneyland.

If you haven't been before, or not for a while at any rate, here are some useful tidbits of information: Disneyland is 20 miles south of downtown L.A., right off I-5 in the city of Anaheim—you can see the Matterhorn from the freeway. The park is open daily at least 10 AM-6 PM, including winter weekends; in summer, it remains open until midnight. Admission to the park, which includes all rides, costs around $39 for one day, $68 for any two out of five days; kids under 12 save 20%.

The phenomenon of Disneyland has been done to death by all sorts of social critics but the truth is, it can be great fun—provided you visit out of season and get there early to avoid the crowds, and really immerse yourself in the extroverted, mindless joy of it all. Most of the rides are great, each in different ways (I like "Pirates of the Caribbean" best), but there can be little forgiveness for "It's a Small World." Avoid it like the plague, or risk having the song ringing in your head for days afterward.

Disneyland opened in 1955, when there was nothing around; now it's surrounded by motels, where it's well worth staying overnight so you can get an early start, go "home" for a while, and come back for the nightly fireworks show. A highly recommended place to stay is the **West Coast Anaheim Hotel**, a block from Disneyland at 1855 S. Harbor Boulevard (714/750-1811), offering spacious modern rooms (and a nice pool) from $65 per night, with free parking and free shuttles every half-hour to and from Disneyland.

For further park details, including opening hours, call Disneyland (714/781-4565); for lodging and other information, call the **Anaheim Convention and Visitors Bureau** (714/758-0222).

If you've already done the Disneyland thing, there is one other Orange County attraction you really shouldn't miss: the Richard Nixon Presidential Library (Mon.-Sat. 10 AM-5 PM, Sunday 11 AM-5 PM; $4.95; 714/993-3393), 18001 Yorba Linda Boulevard, 10 miles northeast of Disneyland off Hwy-91. The library is built on the very ground where the former president was born in 1914; it's also where he and his wife Pat are buried, side by side next to the restored craftsman-style bungalow where Nixon grew up. No matter what your feelings toward him, the spare-no-expense displays do a fascinating job of putting his long career into the distorted perspective you'd expect from the only president ever forced to resign from office. (If you've been to other presidential libraries, you may have noticed that not all are as well funded as this one. That's because the library was paid for by Nixon's friends and receives no federal money—no doubt this is how it gets away with presenting Watergate as a liberal plot to take over the country.) If you can take the show at face value, highlights are many, such as the grainy pictures of the pumpkin patch where Alger Hiss supposedly concealed the microfilm that Nixon and Joe McCarthy used to put him in prison as a Communist spy, next to photos of Nixon and JFK as chummy freshman U.S. senators sharing sleeping compartments on a train. Particularly intriguing is the grand display of Christmas cards, exchanged by the Nixons with some very unlikely figures: Khrushchev and sundry Soviets, as well as every king, queen, and tin-pot dictator you could name. The best-selling item in the gift shop? Postcards of Nixon greeting Elvis Presley, also available as place mats, china, and fridge magnets.

Visiting the Nixon Library also gives you a chance to have a look at one of nation's newest and most high-tech toll roads. Inaugurated in late 1995 along the median strip of the Riverside Freeway (Hwy-91), a new lane was added for drivers willing to pay a variable toll (25 cents to $2.50, depending upon time of day), which is charged through the use of radio transponders affixed to the windshield. But be warned: driving in the toll lanes *without* one of these transponders can get you a ticket very quickly.

Newport Beach

Back on the coast, if you want to get a sense of what wealthy Orange Countians do to enjoy themselves, spend some time along the clean white strands of Newport Beach. Located at the southern edge of Los Angeles's suburban sprawl, Newport started life as an amusement park and beach resort at the southern end of the L.A. streetcar lines. In the 1930s and 1940s, thousands of Angelenos spent summer weekends at the **Balboa Pavilion**, at the southern tip of the slender Balboa peninsula, where a few remnants of the pre-video game amusements survive—a Ferris wheel, a merry-go-round, and those odd "Pokerino" games in which you win prizes by rolling rubber balls into a series of numbered holes.

Midway along the peninsula, near 23rd Street, Newport Pier is flanked by another holdout from the old days: the **dory fleet**, where almost every day small boats set off to catch rock cod and more exotic fish that, starting around noon, are sold straight from the boats at an outdoor market right on the sands.

A mile south of Balboa Pavilion, next to the breakwater at the very southern end of Balboa peninsula, **The Wedge** is one of

To return to Hwy-1 from Balboa peninsula, you can either backtrack around the harbor or ride the **Balboa Ferry**, which shuttles you and your car from the Pavilion across the harbor past an amazing array of sailboats, power cruisers, and waterfront homes.

the world's most popular and challenging bodysurfing spots, with well-formed waves often twice as high as anywhere else on the coast.

Crystal Cove State Park

Midway between Newport and Laguna Beaches, amidst the ever-encroaching Orange County sprawl, Crystal Cove State Park (daily dawn-dusk; $6 per car) protects one of Southern California's finest chunks of coastline. With three miles of sandy beaches and chaparral-covered bluff lined by well-marked walking trails, it's a fine place to enjoy the shoreline without the commercial trappings. Originally home to Native Americans, the land here was later part of Mission San Juan Capistrano and, until 1979 when the state bought it, the massive Irvine Ranch, which once covered most of Orange County.

The main parking area for Crystal Cove is at **Reef Point** near the south end of the park, where there are bathrooms and showers plus excellent tidepools, a fine beach, and a well-preserved collection of 1920s beach cottages. There is also a large section inland from Hwy-1, through the oakland glade of **El Moro Canyon**, which gives a vivid sense of Orange County's rapidly vanishing natural landscape.

During the annual **"Pageant of the Masters,"** Laguna Beach residents re-create scenes from classical and modern art by forming living tableaux, standing still as statues in front of painted backdrops. Held every summer, it's a popular event and proceeds go to good causes, so get tickets ($10-40; 949/494-1145 or 800/487-3378) well in advance.

Laguna Beach

Compared with the rest of Orange County, Laguna Beach (pop. 23,200) is a relaxed and enjoyable place. Bookstores, cafes, and galleries reflect the town's beginnings as an artists' colony, but while the beach and downtown area are still very attractive, the surrounding hills have been covered by some of the world's ugliest tracts of "executive homes."

Right across Hwy-1 from the downtown shopping district, which is full of pleasant cafes and a wide range of art galleries, Laguna's main beach (called simply Main Beach) is still the town's main draw, with a boardwalk, some volleyball courts where the standard of play is very high, and a guarded swimming beach with showers.

Many other fine but usually less crowded and quieter beaches are reachable from Cliff Drive, which winds north of downtown Laguna past cove after untouched cove; follow the signs reading "Beach Access."

Adjacent to the beach, right on Hwy-1, is **Greeter's Corner Cafe**, locally famous thanks to an elderly gentleman named Eiler Larsen, now deceased, who used to stand out front and wave at the passing traffic. The food is fine, and you can eat outside on the broad deck overlooking the beach. Another place worth searching out is the small **Taco Loco**, 640 S. Hwy-1 at the south end of the downtown strip, where the ultra-fresh Mexican food includes your choice of three or four different seafood tacos, from shark to swordfish, in daily-changing specials from about $1.50 each.

Places to stay are expensive, starting at around $100 a night, and include the centrally located, somewhat older **Hotel Laguna**, 425 S. Hwy-1 (949/494-1151), and the beachfront **Laguna Riviera Hotel and Spa**, 825 S. Hwy-1 (949/494-1196). On an oceanside bluff six miles south of Laguna Beach, the **Ritz Carlton Laguna Niguel** (949/240-2000 or 800/241-3333) is California's only Mobil five-star rated resort, with everything you could want from a hotel—all yours for $350 a day.

South of Laguna Beach, Hwy-1 follows the coast for a final few miles before joining up with the I-5 freeway for the 40-mile drive into San Diego.

San Juan Capistrano

Of the 21 missions along the California coast, Mission San Juan Capistrano (daily 8:30 AM–5 PM; $5; 949/248-2049) has been the most romanticized. When the movement to restore the missions and preserve California's Spanish colonial past was at its apogee in the late 1930s, its main theme tune was Leon Rene's "When the Swallows Come Back to Capistrano," popularizing the legend that these birds return from their winter migration every St. Joseph's Day, March 19th. After wintering in Goya, Argentina, they do come back to Capistrano, along with several thousand tourists, but the swallows are just as likely to reappear a week before or a week after—whenever the weather warms up, really.

see the swallows

Many visitors to the chapel at San Juan Capistrano are terminally ill patients saying prayers to **St. Pereguin,** the patron saint of medical miracles.

The mission, which has lovely, bougainvillea-filled gardens, stands at the center of the small, eponymously named town, a short detour inland along I-5 from the coast. Besides the birds, the main attractions include the small **chapel**, the last surviving church where the beatified Father Serra said Mass, widely considered to be the oldest intact church and perhaps the oldest building of any kind in California; and the ruins of the massive **Stone Church**, a finely carved limestone structure that collapsed in an earthquake in 1812, just six years after its completion.

To get a sense of the huge scale of the Stone Church, a full-sized replica called the New Church has been constructed behind the mission, and now serves as the official mission church, open to visitors except during religious services. Across the street from the New Church, the Michael Graves-designed local **library** gives an intriguing postmodern take on the mission style.

In the block between the Mission and the I-5 freeway, the **Walnut Grove Restaurant** and **Mission Inn Motel** are two of the few survivors of old-style San Juan Capistrano, holding out against the relentless suburbanizing that has leveled many of the surrounding historic commercial structures. Another unique spot is the **Coach House**, 33157 Camino Capistrano (949/496-8930), one of Southern California's best small clubs for listening to live music.

San Clemente is also the site of "La Christianita," which in 1769 was the first baptism in Alta California. The event is remembered by a plaque in the civic center parking lot, a block east of I-5.

San Clemente

At the southern tip of coastal Orange County, San Clemente marks the midway point between San Diego and Los Angeles. A sleepy and unremarkable community, San Clemente is probably best known as the site of Casa Pacifica, the one-time "Western White House" of former president Richard Nixon, who lived here following his election in 1968 until after his impeachment in the mid-1970s. The white-walled, mission-style house at the south end of Avenida del Presidente (the western frontage road to the I-5 freeway) is more easily visible from the beach below, though the 25 acres of trees have grown up to obscure it in recent years.

San Clemente also has a handy **HI Hostel**, just a short walk from the beach at 233 Avenida Granada (949/492-2848).

The northwest corner of San Diego County is taken up by the U.S. Marines Corps' massive **Camp Pendleton** training base, which fills 125,000 acres, running for 20 miles along the coast and 15 miles inland.

Alongside the prominent nuclear power plant at **San Onofre,** one of Southern California's better surfing beaches has been home to the friendly, family-run **Pascowitz Surf Camp** (714/361-9283) every summer since 1972.

Mission San Luis Rey de Francia

In the sun-bleached hills above the blue Pacific, four miles east of the ocean off the I-5 freeway along Hwy-76, Mission San Luis Rey de Francia (Mon.-Sat. 10 AM-4:30 PM, Sunday noon-4:30 PM; $3) was among the largest and most successful of the California missions. Its lands have been taken over by Camp Pendleton, and most of the outbuildings have disappeared, but the stately church at the heart of the complex survives in fine condition, worth a look for the blue-tinted dome atop the bell tower and for the haunting carved stone skull that looks down from the cemetery gate.

Oceanside

At the southern edge of 125,000-acre Camp Pendleton Marine Corps Base, Oceanside (pop. 130,000) is the largest city between Los Angeles and San Diego but offers little to attract the casual visitor—apart from guided tours of Camp Pendleton's amphibious-assault training exercises, and the state's longest fishing pier. But if you're in the mood to shop for camouflage gear, watch the muscle cars cruise Hill Street, get a $3 G.I. Joe haircut, or drink beer with a gang of young recruits, this is the right place.

South from Oceanside, all the way to San Diego, a very pleasant alternative to the often-clogged I-5 freeway is the old alignment of US-101, now signed as County Road S21 (and occasionally, "Coast Highway 101"). Slower than the freeway but still in regular use, the old road is now the main drag of quaint beachfront towns like Carlsbad, Leucadia, Encinitas and Del Mar. If you have the time, it's a great drive, in sight of the ocean for most of the way.

Carlsbad: La Costa and Legoland

Named for the European spa town of Karlsbad, in Bohemia of what's now the Czech Republic, Carlsbad (pop. 65,000) was established in the 1880s and had a brief heyday as a spa town until the 1930s. A few remnants of the historic resort area, including the circa 1887 landmark **Neiman's Restaurant**, still survive along old US-101 in the center of town, but these days Carlsbad is best known as the home of **La Costa Resort and Spa**, (760/438-9111 or 800/854-5000), a 500-room complex of luxurious rooms, health spas, golf courses and tennis courts covering 400 acres of hills on the inland side of I-5.

Carlsbad's other main attraction, from its opening in early 1999, is the first American outpost of the popular European children's theme park **Legoland** (adult $32, children $25; 760/438-LEGO or 760/438-5346). Built out of more than 30 million Lego bricks, and covering 128 acres above the Pacific Ocean, the park is divided up into three main areas, including "MiniLand," where miniature landscapes modeled on New York, New Orleans, New England and the Northern California coast have all been constructed using the trademark plastic bricks.

For information on visiting Carlsbad, contact the **visitors bureau** (760/434-6093 or 800/227-5722).

South Carlsbad State Park, three miles south of town, is one of the nicest and most popular places to camp on the Southern California coast, its spacious campsites (with hot showers) spread out along a sandstone bluff above a broad beach. However, swimming can be dangerous, because of strong riptides. If you don't want to camp, or pay the $6-a-day-parking fee, leave your car at the park entrance, which is well marked on a surviving stretch of the old US-101 highway.

> A long but worthwhile detour inland from San Luis Rey brings you to the least visited but perhaps most evocative of all the California missions, **Mission San Antonio de Pala**. Located on the Pala Indian Reservation, 20 miles east of San Luis Rey along Hwy-76, then another 100 yards north along a well-marked side road, Mission San Antonio de Pala is the only California mission still serving its original role of preaching to the native people, and gives an unforgettable impression of what California's mission era might have been like.

Del Mar and Torrey Pines

Most of the time Del Mar (pop. 4,860) is a sleepy little upscale suburb of San Diego, with big houses backing onto a fine, four-mile-long beach. In late summer it comes to life for the thoroughbred racing season at beautiful **Del Mar Racetrack** (built by Hollywood types like Bing Crosby, and seen in *The Grifters* and many other Hollywood movies); call for details (760/755-1141). The waves here are well suited to bodysurfing, but the sands can be hard to reach in summer because of a lack of parking—weekdays it's less of a problem.

> Some of the best views of the Southern California coastline can be had from the windows of the frequent "Coaster" commuter trains, which run right along the shore between San Juan Capistrano and Del Mar. The full trip between San Diego and Los Angeles takes about two hours; for details, call MetroLink (213/808-5465).

South along the Camino Del Mar coast road from Del Mar, hang-gliders, tidepoolers, surfers, and beachcombers flock to the nearly 2,000 acres of bluffs and beaches protected in Torrey Pines State Reserve. Named for the long-needled pines that grow naturally only here, the reserve is crisscrossed by hiking trails leading down steep ravines between the bluffs and the sands.

Overlooking the Pacific from atop a bluff at the south end of the reserve, the **Salk Institute** is one of the world's most important centers for research in the life sciences. Founded by the late Jonas Salk, designed by Louis Kahn, and modeled in part on the gardens of the Alhambra in Granada, the institute is open for **tours** (Mon.-Fri. 10 AM, 11 AM, and noon; free; 760/453-4100).

Stretching inland and south from the Salk Institute the hills are covered with faceless business parks around the spacious campus of **University of California at San Diego** (UCSD), beyond which spreads La Jolla and the greater San Diego area.

Besides hang-gliders, Torrey Pines is prime air space for remote-controlled **model gliders,** which float gracefully in the nearly constant onshore breeze. The primary launching spot is the small city park at the south end of Torrey Pines State Reserve.

Between La Jolla and San Diego, at Belmont Park (619/491-2988), the Giant Dipper wooden roller coaster survives as the sole remnant of a 1920s beachfront amusement park.

San Diego is also the beginning of our cross-country US-80 "Southern Pacific" route, described beginning on page 738, which runs east across Arizona all the way to Tybee Island, Georgia.

Driving San Diego

From La Jolla south, the US-101 highway is buried by the I-5 freeway. Old US-101 can still be followed, however, by following Pacific Highway past Mission Bay and Lindbergh Field toward San Diego Bay, where it becomes Harbor Drive—where the Tijuana Trolley now runs. Southbound automobile travelers must take I-5 in order to pass through the official border crossing at San Ysidro/Tijuana.

SAN DIEGO SURVIVAL GUIDE

SET ALONG A HUGE PACIFIC OCEAN HARBOR at the southwestern corner of the country, just a few miles from the Mexican border, San Diego embodies the Southern California ideal. Like most of California, San Diego was first settled by Spanish missionary Franciscan friars in the late 1700s, but it remained a small village of farmers and ranchers until the arrival of the transcontinental Southern Pacific Railroad in 1882, which brought middle-class Midwestern masses to the coast by the thousand. For a while, around the turn of the century, it rivaled Los Angeles as a  boom-town based on wild real estate speculation, but while L.A. continued to expand by leaps and bounds San Diego grew more slowly. San Diego's economy has long been based around the U.S. Navy, and as recently as the 1960s extensive tuna-fishing fleets filled the rest of the busy harbor, which more recently hosted the America's Cup yachting races.

Despite a metropolitan population of 2.5 million people, San Diego still feels very small and anything but urban. For visitors and residents alike, the main attractions of San Diego are the city's usually sunny climate and its miles of clean and uncrowded beaches, such as Pacific, Mission and Ocean Beaches, rather than any great historic or cultural sights. The main things to see in San Diego are in **Balboa Park**, a lushly landscaped 1,150-acre spread on downtown San Diego's northwest edge, which was laid out and constructed as part of the 1915 International Exposition celebrating the completion of the Panama Canal. The many grand buildings, all built in gorgeous Spanish Revival style by architect Bertram Goodhue, have been preserved in marvelous condition, and now house sundry museums, ranging from automobiles to fine art to a functioning replica of Shakespeare's Globe Theatre. A passport ($21), available from the **visitor center** (619/239-0512), allows entrance to any eight of the park's dozen museums. Balboa Park is also the location of the **San Diego Zoo** ($15; 619/231-1515), one of the largest and most popular in the world.

To see the different sides of San Diego, head to its contrasting corners. The richest district, La Jolla, is on the coast northwest of the city
(continues on following page)

proper The recently renovated Museum of Contemporary Art, overlooking the ocean at 700 Prospect Avenue, plus great surfing (head to
Windansea for the best waves), beachcombing and skin diving in the
famous coves, not to mention the tons of good cafes, restaurants and
art galleries, have long made La Jolla an all-around great day-out.
Another side of San Diego is revealed by a trip south of the Mexico
border to lively **Tijuana**, easily reach-
able via the "Tijuana Trolley" from
downtown.

The **San Diego Padres** (619/283-
4494) play at concrete Qualcomm
Stadium, off I-15 at the Friars Road
exit.

Practicalities

The city of San Diego bends diagonally around its natural harbor,
which makes orientation occasionally confusing. The main airport,
Lindbergh Field, is on the waterfront just north of downtown—and
has one of the swiftest final approaches of any American city airport.
By road, the I-5 freeway runs right through downtown San Diego,
between Mission Bay and the Mexican border, while the I-8 freeway
comes in from the east via Mission Valley.

Because it is small and relatively compact, San Diego is easy to get
around. Downtown is walkable, and on a bike you could see most
everything in a day. Buses operated by San Diego Transit ($1; 619/234-
1060) fan out from downtown, while the light rail "Tijuana Trolley"
($2) runs south from downtown to the Mexican border.

Places to stay are generally modern, clean, and comfortable, though
rates vary with seasons and conventions. The cheapest ($15 a night)
beds are at the **HI San Diego Hostel**, in the historic downtown
"Gaslamp District" at 521 Market Street (619/525-1531); there's a second **HI Point Loma Hostel** northwest of downtown, near Sea World at
3790 Udall Street (619/223-4778). Near the beach and Point Loma,
the **Ocean Villa Motel**, 5142 W. Point Loma Boulevard (619/224-
3481), has ocean-view rooms for around $60. For top of the line ac-
commodations, or just to appreciate the historic architecture, head to
the wonderful old **Hotel Del Coronado**, across the bridge from downtown at 1500 Orange Avenue (619/522-8000). Rising up in turreted
glory, this fabulously grand Victorian-era resort hotel still caters, as it
always has, to the four-star trade. (It's also where the Man Who Would
Be King, England's Edward VIII, first met his femme fatale Mrs. Simpson, whose husband was commander of the local navy base.) Rooms
from under $200.

Though you may feel the need to duck when planes land at nearby Lindbergh Field, for breakfast there's the **Hob Nob Hill,** 2271 First Avenue, a classic old coffee shop, with pecan waffles worth driving all night for. In La Jolla, **The Spot,** 1005 Prospect Avenue, two blocks from La Jolla Cove, is a longtime local favorite that serves hefty portions of burgers, BBQ ribs and chicken, plus pizzas, at moderate prices. San Diego's most popular old-style Mexican place is, appropriately enough, the somewhat ersatz **Old Town Cantina,** 2489 San Diego Avenue near the "Old Town" historic park.

The best range of information is available from the **San Diego International Visitors Center,** 11 Horton Plaza (619/236-1212), downtown at 1st and F Streets. The main daily paper is the *San Diego Union-Tribune,* and local issues and events are covered in the *Reader* and other free weekly papers.

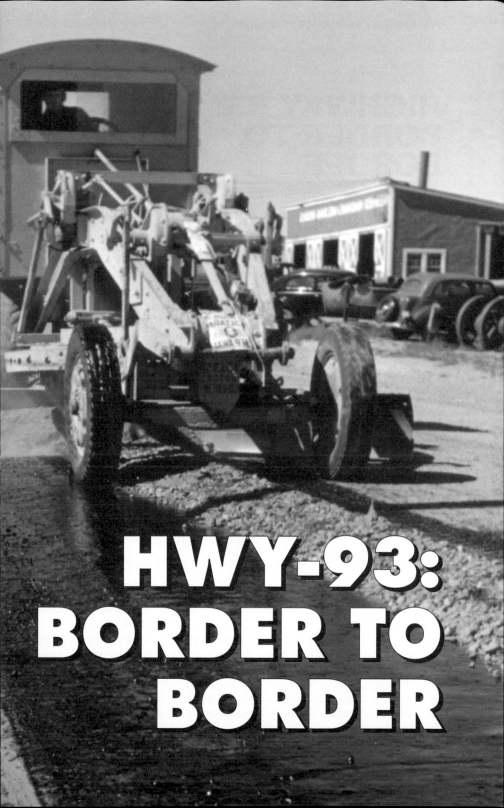

HWY-93: BORDER TO BORDER

HIGHWAY 93: BORDER TO BORDER

The western half of North America is often described as a land of contrasts, and no route across it gives a sharper sense of the region's extremes than Highway 93. Starting in the north, across the Canadian border at Jasper National Park in the heart of the Rocky Mountains, and winding up south-of-the-border in the Sonora Desert twin towns of Nogales, this route, which retains the number "93" despite the different international jurisdictions, traverses some of the wildest and ruggedest lands imaginable: mighty mountains, glaciated valleys, raging rivers, and two very different deserts. Besides offering up-close looks at mile after mile of magnificent and almost completely untouched wilderness, US-93 also takes you right through the neon heart of what is surely the most extreme (and most extremely visual) example of our contemporary "civilization": Las Vegas.

The route divides into two almost unrecognizably different halves. The northern section, from the Canadian Rockies wonderland of Banff and Jasper south as far as Sun Valley, Idaho, is pure alpine majesty. Passing the western flanks of Glacier National Park, US-93 runs along river valleys through diverse communities where skiing, hiking, and sightseeing have replaced mining and lumbering as the economic engines. South of Kalispell, the highway winds across the Flathead Indian Reservation along the western shores of Flathead Lake to Missoula, located at the heart of the bountiful country captured in *A River Runs Through It*. Western Montana's natural beauty reaches a peak in the Bitterroot Valley, which stretches south from Missoula all the way to the Idaho border. Besides scenery, the valley also abounds in history, holding many key sites pertaining to the explorers Lewis and Clark, the first whites to set foot in the region, and other sites related to the epic struggle of Chief Joseph and the Nez Percé tribe.

As you pass over the Bitterroots into Idaho across the Continental Divide, the scenery remains impressive as US-93 winds along the banks of the Salmon River, all the way to its source in the serrated Sawtooth Mountains, then drops down swiftly into Sun Valley, the oldest and most upscale ski resort in the country.

South of Sun Valley, however, everything changes very suddenly. Roaring rivers and mountain forests give way to lava flows and empty deserts as US-93 races across the inhospitable landscape of the Snake River plain. This was the most difficult portion of the historic Oregon Trail, though the biggest difficulty facing today's travelers is the struggle to stay alert—there's very little to look for, apart from acres of potato farms reclaimed from the arid desert. The one real sight is the Snake River itself, which has carved itself into a deep gorge near Twin Falls.

Continuing south into Nevada, US-93 embarks on what is truly, if not officially, the "Loneliest Road in America," traveling across 500 miles of Great Basin desert. Though not for the faint-hearted (or those with unreliable cars!) it's an unforgettably beautiful journey; after hours (or days) of existential solitude, you drop down into the frenetic boomtown of Las Vegas.

Crossing Hoover Dam into Arizona, the route crosses old Route 66 west of the Grand Canyon, then races southeast across the lush Sonora Desert—known as the "world's greenest desert" because of its abundant flora and fauna—through Phoenix and Tucson to the Mexican border. This last stretch is among the most fascinating 200 miles of highway in the country, taking you past such intriguingly diverse and unique sights as the controversial Biosphere II scientific research center, the country's only intact Cold War-era missile silo, and a pair of centuries-old churches, two of the most captivating pieces of architecture in the western U.S.

ALONG THE CANADIAN ROCKIES

At its northernmost extreme high up in the Canadian Rockies, Highway 93 passes through some of the most famous vacation areas in North America: the Canadian national parks of Banff and Jasper. Popular with skiers in winter, and hikers and sightseers in summer, these alpine resorts date back over 100 years, and remain among the most beautiful places on earth. Between Jasper and Lake Louise, Hwy-93 is known as the Icefields Parkway, an amazing drive, with endless panoramas of glaciers and towering peaks, and dozens of turnouts and trailheads to tempt you out from behind the wheel. Over 140 miles (225 km) long, the Icefields Parkway runs right alongside the Continental Divide, the rugged crest that separates the Atlantic and Pacific watersheds. South of the Icefields Parkway, our route passes through the world-renowned resort towns of Banff and Lake Louise, taking in their unforgettable alpine scenery—and historic landmark hotels.

Southwest from Lake Louise, Hwy-93 winds through Kootenay National Park, another incredible assembly of mountain scenery, before dropping down out of the mountains for the run south to the border, following the broad Kootenay River all the way to Montana.

Prices in the Canadian sections are given in Canadian dollars, which at time of writing were worth about 65 cents in American money—i.e., many things are cheaper in Canada than in the U.S., though high taxes tend to more than make up for the difference in exchange rates. NB: the colloquial Canadian equivalent of "buck" (for a dollar) is "loonie," thanks to the image of a loon (a bird) on the dollar coin.

Jasper Townsite

The northernmost point on Hwy-93, at the junction of the Icefields Parkway with the cross-country Yellowhead Highway (Hwy-16), which links Edmonton with Prince Rupert, the town of Jasper (pop. 3,800) preserves its frontier character intact. Unlike Banff, which exudes wealth and comfort, Jasper (which is officially referred to as "Jasper Townsite" to differentiate it from Jasper National Park) is a rough-and-ready, workaday sort of place. Founded on fur trading and mining, Jasper boomed when a cross-Canada railroad came through in 1911, but since the establishment of the national park in 1930 Jasper has served primarily as a handy base for exploring the wilds that surround it.

The main attractions are covered below under the Jasper National Park heading, but a few others are located very close to town. First and foremost of these is probably the **Jasper Tramway** (daily 8 AM-10 PM; $17; 780/852-3093) which lifts passengers 3,500 vertical feet (1,067 meter) in under 10 minutes, up the steep north face of the Whistlers. From the upper terminal of the tramway, you can follow a half-mile (0.8 km) path to the 8,100-foot (753-meter) summit for a breathtaking panorama, south to the Columbia Icefield, and (on a clear day . . .) northwest to Mount Robson, the highest point of the Canadian Rockies, at 13,006 feet (3,964 meters) above sea level.

The other big draw is **Maligne Canyon,** a 100- to 150-foot-deep (30-46-meter) limestone canyon that's so narrow in places that squirrels can leap from rim to rim. Trails lead around and across it, and in winter you can join an unforgettable guided tour ($28; 780/852-3370) and wander along the bottom of the narrow, ice-covered gorge. Beyond Maligne Canyon is one the prettiest lakes in the Canadian Rockies, Maligne Lake. Hiking trails lead along the shore and to panoramic viewpoints, but it is the **cruise** ($31; 780/852-3370) to Spirit Island that attracts most visitors.

Jasper's compact center, sandwiched between the west bank of the Athabasca River and a wide bench of land dotted with forest-encircled lakes, holds all the cafes and gift shops you could want within a block of the main drag, Connaught Drive (Hwy-93). The **Soft Rock Cafe,** 622 Connaught Drive, has cinnamon buns, great fresh-fruit waffles, and anything else you need to start the day off right; **Jasper Pizza Place,** two blocks north at 402 Connaught Drive has wood-fired ovens and walls covered in photos of Jasper in the early days. Another lively spot is the bar and grill on the ground floor of the **Athabasca Hotel,** 510 Patricia Street (780/852-3386), which also has Jasper's least expensive in-town lodging. Jasper's most expensive place to stay is the **Jasper Park Lodge** (780/852-3301), third of the trio of mountain resorts built by the Canadian Pacific Railway but now a mostly modern resort offering 450 rooms, plus golfing and horseback riding, on a lovely site across from town on the other side of the Athabasca River.

Budget travelers may want to take advantage of the hostels around Jasper, including the 80-bed **Jasper International Hostel,** five miles (eight km) south of Jasper on the road to the

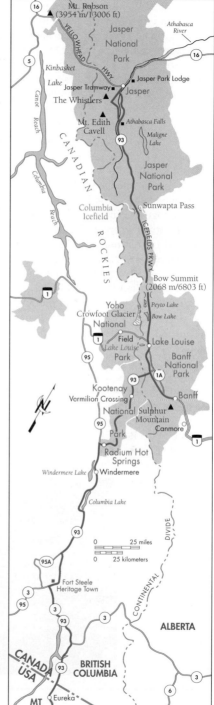

Jasper Tramway, and the smaller and more rustic **Maligne Canyon Hostel**, a short walk from the canyon. Reservations for either hostel, and for other hostels in Jasper National Park, can be made by phone 780/852-3215. There are also two large **campgrounds**, Whistlers and Wapiti, along Hwy-93 on the south side of Jasper, with over 1,000 sites, some with RV hookups.

For details on hiking and camping options, or to purchase the required entrance passes and backcountry camping permits, go to the Parks Canada **information center** (780/852-6176) in a lovely old stone building off Connaught Drive in

---

THE LAST FRONTIER

The Canadian Rockies are farther north than anything else in *Road Trip USA*, but for indefatigable adventurers there's at least one additional destination: Alaska, "The Last Frontier." It's a mere 2,500 miles from Jasper to Anchorage, via the legendary **Alaska Highway**. Running from the oil- and gas-producing center of Dawson Creek (no connection with the TV show) in British Columbia, the Alaska Highway was constructed in 1942, in just nine months, an amazing engineering feat fueled by fears of a Japanese invasion during WW II. Much improved in the years since, it's now paved all the way but is still quite an adventure, with endless miles (and miles, and miles) of forests, rivers, and mountains.

If you're going, you should plan ahead carefully (and buy a copy of Moon's excellent *Alaska-Yukon Handbook*) and keep a lookout for few places you won't want to miss. One of these is roughly midway, in Watson Lake right on the BC/Yukon border right along the highway: the world-famous **Signpost Forest**, a collection of over 20,000 city limits signs from around the globe. The "forest" was started in 1942 by Carl Lindley, a U.S. soldier working to build the highway. When ordered to fix an official road sign, he added another of his own making, pointing the way and the distance to his home in Danville, Indiana. Others followed his lead, and over the years, have added sign upon sign to create the current collection.

Next to the Signpost Forest is the very helpful **Alaska Highway Interpretive Center** (daily 8 AM-8 PM in summer; 867/536-7469) with practical information and historical exhibits.

Athabasca Park; for more complete information, including listings of rooms available in private homes, talk to the folks at the Jasper **visitor center,** which shares the space (780/852-3858).

Jasper National Park

Running from Jasper Townsite all the way to Lake Louise, 144 miles (232 km) to the south, this section of Hwy-93 is known as the Icefields Parkway. Like many roads in American national parks, the Icefields Parkway was initially built as a relief project during the Great Depression and was completed in 1940. Without a doubt one of the world's great drives, this sinuous ribbon winds along the banks of a series of icy rivers between glaciers and towering Rocky Mountain peaks, with almost no development to mar the views. The northern half of the highway passes through Jasper National Park, alongside the milky green Athabasca River.

While the Icefields Parkway makes a great drive, a worthwhile detour follows an older alignment of the highway, Hwy-93A, which runs parallel and slightly to the west. One of the best concentrations of scenery surrounds Mount Edith Cavell, easily reached by Mount Edith Cavell Road that turns off Hwy-93A about four miles (six km) south of Jasper Townsite. From the winding road you can choose from fairly short day-hikes up to wildflower-rich alpine meadows, with views of Angel Glacier, or longer overnight treks into the backcountry, including the park's only off-road accommodations, the **Tonquin Valley Lodge** (780/852-3909), a 15-mile (24 km) hiking or cross-country skiing trip from the trailhead. Right at the trailhead there's the handy **Mt. Edith Cavell hostel** (June-Nov. only; $10 per person; 780/852-3215).

About 15 miles (24 km) south of Jasper Townsite, Hwy-93A and the Icefields Parkway rejoin at **Athabasca Falls,** where the river is forced through a narrow gorge and over a cliff into a cauldron of roaring water; numerous viewpoints above and below the falls let you get up-close and personal with the thundering torrent. There's a rustic **hostel** a short walk away from the falls.

At the southern end of Jasper National Park, 60 miles (97 km) south of Jasper Townsite, the massive Columbia Icefield rises high above the west side of the Icefields Parkway.

The Icefields Parkway is kept open year-round, but gas, food, and lodging services are available almost only near the towns of Banff, Jasper and Lake Louise. Wide shoulders and frequent hostels (780/852-3215) along the Parkway make it an excellent bicycling route, too.

The four contiguous Canadian Rockies National Parks—Jasper, Banff, Yoho, and Kootenay, along with neighboring wilderness areas—jointly protect a 7,000-square mile (18,000-square km) area that has been declared a UNESCO World Heritage Site for its ecological importance.

Passes are required for each person entering any of the Canadian Rockies national parks and are available at park gates and at visitor centers. They're valid for one day ($5) or all year ($35).

Columbia Icefield

Rising to the west of Sunwapta Pass, the dividing line between Banff and Jasper Parks, the massive Columbia Icefield is what the Icefields Parkway is all about: the largest icefield and most accessible glacier in the Canadian Rockies, seemingly endless square miles of solid ice sitting high atop the Continental Divide. Visibly shrinking throughout the 20th century, the icefield is still immense, and you can get an up-close look by joining the very popular "Snocoach" tours ($23.50; 403/762-6767), operated by the Brewster company, which leave every 15 minutes and travel out onto Athabasca Glacier.

THE BREWSTER BOYS

Few guides in the Canadian Rockies were as well known as Jim and Bill Brewster. In 1892, aged 10 and 12 respectively, they were hired by the Banff Springs Hotel to take guests on a tour of local landmarks. As their reputations grew so did their business, which expanded to include a livery and outfitting company, a pair of hotels, and a ski lodge. Today, their legacy lives on in Brewster, where their tour and transportation company has become an integral part of the Canadian Rockies experience for many visitors. The Brewster company operates a fleet of tour buses, a Banff hotel, and the famous "Snocoaches" that take tourists out onto the Columbia Icefield.

Overlooking the icefield from across the Icefields Parkway, the modern **Columbia Icefield Center** (daily 9 AM-11 PM May-Oct.; free), a mini-museum of glacial lore, operated by Parks Canada. If you want to experience the icefield up close, buy a ticket and take one of the Snocoach tours; don't simply walk across the highway and clamber up, since it only takes one false step to fall to your death into one of the very deep but invisible crevasses that crisscross the glacier.

Banff National Park
Roughly midway along the Icefields Parkway, the Columbia Icefield and Sunwapta Pass mark the boundary between Jasper and Banff National Parks, and the dividing line between the Arctic and Atlantic watersheds. South of the pass, the first worthwhile stop is the **Weeping Wall**, a 350-foot cliff of gray limestone down which a series of waterfalls tumble. Frozen in winter, it's a prime spot for ice-climbing thrill-seekers.

Though it may well sound like empty hyperbole, the list of candidates for the most beautiful sight in Banff National Park, and perhaps the entire Canadian Rockies, has to include jewel-like **Peyto Lake**, an iridescently glowing blue-green glacial lake that reflects the snow-capped surrounding peaks. The often mirror-smooth waters of this small, oblong lake change color from a deep blue to jade green as the proportion of glacial silt in the water increases with the snowmelt from summer to fall. The short trail to the usually crowded Peyto Lake overlook starts from the parking area along the Icefields Parkway at 6,500-foot Bow Summit.

Bow Summit is one of the highest points reached by road in Canada; south of here, the Icefields Parkway drops down into the Bow Valley, which is dominated by the sparkling waters of Bow Lake and the views across it to Crowfoot Glacier. At the north edge of the lake, historic **Simpson's Num-Ti-Jah Lodge** (403/522-2167) is a giant octagonal log cabin, with well-priced rooms and a small coffee shop, that marks the start of a popular trail to **Bow Glacier Falls**, a fairly level, two-mile (three-km) one-way hike to this spectacular waterfall.

From the lodge, the Icefields Parkway winds along the east shore of Bow Lake, then along the banks of the Bow River, which flows south through Lake Louise, Banff and on through Calgary, eventually ending up in Hudson Bay.

Detour: Yoho National Park

From the village of Lake Louise, the Trans-Canada Highway cuts off from Hwy-93, running west through Kamloops toward Vancouver. The first 25 miles (40 km) of this highway, west from Lake Louise and the Icefields Parkway, passes through Yoho National Park, the smallest and least-known, but perhaps most feature-packed of the contiguous Canadian Rockies parks. It's impossible to do justice to the park in a paragraph or two, but if you like the other parks, and particularly if you enjoy backpacking, think about spending some time here, too.

Though the communities associated with the national parks are referred to in various ways, their official names are: Jasper Townsite, Lake Louise Village, and the Town of Banff.

From Lake Louise, Trans-Canada Hwy-1 climbs quickly over Kicking Horse Pass before reaching the **Spiral Tunnel Viewpoint**, where you can learn about the amazing engineering feat that allowed trains to travel through this rugged region. Five miles (eight km) farther, the next swing north takes you up, and up, and up, along a *very* tight series of hairpin turns, to **Takkakaw Falls**, perhaps the most impressive waterfall in the Canadian Rockies. You can see the 1,400-foot (427-meter) falls from the parking lot, but a short trail leads to the Yoho River, where you can appreciate the view in all its rainbow-refracting glory.

Farther west along Trans-Canada Hwy-1, about a dozen miles (20 km) from the Icefields Parkway in the railroad hamlet of **Field**, you come to the Yoho National Park **information center** (250/343-6324), which can tell you all about the park's natural attractions. Three miles (five km) west of Field, a turnoff to the north leads high up into the mountains to the **Emerald Lake Lodge** (250/343-6321 or 800/663-6336), a rustic, upscale resort that dates back to 1902. Sitting on the shores of one of the Canadian Rockies' most magnificent lakes, the lodge is open year-round, offering food and lodging ($165-400 a night, depending on season) as well as swimming, boating and horseback riding.

Besides the summer sightseeing, the Lake Louise area offers world-class downhill skiing: three mountains (over 3,000 vertical feet, 900 vertical meters) are yours for the price of a **Larch Mountain** lift ticket ($45; 403/522-3555). One of the lifts operates throughout the summer as well, offering a grand Canadian Rockies panorama.

Lake Louise

The sight of Lake Louise, spreading in a deep aquamarine pool at the foot of silvery snow-capped peaks, is worth traveling around the world to see. Which is exactly what many people do: if you come here in summer, you'll be among an international gaggle of tourists for whom Lake Louise really *is* the Canadian Rockies. A small village with the same name sits along Trans-Canada Hwy-1, but the 1.5 mile-long (2.4 km) (and very cold) lake itself is about two miles (three km) west, at the end of Lake Louise Drive.

Originally built by the Canadian Pacific Railway, the Banff Springs Hotel, Chateau Lake Louise, and Jasper Park Lodge (and some 25 others across Canada) are all owned and operated by the same company. For rates and reservations, call 800/441-1414.

Like the town of Banff to the south, Lake Louise was developed over a century ago as a tourist resort by the Canadian Pacific Railway. As in Banff the landmark here is a magnificent hotel, the **Chateau Lake Louise** (403/522-3511), which stands 10 stories high above the lakeshore. Taking on a Swiss Alps-theme—staff wear lederhosen, while yodelers and harmonica players perform in the hotel lobbies and bars, and all day long a funny old man stands along the shore blowing a 15-foot alpine horn which echoes back and forth in the canyons across the lake—the 520-room Chateau Lake Louise has every service and comfort you could want, at rates ranging in the neighborhood of $200-350 per night.

The Icefields Parkway drops down into Bow Valley.

Of course, there's no charge to explore the hotel or walk along the lake and enjoy the views. You can rent canoes and paddle out onto the lake, and from the hotel a popular trail climbs over 1,000 feet (305 meters) in about two miles (three km) to Bridal Veil Falls, continuing a short way farther to **Lake Agnes**, where a rustic teahouse serves sandwiches (and teas!).

Immediately below the lake, the family-owned, summer-only **Paradise Lodge and Bungalows** (403/522-3595) is smaller and friendlier, with cozy log cabins and modern lodge rooms (many with fireplaces) running $135-250 per night.

Back down in Lake Louise Village, at the northwest end of Village Road, the **Lake Louise Hostel** (403/522-2200) is a very large, modern log-built lodge, with $20-24 dorm beds and the very nice **Bill Peyto's Cafe**, the area's least expensive place to eat, open daily 7 AM-9 PM. There are gas stations, gift shops, a grocery store, cafes, and the popular **Laggan's Mountain Bakery** great pastries and coffee), in the hard-to-miss Samson Mall. There's also a large **campground** along the Bow River a half-mile (0.8 km) south of town; one section has electricity hookups. The whole place tends to fill up most days despite having over 400 campsites total.

While Trans-Canada Hwy-1 is faster, the **Bow Valley Parkway** is a more scenic alternative between Banff and Lake Louise. Running parallel and to the east, it also gives access to some very nice spots, including the waterfalls of Johnston Canyon, where a small resort (403/762-2971) has inexpensive rooms in a quiet, woodland setting.

Because the Town of Banff is located within the confines of Banff National Park, development has been limited—so much so that summertime accommodations here can be hard to come by, and very expensive.

Smaller, less-visited, but every bit as spectacular as Lake Louise, **Moraine Lake** sits at the end of a summer-only road, six miles (10 km) south of the midpoint of Lake Louise Drive. Despite the name, Moraine Lake is not in fact formed by a glacial moraine, but by a rockfall; nevertheless it's a gorgeous spot, the placid lake reflecting the jagged surrounding peaks. From the lakeside, a two-mile (three-km) trail climbs up to Larch Valley, for fall color extraordinaire courtesy of the namesake trees, which are prolific here.

Town of Banff

Fifteen miles (24 km) southeast of Lake Louise, Hwy-93 and the Trans-Canada Hwy-1 diverge, with Hwy-93 cutting due south through Kootenay National Park across southeastern British Columbia toward the U.S. border. That is the route we follow, all the way south to Mexico eventually, but anyone in his or her right mind will want to make the 15-mile (24 km) trip southeast along Hwy-1 to visit the beautiful Town of Banff, home of the landmark Banff Springs Hotel, the biggest and most impressive of the grand old Canadian Pacific hotels. When it opened in 1888, this was the largest hotel in the world—with a grand total of 250 rooms; over the years the hotel has been rebuilt and expanded to its present 846-room size, most of which are booked up months in advance. Spreading between the hotel and Hwy-1, the town of Banff has grown into the tasteful but bustling commercial center of the Canadian Rockies, with a year-round population of some 7,000 people, plus many times that many visitors daily during the peak summer season. Though the commercialism can detract from the natural splendor, Banff is definitely a very pleasant place to while away some time.

For the most spectacular introduction to Banff, head past the Banff Springs Hotel to the south end of Mountain Avenue, where the **Sulphur Mountain Gondola** (daily 7:30 AM-9 PM; $12; 403/762-2523) will take you up 2,300 feet (700 meters) for a grand view over the entire Bow Valley. The "springs" in the Banff Springs Hotel's name refer to actual hot springs; to take a soak, visit the **Upper Hot Springs** ($7; 403/762-1515), at the foot of the Sulphur Mountain Gondola. The original hot springs that spurred the growth of Banff have been closed and converted into the **Cave and Basin Centennial Centre** (daily 9 AM-6 PM; $2.25; 403/762-1557), west of town at the end of Cave Avenue, where exhibits detail the underlying geology that makes hot springs happen.

calm, spectacular Moraine Lake

The main drag of town, Banff Avenue, has all the cafes, restaurants and shopping you could want (for suggestions, see Banff Practicalities below), but if the weather's bad (and if it's not, you really ought to be outdoors, enjoying Mother Nature!), you can learn about Banff and the Canadian Rockies in a trio of museums. Best first stop is the **Banff Park Museum** (daily 10 AM-6 PM; $2.25) near the river at the foot of Banff Avenue, a Victorian-era remnant (it was built in 1903) that displays the taxidermied remains of typical park wildlife. Around the corner, a half-block down from pleasant, riverside Central Park at 111 Bear Street, the **Whyte Museum of the Canadian Rockies** (daily 10 AM-6 PM; $3) has an expansive collection of historic books, postcards, paintings and photographs, all capturing various aspects of the mountains and their inhabitants. Last but not least, the stockade-like **Luxton Museum** (daily 9 AM-9 PM; $5), across the river at 1 Birch Street, details the cultures of the native peoples who inhabited the Canadian Rockies long before there were any Canadians. Inside there's an intricately decorated teepee, bows and arrows and other hunting equipment, and some peace pipes; the museum gift shop is also worth a browse.

Town of Banff Practicalities
So long as you plan ahead, and can afford to enjoy some of Canada's most expensive hotels and restaurants, the Town of Banff makes a great place to visit.

Throughout the summer hotels are booked up solidly well in advance, and summer rates average around $150 for a basic room. (Winter rates are usually less than half that.) The cheapest rooms are at the $80-a-night **Spruce Grove Motel**, 545 Banff Avenue (403/762-2112). A dozen other places are all within a short walk of downtown, where the new **Brewster Mountain Lodge**, 208 Caribou Street (403/762-2900) has spacious rooms starting around $170 a night in summer. Rooms at the landmark **Banff Springs Hotel** (403/762-2211 or 800/441-1414), when available, start at around $175 a night and climb quickly into the $300-500 range.

Restaurants are plentiful, good, and wide-ranging—over 100, which works out to one for every 70 residents. One of the most popular places, with locals and visitors alike, is **Melissa's**, 218 Lynx Street (daily 7 AM-10 PM; 403/762-5511) on the west side of downtown. Housed in a 1928 log building, Melissa's serves great pancakes (with real maple syrup) and beefy burgers, and has a nice bar and outdoor deck. Along with two good Italian places (**Guido's** and **Giorgio's**, at 116 and 219 Banff Avenue, respectively), downtown Banff also has many Japanese places, a Greek cafe, and the ever popular **Wild Bill's Saloon**, which has food and drink (mostly the latter).

Parks Canada operates three **campgrounds** along Tunnel Mountain Road, two miles (three km) east of downtown, which have over 1,000 sites altogether; all the campgrounds have hot showers, and many sites have full or partial RV hookups. Also on Tunnel Mountain Road is the large **HI Banff International Hostel** (403/762-4122).

For comprehensive information on Banff, head to the large **visitor center**, downtown at 224 Banff Avenue, which is home to both the commercially-oriented Banff/Lake Louise Tourism Bureau (403/762-8421) and the rangers of Banff National Park (403/762-1550).

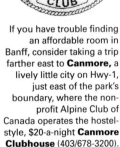

If you have trouble finding an affordable room in Banff, consider taking a trip farther east to **Canmore,** a lively little city on Hwy-1, just east of the park's boundary, where the non-profit Alpine Club of Canada operates the hostel-style, $20-a-night **Canmore Clubhouse** (403/678-3200).

One of many cultural events that take place in Banff is the **Banff Mountain Film Festival** (403/762-6675), where the world's best adventure travel and mountain-climbing films are shown every November.

Kootenay National Park

Though Banff and Jasper seem to get all the attention, neighboring Kootenay National Park draws a breed of traveler who prefers to experience wilderness without having to wait in line. Originally known as the "Highway Park," since the land was deeded to the federal government in exchange for it building (and paying for!) the 65-mile-long (105-km) Banff-Windermere Road that now runs through the heart of the park. Completed in 1922, this was the first road over the Canadian Rockies, and linked the prairies and the west coast of British Columbia for the first time. Fortunately for visitors, Hwy-1, which runs through Yoho to the north, now carries most of the through traffic.

Kootenay National Park spreads for five miles (eight km) to either side of the highway. As in all the Canadian Rockies parks, grizzly bears still roam the Kootenay backcountry, and mountain goats, bighorn sheep, and moose are regularly seen along the roadside. A number of stops along the way offer great short hikes. Two of the most enjoyable, **Marble Canyon** and **Paint Pots**, are at the north end of the park, well-signed along the north side of the highway. Marble Canyon is an amazing sight (and sound): a 100-foot-deep, very narrow slot canyon carved in the shiny white dolomite limestone by the thundering cascade of Tokumn Creek. A half-mile (0.8 km) trail leads back and forth on a series of man-made and natural bridges over the gorge. Two miles (three km) south, the Paint Pots are much more sedate, displaying a handful of brightly colored mud puddles dyed varying shades of red and yellow by oxidizing minerals in the natural springs.

At Vermilion Crossing at the center of the park, about 15 miles (24 km) south of the Paint Pots and 40 miles (64 km) from Radium, you'll find the park's only overnight accommodations at **Kootenay Park Lodge** (403/762-9196), which has a handful of $60-90-a-night cabins, a restaurant, a gas station and a general store. From here south, the road follows the broad banks of the Vermilion and Kootenay Rivers before cutting west over Sinclair Pass, where a viewpoint offers a stunning high country panorama. At the southern end of the park, the road winds through the narrow gorge of Sinclair Canyon before running suddenly into the roadside sprawl of Radium Hot Springs.

You can drive through Kootenay without charge, but if you want to stop *en route* you need to buy a park pass ($5 per person per day) from the entrance stations. Park maps, and details of Kootenay's hiking and camping options, are available from the very helpful **information center** (250/347-9615)at the park's west gate near Radium Hot Springs, or from the Parks Canada centers in Banff and Jasper.

**CANADIAN ROCKIES
HOT SPRINGS**

Radium Hot Springs

At the west edge of Kootenay National Park, the town of Radium Hot Springs is a swift change from the natural idyll. Block after block of motels, cafes and gas stations line Hwy-93, and apart from satisfying your fuel-and-food needs there's not a lot here. Fast food places surround the Hwy-93/95 junction at the center of town, and the one good place to eat is **The Springs** restaurant, west of town on the golf course. Motels here include the $55-a-night **Valley View** (250/347-9565) and the upscale **Springs at Radium Golf Resort** (250/347-9311 or 800/667-6444)

The actual hot springs from which the town takes its name are just east, inside the park boundary in a heavily developed complex (daily 9 AM-11 PM; $7), with two pools (a small one at 103° F, another at 84° F), and an artery-clogging cafe. Unfortunately, the water is heavily chlorinated, and there are no "natural" springs left.

If you're passing through Radium Hot Springs, be sure to stop for a look at the amazing array of signs and sculptures outside Swiss-born artist Rolf Heer's **Radium Wood Carvers** on a hill just east of the Hwy-93/95 junction.

Fort Steele Heritage Town

South of Radium Hot Springs, Hwy-93 runs along the western foot of the Rocky Mountains, but the natural beauty of the national parks doesn't really return until you cross the border and visit Glacier National Park, a good 200 miles (322 km) away. That said, it's a wide-open drive, passing a few towns, some golf resorts and two big lumber mills, following the banks of the Kootenay River all the way.

The one real attraction along this stretch of road is the resurrected frontier community of Fort Steele, roughly midway between Radium and the border crossing. Containing more than 60 preserved and reconstructed buildings, Fort Steele Heritage Town (daily 9:30 AM-5:30 PM; $6; 250/489-3351) re-creates the boom-town that stood here from 1890 until 1898, servicing the silver, gold and lead mines of the East Kootenays. Along with the buildings, which house interpretive exhibits as well as an ice cream store, a bakery and restaurant, and a general store selling top hats and other period essentials, you can enjoy theater performances or ride on a steam train—though there are extra charges for these activities.

ACROSS MONTANA

From the Canadian border, US-93 runs south and east along the Tobacco River valley, then cuts through the Flathead National Forest to the logging and ski resort towns of Whitefish and Kalispell. Continuing south along the shores of Flathead Lake, the route passes through the college town and cultural nexus of Missoula, south of which US-93 passes through some of the most beautiful terrain in the country, winding through broad valleys at the foot of the Bitterroot Mountains, past alpine lakes and snowcapped peaks all the way south to the Idaho border.

From the U.S./Canada border, which is open 24 hours every day, a scenic two-hour drive north will put you in **Banff and Jasper National Parks,** covered in more detail on pages 119-120.

For a truly unusual experience, spend the night in the former U.S. Forest Service **fire lookout** atop Webb Mountain, 20 miles southwest of Eureka. For details and rental rates, contact the U.S. Forest Service ranger station in Eureka (406/296-2536).

Hwy-37 is an official "Scenic Byway" that winds along the Kootenai River and Lake Koocanusa from Eureka to the town of Libby, where it intersects US-2.

Eureka

Like British Columbia, Montana's northwest corner, where Canadian Hwy-93 ends and US-93 begins, is an isolated land of dense forests, broad rivers, and glaciated valleys. Besides providing natural habitat for herds of moose, elk, bison, and bighorn sheep, not to mention mountain lions, wolves, and grizzly bears, the thick groves of cedars, pines, and firs support the Northwest's other endangered species—the logger—whose angular clearcuts and mono-crop tree plantations are also apparent as you pass through the region.

The first sizeable town, 15 miles south of the border, is Eureka (pop. 1,200), a sleepy little place with a pair of gas stations, a couple of cafes (choose from Cafe Jax, the Bullwinkle Bistro, and the Sunflower Bakery, all on Main Street) and a fascinating historical village of pioneer buildings moved to a small park along US-93 at the south end of town. There's very little obvious visitor-oriented development in the area, though **Huckleberry Hannah's,** west of Eureka off Hwy-37, then north to 100 Sofie Lake Road (406/889-3381), is a quiet and comfortable country B&B, very near the international border.

Whitefish

A major division point on the historic Great Northern railroad, whose tracks are still in use by Amtrak and the Burlington Northern Santa Fe, Whitefish (pop. 4,300) was originally known as Stumptown because of the intensive logging operations centered here. Despite its proud industrial history, the blue-collar base has long since been eclipsed by tourism, and the city now calls itself the "Recreational Capital of Montana," with alpine lakes, fishing streams, hiking trails, great skiing and endless mountain scenery right on the doorstep. The main attraction in Whitefish, for skiing in winter and hiking and mountain biking in summer, is **Big Mountain**, the 6,770-foot peak (with a 2,170-foot vertical drop) that looms over the northwest shore of Whitefish Lake.

Besides giving access to the surrounding great outdoors, Whitefish is a pleasant place to stop and stretch your legs, and has everything you could want from a resort town—without the rampant tourist-pandering and real estate speculation that has ruined so many other places. A small **museum** (daily 10 AM-5 PM; free) inside the rustic Great Northern train station, which stands in a pleasant park at the north end of Central Avenue, gives a historical overview of Whitefish. Across the lobby the **chamber of commerce** (406/752-6166) has brochures, maps, and other information. Across the park is a new theater, a new library, and a new home for **Black Star Brewing**, whose hoppy products you can sample in a small tasting room, or in any Whitefish bar.

The heart of town is a few blocks of Central Avenue, running south from the railroad tracks to Montana's one and only Frank Lloyd Wright building, an early 1950s bank and office complex

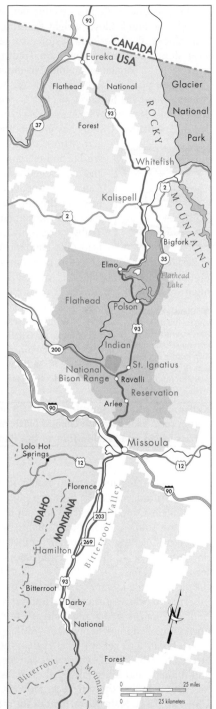

on the east side of Central Avenue between 3rd and 4th Streets called, directly enough, the **Frank Lloyd Wright Building**. In between you'll find some great bars and saloons, **Bookworks** bookstore, art galleries, the irresistible **3 Bar 2** Western wear shop, and the **Big Mountain Trading Company**, 225 Central, a pawn shop where you can bargain for anything from saddles to CDs.

The best place to start the day in Whitefish is along 3rd Street, east of Central Avenue, where the **Buffalo Cafe**, 516 E. 3rd Street, is a popular breakfast and lunch spot, locally famous for its *huevos rancheros;* next door, **Out of the Blue Bakery** on 3rd and Spokane (US-93) has great coffee and fresh pastries. Back on Central,

across from the FLW Building, the **Whitefish Times** is an erudite and relaxing coffeehouse, with magazines and books and overstuffed sofas. Lunch and dinner places line up along Central Avenue, where you can get great burgers and cheap beers at the rowdy **Bulldog Saloon**,144 Central Avenue, Mexican food at **Serrano's**, wood-fired pizza at upscale **Truby's**, or simply quaff a beer or two at **The Palace**, Whitefish's oldest and most ornate bar—all in the same block.

Besides the extensive resort accommodations available year-round at the Big Mountain resort (406/862-3511 or 800/858-5439), where rooms range from $85 a night on up, you can choose from numerous motels (**Comfort Inn** and **Super 8** among them) along US-93 south of town. Two more accommodation options are walkably close to downtown: the attractive and comfortable **Garden Wall B&B**, a craftsman-era cottage at 504 Spokane Avenue (406/862-3440), and the tidy **Non-Hostile Hostel**, 300 E. 2nd Street (406/862-7383), where bunk beds in a converted Elks lodge go for $15 a night.

In the Whitefish/Kalispell area, tune to 103.9 FM for classic country tunes. Rockers may prefer 99.7 FM, which cranks out hits from the likes of Thin Lizzy and Smashing Pumpkins.

Kalispell marks the junction of US-93 and the transcontinental route US-2, which runs east through Glacier National Park (see pages 466-467) and west across Idaho and Washington to the Pacific Ocean.

Kalispell

The nearest thing to an urban center in northwestern Montana, Kalispell (pop. 12,000) spreads across the northern Flathead Valley at the junction of the Stillwater, Whitefish, and Flathead Rivers. Cut by two main thoroughfares, east-west US-2 and north-south US-93, it ain't quaint by any stretch of the imagination; at first glance it looks like yet another lumber mill-and-mining town, but the historic downtown area is full of interesting spots, such as the engaging **Hockaday Center for the Arts** (Tues.-Fri. 10 AM-5 PM, Saturday 10 AM-3 PM; $1 donation), housed in the old Carnegie Library on 3rd Street, two blocks east of Main Street (US-93). Another few blocks east stands the impressive, perfectly preserved **Conrad Mansion**, built by pioneer trader and Kalispell founder Charles Conrad in 1895 and now open for guided tours (daily 10 AM-5:30 PM, mid-May to mid-Oct. only; $5).

Breakfasts don't get much better than those served at **Trattoria on Main**, 34 Main Street (406/755-5000), where you can also get good cheap Italian food for lunch and dinner—and killer milk shakes. Kalispell also has an above-average range of taverns, including the venerable **Moose's Saloon**, near the junction of US-2 and US-93 at 173 N. Main Street, famous for pizza and occasional live music.

There are the usual national motels (including a Motel 6, a Super 8, a Red Lion and a Best Western), but *the* place to stay in Kalispell is the Kalispell Grand Hotel, 8 W. 1st Street (406/751-8100 or 800/858-7422), a conveniently located historic downtown hotel with nice, clean rooms from around $55 a night.

For more information, contact the visitor center (406/752-9091 or 800/543-3105), on Main Street (US-93) at the south edge of town.

Flathead Lake

The largest natural freshwater lake west of the Mississippi River, deep-blue Flathead Lake is a magnet for outdoor recreation in western Montana. US-93 winds along the lake's hilly western shore, passing through a number of state parks and small resort communities that enjoy grand views of the Rocky Mountains to the east and the green foothills of the Flathead National Forest to the west.

Chief Charlo

Along US-93 at the north end of the lake, Somers is a neat old timber town with some well preserved turn-of-the-century buildings, one of which holds Tiebecker's Pub, a beer bar and good restaurant. South of town is another treat: the Osprey Inn B&B (406/857-2042), located right on the lake and named for the eagle-like birds that build huge nests atop local telephone poles. From Somers, you can detour east onto Hwy-82 for a trip along the eastern shore of Flathead Lake, where you can enjoy the upscale resort town of Bigfork and the acres of cherry orchards that line the lakeshore.

Polson: Miracle of America Museum

The southern half of Flathead Lake is surrounded by the Flathead Indian Reservation, home to a mixed population of Flathead Salish, Kootenai, and Caucasians, who make up around 80% of the reservation's population. The large reservation covers a 1.2 million-acre area, roughly 35 by 65 miles, hemmed in by the Mission and Cabinet Mountains, but it's mostly prairie and riverside wetlands, apart from a few small towns.

The largest of these towns, Polson, at the bottom end of the lake where the Flathead River flows south, is a predominately white retirement community, with 24-hour gas stations, the area's only ATMs, a Safeway supermarket, and chain motels like Days Inn and Super 8 as well as the more deluxe lakefront Best Western KwaTaqNuk Resort, 303 Hwy-93 East, (406/883-2448 or 800/882-6363), owned and operated by the Salish-Kootenai tribe, with two pools, an on-site casino, a boat dock and direct access to the lake.

Just two miles south of Polson along US-93, the bizarre but fascinating Miracle of America Museum (Mon.-Sat. 8 AM-5 PM, Sunday 2-6 PM; $2; 406/883-6804), which calls itself "Western Montana's Largest Museum," displays a mixed bag of kitchen appliances, toys, tractors, armored tanks and framed newspaper clippings to give a unique (to say the least!) view of America's industrial, military, and cultural history.

Elmo, at the north edge of the Flathead Reservation, hosts the annual **Standing Arrow PowWow** on the third weekend in July; Arlee, at the southern edge of the reservation, hosts the **4th of July PowWow,** one of the most popular Native American gatherings in Montana. For more information, call the Confederated Salish and Kootenai Tribal Council (406/675-2700), or stop by the People's Center in Pablo, four miles south of Polson.

If you like things like a motorized toboggan or a collection of tractor seats, count on spending an hour at least—twice that long if you also like music, because the museum doubles as the Montana Fiddler's Hall of Fame.

St. Ignatius and the National Bison Range

The wildly angular Mission Mountains, rising to the east of the Flathead Reservation, were named for a Catholic mission established in the 1850s at St. Ignatius, a small town midway between Polson and Missoula. Like most reservation communities, it's a poor and fairly depressed place, worth a look for the imposing **St. Ignatius Mission church** (daily 9 AM-5 PM, longer hours in summer; donations), just east of US-93. Built by Flathead laborers in 1891, the church holds over 50 religious frescoes painted by Fr. Joseph Carignano, the mission cook.

Along with the church, St. Ignatius holds the **Flathead Indian Museum and Trading Post** (daily 9 AM-6 PM; 406/745-2951), a large gift shop, motel, and drive-through espresso stand right on US-93.

West of St. Ignatius, 18,500 acres of natural rolling prairie have been set aside since 1908 as the National Bison Range, protected home of the 500 or so resident bison (a.k.a. buffalo) along with deer, elk, pronghorns, and mountain goats. Allow around two hours to drive a complete circuit of the park; the entrance and visitor center are on the west side of the reserve, off Hwy-200 six miles west of the crossroads town of **Ravalli.**

On US-93 in Ravalli, the **Bison Inn** has good food for breakfast, lunch, and dinner; the house specialty is (you guessed it) buffalo burgers, and in summer, huckleberry milk shakes.

Missoula

Spreading along the banks of the Clark Fork of the Columbia River at the mouth of Hell Gate Canyon, Missoula (pop. 43,000) is an engaging mix of college-town sophistication and blue-collar grit. The two industries that built the city, railroads and lumber mills, have both diminished considerably since their turn-of-the-century

---

A RIVER RUNS THROUGH IT

In recent years Missoula has become something of literary center, thanks in part to the late Norman MacLean, whose novella *A River Runs Through It* rhapsodizes over the surrounding Rocky Mountain country and the larger-than-life lives lived there. The book, which was faithfully adapted into a film by Robert Redford, makes a great traveling companion, full of vivid description and insightful humor—MacLean writes that while growing up he soon discovered that the world is "full of bastards, the number increasing rapidly the farther one gets from Missoula, Montana." He lovingly uses the art of fly-fishing as an essential metaphor for a life well lived.

heyday but still form the foundation of the local economy. The University of Montana campus has given Missoula a literate and left-leaning air not usually found in this neck of the woods.

The mountains, rivers and canyons around Missoula are Montana at its best, and downtown Missoula, stretching along the north bank of the river, contains a large number of elegant turn-of-the-century brick buildings housing a buoyant range of businesses, from department stores to bike shops. Missoula's other social nexus, the **University of Montana** campus, spreads south of the river at the foot of dusty brown Mount Sentinel (the one marked with the large "M") and the Sapphire Mountains. It's a pleasant place to walk around—in summer at least, when cyclists and roller-bladers outnumber pedestrians on the many paths—keeping an eye out for posters advertising local events. The area west of the university is very quiet and residential, but holds one key Missoula stop: **Freddy's Feed and Read** at 1221 Helen Avenue, a combination health-food deli and bookstore that has been a local institution since the mid-1960s.

Missoula's number one attraction, the **Smokejumpers Aerial Fire Depot** (Mon.-Fri. 9 AM-4 PM, mid-June to mid-Sept.; donations), is seven miles west of town at the end of Broadway. Displays include dioramas, old photographs, and antique fire-fighting gear; hourly guided tours are led by the very people who jump out of airplanes to battle raging forest fires.

Thanks to the student population, Missoula has a wider than usual range of places to eat. Start the day at the **Mammyth Bakery**, 131 W. Main Street, which has great pastries. Down the street, the landmark **Missoula Club**, 139 W. Main Street, is a perfectly preserved 1940s burgers-and-beer bar; for an even grittier Missoula scene, it's hard to beat the round-the-clock **Oxford Club**, corner of Pine and Higgins, where the brave try the eggs-and-brains, and everyone else drinks too much Bud. Along US-93 a half-mile south of downtown, the **Stop-n-Go** is a good old-fashioned drive-in amidst the franchised fast-food outlets.

There's no shortage of accommodations in Missoula, though it's always a good idea to book a room in advance. The nicest place to stay is **Goldsmith's**, a very comfortable B&B along the river at 809 E. Front Street (406/721-6732), but travelers on a tight budget will appreciate the **Birchwood Hostel**, 600 S. Orange Street (406/728-9799). A half-dozen motels line I-90 and US-93 (which follows Broadway west of Missoula, and Brooks Street south of town), including the usual national chains, most central of which is a **Travelodge**.

For more information on visiting Missoula and the surrounding country, contact the **visitor center**, across the river from the university at 825 E. Front Street (406/543-6623 or 800/526-3465), or the U.S. Forest Service **ranger station**, 340 N. Pattee Street (406/329-3511), which is headquarters for the entire region.

East of Missoula, scenic Hwy-200 runs along the Clearwater River to Clearwater Junction, where a giant steer welcomes travelers to town.

Missoula is also the national headquarters of the bicycling advocacy group **Adventure Cycling Association,** formerly known as Bikecentennial. They have a number of cycling and mountain-biking maps and guides to Missoula as well as the rest of the U.S. available at their office, 150 W. Pine Street (406/721-1776).

If you're a fan of hot springs, or want to unwind after a day cross-country skiing, you won't want to miss the idyllic **Lolo Hot Springs Resort** (406/273-2290), in the mountains 26 miles southwest of Missoula via scenic US-12. Moose wander through the wooded grounds, and the hot springs, where Lewis and Clark soaked themselves, have been extensively but attractively developed.

The Bitterroot Valley

South of Missoula toward the Idaho border, US-93 runs along the banks of the beautiful Bitterroot River through a broad valley bordered by parallel ridges of 8,000-foot peaks. Once you get past the log-home manufacturers and tract-house suburbs of Missoula that increasingly fill the valley's northern end, the US-93 roadside is lined by groves of cottonwood trees and occasional hamlets like **Florence**, where **Glen's Mountain View Cafe** (406/273-2534), tucked away just west of the highway, is renowned throughout Montana for its incredibly good double-crusted fresh berry pies.

South of Florence, a well-marked alternative route, the **East Side Highway** (Hwy-203 and Hwy-269), runs parallel to US-93 a half-mile to the east, passing rolling ranch lands, pioneer homesteads—some of which are among the oldest in the state—and occasional prefab trailers. This side of the valley is mostly open countryside, with a few small hamlets like **Stevensville**, Montana's oldest town. It was founded by Jesuits in 1841 around the still intact **St. Mary's Mission** (open Wed.-Sun. 10 AM-4 PM daily in summer; $2), at the end of 4th Street, two blocks west of Main.

At the north end of the Bitterroot Valley, where Lolo Creek empties into the Bitterroot River, Lewis and Clark set up camp at what they called **Traveler's Rest** in September 1805 and again on their return in July 1806. A marker along US-93, a mile south of the US-12 junction, gives more of the story.

Hamilton

The Bitterroot Valley's sole sizeable town, Hamilton (pop. 2,700), stands at the southern end of the valley, where US-93 and the East Side Highway rejoin. Hamilton was laid out in the 1890s as a planned community by the multimillionaire "Copper King" **Marcus Daly**, whose 50-acre estate, **Riverside** (Tues.-Sun. 11 AM-4 PM; $5, grounds only $1) is an elegant 42-room Georgian mansion set in lushly landscaped gardens.

Hamilton's other main draw is the large **Ravalli County Museum** (Mon.-Fri. 10 AM-4 PM; free), housed in a 100-year-old former courthouse on the corner of 3rd and Bedford, two blocks south of Main Street. Besides an above-average collection of fishing flies, pioneer clothing and Native American artifacts, the museum has an entire room dedicated to Rocky Mountain spotted fever ticks—Hamilton, home of the Rocky Mountain National Laboratory, was where the disease was discovered— and you owe it to yourself to study the 2-foot-tall tick model and the diagrams tracing the tick's life cycle.

Hamilton has some great places to eat, like the very popular **Coffee Cup Cafe** and the newer **Stone Point Bakery**, both on US-93 on the south side of town. Downtown, the **Wild Oats Cafe**, upstairs at 217 W. Main Street, has healthy wholefood sandwiches at lunchtime, and the more upscale **Banque** serves steaks, etc., in an old bank at 225 W. Main Street. Best burgers: **Nap's Grill**, 220 N. 2nd Street.

One of many highway motels in Hamilton, the **Best Western Hamilton** is on US-93 at 409 S. 1st Street (406/363-2142). Besides its convenience as a stopover, Hamilton is also the gateway to outdoor activities (hunting, fishing, and riding, mainly) in the Bitterroots; contact the **visitor center** (406/363-3131).

The Bitterroot Mountains

South of Hamilton, the serrated peaks and forested foothills of the Bitterroot Mountains close in along US-93 as the valley narrows sharply, the towns shrink in size, and woodlands (and campgrounds) replace farmlands (and commerce) along the roadside. Just 17 miles south of Hamilton, the pioneer village of **Darby** has a couple of cafes, a log-cabin public library, and an only-in-Montana combination: a liquor store that sells secondhand books and used fishing flies. Darby also has a helpful **ranger station** (406/821-3913), the best source of information on hiking and camping in the Bitterroots.

The 150 miles of mountain scenery between Hamilton, Montana, and Sun Valley, Idaho, are perhaps the prettiest and least disturbed parts of the Pacific Northwest.

South of Darby, US-93 cuts away from the Bitterroot River at the hamlet of **Sula**, beyond which the highway continues its slow climb up through seven miles of sub-alpine landscape to another of Montana's many pleasant resorts, **Lost Trail Hot Springs**, 8321 Hwy-93 South (406/821-3574 or 800/825-3574), open year-round with an attractive variety of moderately priced

*The **Big Hole National Battlefield,** where 800 Nez Percé warriors, women, and children were attacked by the U.S. Army on August 9, 1877, lies east of the Continental Divide, 20 miles east of Lost Trail Pass via Hwy-43.*

rooms and cabins, as well as a good on-site restaurant. Lost Trail is especially popular with cross-country skiers, who can traverse many miles of nearby trails, including the route followed by Chief Joseph and the Nez Percé in 1877 while fleeing from the U.S. Cavalry.

From Lost Trail Hot Springs, US-93 climbs up to 6,995-foot **Lost Trail Pass**, which Lewis and Clark crossed in 1805 on their return from the impassable Snake River, and which now marks the border with Idaho. The pass also serves as a 600-acre downhill ski area (406/821-3211), with inexpensive (under $20!) lift tickets and 1,200 vertical feet (366 meters) of groomed runs.

ACROSS IDAHO

In 1938, the WPA *Guide to Idaho* described the state's section of US-93 as "miles of beautiful mountains, ranging from soft flanks voluptuously mounded to the lean and glittering majesty of toothed backbones." Though the official US-93 route was redirected around the mountains, not much else has changed since then: the old road is still in place, and still gives an un-matched tour of the best of what Idaho has to offer.

Entering the state through a historic pass in the beautiful Bitterroot Mountains, the route drops down to follow the mighty Salmon River to its headwaters over 100 miles away near the frontier resort of Stanley, high up in the Sawtooth Mountains. South of the Sawtooths the route plunges into the plush resort community of Sun Valley, then races across the Snake River plain through Twin Falls to the Nevada border.

Across Idaho, towns and services are few and far between, and during the peak summer season it's a good idea to make arrangements for accommodations well in advance.

Salmon River: North Fork

Beginning at the Montana border, atop Lost Trail Pass, US-93 winds steeply downhill through the 1.7-million-acre Salmon National Forest. Another 26 miles south of the pass, US-93 passes by the village of North Fork—where the **North Fork**

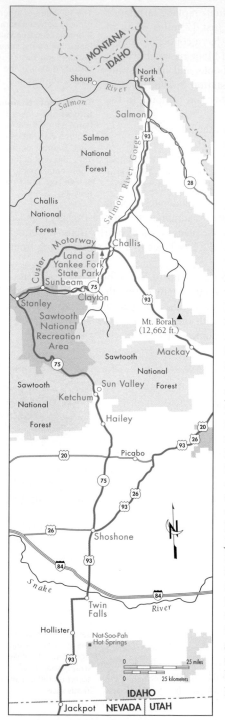

General Store (208/865-2412) is a combination cafe/motel/post office that has everything a traveler could want, from great pies to an RV park. Here US-93 crosses the Salmon River, which is often called the "River of No Return" because, without a jet boat to help you along, it is navigable only in a downstream direction. Running swiftly for nearly 300 miles west through the heart of the most extensive wilderness left in the lower 48 states, the Salmon River has carved one of the deepest gorges in North America, a full 1,000 feet deeper than the Grand Canyon.

From North Fork, a paved road leads 17 miles west along the riverside to the tiny hamlet of **Shoup**, beyond which a number of rough roads and hiking trails lead to ghost towns and the Frank Church Wilderness, deep in the rugged mountains.

Salmon

Surrounded by ranch lands in a broad valley between the Bitterroot and Yellow-jacket Mountains, Salmon (pop. 2,941) is a picturesque place that has turned increasingly to tourism and outdoor recreation as its timber and ranching industries have faded. Not surprisingly, it makes a better base from which to explore the surrounding scenery than it does a destination in itself. Main Street, which US-93 follows through town, holds the most popular places to eat: **Johnny B's Cafe**, open daily for breakfast, lunch, and dinner at 507 Main Street, and the **Salmon River Coffee Shop**, 606 Main Street. Just off US-93, the quiet **DeLuxe Motel**, at 112 S. Church Street (208/756-2231), offers inexpensive rooms. Rafting, hunting, and fishing guides are all over; the **visitor center**, next to City Hall at 200 Main Street (208/756-2100), has complete lists.

Salmon River Gorge

South of Salmon, US-93 continues beside the Salmon River, climbing slowly through a landscape that alternates from open meadows to sheer canyons. Nearly 100 miles later the route arrives at the river's headwaters high up in the Sawtooth Mountains. Apart from a few cottonwoods, there are few trees and no real towns along this stretch of US-93, and traffic still has to stop for the occasional cattle drive, but it's a very pretty drive, and you can stop almost anywhere for a quick walk or picnic along the river. The appearance of the Salmon River canyon varies tremendously, but for most of the way it is dry and brown—a real shock compared to the dense green forests of Montana, just an hour to the north.

Around Salmon, tune to **KSRA 92.7 FM** or **960 AM,** for country music, ABC News and reports on life in the Salmon and Big Hole region.

Challis and the Land of Yankee Fork State Park

The only town for 50 miles in any direction, Challis is an old mining camp that has grown into a miniature version of Salmon—albeit without the water or the tourists. Apart from boasting the all-time Idaho record for least rain in a year (seven inches), Challis is a very quiet market center for local cattle ranchers, with more bars—and barber shops—than you'd expect of a town this small.

On the south side of Challis, at the junction of US-93 and Hwy-75, the excellent, modern Land of Yankee Fork State Park visitor center (open daily 8 AM-6 PM in summer, Mon.-Sat. 9 AM-5 PM rest of year; 208/879-5244) has extensive displays of local mining history and maps to guide visitors to many evocative ghost towns and other relics sprinkling the surrounding hills. Gold was first discovered in the region in the 1870s, and nearby mines and mining camps boomed for the next 25 years, though by 1905 the last mine had closed. A few gold mines have reopened in recent years, though all of these are hidden away in isolated areas and protected behind high-security walls and fences; none is open to the public.

In 1805, explorers Lewis and Clark became the first Americans to cross the Continental Divide when they climbed over **Lemhi Pass,** 25 miles southeast of Salmon. Hoping to follow the Salmon River west to the Pacific, they found it was impassable and continued north over Lost Trail Pass, roughly along the route of US-93.

About eight miles south of Salmon, a roadside sign marks the point where US-93 crosses the 45th Parallel—halfway between the North Pole and the Equator.

45TH PARALLEL HALFWAY BETWEEN THE EQUATOR AND NORTH POLE

US-93: Mackay and the Lost River Valley

At Challis, our main route follows the 1940s alignment of US-93, heading west into the Sawtooth Mountains, but today's US-93 swings southeast toward Arco and the Craters of the Moon National Monument through the Lost River Valley. The scenery here remains spectacular, with the mountains towering

grizzled old miner in the Land of Yankee Fork

On October 28th, 1983, one of the most powerful earthquakes ever to hit North America rumbled the Lost River Valley, instantly dropping the valley floor as much as 14 feet, and forming dramatic escarpments still visible in places throughout the region.

The USFS operates a number of nice campgrounds along the Snake River; for details, contact the **ranger station** (208/879-4100) in Challis.

over the ranches of the valley floor, but it can't compare with the glories of the old road route.

But if you're in a rush, or there's been a recent storm blocking the mountain passes, or you just want to see another corner of Idaho, US-93 will be there for you. Mountaineers follow US-93 on their way to climb 12,662-foot Mount Borah, the highest point in Idaho and a demanding though not technically difficult summit to reach. The trailhead is at the end of the well-signed "Borah Peak Access" road, roughly half-way between Challis and Mackay. For details, contact the USFS ranger station (208/588-2224) in Mackay.

The rough and ready town of Mackay (pop. 575, pronounced makkey) is the valley's hub, with a pair of motels including the **Wagon Wheel** (208/588-3331), where rooms with kitchenettes go for as little as $30 a night. Mackay also hosts an annual rodeo, the Custer County Fair, and a mountain bike race, but it's best known for its famous **free barbecue** at the end of September, when hundreds of people come here for massive amounts of free food ("Tons of Meat—Mackay's Treat" say the signs) and general fun and games.

South of Mackay, US-93 continues to Arco, then elbows west through the eerie Craters of the Moon, rejoining Hwy-75 at Shoshone.

Clayton and Sunbeam

Though US-93 swings to the southeast from Challis, the original alignment, now Hwy-75, winds west into the mountains through the 2,000-foot deep canyon carved by the Salmon River. You're deep in the forest by the time you reach Clayton (pop. 26), a riverside wide spot with a gas station, a biker-friendly tavern, and the popular Rocky Ridge Cafe. Farther west, some 50 miles upstream from Challis, you come to the small but pleasant year-round resort of Sunbeam, which overlooks the confluence of the Yankee Fork and Salmon Rivers. There's a cafe and campground at the junction, and just a half-mile upstream you'll find the area's greatest attraction: the natural **hot springs**, steaming wildly on cold days and forming rock pools of varying temperatures in the Salmon River, marked by a stone bathhouse built during the New Deal 1930s but no longer in use.

From Sunbeam, it's only another 15 miles to Stanley, heart of the glorious Sawtooth mountains.

The Custer Motorway

If you're here in summer and have a few hours to spare, take the rough (no RVs, please!) but very scenic alternative to Hwy-75, built by the Civilian Conservation Corps in the 1930s and called the Custer Motorway, which winds west from Challis into the Yankee Fork mining district, passing the remains of old stagecoach stations and stamp mills before reaching the ghost town of **Custer**. Undergoing restoration as the centerpiece of the Land of Yankee Fork State Park, Custer now consists of a half-dozen mining shacks and log cabins, the Empire saloon, and the small but engaging **Custer Museum**, housed in the old one-room schoolhouse. Beyond Custer, a well-maintained gravel road follows the Yankee Fork of the Salmon River south to Hwy-75, passing an abandoned gold dredge and other relics of mining operations, past and present, before rejoining the highway at Sunbeam, on the banks of the Salmon River.

Further details, and free maps of Custer and the Custer Motorway, are available from the Land of Yankee Fork State Park visitor center in Challis (see above).

Stanley

Set in a broad basin at the eastern foot of the angular Sawtooth Mountains, 58 miles west of Challis, Stanley is a tiny (pop. 71; elev. 6,260 feet), isolated town that makes an excellent base for exploring the surrounding two-million-plus acres of alpine forest. In summertime, the population swells to around 500, including visitors, so although it's just 60 miles north of busy Sun Valley there's still plenty of room to move. Hikers and mountain-bikers, and cross-country skiers in winter, should have no trouble finding solitude in the 10,000-foot peaks; the **ranger station** (208/774-3681), four miles south of town on Hwy-75, can supply details of trails and campgrounds as well as rafting trips along the Middle Fork of the Salmon River.

The **Knotty Pine Restaurant**, on Hwy-75 in "lower" Stanley, has good food (and great pies) and low prices, while a trio of more characterful places stand along Ace of Diamonds Avenue, the main street of Stanley proper, southwest of the Hwy-21/75 junction: the budget beers-and-burritos at the **Rod & Gun Club Saloon**, the cafe in the historic **Sawtooth Hotel**, and the **Kasino Club**, 21 Ace of Diamonds Avenue, in ascending order of price and healthiness.

If you're not camping, a popular, locally owned and semi-historic accommodation is **Danner's Log Cabins** (208/774-3539), along Hwy-21 at the center of town. If the log cabins are full, the modern **Mountain Village Resort** (208/774-3317) at the junction of Hwy-75 and Hwy-21 offers motel rooms, a decent restaurant, and a gas station, and the atmospheric **Sawtooth Hotel** (208/774-9947) has rooms with shared baths for around $35-50.

Sawtooth National Recreation Area

Stanley and Sunbeam both stand along the northern border of the 750,000-acre Sawtooth National Recreation Area, which extends south for over 20 miles of untrammelled meadows, forests, and lakes, and includes the headwaters of many major Idaho rivers. It also holds one of the nicest places to stay in the Rockies: the historic **Redfish Lake Lodge** seven miles south of Stanley on Hwy-75 (May-Sept. only; 208/774-3536), on the east shore of Redfish Lake, which has rustic, log-walled rooms in the main lodge from around $50 a night, and spacious cabins for about twice that. The lodge also has a very good restaurant.

There are two main **visitor centers** for the Sawtooth NRA: a summer-only one near Redfish Lake, and the headquarters (208/726-7672) on the north side of Ketchum.

South of Redfish Lake, Hwy-75 switchbacks steeply up to 8,752-foot **Galena Summit**, which gives a grand view over the surrounding mountains, before dropping steeply down toward Sun Valley along the headwaters of the Wood River. About two miles south of the pass, 25 miles before you reach the resort area, there's one last stop worth making: **Galena Lodge** (208/726-4010), which dates back to the mining era of the 1880s and has been resurrected as a cross-country ski lodge, with food service, ski or snowshoe rentals and trail passes for around $15 a day. The lodge also maintains a system of backcountry "yurts," tent-like structures with wood burning stoves, bunks for up to six people—and dinner delivered to your door.

Redfish Lake takes its name from the millions of red-fleshed sockeye salmon found here by pioneers. These migratory fish travel over 2,000 miles roundtrip, from their spawning grounds at Redfish Lake to the Pacific Ocean and back via the Columbia and Salmon Rivers, but their numbers are so depleted that the run is now on the verge of extinction.

Sun Valley

The first, and still among the most famous, destination ski resorts in the U.S., Sun Valley was developed by Union Pacific railroad tycoon Averill Harriman in the 1930s. Harriman built a large mock-Tyrolean chalet, the **Sun Valley Lodge**, 1 Sun Valley Road (800/635-8261), and began to cultivate Sun Valley's exclusive reputation—reinforced by high prices for lift tickets rapidly approaching $50 a day—and five-star facilities, including golf courses, tennis courts, and gourmet restaurants. Though Colorado's Vail and other resorts now compete for the top-dollar trade, Sun Valley still attracts well-heeled clientele, if the Lear jets and Gulfstreams parked at the local airport are any indication. (The airport is also served by Horizon Air, 800/547-9308.)

Ernest Hemingway

Ernest Hemingway is probably the most famous name associated with Sun Valley. Hemingway first came here in the 1930s, and worked on *For Whom the Bell Tolls* while staying at the Sun Valley Lodge. He returned in 1960, and a year later shot himself; he's now buried in a simple plot in the middle-rear section of Ketchum's small cemetery. Hemingway is also remembered by a small and surprisingly kitschy **memorial** along Trail Creek, a mile east of the resort.

While the resort itself isn't huge, Sun Valley has come to stand for the larger area, including the towns of Ketchum and Hailey and much of the nearby wilderness. Somewhat surprisingly, the Sun Valley area is quite barren and treeless—ideal for skiing, perhaps, though not particularly beautiful. Besides skiers in winter, Sun Valley also draws golfers in summer and fall, not to mention anglers, who rate the Wood River as one of the nation's best.

For further information on visiting the Sun Valley area, especially regarding accommodations, contact the **Sun Valley Chamber of Commerce** (800/634-3347). For details on hiking, camping, cross-country skiing, or mountain biking in the nearby forests, stop by the Sawtooth National Forest **ranger station** (208/622-5371), a mile east of Ketchum on Sun Valley Road.

Ketchum

Though both places preexisted Sun Valley, the two old mining and sheep-ranching towns of Ketchum and Hailey have more or less lost themselves in the upmarket resort aura of their famous neighbor. Ketchum (pop. 2,500), the more touristy of the two, has wall-to-wall art galleries and T-shirt shops lining its traffic-jammed streets. It also supports dozens of very expensive resort hotels and restaurants that cater to Sun Valley's country club set, plus a handful of more interesting and affordable places along the 200 block of N. Main Street. Here you can choose from beer-and-burger bars like **X's Taphouse** and **Whiskey Jacques'**—the latter also serving good pizzas—or the Harley-friendly **Casino**, housed in one of Ketchum's oldest buildings. There's a very good coffee house, **Java on Fourth**, a block west of Main Street at 191 4th Street.

Most central and affordable of Ketchum's accommodations is the **Bald Mountain Lodge**, a rustic former hot springs resort at 151 S. Main Street (208/726-9963 or 800/892-7407), where doubles start at $50 a night. For more listings, stop by the handy visitors bureau, at 4th and Main (208/726-3423 or 800/634-3347).

Hailey

Hailey, 10 miles south of Ketchum and linked by a popular rail-trail bike path, was founded originally in the 1880s as a supply center for local silver and lead mines, and is now the home base of all those workers who make the resorts run smoothly and ski in between shifts. Hailey feels much more friendly and low-key than Ketchum or Sun Valley, and the eating options are much more down-to-earth, especially at diner-style haunts like the **Sunrise Cafe**, 106 N. Main Street. When the sun goes down, you can hang out with the local ski bums and bikers at the venerable **Hailey Hotel**, 201 S. Main Street (208/788-3140) which has a lively bar downstairs and the region's cheapest beds—around $35 a night with shared bath.

In contrast to the civic love affair Sun Valley has with the legacy of Ernest Hemingway, Hailey takes little notice of the fact that it was the birthplace (in 1885, in a house that still stands at Pine Street and 2nd Avenue) of another noteworthy literary figure, **Ezra Pound**. His parents were here working for the U.S. government, but fled the snowy winters just two years later.

Shoshone marks the junction of US-93 with our cross-country "Oregon Trail" route, which runs along US-20/26 between Boise and the Craters of the Moon National Monument. See pages 540-548 for more.

Shoshone: Ice Caves

South of the Sun Valley area, Hwy-75 runs across 60 miles of south-central Idaho's rocky black lava flows. Halfway between Sun Valley and Twin Falls, eight miles north of the town of Shoshone, the **Shoshone Ice Caves** (daily 8 AM-8 PM in summer only; $5) present a series of lava tubes developed into a low-key tourist trap. Just west of the highway, their constant 50° temperatures do make a pleasant contrast to the often scorching summer heat—the "ice" in the name is caused by air currents flowing through the tubes, which causes subterranean water to freeze—and the gift shop and mineral museum will satisfy anyone's needs for tourist trap trash. Just down the road, **Mammoth Cave** is much more basic; for serious spelunkers, there are over a dozen unaltered lava tubes nearby. Contact the BLM office in Shoshone (208/886-2206) for details.

The only town along this stretch of road, Shoshone (pop. 1,249) is a ranching and railroad center that marks the junction of Hwy-75 with US-93. Some of its buildings have been constructed from local volcanic rock, and though it's a fairly timeworn place, Shoshone looks great at sunset, when its steel water tower glows and places like the **Frosty Isle Drive-In** on the north side of town, or the neon-

Many of Idaho's famous **potatoes** are grown in the "Magic Valley" area around Twin Falls; harvest season is late September. To learn everything you ever wanted to know about spuds, take a trip east via US-26 to Blackfoot, Idaho and the World Potato Exposition, 130 N.W. Main Street (208/785-2517).

signed **Manhattan Cafe** along the railroad tracks, all look especially appealing. One of Shoshone's most notable old buildings is the stately **McFall Hotel**, on the north side of the tracks, which dates from 1896 and is being painstakingly restored to its original glory. At the very least stop in for a look at the bar, or inquire about a room (208/886-7016).

Twin Falls

Named for a pair of 200-foot cascades in the Snake River, both of which have long been diverted for irrigation or to generate electricity, Twin Falls (pop. 27,750) is the heart of the extensive "Magic Valley" of highly productive irrigated croplands that cover half a million acres of south-central Idaho. Best known to people outside Idaho as the place where, in 1974, daredevil Evel Knievel tried and failed to ride a rocket-powered motorcycle across the Snake River canyon, Twin Falls is both a busy highway town—with a barrage of

---

EVEL KNIEVEL AND THE SNAKE RIVER CANYON

No one who lived through the 1970s could forget the name Evel Knievel, the ultimate thrill seeker who became rich and famous performing dangerous and virtually impossible feats on a motorcycle. Born in Butte, Montana in 1939, Knievel dropped out of high school and worked a dozen different jobs before finding his true calling as a motorcycle daredevil. In 1965 he made his first jump, flying over a caged mountain lion and boxes of rattlesnakes at Moses Lake, Washington. Within a few years he hit the big time: leaping over the fountains at Caesar's Palace and jumping 50 cars at the L.A. Coliseum. Though he broke nearly every bone in his body as a result of his numerous crash landings, Knievel's feats were always bigger, better, and more dangerous than the last; as he liked to say, "Where there's little risk, there's little reward."

Banned by the government from attempting a leap over the Grand Canyon, Knievel set his sights on the Snake River Canyon in southern Idaho, even leasing the land so no one could stop him, then building a massive ramp and working out the details of his custom-made, rocket-powered Harley-Davidson X-2 Skycycle. On September 8, 1974, some 30,000 people turned out, along with many millions more watching on TV, for Evel's big leap. Unfortunately, one of his parachutes deployed on takeoff, and he floated gently down into the bottom of the gorge, safe and sound, and proud of having the guts to try—even if he didn't quite make it.

backlit and neon signs along US-93—and a quiet farming community, with little to offer travelers apart from a chance to fill the gas tank, eat, or get a night's sleep. For breakfast or a lunchtime burger, head to Kelly's Diner, 110 N. Main Avenue, or the 24-hour **Depot Grill**, at 545 S. Shoshone Street along downtown's diagonal main drag. Sleep at your choice of two **Best Westerns**, a **Comfort Inn**, an **Econo Lodge**, a **Super 8**, or any of a dozen others.

The one unique attraction of Twin Falls, the site of **Evel Knievel's** aborted motorcycle jump, is a mile north of town on US-93, south of the I-84 freeway. There's a large parking area and a visitor center at the south foot of the delicate Perrine Memorial Bridge, and it's well worth stopping for, not only to see the remains of his launch pad (a triangular pile of dirt, 500 yards east of the bridge) or the stone monument that calls him "Robert 'Evel' Knievel—Explorer, Motorcyclist, Daredevil." The views down into the 500-foot-deep gorge, the floor of which has been irrigated and filled with a bright green golf course, are also impressive, especially at sunset when the whole scene takes on an otherworldly glow.

Though the town can make a good jumping-off point for Sun Valley and the mountain wilderness farther north, there's not a lot to *do* in Twin Falls. The waterfalls for which the town is named are barely visible, since their flows have been diverted. **Shoshone Falls**, however, taller than Niagara, may still impress, especially in spring; check them out from the park at the end of Falls Avenue, seven miles east of US-93.

Nat-Soo-Pah Hot Springs

South of Twin Falls, there's a whole lot of nothing in the 47 miles before you reach the Nevada border at Jackpot. One place worth a stop is the summer-only Nat-Soo-Pah hot springs (208/655-4337), halfway to Nevada, where you'll find a giant (125 by 50 foot!) spring-fed swimming pool, a tree-shaded picnic area and snack bar, and a $10-a-night campground. Nat-Soo-Pah is about a mile south of Hollister, then three miles east on a well-signed road. There are a number of other natural springs in the area, so if you enjoy being in hot water, southern Idaho is great place to explore.

ACROSS NEVADA

US-93 runs south along the eastern edge of Nevada for 520 miles, 500 of which take you through an exceptional degree of desolation—endless straight and narrow valleys, two-car traffic jams, and towns few and far between. From the gambling oasis of Jackpot on the Idaho border to where the highway crosses into Arizona atop Hoover Dam, US-93 is at least as lonely as its Nevada sibling US-50, the official Loneliest Road in America.

Towns like Wells, along I-80 in the northern half of the state, are big events; south of here it's 130 miles to the next watering hole, Ely, beyond which the old mining camp of Pioche and the desert hot springs resort of Caliente are the only wide spots in the road before you hit the staggering city of Las Vegas.

Jackpot lies within the **Columbia Plateau** physiography of southern Idaho. This geographical anomaly is the only bit of land in Nevada that falls outside its two eminent deserts: the Great Basin, encompassing the top three-quarters of the state, and the Mojave, which covers the bottom quarter.

Jackpot

In every respect but one, Jackpot belongs more to Idaho than Nevada—a somewhat incongruous introduction to US-93 in the Silver State. Jackpot's visitors and workers mostly come from Idaho, as do its power and water; even its clocks are set to Idaho time. The one little exception, however, is pure Nevada: border-town gambling. Jackpot was founded in 1956, mere months after Idaho banned slot machines, which didn't, to be sure, reduce the demand. In fact, Jackpot has thrived, as a pit stop in any of the town's casinos will attest. Jackpot is compact enough to give long-distance travelers just enough lights, action, and comfort to satisfy more immediate needs and then send them on their way again.

Cactus Pete's (775/755-2321) is the 10-story tower you can see for miles; along with the big casino, it has a great snack bar, a buffet, gourmet restaurant, showroom, lounge, and rooms for around $40 a night. **The Horseshu** (775/755-7777) across the street has a good coffee shop with typical Nevada meal deals, or stock up for the road at the supermarket next door. If you're heading south from Jackpot, be sure to fill the tank before hitting the road; the next gas is over an hour away.

Wells

Some lone peaks, a stretch of badlands and buttes, and a couple of north-south-trending ranges usher US-93 down a long basin toward the little junction town of Wells (pop. 1,250). Just under 70 miles from Jackpot at the interchange of US-93 and the I-80 freeway, Wells was named by the Central Pacific Railroad, which chose the site for a depot and town to make use of the plentiful springs in the hills a few miles northeast. The old downtown—take a right on 6th Street and another right at the light—is the most intact abandoned "**railroad row**" on the entire mainline across northern Nevada. Wells provides an explicit illustration of the West's transition from rail to road to superhighway: the newest action in town is at the east and west exit ramps of I-80; the "strip" between the exits is 6th Street (old US-40), the pre-interstate vintage 1950s and even 1960s, but now derelict around the edges; commerce along the 125-year-old tracks is, of course, extinct.

Wells is situated at the northeastern base of the scenic **East Humboldt Range.** To get into the mountains, go under Wells's west exit ramp and follow the signs; the paved road climbs to 8,400 feet, passing one campground and terminating at another. For details, contact the U.S. Forest Service **ranger station** (775/752-3525) at the west end of town.

Continuing down US-93 affords a different view of the East Humboldts. Ten miles south of Wells you can take a right on Hwy-232, which makes a loop through luxuriant Clover Valley at the eastern base of the mountains, one of the most bucolic basins in Nevada. About six miles in from the highway is a right turn onto a rough dirt track. Look up to see **Hole-in-the-Mountain Peak.** Tallest peak in the East Humboldts (11,276 feet), it features a 30-by 25-foot natural window in the thin rock 300 feet below its summit, which gives you a spectacular little patch of blue (or silver, orange, or purple, depending on the time of day) right through the top of the range. Compelling.

BONNEVILLE SPEEDWAY

Located in the middle of nowhere, west of the Great Salt Lake on the Utah/Nevada border, the vast salt flats of Bonneville cover some 150 square miles. Since the 1930s, Bonneville's broad, hard, flat and unobstructed surface has made it a mecca for efforts to set ever faster land speed records. The earliest speed records were set at Daytona Beach, Florida (see page 424), but as top speeds increased racers needed more room to maneuver safely. In 1931, Ab Jenkins set Bonneville's first world record in his bright red Mormon Meteor, and racers have converged on Bonneville's 10-mile-long drag strip in pursuit of record-breaking speed ever since.

Craig Breedlove, in his car "Spirit of America," was the first to exceed the 400, 500 and 600 mph marks, but in recent years, problems with water dissolving the salt have made Bonneville less than ideal; racers like Richard Noble, whose team set the current record of 763 mph in 1996, have opted for the Black Rock Desert, 150 miles north of Reno, Nevada. Still, every summer hundreds of thrill-seekers descend on Bonneville, racing their hot rods in a series of time trials.

Mormon Meteor, The World's Greatest Unlimited Speed Record Maker, Bonneville Salt Flats, Utah

PUBLISHED BY SPECIAL PERMISSION OF AB. JENKINS

Holding All Speed Records from 10 Miles to 7,154 and from One Hour to 48 Hours

The Days Run Completed

Between Wells and Ely, US-93 bends away from the heart of the Ruby Mountains, running southeast through Steptoe Valley on a marathon drive down an elongated basin, hemmed in by the Schell Creek Range on the east and the Egan Range on the west. The only signs of civilization on this stretch are two **roadhouses**: one at **Lages** (78 miles south of Wells), the other at **Schellbourne** (40 miles north of Ely).

Wendover

At the I-80 freeway, US-93 becomes the hypotenuse of an alternative route, which runs for 60 miles southeast to the Utah border at Wendover, then another 60 miles southwest to rejoin the mainline US-93 at Lages. Wendover, like Jackpot, is a thriving Nevada border town, with five major casinos and as many new golf-course-view subdivisions. Wendover's claims to fame include **Wendover Will**, the huge cowboy outside the Stateline casino who welcomes you to Nevada along the Utah state line; the **Bonneville Salt Flats** and speedway, where most of the world's land-speed records have been set over the past 80 years; and **Wendover Air Force Base**, where in 1945 the crew of the *Enola Gay* trained to drop an atomic bomb on Japan.

The Ruby Mountains and Elko

It's a long, solitary, 140 miles from Wells to Ely. US-93 shoots down Clover Valley to the southern edge of the East Humboldts where Hwy-229, a maintained gravel road, cuts off southwest toward the Ruby Mountains, also known as the Nevada Alps. This is one of Nevada's most scenic ranges: 100 miles long, with more than a dozen peaks over 9,000 feet.

For a sample of the sort of versification you might hear at Elko's Cowboy Poetry Festival, see the "Cowboys' Christmas Ball" poem on pages 206-207.

The best access to the Ruby Mountains is through the engaging small city of Elko, 50 miles west of Wells via I-80. Besides maintaining its Basque culture, Elko hosts the very popular **Cowboy Poetry Festival** every January, a Cowboy Music Gathering the last weekend in June, and a 4th of July celebration. Take advantage of some of the fine restaurants like the **Star Hotel** (775/738-9925), near the railroad tracks at 246 Silver Street, which is worth the drive for the delicious lamb chops and other dishes.

For more information, contact the **Elko Convention and Visitors Bureau** (800/248-ELKO or 800/248-3556).

The McGill smelter's last sky-scraping smokestack was felled in September 1993. At 750 feet tall, it was until then the highest structure in Nevada.

McGill

Tiny McGill, 128 miles south of I-80 and 12 miles north of Ely, is the classic Nevada company town, its workaday life revolving for the first 50 years of this century around a giant copper smelter. Mining company officials lived in the fancy houses around the "Circle" at the top of the hill just below the factory, while workers were housed according to their ethnic origins. The saloon and jail were conveniently built right next door to each other, and steam from the copper furnaces was piped to heat the town's houses. The company's been gone for more than 15 years, but the layout remains, along with acres of fenced-off brick factory buildings painted with fading signs encouraging workers to behave safely.

A few of McGill's buildings have been converted to current uses, but most are closed. US-93, which runs at the foot of town, attracts most of the businesses, including **Marie's Cafe**, the town's main place to eat, a Frosty stand (for burgers and shakes), and the **McGill Club**, right on US-93 down the street in the old Cyprus Hall. "The Oldest Back Bar in the State," the latter is considered one of Nevada's

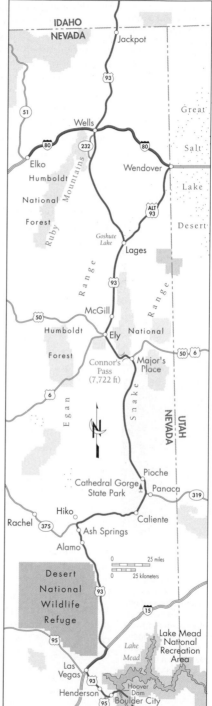

finest by connoisseurs of Silver State licensed establishments. (The McGill jail, however, is now in Ely.)

Ely marks the junction of US-93 and US-50, the legendary "Loneliest Road in America." Ely is described in that chapter on pages 671-672.

Connors Pass and Major's Place

Southeast of Ely, US-93, spliced together with US-50 and US-6 into a single two-lane highway, continues for 25 miles before crossing the narrow waist of the Schell Creek at Connors Pass (7,722 feet elevation), one of only two fractions of US-93 in Nevada that climb above the tree line. (Unlike most of the rest of the country, tree line in Nevada has a lower, as well as an upper, limit: no trees grow below roughly 4,000 feet.) As you ascend toward the pass, the air cools and freshens, the single-leaf piñon and Utah juniper appear and thicken, and, cresting the summit, the mighty Snake Range, including 13,061-foot Wheeler Peak, comes into view.

At Major's Place (where there's a roadhouse), US-93 splits off from US-50 and US-6, the latter two heading east toward Utah, while US-93 cuts south, heading 80 long, solitary miles to the next contact with humans at Pioche. Once again, the highway rolls along taffy-pulled Spring and Lake valleys, ushered on its way by the Schell Creek, Fairview, Bristol, and Highland ranges on the west, and the Snake and Wilson Creek ranges on the east.

Pioche

The only places that are more than a ghostly outline of civilization in the nearly 300 miles of Great Basin desert that US-93 crosses between Ely and Las Vegas are the wildly different towns of Caliente, Panaca, and Pioche.

The oldest and most northerly of the three, Pioche (pop. 800; pronounced pee-OACH), is a one-time mining boomtown that had its heyday well over a century ago. Being so remote—back then exponentially more than now—during the 1870s Pioche descended to a level of anarchy that rivaled Bodie and Tombstone, and over 75 men were killed before anyone died of natural causes.

Corruption, too, was the order of the day, and you can tour Pioche's "Million Dollar" **Lincoln County Courthouse** on LaCour Street for a graphic example of it. Designed in 1871 at an estimated cost of $26,000, the courthouse wasn't completed until 1876, to the tune of $88,000. Then, unable to pay off the principal, the county commissioners kept refinancing the debt, while interest accrued, year after year; by the time it was paid off in 1937, the courthouse had cost a million bucks and been replaced by a more modern structure. Now restored, the old courthouse is open for self-guided **tours** (daily 10 AM-4 PM; donations; 775/962-5182) of the offices, the courtroom, and the old jail.

The eclectic **Lincoln County Museum** (daily 10 AM-4 PM; free), on Main Street at the center of town, is another good stop, as are nearby historic buildings such as the **Thompson Opera House** and the **Commercial Club**. The rusting remains of the **aerial tramway** that ran through Pioche, carrying ore to the stamp mills, can be explored—cables, cars, and all—from various points in town. Two state parks to the east (Echo Canyon and Spring Valley, 12 and 20 miles respectively) round out your Pioche-area sightseeing.

Pioche also has a motel, the **Pioche Motel** on Lecour Street (775/962-5551), as well as **Nancy's** restaurant and the **Silver Cafe**, a Chevron station, and a used book store.

Panaca and Cathedral Gorge

Panaca, 11 miles south of Pioche and a mile east of US-93 on Hwy-319, was founded in 1864 by Mormon farmers in what was then a part of Utah, attracted to the valley by the plentiful water of Panaca Spring. The mining strikes at nearby Bullionville and Pioche disturbed their peace briefly, but Panaca—which has a single gas station/minimart, plus a school and lots of houses—has a strong sense of tranquility and timelessness rarely felt in the rest of Nevada.

Just west of US-93, a mile north of Panaca, **Cathedral Gorge State Park** is a mini-Grand Canyon of eroded mud. A lake once covered this deep gully, and silt and clay were washed to the bottom by streams and creeks. The lake dried up, exposing the sediments, and erosion (which never sleeps) sculpted them into the fantastic procession of formations that you see today. The **campground** ($7 per site; 775/728-4467) here has shade trees, flush toilets, even showers.

Cathedral Gorge

Nevada's one and only national park, **Great Basin National Park**, stands along the slopes of Wheeler Peak, 30 miles east of US-93. For details, see page 673.

Note that there are **no services**—no gas, no food, no lodging or organized camping, not even a video rental store—for the long haul between Major's Place and Pioche.

Panaca Spring, a fine local **swimming hole** with warm, sweet water, is found just outside town: take 5th Street north past the baseball diamond and a rusty old steam engine, toward a big cottonwood tree about a half-mile beyond where the pavement ends.

Caliente

To Pioche's mining and Panaca's farming, Caliente (pop. 1,100), 15 miles south, adds railroading. This small town was built around the San Pedro, Los Angeles, and Salt Lake Railroad tracks in the early 1900s, a short while before Las Vegas itself was founded. The **Union Pacific Depot**, which was built in 1923 and still gets Amtrak service on the Las Vegas-to-Salt Lake City line, is the nerve center of Caliente, being restored to house government offices and an art and local history gallery.

The town supports two gas stations and a half-dozen motels, the best of which is the **Hot Springs** (775/726-3777), off US-93 on the north side of Caliente. Here your room comes with use of Roman baths, whose fire-hydrant faucets fill the five foot-square, four foot-deep tubs in three minutes flat with 115° water. Roadfood, however, is limited to three choices: the **Knotty Pine** coffee shop and casino; the

---

THE EXTRATERRESTRIAL HIGHWAY

West of US-93, stretching nearly to Death Valley and the California border, the U.S. government has turned the 3.5-million-acre expanse of Nellis Air Force Range into its most top-secret laboratory and testing ground. H-bombs, U-2 spy planes, Stealth bombers, you name it—this is where projects no one is supposed to know about exist.

It's not so surprising that, like Roswell, New Mexico, this lonely corner of the world has become the focus of an ongoing controversy pitting government secrecy against allegations that the Air Force has been using a corner of the base known as Area 51 to study UFOs and extraterrestrials. Fueled in part by tabloid stories claiming an E.T. like creature is being kept alive at Area 51 in a high-security compound underneath Groom Lake—and also by local businesspeople's realization that UFO tourism could mean big money—the hoopla has focused on the tiny village of Rachel, which has become to UFO-spotters what the grassy knoll is to JFK conspiracy theorists.

Much of the controversy surrounding Area 51 is pretty silly, but for a serious study of the phenomenon read *Dreamland: Travels inside the Secret World of Roswell and Area 51*, by Phil Patton.

Rachel (pop. 99), the only community along the 100-mile stretch of Hwy. 375 (now officially known as the Extraterrestrial Highway, promoted by the state along the lines of the "Loneliest Road" campaign), is a block-long strip that holds the **Area 51 Research Center**, a mobile home that doubles as command post for UFO-spotters. The more lighthearted **Little A-Le-Inn**, is a typical bar and grill where you can munch on "Alien Burgers," down drinks like the "Beam Me Up, Scotty" (Jim Beam, 7UP, and Scotch) or peruse UFO-related key chains, fridge magnets, and T-shirts. The A-Le-Inn also has rooms (775/729-2515) for around $30 a night.

Branding Iron cafe, across from the depot; and Carl's Sandwich and Burger Shop, next to the post office on US-93, which does a fine cheeseburger.

South from Caliente, US-93 bends due west for 43 miles. Newman Canyon just outside of town has high, sheer, smooth, volcanic-tuff walls similar to Rainbow Canyon's. You twist and climb out of the canyon to cross the Delmar Range at Oak Springs Summit (6,237 feet), where the juniper trees are a welcome change from the low desert scrub. Beyond is an even rarer sight, not only for this highway but for any highway: a little interface zone in which the junipers grow right next to Joshua trees. This is the first indication of the change from Great Basin desert, which lies to the north, to the front edge of the Mojave Desert, which spreads south and west. Pahroc Summit is next (just under 5,000 feet), then Six Mile Flat, and then Hiko, where Hwy-375 heads northwest to US-6 and Tonopah.

Rainbow Canyon, south of Caliente on Hwy-317, is one of Nevada's most scenic and least-known drives: colorful, high volcanic-tuff cliffs, railroad trestles, and idyllic farms and ranches line Meadow Wash. The pavement ends after 21 miles, but in dry weather you can continue 38 miles through Kane Springs Valley to connect back up with US-93.

Ash Springs and Alamo

From the Hwy-375 junction, US-93 turns due south again and enters some unexpectedly lush country, in the midst of which three large and faithful springs provide plentiful water for alfalfa farms and cattle ranches, as well as for the only bona fide lakes that US-93 encounters in more than 400 miles of its Nevada leg. Ash Springs—consisting of a single combination gas station, restaurant, and bar called "R Place"—is named after the nearby water source, which is believed to be part of a vast aquifer underlying much of eastern Nevada; earthquakes have thrust this particular water to the surface.

Twelve miles south of Ash Springs is Alamo, whose two motels, two truck stops, and 24-hour "Del Pueblo" Mexican restaurant are the only real services between Caliente and Las Vegas. Four miles south of town is Upper Pahranagat Lake; an old road runs along the eastern shore, with camping and picnic sites and big cottonwoods—one of the most idyllic spots on the whole Nevada portion of US-93. The water is close enough to the source at Ash Springs that it's relatively warm year-round. Lower Pahranagat Lake, a bit farther south, freezes in the winter.

Upper Lake is also home to the administration and maintenance facilities for the **Desert National Wildlife Refuge,** at one and a half million acres the largest refuge in the Lower 48. Elusive desert bighorn sheep enjoy protection within this huge habitat, alongside of which US-93 travels for the length of the aptly named Sheep Range. The road descends gradually into rocky and barren desert until finally, 70 miles from Alamo and 125 miles from Caliente, US-93 merges with the I-15 freeway for the high-speed haul into the Big Glow, Las Vegas.

Driving Las Vegas

If you time the drive into Las Vegas so you arrive around dusk, the western sky sports a purple sunset, while the horizon shines brightly from a billion amber street lights stretching from one end of the valley to the other. But wait: you're still more than 30 miles out! The downtown and Strip skylines are clearly discernible for a full half hour before you get to Ground Zero, but it's as if those 500 miles of two-lane byway are reluctant to give you up. Even though the roadway widens to four-lane

(continues on page 152)

LAS VEGAS SURVIVAL GUIDE

LAS VEGAS IS THE BIGGEST, BRIGHTEST, AND brazenest boomtown in the history of the world, and this is its biggest boom. In the past decade, five mega-resorts and another dozen major hotels have opened in Las Vegas, which can now claim nine of the 10 largest hotels in the world. With over 100,000 rooms, the city has as many as New York and Chicago *combined*. Twenty-five million visitors lose five billion dollars in the casinos here every year, and as more and more resorts are catering to general "vacation fun," rather than just gambling, there's no end in sight—so long as the water supply holds out.

Still, gambling is the biggest game in town, and here are a few of the many places you can "play:"

Binion's Horseshoe, 1238 Fremont Street (702/382-1600 or 800/237-6537). The quintessential old-time gambling joint, which hasn't changed much from the good old gangster days. Home of the World Series of Poker, with its $1,000,000 prize.

Caesar's Palace (702/731-7110 or 800/634-6661). Long before there was a Mirage, a New York, New York, or a Bellagio, there was Caesar's Palace. From the day it opened in 1966 as the first "themed" hotel in Las Vegas, Caesar's Palace has been the classiest and most famous place in town.

El Cortez, 600 Fremont Street (702/385-5200 or 800/634-6703). The oldest (1941) casino still in operation, once owned by Bugsy Siegel.

Hard Rock Hotel/Casino, 4555 Paradise Road (702/693-5000 or 800/473-7625). For anyone under 50, this is the coolest place in town. Off the Strip and small by Vegas standards, but where else can you play Jimi Hendrix slot machines (a line of "Purple Haze" pays $200) while listening to nonstop classic rock 'n' roll?

Luxor, 3900 Las Vegas Boulevard South (702/262-4444 or 800/288-1000). The most distinctive, housed inside a mammoth (29 million cubic foot) glass pyramid at the southern end of the Strip. Above the casino, stage sets of city streets hold high-tech attractions: motion simulators, 3-D and IMAX movies, and "Virtual Reality" arcade games.

MGM Grand, 3799 Las Vegas Boulevard South (702/891-7777 or 800/929-1111). The biggest, with the world's largest gaming hall—at 171,000 square feet, it could encompass 85 four-bedroom houses—and the rest of the place is huge, too: 5,000-plus rooms, 23 eateries, an arena and showroom, a monorail, and an amusement park.

(continues on next page)

The Mirage, 3400 Las Vegas Boulevard South (702/791-7111 or 800/627-6667). The most opulent, with a rainforest, a 50,000-gallon aquarium, white tigers on display (this is the home of Siegfried and Roy), and the most "Beautiful People."

Treasure Island, 3300 Las Vegas Boulevard South (702/894-7111 or 800/944-7444). The free pirate show, right on the Strip in front of the casino, plays every 90 minutes starting at 1:30 PM. Not to be missed.

Las Vegas Stars, 850 N. Las Vegas Boulevard (702/386-7200). Not a casino, but Cashman Field, home of the Class AAA farm club of the San Diego Padres. Games are broadcast on KBAD 920 AM.

the Luxor

Practicalities

McCarran International Airport (LAS), one of the 10 busiest in the country, is only a couple of miles east of the Tropicana/Strip intersection. The local bus is $1, low in cost but high in adventure. Limos and shuttles will take you to your hotel or motel for under $5. Taxis from the airport are about $10 for Strip destinations, $15 for downtown. There are also all the usual rental car companies. (If you'd like to pretend that the whole thing is a hallucination, a mere mirage in the Mojave Desert, you can barrel straight through Las Vegas on the freeway. But don't turn your head! It's an illusion only if you see it with one eye.)

If you're going to brave a tour through the belly of the beast, your exits are all off I-15: Main Street for downtown; Sahara, Spring Mountain, Flamingo, and Tropicana (these are names of streets as well as casinos) for "The Strip."

If you're staying overnight, you'll enter the wacky and somewhat wicked world of Las Vegas lodging. Rates, depending on the time of year, time of the week, and sometimes even the time of day, can be as low as $19 for a decent hotel room, or as high as $229 for a dive. If you want to stay in a hotel, you should try to make reservations at least a week in advance.

If you're blowing in without a reservation, it's wisest to stop at a pay phone, look under "Hotels" in the Yellow Pages, and call around. You'll quickly find out if: the town is sold out, has a few rooms at top dollar, or can put you up reasonably. Don't even bother with this on a Friday or Saturday, or during a big convention (like Comdex, when every room within 100 miles is booked up), or a boxing match, when the town is *always* sold out. A final note: if you'll be schlepping a lot of luggage, Las Vegas hotel rooms are a *long* way from parking spaces in the high-rise garages and huge lots, but parking is free.

One of the most comfortable, reasonably priced places to stay is **Circus Circus**, 2880 Las Vegas Boulevard South (702/734-0410 or 800/634-3450), which has cheap rooms (doubles from $25 a night) at the center of the Strip, with a carnival midway, circus acts, and low-stakes table games. **Excalibur**, 3850 Las Vegas Boulevard South (702/597-7777 or 800/937-7777), is 100% over-the-top Vegas kitsch, in the form of a turreted castle dwarfed by one of the world's largest hotels—4,032 rooms, usually around $50 a night. Across the Strip, the **Tropicana**, 3801 Las Vegas Boulevard South (702/739-2222 or 800/468-9494), is a real desert oasis, with lots of swimming pools (including one that's 300 feet long) and spacious, 1950s-style rooms and public areas. The **Desert Inn**, 3145 Las Vegas Boulevard South (702/733-4444 or 800/634-6906), where Howard Hughes lived during his recluse years, is now owned (along with half of Vegas, it seems) by the ITT-Sheraton conglomerate, but the "DI" is still the same as it always has been: a sedate, high-roller haven amidst the glitzy bustle of the Strip.

Finally there's **Motel 6**, 195 E. Tropicana Avenue (702/798-0728); "The World's Largest Motel 6," and also the most expensive, at $45 a night (or more) for each of the 880 rooms.

For great cheap food, try the snack bars downtown, especially at the Horseshoe, Golden Gate, and El Cortez; on the Strip, at the Boardwalk, Westward Ho, and Slots A Fun. Fast-food courts are found at the Riviera, Caesar's, and MGM, and there's a neon McDonald's on the Strip. The best all-you-can-eat buffet is at the Rio Suites Casino, away from the Strip at 3700 W. Flamingo Road, west of I-15; Main Street Station, Texas Station, and Fiesta (in that order) also have good buffets. Every major hotel has a 24-hour coffee shop; the Desert Inn, the Mirage, Binion's Horseshoe, Caesar's, and Gold Coast are good ones.

For more information, the main Las Vegas **visitor center** is next to the Convention Center at 3150 Paradise Road (702/892-0711). The *Las Vegas Review-Journal* is the big morning daily; the *Las Vegas Sun* the smaller afternoon paper.

Radio station **KBAD 920 AM** broadcasts all the hits of the 1940s and early 1950s, plus play-by-play of the Las Vegas Stars baseball games.

freeway, the halcyon trip down Nevada's nothingness lingers till the last possible moment, and then the transition is insanely abrupt: the deep desert, then wham bam, Sin City.

Almost everybody who drives into Las Vegas comes by way of the I-15 freeway, which runs between Los Angeles and Salt Lake City, and which connects with US-93 some 20 miles northwest of the Strip. From the south and Hoover Dam, use the new I-515 freeway, which carries US-93 and US-95 on a snaking S-figure between Henderson and Fremont Street in downtown Las Vegas.

Las Vegas has to be the easiest city in the world to drive around: everything lines up along, or in relation to, one big road—**The Strip**, the 10-mile barrage of bright lights and architectural extravagance that stretches along Las Vegas Boulevard, running parallel to I-15 southwest from the compact downtown area. (Other roads in Las Vegas are named after the big hotels near their junction with The Strip, hence you have "Sahara Avenue," "Desert Inn Road," "Flamingo Road," and "Tropicana Avenue," one after another from downtown.)

US-93 actually bypasses The Strip, veering southeast along Fremont Street and the Boulder Highway—or along the I-515 freeway—but it's all but required that you drive at least a little of The Strip before you can say you've been to Las Vegas.

Henderson

Southeast of Las Vegas, US-93 joins courses with US-95 along Nevada's newest freeway, I-515, which connects Las Vegas with the rapidly growing industrial city of Henderson. Henderson itself is relatively young, even by Nevada standards. In 1941, the War Department selected this site, due to its proximity to unlimited electricity generated by then six-year-old Hoover Dam, for a giant factory to process magnesium, needed for bombs and airplane components. Ten thousand workers arrived and within six months had built the plant and a town for 5,000 people. After the war ended, the factory was subdivided for private industry, and since then, Henderson has grown to be the third-largest city in Nevada, behind Las Vegas and Reno—the only three population centers in Nevada with more than 100,000 residents.

Though it doesn't even try to compete with the attractions of Las Vegas, Henderson does have two large and three small casinos (including the world's largest bingo parlor), and the very good **Clark County Heritage Museum** (daily 9 AM-4:30 PM; $1) located two miles south of town at 1830 S. Boulder Highway. For kids, take the tour of **Kidd's marshmallow factory** (call for directions; 702/564-5400).

South of Henderson, US-93/95 climbs up and over 2,367-foot Railroad Pass, and just beyond is the junction where US-95 cuts south, heading along the Colorado River to Laughlin, Nevada, Needles, California, and Yuma, Arizona. US-93 continues east, and a little north, to Boulder City.

Boulder City

Like Henderson, Boulder City (pop. 12,600) was founded and built by the federal government to house workers at Hoover Dam, what was then the largest construction project ever undertaken. Though the dam was completed in 1935, Boulder City continued under the feds' ownership and management for another 25 years; in

1960, an Act of Congress conferred independent municipal status on the town. Long-time residents purchased their houses and alcohol consumption was permitted for the first time in the town's history, though gambling remained forbidden. To this day, a full quarter century since "independence," Boulder City remains the only town in Nevada that expressly prohibits gambling, which may explain why it feels more like the Midwest than a suburb of Sin City.

If you're interested in the men and machines involved in building the dam, the **Boulder City/Hoover Dam Museum**, well signed at 441 Nevada Highway, is worth a look. The museum is hoping to move across the street into the historic (and newly restored) **Boulder Dam Hotel** (702/293-3510); the hotel also has a good dining room. There is a handful of motels and fast-food outlets in town, but the real draws are just below Boulder City—at the dam, of course, and the lake behind it.

If you like what you see and hear on the main Hoover Dam tour, ask about the special "hardhat" tour ($25; 702/293-8321) that takes you behind the scenes and shows off the project's inner workings and impressive engineering.

Hoover Dam marks the border between Nevada and Arizona, and between the Pacific and Mountain **time zones,** so set your clocks and watches accordingly (and remember, Arizona does not use daylight saving time). Heading south, you'll pass no towns or services for some 75 miles, until you reach Kingman on old Route 66, so stock up and fill up in Boulder City before proceeding.

Hoover Dam and Lake Mead

Approaching Hoover Dam from the Nevada side, in the eight miles from Boulder City you pass a Nevada Welcome Center, a National Park Service visitor center for Lake Mead National Recreation Area, the Gold Strike Casino, and a peculiar parade of electrical generators, transformers, and capacitors all secured by cyclone fencing topped by razor wire and barbs to keep out intruders.

Continuing along past the bronzed glass of the new **visitor center** (daily 8:30 AM-5:30 PM; 702/294-3523), which finally opened in 1995, 10 years behind schedule and $100 million over budget, US-93 rolls right over the top of the gargantuan wedge of Hoover Dam: nearly a quarter-mile across, 726 feet high, 660 feet thick at the base, all accomplished with a mere seven million tons (that's only 14 billion pounds) of concrete. Very popular 45-minute **tours** of the dam (daily 8 AM-6 PM in summer, 9 AM-3 PM rest of year; $6) leave from the small ticket office at the top, and food is available at the irresistible **Hoover Dam Snacketeria.**

Meanwhile, Lake Mead, the largest man-made lake in the western hemisphere, contains roughly 30 million acre-feet, or just over nine *trillion* gallons. It irrigates some 2.5 million acres of land in the U.S. and Mexico, and supplies electricity, from 17 electrical turbines inside the dam's base, to millions of people. The lake is a very popular recreation site, with thousands of water-skiers and fisherfolk flocking to its 500 miles of shoreline year-round.

ACROSS ARIZONA

Coming into Arizona across the top of Hoover Dam, US-93 cuts southeast across the length, and half the breadth, of the state, covering nearly 500 miles of desiccated desert. Starting at the Nevada border, US-93 makes a diagonal beeline toward the old Route 66 town of Kingman, one of the few watering holes in Arizona's northwest quarter. From Kingman, the route follows the anodyne I-40 freeway east, then cuts south across another huge stretch of desert, passing through the dude-ranch resort town of Wickenburg before reaching the suburban outskirts of Phoenix, the state's capital and largest city. From this sprawling megalopolis, the route bends east into the mountains, following backroads past the controversial Biosphere II "space station" before hitting Tucson, another hugely horizontal city. South of here you'll enjoy the most feature-packed part of the trip, passing by the historic Spanish colonial communities of Tubac and Tumacácori before winding up at the enjoyable twin border town of Ambos Nogales.

Lake Mead Recreation Area

Most people visit Lake Mead, which covers some 160,000 acres and includes over 500 miles of shoreline, from the extensively developed Nevada side. The only access on the Arizona side is from **Temple Bar**, 19 miles south of Hoover Dam, then another 27 miles northeast on a good paved road; a small marina has boat rentals and a motel (520/767-3211 or 800/752-9669).

Stretching to both sides of Hoover Dam, the Lake Mead Recreation Area also incorporates the smaller Lake Mojave, clearly visible from US-93 and accessible at **Willow Beach** on the Colorado River, 14 miles south of Hoover Dam and four miles west of US-93.

South of Hoover Dam, US-93 runs parallel to the older version of the highway, with numerous old bridges and sections of gravel roadway standing along the modern four-lane freeway.

Detour: Laughlin, Nevada

From Hoover Dam via US-95, and via Hwy-68 from US-93 just north of Kingman, a detour heads west to the Nevada side of the Colorado River, to Laughlin, Nevada, a booming gambling resort that seems even more mirage-like than Las Vegas. Lacking the glitz and pizzazz of Las Vegas, but with cheaper rooms (under $20 is not uncommon) and the almost unheard-of attraction of river views from the casino floors, Laughlin epitomizes the anything-goes character of Nevada gaming.

Laughlin is one of the hottest inhabited places in the country, with an all-time high temperature of 125° F registered here in 1994.

The history of Laughlin—or rather, the lack of it—is impressive even by Nevada standards. Starting with a run-down bait shop he bought in the mid-1960s, Michigan-born entrepre-

neur Don Laughlin envisioned the fantasyland you see today, opening his **Riverside Hotel** (800/227-3849), which is still a local favorite, in the late 1970s, and drawing visitors from all over Arizona and Southern California. Laughlin's independent mini-empire was eclipsed in the 1980s by the big shots: Harrah's built the luxurious **Del Rio** (800/447-8700), Circus Circus opened the steamboat-shaped **Colorado Belle** (800/458-9500), and the **Flamingo Hilton** (800/352-6464) added another 2,000-room palace in 1990. Fortunes have ebbed and flowed ever since, but Laughlin is still well worth a look or an overnight stay.

For further information, contact the Laughlin Chamber of Commerce (702/298-2214 or 800/227-5245).

Chloride

Back on US-93, marked by a big "C" inscribed in the hillside above it, the near-ghost town of Chloride (pop. 352), 53 miles south of Hoover Dam and 15 miles north of Kingman, then four miles east of the highway on a paved, well-marked road, is the oldest and among the most evocative former mining camps in Arizona. Following the discovery of silver here in the 1860s, mining activities continued through the 1940s; the town is now preserved by its dedicated residents.

A couple of stores and cafes still cling to life, and occasional festivals and flea markets draw sizeable crowds of visitors. Mostly what there is to see are the odd bits of "folk art" so often found in the American desert: strange sculptures made of rusting metal and odd bits of junk, plus comical tributes to the mythology of the Wild West, like a fake "Boot Hill" cemetery with laconic epitaphs and hand-painted signs playing up the apocryphal legacy of the local "Hangin' Judge" Jim Beam.

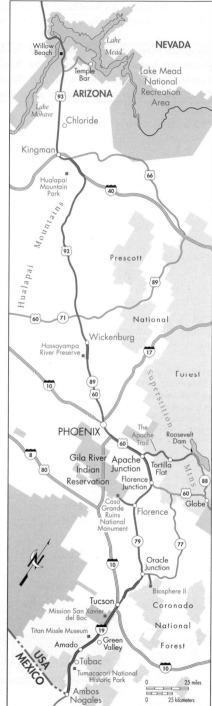

From Chloride, it's another 15 miles along arrow-straight US-93 to Kingman, which is covered in the Route 66 chapter on pages 806-807.

Kingman marks the intersection of US-93 and Route 66. Before the I-40 interstate bypassed it in the 1970s, Kingman was a vital desert oasis on the famous Route 66. For more on the "Mother Road" and Kingman, see the Route 66 chapter beginning on page 794.

Hualapai Mountain Park

East from Kingman, US-93 follows I-40 for over 20 miles before turning south again, but parallel to the freeway a well-marked 14-mile road leads up from the desert to Hualapai Mountain Park, where pines and firs cover the slopes of the 8,417-foot peak. Hiking trails wind through the wilderness, and there's a **campground** ($6) and a few rustic **cabins** ($25) built by the CCC during the New Deal 1930s.

For detailed information or to make reservations, contact the **ranger station** (520/757-3859), near the park entrance.

Wickenburg

In the middle of the Arizona desert, 60 miles northwest of Phoenix and 130 miles from Kingman, Wickenburg (pop. 4,500) grew up as a gold-mining camp in the 1860s and has survived as a low-key resort community. A few crusty prospectors still search for a strike, and cowboys are often seen riding through town, which makes Wickenburg a pleasant place to get a feel for the Old West, especially during the winter months when temperatures are mild and the sun shines nearly every day.

North of Wickenburg, US-93 is known as the "Joshua Tree Parkway" because it passes through many miles of cactus forest, the center of which is 30 miles from town.

Wickenburg's reliably good winter weather accounts for the number of **dude ranches** dotting the surrounding desert, most of which are intended for long stays (a week at least) rather than passing travelers; for a complete list of properties, or further information, contact the **visitor center** (520/684-5479) in the old railroad depot on Frontier Street, a block west of US-93.

At Wickenburg, US-93 officially comes to an end, replaced from here south to Phoenix by joint US-60/89.

Two blocks south along Frontier Street and the railroad tracks, at the US-60/US-93 junction and Wickenburg's only stoplight, the **Desert Caballeros Western Museum** (Mon.-Sat. 10 AM-4 PM, Sunday 1-4 PM; $2.50) gives a broad overview of regional history, and contains a surprisingly good collection of Western art and sculpture.

Most of the places to eat are lined up along east-west US-60 (Wickenburg Way); try the **Gold Nugget** coffee shop at 222 E. Wickenburg Way, across from the **Best Western** (520/684-5445 or 800/528-1234).

the Santa Fe Depot,
Wickenburg

Hassayampa River Preserve

One of Arizona's very few stretches of riverside ecology preserved in its natural state, the Hassayampa River Preserve, three miles southeast of Wickenburg on US-60/89, is a great place to break a journey. For most of its way, the Hassayampa River runs underground, but here it rises to irrigate a dense forest of willows and cottonwood trees, which in turn shelter an amazing variety of birds—over 200 species, from songbirds to raptors, are listed in the preserves' birders' guide.

South of Wickenburg and the Hassayampa River Preserve, the highway crosses over the canal of the **Central Arizona Project,** which provides Colorado River water to Phoenix and Tucson.

The Nature Conservancy, which owns and operates the preserve, runs a small **visitor center** (Wed.-Sun. 8 AM-5 PM in winter, 6 AM-noon in summer; $5 donation; 520/684-2772) where you can pick up trail guides and maybe join a guided walk.

SPRING TRAINING: CACTUS LEAGUE BASEBALL

The coming of the Arizona Diamondbacks to downtown Phoenix in 1998 culminated a long but limited history of baseball in the Grand Canyon State. Though it never before had a major league team of its own, Arizona has, since 1947, when the Cleveland Indians and New York Giants first played at Tucson's HI Corbett Field (now home to the Colorado Rockies), welcomed out-of-state teams for pre-season spring training. Every February and March, hundreds of ball players at all levels of the game come here to earn or keep their places on professional teams, and the daily workouts and 20-odd exhibition games of what's known as the **Cactus League** attract thousands of hard-core baseball fans as well.

The metropolitan Phoenix area hosts the bulk of the teams and the tourists, but Tucson gets a fair share as well. Though they're not necessarily played to win, Cactus League games are played in modern 10,000-seat stadia that approach the major leagues in quality, and the smaller sizes allows an up-close feel you'd have to pay much more for during the regular season. (And your chances of snagging balls during batting practice are infinitely better, too.)

Tickets for games cost $5-15, and are available through Ticketmaster (520/784-4444) and at the stadium box offices. Here is a list of teams and their springtime homes:

Anaheim Angels play in Tempe (602/350-5205).

Arizona Diamondbacks play in Tucson (888/683-3900).

Chicago Cubs play in Mesa (602/964-4467).

Chicago White Sox play in Tucson (888/683-3900).

Colorado Rockies play in Tucson (520/327-9467).

Milwaukee Brewers play in Phoenix (602/247-7177).

Oakland Athletics play in Phoenix (602/392-0217).

San Diego Padres and **Seattle Mariners** play in Peoria (602/878-4337).

San Francisco Giants play in Scottsdale (602/990-7972).

PHOENIX SURVIVAL GUIDE

THE MILLION-PLUS PEOPLE WHO
have settled in the "Valley of the
Sun" in and around the Arizona
capital, Phoenix, have nearly succeeded in obliterating any sense
that the land here ever was, and
still is, a desert. Golf courses,
swimming pools, lakes, and waterfalls are everywhere, with only
a few carefully coiffed cacti remaining to testify to the natural
state of things.

Phoenix really is a sprawling mess, expanding by many acres every day,
with no end (or beginning or middle, for that matter) in sight, but there is
something oddly charming about the place—an anything-goes, Wild West
spirit manifest in the city's ongoing ability to grow and thrive despite the almost total lack of natural advantages.

The best thing about visiting Phoenix is the chance to explore the marvelous **Heard Museum**, 22 E. Monte Vista Road (Mon.-Sat. 9:30 AM-5 PM,
Wednesday till 9 PM, Sunday noon-5 PM; $5), among the best museums any-
where devoted to the native cultures of the Southwestern U.S. The permanent
galleries trace the history and diversity of prehistoric peoples and contemporary tribes, while changing exhibitions focus on specific themes. Don't miss
the amazing collection of Hopi katsina dolls, collected by hotelier Fred Harvey
and the late U.S. Senator Barry Goldwater.

Another treat: **Taliesin West**, 108th Street at the east end of Cactus Road
(daily 9 AM-4 PM; $10; 602/860-2700), where every winter from 1937 until his
death in 1959, Frank Lloyd Wright lived, worked, and taught, handcrafting
the complex of studios, theaters, and living quarters that survives as an architecture school. This monument to Wright's social and aesthetic ideals is located on a beautiful foothill site, once all alone but now at the edge of Phoenix's
ever-encroaching suburban sprawl.

It's altogether appropriate that a city named for the mythological symbol of
rebirth from the ashes should be home to the **Hall of Flame**, 6101 E. Van
Buren Street (Mon.-Sat. 9 AM-5 PM, Sunday noon-4 PM; $4), which displays one
of the world's largest collections of fire fighting equipment in a series of air-
conditioned industrial sheds in Papago Park. Across the street, the headquarters of the **Salt River Project** hold a lobby full of displays tracing the
2,500-year history of Phoenix's water supply, from prehistoric Hohokam
canals to Mormon times and today.

Last but not least, there's "BOB," the Banc One Ballpark, downtown home
of the **Arizona Diamondbacks** (602/514-8400). It's the only major league ballpark with its own outfield swimming pool.

Practicalities

Phoenix, which is the sixth-largest city in the U.S., sits at the junction of the east-west I-10 freeway and north-south I-17 freeway from Flagstaff, with other state-of-the-art local freeways, such as the Hwy-202 Loop, Hwy-51, and the US-60 "Superstition Freeway" completing the high-speed overlay. Note that Phoenix proper is surrounded by a half-dozen legally independent communities—upscale Scottsdale, Mormon Mesa, studenty Tempe—differentiated only by the design of their streets signs. Phoenix's busy Sky Harbor International Airport is just over a mile southeast of downtown and has all the shuttle services and car rental companies you could need.

Though there is a skeletal bus service, trying to get around town without a car is hazardous to your health. In a word, *drive.*

There are tons of highway motels in and around the Valley of the Sun, and a number of gorgeous winter resort hotels. A prime example of the latter, **Biltmore Hotel**, 24th and Missouri Streets (602/955-6600 or 800/528-3696), is an absolutely beautiful, Frank Lloyd Wright-style resort complex tucked away on spacious grounds on the far north side of Phoenix. Stop by for a look, or maybe a meal or a drink, if you can't manage the $250-a-night (and up!) rates. More reasonably priced places to sleep include **Holiday Inn-Old Town Scottsdale**, 7353 E. Indian School Road (602/994-9203 or 800/695-6995), near Scottsdale's Center for the Arts, with rooms for $50-150, depending upon season. Downtown, the **San Carlos Hotel**, 202 N. Central Avenue (602/253-4121 or 800/528-5446) is a well-maintained older hotel, where rooms cost $50-100 a night. The **HI Phoenix Hostel**, 1026 9th Street (602/254-9803), has dorm beds for around $15 a night.

The classic road food stop in Phoenix is the **Tee Pee**, 4144 E. Indian School Road, a characterful and always crowded place serving huge and very cheap plates of old-style Ameri-Mexican food. Other Mexican places range from **Such Is Life**, 3602 N. 24th Street, which specializes in southern Mexican food, with especially delicious *mole* sauces. For something a bit hotter, brave the salsa at **Los Dos Molinos**, 8646 S. Central Avenue, in the old Tom Mix house.

The Phoenix area **visitors bureau** puts out the usual hotel and restaurant listings and other practical information for travelers; contact them downtown at 400 E. Van Buren Street (602/254-6500). The main newspaper is the Arizona *Republic.*

Across the Valley of the Sun

From the northwest, our US-93 route arrives in ever-growing metropolitan Phoenix, also called the "Valley of the Sun," by way of US-60/89, which passes through the retirement communities of Sun City and Sun City West. From the western outskirts of Phoenix, the most direct route follows Grand Avenue all the way to the downtown area, where you can follow the old main road, Van Buren Street, or hop onto the freeway system and hope you don't get too lost—it's a crazy and confusing city, so spread out it can seem to take forever to get anywhere.

Our "old roads" route picks up again at Apache Junction, on the far east edge of metropolitan Phoenix.

The Apache Trail and the Superstition Mountains

East of Phoenix, US-60 runs as a four-lane freeway through the shopping-mall sub-urbs of Tempe and Mesa, but the sprawl ends suddenly around Apache Junction, which marks the beginning of the scenic Apache Trail. Winding along the Salt River, and named for the tribe that dominated the area a century ago, the Apache Trail was created in the early 1900s as a supply road during the construction of Theodore Roosevelt Dam; it now passes by a series of attractive state parks and odd little towns, while giving access to the beautiful Superstition Mountains.

From the US-60 freeway, take Idaho Road (exit 11) north onto the well-signed Hwy-88. After five miles the suburbs give way to the wild desert of **Lost Dutchman State Park** ($3 day-use fee), named for a legendary gold mine located nearby. Two miles farther is the overlook for the 4,535-foot phallus of Weaver's Needle, beyond which the road passes several reservoirs before reaching the entertaining tourist-trap hamlet of **Tortilla Flat** (pop. 6), 18 miles from US-60 and named after the Steinbeck novella—which has nothing to do with Arizona, but who cares?

Beyond Tortilla Flat, which has a good cafe, a saloon with frequent live music, and a small motel, the road turns to dirt, and twists and turns through spectacular desert country for the next 27 miles to Roosevelt Dam, then heads southeast to join US-60 near Globe, at the western edge of the San Carlos Apache Indian Reservation, 50 miles east of Phoenix.

cliff dwelling

For information on the Apache Trail, or on hiking and camping in the Superstition Mountains, contact the U.S. Forest Service **ranger station** in Mesa (602/835-1161).

Hwy-79: Florence and Casa Grande Ruins National Monument

From Apache Junction, US-60 runs southeast for 15 miles to Florence Junction, where Hwy-79 (old US-89) cuts off to the south at **Florence**. One of Arizona's oldest towns, but now best known as the site of the state's largest

shell finger ring

copper bells

prison, Florence has a pleasant, non-touristy Main Street of bars, general stores, and junk shops, parallel to and a half-mile west of the highway. The penal history is documented in gruesome detail at the **Pinal County Historical Museum** (Wed.-Sun. noon-4 PM; donations), 715 S. Main Street, where an actual hang-man's noose and chairs from the retired gas chamber are displayed along with photos of people put to death.

While the route described here is far more scenic, the **I-10** freeway between Phoenix and Tucson is considerably faster.

The most popular destination around Florence is the **Casa Grande Ruins National Monument** (daily 8 AM-5 PM; $4 per car), eight miles west of town off Hwy-287, which preserves some of the state's largest and most perplexing prehistoric remains. A small **visitor center** at the entrance gives some background on the Hoho-kam people who, approximately six centuries ago, built the four-story "big house" and the surrounding village, but no one knows what it was used for, or why it was abandoned.

Tom Mix monument

Biosphere II

One of the most ambitious, controversial, and just plain bizarre schemes to hatch in recent years, Biosphere II stands in the Arizona desert at the northern foot of Mount Lem-mon. Developed by a New Age group called "Synergia Ranch," and funded by the Texas billionaire Ed Bass, Biosphere II was originally intended to simulate the earth's entire ecosystem, in order to test the possibility of building self-sustaining colonies on other planets. A crew of four "biospherians" spent two not entirely self-sustained years sealed inside, emerging in 1993, when another crew took their place.

Amidst allegations of corruption and deceit, the founders of Biosphere II were unceremoniously fired by Mr. Bass in 1994, and the project has since been redirected to focus on pure re-search—though the Biosphere II is still a sealed system, there are no longer any people locked inside, and scientists study the effects of "greenhouse gases" and other ecosystem changes.

Cowboy actor **Tom Mix** died on October 12, 1940, when he crashed his 1937 Cord Phantom into a ditch along Hwy-79 and was decapitated by his suitcase. The site is marked by a riderless horse, in a rest area 19 miles south of Florence.

South of Florence, Hwy-79 follows the **Pinal Pioneer Parkway,** the old main road between Phoenix and Tucson. The route is now lined by a series of signs pointing out palo verde trees, saguaros, and other desert flora.

BIOSPHERE 2

Media attention and tourist traffic have died down considerably, but you can still visit the very pretty site and take a self-guided **tour** (daily 9 AM-4 PM; $12.95, kids under 5 free).

Located in a lovely desert canyon, the Biosphere facility (which was originally constructed in the 1970s as a corporate retreat for Motorola, and is now managed by Columbia University) also offers good meals in a small cafe and comfortable and inexpensive accommodations—rooms cost $50-80 a night depending upon the time of year, and there are tennis courts and a swimming pool. To reach Biosphere II, follow Hwy-79 to Oracle Junction, 25 miles north of Tucson, then turn east onto Hwy-77 for six miles; at the Biosphere II signs, turn south and follow the driveway for just over two more miles to the parking area, ticket booth, and gift shop.

The environmental activist and author **Edward Abbey,** who died in 1989, spent his last years living in the Arizona desert near Oracle Junction.

For more information on Biosphere II, call 520/825-6200 or 800/828-2462.

Tucson marks the junction of the US-93 route with our cross-country "Southern Pacific: US-80" route, which begins on page 738.

Across Tucson

From Oracle Junction, Hwy-77/Oracle Road winds around the western Catalina Mountains, following a series of one-way surface streets into compact downtown Tucson, which fills the area between the I-10 freeway and 6th Avenue, the main highway before the interstate was built. South of town, 6th Avenue becomes the Old Nogales Highway, the old road south to Mexico. Running past the small Tucson airport, the Old Nogales Highway holds a few funky old motels, the Indian-run Desert Diamond Casino, and **Jimmy's Diner**, an old railroad dining car serving up cheap breakfasts and BBQ beef sandwiches to an eclectic clientele.

Continuing south, the Old Nogales Highway veers in various alignments among extensive pecan groves and repeatedly crisscrosses the I-19 freeway, offering a slower (and frequently dead-end) alternative to the fast lane.

Mission San Xavier del Bac

Among the most strikingly memorable of all the Spanish colonial missions in the Southwest, Mission San Xavier del Bac was built over 200 years ago and still serves the native Tohono O'odham (aka "Papago") people. Known as the "White Dove of the Desert" because of the gleaming white plaster that covers its adobe walls, balustrades, and twin bell towers—one of which is domed, the other not—this landmark edifice was designed and built by Franciscan missionaries beginning in 1778; outbuildings date to the mid-1750s, and the mission was originally founded in 1700 by the Jesuit priest Eusebio Kino, who also established the mission farther south at Tumacácori.

Rising up from the flat desert plain, San Xavier presents an impressive silhouette, but what's most unforgettable is the Mexican folk-baroque interior, covered in intensely wrought sculp-

Mission San Xavier del Bac

tures and paintings of saints and religious imagery. Currently under restoration by a team brought in from Italy, these paintings and figurines are among the country's finest example of folk art, using painted mud to simulate marble, tiles, and crystal chandeliers.

The mission (daily 8 AM-6 PM; donations; 520/294-2624) is well signed and easy to reach, just 10 miles south of downtown Tucson off I-19 exit 92, then a half-mile west. Across the plaza from the church is a small Tohono-owned and -operated complex of craft galleries, plus a very good taco stand.

Titan Missile Museum
In just 15 miles south of San Xavier, you can travel from the colonial 1700s to the Cold War 1960s by stopping at the Titan Missile Museum, the only Intercontinental Ballistic Missile (ICBM) silo preserved intact and open to the public anywhere
(continues on page 166)

TUCSON SURVIVAL GUIDE

THOUGH IT'S LESS THAN HALF THE size of Phoenix, Tucson is at least twice as nice a place to visit. With more palpable history than anywhere in the Southwest outside New Mexico, a lively university community, and some of the most beautiful desert landscapes anywhere on earth, Tucson is well worth taking the time to get to know. It also makes an excellent

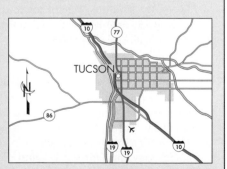

jumping-off point for visiting the Wild West towns of Tombstone and Bisbee to the east along old US-80 in the state's southeast corner.

(continues on next page)

However, with daytime temperatures averaging over 100° F, Tucson is hotter than heck during the summer months (early May to late September), so try to visit during the rest of the year. Spring is especially nice, with wildflowers blooming and spring training baseball bashing away, but this is also the most expensive time to be here—room rates in March are easily double those the rest of the year.

Many of Tucson's biggest attractions (Biosphere II, Mission San Xavier del Bac, the Arizona Desert Museum, and Saguaro National Park) are outside the city limits and covered under various road trips (above, and on pages 747-748, respectively), but the downtown area is worth a wander, especially for the many historic buildings that have been spared the redeveloper's wrecking ball. Most prominent of these old adobes is the **Fremont House**, 151 S. Granada Avenue next to the Convention Center, built in 1858 and later rented out to frontiersman John Fremont during his term as Governor of the Arizona Territory in 1878.

East of downtown, the nicely landscaped 350-acre University of Arizona campus, which spreads between Speedway Boulevard and 6th Street, holds the engaging historical exhibits of the **Arizona State Museum** (Mon.-Sat. 10 AM-5 PM; Sun. noon-5 PM; donations; 520/621-6302) and one of the country's pre-eminent photography collections in the **Center for Creative Photography**.

In the foothills of the Santa Catalina Mountains that rise north of Tucson, **Sabino Canyon** (daily 8:30 AM-dusk; 520/749-2861), with its seasonal waterfalls and a (nearly) year-round creek, is a great place to stretch your legs while getting a sense of how pretty and vibrant the desert can be. Sabino Canyon is 17 miles east of downtown, well signed off Tanque Verde Road.

Southeast of Tucson, off I-10 at the Kolb Road exit, **Davis-Monthan Air Force Base** holds one of the very strangest sights in the entire Southwest desert: rows and rows and rows of surplus military aircraft, lined up for what seems like miles. You can glimpse them from the highway, but for the full experience you have to sign up for one of the very popular tours (9 AM on Mon. and Wed. only; free; 520/228-3358).

Also on the southeast side of town, the **Tucson Sidewinders** (520/325-2621), the Class AAA farm club of the Arizona Diamondbacks, play at Tucson Electric Park, off I-10 at Ajo Way.

Practicalities
The main I-10 freeway runs diagonally from northwest to southeast along usually dry Santa Rita River at the western edge of town. Tucson stretches east from here for over 10 miles, and north toward the foothills of the Santa Catalina mountains. The main east-west route across town is Speedway Boulevard, along with numerous parallel roads.

Tucson's very small **airport** is south of I-10, eight miles from downtown, with all the usual shuttle and car rental companies. It's all but impossible to get around town without a car, though Gray Line (520/622-8811) and other companies offer bus trips to the more popular tourist attractions.

In addition to the usual highway motels, Tucson has some characterful places to stay, from restored downtown hotels to luxurious vacation resorts. One of the latter is the **Hacienda del Sol**, 5601 N. Hacienda del Sol Road (520/299-1501), a historic guest ranch, built as a posh girl's school in the 1920s, and now a quiet, intimate getaway, with a pool, tennis courts, great sunset views, and one of Tucson's best restaurants (The Grill). Another historic property, the **Arizona Inn**, 2200 E. Elm Street (520/325-1541 or 800/933-1093), is perhaps *the* classic Arizona resort, little changed since the 1920s when it was a favorite winter haunt of the Rockefellers and other elites. The Arizona Inn offers very comfortable accommodations on lovingly landscaped grounds, near the University campus; room rates are reasonable, especially off-peak, when they drop to under $100 a night.

Downtown holds many more accommodation options, starting with the lively **Hotel Congress** at 311 E. Congress Street (520/622-8848 or 800/722-8848). This youth-oriented hotel and hostel doubles as a cafe and nightclub, right at the heart of downtown; dorm beds $15, rooms $50. Many steps up on the price and comfort scale is **El Presidio Inn**, 297 N. Main Street (520/623-6151), an intimate bed-and-breakfast in lovely old adobe home at center of town.

One of the most enjoyable places to eat in all of Arizona is the quirky **Cafe Poca Cosa**, right downtown at 88 E. Broadway (in the Clarion Hotel). Adventurously creative Mexican food, served up in large portions at low prices, is the specialty here—try anything in a *mole* sauce, and you won't be disappointed. Across the street at 20 S. Scott Avenue, the restaurant's original location is now **Little Cafe Poca Cosa**, open for breakfast and lunch versions of the same delicious stuff. On the west side of downtown is **El Charro**, 311 N. Court Avenue, "the oldest family-operated Mexican restaurant in the USA," so they say, serving up inexpensive food (and margaritas) since 1922 in a turn-of-the-century downtown house. The same neighborhood also holds **Janos**, 150 N. Main Avenue (520/884-9426), possibly the best restaurant in the state, serving delicious (and very expensive) *nouvelle cuisine* in a landmark adobe home. Reservations strongly recommended.

For more all-American food you may have to head east of downtown, perhaps to the **Big A Restaurant**, 2033 E. Speedway Boulevard next to the University of Arizona, *the* place to eat burgers, drink beer and watch sports on TV. Also great, for food, if not the ambience, is **Jack's Original BBQ**, 5250 E. 22nd Street, a bare-bones barbecue place with succulent meats, tasty sweet potato pies, and the best beans west of Texas.

The **Metropolitan Tucson Visitors Bureau**, 130 S. Scott Avenue (520/624-1817 or 800/638-8350) has tons of information on Tucson and the surrounding regions. There are two daily newspapers (the morning *Daily Star* and the afternoon *Tucson Citizen*), while the free *Tucson Weekly* has the best listings of nightlife and current events.

in the world. On the north side of the sprawling stucco retirement community of Green Valley (pop.

13,231), just west from I-19 off exit 69 on Duval Mine Road, the silo was in active use from 1963 until 1982, was declared a National Historic Landmark in 1994, and is now open for **tours** (daily 9 AM-5 PM; $5; 520/625-7736). The tours, which take around an hour, involve donning a hard hat and descending downstairs into the control room of the hardened silo, which still contains a 110-foot-tall Titan missile. Also on display are a partly dismantled rocket engine and a "re-entry vehicle," which would have held the nuclear-tipped warhead.

Tubac

Tortuga Books

Another good place to stop between Tucson and the Mexican border is Tubac, 45 miles from Tucson, just east of I-19 at exit 34. One of the first European outposts in what's now Arizona, Tubac was established as a Spanish presidio (fort) in 1751, and a century later boomed with the opening of gold mines nearby. The town's lively history is recounted at the **Tubac Presidio State Historic Park** (daily 8 AM-5 PM; $1) on the east side of town, from where you can walk a short (4.5-mile-long) portion of the **Anza Trail** south to Tumacácori and get a real sense of what it was like on the Spanish colonial frontier.

Scattered around a dusty central plaza, just west of the presidio park, Tubac has developed into a small but diverting arts-and-crafts colony, with local artists frequently showcased in the **Tubac Center for the Arts** (Tues.-Sat. 10:30 AM-4:30 PM, Sunday 1-4:30 PM; free) on the north side of the plaza. A short walk south of the plaza, an excellent bookshop, **Tortuga Books**, and the popular **Cafe Fiesta**, which has very good salads and sandwiches, share space in the Mercado del Baca shopping complex at 19 Tubac Road.

Between Tubac and Tumacácori (two-ma-CA-coree), the Anza Trail follows a brief portion of the route taken in 1775 by explorer **Juan de Anza,** who led a group of colonists across the deserts to establish the city of San Francisco in 1776.

The I-19 freeway south of Tucson toward the Mexican border gives all distances in **metric** measures. The speed limit, however, is still the same old 65 mph.

In Amado, just west of I-19 at the Arivaca Road exit, a huge concrete cow's skull marks the entrance to a small cantina, one of a long series of businesses that have tried to make a go of this unique location. Across the highway is the popular **Cow Palace** restaurant, which is open daily 8 AM-9 PM.

Tumacácori National Historic Park

The preserved ruins of an impressive Spanish colonial mission stand at the center of Tumacácori National Historic Park (daily 8 AM-5 PM; $1), 19 miles north of Nogales, and just three miles south of Tubac, off I-19 exit 29. The site was used by missionaries as early as 1691, but it wasn't until 1800 that they set to work building ing the massive adobe church.

Though never finished, thanks to Apache raids and the Mexican Revolution, Tumacácori stands as an impressive reminder of the religious passion of the friars and their efforts to convert local tribes.

Directly across the highway from Tumacácori is a rare sight —a Greek cafe—and a half-mile north is **Wisdom's**, which serves reliable Mexican and American food.

Tumacacori mission

Ambos Nogales

Arizona's busiest border crossing, Nogales is also perhaps the most pleasant of all the "international" cities along the U.S./Mexico border. Despite being divided by an ugly corrugated steel fence, it gets promoted as *Ambos Nogales,* "Both Nogales." The twin cities are economically co-dependent, especially post-NAFTA, but the influx of illegal immigrants caused a crackdown by the Border Patrol (sometimes referred to as "Operation Gatekeeper") with as many as 500 arrests and deportations every day. The devalued peso has meant that fewer Mexicans can afford to come across and shop at Safeway, but Americans still while away evenings drinking cut-price beer in south-of-the-border cantinas. Apart from the intriguing little **Pimeria Alta Historical Society Museum** (daily 9 AM-5 PM; donations), which documents cross-border history in the storefront-sized Old City Hall on Grand Avenue, 400 yards north of the border crossing, there are few real sights to see, but if you just want to spend an hour or two shopping for souvenirs and practicing your Spanish, Nogales Mexico is a painless place in which to do it. (However, it's an ironic truth that shopkeepers south of the border speak better English than they do on the U.S. side.)

Jazz bassist and composer **Charles Mingus** was born in Nogales on April 22, 1922, but soon after moved to L.A. with his father, a railroad worker.

To save hassle (and time) crossing the border, drivers should park on the streets or in the $4-a-day lots on the U.S. side, and walk across. Border formalities are minimal, and U.S. dollars are accepted on both sides. Though prices on the Mexican side aren't dirt cheap, they are usually around 20 percent lower than in the U.S.

From Nogales, Mexican Highway 15, the primary route along the Gulf of California and the Pacific coast, heads south through Hermosillo and Guaymas to Mazatlan, Guadalajara and beyond. There's also good bus and train service to and from Nogales from the rest of Mexico, but the stations are a half-mile south of "The Line."

US-83: THE ROAD TO NOWHERE

US-83: THE ROAD TO NOWHERE

What was once the only entirely paved route from Canada to "Old Mexico" (as hard-to-find postcards along the route still say), US-83 is still likely the shortest—from Swan River, Manitoba, dead south to Browns-ville, Texas, and beyond to Matamoros, Mexico, seemingly without turning once. Its grim moniker, "The Road To Nowhere," is alternately unfair, and then again not severe enough, for the route navigates some of the widest and most aesthetically challenged land-scapes in the country: the yawn-inducing rolling grasslands of the northern Great Plains, the beefy expanses of western Nebraska and Kansas, and the mesmerizing heat of the Texas/Oklahoma Panhandle, before following the lower Rio Grande south to the Gulf of Mexico. Yet on US-83 you'll also take in some phenomenal country: verdant farm-land dotted with truly small towns, endlessly shifting prairie grassland, scrubby canyons, winding Missouri River roadways, and plain, isolated, where-the-hell-am-I agricultural expanses.

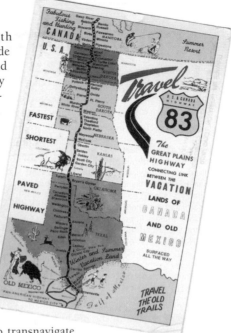

Following roughly along the 100th Meridian, US-83 marks the historic divide between the "civilized" eastern U.S. and the arid western deserts. Physiography aside, this route's cultural landscape centers around small but self-sufficient farm or cattle communities that date back to the last days of the Wild West and that are far enough off the tourist trail to retain an unselfconscious, aw-shucks quaintness. For endless miles in every direction, telephone and power poles provide some of the only signs of life between the highway and the distant horizon, though the towns—where average speeds drop suddenly from 70 mph to radar-enforced 25 mph or slower—are spaced just often enough along the highway to serve your food-and-fuel needs.

Perhaps best of all, US-83 manages to transnavigate this broad, odd nation, albeit north-to-south, without once grazing a conventional tourist attraction. Here in the nation's heartland, conversations over a daybreak breakfast, afternoons spent cooling off by municipal swimming pools, and twilight American Legion baseball games provide the stuff of truly memorable Road Trip diversions, and for that reason alone, US-83 remains a must-do long-distance byway.

US-83 HIGHLIGHTS

ACROSS NORTH DAKOTA

Beginning at Canada's Manitoba border, US-83's route across North Dakota is a 285-mile-long rehash of childhood back-of-station-wagon dreamscapes: epic plains too green or golden-hued for your eyes to process rationally, and endless cultivated fields punctuated by umpteen farmers' cooperatives, storage bins, silos, and grain elevators. Hay bales of all shapes and sizes dry perilously close to the roadside, and Stetsoned figures in dusty pickups or mighty tractors amiably lift their index fingers off steering wheels in back-forty greetings.

A half-hour side trip east from US-83 along Hwy-5 brings you to the town of Bottineau, where a giant turtle named "Wee'l" has been constructed out of old tractor wheels. For a picture, see "Roadside Giants of North Dakota" on page 480.

US-83 doesn't really follow a straight plumb-line south—it just seems that way. After meandering from the border across the fertile residuals of ancient Lake Souris near lonely Westhope, the route seems to fall straight down the map while crossing the drift prairie south to Minot. Continuing south across the neck of giant Lake Sakakawea, US-83 winds across slightly more ambitious hills and plateaus along a historic and hardly changed stretch of the mighty Missouri River to Bismarck, the state capital and a better-than-expected place to spend some time. South of Bismarck US-83 cuts away from the riverfront through a pastry-rich pastoral landscape settled around the turn of the 20th century by German immigrants—including the parents of dance-*meister* Lawrence Welk—while a recommended detour follows the Missouri River across the huge, historic Standing Rock Indian Reservation that stretches into South Dakota.

Westhope

US-83 begins winding its way from the Canadian border at the small U.S. entrance station (open 9 AM-10 PM only) six miles north of Westhope (pop. 575). Westhope, named by an optimistic Great Northern Railway official, is a good example of North Dakota's small agrarian towns. A few motels, cafes, and gas stations, a sparse two-block-long downtown, and that's about it. The Gateway Inn motel/lounge (701/245-6441) has tourist information on the area.

Six miles south of Westhope, US-83 zigzags west along Hwy-5 for five miles before sharply banking south. The next 37 miles to Minot are a straight shot south, passing nothing save two sweeping wildlife refuges and a solitary, nay, lonely Domino's Pizza, all by itself apart from occasional A-10s thundering overhead to and from Minot Air Force Base.

Minot

Snug in the Souris River Valley at the junction of US-2 and US-83, Minot (pop. 34,544; rhymes with "Why not?") grew so rapidly after the Great Northern Railroad came through in 1887 that it was dubbed "Magic City," though perhaps "Event Capital" would be more apropos today, for despite the city's importance in other areas, most people visit during the huge State Fair (third week in July), and during October's burgeoning **Norsk Hostfest**, "North America's Largest Scandinavian Festival." The fairgrounds, along the grandly named Burdick Expressway (Business US-2) a half-mile east of downtown, also hold the small **Pioneer Village and Museum** (daily 10 AM-6 PM, summer only), the usual assembly of turn-of-the-century buildings and artifacts gathered from all over the county.

What look like high-security parking lots in the fields around Minot may actually be underground missile silos under the command of Minot Air Force Base.

In summer, when daytime highs hover in the mid-90's, Minot's most enticing attractions are the expansive gardens of **Roosevelt Park**, along the banks of the Souris River between the fairgrounds and downtown Minot. Named, liked everything else in North Dakota, for Teddy Roosevelt—there's a larger-than-life statue of him, astride a horse in full Rough Rider regalia—the shady green space also holds a large **swimming pool** (daily 1-10 PM in summer; $2) with a 350-foot-long water slide, a rideable miniature train ($2), and a 20-acre **zoo** (daily 10 AM-8 PM in summer, 8 AM-4 PM rest of the year; $3), with some obscure animals and a Northern Plains habitat.

In the 1880s, Minot was one of the spots where scavenging "plainscombers" collected enormous piles of buffalo bones to be used in making fertilizer.

Along with the usual crossroads barrage of franchised fast-food places, Minot supports a couple of breakfast and lunch-only cafes, including **Charlie's Main Street Cafe** at 113 S. Main Street, and **Gladys' Place** at 300 E. Central Avenue. Charlie's is right downtown, its fluorescent-lit pink vinyl booths full of gossiping Minot ladies, while Gladys' is three blocks east, near the train tracks and grain elevators, its fluorescent-lit brown vinyl booths full of gossiping Minot men; the food's good at both, and you get a pot of coffee when you order a cup. Another attraction of Minot is the wide range of cowboy hats and western wear you can look at or buy in the downtown stores.

In range for an hour or more in all directions, Minot's **KRRZ 1390 AM** broadcasts oldies from the 1950s and 1960s, along with Minnesota Twins baseball games.

East of Minot on US-2, the town of Rugby is nearly the **geographical center of North America.**

After dark, choose from any of over a dozen haunts, from bingo parlors and low-stakes casinos to country-western honky-tonks like **Tilly's**, housed in an old Standard Oil service station at 720 N. Broadway (US-83), or low-key beer bars like the **Blue Rider**, 118 1st Avenue SE, a smoke-free pub with what may be rural North Dakota's best selection of bottled brews—look for the "Grain Belt Beer" sign.

Motels are scattered along the congested arteries of both US-83 and US-2, so (except perhaps during the state fair) you shouldn't have trouble finding a place to sleep. The nicest place to stay is the **Best Western International Inn**, on US-83 at 1505 N. Broadway (701/852-3161 or 800/528-1234); less expensive local motels include the clean and quiet **Fairview Lodge**, across from the fairgrounds at 1900 E. Burdick Expressway (701/852-4488 or 800/836-2047).

The Minot **visitor center**, on US-83 south of downtown at 1040 S. Broadway (701/857-8206 or 800/264-2626), has more complete listings and detailed information on events and activities. Being so central to the state, Minot hosts everything from chili cook-offs to the state softball championships, and there's usually *something* going on.

Minot marks the junction of US-83 and US-2, which runs across the country from Seattle all the way to Acadia National Park in Maine. The US-2 route is covered in the "Great Northern" chapter, beginning on page 446.

Lake Sakakawea and Garrison

Nearly 200 miles long and with 1,600 miles of shoreline along the dammed Missouri River, Lake Sakakawea is one of the largest man-made "lakes" in the U.S. There are countless things to do on the water, most of them involving fishing; in summer, a 24-hour fishing hotline (701/463-7376) has details of what's biting where.

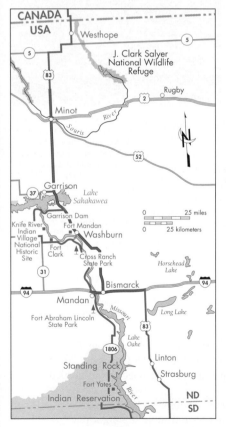

The pleasant town of Garrison (pop. 1,530), on the north shore of the lake and six miles west of US-83 on Hwy-37, serves as lake headquarters. Besides boasting a pair of red-roofed water towers labeled "Hot" and "Cold," Garrison has what may be the country's only neon-signed City Hall. In the city park you'll find the **North Dakota Fishing Hall of Fame and Museum**, (Friday 4-8 PM, Saturday noon-8 PM, and Sunday noon-4 PM, June-Sept. only), marked at the north end of Main Street by a photogenic fiberglass statue of "Wally-the-26-Foot-Walleye."

Garrison Dam

South of the extended bridge across Lake Sakakawea, and 12 miles west of US-83 via Hwy-200, the Missouri River backs up behind wide but low-slung Garrison Dam, the third-largest earth-filled dam in the U.S., which you can explore during hourly public **tours** (daily 7:30 AM-3:30 PM in summer; free). The power-house is enmeshed within a labyrinth of huge power stanchions, high-voltage lines, and transformers. You can also visit the adjacent **fish hatchery** (same hours as the dam) on the downstream side of the dam, where tanks hold hundreds and thousands of walleye, bass, and northern pike, plus rainbow and brown trout.

South of the turnoff to Garrison Dam, roadside interest along US-83 focuses on leviathan testimonials to engineering prowess. Huge tractors and bulldozers raise clouds of dust at the extensive **coal mining** operations around Underwood—the whole area on both sides of US-83 has been strip-mined and restored, though current operations are hard to get a good look at—and most of the valuable black rock ends up at electricity generating plants like the 1,100-megawatt **Coal Creek Station**, six miles north of Washburne and two miles off the roadway but *readily* apparent. This is the largest lignite-fired coal plant in the country, and one of the few that's open for **tours** (Mon.-Fri. 8 a.m.-3 PM; free; 701/442-3211, ext. 810); you can also get an up-close gawk at their **four-mile-long coal conveyor belt**, which passes over the highway in a tube.

However, unless you have an abiding interest in fossil fuels, a more interesting alternative to driving this stretch of US-83 is to follow the river's western bank south of Lake Sakakawea, where it reverts to its naturally broad and powerful self for the next 75 miles. Between Garrison Dam and Washburn, scenic Hwy-200 passes two of North Dakota's most significant historic sites, Fort Clark and the Knife River Indian Villages, both of which, though small, saw key scenes of the late 18th- and early 19th-century interactions between Native Americans and interloping European traders and explorers.

The land flooded by Lake Sakakawea had previously been the prime grazing lands of the **Fort Berthold Reservation,** but the Mandan and other Native American tribes living there received almost nothing from the US government in compensation.

Lake Sakakawea is one of many places in the northwestern U.S. named for the legendary Shoshone Indian woman, also known as **Sacagawea,** who accompanied the Lewis and Clark expedition across the Rocky Mountains.

Knife River Indian Village National Historic Site

Downstream from Garrison Dam along the west bank of the Missouri River, the Knife River Indian Village National Historic Site (daily 8 AM-6 PM in summer, daily 8 AM-4:30 PM in winter; free) is one of North Dakota's most fascinating historic places, and the only federally maintained site devoted to preservation of the Plains tribes' cultures. Standing above the Missouri floodplain, on the site of what was the largest and most sophisticated village of the interrelated Hidatsa, Mandan, and Arikara tribes, the park protects the remains of dozens of terraced fields, fortifications, and earth lodges, remnants of a culture that lived here for thousands of years before being devastated by disease within a few short decades of European contact.

A highlight of the park is an **earth lodge**, reconstructed using traditional materials, which gives a vivid sense of day-to-day Great Plains life. Measuring over 50 feet

Knife River Indian Village

across, and 12 feet high at its central smoke hole, the earth lodge looks exactly as it would have when the likes of George Catlin and Karl Bodmer were welcomed by the villagers during the 1830s. Just north of the earth lodge spread circular depressions in the soil—which is all that remains of the Hidatsa community where in 1804 the Lewis and Clark Corps of Discovery was joined by the French fur trapper Charbonneau and his wife Sacagawea.

The modern **visitor center**, well signed off Hwy-200 at the south edge of the park, has high-quality reproductions of the drawings and paintings that Catlin, Bodmer, and others made of the Knife River Indian Villages, along with archaeolog-

---

THE LEWIS AND CLARK EXPEDITION

Following the instructions of President Thomas Jefferson, Meriwether Lewis and William Clark set off across the continent in 1804 to explore the vast territory recently acquired from France in the Louisiana Purchase. Part of their mission was to find a viable trade route from the Mississippi River to the Pacific Ocean.

Sharing command of what was officially known as the Corps of Discovery, which included 33 soldiers and experienced "mountain men," plus the legendary Sacagawea, her husband Toussaint Charbonneau, and their infant Pomp, not to mention Lewis's Newfoundland dog, Seaman, Lewis and Clark blazed a route up the Missouri River, crossed the Rocky Mountains, and made their way west down the Columbia River, returning to St. Louis after two and a half years and over 8,000 miles of unprecedented travel.

Along with their copious journals, many good books have been written documenting the Lewis and Clark expedition and tracing their route, which has been declared the Lewis and Clark National Historic Trail. Much of the land they traversed has been altered beyond recognition, though numerous historic sights along the way have been preserved or protected as parks or museums; the best of these are described more fully elsewhere in this book.

Jefferson National Expansion Memorial is an excellent museum underneath the Gateway Arch in St. Louis. See page 258.

Sergeant Floyd Monument is a stone obelisk marking the grave of the only expedition member to lose his life, from appendicitis. See page 565.

On a Slant Indian Village has been reconstructed atop the remains of a Mandan village. See page 181.

Fort Mandan, where the expedition spent the winter of 1804-05, has been reconstructed downstream from the original site. See page 178.

Knife River Indian Village, along the banks of the Missouri, holds the remains of the Hidatsa village where Sacagawea lived before joining the Corps of Discovery. See page 175.

Lemhi Pass, on the Idaho/Montana border, is where the expedition first crossed the Continental Divide. See page 135.

ical and anthropological summaries that help to bring to life these intriguing Native American peoples. The center also has **information** (701/745-3309) on the many annual events, festivals, and powwows held at Knife River throughout the year, including the Northern Plains Indian Culture Fest, late in July.

A half-mile south of the visitor center, the tiny town of **Stanton** (pop. 517) has two cafes, two bars, and two gas stations along its three-block main drag. The Mercer County Courthouse, at the center of Stanton, displays arrowheads and other Indian artifacts.

The River of No Return is an impassable portion of the Salmon River. See page 134.

Traveler's Rest, in the Bitterroot Valley south of Missoula, was such an idyllic spot that the Corps of Discovery camped here on both the outbound and return legs of their journey. See page 132.

Fort Canby, overlooking the mouth of the Columbia River, has a small museum on the spot where the expedition first saw the Pacific Ocean. See page 38.

Fort Clatsop, a full-scale reconstruction of the wooden fort where the expedition spent a miserable winter in 1805-06, sits in lush forest along the Oregon coast. See page 41.

Tillamook Head, rising high above the Pacific Ocean, is the farthest point the expedition reached. See page 43.

**THE LEWIS AND CLARK EXPEDITION
1804–1806**

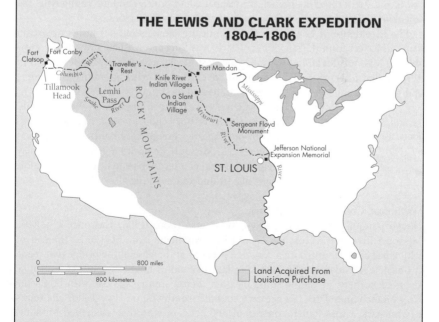

Fort Clark

Seven miles downstream from the Knife River site, well signed off Hwy-200, Fort Clark Historical Site (daily 8 AM-4:30 PM April-Oct.; free) is as eerily isolated as can be. One of three major fur-trading posts on the upper Missouri River, Fort Clark was founded by the American Fur Company circa 1831, primarily to trade with the Mandan Indians. The fort was visited by other tribes as well as the usual roll-call of adventurers, explorers, and frontier luminaries such as Prince Maximilian, George Catlin, and Karl Bodmer; unfortunately, the steamboats that plied the waters to bring supplies also brought smallpox, and in one tragic winter in 1837 the Mandan tribe's population was cut from 1,600 to 100. After the fur trade declined, Fort Clark was abandoned in 1860.

Today the tranquil site, approached on a narrow gravel-and-dirt road, is devoid of anything—a somber, quiet, unretouched piece of history stretching out on a grassy, flat-topped bluff overlooking the Missouri River. A walking trail has markers designating the locations of eight original buildings; depressions from an earth lodge village are still apparent.

Fort Mandan

Back on the east bank of the Missouri River, north of Washburn and two miles west of US-83, Fort Mandan is a very rustic reconstruction of Lewis and Clark's winter quarters in 1804-05. Arriving here at the end of October after a tediously difficult six-month slog upstream from St. Louis, the expedition set up camp, which consisted of rough-hewn log cabins arranged to form a triangular palisade, surrounded by an 18-foot-high wall. Here the 44 men spent the winter, making friendly contact with nearby Indian tribes, most significantly those of the Knife River site—where Lewis and Clark hired the French fur trapper Charbonneau and his young wife, the legendary Sacagawea, who helped guide them across the Rockies.

The actual site of Lewis and Clark's encampment, some 10 miles upstream across the river from the site of Fort Clark, was long ago washed away by the ever-shifting Missouri River, but the full-scale, historically accurate replica fort, built in 1969 by local history buffs, is open all day and night with no admission charge, and gives a strong sense of the deprivations and discomforts suffered by the Corps of Discovery on their two-year expedition across the continent. The fort also has a basic **visitor center** (1-5 PM; free) and an adjacent park with outstanding though bare-bones camping ($5) right along the restless Missouri River. It's a great place to play Tom Sawyer, and on summer afternoons you'll see barefoot kids, shirtless in overalls, fishing and mucking along the banks.

As it flows across the south-central corner of North Dakota, the Missouri River also marks the dividing line between the central and mountain time zones.

Washburn: Cross Ranch State Park

Now a tranquil little highway town, Washburn (pop. 1,506) was once a frenetic Missouri River ferry crossing, served by steamboats from St. Louis, the last of which has been mounted on a concrete pedestal at the base of the bridge that made it obsolete. Besides nearby Fort Mandan, two miles to the northwest, and nice riverside scenery, including some pleasant, dense spinneys, Washburn holds the **Cross Ranch State Park** ($2 per car), six miles southwest on Hwy-1806. The state's newest park, Cross Ranch consists of 560 acres of cottonwood-shaded Missouri

River bottomland, and includes the remains of the ghost town of Sanger, numerous hiking trails, canoe rentals, and fine camping, with sites for RVs and for backpackers. There's also a fully furnished **log cabin**, in which you can stay for $35 a night; for details phone the **visitor center** (701/794-8741), which also has information on the annual Missouri River Bluegrass Festival, held Labor Day weekend.

Adjacent to the state park along Hwy-1806, and owned by the Nature Conservancy, the **Cross Ranch Nature Preserve** (daily dawn-dusk; free) has one of the richest surviving native Missouri River valley ecosystems, including floodplain prairie and riparian forest, plus a resident herd of bison and some undisturbed Native American archaeological sites.

In winter, the steps of the North Dakota state capitol are so treacherously icy that workers pile snow onto them to prevent people from walking up them.

From Washburn, a bridge across the Missouri River carries Hwy-200 northwest on a scenic loop past Fort Clark and the historic Knife River Indian Villages (see above for more).

Thirty miles west of Bismarck, the "World's Largest Cow" stands along I-94 in New Salem.

Bismarck

Like many towns across the Great Plains, Bismarck (pop. 49,300) was named after a wealthy European, in this case the chancellor of the German Empire, in order to lure much-needed capital investment. The town grew exponentially following booms in the railroad industry, gold, and, most recently, oil and synthetic fuels; but it's still economically and culturally dependent upon its status as North Dakota's state capital. It's one of the smallest of the 50 in the U.S., but as state capitals go Bismarck rates quite highly for its size, with thousands of parkland acres, well-preserved historic districts, and an old-time boat ride along the Missouri River.

Bureaucratic Bismarck seems intent on glossing over its bawdy historical peccadilloes by building monuments to modernity like the capitol building, 19 stories of angular art deco nicknamed the "Skyscraper of the Prairies." The white limestone and classical symbolism seem out of place on the plains, but free **tours** (daily 8-11 AM and 1-4 PM) highlight the ornate interior's woodwork, stonecarving and metalsmithing.

On the grounds you'll find the usual memorial statues of noteworthy North Dakotans, starting with a large statue of **Sacagawea**, the guide of Lewis and Clark, carrying her newborn baby Baptiste and looking sternly forward; nearby is another popular subject, a **buffalo**, here rendered out of rusty steel reinforcing rod. A short walk away, the **North Dakota Heritage Center** (Mon.-Fri. 8 AM-5 PM, Saturday 9 AM-5 PM, Sunday 11 AM-5 PM; donations; 701/328-2666), has an informative array of historical and cultural exhibits, tracing the development of North Dakota from its geological underpinnings to its contemporary industries.

Though Bismarck is the state capital, the selection of places to eat is on the meager side, with a few old buildings turned into ersatz but suddenly upscale pubs-cum-restaurants like **Peacock Alley**, 422 E. Main Street, serving predictable pasta and Cajun dishes. A block away, off the corner at 208 E. Broadway, the **Green Earth Cafe/One World Coffeehouse** is a hip haunt which, as the name implies, is a hangout for the city's otherwise invisible leftist fringe, sponsoring readings or performances of a disparate range of industrial, folk, and jazz music.

Between the two state capitals of Bismarck, North Dakota, and Pierre, South Dakota, the Missouri River has been dammed to form 200-mile-long **Lake Oahe.**

Follow US-83 south of Bismarck to visit Strasburg, North Dakota, birthplace of **Lawrence Welk,** whose childhood home still stands along the highway.

In his best-selling travelogue *Travels with Charley,* writer John Steinbeck wrote about Bismarck: "Here is where the map should fold. Here is the boundary between east and west. On the Bismarck side it is eastern landscape, eastern grass, with the look and smell of eastern America. Across the Missouri on the Mandan side it is pure west, with brown grass and water scorings and small outcrops. The two sides of the river might well be a thousand miles apart."

Along with the clusters of motels on the northern fringes of US-83 and along I-94, accommodation options include a **Best Western Fleck House Motel,** in downtown proper at 122 E. Thayer Street (701/255-1450), with cheaper-than-usual rooms from $35 a night.

For further information, contact the Bismarck **visitor center,** 523 N. 4th Street (701/222-4308 or 800/767-3555).

Missouri River Tour: Hwy-1806

An outstanding alternative to US-83 between Bismarck and the South Dakota border is the narrow but well-maintained Hwy-1806, which meanders along the Missouri River taking in great hillocks and easy bluffs off to the left, or scintillating blue water ribboning beneath stark-white, standing-driftwood trees. Round a bend and you'll see a lagoon or a morass. Or admire a great panorama of 2,000-foot buttes to the west, all the way across the state line. Be sure to fill up on gas and supplies before you set off since it's a 100-mile drive with few services along the way.

Mandan and Fort Abraham Lincoln State Park

Cross-river sibling to the state capital, Mandan (pop. 15,177) is a shipping and warehousing center that grew up swiftly in the years after 1882, when the Northern Pacific railroad completed a bridge from Bismarck. Everything in Mandan, from cafes to beauty parlors, seems to be named after Lewis and Clark, but there's not a lot to see in town apart from two statues, one a 25-foot-tall

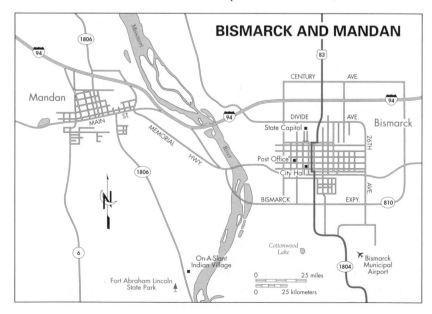

Indian figure carved from a cottonwood tree standing at 601 S.E. 6th Avenue, the other the requisite Teddy Roosevelt, in front of the train station on Main Street. These aside, the real reason to stop in Mandan is to enjoy a sandwich and a milk shake (or a rare cup of espresso!) at the lunch counter of the truly marvelous Americana-rich **Mandan Drug**, 316 W. Main Street.

Heading south along Hwy-1806 from Mandan along the west bank of the Missouri River, the first place you'll reach is sprawling Fort Abraham Lincoln State Park, (daily 8 AM-dusk; $3 per car), which was originally established by the Northwest Company as a fur-trading post in 1780. It eventually fell into the hands of the U.S. Army, which in 1872 changed the fort's name to the present one. Soon afterwards, General Custer arrived to take over the reins of command, and in 1876 the fort was placed squarely on the map and in the national press as the departure point for the doomed general and his 250 men, who met their

Theodore Roosevelt, Roughrider

demise at Little Big Horn. Abandoned in 1891, the fort was dismantled by settlers who salvaged the wood and bricks to build their own homes, and most everything here today is a reconstruction.

The modern park covers nearly 1,000 acres, and contains a number of barracks, stables, and stores, plus a replica of Custer's house (daily 9 AM-9 PM in summer, daily 1-5 PM rest of year; $4), where paid sycophants will lead you around, calling you "General" while conducting guided tours. Best of all is the **On-A-Slant Indian Village**, near the north end of the park, an excavated Mandan village dating from the mid-17th century, where you can explore four full-scale earth lodges re-created by the Civilian Conservation Corps in 1933-34. An adjacent **museum** (daily 9 AM-9 PM in summer, 9 AM-5 PM rest of the year; $3) gives an overall history of the region, from prehistoric times up through Custer's ill-fated adventure.

If you like the idea of *not* driving for a change, the **Fort Lincoln Trolley** (daily 1-5 PM in summer; $4) runs along the river between Mandan and Fort Abraham Lincoln, departing every hour or so for the 4.5-mile trip, leaving Mandan from a depot at 2000 S.E. 3rd Street.

US-83: Linton, Strasburg, and the Lawrence Welk Birthplace

While the scenery is superior along the Hwy-1806 detour, the trek south of Bismarck along US-83 is redeemed by one totally unique Road

George Armstrong Custer

Trip destination: the **Ludwig Welk Farmstead** (daily 10 AM-6 PM in summer, by appointment rest of year; $3; 701/336-7519), boyhood home of Lawrence Welk. Located a mile north of the town of Strasburg, then 2.5 miles west from US-83 following well-signed dirt roads, this is the preserved homestead where the world-famous band leader and accordion player was born in 1903.

Though the Lawrence Welk connection is the main draw for most visitors, the farm is intended as a memorial to his parents, who as part of an exodus of Bavarian-born Catholic farmers fled Ukraine during the 1870s and 1880s when exemptions from military service were threatened. The promise of land brought the Welks in the 1890s. The clapboard house that stands today began as a sod house—the mud walls can still be seen in places—and is now full of odds and ends of furniture and memorabilia donated by the Welk family, who still own the land. Hand tools, a windmill, and farming implements are arranged around the yard, while in the hayloft a mannequin dressed as young Lawrence squeezes out polkas on the accordion—apparently, his early playing was so bad that he was banned from practicing in the house, though now his recordings are broadcast non-stop from a *M*A*S*H*-like speaker system strung around the grounds.

Much of southern North Dakota is still predominantly populated by descendants of the original wave of these immigrant "Germans from Russia" who homesteaded the region in the 1890s. Their influence is clearly apparent in the town of Linton (pop. 1,410), on US-83 18 miles north of the Welk homestead, where the **Model Bakery**, 117 N. Broadway, bakes up delicious, creamy custard kuchen and Germanic cakes and cookies Tues.-Fri., while in Strasburg (pop. 600), Welk's parents are buried in the cemetery behind the absolutely huge Catholic church that dwarfs the tiny town.

The primary tourist attraction on the Standing Rock Indian Reservation is the **Prairie Knights** casino, on Hwy-1806, 44 miles south of Mandan. To sample this little bit of Las Vegas-on-the-Plains, contact the resort (800/425-8277).

Both Linton and Strasburg also have the only-in-North-Dakota attractions of what must be the **world's smallest bowling alleys**: one is tucked away in back of the **Linton Cafe** at 105 N. Broadway (701/254-9077), while Strasburg's four-laner is behind the **Pin Palace Cafe** at 714 Main Street (701/336-9616).

Standing Rock Indian Reservation: Fort Yates

Genuinely huge hills start to appear around the Standing Rock Indian Reservation, home to approximately 4,500 Sioux, spreading across the state line with a total of 880,000 acres. For outsiders, the main draw to the reservation, besides the fantastic roadside views and the glitzy Prairie Knights casino, is the original burial site of **Sitting Bull** in Fort Yates (pop. 183), the reservation headquarters. Though Sitting Bull was originally buried here, two miles west of Hwy-1806, the unimpressive site, marked by a boulder on a dusty side road, is certainly not what one would expect for the great warrior. He is now more suitably interred near Mobridge, South Dakota (see page 184).

The border between North and South Dakota is marked every half-mile by 720-stone monuments, each seven feet tall but half-buried in the ground. They were erected by the federal government in 1892; one stands right alongside Hwy-1804, on the eastern shore of Lake Oahe.

Across from the agency headquarters is another site sacred to the Sioux, the **Standing Rock** from which the reservation takes its name. In the correct angle of sunlight, the stone resembles a seated woman wearing a shawl. Legend holds that the woman, jealous of her husband's second wife, refused to move when the tribe decamped; a search party later found her, turned to stone.

South of Fort Yates the scenery is magnificent, particularly in the early morning and evening. Flawless blacktop winds through valleys and up ambitious, swooping hills of grazing land, and you won't even realize you're in South Dakota until you notice the gold border on the highway signs near Kenel, South Dakota.

ACROSS SOUTH DAKOTA

Two hundred and fifty-four miles of US-83 cut through eastern South Dakota's broad expanse, crossing mostly level but never slate-flat topography, and passing through what's known as the "Great Lakes" region of the state, most evident in and around Pierre. Instead of a multi-lane, transcontinental highway, US-83 across South Dakota resembles a country road, giving an up-close-and-personal look at farming and grazing lands, with an occasional jutting hill, ravine, or serpentine creek bed to break up the monotony. Classic South Dakota—no pretensions.

To either side of the North Dakota border, US-83 is little more than a beeline across the plains. Sadly, the Missouri River is well out of eyeshot, so we highly recommend following a scenic detour across the river through the huge Standing Rock Indian Reservation, linking up with US-83 again at Mobridge. After that you'll pass through small farm towns before reaching the state capital, Pierre, at the center of South Dakota.

Wild pheasants and other beautifully plumed game birds scurry about in the grassy verges along US-83 across the Dakotas.

Standing Rock Indian Reservation

Since US-83's route across northern South Dakota doesn't offer much stimulation for the senses, if you've got the time to spare, detour west along the Missouri River, leaving North Dakota via the "Lewis and Clark Highway," Hwy-1806. This scenic route brings you across the middle of Standing Rock Indian Reservation, which falls mainly in South Dakota but stretches about 30 miles over the border.

On Hwy-1806, at tiny Kenel, you veer a bit to the west, away from the muddy Missouri River and toward imposing 2,200-foot Rattlesnake Butte. You'll cross over huge bays on sweeping bridges, then roll into **Mobridge** (pop. 3,800), the biggest town

The town's name, **Mobridge,** stems from a hasty telegraph message transmitted in 1906 by an operator who needed a quick and clear reference to the area. He chose, at random, *Mo* for the Missouri River, and *bridge,* referring to the one then under construction by the Milwaukee Railroad.

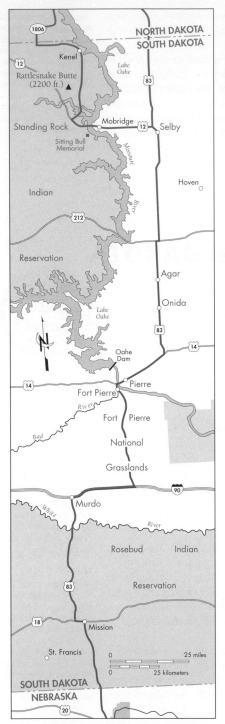

between the North and South Dakota capitals. Mobridge, once a village of the Arikara tribe, is heavily dependent on the anglers who come to pluck the lunkers, walleye, and even 20-pound northern pike from Lake Oahe, here many miles wide.

In the way of food, Mobridge has nothing special. Try the traditional square meal at **Wrangler Motor Inn** (605/845-3641). Located a half-mile west on US-12 at 820 W. Grand Crossing, the Wrangler is the best stop on the stretch, with two dining rooms, a coffee shop, and rooms from $45, as well as a heated pool. The **Super 8**, also on US-12 West (605/845-7215), is cheaper.

Sitting Bull Memorial

Driving six miles west of Mobridge on US-12 and then four miles south on a paved road, you'll find Sitting Bull's final resting place, after his body was disinterred in 1953 from Fort Yates in a controversial, surreptitious move. Whatever injustice or disrespect exhuming his body may have incurred, this magnificent view, high atop a palisade hilltop, is at least worthier than the previous site. The massive granite bust that serves as Sitting Bull's tombstone was carved by the late Korczak Ziolkowski, the sculptor who began the quixotic Crazy Horse Mountain carving near Mount Rushmore.

US-83: Selby, Agar, and Onida

Southeast of Mobridge you rejoin US-83 at diminutive Selby (pop. 707), the kind of sleepy, Middle American hamlet with children riding bikes home at dusk, teenagers rumbling down Main Street in their muscle cars, and a classic cafe on the main downtown drag serving cracked-mug coffee. On the northwest edge of town, near the US-12 and US-83 intersection, you'll find oasis-like **Lake Hiddenwood State Park** ($3), with picturesque deep swales and oak and

cedar trees surrounding a—as the name implies—secluded swimming hole. If you mentally transport yourself back a century and
a half when explorers crossed these bone-dry parts and stumbled
accidentally onto this lushness, the name's quite apt.

On the walls inside the
Scherr-Howe Arena, 212
Main Street in Mobridge,
bold 16- by 20-foot **murals**
depict Sioux history and
culture. View them Mon.-Fri.
8 AM-12 PM and 1-5 PM; free.

Between Selby and Pierre, there's nothing of dramatic importance. Highway hypnosis is kept at bay by the **Bangor Monu-
ment**, a roadside marker, five miles south of Selby, standing on the site of the
vanished town of Bangor (a free book to the first reader who can tell us why Bangor
merited a marker!); farther south, then 13 miles east of US-83, the **Cathedral on
the Prairie** looms over the hamlet of Hoven (pop. 522). Neither are jaw-dropping
in any way.

And then, finally, a town . . . or at least some grain elevators. Agar (pop. 82;
"Home of the 1977 State B Track Champions") is a classic, single-sidewalk leg-
stretch where the Pepsi machine is as large as the filling station it rests against. The
same goes for little Onida (pop. 761), with a handsome onion-domed courthouse,
a bright yellow, purple-capped water tower, and a cute city park complete with
swimming pool and horseshoe courts. You'd hardly guess that this was once a
thriving homesteader boomtown, full of transplanted New Yorkers who named it
after Oneida, with no apparent rea-
son for the spelling alteration; eat at
Niehoff's Cafe downtown, or at the
Fireside Lounge, a steakhouse and
bar right on US-83.

Sioux Horse Effigy

Pierre

The second smallest and by far the sleepiest state capital in the country, Pierre
(pop. 12,906; pronounced Peer), is an odd amalgam of South Dakota characteristics. Part farm town, part railroad town, and best of all, part river town, Pierre accurately embodies South Dakota's dominant activities. Located at nearly the
geographic center of the state, quiet, easy Pierre is filled with natural attractions,
totally lacking in the usual power-broker trappings of other state capital cities.

Pierre's one not-to-be-missed stop is the excellent **South Dakota Cultural Heritage Center** at 900 Governor's Drive (Mon.-Fri. 9 AM-4:30 PM, Saturday and Sunday 1-4:30 PM; free), built into the side of a hill on the north side of town; it is
designed to be a modern evocation of a traditional Native American dwelling. Inside, the museum has the usual interpretive historical displays of native and pioneer cultures, with a focus on the Sioux tribes and the battles for the Black Hills
region. A glass case holds the actual lead plate which the brothers Louis-Joseph
and Francois Verendrye, the first Europeans to explore what's now South Dakota,
left behind when they claimed the entire territory for France in 1743.

At the center of town, the state **capitol** grounds are a verdant island of tranquillity with an arboretum, walking trails and the **Fountain Memorial**, dedicated to Ko-
rean and Vietnam War veterans. The fountain sits on a lake that is home to
thousands of migrating winter waterfowl.

Also worth a look is the **South Dakota National Guard Museum**, 303 E. Dakota,
(Mon.-Fri. 1-5 PM; free), which you can't miss because of the Sherman tank, the A-
70 Corsair and the artillery pieces on the boulevard. You can also see General
Custer's dress sword here. For travel-weary road hogs, the coolest museum is the

hands-on **South Dakota Discovery Center and Aquarium**, (Sun.-Fri. 1-5 PM, Saturday 10 AM-5 PM; $3), in the old Pierre Municipal Power & Light building at 805 W. Sioux Avenue, with loads of science exhibits.

Museums aside, nature is really what draws folks to Pierre. Bordering the town to the south is long **La Framboise Isle Nature Area**, a perfect place to while away time, recuperating from the drive along the beautiful bay.

If you look under "Hotels" in the Pierre Yellow Pages, you'll find only one listing (and that's a Days Inn!), but there are the usual assorted motels on US-83 as it swoops in from the north and follows the wide landscaped boulevards beyond downtown. Along US-83, west of the state capitol building, lots of locally owned places offer single rooms from the bottom-barrel $20 range on up; the **Governor's Inn**, 700 W. Sioux Avenue (605/224-4200 or 800/341-8000), is at the top end of the price and comfort scale. Finally, this same can't-miss-it main drag holds that noteworthy **Days Inn**, 520 W. Sioux Avenue (605/224-0411) with single rooms from $30.

The downtown hole-in-the-wall **D&E Cafe**, 115 W. Dakota Avenue, seemingly lifted out of celluloid cliché into real life, includes original smoky floors and walls with forgotten wainscoting abused by multiple coats of coffee-brown paint. The food is classic short-order with gum-cracking service on the side. Pierre's subtle upward spin has allowed the **World of Donuts**, 200 E. Dakota Avenue, to transform itself into a rather ambitious coffee shop at nightfall.

The gregarious staff at the **chamber of commerce** (800/962-2034), 108 E. Missouri Avenue, is chock-full of helpful information.

Houck's Buffalo Ranch, 25 miles northwest of Pierre on Hwy-1806, is a 53,000-acre spread supporting about 3,000 head of bison, some of whom were seen in the movie *Dances with Wolves*.

As you cruise along the I-90 freeway, keep an eye out for **Wall Drug** signs, advertising the world-famous site that is 100 miles to the west of US-83. If you go as far as Wall, you might as well continue on to Mount Rushmore and the even bigger Crazy Horse memorial, in the Black Hills 50 miles farther west.

Fort Pierre

South of Pierre, US-83 crosses the Missouri River, then takes you into Fort Pierre (pop. 1,900). It's not much now, but it has a rich history. As far back as 1817 it was known as Fort Pierre Chouteau, an American Fur Company trading post; and before that it was Ree and Arikara tribal lands. Located at the mouth of the Bad (Teton) River, Fort Pierre once was a thriving port. But it is better known as the site where Joseph La Framboise, a French fur trader, out of necessity stopped and erected a driftwood shelter, establishing the area's first white settlement.

Visit the old fort, now a National Park Service landmark spread out over 1.3 acres near town. At 115 N. Main Street in the center of town you'll find the **Verendrye Museum** (9 AM-6 PM May-Sept.), which has collections of South Dakota pioneer artifacts and a duplicate of the plate the Verendrye brothers, the first white men to enter South Dakota, planted here in 1743 to claim the land for France. The original plate is in the state Heritage Center in Pierre; the Verendrye brothers themselves are commemorated with a monument in small Centennial Park, off US-83 at the center of town.

Immediately south of Fort Pierre, typical South Dakota topography resumes: rolling black and green hills, and twisting creek beds beneath sharp vertical drops of million-year-old geology. Barely out of the city are the **Gumbo Buttes** to the east, with shale deposits smacking more of northern Montana's scrape marks from open-pit mines.

Fort Pierre National Grasslands
Spreading across the plains south of Pierre along both sides of US-83, the 116,000 acres of the Fort Pierre National Grasslands are home to deer, pronghorn, jillions of waterfowl, and one of the most pervasive stretches of **prairie dog towns** in the region. The area doesn't offer developed campsites, but it does have great fishing at some of the hundreds of small dams dotting the landscape.

Murdo
One of the duller stretches of US-83 is this 20-mile leg along the mind-numbing I-90 artery between the Fort Pierre grasslands and Murdo (pop. 700). Once a stop on the legendary Texas Cattle Trail and also used by stagecoaches, the town was named for cattle baron Murdo McKenzie, whose ranch pushed through some 20,000 head of cattle a year. The town of Murdo today still lives on the cattle industry. Stop by the unique **doll museum** (daily 9 AM-10 PM June-Aug., 1-10 PM in May and Aug.; $2), two blocks east of US-83 on US-16.

The one place that's definitely worth a stop is smack-dab at the diesel-blue polluted confluence of US-83 and I-90, where nostalgists will find the **Pioneer Auto Museum and Antique Town** (daily 7 AM-10 PM June-Aug., daily 8 AM-6 PM April-May and Sept.-Oct.; $5.25); pricey, maybe, but it's a 10-acre, 39-building collection of about 250 antique cars, with tons of other great items. Classic cars include a rare Tucker (the 1940s car with the central pivoting headlamp; George Lucas made a movie about it). There's also a nifty White Co. motor home from 1921, one of the earliest RVs, and, star of the show, Elvis Presley's 1976 Harley-Davidson Electra Glide 1200 motorcycle. Pure Americana.

The public swimming pool across the street, and the **Tee Pee Restaurant** down the road at 303 5th Street ("We Will Sell No Coffee Over a Half-Hour Old") can round off your Murdo visit.

Rosebud Indian Reservation
Nothing much south of I-90 and Murdo until you come across a picturesque dale while crossing the White River, sheltering the first grove of trees in too long a time. South of White River, US-83 crosses the Rosebud Indian Reservation. After the signing of the Fort Laramie Treaty in 1868, the Sicangu Lakota, under the guide of Spotted Tail, were moved five times before finally being settled on this reservation. It's one of the smallest reservations on this route. The first town you'll encounter is **Mission**, the reservation's trading center. It's a strip of gas stations and a Rosebud/Sioux arts and crafts center. The heart of the reservation is the tribal headquarters (605/747-2381), five miles west on US-18, then 10 miles southwest on BIA Road in **Rosebud**. Most of the reservation's activities are centered here, including **rodeos** and **powwows**, often held on Saturdays and Sundays in the

summer. The biggest powwow is the **Rosebud Sioux Tribal Fair and Powwow** in late August, where you can consume a traditional buffalo dinner.

Another eight miles southwest is tiny **St. Francis**, which has the **Buechel Memorial Lakota Museum** (daily June-Sept.; free), a museum dedicated to the Teton Sioux culture and begun by Fr. Eugene Buechel, a German Jesuit, avid botanist, and dedicated student of the culture.

Back on US-83, and another 23 miles south of Mission, is the tribe's most recent economic endeavor, the **Rosebud Casino**.

ACROSS NEBRASKA

The 257 miles from South Dakota to Kansas encompass two distinct regions: typical Midwestern wheat and cattle ranches, and the fascinating grass-coated sand dunes of central Nebraska's Sand Hills region. Contrary to popular belief, Nebraska isn't mostly corn; it's beef, lots and lots of it. US-83 passes by more cattle than it does people, with scant few communities along the way.

The **Sand Hills** of northwestern Nebraska form one of the largest areas of rolling dune geology in the world. They're also the largest tract of mid- to tall-grass prairie in North America, and, in the right light (sunrise or sunset), at the right time of year (spring especially) they are absolutely beautiful.

Thanks to its cupidic name, Valentine is a popular place to send cards for delivery on February 14.

The powers that be don't neglect to mention your entrance into Nebraska, and it's a good thing, for the subtle changes in the topography (or the quality of the roadbed) won't necessarily be enough to clue you in. Your first stop south of the border is Valentine, then you cross the rolling Sand Hills region toward the railroad town of North Platte, former home of "Buffalo" Bill Cody. From North Platte it's a straight shot south across acres of corn to Kansas.

Valentine

Just west of the 100th Meridian, the small town of Valentine (pop. 2,826) is a center of the extensive cattle ranching industry of the Sand Hills region, and the kind of tiny but prideful town that makes road tripping fun. Seat of enormous Cherry County and situated at the northern edge of the 19,300-square-mile Sand Hills region, Valentine, which takes its name from a U.S. congressman, is a broad, well-maintained place that pays its bills with beef cattle fed to tenderness on the 800 species of grasses coating the region.

Considering the long stretches of road ahead, it's prudent to check out what the town's got, and there's quite a bit. Downtown—where the streetlights are hung with red and white banners emblazoned with the unsurprising town motto "Valentine, Heart of the Sand Hills"—the facade of the First National Bank holds the **largest brick mural** in Nebraska, with 1,200 square feet of images of longhorn cattle and the building of the transcontinental railroad built out of dark brown bricks. Of Valentine's **museums**, the most intriguing is **Sawyer's Sand Hills Museum** (daily 9 AM-6 PM in summer), on US-20 four blocks west of US-83. The museum offers a broad display, including some legitimately historical stuff, as well as a two-headed calf and a great collection of antique cars that still run. The **Cherry County Historical**

Society Museum, next door to the pharmaceutically clean and well-stocked **visitor center** (800/658-4024) at the US-20/US-83 junction, is much more traditional. Four miles southeast of Valentine on US-20/83, an absolutely HUGE old railroad trestle bridges the broad Niobrara River.

Nature lovers score well in this town. Seasoned canoeists and keen trout anglers will want to tackle the rough **Snake River** some 15 miles southwest of town, near the short but powerful **Snake River Falls**. A 22-mile stretch of the more sedate **Niobrara River**, east of the Fort Niobrara Wildlife Refuge, offers top-notch canoeing and tubing and in fact is one of *Backpacker* magazine's best picks. The **Fort Niobrara Wildlife Refuge** is a residual of old Fort Niobrara, known for never fighting a battle during its 27 years on the Wild West prairie. Today elk, bison, and Texas longhorns roam its 19,122 acres of gorgeous, rolling dune prairie. There are many miles of hiking trails along the wild Niobrara River, which downstream tumbles over 60-foot **Smith Falls**, centerpiece of Nebraska's newest state park, off Hwy-12, 15 miles northeast of Valentine.

Valentine has the usual motels scattered along US-20 and US-83, including the **Trade Winds Lodge** (402/376-1600 or 800/341-8000), with doubles from $35. The place most people go for a sit-down meal is the **Peppermill**, 112 Main Street, featuring steaks, seafood, and alfresco dining in summer; a few adequate **cafes** are sprinkled about, including the **Home Cafe** at the US-82/US-20 junction, at the south end of town.

For details on camping, eating, sightseeing, sleeping and anything else in and around Valentine, contact the visitor center at 239 S. Main Street (402/376-2969 or 800/658-4024).

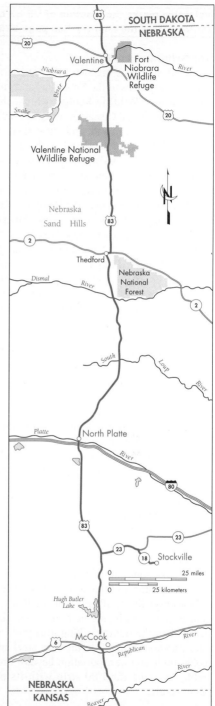

Valentine marks the junction of US-83 and US-20, one of our west-east routes across the country. See page 526 for more.

The Nebraska Sand Hills
South of Valentine are two fine natural areas, preserving and highlighting the unique ecosystems of the Nebraska Sand Hills. South along US-83 is the large **Valentine National Wildlife Refuge**, which, thanks to water seeped from the world's biggest aquifer, the Ogalala Aquifer, is home to both native rolling dune prairie and lowlands of lake, marsh, and sub-irrigated meadow. Lots of curlews, sandpipers, terns, and mule deer are found on the drives and hikes through the vaulted hills and long spiny grasses, and along the lakeshores.

Beyond this, the Sand Hills occasionally flatten out into simple, absolutely open range, with perhaps a ridge jutting out. The aspect of the land here shows itself as much more scabrous than the Dakotas. Mauve, tan, and cream cows fleck the land, as do a few windmills: great, stark, American Gothic windmills, not the pseudo-efficient energy spinners seen elsewhere.

US-83 joins with Hwy-2 approximately 30 miles after leaving the Valentine Wildlife Refuge. Swinging east will take you to the one of the three huge **Nebraska National Forest** districts, among the largest man-made forest tracts in the world (20,000 acres total) and one of the oldest extant U.S. Forest Service nurseries. There's no visitor center per se, but ranger stations provide information.

Thedford and Scenic Hwy-2
Sleepy little Thedford (pop. 243) stretches west of US-83, lining up along the Burlington Northern railroad tracks. The town is not much more than a few little houses, some loud cicadas, a Rodeway Inn motel, and the **Arrow Cafe**, a combination Conoco station and roadfood restaurant, though it does mark the junction of US-83 and scenic Hwy-2, which runs west-east across the heart of Nebraska, abounding in wildflowers, ultra-quaint but totally unselfconscious small towns, and pastoral beauty from horizon to horizon. At the south edge of the Sand Hills, 100 miles west of Thedford at the end of Hwy-2, the totally unique **Carhenge**—the finest Detroit wheels, stacked on top of each other to form a steel Stonehenge—stands just outside the town of Alliance. For a photo and further details, see page 562.

South of Thedford, US-83 jumps and descends for another 65 miles toward North Platte with very, very little to occupy your time other than scenic overlooks along the Dismal and South Loup Rivers.

North Platte
It can take some time getting into North Platte, but despite the heavy-industrial initial appearances there is a lot here to enjoy. The northern approach along US-83 crosses over the North Fork of the Platte River, taking a leisurely little swoop up and over it, passing scenic bluffs, then flash back through a living history of the days when the train was king. Rusty old weed-filled tracks and abandoned shops and warehouses lie off to the side, steel and brick remnants of North Platte's blue-collar trade and transportation heyday. From the south the entrance is less memorable, crossing the I-80 strip with its plastic signs and anonymous franchise architecture.

Originally the site of a Union Pacific construction camp, North Platte nearly expired when the workers decamped for Colorado; but the 300 permanent residents were spared when the railroad chose it as a division point, securing the town's future. The city is still proud of its **Bailey Yard**, recently decreed by the *Guinness Book of World Records* as the largest railroad classification yard in the world. You can view it from a high platform three miles west of town on Front Street. (Get directions from the visitors bureau, as it can be hard to find.) Many of the city parks feature railroad displays, including 90-acre **Cody Park** along US-83. Within the confines rests **Big Boy**, one of the world's largest steam locomotives.

Before the railroad came through, North Platte was a key stop on both the Oregon Trail, which followed the Platte River west past Scotts Bluff and into Wyoming, and the Pony Express. At the dawn of the Automobile Age, North Platte played a starring role

Buffalo Bill

along the historic Lincoln Highway, the first transcontinental road, which followed the Oregon Trail route west along what's now US-30, ending up eventually in San Francisco.

But North Platte is most widely known as the home of Buffalo Bill Cody. The huge **Buffalo Bill Scout's Rest Ranch**, (daily 10 AM-8 PM June-Sept., Mon.-Sat. 9 AM-5 PM and Sunday 1-5 PM April-May; $2.50 per car), four miles northwest via US-30 and Buffalo Bill Avenue, is a state historical park with original dwellings. Cody's house, and some outbuildings, look much the way they did when Buffalo Bill lived here, from 1879 to 1913. This is where Buffalo Bill originated his rodeo with the "Old Glory Blowout" in 1882 and later housed his Wild West Show when not on the road. Tours are available, and the buffalo stew cookouts ($5) are popular. The town still whoops it up with the **Buffalo Bill Rodeo** in June.

Besides Buffalo Bill memorabilia, North Platte has an interesting WW II canteen mock-up, a great Railroad Town, and an eight-million-year-old, 200-pound, fossilized land tortoise, all on display at the **Lincoln County Museum** (daily 9 AM-8 PM in summer), 2403 Buffalo Bill Avenue, adjacent to the Scout's Rest Ranch.

Downtown North Platte, on the south side of the railroad tracks, has largely been superseded by the surrounding Interstate sprawl, but the brick-paved streets here still hold some grand old buildings and a few nifty old neon signs, including one for the landmark **Fox Theater**, at 5th and Bailey streets.

There is a dearth of good, inexpensive restaurants with any sort of character in North Platte, but 12 miles west, along US-30 in the town of Hershey, **Butch's** (308/368-7231) serves some of the country's best prime rib and pork chops, so tender you can cut 'em with a fork. Interstate 80 also whips through North Platte, so including the road you're on, there's no shortage of fast-food or places to stay, including a **Motel 6** (308/534-6200) on the south side of town at the US-83/I-80 junction. Unfortunately, most of the old Lincoln Highway motels along US-30 are run-down, rented out by the week or month if still in business at all.

On the north side of I-80 and the US-83 junction is the giant **Buffalo Bill Trading Post,** a massive postcard and souvenir store with a very good selection of books on Western Americana and, best of all, a free miniature working model of Buffalo Bill's Wild West Show, complete with dancing bears, jumping horses and cowboys and Indians.

South of North Platte on US-83, you'll pass a country road, going east and south, that leads to the **Sioux Lookouts,** one of the highest points above the Platte Valley.

In between downtown and I-80, on the median between the two one-way halves of US-83, you can find out more about the town and region at the North Platte visitor's bureau (Mon.-Fri. 10 AM-5 PM; 308/532-4729 or 800/955-4528) at 502 S. Dewey Street.

Stockville: Dancing Leaf Earth Lodge

There's nothing much, community-wise, for the 70-odd miles along US-83 between North Platte and McCook, but the road and rolling landscape will definitely hold your interest. You're privy to the few acres of genuine Nebraska corn, which eventually fold into encroaching knobby little rises, hollows full of oaks, or open range. Though there are no real sights to look out for, a detour east of the highway brings you to one truly unique place: the Dancing Leaf Earth Lodge. An as-authentic-as-possible recreation of a Native American dwelling, located amongst cottonwood trees along the banks of Medicine Creek, midway between North Platte and McCook in the town of Stockville, the 20-by-20-foot lodge is the heart of a "cultural learning center" that endeavors to give visitors a total immersion into the lifeways and spirituality of ancient Plains Indians. Constructed by hand from willows and grasses and plastered with thick mud, the two earth lodges stay cool in summer and warm in winter, and provide primitive but comfortable accommodations and an unforgettable experience of what life might have been like before the arrival of European cultures.

Families and groups are especially welcome at the Dancing Leaf, where rates, including buffalo stew dinner and a soothing session in the sweat lodge, start at $90 a night for three people. The lodges each sleep a maximum of 15 people, and guests need to bring sleeping bags. Even if you don't stay overnight, tours of the lodges and nearby archaeological remains, plus informal instruction in tool-making, basket-weaving, hunting, fishing and cooking, are also available from the hosts, Les and Jan Hosick, who can be contacted by phone 308/367-4233 or mail to P.O. Box 121, Stockville NE 69042.

McCook sits at the crossroads of US-83 and US-6, which used to be the longest cross-country highway in the US, running from the tip of Cape Cod all the way to Long Beach, CA.

South of McCook, US-83 turns grandly scenic (it's even marked as such on some maps). Just north of the Nebraska/Kansas state line, the highway crosses the Beaver River, passing over an old trestle bridge.

McCook

Fifteen miles north of the Kansas border, patches of corn grow in the fertile loam of the undulating Republican River Valley around McCook (pop. 8,100), the market center for much of southwest Nebraska. With the arrival of the railroad, the town (which is still served by Amtrak's Zephyr and numerous freight trains) grew into a farm trade center, and now is a sedate, content-enough place, with at least two good excuses for a brief stop, both of them on the hill above downtown. **The Museum of the High Plains**, in a large modern building at 421 Norris Avenue (Tues.-Sat. 1-5 PM, Sunday 1:30-5 PM; free), includes excellent fossil collections, some WW II prisoner-of-war artwork, a room dedicated to Sen. George Norris, and an old drugstore replicated in the very building where Kool-Aid was developed.

Up the street, the **George W. Norris Home** (Wed.-Sat. 10 AM-noon and 1-5 PM, Tuesday and Sunday 1:30-5 PM; $1), 706 Norris Avenue, is devoted to McCook's favorite son, the Nebraska senator who founded the Tennessee Valley Authority and promoted rural electrification during the New Deal 1930s. Norris also authored the 20th Amendment to the Constitution, which ended the traditional "lame duck" sessions of Congress and moved the date of presidential inaugurations from March to January.

In between the two museums, at 602 Norris Avenue, stands Nebraska's only Frank Lloyd Wright-designed house, still a private residence and not open for tours.

Most of McCook's limited food and lodging options line up along B Street, the US-83/US-6 route; for details, contact the McCook **visitors bureau,** 305 E. 1st Street (308/345-3200 or 800/657-2179).

ACROSS KANSAS

Kansas is no mere geographical expression, but a "state of mind," a religion, and a philosophy in one.
—Carl Becker, *Kansas* (1910)

I like Kansas—that is, natural Kansas—better than I had expected to . . .
—Horace Greeley, *An Overland Journey* (1859)

The clichés have told you wrong: US-83 across much of Kansas—surprise, surprise—is actually a treat, not at all the interminable tedium of grainfield stretches you might expect. Yes, the physiography through most of the intrastate span is still predominantly flat, dry Northern High Plains, but it's compensated for, particularly in the north, with extensive irrigation that coaxes lusher patches of vegetation out of the dark rich soil.

US-83 ushers you along gaping, horizon-filled stretches broken by isolated lakes and occasional oases such as Oberlin or Oakley, home of the nearly famous Prairie Dog Town. Continuing south across the windblown plains and limestone hills, US-83 passes through the cow towns of Scott City and Garden City before crossing the Arkansas River into the baked-clay watercolor that stretches south into Oklahoma and Texas. One final Kansas stop is perhaps the best: Liberal, self-declared home of Dorothy from *The Wizard of Oz.*

Oberlin
Funky little Oberlin, 12 miles south of the Nebraska state line, is definitely worth a stop. A picture-postcard town, with awnings covering storefronts along the two blocks of red-brick downtown streets, it has a mini-cinema (called the Sunflower, of course) playing Hollywood hits and a Social Realist sandstone statue of pioneering family marking its north edge.

The peace and quiet of today's Oberlin is in stark contrast to its past: Oberlin was the site of the last Indian raid in Kansas on September 29, 1878, after a fierce skirmish had erupted between Chief Dull Knife's Northern Cheyenne, heading to regain their lands in the Dakotas, and an infantry contingent from Fort Dodge at what today is Lake Scott State Park, near Scott City 80 miles to the south. The Oberlin cemetery contains a memorial to the 19 settlers who were killed in Cheyenne attacks, and the town has the late-September **Mini-Sapa Days**, a two-day festival commemorating the event. Downtown along S. Penn Avenue, the worthwhile **Decatur County/Last Indian Raid Museum** (Tues.-Sat. 10 AM-noon and 1-5 PM, Sunday 1:30-4 PM, April-Nov., opens one hour earlier in summer; $3; 913/475-2712), has eight preserved buildings, including a sod house.

> Traveling US-83 across the Midwest, you'll notice that most of the roadside services are found along the east-west crossroads, especially the major old transcontinental highways like US-6, US-30, or US-40, or today's interstate superslabs. North-south travelers have always been a rare species.

Colby

Out of Oberlin, US-83 sweeps through beautiful farmlands, often paralleling railroad tracks, and passes through low, one-horse towns with towering feed elevators. The road banks sharply west and then south, at which point you can either continue on US-83 until the road crosses I-70 near Oakley, or head west along US-24 to the I-70 junction at ambitious Colby, which calls itself "The Oasis of the Plains." The town is simply a service center for the wheat belt, but it does have the fairly huge **Prairie Museum of Art and History** (Mon.-Fri. 9 AM-5 PM, plus Saturday and Sunday 1-5 PM, closed Monday in winter; $4) at 1905 S. Franklin Street. The museum is a sprawling, 24-acre complex that includes rare porcelains, china dolls, assorted historical stuff, a complete home decorated as it would have been in the 1930s, and the **Cooper Barn**, one of the largest barns in the state.

Oakley

Back on US-83, amid the olfactory assault of I-70, stands possibly the most bizarre tourist trap the highway has to offer: **Prairie Dog Town** (daily 8 AM-8 PM, May-Oct.; $4.95 adults, under-10s $2.95). This collection—"Home of the 8,000-lb. Prairie Dog," as the old roadside signs say—is a combination petting zoo and freak show, with collections of the eponymous little dogs as well as dozens of birds, snakes, bobcats, bison and other Great Plains critters, many taken in as orphans. There's even a six-legged cow.

The rest of Oakley (pop. 2,045), south and west of I-70, and lined up along historic US-40, turns out to be an old, big-time ranching and railroad town, neither ugly nor picturesque, featuring lots of utilitarian architecture, massive diesel engines, farm supply stores and railroad tracks. It's unassuming but important, situated as it is at the junction of three major highways.

Right off US-83, the **Fick Fossil Museum** (Mon.-Sat. 9:30 AM-noon and 1-5 PM, Sunday 2-4 PM, longer hours in summer; free), at 700 W. 3rd Street, features some unique exhibits: 11,000 fossilized shark teeth, a sod house, collections of pressed wildflowers, and some perfectly garish mosaics, including the Great Seal of the President of the United States, made entirely out of the aforementioned shark's teeth. It was created by—who else?—Mrs. Fick. The local history and paleontological exhibits are quite good, too.

Along the interstate, the usual 24-hour, truck-jockey hash is dished out at the **Mitten Cafe** or the **Jones Corner Cafe** (right next to Prairie Dog Town), and

the I-70 Business Loop (old US-40) offers the usual array of cafes and motels,
including a nice **Best Western**. The favorite local place to go for dinner and a
drink is the very friendly **Scotts Bluff**, a
private club with great steaks and sandwiches at 310 S. Freeman Avenue (785/
672-8892). Oakley is a "dry" town, but
motel guests get complimentary "membership" at the Scotts Bluff, and there's
no better place to hang out and over-
hear cowgirls, cattlemen and assorted
other bull-shippers shooting the breeze
over a beer or two.

Chalk Pyramids/Monument Rocks
South of Oakley, the road bolts straight
for over 20 miles, passing between an
enormous sea of yellow flowers (in early
summer) on one side and expanses of
open range on the other. Later, the
scenery peters out into a prickly dry,
faint yellow, rocky desolation that sig-
nals the fringes of the Smoky Hills
region.

The prime topographical feature of
the Smoky Hills is the surreal Chalk
Pyramids, also known as Monument
Rocks; they are referred to in the old
WPA *Guide to Kansas* as the "Kansas
Pyramids." Whatever you call them,
these highly eroded geological formations, which reach heights of 70 feet
above the plains, are composed of layers of ancient seabed from the Creta-
ceous period and were originally formed
80 million years ago. The impressive
spires, karst-like formations, and shaley
cliffs farther on have yielded thousands
of excellent fossils of sharks, shark's
teeth, fish, and reptiles. The pyramids
are on private land but access is not restricted; however, there are no facilities.
To get there, drive 26 miles south of Oakley, or 18 miles north from Scott City,
then east from US-83 for 6.5 miles, then
2.5 miles north.

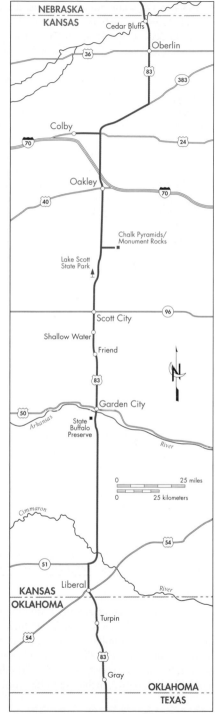

You can get some good maps and directions to the Rocks themselves at the friendly **Keystone Gallery**, "conveniently located in the middle of nowhere" at 401 US-83 in Scott City (316/872-2762); the gallery also has a display of fossils from the Rocks, and you can enjoy a sampling of local art and sculpture as well.

Lake Scott State Park and Scott City

Midway across Kansas, 35 miles south of Oakley and the I-70 freeway, Lake Scott State Park (daily dawn-dusk; $4 per car) is a true spring-fed oasis sheltering cottonwoods, ash, hackberry, and willow in vacuous, high-sky rangeland. Beyond offering a lovely and relaxing spot in which to unwind, Lake Scott includes Kansas's most intriguing historical site, *El Cuartelejo* ("The Old Barracks"), the only Pueblo Indian community in Kansas and the farthest north of any in the country. Originally settled in the 1660s by Taos Pueblo people fleeing the Spanish in New Mexico, the area became home to the Picuris about 30 years later.

Both migrant groups joined with the local Plains Apache clan, but the oasis and the ruined pueblo buildings continued to be used for occasional nomadic squatting by the Pawnee and later by Spanish and French explorers and traders before eventually eroding away. In the late 1880s the site was discovered accidentally by Herbert Steele, who stumbled onto the extensive irrigation ducts leading from spring areas to crop patches. Further excavation eventually revealed the pueblo sites, now considered the first permanent-walled structures in the state. The park has a few other historical points of interest, including a marker on the site of the fateful last battle between the U.S. Cavalry and escaping Cheyenne Indians led by Chief Dull Knife. The park also has herds of elk and bison, and visitors can see the preserved home of Herbert Steele, full of pioneer furniture and farming implements.

South of Lake Scott State Park, US-83 continues across the High Plains, with not a whole lot to disrupt the continuity until Garden City, another 45 miles south. The only town of any size is Scott City (pop. 3,800), with its miles and miles of cattle fencing, feed lots, innumerable cattle companies, and big American flags greeting you (or waving good-bye) at the town limits. It's a hardy, industrious place, with everyone busy working. Hard.

South of Scott City are two mere blip-stop towns, both inappropriately named: Shallow Water and Friend.

Garden City stands at the junction of US-83 and coast-to-coast US-50, which is covered beginning on page 654.

Garden City

Though it has a classic red-brick downtown and a decent little zoo, Garden City (pop. 24,100) is better known for its huge public **swimming pool**: 337 feet by 218 feet, with over 2.5 million gallons of water. It's near the Arkansas River in Finnup Park, S. 4th Street, and it's free! The classic Windsor Hotel downtown is a hotel no longer, but after its construction in 1886 this "Waldorf of the Prairies" drew lots of cowpoke-luminaries, including Buffalo Bill Cody.

Elsewhere in the brick-paved downtown, which unlike many Midwest towns shows few signs of businesses fleeing to the highway frontages, you can window-shop (or even buy something) at the department stores and antique shops, see a movie at the classic State Theatre on Main Street, or get a bite to eat at cafes like **Herb's Hamburgers** (good burgers) or **Traditions**, on Grant Street a block west of Main.

Garden City also supports the usual gas stations, motels, and fast-food but, best of all, the 4,000-acre **State Buffalo Preserve**, which may be viewed along the west side of US-83, south of town for about five miles.

Farther south, across the often dry-as-a-bone Arkansas River, oil pumps languidly dip their heads. This is where stereotypical Kansas landscape comes in: either stark desolation or—thanks to money and modernity—vast irrigation efforts. Prior to the advent of reliable irrigation from the Ogalala Aquifer, overeager farmers almost ruined the region's fortunes plowing up the fragile buffalo grass for a one-season crop, before the wind blew the topsoil away. The hills that stood here prior to the Dust Bowl are gone completely now, and the landscape is endless, see-forever plains, marked by grain elevators a deceptive 10 miles away.

At the Brookover feed lot along US-83 on the northwest side of Garden City, a huge sign standing atop a pair of grain elevators reads: "Eat Beef Keep Slim." From the comfort of your car you can hear the hundreds of cattle burping and mooing up a storm.

Garden City's **91.1 FM** is a High Plains public radio station, with NPR news and diverse music and features, all commercial-free.

Liberal

First, the name. It's said that a munificent early settler came and dug a well, and whenever a dusty emigrant would offer money for a drink or the chance to wash his neck, the settler would say, "Water is always free here." One day the reply came, "That is mighty liberal." Bob Dole probably wouldn't approve of the word choice, but the name stuck, and now the town's stuck with it.

Second, the adjectives: hot; dusty; treeless; flat. The approach into town reveals the drab side of Liberal's oil, gas (the town lies on the eastern edge of an enormous natural gas field), and meatpacking industries.

But the sights do improve. Honest. There is one significant draw, the top-notch **Mid-America Air Museum** (Mon.-Fri. 8 AM-5 PM, Saturday 10 AM-5 PM, Sunday 1-5 PM; $5; 316/624-5263), at 2000 W. 2nd Street, on the site of old Liberal Army Airfield. It's one of the largest air museums in the U.S. and has amassed an astonishingly diverse collection of aircraft covering the entire history of flight, including military fighters and bombers from WW II and the Korean and Vietnam Wars.

Otherwise, there's a lot of **Ozmania** in town. Though there's not even the most tenuous connection between Liberal and the film or the book, apart from them all being set in Kansas, an annual **Oztoberfest** blowout is held at the so-called **Dorothy's House**,

Garden City was founded in 1879 by **C.J. "Buffalo" Jones,** one of many larger-than-life characters who populated the Wild West. One of his many achievements was the capture and preservation of a small herd of buffalo, the descendants of which populate the Buffalo Preserve on the south side of town.

THE DUST BOWL

Though it may not have been the biggest migration in U.S. history, it was certainly the most traumatic—entire families packing up their few belongings and fleeing the Dust Bowl of the Depression-era Great Plains. Beginning in 1933 and continuing year after year until 1940, a 400-mile-long, 300-mile-wide region roughly bisected by US-83—covering 100 million acres of western Kansas, eastern Colorado, and the "Panhandles" of Oklahoma and Texas—was rendered uninhabitable as ceaseless winds carried away swirling clouds of what had been agricultural land.

The "Dust Bowl," as it was dubbed by Associated Press reporter Robert Geiger in April 1935, was caused by a fatal combination of circumstances. This part of the plains was naturally grassland and had long been considered marginal at best, but the rise in agricultural prices during and after WW I made it profitable to till and plant. Farmers invested in expensive machinery, but when the worldwide economic depression cut crop and livestock prices by as much as 75%, many farmers fell deeply in debt. Then, year after year of drought hit the region, and springtime winds carried away the fragile topsoil, lifting hundreds of tons of dust from each square mile, and dropping it as far east as New York City.

By the mid-1930s, many of the farmers had been forced to abandon their land, and while some were able to rely upon a series of New Deal welfare programs, many more fled for California and the Sunbelt states. In this mass exodus, as recorded by photographers like Dorothea Lange, and most memorably in John Steinbeck's 1939 novel *Grapes of Wrath,* some 100,000 people each year packed up their few possessions and headed west, never to return.

Nowadays, thanks to high-powered pumps that can reach down to the Ogalala Aquifer, much of what was the Dust Bowl is once again fertile farmland, no longer as dependent on the vicissitudes of the weather. Much of the rest of the land was bought up by the U.S. government, and some four million acres are now protected within a series of National Grasslands that maintain the Great Plains in more or less their natural state.

also known as the **Coronado House**, (Mon.-Sat. 9 AM-6 PM, Sunday 1-5 PM June-Aug., fewer hours rest of the year; $2), a block north of US-54 at 567 E. Cedar Street. This combination historical museum and re-creation of the movie's Kansas sets displays a mock-up of Dorothy's bedroom from the movie, a mini-Yellow Brick Road lined by models of the film's animalian heroes, as well as a horse bit from the expedition of Don Francisco Vasquez de Coronado and his troops, who passed through in 1541 searching for the fabled Seven Cities of Cibola.

Outside of town the majestic **Rock Island Line Railroad Bridge** crosses the Cimarron River. The "Mighty Sampson," at 1,200 feet long and 100 feet above the river, is among the largest of its kind.

The city's most unusual attraction happens annually on Shrove Tuesday (aka Mardi Gras), when it holds its annual, international, soon-to-be-famous **Liberal Pancake Race**, a competition between local housewives and their counterparts from Olney, England. They race a 415-yard, S-shaped course, each flipping a pancake along the way. The Olney event purportedly dates from 1445 when a woman rushed to church with her pan still in her hand; the Liberal race has taken place since 1950.

US-54 and US-83 claim the majority of places to stay, including the $30-a-night **Travelers Lodge** (316/624-6203), on US-54 almost a mile northeast of the US-54/83 junction. US-54 is also known as Pancake Boulevard—doubtless because the strip lacks places to eat that aren't boisterous, family-style, and faux-western. The local **chamber of commerce**, 505 N. Kansas Street (316/624-3855 or 800/542-3725), likes to describe it as "fast-food alley."

ACROSS OKLAHOMA

On its beeline to Texas, US-83 doesn't just cross Oklahoma; it forsakes it, merely nipping the panhandle for a 37-mile dash. When crossing the border three miles south of Liberal, among the first things you see are a trailer park, a couple of bars, and a bingo hot-spot. They're inauspicious sights at best. And that's not even mentioning the slate-flat, wicked badlands, with heat bad enough in summer to occlude your vision of the blistering pavement, and preclude a drive at top speeds. After a while you're unable to conjure up synonyms for "endless," though there's plenty of time for it. Even the historical marker you think you eventually see winds up being in Texas.

The first town you come up to is diminutive **Turpin**, comprising a Phillips filling station now usurped by a Shamrock, farm equipment places, and a motel or two *sans* signs. Oh yes—there's a stop sign at Balko, where US-83 crosses US-412.

And that's it. *Finito.* You keep stretching the atlas over the steering wheel (no danger in these parts), wondering where the hell **Gray** is, and why you care. It's supposed to be on this highway. You're sure of it. But for some reason it never appears. Before you know it, Texas looms outside the windshield, and damn if the aspect of the land doesn't change literally at the state line. Suddenly, there are lots of trees, and hills, and that historical marker you've been dreaming of.

ACROSS TEXAS

The old WPA *Guide to Texas* says that "no other route across Texas offers such differences in topography, produce, climate and people" as does US-83, which is still very true today. Starting at the Oklahoma border on the southern edge of the Great Plains, your route winds along the foot of the Cap Rock escarpment, then opens out onto the cattle country of Edwards Plateau where numerous river canyons provide respite from the mesquite scrub land, and finally ends up some 900 miles later at the Gulf of Mexico. Besides diverse landscapes, US-83 also passes through a virtual survey of Texas history: the prehistoric pictographs of Paint Rock; Mexican-American battlegrounds along the Rio Grande; 100-year-old frontier towns built of red brick around their central courthouses; and the modern Gulf Coast resort of South Padre Island. As you'll soon learn if you're perusing other Texas travel literature, this section of the state is, for the most part, ignored. Thus, you're definitely among an elite company, traveling along truly unbeaten paths.

In its 900-plus-mile crossing of Texas, US-83 is known as the Vietnam Veterans Memorial Highway. It forms the **longest stretch of US highway** through any of the lower 48 states.

Many of the smaller, usually dirt, roads in Texas are labeled "FM," for farm-to-market, or "RM," for ranch-to-market, before their route numbers, i.e., "FM-1208." For simplicity's sake we have labeled them "Hwy-."

Perryton

After passing by wheat fields and ranch lands, then negotiating a verdant allée of foliage, you arrive at medium-sized, agreeable Perryton (pop. 7,607), seven miles south of the Oklahoma border. The town was formed in 1919 when the Santa Fe Railroad came through; people in nearby towns simply picked up their stuff—buildings included—and shifted them here. Ochilton, eight miles south off US-83/Hwy-70, was one such town, before some 600 people moved the whole infrastructure. If you ignore the industrial oil-well litter on the outskirts, Perryton's not bad-looking, with spacious tree-lined streets. The self-styled "Wheatheart of the Nation," Perryton is also the hometown of Mike Hargrove, former American League Rookie of the Year, and now manager of the Cleveland Indians.

Canadian

South from Perryton, the landscape changes radically from the plains stretches, offering instead classic ranches with miles of fencing and great white gates à la *Dallas*, a few oil wells, small canyons with innumerable creekbeds, and craggy, fluted bluffs peppered with veldtlike vegetation.

Canadian (pop. 2,417) offers an auspicious view as you descend toward it. You plow through an imposing tunnel of trees and then cross the namesake river, once an important route for early explorers; the crossing itself runs alongside anachronistic railroad trestles. Besides sustaining the only trees for miles, contemporary Canadian also has the interesting **River Valley Pioneer Museum** (Mon.-Fri. 9 AM-noon and 1-4 PM, Sat.-Sun. 2-4 PM) on US-83 at 118 S. 2nd Street.

For food, within a block of the chamber of commerce you can choose between great doughnuts at **Ma Beasley's**

A few miles north of Canadian, 10 miles east of the US-83/US-60 junction, and via a good paved road, you'll find the **Lake Marvin National Grassland**, which maintains one of the few surviving portions of the natural landscape that once covered the Great Plains—where the deer and the antelope once played and millions of buffalo roamed.

Donut Shop, 316 Main Street (Mon.-Fri. 5:30 AM-noon), and some lunch stands complete with the quintessential advertisement proclaiming "Good Eats." There are lots of seedy-looking motels on the north side of town, but a couple of blocks east of the chamber of commerce is an alternative place to stay, the **Emerald House Bed and Breakfast**, 103 N. 6th Street (806/323-5827).

Four miles south of Canadian, along the east side of suddenly four-lane highway that jointly carries US-60 and US-83, a huge **brontosaurus** stands atop a high bluff. Her name is Aud; don't ask me why.

At Shamrock, US-83 crosses the legendary Route 66, whose full L.A.-to-Chicago odyssey is covered beginning on page 794.

Shamrock

Once a major oil pumping and refining center, Shamrock is a dusty, rusty old industrial town, off I-40 and a mile south of historic Route 66, which survives as the "Business Loop" of I-40 through town. Though it's not a particularly lovely place, Shamrock at least ranges from grimly ugly and stifling near the highway to decompressively sedate in the town proper. Playing up the Irish connection, Elmore Park in town exhibits a sliver of the reportedly genuine **Blarney Stone**, encased in a hip-high hunk of green concrete, but there's no green beer or other St. Patrick's Day celebrations to speak of—Shamrock is a dry town.

The old brown-brick Reynolds Hotel, east of US-83 at 206 N. Madden Street, holds the better-than-you-might-expect **Pioneer West Museum** (Mon.-Fri. 9 AM-noon and 1-5 PM; free), with two dozen rooms full of bygone goodies, including the complete interiors, fixtures and fittings of a dentist's office, a barber shop, and general store. There's also an exhibit honoring Apollo astronaut Alan Bean, who lived nearby in his youth.

The town doesn't exactly enjoy an overabundance of cuisine, but it does have a couple of restaurants and cafes, including the **U Drop Inn**, a classic greasy spoon cafe at the northeast corner of US-83 and old Route 66. (The building looks great, but the food

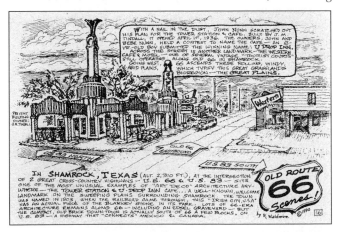

hasn't always matched; in fact, the cafe has gone through a series of owners in recent years, none of whom has had much success.) Also along the highways you'll find gas stations and some of the cheapest sleep around, with fleabag motels advertising singles from $14 a night.

Wellington and the Rocking Chair Mountains

South of Shamrock, US-83 passes over the Salt Fork of the Red River, which definitely deserves its name, running a muddy red throughout the rainy season. West of the highway rise the **Rocking Chair Mountains,** named after a large cattle ranch established west of here in the 1880s by a group of aristocrats, mainly younger sons of noble Scottish families. The only visible sign of their Hibernian legacy survives as place-names like Aberdeen, Clarendon, and **Wellington** (pop. 2,450), 25 miles south of Shamrock. Wellington is now a major market town for the surrounding cotton plantations, and during the harvest the gins run round the clock. The center of town is west of the highway, but the US-83 frontage holds four gas stations, four cafes (including **Miss Piggie's BBQ** and the popular **Roberson Family Restaurant**), alongside a dilapidated Quonset-hut machine shop, another boarded-up structure, and the usual piles of small-town jetsam.

Childress

A vintage Texas town built around an old Spanish *zócalo,* Childress (pop. 5,055) is an important shipping and supply point for surrounding grain and cattle ranches, and serves as the market town for area cotton farmers. Located at the junction of US-83 and US-287, Childress was named after George Childress, the author of the Texas Declaration of Independence; it is also the hometown of eight-time world champion calf roper Roy Cooper.

A historical marker in Childress Park tells the story of the **Goodnight Trail,** *the famed frontier cattle trail that passed through town.*

The once picturesque downtown still houses the small but engaging **Childress County Heritage Museum** (Mon.-Fri. 9 AM-5 PM, Saturday 9 AM-1 PM; free) at 10 3rd Street NW (follow the signs). The downtown is one short step from dry, depressed implosion—the result of every business relocating to the congested, annoying fringe highways—but the elaborate 100-year-old facades provide ample opportunities for nostalgic photography and aimless wandering. Depending on your time of arrival, the brick-cobbled streets and empty shells of formerly grand buildings smack more of a ghost town, but there are a few good antique shops taking advantage of the historic charm.

The restaurant of choice in Childress is **Pardner's Steakhouse,** at the US-83/287 junction, where along with slabs of beef you can enjoy walls of memorabilia belonging to favorite son, calf-roping rodeo cowboy Roy Cooper. Virtually every motel in town lines US-287 (Avenue F) east and west of the junction with US-83, and thanks to their highway-side location, they all suffer from a lack of quiet and privacy. The **Econolodge** (817/937-3695), right on US-287, offers doubles from $42, and there are many cheaper local options.

Paducah

South of Childress, US-83 passes through a magnificent landscape of rich red and gold canyonlands covered with vast groves of trees. Paducah, 30 miles south of Childress at the junction of US-70, is a modest cotton town proudly arrayed around a New Deal-era central courthouse modeled after an Egyptian temple. Brick-paved streets front abandoned stores and the huge old Cottle Hotel, which stands as a dormant reminder of better times, when harvest season or round-up would bring hundreds of transient field hands, cowboys, and card sharps into town. Nowadays Paducah offers little in the way of restaurants other than a doughnut shop and

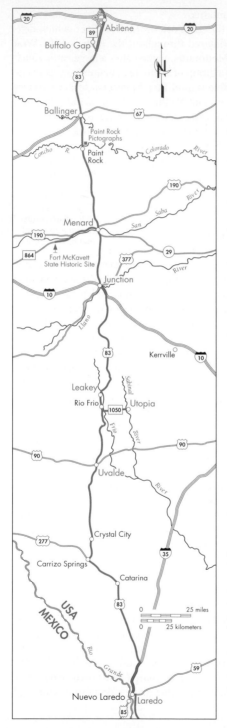

Cracker's Steakhouse. You can find a room at three motels west of US-83 along US-70; other options will require more than an hour's drive, so if it's quitting time, check out **The Town House**, the best of the lot.

West of Paducah along US-70 spreads the **Matador Ranch**, once one of the largest in Texas, with 450,000 acres of fenced pasture, and thirsty gullies amid semiarid canyons dotted with cedars and mesquite.

Hamlin and Swedona

Deep in the heart of Texas, surrounded by miles and miles of green grass, red earth, mesquite and juniper trees, windmills, pump supplies, and peanut driers, the tidy town of Hamlin ("Home of the Pied Pipers"; pop. 2,791) is full of charming folks and streets lined by locust trees. There's not much here, but on the north side of town the blue-roofed **Hatahoe Restaurant**, despite its ominous chainlike appearance, serves copious, cheap, and quite good meals. Standing next to the only stoplight in town, *this* is the place to meet the area's characters over breakfast.

Seven miles west of Hamlin on Hwy-92 stood Swedona (swee-DOAN-ya), a farming community founded by Swedish immigrants in 1877 that held fast to the ways of the Old Country for over 50 years. All that remains today is a tranquil cemetery.

Anson marks the junction of US-83 and US-80, part of the cross-country "Southern Pacific" route which is described more fully beginning on page 738.

Anson

Eighteen miles southeast of Hamlin, at the junction of US-180, sits Anson, named in honor of Dr. Anson Jones, the last president of the Republic of

Texas. Anson was also a stop on the legendary Butterfield Stage U.S. Mail route that ran between St. Louis and San Francisco from 1858 to 1861, but these days it feels more like a stage set for *The Last Picture Show,* with handsome blocks of brick-fronted buildings forming a square around the stately Jones County Courthouse, at the center of town. Anson is still a center for the local cotton industry, but its main claim to fame is the **Cowboys' Christmas Ball,** described in an 1890 poem by William Lawrence "Larry" Chittenden and recently re-awakened by the involvement of country-folk singer Michael Martin Murphey, who did a Christmas show here in 1995.

You can see almost all of Anson by driving through on US-83, but if you want to learn more, stop by the **Anson Jones Museum** (Wed.-Sun. 2-4:30 PM), a block southeast of the courthouse. For more information, contact the Anson **visitors bureau** (915/823-3259).

The only real alternative to all-news, Tejano, or twangy country-western on your radio dial is Abilene's **102.7 FM,** which plays a mixed bag of 1970s hits—Jefferson Airplane, CCR, and the odd New Wave tune.

Abilene

At the junction of US-83 and I-20, Abilene sits approximately in the geographic center of Texas and has a population of over 100,000. Abilene's fundamentalist Christian seminaries and the tame (for Texas) demeanor of its citizens have earned it the much-used nickname, "Buckle of the Bible Belt." Originally named after the raucous cowboy town of Abilene, Kansas, Abilene, *Texas,* grew from nothing once the Texas and Pacific Railway came through in the 1870s. Then as now, cattle played a predominant economic role, though Abilene's economy has diversified into less classic Texas endeavors, such as the unavoidable military airbase and petroleum refinery. Abilene supports big-city amenities, including a symphony, though its indigenous fundamentalism precludes more libertine nocturnal notions; in 1925, the town fathers made it a misdemeanor, in the eyes of the law, to "flirt in a public place"!

Abilene's downtown area, marked by a pair of 10-story towers, is not quite gentrified, but obviously galvanized for the attempt. The grand old Grace Hotel, now refurbished and known as the **Museums of Abilene** (Tues.-Sat. 8 AM-5 PM and Thursday 5 PM-8:30 PM; $2, but free on Thursday; 915/673-4587), at 102 Cypress Street, houses an art museum, an engaging historical museum, and a children's museum. It's air-conditioned and well worth a look.

If you choose to spend some time in Abilene, you won't want for excursions. The **Abilene Zoo** (daily 9 AM-5 PM, plus Sat.-Sun. 9 AM-7 PM in summer; $2) yields the **Discovery Center,** which features a great exhibit on southwest habitats, comparing veldts and plains of places as diverse as Africa and the United States. West of town is the **Dyess Air Force Base** and its **Linear Air Park,** a collection of aircraft from WW II to Desert Storm; it's free and you paid for it, so you may as well check it out.

The best place for food is the upscale **Cypress Street Station,** at 158 Cypress Street next to the museums in the heart of downtown Abilene. Also worth searching out are **Mama Ruth's** at 1232 Grape Street, northwest of downtown in the Merchant Park Mall, open 24 hours for time-honored home cooking; and the classic Texan BBQ of **Joe Allen's,** on Treadway Boulevard (US-83 Business) at S. 13th Street (915/672-6082), south of downtown in a unpromising industrial district. Open 11 AM-9 PM every day, Joe Allen's interior looks straight out of some beer

COWBOYS' CHRISTMAS BALL

All along US-83, but especially in the Panhandle area of northern Texas, you pass through town after time-worn town that have clearly seen more prosperous times. Stately courthouse squares, massive old hotels, and blocks of all-but-abandoned storefronts testify to the depopulation of many rural areas in the wake of agricultural mechanization and a myriad of related economic and social changes. Looking at the photogenic remains of these once bustling towns, it's hard not to imagine what life would have been like here during harvest, round-up or holiday festivities, when every able-bodied man, woman and child for miles would come to town to buy supplies, sell their goods and socialize with friends and neighbors. An entertaining poem, written about Anson, Texas in 1890 by William Lawrence "Larry" Chittenden, captures the vitality of these occasions and gives a strong sense of the creative phraseology that animates "Cowboy Poetry" to this day.

Here's a taste:

> Way out in Western Texas, where the Clear Fork's waters flow,
> Where the cattle are a-browsin' and the Spanish Ponies grow;
> Where the Northers come a-whistlin' from beyond the Neutral Strip;
> And the prairie dogs are sneezin', as though they had the grip;
> Where the coyotes come a-howlin' round the ranches after dark,
> And the mockin' birds are singin' to the lovely medder lark;
> Where the 'possom and the badger and the rattlesnakes abound,
> And the monstrous stars are winkin' o'er a wilderness profound;
> Where lonesome, tawny prairies melt into airy streams,
> While the Double Mountains slumber in heavenly kinds of dreams;
> Where the antelope is grazin' and the lonely plovers call,
> It was there I attended the Cowboys' Christmas Ball.
>
> The town was Anson City, old Jones' county seat,
> Where they raised Polled Angus cattle and waving whiskered wheat;
> Where the air is soft and balmy and dry and full of health,
> Where the prairies is explodin' with agricultural wealth;
> Where they print the Texas Western, that Hall McCann supplies
> With news and yarns and stories, of most amazin' size;

commercial (and they have galvanized tubs full of iced Texan Shiner Bock beers, as well as the other usual suspects); the food is excellent, especially the ribs, and they also serve mesquite-grilled staples such as chicken, sausage, or brisket, plus rib eye steaks cut to order, as thick as you want 'em.

With most of the options lined up along I-20 or the older US-80 strip along the railroad tracks, Abilene motels include a **Motel 6** (915/672-8462) at 4951 W. Stamford, off I-20 at exit 282, not far from the junction with US-83; and the plusher **Kiva Inn** (915/695-2150) at 5403 S. 1st Street.

Where Frank Smith "pulls the badger" on knowin' tenderfeet,
And Democracy's triumphant and might hard to beat;
Where lives that good old hunter, John Milsap, from Lamar,
Who used to be sheriff "back east in Paris, sah."
'Twas there, I say, at Anson with the lovely Widder Wall,
That I went to that reception, the Cowboys' Christmas Ball.

The boys had left the ranches and come to town in piles;
The ladies, kinder scatterin', had gathered in for miles.
And yet the place was crowded, as I remember well,
'Twas gave on this occasion at the Morning Star Hotel.
The music was a fiddle and a lively tambourine,
And viol came imported, by the stage from Abilene.
The room was togged out gorgeous—with mistletoe and shawls,
And the candles flickered festious, around the airy walls.
The wimmen folks looked lovely—the boys looked kinder treed,
Till the leader commenced yellin', "Whoa, fellers, let's stampede,"
And the music started sighin' and a-wailin' through the hall
As a kind of introduction to the Cowboys' Christmas Ball.

The dust riz fast and furious; we all jes' galloped round,
Till the scenery got so giddy that T Bar Dick was downed.
We buckled to our pardners and told 'em to hold on,
Then shook our hoofs like lightnin' until the early dawn.
Don't tell me 'bout cotillions, or germans – no, sir-ee!
That whirl at Anson City jes' takes the cake with me.
I'm sick of lazy shufflin's, of them I've had my fill;
Give me a frontier break-down backed up by Windy Bill.
McAllister ain't nowhere, when Windy leads the show;
I've seen 'em both in harness, and so I ought ter know.
Oh, Bill, I shan't forget yer, and I oftentimes recall
That lively gaited sworray – the Cowboys' Christmas Ball.

—Larry Chittenden
From *Songs of the Cowboys*, compiled by Jack Thorp

For more complete information, contact the **visitors bureau** at 1101 N. 1st Street (915/676-2556) in a refurbished old train depot at the south end of downtown.

Buffalo Gap

If you're passing through Abilene, don't miss the restored frontier town of Buffalo Gap (Mon.-Sat. 10 AM-6 PM, Sunday noon-6 PM; $4; 915/572-3365), 14 miles southwest of town via Hwy-89. It's not completely a tourist trap; cowpokes still reside here, and a courthouse and jail are just two of 20-odd buildings dating from the late 1800s. Other buildings are done up as Wild West souvenir stands, and two

hold good restaurants: **Judy's Gathering Place** for stylish Mexican food, and the **Perini Ranch** for steak and chicken.

Ballinger

The first large town you come to, 53 miles south of Abilene among the rolling sheep-herding hills of the fantastic Edwards Plateau, is Ballinger (pop. 3,975). It's a lively little town with many of its brick and sandstone buildings dating from its inception in 1886 as Hutchins City, when the railroad came through. Standing along the banks of the Colorado River, the town now supports itself with agriculture. Catercorner to the **Coppini Cowboy Statue** on the courthouse square, Ballinger has the incredibly cheap and always packed **Texas Grill**, open 24 hours at the corner of US-83 and Hwy-67.

South of Ballinger along US-83, keep an eye out for the massive stainless steel cross, set on a hill east of the highway.

Paint Rock Pictographs

Fifteen miles south of Ballinger, a dirt road leads west to the Paint Rock Pictographs, the largest concentration of prehistoric drawings in Texas, with well over 1,500 brightly colored images covering a limestone bluff over the Concho River. These images explain the name of the tiny town of **Paint Rock**, a mile south where US-83 crosses the Concho River. In town, the first building you come to (there are only two or three all told) holds **Paint Rock Excursions** which offers guided tours of the pictographs, the only way to see them. The pictographs are on land that's been owned by the Sims family since the 1870s, and since the Sims give the tours, they know what they're talking about. Tours are offered year-round, by advance reservation ($6 adults, $3 children; call 915/732-4418, between 6 and 10 PM).

Menard

US-83 winds through another 40 miles of scrubby hills before reaching the fascinating old wool-products market town of Menard (pop. 1,775; pronounced MAY-nurd), standing in a lush valley along the San Saba River. A trading post and stop on the old cattle trails, Menard was originally founded by Franciscan missionaries in 1757, and many of its early structures survive or have been restored.

It's an eerily picturesque little town, with huge trees and a wide, wide bridge over the river. **Menardville Museum**, housed in the old Santa Fe railroad depot, contains a 150-year-old wooden bar from the now-defunct Legal Tender Saloon. A block south of the main drag, the **Historic Ditch Walk** follows the 10-mile Vaughn Agricultural and Mechanical Canal, a fancy name for an irrigation ditch that has served local farmers since 1876. The canal features remains of the old waterworks and colorful flower plantings, and the walk passes the 1899-vintage **Sacred Heart Catholic Church**.

Several historic limestone buildings in town date to the turn of the century. The Luckenbach Building (built in 1903) contains the **Burnham Brothers Co.** (915/396-4572), the oldest U.S. retailer of game calls, from simple wooden instruments to state-of-the-art computerized devices that lure turkey, deer, elk, duck, and other game.

Menard hasn't much in the way of places to eat, but **Decker's**, a small-town hole-in-the-wall store/cafe right on US-83 at 210 Frisco Street, sells great barbecued brisket plate lunches. The **Menard Country Store**, on US-83 at the south end of town, offers fresh pastries, cakes, breads, jams, and candies, as well as handicrafts marketed by the Menard Area Arts and Crafts Club.

Places to stay include a pair of highway motels: the **Motel 83** (915/396-4549) and the **Hilltop** (915/396-2075).

During Menard's annual **Jim Bowie Days** in late June, visitors and residents gather for arts and crafts shows, mock gunfights, live music, and the outdoor production of *Song of Silver,* a musical patterned after Bowie's life story.

San Saba Mission

Two miles east of Menard, off US-190 on the banks of the river, the cemetery and a few buildings are all that's left of the San Saba Mission, abandoned in 1758 after repeated Comanche attacks. Next to a golf course along Hwy-29, two miles west of town, the Spanish presidio that failed to protect the mission has been fully restored. The rebuilt chapel now houses a small museum, and portions of a later stone fort, named **Real Presidio de San Saba**, also survive intact. A simple inscription, "BOWIE," on the stone gate is thought to have been carved by Jim Bowie of Alamo fame. Bowie lived at the presidio ruins while searching for buried Spanish silver during the early 1800s.

Fort McKavett State Historic Site

Twenty-three miles west of Menard via US-190 and Hwy-864, Fort McKavett (Wed.-Sun. 8 AM-5 PM from Labor Day to Memorial Day, daily 9 AM-6 PM rest of the year) was established in 1852 as the "Camp on the San Saba" by the 8th Infantry. It was soon renamed in honor of a U.S. Army colonel who was killed in the Battle of Monterrey during the war with Mexico. As with other west Texas forts, Fort McKavett served as a first line of defense against Comanche raids along the Texas frontier and provided protection for travelers along the Upper San Antonio-El Paso Trail. Temporarily abandoned in 1859, the post was reestablished in 1868 by the 4th Cavalry after local residents lobbied for Army protection against renewed attacks. The cavalry was soon replaced by the 38th Infantry, a company of African-American troops. All four of the Army's black units, who came to be known as "Buffalo Soldiers" by the Indians, eventually served at McKavett, including the famous 9th and 10th cavalries. Fourteen of the original 40 buildings have been restored, including the officers' quarters, barracks, hospital, school, bakery, and post headquarters. Seven other buildings lie in ruins, and the rest are gone. The hospital ward serves as a visitor center and contains interpretive exhibits explaining the natural and military history of the area. A nature trail leads to the old fort kiln and the "Government Springs."

the Coppini Cowboy Statue

Junction

After passing through the attractively rugged but shallow canyonlands south of Menard—which make US-83 into a roller coaster of a road, by Texas standards—the two-lane road crosses high-speed I-10 at the aptly named town of Junction.

Once a major crossing where the east-west Chihuahua Trail met a branch of the north-south Chisholm Trail (now I-10 and US-83 respectively), Junction (pop. 2,799) sits at the edge of Texas's famed Hill Country, where the Edwards Plateau crumbles into limestone canyons and cliffs along the Balcones Escarpment. As in the areas to the immediate north, wool and mohair production are the main means of local livelihood, supplemented by pecan farming.

Places to eat line Main Street (US-83) through town—try the **Milky Way Drive Inn**, 1619 Main Street, or **Isaak's**, which is open daily 6 AM-10 PM at 1606 Main Street. Four motels just south of I-10 offer inexpensive to moderately priced rooms, including the well-maintained **Carousel Inn** at 1908 Main Street (915/446-3301).

To continue south along US-83, you can wind along Main Street or follow I-10 southeast for one exit, roughly two miles, to rejoin the old road.

Leakey and the Frio Canyon

Below Junction, US-83 continues southward through 55 beautiful miles of rolling ranches and native pecan orchards, entering a verdant, spring-filled region that was one of the last strongholds of the Lipan Apaches and Comanches. The rolling hills around Leakey (pop. 420, pronounced LAY-key) hold limestone caves, some of which the Confederates mined for saltpeter —an essential ingredient of gunpowder—during the Civil War. At 1,600 feet above sea level, this is one of US-83's prettiest reaches through Texas, as the road follows the clear, cold Frio River through 17 miles of cypress, pecan, live oak, cedar, walnut, wild cherry, piñon, and mountain laurel. Some areas also have bigtooth maple and sycamore, a major tourist attraction in the late fall when the leaves change color.

Farther south along the eponymous river, which suffered from major floods in the summer of 1998, the hamlet of **Rio Frio** (pop. 50) boasts the largest live oak tree in Texas. The centuries-old tree stands alongside Hwy-1120 on the east side of the Frio River.

US-377 traces a 22-mile scenic route along the Llano River southwest of Junction, bisecting typical Edwards Plateau tableaus of limestone arroyos studded with mesquite, oak, prickly pear, and yucca. **South Llano River State Park,** four miles southwest of Junction off US-377, protects 507 wooded acres and abundant wildlife (white-tailed deer, Rio Grande turkey, javelina), and offers facilities for picnicking, camping, hiking, canoeing, and swimming.

From Junction, I-10 continues southeast to San Antonio, passing through the Hill Country town of Kerrville, which hosts the very popular **Kerrville Folk Festival** around Memorial Day. For information, call 830/257-3600 or 800/435-8429.

You'll find a dozen or more camps and lodges between the highway and the river, which is popular for fishing and tubing. The tin-roofed, wooden-sided **Welcome Inn Motor Hotel** (830/232-5246) on US-83 in the center of town provides comfortable motel rooms and cabins; Leakey's best local eating is right across the road at the **Frio Canyon Cafe, Feed Store, and Exxon.**

About 10 miles south of Leakey along US-83 on the Frio River, the very pretty 1,420-acre **Garner State Park** (830/232-6132) offers campgrounds, cabins, hiking trails, canoe rentals, swimming, and a popular outdoor dance terrace.

Utopia

Fifteen miles east of Rio Frio via Hwy-1050, on the Sabinal River, the town of Utopia gained momentary fame when it appeared in television ads created by a national burger chain. Seven churches and a population of only 360 represent a legacy left by frontier circuit preachers who found this spot a heavenly place to hold camp meetings and save souls. The **Sabinal Canyon Museum** (Saturday 10 AM-4 PM, Sunday 1-4 PM) on Utopia's main street displays local arts and crafts, including antique handmade quilts, historic photos, farm implements, arrowheads, spurs, and other artifacts that outline Bandera County history.

Uvalde

Forty-one miles south of Leakey, US-83 crosses US-90 (the former San Antonio-El Paso Trail) at Uvalde, founded in 1855 and still centered around a broad square that originally served as a wagonyard for teamsters and travelers. Now a mostly Hispanic town of 15,000 residents, with a wide variety of buildings lining lushly verdant streets, Uvalde was the home of Billy the Kid's killer Pat Garrett during the 1890s; the corrupt lawman's house site is marked off US-90 a half-mile east of US-83. Another Western legend, celluloid cowgirl Dale Evans, hails from Uvalde.

The town's most famous native son, John Nance "Cactus Jack" Garner, served as Franklin Delano Roosevelt's first- and second-term vice president (1933-41); after retiring from politics, he returned to Uvalde and lived here until his death in 1967 at age 98. His home at 333 N. Park now contains the **Ettie R. Garner Museum** (Mon.-Sat. 9 AM-noon and 1-5 PM; 830/278-5018), a repository of memorabilia from Garner's political career. The 1891 **Grand Opera House** (Mon.-Fri. 9 AM-3 PM; free; 830/278-4184), on the square at 100 W. North Street, has been restored to a 390-seat live performance venue; it's open for free guided tours.

A number of motels line US-90 (Main Street) east of the town square, including the economic **Inn of Uvalde** (830/278-9173), a **Holiday Inn**, a **Best Western**, and the **Amber Sky Motel** (830/278-5602) at 2005 E. Main Street. Friendly **Jerry's Restaurant** (830/278-7556) at 539 W. Main Street features a classic, small-town South Texas menu of fajitas, *migas* (eggs scrambled with chiles, onions, and tortilla strips), catfish, steaks and oysters. It's open Mon.-Sat. 6 AM-10 PM, Sunday 11 AM-2 PM.

Five miles west of Uvalde on US-90, a large roadhouse-style dance hall called **The Purple Sage** (830/278-1006) offers two floors of bars, live country-western swing bands, and dance floors. It's open weekends only; minors are admitted.

From Uvalde, US-90 runs 75 miles east to **San Antonio,** home of the Alamo and the prettiest city in Texas. For visitor information, contact the San Antonio visitors bureau (210/270-8748 or 800/447-3372).

South of Uvalde

As US-83 continues south from Uvalde, the highway descends farther onto the mostly flat Rio Grande Plain, entering a subtropical zone of seemingly endless chaparral. Amidst "brush country"—marked by a mixture of thorny cacti, mesquite, dwarf oak, black bush, and huisache—spread large irrigated farms known as the "Winter Garden of Texas" for the bounty of spinach and citrus crops they produce. Forty miles south of Uvalde sits **Crystal City** (pop. 8,245), the Zavala County seat and self-proclaimed "Spinach Capital of the World," where a **statue of Popeye** stands on the town square. Three miles south of Crystal City, the seasonal **Espantosa Lake** once served as an important water stop along the colonial mission trail between Mexico and Texas.

CRYSTAL CITY, TEX

POPEYE

ERECTED MARCH 26,1937 COURTESY E.C.SEGAR

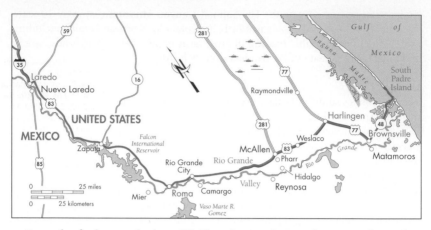

Ten miles farther south along US-83 is **Carrizo Springs** (pop. 5,745), another farming center and county seat of underpopulated Dimmit County. Twenty-five miles on, the flyspeck hamlet of **Catarina** (pop. 45) marks the end of the farmlands and the return to the range.

To get a taste of South Texas culture, tune in to "Tejano 102," **KUVA 102.3 FM,** for nonstop Tejano and traditional country-western tunes.

Eighteen miles north of Laredo, US-83 merges with I-35, then crosses the Rio Grande to meet Mexico 85 (the Pan-American Highway), forming a continuous road between the USA and the Panama Canal, via Mexico and Central America.

Nuevo Laredo, the quintessential Mexican border town, offers everything from elegant dining to street vendors to cut-rate liquor stores, plus two leafy public plazas, all within walking distance of the International Bridge and downtown Laredo. Unfortunately, it also has all the unsightly *maquiladora* assembly plants typical of border towns.

Laredo

Founded as the first nonmissionary, nonmilitary Spanish settlement in North America in 1755, Laredo (pop. 122,900) is surrounded by the oldest ranch lands in the United States. With a population that is about 90% Hispanic, the city is growing rapidly due to its position as the largest international trade center along the U.S.-Mexico border.

At the heart of downtown Laredo, a block north of the Rio Grande, is the **Villa De San Agustín Historical District**, site of the original 1755 Spanish settlement of Villa de San Agustín. Numerous historic buildings surround the plaza, including a small stone building next to La Posada Hotel that served as the capitol of the short-lived Republic of the Rio Grande. It now houses a **museum** (Tues.-Sun. 10 AM-noon and 1-5 PM) containing a collection of memorabilia from the separatist movement of 1840.

Stay the night at the historic **La Posada Hotel**, right downtown (956/722-1701), or choose from the many chain motels lining I-35.

Southeast from Laredo: Roma

South of Laredo, US-83 follows a route parallel to the Rio Grande that was originally cut through the dry chaparral by Gen. Zachary Taylor's soldiers during the 1846-48 Mexican-American War. The 1953 construction of 87,000-acre **Falcon International Reservoir** submerged the town of **Zapata**, the new version of which lies 49 miles southeast of Laredo, followed by Roma (89 miles) and Rio Grande City (109 miles). Both the U.S. and Mexico use the dam and reservoir for hydroelectric power, flood control, and recreation along US-83. Camping is possible at **Falcon State Park** on the lake's southeast shore.

US-83 continues southeast along the Rio Grande, passing through several Texas border towns held together by a common historical and cultural thread: all were settled by Spanish colonists in the mid-18th century as part of the famous José de Escandón land grant.

CROSSING THE BORDER

At dozens of sleepy little towns across Southern California, Arizona, New Mexico, and Texas, the temptation to nip across the border and see something of our southern neighbor can be strong. It's only a hop and a skip away, and the crossing is usually simple and hassle free, but before you go it's good to know a few things about international customs—small "c" and big "C," as the U.S. Customs Service is not something to take lightly.

All that a U.S. citizen needs to cross the border for 72 hours or less (and be re-admitted to the U.S. after your visit!) is proof of citizenship—a passport basically—and the burden of proof is on the traveler. Often, you can get by with just a driver's license, or simply an American-looking face, but this is risky business and you could well be turned back. To stay longer or to travel beyond the border areas, you need a *tarjeta de turística* (tourist card), which is available free of charge from Mexican tourist offices, consulates, or government offices at the ports of entry.

If you're thinking of heading south to stock up on Mexican beers or a rug or other handicraft, the much ballyhooed NAFTA treaty did nothing to change what you can bring back from Mexico: all merchandise is subject to a $400 duty-free limit, above which U.S. customs will charge a 10% duty based on fair retail value. Alcohol imports by individuals are limited to a whopping liter every 30 days—about two cans of beer—and it is illegal to import Mexican versions of trademarked items (perfumes, watches, even cans of Coke!) that are also sold in the United States. So don't risk having to leave something behind at the border—ask before you buy.

The most important advice I can offer is that, because of insurance and other legal concerns, you should leave your car on the U.S. side of the border and cross into Mexico on foot. If you do want to drive across, be sure you have a policy that specifically covers travel in Mexico—the AAA is a good source, since these policies must be written by Mexican companies, and they have reciprocal contacts. Insurance is essential because if you are involved in any kind of collision in Mexico, even a tiny fender bender, the police are required to impound the cars and hold the drivers in jail until the responsibilities are decided—not how you want to spend your time. Also, if you're tempted to cross the border simply to fill up on cheap Mexican gas, be aware that, because of a different rating method, the 92 octane unleaded ("Magna Sin" in Mexico) is the same as 87 octane gas in the U.S.

For more detailed information on traveling across the border, pick up a copy of Joe Cummings's excellent *Northern Mexico Handbook* (800/345-5473).

If it's fruit, you'll find it here.

The surviving 19th-century Spanish- and French Creole-style architecture in **Roma**, 40 miles southeast of Zapata, once the end of the line for steamboats sailing up the Rio Grande from the Gulf of Mexico, inspired director Elia Kazan to use the town as a film location for the 1952 movie *Viva Zapata!* starring Marlon Brando and Anthony Quinn. Across the river in the Mexican state of Tamaulipas, the narrow sandstone streets, old churches, and plazas of **Mier** haven't changed much since the Spanish era.

Farther along US-83 comes **Rio Grande City**, another former riverboat terminal. Among the historic buildings downtown is the renovated **LaBorde House**, 601 E. Main Street (956/487-5101), a Creole-style inn designed by Parisian architects in 1899. Rooms are moderately priced and meals at **Che's**, the hotel restaurant, are good. Other restaurants to look for in the area include the family-run **Caro's** (956/487-2255) at 205 N. Garcia, an inexpensive northern Mexican-style cafe.

Across the river from Rio Grande City is the small Mexican town of **Camargo** (established 1749), José de Escandón's first Nuevo Santander settlement. A Catholic **church** on the plaza dates to the early 1750s.

The Rio Grande Valley

Southeast of Rio Grande City the river and US-83 curve eastward toward the Gulf of Mexico through a broad delta region known as the Rio Grande Valley, despite the fact there are no nearby mountains to make it a true valley. Citrus orchards, interspersed with date palms planted as windbreaks, line the highway, while lush plantings of bougainvillea and poinsettias drape many of the houses in the string of towns that appear every few miles all the way to the Gulf. The population of the valley, which sits at the same latitude as the Florida Keys, swells with the arrival each winter of over 100,000 "Winter Texans" fleeing the colder midwestern states. This "snowbird" presence means there's a high concentration of RV and mobile home parks throughout the area, and some of the lowest daily, weekly, and monthly rates in the nation. The McAllen **Chamber of Commerce** (956/423-5440) has lists of over a dozen of these, catering to overnight and long-stay visitors.

The westernmost, oldest, and largest of the valley towns, **McAllen** (pop. 90,000) started out as a terminus for a 1904 railway line parallel to the Mexican border.

Eight miles from the center of McAllen across the Rio Grande is the Mexican city of **Reynosa** (pop. 375,000), a popular tourist destination for valley visitors. McAllen in return receives many Mexican visitors.

The McAllen area's unique attraction is **Los Ebanos ferry**, the last hand-pulled ferry across the Rio Grande. To get there, drive west from McAllen on US-83 to Hwy-886 (between Havana and Sullivan City), then turn left (south) and follow the mazelike road until you hit the river. In service daily 7 AM-3 PM, the ferry can carry three cars and a small number of pedestrians on each crossing. The fare is $1 per auto; pedestrians may ride for US 25 cents per person. On the Mexican side, it's two miles to **Díaz Ordaz**, a small cotton- and sorghum-farming center.

McAllen holds a large number of motels and restaurants on and off US-83, though the steady tourist trade makes it the valley's most expensive town to overnight in. In nearby **Pharr**, **Armando's Taco Hut** at 106 N. Cage (956/781-1091) offers good, inexpensive Tex-Mex food, a great Tex-Mex jukebox, and occasional live *conjunto* music; open daily 7 AM-3 AM. Over in Reynosa, **Sam's** (2-00-34) at Allende and Ocampo is famous throughout the area for its inexpensive steak dinners, Mexican platters, and border specialties such as quail. It's open daily 11 AM-midnight.

About eight miles southwest of McAllen via Hwy-374 (west) and Hwy-2062 (south), **Bentsen-Rio Grande Valley State Park** (956/585-1107) preserves 588 acres of Rio Grande delta riparian woodlands and *matorral* (thorn scrub). Camping and picnicking facilities are available.

> South of McAllen on the Mexican border, the town of Hidalgo has proclaimed itself the **"Killer Bee Capital of the USA,"** and has a larger-than-life statue of one at the center of town to prove it.

Harlingen

From McAllen, for the second time in its 2,000-mile journey from the Canadian border, US-83 continues as a full-fledged, multi-lane freeway through San Juan, Alamo, and Weslaco, ending up 30 miles east in Harlingen. At the junction of US-83 and US-77 you'll find a **Texas Travel Information Center**, the best source of tourist information for this part of the state.

Harlingen's **Rio Grande Valley Historical Museum Complex** (Tues.-Fri. 9 AM-noon and 2-5 PM, Sunday 2-5 PM), three miles north of town at Boxwood and Raintree in the Harlingen Industrial Air Park, contains exhibits interpreting the history of the valley from the time of the Karankawa and Coahuiltecan peoples. At the nearby **Iwo Jima Memorial** stands the sculpture (originally plaster, now protected in fiberglass) from which the famous bronze statue of the flag-raising Marines (installed at the Marine Corps Memorial in Arlington, Virginia) was made. There's also a small museum (Mon.-Fri. 10 AM-4 PM; donations; 800/365-6006), documenting the experience of Iwo Jima veterans.

> Boosted by controlled watering and mild year-round temperatures, the rich alluvial soils of the Rio Grande Valley produce 56 varieties of fruits and vegetables, including citrus, sugarcane, onions, cucumbers, tomatoes, cabbage, and 99% of the aloe vera grown in the United States.

the original Iwo Jima Memorial sculpture

A gaggle of chain motels and restaurants lines US-77/83 through Harlingen, including **Best Western**, **Ramada Inn**, **La Quinta**, **Rodeway Inn**, and **Motel 6**. Vela's at 603 W. Tyler serves inexpensive, authentic Valley-style Mexican food 24 hours a day. Rustic **Lone Star Restaurant** at 4201 W. Business 83 (956/423-8002) cooks mesquite-grilled steaks, barbecue, and Mexican dishes; it's open daily for lunch and dinner.

Of the valley's 22 radio stations, 12 broadcast a portion or all of their programming in Spanish. Radio station **KIWW 96.1 FM** broadcasts Tejano music; for country-western, tune in **KFRQ 94.5 FM**.

Raymondville, 23 miles north of Harlingen via US-77, has been a boot-making center since at least the turn of the century. Family-run **Armando's Boot Co.** (169 N. 7th) and **Torres Custom Boots** (246 S. 7th) offer some of the best prices in the state for custom-made cowboy boots.

Brownsville

South of Harlingen, US-83 merges with US-77 for the final 26 miles to Brownsville, where you may well feel like you've unknowingly crossed the border into Mexico. One of the most historic cities in Texas, Brownsville retains its Spanish and Mexican heritage more than most places, particularly in the architecture of the downtown district around **Elizabeth Street**, which runs northwest from the 24-hour border crossing at **Matamoros, Mexico**. U.S.-Mexico trade supports the local economy via a Union Pacific rail terminus connected with Mexico's national railway over the Rio Grande; also, a 17-mile deep-sea channel in the river delta links the city with the U.S. Inland Waterway System and the Gulf of Mexico.

Besides the historic downtown, another must-see is the well-endowed **Gladys Porter Zoo** (daily 9 AM-5 PM; $6; 956/546-7187) at Ringgold and 6th Streets, named by zoo professionals as one of the country's 10 best zoological facilities.

Virtually every fast-food place in the city, even McDonald's and Dairy Queen, serves tacos of some kind. For Tex-Mex meals, one of the popular places in town is **Los Camperos Char Chicken** (1440 International Boulevard, open daily for lunch and dinner), where the house specialty is smoked, charbroiled chicken served with corn tortillas and red and green salsas. **Antonio's** (2921 Boca Chica Boulevard, in Strawberry Square) and **Miguel's** (2474 Boca Chica Boulevard) make the best fajitas in the Rio Grande Valley. Both restaurants are open Mon.-Sat. for lunch and dinner, Sunday for dinner only. Across the border in Matamoros, dark and velvet-lined **The Drive Inn** at Calle 6 and Hidalgo has been a border institution since 1916 for steak, continental, seafood, and Mexican.

Several modern hotels, from the **Motel 6** to the **Sheraton Plaza Royale**, representing all budgets, cluster along the highway just north of the city.

Sabal Palm Grove Sanctuary

The last remaining grove of endangered Sabal palms in the Rio Grande delta (they are the only palm tree native to the continental U.S.) is protected for future generations in the 172-acre Sabal Palm Grove Sanctuary, which is run by the National Audubon Society and located about five miles southeast of Brownsville. Densely packed with the endangered palms, which grow to nearly 50 feet, the sanctuary is one of the only places where you can get a sense of the natural ecosystem of the Rio Grande delta. Bird-lovers flock here to catch a glimpse of the rare green jays, as well as the colorful parakeets and hummingbirds that make their homes in the dense jungle-like growth.

To reach the reserve from Brownsville, take Boca Chica Boulevard (Hwy-4) east, then turn right (south) on Hwy-3068. From the end of the road, turn right (west) on Hwy-1419 and follow the marked road to the sanctuary. The visitor center (daily 8:30 AM-5 PM; $3; 956/541-8034) has maps and natural history guides to the sanctuary, which is open daily from dawn to dusk.

One of the first white-hunter-in-the-African-jungle movies, *Life Along the Delta,* was filmed in 1930 in what is now the Sabal Palm Grove Sanctuary.

South Padre Island

Twenty-six miles northeast of Brownsville via Hwy-48 and the Queen Isabella Causeway, South Padre Island provides a strong contrast to the sleepy, historic towns of the Rio Grande Valley. Only the southernmost five miles of this 30-mile Gulf of Mexico barrier island are developed; sand dunes and tidal marshes dominate the remainder. Sportfishing in the Laguna Madre, the protected bay that lies between Padre Island and the mainland, is excellent.

In the developed zone, multi-story hotels and condominiums line white-sand beaches on both the Gulf and Laguna Madre sides of the island. Rooms are easy to come by except during the annual Spring Break (March-April) when college kids from all over Texas and the Midwest fill the hotels and beaches with round-the-clock revelry.

Call the helpful **South Padre Visitor and Convention Bureau** (956/761-6433 or 800/343-2368) for a listing of hotel, condo, and beach home properties.

THE GREAT RIVER ROAD

THE GREAT RIVER ROAD

Old Man River, Father of Waters, "body of a nation," Big Muddy: by any name the mighty Mississippi River cuts a mythic figure across the American landscape. Who hasn't read Mark Twain or listened to *Showboat* and not dreamt of a trip down the Mississippi? If you're tired of waiting for somebody to buy you passage aboard the *Delta Queen* or to help you paddle among the 1,500-ton barges, then do what Huck Finn would have done if he'd had a driver's license: tag alongside the Mississippi on the Great River Road.

Created in 1938 from a network of federal, state, and local roads, the Great River Road—also known as the River Road, and commonly abbreviated to "GRR"—forms a single route along the Mississippi from head to toe. Designed to show off the 10 states bordering the Mississippi from its headwaters to its mouth, the GRR is nothing if not scenic, and anyone who equates the Midwest with the flat Kansas prairie will be pleasantly surprised. Sure, farms line the road, but so do upland meadows, cypress swamps, thick forests, steep bluffs, and dozens of parks and wildlife refuges.

Of course it isn't all pretty. There's enough industry along the Mississippi for you to navigate the river by the flashing marker lights on smokestacks, and a half-dozen major cities compete with their bigger cousins on the coasts for widest suburban sprawl and ugliest urban clutter. A pandemic of tacky strip malls has infected the region, too, but apart from the astounding growth in casinos (you'll never be more than 100 miles from a slot machine from one end of the Mississippi to the other) the GRR resists the developers' bulldozers because its meanders are shunned by a century increasingly drawn to the straight, fast, and four-lane.

If the rivers were being named today, the Mississippi River would flow into the Missouri River and not vice versa, since the Missouri is by far the longer of the two.

A full 50% longer than the comparable route along the interstates, the GRR changes direction often, crosses the river whenever it can, dallies in towns every other road has forgotten, and

NAVIGATING THE GREAT RIVER ROAD

The GRR is identified by a green pilot's wheel with a steamboat pictured in the middle. Quality and quantity of route markers vary considerably from state to state: some states, like Minnesota and Illinois, are well marked, with advance warning of junctions, confirmation after turns, and reminders on remote backroads. Other states, like Louisiana and Mississippi, seem committed to hiding GRR signs miles from where they would serve any conceivable good. Missouri is terribly inconsistent, and Tennessee doesn't seem to have joined the program at all. Without a guide or a map, you simply cannot travel the length of the GRR just by following the signs.

There are variations—signposted as "Alternate" or "State Route"—and spurs, denoted by a brown pilot's wheel, which lead to various points of interest.

For a schematic map of the entire GRR and a guide to local happenings in each of the states along the route, send a $1 donation to the **Mississippi River Parkway Commission**, Pioneer Building, Suite 1513, 336 N. Robert Street, St. Paul, MN 55101.

altogether offers a perfect analog to floating downstream. If the road itself isn't your destination, *don't* take it. For those who do travel it, the GRR spares you the fleets of hurtling 40-ton trucks, creeping RVs, and that endless parade of interstate billboards, and rewards you with twice the local color, flavor, and wildlife (two- and four-legged) found along any alternate route. Lest these tangibles be taken too much for granted, every so often the GRR will skip over to an interstate for a stretch to help you sort your preferences. Savor, and enjoy.

GREAT RIVER ROAD HIGHLIGHTS

ACROSS MINNESOTA

The Great River Road begins in Lake Itasca State Park and stairsteps along occasionally unpaved but well-graded back-country roads through a mix of northern boreal forest, tree farms, and hayfields, all the while staying as close to its namesake as possible. By Grand Rapids, only 130 road miles from its source, the Mississippi has been transformed from a grassy brook barely deep enough to canoe to an industry-sustaining river fed by a half-dozen of the state's 10,000 lakes. Farther south, the red and white pines, paper birch, and big-tooth aspen give way to more farms while the route breaks from the surveyor's section lines to curve with the river across the glacially flattened state. By St. Cloud, the GRR enters an increasingly developed corridor that culminates in the hugely sprawling "Twin Cities" of St. Paul and Minneapolis, south of which the road slips into rural Wisconsin.

Throughout the upper Midwest, Friday night is the traditional night for a fish fry. Look for the backlit signboards or hand-lettered banners stuck out in front of the local VFW post or social club for a sample of the truly local variety.

Given the extremely rural quality of most of Minnesota north of the Twin Cities, night drivers must be particularly careful of wildlife—fox, deer, raccoon, skunk—wandering onto the road.

Lake Itasca State Park

The GRR begins here among the cattails and tall pines, in the park that protects the headwaters of the mighty Mississippi River. The small, clear brook tumbling out of the north end of Lake Itasca will eventually carry runoff from nearly two-thirds of the United States and enough silt to make the muddy plume at the river's mouth visible from space. But at its headwaters, 2,550-odd meandering miles from the Gulf of Mexico, you can not only wade across the Mississippi, you can see the bottom. Here, drinking the river water won't cause cancer—an increasingly rare claim, unfortunately.

The Mississippi's humble beginnings were the object of chest-thumping adventurers and the subject of not-so-scholarly debate for decades before explorer Henry

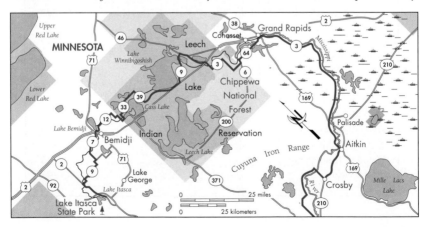

Rowe Schoolcraft, led by Ojibwa native Ozaawindib, determined this lake to be the true source of the nation's most legendary river in 1832. Schoolcraft's story, the tale of the battle to protect the park against logging, and lots of other Mississippi facts are found at the **interpretive center** just inside the park's north entrance (open year-round; $4 per car). Skeptics will also find out why professional geographers don't consider the two smaller lakes and the five creeks that feed Itasca competition for the headwaters title.

If you're practicing your Lake Wobegon language skills, be sure to say "You bet" in place of "You're welcome."

The first time you see the super grades of gas selling for the same price as the regular grade, you may think it's a mistake, but no: the high grades of gasoline are mixed with 10% ethanol, making them as cheap as regular in this grain-rich state.

The fact that the lakeshore has been "improved" from its naturally marshy state, the surrounding old-growth pine forest—the most extensive stand of virgin timber left in the state—and outdoorsy amenities such as paved bike trails and boat launches all contribute to Itasca's popularity; rangers and bulletin boards at either entrance can explain what's going on when. Bike and boat rentals are available spring through fall opposite the park's headquarters. If you plan to camp (800/246-CAMP or 800/246-2267 for site reservations, advised but not required), be sure to pack repellent for ticks and mosquitoes. Other accommodations include the grand turn-of-the-century **Douglas Lodge**, where rooms cost $50-80 a night, and assorted

THE LEGENDS OF PAUL BUNYAN

Like most other myths of the American frontier, the legend of Paul Bunyan is obscured in the mists of time. The source of the many legends describing Paul's life—such as that when he was born it took five storks to deliver him and it took a whole herd of cows to keep him fed; that at just a week old he was big enough to wear his father's clothes; that he once bent a crowbar and used it as a safety pin to hold his pants together; that he was able to fell trees an acre at a time, and he used to whistle through a hollowed-out log—are impossible to trace, though their widespread popularity is due primarily to a public relations man at the Red River Lumber Company, William Laughead.

Beginning in 1914, and continuing for the next 20 years, Laughead and the lumber company, which was owned by the Walker family (founders of the Walker Art Center), published a series of illustrated booklets, recounting the stories already in general circulation around the logging camps. The booklets, bearing the full title, *The Marvelous Exploits of Paul Bunyan as Told in the*  *Camps of the White Pine Lumberman for Generations, During Which Time the Loggers Have Pioneered the Way through the North Woods from Maine to California, Collected from Various Sources and Embellished for Publication,* map the "Paul Bunyan Belt" in towns that constructed statues of Paul and Babe, his big blue ox. The first large statue of Paul and Babe was built in 1937 in Bemidji, where they now stand along the lake; statues were later built in Klamath, California, Brainerd, Minnesota, and Bangor, Maine; and many other logging towns.

lakeside cabins (all 800/246-CAMP or 800/246-2267), while just steps from the bike path and beach you'll find the immaculate, friendly, and bargain-priced HI Mississippi Headwaters Hostel (year-round; 218/266-3415), which has rooms for families and couples as well as single travelers. When not fishing or foraging for your meals, consider the Douglas Lodge dining room, where the menu includes regional blueberries, wild rice, and walleye pike.

Lake Itasca is near one of those special junctions of the Pie Belt and Blueberry Territory; come summer this is a marriage made in heaven. The town of Lake George, just east of the park, opens the pearly gates to its Blueberry Festival the last weekend of every July.

Explorer Henry Schoolcraft christened Lake Itasca with syllables from the Latin *veritas caput,* meaning "true head." The native Ojibwa called it "Omushkos," their word for elk, while the French trappers knew it as Lac La Biche, or Elk Lake.

Between Bemidji and Grand Rapids, the Great River Road follows a slower but more scenic parallel to trans-continental US-2, whose route across Minnesota is detailed on pages 482-485.

Bemidji

Walleye pike is a mild white fish sought by Midwest anglers from May through the cold of February. The walleye found in Minnesota restaurants all come from Red Lake, site of the only commercial walleye fishing allowed by law, and generally disappear from menus after October, when the lakes start freezing over.

Under a century ago, the northern forests of Minnesota were chock-full of lumber boom camps, with hundreds of mills and lumber works whining night and day, and dozens of saloons, brothels, and boardinghouses catering to the rough-and-tumble logging trade. The ravenous cutting wiped out the stands— virtually nothing remains of Minnesota's primeval pine forests— and the camps disappeared as quickly as they sprang up, but the woods have repeatedly grown back, to be harvested on a more sustainable basis while still providing an eye-pleasing backdrop to the region's literally thousands of lakes.

From its boomtown roots, Bemidji (pop. 11,245) has long since settled down into a picturesque community—i.e., looking just as it did when Hubert Humphrey first ran for Congress—its compact and charismatic business district filling a half-dozen blocks along the south shore of lovely Lake Bemidji. With three large mills still busily turning trees into wood products, Bemidji is a typically industrious lumber town, remarkable mainly for having assisted in the birth of that well-loved legendary duo of logging lore, Paul Bunyan and his blue ox, Babe (see special topic, The Legends of Paul Bunyan).

The main course of US-2 wraps around downtown Bemidji, so be sure to follow the Business Loop (old US-2), which passes up and over both the Mississippi River and Lake Bemidji while winding to downtown and a park where the town's big tourist draw, leviathan statues of Paul Bunyan and Babe the Blue Ox, have stood along the lakefront since their construction in 1937. Nearby there's a recently re-modeled visitor center (218/751-3541 or 800/458-2223), boasting a fireplace made with stones from every US state (apart from Alaska and Hawaii, which weren't states when the fireplace was first built) and sharing space with a small museum ($1.25) of taxidermied wildlife and odd historical items—including Paul Bunyan's ax and oversized underwear.

Along with Paul and Babe, Bemidji offers endless opportunities for water-skiing, canoeing, fishing, ice-fishing and autumnal leaf-peeping. It also has more than enough cafes to detain the most discerning road-tripping traveler. Top of the list is the **Maid Rite Diner**, across from the lake near the information center; a classic diner, it's open from 7:30 AM for hearty meals and homemade rhubarb pies. Other good places are in the main business district, two blocks inland from the lake: **Griffey's Bakery**, at 123 N. Beltrami Avenue in Union Square and the **Coachman's Cafe**, 509 N. Beltrami Avenue. The only cafe still open after 5 PM is **Clementine's Eatery**, 205 N. 2nd Street, with regional specialties including (sometimes) fresh walleye pike. Dinner is a different story, and apart from the franchised chains lining US-2, your options are few. Best bet for dinner is **Union Station**, in the old railway building at 128 W. 1st Street, a bar and restaurant serving pastas, steaks, the ever-present walleye, and the best wild rice salad around. **Tutto Bene**, at 300 N. Beltrami Avenue, is a slightly upscale Italian place, with a pleasantly cool outdoor terrace; for late-night dining, **Dave's Pizza** at 15th and Irvine is open till 11 PM, until midnight on weekends.

Motels include the family-oriented **Edgewater**, appropriately situated on the lake at 1015 Paul Bunyan Drive (218/751-3600 or 800/776-3343), with its own beach and complimentary canoes available to guests; the national chains (**Best Western**, **Comfort Inn**, **Holiday Inn**, and **Super 8**) line US-2 west of downtown, away from the lake.

Chippewa National Forest

The scenery along US-2 between Bemidji and Grand Rapids turns on the color jets as the numbing agricultural morass gives way to the edges of the enormous— 663,000 acres—Chippewa National Forest, a conglomeration of over 700 lakes, state parks and forests, recreation areas, U.S. Army Corps of Engineer dams, as well as some nifty driving highlights. It's also home to quite a few bald eagles.

Cass Lake, where the native Ojibwa tribe hosts summertime powwows, is on US-2 at the western end of the forest, and includes the **U.S. Forest Service headquarters** (218/335-8600) in addition to a bald eagle nesting site. **Deer River**, at the eastern edge of the forest, is handy mostly for cheap coffee and gas. In between, a 50-foot-long fish stands alongside the popular **Big Fish Supper Club** (218/665-2333) on US-2 at the hamlet of Bena, while most of the forest lands account for the **Leech Lake Indian Reservation**.

Big Fish Supper Club

Bemidji to Grand Rapids: The Great River Road

Leaving downtown Bemidji along the edge of the lake, the GRR makes a series of backcountry loops through tree farms and the first national forest, crossing US-2 twice before snaking into Grand Rapids 100 miles later. As opposed to the busy and monotonous US-2, from which you see lots of scraggly jack pine and nary a body of water, the GRR hugs the red pine- and aspen-wooded shores of six lakes and crosses the ever-widening Mississippi eight times. Numerous signs point to unseen resorts, which in Minnesota don't offer luxury so much as proximity to good fishing. Fishing is serious business hereabouts, as is evident from the frequency of signs advertising Leeches-Minnows-Nightcrawlers.

Grand Rapids

Navigational headwaters of the Mississippi River, Grand Rapids (pop. 7,976) is a small Frank Capra-esque kind of place, known for its four large in-town lakes (there are over 1,000 in this part of the state) and a great bridge over the river. The city can be a bit confusing in its layout, but its small size makes sightseeing manageable.

The city sits along the western edge of the famed Mesabi Iron Range and includes viewing sites at a handful of **open pit mines.** The iron mines are a thing of the past, but Grand Rapids is still a major lumber town, and you can tour the impossible-to-miss **Blandin Paper Mill** (Monday, Wednesday, and Friday, May-Sept. only; 218/327-6226; free). One of the country's largest mills, Blandin owns most of the surrounding forests and turns the trees into the stock onto which magazines like *Time* and *Sports Illustrated* are printed.

Three miles southwest of Grand Rapids, well signed along the Great River Road and equidistant via US-169 or US-2, the fine **Forest History Center** (Mon.-Sat. 10 AM-5 PM, Sunday noon-5 PM in summer, daily noon-4 PM rest of the year; $3), is a living-history replica of a 19th-century logging camp, complete with nature trails through the surrounding woods and energetic lumberjacks rolling logs and telling tall tales.

In the center of town, the **Central School Heritage and Arts Center** (Mon.-Sat. 9 AM-5 PM June-Sept.; rest of the year, 9:30 AM-5 PM; $3) is housed in a squat, three-story Victorian Romanesque-style grade-school building at the crossroads of US-2 and US-169. Here you'll find the county historical museum, with the usual "Main Street" of banks, stores, services, and pell-mell displays of farm equipment and logging gear.

Upstairs, however, is the real draw: the self-proclaimed "World's Largest Collection of Judy Garland Memorabilia," she of ruby-slipper fame having been born in Grand Rapids on June 10, 1922. Truly a cradle-to-grave biographical assembly, the collection displays everything from her first crib to photos of her early performances as part of the Gumm Sisters, a family vaudeville group, to fading images of the London house where she died of an overdose of sleeping pills on June 22, 1969, and a final shot of her tomb in Hartsdale, New York. There are posters from most of her movies, and a copy of her costume from *The Wizard of Oz,* complete with ruby slippers. In front of the building, right along US-2, is a miniature "Yellow Brick Road" dedicated by some of the surviving "munchkins" who worked on the picture.

The Central School also holds a unique place to eat: the school cafeteria, now a pleasant if somewhat frilly restaurant called the **First Grade**, specializing in homemade soups and sandwiches—and great pies.

The Grand Rapids **visitor center** (218/326-1251 or 800/ 472-6366), downtown at N.W. 3rd Street in the circa 1898 Great Northern Railroad depot, includes a 24-hour enclosed kiosk with information and a phone hookup to local **motels**.

Grand Rapids is very proud of its most famous daughter, **Judy Garland,** and whoops it up every July with a festival in her honor.

Some of the best pies in the land of great pies can be had 20 miles north of Aitkin in the riverside town of Palisade (pop. 150), where the wonderful **Palisade Cafe** on Main Street (Hwy- 3) sells all sorts of fresh homemade pies.

Aitkin

South of Grand Rapids the land rivals Kansas for flatness, yet the mix of farms and forest continues to lend visual interest to what could otherwise be achingly monotonous. The GRR alleviates boredom with its sinuous irregularity, the curves always hinting at the proximity of the Mississippi. For most of the way the river itself remains hidden, although regular signs for boat landings confirm its presence, and on occasion its broad channel and tree-lined banks roll into view.

For nearly 70 miles south of Grand Rapids you will have this rural road to yourself; then at the single stoplight in Aitkin (pop. 1,770), the GRR joins busy Hwy-210, at the edge of the mid-state lakes region. Aitkin is best known as the site of the annual **Fish House Parade**, in which ice fishermen show off their one-of-a-kind refuges from the winter cold; this unique event is held every year, on the Friday following Thanksgiving. Year-round, Aitkin is a nice, all-American town, with a still-in-use 1930s movie palace (The Rialto), a very good bakery (Aitkin Bakery), and, next door, the great lunch counter inside **Ziske's Grocery**, 24 NW 2nd Street (218/927-2147), *the* place to stop and get a feel for Aitkin life.

Crosby

Watch your compass needle for signs of deflection as you proceed to the small but tidy town of Crosby, the center of Minnesota's "forgotten" iron range, the Cuyuna. The flood-prone mines have died out, but the surrounding landscape still bears evidence of mining's heyday, with lakes and hills created by subsidence and strip mining, and also by contemporary gravel quarrying. Crosby itself has a nice park fronting onto Serpent Lake, complete with a brightly colored Chinese dragon, while **Croft Mine Historical Park**, well posted on the edge of Crosby, profiles the iron-mining industry and an era, covering immigration and labor issues as well as the actual

mining process. Machinery, period buildings, a gift shop, and a simulated underground tour round out the site's features (daily 10 AM-6 PM, Memorial Day-Labor Day; grounds and museum free, tour $3.50).

Between Grand Rapids and Brainerd, the official GRR takes a slow and somewhat scenic route along country lanes, though you'll save many hours (and not miss *that* much) by taking US-169 and Hwy-210.

The 4th of July in Brainerd is quite an event, with all the usual marching bands, rock bands and parades—plus a **rubber duck race** down the Mississippi River.

As seen in the movie *Fargo*, Brainerd also possesses a very large statue of Paul Bunyan and his Big Blue Ox, Babe, standing in the parking lot of an amusement park at the junction of Hwy-210 and Hwy-371.

Brainerd

South of Crosby, the GRR leaves the truck traffic and takes to the cornfields and sumac-laced forests again, passing as many barns as houses, the occasional lakeside hideaway, and some rural town halls; for a thumbnail overview of the area's settlement history, keep an eye peeled for the historical markers along the way. After about 30 miles our route crosses the lake-sized Mississippi River and rolls into the geographical center of the state: Brainerd, the medium-sized Minnesota town that played a starring role in the offbeat Coen brothers movie, *Fargo*.

That huge Potlatch paper mill along the banks of the river notwithstanding, the economy of this part of the state benefits greatly from recreation. In Minnesota this means lakes: over 400 within a 50-mile radius, with over 150 resorts or campgrounds on their shores. Brainerd, the commercial center of it all, began life in 1871 when the Northern Pacific Railroad chose to cross the Mississippi River here; the rail yards are still in the heart of town beneath the giant water tower, which resembles a Las Vegas-style medieval keep. Unfortunately the historic downtown has been badly "malled" by outlying shopping plazas, and the visual clutter of the strip along Hwy-210 (Washington Street) obscures the signs for the GRR, which winds along River Road on a grand tour of Brainerd's scenic backside.

Among the discount merchandisers, pawn shops, and empty storefronts of downtown there are still a few points of light, such as **The Front Street Cafe**, at 616 Front Street across the tracks from that faux piece of Camelot. With free seconds on soups, mile-high meringue on the pies, and unbelievably low prices—plus a collection of commemorative plates to which words cannot do justice—the Front Street Cafe sets a hip standard for square meals.

Across from the water tower, on Hwy-210 at 601 Washington Street, is the **Sawmill Inn**, a solid meat-and-spud place. The **Magic Skillet**, good for ribs and breakfasts, is at 123 Washington, and elsewhere along Hwy-210 are all the familiar names in fast food. The usual Midwestern restaurant rules still apply: eat dinner early, or do without.

Finally, don't be put off by the unprepossessing location of the **West Side Cafe:** the fact that it's in a gas station (the big Conoco at 801 W. Washington Street, a half-mile west of the Mississippi River) doesn't detract a whit from the fact that it serves some of the best pies for miles around, in a setting akin to an old Woolworth lunch counter. From seasonal rhubarb to tangy cherry to unusual carrot, none is too sweet, and the superb flaky crusts are baked to a full golden brown—for a dollar and change, it doesn't get much better than this. They're open daily 6 AM-10 PM and serve unlimited cups of coffee for 70 cents an hour—with weekly rates available on request.

Super 8, Days Inn, Best Western, and **AmericInn** motels are all clustered on Hwy-210 heading west out of Brainerd, while there's an **Econo Lodge** and a **Holiday Inn** right on the GRR (Hwy-371) on the town's southern outskirts. The cheapest decent sleep in town is the aging **Riverview Motel**, 324 Washington Street (218/829-8871), smack-dab in the tacky commercial stretch just west of the Mississippi crossing.

For a free vacation planner and complete guide to the area's family-oriented resort accommodations—or simply the latest local weather report—contact the Brainerd Lakes Area Chamber of Commerce's automated **information system** at 800/450-2838.

Crow Wing State Park and Little Falls
South of Brainerd the GRR speeds along Hwy-371, which yearns to be an interstate for the 30-odd straight miles it takes to reach Little Falls. Exceedingly flat and awash in a sea of corn, it gives no hint of the Mississippi except at Crow Wing State Park (open year-round; $4), with trails, picnic area, and camping beside the confluence of the Mississippi and Crow Wing Rivers. Native Americans, missionaries, fur trappers, and lumberjacks made this a thriving and mostly inebriated 19th-century townsite, but the forced removal of the Indians and the shift of trade to the rail crossing upstream turned Crow Wing into a ghost town; only cellar holes and old cemeteries remain.

At Little Falls the GRR neatly misses the fast food and gas claptrap that has sprung up on the Hwy-371 bypass, proceeding instead through the heart of town, which would probably still be recognizable to Charles Lindbergh, who spent his boyhood summers here. Running along the west bank of the river, the GRR passes by the **Charles A. Lindbergh House and History Center** (daily 10 AM-5 PM, May 1-Labor Day, weekends only rest of the year; $4) a mile south of town; the house, which sits on a beautiful stretch of the Mississippi, bears the unusual distinction of having been restored with the meticulous guidance of the aviator himself. Lindy wanted the site to honor his father, a five-term U.S. congressman, as well as himself, and so it does; exhibits also illustrate the junior Lindbergh's life and achievements after his historic solo flight across the Atlantic.

South of Little Falls the GRR continues on its meandering way, but you can switch over to the uglier but much faster **US-10** or **I-94** freeways for the ride into the Twin Cities without missing anything significant.

St. Cloud and Monticello

South of Little Falls the GRR again resorts to some unpaved rural sections, wide and well graded as always. Agriculture continues to dominate the landscape, but as our route approaches industrial St. Cloud (pop. 48,812), the loss of farms to suburban housing foreshadows what is to come downriver. Much of the development retains that raw look of Monopoly houses dropped on the land; if trees are in the way, it is apparently easier to bulldoze them than build around them.

Bookended by a big paper mill at one end, and an ancient-looking prison and huge highway shopping malls at the other, St. Cloud is plainly a commercial and industrial center amid the cornfields. Our route nips across the Mississippi to pass

TWIN CITIES SURVIVAL GUIDE

THE TWIN CITIES SHARE THE MISSISSIPPI RIVER AND A DUSTY OLD RIVALRY THAT'S stoked by sports fans, high schools, and barflies giving advice to out-of-towners. In general, Minneapolis has more fashion, culture, and reflective glass, while St. Paul has a greater small-town feel, fewer tourist attractions, and more enjoyable baseball. Together, the Twin Cities are a typically sprawling American metropolis with an atypically wholesome reputation: safe, liberal-minded, welcoming of strangers, and inclined to go to bed early. Such sensibility might be boring—unless you're looking for somewhere to raise kids—but don't fret, there's enough to keep the visitor fully entertained.

The best place to stop and get a feel for the Twin Cities is at the **Minneapolis Sculpture Garden** on Lyndale Avenue along I-94 (daily 6 AM-midnight; free; 612/375-7577). Dominated by Claes Oldenburg and Coosje van Bruggen's giant *Spoonbridge and Cherry,* this is one of the city's finer urban oases, with over 40 works of art ranging from Henry Moore to Jenny Holzer. Running over the I-94 freeway, a sculptural footbridge adorned with words from a John Ashbery poem connects the sculpture garden to Loring Park and the pedestrian greenway to downtown.

Next door to the garden is the **Walker Art Center** (Tues.-Sat. 10 AM-8 PM, Sunday 11 AM-5 PM; free on Thursday, otherwise $4; 612/375-7622), rightfully renowned as one of the nation's finest contemporary art museums.

The major league Minnesota Twins (612/33-TWINS or 612/338-9467) play indoors at the often-empty Hubert Humphrey Metrodome, off I-35W at the 3rd Street exit. The unaffiliated, independent, and generally anarchic **St. Paul Saints** play outdoors at usually sold-out Midway Stadium, 1771 Energy Park Drive (651/644-6659), north of I-94 at the Snelling Avenue exit.

Sauk Rapids, around whose hydropower the city grew; a small city park offers a closer view. Almost any view of the river from Sauk Rapids south to the Twin Cities will include something industrial, so it should come as no surprise that the Mississippi downstream from St. Cloud is contaminated by toxic metals and carcinogens like mercury, cadmium, lead, zinc, and polychlorinated biphenyls (PCBs). More surprising is the public disregard for these findings; despite muted cautionary pronouncements, people routinely fish for their dinners from downstream waters, and neither the EPA nor local governments seem willing to risk publicizing the real dangers with any sort of widespread ban.

Across the Mississippi from Monticello, 2.5 miles downstream from Elk River off US-10, the Oliver H. Kelley Farm preserves the 40 acres where the Patrons of Husbandry, an agricultural education and lobbying organization better known as **"The Grange,"** was founded in 1867.

The GRR follows 9th Avenue through St. Cloud before hitching along divided

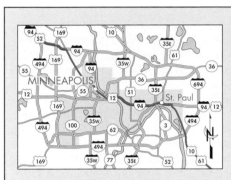

Practicalities

The Twin Cities are on opposite sides of the Mississippi River, at the crossing of the I-35 and I-94 freeways. Located seven miles south of downtown, the **Minneapolis-St. Paul International Airport** is served by 10 major airlines, with Northwest Airlines exercising the home field advantage. City buses, limousines, taxis (approx. $25 to either downtown Minneapolis or St. Paul), and all the usual car rentals are available from the terminal.

Drivers here, like all Minnesotans, are friendly and helpful, and the city grids are easy enough to navigate by car, although street **parking** becomes more scarce as you approach the downtown areas. Check meter hours, too—oddly enough, some run until midnight. There are many parking garages ("ramps"), but do compare as rates vary considerably.

If you're traveling on an expense account, downtown Minneapolis has a dozen hotels catering just to you. Otherwise, look to the interstate beltways for the budget chains, particularly I-494 between the airport and Bloomington's 100-acre Mall of America, the nation's largest. In downtown Minneapolis, the **Regency Plaza Best Western,** 41 N. 10th Street (612/339-9311 or 800/423-4100), is one of the least expensive of the downtown hotels. Free parking, too; doubles $66-72. In contrast, the **Hyatt Regency,** 1300 Nicollett Mall (612/370-1234 or 800/228-9000), offers luxury with good city views and possibly the city's best steakhouse on the premises—everything you'd expect from the highest-priced hotel in town, doubles here range $95-195. In St. Paul, the **Saint Paul Hotel,** 350 Market Street (651/292-9292 or 800/292-9292), across from the beautiful **Ordway Music Theatre,** is a 1910 gem, built for the city's rail and mill tycoons, doubles here range $105-160.

(continues on next page)

St. Cloud was also home to the early automobile manufacturer, PAN Motor Company, which produced touring cars for a few years after WW I. four-lane Hwy-75 at the city's southern perimeter, whizzing past acres of giant malls until crossing paths with our first interstate, I-94. Turning quickly away from the high-speed traffic, the GRR picks up a leisurely rural route again. While the interstate cuts a straight swath across the landscape, the GRR rolls through undulating farm-covered hills over which swallows perform their afternoon aerobatics, scooping insects out of the air.

Cream of Wheat is one of the many cereals made in Minneapolis.

In Minneapolis, the traditional dominance of meaty northern and eastern European cuisine is being challenged by a bumper crop of Vietnamese places (there's a large ethnic Hmong population here), while numerous local coffeehouses prove the West Coast doesn't have a monopoly on either good cappuccino or cool atmosphere. The latter abounds at **Buca,** 15 South 12th Street, a cozy basement labyrinth where the decor is tongue-in-cheek—garlic braids, pyramids of olive oil cans, a zillion photos of everyone from grinning JFK to Sophia Loren in her underwear—but the menu is serious Southern Italian comfort food. **Nye's Polonaise Room,** just over the bridge from downtown at 112 East Hennepin Avenue, is a dimly lit, plush-boothed, 1950s power broker restaurant that could have witnessed the birth of the three-martini lunch. It's surf and turf solid, with sing-along piano entertainment nightly. For a touch of Ukraine, **Kramarczuk's Sausage** 215 East Hennepin Avenue, two blocks east of the river, has fat wursts, borscht, *varenyky, nalesnyky,* and *holubets* (aka dumplings, crepes, and cabbage rolls), as well as other Eastern European market food served cafeteria style beneath coffered tin ceilings and the gaze of giant Miss Liberty holding aloft her lamp.

In St. Paul, Lowertown is the newly gentrified dining area, amid historic old warehouses on the single-digit streets by the river. The best road food place is the 24-hour **Mickey's Dining Car,** right downtown at 36 7th Street opposite the bus station. Haute cuisine it ain't, and half the regulars treat it as a social service agency, but this 1937 O'Mahony is a fine example of what has become an endangered species since the proliferation of double arches. The onion rings and blueberry pancakes are good, but pass on the food-service pies. Try the mulligan stew, if you dare.

The **Greater Minneapolis Convention and Visitors Association,** 40 South 7th Street (612/661-4700), can provide more information on hotels, restaurants, and attractions. The *Minneapolis Star Tribune,* the largest-circulation daily newspaper, provides a decent roster of Twin Cities dining and entertainment suggestions in its Friday and Sunday editions. *City Pages,* one of two free weeklies found in cafes and newsboxes all over, offers by far the most intriguing and complete club, movie, museum, and restaurant listings.

When members of Lt. Zebulon Pike's 1804-05 expedition up the Mississippi first laid eyes on this land, it was covered in dense forest—try to imagine *that* as you drive the 30 miles to our fourth junction with I-94, Monticello. With the Twin Cities beltway only 25 miles away, this is a good opportunity to hop over to the interstate and simply make a beeline into or around Minneapolis and St. Paul, before the sudden sprouting of housing subdivisions and smokestack industries south of Monticello make the thought of virgin forest even more wildly improbable.

The Burma-Vita Company, based just west of Minneapolis, began erecting advertising signs along Hwy-61 near Red Wing and Hwy-65 near Albert Lea back in 1925. Over the next 38 years these signs and their witty rhymes appeared in nearly every state in the U.S. and made **Burma-Shave** one of the most recognized brand names in American business.

Driving the Twin Cities

Interstate-94 runs right through the heart of the Twin Cities, linking up with the GRR north of Minneapolis and east of St. Paul. For better or worse, this is pretty much the closest you'll get to a riverside highway, so if you were hoping to follow the river through town (by car, at least) you're out of luck.

On the Minnesota side of the Mississippi River, US-61 runs as a very fast and fairly scenic freeway, four-lane almost all the way south to La Crosse, Wisconsin.

ACROSS SOUTHWESTERN WISCONSIN

On an island near Red Wing, Minnesota, the **Prairie Island Nuclear Power Plant** is the northernmost of a half-dozen nuclear generating stations located along the Mississippi.

Heading out of St. Paul along the industrialized Mississippi riverbanks, the GRR crosses the St. Croix River at Prescott, Wisconsin, and wends south on Hwy-35 across a portion of the glacial plain whose rolling hills, sown in corn, account for an important part of the nation's breadbasket. The fertile soil here, as throughout the Midwestern grain belt, is a product of *drift:* pulverized soil left by mile-thick ice sheets scouring the ancient sediments of an inland sea for about two million years. Farther south, however, the GRR enters a very different landscape,

Between Minneapolis and La Crosse, Winona State University's **KQAL 89.5 FM** plays an excellent range of commercial-free pop music, including the Meat Puppets and early Hüsker Dü.

known as the **Driftless Region,** an area of limestone bluffs and rocky uplands bypassed by all that rototilling glaciation. Stretching south into Illinois, and covering an area four times the size of Connecticut, the Driftless Region affords dramatic views, wildlife habitat, and a setting for one of the more painful episodes in Native American history: the devastating **Black Hawk War.**

The GRR follows two-lane Hwy-35 from Prescott south for nearly 100 miles, staying within closer view of the Mississippi for longer stretches than almost anywhere else on the route. The Corps of Engineers is a regular presence on the river

from here south to the Gulf, most visibly with their locks and dams, but also with their dredges. It may not look shallow, but up here along Wisconsin's "west coast" the Mississippi doesn't naturally have the minimum nine-foot depth required by the "tows," those giant rafts of barges you'll see being pushed along the river.

Hwy-35: Main Street USA

At **Maiden Rock**, about 50 miles southeast of St. Paul, Hwy-35 enters the heart of the **Driftless Region**, picking its way between steep bluffs and the wide Mississippi. Small towns, populations numbering only in the hundreds, cling to the margin, competing for the distinction of having the longest Main Street in the nation, if not the world; for some of these long hamlets the GRR is nearly the *only* street. These towns wear their age well, too busy with fishing or loading up barges to make themselves pretty for tourists, or to tear down every old building that no longer seems useful. Most of these towns have at least a gas station, open late, and a roadhouse with Old Style or Pabst neon in the windows, open even later. Along with the riverside scenery, most also have a single tourist attraction: Amish crafts in **Stockholm** and a cheese factory in **Nelson**. Seven-mile-long **Alma** has an observation platform and small cafe over Lock and Dam No. 4, where you can watch river traffic "lock through," and in **Pepin**, an hour north of La Crosse, midway between Maiden Rock and Alma, there's a replica of Laura "Little House on the Prairie" Ingalls Wilder's log cabin home, a museum dedicated to her, and one of the region's best restaurants: the **Harbor View Cafe**, near the marina (surprise, surprise).

The river itself meanders little here, or what meanders used to exist have been flooded out by the staircase of Corps lakes and dams; instead of oxbows there are islands and sloughs, swampy backwater inlets and channels. As the valley widens —a product of the river's ancient restlessness—our narrow roller-coaster ride past tiny hamlets and scenic waysides (rest stops) begins to level out, but the bluffs continue to dominate the horizon on both sides of the Mississippi.

Trempealeau

At the sleepy hamlet of Trempealeau (pop. 1,039), the GRR would have you zigzag right through town, but detour a block down toward the river's edge to find the **Historic Trempealeau Hotel, Restaurant & Saloon** (608/534-6898), sole survivor of an 1888 downtown fire—maybe that's why the whole joint is smoke-free. The hotel dining room offers a surprisingly eclectic menu, from steak and seafood to Tex-Mex and vegetarian dishes; just head for the "Delicious Food" neon sign. The hotel also sponsors an excellent annual outdoor music series beginning with a Reggae Sunsplash the second weekend of May and featuring bands you've heard of throughout the summer (Steppenwolf and Asleep at the Wheel have appeared more than a few times). They rent canoes and bicycles to hardy souls desiring to try either the **Long Lake Canoe Trail** or the 100-mile network of **paved bikeways** that passes through town. Finally, the

hotel does rent rooms, too; all 12 share bathrooms and cost just $27 a night.

Shortly south of Trempealeau the GRR crosses US-53. Consider taking this interstate-wannabe into La Crosse to avoid the uninteresting 12 miles of stop-and-go traffic through Holman and Onalaska, La Crosse's northern abutters.

La Crosse

La Crosse (pop. 51,135) was named by fur traders who witnessed local Winnebago Indians playing a game strikingly similar to French lacrosse. It's an attractive place, but you wouldn't know that coming into town—mile after mile of food-gas-lodging establishments compete for attention. Successfully run the gauntlet and your reward will be finding the century-old downtown, the tidy residential neighborhoods, and the leafy University of Wisconsin-La Crosse campus.

Two miles east of downtown at the end of Main Street, **Grandad Bluff**, a lofty 590 feet over the city, gives a grand view of the Mississippi and the two states along its opposite shore. The view is a balm to any aesthete jangled by the commercial neon carpet that welcomes travelers, too, for La Crosse actually looks rather attractive from above. Listen closely and you might hear the University of Wisconsin marching band practicing below.

La Crosse-based Heileman is widely recognized around the upper Midwest for its Old Style brand beer. The **G. Heileman Brewery**, right on the GRR at 1111 S. 3rd Street (608/782-BEER or 608/782-2337; or 800/433-BEER or 800/433-2337), has

giant fermentation tanks painted to look like the world's largest six-pack. Free brewery tours are available daily 10 AM-3 PM, and a drinking fountain and tap in the parking lot serve up fresh cold water straight from the source, 600 feet below the tarmac.

Slap *Spartacus* on the theater marquee and the heart of downtown could easily be mistaken for a giant Eisenhower-era time capsule. Within this classic commercial center a couple of coffeehouses have sprung up. **Brew Note**, at 327 Jay Street next to Deaf Ear Records, may be a little too polished, but it does have the obligatory poetry nights, good healthful food, and is open late.

Diners seeking less dainty fare should take the big blue Cass Street bridge (US-61) over the Mississippi to Dr. J's Auto Clinic, just across the state line in La Crescent, Minnesota. Behind the good doctor (and almost invisible from the highway) sits **Sabatino's 24-Hour Diner**, home of carbohydrates prepared to order, and well deserving of its reputation for tasty Frisbee-sized omelets. Equally heart-stopping omelettes, plus melt-in-your-mouth doughnuts, are on the menu at **Mr. D's**, at State and West streets, and for good ol' drive-in burgers, root beers and milk shakes, nothing beats **Rudy's**, northeast of downtown at 10th and La Crosse streets, where roller-skating car-hops feed you 10 AM-10 PM daily, March-Oct.

Chat with anyone who spends time on the river from La Crosse south and you'll quickly learn about zebra mussels, an invasive species of freshwater clam from Europe that is becoming the kudzu of the Mississippi, carpeting boat hulls, intake pipes, native clams, and even live crawfish.

The Pearl, a polished-to-perfection confectionery at 207 Pearl Street, offers more adult indulgences like fluorescent Blue Moon ice cream while the Andrews Sisters harmonize in the background. If a double scoop of cookie dough isn't your idea of lunch then try something wholesome, fresh, and filling from the deli of the **People's Food Coop**, on 5th Avenue between Cass and King. Wash it down afterward with one of the 200 bottled beers or 10 microbrews on draught at the **Bodega Brew Pub**, at 122 S. 4th Streets, right downtown.

For accommodations, look to exits 2, 3, and 4 off I-90 for the budget national chains. **Best Western, Holiday Inn, Radisson Hotel**, and **Courtyards By Marriott** are also scattered around town, while local motels line South Avenue (the GRR, sometimes aka Mormon Coulee Road), such as the ranch-style **Redwood Motel**, 3305 South Avenue (608/788-0900).

For a complete lodging and attractions guide, with map, call the La Crosse Area Convention and Visitors Bureau (608/782-2366 or 800/658-9424) or visit their **information center** in leafy green Riverside Park, where a 25-ton, 25-foot-tall statue of Hiawatha greets river traffic with arms crossed and a politically incorrect plaque reading "Me Welcome You to Visitor Center."

Detour: Spring Green
Frank Lloyd Wright's famous country house and studio, **Taliesin** (tally-ESS-en), is in Spring Green, 70 miles east of Prairie du Chien via Hwy-60. Fully guided tours

BLACK HAWK WAR

Black Hawk was a leader of the Sac and Mesquakie Indians in northern Illinois during the feverish era of westward expansion into the newly opened Louisiana Purchase. As an ally of the British in the War of 1812, Black Hawk had done his best to force American settlers off the western frontier. By the time war hero Andrew Jackson rode his Indian-fighter reputation into the White House 16 years later, Black Hawk had been reduced to vain protests against the swindling and starvation of his tribes, which had been forced to leave their rich Illinois cornfields for unfamiliar Iowa plains. Under Jackson, Native American genocide became a national obsession; amid such blind inhumanity an act as simple as searching for some empty land back in Illinois on which to plant corn became an "invasion" and act of war.

It was springtime on the upper Mississippi, in 1832, and while Sac-Mesquakie women and children tried to sow a crop, newspapers demanded the extermination of every Indian in the territory. Jackson sent in the army to round up the Sac-Mesquakie, but they botched the job: when Black Hawk tried to surrender he was fired upon; when he fought back, they ran. The war was on, and for the next three months Black Hawk's people were pushed north. Indians who surrendered were killed. Some of the Sac-Mesquakie followed Chief Keokuk, who was promised all that had once been promised to Black Hawk; Keokuk took the promises and ended up on a reservation in Iowa. The war ended at the Battle of Bad Ax, near present-day **Victory**, on August 1, 1832, but it wasn't a battle so much as a butchering. Caught by a gunboat and the army as they tried to cross the Mississippi, Black Hawk and his men came forward under a white flag. When the Indians identified themselves, the gunboat promptly opened fire. For the next eight hours the volunteer militias used axes, guns, cannon, and clubs to cut down the Indian warriors while women and children who succeeded in swimming the river were slaughtered on the other side. By various accounts some 90% of Black Hawk's people were killed. The Mississippi, survivors said, ran red with their blood. Black Hawk himself, captured and imprisoned, was paraded around the U.S. in chains; after he died his skeleton was displayed in the governor's mansion in Iowa, like a trophy.

If there is any doubt about the esteem 19th-century Americans had for Indian fighters, consider that among the officers sent against Black Hawk were these men: William Henry Harrison, Zachary Taylor, Abraham Lincoln, and Jefferson Davis.

of the private residence and architecture school are offered daily May-Oct.; ticket prices range $7-35, depending on what's included in the tour (call 608/588-7900 for info and reservations). Spring Green is also home to the state's biggest tourist trap, the incredible **House on the Rock** (daily 9 AM-dusk; $14; 608/935-3639) with its "World's Largest" merry-go-round, kitschy collections of everything from dolls to replicas of the Crown Jewels, and the eponymous house, standing atop a 450-foot-high rock.

Prairie du Chien

For most of the nearly 60 miles between La Crosse and Prairie du Chien, the GRR (Hwy-35) is again confined to the margin between the tall gray and yellow bluffs and the impressively wide, lake-like Mississippi. At times the roadway is so narrow that the few houses have to climb three stories up the irregular wooded slopes, while the rail bed on your right is suspended over the water on viaducts. About halfway along there's a maze of small islands around the mouth of the Bad Ax River, with the occasional blue heron poised like a Giacometti sculpture in algae-covered sloughs. Dotting the curves alongside the road are a series of historical markers old enough to be artifacts themselves; most are related to the **Black Hawk War.**

If it's summertime and you want an up-close look at the Mississippi, continue south with the GRR on the Wisconsin side about 30 miles to **Cassville,** a historic frontier town that holds one of the river's few surviving **car ferries** (daily 9 AM-9 PM, Memorial Day-Labor Day, weekends only in May and October; $5 per car; 608/725-5180 for 24-hour information).

Named by early 19th-century French voyageurs for the abundant native prairie dogs, Prairie du Chien (pronounced duh-SHEEN) could be re-christened Prairie du Kwik-Stop or Prairie du Pabst by the modern traveler cruising through downtown's West Blackhawk Avenue. The town's main attraction is the posh **Villa Louis** (daily 9 AM-5 PM, May-Oct.; $5), which embodies the wealth that could be made in the fur trade back when every European dandy's head sported beaver-pelt hats. Built by the state's first millionaire, the house boasts one of the finest collections of domestic Victoriana in the country; signs point you to it from all over town.

ACROSS NORTHEASTERN IOWA

In its 140-mile course across Iowa, the GRR passes swiftly but unmistakably across the cultural and geographic North-South Divide. Separated by the Mississippi River from the rough topography of Wisconsin's Driftless Region, the southeastern corner of Iowa offers instead a taste of the state's trademark rolling plains covered with corn and soybeans. Menus are different, too: cattle here are raised for meat instead of milk, and Iowa is a leading producer of hogs (one of the state lottery games is called "Bring Home the Bacon," while radio ads encourage you to "eat more pork—the other white meat"). So say good-bye to walleye and hello to BBQ. Twangy country music, too, is no longer a novelty on the FM radio dial, and posters advertising local rodeos appear in store windows.

South of Prairie du Chien, across from McGregor, Iowa, is the spot where **Louis Joliet** and his Jesuit companion **Jacques Marquette** caught their first sight of the Mississippi after coming down the Wisconsin River in 1673 while searching for a route to the Orient.

Running along the western bank of the Mississippi, our route tends to the tops of the bluffs, too, rather than to their base, which means the river is often spied from a distance and seems unrelated to the rolling landscape; fortunately it continues to guide the curves of the road. Other than Dubuque, our route passes through towns so far from the beaten path they don't even rate a fast-food strip or Wal-Mart—appreciate this while it lasts.

McGregor and Effigy Mounds

Immediately across the pair of long bridges from Prairie du Chien, near the foot of the "original" Pike's Peak—Zebulon Pike came up the Mississippi before he went out to Colorado—McGregor is a river town whose enticing old saloons may tempt you to stop and watch boat traffic, if you manage to turn a blind eye to the garish Pink Elephant advertising the **Miss Marquette Riverboat Casino** complex. North of McGregor, right along the riverbank, the **Effigy Mounds National Monument** (daily 8 AM-5 PM; $2) preserves 1,500 acres of burial mounds shaped like birds and animals, traces of a native culture that lived along the Mississippi around 500 B.C.

McGregor was the hometown of the five children who grew up to found the **Ringling Brothers** circus.

The slogan of McGregor's tourism promotion effort is "Intriguing Stores on Historic Shores."

Guttenberg

Atop the bluffs, tidy frame farmhouses dot the landscape, with white barns, silos, and farmland aroma accompanying US-18 and US-52 as they loop inland south toward Guttenberg (pop. 2,300), another postcard-pretty old river town whose downtown lines the Mississippi. In fact, it's one of the few Mississippi riverfronts where the river itself is not hidden away behind levees, and a long green riverside park makes the downtown area a particularly pleasant place to stroll.

Forty-six miles west of McGregor is the town of Spillville, where **Antonin Dvorak** completed his symphony, *From the New World,* in 1893. The Main Street house where he stayed now leads a double life: displays on Dvorak are upstairs, while downstairs is an incredible show of carved wooden clocks. For details, phone 319/562-3569.

Guttenberg is indeed named in honor of Johannes Gutenberg, 15th-century inventor of printing from moveable type. Local legend has it that an official of French descent purposely added the extra "t" after German residents won a vote to change the town's name from the original Prairie la Porte. Germanic surnames still predominate the local phone book, and the two main streets, which run perpendicular to the Mississippi, are named Schiller and Goethe.

On the north side of town, near the Phillip's 66 station and reliable **Rausch's Cafe**, the GRR takes another look at the prairie's geological underpinnings as it cuts down to the river's edge. For a quick marine biology lesson, the **Upper Mississippi Fisheries Aquarium** at Lock and Dam No. 10 downtown displays live specimens of most of the river's fish species and includes a number of invertebrates (daily 8 AM-9 PM, May-Sept.; free; 319/252-1156).

You can take the Cassville ferry across the Mississippi some 10 well-signed miles southeast of Guttenberg, or stay in Iowa and cruise through the Germanic eyeblink towns on the rolling uplands between Guttenberg and Dubuque. There are great views to be had, especially in the first few miles south of Guttenberg; midway along, tiny **Balltown** in particular is worth a stop to sample the food and decor at **Breitbach's** (319/552-2220), a bar and restaurant that's so old President Millard Fillmore issued the permit allowing it to open.

Dubuque marks the junction of the Great River Road and our cross-country route US-20: The Oregon Trail, which is covered in full detail beginning on page 446.

Dubuque

After miles of Iowa prairie and river towns the GRR rolls into Dubuque (pop. 57,546), named for the 18th-century French voyageur, Julien Dubuque, who unsuccessfully mined for lead on land acquired from the Spanish. Finding lead wasn't the problem— Indians had dug lead by hand as early as 1680 for trade with the English— but getting it to market was. After the steamboat's invention and forced removal of native tribes in the late 1820s, mineral wealth became a major catalyst to settlement of the tri-state area around Dubuque, as town names like Potosi, Mineral Point, New Diggings, and Lead Mine attest. During the Civil War, just five counties around here supplied all the lead for the entire Union war effort.

The **Iowa Welcome Center** (800/79-VISIT or 800/798-4748), down on the waterfront, stands next to Dubuque's newest source of wealth, the **Casino Belle**, another of the long parade of riverboat casinos found all the way down to the Gulf of Mexico. On the inland side of the compact downtown, a good view of the city and the Mississippi valley can be had at the top of the **Fenelon Place Elevator**, a small funicular cable car that proudly holds the title of "world's steepest, shortest scenic railway" (daily 8 AM-10 PM, April-Nov.; 75 cents one-way). If a tall lanky fellow is at the controls of the 15-hp motor up in the head house, and you're a baseball fan, you might have fun trying to stump him with questions about the Minnesota Twins, his favorite team. He purports to know their starting lineups for every year back to 1961.

Not able to wholly give in to sin, Iowa initially required its riverboat casinos to be "low stakes," meaning that players were restricted to $200 per excursion aboard the boat. Once neighboring Illinois floated its own no-limit game boats, Iowa had to amend its law to keep the golden goose from roosting somewhere else.

Dubuque is a very meat-and-potatoes place when it comes to food, and plan to dine early to catch restaurants before they close. Basic coffee shop breakfasts, lunches, and dinners are on the menu at **Dottie's Cafe**, downtown at 5th and Central, while the landmark **Bridge** steakhouse (319/557-7280), on Main Street at the foot of the US-20 bridge (look for the neon "Good Food" sign), is a step or two up in price and quality. Near the Fenelon Place elevator, **Shot Tower Pizza** has an upstairs deck and beer by the pitcher. For entertainment, check out Main Street bars like **Loie and Admiral's High Hat Lounge**, which has live music most nights.

The classic old hotel in town is the **Julien Inn**, 200 Main Street (319/556-4200 or 800/798-7098), providing rooms at $30-50, while the **Redstone Inn**, 504 Bluff Street (319/582-1894), offers comfortable B&B rooms in a stately downtown mansion. The usual chain motels line US-20 west of the river.

South of Dubuque, the GRR follows US-52 back up the bluffs past Julien Dubuque's original lead workings and across 45 miles of upland farms and wooded bottoms until the next Mississippi crossing at Sabula.

The ball field created for the movie *Field of Dreams* has become a minor tourist mecca for rural **Dyersville,** 35 miles due west of Dubuque via US-20. For details, see page 568.

St. Donatus

Fifteen undulating agricultural miles south of Dubuque, the tiny hamlet of St. Donatus is widely advertised as a historic and picturesque Luxembourg village, but the only historic or picturesque feature is the handsome masonry of the Gehlen House and barn, opposite the Kalmes general store and restaurant. Upon much closer inspection (or guidance from the tourist informants in the Gehlen House) you could find some 80 other limestone structures built by immigrant Luxembourg masons before the middle 1800s, but their impressive handiwork is invisible to all but the most practiced eye, covered up by protective stucco. Most of the buildings are scattered around the countryside, too, but a few are found west of the Gehlen House; follow the signed turn to Lower Town.

A highly recommended 15-mile side trip is to **Galena,** southeast of Dubuque via US-20. Spawned by the early 19th-century lead rush, Galena was the early social and cultural capital of the Upper Mississippi, and is now one of the best preserved historic towns in the country. For more, see pages 569-571.

Other eye-catching structures are the Catholic church and **Pieta Chapel** atop the adjacent Calvary Hill; if you wish to make a pilgrimage up the Way of the Cross, start behind the church burial ground, east of the Kalmes Store. The plain brick construction of the 14 stations belies the fact that this is the oldest outdoor Calvary in the United States. At the top of the hill is an 1885 reproduction of the du Bildchen chapel in Luxembourg, left unlocked for the devout. Appropriately, the hill is home to a flock of sheep awaiting the return of their shepherd; they do keep the brush down, but their habits mean you should be shod in something other than Birkenstocks or polished wingtips when making the trek up to the chapel. Nice view from the top—the other set of spires across the valley belongs to the German Lutheran St. John's Church.

Sabula takes its name from the Latin *sabulum,* meaning "sand."

Bellevue and Sabula

The GRR (US-52) returns to the Mississippi valley at Bellevue, with its lengthy Main Street and Riverfront Park beside Lock and Dam No. 12, and stays in sparsely populated wooded lowlands until it reaches the junction of US-67, marked by the first stop sign south of Dubuque. The **Kalmes Restaurant and Tavern**, a focal point of the community since 1850, is so packed on weekend evenings you'll wonder if they're giving away food: but no, Iowans are just friendly and sociable as a rule. Belly up to the bar and see for yourself.

From the end of November to the beginning of March, the American bald eagle nests along the middle and upper Mississippi. The best place to catch sight of one is below any of the dams, where turbulence keeps the river from icing over and fish injured or stunned by the dams make easy prey for the great bird.

Follow US-52 southeast into Sabula, an island of a town created by the Corps of Engineers when the pool above Lock and Dam No. 13, 16 miles downstream, flooded out the surrounding plains. Sabula's encompassing levees provide fine wetlands birdwatching. From Sabula, cross the narrow causeways and Mississippi bridge into Illinois to be guided by the GRR's familiar pilot's wheel down to the Quad Cities.

ACROSS ILLINOIS, IOWA, AND MISSOURI

Our route along the middle Mississippi starts in northwestern Illinois, just below the Driftless Region, and proceeds through sandy floodplain and fertile prairie, nipping back and forth across the ever-locked and dammed Mississippi between Illinois, southern Iowa and the generally more developed Missouri uplands. Here, small towns bypassed by much of the 20th century are more likely to be forlorn than quaint, a prelude to those southern states in which local ordinances appear to require the public display of rusty appliances. With a few exceptions— such as the historic Mormon town of Nauvoo or Mark Twain's hometown of Hannibal— our route now mostly runs through communities whose best years may have passed. This stretch of the GRR also includes one of the most dramatic sections of the entire route: the 25 miles around Grafton, Illinois, at the northern doorstep of St. Louis.

South of St. Louis, I-55 is the recommended route, as it bypasses a long string of auto dealerships, appliance stores, shopping centers, and other prefab conveniences lining old US-61. Passing through the old river town of Sainte Genevieve, the GRR crosses the Mississippi once again, ambling back to the corn, soybeans, and cicadas of Southern Illinois. Accents, "Bar-B-Q" signs, and Baptist churches leave no doubt that our route has entered the South; in summer the heat and humidity confirm this with a vengeance. Fortunately, after leaving the "American Bottom" the GRR skirts the edge of the Shawnee National Forest, whose shade brings up to 25° relief from the temperatures along the roadside fields on a sunny July day. Occasional levees, raised roadbeds, and brackish seasonal ponds are reminders that the mile-wide Mississippi is only temporarily out of sight of the GRR, which finally crosses into Kentucky beside the giant turbid confluence of the Mississippi and Ohio Rivers at Cairo.

Savanna

Across the Mississippi from Iowa, Savanna, Illinois, is an unlovely old railroad town that has grown into an unlovely antiques center, offering three antique mini-malls along the main drag. Savanna maintains a few pretty Victorian mansions up on the heights, but for a truly attractive vista take a detour in

---

The Illinois Bed & Breakfast Association offers a free guide to selected B&Bs around the state; request one directly from the IBBA at P.O. Box 295, Mossville, IL 61552.

Hanover, Illinois, 20 miles north of Savanna on Hwy-84, is home to **Whistling Wings,** the world's largest mallard duck hatchery (Mon.-Fri. 9 AM-5 PM, Saturday 9 AM-noon; free; 815/591-3512). Over 200,000 mallards are raised annually for sale to refuges, restaurants, researchers, and individuals whose gardens lack that certain quack.

Thomson, 20 miles south of Savanna on Hwy-84, is the self-proclaimed **Watermelon Capital of the World,** and celebrates its "Melon Days" festival every Labor Day weekend. Country music, carnival rides, watermelon-eating contests, and free watermelon are the traditional highlights.

The Illinois side of Lock and Dam No. 13, accessible from the GRR just north of Fulton, is considered one of the best spots for bald eagle sightings

the opposite direction from Savanna, *north* from the end of the Iowa bridge to nearby **Mississippi Palisades State Park**, with its great eroded bluffs and fine river views.

Between Savanna and the interstate beltway around the Quad Cities are nearly 50 flat miles of river valley, dotted with small historic river and railroad towns vandalized by new commercial and residential construction. Agriculture is conspicuous, too, and the sandy soils between Savanna and Thomson are particularly known for their melon crops. While the Mississippi for the most part stays invisible from the GRR, the industry on its banks is clearly evident, especially at night. River access is at hand via a handful of **recreation areas** in the **Upper Mississippi National Fish and Wildlife Refuge**.

Le Claire, Iowa

On the northeastern edge of the Quad Cities, just off the I-80 freeway, lies the little town of Le Claire, famous once for its river pilots but now best remembered as William F. "Buffalo Bill" Cody's home. The **Buffalo Bill Museum**, on the waterfront, is dedicated to Cody's life (daily 9 AM-5 PM, May 15-Oct. 15, weekends only the rest of the year; $1). More interesting are the paddle wheelers that tie up alongside the small, gun-filled museum, one of which, the *Julia Belle Swain,* offers overnight cruises up to Galena, Illinois (800/331-1467 for info and reservations). **The Faithful Pilot** at 117 N. Cody Road (319/289-4156), on Le Claire's main street (US-67), is one of the best restaurants in the entire Quad City region, with creative, high-quality cuisine, a good wine list, and fine microbrews, all at prices you'd expect. The small bar at the back has views of the river, and the friendliest bartender along its banks.

The welcome sign for Le Claire alludes to a "famous green tree," a sight familiar in Mark Twain's day, but now long gone. The tree was the gathering point for the specialized "rapids pilots" who would guide boats through the 14-mile-long Moline Rapids that began below Le Claire.

The names Black Hawk, Marquette, and Joliet continue to crop up, as this stretch of the Mississippi was their prime stomping grounds. South of the Quad Cities you'll see more of Abraham Lincoln, too, as the GRR shares the road with Illinois's Lincoln Heritage Trail.

The Quad Cities

Straddling the Mississippi at its confluence with the Rock River, the Quad Cities—Moline, Rock Island, Davenport, and Bettendorf —encompass an enormous sprawl of some 400,000 residents on what was once the home of the Sac-Mesquakie Indian nations, Saukenuk. While much of the cityscape is dominated by heavy industry, particularly on the Iowa side, points of interest are sprinkled throughout. Like a parking lot with flowers growing up through the cracks, look closely and you'll find a vital arts community, a gay/lesbian community, and even some excellent restaurants that break the typical Midwestern meat-and-potato mold.

If there's a must-see stop in the Quad Cities, it's the headquarters of tractor manufacturers **Deere & Company**, located on a rural stretch of John Deere Road (Hwy-5) in southeast Moline. Architect Eero Saarinen's award-winning building fits well amid spacious lakes and landscaping, but the highlight is the product display floor's giant three-dimensional historical collage, **Reflections of an Era**, by Santa Fe artist Alexander Girard. Check out a new John Deere tractor, too; the display floor is open daily 9 AM-5:30 PM.

Along the river at the heart of the Quad Cities, adjacent to downtown Rock Island, is the former namesake of that city, now called Arsenal Island for the U.S. Army facility based there. Despite the look of the gatehouse at the southern entrance, the island is open to the public; besides an arsenal museum and Civil War cemeteries, there's a very good **Corps of Engineers visitor center** (daily 9 AM-9 PM in summer, till 5 PM rest of the year; free) on the island right next to Lock and Dam No. 15, where the operation of the locks can be seen from a penny-pitch away.

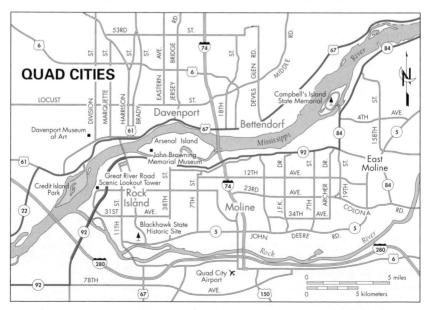

The first railroad bridge over the Mississippi linked Rock Island and Davenport in 1856. The railroad was promptly sued by a steamboat company whose craft was mortally attracted to the bridge piers. The plaintiffs argued that bridges violated their navigation rights; the defense lawyer's elegantly simple—and successful—rebuttal was to claim that a person has as much right to cross a river as to travel upon it. That lawyer was Abraham Lincoln. Today the railroad crosses the river on the upper deck of the old iron Government Bridge, which swings open for the tows entering the locks; cars crossing between Rock Island and Davenport can ride the humming lower deck for free or take the modern concrete highway span below the dam for a 50-cent toll.

Davenport celebrates the music legacy of native son and cornetist **Leon Beiderbecke** with the annual Bix Beiderbecke Memorial Jazz Festival, held at the end of July. A statue of Bix stands along the river, next to wonderful old (circa 1930) **John O'Donnell Stadium,** where the minor league Quad Cities River Bandits (tickets $3-6; 319/324-2032) play their home games.

The **Davenport Museum of Art,** 1737 W. 12th Street (open Tues.-Sun. till 4:30 PM; free, but donation suggested), has a good regional collection featuring Thomas Hart Benton and Grant Wood, along with parodies of Wood's most famous painting, *American Gothic.*

Quad Cities Practicalities

The average Quad City restaurant features steaks, burgers, fried catfish, and spaghetti (*not* pasta), or onion rings and chili dogs. If these selections tickle your palate, you'll have a surfeit of choices. Otherwise, except for Bettendorf, the downtown of each of the Quad Cities has a pocket of worthwhile restaurants and, yes, even coffeehouses.

The area code for Davenport, Iowa is 319, while that for Moline, Illinois is 309. Confusing, huh?

In downtown Davenport, for example, look to Harrison and Brady Avenues within the first few blocks of both the casino landing and convention center to find several eateries, including **Theo's Java Hut** (221 Brady), the **Smile Coffeehouse** (330 N. Harrison), or, for more substantial fare, the **Thai House Restaurant,** at 332 N. Harrison Avenue.

Downtown Moline is but a half-dozen blocks along 5th Avenue between I-74 and 14th Street; among its offerings are **Le Mekong** (1606 5th Avenue), the **Caffé Piccalo** at 421 14th Street, and for replenishing your backseat car buffet, **Heritage Natural Foods** up at 1317 6th Avenue near 14th Street. Also in downtown Moline is the extraordinary **Lagomarcino's** (1422 5th Avenue), a soda fountain that still uses those conical paper cups in solid metal holders and serves drinks like "phosphates" in a setting virtually unchanged since it opened in 1908. Order a strawberry shake here and the flavor will come from scoops of real strawberries ladled over freshly made vanilla ice cream.

Rock Island's old downtown, 2nd Avenue, has experienced something of a revival with

THAT DIRTY WATER

If you're wondering how a major industrial corridor can coexist with critical wildlife habitat, the answer is that it can't, though most people are unaware of how serious the conflict is. The return of the bald eagle from the brink of extinction is undeniably good news; so is the enormous reductions in raw sewage and mercury releases over the last 20 years. But nearly 300 million pounds of toxic chemicals are still dumped into the Mississippi every year, and over a billion gallons of wastewater from cities and factories are discharged into the river *daily*.

Defenders of the status quo argue that the river does a fine job of dilution, as shown by how infrequently water quality standards are compromised. This conveniently ignores the fact that many toxins are bioaccumulated: whether a mother eats a single heavily contaminated fish during pregnancy or several years' worth of slightly contaminated fish prior to conceiving, the damage to the fetus can be the same. Pollutants also are very persistent, settling into river sediments only to be re-released through dredging or boat traffic. Such "sediment loading" isn't even considered by the states or the EPA when assessing water quality, nor have assessment criteria been updated to include over 1,000 compounds recognized in the last 20 years as toxic or hazardous to human health. Monitoring is also very haphazard, with half of the states bordering the Mississippi routinely failing to submit the data required to determine whether EPA-determined Maximum Contaminant Levels have been exceeded or not.

The river's health is reflected in its dependents. Filter-feeders like freshwater mussels are considered good barometers; of the 37 species found in the Mississippi, 22 are in decline and 11 are endangered or extinct on the upper portion of the river. Fish kills—die-offs caused by oxygen-depleted water or pollutants—number in the hundreds each year, and species such as largemouth bass, striped bass, and sturgeon are all in decline. Plenty of the surviving fish store an alphabet soup of toxins in their fatty tissue. DDT, banned in 1972, is *still* found in significant quantities in bottom-feeding species like catfish.

Meanwhile, millions of residents from the Twin Cities to New Orleans still obtain their drinking water from the Mississippi, and both commercial and recreational fishing are widely practiced.

the appearance of a riverboat casino a block away; one pleasant result is "the District," centered around the 2nd Avenue pedestrian mall. At the 17th Street end is the **Quad City ArtsCenter Gallery** (Tues.-Sat. 10 AM-6 PM; free; 309/793-1213), where there's always something free and interesting happening on Friday evenings, Sept.-May. A block away at 1806 2nd Avenue is **All Kinds of People Espresso Bar & Bookshop,** serving fine yuppie sandwiches, soup, baked goods, and beverages (including microbrews), at not-so-yuppie prices; travelers may feel like they've found a magic doorway back to the Beat Generation when they see the book and journal selection in the back. Neighbors include **Tony's Taco House,** with an authentic lineup of dishes right down to the *menudo,* and the **Blue Cat Brew Pub,** around the corner at 113 18th Street, with salads, seafood, and desserts that go way beyond your average pub fare and beers that range from traditional to an esoteric orange coriander concoction. While the Blue Cat's kitchen is open until way past your proper bedtime, hungry night owls on weekends may also want to try nearby **Ruby's Creole & Cajun Restaurant** (1700 3rd Avenue), under the old "Dutch Inn" sign: between Friday 6 AM and Sunday 10 PM they never close.

For a truly regional diner experience, look in the phone book or ask directions to a **Maid-Rite Cafe** (there are seven in the area, three in Moline). A strictly upper Midwest phenomenon whose faded logo "Since 1926" can often be seen on old brick buildings or historic commercial storefronts up through Minnesota, the local Maid-Rites are unusually bright and polished, and come heartily recommended.

There are some 35 **motels** in the Quad Cities, including all the major chains, most with locations on both sides of the Mississippi. In Illinois the major clusters are both off I-74, one next to the airport and the other by John Deere Road; the same smorgasbord is replicated in Iowa off I-80's exit 295A (US-61 south) and at the Bettendorf/Davenport line off I-74's Kimberly Road (US-6 West) exit.

If you want extra printed information to orient yourself, there are two **Welcome Centers** nearby: one on I-80 eastbound, the other off I-80 westbound, across the Mississippi. The Quad Cities visitors guide and B&B brochure are particularly recommended. To obtain info in advance call the Quad Cities Convention and Visitors' Bureau recorded **information line** (800/747-7800).

Beer aficionados should keep an eye out for a wheat beer called Millstream, brewed in Amana, Iowa. As it's not widely distributed, it's a rare find, well worth sampling. **Amana** itself, some 80 miles to the west of Le Claire via I-80, is a long way from the GRR, but is a neat place: a utopian agricultural community established in the 1850s that later gave birth to the Radarange, the first commercial microwave oven. Call 800/245-5465 for details.

For a complete rundown on arts and entertainment in Dubuque, Galena, and the Quad Cities, pick up a free copy of the monthly *River Cities' Reader*.

Through the Yellow Banks

For nearly 100 miles south of the Quad Cities, the GRR picks its way along a series of back roads through Illinois floodplain and prairie, most of which is under cultivation. Frequent small towns serve as reminders of the need for frequent stops by early stages, steamboats, and railroads. Most of the towns seem not to have changed much since the last steamboat or train whistle blew, although now there's neon in the bars, vinyl and aluminum siding on the houses, and farmers with high-powered four-by-fours on the roads. All the big towns sit on the opposite side of the Mississippi, a product of the enormous 19th-century expansion of the American frontier. On the west bank were all the embarkation points for settlers heading across the great prairie and Plains trails—the Oregon, the Mormon, the Santa Fe—so it was around those places that supply towns grew. Illinois could only sit and watch.

Nearly 45 miles south of the Quad City beltway, the GRR passes tiny **New Boston**, at the mouth of the Iowa River. The town is a historical footnote these days, having been surveyed by the young Abraham Lincoln after his stint in the army—a tour of duty during which his only combat was against mosquitoes, he later recalled.

Along the river farther south, near **Keithsburg** a sign welcomes travelers to Yellow Bank country, named for the deep layer of sand exposed in the river valley in this region. Because of this deposit, visitors can find sandburs and even cactus in the Big River State Forest south of town. Keithsburg used to be one of a number of button manufacturing centers located along the middle Mississippi: freshwater clams were dredged from the river bottom and their shells were used for making pearl buttons. Clamming is still the commercial occupation of a few hardy divers, although now the shells are almost exclusively used for "pearl seed," the sand-sized implant injected into commercial pearl oysters in the Pacific.

In Oquawka, Illinois, 10 miles northeast of Burlington, Iowa, a roadside marker points out the spot where in 1971 a circus elephant (named Norma Jean Elephant!) was killed by lightning.

Burlington and Niota

Across the Mississippi River via an austere modern suspension bridge, Burlington was the frontier capital of Iowa, founded in 1808 and holding many Victorian homes and commercial buildings. It also has a riverboat casino, a great Maid-Rite diner, and very busy downtown rail yards—home base of the Burlington Northern Railroad conglomerate.

At Niota, the ghost of a town that marks the next crossing south of Burlington, a nifty old double-decker swing bridge (trains below, cars on top) crosses the Mississippi, landing on the west bank next to a huge old state prison at the historic town of Fort Madison.

Nauvoo

Founded in 1839 by the Church of Jesus Christ of Latter-day Saints (LDS), the town of Nauvoo—a Hebrew word for "the beautiful location"—was named by Mormon leader Joseph Smith. Though the Mormons were forced to flee to Utah in 1846, today Nauvoo is a top destination for Mormon pilgrims, and the church has sponsored a massive historic preservation of old Nauvoo. Even if you're just passing through, you'll have plenty of opportunities to learn about Mormon history and religion, and the restored townscape is a non-commercial reminder of what frontier America looked like in the years before the Wild West was finally won.

A public park at the south end of the business district marks the site of the original Nauvoo temple, which when construction began in 1841 was the largest building west of Philadelphia. Now remembered by a scale model—which looks distinctly odd juxtaposed against the neighboring water tower—and a few exposed foundations, the temple had a remarkable series of stone capitals carved with sunburst motifs, one of which is displayed in a glass case. Other interesting historic Mormon-related sites include the store run by Joseph Smith and the home of Brigham Young. The home and workshop of Jonathon Browning, inventor of the repeating rifle, has been restored along Main Street, south of the present downtown area.

For a map of the town and visitor information, stop by either the huge **LDS Visitors Center** (daily 9 AM-9 PM in summer, till 5 PM rest of the year; free; 217/453-2237 or 800/453-0022)—don't miss the archaeology exhibit on the second floor—or the more modest Reorganized Latter-day Saints-operated (RLDS) **Joseph Smith Historic Center**, down by the river at the corner of Hwy-96 and Water Street (daily 9 AM-5 PM; free; 217/453-2246). (The LDS is formed by Mormons who went to

---

MORMONS IN ILLINOIS

If you're passing through Nauvoo, you'll have plenty of opportunities to learn about Mormon history and religion. Nauvoo is Mecca for Mormons, or "Latter-day-Saints" (LDS) as church members prefer to call themselves. In 1839, the Mormons purchased a large tract of swampy land along the Mississippi River, then set about draining swamps and building a city. Within a few years Nauvoo was not only the largest LDS settlement in America, but the 10th-largest city in the U.S. The emergence of such a powerful little theocracy generated resentment among outnumbered neighbors, and even some internal dissent. The friction escalated to violence on both sides, finally culminating in the 1844 arrest of Joseph Smith, Jr., church founder and president, for having sanctioned the destruction of printing presses used by some church members to question his leadership. While in the nearby Carthage jail, Smith was lynched by a mob and so became one of the Mormons' first martyrs. Amid ensuing disputes over church succession and renewed hostilities with non-Mormon neighbors, most residents followed Brigham Young across the Mississippi on the famous exodus to Salt Lake City.

Given Smith's martyrdom, the fact that he's buried here, and the Brigham Young migration's roots in the town, little wonder that Nauvoo attracts Mormon pilgrims by the busload. The Utah-based LDS have sponsored a massive restoration of old Nauvoo buildings, and the town now ranks as one of the capitals of historic preservation in the United States. Most of old Nauvoo is operated essentially as a big museum, totally free and open to the non-LDS public.

Utah, the RLDS by those who stayed behind.) At either, you'll learn Mormon interpretations of local history and find about crafts demonstrations and guided tours in restored 19th-century properties. The town operates its own info center, too,

The annual **Nauvoo Grape Festival,** held each Labor Day weekend, celebrates the wine business that arose after European immigrants moved onto farms abandoned by the Mormon exodus. As the town also acquired a blue cheese industry early this century after Prohibition shut down the beer-making trade, the centerpiece of the festival features "the Wedding of the Wine and Cheese," a medieval-style pageant borrowed from Roquefort, France.

Restaurants and lodging are all clustered along Mulholland Street (Hwy-96, a.k.a. the GRR) within a few blocks of the water tower. The **Hotel Nauvoo,** 1290 Mulholland (217/453-2211) is particularly well regarded for its belt-straining buffets. For picnic supplies, try the **Nauvoo Mill and Bakery** (Mon.-Sat. 8 AM-5 PM), near the Shell station.

For more complete practical information, contact the Nauvoo Chamber of Commerce (217/453-6648), uptown opposite the historic Hotel Nauvoo.

Warsaw

For a scenic dozen miles south of Nauvoo the GRR returns after long absence to the banks of the Mississippi, shaded by native hickory and oak, and then sidesteps

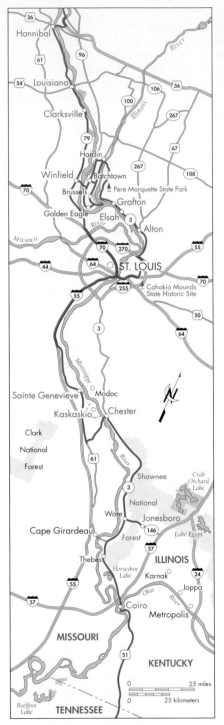

yet another opportunity to enter Iowa, this time via US-136 west to Keokuk. Staying on the east bank, we follow a series of farm roads past gravel pits and fields for most of the 40-mile run down to Quincy.

First stop south of Nauvoo is what used to be the town of Warsaw. Patrons of the bars along the main drag probably think it still *is* Warsaw, but blocks of empty windows and shuttered doorways tell a different story. At the end of town the GRR threatens to turn amphibious as it rolls down past a towering grain elevator to the Mississippi's edge, bends south along the base of the bluffs past old house trailers, scruffy fields full of wildlife—including wild turkeys and river turtles waddling along the roadside—and old kilns visible in the limestone, and passes finally into cornfields planted in the fertile floodplain of the river.

Unfortunately, though the roads are good and the scenery fine, it is on this stretch that the first serious disappearance of the trusty GRR pilot's wheel occurs; a hint, perhaps, of what awaits farther south. You can't go far wrong, though: where the pavement dead-ends there's an opportunity to turn left, and all roads lead eventually to Hwy-96, which will bring you into Quincy on the (still unsigned) GRR.

Quincy

Midway between the Quad Cities and St. Louis, Quincy (pop. 39,681) is a modest-sized city, Germanic enough in its heritage to consider Pizza Hut an ethnic restaurant. A bastion of abolitionists before the Civil War, Quincy was also home to anti-abolitionist Stephen Douglas, the incumbent Illinois senator whose campaign debates with Abraham Lincoln put that tall country lawyer on the path to the White House.

The GRR follows the riverfront and again the pilot's wheel is missing, but the giant span of the Bayview bridge over the Mississippi will leave no doubt as to which way to turn to stay on track. However, most of the city perches on the tall bluffs above the GRR and is worth a drive-through if only to sample its textbook variety of residential architecture. Check out the **Gardner Museum of Architecture and Design** (Tues.-Sun. 1-5 PM; $2), in the old public library downtown on Maine and 4th, for an overview of both those topics. Then take a walk or drive through the East End, an area roughly bounded by Maine and State Streets between 16th and 24th. Filled with historic mansions along quiet tree-canopied streets, it's the perfect place to practice distinguishing Queen Anne from Tudor, prairie from gothic.

If you have thus far avoided the tried-and-true cooking of the **Maid-Rite** chain, Quincy gives you two chances to fix this oversight: the one that opens for breakfast is out on Broadway near 31st Street, near the strip of national fast-food chains, while the one with only lunch and early dinner hours is at 507 N. 12th Street. For something even more strictly local and down-home, slide back down to the waterfront under the bridge for some fried fresh fish at the **Sky Ride Inn** on Front Street, marked by a multicolored neon sign.

If you plan to spend the night, you'll find the **Holiday Inn, Travelodge**, and **Days Inn** downtown, while **Comfort, Fairfield**, and **Super 8** sit a few miles out on Broadway between the Quincy Mall and the local interstate-equivalent, Hwy-336. If you prefer antiques to HBO in your room, there are a couple of reasonable B&Bs; the **Kaufmann House**, in the heart of the historic mansions at 1641 Hampshire Street (217/223-2502), has doubles for $45-65.

For more information call the friendly and helpful **Convention and Visitors Bureau** (800/978-4748) or drop by their tourist information center in the **Villa Kathrine**, the you-won't-miss-it turn-of-the-20th-century Moorish residence on the bluffs overlooking the Mississippi, just beside the Gardner Expressway (Hwy-57).

Following Hwy-57 south through Quincy's industrial margin, the GRR merges into high-speed Hwy-336, then cuts west along US-36 across the mile-wide Mississippi into Hannibal.

Hannibal

It doesn't take a literature professor to figure out who Hannibal's most famous resident was: his name prefaces half the signs in town, and the names of his characters preface the other half. Cross the Mark Twain Memorial Bridge onto Mark Twain Avenue and if not bound for the Huck Finn Mall or Mark Twain Lake (or the Tom N' Huck Motel), turn onto 3rd Street (the GRR) near the Hotel Clemens and park yourself in the heart of historic old Hannibal. Visit the **Mark Twain Home** and newly relocated **Mark Twain Museum**, both at 208 Hill Street; take a very expensive ride on the almost miniature *Mark Twain* riverboat, docked at the Center Street Landing; browse through books by and about Twain at the Becky Thatcher Bookshop,

Warsaw lends its name to a variety of **geode** found locally in profusion; inside, Warsaw geodes grow calcite crystals. Across the Mississippi, Keokuk geodes grow quartzite crystals inside their stony spheres.

The Mississippi is the backbone of the North American Flyway: winter migration brings millions of Canada geese, snow geese, and canvasback ducks through its valley. Some 60% of all bird species in the U.S. are found along the GRR, including an ever-growing population of bald eagles.

Drop the top on your convertible and maybe you can land yourself a travel companion during the World Free Fall, an annual skydiving event that fills Quincy's skies with thousands of jumpers from all over the planet. Held at Baldwin Field between the first two weekends in August, the Free Fall is the legacy of one **Thomas Baldwin**, whose pioneering parachute jump from a balloon into a Quincy park in 1887 earned him two world exhibition tours.

Mark Twain

Twain was a bit of an impractical investor, losing lots of money on lots of harebrained schemes while missing at least one spectacular opportunity, the telephone. Or so hindsight teaches us—but how much would *you* invest in a new invention by a guy who flies tetrahedral kites and makes devices to detect metal in the body? Twain said no, so Alexander Graham Bell took his invention to J.P. Morgan instead.

The Twain mania is so overwhelming that little is made of Hannibal's other famous sons. Baseball lovers searching for some mention of **Joseph Jefferson "Shoeless Joe" Jackson** will look in vain; there is none. Neither is there any mention of **Bill Lear,** inventor of the Lear jet, as well as the eight-track tape, who was born here in 1902.

211 Hill Street; or eat Mark Twain Fried Chicken at the **Mark Twain Dinette,** 400 N. 3rd Street. Not to detract from the credit due him, but don't look for any subtlety or modesty surrounding Mark Twain's achievements here.

Most of the Twainery is located downtown, within a few blocks of the river and pedestrianized Hill Street, and enjoyment requires at least a passing familiarity with (and fondness for) *Tom Sawyer,* Twain's fictionalized memoir of his boyhood here. Otherwise many of the enshrined places and allusions will mean little. South of downtown along the GRR (Hwy-79), we pass Hannibal's most hyped attractions: the **Mark Twain Cave,** (daily 8 AM-8 PM in summer, 9 AM-4 PM rest of year; $8) where costumed guides spin tales about Tom and Huck on an hour-long tour; and the family fun fair (and shopping mall) of **Sawyer's Creek.**

Hannibal being in the heart of the Midwest, its menus tend toward meat and starch, fried or charbroiled. Fancy fried chicken will be called "Cordon Blue"; fancy fried shrimp, "tempura." To immerse yourself fully in the Mark Twain experience, try the memorial chicken (or any of the other dishes) served all day at the Mark Twain Dinette on 3rd and Hill, adjacent to the Mark Twain Home in what looks suspiciously like a converted A&W.

Otherwise the **Riverview Cafe** (daily 11 AM-8 PM), in Sawyer's Landing along Hwy-79 south of town and atop the bluff, has possibly the best kitchen in town, with a view that may indeed be worth the slightly higher prices (some entrees are over $10). Don't let the surrounding kitsch of Sawyer's Creek arcades and gift shops keep you from venturing in. Meanwhile, dessert fans may wish to step into the **Ole Planters Restaurant** at 316 Main Street downtown to sample the German chocolate pie, a specialty of the house. This species, like rhubarb, is predominantly found in pie cases along the middle Mississippi, so if you're planning a scientific sampling, start now.

Consistent with its status as a national tourist attraction, Hannibal has plenty of motels, B&Bs, and campgrounds. The **Hotel Clemens** at the base of the bridge is a Best Western; an **Econo Lodge** and **Travelodge** are a short distance away on Mark Twain Avenue (US-36). On US-61 southwest of town are **Days Inn, Super 8,** and **Holiday Inn,** along with some local motels.

For a complete list of lodgings, restaurants, and tourist traps, pick up a free guide from the **visitor center,** 320 Broadway (314/221-2477).

Since Missouri slacks off on maintaining GRR signs where they're needed, staying on course begins to require more effort for the next 75 miles, until we cross back into Illinois. As you leave Hannibal, for instance, the familiar pilot's wheel can

*Mark Twain
Outdoor Theatre*

be found on Main Street, but it won't point you to the right way out of town. So sidestep up to 3rd Street and follow scenic Hwy-79 south through Louisiana all the way to the town of Winfield.

Louisiana and Clarksville

For the first 20-odd miles south from Hannibal, the GRR ascends and descends the densely wooded tops of bluffs, pausing at scenic turnouts for views across the Mississippi Valley, here many miles wide. In October, the upland forests are blazing with fall color that compares with any outside New England, and if you roll down the windows or stop to stretch your legs during the summer, listen for the omnipresent buzz of cicadas in the tangled undergrowth, sure signs of our ineluctable march south.

Another icon of the lower Mississippi, one that has extended its range north, like the cicadas (and the fire ant), is the huge and pungent Hercules Chemical plant on the south side of the town of Louisiana (pop. 3,967). The town itself, like a Hannibal without Mark Twain, is full of 100-year-old brick cottages and warehouses, but looks like it has just about lost the battle against extinction—its Dairy Queen closed and up for sale, 15-year-old cars everywhere and thrift stores lining up downtown—just the kind of place *aching* to attract a glittering riverboat casino.

A short ways farther south, Clarksville (pop. 480) is another town with more of a past than a future, but some optimistic restorers of the riverfront historic block are counting on tourism to improve the town fortunes. Along 1st Street, down by the river and the railroad tracks **Mississippi Landing**, offers art and espresso.

A caveat for vegetarians: while restaurants throughout the Midwest persistently equate iceberg lettuce with salad, as you progress south they also are seized by the belief that a salad is naked unless dressed with a pile of ham julienne and bacon dressing.

Besides holding title to the **highest point along the Mississippi River**, 600-foot **Pinnacle Peak**, with a rusty old "Sky Ride" chair lift to the top ($5), Clarksville boasts what may be the largest concentration of **bald eagles** in the lower 48 states. In winter months they feed by the hundreds on fish below Lock and Dam No. 24 on the northern edge of town.

Winfield

Swinging away from the river south of Clarksville, the GRR re-enters the corn belt in great straight stretches of road over prairie still hilly enough that you can play peek-a-boo with approaching traffic over the miles of ups and downs, passing towns that often comprise little more than a few houses around a gas station and a grain elevator on a rarely used railroad siding.

If you've been keeping track, you'll have noticed the lock and dam numbering skipped No. 23 between Hannibal and Clarksville. There are 29 Corps of Engineers-operated locks and dams on the Mississippi, from the unnumbered ones in the Twin Cities to No. 27 at St. Louis.

Though it looks a lot like all the other riverside roadside towns along this stretch of the Mississippi, Winfield (pop. 592), 25 miles south of Clarksville, has the singular attraction of what's perhaps the best cafe in this neck of the woods: **Alice's Home Style Restaurant**, right on Hwy-79 at the center of town, next to the only stop sign. A classic "everybody knows everybody" cafe, Alice's serves up meals big enough to sink one of those barges, so beware: turkey and gravy with beans, mashed potatoes, big floury biscuits, and coffee or iced tea is a typical lunch, at a price that leaves enough out of a five-dollar bill to give a good tip. For an extra $1.50, tuck into one of the fresh-daily slabs of pie, with crust so short you'll find it in Webster's under "flaky."

At the north end of Winfield, 100 yards from Alice's, there's a clearly visible sign for the **ferry** (Mon.-Fri. 5 AM-8 PM, weekends 8 AM-9 PM, year-round; $3.50), which crosses the Mississippi about three miles east of town, just below Lock and Dam No. 25. There's no fixed departure times: the operator leaves when all the customers waiting are aboard, or when the ferry is full, and returns when he has a fare to bring back or when he spots you waiting—so drive right up to where you can be seen, and if it's after dark, keep your lights on.

If the ferry isn't running, St. Louis's suburban edge is 20 miles south along Hwy-79.

Calhoun County

Crossing the river from Winfield, Missouri, our route cuts across peninsular Calhoun County, one of Illinois's best-kept secrets. Cut off from the rest of the state by the Illinois River, connected to neighboring Missouri by ferry only, Calhoun is a world of its own. A third of the state's substantial peach crop is grown here on farms that have changed hands only a few times, if at all, since they were given out as land grants to veterans of the War of 1812; bypassing the summer farm stands, especially when the baseball-sized, plum-sweet tomatoes are in season, borders on criminal. Urban St. Louisians keep weekend getaways here, too, alongside shacks and trailers that accumulate debris like the Corps' dams accumulate Mississippi mud.

From the end of the ferry access road, detour north to **Batchtown** a couple of miles away, stopping at **Friedel's Grocery** for a shake or malt as whim or muggy weather may demand. About three miles east of Batchtown you'll come to a junction with Hwy-1, which runs south to the state-run **Brussels Ferry** (frequent and free, 24 hours every day—flood or ice notwithstanding) across the mouth of the Illinois River. If the ferry is closed, there's a bridge at Hardin 14 miles upstream; if the ferry is open, as is most likely the case, follow the clearly signposted route through the town of **Brussels**, whose public phone booth is possibly the town's sole civic improvement since the Coolidge administration. A handful of cafes and bars is evidence of the county's popularity with savvy weekenders from St. Louis; in summer, look for the small roadside trailer selling fresh fish, $2-3 a fillet, fried while you wait. The most popular haunt is the venerable **Wittmond Hotel** (618/883-2345) across from the water tower and post office at the heart of Brussels. The dining room here serves delicious, all-you-can-eat family-style meals (very popular on Sunday). They also rent rooms ($40 a night), have a timeless bar, and have an even more ancient-looking general store—complete with dusty old merchandise that looks like it dates back to when the enterprise opened in 1847.

Besides the Brussels Ferry, the privately operated "Golden Eagle" paddle wheel ferry service runs across the Mississippi River between **Golden Eagle,** Illinois, and the Missouri shore, landing outside St. Charles. For current hours and fares, phone 618/883-2217.

The Illinois River

The Brussels ferry ride takes all of two or three minutes to cross this narrow reach of the Illinois River, along which Marquette and Joliet returned to Canada after their failure to find a westward-flowing river to the rich lands of Cathay and the Far East. René-Robert Cavelier, Sieur de La Salle, came down the Illinois eight years later in 1681, on the first expedition to specifically target the Mississippi. It was La Salle who claimed the Mississippi territory for his sponsor, King Louis XIV of France, and who went all the way down to the Gulf of Mexico (Marquette and Joliet turned back after the confluence of the Arkansas River). In more recent times the Illinois River was associated with the outbreak of typhoid fever in St. Louis, after engineers in typhoid-ridden Chicago took the sewage-laden Chicago River flowing through their city into Lake Michigan, reversed it, and made it flow backwards into the Illinois. This sort of give-it-to-the-next-guy attitude has prevailed along the Mississippi to this day. The Illinois River, for example, continues to add Chicago effluent to the Mississippi.

The familiar 12-spoke pilot's wheel waits at the end of the ferry off-ramp, ready to guide us the 50-odd miles south to St. Louis.

Illinois recently ranked highest in the nation for industrial discharges of toxic materials into publicly owned sewage treatment facilities, and third highest in the nation for direct discharges of toxics into surface waters. Stretches of the Illinois River in particular are known for their very high levels of PCBs.

Pere Marquette State Park

If you're equipped for some hiking or biking, Pere Marquette State Park is a worthwhile three-mile detour from the ferry landing. The handsome **park lodge**, built by the Civilian Conservation Corps in the late 1930s, is noted for its 700-ton stone fireplace, massive tree-trunk roof supports, decorative ironwork, and outsized chess set in front of the ox-sized hearth that definitely can create a congenial chalet atmosphere, particularly if you time your arrival for evenings, mid-week, or off-season to avoid the crowds. Cabins and lodge rooms are available for the same reasonable rates ($65-a-night doubles; 618/786-2331). Expect holiday and fall foliage weekends to be booked up to a year in advance; camping ($8; 618/786-3323) and tent rental are available.

The 20-mile **Sam Vadalabene Bike Trail** between Pere Marquette State Park and Alton is unquestionably the best venue for appreciating the scenery, even for a short walk, for here the GRR becomes a fast divided highway whose drivers don't appreciate slowpokes.

Grafton

Travelers coming from the north may have wondered why there has been so little evidence of the disastrous 1993 floods so far along our route; it's because the GRR has so far avoided all the upstream areas that were hit hard. That is about to change: resume following the GRR downstream from the Brussels Ferry and in just a few miles you'll pass through Grafton—or rather, what's left of it. Most of low-lying Grafton was flooded out by the Mississippi, forcing residents to relocate to higher ground. The few who have rebuilt according to new code requirements illustrate the river's mammoth rise as dramatically as their neighbors' mud-streaked walls, with new houses perched atop great concrete and steel stilts. Stop in any of the cafes, fish shacks, or galleries at the higher, southern end of town and you can pry stories about the "Flood of '93" from just about anyone. For unusual local flavor, stop by the **Chateau Ra-Ha Winery** at 230 E. Main Street to sample their specialty, mead, made with local honey.

*Atop the bluffs over Elsah is the very Tudor campus of **Principia College,** the world's only Christian Science institution of higher education (public welcome Mon.-Sat. 9 AM-5 PM).*

South of Grafton the GRR enters what is widely considered one of its most scenic stretches: towering limestone bluffs, their curving faces pocked with caves and overhangs, push the road to the edge of the lake above Lock and Dam No. 26.

Elsah

Speeding along, it's easy to miss the turnoff for Elsah, four miles south of Grafton, but even if you have to turn around and come back, it's worth it to check out this tiny hamlet tucked away in a cleft in the palisades. Listed in the National Register of Historic Places in its entirety, Elsah is an elegant architectural gem, with 19th-century cut stone and clapboard buildings and narrow lanes redolent of some idyllic English country village. Two small B&Bs and the **Green Tree Inn** (618/374-2821; $77-117 with tax) offer what most people would consider romantic getaways; the inn even has a tandem bike for guests. For meals there is only **Elsah's Landing Restaurant** (Tues.-Sun. 11:30 AM-7:30 PM), but the monopoly is well deserved: its made-from-scratch ethic pays off in all departments, with pies alone worth staying overnight for.

South of Elsah, before the bluffs give way to grain elevators at Alton, you'll catch a glimpse of the **Piasa Bird** (PIE-a-saw) high on the wall of an old roadside quarry. Marquette and other early explorers mention a pair of huge pictographs on the cliff face, representations of the Illini Indians' legendary "bird that devours men." Faded by the 1840s, the original site was destroyed by quarrying. The current 20-by-40-foot replica, based on various eyewitness descriptions, resembles something from the notebook of an adolescent Dungeons and Dragons fan.

Alton

At Alton, 20 miles northeast of St. Louis, the riverfront turns decidedly urban. The GRR races along the water, past tugboat docks, the tacky but hugely lucrative *Alton Belle* casino boat (the first in Illinois when riverboat gambling was made legal in 1991), sulphurous chemical plants, and spacious tank farms, all under the shadow of the great protective levee and a thicket of high-tension power lines.

Inland from the GRR, however, the town is surprisingly peaceful and quiet, its red-brick streets lined by mature trees and a range of modest but well-maintained

19th-century houses. Near 5th and Monument Streets at the south end of town, high on a hill above the riverfront, Alton's cemetery is dominated by a large column topped by a winged figure—a monument to one of Alton's most important individuals, the abolitionist newspaper editor **Elijah Lovejoy.** Widely considered to be the nation's first martyr to freedom of the press and freedom of speech, Lovejoy, a newspaper publisher and preacher, was lynched in Alton in 1837 by a mob of pro-slavery Missourians.

Around Alton, keep an eye out for the signs to the **Lewis & Clark Historical Site** to get a glimpse of the confluence of the Missouri and Mississippi Rivers rolling together in a muddy tide between swampy wooded banks. The merging of the rivers was violent enough to frighten early navigators, but dynamited rapids and upstream dams have changed all that. Despite considerable flood damage in recent years, the riprap-lined gully of what might once have been a pretty creek, and the rather forlorn condition of their memorial, the winter campsite of Meriwether Lewis and William Clark's Corps of Discovery is a peaceful place with simple tablets commemorating highlights of the journey that began here on May 14, 1804. For more on their epic trek, see pages 176-177.

Twelve miles south of Alton, the GRR briefly joins I-270 eastbound toward Effingham before exiting onto Hwy-111, a route illustrating the steady creep of suburban mini-malls into the Illinois cornfields.

A life-sized statue of **Robert Pershing Wadlow,** the world's tallest human, stands on the campus of the Southern Illinois University Dental School, on College Avenue (Hwy-140), a mile or so east of the river. The Alton-born "gentle giant" was 8 feet 11³/₄ inches when he died at age 22.

The GRR across St. Louis

The Great River Road has many routes in, around and across St. Louis, and they're all so poorly marked that you're sure to get lost trying to follow any of them. Most pass through rusty old industrial districts of dubious interest like Granite City and East St. Louis, so to do the city justice (and have some fun), follow a more direct route instead. From Alton, US-67 crosses just below Dam 26, taking first the Clark Bridge (over the Mississippi) and then the Lewis Bridge (over the Missouri River). No prizes for guessing what *those* names refer to, since you enter the city on Lewis and Clark Boulevard (Hwy-367).

Where the Great River Road hops onto the I-55 freeway for its final approach into St. Louis, a clearly marked "GRR Spur" leads to Cahokia Mounds, the remains of the largest prehistoric American city north of Mexico. For more, see page 843 in the Route 66 chapter.

A good non-freeway main route across St. Louis is Kings Highway, which runs north to south past many of the city's main destinations, including Forest Park and the Missouri Botanical Gardens, before ending up at Gravois Avenue, part of old Route 66. From here, numerous roads give direct access to I-55 and US-61, both of which link up with the scenic GRR route south to Sainte Genevieve.

St. Louis is the only city where three of our Road Trip USA routes coincide—the Great River Road, US-50, and Route 66. For details on US-50, see page 654; for details on Route 66, see page 794.

(continues on page 260)

ST. LOUIS SURVIVAL GUIDE

FOUNDED BY FRENCH FUR TRAPPERS in 1764, for most of its first century St. Louis served as a prosperous outpost of "civilization" at the frontier of the Wild West. It was the starting point for the explorations of Lewis and Clark, and much later Charles Lindbergh, whose *Spirit of St. Louis* carried him across the Atlantic. Unfortunately, like many other American cities, St. Louis has suffered from years of decline and neglect, and seems perpetually on the verge of a comeback. Although it has all the cultural and institutional trappings of a major city, not to mention the landmark Gateway Arch, St. Louis is at heart a city of small neighborhoods, such as bluesy Soulard south of downtown, or the collegiate West End district near verdant Forest Park, the parts brought together in mutual appreciation of its flagship product, Budweiser.

One thing you have to see when in St. Louis (you literally cannot miss it) is the **Gateway Arch**, on the riverfront at the foot of Market Street (daily 9 AM-6 PM, longer hours in summer). Rising up from the west bank of the Mississippi River, Eero Saarinen's stunning 630-foot stainless steel monument still dominates the city skyline, despite the disrespectful rise of nearby office towers. Under the legs of the Arch, which is officially called the Jefferson National Expansion Memorial, the free and fascinating **Museum of Westward Expansion** chronicles the human wave that swept America's frontier west to the Pacific. A small elevator-like **tram** ($5) carries visitors up the arch to an observation chamber at the very top.

West of downtown around the Washington University campus Forest Park's 1,300 beautifully landscaped acres hold a number of buildings that date back to the 1904 World's Fair, St. Louis's world-class swan song. A fine art museum, a history museum, and a science museum fill the old fair buildings. Southwest of downtown, on Shaw Boulevard off I-44, the **Missouri Botanical Garden** is the other most attractive acreage in the city, with a particularly nice Japanese garden and the "Climatron," a geodesic conservatory. Above the botanical gardens rises **The Hill**, a close-knit working-class neighborhood of small frame houses with Italian flags flying from porches, red-white-and-green fire hydrants, and restaurants that set a standard for Italian food in America. This is Yogi Berra's home turf, so come and pay your respects.

The world's largest brewery, and home of those famous Clydesdales, the Anheuser-Busch Brewery, above I-55 at 1127 Pestalozzi Street, is open for free tours (and quick samples) every day but Sunday.

Mark McGwire hits home runs for the St. Louis Cardinals (314/421-2400) who play at character-less concrete Busch Stadium, right downtown.

Practicalities

St. Louis sits amid a fat web of major Interstates (I-55, I-70, I-64, I-44), federal highways (US-40, US-50, US-61, US-67), and the Great River Road. Old Route 66 used to pass through here, too, a fact remembered in song more than on street signs. Most major airlines serve Lambert-St. Louis International Airport, 14 miles west of downtown, although locally- based TWA dominates the flight schedule. A light-rail system connects the main terminal to downtown and The Arch, and you'll find numerous shuttles, taxis ($18-20 to downtown), and rental car facilities.

Freeways and high-speed arteries reminiscent of L.A. make a car handy for navigating the St. Louis area—unless you have oodles of money for cab fares. Thanks to the city's sad history of replacing old buildings with blacktop, you'll find plenty of parking lots around downtown St. Louis.

St. Louis doesn't have that much of a tourist trade (the muggy weather here in summer keeps sensible people far away) so places to stay are pretty cheap. Days Inn at the Arch, 333 Washington Avenue (314/621-7900 or 800/325-2525), is usually the least expensive downtown motel; doubles $50-90. At the other end of the price and aesthetic spectrum, the Hyatt Regency at Union Station, 1820 Market Street (314/231-1234 or 800/233-1234), is the most expensive bed in the city, at around $200 a night. The opulently restored lobby, formerly the great rail center's vaulted waiting room, is worth seeing even if you aren't a guest.

For food, "The Hill" is hard to beat: Favazza's, at 5201 Southwest Avenue, is one of a handful of reliable (if not exactly trend-setting) places; industrial-strength Italian food doesn't get better than this. Wherever you go, try the toasted ravioli, a local treat. Across I-55 from the Budweiser factory, the wild Venice Cafe, 1903 Pestalozzi Street, matches anarchic Gaudi-meets-the-Merry-Pranksters decor with a menu that leans heavily toward Jamaican jerk chicken, served up indoors—where poets linger over bottles of beer—or in the backyard garden.

No one leaves St. Louis without cruising old Route 66 southwest from downtown to Ted Drewe's, 6726 Chippewa Avenue (314/481-2652), a local institution famous for its many flavors of "concrete"—a delicious frozen dairy-and-egg custard concoction so thick you can turn it upside down and not spill a drop.

The St. Louis Convention & Visitors Commission (314/241-1764 or 800/916-0092) operates a well-stocked information center downtown at 308 Washington Avenue, near the river and I-70. The city's daily newspaper, the Post-Dispatch, has entertainment and events ideas, while the free alternative weekly, The Riverfront Times, has the most comprehensive club and event listings.

Sainte Genevieve

To avoid the worst of the suburban commercialization south of St. Louis, take I-55 as far as exit 162, where you can rejoin the GRR by picking up US-61 south; if you don't blink you may even catch sight of one of Missouri's rare pilot's wheel signs as the busy road ascends a ridge with a fine western panorama. About 55 miles south of St. Louis's I-270/255 beltway, the GRR comes to the modern commercial out-skirts of Sainte Genevieve, one of several French trading posts established along the Mississippi in the wake of La Salle's 17th-century expedition. The town's new trade is tourism, as the B&Bs, "fine dining," and shops clearly illustrate. The beau-ty of Sainte Genevieve's restored 18th- to 19th-century remnants, including a brick belle of an old hotel, is marred only by the intermittent appearance of vinyl siding, AstroTurf front steps, and metal screen doors of their better-kept neighbors. **Sara's Ice Cream**, down toward the water at Merchant and 1st streets, provides yet more tasteful distractions.

Since US-61 doesn't enter town, follow the small blue "Tourist Information" signs down to the old waterfront to find the area's historic places, and visit the **Great River Road Interpretive Center**, 66 S. Main Street (daily 9 AM-4 PM; free; 314/883-7097 or 800/373-7007) to get the skinny on the town's past and present.

The **Mississippi River-Modoc Ferry** (Mon.-Sat. 6 AM-6 PM, Sunday 9 AM-6 PM; $6; 314/883-7382) to Modoc, Illinois, is almost three miles out of town: follow Main Street north until it dead-ends at the ferry landing. Since the operator likes to knock off work early, plan on arriving before 5:30 PM. Twelve rural crop-lined miles from the Modoc Ferry we rejoin the GRR heading south on Hwy-3 to Chester; being Illinois, the (mostly) paved farm lanes have signs where necessary to keep you informed and on track.

If you were to camp under the protective overhangs of the Modoc limestone bluffs, you'd be continuing a long tradition: indigenous people began camping here roughly 10,000 years ago.

Kaskaskia

Fifteen miles south of Sainte Genevieve, signposted off US-61, is old Kaskaskia, the first Illinois state capital and the only Illi-nois town now *west* of the Mississippi, thanks to an 1881 flood. "Town" is a gener-ous overstatement: consisting of a church and a handful of farmhouses to begin with, the community has been all but washed away numerous times in its 250-year history, most recently in the 1993 Great Flood. Cut off from the Missouri shore by huge levees and a swampy river channel, Kaskaskia is a ghost with an illustrious past: it was here during the American Revolution that George Rogers Clark and his tiny force of Kentucky **"Long Knives"** launched their attack against British control of the huge, formerly French territory between the Mississippi and Ohio River val-leys, a campaign so stunningly successful that it effectively doubled the size of the U.S. during the Revolution. After capturing Fort Kaskaskia (now across the river), the victorious Americans rang the 600-pound bell that hung in the French Catholic church; this bell, now in its own spartan iron-barred chapel, is called "the Liberty Bell of the West."

Chester

The GRR neatly skips around Chester, "Home of Popeye," via a pleasant riverbank detour, returning to Hwy-3 on the downstream side of town. Unless a doughnut stop is required at **Bill's**, a joint on Main Street this loop is preferable to town. **Pop-**

eye first appeared in print in 1929, and a memorial to local boy Elzie Segar, creator of the spinach-guzzling scrapper, stands in a picnic area beside the bridge to Missouri; if you miss it, you'll have to turn around on the other side of the Mississippi. Chester locals Frank "Rocky" Fiegel and William "Windy Bill" Schuchert were the inspiration for Popeye the Sailor and Wimpy the Hamburger Fiend. If you pass through on the second weekend of September, drop by Popeye's birthday party, with its big flea market of all the Popeye collectibles you never imagined existed.

South of Chester, the GRR passes by a number of old barns painted with fading signs advertising "Meramec Caverns - US-60 - Stanton MO."

Hwy-3: Shawnee National Forest

No town of any consequence impedes the GRR's 90-mile leg along the southern tip of Illinois. The roadside landscape continues to be cultivated, heat-loving corn and leafy soybean mixed now with milo, an animal feed crop whose Grape-Nuts clusters resemble grain sorghum. The bluffs of the Shawnee National Forest, whose recreational offerings are invitingly sign-posted with names like Oakwood Bottoms, Turkey Bayou, and Pine Hills, appear a couple of miles to the east, and follow the GRR through the old river valley. Much of the forested uplands are a botanical crossroads: glacier-borne northern species like the sumac and partridge berry; warmth-seeking southern species like the short-leaf pine; eastern species held back by the Mississippi, such as Virginia willow and silver bell; and western species with a toehold in the east, like Missouri primrose and Ozark coneflower. All count Southern Illinois as the edge of their natural ranges.

Shawnee National Forest contains some significant stands of old-growth forest which, like the spotted-owl habitat in the Pacific Northwest, were sold off in the 1980s to logging companies by the U.S. Department of Agriculture. Unfortunately for the trees, local loggers were spared much scrutiny since the national media never picked up the story.

Jonesboro

Just under 50 miles south of Chester, amid grainfields maintained by private duck-hunting clubs, the GRR is intersected by Hwy-146 at the village of Ware. Eight miles east of this junction is the small town of Jonesboro, whose **Dixie Bar-B-Q**, at 205 W. Broad Street, on the left before the courthouse rotary, is definitely worth a side trip. Jonesboro's Forest Service **ranger station** is also worth a visit for a guide to the Shawnee's attractions, or request one in advance from the **Southern Illinois Tourist Council** (800/342-3100).

George Rogers Clark's fame as a war hero, Indian fighter, and explorer put him at the top of Thomas Jefferson's short list for leading an expedition into what became the Louisiana Purchase, but the aging (and, some say, alcoholic) Clark nominated his younger brother instead. Thus did **William Clark** join Meriwether Lewis for their historic journey to the Pacific. For more on Lewis and Clark, see pages 176-177.

When John James Audubon passed through this region in the early 1800s, he recorded seeing thousands of bright green, red, and yellow-striped parakeets. They are all long extinct; gone, too, are the panther and the black bear.

Absent-minded and lead-footed drivers beware: some cash-strapped counties of Southern Illinois are known to use speed traps to help make ends meet.

In September 1858 Jonesboro hosted the third of the seven senate campaign debates between challenger Abe Lincoln and incumbent Stephen Douglas, who tried to portray Lincoln as being out of touch with people over the issue of slavery. Although Illinois was a designated free state, this area had strong sympathies with the South.

Keep a sharp lookout to spot the historic markers near Hwy-146 that give brief mention to the **Trail of Tears**, the 1838 winter death march of the Cherokee nation. Six years after wiping out Indians of the upper Mississippi in the Black Hawk War, Pres. Andrew Jackson ordered the "Five Civilized Tribes" of the Cherokee removed to the arid plains of Oklahoma from their lands in the fertile Tennessee River valley. Five thousand people died along the thousand-mile journey, which passed through the state near here. On the Missouri side of the river, 10 miles north of Cape Girardeau, the 3,400-acre Trail of Tears State Park preserves the scene of this tragedy, with interpretive plaques marking the wooded bluffs.

Back on Hwy-3, just north of I-57 and the town of Cairo, the GRR passes **Horseshoe Lake Conservation Area**, an example of what happens when the river shifts to a new channel and leaves an oxbow lake behind. Now prime winter habitat for over a million migrating geese and ducks, its tupelo gum trees, bald cypress, and swamp cottonwoods foreshadow the scenery found downstream among the bayous of the Mississippi Delta.

Cape Girardeau, on the Missouri side of the Mississippi River, was the boyhood hometown of radio talk-show host **Rush Limbaugh.**

The town of **Metropolis,** Illinois (pop. 6,700), along the Ohio River 25 miles northeast of Cairo but most easily accessible via Paducah, Kentucky, takes pride in its adopted superhero son, Superman. A statue of him, and a quick-change telephone booth, stands near the offices of the *Daily Planet* newspaper, and every June a festival celebrates his crime-fighting efforts. For more information, contact the Super Museum, 517 Market Street (618/524-5518).

Cairo

"A grave uncheered by any gleam of promise," was but one of Charles Dickens's unsympathetic descriptions of Cairo (CARE-oh), the town that presides over—and sometimes under—the meeting of the Mississippi and Ohio Rivers. Routinely submerged by floodwaters until the Corps of Engineers ringed the town with a massive stockade of levees and huge steel floodgates, Cairo's star shone briefly in the steamboat era and during the Civil War, when General Grant quartered his Army of the Tennessee here and Union ironclads were berthed along the waterfront. A few Victorian mansions built by boat captains remain, but otherwise the GRR's passage through town is best enjoyed with your eyes stuck firmly to the road.

What *is* worth seeing is the confluence of the two mighty rivers. Unless there's a flood in progress, do your watching from a small platform in **Fort Defiance State Park**, at the foot of the bridge that carries US-60 between Missouri and Kentucky, lasting but a quarter-mile in Illinois. Just don't expect the vista to be a pastoral one: as you stand on the spongy park lawn with a mighty river on either hand, the horizons are dominated by billowing smokestacks, the foreground by barges and huge diesel-burning tows plowing up and down the brown tide. The unleaded you bought in Minnesota probably passed by here, and the flour for the bread you'll eat in Louisiana probably has, too.

There's a cluster of gas and food stores and a **Days Inn** at Cairo's northern edge, where I-57 crosses the GRR.

TRUTH – JUSTICE – THE AMERICAN WAY

ACROSS KENTUCKY AND TENNESSEE

With its crossing of the Ohio River from Cairo, the GRR enters the Lower Mississippi Basin, a long floodplain whose wetlands acted as a natural reservoir for floodwaters until the Corps of Engineers came along in the 1930s and hemmed it in with a thousand miles of levees, revetments, and wing dikes. Problem is, channeling and controlling the river has had exactly the opposite effect: flood crests are higher with two-thirds of the basin's carrying capacity cut off by the Corps, and people are sleeping closer to the restless giant now that wetlands have been drained and opened for development. But if it wasn't for the false security of the levees abutments along the river, the area would have no security at all.

Most of the GRR's 60-odd Kentucky miles are quite scenic, populated by only a handful of small towns, none of which has been overrun by tacky commercial strips. Upon crossing the Tennessee line the route promptly loses all trace of GRR signage, swallowed up, perhaps, by the nearby New Madrid Fault. Rising up off cultivated bottomlands around earthquake-created Reelfoot Lake, the GRR rejoins four-lane US-51 as it traverses the last 80 miles to downtown Memphis along developed

In the south, drive like a Southerner: no matter what your speed, keep one arm dangling outside your rolled-down window, to be lifted up in lazy acknowledgment of passing vehicles and porch sitters. Single-handed driving won't be a problem: the arrow-straight roads are designed not to tax anybody's steering skills.

Assimilation through driving, Part II: Drive an American car, preferably a pickup, sport-utility, or huge sedan of any vintage in any condition. Driving a Honda, Saab, Volvo, or any foreign car with the stickshift on the floor will clearly identify you as someone from another planet, like Chicago.

uplands: southern short-leaf pine woods and cotton fields mixed with mobile homes, suburban ranch houses, and gas stations that double as the local video stores.

Wickliffe to Hickman

Skipping from the banks of the Ohio through small, thoroughly industrial Wickliffe, the GRR stays with US-51 southbound for about 16 miles, passing an "alternate" GRR turnoff that simply saves a visit to the center of staid old **Bardwell**, a town that grew up on the railroad rather than the river. Leaving the federal highway for a spell, our route takes an attractive 40-mile meander away from the river through wooded hill country, returning to the edge of the Mississippi at Hickman.

West from Hickman, there's a small toll ferry to Missouri, if you desperately need to fetch something left behind. Heading south it's just another dozen rural miles to the Tennessee line.

Reelfoot Lake Area

Leaving Kentucky, the GRR enters a 40-mile stretch of low-lying bottoms, picking up Hwy-78 south. After passing the roadhouse bars and bait shops near Reelfoot Lake, a major recreation area and wildlife refuge created by the first New Madrid earthquake's sudden and massive

(continues on page 268)

THE NEW MADRID EARTHQUAKE OF 1811

The strongest earthquake recorded in North America struck the Mississippi region on December 16, 1811. The Richter Scale wasn't around to measure it, but the New Madrid (MAD-rid) quake, named for the river town just across the Mississippi in Missouri, was felt in Boston, Detroit, and New Orleans. Fatalities are presumed to have stayed low because of the sparse frontier population, but there were sufficient witnesses to tell of geysers of mud and stone, great chasms splitting open and swallowing acres of fields and forest, tornado-like winds, and towns reduced to kindling. The Mississippi, it is said, ran backward. Louisville recorded some 1,800 aftershocks through the winter, before another massive quake on February 7, 1812, again caused fearful settlers to wonder if Judgment Day had come.

Among the witnesses to the catastrophe of the first New Madrid quake were the crew of the *New Orleans*, the first steamboat on the Mississippi, which was making its maiden voyage from Pittsburgh to its namesake city. As it turned out, only the fact that the river was in flood made the voyage possible at all, for the paddle wheeler's draft was too deep to return upstream.

The cause of the quake, the **New Madrid Fault** that runs from Arkansas up the Ohio River valley, is still active, minimally enough to generate predictions that California isn't the only place that should worry about The Big One. A strong sulphur odor is said to precede temblors in this area.

IN SEARCH OF ELVIS

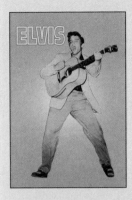

Scratch the surface of Memphis, and you'll always turn up a little Elvis, like pennies and pocket lint in an old sofa. That guy behind the counter? His mom used to give piano lessons to Elvis's step-brothers. That woman at the next table? Her after-school job was in the Libertyland amusement park Elvis would rent out in its entirety just so he could ride the Zippin' Pippin' roller coaster for hours on end. A frequent Graceland visitor during the Elvis years collected fuzz from the shag carpet to give to friends; maybe the woman paying for her coffee still has her tuft. Even the owner of the greasiest old pizza joint will tell you how Elvis would come in with his band, "back when he was *nothin'*." Get used to it: Elvis is *everywhere*.

The font of all this meta-Elvisness is, of course, **Graceland** (daily 9 AM-5 PM, 8 AM-7 PM in summer; $5-19; 901/332-3322 or 800/238-2000), on Elvis Presley Boulevard (US-51) about a mile south of I-55 (exit 5B) amid a clutter of burger joints and muffler shops. At age 21, flush with his early success, Elvis paid $100,000 for Graceland, which was one of the more fashionable houses in Memphis in 1957, and seeing what happens when Elvis's poor-white-boy taste and Hollywood budget run amok is well worth the admission fees, which vary depending upon how much of the place you want to see. You can buy tickets to each part of the Graceland complex, or splurge on a combination "Platinum Tour" ticket that gives admission to the mansion as well as the other "collections," such as the King's private jet or his car collection (many of his cars, including his famous pink 1955 Cadillac, are arrayed as if at a drive-in movie—with a big screen playing his race car scenes from *Viva Las Vegas* on a continuous loop), my personal favorite stop in the whole shebang.

A visit to Graceland says very little about Elvis's music (though there is a room showing off an 80-foot wall full of gold and platinum records), but speaks volumes about his mystique. Elvis is buried on the property, alongside his father and mother, in the Meditation Garden.

One place where you *won't* find Elvis (except on a few overpriced postcards) is east of downtown at the **Java Cabana**, 2170 Young Street, a block east of Cooper. As renowned headquarters of the First Church of the Elvis Impersonator, the Java Cabana would consider it *heretical* to mount any true likeness of Elvis himselvis on its walls—and dangerous, too, given the threat of legal action from Presley Enterprises if it did. The decor, of course, appropriately reflects the nature of the shrine, with a 24-hour coin-operated "blessed vista" in the front window and the Viva Memphis! Wedding Chapel in the back, presided over, with advance arrangements, by a nondenominational Elvis impersonator. Naturally, the cafe's "congregation" is a gregarious mix of Medici and Kerouac improvising their own Eucharist over cappuccino, kosher pastries, Scrabble, and cigarettes. (Poetry night is Thursday.)

MEMPHIS SURVIVAL GUIDE

MEMPHIS'S GIFTS TO AMERICAN culture include: the supermarket, the drive-in restaurant, the Holiday Inn, Elvis Presley, and Federal Express, and if you detect a pattern here you'll understand why the city is at once entertaining kitsch and supremely captivating. This is not to say Memphis lacks a coherent character—just the opposite—but its charms are like  home brew or overripe cheese: musty, sharp, and lingering, with unpredictable side effects. Ever-sprawling development continues to deprive Memphis of its historical vitality, but once you learn your way around, you'll find that Memphis is generally a very welcoming and very affordable city, especially when it comes to good food and live music, both of which it still pumps out in abundance.

Beale Street, downtown between 2nd and 4th Streets, has been Memphis's honky-tonk central ever since native son W.C. Handy set up shop in the early 1900s with the blues he'd learned in Mississippi. Beale Street has been sanitized for your protection, turning it into a new! & improved! version of its old self; slap an adhesive name tag on your lapel and you'll fit right in with the tour bus crowd strolling at night along the block of clubs (including B.B. King's at 143 Beale, marked by a neon guitar), curbside bars, and T-shirt mongers. It's marginally better by day: check out the line of voodoo potions and other necessities in the justly famous **A. Schwab's Dry Goods Store**, 163 Beale Street, which hasn't changed much since it opened in 1876, or step into the enlightening **Center for Southern Folklore** (Mon.-Sat. 9 AM-5:30 PM, Sunday 1-5:30 PM; $2; 901/525-3655), at 130 Beale Street, to brush up on your musical history and Deep South appreciation.

The original **Sun Records** studios (daily 10 AM-5:30 PM; $8), where Elvis recorded his first tracks, are a short walk northeast at 706 Union Avenue.

If there's one place that shouldn't be missed, it's the eloquent **National Civil Rights Museum**, 450 Mulberry Street (Monday and Wed.-Sat. 10 AM-5 PM, Sunday 1-5 PM, closed Tuesday; $5; 521-9699), south of Beale Street behind the restored facade of the Lorraine Motel, where Dr. Martin Luther King, Jr., was assassinated in 1968. Aided by extensive video newsreels and life-sized dioramas, exhibits let you step as far as you like into the powerful history of the Civil Rights Movement—whether by listening to the recollections of those at the front lines of the struggle, or by joining Rosa Parks at the front of a bus and having the tape-recorded driver angrily tell *you* to move to the back or face serious consequences.

On the north side of downtown, **Mud Island** (daily 10 AM-7 PM April-Nov.; $4; 576-7241) is a real island in the middle of the Mississippi River, connected to Front and Adams Streets in downtown Memphis by a pedestrian bridge and a monorail. This 50-acre island holds a giant scale, five-block-long mock-up of the Mississippi River, with the role of Gulf of Mexico played by a huge, 1.3 million gallon public swimming pool. The excellent **Mississippi River Museum** tells all you could want to know about the geography and history of Ol' Muddy and has a very good music section to boot. The island is even more worth a visit for the chance to see the odd sight of the **Memphis Belle**, the blonde-bombshell-emblazoned B-17 bomber that saw action during World War II.

The minor league Memphis Chickasaws, aka the "Chicks," were bumped up to a Class AAA farm club for the St. Louis Cardinals, and renamed the **Redbirds** (901/721-6000). They play at municipal-feeling Tim McCarver Stadium, east of downtown off Central Avenue, across from the wonderful old **Libertyland** amusement park ($7-17; 901/274-1776) home of Elvis Presley's favorite roller coaster, the rickety wooden "Zippin' Pippin."

For more on **Elvis Presley**, including details on visiting Graceland, see **In Search of Elvis** on page 265.

Practicalities

Home base of Federal Express, Memphis is generally well connected to the outside world. The main airport, Memphis International (aka M.I.A.), is a Northwest Airlines hub, and is located across I-55 from Graceland, around seven miles south of downtown. The usual car rental firms have locations there; the ride downtown costs around $10 by shuttle van, closer to $20 by taxi. Getting around Memphis is best done in a car, not least because parts of town can suddenly switch from very safe to potentially dangerous in between the main tourist areas.

Food is one area where Memphis still surpasses just about any other American city, with bigger portions and better prices than you can find anywhere else. **Buntyn Restaurant**, 3070 Southern Avenue (Mon.-Fri. 11 AM-8 PM; 901/458-8776), east of the Mid-South Coliseum invites you to sit down to the kind of cookery that has made the South famous: veggies boiled with fatback pork, excellent batter-fried chicken, heaps of mashed potatoes with thick brown gravy, and sweet pies with crusts as white as snow. Other similarly traditional Southern places in Memphis include the **Arcade**, 540 S. Main Street, and the neighborly **Barksdale**, east of downtown at 237 S. Cooper Street. **Rendezvous Ribs**, 52 S. Second Street (901/523-2746), in the alley behind the Days Inn downtown, is a cavernous place, frequently ranked as one of the best rib joints in a city that considers itself the pork BBQ capital of the known universe. Some of the many other candidates for best BBQ in town are the **Cozy Corner**, at 745 N. Parkway, and the **Interstate BBQ**, 2265 S. 3rd Street.

Like the city's food, **accommodations** are priced more reasonably than you might think. The whole alphabet of major chains—from Best Western to Super 8—is spread around the I-240 beltway, and again along I-55 in neighboring Arkansas. One time *not* to try to find a cheap room is mid-August,

(continues on following page)

when the city is flooded with Elvis fans coming to honor their King during "Dead Elvis Week" (officially, Elvis International Tribute Week). While sightings of Elvis-related camp can reach comedic heights, it is not a good time to try to compete for motel rooms.

One convenient place to stay is the **Days Inn Downtown**, 164 Union Avenue (901/527-4100), with standard rooms from under $100. Across the street, **The Peabody**, 149 Union Avenue (901/529-4000, 800/PEABODY or 800/732-2639) is Memphis's premiere downtown hotel, whose sparkling lobby is home to the Mississippi's most famous mallards: twice daily at 11 AM and 5 PM the red carpet is rolled out for the Peabody Ducks to parade (waddle, really) to and from the fountain, to the delight of kids and flash manufacturers; doubles cost $175 and up. If you're planning a vigil at Graceland, consider the rather plain **Wilson World-Graceland Motel**, 3677 Elvis Presley Boulevard (901/332-1000 or 800/945-7667). Owned by his heirs and across from his former lair, it features a 24-hour in-room Elvis movie channel; doubles run $55-65 a night.

For tourist **information** contact the friendly and thorough Memphis Convention and Visitors Bureau, 47 Union Avenue (901/543-5300 or 800/873-6282), or drop by their information booth at 340 Beale Street.

Columbus, Kentucky (pop. 500) fancied itself a candidate for the new U.S. capital after Washington, D.C. was sacked and burned by the British in the War of 1812. At that time the town was very nearly the geographical center of the U.S.

landscaping, the route's dullness is broken only by a couple of one-horse towns and glimpses of smokestacks along the unseen Mississippi. A few miles before rejoining US-51 southbound at the gas-food-lodging fringe of **Dyersburg**, the GRR finally climbs out of the river valley and back onto more varied terrain. Unfortunately US-51 does its level best to mimic an interstate, cutting across contours rather than conforming to them and generally rendering the final 78 miles to downtown Memphis a forgettable blur.

In late September **Fulton, Kentucky** hosts the International Banana Festival to celebrate its bygone days as "Banana Capital of the World," when 70% of all the bananas shipped to the U.S. used to be landed there. A highlight of the festival is the one-ton banana pudding.

Driving across Memphis

Fans of Pop Culture kitsch will love what the GRR offers you in Memphis: the main road from the north (US-51) is Danny Thomas Boulevard; south of downtown, this turns into Elvis Presley Boulevard, and runs right past the gates of Graceland. (However, if you're continuing on to the Mississippi Delta, from Graceland you should switch onto US-61, which runs about two miles to the west.)

ACROSS MISSISSIPPI

Between Chickasaw Bluff in Memphis and the Mississippi state line the GRR enters what's known as the Mississippi Delta. In one sense we've already been in it, for ecologically the delta is the vast alluvial plain between Cairo and the Gulf coast, but "The Delta" of popular myth is much more circumscribed, encompassing just 250 miles of King Cotton's realm between Memphis and Vicksburg; in his historical book *Where I was Born and Raised* writer David Cohn contends that the Mississippi Delta "begins in the lobby of the Peabody Hotel in Memphis and ends on Catfish Row in Vicksburg." As important as its proper boundaries is its dual legacy as a great Civil War battleground and cradle of nearly every American musical style from gospel, blues, and jazz to country and rock 'n' roll. The backbone of our route, US-61, is also legendary as the path of the Great Migration, the post-Depression exodus to the industrialized northern U.S. of some five million black sharecroppers displaced by the mechanized cotton harvester.

As the GRR—sans the familiar pilot's wheel—drops like a plumb line across the cotton fields, we recommend side trips to landmarks of this rich cultural heritage. Where the Delta ends at the foot of Vicksburg's bluffs our route begins mingling with ghosts from the South's plantation and Civil War past, briefly detouring along the pastoral Natchez Trace Parkway until reaching the antebellum confection of Natchez itself. The GRR finally rolls into Louisiana amid thick pine woods along US-61.

Monday is traditionally red-beans-and-rice day at most true Southern home-style, barbecue, or soul-food restaurants, because Monday is traditionally wash day, and beans are a good dish to let sit and cook all day while you scrub your laundry.

If you need to do some of your own laundry in Mississippi or Louisiana, it isn't a laundromat you'll be searching for, but a washerette or washeteria.

To Northerners, it was the Civil War. South of the line where most people start calling you "Ma'am" or "Sir" it was once the "War Between the States." In the heart of Dixie it was the "War for Southern Independence." (In places Yankees fear to tread, it was called the "War of Northern Aggression.")

The word Mississippi comes from the Algonquian *misezibi* meaning "water from land all over," or "great water."

Northwest Mississippi: Casino Country

Leaving Memphis via US-61, the unsigned GRR enters De Soto and Tunica Counties, the place-names memorializing Hernando de Soto, the first European to see the Mississippi, and the combative Tunica tribe who forced the Spanish conquistador's mosquito- and snake-bitten expedition to cross the river hereabouts in 1542. Outfitted with cannons, priests, slaves, pigs, war dogs, and 1,000 soldiers, De Soto spent years marching through southern swamps in quest of gold—but he was 450 years too early. Tunica County, long one of the most destitute places in America, only became a gold mine in 1992 after the state legalized gambling. Several billion dollars of investment later, every big name in casinos lines the levee, glittering palaces plunked down amid the cotton bolls. Bugsy Siegel would be proud.

To aid the influx of people anxious to part with their money, US-61 is being turned into a high-volume, four-lane highway for some 50 miles from the Tennessee

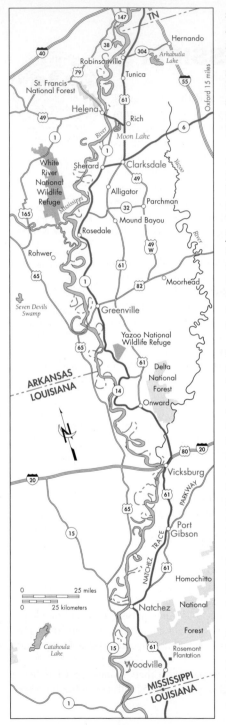

state line to the US-49 bridge from Arkansas. Motels, fast-food places, and gas stations are popping up like mushrooms after a spring rain, while the sorry-looking shacks that used to house the county's African-American sharecroppers are being torn down, as if deleting the symbols will amend the history of peonage.

Turn off the GRR toward the Commerce Landing casinos to find the vestiges of **Robinsonville,** once home to blues guitarist **Robert Johnson,** whose skill is said to have come from the Devil. **The Hollywood** restaurant on Hwy-304 just opposite the post office has live blues some weekend nights, and gen-u-wine down-home good cookin' daily (lunch Mon.-Fri., dinner Thurs.-Sun.). Skeptics who doubt the ingenuity of Southern cuisine should come try the deep-fried dill pickle slices.

As "improvements" on behalf of the casinos strip the land of its relics, detour toward **Hernando** on Hwy-304 to visit what's being lost. About 10 miles east of the GRR, just past the junction with Hwy-301, is a small sign for **Country Charm,** a weekends-only antique shop and museum whose collection includes a set of buildings the Delta is trying to forget: a shotgun shack, dog-trot house, pole barn, and slave cabin. Owner Beth Farnell will happily share her appreciation of these rough utilitarian structures, scavenged locally and restored with obvious dedication. Stand inside them, imagine life inside them, and soon, the birth of the blues in the Delta will start to make a whole lot of sense.

Following US-61 southbound, the GRR skirts the edge of **Tunica,** passing the classic grits-and-gravy, steak-and-potato **Blue & White Cafe,** before making a 35-mile beeline through the cotton fields and casino billboards to Clarksdale.

Moon Lake

Twenty miles south of Tunica's casinos, just west of US-61, Moon Lake was home to one of the South's most famous Prohibition landmarks, the **Moon Lake Club**. Unlike speakeasies associated with thugs and tarts, this club was a family destination where parents could dance and gamble while the kids played by the lake. In a place and time when

planes were still so rare the sound of their engines could interrupt work and empty classrooms, the club flew in fresh Maine lobster and Kansas City steak for its clientele of rich white Memphians.

Moon Lake has a literary history, too, appearing in a number of Tennessee Williams's dramas. Williams knew it well: not only was the club property owned by a cousin, but as a boy he had been a frequent guest, accompanying his grandfather, the Reverend Dakin, on parish calls throughout the county. The club was finally shut down by its own patrons after they learned the gambling franchise was tied to the Chicago mob, but the building still stands on Moon Lake Road, south of US-49. Now a mere ghost of its former self, it's called **Uncle Henry's Place**, a homey seafood restaurant (by reservation only, 601/337-2757), characterful B&B, and annual host of the Clarksdale **Tennessee Williams Festival** opening night dinner held in mid-October.

St. Louis likes to claim **Tennessee Williams** as a native son, but while the family did indeed move there when Tom was in fourth grade, the Mississippi-born playwright hated St. Louis "with a purple passion."

According to blues legend, mediocre musician **Robert Johnson** traded his soul to Satan at "The Crossroads" of Highways 49 and 61 to become king of the blues guitar. Seventy years ago in Johnson's day, of course, *any* guitar-pickin' "musicianer" was thought to be in cahoots with the Devil.

Helena, Arkansas

About a dozen miles west of the GRR and Moon Lake via US-49 is Helena, Arkansas, "the most deadly place on the river" to Union regiments in the Civil War stopped in their tracks by the festering malarial swamps that once surrounded the town. It began building a more sanguine reputation as the self-proclaimed "Buckle on the Blues Belt" when a local station began broadcasting a flour company-sponsored live blues show back in the early 1940s. Now the second weekend of each October the **King Biscuit Blues Festival** (call 501/338-9144 for info) attracts fans by the tens of thousands to hear one of the best lineups of live gospel and blues in the nation. The **Delta Cultural Center** (daily till 5 PM; free) in the renovated train depot downtown is an equally compelling reason to visit this small river town, with its fine historical displays on the lives of Delta inhabitants that neither deny nor ignore the shameful episodes. For the best burger in town—the "bluesburger," of course—look no farther than **Casqui's**, across the street from the depot.

Another Moon Lake landmark, now gone, was country star Conway Twitty's roadhouse, the kind of place so rough that if you came in without a gun, they'd issue you one.

Thomas Harris, author of *The Silence of the Lambs,* hails from the tiny hamlet of Rich, just east of the junction of US-61 and US-49.

Clarksdale

The blues were born in the Delta, but they grew up in Clarksdale, 15 unswerving miles south along US-61 from the US-49 junction to Helena. The census rolls for this small town read like a musical hall of fame: Ma Rainey, W.C. Handy, Bessie Smith, Sam Cooke, Ike Turner, Muddy Waters, Wade Walton, John Lee Hooker, Big Jack Johnson, and many others whose achievements are described—and may be heard—in the **Delta Blues Museum** (Mon.-Sat. 9 AM-5 PM; free; 601/624-4461 or 627-6820) in the **Carnegie Public Library** at 114 Delta Avenue, on the corner of 1st Street. The museum offers maps of blues landmarks around town and around the state, a calendar of blues events, and all sorts of helpful information. In short, this is the best place to start your journey through the Delta Blues world.

Ever since W.C. Handy traded his steady gigs in Clarksdale for a career on Beale

---

GETTING THE BLUES

If serious blueshounds sniff around enough, they will find the kind of swaggering, sweaty, Saturday-night juke joint that will always be synonymous with real Delta blues. You know the place: Budweiser on ice in a plastic cooler, clouds of cigarette smoke, some rough customers, hot dancing, and honest gut-wrenching blues played with an intensity that rattles your fillings. Yes, such places exist, but they don't run display ads in the local paper, or make the list of area attractions given out by local chambers of commerce. Given the state's deep racial divide you won't find many white chamber-of-commerce types in these predominantly black joints.

The really homegrown variety announces itself with hand-lettered signs on telephone poles and laundromat bulletin boards, if at all. They have no phone numbers, no advance tickets (usually); and you have to show up to find out who, if anyone, is playing. Ask around: the convenience store clerk, the men hanging around the commissary in one of the small towns off the main road, the person next to you at the barbecue counter. Keep in mind the blues are rooted in a condition of the Delta's black community that is no bed of roses; voyeurs slumming as tourists to hardship will be politely stonewalled at best. Even a juke-joint guide who trusts he or she is not being put inside a fishbowl for your entertainment may still hesitate to tell you where to go, since some places have legitimate reputations as low-life dives. But with perseverance, the proper attitude (and especially for women, a companion), you'll find what you're looking for. Once you get there, out-of-towners needn't worry about the reception: blues musicians welcome an appreciative audience, period.

Weekends, again mostly Saturday nights, are also about the only time you'll catch blues in the more commercial juke joints and clubs, simply because so many musicians have other jobs during the week. If you really want to be sure of hearing some blues, time your travels to coincide with one of the blues festivals happening throughout the summer months.

Street in Memphis, the Mississippi Delta has exported its blues musicians to places where they receive wider recognition and a living wage, but come Friday or Saturday night and you'll see Clarksdale still cooks up some good hot blues. Try **Red's South End**, 395 Sunflower Avenue (601/627-3166), **Margaret's Blue Diamond Lounge**, 381 W. Tallahatchie Avenue in a very dilapidated part of town (601/627-4060); or the **Rivermount Lounge**, 911 Sunflower (601/627-1971); all of which book live blues along with R&B, disco, and rap. If you're in town during the

Mississippi law doesn't require casinos to be riverboats, it merely requires them to float. All appearances to the contrary, the giant Las Vegas-style casinos in Tunica County are indeed floating, mostly in ponds dredged specifically to meet the letter of the law.

first weekend in August it would be a shame to miss the **Sunflower River Blues Festival**, staged at venues around town.

At time of writing, blues-rich **Stackhouse Records** had closed the doors of its long-time home behind the steamboat facade at 232 Sunflower Avenue. This was

---

For a spine-tingling Delta experience of another order, it is still possible to find that private front-porch recital by a legendary bluesman too old or rooted on his farm to do tours, or that demonstration of a diddley-bo by a fellow who makes them, or that master lesson for an aspiring musician. These sessions carry their own etiquette for tipping or gift-giving, so some familiarity with Southern protocol helps. Persistence pays off here, too, but the best advice for would-be pilgrims and apprentices is to make the **Delta Blues Museum** in Clarksdale, Mississippi an early stop on your tour.

The following is a partial list of annual Delta blues festivals, all in Mississippi unless otherwise noted.

Muddy Waters Day, Clarksdale (601/624-4461), first Saturday in April

Robert Johnson Day, Clarksdale (601/624-4461), first Saturday in May

Mississippi Crossroads Blues Festival, Greenwood (800/748-9064), last Saturday in May

B.B. King Homecoming, Indianola (601/887-4454), first Saturday in June

Eureka Blues Festival, Eureka Springs, AR (501/253-9344), first weekend in June

Bentonia Blues Festival, Bentonia (601/755-2278), first Saturday in July

Sunflower River Blues and Gospel Festival, Clarksdale (601/624-4461), first weekend in August

Northeast Mississippi Blues and Gospel Folk Festival, Holly Springs (601/252-4661), second Saturday in September

Mississippi Delta Blues Festival, Greenville (800/467-3582), mid-September

King Biscuit Blues Festival, Helena, AR (501/338-9144), second weekend of October

The old Afro-American Hospital at 615 Sunflower Avenue is where vocalist **Bessie Smith** died in 1937 after a car accident out on US-61. The apocryphal version of this tragedy, dramatized by Edward Albee, suggests the singer might have survived if she hadn't been denied admission to white hospitals, but at least one doctor from the old Afro-American Hospital has disputed this.

also the headquarters of the Rooster Blues record label, and a good place to find out about local goings-on, so hopefully they'll have found a new home by the time you visit. Ask at the Delta Blues Museum; they'll know the story.

Clarksdale has plenty of fast food, but the barbecue is better: try the **Ranchero**, 1907 N. State Street on US-61, or **Abe's Bar-B-Q**, 616 State Street (at the junction of US-61 and US-49) at the center of town, cooking up tangy 'cue since 1924. For a surprising dose of Lebanese-Italian food amid the pork palaces, check out **Chamoun's Rest Haven** (closed Sunday), at 419 S. State Street, on US-61 just south of the Big Sunflower River.

US-61, a.k.a. State Street, is also where you'll find Clarksdale's motels, from a **Days Inn** across from the Ranchero to a **Comfort Inn** at the southern end of town. Least expensive is the **Plantation Inn** (601/624-6541), across from the Rest Haven, with doubles from $30.

Detour: Oxford

Do you need a break from the Delta yet? Has counting pickup trucks, propane tanks, and barbecued ribs induced a bad imitation drawl? How far would you detour for a well-stocked bookstore, a movie with subtitles, a restaurant that doesn't immerse everything in boiling oil? Sixty-two miles east of Clarksdale on Hwy-6 is the college town of Oxford, whose cultural amenities, though common to college towns from Amherst and Boulder to Madison and Santa Barbara, set it in a world apart from the rest of Mississippi. The college in question is "Ole Miss," otherwise known as the University of Mississippi, whose pleasant campus holds such treasures as B.B. King's entire personal collection of records, posters, photos, and more in the **U of M Blues Archive** (Mon.-Fri. 8:30 AM-5 PM; 601/232-7753; appointments required to listen to music), in Farley Hall across from Barnard Observatory. The renovated antebellum observatory actually houses the **Center For The Study of Southern Culture** (Mon.-Fri. 8:15 AM-4:45 PM; 601/232-5993), which sponsors exhibits, lectures, and screenings.

Elsewhere under the leafy old oaks you'll find a large collection of primitive **Southern folk art** in the University Museums (closed Monday), and a collection of William Faulkner first editions in the J.D. Williams Library. Faulkner was a resident of Oxford for most of his life; readers of his novels will recognize in surrounding Lafayette County (luh-FAY-it) elements of Faulkner's fictional Yoknapatawpha. A statue of him was recently placed in the square at the center of Oxford, and **Rowan Oak** (Tues.-Sat. 10 AM-noon and 2-4 PM, Sunday 2-4 PM; free), his house on Old Taylor Road off S. Lamar Avenue, remains as he left it when he died in 1962, with the bottle of whiskey next to the old typewriter in his study almost, but not quite, empty. Visit his gravesite by following the signs from the north side of the courthouse square; near the cemetery entrance lie other family members who didn't affect adding the "u" to their surname, including the brother whose untimely death Faulkner mourned in his first novel, *Soldier's Pay*.

When respects have been paid to Southern culture and it's time to eat, take a 10-mile trip north on Hwy-7 to tiny **Abbeville** and sit down to fine fried catfish and other solid Southern dishes at the counter inside **Ruth & Jimmie's** nationally famous gas station-bait shop-grocery-and-cafe. You can't miss it; they're open for breakfast 7-

9 AM and lunch 11 AM-2 PM, every day but Monday. Or, for a full Southern country breakfast (try the red-eye gravy) or lunch in town, **Smitty's**, at 208 S. Lamar just south of the square, is the place. (That gravy gets its name from the coffee mixed in with the ham drippings.) Also in Oxford, on Harrison Avenue in what doubles as the lobby of an art-house cinema, **Hoka Theater & Cafe** serves vegetarian bar food for the undergraduate crowd at undergraduate prices amid a decor that is vividly political, playful, and about as subtle as MTV. They have Ben and Jerry's ice cream, too.

Accommodations in Oxford include a **Holiday Inn** north of the courthouse, and other motels by the exits along Hwy-6.

The **Oxford Tourism Council** (601/234-4651) will happily provide more information and a calendar of cultural events; they also operate a **visitor center** in a tiny cottage next to City Hall on the central square. Another good source of information and other new and used reading matter is **Square Books**, on the south side of the same square.

Highway 1

The official Great River Road actually bypasses Clarksdale along rural Hwy-1, which winds nearer to the river; to rejoin this riparian route, turn west on Hwy-322 toward **Sherard**, south of where the GRR races across one straight section after another, as if its engineers couldn't wait to get out of the Delta. The monotony of cotton is broken only by the occasional soybean, milo, and catfish farm; next to agriculture, "pond cat" is one of the Delta's hottest products.

The passing towns are mostly anonymous down-on-their-luck affairs filled with shotgun shacks, low-slung Creole-style bungalows, and old trailers that some people have nicknamed "doghouses" without any attempt at irony. What look like oil drums mounted on garden carts in the odd front yard are smokers, for doing barbecue just right; their presence sometimes implies the proximity of a social club or juke joint that may do only weekend business. Local stores, if they exist, are where men in overalls sit and stand in clusters, keeping an eye on the world. Some of these places are reputed to have backroom card games that would make any of the new casinos weep with envy. In autumn when the cotton is ready for harvest, huge truck-sized bales sit in the cleared muddy margins of the fields, and white fluff accumulates in drifts on the narrow loose shoulder, swirling in small eddies in your wake.

Meanwhile the Mississippi River does its snaky shuffle off to the Gulf of Mexico behind a continuous line of levees, a bayou here and cut-off lake there as proof of past indirections. Unlike the spreading deltas of the Orinoco or Nile, the Mississippi cuts a deeper channel as it rolls south, the deceptively unruffled surface hiding a flow four times greater than at the St. Louis Arch.

Holly Springs, 30 miles north of Oxford, is home to "the world's number one Elvis fan," Paul MacLeod, and his equally dedicated son, Elvis Aaron Presley MacLeod, who devote their lives to documenting every Elvis reference they find in newspapers, in magazines, or on TV. For a $5 donation you can visit their ever-vigilant 24-hour Elvis media monitoring station and artifact-filled shrine, **Graceland Too**, at 200 East Gholson Avenue.

The most famous shotgun house in Mississippi is the one in which **Elvis Aaron Presley** was born on January 8, 1935, in Tupelo, a half-hour east of Oxford. The name for these long and narrow three-room wooden boxes refers to the alignment of its doorways: a shot fired through the front door will pass clear through to the back without hitting a wall. Tupelo is also the birthplace of blues master **John Lee Hooker.**

Before yielding to any temptation to simply drive down a dirt farm lane for a peek at the river that General Grant called "too damned muddy to drink, too wet to plow," keep in mind that Mississippi mud is as tenacious as it gets. If you've never had the pleasure of using gasoline to burn caked mud off your tires—after a tractor has pulled your car out—sink an axle into Alligator clay (named for a hamlet south of Clarksdale) and you might get a chance.

Greenville

Shortly after passing the 1,000-year-old Winterville Mounds and less-ancient Hub Cap City, two landmarks illustrating the range of human activity in the Delta from prehistory through the present, the GRR enters Greenville, one of the largest river ports in the state, its levees now lined by floating casinos. Hwy-1 through Greenville takes top honors for the least attractive strip of gas stations and mini-marts yet encountered along the GRR, with a close second going to the intersecting Hwy-82 that enters town from the east.

Like Scripture verse quoted by a used-car salesperson, Greenville's covers don't do justice to its text, for the city has some fine cultural traditions, from the anti-Ku Klux Klan editorializing of Hodding Carter's *Delta-Democrat Times* during the 1950s and 1960s to the hot tamales at **Doe's Eat Place**. In the big white building at 502 Nelson Street (follow N. Broadway to the brick churches, then turn toward the river), Doe's is known throughout the state for its good food and honest prices, and for the fact that you have to enter through the kitchen. The presence of tamales on menus all the way down to Natchez, and at roadside stands along US-61, is one of the more unusual Delta idioms, although this being the South the corn husks with their tasty corn meal and meat fillings are cooked in hot oil rather than steamed as they might be in East L.A. or El Salvador.

Second to Clarksdale in the Delta blues galaxy, Greenville's **blues clubs** (Boobah Barnes Playboy Club, for example) are all located around Thompson Avenue in a part of town that will make your mother's heart skip a beat; come in mid-September during the annual **Mississippi Delta Blues Festival** and at least there will be the strength of overwhelming numbers to soothe her arrhythmia.

For **accommodations**, look along Hwy-82 near the junction with US-61, east of town: **Days Inn, Best Western, Ramada,** and **Hampton** are all there.

For more information contact the Greenville **visitor center** at 915 Washington Avenue (601/378-3141).

About 30 miles east of the GRR on Hwy-32 is **Parchman,** infamous home to the state prison farms, memorialized in songs like bluesman Bukka White's "Parchman Farm." The "Midnight Special," another oft-heard allusion in Delta blues lyrics, was the weekend train from New Orleans that brought visitors to the prison.

East of the GRR on Hwy-61 is small **Mound Bayou,** the oldest black town in the state. A man named Isaiah Montgomery, inspired by Booker T. Washington's prescriptions for black self-improvement, founded the all-black community in 1888 with support from his former employer, Jefferson Davis.

Across the Mississippi from Rosedale in a cotton field off Hwy-1 is **Rohwer, Arkansas,** where 8,500 Japanese-Americans were forced from their California homes and imprisoned for the duration of WW II.

About 30 miles east of Greenville, Moorhead is known in blues geography as the place "where the Southern crosses the Dog," an allusion to the Southern and Yazoo-Delta (a.k.a. "Yellow Dog") Railroads.

Highway 1 Revisited

Between Greenville and Vicksburg the GRR continues along Hwy-1 through the cotton-rich bottoms, the landscape as unvarying as the country music that dominates the radio dial. Before the Civil War this land was nearly uninhabitable hardwood forests and fever-riddled swamps, home to snakes, panthers, and mosquitoes. After Reconstruction the valuable oaks, sweetgum, and hickory were logged off, the swamps drained, and levees built; now just the snakes and mosquitoes remain.

At the junction with Hwy-14 the GRR turns abruptly west to mosey for 30 miles amid second-growth forest—dense woodlands that are the edge of the lower Yazoo River basin, valuable habitat for the wood stork, bald eagle, and Louisiana black bear. The GRR rejoins US-61 again in the hamlet of **Onward**, where a historical plaque marks the "birthplace of the Teddy Bear," and the funky old general store next to the Fina station has a mechanical bear that does a little dance in exchange for your quarter.

After the rigid flatness of the Delta, the final stretch south to Vicksburg rolls through low hills whose slopes seem downright dramatic, but don't let the novelty of a little scenery distract you from taking the US-61 Business turnoff, shortly after the highway grows to a fast four lanes.

Vicksburg stands at the junction of the Great River Road and our "Southern Pacific" tour along US-80, which runs from San Diego to Savannah, and is described on pages 738-791.

Vicksburg

The "Red Carpet City of the South" didn't roll one out for the Union army during the Civil War; rather, the city so stubbornly opposed Union efforts to win control of the Mississippi River that Vicksburg became the target of one of the longest sieges in U.S. military history. After the war ended, Vicksburg suffered once again in 1876, when the city woke up to face a mud flat of flopping fish after the Mississippi River found itself a new streambed—overnight. Thanks to the diligence of engineers who redirected the Yazoo River, Vicksburg has its waterfront back, now complete with several modern-day sharks, whose slot machines and roulette wheels spin 24 hours for your entertainment.

Though the engineering feat is impressive, it's the story of the campaign to split the Confederacy in half along the great river that dominates history. The battle for Vicksburg reached its dramatic conclusion in 1863 amid the strategic heights and ravines of the 1,800-acre **National Military Park** ($4 per car). Without a historical informant the old battlefield is merely an extensive collection of ornate monuments to the soldiers who died fighting over these grassy earthworks that spring. A visit becomes emotionally compelling after some accounting of the 47-day Siege of Vicksburg—the anecdotes of individual valor, of odd courtesies amid the bloodshed, of the tragedy and humanity that lie in such unequal measure behind the 16 winding miles of stone. Audiotape tours may be rented from the visitor center (daily except Christmas 8 AM-5 PM) for $4.50, with narration and sound effects, or you can hire a guide ($10 per hour, two-hour minimum, three hours recommended) to accompany you in your car and explain everything from battle strategies to the symbolism of the monuments. The advantage to a live guide is the opportunity to ask questions and to delve into whatever suits your curiosity, be it stories of the many women who fought incognito, or of the immigrants who enlisted to win citizenship, or of General Grant's legendary difficulties with drink. The **Vicksburg Convention and Visitors Bureau** (601/636-9421 or 800/221-3536) keeps a list of these very worthwhile guides.

Late in the year when the pecan crop is in, you can buy pecans from vans or shacks beside the highway. But buy pre-shelled ones, or spend hours struggling with a nutcracker.

AN EXHIBIT OF JIM HENSON'S DELTA BOYHOOD

The town of Leland, eight miles east of Greenville on US-82, was the boyhood home of Muppet-master **Jim Henson.** There's now a small and suitably warm-spirited museum, on the north side of US-82 at Deer Creek, honoring him, Kermit the Frog, and his other creations.

You won't notice many people lolling about on grassy lawns or parks in the southern Delta, for the simple reason that this has become the realm of the fire ant, whose stinging bite would shame a wasp into adopting some other line of work.

Many of the city's posh **antebellum houses** survived the Civil War with varying degrees of damage, and during the post-war Reconstruction several additional mansions were added to the bluffs overlooking the river. Most of these homes are open to the public (average $5), and during the fortnight-long "Pilgrimages" in late March and mid-October, slightly discounted multiple-house tours are available. The architecturally varied mansions, many of which double as B&Bs, and their copious inventories of fine antiques are more fascinating to decorative arts aficionados than to history buffs, who may find tours illuminating more for what is omitted than included. Stories of deprivation and Union plundering, cannonballs in parlor walls, and other wartime relics are religiously enshrined, yet never a word is spoken about slavery. The most famous of these homes is **Cedar Grove**, 2300 Washington Street, which ironically was built for a cousin of General Sherman, who used it as a military hospital, while **Anchuca**, 1010 E. 1st Street, preserves a more complete picture of antebellum life, with well preserved gardens and slave quarters. Dozens more, including some dating from the 1870s up through the early 1900s, are found throughout Vicksburg's pleasantly cobblestoned residential areas.

The downtown commercial district, on the bluffs above the river, offers another, more contemporary glimpse into Southern culture. If you've ever tried to imagine a world without Coke, step into the **Biedenharn Museum of Coca-Cola Memorabilia**, smack downtown at 1107 Washington Street, and see where one man's ingenuity slew all hopes for such a world. Here in 1894 Joseph Biedenharn conceived of putting the strictly regional soda fountain drink into bottles, the better to reach new markets; the rest, as they say, is history. Toast worldwide domination with

BIRTH OF THE TEDDY BEAR

The original Teddy Bear was inspired by a cub from the woods near Onward, Mississippi: tied by a noose to a tree in the canebrakes, the cute fellow was found by President Teddy Roosevelt while hunting here in 1903. His refusal to shoot the defenseless animal, publicized in an editorial cartoon, garnered such popular approval that a New York firm requested the president's permission to name a stuffed toy after him. The only rub is, T.R. didn't actually refuse to shoot—because, in fact, he wasn't there. But neither was the cub! According to members of the hunting party, the president's guide, Holt Collier, an African-American veteran of the Confederate cavalry, was challenged to prove he could lasso a bear. So he did, when one came along through the swamp —an old and rather weak one, as it turned out, that splashed around in a slough before they cut him loose. T.R., however, having tired of waiting for game, had returned to camp and missed the whole episode.

To escape from Vicksburg's indoor onslaught of Louis XV marquetry and Chippendale claw feet, stop by **Margaret's Grocery** right on the GRR (old US-61) on the north side of town, at 4535 N. Washington Street (601/638-1163), where an assemblage of huge hand-lettered signs preach Biblically inspired words of wisdom at passersby. It's no longer a store, but is open as an informal "Welcome Center;" for details, see **Deep South Roadside Shrines** on pages 774-775.

some of the classic stuff, straight up or over ice cream, or pay $2 to view galleries full of old promotional serving trays and the like.

Vicksburg Practicalities

For a traditional Southern feast, sit down to the communal round table at **Walnut Hills**, 1214 Adams Street at Clay and dig into the endless supply of classic regional dishes, from fried pork tenderloin to okra; given the fresh ingredients and depend-

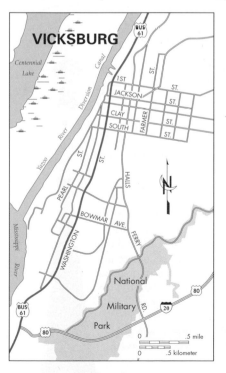

ing on how much of a pig you can be, the moderate prices are a great value. An equally rib-stuffing meal at an even more amazing price is found weekdays at lunch in the friendly **Kitchen in the Garden**, a hole-in-the-wall tucked away at the north end of 5th Street, just off Main Street E. "Down-to-earth soul food" is the credo here, and it's no lie: try the fried chicken or fish for a real treat, and savor how pork fat makes greens so tasty. Many of the side vegetables come out of a can, but you can't expect Julia Child at these prices. The place is also open in the evening, when it attracts a rowdier crowd— which may explain why some of the seating is so rickety.

Reavey's Bar-B-Q at the corner of 1st Street N and Clay serves some of the city's finest pork and beef ribs, while deep-fried tamale addicts should seek out **Solly's Hot Tamales**, on US-61 Business at 1921 Washington Street.

Ruins of Windsor

One of the most unusual sights in the Vicksburg Military Park is the **USS Cairo,** an ironclad, paddlewheel battleship that sank during the Civil War. Preserved for a century by the Mississippi mud, it was recovered and restored, and is now on display as a museum.

Vicksburg's street signs are small white croquet poles stuck into the grass at street corners, lettered vertically with a stencil; they must have cost a fortune to have escaped replacement by something useful. Rather than wonder at their illegibility, obtain a map from the visitor bureau.

The icon of Southern gentility and refreshment, the **mint julep,** was allegedly born in Vicksburg: water from fragrant Mint Springs in what is now the National Military Park was mixed with good Kentucky bourbon brought to town by riverboat captains. It goes without saying that Kentuckians and Tennesseans consider this to be pure fiction.

Vicksburg motels, found at the south edge of town along I-20 between the Mississippi River and the Military Park, include a wide selection of the national chains and their local imitators. One of the nicest is the **Park Inn,** at the I-20/ US-61 junction (601/638-5811), which has a pool, a bountiful free breakfast buffet—and live parrots squawking in the lobby. Or, for only $85-150, you can play Rhett and Scarlett for a night, pampering yourself with canopied beds and frocked shower curtains in one of the 10 camellia-draped tour homes that double as plush B&Bs. Any will have you whistling "Dixie," but true history buffs will want to request the Grant Room at **Cedar Grove** (800/862-1300), still furnished with the very bed the general used after Union forces occupied Vicksburg. The staff claims ol' Sam was a bedridden drunk for his entire stay, but pay no attention—he was probably a poor tipper at the bar, and folks around here bear grudges for generations over things like that.

For thorough and concise information on lodging and attractions, call the friendly **Vicksburg Convention and Visitors Bureau** (800/221-3536) or visit their **tourist information center** opposite the entrance to the National Military Park. If your visit falls during Pilgrimage, don't expect easy pickings on rooms: most B&Bs are booked up to *two years* in advance for those weeks.

Port Gibson

Neither the weather nor the road seems to take any notice of the fact that you leave the low-lying Delta bottoms as the GRR heads south from Vicksburg along a wooded stretch of US-61; trees or no trees, summer humidity will still glue your clothes to your car seat. Relief comes after 30 miles in Port Gibson, the town General Grant found "too beautiful to burn."

The Union Army spared Port Gibson during the Civil War, and decades of economic doldrums have discouraged the Wal-Mart sprawl that at times seems to have enveloped the rest of the South. Fine homes still grace the pleasantly shaded main drag, but most eye-catching is the giant Monty Python prop known as the Church of the Golden Hand because its steeple is topped by a gold-leafed hand, its index finger pointing the way to Heaven.

Actually, this is the circa 1859 First Presbyterian Church, whose interior is lit by the gasoliers of the famous steamboat *Robert E. Lee*, the record-setting winner of the Great Steamboat Race of 1870. Newspapers of the day reckoned that millions of dollars were wagered on the outcome of the New Orleans-to-St. Louis race, which attracted international attention. The *Lee's* three-day, 18-hour, and 14-minute victory was an upset for the favored title holder, the *Natchez*.

Across the street from the Golden Hand, next to an Exxon station, stands another unusual building, **Temple Gemiluth Chassed**, an elaborate Moorish-arched temple built in 1891 by Port Gibson's then-large and prosperous Jewish community.

From Port Gibson, you can follow a quietly scenic 50-mile detour southwest to Natchez, first through the kudzu-draped woodlands along Bayou Pierre, and then along the serene Natchez Trace Parkway. The looping first part of this route follows Hwy-522 past nearly invisible old Indian mounds, abandoned homesteads, and picturesque old cemeteries rotting in the woods. Spot the giant stone columns poking through the treetops on the left near the old townsite of Bruinsburg and you'll have found the **Ruins of Windsor:** once the state's most lavish Greek revival mansion and landmark to river pilots, it was reduced by an 1890 fire to its bare Corinthian ribs.

> While Vicksburg's surrender allowed President Lincoln to declare that "the Father of Waters now flows unvexed to the sea," local whites stayed vexed for over 80 years: because surrender occurred on July 4, until the end of WW II Independence Day in Vicksburg was celebrated only by African-Americans.

Natchez

Before the Civil War, Natchez (pronounced NATCH-iss, rhymes with "matches") had the most millionaires per capita in the U.S., and it shows. If luxurious antebellum houses make your heart beat faster, Natchez (which has more than 500 antebellum structures inside the city limits) might just put you in the local ICU, with its innumerable white columns and rich smorgasbord of Italian marble, imported crystal, sterling silver, painted china, plush drapery, petit point, Hepplewhite, and ivory. That so much antebellum finery still exists is because Natchez, unlike Vicksburg, surrendered to Grant's army almost without a fight. Anti-Yankee sentiment may in fact run higher now than during the war, for Natchez was vehemently opposed to the Confederacy, and outspokenly against Mississippi's secession from the Union. For a town that was second only to New Orleans as social and cultural capital of a region with two-thirds of the richest people in America, most of whom owed their wealth to slave-picked cotton, you might call support of the Union a little incongruous. Of course, such apparent contradictions should come as no surprise from a community raised with genteel cotillions and the Mississippi's busiest red-light district side by side, although visitors won't find much evidence of the town's seedy past any more. (The most famous brothel in the South, Nellie's, finally closed after a 1992 fire killed the octogenarian owner.) Once-disreputable Natchez Under-the-Hill, eroded by Mississippi floods and community standards, is today but a single gentrified block of bars, restaurants, and shops, where gambling has been cleaned up and packaged aboard a permanently moored riverboat (the *Lady Luck;* 800/722-5825) and the visiting *American Queen*, which frequently docks here.

As befits the place that originated the concept, the annual Natchez Pilgrimages (held in late Spring, October and at Christmas) are twice as long as the typical 10-15 days done elsewhere. The number of **antebellum mansions** open to the public more than doubles, hoop skirts and brass-buttoned waistcoats abound, and musical diversions like the **Confederate Pageant** are held nightly. If you have patience for wistful recollections of the storied past, you can sample over a dozen of the architectural cupcakes year-round ($4-6 each, or selected multiple-house tickets from Natchez Pilgrimage Tours; 800/647-6742). Among the most fascinating is the one that didn't get finished: **Longwood**, the nation's largest octagonal house, capped by a red onion dome. Its grounds are fittingly gothic, too, with moss-dripping tree limbs, sunken driveway, and the family cemetery out in the woods.

Southern history doesn't merely comprise those Greek revival heaps and their *Gone With the Wind* stereotypes. Natchez, for example, had a large population of free blacks, whose story is told in downtown's **Museum of Afro-American History and**

Mammy's Restaurant, Natchez

Culture (call for hours; 601/445-0728), in the old Post Office on Main Street, where you'll also find interesting Black Heritage walking tour brochures. Large Jewish sections in the **City Cemetery** (follow signs for the National Cemetery, and the city's is along the way) also furnish evidence of the South's tapestried past. The marble statuary and decorative wrought iron offer a pleasant outdoor respite for weary mansion-goers, too.

One last Natchez landmark deserves special mention: **Mammy's**, a roadside restaurant in the shape of a five-times-larger-than-life Southern woman, whose red skirts house the small dining room and gift shop. Having survived many incarnations and abandonments, Mammy's is once again open for business, offering rather refined lunches (cups of tea and dainty sandwiches) from 11 AM to 2 PM Mon.-Saturday. She can be found along the east side of four-lane US-61, roughly five miles south of town.

For an overview of a nearly vanished Southern culture, spend some time at the **Museum of the Southern Jewish Experience** (601/362-6357). Based in Utica, an hour to the northeast, the museum has a branch exhibit in the basement of Temple B'nai Israel in Natchez (by appointment only; 601/445-5407).

Historic downtown Natchez was hit by tornado-strength winds in February 1998, which caused some $30 million worth of damage, almost all of which has been repaired.

Natchez Practicalities

Have you noticed how you usually have to pay a premium to avoid fried food in the South? Not so at **Pearl Street Pasta**, 105 S. Pearl just off Main Street, whose short dinner-only menu is eclectic, reasonably priced, and laced with vegetables that haven't been boiled to oblivion. For more big-city sophistication at moderate prices, head straight to **Liza's Contemporary Cuisine**, at 657 S. Canal Street next to the Best Western. The seasonal menu adds a dash of California to the Deep South, with flawless results. Veal with wild mushrooms and smoked garlic, grilled eggplant and shiitake, grilled quail with collard cornbread dressing, tuna with ginger wasabi . . . you get the picture.

If you prefer fried catfish, po' boys and chocolate shakes, head down to **The Malt Shop**, where Martin Luther King Street (US-61 Business) dead-ends into Homochitto Street. More creole food is served up downtown at **Big Easy's**, 112 N. Commerce Street.

NATCHEZ TRACE PARKWAY

A mile or so south of Port Gibson, US-61 and the GRR cross the much more relaxed Natchez Trace Parkway, which like the Blue Ridge Parkway is a scenic route managed by the National Park Service. The Parkway follows the route of the old **Natchez Trace**, a pre-Columbian Indian path that grew into the major overland route between the Gulf Coast and the upper Mississippi and Ohio River valleys in the years before steamboats provided a faster alternative. The Natchez Trace appeared on maps as early as 1733, and from the 1780s to the 1820s, when steamboats made it obsolete, the Natchez Trace was one of the nation's most traveled routes. Farmers and craftspeople in the Ohio River Valley would transport their products by raft downstream to Natchez or New Orleans, then return on foot, staying at the dozens of inns along the route while doing battle with swamps, mosquitoes, and bands of thieves.

The entire 430-mile length of the Parkway, which runs from Nashville south to the edge of Natchez, with a short break around Jackson (see pages 773-774), is well paved and makes a delightful driving route, with places of interest marked every few miles. Just north of Port Gibson at mile marker 41.5, the **Sunken Trace** preserves a deeply eroded, 200-yard-long section of the trail, the canopy of moss-laden cypress trees offering one of the most evocative five-minute walks you can imagine. Between Port Gibson and Natchez, sights along this short (and eminently bicycleable) stretch range from the prehistoric **Emerald Mound**, which dates from around A.D. 1400 and offers a commanding view of the woodlands, to **Mount Locust** at mile marker 15.5, a restored Trace roadhouse—the place to pick up parkway information, and if you're fortunate, to get a tour guided by park ranger Eric Chamberlain, who was born in the house and whose family lived there for five generations.

The National Park police keep the parkway under very thorough radar surveillance, by the way, so try to stay within the posted speed limit, a maximum 45 or 50 mph.

Natchez is almost the southern extremity of the Tamale Belt, and if this prospect gives you the DTs then sit down to a paperboard dish of them (a dozen for under $6) at **Fat Mama's** in a little log cabin at 500 S. Canal Street. Be warned, the delicious little things are greasy enough to wink back at you. The **Local Color Delicatessen**, 201 N. Pearl at Franklin Street, offers good bargain-priced sandwiches, salads, gumbo, and the like, accompanied by occasional evening live music and the best jukebox in town. (Rescued from Nellie's brothel after the fatal fire, it'll still croon you some Elvis for a quarter while you peruse news clippings about the former madam's distinctive career or a copy of her will, all preserved under the glass tabletops.) More local color can be found at either **The Corner Bar**, on Main and Canal, or **The Saloon**, in Natchez-Under-the-Hill, with its fine view of the Mississippi. Like New Orleans and Las Vegas, Natchez has no closing law, but in fact most bars do close when the last paying customers roll on home.

Across the Mississippi from Natchez, the town of **Ferriday, Louisiana,** was where rocker Jerry Lee "Great Balls of Fire" Lewis and his cousin, evangelist Jimmy Swaggert, grew up.

There are no cotton fields around Natchez, because all the cotton that paid for these mansions was grown across the river in the Louisiana bottomlands.

Accommodations include a half-dozen familiar names from budget to executive, scattered along US-61 and US-84 both north and south of downtown. As could be expected from a major tourist destination with so many fine homes, Natchez is also brimming with B&Bs, varying from white-columned manors like **Dunleith,** 84 Homochitto Street, to intimate cottages, with only one or two bedrooms. By New England or California standards most put luxury within the realm of affordability, and even the tacky or tasteless bits thrown in with the genuinely historic elegance make a nice departure from retro-Victorian pomp. Southern style, suffice it to say, is in a league of its own.

As an example of local value, consider the circa 1890 **Highpoint,** on the north side of downtown at 215 Linton Avenue (601/442-6963 or 800/283-4099): $80-95 fetches your choice of three spacious rooms, a generous "plantation" breakfast, evening mint juleps, and friendly hosts whose political, Southern, and Confederate connections would make any storyteller green with envy. Reservations for most of the other 30-odd B&Bs in town can be made through **Historic Inns of Natchez** (800/256-INNS or 800/256-4667) or **Natchez Pilgrimage Tours** (800/647-6742). Keep in mind the enormous popularity of Pilgrimage requires seriously advanced bookings during those times.

For an illustrated B&B guide and other useful information contact the **Natchez Convention and Visitors Bureau** (601/647-6724 or 800/99-NATCHEZ or 800/996-2824), which operates information centers downtown at 422 Main Street, and a larger one near the Mississippi River bridge (US-84) at 640 S. Canal Street.

Woodville: Rosemont Plantation

Rolling and curving past hay fields and woods, the distinctively red earth of southern Mississippi crowding the soft shoulders, the GRR passes quickly over the 45 miles between Natchez and the Louisiana state line. About 10 miles north of the border, an unprepossesing intersection of gas stations marks the turnoff west for Woodville (pop. 1,393), where a lovely old courthouse sits at the center of a green square full of stately old oak trees, and a trio of historic churches line the somnolent streets.

You won't see it from the highway, but just across the Mississippi is possibly the most significant piece of engineering anywhere along its length: the Old River Project. More than mere flood control, the project is designed to keep the Mississippi going down to Baton Rouge and New Orleans, rather than finding a new route to the Gulf via the Atchafalaya River. This actually happened during the 1948 flood, and there are hydrologists who predict it is only a matter of time before it will happen again—a potential catastrophe for downstream cities along both rivers.

The biggest attraction of Woodville, however, is a mile east of the GRR on US-24, where a small sign along the highway marks the entrance to **Rosemont Plantation** (daily 10AM-5 PM Mar.-Dec.; $6), the boyhood home of Confederate President Jefferson Davis. Built in 1830 with wooden pegs holding together hand-hewn posts and beams, the house is surrounded by a grove of live oaks and a large rose garden, planted by Davis's mother, after which the plantation takes its name.

A few other plantations still survive around Woodville, and all along the GRR south to New Orleans, but the hand of humanity around here and into Louisiana leans more toward utilitarian, or plain ugly. Logging used to be a major industry hereabouts before WW I and again in the decade following WW II, when portable "woodpecker" sawmills buzzed through these hills and logged off whatever virgin pine and hardwoods had been left by earlier loggers. The local timber industry now runs toward pulpwood rather than saw timber, as that second- and third-growth slash pine forest alongside the road no longer supports much of the valuable but slow-growing ash, hickory, and oak. To get a better impression of what this land used to look like back in the days of the ivory-billed woodpeckers, continue west from the GRR/Woodville intersection and follow the Pinckneyville Road about 13 miles to the **Clark Creek Nature Area**. A short trail leads up to attractive **Tunica Falls** through woods that botanically have more in common with the Ozarks and Appalachians than the rest of the lower Mississippi valley. The folks at old Duck Pond Grocery (601/888-4426), a throwback to an era of small town stores, can give directions to the trailhead if needed.

ACROSS LOUISIANA

As the GRR approaches its southern end, land and river begin to merge. The Midwestern humidity pales next to Louisiana's semi-tropical climate (when was the last time your windshield fogged up driving with all your windows *open?*); bring a snorkel. Spanish moss drips from trees and snakes slither across the road. With giant levees on one side and standing water on the other, it's easy to imagine the land is sinking—and indeed, by the time you roll off elevated I-10 into New Orleans, you will be four to six feet *below* sea level.

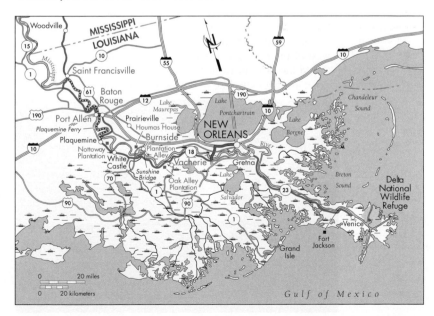

For free highway maps or other tourist information, stop at the **Louisiana Tourist Information Center** on US-61 south of the Mississippi state line.

In general, roads along the GRR are good, though they vary from four-lane freeway to unpaved track, and Minnesota's unpaved roads are smoother than Louisiana's paved ones.

About five miles southeast of St. Francisville on Hwy-965 is the **Oakley House,** where in 1821 John James Audubon came to work as a resident tutor while he completed the final 80 illustrations for his *Birds of America* series. His wife Lucy also tutored local women to help pay for the publication of his work

A dozen miles west of St. Francisville and the Great River Road along Hwy-1, the small town of **Morganza, Louisiana,** was the place where the character played by Jack Nicholson was beaten to death in his sleeping bag in the classic 1960s road movie, *Easy Rider.*

From the St. Francisville ferry to the interstate bridge just west of New Orleans, we cross the Mississippi four times, threading along rough back roads along the notorious "Chemical Corridor" of industrial giants whose toxic discharges have produced another sobriquet: Cancer Alley. Here, too, you can see a series of fine antebellum plantation homes, some crowded so close to the petrochemical plants that they have become gilded anachronisms in the pipefitter's forest. The Great River Road across Louisiana is not without its charms—a vividly painted church out in a field, or exquisitely gnarled and bent live oaks festooned with epiphytes—but these are all too often overshadowed by the specter of a land being poisoned for profit.

St. Francisville

Louisiana is divided into parishes rather than counties, a subtle reminder of the French Catholic settlement of the state. Midway across West Feliciana Parish, turn west off US-61 at St. Francisville, an 18th-century settlement that grew up around the graveyard of an order of Capuchin monks in what was then Spanish West Florida. As you follow signs for Hwy-10 west to the ferry and pass houses whose contents spill out like the ragged stuffing of an old sofa and vintage cars in less-than-vintage condition, it takes a leap of faith to believe this place is a weekend resort for downstream urban dwellers, but in fact the surrounding mossy woods hide a number of "romantic getaways" and "executive retreats," some at prices that assume a dowry or expense account. Pick up an anecdotally rich walking tour brochure at the **West Feliciana Historical Society Museum** on Ferdinand Street (Hwy-10), and follow Royal Street, a block west of the museum, for a sample of the architectural charms that draw visitors to this curious little town. The **Magnolia Cafe**, in what looks like an old gas station at the corner of Com-

Greenwood Plantation, St. Francisville

merce and Ferdinand streets, is the best reasonably priced lunch stop, with some of the best-tasting po' boys in the state that invented them.

From St. Francisville, snake west along Ferdinand Street (Hwy-10) for about a mile until it dead-ends at the large car ferry (on the hour and half-hour; $1) that shuttles across the Mississippi to Pointe Coupee Parish. If you've just missed the boat, head back into town or sit put, admiring the belching chemical plants and rusting barges or watching people catch crawfish along the muddy banks. Lest you consider skipping the ferry and proceeding to Baton Rouge via US-61, be advised that US-61 is a sorry route: oil storage tanks, trailer parks, an auto-part-pawn-shop-mini-mart strip that defies all pejoratives, and finally, adding insult to injury, the once-but-never-again "Scenic Highway" has a grandstand view of the Exxon refinery.

After disembarking on the west bank of the Mississippi, cross the steep revetment by the ferry landing and take the first left onto rough-paved Hwy-981 toward Port Allen.

Acadiana: Port Allen

In rural counterpoint to the tank farms on the east side of the river, the landscape in this corner of Acadiana, the extended swath of southwest Louisiana settled and still inhabited by descendants of French-speaking Catholics exiled from the Canadian province of Acadia in 1755, is filled with sugarcane plantations and contentedly grazing cattle—at least for the first 32 miles south of the St. Francisville ferry. Stay within the shadow of the levee, turning as necessary, until you pass under the huge steel arches of the US-190 bridge and into Port Allen. A few miles of handsome Creole-influenced plantation homes, and even a nice splash of art deco, precede the junction with Hwy-1, but for the most part this is a heavily industrialized district, better known as West Baton Rouge.

Our route crosses over the Mississippi on I-10, whose bridge looms on the horizon; as you take the approach ramp from Hwy-1 be sure to follow signs for the city, not the port, of Baton Rouge. If you want to bypass Baton Rouge altogether, follow Hwy-1 south from Port Allen to Plaquemine, then follow the GRR along what's left of the much-hyped "Plantation Alley."

Baton Rouge

From the lofty vantage point of the I-10 bridge, Baton Rouge appears to be a largely industrial city, its skyline dominated by smokestacks, distilling columns, and the nation's tallest state capitol—essentially a 34-story monument to the populist demagoguery of Huey Long. Closer inspection yields little evidence of anything particularly attractive, with the sole exception of the **Old State Capitol** (Mon.-Sat. 10

Along with po' boys and boiled crawdads, Louisiana's roadsides offer another local specialty, the daiquiri bar. Like a high-octane version of a Dairy Queen Slush, daiquiris come pre-mixed in a variety of sticky fruit flavors and sizes up to the quart that kicks: yes, an eye-crossing 32-ouncer. If that isn't enough, many of these bars have drive-up windows. In the eyes of the law, that piece of masking tape across the cup's lid makes it a "sealed container"; seems the law doesn't care about the straw.

According to the EPA, Louisiana is number one in the nation for reported toxic dumping. Yet the state regularly fails to monitor or report on toxic and radiological contaminants in its public water supplies—meaning that companies report what they've dumped, but no one knows where it goes.

The bridge that now carries US-190 over the Mississippi was built during the gubernatorial reign of the notorious "Kingfish," **Huey P. Long.** The structure was designed to be low enough to prevent oceangoing freighters from passing, thus snuffing out the chances of Vicksburg and other upstream cities to compete with the port of Baton Rouge—now the nation's fifth busiest.

AM-4 PM, Sunday noon-4 PM; $5), that clearly visible white gothic set piece from *Ivanhoe* —the only thing missing is a moat. Inside the restored 1847 edifice are engaging computer-aided history exhibits, curated by the resident Center for Political and Governmental History. Practice your stump speeches from a podium whose TelePrompter will cue you with famous sound bites from Louisiana politicians, or sit in a facsimile of a studio control room and search a digitized video database of newsreels and oral history clips. Study the unresolved 1935 Huey Long assassination: was the patronage-dealing, vote-buying potentate the target of premeditated murder, or was then-senator Long the victim of his five trigger-happy bodyguards' "friendly fire," aimed at a man who merely punched the boss? Review the evidence and draw your own conclusions.

Another lesson in Louisiana history can be yours at the wonderful **Rural Life Museum** (daily 8:30 AM- 5 PM; $5; 225/765-2437), managed by Louisiana State University and located at 4600 Essen Road, east of downtown off I-10 exit 160. This expansive collection of shotgun houses, barns, farming equipment, riverboats, donkey carts, hand tools and appliances—basically, anything that might have been seen in the state 100 years ago—was assembled on a former plantation by artist Steele Burden. The rest of the plantation is now a picturesque garden, which covers 25 acres.

Baton Rouge Practicalities

If you're looking for a place to eat and absorb a little Baton Rouge ambience, the **Pastime**, a few blocks from the Old State Capitol at 252 South Boulevard, right under the I-10 interchange, is one of those windowless smoky sports bars ideally suited for discussing political chicanery over po' boys, fried fish, and beer. Best pizzas in town, too; try the one topped with crawfish tails for some local flavor. Another excellent place to eat a fine meal and get filled in on local lifeways is world-famous **Jay's Barbecue**, 4215 Government Street, open 10 to 10 every day but Sunday for real good ribs, beef, pulled-pork sandwiches—and, if you're lucky and ask nicely, smoked alligator.

Another bunch of good eating and drinking prospects are clustered around the Highland Avenue entrance to Louisiana State University, a couple of miles south of I-10. **Louie's Cafe**, 209 W. State across from the Super Fresh shopping plaza (between a Kinko's and a Subway), is all-around exceptional: exceptional prices for exceptional portions of exceptionally good diner-style food. Since it's open 24 hours, there's no excuse to miss it. Facing the LSU gates at 3357 Highland is **The Chimes**, a restaurant and oyster bar (serving daily to midnight) with "100 beers from 24 countries" and frequent live music. Several other bars in the vicinity offer music with some regularity, but undergraduate projectile vomiting is a serious hazard (Louisiana's drinking age is still 18). Assess the sidewalk in front for a rough measure of how well a bar's patrons know their limits: if the volume of broken beer bottles and discarded "hurricane" cups is high, don a wet suit or go elsewhere. Down the street from the Chimes is **Highland Coffees**, at 3350 Highland, a genteel oasis amid the spilled beer, with the aroma of on-site roasting, *The New York Times,* and classical music to accompany that double tall *mochaccino.* Baton Rouge has an unusual number of Lebanese places, two of which bracket the gauntlet of bars on W. Chimes Street:

The popularity of collegiate football shouldn't be underestimated in Baton Rouge: motel "No Vacancy" signs light up all over town whenever the LSU Tigers play a home game in the fall.

the slightly upscale **Cafe Mediterranean** near Highland, and the more downscale **Arzi's**, at 276 W. Chimes. Like any sensible restaurant adjoining a campus teeming with hungry students, both are open daily, usually till 10 PM.

While there's a **Ramada Inn** on Nicholson Drive near LSU, most of the conveniently located accommodations cluster around exit 151 on I-10, two miles west of the Mississippi in Port Allen. **Days Inn, Holiday Inn, Motel 6**, and a pair of local mid-range motels are all there.

The Baton Rouge **visitor information center**, in the State Capitol complex (225/383-1825 or 800/527-6843) should be able to satisfy your informational and glossy brochure needs.

Plantation Alley: Nottoway

To 19th-century passengers aboard the packet steamboats traveling the lower Mississippi, the great mansions adorning the river bends between Baton Rouge and New Orleans must have made an impressive sight. The houses are no less grand today but, sadly, their surroundings are. Petrochemical companies are the new masters of the stricken land and its neglected towns, and no amount of antebellum finery can hide it. People in the tourist business try to pretend it's still Plantation Alley, but to everyone else it's become known as the Chemical Corridor. From here to New Orleans, if you don't have a stomach strong enough to bear miles of industrial blight, hop on the I-10 freeway and head straight into New Orleans.

Our 100-mile traverse of Plantation Alley via the GRR begins on Nicholson Avenue (Hwy-30) southbound out of Baton Rouge. The LSU campus and stadium are quickly replaced by a rural landscape of cows, cricket oil wells, and high tension lines. Keep an eye peeled for the **Plaquemine Ferry** turnoff (Hwy-327), about eight miles south of I-10. It's about another eight miles to the small ferry itself (daily every 30 minutes, 5:15 AM-8:45 PM; $1), whose looping path across the Mississippi illustrates just how strong that current really is.

On the western shore of the Mississippi, in the dreary town of Plaquemine (PLACK-uh-minn), pick up divided Hwy-1 for a straight 25-mile shot south through the cane fields. En route, the white-walled enclosure surrounding **Nottoway** (daily 9 AM-5 PM; $8; 225/545-2730), whose 64 rooms place it among the largest plantation homes in the South, comes into view on the left, about two miles north of the town of **White Castle**. With over an acre of floor space, be glad you don't have to pay Nottoway's air-conditioning bills or do the dusting. A quick climb up the levee affords a panorama of both the gigantic house and the river. B&B rooms are available, but rates run around $200 a night.

For a dramatic perspective of the Mississippi, turn onto Hwy-70, which runs between the GRR at Donaldson and I-10 exit 182. A quick link between "Plantation Alley" and New Orleans, Hwy-70 crosses the Mississippi River, with its conga line of oceangoing freighters extending as far as the eye can see, on the **Sunshine Bridge,** which was named in honor of "Singing Governor" Jimmy Davis's most famous song, "You Are My Sunshine."

Stately **Houmas House,** was used as the setting for Robert Aldrich's 1965 gothic Southern horror film, *Hush, Hush, Sweet Charlotte,* starring Bette Davis, Olivia de Havilland, Joseph Cotten, and Bruce Dern.

To get a real feel for Louisiana's extensive bayous, you have to get out of the car. A number of outfits offer **"swamp tours,"** including Alligator Bayou in Prairieville (225/642-8297 or 888/379-2677) and Chacahoula Bayou Tours (225/436-2640).

Burnside: Houmas House

If you haven't had your fill of Greek Revival and wrought iron, cross the bridge (return toll $1) to the east bank of the Mississippi and turn briefly north to find Houmas House (daily 10 AM-5 PM; $8; 225/473-7841), in Burnside at 40136 River

NEW ORLEANS SURVIVAL GUIDE

WORLD FAMOUS PARTY TOWN EXTRAordinaire—with great music, great food, bars with no closing times, and uniquely (for America) you can drink on the street—New Orleans really needs no introduction. The question here is not why you should go, but why on earth would anyone ever leave? With deep roots going back to the earliest days of European settlement in

North America, New Orleans is proud of its multicultural heritage, its people, its beautiful, ornate buildings, and especially its food, all reflecting a uniquely diverse and tolerant culture. After visiting New Orleans, anywhere else in the country can suddenly seem deeply WASPish and Puritanical, and the generally free-for-all spirit of the "Big Easy" is still as irresistible as ever. Spend even a little time here, and soon you, too, will be saying, "Laissez les bon temps rouler!" Let the good times roll!

The focus of New Orleans, for visitors and locals alike, is the Vieux Carre, the **French Quarter.** Yes, it's a huge tourist attraction, but it's also the heart of old New Orleans. Centering on Bourbon Street, now lined with tacky souvenir stalls and strip clubs catering to conventioneers, this square mile is full of wrought-iron balconies on picturesque brick buildings; despite the name, only one surviving structure dates from the time when New Orleans was under French colonial control.

At the center of the quarter is Jackson Square, where a statue of Andrew Jackson stands in front of St. Louis Cathedral, which was rebuilt in 1850 on top of an original foundation dating back to 1724. **Walking tours** of the French Quarter are offered under the auspices of the Louisiana State Museum, which preserves a number of French Quarter buildings, including the old **U.S. Mint,** 400 Esplanade (Tues.-Sun. 10 AM-5 PM; $3), which holds excellent collections tracing the history of two New Orleans institutions: jazz and Mardi Gras.

Road, another of Louisiana's grandes dames, now cheapened by the monstrous sprawl of a neighboring Du Pont plant. Once the seat of a massive, 20,000-acre sugarcane plantation, Houmas House was built in stages starting in the late 1700s, with a grand Greek Revival mansion added around 1840.

Back on the west bank of the Mississippi, river, levee, and the Great River Road (Hwy-18) follow wide tacks across the humid sea of cane fields, tank farms, and towns frayed with stubborn neglect. With many houses now on stilts and all the cemeteries aboveground, you can almost feel the impounded water rising around you, and in fact, Hwy-18 would be fit only for ducks if the levees were breached. If you get caught in one of Louisiana's typical frog-strangling monsoons, you'll get a taste of what that would be like.

After dark, one French Quarter stop you have to make is **Preservation Hall**, 726 St. Peter Street (nightly from 8 PM), for the redolent ambience and the live traditional Dixieland jazz—flowing free, at the source.

Practicalities

New Orleans International Airport is in Kenner, a dozen miles northwest of town via US-61 or I-10, and is served by most U.S. airlines. Shuttle buses run into town for around $10; taxis can cost twice that much. By road, the I-10 freeway loops south around Lake Pontchartrain through the heart of New Orleans, absorbing the north-south traffic of I-55; the two highways intersect 20 miles west of downtown forming the final miles of the Great River Road. To reach the French Quarter and the heart of old New Orleans, follow I-10 and get off between exits 234 and 236; park the car, and stroll. Street parking is rare, and the small print on the signs can set you up for a ticket or a tow; play it safe

boiled crawfish

and park in one of many lots, which typically charge around $10 a day.

The famous "Streetcar named Desire" is now on display in the courtyard of the old U.S. Mint in the French Quarter, but the rattling St. Charles Avenue streetcars still trundle around the clock (once an hour after midnight), and cost $1 each way.

New Orleans has some of the best and most enjoyable places to eat in the world, so plan to take the time to enjoy yourself here. In the French Quarter, the **Acme Oyster Bar**, 724 Iberville Street, is the place to go for the freshest $1-a-pop bivalves, but it closes early by New Orleans standards—around 10 PM nightly. **Felix's** across the street is open later and is much less frenetic. At the other end of the spectrum is expensive, formal **Antoine's**, 713 St. Louis

(continues on next page)

Vacherie: Oak Alley

Traveling along the GRR, moldering concrete mausoleums, houses with loud colors and louvered French doors, insouciant pedestrians along the levee (not to mention the dangerous large potholes), all may arrest your attention briefly, but Oak Alley (daily 9 AM-5 PM; $8; 225/265-2151), north of Vacherie on Hwy-18, about 15 miles south of the Sunshine Bridge, will probably stop you in your tracks. This place is to antebellum plantations what Bora Bora is to islands, or the Golden Gate is to bridges: even if you've managed to avoid seeing its image on tourist

Because the Mississippi in its natural, pre-Corps state created a raised channel for itself between embankments of silt, the river sits *higher* than a third of Louisiana. Which is why down here, the Mississippi cannot drain the surrounding land of its water.

Street, one of the oldest restaurants in the world, serves classic French-Creole cuisine to a who's who of New Orleans society. Another very popular spot is **K-Paul's Louisiana Kitchen**, 416 Chartres Street, where Chef Paul Prudhomme, who popularized Cajun-style "blackened" food all over the country, saves the very best examples for his own place. Lines stretch down the block, but they do take a few reservations (504/524-7394). One more place that merits a meal or two: **NOLA**, 534 St. Louis Street, a comparatively casual setting for celebrated chef Emeril Lagasse's finely crafted Creole fare.

No visit to New Orleans is complete without a stop for coffee and beignets (and some serious people-watching) at busy **Cafe du Monde**, 800 Decatur Street, open 24 hours a day on the Mississippi side of Jackson Square.

Except during Mardi Gras or Superdome football games, places to stay in New Orleans aren't all that expensive. The **Clarion Hotel**, 1500 Canal Street (504/522-4500 or 800/824-3359), has 15 floors of bland but comfortable rooms within walking distance of the French Quarter; doubles cost around $100. In the French Quarter, the **Dauphine Orleans Hotel**, 415 Dauphine Street (504/586-1800 or 800/521-7111), is a medium-sized modern hotel just a block off Bourbon Street, with a pool, free newspapers, and Continental breakfast. Doubles cost $115-175. More characterful, the **Olivier House**, 828 Toulouse Street (504/525-8456) is a quirky, family- run hotel, filling a pair of French Quarter townhouses; doubles start at around $90. Another good bet: **Place d'Armes Hotel**, 625 St. Ann Street (504/524-4531 or 800/366-2743), right off Jackson Square at the heart of the French Quarter, with rooms facing onto a quiet courtyard; doubles from $80.

The best budget options are the **HI-New Orleans Hostel**, with $15 bunks and some private rooms, a block from the St. Charles streetcar line at 2253 Carondelet Street (504/523-3014), and the **YMCA**, 920 St. Charles Avenue (504/568-9622), where private rooms with shared bathrooms, plus use of pool and gym—the better to work off those high-calorie feasts—go for around $40.

The best visitor information is provided by the **New Orleans Metropolitan Convention and Visitors Bureau**, at the base of the Superdome at 1520 Sugar Bowl Drive (504/566-5011) and also at 529 St. Ann Street in the French Quarter (504/566-5031). The main daily paper is the *Times-Picayune,* which has a Friday tabloid listing entertainment and events for the upcoming weekend.

brochures, it will look familiar —or rather, it will look exactly like it ought to. Plus, no cooling tower or gas flare mars the immediate horizon. For the full effect of the grand quarter-mile-long *allée* of arching live oaks, which were planted in the 1700s, nearly a century before the current house was built in the late 1830s, drive past the entrance a short ways. Besides the obligatory tour, there's lodging and a restaurant in buildings on the grounds in back of the main house.

If the meal you ate in New Orleans or Baton Rouge is but a doubtful memory, stop by the **Corner Drive-Inn** in Vacherie, a few miles past Oak Alley. It's a gas station-convenience-store-cafe offering authentic and cheap Vietnamese dishes, most of which aren't found on the menu, so ask. If you prefer standard American fried food, they have that, too.

South of Vacherie, scattered housing begins to invade the sugarcane, and traffic starts to pick up as the route works its serpentine way past a pair of ferry landings, a nuclear power plant, and a huge Union Carbide factory with a cemetery felicitously occupying its front yard. By the time the GRR is within sight of the giant I-310 bridge, the tentacles of New Orleans's bustle are definitely apparent. This is it! The Great River Road is at its end. Hop on the interstate eastbound and inside of 25 miles you can be hunting for parking in New Orleans's Vieux Carré, or searching for a Sazerac to celebrate the end of your journey.

Driving New Orleans

Assuming you resisted the industrial-strength charms of US-61 and opted to take the I-10 freeway into town, stay on it until you reach downtown, then get off and park the car as soon as can, and get out and walk. New Orleans rivals Boston for the discomfort it causes drivers, and there are no driving routes that let you see anything you can't see better on foot—or from the St. Charles trolley. Parking in and around the French Quarter is a nightmare, but there are many $10-a-day lots in the neighboring Central Business District, or CBD.

Hwy-23: To the Gulf

From downtown New Orleans, if you really really want to follow the Mississippi River all the way to its mouth at the Gulf of Mexico, you can. (Well, almost . . .) From the Superdome, take the US-90 bridge south across the river to Gretna, where you can join the Belle Chasse Highway (Hwy-23), which follows alongside the river for about 75 miles, ending up at Venice, still a dozen miles from the Gulf, on the fringes of the Delta National Wildlife refuge. Apart from swamps and giant freighters, the main sight along the route is old **Fort Jackson** (daily 7 AM-6 PM; donations; 504/657-7083), six miles northeast of Venice, which was built in the 1830s to protect the river from invasion.

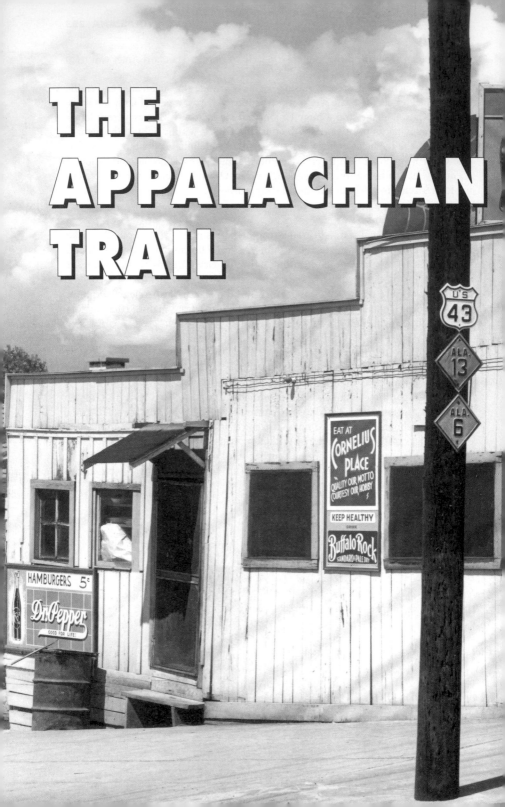

THE APPALACHIAN TRAIL

THE APPALACHIAN TRAIL

The longest and best-known hiking trail in the country, the Appalachian Trail winds from the north woods of Maine all the way south to Georgia. Dozens of guidebooks cover the hiking trail, but until now there has been no description of how to follow the route in a car. The following scenic roads come fairly close to paralleling the pedestrian route, taking in a number of fascinating cities, towns, and historic sites along with the—almost—continuous natural beauty. Best of all, with very few exceptions, the route follows magnificently scenic two-lane roads all the way from the top of New England to the heart of Dixie. Though the Appalachian Trail runs within day-hiking distance of over 50 million people, most of the route is intensely solitary, as only some 200 people manage to hike the entire 2,144-mile trail each year.

The Appalachian landscape, notorious for harboring an almost Third World level of economic deprivation, also holds some of the wealthiest areas in the entire country, the contrasting worlds often within a few miles of one another. Every resort and retirement community seems to have its alter-ego as a former mill town, all of them now as dependent upon three-season tourism as they once were upon the land and its resources.

The Appalachian Trail driving tour starts atop rugged Mount Washington in the heart of New Hampshire's Presidential Range of 6,000-foot peaks, the tallest mountains in New England and some of the hardest and most durable rocks on earth. From the mountains the route winds through the idyllic charms of rural New

England, taking in the Connecticut River Valley with its summer homes and liberal-arts college communities.

On to the Berkshires, the summer destination of the Boston-New York culture vultures and intelligentsia for most of two centuries. As you approach within commuting distance of New York City, towns become even more prissy and pretty, as evidenced by the Litchfield Hills antique shops.

Skirting the Big Apple, our route ducks down through the Delaware Water Gap to enter the suddenly industrial Lehigh Valley, former land of coal and steel that's now struggling to find an economic replacement. South of here, you pass through the heart of the world-famous Pennsylvania Dutch Country, where the simple life is under the onslaught of package tourism. Then it's on to Gettysburg and Harpers Ferry, polar opposites of the Civil War—Harpers Ferry, the beginning, Gettysburg, the beginning of the end.

Driving north to south, you could follow the fall color in leisurely moves south; heading south to north, you'd be assured of catching the peak season at least somewhere.

South from Pennsylvania, nearly to the end of the route in Georgia, the Appalachian Trail runs through continuous nature, with barely a city to be seen. Starting with Virginia's Shenandoah National Park, then following the Blue Ridge Parkway across the breathtaking mountains of western North Carolina, it's All-American scenic highway all the way, with recommended detours east and west to visit such fascinating historic sights as Thomas Jefferson's home, Monticello, outside Charlottesville, Virginia; the most opulent mansion in America, Asheville's Biltmore; the real-life town that inspired TV's Mayberry RFD—Mount Airy, North Carolina; or the whitewater that was used to film *Deliverance*, north Georgia's Chattooga River.

All in all, the Appalachian Trail is an amazing drive, whether or not you come for fall color.

APPALACHIAN TRAIL HIGHLIGHTS

ACROSS NEW HAMPSHIRE

"Live Free or Die" is the feisty motto of tiny New Hampshire, the state that hits the national limelight every four years when its political primaries launch the horse race for the White House. During the presidential campaign's opening stretch, locals have to turn into hermits to avoid having their votes solicited by every candidate running and their opinions polled by every reporter. Some of New Hampshire's million residents take the state's motto to heart, however, and when you see the ruggedness of the landscape you'll appreciate how easy it is to find isolation from the madding crowd.

Despite its apparent brevity, the route across New Hampshire provides a hearty sampling of the topographic spectrum from its start at New England's highest peak, Mount Washington, to neighboring Vermont amid the rolling farmland of the Connecticut River valley.

Mount Washington and Pinkham Notch

The star attraction of the White Mountains' Presidential Range, 6,288-foot Mount Washington stands head and shoulders above every other peak in New England. East of the Mississippi, only Mount Mitchell in North Carolina's Blue Ridge and Clingman's Dome in Tennessee's Great Smokies are taller. Despite its natural defenses —such as notoriously fierce storms that arise without warning—Mount Washington is accessible to an almost unfortunate degree. The **Mount Washington Auto Road** (weather permitting, mid-May to mid-Oct; $15 car and driver, $6 each additional adult; 603/466-3988) was first built for carriages over a century ago and switchbacks up the eastern side, while the **Mount Washington Cog Railway** ($39; 603/846-5404) climbs straight up from Bretton Woods at the mountain's western foot.

The best way to appreciate the mountain's granite cliffs, steep ravines, tumbling cataracts, and fragrant pines is on foot. Besides the **Appalachian Trail**, hikers will find a smorgasbord of routes to the summit, including the country's oldest continuously maintained hiking trail, the **Crawford Path**, in use for over 175 years. One-day ascents of Mount Washington are possible, most popularly by the **Tuckerman Ravine Trail** from the east. But don't be deceived by short trail lengths, as the elevation gain and frequent rough terrain can be quite taxing. The Tuckerman route mustn't be confused with the roughly parallel Huntington Ravine Trail, whose exposed ledges and steep pitches are strictly for vertigo-resistant hikers skilled at free climbing.

Beset by tundra conditions more typical of terrain a thousand miles to the north, the Presidentials are noted for their alpine gardens and *krummholz*, wind-stunted trees that try to eke out a

In New England, locals call their highways "routes," and we've followed suit, using Route as a generic term (Route 100 for example, rather than Hwy-100). The Interstates (I-93) and federal highways (US-3) are abbreviated as usual.

Fall foliage is at its best when warm clear days are followed by cold nights that stop the essential pigment-producing sugars from circulating out of the leaves. Sugar production is low on cloudy days, while warm nights allow the sugars to disperse before the brightest colors are produced. For New Hampshire Fall Foliage Reports (Sept.-Oct. only), call 800/258-3608.

MOUNT WASHINGTON WEATHER

A mountain barely over 6,000 feet hardly deserves the same cautious respect as the 20,000-footers in the Patagonian Andes, yet people die from exposure on the flanks of Mount Washington every year. Easy access invites complacency, and a tendency to ignore trailside warnings advising retreat if you're unprepared for bad weather. But respect the facts of nature: simply put, the Presidential Range of the White Mountains experiences some of the worst weather in the world, rivaling both Antarctica and the Alaska-Yukon ranges for consistently raw and bone-numbing combinations of gale-force winds, freezing temperatures, and precipitation. Lashings by 100-mph winds occur year-round on Mount Washington, whose summit holds the title for highest sustained wind speed on the face of the planet (231 mph in April 1934). Cloudy days outnumber clear ones on the peak, where snowstorms can strike any month of the year. Even in the balmiest summer months the average high temperature at the summit hovers around 50° F. Compounding the weather's potential severity is its total unpredictability: a day-hike begun with sunblock and short sleeves can end up in driving rain and temperatures just 10° above freezing, or worse, in a total whiteout above tree line, even as a group of hikers a couple miles away on a neighboring peak enjoys lunch under blue skies and warm breezes.

The bottom line is, listen to what your mother always told you: be careful, and don't take chances. Learn to recognize and prevent hypothermia. Figure out your trail maps and compass *before* you get caught in pelting sleet above tree line. Better to feel foolish packing potentially unnecessary wool sweaters and rain gear for a hike in July than to have your name added to the body count.

living among the boulders and ice-shattered rock above timberline. Hikers seeking these sorts of wilderness should consider ascending a neighboring peak rather than Washington's fully developed summit. Some of the alpine areas on Mount Washington are off-limits to visitors, due to their fragility beneath too many hiking boots. As a general rule in any wilderness area, be mindful of the stress plants constantly face from the weather, and try not to tread on the vegetation above tree line.

Without a doubt you can pick up the best **hiking information** for Mount Washington and the rest of the White Mountains at the **Pinkham Notch Camp,** on Route 16 south of the Auto Road. Operated by the venerable Appalachian Mountain Club (AMC), the year-round trailhead facility offers topographical maps, guidebooks, weather updates, and precautionary advice, as well as limited gear. The camp also offers snacks, a cafeteria, a 24-hour hikers' pack room with bathrooms and showers, scheduled shuttle van service, and the **Joe Dodge Lodge** ($30-35 bed only, $47-52 bed and board; 603/466-2727), a modern hostel with shared bunk rooms, a few private doubles, and great views from the library. For extended stays be sure to inquire about the significantly discounted package rates, or consider AMC membership ($40 yearly), which yields up to an additional $7 discount on all overnight stays—including package prices—at any AMC property.

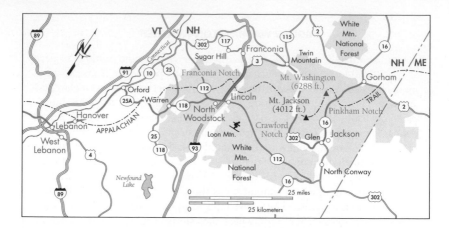

If you're serious about hiking in the region, you won't want to be without the *AMC White Mountains Guide,* the most trusted source of trail and campsite descriptions and site-specific hiking advice since 1907. It's available at the Pinkham Notch Camp, or you can order it in advance by phone (800/262-4455) or by writing to AMC Books, P.O. Box 298, Dept. BC, Gorham, NH 03581-0298.

Mount Washington Valley: Gorham and Jackson

North of 2,032-foot Pinkham Notch and the Auto Road, Route 16 descends gradually to intersect US-2 in the plain town of Gorham (pop. 3,173), whose main drag offers rather predictable, if unfranchised, fast food and family dining. If you're hungry for information, the **White Mountains National Forest Ranger Station** on Route 16 just south of town can provide recreation tips. For more basic needs like lodging referrals you can call the friendly **Northern White Mountains Chamber of Commerce** (800/992-7480) and get a list of motel phone numbers.

Dropping sharply away to the south of the Notch is the Ellis River, along whose banks sits the northern gateway to the Mount Washington valley, resort-dominated Jackson (pop. 678). Given the number of lodgings among the attractive century-old clapboard homes, it seems the principal village occupation is innkeeper. The quantity of porches, gables, and chimneys hint at standard country B&B charms: lazy piazza breakfasts in summer, nooks and crannies brimming with cabbage roses and cotton voilé, and crackling fires in your room at New Year's. A covered bridge beside Route 16, taverns filled with antiques, and winter sleigh rides complete the postcard image of Merry Olde New England. Reservations for Jackson's numerous B&Bs and country inns, which range in price $50-200, may be made by calling **Country Inns of the White Mountains** (800/562-1300), the **Jackson Resort Association** (800/866-3334), or the **Mount Washington Valley Visitors Bureau** (800/367-3364).

South of Jackson you leave Route 16 and pick up US-302, which heads west from **Glen,** a cluster of restaurants, a grocery store, and a bank ATM. If you're overdue for a little retail therapy you might consider continuing south on Route 16 to **North Conway,** one of the cornerstones of New England's factory-outlet circuit. City dwellers be warned: horrible flashbacks to your homeward commute may result if you venture into the shopping mall zone, where half-hour crawls along a five-mile stretch of highway are not unheard of on holidays, weekends, afternoons, summers, springs, or autumns.

Crawford Notch

US-302 between Glen and Twin Mountain passes through Crawford Notch, another of the White Mountains' high passes and centerpiece of the Crawford Notch State Park. After running a gauntlet of rental condos that crowd the base of the ski slopes near Glen, the road ascends the south side of the Notch and closely follows the Saco River through new-growth forest; the oaks and white pine of the lower valley give way to more birch and spruce as you gain elevation. Come autumn, the entire White Mountains National Forest is a riot of color: the northern oaks' dark reds, the birches' and aspens' golden yellows, purples from the white ashes and sumacs, and most brilliant of all, the blaze of orange from countless sugar maples, which set New England's fall foliage apart from the crowd. From mid-September through Columbus Day weekend, be prepared to slow down and take it easy on the roads as the so-called "leaf-peepers" drive like grandmothers. If you don't want to face a lot of No Vacancy signs, book your fall weekend accommodations as far in advance as possible, since throughout New England autumn ranks as the year's busiest season for motels and inns.

Crawford Notch offers good **day-hikes** to various waterfalls and vantage points such as **Frankenstein Cliff**, named for an artist whose work helped popularize the White Mountains, and 200-foot **Arethusa Falls**, the state's highest waterfall. During high spring runoff or after storms, Arethusa and nearby Ripley Falls on Avalanche Brook are among New Hampshire's most dramatic sights. **Camping** is available at the state-run **Dry River Campground** (mid-May to mid-Oct.; $12; 603/271-3628), a primitive tent-only facility opposite the trailheads to both Frankenstein Cliff and Arethusa Falls, or along the Saco River at the private wilderness campground affiliated with the **Carter Notch General Store** (May-Oct.; 603/374-2779; $18-20). A modest step up from tents is the $18-a-night **AMC Crawford Hostel** (603/466-2727), whose large, spartan (but heated) bunk rooms, fee showers, and self-service kitchen are open year-round beside US-302. **Information** about trails in the area may be found at the hostel, along with some minor supplies, although **Pinkham Notch Camp** is still the overall best resource for hikers in the region.

North of Crawford Notch the highway joins the Ammonoosuc River headwaters as they flow toward the Connecticut River, passing **Bretton Woods** and the access road for the Mount Washington Cog Railway. The giant **Mount Washington Hotel** (800/258-0330) dominates the surrounding plain, its Victorian luxury no longer standing in such grand isolation below the peaks of the Presidentials now that a ski resort sits across the highway, and motels and condos squat around its skirts. Built at the turn of the century by Pennsylvania Railroad tycoon

Besides factory outlet stores, North Conway is also home to New Hampshire's most popular scenic **railroad,** running steam engines in summer and during the "Fall Color" season. Call 603/356-5251 or 800/232-5251 for schedules and fares.

Parking along New Hampshire highways is illegal, so don't be tempted to leave your car beside the road while you take a hike up that nearby hill—you may return to find it's been towed to some town 20 miles away.

Built in 1869, the **Mount Washington Cog Railway** has a maximum grade of 37.5%, surpassed by only one other non-funicular railway in the world, in the Swiss Alps. Burning a ton of coal with each trip, the cinder-spewing engines take over an hour to ratchet up the three-mile track. Trips run from mid-May to mid-Oct. and cost $39; phone 603/846-5404 or 800/922-8825 for further information.

HIGH MOUNTAIN HUTS AND LODGES

From Mount Greylock, Massachusetts' highest peak, to Maine's Acadia National Park, the Appalachian Mountain Club maintains trails; operates a network of accommodations; sponsors educational programs; publishes maps and guides for hikers, canoeists, and kayakers; and in general has made itself synonymous with backcountry recreation in New England for well over a century. Many of their overnight properties are lean-tos and tent platforms, but some, like the High Mountain Huts, are complete mountaintop hostels. Eight staffed alpine cabins are strung out roughly a day's hike apart along the Appalachian Trail between Lonesome Lake, west of Franconia Notch, and Carter Notch, east of Route 16. Several are easily accessible, but others are a strenuous hike from the nearest trailhead; some are below tree line, while others lie well up in the clouds. All offer bunk rooms, cold-water bathrooms, and two hot meals a day during their full-service periods. None have heat or showers. Most are open only during the summer months, but two are open on a self-service basis year-round. Adult rates run from $18 (winter, self-serve) to $62 per person (peak times, including breakfast and dinner), although package stays and member discounts are available. Despite their price, the huts require reservations months in advance (603/466-2727).

For detailed descriptions of the huts and their access routes, consult either the *AMC White Mountain Guide* or *High Huts of the White Mountains*, available from AMC Books (800/262-4455).

Joseph Stickney, the Mount Washington Hotel received its most lasting recognition as host of the 1944 United Nations International Monetary Conference, the historic meeting of financiers from 44 nations that established the World Bank and pegged the price of gold to the U.S. dollar. Since it recognized the U.S. as the strongest postwar economy and chose the dollar as the global standard for trade, the conference was perhaps even more influential than military victory in guaranteeing the longevity of U.S. dominion over the postwar world. Wander around the hotel's public areas and enjoy the grandeur (or a meal or a drink), but room rates are definitely in the "if you have to ask, you can't afford it" category.

Franconia

Between the junction of US-302 and US-3 at **Twin Mountain** and the merging of US-3 with I-93 above Franconia Notch, you'll find the aging face of the area's long association with tourism: a variety of motel courts and "housekeeping cottages" at least as old as you are. Despite their outward dowdiness, several make a virtue of the rustic, but given their prime location most are hardly the bargains you might hope for, with rates running $40-80 a night. More interesting and historic lodging may be had on a 200-acre working farm in Franconia (pop. 811), where since 1899 the friendly Sherburn family's **Pinestead Farm Lodge**, on Route 116 south of town, has offered simple rooms and warm hospitality at reasonable rates ($35-40 with shared bath and kitchen; 603/823-8121).

Dating back to the same era is **The Homestead** ($50-90 double; 800/823-5564), a country inn just west of Franconia on Route 117 in **Sugar Hill.** The township is aptly named: the sugar bush (groves of sugar maples) on Hildex Maple Sugar Farm, also on Route 117, contributes its unforgettable essence to breakfasts at the very popular **Polly's Pancake Parlor,** located in the farm's thrice-expanded 1830 carriage shed (open weekends only April to mid-May and late Oct., daily otherwise). Warning: after trying real maple syrup, you may never be able to go back to Aunt Jemima's or Mrs. Butterworth's again.

Possibly the most famous farm in the vicinity is **The Frost Place** (Sat.-Sun. 1-5 PM Memorial Day-June, Wed.-Mon. 1-5 PM July-Columbus Day; $3) on Route 116 south of the Franconia village intersection. Besides displays of Robert Frost memorabilia from his 11-year residency here and the property's 1.5-mile Poetry Trail, there's a regular program of readings by the current poet-in-residence.

Franconia Notch

Franconia Notch is the tourist Grand Central of the White Mountains, in part because of the accessibility offered by I-93, which barrels through here, passing some of the most scenic country in the interstate system. "The Old Man of the Mountains," the state's mascot to judge from the tourist brochures, is found here in the granite cliffs of the Notch, along with a host of other tourist attractions—an aerial tram, the state's own "little Grand Canyon," covered bridges, a powerful waterfall called The Flume, even a trading post with trained bears. The combined admission fees to these attractions will sorely test budgetary restraint. Weaving under the interstate like the opposite strand of a DNA double helix is US-3, the old route through the Notch is lined with stores and motels whose tackiness belongs to such a bygone era, it's almost historic. Of course, nature upstages all the gift shops and game rooms and requires no admission fee; for **trail information** consult with the AMC staffer on duty at the Franconia Notch State Park's **Lafayette Campground** (mid-May to mid-Oct.; no hookups; $14) near exit 2 of the Parkway.

The main draws in Franconia Notch start with the most famous: **The Old Man of the Mountain,** a series of five granite ledges, 1,200 feet above the valley, that viewed from certain angles seem to resemble an old man's profile. An "Old Man Viewing Area" is well signed off I-93. The other well-known feature of Franconia Notch is at the south end, five miles south of the Old Man, where **The Flume** is a granite gorge, 15 feet wide and nearly 100 high, carved by roaring waters. From a large **visitor center** (603/745-8391), where you pay the admission fee ($8), a short bus ride drops you (and many others) near the start of

Among the peaks of the southern Presidential Range overlooking Crawford Notch is Mount Jackson, named for neither the seventh U.S. president, Andrew, nor for the Confederate general, Thomas "Stonewall," but for a former state geologist, Charles.

North of Bretton Woods, a turnoff for the National Forest's tiny Zealand Campground leads to the trailhead for **Zealand Notch.** The trail passes through what's considered New England's finest example of forest regeneration, an area recovered from devastating turn-of-the-century fires.

For additional lodging and dining suggestions along the north side of White Mountains National Forest, check out the description of US-2 between Gorham and Lancaster on pages 517-518.

Take those moose crossing signs seriously—dozens of collisions occur annually, and you can bet a car won't fare too well if it hits an animal that weighs well over half a ton.

Technically speaking, the six-mile stretch of I-93 that passes through the narrowest part of Franconia Notch isn't interstate at all, but the so-called **Franconia Notch Parkway.** Although divided and with limited access, it's only a single lane in each direction, with a speed limit of 45 mph.

Running east from Lincoln, over the mountains to Conway, the **Kancamagus Highway** (Route 112) is one of the most incredible drives in the White Mountains. Just east of the crest, and an easy half-mile walk from the well-signed parking area, Sabbaday Falls is a lovely little waterfall roaring through a narrow gorge.

If you spot some beefy guys in skirts heaving telephone poles around at the base of Loon Mountain, you've probably stumbled across Lincoln's annual Highland Games, held the third weekend of September. Fortunately you don't have to toss a caber or know how to skirl to take part in the festivities. For info and advance tickets,

the wooden boardwalk which runs the length of the 800-foot-long gorge. Though less famous than the Old Man and The Flume, in between the two sits my favorite Franconia Notch stop: **The Basin,** where a lovely waterfall in the thundering Pemigewassett River has polished a 25-foot-round pothole. Thoreau visited it in the 1820s, and thought it was remarkable; it's still a peaceful place to sit and picnic and be soothed by the natural white noise.

Cyclists will appreciate the nine-mile paved bike path through Franconia Notch, from just north of Cannon Mountain south to the Flume Visitor Center. Basically downhill all the way (north to south), the path is free of both pedestrians (the hiker's Pemi Trail is parallel but totally separate) and 'bladers (discouraged, as the grade has too many steep spots to be safe for most skaters). Check ahead for bike availability if staying at a local inn, or rent from the folks at the Cannon Mountain aerial tram ($8 an hour or $25-29 a day, depending on style rented; includes helmet and lock).

Just south of Franconia Notch along US-3, a barrage of tacky tourist attractions and old-fashioned roadside Americana awaits you. Classic motor courts line the highway around **Clark's Trading Post** (daily 10 AM-6 PM; $7), where you can "See Live Bears," ride on a real old wood-burning railroad, and generally enjoy a slice of good ol' cornpone kitsch.

Lincoln and North Woodstock

Tiny North Woodstock (pop. 700) is a good example of what White Mountains towns used to look like before vacation condos popped up like prairie dog colonies; neighboring Lincoln (pop. 1,229) is the portrait of "after." The former is a handful of mostly unpretentious businesses at the junction of US-3 and Route 112, while the latter seems to be nothing but a strip of ski-clothing stores, malls, and motels at the base of the Loon Mountain ski resort. When Loon's condo-covered foothills fill to capacity during fall and winter holidays, the weekend population can mushroom more than twentyfold to over 30,000.

As a rule, the Granite State isn't known for offering outstanding dining, certainly not like the Green Mountain State next door, which gives Northern California a run for its money in the small-town nouvelle-cafe department. The Lincoln area is typical, with its choice of aprés-ski pub grub, local pizza-and-grinder parlors (submarine sandwiches are called "grinders" in this state), and family dining on "Yankee soul food" like turkey, prime rib, and spaghetti with meatballs. New Orleans chefs aren't exactly quaking in their toques over the competition from the high-toned inns up here, either, but if you can set aside visions of Emeril's and K-Paul's, it's quite possible to enjoy satisfying home-style cooking in casual surroundings. Lincoln's **Country Mile** (closed Wednesday) opposite the Millfront Marketplace, for example, serves a fine breakfast, with from-scratch pancakes and breads. **Peg's Restaurant** on the main drag in North Woodstock also offers a decent breakfast

---

YOU CAN'T GET THERE FROM HERE

One of the first things first-time visitors to New England notice is its compact size: a crow flying 100 miles from almost any treetop outside of Maine will end up in the next state, if not Canada. But map distances bear absolutely no relation to travel time, thanks to the mountain ranges pitched up across northern New England.

So if you're sitting in your motel room in New Hampshire or Vermont wondering how far to drive for dinner, look to towns north or south. As a rule these will share the same valley since the Taconic, Green, and White Mountains are generally aligned north-to-south, like compass needles. In contrast, that next town to the east or west may as well be on the opposite side of the state so far as convenience is concerned. Whether winding along erratic streambeds or stitching their ways up the sides of passes between high peaks, east-west roads tend to be a slow grind in even the best weather, truly as tortuous as the wiggling lines on the map suggest. Heavy vehicles, cautious drivers, and foul weather make the going doubly difficult. Keep this in mind as you consider outings and side trips or you, too, will learn to say, "You can't get there from here."

---

and lunch (daily 5:30 AM-4 PM), while **Frannie's Place,** on US-3 seven miles south of Route 112, is worth a detour, particularly on nights when they feature the "All-U-Can-Eat" fish fry. Other dining options are easily found all along Route 112 from North Woodstock to the Loon Mountain base lodge.

Accommodations also line Route 112 in Lincoln and US-3 in North Woodstock, just south of exit 1 on the Franconia Notch Parkway. The rates remind you that, fast food aside, the area is first and foremost a resort destination: even the oldest, most rustic motel courts begin at $35, and during the busiest holidays rates typically double. The only year-round bargain—for singletons especially—is the nearest local equivalent to a home hostel: **The Cascade Lodge** (603/745-2722) in North Woodstock next to the handsomely restored Woodstock Inn. Resembling an old rooming house with its simple bedrooms and small shared baths down the hall, the Cascade becomes most like a hostel in summer when single "thru hikers" coming down off the Appalachian Trail stop for a hot shower and dry bed. During the summer they're "stacked like cordwood" in the doubles and triples of the old house by the cheerful, chatty, and chain-smoking owner, Bill Robinson. Rates are $21.50 a person B&B, or $18 a person lodging only.

The **information center** next to the I-93 overpass on the west side of Lincoln offers plenty of brochures for area motels and B&Bs, and the chamber of commerce operates a free phone reservation service (800/227-4191).

Down to the River

Between Lincoln and the Connecticut River, our route follows a succession of small state roads—Route 112 west, Route 118 south, and Route 25A west again—through some very charac-

For some reason (unmarried couples traveling Dutch? a ploy to fool the computationally illiterate comparison shopper?) most lodgings in the White Mountains advertise rates on a per-person rather than per-room basis, even though the minimum rates are almost always for two people.

teristic New Hampshire landscape. Instead of "shoppes" and "pubs," you'll pass snowmobile dealers and mobile homes, old pickup trucks and shingles slung below mailboxes advertising homemade maple products, roofing contractors, mechanics. Houses nestled among the hardwoods spend nearly half the year wearing their insulation on the outside, the brunt of winter kept at bay with plastic swaddling and huge piles of split cordwood ready to stoke the stoves. Leaving the steep slopes of the national forest, the route starts to level off among small farms and hamlets composed of little more than a church, some houses, and a place to drop off the mail.

Join the Army, take home a missile: that Titan rocket in the middle of wide-spot-in-the-road Warren, on Route 118/25, is a keepsake from a local gent's career in the Army's Missile Command down in Redstone, Alabama.

A few miles west of the clearly signposted Appalachian Trail crossing, Route 25A passes the **Sugar House** at Mount Cube Farm. When the maple sap begins to run in early spring, this rudimentary wooden shed is transformed by the heady aroma of boiling syrup—a bright event in what is otherwise known as Mud Season. This rite of spring depends entirely upon the weather: warm days and cold nights keep the sap flowing, while too much cold or warmth shuts it off. Generally the sugar season lasts from mid-March through April. If you spot the steam from the evaporator, stop by for a sample or, come summer, enjoy a full breakfast of fresh pancakes swimming in that New England elixir (Thurs.-Sat., 4th of July weekend to Columbus Day weekend; 603/353-4709).

About 35 miles from Lincoln our route hits the banks of the Connecticut River in small **Orford**, turning south on scenic Route 10 to Hanover, 15 miles downstream.

Hanover

Dartmouth College is the principal resident of attractive little Hanover (pop. 9,212) and it shows. Even people who attended schools cloned from office parks recognize Baker Library's tall clock tower and Georgian brick symmetry as the visual expression of all that's collegiate. When school is in session the cafes hum with undergraduate discourse, the downtown teems with students, and a varsity air envelops the historic campus and its sturdy neighbors. Between terms, however, the town's metabolism drops toward hibernation levels—which means there's no line for espresso.

That there *is* espresso at all is attributable to the Ivy League influence, just like the local architecture, dress, and cultural diversions. Concerning the last, Dartmouth's **Hood Museum of Art** (closed Monday; free; 603/646-2900) and **Hopkins Center** (603/646-2422 for schedule and tickets), both facing the south side of expansive Dartmouth Green, remain the uncontested local hotspots for fine art, performing arts, and film.

A predominantly undergraduate student body and a state drinking age of 21 means that double tall cappuccinos and lattes have replaced yards of beer for the majority of Hanover's young scholars. Which is why the **Dirt Cowboy Cafe** at the head of S. Main Street is usually a live wire until their 2 AM closing, tendrils of cigarette smoke and conversation weaving amid the earnest note-takers and book-readers seated beneath the latest local artist's showing. If you prefer French Press over Krups Drip, **Rosey's Cafe** is the coffeehouse for you, at the corner of Lebanon and S. College Streets at the downstairs rear of the Rosey 'n' Jeke's clothing store; their

The
Hanover Inn

With the Dartmouth Outing Club responsible for maintaining hundreds of miles of trails, including over 75 miles of the Appalachian Trail, a part of which runs right through the campus, it's no surprise that Hanover is something of a hiking center, too. Various hiking maps and guides are available from the Outing Club's office in Robinson Hall (603/646-2428) and the Dartmouth Bookstore on S. Main Street.

mocha in particular is more European (bitter chocolate, not semisweet) than those offered by cafes bowing to the American sweet tooth.

Espresso, yes, and sandwiches too: on S. Main across from the Ledyard Bank, **Patrick Henry's** offers decent soup-salad-sandwich fare in a mellow, fraternity-free setting. If you prefer thick-crust pizzas and calzones garnished with everything from kielbasa and sauerkraut to pesto chicken, try **Foodee's** at 45 Lyme Road, a New Hampshire-based chain whose local outlet is just north of town on Route 10 in that modern building next to the Exxon station. When it comes to Italian, though, the last best word on the subject is the menu at **Café Buon Gustaio**, 72 S. Main Street, whose cuisine earns top honors and commands top dollar for both preparation and presentation (Tues.-Sun. dinner only).

A few years after New Hampshire and the other 12 American colonies began their revolt against mother England, Hanover and a handful of neighboring towns divorced themselves from the state to join Vermont, but the short-lived association fell apart in 1782, leaving the towns independent for four years before they reunited with New Hampshire.

For accommodations around Hanover, there's the stately, Dartmouth-run **Hanover Inn** facing onto the Green (603/643-4300); for affordable rooms, however, look under West Lebanon and White River Junction, below.

In the basement of Baker Library is a set of frescoes by **José Clemente Orozco:** "An Epic of American Civilization," painted 1932-34. These dramatic murals are the Mexican artist's only commissioned work in the U.S.

Lebanon and West Lebanon

Three miles south of patrician Hanover is the commercial busybody of West Lebanon, with its shopping plazas, traffic tie-ups, and familiar fast-*everything* clustered around I-89's two local exits. Sitting rather quietly a couple of miles east is the historic heart of the township, Lebanon (pop. 12,183), with a town green so spacious it seems more like the outskirts of a city park than the center of a town. Near the northwest corner is the main commercial block, or what's left since the malls arrived. It's kept alive in part by a pair of establishments well worth the detour from Hanover or West Lebanon: **Sweet Tomatoes**, facing Coburn Park (lunch weekdays till 2 PM, dinner nightly from 5 PM), an ever-popular trattoria whose gourmet pasta and wood-fired pizzas pull in crowds from miles around; and **The Bean Gallery** just opposite, a very shiny, black, smoke-free temple to art and espresso, open from very early to very late every day but Sunday.

Resources to consider when planning your trip: the White Mountains Attractions Association (800/FIND MTS or 800/316-3687 outside New Hampshire, or 603/745-8720); Chambers of Commerce Statewide Reservation Service (800/ENJOY NH or 800/365-6964); and Weekly NH Events (April-Aug. only; 800/258-3608).

Back along the bonny banks of the Connecticut River in West Lebanon are more restaurants of note, such as the **Bangkok Garden** Thai restaurant in the K-Mart Plaza on Route 12A (lunch daily to 3 PM, dinner Mon.-Sat. from 5 PM), or, on the south side of the I-89 overpass, **The Seven Barrels**. One of the brewpubs on the region's growing list, the "Seven Bs" has a good line of beers and a liberal sampling of English pub-grub— bubble and squeak, toad-in-the-hole, and fish 'n' chips.

Also well worth a visit is the **Four Aces Diner**, on US-4 just uphill from the old bridge to Vermont, with very good from-scratch diner fare at down-to-earth prices (Sun.-Mon. to 3 PM, Tues.-Wed. to 8 PM, Thurs.-Sat. to 9 PM; 603/298-9896). This classic 1950s Worcester diner, built into the side of a red clapboard mill, does all its own baking and has a soda fountain, too.

With I-89 passing through the town and I-91 just across the river in Vermont, there are several budget and chain **motels** on both sides of the Connecticut River. Take your pick of **Radisson, Super 8, HoJo's, Comfort, Days,** and **Holiday Inn** between I-91's exit 11, just north of the I-89 interchange in Vermont, and I-89's exit 18 (Route 120) in Lebanon.

ACROSS VERMONT

Vermont is quintessential New England: picturesque villages still served by cluttered country stores, small farms nestled among the granite ridges of the Green Mountains, and needle-sharp white church spires rising above forests ablaze with autumn colors. Precocious from birth—its constitution was the first in the U.S. to prohibit slavery and establish public schools—Vermont is known for such a strong liberal tradition that even the state's Republicans are moderates.

Before Vermont joined the U.S. in 1791 as the 14th state, it spent 14 years as the independent Republic of New Connecticut. Its name comes from the French *verd mont,* meaning "green mountain," and appeared on maps as early as 1780.

From the Connecticut River, the route follows the contours of the land, keeping to the valleys between the steep surrounding ridges that carry the Appalachian Trail ever southward, or tagging along fast-running mountain streams that cut east-west. Besides the scenery, highlights include plenty of charming little towns, most of which support the casual restaurant and cafe whose inspired New American cuisine has made Vermont a realm in which portobello mushrooms, balsamic vinegar, and tiramisu are, if not basic currency, at least fairly common coin.

White River Junction

Turn-of-the-century White River Junction (pop. 2,582) used to echo with the sounds of some 50 trains a day beating their metallic castanets over five separate rail lines. The demise of the railroads and arrival of the interstate cloverleaf on the outskirts effectively mothballed the downtown area, but like good vintage clothing, the historic center has been rediscovered by an art-smart crowd that doesn't mind the holes and missing buttons. Exclusive galleries and expensive boutiques aren't invading the old brick storefronts around the tracks; on the contrary, the town looks like it's still expecting the New Deal to come pay a visit, though **River City Arts** (802/296-2505) is somehow able to keep the **Briggs Opera House** alive with music and theater.

If you're looking for lodging with more character than that of the chain motels along the Interstates, consider downtown's **Hotel Coolidge** (800/622-1124). Despite a passing resemblance to something from *Barton Fink*, it's a good value, with rooms from $60, and HI-hostel bunks for $21. If you prefer luxurious country inns and B&Bs, continue to Woodstock for the largest selection in a small area.

About 20 miles up the White River valley on Route 14 is the township of South Royalton, birthplace in 1805 of Mormon founder **Joseph Smith.** A huge solid granite monument and visitor center (daily 9 AM-5 PM) mark the spot, along with about 80,000 lights between Thanksgiving and Christmas.

Vermont has a statewide system of color-coded roadside commercial signage that makes it easy to find B&Bs and other services off the main roads, although the sign space is paid for and therefore shouldn't be mistaken for a comprehensive guide to what's out there.

Quechee and Woodstock

After White River Junction the route along US-4 enters the valley of the Ottauquechee River (auto-kwee-chee) near Quechee, a second-home community to country-clubbing executives from Connecticut and Boston. You'll cross **Quechee Gorge** almost without warning, but adjacent parking gives you a chance to take a second look at the dramatic little canyon or to stretch your legs along the rimside hiking trails before continuing the drive upstream. West of the gorge, turning north off the highway into old Quechee lets you enter a quaint old town, with a lumber mill-cum-art gallery, and a Norman Rockwell-esque rope swing under a covered bridge, from which local youths drop into the river below.

"The good people of Woodstock have less incentive than others to yearn for heaven," said a 19th-century resident. It's a sentiment readily echoed today. Since its settlement in the 1760s, Woodstock (pop. 3,212) has become an exceedingly well-preserved example of small-town New England, its classic village green, for example, still ringed with the tidy federal-style homes built by wealthy professionals of the newborn American republic. Now the historic village is home to wealthy retirees and inheritors, old money whose presence affords niceties like well-stocked wine racks at the general store, excellent performing arts at the Town Hall Theater, and the wherewithal to refuse any compromising commercial development. Having financially generous, conservation-minded residents like Laurance Rockefeller around hasn't hurt, either. To put it mildly, expansion of the tax base is *not* a pressing issue for this community.

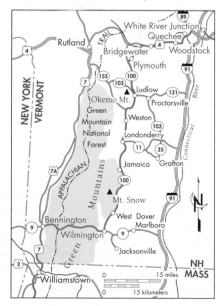

During summer and fall, walking tours are an excellent way to take stock of the town's history and architecture; call or visit the **Information Booth** (802/457-1042) on the Green for a schedule. Hiking trails lead up both the summits overlooking the town. A community blackboard at the corner of Central and Elm, a.k.a. the Town Crier, lists local events and activities all year.

Notice, as you approach Woodstock Village Green, that there are no overhead power lines on the two main downtown streets, Central and Elm. Laurance Rockefeller paid to have the lines buried back in 1973.

If you've admired the rolling fields and weathered wooden fences, savored the local apples and sharp cheddar, enjoyed the scent of mown hay or boiling maple sap, you'll appreciate an even closer look at New England's farms with a visit to the **Billings Farm & Museum**, on Route 12 north of the village (daily 10 AM-5 PM May-Oct., weekends 10 AM-4 PM Nov.-Dec. and Dec. 26-31; 802/457-2355; $7). Frederick Billings, better known as the builder of the Northern Pacific Railroad, began this working dairy farm in the late 19th century. Its restored farmhouse and huge barns illustrate the rural life in galleries, demonstrations, and hands-on activities.

If you prefer undomesticated nature, head up Church Hill Road on the west side of the Green to the **Vermont Institute of Natural Science** (daily 10 AM-4 PM except Sunday Nov.-April; 802/457-2779; $6). The institute devotes itself to environmental education and wildlife rehabilitation, but for casual visitors the highlight of the 77-acre nature preserve is the self-guiding trail through the **Raptor Center**, a set of 26 outdoor habitats for hawks, eagles, owls, and other birds of prey, all permanent convalescents from hunting or accidental injuries.

FRESH BEER HERE

Living in the Upper Valley of the Connecticut River must be thirsty work. Or folks up here have a particularly well-developed appreciation for the finer beers in life. Whatever the reason, several microbreweries and brew pubs flourish within a very small radius of White River Junction.

The Seven Barrels lies on Route 12A beside the I-89 overpass in West Lebanon, New Hampshire. This brew pub offers a good line of beers—British bitter, I.P.A., oatmeal stout, various seasonals—a liberal sampling of English pub grub—bubble and squeak, toad-in-the-hole, fish 'n' chips—and some concessions to modern American palates—veggie burgers, buffalo wings, pasta specials. Usually very crowded.

Catamount Brewing Company offers tours and tastings of their English-style ales and seasonal brews at their modern brewery along US-5 in Windsor, a mile south of I-91.1

The **Long Trail Brewing Company**, aka Mountain Brewers, has a taproom (daily until 6 PM) at the junction of US-4 and Route 100A, west of Woodstock, Vermont, where you can try the state's most popular microbrew, Long Trail Ale. Their flagship ale is named after the route that inspired the Appalachian Trail: the 85-year-old Long Trail, a 255-mile footpath running along the spine of the Green Mountains from Massachusetts to Canada. They also have seasonals, stout, even a kölsch—a light, wheaty ale, perfect for quenching summer thirst.

Windsor covered bridge

Hungry travelers will find plenty of choices around town, although some eateries assume you have a private endowment. The burgers at downtown **Bentley's**, for example, are a tad high-priced, but consider the accompaniments: Vermont microbrews, Oriental carpets, Victorian sofas, and a casual, cheerful, talkative crowd. If you'd pay as much for good vibes as you'd tip for good service, it's worth a visit. For simple—or not-so-simple—deli items, try either **The Village Butcher**, across Elm from Bentley's, or Central Street's natural foods market **18 Carrots**, offering veggie burritos, sandwiches, and softball-sized muffins.

Accommodations run the gamut from $40 motels to $80 B&Bs to $200-a-night inns. Expect stiff increases during high season, which in Woodstock is most of summer and fall, along with the winter holidays. Budget lodgings are found outside the village or in neighboring towns: around the huge Killington ski area about 20 miles west on US-4, for example, summer is considered low season, so prices are set accordingly. Otherwise, the modest **Braeside Motel** (802/457-1366 or 800/303-1366 inside Vermont; $48-88 double) on the eastern outskirts of town is about as budget-friendly as you're going to get.

The local **chamber of commerce** (802/457-3555) can supply a directory of area lodgings in advance or in summer from their booth on the Green.

Vermont holds over a hundred **covered bridges,** several good examples of which are to be seen between Quechee and Bridgewater. Look for the 1836 Taftsville bridge west of Quechee, the Middle bridge in Woodstock, and the 1877 Lincoln bridge west of Woodstock. The nation's longest covered bridge crosses the Connecticut River at Windsor, about 15 miles southeast of Woodstock, with a 460-foot span built in 1866.

For a long-distance "leaf-peepers" update on the progress of Vermont foliage, call the state's fall foliage hotline (24-hour recording, Sept.-Oct. only): 802/828-3239.

If you're in the area around mid-June, check out the **Quechee Hot Air Balloon Festival,** held over Father's Day weekend.

Bridgewater

Although the building still stands, the large woolen mill in Bridgewater (pop. 895) is long gone, the water-powered turbines and textile machines replaced by small shops selling a typically Vermont mix of antiques and ski apparel, New Age books, and gift-packaged Vermont foods. By the map, this tiny town stretched along the banks of the Ottauquechee seems well on the way to the middle of nowhere, but that's what lures visitors to most of the state: the fact that so much of it seems to have contentedly hung back with Rip Van Winkle and missed out on the neon competition for tackiest franchise mall. That said, Bridgewater is a gateway to one of the state's most important Somewheres: the ski resorts of central Vermont.

A jot west on US-4 at **Bridgewater Corners**, the route turns south on Route 100A toward Ludlow. The junction is just beside **Long Trail Brewers**, whose taproom (open daily until 6 PM) is worth a visit if you haven't yet tried the state's most popular microbrew. Their flagship Long Trail Ale is named after the route that inspired the Appalachian Trail: the 85-year-old Long Trail, a 255-mile footpath running along the spine of the Green Mountains from Massachusetts to Canada.

Since the demise of the friendly old Bridgewater Village Diner (due to non-payment of taxes), the best local roadfood place is **Blanche and Bill's Pancake House** (Wed.-Sun. 7 AM-2 PM; 802/422-3816), on US-4 west of the Route 100A junction.

During November and December hikers should be especially alert, as these months are hunting season throughout New England. Most hunters know to stay away from the most popular hiking areas, and are ready to head home by the time you finish breakfast, anyway, but it doesn't hurt to wear bright clothing and avoid practicing your bushwhacking skills during these months.

Plymouth

Running a twisty seven miles south from Bridgewater, 100A passes through beautiful scenery and Plymouth Notch, **birthplace of Calvin Coolidge**, the only U.S. president born on the 4th of July. The small hilltop clutch of buildings is so little changed by this century, it's a wonder there aren't horses with carriages parked behind the visitor center instead of Subarus. Calvin's home (the "Coolidge Homestead"), his father's general store (named for a later owner, Florence Cilley), and his son's cheese factory are three of the ten buildings open to the public (daily 9:30 AM-5 PM, Memorial Day to mid-Oct. $5; cheese factory open year-round, free), along with a mile-long meadow nature trail offering fine views of the Notch and its surroundings. The Coolidge Homestead was restored to its 1923 appearance when Col. John Coolidge administered the oath of office to his vacationing son, the vice-president, after President Harding died unexpectedly in San Francisco.

If you're looking for accommodations out where there are more stars than streetlights, try the **Salt Ash Inn** (doubles $85-165; 800/258-7258), an 1830s stagecoach stop at the junction of Routes 100A and 100 in Plymouth Union. Although Woodstock, Killington, and Ludlow are all within scenic 10- to 15-mile drives, surrounding mountains keep the twin notions of towns and business a world away. Alternatively, for a true night under the Milky Way, pitch your tent in Coolidge State Park (late May-early Oct.; $11) off Route 100A in Plymouth.

"Silent Cal" Coolidge was famous—perhaps unjustly—for being a man of few words. A White House dinner guest is said to have bet that she could make the president address her with at least three words; when confronted with this challenge, Coolidge replied, "You lose."

Route 100

Known as the "Skiers' Highway," serpentine Route 100 manages to pass the base of nearly every major ski resort in Vermont. Joining it midway through the state, our route follows a favorite stretch for cyclists, a mostly level dozen miles through the small farms (some of which sell maple syrup in spring) and posh-looking lakeside resorts of the Black River valley. Route 100 ends up in **Ludlow**, at the foot of Okemo (oh-KEY-mo) Mountain. Any doubts that skiing is the cash cow of the state's most lucrative industry—tourism—are quickly dispelled by just one look at the wall-to-wall inns, sportswear shops, vacation real estate offices, and restaurants along Ludlow's main drag. The town's star attraction is that 3,300-foot peak with its hundreds of acres of ski trails serviced by state-of-the-art *everything*, although seven other ski areas cluster like the Pleiades within a 25-mile radius.

Between the end of ski season and the beginning of fall foliage, Ludlow's pulse nearly flatlines. Flocks of elderly, low-tipping Floridians migrate to the vast strings of condos around Okemo, if anything adding to the summer slowdown. In recent years mountain bikers and inn-to-inn cyclists have become a source of some life, but overall Ludlow, like many other Vermont ski towns, spends the warm months convalescing.

Fortunately yuppie recreation requires yuppie food, so when it comes time to do your pre-ride carbo-loading or aprés-ski whistle-wetting, you won't have to resort to a hamburger that's like the other billions and billions served. **Nikki's**, in the shopping plaza next to Okemo's access road, is your best bet for creative continental cuisine—from the pizza del mar appetizer to the no-holds-barred white chocolate mousse. Good wine list, too. If Momma Valente's homemade lasagna or eggplant parmigiana is more your speed, continue south to the traffic light downtown and let her son welcome you into **Valente's**, next to the park on the corner. Or if you're looking for a decent inexpensive breakfast, try **The Hatchery** across the street.

Accommodations run mostly on the flashy side with either antique-filled Victorian inns or "modern rustic" motels and chalets, but there's also the very reasonable **HI Trojan Horse Hostel** (802/228-5244; $15-20 per person; closed April), with its shared or private rooms in a converted barn beside Route 100 less than a half-mile south of the main street. (They offer canoe rentals in season, too.) Otherwise, for a place to stay expect to shell out anywhere from a summertime low of around $50 to a fall and winter weekend high of over $200.

Turning south out of Ludlow opposite the Black River Brewing Company, Route 100 wanders along the eastern edge of the Green Mountains' high spine through one town after another. With the exception of well-to-do **Weston**, a small place that makes a big business out of its country stores, skiing is clearly the name of the game for most of them: **Londonderry**, below Big Bromley; **Jamaica**, near Stratton Mountain; and **West Dover**, sandwiched between the impressive Mount Snow/Haystack complex. All the ski areas, of course, bubble with the usual superlatives about snowmaking, grooming, and fast chair lifts, while the towns boast colonial frame houses, snowboard shops, cafes, and country inns with discreet hand-

When garnished with Vermont-made Ben & Jerry's, apple pie à la mode is certainly nothing to sneer at, but if you really want to try apple pie the Vermont way, ask for a slab of sharp cheddar on the side instead of ice cream.

President Coolidge recollected in his autobiography "No doubt there have been kings who have participated in the induction of their sons into their office, but in republics where the succession comes by election I do not know of any other case in history where a father has administered to his son the qualifying oath of office. . . It seemed a simple and natural thing to do at the time." His father, when later asked how he knew he could administer the oath, replied, "I didn't know I couldn't."

Okemo and its central Vermont sisters are best for intermediate skiers; though each has a few black diamond trails for experts—Killington more than just a few, if you don't mind sharing them with half the state of New Jersey on weekends—skiers looking for more than a couple of hours of challenging downhill terrain will get more for the price of their lift ticket among the half-dozen ski areas around Stowe and Waterbury, a couple of hours farther north, where Route 100 crosses US-2 and I-89.

Buffalo Brook, which drains into Lake Echo north of Ludlow, was for almost 30 years the site of a gold-mining operation in the mid-19th century.

If your supply of driving music is getting stale, visit the gift shop at the **Weston Priory,** three miles north of town, and pick up a tape of something truly inspirational. To hear the resident Benedictine monks live, consult the bulletin board by the parking lot for a schedule of their public devotional services. From the Route 100/155 junction, take Route 155 north; the priory's driveway is the first left.

If you're fond of sharp cheddar, consider taking a particularly scenic loop south from Ludlow on Routes 103 and 35 or east from Londonderry via Routes 11 and 121 to historic little **Grafton,** arguably the prettiest town in Vermont. The **Grafton Village Cheese Factory** south of town makes some of the sharpest cheddar you'll ever taste. If you don't need tidy gift-wrappable blocks, ask in the Village Store for their "random cuts," irregular chunks sold for a steep discount.

Vermont has been synonymous with skiing since the beginning of the sport, with credit for both the first ski tow and first chair lift in the United States. Less well known is the state's love of tennis: there are more courts per capita here than anywhere else in the nation.

It ain't Texas, or even Cincinnati, but chili fans who find themselves near Mount Snow on the second Saturday of each August should be sure to drop in on the annual **Vermont State Chili Cookoff** (802/464-3333 for details).

carved wooden signs out front. Notice the details of the Vermont landscape: Saabs or pickups in the driveways, cupolas and weathervanes on the barn roofs, and expensive Kubota tractors for mowing the fields that, while no longer belonging to working farms, are nevertheless groomed to postcard perfection.

Wilmington and Route 9

Route 100 leaves its panoramic view of Mount Snow as it descends into Wilmington (pop. 1,968), another picturesque village of 18th- and 19th-century shops and houses built along the Deerfield River. For delicious pancakes served with a half-dozen toppings, stop at earthy **Sonny's Cup 'n' Saucer,** 159 N. Route 100. The chamber of commerce is named after the local ski resort rather than the town, so you know who pays the bills around here. Nevertheless, summers see a fair bit of activity in the galleries and antique shops, along with the occasional bus tour stopping by on its way to the North River Winery down in **Jacksonville,** seven miles farther south on Route 100. For classical music lovers, the **Marlboro Music Festival** marks summer's zenith at Marlboro College, Marlboro, a dozen miles east toward Brattleboro on Route 9. Between mid-July and mid-August several score of the world's finest classical musicians perform here in one of the nation's most distinguished annual chamber music series (for schedule and ticket info, call 802/254-2394).

Heading westward on Route 9 to Bennington, the route crosses the diffuse southern edge of the Green Mountains, which also means it crosses the path of the Appalachian Trail, the only place in Vermont where our route does so. Unlike the well-defined ridges in the northern part of the range, the southern Greens spread out over a fairly wide area, and roadless tracts between the Big Bromley ski area and the Massachusetts state line are quite visible as large blank spots on the map. **Woodford State Park** on Route 9 is a good base for hikes into these areas, either along the AT or tributary trails; besides camping at the park (late May-early Oct.; $13-17), there's a seasonal HI hostel at Prospect Ski Mountain's Greenwood Lodge (late May-late Oct.; 802/442-2547; $14-17 per person), about three miles farther west on Route 9.

Bennington

By far the largest town yet encountered on our route, Bennington (pop. 16,451) is a bustling little manufacturing and commercial center, named for a significant battlefield victory against the British-paid Hessians during the American Revolution, a sweet morale-booster that contributed to the defeat of Gen. "Gentleman Johnny" Burgoyne's army of Redcoats at Saratoga soon after. In the subsequent centuries Bennington's name has become synonymous with art: the decorative arts of the antebellum **United States Pottery Company**; the liberal arts of **Bennington College**, one of the nation's most expensive and exclusive private colleges; and the folk art of Mary Robertson "**Grandma**" **Moses.** The largest public collection of Moses's beguiling work is on display in **The Bennington Museum** (daily 9 AM-5 PM; $6), whose white-columned ivy-covered edifice is found on West Main Street (Route 9) in the graceful old part of town, near the 306-foot obelisk commemorating that 1777 victory (elevator to observation room, mid-April to Nov. 1).

If anyone starts erecting monuments to good dining instead of to old wars, this town would have another tower of stone beside the **Blue Benn Diner**, on US-7 north of downtown. The fact that it's a vintage 1940s Silk City certainly gives this cozy nonsmoking joint character, but what earns the seven-days-a-week (from 6 AM!) loyalty of its patrons is the top-notch short-order cooking: from baked meat loaf and roast pork to broccoli stir-fry and multi-grain pancakes, it's good, it's cheap, and it's served up so fast you'll barely have time to choose between Sinatra or Soundgarden on the wall-box juke at your table. The enchiladas are a match for any in San Antonio, although New Englanders still haven't gotten the hang of eating them for breakfast.

Most of Bennington's **accommodations** are strung along Route 7A to the north and Route 7 to the south of downtown, all local names but for the Ramada and Best Western inns found on 7A. If you are in the market for a distinctive B&B, push on the dozen miles to Williamstown (covered under Massachusetts, below).

An excellent source of **hiking information** is the Green Mountain Club; their *Day Hiker's Guide to Vermont* and *Guide Book of the Long Trail* are both available direct from the GMC, which is on Route 100, 10 miles north of the Ben & Jerry's Ice Cream Factory (RR 1 Box 650, Route 100, Waterbury Center, VT 05677; 802/244-7037). Or, buy a copy from bookshops in Bennington or Wilmington.

Brigham Young, the man who led the Mormon exodus to Utah, was born in Whitingham, less than 10 miles south of Wilmington on Route 100. There's a small commemorative monument and picnic area on the Town Hall Common. For more history on Mormons, see the special topic, **Mormons in Illinois** on page 249 in the Great River Road chapter.

ACROSS MASSACHUSETTS

Hemmed in by the daunting topography of its surrounding mountains, Western Massachusetts is a world apart, blessed with an easygoing small-town character so dissimilar from that of the metropolitan seacoast that locals compare it to southern Vermont, or upstate New York, or anything, in fact, but Massachusetts. Given Boston's perennial neglect of the region, constituents often seem to wish it *were* another state.

Berkshire County might find the political clout it has so long sought if representation were based on culture and the social register rather than population. The region has been a magnet for performing arts and artists for over 150 years, and a playground for the rich and famous for over a century. To better sample this heritage and the associated culinary attractions, our route busies itself with the more populous valley floor. But remember, it never takes more than a few strategic turns to find splendidly rural backroads through woods as deep and undisturbed as those enjoyed by hikers along the Appalachian Trail.

> By the early 19th century, farmland had replaced 75% of Berkshire County's forests. Now forests have reclaimed that 75% and more, but innumerable drystone walls serve as reminders of the once vast cultivated fields.

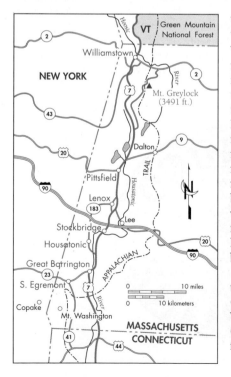

Williamstown

To the visitor it appears as if stately Williamstown (pop. 8,220) is simply a nickname for the immaculate and graceful campus of Williams College—even the main commercial block is basically the corridor between dorms and gym. From their common 18th-century benefactor, Ephraim Williams, to the large number of alumni who return in their retirement, "Billsville" and its college are nearly inseparable. The town-gown symbiosis has spawned an enviable array of visual, performing, and edible arts, yet fresh contingents of ingenuous youth keep all the wealth and refinement from becoming too cloying.

Two of the town's crown jewels are the **Clark Art Institute** on South Street (Tues.-Sun. 10 AM-5 PM; free) and the **Williams College Museum of Art** (Tues.-Sat. 10 AM-5 PM, Sunday 1-5 PM; free) on Main Street opposite Memorial

YE OLDE GENTRIFICATION

From central Vermont to northwest Connecticut you'll occasionally run across resentment toward second-home owners who, popular wisdom suggests, have invaded from out of state, buying up old farms or building expensive new houses on what was once pristine forest or prime grazing land, generally driving up property values and driving out the locals. These invading aliens—typically New Yorkers, or "212s" in the hip parlance of area codes, but Bostonians and Connecticut suburbanites, too—are mocked for their brazen self-importance, their stuffy contempt for small-town ways, their cravings for their hometown newspapers and foodstuffs. To hear waitresses and barflies kvetch about it, you'd think the problem is recent, but in fact it's almost as old as the hills. As far back as the 1850s, after the more arable Ohio Valley had been opened up to homesteading by improved transportation and Indian genocide, New Yorkers and Bostonians were buying up old country farmsteads abandoned by the westward migration. Like their modern successors, those early yuppies fixed up the old houses and embraced the restorative powers of nature. Perhaps some even raised a few local eyebrows with odd fad diets—eating Sylvester Graham's digestive crackers, for example, made from coarse-ground whole wheat—and unholy devotion to new lifestyle gurus like Henry David Thoreau.

The intervening years haven't diminished the importance of the development debate; they merely remind each wave of settlers that it's ingenuous to pretend they can enter the promised land and slam the gate behind themselves. Pressures to develop will continue, too, so long as it's more profitable to grow houses than food, or until self-interest succeeds in capturing all the rural peace and quiet within split-rail fences and picture window frames.

Chapel, that Westminster Abbey knock-off. They make an outstanding pair: the Clark with its extraordinary collection of Impressionist paintings, including over 30 Renoirs; and the WCMA with its emphasis on changing exhibits of contemporary and non-Western art, set within gallery spaces that are themselves artfully conceived.

Another singular collection is stashed away on the second floor of Stetson Hall, the ivy-covered red brick building furthest behind Memorial Chapel's gothic bulk. If you can find it, the **Chapin Library of Rare Books** (Mon.-Fri. 9 AM-noon, 1-5 PM; free) will reward you with a display of all of our nation's important birth certificates: the Declaration of Independence, the Articles of Confederation, an annotated draft of the Constitution, George Washington's copy of the Federalist Papers, and two early versions of the Bill of Rights (one with 17 and the other with 12 amendments).

High-toned continental dining suitable for starched alumni banquets abounds in Williamstown, but if you're looking for truly fresh, interesting food, skip the inns and go to the **Cobble Cafe** on Spring Street (breakfast daily, lunch Mon.-Sat., dinner Tues.-Sat.), a place whose menu, ambience, and wine list will give San Franciscans déjà vu—provided it has reopened since a 1998 fire. A late-night dessert-and-drinks menu accommodates evening patrons of summer's annual **Williamstown Theatre**

Winslow Homer's Saco Bay is part of the collection at the Clark Art Institute.

Festival (413/597-3399 for schedule) as well as anyone looking for some of the best not-too-sweet-or-gooey pecan pie money can buy. Next door, the **Clarksburg Bread Co.** (closed Sun.-Mon.) serves up soups, sandwiches, and a wealth of delicious baked goods until 4 PM. The hands-down best takeout pizza joint is **Hot Tomatoes** on Water Street, but in mild weather the nearby streamside park is well suited to lolling picnickers if you don't fancy perfuming your car with pesto or spicy sausage.

Wild Oats, the food co-op in the Colonial Shopping Center east of town on Route 2 (daily till 6 PM, Thursday till 8 PM), has a big selection of bulk items that will appeal to campers and hikers. Incidentally, the Appalachian Trail crosses Route 2 just 1.5 miles east of Wild Oats' front door.

A drive along Main Street (Route 2) will give you a view of most of Williamstown's accommodations, from the on-campus, $150-a-night **Williams Inn** (413/458-9371) to the small motels out on the eastern edge of town. For a real treat consider **Field Farm** ($125 double; 413/458-3135) on Sloan Road in South Williamstown, five miles south along either Route 7 or scenic Water Street (Route 43). Occupying the 254-acre former estate of Pacific Northwest lumber tycoon Lawrence Bloedel, the main house, designed in 1948, is a striking example of American modern architecture. If you have any love of Frank Lloyd Wright or Charles and Ray Eames, you'll be delighted by this live-in museum of contemporary design, with its huge picture windows, proto-Scandinavian furniture and Lucite fixtures, its walls adorned with selections from Bloedel's extensive 20th-century art collection, plus tennis courts, a swimming pool, nature trails, and breathtaking views of Mount Greylock across the valley.

Additional **information** is available from the Board of Trade's Information Booth at the center of town, or by picking up the latest copy of the free *Guide to Williamstown* from local shop and restaurant vestibules.

Singer sewing machine heir Robert Sterling Clark's huge art collection ended up in Williamstown in part because of the Cold War. In the late 1940s and early 1950s, the threat of a Russian nuclear attack seemed real enough that distance from likely bomb targets was a critical factor in choosing a permanent repository.

Luxurious Cunard Lines used to serve their ocean-going passengers water exclusively from Williamstown, whose Sand Springs thermal mineral waters are as pure as any known on the planet. The 74° spring waters, still used by some hospitals and distributed by a small commercial bottler, have been enjoyed by bathers since at least 1762. The current bathhouse on the site is the Sand Springs Spa (Memorial Day to Labor Day; $7.50 single-day swim pass) on the north side of town, whose genial owners Fred and Helen George bought the place during their honeymoon visit back in 1950.

Mount Greylock

Massachusetts' tallest peak is the centerpiece of 12,500-acre **Mount Greylock State Reservation**, one of the state's largest and most popular possessions. Over 50 miles of trails, including some thigh-burning mountain-bike routes, wander along the reforested slopes, most of which were heavily logged for fuel and pulp back in the 19th century. Rock ledges provide great views of the Hoosic River valley to the east and the Housatonic valley to the south, when the namesake mists aren't keeping the 3,491-foot summit wadded up in a damp ball of dingy cotton. During warm months access is a cinch: century-old Notch Road snakes its way up through the birch and spruce from Route 2 on the north side, while Rockwell Road ascends from Route 7 along the flanks of Greylock's southern neighbors. Combine these roads' 17 miles and you'll enjoy the most scenic driveable mountain ascent in New England, though keep in mind that both roads are narrow and steep, contoured with frost-heaves, enlivened by occasional hairpin turns, and—especially at dusk—prone to wandering wildlife. If you want to see over the forest without your car, climb the 105-foot **War Memorial Tower** on the summit. If the weather is good, you'll have a panorama from New Hampshire to Connecticut.

A stone's throw from the granite tower is the AMC's **Bascom Lodge** (mid-May to late October only; 413/443-0011), a beautiful old stone and timber structure with private rooms, shared bunk rooms and cold-water baths, overpriced at $30-65 but for the location, which is sublime despite the nearby TV relay mast.

One of the few bicycle shops offering rentals along the AT route through Massachusetts is **Spoke Bicycle & Repair,** at 408 Main Street in Williamstown (413/458-3456), which also carries copies of the incomparable *Bike Rides in the Berkshire Hills* by Lewis Cuyler.

Possibly the most detailed and well-written guide to exploration of the Berkshires on foot is Lauren Stevens's *Hikes & Walks in the Berkshire Hills,* usually available in local bookstores and gift shops, or directly from Berkshire House Publishers, Box 915, Great Barrington, MA 01230.

For an up-to-the-day report on the spread of autumn color through the Berkshires during September and October, call for the local foliage report: 800/343-9072 from out of state, or 800/632-8038 within Massachusetts.

Pittsfield

Once-thriving Pittsfield (pop. 48,622) is a classic example of a single-industry city on the skids: having first lost its commercial center to a giant mall in a neighboring town, Pittsfield then watched its major employer, General Electric, proceed to consolidate, cut back, downsize, and otherwise all but lock up and turn out the lights. Compared to the carefully preserved Norman Rockwell simplicity of many of the surrounding small towns, Pittsfield's aging industrial cityscape has made it the place most Berkshire weekenders strenuously try to avoid; despite the fact that its size, and the valley's topography, make this nearly impossible unless you have a resident's familiarity with the backroads. That said, however, there are actually good reasons to pay the place a visit.

Baseball, for example. Catching a home game with the professional minor league **Pittsfield Mets** in Wahconah Park is widely regarded as an exemplar of the American pastime as it used to be: gregarious fans, decent players, and cheap admission ($2.75 general, $3.75 grandstand, $6.75 box seats; 413/499-METS for schedule). Wahconah, built in 1919, has a charm of its own, with plastic owls hanging from the rafters for pigeon scarecrows, a mascot that looks like Mr. Potato-Head with baseball stitching, cheesy sing-alongs, and the famous Sun Delay, when play is suspended until the setting sun stops shining in the batter's, catcher's and umpire's eyes.

HANCOCK SHAKER VILLAGE

West of Pittsfield on US-20, Hancock Shaker Village is a well-preserved remnant of the religious sect known popularly as "Shakers" but formally as the United Society of Believers in Christ's Second Appearing, whose utopian communities flourished in the years before the Civil War. Shakers, as outsiders called them because of their occasional convulsions during worship, were dedicated to a communal life conspicuous in its equality between men and women, a natural corollary to their belief in parity between a male God and a female Holy Mother Wisdom.

The English-born leader of the group, Ann Lee, was in fact regarded by Shakers as the female, and second, incarnation of Christ. Though Puritan theocracy was ending, preaching this gospel did not endear her to many New Englanders in the decade following her arrival just prior to the American Revolution. During that war, Lee and her "children" sought their "Heaven on Earth," as seen in her visions. Mother Ann died near Albany, New York, of injuries sustained from repeated beatings, before any communities based on her precepts could be founded.

Hancock Shaker Village, third among the 24 settlements built in the U.S. by Lee's followers, survived 170 years, outlasting all but two others. It's now preserved as a living museum (daily 9:30 AM-5:30 PM April-Oct.; $13.50; 413/443-0188 or 800/817-1127), with exhibits, tours, and working artisans interpreting the rural lifestyle and famous design skills of the Shakers. Appreciation of the efficiency, simplicity, and perfect workmanship consecrated within the "City of Peace" can quickly fill a couple of days if you let it. For a special treat secure a place at the candlelight Shaker dinners held on Saturday evenings; you can also sample Shaker cuisine in the Village Cafe.

HANCOCK SHAKER VILLAGE

Pittsfield is also a good place to remember the advice, "One-word: plastics" given to Dustin Hoffman in *The Graduate,* perhaps while taking a tour of General Electric's **Living Environments concept house**, located on New York Avenue across from parent GE Plastics. Primarily a laboratory for testing high-tech materials and technologies for home construction and consumer products, the "Plastics House" has attracted so much attention from folks wanting to window-shop the future that weekly reserved tours are offered to benefit the local chapter of the United Way (Thursday afternoons and some Saturday mornings; $6; 413/442-6948 or 800/696-6948 for reservations).

If associating plastics with Pittsfield seems novel, what about whales? Head out to Holmes Road, at the city's rural southern edge, and maybe you, too, will see the resemblance between the leviathan and the imposing outline of Mount Greylock, particularly if you view it from the study window of Herman Melville's **Arrowhead** (daily 10 AM-5 PM Memorial

Day to Labor Day, Fri.-Mon. remainder of the year; $4.50). That salty masterpiece of digression and most unloved of high school reading assignments, *Moby-Dick,* was indeed written in this landlocked locale. While foremost a literary shrine, the spacious farm is also home to the Berkshire County Historical Society, whose well-curated exhibits are always interesting.

Arrowhead

As with its other attractions, when it comes to food Pittsfield has some real out-of-the-way gems. In the acute angle between East and Elm Streets, for example, is the semicircular facade of the **Pittsfield Rye Bakery,** a 1950s flying saucer of glass and blue tile with big bright cases of fresh muffins, bagels, and breads beckoning within. Farther along East Street, past the mammoth GE Polymer Plastics plant, you'll find a pair of Italian places around the corner from one another; both serve good food, sometimes great food, at unusually low prices. The one you won't miss is **elizabeth's borderland café,** in the shocking pink house on East Street, where all the pasta dishes are accompanied by fistfuls of crusty bread and wonderful salads, leaving little room for fine appetizers such as the *bagna caoda,* a must for anchovy lovers. For excellent pasta, pizza and pub grub at a great small-town price, step around the corner to the **East Side Cafe** on Newell Street, a neighborhood bar whose comfort food and convivial atmosphere attract a family clientele.

Serious pilgrims on the path of Ishmael and the great white whale will want to visit the **Melville Memorial Room** on the upper level of the Berkshire Athenaeum—Pittsfield's public library.

Lenox

During the turn-of-the-century Gilded Age, the Berkshires were known as the "inland Newport" because of the opulent "cottages" that dotted the South County landscape, principally around Lenox (pop. 5,100). Some 75 of these giant mansions still stand, built for an era in which "society" was a respectable, full-time occupation for folks with names like Carnegie and Westinghouse. Many of the houses have been converted to palatial inns, spas, or private schools; others are home to orga-

Many an American industrialist's fortune came to rest among the Berkshire Hills, but the county's connection to the nation's wealth goes to the very fiber of the dollar. Crane & Co. of Dalton, just east of Pittsfield, has produced the paper for all U.S. currency since 1879.

nizations whose presence makes Lenox a seasonal epicenter for professional performing arts. Besides **Tanglewood,** the local culture roster includes the **National Music Center** (800/USA-MUSIC or 800/872-6874), the **Berkshire Opera Company** (413/243-1343), and **Shakespeare & Company** (theatrical summer residents of novelist Edith Wharton's 1902 estate, **The Mount;** 413/637-1199). Add the **Jacob's Pillow** dance festival in Becket (413/243-0745) and the **Berkshire Theatre Festival** in Stockbridge (413/298-5576), and you can understand why such a small town is such a big magnet for East Coast culture vultures.

The annual influx of cosmopolitan concertgoers affects everything in southwestern Massachusetts, most obviously the local restaurants, half of which cater to immigrants from Boston and New York. If you aren't counting nickels, try the eclectic American menu at the **Church Street Cafe,** where the tastes from the kitchen and accents from the diners are unmistakably reminiscent of some big city bistro. Other major contenders for the town's gourmet dining crowd lie within the same two-block area.

At the other end of the price spectrum is the mostly takeout **Salerno's Gourmet Pizza**, tucked off Franklin Street at no. 8, whose plain fast-food-style decor masks a practitioner of the delicious *abbondonza* school of pizza. If you prefer food you can eat with a fork, take Main Street north of town to busy US-7/20, where even Italians will grudgingly admit that **Sweet Basil Grille** serves up good Italian fare—one of the few places in the region to make the passing grade. The prices are good when you read the menu, great after you see the portions.

Tanglewood occupies the former Tappan Estate, a Berkshire cottage whose grounds included the Red House, in which Nathaniel Hawthorne wrote *House of the Seven Gables* during his brief Berkshire residency.

Lenox brims with over 20 handsome B&B inns attractively situated amid wide lawns and gardens, including the **Birchwood Inn**, 7 Hubbard Street (800/524-1646), opposite The Church On The Hill; and the **Brook Farm Inn** on Hawthorne Street (413/637-3013), which offers over 700 volumes of poetry in the library, poets on tape, poetry readings on Saturday, and poems

TANGLEWOOD

To cognoscenti, Tanglewood is the name of an expansive hilltop estate whose concert halls and sloping lawns are home to the Boston Symphony Orchestra and a plethora of visiting artists for 10 weeks each summer. To everyone else it's the one-word explanation for the long restaurant lines, flash flood of weekend South County traffic, and consensus of No Vacancy signs. From the end of June through to the beginning of September, anyone looking for a room will be guaranteed maximum frustration; if you want to be sure of a weekend room in and around Lenox during summer, reserve it in early spring, after which any places with the least bit of charm and comfort will have their weekends booked solid. The end of summer also is rather predictable, so there's no excuse for delaying your fall-foliage reservations.

While indoor tickets to Tanglewood performances are available in advance by fax, by mail, or through Ticketmaster (surcharge added), tickets for the lawns surrounding the Music Shed and Concert Hall are only available in person. For $13-20 you can buy an orchestral serenade beneath the stars—an exceptional value if the clouds don't burst (no rain checks are given), especially when accompanied by gourmet victuals from a local deli or restaurant. Which is why you'll see most Tanglewood patrons sensibly outfitted with lawn chairs, blankets, and baskets instead of top hats and tails.

For complete program and ticket info, call Symphony Charge (888/266-1200), or write the Boston Symphony Orchestra, Symphony Hall, Boston, MA 02115. From early June through Labor Day, you may also call the Tanglewood box office (413/637-5165). Once the season begins, weekly program updates are available (413/637-1666).

du jour for perusal before breakfast. Another popular option, right at the center of Lenox, is the **Village Inn**, 16 Church Street (413/637-0020), built in 1771 and featuring clean, comfortable rooms and a very good restaurant at moderate prices—from $55 a night when Tanglewood is *not* in season.

Of course, if you prefer the anonymity of your favorite chain motels you'll find **Suisse Chalet, Quality Inn, Best Western,** and **Super 8** scattered along US-20 between the Pittsfield-Lenox line and the I-90 interchange in neighboring Lee. For a complete list of these local accommodations, or for help with last-minute lodging referrals, call the **Lenox Chamber of Commerce** (800/25-LENOX or 800/255-3669) or visit their office in the Lenox Academy Building on Main Street across from the Post Office plaza.

Stockbridge

If the main street of Stockbridge looks vaguely familiar, perhaps it's because the town made its way onto Norman Rockwell canvases during the final decades of his career, when he lived and worked here. You may dismiss his illustrations as the epitome of contrived sentimentality, but the only people who don't find themselves grinning after a stroll through the unparalleled collection of **The Norman Rockwell Museum**, on Route 183 west of town, have hearts of solid flint (daily 10 AM-5 PM May to Oct. and weekends year-round, otherwise 11 AM-4 PM; $9). The town itself is worth a stroll, too, particularly past the grand houses along Main Street deliberately frozen in an idyllic past.

While most of the large estate homes are not open to the public, one of the county's more extravagant "cottages" is: **Naumkeag** (daily 10 AM-4:15 PM late May to Labor Day, weekends only through Columbus Day; $7, or $5 garden only), an 1885 mansion on Prospect Hill Road less than a mile north of downtown Stockbridge. The mansion amply illustrates why this region was regarded the state's Gold Coast a century ago; even the impressively landscaped grounds are an attraction in their own right.

Sculpture is the highlight of **Chesterwood** (daily 10 AM-5 PM May-Oct.; $7.50), off Route 183 just south of the Rockwell Museum. The residence was the summer home of **Daniel Chester French**, one of the most popular contributors to the *fin de siècle* American Renaissance, remembered best for his statue of the seated president in

Washington, D.C.'s Lincoln Memorial. A tour of French's studio and house, now a property of the National Trust, or a walk around his 122 wooded acres graced with works of contemporary sculptors, quickly confirms why the sculptor once called his seasonal visits "six months . . . in heaven."

Edith Wharton, the first woman to win a Pulitzer Prize for her 1920 novel *The Age of Innocence,* drew upon local people and incidents in many of her works, including two of her most famous: *House of Mirth* and *Ethan Frome.* The house she designed and built for herself in 1902, called The Mount (Tues.-Sun. 10 AM-2 PM in summer only; $6; 413/637-1899), is just south of central Lenox, well signed off Plunkett Street.

That Rockwell painting of the runaway kid with the policeman? The lunch counter setting was inspired by **Joe's Diner** in nearby Lee, a Central Street institution favored by everybody from local factory workers to New York celebrities.

The Stockbridge Indians, a band of Mahicans whose conversion to Christianity occupied some of the town's earliest settlers, were forced from this region in the 18th century. Their descendants now reside in central Wisconsin.

Stockbridge's Main Street hasn't always been the exclusive province of boutiques for coffee, curtains, and AARP members. Once upon a time it was also home to the eatery immortalized as the place where "you can get anything you want" by Arlo Guthrie in his song, "Alice's Restaurant Massacree." The building is now **Naji's,** 40 Main Street, somewhat pricey but serving the only Middle Eastern food for miles.

Monument Mountain was where Herman Melville and Nathaniel Hawthorne first met on an outing arranged by a New York publisher in 1850, the year the two writers took up residence in the area. Melville, who dedicated *Moby Dick* to his friend, was disconsolate when Hawthorne later moved away without notice.

Looking for a distinctive, out-of-the-way B&B? Consider using a booking service such as the friendly and efficient Berkshire Bed and Breakfast Homes ($8 fee upon confirming reservation). Owner Eleanor Hebert represents unadvertised and reasonably priced properties all along our route through the Berkshires, from a working dairy farm in Williamstown to a circa 1815 colonial with pool in Sheffield, and plenty in between. Call 413/268-7244 (Mon.-Fri. 9 AM-5:30 PM) or write P.O. Box 211, Williamsburg, MA 01096 for more info.

Housatonic

The few miles of Route 183 between the museums in Stockbridge and the town line are a prime example of the Berkshires' back-road charms. Wrapping around an old mill dam on the Housatonic River, the road tags along beside the water as the rounded bulk of Monument Mountain rises to the east, followed quickly by the dark brick hulks of the old Monument Mills. "Entering Great Barrington," reads the sign, though the first glance suggests otherwise: if this place ever saw greatness, it was back in the era of steam locomotives. But looks deceive. Properly known as Housatonic, this village is becoming the funky country cousin of Manhattan's gentrified TriBeCa, with a cluster of working artists' studios among those old cotton mills along the river, and storefront galleries in the old commercial block beside the railroad trestle. Before you follow Route 183 south, park by the school yard or the lumber mill and stroll around. The **Front Street Gallery** and **Le Petit Musée** are typically open weekends (noon-5 PM), but serendipity is the operative concept in this town, so take a look anyway if you visit on a weekday in case somebody happens to be around. **Spazi Contemporary Art** and **RiCA**, on the east side of the river above the lumberyard and in the old trolley barn down the road respectively, keep somewhat longer hours (Thurs.-Sun. and Wed.-Sun. noon-5 PM), and can inform you of the open studio schedule for artists who work nearby.

When hunger pangs begin to diminish your art appreciation, step over to **Christina's Just Desserts** (daily to 6 PM) across from the school yard for tasty lunch fare and pastries. Or start a picnic basket with delicious, fresh, crusty sourdough from the **Berkshire Mountain Bakery** (Sun.-Thurs. to 10 PM) less than a mile south of the village on Route 183. To complete the basket, follow the highway another mile south to the **Taft Farms** roadside market. During apple-picking season Taft's wooden crates full of orchard-fresh fruit aren't to be missed.

Jutting up sharply north of the market parking lot, Devil's Pulpit on Monument Mountain is a good spot to enjoy your repast, which will be well earned by the half-hour climb to the rocky ledge with its unspoiled westward views (the eastern vista is scarred by gravel pits). Trailhead parking and picnic tables appear rather abruptly on the downhill side of US-7 north of the Route 183 junction; look for the discreet Monument Mountain Reservation signs (voluntary contribution suggested).

Great Barrington

While most South County towns have been spruced up like precious antiques, Great Barrington, with as many hardware stores as chic boutiques, is like grandma's comfortable old sofa, still too much in daily use to keep under velvet wraps. The town doesn't deplore the few tacky commercial lots around its fringes, perhaps because they can't detract from the handsome buildings at its core: the 1905 Mahaiwe Theater, all marble and gilt trim behind its marquee; the stone churches on wide

Main Street; and imposing Searles Castle, a former Berkshire cottage turned private academy.

The center of Great Barrington has a lot to offer hungry travelers. Fussy early risers seeking their cappuccino and muffins, or picnickers seeking the makings of a great spread, will want to check out **The Berkshire Coffee Roasting Company**, on Main Street, which serves up espresso drinks, teas, and bakery items, with the added benefit of the South County's best let's-hang-out atmosphere. **Bev's Homemade Ice Cream**, around the corner on Railroad Street, is another source of caffeine, light lunch fare, and sugar, too, by the rich and creamy coneful.

Across from Bev's is **20 Railroad Street**, *the* place for burgers, sandwiches, and soups; its lively bar is the closest native example of a honky-tonk.

South Egremont to the State Line

The more pastoral of the two roads into Connecticut follows Route 23/41 into South Egremont, another of those well-preserved villages entirely ensconced in the National Register of Historic Places—which is hardly a rare honor in Massachusetts. While the custom of baptizing property with cute monikers has seized altogether too many New Englanders, this is one place that genuinely deserves appellations such as Huckleberry Hollow, The Birches, and Wheelbarrow Hill Farm.

South Egremont is the northern gateway to the state's remotest corner, the town of **Mount Washington** (pop. 120). Within its wooded boundaries, Bash Bish Falls State Park, Mount Washington State Forest, and Mount Everett State Reservation all provide fine hikes on and off the Appalachian Trail. You can pick up a free trail map covering all three properties at State Forest Headquarters (413/528-0330). Take the signposted turn from Route 41 west of South Egremont Village, and follow the road past signs for Bash Bish Falls and Copake, New York, until you reach the end of the paving nine miles later.

You'll find good day-hikes beside the Connecticut state line off US-7A in Ashley Falls, at **Bartholomew's Cobble**, a designated National Natural Landmark ($3). Geology and weather have conspired to produce an outstanding diversity of flora, over 700 species, within a relatively small pocket of fern-covered boulder outcrops and broad meadows.

Back in South Egremont, **Mom's Country Cafe** at the center of town is a friendly choice for a bite before or after a hike; you'll find country breakfasts, burgers, pasta, and soups. Inexpensive, too. **The Gaslight Cafe**, a few hundred yards farther east, is worth a stop for its pies alone, but you won't be disappointed with by omelets, sandwiches, and salads.

In a class by itself is **John Andrew's**, serving dinner and Sunday brunch at the corner of Route 23 and Blunt Road, almost at the New York line. The small, seasonally adjusted menu may be laced with the familiar—wild mushrooms, baby greens, balsamic this, wild thyme that—but the sum of the parts is without peer. For such

When people think of electricity they think of Thomas Edison and light bulbs, but the roots of your local utility lie here in the nation's first commercial electrical system, created by transformer inventor **William Stanley** for Great Barrington's downtown in 1886.

If you're looking for a last-minute room at a local B&B or inn, save yourself a walk through the Yellow Pages with a single call to the Lodging Availability Hotline of the Southern Berkshire Chamber of Commerce (413/528-4006).

If you want to see for yourself how well suited the Housatonic River is for recreational canoeing, set up a rental with Gaffer's Outdoors on US-7 in Sheffield (413/229-0063; $25/weekdays, $35/weekends, or $35 for van shuttle and six hours of paddling time).

The last battle of **Shay's Rebellion,** an uprising of farmers demanding reforms to prevent foreclosures after the American Revolution dried up English credit, was fought in a field south of the village on Sheffield Road. A small stone obelisk marks the spot, coincidentally adjacent to the AT.

an experience, even $30 a head will seem an absolute bargain; reservations are advised (413/528-3469; closed Wednesday off-season).

Besides South Egremont's pair of 200-year-old inns—The **Weathervane** (413/528-9580) and the **Egremont** (413/528-2111) —accommodations in the vicinity include several B&Bs, three of which lie along Route 41 in adjacent Sheffield, en route to Connecticut. If you want to linger over the excellent hiking without resorting to a tent, consider the **Race Brook Lodge** on Route 41, roughly six miles south of Route 23 (413/229-2916). With a connecting path up to Mount Race right outside the front door, this cheerfully rustic "chintz-free zone" makes a perfect base for loop hikes along the AT.

ACROSS CONNECTICUT

Anyone who drives its interstates will appreciate why Connecticut enjoys a solid reputation among New Englanders as "the drive-through state," a dubious distinction it shares with New Jersey. The high-speed route between Boston and New York City, I-95, is something endured rather than enjoyed, but our route through the scenic northwest corner is as different from the grim coastal megalopolis as a tulip is from a truck tire. Like the neighboring Berkshires, Connecticut's Litchfield Hills are a traditional retreat for discerning city dwellers. The area is rich in forests, farms, and picturesque little towns laden with antiques. Fast food and discount shopping are as alien to this landscape as affordability, so if your purse strings are tight you'll want to keep moving; otherwise, linger a while and enjoy some of the rural charm so prized by those people you see on the cover of *Business Week*.

For further information on activities and services, or for a brochure of local auto tours, contact the helpful folks at the Litchfield Hills Travel Council (P.O. Box 968, Litchfield, CT 06759; 860/567-4506).

Salisbury and Norfolk

After extensive touring around New England, you risk taking white columns, wide porches, picket fences, and the obligatory Congregational steeple for granted. Prim little Salisbury, for example, at the junction of Route 41 and US-44, may elicit reveries about what small-town America would look like if strip malls ceased to exist. Spend an afternoon sipping cardamom-scented tea in tiny **Chaiwalla**, at the head of Main Street (US-44), or step over to Academy Street to nosh on a stylish lunch at the **Harvest Bakery** while regulars banter with the owner as they stock up on the delicious breads and desserts, and see if you don't conclude that franchising of fast food should be declared a misdemeanor.

Interestingly, Salisbury was once a heavily industrialized center of 18th-century iron mining and manufacture, with ore pits, forges, and blast furnaces nestled amid hills whose forests were chewed down to the rocky soil by the incessant appetite of the wood-burning smelters. That this Pittsburgh of the American colonies has become tidy and quaint 200 years later could suggest a moral about resilience and resurrection, but perhaps more germane is that Salisbury looks the way it does now because residents were willing to question whether land development is an inalienable right.

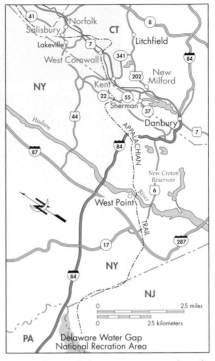

About 15 miles east of Salisbury on US-44 lies another pearl, Norfolk, even more manicured than Salisbury, which at least has an auto-body shop and lopsided old American sedans amid the imports on the roads. If any town has capitalized on being far removed from trading floors and board meetings, it's this one: with three public parks and the largest private forest in the state, Norfolk has considered its sheer scenic beauty a stock in trade for nearly a century. Between late June and early August, residents and their guests enjoy the Yale School of Music's **Norfolk Chamber Music Festival** on the Ellen Battell Stoeckel Estate opposite the village green; phone for schedule and ticket information (860/542-5537 during the festival season, or 203/432-1966 Sept.-May).

If good beer is a stronger incentive than sonatas or waterfalls, you'll want to make a beeline for **The Pub**, in the handsome commercial brownstone at the center of town. With over 150 excellent brews from around the world, it almost wouldn't matter whether the grub's any good, but fortunately it is. The Cajun specials (Wed.-Thurs.) are a particularly good value.

As befits such an oasis as Norfolk, there's a handful of **B&Bs** in town costing $120 a night or more, and mostly catering to couples in search of the consummate we-deserve-it getaway. Bask in the rich Tudor woodwork and Tiffany windows of the **Manor House** (860/542-5690) while sipping tea by the fireplace—or between naps in your jacuzzi, if your credit can stand it. Don't feel up to masquerading as English gentry? Perhaps **Angel Hill** (860/542-5920) is the tonic you need, although if L-O-V-E sets your teeth on edge you may not appreciate how closely the place resembles Cupid's lair. A whimsical and flirtatious abundance of cherubs, angels, and hearts are accompanied by all the paraphernalia of romance: flowers, candy, liqueurs, cassettes of Enya, and books of famous love letters.

West Cornwall

Rivers are consistently some of the most attractive driving companions you could ask for, a fact proven once again as US-7 rejoins the Housatonic south of Lime Rock. The highway's scenic miles are further enhanced by the sudden appearance

Collin's Diner
in Cornwall

Salisbury's Lakeville Furnace was the armorer of the American Revolution, supplying George Washington's troops with almost their entire arsenal of artillery and ammunition for the duration of the war.

LIME ROCK PARK

On Route 112 a couple of miles west of US-7 you'll find **Lime Rock Park** (860/435-0896 or 800/RACE-LRP), a stock-car racetrack made famous in part by classic car rallies, the Skip Barber Racing School (800/221-1131) and the occasional appearance of celebrity drivers like Paul Newman and Tom Cruise. The sharp twisting descent from nearby Lakeville to the raceway is one of the prettiest back-road drives in the area.

of a barn-red covered bridge, the one-lane gateway to idyllic West Cornwall. This is the kind of place that would tar and feather the first vinyl siding salesperson to walk into town, lest harm befall its antiquarian bookshop or other clapboard buildings bearing signs from previous commercial lives (though the old meat market is now a video store).

South of town, **Housatonic Meadows State Park** offers riverside **camping** (mid-April to mid-Sept.; $10), perfectly situated for anyone considering a canoe or kayak rental from adjacent **Clarke Outdoors** (860/672-6365). Bring mosquito repellent if you're planning to spend time near the water.

Kent

Like many of its Litchfield neighbors, 19th-century Kent (pop. 2,918) had a thriving iron industry until competition from larger Pennsylvania mines—with better access to post-Civil War markets—forced the local furnace to close. Now it's a bustling upscale market town, its main street (US-7) lined with antique shops, galleries, and boutiques. The "New York-Paris-Kent" art gallery in the old Pullman car behind the ice cream shop-née-depot, the gallery of African and Asian artifacts upstairs from the Foreign Cargo store, and the estate jewelry at Pauline's Place on the north side of town are examples of what's replaced blacksmith shops and wheelwrights.

But not every price tag around here ends in triple zeros. For proof, step into **The Villager** smack in the heart of town, where your scrambled eggs and burgers come as plain as you like or gussied up with Andouille sausage or avocado and salsa. "Reliable" is the word that comes to mind for an oasis like this: open daily, with prices that are rarely seen these days outside of the Midwest.

Camping is available for $10 a day all summer in state parks alongside Route 341 on either side of Kent: to the west in **Macedonia Brook State Park** (860/927-

3238); and to the east in **Lake Waramaug State Park** (860/868-2592), whose campsites share the water's edge with a handful of posh inns and exclusive homes.

New Milford

The AT crosses the New York state line near Bull's Bridge south of Kent, and so should you—on Route 55 or Route 37—if you want to enjoy a passing landscape that offers more fields and trees than guardrails and parking lots. Technically speaking there's still a large swath of New England between New York and New Milford, but most of this has more in common with the Indianapolis Beltway than with the Vermont countryside.

The infidels of prefab modular construction may be pounding at the gates, but aptly named Milford Green is still framed by a well-preserved backdrop of classic 19th-century architecture, from the church to the hardware store. New Milford also is a good place to grab a bite of Eastern European, Greek, or Tex-Mex food, on block-long Bank Street or around the corner on Railroad Street. Mellow **Bank Street Coffee House**, tucked below street level, can satisfy cravings for steaming latte or icy granitas. If you crave a memorable meal, check out **The Bistro Cafe** across from the black-glass white-tile art deco cinema, serving nori-wrapped tuna and oven-roasted duckling among the $15-and-up entrees of New American food. If you seek a feast for the senses, it doesn't get much better than this.

For accommodations, try the **Homestead Inn** (860/354-4080) at the north end of the Green, within walking distance of dinner or a movie.

Between Danbury, Connecticut, and Port Jervis, New York, the Appalachian Trail runs parallel to our US-6 route, which is described on pages 616-651.

Cyclists looking for itineraries among the Litchfield Hills—or anywhere else in the state, for that matter—should obtain a copy of *The Connecticut Bicycle Book* from The Coalition of Connecticut Bicyclists (P.O. Box 121, Middletown, CT 06457; 860/287-9903).

One place to rent a bike in the Litchfield Hills is the friendly and knowledgeable **Cycle Loft,** located among the shops of the Litchfield Commons on Route 202 in Litchfield (860/567-1713; $6 an hour or $20 a day).

Wander amid the century-old ghosts of the region's iron industry at **Mine Hill Preserve,** the state's largest set of ore pit and furnace ruins, just off Route 67 between New Milford and Route 199. To get there, turn north on Mine Hill Road, immediately west of the Shepaug River bridge.

The I-84 freeway northeast of New York City is a real pain in the driver's seat, with lots of left exits, sudden shrinkings from three to two lanes, frequent construction, constant changes in speed limits, and too much traffic.

NEW YORK CITY SURVIVAL GUIDE

NEW YORK CITY IS EITHER THE BIG APPLE OR THE Great Satan. Some people avoid it like the plague, denying themselves the incredible variety of food and culture; others can't bear to leave the glorious buzzing mosaic that makes New York unique in the world. Love it or hate it, New York *is* New York, and this great metropolis is undeniably the capital of the capitalist world, with the best museums, the best shops, the best sights, and the best restaurants in the world. Like every great city, New York has its share of crime and decay, but these are greatly exaggerated by the magnifying glass of the world media located here. New York's critics seem to forget  that over seven million people live here, the vast majority of them normal and leading normal lives—well, as normal as normal can be on a tiny island packed with way too many people.

There's not much point in us recommending a select few of New York's huge spectrum of attractions, so we'll get straight on to offering some practical help. (And if you want to see the city but would rather not deal with its traffic, hassles and high hotel rates, see the special topic, "To See, or Not To See, New York City" on page 332.)

Practicalities

There are three major airports in the NYC area, LaGuardia and John F. Kennedy, both in Queens, and Newark, across the Hudson in New Jersey. By road, the main routes are I-95 entering from the southwest and northeast; I-87, the New York State Thruway, from the north; and from the west, I-80 and I-78.

If you value your sanity and your shock absorbers, park your car in a long-term lot (not on the streets; city parking regulations are arcane and the fines huge) and walk or take public transportation. Although much-maligned in the media, New York's subway system, one of the most extensive in the world, is inexpensive ($1.50, payable with tokens, cash, or handy *Metrocard*), relatively safe and usually the fastest way to get around town. City buses are generally slower, but you see more of the sights and you can ask for a transfer onto any of the bus lines that cross your route. Taxis are ubiquitous—except when you want one—and inexpensive by the standards of most world-class cities. Unfortunately, the classic wisecracking New York cabbie, a near-mythological figure, has been replaced by recent immigrants, many of whom barely speak English and likely know less about the city than you do.

The key to a successful visit to New York City is finding a place to stay. Ideally, you'll have friend or a rich aunt, but failing that here are few suggestions, most in the low-to-moderate range. It's hard to beat the **Holiday Inn**, 138 Lafayette Street (212/966-8898), for convenience: equidistant from Chinatown, Little Italy, SoHo, and TriBeCa, this hotel gives you downtown chic at bargain rates; doubles start at $120. A much more stylish alternative, the **Carlton Arms Hotel**, 160 E. 25th Street (212/679-0680), was redecorated in the 1980s by a squad of cutting edge artists, including Keith Haring, which makes it interesting, to say the least; doubles from $99. Heading uptown, the **Pickwick Arms Hotel**, 230 E. 51st Street (212/355-0300), is a rare find: an inexpensive (under $60 for a single with shared bath), clean and pleasant place to stay, in the heart of Manhattan.

Apart from hotels, B&Bs are another option, which in Manhattan tends to mean renting a private studio apartment, or a room in someone's apartment; **B&B Manhattan** (212/472-2528) has a good reputation and given enough notice can probably set up a room for around $90-110 a night. There's also a very large and popular **HI Hostel**, 891 Amsterdam Avenue at 103rd Street (212/932-2300), with dorm beds for $25 a night.

Eating out is another way to blow a lot of money very quickly, but there are some great places where you can get both a good meal and a feel for New York without going bankrupt. One such place is **Katz's Delicatessen**, 205 E. Houston Street, a Lower East Side landmark that's been serving up man-sized sandwiches (including great pastrami) "since 1888." (For movie buffs, Katz's is where Meg Ryan did her famous fake orgasm scene in *When Harry Met Sally*.) And if you like diners, check out the **Empire Diner**, 210 10th Avenue at 22nd Street in the Chelsea neighborhood—all black enamel and gleaming stainless steel, and open 24 hours, 7 days a week. The well-prepared food is the usual burgers and meat loaf, etc., enlivened by frequent live jazz.

The **New York Convention and Visitors Bureau**, near Central Park at 2 Columbus Circle (212/397-8222), will overwhelm you with suggestions; there are also tourist information booths at Grand Central Station, and on 42nd Street between 7th and 8th Avenues. The *New York Times* is the paper of record, but the *Daily News*, followed by *Newsday* and the *New York Post*, generally have livelier local coverage.

The New York Yankees (718/293-6000) play at Yankee Stadium, in the Bronx off I-87. The New York Mets (718/507-8499) play at Shea Stadium in Queens.

TO SEE, OR NOT TO SEE, NEW YORK CITY

In the northeastern U.S., all roads seem to converge upon—and become grid-locked in—New York City. However, there are a number of painless ways to deal with the city without driving miles out of the way, or driving yourself mad. Your primary resource is up-to-date information. Every Friday, the *New York Daily News* runs the "Gridlock Sam" column delineating all highway construction expected to cause delays. For minute-by-minute updates, tune in to one of the news radio stations such as WCBS (AM 880), which has traffic reports every 10 minutes on the eights (9:08, 12:38, etc.).

The best way to experience New York in passing is on I-95; this gives you a brief glimpse of the city's gritty glamour and a distant view of Manhattan's spires to the south. Unfortunately, the section that passes through the city, known as the Cross Bronx Expressway, is one of the worst stretches of road in the country. The many dangers include potholes, endless traffic jams, poor lighting, and frequent accidents caused by far too many cars and trucks. Nevertheless, the vast majority of vehicles pass through unscathed. For the smoothest, fastest trip, your best bet is to brave the Cross Bronx between midnight Saturday and 10 AM on Sunday mornings.

If you want to see the Big Apple but would rather take public transportation than confront the city streets on your own, a number of outlying suburbs make good bases from which to see the city. From Connecticut and New York State, you can take the New Haven train line or the Harlem-Hudson line heading to Manhattan's Grand Central Station. For public transit from New Jersey, you must rely on numerous bus lines to the Port Authority bus terminal (8th Avenue and 42nd Street) or the PATH trains to Manhattan from Jersey City, Hoboken, or Newark. And if you plan to stay a while, see the New York City Survival Guide in this chapter.

Some of the more useful outlying towns are:

White Plains

Just over the border from the Bronx, heavily suburban Westchester County contains a number of small cities with good hotels, access to transportation, and a few tourist attractions of their own. White Plains, which lies along I-287 (running between I-95 and the Tappan Zee Bridge), is a corporate center filled with glass-walled office buildings. By train, it is about 45 minutes to Manhattan's Grand Central Station, and seven different highways lead from I-287 to various parts of the city. The New York State Thruway (I-87) will take you to FDR Drive on Manhattan's east side, while the Saw Mill River Parkway becomes the Henry Hudson Parkway running down the west side of Manhattan. Most hotels in the White Plains area cater to the expense account set and thus are not cheap. This includes the **Holiday Inn Crown Plaza** (914/682-0050) and the **Stouffer Westchester** (914/694-5400).

Tarrytown

On the bank of the Hudson River, Tarrytown offers good access by train and highway and a number of nearby tourist attractions. It lies on US-9 about a mile north of I-287; take the last exit before the Tappan Zee Bridge. During the 19th century, many robber baron industrialists built their mansions in these green hills, and some of them are now museums open to the public. The most spectacular of these is **Kykuit**, a huge mansion surrounded by gardens on the Rockefeller Family Estate. You can tour the house June-Oct.; reservations are advised (914/631-8200). Tarrytown's most famous citizen was Washington Irving, author of the "Legend of Sleepy Hollow" (set in this area) and many other works. His estate, **Sunnyside**, stands on the river in Tarrytown and contains a large and fascinating collection of memorabilia (open year-round, 914/631-8200). Tarrytown lodgings include the **Courtyard by Marriott** (914/631-1122) and the **Hilton Inn** (914/631-5700).

Fort Lee, New Jersey
Across the Hudson, the state of New Jersey offers many lodging opportunities. I-95 crosses the river over the George Washington Bridge and passes through the city of Fort Lee, the beginning of New Jersey's vast suburbs. Downtown Fort Lee boasts a few office buildings and some moderately priced hotels, such as **Days Inn** (201/944-5000) and **Holiday Inn** (201/461-3100). For public transit into Manhattan, take the New Jersey Transit bus to the Port Authority Bus Station. For the Cloisters medieval museum—the only tourist attraction in upper Manhattan—take the bus to the George Washington Bridge bus station.

Jersey City
Across the river from the tip of Manhattan, Jersey City is an industrial giant with excellent access to the Jersey Turnpike and to Manhattan via the Holland Tunnel. The $120-a-night **Quality Inn-Jersey City** (201/653-0300) stands right at the tunnel entrance and is about a block from the Newport Center Mall PATH station. PATH trains can take you either to the World Trade Center or to 33rd Street and 6th Avenue in Manhattan via Greenwich Village. Jersey City's main tourist attraction is **Liberty State Park,** just onshore from the Statue of Liberty, with a picnic area, a salt marsh nature walk, and the new, high-tech Liberty Science Center, filled with interactive displays popular with children. The park also offers ferry service to the Statue of Liberty and Ellis Island.

Newark
More lodgings can be found around Newark Airport, southeast of Jersey City. This area is more distant from New York but offers good public transportation by bus or PATH train from the Newark train station. Airport hotels include **Courtyard by Marriott** (973/643-8500), **Days Inn** (973/242-0900), and **Holiday Inn** (973/589-1000), all of which have rates around $90 a night. Few tourists visit Newark, a depressed industrial city, but the **Newark Museum** at 49 Washington Street, a few blocks from the train station, is worth a visit, with small but excellent collections of American and European art and the largest display of Tibetan art outside Asia.

ACROSS PENNSYLVANIA

The hikers' Appalachian Trail runs across southern New York and western New Jersey, but our road route avoids the Garden State entirely, crossing instead the natural chasm of the Delaware Water Gap, whose forests, waterfalls, and wildlife are popular with city-dwellers escaping the New York City megalopolis. In its 150-mile length, the route passes through a succession of strikingly different places, starting with the densely populated industrial regions of the Lehigh Valley and the historic little town of Bethlehem, which plays up its Christmas connections more than its role as a formerly vital steelmaking center. Farther south, modern industry gives way to the traditional agriculture of Pennsylvania Dutch Country, world-famous for its anti-technology, Old Order Christian communities. Continuing southwest across the Susquehanna River, you'll follow the route of the old Lincoln Highway through historic York, early capital of the United States, now home to a Harley-Davidson motorcycle plant. The last stop on the Pennsylvania leg of the route is the Civil War battlefields at Gettysburg, just shy of the Maryland border.

The town of **Lackawaxen,** 15 miles northwest of I-84 on the New York/ Pennsylvania border, was long home to writer **Zane Grey,** and also holds an early prototype of the Brooklyn Bridge. For more, see page 627.

Delaware Water Gap National Recreation Area

Totaling some 30,000 acres of forest on both banks of the Delaware River, the Delaware Water Gap National Recreation Area stretches for 35 miles south of the I-84 freeway along two-lane US-209. Established in 1965, the park is still very much under development, though numerous hiking trails lead through hardwood forests to seasonal waterfalls, and the river itself offers abundant canoeing, swimming, and fishing. Though far from pristine, considering the park lies only 50 miles west of New York City, the natural beauty is surprisingly undisturbed.

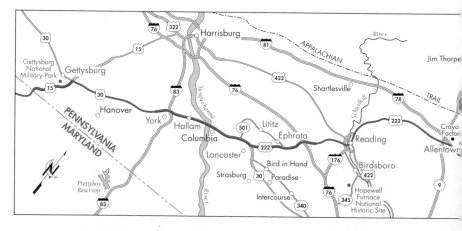

A few remnants of the area's historic agricultural villages have been preserved under the aegis of the park service, but the main attraction is the oddly named Delaware Water Gap itself, a deep cleft carved by the river into the solid rock of the Kittatinny Mountains. Artists, sightseers, and rock-climbers have admired this unique feat of geology for well over 100 years, but unfortunately the natural passageway is crisscrossed by all manner of road and railroad, including the six-lane I-80 freeway that runs right through it.

The tiny tourist town of **Delaware Water Gap**, south of I-80 at the far southern end of the park, provides the best views of the gap. A **visitor center** (908/841-9520 or 717/588-2435) sits along the river, just off I-80 at the first/last New Jersey exit, and offers exhibits on the geology and history of the region, as well as information on sundry recreational opportunities. **Pack Shack Adventures** (717/424-8533) rents canoes for $45 a day.

There's not much in the way of developed accommodations in the park, though there is a handy **youth hostel** in Layton, New Jersey, four miles east of Dingman's Ferry via Hwy-560. At the southern edge of the Delaware Gap park, the most extensive tourist facilities cluster along the I-80 freeway in the towns of **Stroudsburg** (pop. 5,312) and **East Stroudsburg** (pop. 8,781), where you can choose between **Best Western** and **Super 8**; there's also a nice **Ramada Inn**, with two pools, off I-80 in Delaware Water Gap. Good food, however, is hard to come by.

A 25-mile stretch of the Appalachian Trail cuts along a 1,200-foot-high ridge at the southeast corner of the park, crossing the Delaware River on an old bridge at the town of Delaware Water Gap.

The **Pocono Mountains,** which rise to the west of the Delaware River, hold Pennsylvania's odd version of the traditional honeymoon resort, featuring champagne glass-shaped jacuzzis in the rooms, plus archery ranges so you and your beloved can play Cupid with real arrows. Most of the resorts are run by Caesar's World (800/233-4141) and are outrageously priced—$350 a night is not unusual.

Bethlehem

South of the Delaware Water Gap, Hwy-611 runs along the Delaware River until its confluence with the Lehigh River, five miles west of the remarkable small city of Bethlehem (pop. 71,400). Famous for its Christmas festivals, and as a fun place from which to mail Christmas cards, Bethlehem was originally established in 1741 by a group of Moravian missionaries. The missionaries' original circa 1803 chapel still stands at the heart of the compact, gas-lighted downtown district, its cemetery full of 200-year-old headstones laid flat so as not to offend God. Another engaging historic

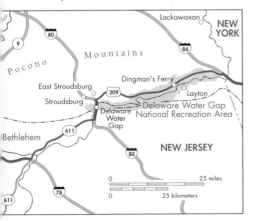

site is the **Sun Inn** (610/866-1758) at 564 Main Street, a well-preserved former tavern "where the leading figures of the Revolutionary era were entertained," says a plaque on the wall; it's now an expensive German restaurant but also offers guided tours ($2).

Across the Lehigh River from the tidy homes and shops of downtown Bethlehem stand the rusting remains of the **Bethlehem Steel Company.** Famous for fabricating engineering marvels such as the towers of the Golden Gate Bridge—cast here in sec-

Crayola Crayons 1903

Every May, Bethlehem hosts a hugely popular **Bach Festival** rated as one of the best in country. For details, contact the visitor center (610/868-1513).

The town of **Jim Thorpe,** in the Lehigh Valley 30 miles northwest of Allentown off the Pennsylvania Turnpike (Hwy-9), 10 miles north of the Appalachian Trail, is a former coal-mining town with many 19th-century buildings. The town changed its name from Mauch Chunk in 1954 to honor the great Olympic athlete Jim Thorpe, whose remains lie in a granite mausoleum along Hwy-903 on the northeast side of town.

tions, then shipped through the Panama Canal and assembled in San Francisco—the mill was closed down in the 1990s, despite the best efforts of local preservationists.

Two more historic American manufacturers, both with happier presents, are in the nearby area. Oldest is the venerable **Martin Guitar Company,** in business since 1833, which operates out of nearby Nazareth. Tours of the family-owned factory, at 510 Sycamore Street, are given weekdays (1:15 PM; free; 610/867-0173), and include both a look inside a luthier's workshop and displays of classic Martin guitars. The other is even more fun: the **Crayola Crayon Factory** (Tues.-Sat. 9:30AM-5PM; 610/515-8000), where you can watch the colorful crayon being made and packaged, then scribble away to your heart's content.

The Bethlehem **visitor center,** 52 W. Broad Street (610/868-1513 or 800/360-TOUR or 800/360-8687) offers walking-tour maps of local historic sites and can also provide listings of restaurants and places to stay. Nearby, the sidewalk tables outside **Viennese Pastry,** 500 Main Street, are a great place to enjoy a wickedly rich piece of cake or a light lunch; for dinner, try the aforementioned **Sun Inn** at 564 Main Street. Near Lehigh University, on 4th Street across the river from downtown, **Godfrey Daniel's Coffee House** (610/867-2390) hosts a range of live folk and jazz music most nights.

The large **Hotel Bethlehem** (610/867-3711 or 800/545-5158), on Main Street overlooking the river, is centrally located, with doubles costing around $80 a night. There are also the usual national chains, including an **Econo Lodge** and a **Comfort Inn** off US-22, both with rooms for under $50 a night.

Allentown

The seat of Lehigh County, Allentown (pop. 105,100) spreads west of Bethlehem, across a bend in the Lehigh River. The downtown area is large and lacks focus, though it does provide two very worthwhile stops, the bigger and better of which is the **Allentown Art Museum** (Tues.-Sat. 10 AM-5 PM, Sunday noon-3:30 PM; $3.50) at 5th and Court Streets. Here you'll find a good general collection of paintings and photography as well as an entire library moved from the Frank Lloyd Wright-designed Little House. Allentown's other main attraction lies two blocks west at Church and Hamilton Streets: the **Liberty Bell Shrine** (Mon.-Sat. noon-4 PM; free), an old church which houses a replica of the famous bell that was hidden here for safekeeping during the Revolutionary War battles at Philadelphia.

ROADSIDE AMERICA

One of the quirkiest, kitschiest tourist attractions in the U.S., Roadside America (daily 10 AM-5 PM, 9 AM-6 PM in summer; $4; 610/488-6241) stands alongside the I-78 freeway, 20 miles northwest of Reading in the village of Shartlesville. Built by Reading native Laurence Gieringer over 60 years ago, Roadside America is a giant $3/8$-to-the-inch scale model of bygone Americana, fleshed out with animated scenes that trace a typical day in the life of the country—circa 1941, when Roadside America first opened to the public. As you walk around the edges of the 8,000-square-foot exhibit, you can push buttons to make wheels spin, lights flash, and pumps pump, and you'll see a little of everything rural: an 1830s New England village featuring a church and choral music; a canyon and lake complete with waterfalls and resort cabins; a model of Henry Ford's workshop in Dearborn, Michigan, where he built one of the first "horseless carriages"; various turnpikes, canals, highways, and railroads; a coal mine; and a mock-up of the San Francisco Bay Bridge, the closest Roadside comes to a city scene.

Though it's definitely a fine example of kitsch, Roadside America is also an oddly compelling place, and only the hardest-hearted road-tripper will be able to hold back the tears when, every half-hour or so, the sun sets and Kate Smith bursts into "God Bless America."

Allentown boasts one unique place to eat: **Yocco's The Hot Dog King**, 625 Liberty Avenue, which has been serving up wieners (and a few burgers) bathed in a top-secret chili sauce since 1922. Streamlined **Tom Sawyer Diner** is open 24 hours every day on the south side of town, near where US-222 crosses the I-78 and Hwy-9 freeways; many more area diners have, alas, been "modernized" and covered in charmless brick or plaster. Because it's the business center for the surrounding area, Allentown has lots of accommodation options, including **Comfort Inn**, **Days Inn**, **Econo Lodge**, and most other national chains.

Midway between Allentown and Reading, every June and July the week-long Kutztown Folk Festival celebrates the arts, crafts, and culture of the local Pennsylvania Dutch communities, which are less austere than their Lancaster County counterparts.

Reading

Standing along the eastern banks of the Schuylkill River, Reading (pop. 78,380) is more interesting than its frightening title "Factory Outlet Shopping Capital of Southeastern Pennsylvania" would lead you to expect. Ornately turreted row houses line 5th Avenue (US-222 Business) through the residential districts, and downtown holds a number of well-maintained businesses and signs from the first half of the century, but there is very little for visitors to search out; perhaps the best place to stop is along US-222 on the north side of town, where **Schell's Hot Dogs, BBQ and Miniature Golf** offers almost everything a roadtripper could ask for. (Well, almost.)

The Monopoly "Chance" card "Take a Ride on the Reading—Collect $200," commemorates the railroad that formerly ran between Reading and Philadelphia.

Birdsboro and Hopewell Furnace

For history buffs, two worthwhile places to visit sit southeast of Reading along the Schuylkill River. The closer of these is at Birdsboro, 10 miles from town and a mile north of US-422. The **Daniel Boone Homestead and Birthplace** marks the site where the great frontiersman was born in 1734. Back in Birdsboro on US-422, **Gregory's Diner** is open daily 5 AM-10 PM, for the usual fare plus very good pies.

Well worth the winding five mile drive south of Birdsboro via Hwy-345, the **Hopewell Furnace National Historic Site** (daily 9 AM-5 PM; $2) preserves intact an entire iron-making community that thrived here from the colonial era until the mid-1840s. Park rangers fire up the furnace and demonstrate the primitive foundry (melting aluminum rather than iron to take the "heat" off the ancient tools), and exhibits trace the iron-making process—mining the ore, making charcoal, and fabricating the finished product, which here at Hopewell was primarily pig iron and stoves.

Ephrata Cloister

Ephrata and Lititz

South of Reading, US-222 runs along the western edge of the Amish and Mennonite-influenced Pennsylvania Dutch Country. The heart of this region is due east of Lancaster, but the area north of Lancaster also holds a number of related sites often missed by visitors. The most appealing of these is the **Ephrata Cloister** (Mon.-Sat. 9 AM-5 PM, Sunday noon-5 PM; $5), at 632 W. Main Street just west of the town of Ephrata. Founded in 1732 by a communal society of religiously celibate German Pietists, the Ephrata Cloister consists of a half-dozen well-preserved 250-year-old wooden buildings, which housed dormitories, bakeries, and a printing shop where the commune produced some of the finest illustrated books of the colonial era. Across Main Street from the entrance, the **Cloister Restaurant** serves very good home-style food for breakfast, lunch, and dinner in an overgrown 1940s diner.

West of Ephrata, eight miles north of Lancaster via Hwy-501, the tiny town of Lititz (pop. 8,280) is dominated by the huge **Wilbur Chocolate** candy factory at 48 N. Broad Street, which liberally perfumes the air with the smell of hot chocolate. Lititz also holds the nation's oldest operating pretzel factory, the **Sturgis Pretzel House** at 219 E. Main Street (Mon.-Sat. 9 AM-5 PM; $1.50), where you can twist your own; and the small but high-quality **Heritage Map Museum** (Mon.-Sat. 10 AM-5 PM; $3.50), which displays original maps from the 15th-20th centuries, and publishes and sells copies, too. Lititz is the final resting place of John Sutter, who owned huge chunks of pre-gold rush California and who died here in Pennsylvania while battling the Washington, D.C. bureaucracy to receive compensation for his confiscated land.

A word to the wise: in Dutch Country, remember that anything claiming to be "authentic Amish" definitely isn't. Also, please respect the Amish you see and refrain from taking photographs. Drive carefully, too.

Two of the main tourist stops in the Dutch Country region are the towns of **Intercourse** *(source of many snickeringly allusive postcards) and* **Paradise** *(the Paradise post office, just north of US-30 at the east end of town, is a popular place to mail from).*

Back on US-222, two miles northeast of Lancaster, the state-run and well-posted **Landis Valley Museum** (Tues.-Sat. 9 AM-5 PM, Sunday noon-5 PM; $7) is a popular 40-acre "living history" park preserving and interpreting traditional rural lifeways of eastern Pennsylvania.

Lancaster

The only place approaching an urban scale in this part of Pennsylvania, Lancaster (pop. 55,600) is the region's commercial center, a bustling city that, for a single day during the Revolutionary War, served as capital of the country. Though most visitors view it as little more than a handy base for exploring nearby Pennsylvania Dutch Country, Lancaster does have a couple of attractions in its own right, such as the red-brick, pseudo-Romanesque **Central Market** at King and Queen Streets in the center of town. It hosts the nation's oldest publicly owned, continuously operating Farmer's Market, currently held all day Tuesday and Friday, as well as Saturday mornings. A block south on Queen Street, the ground-floor windows of the local newspaper trace local history through headlines, starting back in 1794 and continuing up through the present day.

Midway between Lancaster and York, the town of Columbia holds what is arguably the country's best collection of timepieces in the **Watch and Clock Museum** (Tues.-Sat. 9 AM-4 PM, Sunday noon-4 PM; $3) at 514 Poplar Street. Also in Columbia is a beautiful multi-arched concrete bridge that used to carry the old Lincoln Highway (US-30) across the broad Susquehanna River.

HAINES *The Shoe Wizard* SHOE HOUSE YORK, PA

Hallam: The Shoe House

Many oddball attractions grew up along the old Lincoln Highway, the great cross-country highway that ran coast-to-coast beginning in 1915, and one of the best beloved is the **Haines Shoe House**, which stands above the modern four-lane US-30 freeway, outside the town of Hallam. This landmark of programmatic architecture was built in 1948 by Mahlon "The Shoe Wizard" Haines, who owned a successful shoe company which proudly claimed to make boots "hoof-to-hoof," from raising the cattle to selling the finished products. The seven-room structure is shaped like a giant cartoon boot, and can be reached by following Hwy-462 (the old Lincoln Highway, which runs just south of current US-30), to Shoe House Road, then winding north for a quarter-mile. (The turnoff is easy to miss, so keep an eye out for the "Shoe House Mini-Storage," which stands on the corner.) Since 1995 the Shoe House has been operated as an antique store (closed Monday and Tuesday), and if you're lucky the owners will be there and let you tour the interior.

East of Hallam, on US-30, **Jim Mack's Ice Cream** has been attracting fans for its ice cream—and its adjacent mini-golf course, and mini-zoo, complete with farm animals and a pair of rather pathetic-looking brown bears.

York

Though it doesn't look like much from the highway, bypassed by both US-30 and the I-83 freeway, the medium-sized town of York (pop. 42,192) claims to be the first capital of the United States: late in 1777, the Articles of Confederation were adopted here by the 13 newly independent former colonies, and (arguably) it's in that document that the name "United States of America" was first used. A significant number of historic buildings still stand in the quiet, low-rise downtown area, including the medieval-looking, circa 1740 **Golden Plough Tavern** and other colonial-era structures along Market Street at the west edge of the business district.

THE PENNSYLVANIA DUTCH COUNTRY

East of Lancaster, toward Philadelphia, the old Lincoln Highway (US-30) runs through the heart of what has become internationally famous as the Pennsylvania Dutch Country. This is a very pretty, almost completely rural region, unremarkable apart from the presence here of various "Old Order" Anabaptist Christian sects, including Amish and Mennonite groups, who eschew most of the trappings and technological advances of the twentieth century, including cars, electricity, and irrigation, and retain their simple ways. Long before the Peter Weir movie *Witness* gave their low-tech lifestyle the Hollywood treatment, visitors have been coming here to see these anachronistic descendants of German immigrants (Deutsche = Dutch) who settled here in the early 1700s, and to whom all outsiders are known simply as "English."

The best way to get a feel for the Amish and Mennonite ways of life is to follow back roads, by bike if possible, through the gently rolling countryside of Lancaster County, keeping an eye out for their horse-drawn buggies (Amish ones are gray, the Mennonites' are black). You can buy produce, breads, cakes, or "Shoo Fly Pie" from the many roadside stands marked by hand-lettered signs. For a thorough overview, stop at **The People's Place** (Mon.-Sat. 9 AM-5 PM; $3), 3513 Main Street in Intercourse (so named because it sits at the junction of two roads), which presents a multimedia show outlining the beliefs and culture of the Amish and Mennonite peoples along with displays of quilts and other handicrafts. More amusing is the restored one-room **Weavertown Schoolhouse**, populated by "authentic" audio-animatronic Amish schoolkids, along Hwy-340 a mile east of the town of Bird-in-Hand, 2.5 miles west of Intercourse.

Most of the many Amish-style restaurants in the region are huge and forbiddingly full of bus-tour hordes; one exception is **Stoltzfus Restaurant** (Mon.-Sat. 11 AM-8 PM, May-Nov. only; 717/768-8156) on Hwy-772 a mile southeast of Intercourse. A less Amish but very good roadfood place is **Jennie's Diner**,

For all its historic importance, York is best known for its industrial prowess, which is saluted in a pair of unique attractions. The smaller of these is the oddly combined **Weightlifting and Softball Hall of Fame** (daily 9 AM-3 PM; free), 3300 Board Road off I-83 exit 11, basically a showcase for the sporting goods manufactured by the York Barbell Company. Much more compelling, and perhaps the best reason to visit York, is the **Harley-Davidson assembly plant and museum**, a mile east of town off US-30 on Eden Road. The popular guided tour (Mon.-Fri. 10 AM

and 1:30 PM except July; free; 717/848-1177) takes about two hours. It begins with a brief history of the company, which is the only American producer of motorcycles still in business. The tour then takes you past a lineup of some 40 Harleys past and present, culled from the corporate collection of over 200 motorbikes. You then proceed to the shop floor for a close-up look at the bikes being put together: sheets of steel are pressed to form fenders and fairings, and, once assem-

open 24 hours every day on the north side of US-30, just east of the Hwy-896 intersection.

Though it won't give you any great insight into the Amish, one unique place to stay is the **Red Caboose Motel and Restaurant** (717/687-5000), a mile east of Strasburg on Paradise Lane. All the rooms are built inside old railroad cars, and the on-site restaurant simulates a train journey, with whistles blowing and a gentle rocking vibration to ease your digestion.

For complete listings of attractions, restaurants, and hotels, or to pick up handy maps or other information, stop by the helpful Pennsylvania Dutch **visitor center** (daily 9 AM-5 PM, longer hours in summer; 717/299-8901, 800/PA-DUTCH or 800/723-8824), on US-30 between Dutch Country and Lancaster.

bled, each bike is "road-tested" at full throttle on motorcycling's equivalent of a treadmill. A souvenir store is stocked with all manner of things with the Harley-Davidson logo, from T-shirts to leather jackets.

Downtown York has a handful of cafes and restaurants, and on the west edge of town, where the US-30 bypass rejoins the old Lincoln Highway (Hwy-462), **Lee's Diner** (717/757-4598), 3608 E. Market Street, is a classic early 1950s Mountain View pre-fab diner, still serving up hearty roadfood.

The town of **Hanover**, south of US-30 between York and Gettysburg, is a prime producer of snack foods, from the famed pretzels baked by Snyder's of Hanover. Free factory tours are given at Utz Quality Foods, 900 High Street.

Gettysburg

Totally overwhelmed by the influx of tourists visiting its namesake battleground, the town of Gettysburg (pop. 7,025) has survived both onslaughts remarkably unscathed. Despite the presence of sundry tourist attractions—wax museums, various multimedia reenactments of the battle and President Lincoln's Gettysburg Address,

---

THE LINCOLN HIGHWAY

The main east-west route through Pennsylvania Dutch Country, US-30 is also one of the best-preserved stretches of the old Lincoln Highway, the nation's first transcontinental route. Planned and named in 1915, linking New York City's Times Square with the Panama Pacific International Exposition in San Francisco, the Lincoln Highway followed over 3,000 miles of country road across 12 states. A thousand miles of the original "highway" were little more than muddy tracks, scarcely more visible on the ground than they were on the still nonexistent road maps, but by the early 1930s the road was finally fully paved, following present-day US-30 as far as Wyoming, then bending south to follow what's now US-50, "The Loneliest Road in America," along the route of the Pony Express across Nevada and most of California.

Originally marked by telephone poles brightly painted with red, white, and blue stripes and a large letter "L," in 1928 the Lincoln Highway was blazed by more discreet concrete mileposts carrying a small bust of Lincoln—3,000 of these were placed, one every mile, by Boy Scout troops across the land, but only around a dozen still stand. As with the later Route 66, the Lincoln Highway was replaced by the interstates, but it does live on, in folk memory as well as the innumerable "Lincoln Cafes" and "Lincoln Motels" along its original route.

For a more thorough discussion of this old road's significance and legacy, read Drake Hokansen's excellent *Lincoln Highway: Main Street Across America* (University of Iowa Press, 1987), and become a member of the Lincoln Highway Association, P.O. Box 308, Franklin Grove, IL 61031 (815/456-3030). For help finding the many roadside landmarks that survive in the Keystone State, pick up a copy of *Pennsylvania Traveler's Guide to the Lincoln Highway* by Brian A. Butko (Stackpole Books, 1996). And if you like what you see here, take a trip west to Iowa, another state with substantial reminders of the Lincoln Highway heyday (see page 568 for more).

LINCOLN

L

HIGHWAY

A 230-acre farm on the southwest fringe of the Gettysburg battlefields was home to U.S. Army general and later president **Dwight D. Eisenhower** and his wife Mamie, and is now open for guided tours (daily 9 AM-4 PM; $4; 717/334-1124) that leave from the Gettysburg visitor center.

even a Lincoln Train Museum displaying over a thousand model trains that include a scale replica of the one Lincoln rode here in—once the day-tripping crowds have dispersed Gettysburg is actually a very pleasant place, with rows of brick-fronted buildings lining Baltimore and York Streets out from the circle at the center of town.

There are, not surprisingly, quite a few places to eat, including the atmospheric and inexpensive **Dobbin House**, south of town at 89 Steinwehr Avenue, serving above-average pub food in Gettysburg's oldest building. The same building doubles as the **Gettystown Inn** (717/334-2100), a moderately priced and pleasant B&B. The dozens of other places to stay include all the usual national chains, with a very special Best Western housed in the circa 1797 **Gettysburg Hotel** (717/337-200 or 800/528-1234) on Lincoln Square right at the center of town.

Gettysburg National Military Park

Site of the most famous two-minute speech in U.S. history, and of the bloody Civil War battle that marked the high tide of Confederate fortunes, Gettysburg National Military Park surrounds the town of Gettysburg, protecting the scenes of the struggle as they were July 1-3, 1863, when 50,000 of the 165,000 combatants were killed or wounded. Over a thousand monuments mark the various historic sites around the 6,000 acres of rolling green pasture that form the park, and tape-recorded **tours** ($12) or park-approved **Battlefield Guides** ($20 per car) take you along a well-marked route past such places as Little Round Top, The Angle, and Cemetery Ridge, site of fabled Pickett's Charge.

Most of the guided tours start and finish at the **visitor center** (daily 8 AM-5 PM; free) on Taneytown Road a mile south of town, in the shadow of a hideous Erector Set excrescence, the 310-foot-tall National Tower. In the visitor center, an extensive museum (free) puts the battle into context and displays a huge array of period weaponry. You can learn more by watching the battle unfold on the **Electric Map** ($2.50), which looks a lot like a boxing ring, or by studying the circular **Cyclorama** (free, $2 for sound and light show), a 26- by 356-foot painting that accurately portrays the events of the final day's battles. Across the road, the **Gettysburg National Cemetery** is the place where President Abraham Lincoln delivered his famous address on November 19, 1863.

Robert E. Lee,
Confederate commander
at Gettysburg

George Gordon Meade,
Union commander

Abraham Lincoln,
November 8, 1863

ACROSS MARYLAND

Crossing the Mason-Dixon Line from Gettysburg into Maryland on US-15, our route veers west into the Appalachian foothills of Catoctin Mountain Park, site of the presidential retreat Camp David. The landscape here is quite rugged, and signs of life few and far between—an oasis of peace and quiet, under an hour by road from Baltimore or Washington, D.C. Winding south through the mountains of the Maryland Panhandle, the thin strip of land that stretches for some 75 miles between Pennsylvania and West Virginia, this route again meets the hikers' Appalachian Trail, then detours to visit the battlefield of Antietam, the well-preserved site of the worst carnage of the Civil War.

The Maryland state motto, *Fatti Maschi, Parole Femine,* is translated roughly as "Manly Deeds, Womanly Words."

In Gathland State Park, on the Appalachian Trail east of Gapland off Hwy-67, the 50-foot terra-cotta arch of the **War Correspondents Memorial** was erected in the late 1880s in honor of journalists killed while covering the Civil War.

Catoctin Mountain Park: Camp David

US-15 continues south from Gettysburg across the Maryland border, and there's little to stop for until **Thurmont** (pop. 3,500), "Gateway to the Mountains," where the route heads west on Hwy-77 into the green expanse of Catoctin Mountain Park. Fully recovered after centuries of logging activity, the park protects some 10,000 acres of hardwood forest, a handful of 1,500-foot peaks, and the presidential retreat at Camp David, hidden away in the woods and strictly off-limits to visitors; for security reasons it doesn't even appear on park maps. The park **visitor center** (Mon.-Fri. 10 AM-4:30 PM, Saturday and Sunday 9 AM-5 PM; 301/663-9388) along Hwy-77 two miles west of US-15 provides information on **camping** and maps of the many hiking trails, including a short trail from the visitor center to the preserved remains of the Blue Blazes whiskey still, where rangers demonstrate moonshine-making on summer weekends.

Spreading along the south side of Hwy-77, Maryland-run **Cunningham Falls State Park** offers more natural scenery and a very pleasant swimming area in Hunting Creek Lake. There's a snack bar and boats for rent.

Washington Monument State Park
From Catoctin Mountain Park, our route heads south on undivided Hwy-6 and two-lane Hwy-17 along the hikers' Appalachian Trail, winding up at Washington Monument State Park between the I-70 freeway and the small town of **Boonsboro**. A 35-foot-tall, bot-tle-shaped mound dedicated to the memory

the "original" Washington Monument

of George Washington stands at the center of the park; Boonsboro citizens com-pleted the monument in 1827, making it the oldest memorial honoring the first U.S. president.

Atop a hill south of the park, across an old alignment of the National Road (US-40), the **South Mountain Inn** (301/432-6155) has operated as a tavern and inn since 1732, and now serves dinner nightly and lunch on weekends.

Antietam National Battlefield
Between Boonsboro and the Potomac River, which forms Maryland's bor-der with West Virginia, Antietam National Battlefield preserves the hallowed ground where over 23,000 men were killed or wounded on the bloodiest day of the Civil War—September 17, 1862. Atop a shallow hill at the middle of the park, a scant mile north of **Sharpsburg** off Hwy-65, the **visitor center** (daily 8:30 AM-5 PM; $2; 301/432-5124) offers films, museum exhibits, and interpretive programs that put the battle into military and political context. Though there was no clear winner, Antietam is said to have convinced Lin-coln to issue the Emancipation Proclamation, officially freeing slaves in Confederate states and effectively putting an end to British support for the southern side.

The attractive and historic city of Frederick, 25 miles south of Thurmont at the junction of I-70 and US-15, holds the shocking pink 1950s **Barbara Fritchie Candystick Restaurant,** on the old National Road (US-40), a mile east of I-70. Look for the giant candy cane out front. Frederick is also home to the **Frederick Keys** (301/662-0013), a Baltimore Orioles farm club who play at a modern stadium off I-70, exit 54.

Clara Barton, who tended the wounded during and after the Civil War's bloodiest battle at Antietam

ACROSS WEST VIRGINIA

In its short run across the eastern tip of West Virginia, US-340 passes through one of the most history-rich small towns in the U.S.: **Harpers Ferry,** located at the confluence of the Shenandoah and Potomac Rivers. Lovely mountain scenery surrounds Harpers Ferry, especially during early autumn when the hardwood forests rival Vermont's for vibrant color. South of Harpers Ferry, the hikers' Appalachian Trail runs directly along the Virginia/West Virginia border, east of the Shenandoah River atop the roadless crest of the Blue Ridge Mountains. The best route to follow by car, US-340 swings to the west through the historic mountain resort of **Charles Town** before entering Virginia.

Harpers Ferry is the national headquarters of the **Appalachian Trail Conference,** the nonprofit group that oversees the entire 2,144-mile footpath. For information, contact them at P.O. Box 807, Harpers Ferry, WV 25425 (304/535-6331).

Harpers Ferry

Climbing the steep slopes of the Blue Ridge Mountains, Harpers Ferry (pop. 300) embodies the industrial and political history of the early United States. Now protected as a national park, its many well-preserved wood, brick, and stone buildings are palpable reminders of early American enterprise: besides the country's first large factory, first canal, and first railroad, scenic Harpers Ferry saw John Brown's rebellion against slavery, and was later a strategic site during the Civil War.

Small museums, housed in separate buildings along Shenandoah and High Streets along the riverfront in the "Lower Town," trace the various strands of the town's past. From the Shenandoah River, the Appalachian Trail winds south down what the third president called "one of the most stupendous scenes in Nature," Jefferson's Rock. Crossing the Potomac River to the north, the AT climbs up to Maryland Heights for more spectacular vistas.

Especially in summer, when cars are banned from lower Harpers Ferry, the best first stop is the small **visitor center** (daily 9 AM-5 PM; $2; 304/535-6029) above the town along US-340. Park here and take one of the frequent free trams down to the historic area. Although most of Harpers Ferry is preserved as a historic site, the eastern portions along the Potomac riverfront are still in private hands, and here you can indulge your taste for fast food, wax museums, and schlocky souvenirs. There's also an **Amtrak/MARC** station, with trains serving Washington, D.C. on a very limited schedule.

Back up the hill along US-340, near the visitor center, a **Comfort Inn** has comfortable rooms for around $50 a night. Across the Potomac River in Knoxville, Maryland, a two-mile walk brings you to the **HI Harpers Ferry Lodge**, 19123 Sandy Hook Road (301/834-7652), which has hostel-style dorm beds for under $15 a night.

Charles Town is home to a sanctuary for those once-trendy yuppie pets, Vietnamese pot-bellied pigs. If you want to scratch their stomachs, or offer a donation for their upkeep, call 304/725-PIGS or 304/725-7447.

Charles Town

Founded in 1786, the former colonial resort of Charles Town (pop. 3,122) was named in honor of George Washington's younger brother Charles, who surveyed the site on behalf of Lord Fairfax. Many of the streets are named after other family members, over 75 of whom are buried in the cemetery alongside the **Zion Church**, on Congress Street on the east side of town. Charles Town, which shouldn't be confused with the West Virginia state capital, Charleston, later played a significant role in John Brown's failed raid on Harpers Ferry; after Brown was captured, he was tried and convicted of treason in the Jefferson County Courthouse at the corner of George and Washington Streets. A small **museum** (Mon.-Fri. 9 AM-5 PM; free) operates inside the old courtroom.

South of Charles Town, US-340 winds along the western slopes of the Appalachians for a dozen miles before entering Virginia east of Winchester.

East of Winchester, Virginia, this Appalachian Trail route crosses the transcontinental US-50 highway, which is covered beginning on page 654.

ACROSS VIRGINIA

The Appalachian Trail covers more ground in Virginia than it does in any other state, following the crest of the Blue Ridge Mountains from Harpers Ferry in West Virginia all the way south to the Tennessee and North Carolina borders. In the northern half of the state, the road route closely follows the hikers' route, and the two crisscross each other through the sylvan groves of Shenandoah National Park. Midway along the state the two routes diverge, and hikers turn west while the motor route follows the unsurpassed Blue Ridge Parkway along the top of the world.

Most of the time the route follows the mountain crests, though in many places you'll find fascinating towns and cities a short distance to the east or west. Best among these is Charlottesville, a history-rich Piedmont town that's best known as the home of Thomas Jefferson and the University of Virginia. Other suggested stops include the Shenandoah Valley town of Lexington, the "natural wonder" of Natural Bridge, and the engaging city of Roanoke.

Dinosaur Land

Located at the intersection of US-340 and US-522, eight miles southeast of Winchester near the hamlet of White Post, Dinosaur Land (daily 9 AM-5:30 PM; $3) displays an entertaining and marvelously kitschy collection of manmade sharks, cavemen and, of course, dinosaurs. It's especially fun for kids, who are welcome to climb on and around the concrete menagerie, and wry-humored adults will enjoy searching through the very large gift shop, which has all manner of cheesy souvenirs.

White Post, by the way, got its name from, you guessed it, a white post, placed here by a young surveyor named George Washington. The post marked the road to the country estate of Lord Fairfax, which was destroyed in 1858.

Front Royal

The town takes its name, perhaps apocryphally, from a Revolutionary War drill sergeant who, since his troops were unable to tell their left from their right, was forced to shout out "Front Royal Oak" to get them to face the same way. Front Royal (pop. 11,880) sits just south of I-66 at the entrance to Shenandoah National Park. Because of its key location, Front Royal has grown unwieldy in past decades but retains some semblance of its 19th-century self along Chester Street, a well-maintained historic district at the center of town, a block east of US-340.

You'll find walking-tour maps and other information at the **visitor center**, 414 E. Main Street (540/635-3185 or 800/338-2576), which is housed in an old train depot. The usual battery of fast-food franchises line US-340 from the freeway south through town, as does **Sandy's Diner**, just south of the Shenandoah River bridge, and motels like the **Twin Rivers**, 1801 Shenandoah Avenue (540/635-4101), a mile south of I-66/Hwy-7.

At the foot of the Blue Ridge Mountains, 26 miles southeast of Front Royal via US-522, pristine colonial **Washington** (pop. 200) was surveyed by the future father of the U.S., George Washington, who named many of the streets after friends and family. The main attraction here is the **Inn at Little Washington** at Main and Middle Streets (540/675-3800), one of the few Mobil five-star resort

Fall foliage in the Blue Ridge Mountains can be stunning, though it is not usually as intense as it is in New England.

hotels in the country, though with room rates starting at over $300 a night and dinners averaging $100 a head, it's definitely a special-occasion place to stay or eat. It's worth it though: a critic for *New York Times* said his dinner there was "the most fantastic meal of my life."

Shenandoah National Park

One of the most popular national parks in the east, especially during the fall foliage season when seemingly everyone in the world descends upon the place to "leaf-peep," Shenandoah National Park protects some 195,000 acres of hardwood forest along the northernmost crest of the Blue Ridge Mountains. Though the landscape looks natural now, it was in fact heavily cultivated until the 1920s; when the soils were depleted, farmers moved out, and the government began buying up all the land to return it to its original state.

Most people experience the park by driving spectacular **Skyline Drive** ($10 per car). A helpful brochure is handed out at booths along the route (one at either end and two mid-way). The drive opened in 1939 and runs (at 35 mph!) over 100 miles between the I-66 and I-64 freeways, giving grand vistas at every bend in the road. While such scenic driving is definitely memorable, by far the best way to really see the park is to get out of the car and walk along the many miles of trails that lead through the dense green forests to innumerable waterfalls and overlooks. If you have more time, the AT runs alongside Skyline Drive. It's accessible from dozens of different spots and feels miles away even when only a short walk from the roadway.

All of the Skyline's concession services—gas, food, and lodging—are

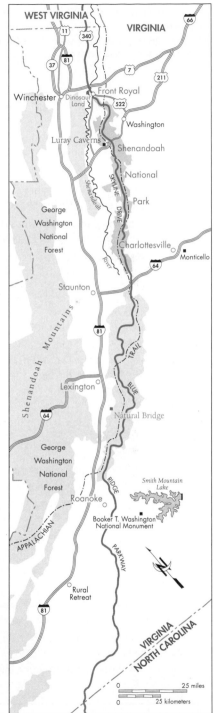

operated by **ARA Virginia Skyline Inc.** (800/999-4714). Sites at the more popular **campgrounds** can be reserved in advance through MISTIX (800/365-CAMP or 800/365-2267). A few backcountry **cabins** are operated by the Potomac Appalachian Trail Club (540/242-0315), which also offers the best information on hiking in the park.

SKYLINE DRIVE

Mileposts, arranged in mile-by-mile order from north to south, mark the best places to stop along Skyline Drive in Shenandoah National Park:

Mile 0.6: **Front Royal** entrance station.

Mile 4.6: Climbing swiftly up from Front Royal in the north, the road reaches the main **visitor center** at Dickey Ridge, where you'll find a short nature trail.

Mile 21: On the shoulder of 3,474-foot **Hogback Mountain**, an overlook gives great views west over the meandering Shenandoah River. Access to the AT.

Mile 22.2: **Matthews Arm** campground.

Mile 24: Elkwallow **gas station** and store.

Mile 31.5: **Thornton Gap** entrance station; nearby Panorama restaurant deserves its name.

Mile 32.4: **Mary's Rock Tunnel**, a 13-foot bore cut through the granite in 1932; access to the AT.

Mile 41.7: **Skyland**, an early resort that preceded the establishment of the park, stands at 3,680 feet, the highest point on Skyline Drive. The lodge (540/999-2211 or 800/999-4714) has a dining room and other facilities, and offers horseback rides. Access to the AT.

Mile 50.7: Under a mile from the well-marked trailhead, **Dark Hollow Falls** drops over a 70-foot cliff.

Mile 51: **Byrd Visitor Center**, the other main visitor center in the park, marks the turnoff to **Big Meadows**, where there's a lodge (540/999-2221 or 800/999-4714), a campground, a **gas station**, and access to the AT.

Mile 56.4: A short steep hike scrambles up to the 3,300-foot-high summit of **Bearfence Mountain** for a 360-degree panorama.

Mile 65.7: **Swift Run Gap** entrance station.

Mile 79.5: **Loft Mountain** wayside area has a campground, showers (15 minutes of hot water for $1 in quarters), cabins, a store, a **gas station**, and access to the AT.

Mile 84.1: A parking area marks the trailhead for the rewarding two-mile hike to **Jones Run Falls**, tumbling over a mossy 45-foot cliff. Access to the AT.

Mile 98.9: Near the southern end of Skyline Drive, **Calf Mountain** provides a grand panorama over the Shenandoah Valley.

Mile 104.6: Rockfish Entrance Station. Skyline Drive ends at I-64, at mile 105.4.

Charlottesville

From the southern end of Shenandoah National Park, it's a quick 20 miles east on I-64 to Charlottesville (pop. 40,341), a richly historic college town that's one of the most enjoyable stops in the state. From the rolling green lawns of the University of Virginia campus to neoclassical Monticello on the hills above it, the legacy of Thomas Jefferson dominates Charlottesville. Jefferson lived and worked here for most of his life— when he wasn't out founding the country or serving as its president.

West of the compact downtown district, the **University of Virginia** campus was Jefferson's pride and joy. Not only did he found it (in 1819) and fund its early years, he planned the curriculum and designed the original buildings, a quadrangle of red brick Palladian villas that the American Institute of Architects declared the most perfect place in the country. Edgar Allan Poe lived and studied here briefly before dropping out in 1826. Poe's room, appropriately, is No. 13 in the West Range, and it's decorated to look like it did a century ago, with a few period belongings visible behind the glass door.

Charlottesville's other key site is Jefferson's home, **Monticello** —the domed building that fills the back of the nickel coin— well-signed off I-64 exit 121. Recently restored and open for tours (daily 9 AM-5 PM, from 8 AM in summer; $9; 804/984-9822), Monticello embodies the many different traits of this multifaceted man. The house was designed and built by Jefferson over a period of 40 years (1769-1809), and holds various gadgets he invented—including a double-pen device that made a copy of everything he wrote—and odd things he collected over the years, from elk antlers to recipes for home-brewed beer. Jefferson died here at Monticello on the 4th of July, 1826, and the grounds, which in Jefferson's time formed an extensive plantation worked by slaves, hold his mortal remains in a simple tomb beyond the vegetable gardens.

Down in the valley below Monticello, **Michie Tavern** (9 AM-5 PM; $6 adults, $2 children) is a touristy but interesting inn that opened in 1784 and was moved to the present site in the 1920s. Admission includes a tour of the parlors, bars, and upstairs rooms, as well as a dairy and a grist mill; it's also a restaurant serving "Olde Worlde foode" for the bus-tour hordes, at $10 a head for a "colonial buffet" lunch. (Just so you know, Michie is pronounced MICK-ee, as in Mantle.)

Like most college towns, Charlottesville provides a broad range of good places to eat, from bare-bones cafes like the **White Spot** at 1407 University Avenue, right across from campus, to more upscale places ranged along Elliewood Street around the corner. Among the nicest places to enjoy a meal is the lovely **Ivy Inn**, serving up New American food in a circa 1804

Halfway through Shenandoah National Park, US-211 runs west down to **Luray Caverns** (daily 9 AM-4 PM, till 6 PM in summer; $13 adults, $5 children; 540/743-6551), the largest and most impressive of the many caverns in the limestone Blue Ridge region—a single room measures 300 by 500 feet and is over 140 feet high. It also boasts the "World's Only Stalacpipe Organ," where rubber mallets make music by banging on the stone stalactites.

Pollution from metropolitan areas and from so many car-borne visitors has caused serious problems at Shenandoah National Park, both for the trees—many of which have been poisoned—and for the views people come to see. On an average summer day visibility is impaired and the surrounding valleys are often shrouded in smoggy haze.

Along with multicolored leaves, the autumn months bring hundreds of hawks, eagles, and other birds of prey to the mountains on their annual migration. You'll spot the greatest numbers of raptors in late September, when birdwatchers congregate for a "Hawk Watch" in the parking lot of the Holiday Inn, off I-64 along the crest.

In the middle of Charlottesville, in Midway Park at Main and Ridge Streets, there's a memorial to the explorers Lewis and Clark, both of whom were born in the region.

To get a sense of life in the Shenandoah Valley, tune to **WSVA 550 AM** in Harrisonburg, which broadcasts updated farm and livestock prices every hour on the hour, and Rush Limbaugh for lunch.

federal-style house at 2244 Old Ivy Road off US-250, west of the football stadium. After dark, head to the downtown pedestrian mall, where you can enjoy Virginia's original brew pub (**Blue Ridge Brewing**, at 709 W. Main Street), or listen to great live music at **Miller's**, 109 W. Main Street, where alt-rock pop star Dave Matthews used to tend bar.

Most of Charlottesville's motels line up along Emmet Street (Business US-29), including the well-placed **Best Western Cavalier Inn** at 105 Emmett Street (804/296-8111), with doubles for around $55 a night. For more detailed information on visiting Charlottesville, contact the **visitor center** (804/293-6789), which is hard to miss on Hwy-20, off I-64 at exit 121.

Staunton

West of the mountains from the south end of Shenandoah National Park on I-64, tidy Staunton (pop. 24,461, pronounced STAN-ton) was founded in 1732 as one of the first towns on the far side of the Blue Ridge. Unlike much of the valley, Staunton was untouched during the Civil War, and now preserves its many 18th- and early 19th-century buildings in a sizeable historic district around the boyhood home of Staunton's favorite son, Woodrow Wilson. Son of a Presbyterian minister, Wilson was born in 1856 in a stately Greek Revival townhouse at 18-24 N. Coalter

---

THE BLUE RIDGE PARKWAY

Starting at the southern end of Shenandoah National Park, and winding along the crest of the Blue Ridge Mountains all the way to Great Smoky Mountains National Park, some 469 miles away, the Blue Ridge Parkway is one of the country's great scenic drives. This is especially true during autumn, when the dogwoods and gum trees turn deep red, and the hickories yellow, against an evergreen backdrop of pines, hemlocks, and firs. Spring is wildflower time, with abundant azaleas and rhododendrons blooming orange, white, pink and red throughout May and June, especially at the higher elevations.

First proposed in the 1920s, the Parkway was constructed 1935-67, when it grew from a network of local roads to the current route, along which billboards and commercial traffic are both banned. While the Parkway avoids towns and commercial areas to concentrate on the scenery, many interesting towns and other places along the way are well worth a detour.

For ease of use, the following description is divided into three main sections, starting with the drive between Shenandoah National Park and Roanoke. The Roanoke-to-North Carolina section begins on page 356, and the final run south to the Great Smoky Mountains is on page 358.

Mile 0: **Rockfish Gap**, at the southern end of Shenandoah National Park's Skyline Drive, marks the northern start of the Blue Ridge Parkway. I-64 and the AT cross here as well.

Mile 6.1: **Humpback Rocks** has a short (45 minute) trail leading through a reconstructed historic farmstead and a visitor center (540/943-4716), ending with a 270-degree view over the mountains. AT access.

Street, now established as the **Woodrow Wilson Birthplace and Museum** (daily 10 AM-4 PM, 9 AM-5 PM in summer; $6), with galleries tracing his life as a scholar—he was president of Princeton University—and as U.S. President during WW I.

President Woodrow Wilson

They may not have guided their country through a world war, but Staunton's real favorite sons are the Statler Brothers, the Staunton-born country singers and Grand Ole Opry stars who still live and run their corn-pone careers from town. At the **Statler Complex** (tours at 2 PM Mon.-Fri. only; free; 540/885-7927), at 501 Thornrose Avenue, off US-250 about a mile northwest of downtown, the Statlers display mementos, awards and album covers in the halls and classrooms of the school they attended in their youth. Best of the displays is a room chock-full of gifts sent to them by their fans, but you can only see these if you join the once-a-day guided tour.

Staunton is also the home of the unique **Museum of American Frontier Culture** (daily 9 AM-5 PM; $8; 540/332-7850), right off I-81 on the east side of town. A rural version of Williamsburg, this living history museum consists of four resurrected working farms, incorporating buildings brought over from Germany, England, and Ireland. The fourth farm, dating from antebellum Virginia, shows how various "Old World" traditions blended in America. The farms are inhabited by interpreters

---

Mile 29: **Whetstone Ridge** has a summer-only restaurant ($4 burger-and-fries), plus a gift shop and short nature trail.

Mile 34.4: **Yankee Horse** parking area has an exhibit on an old logging railroad, part of which has been restored, and a short trail to Wigwam Falls. AT access.

Mile 45.6: Junction with US-60, which runs west to the town of **Buena Vista** where there are motels and a great old general store, and to Lexington (see below).

Mile 63.6: Visitor Center (804/299-5496), exhibits and trails along the **James River and Kanawha Canal**. Lowest point on Parkway, at 649 feet; it is also the junction with US-501, which runs west along the James River for 15 miles to **Natural Bridge** (see below).

Mile 76.5: Great views over both valleys from the **highest point** on Parkway in Virginia, at 3,950 feet.

Mile 84-87: The most popular—and most developed—stretch of the Parkway, the **5,000 Peaks of Otter** section includes a visitor center (540/586-4357), gas station, restaurant, and very pleasant lodge (540/586-1081), which is open year-round. Three peaks rise above a small lake, and give great sunrise and sunset views; many good trails, including a two-mile loop to Fallingwater Cascades, let you escape the sometimes sizeable crowds.

Mile 100: **Curry Gap**, the last access to the AT, which cuts off west across the valley, then south into Tennessee.

Miles 105-122: The city of **Roanoke** (see page 355).

While in Staunton, check out the wares available at the **Jolly Roger Haggle Shop,** a fascinating junk shop ("over 1,000,000 items") across from the train station at 27 Middlebrook Avenue.

Mountain passes throughout the Blue Ridge are known as "gaps."

dressed in (very clean) period costumes busily husking corn, spinning wool, or working in the fields.

Staunton holds one of the best places to eat in the Shenandoah Valley, on US-250 just east of I-81 exit 222, near the frontier museum: the **Mrs. Rowe's Family Restaurant** (540/886-1833), which has been serving excellent, home-style cooking, from pork chops to banana cream pies, for the past 50 years. It's open every day (since 1947) for breakfast, lunch and dinner—go for their world-famous fried chicken, which is well worth the 25-minute wait for it to be prepared to your order

All the usual motels cluster around the I-64/I-81 junction, but you'll find the region's most pleasant accommodations at the rambling Victorian-era **Belle Grae Inn,** 515 W. Frederick Street (540/886-5151) in the center of Staunton, with B&B rooms from $90 a night.

Lexington

Founded in 1778, and named for the then-recent Revolutionary War battleground, photogenic Lexington (pop. 6,959) is home to an estimable pair of Virginia institutions, the gender-embattled Virginia Military Institute, and Washington and Lee University, which meld into one another at the center of town. Numerous old brick buildings, including a typically southern lawyer's row around Courthouse Square, still stand around the town, which you can tour on foot or in one of the horse-drawn carriages ($10/hr) that leave from the downtown visitor center.

Animated by an unusually crew-cut version of typical college-town energy, Lexington is redolent with, and proud of, its military heritage. Generals, in fact, have become the town's stock-in-trade: from 1859 until his death in 1863, Gen. **Thomas "Stonewall" Jackson** lived at 8 E. Washington Street, now a small museum (Mon.-Sat. 9 AM-5 PM, Sunday 1-5 PM; $5); he is buried in the small but well-tended cemetery a short distance west of downtown. General **Robert E. Lee** spent his post-Civil War years teaching at Washington and Lee, which was named after him (and his wife's ancestor George, yet another famous general). Lee is entombed in a crypt below the chapel, under a famous statue of his recumbent self, with his trusty horse Traveller buried just outside. Another influential old war-horse, Gen. **George C. Marshall,** is honored in a large eponymous museum (daily 9 AM-5 PM; $3) on the VMI campus; the museum traces General Marshall's role in WW II and salutes his Nobel Prize-winning "Marshall Plan" for postwar reconstruction.

If you've tired of fried food and meat, Lexington offers respite from the usual road fare: the **Blue Heron Cafe,** serves healthy and delicious soups and sandwiches at 4 E. Washington Street, in the center of town. For truly fine "New American" dining, try the smoke-free **Wilson-Walker House,** 30 N. Main Street (540/463-3020).

There are a number of comfortable and captivating places to stay in and around Lexington, such as the **Alexander Winthrow House,** 3 W. Washington Street (540/463-2044), or the **Llewellyn Lodge,** 603 S. Main Street (540/463-3235 or 800/882-1145), both friendly B&Bs within easy walking distance of the campuses and the historic town center.

For walking-tour maps, more general information, or further listings, contact the Lexington **visitor center,** 106 E. Washington Street (540/463-3777).

Natural Bridge

For NPR news and non-commercial arts programming, tune to **WVTF 89.1 FM** in Roanoke.

Held sacred by local Monacan Indians, and bought from King George in 1774 by Thomas Jefferson, the 215-foot-high notch of Natural Bridge is a remarkable piece of geologic acrobatics. Spanning some 90 feet, the thick stone arch bridges Cedar Creek at the bottom of a steeply walled canyon. To see the Natural Bridge, which is heralded as one of the "Seven Natural Wonders of the World" (others on the list include Niagara Falls, Yellowstone, and Giant's Causeway in Northern Ireland), you have to buy a ticket (daily 8 AM-dusk; $8; 800/533-1410) from the unbelievably huge souvenir shop that fills the bottom of the old hotel. Natural Bridge is the focus of a once-plush resort complex that has definitely seen better times but still offers some 200 rooms in two hotels, as well as a wax museum ($7) of Virginia history in which you can watch the wax figures being made, dressed, and posed.

Not surprisingly, wonderfully tacky Roadside Americana surrounds Natural Bridge. Look out for an "Enchanted Castle" and a family of dinosaurs lining US-11 on the way in from I-81.

Roanoke

Apart from Asheville at its southern end, Roanoke (pop. 96,397) is the only real city that can claim it's actually *on* the Blue Ridge Parkway. With block after block of brick-fronted business buildings, most of them adorned with neon, metal, and painted signs that seem unchanged since the 1940s, Roanoke contrasts abruptly with the natural verdance of the rest of the Parkway, but you may find it a welcome change after so many trees. Once a busy, belching, industrial Goliath supported by the railroads, Roanoke has evolved into a sophisticated, high-tech city—the commercial, cultural, and medical center of southwest Virginia.

Roanoke's main visitor attractions lie right downtown in the **Center in the Square** complex, a restored warehouse that holds a wide variety of cultural offerings, including theaters, an art museum, a science museum, and a local history museum (Tues.-Sat. 10 AM-5 PM, Sunday 1-5 PM; $2). Also worth a look is the **Virginia Museum of Transportation,** 303 Norfolk Avenue (Mon.-Sat. 10 AM-5 PM, Sunday noon-5 PM; $5), which displays lots of old cars and trucks, steam and diesel locomotives, and horse-drawn carriages, plus a complete traveling circus—minus the performers, of course.

On Mill Mountain high above Roanoke, the 100-foot-tall "**World's Largest Man-Made Star**" shines nightly, lit by 2,000 feet of neon tubing. You can drive up to it and get a grand view over Roanoke. Near the foot of the mountain, along the Roanoke River, the front yard of a small house at 605 Riverland

Southeast of Roanoke, the **Booker T. Washington National Monument** (daily 9 AM-4:30 PM; free; 540/721-2094) preserves the site of the plantation cabin where the influential African-American leader was born. Other buildings on the 225-acre site, 20 miles from Roanoke via Hwy-116 and Hwy-122, have been reconstructed.

THE BLUE RIDGE PARKWAY: ROANOKE TO NORTH CAROLINA

South from Roanoke, the Blue Ridge Parkway winds another 100 miles before crossing the North Carolina border. This midsection of the Parkway, especially the first 25 miles south of Roanoke, runs at a lower elevation across a more settled and cultivated landscape than the rugged ridge tops followed elsewhere. In place of the spectacular vistas, you'll see many more houses and small farms, a few pioneer cabins (preserved and not), miles of split-rail fences, and some picturesque cemeteries. The southern reaches, approaching the North Carolina border, get better and better.

Miles 105-122: The city of **Roanoke** (see above).

Mile 154.5: A two-mile loop trail leads to a pioneer cabin overlooking the **Smart View** for which it's named. Blooming dogwoods abound in May.

Mile 165.2: At **Tuggles Gap**, the junction with Hwy-8 has a motel, a restaurant, and a gas station, also a small cemetery right along the Parkway.

Miles 167-174: The 4,800-acre **Rocky Knob** area contains a campground, a visitor center near the Meadows of Dan at Mile 169, and a 10-mile roundtrip trail at Mile 167.1 leading down through Rock Castle Gorge.

Mile 174: East of the Parkway along Greenwood Road, you'll find the summer-only **Rocky Knob Cabins** (540/593-3503).

Mile 176.1: A short trail leads to **Mabry Mill**, in use 1910-35. In summer, interpreters demonstrate blacksmithing and milling skills. A coffee shop (open May-Oct. only) sells old-fashioned pancakes made from stone-ground flour, plus country hams and hamburgers.

Mile 177.7: Junction with **US-58**, marked by gas stations and the clean, quiet **Blue Ridge Motel** (540/952-2244), which also has a good restaurant.

Mile 189: Near the midpoint of the Parkway, atop Groundhog Mountain, the **Doe Run Lodge** (540/398-2212) offers spacious, modern, chalet-style cabins (with a pool and tennis courts) and a "fine dining" restaurant.

Mile 199-200: Junction with US-52, · which runs south to Mount Airy, NC (see below), and with I-77 freeway, running south to Charlotte.

Mile 216.9: Virginia/North Carolina border.

Drive holds **Miniature Graceland**, a roughly scale model of the King's Memphis home (complete with wrought iron gates and a pink Cadillac) which you have to see to believe.

The town's most popular place to eat is **The Roanoker**, "The Home of Good Food since 1941," which serves traditional Virginia dishes and also does a tasty bowl of chili, a mile south of downtown off US-220 (Wonju Street exit) at 2522 Colonial Avenue (540/540/344-7746). There are also a number of good cafes downtown, like the unexpectedly world-beat cuisine at **Carlos' Brazilian and International**, 312 Market Street near Church (540/345-7661). If you're planning a picnic up in the mountains be sure to stop first at the historic **Farmer's Market** (Mon.-Sat. 8 AM-4 PM; free), downtown next to the Center in the Square, and active since 1874.

On the west edge of Roanoke, near I-81 on Hwy-311 in Salem, excellent home cooking (fresh biscuits, fried chicken, incredible fresh fruit cobblers) is served Thurs.-Sat., for lunch and dinner, at **The Homeplace** (540/384-7252).

Places to stay range from the usual interstate motels, lined up along Orange Avenue (US-460) to $80-a-night B&Bs like the **Walnut Hill**, 436 Walnut Avenue (540/427-3312). The handy **visitor center**, downtown at 114 Market Street (540/345-8622 or 800/635-5535), offers lots more listings and information.

> The soft drink Dr. Pepper, which originated in Waco, Texas, was named for a pharmacist who worked in the town of Rural Retreat, Virginia, along I-81 near its intersection with the AT.

> The border between Virginia and North Carolina was surveyed in 1749 by a team that included Thomas Jefferson's father, Peter.

ACROSS NORTH CAROLINA

Running along the crest of the Blue Ridge Mountains at the far western edge of the state, this route across North Carolina takes in some of the most beautiful scenery east or west of the Mississippi. Though not as immense as the Rockies or other western landscapes, this part of North Carolina abounds with rugged peaks and deep valleys, pastoral meadows, and ancient-looking mountain villages, some dating back to colonial times. It's all linked by the magnificent Blue Ridge Parkway, perhaps the country's greatest scenic drive.

The region's sole city, Asheville, is a proud old resort dominated by the ostentatious Biltmore Estate, "the world's largest private house," but everywhere else nature predominates—especially in the majestic Great Smoky Mountains National Park in the state's far southwestern corner.

Mount Airy: Mayberry RFD
Along the Virginia/North Carolina border, 12 miles southeast of the Parkway via US-52, Mount Airy (pop. 7,156) was the boyhood home of **Andy Griffith**, who based much of his long-running TV show *The Andy Griffith* (*continues on page 360*)

the sheriff's car, parked outside the Mayberry Motor Inn

THE BLUE RIDGE PARKWAY: VIRGINIA TO THE SMOKIES

The highest and most memorable parts of the 469-mile Blue Ridge Parkway are the mountainous miles leading along the backbone of North Carolina. Following the southern Blue Ridge Mountains as they fade into the taller and more massive Black Mountains, the Parkway skirts three other mountain ranges before ending up at Great Smoky Mountains National Park on the Tennessee border. Spring flowers (including massive rhododendrons), fall colors, songbirds and wild turkeys, numerous waterfalls and occasional eerie fogs that fill the valleys below, all make this an unforgettable trip no matter what the time of year. Take your time and drive carefully, however hard it is to keep your eyes on the road.

A couple of worthwhile detours—to the mountain hamlets of Blowing Rock and Little Switzerland, and to the city of Asheville—are covered in greater detail in the main text. From north to south, here are the mile-by-mile highlights along the North Carolina portion of the Blue Ridge Parkway:

Mile 216.9: Virginia/North Carolina border.

Mile 217.5: A very easy half-mile trail leads to the top of 2,885-foot **Cumberland Knob**. A visitors center (336/657-8161) marks the location where New Deal Civilian Conservation Corps workers began construction of the parkway in 1935.

Miles 238.5-244.7: **Doughton Park**, named for one of the politicians who made the Parkway possible, has a gas station, a nice cafe (daily 7 AM-7 PM in summer), a campground and the small **Bluffs Lodge** (336/372-4499) at Mile 241. Starting at the historic Brinegar Cabin (Mile 238.5), the four-mile Cedar Ridge trail is one of many rewarding day hikes, all of which offer great views.

Mile 260.6: An easy mile-long trail leads to the top of **Jumpinoff Rocks** for a sweeping view.

Mile 285.1: **Boone's Trace**, a pioneer trail first blazed by Daniel Boone, crosses the mountains at this point, marked by a stone and a plaque.

Mile 291.9: Junction with US-221, which leads south to the lovely little mountain town of **Blowing Rock** (see below for more), two miles off the Parkway.

Miles 292-295: **Moses H. Cone Memorial Park** is a 3,600-acre former private estate, with many miles of mountaintop hiking trails. At Mile 294, Southern Highlands Crafts Guild members demonstrate various Appalachian crafts throughout the summer, on the front porch of the former Cone mansion, which is now the nonprofit Parkway Craft Center (daily 9 AM-5:30 PM, May-Oct. only; free; 828/295-7938).

Mile 304: The marvelous engineering feat of the **Linn Cove Viaduct** carries the Parkway around rugged Grandfather Mountain. Completed in 1987, this was the last part of the Parkway to be built. A small visitor center (open May-Oct. at Mile 304.6) has general information and exhibits on the viaduct's construction, which included pre-cast, post-stressed concrete box girders cantilevered in spans of 180 feet. Dense walls of rhododendrons border the Parkway south of the viaduct.

Mile 305.1: US-221, which used to carry the Parkway before the viaduct was built, leads a mile south to 5,837-foot **Grandfather Mountain**, the highest peak in Blue Ridge, now a private park (daily 8 AM-5 PM; $10 adults, $5 children) with trails, a zoo and the famous "Mile-High Swinging Bridge."

Mile 308.2: A half-mile nature trail leads to 3,995-foot **Flat Rock** for a view of Grandfather Mountain.

Mile 316.3: **Linville Falls** crashes through a rugged gorge; short trails lead to scenic overlooks. Visitor center and campground (828/259-0701).

Mile 331: At the junction of Hwy-226, the **Museum of North Carolina Minerals** (daily 9 AM-5 PM; free) displays all kinds and sizes of local gemstones, which you can watch being polished.

Mile 334: Junction with Hwy-226, which leads south to **Little Switzerland**, a resort community described more fully below.

Mile 339: **Crabtree Meadows** has rhododendrons, a gas station, and a nifty Flintstones-modern coffee shop (May-Oct. only).

Mile 355.4: West of the Parkway, the 1,650 acres of **Mount Mitchell State Park** include a mountaintop observation tower, a tents-only campground, snack bar, and a visitor center (daily 8 AM-dusk; free; 828/675-4611). Drive to within 200 yards of the weather-beaten 6,684-foot summit, the highest point east of the Mississippi River.

Mile 364.6: Best seen in late spring when the rhododendrons are in full bloom, the lush greenery of **Craggy Gardens** feels like an Appalachian Shangri-la. Nature trails lead from the visitor center (daily 9 AM-5 PM April-Oct.; free).

Mile 382: You can check out exhibits and demonstrations of Appalachian arts and crafts in the **Folk Art Center** (daily 9 AM-5 PM; free; 828/298-0293).

Miles 383-395: The historic mountain resort city of **Asheville** (see below) lies west of the Parkway.

Mile 407.8: Originally part of the 100,000-acre Biltmore Estate, the slopes of 5,721-foot **Mount Pisgah** were among the first places in the U.S. where sustainable forestry was practiced. A small "Cradle of Forestry in America" exhibit, focusing on the work of Gifford Pinchot, Biltmore gardener and founder of the U.S. Forest Service, is housed in a visitor center off the Parkway at Mile 412.

Mile 422: At **Devil's Courthouse**, climb the bare rock summit for a 360-degree panorama.

Mile 431: A self-guided nature trail leads through a first-growth spruce and fir forest, from the **highest point on the Parkway**, at 6,047 feet.

Mile 469: **Southern end** of Blue Ridge Parkway, at the junction with US-441 and the entrance to Smoky Mountains National Park.

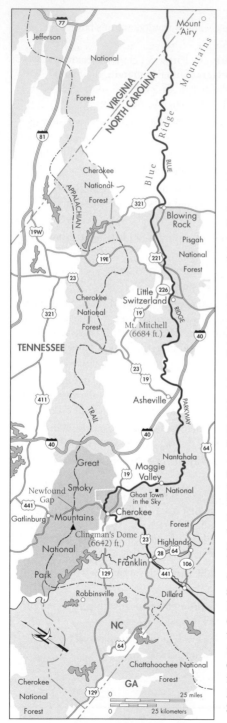

Show and the spinoff sitcom *Mayberry, RFD* on the region. If you have fond memories of Opie, Andy, Barney, and Aunt Bea, you'll definitely want to visit Mount Airy, which has effectively re-created itself in the image of the show. Eat at the very popular **Snappy Lunch**, 125 Main Street in the compact down-town business district, and admire the 8x10 glossies of Mayberry actors and their local lookalikes at Floyd's Barber Shop, next door. Or head a few blocks west to **Aunt Bea's BBQ**, on US-52, and stay the night at the comfortable, clean and inexpensive **Mayberry Motor Inn** (336/786-4109) across the highway— just look for the black-and-white May-berry sheriff's car parked out front.

The Mayberry mania reaches a peak during Mayberry Days in late Septem-ber; details on this can be had from the Mount Airy **visitor center**, 615 N. Main street (336/789-4636 or 800/576-0231).

Blowing Rock

A quick two miles south of the Blue Ridge Parkway via US-221 from Mile-post 291.9 lies the delightful little re-sort community of Blowing Rock (pop. 1,257)—the place to stop if you're only stopping once. The cool summer tem-peratures have been attracting visitors for centuries, and once you get past the hideous factory outlet mall that welcomes you to town, quaint old Main Street is a great place to stretch your legs while taking in the eclectic range of late Victorian buildings, including some delightful churches. Blowing Rock takes its name from a nearby cliff overlooking John's River Gorge, where updrafts can cause lightweight objects to be blown upwards rather than down; this effect, which earned Blow-ing Rock a mention in *Ripley's Believe It or Not!* as the only place "Where Snow Falls Upside Down," also inspired the Native American legend of a Cherokee brave who, rather than be forcibly separated from his Chickasaw lover, leapt off the cliff, only to be blown back into the arms of his sweetheart.

North Carolina's oldest tourist attraction, the **Blowing Rock** itself, two miles east of town via winding US-321 (daily 9 AM-5 PM, 8 AM-8 PM in summer; $4), is worth the admission, whether or not the "magic wind" is blowing. Check out the tremendous views from a platform suspended 3,000 feet above the valley below. The nearby area also offers a couple of enjoyable tourist traps, including an apparently gravity-defying "**Mystery Hill**" just off the Parkway, and the scenic, coal-fired steam trains of the **Tweetsie Railroad** four miles north of town on US-321.

Downtown Blowing Rock has a number of good places to eat lined up along the quaint few blocks of Main Street downtown. For good food at fair prices, and a front deck that overlooks the town, it's hard to beat the **Speckled Trout Cafe**, open for breakfast, lunch and dinner at the north end of Main Street. Across US-321 from the Blowing Rock, the storybook **Green Park Inn** (828/295-3141) is a large historic resort hotel built in 1882, with a golf course and rooms in the $100-150. More modern conveniences are available at the **Cliff Dwellers Inn** (828/295-3121), right off the parkway on US-321.

Little Switzerland

Another classic mountaintop vacation spot, located midway between Blowing Rock and Asheville, Little Switzerland was founded in 1910 around the **Switzerland Inn** (828/765-2153 or 800/654-4026), a stately old chalet-style resort that also operates a very popular restaurant right off the Blue Ridge Parkway at Milepost 334.

The inn stands on a crest, but the rest of Little Switzerland sits in the deep canyon to the east, spread out along Hwy-226 and a number of smaller side roads. The main stop is **Emerald Village** (daily 9 AM-6 PM April-Nov.; $4), on McKinney Mine Road 2.5 miles from the Parkway, where you can tour an old gemstone mine (above and below ground) and museums displaying everything from gemstones to mechanical music makers.

Asheville

What the English country town of Bath was to King George's London, the mountain resort of Asheville (pop. 61,607) was to the pre-jet set, pre-air-conditioned Deep South. When summer heat and humidity became unbearable, the gentry headed here to stay cool while enjoying the city's many grand hotels and elaborate summer homes.

The presence here of the world's biggest vacation house, the Vanderbilt family's **Biltmore Estate** (daily 9 AM-5 PM; $22.95; 828/255-1700 or 800/543-2961), is a testament to Asheville's primary position in the resort pantheon. The estate now covers 8,000 acres on the south side of town, though at one time it stretched up to

In the valley below Mount Mitchell, off I-40 northeast of Asheville, **Black Mountain College** was a lively intellectual and artistic nexus during the 1930s and 1940s, when the likes of Charles Olson hung out here.

The hikers' Appalachian Trail winds west of the Blue Ridge Parkway along the North Carolina/Tennessee border.

A dozen miles west of the Blue Ridge Parkway via US-321 and Hwy-194, the village of Valle Crucis holds the circa 1883 **Mast General Store** (828/963-6511), a one-of-a-kind survivor that sells a little of everything, from gasoline to Gore-Tex parkas.

You can spot the wild mountains southeast of Asheville in numerous movies including *Last of the Mohicans,* much of which was filmed around Chimney Rock near the oddly named town of Bat Cave.

For good commercial-free music and NPR news in and around Asheville, tune to **WNCW 88.7 FM**

Thomas Wolfe

the Blue Ridge Parkway. Surrounded by a series of flower gardens planned in part by Frederick Law Olmsted, the estate centers on a truly unbelievable French Renaissance-style mansion built in 1895. The 250-plus rooms hold everything from a palm court and a bowling alley to Napoleon's chess set to paintings by Renoir, Singer Sargent, Whistler, and others. Signs aplenty direct you to the estate, which stands just north of the I-40 exit 50 off Biltmore Avenue, across from the Historic Biltmore Village shopping mall that originally housed the estate's staff and workshops—a "model village" designed in gothic style by Richard Morris Hunt.

The rest of Asheville can't compete with the nouveau riche excess of the Biltmore Estate, and in fact it's a surprisingly homespun city, with a downtown commercial district filled with 1930s-era storefronts housing thrift stores and off-beat art galleries. One truly worthwhile place to see in downtown Asheville is the nondescript old boardinghouse where author Thomas Wolfe grew up from 1900-20, preserved exactly as it was when Wolfe lived here—peeling paint, creaking floorboards, dodgy wiring, and all. The rambling house, officially the **Thomas Wolfe National Historic Site**, 48 Spruce Street (Mon.-Sat. 9 AM-5 PM, Sunday 1-5 PM; $1) across from the monstrous modern Radisson Hotel, is perhaps the most evocative of all American literary sites. In the details and, more importantly, in general ambience, it's identical to the vivid prose descriptions of the house he called "Dixieland," the primary setting of his first and greatest novel *Look*

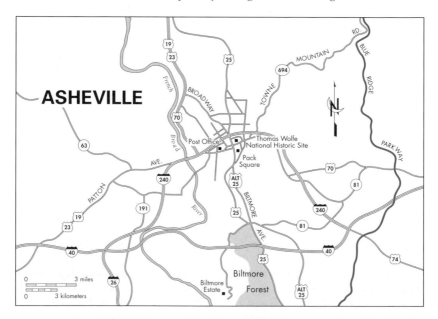

Homeward, Angel. After Wolfe's death from tuberculosis in 1938, the house was made into a shrine to Wolfe by his family, who arranged it to look as it did during his youth; one room contains his desk, typewriter, and other mementos of his life and work.

Two blocks south of the Wolfe memorial, where Broadway becomes Biltmore Avenue, **Pack Square** is the center of Asheville, surrounded by the county courthouse, the city hall, a small art museum, and the public library. This is where Thomas Wolfe's father ran a stonecutting shop, on whose porch stood the homeward-gazing angel, now recalled by a statue standing on the square's southwest corner.

Asheville Practicalities

The streets around Pack Square hold a few good places to eat, including a trio of bistro-type places with outdoor dining areas, lined up side by side around the **1896 Bistro**, at 7 S. Pack Square (828/251-1300). There are more good places around the art deco-style Grove shopping arcade west of the square, including the **Laughing Seed Cafe**, serving health-conscious "international vegetarian cuisine" to a weirdy-beardy hacky-sack slacker crowd at 40 Wall Street (828/252-3445). Best coffee is at **Bean Streets**, on Broadway a block north of Pack Square, and good beers (and free evening films) are available at **Two Moons Brew & View**, 675 Merrimon Avenue (828/236-2799), north of downtown near the UNC-Asheville campus. Live music is another Asheville specialty: the welcoming pub-cum-performance space **Be Here Now**, off Pack Square at 5 Biltmore Avenue (828/258-2071), gets nationally known indie rock, jazz, and bluegrass bands, while the **Fine Arts** cinema across the street shows the latest art-house releases.

The usual chain hotels cluster along the Interstates, and some more characterful older, neon-signed motels line old US-70 between downtown and the Blue Ridge Parkway. For a true taste of Americana, you may prefer the classic 1930s **Log Cabin Motor Court**, six miles north of Asheville off US-70 at 330 Weaverville Highway (828/645-6546).

If the Vanderbilts came to Asheville today, they'd probably stay at **Grove Park Inn Resort**, 290 Macon Avenue north of I-90 (828/252-2711 or 800/438-0050), a lovely rustic inn built in 1913 in the hills above downtown Asheville. Newer wings contain the most modern four-star conveniences, but the original lodge boasts rooms filled with authentic Roycroft furniture, the largest collection anywhere, making the Grove Park a live-in museum of arts-and-crafts style.

Asheville's long-standing relationship with visitors explains why the local minor league baseball team is called the **Asheville Tourists**. They play at retro-modern McCormick Field, a mile south of downtown; call 828/258-0428 for tickets or further information.

Novelist **F. Scott Fitzgerald** lived at Asheville's Grove Park Resort while visiting his wife Zelda, who had been committed to the Highland Hospital sanitarium, where she died in a fire in 1948.

Another of Asheville's literary lights was the short story writer **O. Henry**, who is buried in the Riverside Cemetery on Birch Street. Thomas Wolfe is buried here as well.

For further information on the Asheville area, contact the **visitor center**, 151 Haywood Street off I-240 exit 4C (828/258-6109 or 800/257-1300).

Maggie Valley

The Blue Ridge Parkway swings south from Asheville through Transylvania County on the approach to Great Smoky Mountains National Park, though you'll save an hour or more by following the I-40 freeway to the junction with US-19, which links up with the south end of the parkway. This stretch of US-19, winding through the Maggie Valley over the foothills of the Great Smokies, is a very pretty drive, and absolutely packed with roadside Americana—miniature golf courses, trout farms, souvenir shops, lookout towers alongside pancake houses, BBQ shacks . . . you name it, it's here.

One of the best of many great places to stop in Maggie Valley is the **Ghost Town in the Sky** (daily 9 AM-5 pm; $19; 828/926-1140 or 800/446-7886), a real, old Appalachian "ghost town" that's been made into an amusement park, with roller coasters, bumper cars, and all the usual suspects—high on the side of the Great Smoky Mountains. Staged gunfights, and shows featuring can-can dancers and Cherokee Indians, completes the unique spectacle.

Cherokee

West of Maggie Valley, the Blue Ridge Parkway and US-19 join up 40 miles west of Asheville at touristy Cherokee (pop. 5,971), commercial center of the 56,000-acre **Cherokee Indian Reservation**, which was established here by a small band of Cherokee Indians in 1866, long after the rest of this once mighty tribe had been forcibly exiled to Oklahoma on the Trail of Tears. Cherokee, which is home to the state's newest (and only) casino, the $100 million Harrah's, is a last gasp of commercialism at the edge of the national park, a traffic-clogged gauntlet of places where you can See Live Bears, Eat Boiled Peanuts, or Pan For Gold. Amidst the tourist-taunting sprawl, however, you'll find a couple of worthwhile stops, first of which is the **Qualla Arts and Crafts Shop** on US-441 a half-mile north of town, where you can buy or just admire the fine craftsmanship of Cherokee basketry and jewelry. Across the street, the **Museum of the Cherokee Indian** (daily 9 AM-5 PM, longer hours in summer; $4) traces tribal history, from the pre-conquest achievements—the Cherokee used a natural version of aspirin centuries before western chemists "discovered" it, for example—to their forced removal after gold was discovered here in the 1830s.

The Cherokee **visitor center** on Main Street (828/497-9195 or 800/438-1601) provides information on places to eat and on the Cherokee area's many motels and campgrounds.

For many years, Cherokee Chief Henry was known as **"The World's Most Photographed Indian,"** his image gracing countless postcards.

Just over the mountains on the Tennessee side of the Great Smokies, Dolly Parton owns, runs, and stars at **Dollywood** (800/DOLLYWOOD or 800/365-5996), the country's biggest autobiographical theme park.

One of the nicest places to stay near the Great Smokies is the mountaintop **Snowbird Mountain Lodge,** 275 Santeetlah Road (828/479-3433), south of Cherokee between Robbinsville and the first-growth hardwoods of Joyce Kilmer Memorial Forest.

Great Smoky Mountains National Park

The most popular park in the U.S., Great Smoky Mountains National Park offers a taste of wilderness to some nine million visitors annually. Knoxville, Nashville, and Atlanta are all within a two-hour drive, and day-trippers visit mostly during late October for the annual display of fall color. The park covers 520,460 acres along the 6,000-foot-high crest of the Great Smoky Mountains, so-named for the fogs that fill the deep valleys. Before the park was established its lands were extensively logged—70% of the trees had been clearcut by 1934, when the lands were protected as a national park. Fortunately, the forests have grown back to obscure any sign of past degradations, and the uncut portions form the most extensive stands of primeval forest in the eastern U.S.

Biologists estimate that some 500 native black bears live in the backcountry (and campgrounds!) of Great Smoky Mountains National Park.

The Appalachian Trail runs along the crest of the Great Smoky Mountains, crossing Newfound Gap Road at the center of the park.

The main route through the park is Newfound Gap Road (US-441), which runs northwest from Cherokee to the even more tourist-traveled Gatlinburg and Pigeon Forge in Tennessee. The road winds steeply through dense forests packed with magnificent giant hardwoods, flowering poplar, dogwood, azalea, and rhododendron, and evergreen pines and firs at the highest elevations. Where the highway reaches the crest, a spur road runs parallel to the Appalachian Trail five miles west to 6,642-foot **Clingman's Dome**, the highest point in the park, where you can take a short but steep trail up to a lookout tower.

One of the most extensive "natural" areas—unlogged, old-growth forest, full of the park's oldest and tallest trees—lies at the very center of the park, off Newfound Gap Road on the north side of the crest. Starting at the popular Chimney Tops Picnic area, the well-marked, three-quarter-mile **Cove Hardwood nature trail** winds through a sampling of the park's most stately maples and other broad-leafed trees— the ones responsible for the best of the fall colors.

Along Little River Road, west of the Sugarlands Visitor Center off US-441 at the park's northern entrance, stands another group of ancient trees. Midway along, trails lead to two marvelous waterfalls, Laurel Falls and Meigs Falls. Little River Road ends up at **Cades Cove**, where the preserved remnants of a mountain community that existed here from the early 1800s until the 1930s give a strong sense of Appalachian folkways. A church and a number of mills still stand, and interpretive staff offer guided walks and other programs explaining the history and culture of these "hillbilly" people—some 6,000 of whom used to live within the park

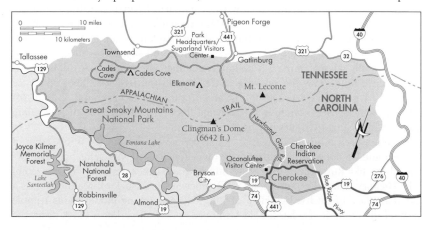

boundaries. **Bike rentals** are available at the Cades Cove campground, and you'll find plenty of opportunities for rides along the old country lanes.

Another popular park destination is **Grotto Falls**, southeast of Gatlinburg via the Roaring Fork Road, where a short flat trail to the tumbling cascade leads through lush hemlock forest—an ideal environment for mushrooms, and for the 27 different species of salamanders that slither around underfoot.

The only beds available in the park are at the historic **LeConte Lodge** (423/429-5704), built in the 1920s atop 6,593-foot Mount LeConte, and located a six-mile hike from the nearest road. There are no phones, no TVs, little privacy and no indoor plumbing, but the $75 nightly rates do come with "family-style" breakfast and dinner. Ten fairly basic **campgrounds** (no showers or hookups) operate in the Great Smokies park, with reservations taken only for the largest and most popular ones at Cades Cove, Elkmont and Smokemount (800/365-CAMP or 800/365-2267). These last three are accessible to RVs up to 35 feet long; for hikers, there are also bear-proofed backcountry shelters along the Appalachian Trail.

The many different salamanders native to the Great Smokies range from the tiny pygmy to the massive hellbender, which grows up to two feet long, head to tail. These crawling critters have earned the Great Smokies a reputation as the "Salamander Capital of the World."

One of the few radio stations you can hear in mountainous western North Carolina, Franklin's **1480 WVFC AM** plays an entertaining combination of local news and contemporary Christian country music.

For more information, or to pick up the handy brochures (35 cents each) describing the park's array of flora, fauna, trails, and other features, stop by either of the two main visitor centers (both 8 AM-4:30 PM, longer hours in summer). North of Cherokee at the south entrance, the **Oconaluftee Visitor Center** (828/497-1900) stands alongside a restored pioneer farmstead, where crafts demonstrations are given in summer. From the **Sugarlands Visitor Center** (423/436-1200), two miles south of Gatlinburg, Tennessee, you can take a short hike to Cataract Falls.

South to Georgia: Franklin

South from Cherokee and the Great Smoky Mountains, US-441 runs through the giant Nantahala National Forest, which stretches all the way to the Georgia border. It's a fast road, mostly divided four-lane freeway, passing through a fairly developed corridor of towns and small cities.

The biggest town in this part of North Carolina, Franklin (pop. 2,873) was founded in the mid-1800s on a shallow ridge overlooking the Little Tennessee River. Along with lumber milling, Franklin's main industry has long been the mining of gemstones—garnets, rubies, and sapphires—from the surrounding hills. Though mining is no longer commercially viable, many of these old mines have found new life catering to rockhound tourists, who for a small fee (around $1 per bucket, in addition to an entrance charge of around $5) can sift through gravelly ores searching for valuable finds. A half-dozen such places line Hwy-28 in the first five miles northwest of Franklin.

Franklin itself is a light industrial center, spread out around the intersection of US-441 and US-64, with a compact downtown area packed with gemstone and jewelry shops like **Ruby City**, 44 N. Main Street, which also has a small free museum. The **Hickory Ranch Restaurant**, at 126 Palmer Street a block off Main Street, is a popular place to eat fried chicken or BBQ while watching model trains rumble around the room; it also has an old-fashioned ice cream parlor. A block away, the

Franklin Motel, 223 Palmer Street (828/524-4431 or 800/433-5507), has clean, comfortable rooms and a swimming pool for under $50 a night.

US-441 races south to Georgia from Franklin, while Hwy-28/US-64 heads southeast through the heart of Transylvania County, known as the "Land of Waterfalls" because of its many cascades. The biggest of these is 13 miles from Franklin and named, for some unknown reason, **Dry Falls**. From the well-signed parking area, follow a short trail that ends up underneath and behind the impressively raging torrent, a powerful white-noise generator you can hear long before you reach it. Another waterfall, known as **Bridal Veil Falls**, is a mile south from Dry Falls. Bridal Veil is much smaller than Dry Falls, but spills right along the road; the overhang is so deep that you can drive underneath it.

Two miles south from Bridal Veil Falls, US-64 enters the resort community of **Highlands** (pop. 900). Here Hwy-106 loops back to the southwest, giving grand panoramic views over the forested foothills before rejoining US-441 across the Georgia border in Dillard.

> Between Franklin and Highlands, US-64 passes by several waterfalls and has been designated a **"Mountain Waters Scenic Byway."**

ACROSS GEORGIA

If Georgia brings to mind endless, flat cotton or peanut plantations, you'll be pleasantly surprised by the mountainous wilds of the state's northern tier. The great Appalachian ridge that runs along the East Coast has its southern foot here, high up in the forests of Rabun County, which packs natural wonders, outdoor adventures, and down-home Appalachian spirit into the state's small, isolated corner. Chattooga River whitewater—made famous by the movie *Deliverance,* and rated among the top 10 river runs in the U.S.—is the biggest draw, and sightseers can take in Chattooga's spectacular waterfalls. Christmas-tree farms, dairies, and car graveyards dot the old-time mountain towns, where rooted residents in homey cabins and old trailers grow corn in side yards and advertise "Mountain Honey for Sale" on hand-painted wooden signs.

Dillard

Just south of the North Carolina border, the highway hamlet of Dillard (pop. 199) is a mini-fiefdom of the Dillard family, whose name dates back to the 1700s in these parts. For generations, the Dillards have run a local hospitality empire based around the sprawling set of bungalows, lodges, and dining rooms all going by the name **Dillard House** (706/746-5348), on a hill above US-441 at the south edge of town. Heading up the complex is the Dillard House restaurant, famous for its all-you-can-eat country cooking: from its glass-walled patio, where diners can enjoy plates of classic country ham, fried chicken, pan-fried

> The hikers' Appalachian Trail crosses the Georgia/North Carolina border roughly 10 miles west of Dillard, then veers southeast, coming to a finale at the 3,782-foot summit of Springer Mountain, where a photogenic sign marks the end (or the beginning, since most of the 200 or so annual thru-hikers travel south to north) of the 2,144-mile trail.

Chattooga River whitewater rafting

The rocky crest of Black Rock Mountain marks the eastern **Continental Divide**—from here waters part to follow a path to either the Atlantic Ocean or the Gulf of Mexico.

trout, vegetables, cornbread, and assorted relishes and desserts. The legendary institution may today impress you as more institution than legend—bus tours dominate the clientele—but you never leave hungry. Rooms are around back—in low-slung lodges scattered near a swimming pool and tennis courts; prices hover around $60.

In addition to the rambling inn, the family oligarchy operates a row of roadside businesses off US-441, selling collectible and keepsake souvenirs.

Black Rock Mountain

At the wind-worn summit of 3,640-foot Black Rock Mountain, a flagstone terrace looks out over a grand Appalachian panorama: if there's no fog, you can see clear to the South Carolina piedmont 80 miles away and as far as the Great Smokies to the north. The highest state park in Georgia now occupies the slope's legendary mountain, offering hiking trails and accommodations in addition to the splendid vistas. Set off in a ring at the top of the mountain, 10 spacious cottages are removed from lowland civilization—no phones, no TVs, just fireplaces and porch rockers. The cottages cost $55-70 a night, sleep up to 10 people, and are availabe for rent year-round—a nice snowy winter retreat. There's also a pair of $12-a-night campgrounds.

Black Rock Mountain State Park is three miles north of Clayton, well-signed to the west of US-441. For information, or for reservations for the cabins or the campgrounds, contact the park **visitor center** (706/746-2141) near the summit.

Foxfire Museum

Tucked away on the west side of US-441 just south of the turnoff to Black Mountain State Park, the modest Foxfire Museum (Mon.-Fri. 10 AM-4 PM; donations; 706/746-5318) displays a crowded collection of Appalachian arts and crafts. The museum is part of a radical (for rural Georgia) cultural and educational movement that began here in the mid-1960s when local schoolteacher Eliot Wigginton, frustrated in attempts to motivate his uninspired high-school students, assigned them the task of interviewing their elders about how things were in "the old days." The students, inspired with the newly discovered richness of their Appalachian heritage, assembled the written interviews into a magazine, which they named *Foxfire* after a luminescent local fungus.

The magazine expanded to a series of *Foxfire* books, and more than eight million copies sold worldwide. The collection exhaustively documented fading Appalachian folkways, and the program's twofold success—educational innovation and folklife preservation—further broadened as the then-emerging back-to-the-land movement seized upon these books as vital how-to manuals for subsistence farming, cookery, animal husbandry, and crafts making from found materials. The Foxfire organization still runs classes and summer programs around the country and on a 110-acre campus in the hills above the museum.

Mountain City

Passing through Mountain City (pop. 784) at the end of the day, drivers watch the monolith of Black Rock Mountain impose an early twilight on the broad valley to its east. Behind scruffy roadside cabins with their lean-to signs, the granite mountain's shadow slowly reaches past grazing black-and-white cows and tractors parked between haystacks.

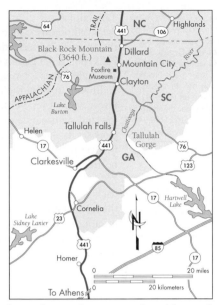

The town itself stretches along US-441 for a few miles south from the Foxfire Museum, but the main attraction is the highway on York House Road, beyond the cows and hay and over the gully bridge, where you'll find trim white **York House** (706/746-2068) banked against the forest wall. This historic inn has been open for business since 1896, and not much has changed since then, except the addition of indoor plumbing in every room; rates run $64-69 for a comfortable room with a continental breakfast.

Clayton

The downhome mountain community of Clayton (pop. 1,613) is the largest town in Rabun County, and a good base of operations for excursions into the wild forest and Chattooga River areas to the east. Main Street, a three-block length of wooden storefronts on a sunny rise just west of US-411, still looks like you could hitch a horse at the curb to do your trading and salooning. The **Old Clayton Inn** (706/782-7722) at the center of town has been open for a century or so, though it's been tidied up considerably in the years since Burt Reynolds and crew stayed here while filming *Deliverance* on the raging Chattooga.

For road-trippers, the best reason to plan a stop in Clayton is to sample the woodstove cookery at the **Green Shutters Restaurant**, just over a mile from town on S. Main Street (old US-441). Three family-style meals a day, accompanied by cinnamon rolls, sweet potato bread, buttermilk biscuits, and corn muffins, are served in a small but cozy downstairs dining room  looking out across a screened-in verandah at apple orchards and pasturelands. Unfortunately, the Green Shutters keeps limited hours (open daily except Tuesday 8-10 AM, 11 AM-2 PM, and 5-9 PM; 706/782-3342), so plan your trip accordingly. If the Green Shutters isn't serving, the **Clayton Cafe** on Main Street downtown slings downhome breakfasts, burgers, and other basic diner fare.

The enthusiastic folks at the Rabun County Chamber of Commerce run a resourceful **visitor center** (706/782-4812) on US-441 north of town.

Following US-76 12 miles west from Clayton brings you to postage-stamp-sized **Moccasin Creek State Park,** Georgia's smallest state park. Nestled invitingly on the shores of Lake Burton off Hwy-197, it offers good fishing, a campground (706/947-3194), and family-style food at LaPrade's across the street.

Slicing through the Appalachian wilderness at the junction of three states, the **Chattooga River** rates among the nation's top 10 whitewater river adventures, attracting some 100,000 visitors a year to Rabun County for rafting, canoeing, kayaking, tubing, swimming, fishing, and riverside hiking. The "Wild and Scenic" river was seen in the movie *Deliverance,* based on the book by Georgia poet and novelist **James Dickey;** ever since the movie was released, authorities have been pulling bodies out of the river—not toothless mountaineers but overconfident river-runners who underestimate the whitewater's power.

In the mountains northwest of Clarkesville, 15 miles along Hwy-17 and Hwy-75, the tiny town of **Helen** (pop. 355) turned itself into a tourist draw in 1969 by remodeling all the buildings in mock-Bavarian decor and repaving the streets in cobblestones.

Tallulah Falls

Balanced precariously over the precipitous gorge that once held the thundering cascades of the Tallulah River, tiny Tallulah Falls (pop. 147) has an illustrious history. As word of the natural wonder spread, crowds were drawn to the breathtaking sight, and by the turn of the century Tallulah Falls was a fashionable resort, with several elite hotels and boardinghouses catering to lowland sightseers. But fortunes changed once the power company set its sights on harnessing water power for hydroelectricity. Over public objections, the completed dam (which sits at the north end of town, directly beneath the new bridge that carries US-441 over the river) slowed the water—and the crowds—to a trickle. Despite the still-impressive sight of the now-dry gorge, the resort ambience faded, and Tallulah Falls reverted to a rustic mountain community. Recently, after decades of talk about restoring the gorge's former glory, the power company agreed to test the waters and send the Tallulah River spilling through the gorge once again.

Tallulah Gorge

The dramatic, sheer walls of Tallulah Gorge have both haunted and attracted people for centuries. The wary Cherokee heeded legends that warriors who ventured in never returned, and many a curious settler had a waterfall or pool named in his honor—posthumously, after an untimely slip.

Tallulah Gorge is best seen from the mile-long scenic route (old US-441), which loops off east of the modern highway. Drivers can pull over at numerous parking areas and take one of several rough trails along the gorge's rim, though the best views are from the historic **Tallulah Point Overlook** (daily 9 AM-7 PM; free), a privately owned concession stand midway along the loop. You can stretch your legs or rent mountain bikes here ($25 a day; 706/754-4318; maps, water bottles, and helmets are included in the price).

Whether or not the waters are flowing, when you take in the sight of Tallulah Gorge, imagine walking a tightrope suspended 1,200 feet above the ground across its breadth. "Professor Leon" managed it (despite a stumble) in 1886; in 1970, the flying Karl Wallenda replicated the feat, walking across on a wire suspended from the Tallulah Point Overlook, where postcards and photos document his effort.

Clarkesville

The charming little town of Clarkesville (pop. 1,151) retains a sophistication dating back to its founding over 150 years ago by lowland Carolina and coastal Georgian plantation families seeking refuge from the oppressive summer heat. Best known as the home of the renowned country resort, Glen-Ella Springs Inn, Clarkesville sits at the lower slope of a river valley that stretches northwest to the faux-Bavarian town of Helen, and is surrounded by countryside perfect for a leisurely drive or bike tour past an old mill here, a covered bridge there, and old-time country stores in wooden cabins.

Clarkesville tucks urbane delights into its rustic country setting, with over 40 buildings, most of them former summer homes, listed on the National Register of Historic Places. Downtown, three blocks of wooden storefronts, centering around a shaded plaza where numerous festivals take place, hold cafes and crafts shops. From a wooden cabin a mile south of town on Washington Street (old US-441), **Adam's Rib** serves a hearty breakfast of homemade biscuits and gravy, country ham, steak and eggs, and hot cakes. Come back at lunch for their buffet or specialty barbecued pork, beef ribs, and chicken.

The **Charm House** (706/754-9347) sits on a small knoll above US-441 at 108 N. Washington Street, and offers B&B lodging in a historic Greek Revival mansion within a short walk of the square. Mid-week rooms cost $95; the $165/night weekend rates include gourmet Southern dinners.

For further listings or more general **information**, contact the chamber of commerce (706/778-4654).

Hundred-year-old **Glen-Ella Springs Inn,** eight miles north of Clarkesville on Bear Gap Road off US-441 (706/754-7295), is northern Georgia's premier country inn. Set on 17 lush acres, the historic two-story lodge holds 16 guest rooms, each of which opens to a porch with rocking chairs; rates run $125-175 a night for two people.

Cornelia, the southernmost Appalachian town, is known for its **Giant Apple Monument** on Hwy-23 downtown, a tribute to the primary local industry.

On US-441 some six miles north of I-85, the tiny town of **Homer** has hosted the "World's Largest Easter Egg Hunt" every Easter Sunday for the past 40 years. For details, phone 706/677-2108.

Detour: Athens

If you've got the time and inclination, one of Georgia's most enjoyable destinations is just a slight veer to the east off our route: Athens, the coolest college town in the South. Famed in recent years for its lively music scene which gave the world the "alternative rock" bands B-52s and R.E.M., Athens is the home of the University of Georgia, whose Greek Revival campus sits at the center of town, bordered on the north by a half-dozen blocks of cafes, bars, and book and record stores. Athens also holds a classic Road Trip destination: **"The Tree That Owns Itself,"** a second-generation mighty oak tree standing on a small circle of land at the corner of Finley and Dearing Streets west of campus, whose legal autonomy earned it a place in *Ripley's Believe or Not!*.

The main music venue is the R.E.M.-related **40 Watt Club**, 285 W. Washington Street (706/549-7871). Good cheap BBQ is available on the east side of town at **Weaver D's**, 1016 E. Broad Street, whose enigmatic slogan "Automatic for the People" was enshrined as an R.E.M. album title.

For listings of hotels or for more general **information**, contact the Athens **visitor center** (706/546-1805 or 800/653-0603).

On to Atlanta: Stone Mountain

From the foothills of northern Georgia, it's only an hour by freeway southwest to Atlanta, the cultural and commercial center of the New South, and a fascinating (and fun) place to explore. Unfortunately, Atlanta is surrounded by miles and miles of mega-freeway sprawl, so you'll have to endure some of the country's craziest driving to get there.

From Athens, Hwy-316 merges into I-85 for the quickest route there, but for a more interesting route follow old US-78 southeast, approaching Atlanta by way of **Stone Mountain**, 16 miles east of downtown. A Confederate Mount Rushmore, Stone Mountain (daily 6 AM-midnight; 770/498-5690 or 800/317-2007) consists of the twenty-times-larger-than-life figures of Robert E. Lee, "Stonewall" Jackson and Jefferson Davis carved into a 800-foot-high hump of granite. At the base are 3,200 acres of the tackier tourist traps going (riverboat cruises, a scenic railroad, a cable car "Skylift" to the summit—all of which charge separate fees), plus the brand new Olympic velodrome, and Atlanta's best **campground.**

ATLANTA SURVIVAL GUIDE

METROPOLIS OF THE SOUTH, WITH A YOUTHFUL and energetic population rapidly approaching three million, Atlanta has emerged as one of the most dynamic communities in the country. State capital of Georgia, and world headquarters of those dual flagships of American culture, Coca-Cola and CNN, Atlanta is the financial and cultural heart of the "New South," having recovered from total destruction during the Civil War (remember *Gone with the Wind*, which was written by Atlanta native Margaret Mitchell?). While not all its residents are as prosperous as Ted Turner, the low wages paid here are matched by proportionally lower rents, and Atlanta rarely feels particularly poverty-stricken or dangerous, certainly not when compared to the post-industrial despair of many northern U.S. cities. In general people here are gracious and welcoming, so much so they could seem like walking parodies of Southern hospitality—if they weren't so genuinely sincere.

Atlanta began as a railroad junction (its original name was simply "Terminus"), and the early streetscape has been preserved and restored in **Underground Atlanta**, a warren of shopfronts underneath the center of the modern city. Abandoned in the 1920s, the buildings here were restored by the Rouse Company in the late 1980s to form a successful shopping and entertainment district, with numerous plaques and artworks commemorating the area's past. Above ground, the **World of Coca Cola** (Mon.-Sat. 10 AM-8 PM, Sunday noon-5 PM; $4) traces the history of the all-American beverage, while two blocks to the east stands the **Georgia State Capitol** (Mon.-Fri. 8 AM-5:30 PM; free). The **High Museum**, which has its main collection uptown, has a smaller gallery downtown in the Georgia Pacific Building at 133 Peachtree Street (Mon.-Fri. 11 AM-5 PM; free), which focuses primarily on folk art and photography.

A mile east of downtown, the **Martin Luther King, Jr. National Historic Site**, 522 Auburn Avenue (daily 9 AM-5 PM; free; 404/331-3920), sits at the heart of the predominantly black "Sweet Auburn" neighborhood. The four-block area holds many important landmarks in the life of Dr. King: his birth-place at 501 Auburn Avenue; the Ebenezer Baptist Church, 407 Auburn Avenue, where he, his father, and his grandfather all served as pastor; and his tomb, emblazoned with the words "Free at Last, Free at Last," sitting on the grounds of the **Center for Non-Violent Social Change**, 449 Auburn Avenue.

On the west side of downtown, the powerhouse **Atlanta Braves** (800/326-4000) play at Turner Field, "The Ted."

Practicalities

Atlanta's airport, **Hartsfield International**, one of the busiest in the country, is a dozen miles south of downtown Atlanta, at the junction of the I-85 and I-285 freeways. All
the usual rental car companies have branches there, and the Atlanta Airport Shuttle vans supplement the Metro Atlanta Rapid Transit Authority (MARTA) **trains**, the latter of which are great if you're traveling light, taking just 15 minutes to take you downtown. Taxis cost around $15.

The I-75/I-85 freeway cuts through the center of Atlanta, while the I-20 freeway skirts its southern edge. Sliced by freeways and spreading Los Angeles-like in a low level ooze of mini-malls and tract houses, Atlanta's outlying areas are impossible to make sense of, but the downtown area is compact and manageable—much better on foot than in a car, as parking can be hard to find. If it's too hot for a lengthy stroll, ride the well organized rail and bus system operated by MARTA, (404/848-4711). Note also that seemingly every other thoroughfare includes the word "Peachtree" in its name, so check twice before getting completely lost.

Centrally located places to stay include **Days Inn—Downtown**, 300 Spring Street (404/523-1144 or 800/325-2525), with clean comfortable rooms at downtown's best rates (doubles from $75), and the **Days Inn—Peachtree**, 683 Peachtree Street (404/874-9200 or 800/325-2525), a historic 1920s building upgraded with all modern conveniences, in a handy Midtown location, across from the landmark Fox Theatre; doubles here cost $60-75 night. The **Westin Peachtree Plaza**, 210 Peachtree Street (404/659-1400 or 800/228-3000), is the world's tallest hotel, rising 73 stories above downtown, packed with all the expected facilities, including a revolving rooftop restaurant. Doubles cost $175-275.

East of downtown, the **Woodruff Inn**, 223 Ponce de Leon (404/875-9449), is a well-maintained c. 1915 Midtown house offering $65-a-night B&B rooms, across the street from Mary Mac's Tea Room. The Woodruff doubles as the **Atlanta International HI Hostel** (404/875-2882), where dorm beds cost around $14—an ideal combination for hungry budget travelers.

(continues on next page)

The Sweet Auburn neighborhood has some very good places, like the **Beautiful Restaurant**, 397 Auburn Avenue (404/233-0080), serving soul food best taken in conjunction with a visit to the adjacent Ebenezer Baptist Church. **Mary Mac's Tea Room**, 224 Ponce de Leon Avenue (404/875-4337), is known throughout the South for its large portions of down-home fare such as jambalaya, catfish, and fried chicken. The menu changes daily, and always includes some great desserts, such as the peanut-rich Carter Custard, named for the globe-trotting former President. On the same street, the **Majestic Diner**, 1031 Ponce de Leon Avenue (404/875-0276), is a large and lively 1940s-style cafe, open 24 hours for great waffles, burgers and one of Georgia's finest cups of java. The place to go at 4 AM, when the bars and clubs of the nearby Virginia Highland and Little Five Points districts close, and people unwind with a piece of apple pie.

One last Atlanta landmark deserves mention: **The Varsity**, 61 North Avenue (404/881-1706), near Georgia Tech alongside I-75, the world's largest drive-in, serving up very good chili dogs, onion rings, and more Coca-Cola than anywhere else on this earth.

The usual barrage of tourist information can be had from the Atlanta Convention and Visitors Bureau, 233 Peachtree Street (404/521-6600). Daily newspapers are the morning *Constitution* and the evening *Journal;* the free weekly is aptly titled *Creative Loafing*, which captures the laid-back feel of Atlanta's alternative arts and entertainment scene.

COASTAL EAST COAST

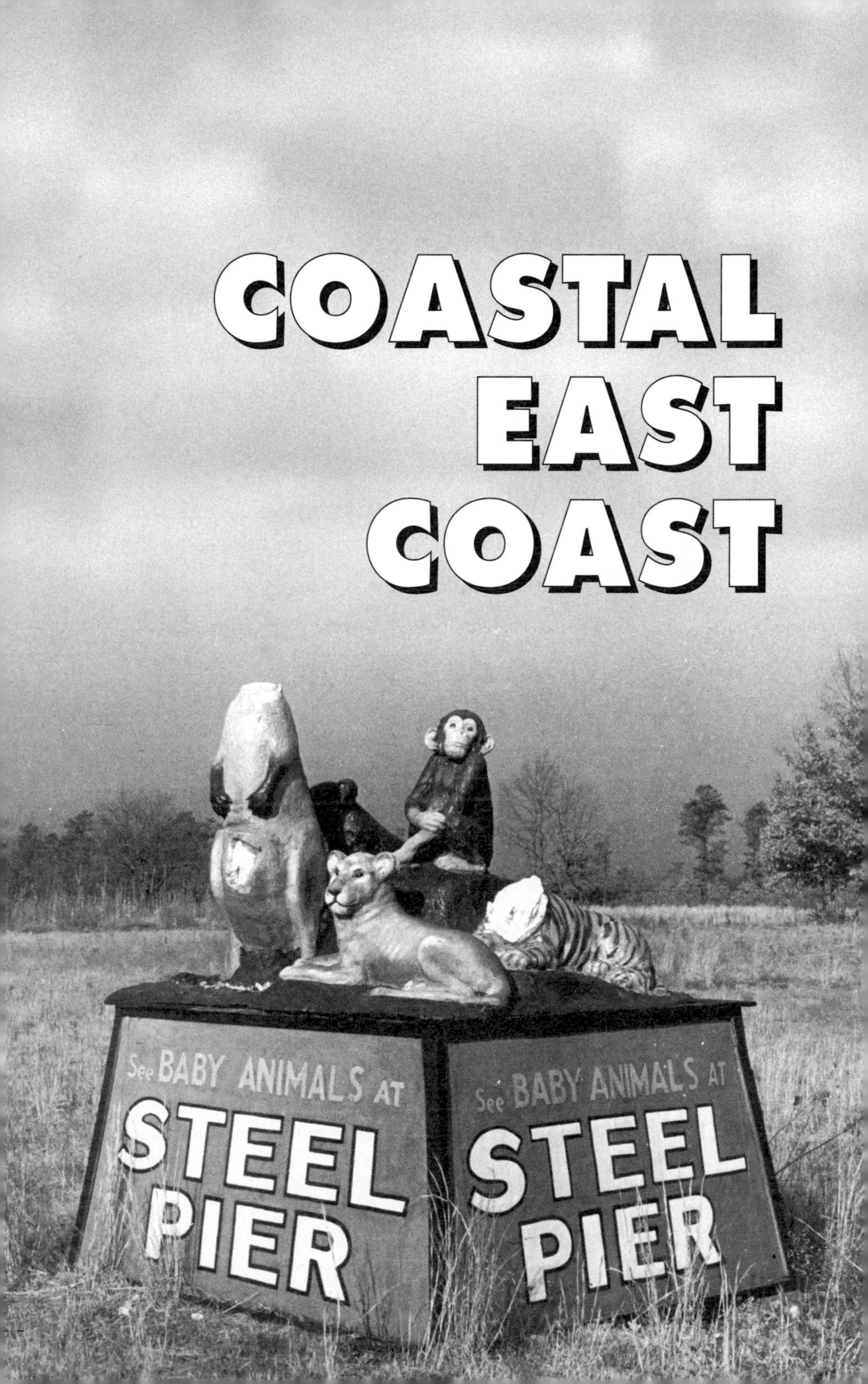

COASTAL EAST COAST

If your impressions of the East Coast come from driving along the I-95 corridor through nearly nonstop urban and industrial sprawl, following our Coastal East Coast route will open your eyes to a whole other world. Alternating between wildly differing beach resort areas and lengthy stretches of pristine coastal wilderness, the route runs along nearly 1,500 miles of two-lane country roads, within earshot if not sight of the Atlantic Ocean almost the entire way. In place of the grimy concrete and soulless nether world of the interstate, this route passes through innumerable quirky seaside towns and timeless old fishing villages, interspersed with huge swathes of beaches, wetlands, and woodlands that have hardly changed since the first explorers laid eyes on them four centuries ago.

Starting in the north at the glitzy casino resorts of Atlantic City, and winding up in the south at wild Key West, the Southernmost town in the USA—this route truly offers something for everyone. Those searching for photogenic lighthouses or beachcombing solitude will love the undeveloped and usually deserted strands that stretch for miles along the low-lying islands that make up most of the coast, much of which, as at Assateague Island or Cape Hatteras, has been protected as national seashore parks. In contrast, the many beach resorts that dot the in-between areas vary from the grand Victorian charms of Cape May to the funky old Coney Island-style attractions of Ocean City and Myrtle Beach, with their boardwalks full of roller coasters, wax museums, and saltwater taffy stands.

Alongside the contemporary attractions are many evocative historic sites, including such unique places as Roanoke, where the first English-speaking colony in North America vanished without a trace in 1587. Lying south of the Mason-Dixon Line for almost all of its length, the route also visits many important Civil War sites, including Fort Sumter, where the first shots were fired, and the vital naval battlegrounds at Hampton Roads at the mouth of Chesapeake Bay. Midway along, we also pass one of the key sites of modern history, the windy sand dunes at Kitty Hawk where the Wright Brothers first proved that humans could fly.

Though this East Coast route will bring you to many well-known sights, its real attraction is the traveling, stopping off for fried chicken or barbecue at one of the hundreds of roadside stands, watching the shrimp boats pull into a sleepy dock and unload their day's catch, or simply chatting with locals at the general store or post office in a town that may not even be on the map.

ALONG THE NEW JERSEY SHORE

Since the New Jersey shore is so close to the major population centers of the East Coast, it's not surprising that New Jersey has among the busiest and most densely developed stretches of coastline in the country. It is surprising, however, that beyond the boardwalk amusements and flashy gambling casinos of **Atlantic City**, the New Jersey shore offers a whole lot more. As with most of the East Coast, the "shoreline" is actually a series of barrier islands separated from the mainland by wildlife-rich estuaries; these provide fishing and birdwatching opportunities, as well as a break from the ceaseless commercial and residential development along the ocean beaches. Bustling in summer, these beach-front communities—starting with **Margate** near Atlantic City, and running south through vibrant **Wildwood** before winding up at the dainty Victorian-era beach resort of **Cape May**—offer something for everyone, all within a 100-mile stretch of shoreline.

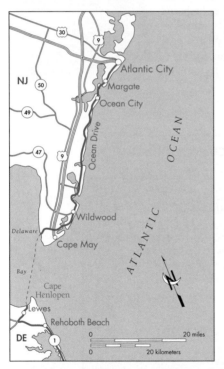

Atlantic City

The world-famous beach resort of Atlantic City has ridden the ups and downs of history. Home of the world's oldest beachfront boardwalk and the first pleasure pier, Atlantic City also spawned the picture postcard and the Miss America beauty contest. Perhaps most significant of all, the street names for Monopoly were taken from Atlantic City, although the city's layout bears little resemblance to the board game (and there's no "Get Out of Jail Free" deals, either).

Atlantic City reached its peak at the turn of the 20th century, when thousands of city dwellers flocked there each weekend. Later on, as automobiles and airplanes brought better beaches and more exotic locales within reach of New York and Philly vacationers, Atlantic City went into a half-century of decline until the 1970s, when **gambling** was legalized and millions of dollars flowed into the local economy from speculating real-estate developers. First and foremost of these was Donald Trump, whose name is emblazoned on four of Atlantic City's five largest casino/hotels, including the massive **Taj Mahal**, which nearly cost him his fortune.

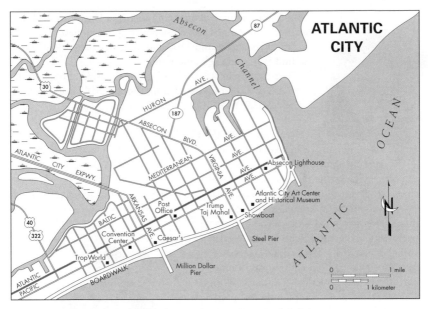

ATLANTIC CITY

These days the boardwalk of Atlantic City (pop. 38,000) has been transformed from a derelict relic into a glitzy gambling resort, attracting some 35 million annual visitors, and millions of dollars daily to its casinos. The clattering of slot machines and the buzz of the craps tables continues 24 hours a day year-round. The **Boardwalk**, backed by a wall of 25-story casino/hotels, is still the main focus, running along the beach for over two miles from **TropWorld** in the south to the **Showboat** (which has free parking). Few of the remaining piers offer much of interest. **Ocean One**, located opposite Caesar's casino at the foot of Arkansas Avenue, is an anodyne shopping mall on the site of the legendary Million Dollar Pier. Only the rebuilt Steel Pier holds the traditional seaside rides and arcade games. It's located opposite Trump's Taj Mahal at the foot of Pennsylvania Avenue. At the heart of Atlantic City, on the Boardwalk a block south of Park Place, stands the stalwart art deco **Convention Center**. The largest auditorium in the world when it was built, the convention center seats 22,000 and still houses a massive pipe organ, the console of which is on display in the lobby.

Besides comprising Atlantic City's main attractions, the casinos hold most of the places to eat, apart from the dozens of fast-food stands along the Boardwalk. That said, a couple of old favorites stand out from the seedy crowd of ramshackle businesses that fill the nearby streets. One is the birthplace of the "submarine" sandwich, the chrome **White House Sub Shop**, open until midnight every day at 2301 Arctic Avenue; at the other end of the aesthetic and budgetary spectrum is **Dock's Oyster House** at 2405 Atlantic Avenue, a white-linen, dinner-only restaurant that's been serving great seafood since 1871. Except for a number of seedy motels and

Large parts of Atlantic City—basically everything outside the casinos—are still derelict and more than a little dangerous. Be careful when exploring the city, and don't wander around after dark.

Heading south from Atlantic City, the 70-mph Garden State Turnpike runs inland while the slower but more engaging **Ocean Drive** follows local roads along the coastline over a series of five bridges, each charging a 50-cent toll.

$75-a-night national chains (**Comfort Inn, Days Inn, Holiday Inn**, etc.), the casinos also monopolize accommodation options —expect to pay around $100 a night, since bargains are hard to find even midweek, midwinter.

For complete listings and more detailed information, contact the Atlantic City **visitors center**, 2314 Pacific Avenue (800/BOARDWALK or 800/262-7392).

Margate: Lucy the Elephant

Immediately south of Atlantic City, tidy Margate (pop. 8,400) fans out along the shore, its solidly suburban streets lined by grand houses. Margate utterly lacks the reckless seaside qualities of its larger neighbor, but does include one classic remnant of the Jersey shore's glory days: Lucy the Elephant (daily 10 AM-4 PM in summer, limited hours rest of the year; $2). The six-story wood-and-tin pachyderm, a curiosity built by real-estate speculators in the 1880s to draw customers to their newly laid out community, looms over the beach at 9200 Atlantic Avenue. The landmark architectural folly was used around the turn of the century as a tavern and a hotel, and now holds a small museum of local history. Visitors walk through the museum on the way up to an observation deck, which is disguised as a canopied seat on Lucy's back.

Ever in need of repair, Lucy is kept alive by donations, and sales of Lucy souvenirs in the small gift shop.

Lucy the Elephant

Ocean Drive: Ocean City and Wildwood

A series of local roads collectively known as Ocean Drive runs along the south Jersey coast, passing through a number of family-oriented beach resorts, starting at Ocean City, "The Greatest Family Resort For a Vacation, or a Lifetime," 10 miles south of Atlantic City. Ocean City (pop. 15,500) was founded as a religious retreat in the late 1870s, and feels oddly suburban away from the beachfront boardwalk area, where the wonderful **Wonderland Pier** (daily noon-midnight, June-Sept. only; free admission, fee for each ride) at 6th Street has over 30 rides, including a giant Ferris wheel, a 1920s carousel, and much more. A block south, you can cool off on a hot summer's day at **Gillian's Water Wonderland**.

To enjoy a day on the sands at many of New Jersey's beaches, you need to buy (and wear) a **beach tag**, which costs around $2 a day and is available at local tourist offices, shops, and fast-food stands.

Vacation homes, marinas, and miniature golf courses line the shore for the next 20 miles, reaching a peak at raucous Wildwood, which houses dozens of nightclubs and New Jersey's biggest beachfront amusement parks. The largest of all,

Mariners Landing on the pier at Schellenger Avenue, has 35 rides including the largest Ferris wheel on the East Coast. At 25th Street is Morey's Pier, which has a miniature-golf course that takes you through the history of the New Jersey shore. A little farther south is Morey's Adventure Pier, which has the USA's only wooden roller coaster built on a pier. All three of these are jointly owned by the Morey family, prime movers behind Wildwood's retro-rediscovery, and an all-ride, all-pier pass costs only $30 for a full day's fun—over 100 rides, at little more than 25 cents a go. Call 609/522-3900 for further information.

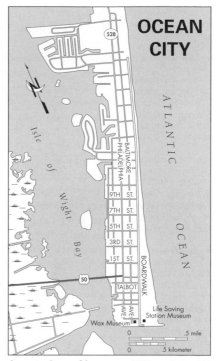

Besides roller coasters, Wildwood also boasts an extensive collection of 1950s roadside architecture—mainly motel after motel, all sporting exuberant Las Vegas-style neon signs—which has inspired Wildwood to bet its future popularity not on casinos but on the public's nostalgic love for the architectural equivalent of lounge music. You can stay the night in one of these classic "Doo Wop" motels—like the Mango Motel, 209 E. Spicer Avenue (609/522-2067), or the Lollipop Motel, 2300 Atlantic Avenue (609/729-2800)—or stop for a meal at the chrome-and-glass Ernie's Diner on Atlantic Avenue a block north of the main pier.

For more details of places to stay and things to do, contact the Wildwood visitor center (800/WW-BY-SEA or 800/992-9732).

Wildwood's local history museum, at 3907 Pacific Avenue, is worth a look for its one unique feature: the **National Marbles Hall of Fame,** featuring thousands of glass balls and more marble-shooting paraphernalia than you've ever seen.

Cape May

A world away from the carnival atmosphere of the other shore resorts, Cape May, the oldest and most serene of the New Jersey beach towns, sits at the southern tip of the state. First settled in the early 1600s, Cape May's glory years ran from the 1850s to the 1890s as an upper-crust summer resort, when it rivaled Newport, Rhode Island, as the destination of choice for the power brokers of Philadelphia and New York City.

A few modern motels and mini-golf courses spread along Cape May's broad beaches, while the compact downtown district retains all its overwrought Victorian splendor. Century-old cottages now house cafes, boutiques, and art

In the mid-1990s, Wildwood tried to cash in on Atlantic City's gambling wealth by signing up a displaced Native American tribe to run a small casino. However, things didn't work out as planned, and the tribe eventually filed suit, claiming legal ownership of the entire city, and all of coastal New Jersey.

To take the pulse of the Jersey shore's nightlife, tune to **WZML 100.7 FM,** which advertises nightly events and plays a proven mix of alternative rock hits, from Lou Reed to R.E.M.

The **Wetlands Institute** (609/368-1211) five miles north of Wildwood, at 1075 Stone Harbor Boulevard, is one of the best places to experience the abundant natural life of the New Jersey shore. An observation tower looking over 6,000 acres of saltwater marshland provides excellent birdwatching opportunities, and there's also a museum with a touch-tank and aquarium.

galleries, and it seems every other building has been converted into a quaint B&B. The town's ornate gingerbread mansions were constructed in the aftermath of a disastrous 1878 fire; among the better examples is the elaborate **Emlen Physick House,** eight blocks north of downtown at 1048 Washington Street, designed by noted Philadelphia architect Frank Furness. It now houses the nonprofit, preservation-oriented **Mid-Atlantic Center for the Arts** and is open as a **museum** of late Victorian life (daily 10 AM-3 PM in summer, weekends only in winter; $5; 609/884-5404).

Pick up walking-tour maps of some of the town's 600 listed historic buildings at the **Cape May Welcome Center,** housed in an onion-domed former church downtown at 405 Lafayette Street (609/884-9562). The center also carries brochures on Cape May's many architecturally magnificent **bed and breakfasts,** including the mansard-roofed **Queen Victoria** at 102 Ocean Street (609/884-8702), the **White Dove,** 619 Hughes Street (609/884-0613), and the **Mainstay Inn,** 735 Columbia Avenue (609/884-8690). Cape May's oldest and most atmospheric place to stay is the Southern gothic **Chalfonte Hotel,** located at 301 Howard Street (609/884-8409). What the Chalfonte lacks in air-conditioning and other modern conveniences it more than makes up for with a bank of rocking chairs, full breakfasts, and huge, down-home dinners.

Places to eat, including a dozen or so bakeries, cafes, restaurants and bars, can be found along the pedestrian-friendly few blocks of Washington Street at the center of town. The best seafood restaurants, naturally enough, are near the marina on the north edge of town, off US-9.

CAPE MAY-LEWES FERRY

Running between the tip of the New Jersey shore and the heart of the Delaware coast, the Cape May-Lewes Ferry carries cars and passengers on a 70-minute ride across Delaware Bay. The trip costs $20 for a car and one passenger, plus $6.50 for each additional passenger. Bikes are $7, $12.50 RT. Schedules change seasonally, with boats leaving about every two hours in summer and every three hours in winter. For up-to-date times and other **information,** call 609/886-9699, 800/64-FERRY or 800/643-3779; **reservations** ($3; call 800/717-7245) are a very good idea but must be booked at least one day ahead of time.

ALONG THE DELAWARE SHORE

Across Delaware Bay from Cape May, the Delaware shore is considerably quieter and more peaceful than New Jersey's. Both shores, originally settled by Scandinavian whalers who established port colonies here in the early 1600s, share a common history. But because the Delaware shore is that much farther from the urban centers, it has been spared the rampant over-development of much of the rest of the coast. Nevertheless, Delaware's statewide population of half a million doubles in summer as visitors from Baltimore and Washington, D.C. descend upon its coastal resorts, from historic **Lewes** to lively **Rehoboth Beach** to the untouched sands of **Delaware Seashore State Park**, stretching south to the Maryland border.

Lewes and Cape Henlopen

Sitting at the southern lip of Delaware Bay, Lewes is a sportfishing center that traces its roots back to 1631, when it was settled by the Dutch West India Company as a whaling port. Though this colony lasted only two years, Lewes calls itself the "First Town in the First State," commemorating its history in the false-gabled brick **Zwannendael Museum** at the center of town (Tues.-Sat. 10 AM-4:30 PM, Sunday 1:30-4:30 PM; free). Lewes also harbors huge sand dunes, a fine stretch of beach, and a **campground** with showers in 3,000-acre Cape Henlopen State Park, east of town at the mouth of Delaware Bay. Expect relative peace and quiet here, since most visitors, arriving off the Cape May ferry, simply rush through Lewes to the beach resorts farther south.

Rehoboth Beach

Fronting on the open Atlantic and just eight miles south of Lewes, Rehoboth Beach, whose biblical name means "room enough," was founded in the 1870s when church groups bought beachfront land, established the town, and extended a railroad line south from Lewes. With its small but lively **Funland Amusement Park**, a tidy boardwalk running along the broad beach, and only a short strip of T-shirt shops and arcades lining Rehoboth Avenue at the center of town, Rehoboth has retained a small-town feel despite the many thousands of bureaucrats and power brokers who descend upon the place during the summer, escaping the sweltering summers of Washington, D.C.

Ever wonder what happens to all those pumpkins that don't get bought by Halloween? In Lewes, they end up as fodder for a unique competition, the "Punkin' Chunkin'," in which the helpless gourds get launched hundreds, even thousands of feet through the air by a variety of mechanical devices. Thousands turn out for the event, which is usually held the first weekend in November; call 302/645-8273 for details.

The town's profusion of very good (and very expensive) restaurants includes the outrageously kitsch **La La Land** at 22 Wilmington Avenue, a block south of the main drag. Unless money's no object, you might prefer to feed at more humble places like **Boudreaux's BBQ**, across the street at 17 Wilmington Avenue. There are also the more mainstream delights of **Thrashers French Fries**, and sundry beer-and-burger stands along the Boardwalk.

Places to stay include a barrage of $100-and-up-a-night B&Bs and motels, and old-fashioned guest houses like the **Gladstone Inn**, 3 Olive Drive (302/227-2641), with rocking chairs on a cozy front porch that's just 20 yards from the beach. Doubles here cost around $65 a night, with a shared bathroom.

For more detailed information, stop in at the Rehoboth **visitor center**, in the old train depot at 501 Rehoboth Avenue (302/227-2233 or 800/441-1329).

Delaware Seashore State Park

South from Rehoboth stretches one of the most pristine lengths of beach on the northern East Coast: Delaware Seashore State Park, which contains 10 miles of open beach with golden-flecked white sand, and acres of marshland estuary, thronged in season with migrating birds—and birdwatchers. (Fishermen, too.) The park's many beaches are all easily accessible from beachfront Hwy-1.

Beachfront resort towns are at either end of the park: **Dewey Beach** in the north draws a younger, collegiate crowd while **Bethany Beach** in the south attracts families. Approaching Maryland, an 1858 lighthouse, on the bay side of the highway, marks the Mason-Dixon Line and state border.

ALONG MARYLAND'S EASTERN SHORE

Maryland, the most oddly shaped of the lower 48 states, shares the broad Eastern Shore peninsula with Delaware and a small piece of Virginia. The inland area along the Chesapeake Bay with its many inlets and tributary rivers is filled with dozens of small colonial-era towns and fishing villages, while the Atlantic Coast is completely taken up by two very different beasts: the gloriously kitschy beach resort of **Ocean City** and the untrammelled wilds of **Assateague Island National Seashore**. Heading inland around Assateague, the highway passes by a number of historic small towns, including captivating **Snow Hill**.

Running west from Ocean City across the Eastern Shore, and across the country to California, the US-50 route is covered on pages 654-735.

Ocean City

About the only place left on the entire East Coast that retains the carnival qualities of classic seaside resorts, Ocean City (pop. 5,146) has by far the best array of old-time fun-fair attractions in the Mid-Atlantic (well, south of Wildwood, New Jersey, at least). On and around the main **Ocean Pier** at the south end of the island, there are enough merry-go-rounds, Ferris wheels, roller coasters (including "The Hurricane," which is illustrated with scenes from Ocean City storms past), mini-golf courses, haunted houses, and bumper cars to divert a small army. A block inland, **Trimper's Amusements**, in business since the 1890s, has two more roller coasters, plus a Tilt-a-Whirl, a 100-year-old Hershell carousel, and a spooky Haunted House.

From the pier north, Ocean City stretches for over two miles along a broad, clean, white-sand beach. A wide, part-wooden boardwalk lines the sands, packed with arcades full of video games and a few nearly forgotten old amusements like skee-ball and pokerino, not to mention midway contests—the kind where for $1 a try you can win stuffed animals and other prizes by shooting baskets or squirting water into clowns' mouths. A ramshackle collection of fortune-tellers, T-shirt stands, and burger-and-beer bars completes the scene, forming a busy gauntlet that is among the nations's liveliest promenades.

On a summer weekend Ocean City becomes Maryland's second-largest city, its population increasing from the resident 5,000 people to upwards of half-a-million. Most of the fun is simply in getting caught up in the garish human spectacle of it all, but there are a couple of specific things worth searching out. For the price of a bumper car ride, you can enjoy the quirky collections of the **Life Saving Station Museum** (daily 11 AM-10 PM in summer, Sat.-Sun. noon-4 PM Nov.-March; $2), at the south end of the boardwalk, where alongside displays of shipwrecks and bathing suits you can compare and contrast bowls full of sand from 100 different beaches around the world. The museum also marks the starting point for the **trams** ($2) that run north along the boardwalk for over two miles to where the modern condos and resort hotels line up along the rest of the island.

Much of Ocean City's charm is decidedly low-brow, but the **food** is better than you might expect, with numerous places offering plates full of shrimp and pitchers of beer for under $10, and fresh-fried chicken or crab cakes available from boardwalk stands like **Dayton Brothers Chicken House**, across from the Life Saving Station. **Thrashers Fries** are available from a number of counters along the boardwalk, and you can top them off with a cone or shake from **Dumser's Ice Cream**, near the Wax Museum at the south end of the boardwalk.

Places to stay are also abundant, but unfortunately often far from cheap, at least during peak times. Of the grand older hotels, only the $80-a-night **Atlantic Hotel**, on the oceanfront at Wicomico Street (410/289-9111, 800/3-ATLANTIC or 800/328-5268) is still open for business; modern motels like the **Comfort Inn**, at Boardwalk and 5th Street (410/289-5155 or 800/282-5155), charge as much as $120 for a double that goes for less than $40 out of season, and upscale resort hotels like the **Sheraton Fontainbleau**, on Oceanfront at 101st Street (410/524-3535 or 800/638-2100) can cost upwards of $200 a night.

For more complete listings of motels, hotels, and restaurants, contact the Ocean City **visitor center**, in the Convention Center at 4001 Coastal Highway (410/289-2800, 800/62-OCEAN or 626-2326).

To go along with its great beaches, Ocean City has a radio station, the excellent **WZBH 93.5 FM,** "The Beach," playing classic rock 'n' roll and broadcasting details of Ocean City's nightclub scene.

Across the Virginia border, the southern half of Assateague Island includes the **Chincoteague National Wildlife Refuge,** noted for its long, wide beach and wild ponies. Access to this part of the island is through the small town of Chincoteague (see below for details).

Paddle a canoe through the wild Pocomoke Swamp with the Pocomoke River Canoe Company, 312 N. Washington Street (410/632-3971), next to the drawbridge in Snow Hill. Sadly, the river has recently suffered from mysterious (and very unsightly) fish kills, so ask before you go.

Assateague Island National Seashore

At one time Assateague Island, the 10 mile-long barrier island on which Ocean City sits, stretched in an unbroken line all the way into Virginia. In 1933 a major storm created the broad inlet that now divides the bustling resort city from the near wilderness of Assateague Island National Seashore. One of the few areas of the Atlantic coast protected from commercial development, Assateague consists of some 10,000 acres covering over 20 miles. Recreational opportunities include hiking, swimming, camping, canoeing, clamming, and birdwatching; swarms of voracious mosquitoes, and a lack of water, keep the crowds to a minimum.

To reach the island from Ocean City, follow US-50 west for two miles and turn south on Hwy-611, which loops around Sinexpunt Bay before arriving at a small **visitor center** (daily 8:30 AM-5 PM; 410/641-3030). The center has a small aquarium as well as maps, guides, and up-to-date information about the national seashore.

Snow Hill and Pocomoke City

From Ocean City, the route turns inland around Assateague Island and Chincoteague Bay, following US-50 west for eight miles, then turning south on US-113 through the dark cypress swamps along the Pocomoke River. Twenty miles southwest of Ocean City, the tiny, 200-year-old town of Snow Hill (pop. 2,200) is worth a stop to take a look at the **Julia A. Purnell Museum,** 208 W. Market Street (Mon.-Fri. 10 AM-4 PM, Sat.-Sun. 1-4 PM, April-Nov. only; $2). The museum features a range of exhibits tracing Eastern Shore history and a unique Flea Circus consisting of dozens of fully dressed fleas. Pick up a walking-tour map of Snow Hill's many significant structures. Dating back to the 1790s, the **Snow Hill Inn** at 104 E. Market Street (410/632-2102) is a charming place to stay, with a small restaurant and three guest rooms.

Fifteen miles southwest of Snow Hill near the Virginia border on US-113, Pocomoke City, founded in 1780, is a prosperous market town with a few surviving historic homes on the Pocomoke River. At Pocomoke City, US-113 turns into US-13 for the final few miles south to Virginia.

ALONG THE VIRGINIA COAST

Virginia's Eastern Shore is among the most isolated regions of the country, and its dozens of small towns and villages remain much as they have for centuries. Everything on the Eastern Shore is on a much smaller scale than on the mainland, and the many stands selling fresh corn and tomatoes along the roadside attest to the important role farming plays in the local economy. Although fast-food places, chicken-processing plants, and a couple of modern malls dot US-13, the main route through Virginia's Eastern Shore, the area is still mostly rural and undeveloped, with business loops turning off through the many well-preserved old towns. The numerous historic sites include colonial-era plantations and archaeological remnants of Native American tribes.

The highlight for most visitors is **Chincoteague**, a small commercial and sportfishing port sitting at the entrance to massive **Chincoteague National Wildlife Refuge**, which faces the Atlantic Coast and offers the only ocean beaches in this part of the state. South of Chincoteague, US-13 runs down the center of the narrow Eastern Shore peninsula, giving access to the Chesapeake Bay waterfront at **Onancock**, then passing through numerous small towns like **Accomac** and **Eastville**, neither of which has changed much since Revolutionary times. Crossing the mouth of the Chesapeake Bay via a 23-mile-long bridge and tunnel brings you to maritime Norfolk and the state's main Atlantic resort, Virginia Beach, before the route turns inland and south into North Carolina.

The Virginia **Welcome Center** at New Church, on US-13 at the northwest corner of the Eastern Shore, has maps and reams of visitor information.

Chincoteague

The drive into Chincoteague (pop. 1,600, pronounced CHINK-a-teeg), a low-key fishing village, takes you across miles of glowing gold and blue marshlands, and through a gauntlet of quirky billboards advertising local motels, restaurants, and sportfishing charters. This mix of natural beauty and tacky tourism aptly reflects the character of the town, which is totally dependent upon summertime visitors but seems to wish that they'd all leave and let the locals go fishing. The main attractions, besides fishing, are the beaches and birdwatching opportunities offered by the nearby wildlife

refuge (see below); however, one thing to do in town, besides eat tons of fresh clams, crabs, and other seafood, is visit the tiny **Oyster Museum** (daily 10 AM-5 PM in summer only; $3), a mile east of town on Maddox Boulevard. Its displays illustrate the history of oystering from the 1600s to the present.

A small bridge along Hwy-175, which runs 10 miles east from US-17, drops you at the heart of town, where casual seafood restaurants like the **Shucking House Cafe** and the **Landmark Crab House** line the small wharves that stretch along the bay. Among the many places to stay are several nice B&Bs, like the **Watson House** at 4240 N. Main Street (757/336-1564 or 800/336-6787), and the circa 1848 **Island Manor House** at 4160 Main Street (757/336-5436). The **Sea Shell Motel** at 3720 Willow Street (757/336-6589) is nice, too.

For more complete listings and other information, contact the Chincoteague **visitors center**, 6733 Maddox Boulevard (757/336-6161).

The classic children's story *Misty of Chincoteague* is set in the area and tells how wild ponies—whose ancestors were sent here by English settlers in the late 1600s—are rounded up from the wildlife refuge on Assateague Island for a forced swim across to Chincoteague. The annual roundup, swim and auction benefits local firefighters and attracts thousands of spectators. The swim takes place the last Wednesday in July, and the auction follows the next day.

Accomac is also home to a huge Perdue Chicken processing plant, right along US-13.

Chincoteague National Wildlife Refuge

The Chincoteague National Wildlife Refuge is one of the largest refuges along the Atlantic flyway, attracting hundreds of species of birds, including egrets, herons, geese, and swans, and thousands of migrating ducks. A continuation of the Assateague Island National Seashore across the Maryland border (see above), the refuge contains hundreds of acres of marshland, excellent beaches, and a number of hiking and cycling trails. The refuge **visitor center** (daily 9 AM-4 PM; 757/336-6577) at Tom's Cove has detailed information on park activities as well as special exhibits on Chincoteague's famous **wild ponies**, which can usually be seen from the Woodland Trail that loops south from Beach Road.

Accomac

The first sizeable town on the Virginia section of the Eastern Shore, Accomac (pop. 525) is centered upon an ancient-looking red-brick courthouse, flanked by a series of wooden sheds converted into professional offices. The old library next door dates from the 1780s, and was used for years as a debtor's prison; the library, courthouse, and surrounding buildings comprise one of the more extensive collections of colonial-era buildings in the country.

After wandering around the town, you may want to head to the family-run **Owl Restaurant**, three miles north of Accomac on the east side of US-13, and choose from Southern standards like ham steaks or fried chicken, or local seafood specialties including Chincoteague clams and oysters. Sample one of their excellent pies for dessert. Conveniently, the Owl is also a motel (757/665-5190).

Onancock and Tangier Island

The picturesque harbor town of Onancock (pop. 1,435, pronounced o-NAN-cock), on the Chesapeake Bay two miles west of US-13 via Hwy-179, is one of the nicest towns on the Eastern Shore. A short walking tour of over a dozen historical homes and churches—and a nifty 1950s movie theater, **The Roseland**, still showing Hollywood pics on weekends—begins at **Kerr Place** at 69 Market Street (Tues.-Sat. 10 AM-4 PM; $3), built in 1799 and now home to the Eastern Shore Historical Society. Another historic curiosity is the 150-year-old **Hopkins and Bros. general store**, on the wharf at 2 Market Street, which sells everything from sweet potatoes to postcards—however, the store was undergoing major renovations at time of writing, so the new and improved version may be very different. A great place to eat in Onancock is **Armando's**, at 10 North Street (closed Monday; 757/787-8044), serving a mix of Italian and South American food that's good enough to plan a weekend around.

Hopkins and Bros. on the wharf is also the place to buy tickets for the ferry across the Chesapeake Bay to Tangier Island, an evocative old place where car culture hasn't wreaked its havoc, and things seem to have hardly changed since colonial times. The few hundred people who live here year-round have a unique and almost indecipherably archaic accent—which some trace back to 17th-century Cornwall, England—and earn their livelihoods catching crabs and the occasional oyster from Chesapeake Bay. Ferries for Tangier Island leave once a day from Onancock Wharf (757/891-2240). Travel time is one hour 15 minutes each way, and the roundtrip cost is $17.50. Visitors returning on the ferry have only about two hours on the island, though **Shirley's Bay View Inn** (757/891-2396) and **Hilda Crockett's Chesapeake House** (757/891-2331) make possible an overnight stay, which is about the only way to have a close encounter with the tourist-shy locals. Hilda's has an all-day (11 AM-6 PM), all-you-can-eat seafood buffet, and more good seafood is available at the **Fisherman's Corner Restaurant** (757/891-2571).

Eastville

You can get a good idea of just how rural and quiet life is on Virginia's Eastern Shore by visiting Eastville (pop. 185), the seat of Northampton County. A mile west of US-17 on a well-marked business loop, Eastville centers on the red-brick courthouse and old county jail, with a handful of even older buildings dating back to the mid-1700s.

The Chesapeake Bay Bridge/Tunnel

One of the more impressive engineering feats on the East Coast is the Chesapeake Bay Bridge/Tunnel, which opened in 1964 at the mouth of the Chesapeake Bay, and was effectively doubled in 1997 by the addition of an extra set of driving lanes. Almost 18 miles long, and charging a $10 toll, the structure consists of one high-level bridge, two deep tunnels, four islands, and many miles of raised causeway. Two miles from the southern end of the bridge, a fishing pier and restaurant operate on a man-made island.

Onancock's **KHI 107.5 FM** plays oldies to suit the living time-warp that is the Eastern Shore.

Stands selling fresh fruit and vegetables—particularly sweet corn and tomatoes—dot roadsides all over the Eastern Shore.

Midway along US-17, the town of Exmore holds the popular **Sally & Bob's Drive-In,** which serves homemade crab cakes and fresh roasted chicken.

Before the Chesapeake Bay Bridge/Tunnel was completed in 1964, ferries linking the Eastern Shore with the mainland docked at **Cape Charles,** west of US-13 eight miles south of Eastville. Barges still use the harbor, ferrying freight trains across the bay.

The two deepwater harbors near Norfolk at the mouth of the Chesapeake Bay, **Newport News** and **Hampton Roads,** are the headquarters of the U.S. Navy's Atlantic Fleet and together form the world's largest naval base.

Virginia Beach

From the toll plaza at the southern end of the Chesapeake Bay Bridge, US-60 heads east along Atlantic Avenue, passing through the woodland waterfront of **Seashore State Park** before winding up at the ocean and Virginia Beach (pop. 394,000), the state's most populous city and its one and only beach resort. Ten-story hotels—so tall they block the afternoon sun from reaching the sands—line the main drag, Atlantic Avenue, which is plastered with large signs banning cars from "cruising" the mile-long array of fun fairs, surf shops, and nightclubs.

Unlike many coastal towns, Virginia Beach also boasts a significant history. Virginia's first colonists landed at Virginia Beach on April 26, 1607, before settling upriver at Jamestown; the site is marked by a stone cross at Cape Henry, at the southern lip of Chesapeake Bay. The **visitors bureau,** on the west side of town at 2100 Parks Avenue (800/VA-BEACH or 800/822-3224), has walking and driving tour maps of Virginia Beach's many historic houses, and can point you toward the area's excellent **Marine Sciences Museum,** at 717 General Booth Boulevard (daily 9 AM-5 PM; $8; 757/425-FISH or 757/425-3474), which has nearly a million gallons of sharks, sting rays, barracudas and sea turtles.

Virginia Beach is home to the **Association for Research and Enlightenment,** at 67th and Atlantic (757/428-3588), which is dedicated to continuing the legacy of early American psychic Edward Cayce, offering classes in ESP—but you already knew that, didn't you?

Dining options tend toward seafood restaurants hidden away in the resort hotels, though the **Maple Tree Pancake Shop,** at 2608 Atlantic Avenue, is a great breakfast stop and the **Jewish Mother Deli,** 3108 Pacific Avenue, serves up good sandwiches, doubling as a popular nightclub.

Perhaps the best reason to stop at Virginia Beach is that accommodations are much cheaper here than elsewhere in the area: beds at **Angie's Guest Cottage HI Hostel** at 302 24th Street (757/428-4690) cost $12-50 a night; a double room at an oceanfront motel costs $35-85, depending upon the time of year. Choose from Best Western, Comfort Inn, Days Inn, Hilton, Holiday Inn, Howard Johnson, Sheraton, or dozens of local places, like the **Idlewhyle Inn,** 2705 Atlantic Avenue (757/428-9341).

Norfolk

During colonial times, Norfolk (pop. 229,400, pronounced NAW-fik) was the largest city in Virginia and one of the busiest ports in North America, though these days it's little more than an adjunct to the massive naval shipyards at Hampton Roads and Newport News. That said, it does hold a couple of worthwhile destinations, including the lovely **Chrysler Museum** (Tues.-Sat. 10 AM-4 PM, Sunday 1-5 PM; $4), on the north side of downtown off Olney Road and Duke Street. The personal art collection of Walter Chrysler, the man who ran one of the "Big Three" car companies and built New York's Chrysler Building, is displayed inside a commodious Italianate building. Norfolk, a staunch Navy town, also holds the final resting place of controversial U.S. Army Gen. Douglas MacArthur, preserved alongside his personal papers (and his 1950 Chrysler Imperial limousine) at the MacArthur Memorial (Mon.-Sun. 10 AM-5 PM, free), inside Norfolk's old City Hall building at Bank and Plume Streets downtown.

Even if you're just racing through, bound for the beach, Norfolk has one place where you really ought to stop and eat: **Doumar's Cones and BBQ**, a half-mile north of downtown at 19th Street and Monticello Avenue (757/627-4163). Besides being a real old-fashioned drive-in, where friendly young ladies take your order and deliver it to your car, this place stakes a claim to having invented the ice-cream cone, since the owner's uncle, Abe Doumar, sold the first ones at the 1904 St. Louis World's Fair. They still sell great handmade cones, very good BBQ sandwiches, and a thirst-quenching limeade. Pass by at your peril. . . .

For a stylish but inexpensive place to stay, try the newly renovated, $75-a-night **Ramada Madison**, 345 Granby Street (757/622-6682).

The **Norfolk Tides** (757/622-2222), Class AAA farm team of the New York Mets, play at beautiful Harbor Park, off I-264 at Waterside Drive, where you can watch big ships sail past during the 7th inning stretch. Games are broadcast on WTAR 850 AM.

From Norfolk, you can take US-17 south across the Dismal Swamp, or follow the faster Hwy-168, which takes you past a feast of roadside fruit stands, BBQ shacks and junk shops, straight down to Kitty Hawk and the Outer Banks of North Carolina.

The Dismal Swamp

Across both sides of the Virginia/North Carolina border, for 30 miles down US-17, stretches a 750-square-mile wilderness known as the Dismal Swamp, a low-lying wetland with rich growths of cypress, juniper, and hardwood trees. Though it once was three times as large as it is now, apart from some hidden lumber mills and a few small farms, most of the swamp seems unchanged since colonial times, when the loquacious William Byrd of Virginia described it as a "vast body of dirt and nastiness" where the "eternal shade that broods over this mighty bog, and hinders the sunbeams from blessing the ground, makes it an uncomfortable habitation for anything that has life. . . . Not even a Turkey Buzzard will venture to fly over it." Byrd's damning description is unfortunately more true now than ever. Because of industrial pollution and the inroads of development, the swamp no longer teems with the birds, bears, raccoons, and opossums that made their home here as recently as 30 years ago. Yet the swamp is eerily beautiful, the sense of decay and desolation counterbalanced by patches of honeysuckle that perfume the otherwise fetid summer air.

DOUGLAS MacARTHUR
6¢ US

US-17 cuts south from Norfolk at the eastern edge of the swamp, running alongside the **Dismal Swamp Canal**, which was cut through in the 1790s as a private venture financed by George Washington and Patrick Henry, among others. The canal remained in active commercial use until the 1920s, though today traffic is limited to a few pleasure boaters and picnickers who stop for lunch in the many pull-outs along the highway.

Stop for a bite at Doumar's.

ALONG THE NORTH CAROLINA COAST

Linking Virginia and the Outer Banks, Hwy-168 is shorter than US-17, but has become a traffic nightmare in summer. The problem intensifies on Saturdays, when rental properties "turn over," and 30,000 cars pack the single-lane highway.

Wild Atlantic beaches, a handful of tiny fishing villages, and some of the country's most significant historic sites make coastal North Carolina a great place to visit. A highlight for many vacationers are the miles of barrier islands that make up the **Outer Banks**, where busy resort towns like **Nags Head** contrast with the miles of pristine beaches protected on the **Cape Hatteras National Seashore**. Besides golden sands, the Outer Banks area includes two evocative historic sites: the dunes at **Kitty Hawk** where the Wright Brothers first took to the air, and **Roanoke Island**, site of the first ill-fated English effort to colonize the New World. Farther south, beyond the quirky small city of Wilmington, a movie-making mecca, the 300-mile coastal route turns inland around **Cape Fear**, heading toward the South Carolina border.

Wright Brothers National Memorial

Kitty Hawk: The Wright Brothers National Memorial
Alternately known as Killy Hauk, Kitty Hock, and Killy Honk before its current name came into general use, Kitty Hawk to most people means one thing: the Wright Brothers' first powered airplane flight on December 17, 1903. Lured by the steady winds that blow in from the Atlantic and by the high sand dunes that cover the shore, Wilbur and Orville Wright first came to the Outer Banks in 1900, and returned every year thereafter with prototype kites and gliders built out of bicycle parts that they fine-tuned to create the world's first airplane. Their tale is truly one of the great adventure and success stories of the modern age, and the site of their experiments has been preserved as the **Wright Brothers National Memorial**. First stop is the **visitor center** (daily 9 AM–5 PM; $2; 919/441-7430), which includes a number of exhibits tracing the history of human efforts to fly. Every hour rangers give engaging talks alongside a full-sized replica of the Wright Brothers' first plane.

Orville and Wilbur Wright

The most affecting aspect of the memorial is the unchanged site where the brothers first flew. Each of the first four flights is marked by stones set on the grassy field. The first flight, with Orville at the controls flying into a 25 mph headwind, lasted 12 seconds and covered just 120 feet—barely more than a brisk walking pace. The 90-foot-high sand dune where Wilbur and Orville first took to the air has been planted over with grasses to keep it from blowing away. A series of paths climb to the top of the dune, where a 60-foot, wing-shaped granite pylon is inscribed with the words:

In commemoration of the conquest of the air by the brothers Wilbur and Orville Wright. Conceived by genius, achieved by dauntless resolution and unconquerable faith.

The park is well posted off US-158, on the inland side of the highway, two miles south of the Wright Memorial Bridge from the mainland. Though the memorial is definitely worth an extended visit, the towns around it are a bit disappointing—both Kitty Hawk and Kill Devil Hills are little more than narrow strips of commercial development. That said, Kitty Hawk does have the very pleasant, $15-a-night **HI Outer Banks Hostel**, 1004 West Kitty Hawk Road (252/261-2294) near the US-158 bridge, housed in a former school and set on 10 wooded acres.

Jockey's Ridge State Park

The windswept 110-foot-high twin sand dunes of Jockey's Ridge State Park (daily 8 AM-sunset; free; 252/441-7132) tower over US-158 between Kitty Hawk and Nags Head. The highest sand dunes on the East Coast, Jockey's Ridge barely survived being bulldozed in the 1970s to form yet another Outer Banks resort; it's now one of the prime hang-gliding spots in the country—remember the Wright Brothers! Jockey's Ridge is also a nice place to wander the short boardwalk nature trail that points out the diverse plants and animal of the dune community. You may want to take your shoes off and scamper around the sands barefoot. If you feel especially daring, **Kitty Hawk Kites** across the highway gives **hang-gliding lessons** ($69; 252/441-4124 or 800/334-4777) and demos equipment to licensed pilots.

Nags Head

The towns of the northern Outer Banks overlap each other and are so of a piece that only a sign tells you you are in Nags Head, six miles south of Kitty Hawk. It is one of the oldest and most popular resorts in the region, with

If you're traveling along the Carolina coast in summer, be aware that the **hurricane** season begins in June and lasts through the end of November. These are deadly serious storms, so take heed of any warnings, and follow the evacuation instructions broadcast over radio and TV networks.

Hundreds of ancient ships and unfortunate sailors met their watery end in the shallow waters off Cape Hatteras. The remains of over 2,000 vessels lie along the entire Carolina coastline; a few are visible from shore at low tide.

Information on the **Cape Hatteras National Seashore** (see below) is available at the main National Park Service **visitor center** (daily 9 AM-5 PM; 252/261-4644), in the town of Kitty Hawk on US-158 at milepost 1.5.

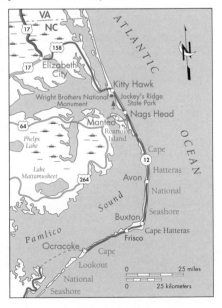

The name **Nags Head** is derived from the practice of Outer Banks pirates who tied lanterns around the heads of their horses to simulate boats bobbing at anchor. The lanterns lured passing ships onto shore, where they ran aground on the offshore sandbars.

Warmed by the Gulf Stream currents, the Outer Banks beaches are some of the best in the world, but the waters do not warm up appreciably until south of Oregon Inlet, and swimming in the northern stretches remains quite invigorating until July.

hotels, vacation homes, and time-share condos perched—often on stilts to protect them from storm damage—directly on the broad Atlantic beaches.

Nags Head is the most commercialized of the Outer Banks areas, and offers the widest range of visitor facilities. Accommodations are plentiful, but so are hordes of tourists. Good places to spend a night or two include the atmospheric but rather pricey **First Colony Inn** (252/441-2343 or 800/368-9390), in the middle of the island at 6720 S. Virginia Dare Trail/milepost 16, which offers a delicious breakfast and afternoon tea. The **Comfort Inn** (252/441-6315 or 800/221-2222), at the south end of Beach Road/milepost 17, has good-value rooms and is also the place to go for 1940s swing—the Big Band Preservation Society plays dance concerts here in the summer. Those fortunate enough to spend a week or more here can find a cottage rental through the **Outer Banks Ltd.** (800/624-7651).

The popular local hangout **Sam & Omie's**, near the east end of US-64 at 7228 S. Virginia Dare Trail/milepost 16.5, has featured

---

THE OUTER BANKS

The geography of the Outer Banks, a series of barrier islands stretching for over 200 miles along the entire coast of North Carolina, has changed dramatically over time, thanks to hurricanes and winter storms, not to mention human hands. Until a series of lighthouses was built beginning in the late 18th century, the islands and the offshore shoals were so treacherous they became known as the "Graveyard of the Atlantic."

Nowadays the same places where pirates once ruled are given over to windsurfing, hang-gliding, sportfishing, and beachcombing, as the Outer Banks have become a tourist destination par excellence. The resident population of 25,000 caters to over six million annual visitors, but unlike its nearest comparison, Cape Cod, the Outer Banks area boasts only a few colonial towns. Unfortunately, substantial development during the 1980s building boom filled up much of the roadside landscape with ugly franchise sprawl. Most of the development has taken place in the north along two parallel roads: US-158, usually called "The Bypass" but also known as "Croatan Highway"; and oceanfront Hwy-12, a.k.a. "Virginia Dare Trail" and "Beach Road." Mileposts on both roads mark distances from north to south. There's plentiful lodging in the many little towns along Hwy-12, including chain motels and hotels such as **Best Western, Quality Inn, Days Inn, Holiday Inn**, and dozens more); gas stations and fast-food restaurants line US-158.

For detailed listings, contact the Outer Banks **visitors bureau** (919/441-8144 or 800/446-6262).

Along the northern Outer Banks, bridges link Nags Head and Kitty Hawk with the mainland, though access to the less developed southern parts of the Outer Banks is limited to ferry boats, all of which carry cars.

inexpensive but well-prepared family fare for over 50 years. The upscale **Penguin Isle**, across the highway from the First Colony Inn, overlooks Roanoke Sound at 6708 US-158/milepost 16, with lovely sunset views and excellent seafood dinners.

Roanoke Island: Fort Raleigh National Historic Site

Raleigh's flag ship, Ark Raleigh

In an area known as Whalebone Junction at the south end of Nags Head, US-64 runs west over a causeway and bridge to Roanoke Island, site of the first English settlement in North America. The legendary "lost colony" was first established in 1585 by Sir Walter Raleigh, but the effort was not a success, and the survivors returned to England. In 1587, a larger expedition of 110 colonists arrived, including 17 women and nine children, but because of war with Spain there was no further contact with England until 1590. By that time the settlers had disappeared without a trace, which prompted numerous theories about their fate. Amidst an eerily dark and ugly forest, the original earthwork fortress is now excavated and reconstructed as the centerpiece of the small **Fort Raleigh National Historic Site**. Exhibits inside the visitor center (daily 9 AM-5 PM, longer hours in summer; free; 252/473-5772) include a few rusty artifacts and dry displays explaining the historical context of the colonial effort. There are also copies of the many beautiful watercolors and drawings of native plants, animals, and people produced by the original expedition's two immensely talented scientists, John White and Thomas Hariot.

The historic port of **Manteo** (pronounced MAN-tee-o, pop. 950), in the middle of Roanoke Island, between Fort Raleigh and the beach resorts of the Outer Banks, was named for the Native American who helped Sir Walter Raleigh and the Lost Colony. Manteo is the only county seat in North Carolina that's located on an island. You can still sense the town's proud seagoing history as you walk along the quiet streets near the tidied-up waterfront. Surrounded by pleasure boats, the main attraction here is the *Elizabeth II* (daily 10 AM-6 PM April-Oct., Tues.-Sun. 10 AM-4 PM rest of the year; $3), a full-sized, square-rigged replica of the type of ship that carried colonists here from England 400-odd years ago. Across the water, **1587** is one of the coast's best restaurants, with a chef who has a deft hand with the region's unsurpassed seafood. The 1587 is located inside the aptly named **Tranquil House Inn** at 405 Queen Elizabeth Street (252/473-1404 or 800/458-7069), where you'll be lulled to sleep in a comfy bed to the sound of gently clanging halyards.

For detailed listings of hotels and restaurants, and comprehensive information on visiting the Outer Banks, contact the **Dare County Tourist Bureau** (252/473-2138), on US-64 and Budleigh Street in Manteo; or try the **Outer Banks Chamber of Commerce** (252/441-8144 or 800/446-6262).

Throughout the summer, a waterfront theater adjacent to Fort Raleigh presents a popular production of *Lost Colony,* which dramatizes the events of the ill-fated settlement. Call for details or tickets ($14 adults, $7 under 11; 252/473-3414 or 800/488-5012).

Cape Hatteras National Seashore

The first piece of coastline to be protected as a national park, Cape Hatteras National Seashore stretches for 75 miles along the Atlantic Ocean. Starting in the north at Nags Head, and continuing south along slender Bodie, Hatteras and Ocracoke islands, the area preserved within Cape Hatteras National Seashore is the largest undeveloped section of coastline on the East Coast, providing an increasingly rare glimpse of nature amidst ever-encroaching development. The few old fishing villages that stood here when the seashore was set aside in the 1930s are unfortunately exempt from the anti-development prohibitions of the National Seashore, and have grown ugly and unwieldy, especially in the wake of the 1980s building boom. Nevertheless, the many miles in between remain almost entirely untouched.

For many visitors, the highlight of the National Seashore is the historic Cape Hatteras Lighthouse, a mile west of Hwy-12 at the south end of Hatteras Island, while others come here to enjoy the warm waters and strong, steady winds—two areas of Pamlico Sound on the inland side of Cape Hatteras have been set aside for windsurfers, dozens of whom flock here on summer days to what's considered one of the finest board-sailing spots in the U.S. And of course, there are miles of open beaches, perfect for aimless strolling.

At the north end of Cape Hatteras, eight miles south of Nags Head, there's a National Seashore **visitor center** (daily 9 AM-5 PM in summer only; 252/473-2111) and

---

HURRICANES!

If you're traveling along the East Coast in late summer, be aware that the farther south you go the more likely you are to encounter one of Mother Nature's most powerful phenomena, the hurricane. All along the Atlantic coastline, hurricane season begins in June and lasts through the end of November, and the threat of a storm can put a sudden end to the summer fun. Hurricanes are tropical storms covering upwards of 400 square miles, with winds reaching speeds of 75 to 150 mph or more. These storms form as far away as Africa, and sophisticated warning systems are in place to give coastal visitors plenty of time to get out of harm's way. Radio and TV stations broadcast storm watches and evacuation warnings, and if you hear one, heed it and head inland to higher ground.

Even more dangerous than the high winds of a hurricane is the storm surge—a dome of ocean water that can be 20 feet high at its peak, and 50 to 100 miles wide. Ninety percent of hurricane fatalities are attributable to the high waves of a storm surge, which can wash away entire beaches and intensify flooding in coastal rivers and bays many miles upstream from the shore. The strongest hurricane recorded in the U.S. was the Labor Day Storm of 1935, which killed 500 people and destroyed the Florida Keys Railroad; more recent hurricanes include Hurricane Hugo, which hit both North and South Carolina in 1989, and Hurricane Andrew in 1992, which killed 54 people and caused more than $25 billion worth of damage across Florida and Louisiana. The deadliest hurricane ever hit Galveston Island, Texas in 1900, killing more than 6,000 people—the worst natural disaster in U.S. history

a nature trail winding along Pamlico Sound at the foot of **Bodie Island Lighthouse**, the first of three historic towers along the Hatteras coast. On the ocean side of Hwy-12, **Coquina Beach** has a broad strand, lifeguards and showers in summer, and the remains of a wooden schooner that was wrecked here in the 1920s.

Continuing south, across the Oregon Inlet (where there's a campground), Hwy-12 runs through the 6,000-acre **Pea Island National Wildlife Refuge**, which was established in 1938 to protect the nesting grounds of loggerhead sea turtles, as well as the coastal wetlands essential to the survival of the greater snow goose and other migratory waterfowl. South of the refuge, a few short barrages of vacation condos and roadside sprawl—go-cart parks, mini-golf courses, and KOA Kampground—line the highway between Rodanthe and Salvo, before the road reaches the heart of the park, where high sand dunes rise for over 15 miles along the undeveloped oceanfront.

> The section of Pamlico Sound known as **Canadian Hole**, between the towns of Avon and Buxton, is rated as one of the best windsurfing spots on the East Coast.

Avon and Buxton: Cape Hatteras Lighthouse

At the rough midpoint of Hatteras Island, the vacation town of Avon stretches for a couple of miles along Hwy-12, before the road hits the Canadian Hole windsurfing area, two more miles south of town. After another few miles of natural dunes, the road bends sharply to the west; continuing south here brings you to the main Cape Hatteras **visitor center** (daily 9 AM-5 PM in summer only; 252/995-4474), and the famous **Cape Hatteras Lighthouse**. At 208 feet, the black-and-white striped lighthouse is the tallest brick lighthouse in the U.S., visible from as far as 25 miles. However, because the ocean here has been slowly eroding away the beach (when the lighthouse was built in 1870, it was a quarter-mile from the waves, which are now a mere 120 feet away from its base), the National Park Service plans, perhaps as early as May 1999, to lift the 3,000-ton lighthouse onto rails, and shift it a quarter-mile inland. Stay tuned to see what happens, since not everyone agrees this $12 million-plus plan is such a bright idea. In the meantime you can climb up the hundreds of step to the top of the lighthouse for a grand view—one that gives the clearest sense of just how narrow, and transitive, the Outer Banks really are.

Farther along, at the end of this road, there's a summer-only, first-come first-served **campground**; and ocean beaches at the very tip of the cape that are among the most spectacular anywhere. South-facing, they tend to pick up some of the most extreme surf—especially when hurricanes hit.

From the Cape Hatteras Lighthouse, Hwy-12 runs west and south through **Buxton**, where you will find the ugly guantlet of motels, gas stations and fast-food restaurants that's the seashore's main commercial center. **Billy's Fish House**, on the main highway next to Buxton High School, and **Bubba's BBQ**, in Frisco farther south, both offer good food at fair prices. Nearby motels like the **Lighthouse View** (252/995-5680 or 800/225-7651) or the **Falcon** (252/995-5968 or 800/635-6911) are reasonably priced and clean.

More restaurants and motels (including a Holiday Inn Express) await you in Hatteras, at the southern end of the island. From here, free **ferries** run across to Ocracoke Island, another mostly unspoiled barrier island where you'll find great beaches and the pretty village of Ocracoke, at the island's southern tip.

> The **ferry** between Hatteras and Ocracoke runs at least every hour on the hour 5 AM-midnight, year-round. It's free and takes about 40 minutes; call 800/BY-FERRY for exact schedules and further information.

BLACKBEARD THE PIRATE

Wandering around the idyllic harbor of Ocracoke, it's hard to imagine that the waters offshore were once home to perhaps the most ferocious pirate who ever sailed the Seven Seas—Blackbeard. The archetypal pirate, even in his day, when piracy was common, Blackbeard was famous for his ruthlessness and violence as much as for his long black beard and exotic battle dress, wearing six pistols on twin gunbelts slung over his shoulders and slashing hapless opponents with a mighty cutlass. His pirate flag featured a heart dripping blood, and a skeleton toting an hourglass in one hand and a spear in the other.

For all his near-mythic status, Blackbeard's career as a pirate was fairly short. After serving as an English privateer in the Caribbean during Queen Anne's War, in 1713 Blackbeard (whose real name was Edward Teach) turned to piracy, learning his trade under the pirate Benjamin Hornigold. Outfitted with 40 cannons and a crew of 300 men, Blackbeard embarked on a reign of terror that took him up and down the Atlantic coast of the American colonies. After five years of thieving cargoes and torturing sailors, Blackbeard was confronted off Ocracoke by forces lead by Lt. Robert Maynard of the Royal Navy, and during a ferocious battle on November 22nd, 1718 the pirate and most of his men were killed. Blackbeard himself was stabbed 25 times, and his head was sliced off and hung like a trophy on the bowsprit of his captor's ship.

Though there is no evidence that he ever buried any treasure anywhere near Ocracoke, Blackbeard's ship was discovered in 1996 off Bogue Bank, and his legend, to be sure, lives on.

Ocracoke

About the only Outer Banks town that hasn't lost its small-scale charm, Ocracoke is a great place to spend an afternoon or two, walking or cycling along unpaved backstreets lined by overgrown gardens and weathered old homes. Since it's easy to reach from the mainland, via ferries from Swan Quarter and from Cedar Island, Ocracoke is a popular destination, but the tourism here is so low-key it still feels like a place you can discover for yourself.

The ferries drop you at the heart of town, but coming in from the north on Hwy-12 you pass through a short strip of real estate agencies and restaurants like **Howard's Pub**, whose rooftop, ocean-view deck is a very pleasant place to eat fresh local seafood and sample one or more of its 200 different beers.

From Hwy-12, a number of small back roads (including the main one, called simply "Back Road," which runs past **Teach's Hole**, a shop dedicated to the pirate Blackbeard) are worth exploring. Just south of the harbor, Point Road runs west to the squat, whitewashed 1823 Ocracoke Lighthouse, while the harbor itself is ringed by restaurants, bike rental stands, and B&Bs like the four-story **Berkeley Manor** (252/928-5911 or 800/832-1223).

Across from the ferry landing, there's a very helpful **visitor center** (252/928-4531) which has complete information on Ocracoke and the rest of Cape Hatteras.

Cape Lookout National Seashore

If you liked the look of Cape Hatteras but want to avoid the crowds, plan a visit to the much wilder Cape Lookout National Seashore, another series of barrier islands, which stretch for 55 miles from Ocracoke to the south near Beaufort. It's accessible only by boat, and there are few roads or services once you're there, but it's a lovely place to hike or camp, collect seashells, or just wander along the peaceful shore. For more information, contact the park **headquarters** at 3601 Bridge Street in Morehead City (252/728-2250).

Beaufort and Morehead City

Known as Fishtown until it was renamed in 1722, the charming 18th-century town of Beaufort (pop. 3,800) has quiet streets lined with churches, cemeteries filled with weather-stained monuments, and whitewashed houses with narrow porches. The nautical-themed shops and restaurants along the water on busy Front Street, three blocks south of US-70, attract tourists and boaters traveling along the Intracoastal Waterway. The spacious **North Carolina Maritime Museum**, 315 Front Street (Mon.-Sat. 9 AM-5 PM, Sunday 1 PM-5 PM; free; 252/728-7317), features many informative exhibits on the region's nautical and natural history, as well as a truly impressive display of over 1,000 beautiful seashells. The museum offers day-long guided field trips to the dunes and marshes, but is perhaps best known for its annual **Wooden Boat Show** held the last weekend in September, and for the **Strange Seafood Festival** in mid-August, when visitors can nibble on marinated octopus and squid, stingray casserole, and more traditional seafood.

Besides the handful of places to eat on the boardwalk like **Clawson's**, 425 Front Street, a burger and seafood place that's been in business "since 1905"; you'll find the best food in Morehead City, three miles west of Beaufort and across the bridge. Try the homemade seafood cocktail sauce and Tarheel hush puppies at the **Sanitary Fish Market & Restaurant**, 501 Evans Street (252/247-3111); it's easy to find amidst the sportfishing boats a block south of US-70.

In Beaufort, B&B rooms are available in restored homes, and hotels like the **Cedars Inn**, 305 Front Street (252/728-7036). Morehead City holds motels like Best Western and Comfort Inn along US-70.

For more information, contact the Carteret County **visitor center** (800/786-6962).

Bogue Bank

More barrier island beach resorts line Bogue Bank, which runs south of Morehead City in a nearly east-west orientation for some 25 miles. None of the half-dozen family-oriented resort towns is particularly compelling, though all have freely

---

The village of Frisco, five miles north of the Hatteras ferry terminal, holds the small but surprisingly good **Native American Museum** (closed Monday; donations), which boasts an extensive collection of artifacts from several tribes, including those from the Cape Hatteras area, and Hopi and Navajo crafts.

Running between Ocracoke on Cape Hatteras, and Cedar Island on the Carolina mainland, the state-run ferry departs approximately every two hours (every three hours in winter) and takes close to two and a half hours each way. The cost is $10 per car. Call 800/BY-FERRY (800/293-3779) for current schedules and further information.

Not surprisingly, Beaufort, North Carolina is often confused with Beaufort, South Carolina. The former is pronounced BO-fort; the latter is pronounced BYOO-furd, and is described on page 410.

accessible—but quite often crowded—beaches. The largest, **Atlantic Beach**, across a bridge from Morehead City, has a boardwalk backed by a go-cart track and small amusement arcade. The **State Aquarium** (Mon.-Sat. 9 AM-5 PM, Sunday 1-5 PM; $3) five miles west of town on Hwy-58, features extensive displays on the local loggerhead sea turtles.

At the northeast end of Bogue Bank stands **Fort Macon State Park** (daily 9 AM-5 PM; free), which centers on a well-preserved pre-Civil War fortress overlooking the harbor entrance. There's a nice dune-backed beach a mile to the west.

Jacksonville and Camp Lejeune

Midway between Beaufort and Wilmington, much of the coastline is taken over by the 100,000-acre U.S. Marine Corps base of Camp Lejeune. Established during WW II, and now home to the crack rapid deployment forces, Camp Lejeune is open to visitors interested in a nose-to-nose encounter with tanks, HumVees, and other lethal machines. Sentries will check you in and out at both ends of the surprisingly scenic 25-mile drive across the base (at an enforced maximum speed of 25 mph).

The characterless city of Jacksonville (pop. 30,000), on US-17 at the northwest corner of Camp Lejeune, is little more than a civilian adjunct to the base, with all the gas stations, fast-food franchises, and tattoo parlors you could want. On the edge of town, just off Hwy-24 (opposite a Sonic Drive-In), the 50-foot-long granite wall of the **Beirut Memorial** remembers the more than 250 Camp Lejeune Marines killed in Beirut in 1983 by a suicide bomber. Alongside a list of their names are the words "They Came in Peace."

Holly Ridge: "Venus Flytrap Capital of the World"

US-17, the inland route across North Carolina, links up with the coastal route on the south side of Camp Lejeune, then continues south along the coast through the odd little community of Holly Ridge. The swamps around the town are an ideal environment for wild irises and azaleas, and for the thousands of insectivorous **Venus Flytraps** that grow wild here, many right along the highway. The flytraps, which Charles Darwin called "the most wonderful plant in the world," do not grow wild in any other part of the world except the seacoast Carolinas.

Worth stopping for in Holly Ridge: the award-winning BBQ of **Betty's Smokehouse Restaurant**, on US-17 on the north edge of town.

Wrightsville Beach

It would be difficult and probably pointless to try to decide which of the hundreds of miles of beaches along the Atlantic Coast is the best, but if you're looking for clean strands and clear blue waters, Wrightsville Beach, 10 miles east of US-17 via US-74 or US-76, is a good bet. It's not all that different from dozens of other coastal resorts, but proximity to the lively city of Wilmington makes it a great place to stop. Places to stay along the beach include a well-appointed **Holiday Inn**, and the comfortable **Blockade Runner Hotel** at 275 Waynick Boulevard (910/256-2251 or 800/541-1161), a half-mile south from the end of US-76; the Blockade Runner also has a good restaurant and nightclub, as well as bicycle rentals.

North Carolina's beaches are prime nesting grounds for endangered loggerhead sea turtles. These huge turtles come ashore mid-May to late August by the light of the full moon. Each female lays over 100 eggs that hatch at the end of summer.

Wilmington

Though it's surrounded by the usual miles of highway sprawl, the downtown business district of Wilmington (pop. 55,530) is unusually attractive and well preserved, its many blocks of historic buildings stepping up from the Cape Fear River waterfront. The largest city on the North Carolina coast, Wilmington was of vital importance to the Confederate cause during the Civil War, when it was the only southern port able to continue exporting income-earning cotton, mostly to England, in the face of the Union blockade. Wilmington also played an important role before and during the Revolution, first as a center of colonial resistance, and later as headquarters for the British troops.

Despite its lengthy and involved military history, Wilmington itself has survived relatively unscathed and now possesses one of the country's more engaging small-town streetscapes. Cobblestoned wharves and brick warehouses line the Cape Fear River, which also provides moorage for the massive 35,000-ton battleship USS *North Carolina* (daily 8 AM-dusk; $5), across the river. A couple of the warehouses, like the **Cotton Exchange** at the north end, have been converted to house boutiques and restaurants. A block inland, **Front Street** is the lively heart of town, a franchise-free stretch of book and record stores, cafes, and other businesses that's

Wilmington waterfront

often used by film crews attempting to re-create a typically American "Main Street" scene.

Thanks in large part to its significant movie-making business, Wilmington has a number of excellent places to eat. **Elijah's**, a seafood grill at 2 Ann Street on Chandler's Wharf, overlooks the Cape Fear River, while the comfortable **Caffe Phoenix** at 9 S. Front Street is an excellent Italian bistro serving fresh pasta dishes and pizzas. Within stumbling distance are bars like the **Ice House** at 115 S. Water Street, which features jazz and blues bands, and the more rough-hewn **Barbary Coast**, 116 S. Front Street.

Rates at Wilmington's many chain motels and hotels are surprisingly low; try the riverfront **Hilton**, or the very nice **Best Western Carolinian** at 2916 Market Street (910/763-4653 or 800/528-1234).

For more information on visiting the Wilmington area, contact the **Cape Fear Convention & Visitor Bureau** in the 100-year-old courthouse at 24 N. 3rd Street (910/341-4030 or 800/222-4757). The free weekly tabloid, *Encore,* available at most shops and restaurants, lists events and entertainment options.

Cape Fear

Though it has lent its name to two of the most terrifying movies ever made, Cape Fear is not at all a scary place. The name was given to it by sailors who feared its shipwrecking shoals. Hundreds of vessels have been wrecked off the cape, including dozens of Confederate blockade-runners sunk during the Civil War embargo of Wilmington harbor.

Between the east and west banks of the Cape Fear River, a **ferry** ($3) runs about once an hour between Fort Fisher and Southport. For current schedules and other information, call 800/BY-FERRY (800/293-3779).

South of Wilmington, US-421 runs along the east bank of the Cape Fear River through typical barrier island beach resort towns like Carolina Beach and Kure Beach. Near the south end of the island, **Fort Fisher State Historic Site** features the earthwork fortification that enabled Wilmington harbor to remain open to blockade-running ships throughout most of the Civil War. The fortress looks more like a series of primitive mounds than an elaborate military installation, but its simple sand piles proved more durable against Union artillery than the heavy masonry of Fort Sumter and other traditional fortresses. A **visitor center** (Mon.-Sat. 10 AM-4 PM, Sunday 1-4 PM, longer hours in summer; free) describes the fort's role, with details of the war's heaviest sea battle, when Union ships bombarded Fort Fisher in January 1865.

On the west bank of the Cape Fear River, Hwy-133 winds up at the pleasure-craft harbor of **Southport**, which is the halfway point between New York City and Miami, attracting sailors traveling the Intracoastal Waterway. It's also the site of the large Brunswick nuclear power plant.

Cape Fear itself is formed by **Bald Head Island**, at the mouth of the Cape Fear River, reachable only by boat from Southport. The **Old Baldy Lighthouse** on the island is the state's oldest, built in 1817.

Hwy-179: Ocean Isle Beach

South of Wilmington, US-17 runs inland, so if you want to stick close to the coast take Hwy-179, which curves between Ocean Isle Beach and Sunset Beach before rejoining US-17 at the South Carolina border. Amid the roadside shrimp stands, one place that's worth searching out is **Big Nell's Pit Stop**, which has attracted Myrtle Beach-bound travelers with huge breakfasts, tasty barbecue, and their roadfood-rated Brunswick Stew. It's about midway between Ocean Isle Beach and Sunset Beach, and open daily 7 AM-3 PM.

SOUTH OF THE BORDER

If the Grand Strand and Myrtle Beach hasn't satsfied your need for roadside kitsch, or if you're bombing along I-95 looking for a place to take a break, head to South of the Border, the world's largest and most unapologetic Mexican-themed tourist trap. Located just south of the North Carolina state line at I-95 exit 1, South of the Border is a crazy place with no reason for existence other than that it marks the midway point between New York and Florida, yet it draws many thousands of visitors every day to a 250-acre assembly of sombrero-shaped fast-food stands, giant video arcades, and souvenir shops, plus a miniature railroad (the "Carolina and Upper Mexico") and innumerable signs and statues of the South of the Border mascot Pedro, including one that's nearly 100 feet tall.

Many roadside businesses suffered when a new Interstate or bypass left them high and dry, but in the case of South of the Border, the opposite is true. It started as a fireworks and hot dog stand along US-301 in the late 1940s, but when highway engineers decided to locate I-95 here, its middle-of-nowhere acres suddenly became prime highway frontage, and owner Alan Shafer made playful use of its location (50 feet south of the state line) to create the pseudo-Mexican "South of the Border" village-cum-roadside rest stop. Though the complex itself is hard to miss, with its sombrero-clad concrete brontosaurus and 20-story "Sombrero Tower" giving a panoramic view of the Interstate, I-95 drivers from both directions get plenty of notice of their approach, thanks to the hundreds of garish billboards that line the road, saying silly things like "Chili Today, Hot Tamale," "You Never Sausage Such a Place," and "You're Always a Wiener at Pedro's," the subliminal messages all but forcing you to pull off and chow down on a hot dog or three and buy some mass-produced keepsake you'll throw away as soon as you get home.

South of the Border is open 24 hours every day, and, along with the myriad of tourist tack, it also has two gas stations and a pleasant, 300-room motel, with two pools and 20 "Sexy Honeymoon Suites." Call 803/774-2411 or 800/845-6011 for room reservations or more information.

ALONG THE SOUTH CAROLINA COAST

Just beyond the border into South Carolina, you suddenly hit the exuberant mega-tourism of the "Grand Strand," a 25-mile-long conglomeration of resort hotels, amusement arcades, and Coney Island-style Americana that centers on **Myrtle Beach**, the state's number one tourist destination. South of here things quiet down considerably, as coastal US-17 winds past the lush lowland marshes, passing through historic **Georgetown** and numerous preserved plantations before reaching **Charleston**, one of the most gracious and engaging cities in the southern U.S.

Myrtle Beach: The Grand Strand

Standing at the center of the Grand Strand, Myrtle Beach (pop. 25,000) is one of the largest and most popular beach resorts in the country, attracting millions of visitors every summer. It's a huge, and in many ways hideous, place, with mile after mile of motels, Wal-Marts, and fast-food franchises lining all the main roads. The beaches, presumably the reason so many people come here, are backed by 20-story towers which form an ugly "Costa del Concrete" along the sand; the beaches themselves are surprisingly narrow and in some places completely submerged beneath the tides.

All of which isn't to say Myrtle Beach should be avoided; in fact, if you want to wallow in beachfront Americana, there are few better places to head. Myrtle Beach grew up around **The Pavilion** amusement park, at the east end of US-501 along Ocean Avenue at 9th Avenue, which started in the 1920s as a dance hall (where the dance craze "The Shag" began). The pay-as-you-ride park, a block inland from the beach, offers a classic array of roller coasters, Ferris wheels, and a circa 1915 merry-go-rounds, plus two go-cart tracks and multiple midway arcade games. From Spring Break until the end of summer, the surrounding blocks are jammed with people showing off their well-formed bodies, though after school starts the resort gets suddenly quiet.

The best places to eat are in Murrells Inlet (see below), but there are also dozens of old-time burger stands like **Peaches Corner** on Ocean Avenue across from The Pavilion. Accommodations in and around Myrtle Beach range from roadside motels to flashy resorts, where the rates are low, but vary depending upon time of year. A beachfront room at the centrally located **Holiday Inn** at 1200 N. Ocean Boulevard (843/448-1691, 800/HOL-IDAY or 800/465-4329), which costs $75 a night in August, may set you back only $30 in October; rates at plusher resorts like **The**

Just south of the state border along US-17, the **South Carolina Welcome Center** in Little River (843/249-1111) has a large selection of maps, brochures, and visitor information.

Myrtle Beach boasts more golf courses, including a bewildering array of miniature golf courses, than anywhere else in the country. Most have castaway or pirate themes; one's based upon the TV show *Gilligan's Island.*

The spring- and summer-blooming **crape myrtle** trees, with long branches of purple and red flowers, gave Myrtle Beach its name.

Carry insect repellent and be prepared for mosquitoes, especially late in the afternoon, almost everywhere along the muggy South Carolina coast.

Breakers, 2006 N. Ocean Boulevard (843/626-5000 or 800/845-0688), range from $25-125 a night.

For complete listings and other information, contact the **visitor center**, 1301 N. King's Highway (843/626-7444 or 800/356-3016).

Murrells Inlet

There *may* be more picturesque places elsewhere in the state, but the relatively unspoiled fishing village of Murrells Inlet, 12 miles south of Myrtle Beach, is definitely worth a stop for the chance to sample its dozens of excellent seafood restaurants. Lining a short Business Loop off US-17, these range from **Flo's Place** at the north end, to the waterfront **Anchor Inn** and **Dockside**, to the rustic **Oliver's Lodge** a mile south. And if you've got the time and inclination to catch your own, sportfishing charter boats run from the marina, or you can put on some waders and head into the waters in search of clams, mussels, oysters, and crabs.

Brookgreen Gardens and Huntington Beach State Park

Well posted off US-17, four miles south of Murrells Inlet, Brookgreen Gardens (daily 9:30 AM-5 PM; $7.50) is a privately owned, 4,000-acre park on the well-maintained grounds of four colonial-era indigo and rice plantations. Oak trees laden with Spanish moss stand alongside palmettos, dogwoods, and azaleas as well as hundreds of sculptures, including many done by the owner, Anna Hyatt Huntington, who developed the site in the 1930s. Alligators and otters play in the simulated swamp and many species of birds fly around enclosed aviaries in a section of the gardens set aside as a wildlife park.

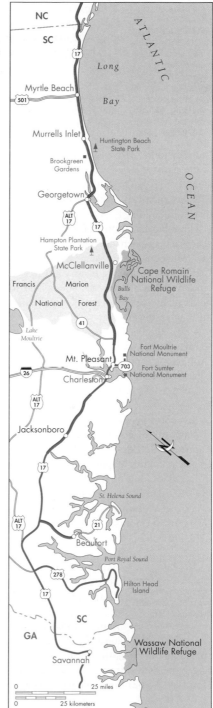

One of the more unusual radio stations in the country, **WLGI 90.9 FM,** is operated by the Ba'hai Faith and broadcasts a commercial-free mix of classic 1970s soul, contemporary jazz, and messages of peace, love, and understanding. To learn more, call 800/22-UNITE (800/228-6483).

Across the highway is the 2,500-acre Huntington Beach State Park ($4 per car), which sits on land carved out of the Huntington estate that is leased to South Carolina. Besides a nice beach, it features the Moorish-style castle "Atalaya," Anna Huntington's studio.

Georgetown

Site of a short-lived Spanish settlement in 1526, the first European outpost in North America, Georgetown later became the rice plantation center of the colonial era. Bounded by the Sampit and Pee Dee rivers and the narrow inlet of Winyah Bay, Georgetown is one of the state's few deepwater harbors and is home to two huge steel and paper mills along US-17. Its downtown district along Front Street is compact and comfortable, with dozens of day-to-day businesses and a few cafes and art galleries filling the many old buildings.

Three blocks south of US-17, at the east end of Front Street, there's a pleasant waterfront promenade, where the clock-towered old town market now houses the **Rice Museum** (Mon.-Sat. 9:30 AM-4:30 PM; $3). A series of dioramas traces South Carolina's little-known history as the world's main rice and indigo producer, a past often overshadowed by the state's later tobacco and cotton trade. The rest of town holds many well-preserved colonial and antebellum houses, churches, and commercial buildings.

Across the Pee Dee River, a mile north of Georgetown on US-17, the **Bellefield Nature Center** (daily 10 AM-5 PM; $3; 843/546-4623) was once the home of New Deal-era statesman Bernard Baruch and his daughter Belle. The plantation buildings have been preserved in antebellum condition, complete with one of very few surviving slave streets. Despite their historic quarters, the nonprofit educational foundation that currently occupies the buildings is more involved with environmental concerns than with regional history.

A couple of good places to eat in Georgetown include the locals' favorite **Thomas Cafe** next to the Rice Museum at 703 Front Street, and the **Chandler's Choice** and **Pink Magnolia,** both of which back onto the marina from Front Street. If you're looking to stay at a good B&B, try the **King's Inn** at 230 Broad Street (843/527-6937); chain motels line US-17.

For more information, or to pick up a self-guided tour map of town, contact the Georgetown County Chamber of Commerce, on the waterfront at 102 Broad Street (843/546-8346 or 800/777-7705).

The original lyrics to Stephen Foster's song "The Old Folks at Home" began "Way down upon the Pee Dee River . . . " though he quickly changed it to the more sonorous "Suwanee."

Hampton Plantation and McClellanville

The Santee Delta region along US-17 between Georgetown and Charleston once held dozens of large and hugely profitable plantations. One of the best preserved of these is now the Hampton Plantation State Park (Thurs.-Mon. 9 AM-6 PM; free), located 15 miles south of Georgetown, two miles west of US-17. Spreading out along the northern edge of Francis Marion National Forest, the 320-acre grounds feature a white wooden Greek Revival manor house (tours Thurs.-Mon. 1-4 PM; $2) that once welcomed George Washington. The manor house was later home to Archibald Rutledge, poet laureate of South Carolina from 1934 until his death in 1973.

South from Hampton Plantation along US-17, a small sign and a flashing yellow light are all that mark the turn-off to the quaint low country fishing village of McClellanville (pop. 383). It's the kind of place where neighbors drift in to sit on barrels and chat at **Graham's General Store**, and stop for a bite to eat at **Buster's**, the roadside cafe that shares the space—it's open every day but Sunday for breakfast, lunch and dinner. A short drive along Pinckney Street, the main road, brings you to the town hall (complete with a hurricane warning tower) and the town dock, where a substantial portion of South Carolina's shrimp and crab catch gets unloaded and shipped to market.

Along US-17 north of Charleston, sellers of African sweetgrass baskets line the highway outside Mount Pleasant, the only place in the U.S. where this traditional handicraft still flourishes. Women sit and weave at their individual roadside stands almost every day, but the weaving may soon be a lost art, as younger women are increasingly reluctant to take on this low-paid work; it takes four to five hours to weave a $20 basket.

Cape Romain National Wildlife Refuge

The unspoiled Cape Romain National Wildlife Refuge, south of McClellanville and five miles east of US-17, is one of the largest and most important sanctuaries for migratory birds in the Atlantic flyway. Thousands of great blue herons, pelicans, terns and ducks join the resident population of wild turkeys, feral pigs, deer, and alligators, which have returned after Hurricane Hugo. The state has been thinking about building a visitor center here, but in the meantime, the refuge's few visitors park on a grassy lot and fish off the small pier, while a few boats take serious bird-watchers to the marshland's several small islands.

Directly across from the refuge entrance on US-17 is the homey **SeeWee Cafe**, a general store turned restaurant serving homemade specialties, including a generous cup of she-crab soup with sherry on the side.

Fort Moultrie National Monument

Sitting at the entrance to Charleston harbor, across from its better-known sibling Fort Sumter, Fort Moultrie (daily 9 AM-5 PM; free) overlooks the Atlantic with good views of passing ships and the city of Charleston. The location alone would make Moultrie well worth a visit, but most come because of its vital role in American military history. Originally built from palmetto logs during the Revolutionary War, and since rebuilt many times, the fort is a testament to the development of coastal defenses. Its well-preserved sections date from every major U.S. war between 1812 and WW II, when Fort Moultrie protected Charleston harbor from roving German U-boats. But the fort is most famous for its role in the events of April 1861, when Fort Moultrie touched off the Civil War by leading the bombardment of Fort Sumter.

Fort Moultrie is easy to reach from US-17: across the Cooper River north of Charleston, turn south onto Hwy-703 at Mount Pleasant, then follow signs along Middle Street to the fort.

Fort Sumter National Monument

Commanding an island at the mouth of Charleston Harbor, Fort Sumter National Monument marks the site of the first military engagement of the Civil War. On April 12, 1861, a month

African sweetgrass basket

after Abraham Lincoln's inauguration and four months after South Carolina had seceded from the United States, Confederate guns bombarded the fort for a day and a half before the federal forces withdrew. The structure was badly damaged, but no one was killed and the fort was held by the Confederates for the next four years, by which time it had been almost completely flattened. It was later used as lighthouse station, and in 1899 a massive concrete battery was inserted into its center. Fort Sumter has been partly restored and is a key stop on any tour of Civil War sites.

The only way to visit Fort Sumter is by tour boat ($8.50; 843/722-1691), which leaves from the north side of Charleston Bay at Patriot's Point, just off US-17 at the foot of the massive bridge across the Cooper River. Other boats to Fort Sumter dock at the City Marina, on the south side of Charleston, off US-17 at 17 Lockwood Drive.

Patriot's Point, where boats bound for Fort Sumter dock along the Cooper River, is also the anchorage of the aircraft carrier USS *Yorktown* (daily 9 AM-5 PM; $5), a floating museum complete with WW II-era fighter planes.

George Gershwin's opera *Porgy and Bess* was inspired by life in Charleston's Creole ghetto, specifically Cabbage Row, now a tidy brick-paved alley off 91 Church Street.

Charleston

Established in 1670 as the capital of South Carolina, Charleston more than any other Deep South city proudly maintains the aristocratic traditions established during the plantation era. Then the elite would flee the heat, humidity, and mosquitoes of their lowland fiefdoms and come here to cavort in ballrooms and theaters. Still ruled by old money, though no longer the state capital, Charleston is both pretentious—with more Gucci and Ralph Lauren-type boutiques than you'd expect in a city of 80,000—and provincial; locals like to say that Charleston is the place where the Ashley and Cooper Rivers meet to form the Atlantic Ocean. It's also surprisingly cosmopolitan, accommodating a historic ethnic mix of French Huguenots, Catholic Acadians, and African-Americans from the Caribbean, who collectively introduced the wrought-iron balconies and brightly colored cottages that give the city much of its charm.

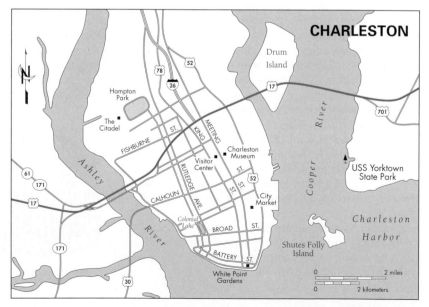

A Grumman E-1B Tracer on the deck of the USS Yorktown, at Patriot's Point.

Having suffered through a devastating earthquake, two wars, and innumerable hurricanes, Charleston has rebuilt and restored itself many times, yet it remains one of the South's most beautiful cities. Impressive neoclassical buildings line the streets, especially in the older, upmarket sections of town south of Broad Street and along the waterfront Battery. Charleston's many small, lush gardens and parks make it ideal for aimless exploring on foot rather than by car.

The Charleston accent is famous throughout the South. The word "garden" here is characteristically pronounced "gyarden," and "car" is "kyar," while the long "a" of Charleston (usually pronounced "Chaaarleston") is as distinctive as JFK's "Harvard."

Many of the mansions and churches are open to visitors, but it's the overall fabric of Charleston, rather than specific sites, that is most memorable. Nevertheless, the 1828 Greek Revival **Edmonston-Alston House** at 21 E. Battery (Tues.-Sat. 10 AM-5 PM, Sun.-Mon. 1:30-5 PM; $7) is definitely worth a look, as is the beautiful spire of **St. Michael's Episcopal Church**, 78 Meeting Street (daily 9 AM-5 PM; donations), which was modeled on the London churches of Sir Christopher Wren. A quarter-mile north, at Church and Market Streets, is the open-air **City Market**, known as the "Ellis Island of Black America," since over a third of all slaves arrived in the colonies here. Once the commercial center of Charleston, the market now houses a range of souvenir shops and touristy restaurants.

Charleston's artsy **Spoleto Festival USA** (843/722-2764) is held in May and June; from June to August, the Class A Charleston RiverDogs (843/723-7241) play at their riverside stadium downtown.

Outside the historic area a half-mile south of US-17, the **Charleston Visitor Center** at 375 Meeting Street (daily 9 AM-5 PM; 843/853-800) is a good first stop; watch the 21-projector multi-image slide show **"Forever Charleston"** (every 30 minutes; $2.50) and pick up a **day pass** ($2) to ride the DASH shuttle buses that loop around town. Across the street from the visitor center, the **Charleston Museum** (Mon.-Sat. 9 AM-5 PM, Sunday 1-5 PM; $6) has general exhibits on regional history and culture.

Thanks to its well-heeled populace and its considerable tourist trade, Charleston supports a number of excellent eateries. Around the City Market, choose from the very popular **Hyman's Seafood**, 215 Meeting Street, which has a variety of basic but good-value fresh fish entrees for around $10; the more sedate (and expensive) places nearby include the stylish, Mediterranean-inspired **Blossom Cafe**, 171 E. Bay

Along US-17 in Jacksonboro, midway between Charleston and Beaufort, the **Edisto Motel Cafe** (843/893-2270) serves up piping hot platters of fresh-fried seafood (shrimp, oysters, scallops, etc.) in a simple, cinderblock roadhouse.

Beaufort is perhaps best known as the home of the massive U.S. Marine Corps Recruit Depot at nearby **Parris Island** (843/525-3650).

Street, and the upscale and usually crowded **Magnolias** next door. Both are open until 11 PM or later. Bakeries and cafes line busy King Street, and there are some very formal places in the plush hotels.

Like its restaurants, Charleston's accommodation options tend toward the luxurious and expensive. Of the dozens of old fashioned but well-appointed bed B&Bs (all of which charge over $100 a night), the elegant **John Rutledge House**, 116 Broad Street (843/723-7999 or 800/476-9741) offers four-star comfort in a converted 1763 house. The romantic, Queen Anne-style **Two Meeting Street Inn** at 2 Meeting Street (843/723-7322) has been welcoming guests for over 50 years. Hotels in and around the historic district are similarly expensive, though you'll find a very handy, $80-a-night **Days Inn** downtown at 155 Meeting Street (843/722-8411). Other chain motels, including **Best Western**, **Econo Lodge**, and **Motel 6**, are along both Savannah Highway (US-17) south of town and the I-26 frontage north of town.

Beaufort

The second-oldest town in South Carolina, Beaufort (pop. 9,500, pronounced BYOO-furd) is a well-preserved antebellum town stretching along a fine natural harbor, 18 miles south of US-17 via US-21. Established in 1710, Beaufort stands on the largest of some 75 islands dotting Port Royal Sound near the Georgia border. Beaufort was established in 1710, and dozens of colonial-era and antebellum homes line its quiet, small-town streets. Only two of these houses, the circa 1790 **Verdier House** and the Greek Revival **Elliott House**, a block apart on Bay Street along the waterfront, are open to visitors, though you can pick up a walking-tour map of the others from the **visitor center** at 1006 Bay Street (843/524-3163).

Though his house isn't on the visitor center map, and his story is seldom told, one of Beaufort's most noteworthy residents was **Robert Smalls**, who was born a slave but rose to become the first black captain in the U.S. Navy; Smalls later served five terms in the U.S. House of Representatives. After Jim Crow laws disenfranchised blacks, Smalls lost his seat and returned to Beaufort, living in his former master's house and taking care of his former master's widow, at 511 Prince Street. After his death in 1915, he was buried in **Beaufort's Baptist Tabernacle Church** at 907 Craven Street, where a small bust marks his accomplishments.

The **Anchorage House**, housed in a circa 1765 building on the water at 1103 Bay Street, offers such low country specialties as a crabmeat casserole and she-crab soup with sherry. Places to stay include the waterfront **Best Western Sea Island Motel**, 1015 Bay Street (843/524-4121 or 800/528-1234); and the state's only four-star B&B, the lovely **Rhett House**, 1009 Craven Street (843/524-9030), where the film *Prince of Tides* was shot on location.

Hilton Head Island

Near the southern tip of South Carolina, Hilton Head Island is the largest ocean island between Florida and New Jersey. It was first settled in 1663, but only since the late 1950s, when a bridge to the mainland was completed, has it really been on the map. Now Hilton Head is a major destination resort in the South, and golf courses and "plantation-style" estates abound here, as do mini-malls and all the trappings of suburban America. Information is available through the Hilton Head Island Chamber of Commerce (843/785-3673).

As recently as 1960, the population of South Carolina's Sea Islands was predominantly African-American—10 to 1 on average. Now, with all the upscale vacation resorts, the proportions have effectively been reversed.

South to Savannah

From Beaufort, a confusing series of narrow, roadkill-strewn two-lane highways—Hwy-170, Hwy-46, and US-17—run across the lowlands around Hilton Head Island toward Georgia. One place along here, the Savannah National Wildlife Refuge, is worth a stop for birdwatchers, but everyone else will probably want to race along to that most gracious of historic southern cities, Savannah, which is just over the Georgia border.

The beautiful city of Savannah marks the junction of our Coastal East Coast route with our Southern Pacific road trip along US-80, which is covered on pages 738-791.

ALONG THE GEORGIA COAST

The marshes and barrier islands that line the Atlantic Ocean along the Georgia coast are among the lesser-known treasures of the eastern U.S. Geographically, the coastline consists of mostly roadless and largely unconnected islands, which makes coastal driving nearly impossible; the nearest north-south routes, I-95 and the older US-17, run roughly 15 miles inland, and only a few roads head east to the Atlantic shore. The lack of access has kept development to a minimum and has also been a boon to wildlife—well over half the coastline is protected within state and federal parks, preserves and refuges.

The "you-can't-get-there-from-here" aspects can make it more than a little frustrating for casual visitors, but if you have the time and inclination, they also make the Georgia coast a wonderful place to explore. The two main car-friendly destinations along the Georgia coast are **Tybee Island** in the north, east of Savannah and forming the end of our cross-country road trip along US-80, and the beautiful and history-rich **Golden Isles**, east of Brunswick. Both are great places to visit, and offer an appetizing taste of the 100 miles of isolated shoreline Georgia otherwise keeps to herself.

*The Class A **Savannah Sand Gnats** (912/351-9150), a Texas Rangers farm club, play at WPA-built Grayson Stadium, off US-80 on the south side of town.*

Savannah

Named "the most beautiful city in North America" by the style-arbiting Parisian newspaper *Le Monde*, Savannah is a real jewel of a place. Founded in 1733 as the first settlement in Georgia, the thirteenth and final American colony, Savannah today preserves its original neoclassical, colonial, and antebellum self in a welcoming, unselfconscious way.

Famous for having been spared by General Sherman on his destructive "March to the Sea" at the end of the Civil War, it was here that Sherman made his offering of "40 acres and a mule" to all freed slaves. Before and after the war, Savannah was Georgia's main port, rivalling Charleston, South Carolina for the enormously lucrative cotton trade. As commercial shipping has tailed off, the harbor is now primarily recreational—the yachting competitions of the 1996 Olympics were held offshore. Savannah, home of writer Flannery O'Connor and songsmith Johnny Mercer, also served as backdrop to the best-selling book *Midnight in the Garden of Good and Evil,* and for numerous movies, most famously *Forrest Gump,* but has resisted urges to turn itself into an "Old South" theme park; you'll have to search hard to find souvenir shops or overpriced knickknack galleries.

At the center of town, midway down Bull Street between the waterfront and spacious Forsyth Park, **Chippewa Square** was the site of Forrest Gump's bus bench (the movie prop was moved to the visitor center and may one day be erected in bronze). **Reynolds Square,** near the waterfront, has a statue of John Wesley, who lived in Savannah in 1736-37 and established the world's first Sunday School here. **Wright Square** holds a monument to Chief Tomochichi, the Native American tribal leader who allowed Oglethorpe to settle here, and **Forsyth Park,** at the south edge of the historic center, is modeled after the Place de la Concorde in Paris, surrounded by richly scented magnolias.

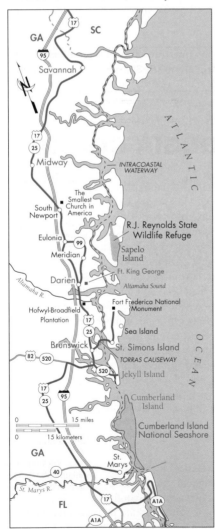

Another great place to wander is **Factor's Walk,** a promontory along the Savannah River named for the "factors" who controlled Savannah's cotton trade. This area holds the Cotton Exchange and other historic buildings, many of them constructed from 18th-century ballast stones. Linked from the top of the bluffs by a network of steep stone stairways and cast-iron walkways, River Street is lined by restaurants and nightclubs, and at the east end there's a statue of a girl waving: this was erected in memory of Florence Martus who for 50 years around the turn of the century greeted every ship entering Savannah harbor in the vain hope that her boyfriend would be on board.

Away from the magnificent mansions and manicured squares, another side of the Savannah story is conveyed at the **King-Tisdell Cottage**, 514 E. Huntingdon Street (Mon.-Fri. noon-4 PM, Saturday and Sunday 1-4:30 PM; $3; 912/234-8000). South of central Savannah in the predominantly black Victorian District, this well-restored, circa 1896 cottage holds a fine museum of African-American culture and history, with changing displays of arts and crafts such as Gullah basketry.

Savannah Practicalities

Savannah's brand-new airport is a delight, but still not served by many flights apart from Delta's frequent hops from Atlanta; it's about 15 miles west of town, right off I-95. Parking in town isn't hard to find, but if you're staying a while, the visitor center sells a $5 visitor's parking pass, which lets you disregard *almost* all the parking restrictions for two days. Getting around is blissfully easy: Savannah is the country's pre-eminent walker's town, with a wealth of historic architecture, and a checkerboard of small squares shaded with centuries-old live oak trees draped with tendrils of Spanish moss—all packed together in one square mile. The sensible and very attractive modified grid plan of Savannah—which was based upon a drawing by draughtsman Robert Cassell, who died, ironically, in an English debtor's prison, the sort of place Georgia was intended to replace—makes finding your way so simple that it's almost fun to try to get lost.

For travel information on the Georgia coast, call 800/GA-COAST (800/422-6278).

For an unforgettable breakfast or lunch, be sure to stop at **Mrs. Wilkes Boarding House**, 107 W. Jones Street, a central Savannah home that's no longer a boarding house but still offers up traditional family-style Southern cooking —varying from fried chicken to crab stews, with side dishes like okra gumbo, sweet potato pie, red, green or brown rice, and cornbread muffins. Worth a trip from anywhere in the state, don't leave Savannah without eating here. On the south side of town on old US-80, **Johnny Harris**, 1651 E. Victory Drive, is Savannah's oldest restaurant, and one of the fanciest BBQ places in the world. Serving great food since 1942, it also has live "Big Band" music most weekends. **Paper Moon**, 152 Whitaker Street at Oglethorpe, is a great little restaurant, with lots of books to go with goodies ranging from sausage ragout and pizza to New York strip steak. Road food fans will want to head a half-mile south of downtown to the **Streamliner Diner**, Barnard and W. Henry Streets, a gorgeously restored 1938 Worcester diner operated by (and across the street from) the Savannah College of Art & Design (SCAD), which has taken over many of the city's older buildings and converted them into art studios and galleries.

One of Savannah's more unusual tourist attractions is the Juliet Gordon Low Birthplace, at 142 Bull Street, a circa 1820 house that was the childhood home of the woman who introduced **Girl Scouts** to America in 1912. Current Girl Scouts gain a merit badge just by walking in the door.

There are also many good places cheek-by-jowl in the old City Market, like the lively **Vinny Van Go Go's** pizza joint on Montgomery Street facing Franklin Square.

Along the Savannah River, which marks the boundary between South Carolina and Georgia, **Eli Whitney** invented the cotton gin in 1793 at Mulberry Grove plantation.

Places to stay in Savannah vary from a budget hostel to quaint B&B inns to stale high-rise hotels, and happily are less expensive than you might expect. For the total Savannah experience, try the **Bed and Breakfast Inn**, 117 W. Gordon Street (912/238-0518), which has very nice rooms for under $90 a night, in an 1853 townhouse off Monterey Square. At the **River Street Inn**, 115 E. River Street (912/234-6400 or 800/253-4229), well-appointed rooms, costing $85-150, fill a converted antebellum cotton warehouse, right on Factor's Walk at the heart of the Savannah riverfront. Nearby, the large **Days Inn**, 201 W. Bay Street (912/236-4440 or 800/325-2525), has standard rooms for under $85, right across from Factor's Walk.

Last, but not least, the **Savannah International Hostel**, 304 E. Hall Street (912/236-7744), has $15 dorm beds in a turn-of-the-century Victorian home, just south of the historic heart of Savannah.

Along US-17 near I-95 exit 12, a small sign on the east side of the highway welcomes travelers to "The Smallest Church in America," a 12-seat cabin that's open 24 hours. Turn the lights out when you leave.

More complete information on the city can be obtained from the **Savannah Convention & Visitors Bureau**, 222 W. Oglethorpe Avenue (912/944-0456 or 800/444-2427). Once in town, the **Savannah Visitors Center**, at 301 W. Broad Street (912/944-0455), in the old Georgia Central railroad terminal just west of the historic center, has free maps and brochures.

US-17: Midway

For a quick taste of the old-style Georgia coast, detour east from I-95 or US-17 along Hwy-99, which loops for 16 miles along the waterfront between Eulonia and Darien. Midway along Hwy-99 is Meridian, where you can catch the passenger ferry for a four-hour tour (reservations required; adults $10, under 18 $6; 912/437-3224) to wonderful Sapelo Island. The island is a sparsely populated, mostly undeveloped and generally fascinating place to spend some time.

The section of US-17 south of the Ogeechee River, off I-95 between exits 14 and 12, offers shunpikers a 24-mile taste of old-style Lowland Georgia; it is a textbook example of how traveling the two-lane highways is superior in almost every way to hustling down the interstates. Midway along, the coincidentally named town of Midway (pop. 900) was founded back in 1754 by a band of Massachusetts Puritans, two of whom (Lyman Hall and Button Guinett) went on to sign the Declaration of Independence as Georgia's self-declared representatives to the Continental Congress. The centerpiece of Midway, then and now, is 200-year-old **Midway Church**, which preserves the original pulpit (and slave gallery); keys for the church are available at the adjacent **Midway Museum** (Tues.-Sat. 10 AM-4 PM, Sunday 2-4 PM; $3)

Though redolent with ghosts of Georgia's past, Midway is still a living, breathing little place, with a great little roadfood restaurant, **Ida Mae & Joe's**, serving up plates of fresh-fried catfish along US-17 just south of town.

Darien: Fort King George

Located near the mouth of the Altamaha River, which formed the rough and frequently fought-over boundary between British and Spanish parts of the New World, Darien (pop. 1,800) looks a lot like most other coastal Deep South towns, but boasts a history to match many bigger or more famous destinations. After a small, 16th-century Spanish mission near here was destroyed by Native Americans, Darien was founded in 1736 by Scottish colonists (many named McIntosh, now the name of the surrounding county) near Fort King George, the first British outpost in what became Georgia. Darien later became a center of the lucrative early

19th-century rice trade, surrounded by plantations where the abuse of slaves inspired British actress Fanny Kemble's book-length indictment, *Journal of a Residence on a Georgia Plantation in 1838-39*, an influential abolitionist text.

Despite the many claims it could make to importance, Darien preserves its past in a matter-of-fact manner. The main attraction is the reconstructed **Fort King George**, a state historic site, a mile east of US-17 on Fort King George Drive (Tues.-Sat. 9 AM-5 PM, Sunday 2-5 PM; $2.50).

A more intriguing place to visit is the **Hofwyl-Broadfield Plantation**, five miles south of Darien along US-17 (Mon.-Sat. 9 AM-5 PM, Sun 2-5 PM; $2), where a well-preserved plantation home is surrounded by 1,200 acres of one-time rice fields that have reverted to cypress swamps. Displays inside the visitor center tell the story of how slaves were forced to labor in the sweltering, mosquito-plagued summer heat, building levees and doing the back-breaking work of planting, growing and harvesting the rice.

A compelling non-fiction account of the pernicious effects of segregation in 1960s and 1970s Darien, Melissa Fay Greene's *Praying for Sheetrock* describes how locals and legal activists used federal lawsuits to overcome the corrupt regimes of local government and law enforcement officials.

Brunswick

A heavily industrialized city, with a waterfront lined by shrimp canneries and pulp mills, Brunswick (pop. 16,500) is a place most travelers pass through as quickly as possible on their way east to the lovely Golden Isles. The one real reason to stop is the fabulous pulled-pork sandwiches at the **Georgia Pig** (912/264-6664), south of town at the US-17/82 junction, east of I-95 exit 6, tucked away next to a Texaco station in a scruffy woodland on the north side of the main road to and from Jekyll Island. Though it looks like it's been there forever, this classic roadside BBQ joint is a comparative newbie, having been open a mere two decades. The bare-bones decor—log rafters, pine picnic tables, and creaking front door —disappears when you bite into the absolutely perfect meat, which is sliced to order after being smoked in a hickory-fired oven that burns right behind the counter.

Every August, the **Sea Island Festival** on St. Simon's Island brings together gospel singers and traditional Gullah craftsmakers. For details, phone 912/638-9014.

The region's cheapest and most unusual accommodation is located two miles west of the Georgia Pig: the **Hostel in the Forest** ($10; 912/264-9738) has dorm beds in a geodesic dome, and a few tree houses, too.

St. Simon's Island

East of Brunswick via the Torras Causeway (toll 35¢), St. Simon's Island is a mini-Hilton Head, with many vacation resorts and a sizeable year-round community. The center of activity on St. Simon's is at the south tip of the island, where the "village" consists of a central plaza and a few blocks of shops, saloons and restaurants along Mallery Street, which leads down to the waterfront pier and a circa 1872 lighthouse. In between the pier and the lighthouse, the **visitor's center** (800/933-2627) has maps and listings of St. Simon's eating, drinking, sleeping, and outdoor recreation options.

Georgia's most famous 19th-century poet, **Sidney Lanier,** settled near Brunswick after contracting tuberculosis as a POW during the Civil War. He wrote his most famous poems, including "The Marshes of Glynn," while he sat under an oak tree that stands along US-17, a mile north of town. The old Sidney Lanier lift bridge, along US-17 south of Brunswick, has been rendered obsolete by a sky-high concrete one alongside.

Around the turn of the twentieth century, 50 members of the Jekyll Island Club, which included such names as Rockefeller, Carnegie, Morgan and Vanderbilt, controlled as much as 20% of the world's wealth.

For the total island experience, splurge on a night or two at one of St. Simon's plush resorts, like the four-star, $400-a-night **Cloister Hotel** (800/SEA-ISLAND or 800/732-4752), which covers adjacent Sea Island with 36 holes of golf courses and 264 Spanish-style rooms. Presidents from Coolidge to Bush have vacationed here, and JFK, Jr. got married here, which should give you some idea of the preppie character of the place.

The one real "sight" on St. Simon's Island is the **Fort Frederica National Monument**, at the northwest edge of the island, which protects the remains of the village surrounding what was once the largest fortress in the British colonies. Built in 1736 and abandoned in 1763, Fort Frederica played a vital role in keeping Georgia British, rather than Spanish; in 1742, a key battle was fought six miles south of the fort, at a site known as "Bloody Marsh."

Jekyll Island

Once a private, members-only resort for New York millionaires, Jekyll Island is now owned by the State of Georgia, which offers a chance for those *not* in control of a Fortune 500 company to enjoy the genteel side of Golden Isles life. A grand hotel, and dozens of palatial vacation "cottages" that would look equally at home in Newport, Rhode Island, are accessible to the general public, after a half-century of catering to the richest of the rich.

At the center of the island, and the best place to start a visit, is the landmark **Jekyll Island Club Hotel**, just north of where the Jekyll Island Causeway (toll $2) meets the island. Majestic oak trees dangling garlands of Spanish moss cover the grounds, and within a short walk are many of the grand mansions, including one built by tire magnate Frank Goodyear that's open for free tours. The nearby stables have been converted into a nice little **museum**, (daily 9:30 AM-4 PM; free) which tells the whole Jekyll Island story.

Less than a mile east, the Atlantic oceanfront is lined by **Beachview Drive** and a five-mile-long beach—with the least developed stretches at the north and south ends of the island. Bike rentals—which really provide the best way to see the island —are available from the mini-golf course midway along Beachview Drive (912/635-2648). Horses can be hired for trail rides at the north end of the island (912/635-9500).

Rooms at the **Jekyll Island Club Hotel** (912/635-2600 or 800/535-9547) aren't *all* that expensive, running $120-250 a night, but the more bargain-oriented can try the many motels that line Beachview Drive: **Comfort Inn, Days Inn**, and **Holiday Inn** are all here, with rooms in the $75-150 range. There's also a nice campground (912/635-3021) at the north end of the island, with sites for tents and RVs (full hookups).

The dining room at the Jekyll Island Club is reasonably priced considering the lush accoutrements, but for regional seafood served up outdoors on a deck overlooking the marshes, try **Sea Jay's Cafe**, across the road from the hotel at Jekyll Harbor Marina.

For more complete information, stop by the **Jekyll Island Welcome Center**, just west of the drawbridge over Jekyll harbor (912/635-3636 or 800/841-6586).

Detour: Cumberland Island National Seashore

Once the private reserve of the Carnegie family, the Cumberland Island National Seashore is a 99% uninhabited barrier island with miles of hiking trails and primitive backcountry camping along beaches and in palmetto forests. Also here is the unique **Greyfield Inn**, the Carnegie family mansion that's now operated (by Carnegie heirs) as an unpretentious (and unair-conditioned) 15-room historic lodge (904/261-6408), that runs around $350 a night for two people, including gourmet meals.

Cumberland Island is only accessible by a twice-daily ferry (outbound at 9 AM and 11:45 AM, returning at 10 AM and 4:45 PM; about $14 roundtrip; 912/882-4336) from the tiny town of St. Marys, on Hwy-40 10 miles east of I-95 exit 1.

Back on US-17, approaching Florida through the back door along this grand old two-lane highway, you pass the remains of dozens of roadside attractions and businesses. Almost everything that once made up Kingland, Georgia is closed, and probably has been since I-95 opened, but under the ever-growing kudzu sit substantial old motels, restaurants, and tourist traps—awaiting some pop-culture-minded archaeologist to uncover their forgotten stories.

ALONG THE FLORIDA COAST

Stretching some 600 miles between the Georgia border and Key West at its far southern tip, Florida offers something for everyone, from unsullied nature to the tackiest tourist traps in the land, and everything imaginable in between. More than anywhere else in the U.S., the Florida landscape has been designed for tourists, and no matter what your  fancy or fantasy, you can live it here, under the semi-tropical sun. The many millions who visit Disney World or flock to fashionable Miami Beach each year are doing exactly what people have come to Florida to do for over a century—enjoy themselves.

Despite the modern gloss of golf course estates and sprawling retirement communities, which tend to overshadow the substantial stretches of wide open beaches and coastal forest, Florida has a lengthy and fascinating history, with significant native cultures and, in **St. Augustine**, some of the oldest signs of European presence in North America, including the legendary Fountain of Youth. At the other end of the state, on the fringes of the Caribbean, **Key West** is a tropical paradise, founded by pirates four centuries ago, and still one of the most lively and anarchic places in the USA. In between, our road trip route passes through such diverse places as **Daytona Beach**, mecca for race car fans and a magnet for college kids on Spring Break; the launch pads and mission control centers of the **Kennedy Space Center**; the multi-cultural melting pots of **Miami** and **Miami Beach**; and, of course, the "Happiest Place on Earth," **Disney World.**

There are three main routes running north-south along Florida's Atlantic coastline, and your travels will likely make use of at least a little of each one. The fastest route is the **I-95** freeway, which races uneventfully along, linking the major cities.

The most scenic route is **Hwy-A1A**, a mostly two-lane highway that runs as close as possible to the shoreline, linking many gorgeous beaches but, because of the very flat topography and the extensive beachfront development, only rare glimpses of the open ocean. In between I-95 and Hwy-A1A runs historic **US-1**, part of the old Dixie Highway, which is lined by reminders of Florida's rich roadside heritage, but also passes through some of the state's less salubrious corners, especially in and around the larger cities. Our suggested route primarily follows coastal Hwy-A1A, but directions from other faster routes are also given—so you can alternate freely and easily among them all.

Amelia Island

Entering Florida from Georgia across the St. Marys River, which flows east out of the Okefenokee Swamp to the Atlantic Ocean, you may want to skirt around the metropolitan sprawl of Jacksonville by following old US-17, or getting off I-95 at exit 129, to Hwy-A1A, which runs due east to the brilliant white beaches and picturesque historic buildings of Amelia Island. The main community on the island is **Fernandina Beach** (pop 10,043), once the main port in northeast Florida. The eastern terminus of the first trans-Florida railroad, and long a popular tourist destination, Fernandina Beach retains many late-Victorian buildings, collected together in a wanderable 30-block historic district along the waterfront.

Among the many nice B&Bs here, you'll find the **Florida House Inn**, 22 S. 3rd Street (904/261/3300 or 800/258-3301), a historic hostelry that's been welcoming travelers since 1857. Florida's oldest hotel, it still rents

rooms (for a reasonable $70-95 a night), and serves tradi-
tional southern family-style meals, all-you-can-eat for
lunch (Mon.-Sat., $7) and dinner (Tues.-Sat.; $12). At the
center of town, the lively **Palace Saloon**, 117 Centre Street,
is another of "Florida's Oldest," with a lovely carved wood
bar, very good burgers, and regular live reggae and other
warm-weather music. For further information on Fernandina Beach, contact the **visitors bureau** (904/261-3248 or
800/226-3542)

FLORIDA HOUSE INN

More history has been preserved at the north end of
Amelia Island, adjacent to Fernandina Beach, where the well-
preserved remnants of a pre-Civil War brick fortress stand in
Fort Clinch State Park (daily 9 AM-5 PM; free), 250 acres of
marshes, sand dunes and coastal hammock forests along the
edge of Cumberland Sound.

South of Fernandina Beach, Hwy-A1A follows Fletcher Avenue along Amelia Island's gorgeous white beaches, passing upscale resorts (including the Ritz-Carlton) before crossing over a
bridge onto Talbot Island. Four miles south of the bridge,
there's a turnoff west to the 3,000-acre **Kingsley Plantation State
Historic Site** (daily 9 AM-5 PM; free), the last remaining antebellum plantation in Florida, where you can explore the elegant
old lodge and remains of more than 30 slave cabins.

Continuing south, Hwy-A1A winds across the dense native
jungles of Little Talbot Island, where a large state park (daily
dawn-dusk; $3.50; 904/251-2320) has hiking and cycling trails,
a nice campground, and a magnificent beach. The scenic road,
which has been dubbed the "Buccaneer Trail," eventually ends
up at the terminal for the ferry to Mayport (every 30 minutes;
cars $2.50, no RVs) across the St. Johns River.

Jacksonville Beach

East of Jacksonville, at the mouth of the St. Johns River, Hwy-
A1A curves around a large U.S. Navy base, past the Bath Iron
Works shipyard and the sizeable fishing port of **Mayport**, where
you can enjoy a quick bite at a seafood shack (try **Singleton's**,
100 yards west of the ferry landing) while waiting for your ferry
boat. From Mayport, Hwy-A1A zig-zags inland south and east,
reaching the water again at Jacksonville Beach, a welcoming,
family-oriented community with the usual gauntlet of cafes,
mini-golf courses and video arcades, and a nice beachfront centering on a small pier.

South of Jacksonville Beach spreads the enclave of **Ponte
Vedra Beach**, where country club resorts replace roadside
sprawl. Hwy-A1A bends inland through here, so if you want to
keep close to the shore (most of which is private) follow Hwy-
203 instead, rejoining Hwy-A1A on the edge of town.

Two men who made
millions in the automobile
industry have had
immeasurable influence
over the evolution of the
Florida coast. Standard Oil
baron Henry Flagler
constructed the first railroad
and built a chain of deluxe
resort hotels from St.
Augustine to Miami, while
Carl Fisher, the developer of
car headlights, promoted
Florida's "Route 66," the
Dixie Highway, and later
helped to found Miami
Beach. Their names
reappear frequently
wherever you travel along
the Atlantic coast.

Of all the American
colonies, only Florida
remained loyal to the British
crown during the
Revolutionary War. After the
war, the British ceded
Florida to Spain, which
eventually swapped it to the
United States in 1821 in
exchange for $5 million in
assumed debt.

Jacksonville, which covers
over 750 square miles, is the
largest city in the
continental U.S. Along I-95
south of Jacksonville you'll
pass the brand-new, $1.5
billion **World Golf Village**
(800/WGV-4746 or 800/948-
4746), a PGA-sponsored Hall
of Fame, IMAX theater and
Sam Snead-approved golf
course.

South of Ponte Vedra, Hwy-A1A passes a pair of beachfront state parks (the marvelous 12,000-acre Guana River and smaller South Ponte Vedra), both of which give access to usually uncrowded sands. About 30 miles south of Jacksonville Beach, across the water from St. Augustine in the town of Vilano Beach, Hwy-A1A passes by a real historic Florida landmark, **Oscar's Old Florida Grill**, at 614 Euclid Avenue, east of the highway at mile marker 52. Built in 1909, and hardly changed since, this funky little shack has great fresh seafood, steaks, and burgers, and you can listen to live bluegrass and other good music while watching the sun set over the Tolomato River, the slow-flowing stream that doubles as the Intracoastal Waterway. Oscar's is closed Monday and Tuesday.

The Fountain of Youth

Between Vilano Beach and St. Augustine, Hwy-A1A cuts inland from the shore, crossing a bridge over the North River, then following San Marco Avenue south past the Fountain of Youth and into the center of St. Augustine. That's right, the Fountain of Youth. Though its efficacy has never been proven in court, there is an actual site where Spanish explorer Ponce de Leon, searching for a fabled spring that would keep him forever young, came ashore in 1513. Now a pleas-

ant 20-acre park, facing Matanzas Bay about a mile north of central St. Augustine, the Fountain of Youth (daily 9 AM-5 PM; $5) preserves a naturally sulphurous spring (which you can drink from using Dixie cups—though there are no guarantees of immortality!), a burial ground, and remnants of a native Timucuan village and an early Spanish settlement.

St. Augustine

If you like history, architecture, sandy beaches, bizarre tourist attractions—or any combination of the above—you'll want to spend some time in St. Augustine. The oldest permanent settlement in the U.S.—though Santa Fe, New Mexico makes a strong counterclaim to this title—St. Augustine was founded in 1565, half a century after Ponce de Leon first set foot here in 1513, looking for the Fountain of Youth. Under Spanish control, the town's early history was pretty lively, with Sir Francis Drake leveling the place in 1586. The British, after trading Cuba for Florida at the end of the Seven Year's War, took control in 1763, and held St. Augustine throughout the American Revolution—during which Florida was staunchly loyal to King George. It served for many years as capital of Florida under both the British and Spanish, but after the Americans took over St. Augustine, the city lost that status to Tallahassee, subsequently missing out on much of Florida's 20th-century growth and development, which has allowed the preservation of its substantial historical remnants.

The heart of St. Augustine is contained within a walkably small area, centered upon the Plaza de la Constitucion, which faces east onto Matanzas Bay. Pedestrianized St. George Street runs north and south from here through the heart of historic St. Augustine, while two blocks west stands the city's most prominent landmarks, two grand, turn-of-the-century hotels—the **Ponce de Leon** and the **Alcazar**—originally owned and operated as part of Henry Flagler's Florida empire but now respectively housing **Flagler College** (daily 10 AM-3 PM; free) and the decorative arts collections of the **Lightner Museum** (daily 9 AM-5 PM; $4). Both are full of finely crafted interior spaces and well worth a look.

Though it's the compact size and overall historic sheen of St. Augustine that make it such a captivating place to spend some time, there are lots of individual attractions hawking themselves as important "historic sites," usually the oldest this-or-that in Florida, or even in the whole U.S.A. The **Oldest Wooden Schoolhouse** (daily 9 AM-5 PM; $2), at 14 St. George Street in the heart of historic St. Augustine, dates from 1750 and now features a push-button wax dummy of a schoolteacher, while the **Oldest Store** (daily 9 AM-5 PM; $4), a block south of the main plaza at 4 Artillery Lane, has 100,000 items, all of them well past their turn-of-the-century

---

HENRY FLAGLER: FATHER OF FLORIDA TOURISM

You can't travel very far along the east coast of Florida without coming under the influence of Henry Flagler, who almost single-handedly turned what had been swampy coastline into one of the world's most popular tourist destinations. After making a fortune as John D. Rockefeller's partner in the Standard Oil Company, in the early 1880s Flagler came to St. Augustine with his wife, who was suffering from health problems. He found the climate agreeable, but the facilities sorely lacking, so he embarked on construction of the 540-room Hotel Ponce de Leon, which opened in 1888. The hotel, the first major resort in Florida, was an instant success, and Flagler quickly expanded his operations, building the first railroad along the coast south to Palm Beach, where he opened the world's largest hotel, the now-demolished Royal Poinciana, in 1894, joined by The Breakers in 1901, and his own palatial home, Whitehall, in 1902.

Meanwhile, Flagler was busy extending his railroad south, effectively founding the new city of Miami in 1897 when he opened the deluxe Royal Palm Hotel (which stood on the waterfront, where the Inter-Continental does today). From Miami, he decided to extend his Florida East Coast Railway all the way to Key West, which at the time was Florida's most populous city, and the American deep-water port closest to the proposed Panama Canal. At a cost of $50 million and hundreds of lives, this amazing railroad was completed in 1912, but lasted only two decades before a hurricane destroyed the tracks in 1935. The remnants of Flagler's railroad were used as the foundation for today's Overseas Highway, US-1, but Flagler himself never lived to see it. In 1913, a year after his railroad reached Key West, Henry Flagler fell down a flight of stairs and died at age 84.

In the 1920s and 1930s, when car travel and Florida tourism were both reaching an early peak of popularity, the roadside landscape was, in the words of the WPA *Guide to Florida*, lined by "signs that turn like windmills; startling signs that resemble crashed airplanes; signs with glass lettering which blaze forth at night when automobile headlights strike them; flashing neon signs; signs painted with professional touch; signs crudely lettered and misspelled. They advertise hotels, tourist cabins, fishing camps, and eating places. They extol the virtues of ice creams, shoe creams, cold creams; proclaim the advantages of new cars and used cars; tell of 24-hour towing and ambulance service, Georgia pecans, Florida fruit and fruit juices, honey, soft drinks, and furniture. They urge the traveler to take designated tours, to visit certain cities, to stop at certain points he 'must see.'" Alas, most of these signs are long gone.

Across the street from the Ripley's Believe It or Not!, a coquina stone ball known as the **Zero Milepost** marks the eastern end of the Old Spanish Trail, one of the earliest transcontinental highways. Marked and promoted from here west to San Diego, the Old Spanish Trail, like the Lincoln Highway and the Dixie Highway, preceded the system of numbered highways (Route 66 et. al.), and provided a popular cross-country link.

sell-by date. At the north end of St. George Street, an original city gate leads across San Marco Avenue (Hwy-A1A) to another must-see tourist trap: the original **Ripley's Believe It or Not!** museum (daily 9 AM-10 PM; $9), an elaborate Spanish revival mansion with the usual freak show and assorted oddities inside. Outside, in the parking lot, is a four-room "tree house," made from a California redwood tree in 1957.

These are fun in a tongue-in-cheek way, but the most impressive historic site is the remarkable **Castillo de San Marcos** (daily 9 AM-5 PM; $2) which dominates the St. Augustine waterfront. Built by Spain between 1672 and 1695, the Castillo saw its first battle in 1702, when British forces laid siege for 50 days but were unable to capture it, though they did once again level the adjacent town of St. Augustine. The Castillo was later used by the British to house American POWs during the Revolutionary War, and by the U.S. to house Native American prisoners captured during the Seminole War of 1835-42, and during the later Indian Wars of the

Oh the sights you can see at Ripley's Believe It or Not! museum

Wild West. Since 1924 it's been a National Monument and is open for walks along the ramparts, and for frequent ranger-guided tours.

St. Augustine Practicalities

One of many attractive things about St. Augustine is the almost total lack of franchised fast-food restaurants, at least in the historic downtown area. Instead, you can choose from all sorts of local places, like the **Florida Cracker Cafe**, 81 St. George Street, a casual seafood grill where you can sample the local delicacy, alligator tail. For fish 'n' chips, try the **White Lion Cafe and Pub**, off St. George Street on Cuna Street, or **Milltop Pub**, at the north end of St. George Street, which has nightly live music and boasts a block-long bar. (Yes, it's a short block.)

Away from the historic core, you can head north up Hwy-A1A to the **Manatee Grill,** north of the Fountain of Youth at 179 San Marco Avenue, a healthy, veggie-friendly place, serving all-organic food for breakfast and lunch only. Farther north and east, across the bridge, in Vilano Beach, there's historic Oscar's Old Florida Grill (see above). Heading south toward St. Augustine Beach, Hwy-A1A passes a series of roadside restaurants: **Capt. Jack's,** 410 Anastasia Boulevard, is a family-friendly, deep-fried fish place, while the **Gypsy Cab Company,** 828 Anastasia, is more urbane —and more expensive. On St. Augustine Beach itself, **Po-Mar's** is a very popular sandwich and beer stand.

Unfortunately for present-day visitors, the grand old Ponce de Leon Hotel, built by Standard Oil baron Henry Flagler in 1888, no longer welcomes overnight guests (though you can take a guided tour of what was once the most opulent hotel in America). Contemporary St. Augustine still offers a wide variety of accommodations, including the only B&B on Florida's Atlantic beachfront, **Coquina Gables,** 1 F Street in St. Augustine Beach (904/461-8727), where you can spend the night in one of three tastefully decorated suites in a historic home, then wake up and watch the porpoises cavorting offshore while enjoying a truly gourmet breakfast. Doubles cost $109-169 a night. In the historic district, the **Kenwood Inn,** 38 Marine Street (904/824-2116), has rooms in a Victorian hotel from around $80 a night.

> While Hwy-A1A passes right through, US-1 bypasses the historic center of St. Augustine, and I-95 is linked from exit 95 via Hwy-16.

For additional listings, maps and general information, your first stop should be the St. Augustine **visitors center,** across from the Castillo (904/825-1000, 800/ OLD-CITY or 800/653-2489).

Alligator Farm

From the heart of St. Augustine, Hwy-A1A crosses over the Matanzas River across the lovely, historic Bridge of Lions to Anastasia Island, bound for the Atlantic beaches three miles to the east.

> About three miles north of Marineland, on the inland side of Hwy-A1A, you can see the 16-foot-thick stone walls of **Fort Matanzas,** built by the Spanish around 1736, never conquered. Now a national historic site, it's open for free tours.

On the way to beach, just two miles south of Old Town St. Augustine on Anastasia Boulevard (Hwy-A1A), sits one of the greatest of Florida's many tourist traps, Alligator Farm (daily 9 AM-6 PM; $10.95; 904/824-3337). Touted as the world's only complete collection of crocodilians, this was the first and is now one of the last of many such roadside menageries. A legitimate historical landmark, Alligator Farm is also a fun and informative place to spend some time—great for kids, and anyone who finds gators and crocs (and turtles, iguanas, monkeys, and tropical birds, all of which are here) to be captivating creatures. Start at the largest enclosure, a mossy pond seething with hundreds of baby 'gators (which you can feed), and be sure to pay your respects to Gomek, the Alligator Farm's mascot, a 23-foot-long crocodile who was taxidermied after his death.

Across from Alligator Farm, a road turns east from Hwy-A1A to **Anastasia State Recreation Area,** the site where the stone for Castillo de San Marcos was quarried, where besides beaches there's an inlet set aside for windsurfing, hiking trails through coastal hammock forests, and a nice campground (904/461-2000) amidst stately live oaks and magnolia trees.

The town of Ormond Beach, which adjoins the north side of Daytona Beach, was also used by early speed-seekers, and prior to that was a winter playground of the rich and famous, richest and most famously John D. Rockefeller, who wintered here for years before his death in 1937, aged 97. His mansion, called **The Casements,** sits along the east bank of the Halifax River at 25 Riverside Drive.

Marineland

Eighteen miles south of St. Augustine, 35 miles north of Daytona Beach, the original sea creature amusement park, Marineland closed (perhaps temporarily, perhaps forever . . .) in 1998, declaring bankruptcy after struggling for years to compete with the much-larger likes of Sea World and Disney World. Marineland, which is credited with the first performing dolphins (and with playing a key role in the sci-fi movie *Creature From the Black Lagoon)* has hardly changed since it was created by *Gone With the Wind* producer Cornelius Vanderbilt Whitney. At time of writing there was still hope of resurrecting the complex as a research center, but the task of preserving and revitalizing the once-modish streamlined concrete architecture is daunting.

Continuing along the coast south of Marineland you start to see roadside fruit stands advertising "Indian River Fruit"—something you'll see a *lot* more of as you travel south. This stretch of Hwy-A1A, around the town of Flagler Beach, is also one of the few where you can actually see the ocean from the road.

Daytona Beach

Offering a heady barrage of blue-collar beach culture, Daytona Beach (pop. 61,900) is a classic road trip destination in every way shape and form. The beach here is huge—over 20 miles long, and 500 feet wide at low tide—and there's a small amusement pier (with a Sky Ride that dangles you over the fishermen below) at the foot of Main Street, but the rest of Daytona Beach is rather rough-at-the-edges, with boarded-up shops and some lively bars and nightclubs filling the few blocks between the beach area and the Halifax River, which separates the beach from the rest of the town.

Besides being a living museum of pop culture, Daytona Beach has long played an important role in Car Culture: in the first decades of the 20th century, a real who's who of international automotive pioneers—Henry Ford, R.E. Olds, Malford Duesenberg and more—came here to test the upper limits of automotive performance. The first world land speed record (a whopping 68 mph!) was set here in 1903, and by 1935 the ill-starred British racer Malcolm Campbell had raised it to 276 mph.

tearing up the track at Daytona International Speedway

The speed racers later moved west to Bonneville Salt Flats in Utah (see page 143), and Daytona become the breeding ground for stock car racing—today's Daytona 500 started out as a series of 100-to-200-mile races around a rough four-mile oval, half on the sands and half on a paved frontage road. The circuit races, both for cars and motorcycles, really came into their own after WW II. In 1947, NASCAR (the National Association for Stock Car Auto Racing) was founded here as the nascent sport's governing body, but the races soon outgrew the sands, and in 1958 were moved to the purpose-built **Daytona International Speedway**, on US-92 six miles west of the beach, right off I-95 exit 87. Except during the run-up to a race, you can take a guided tour (daily 9:30 AM-4:30 PM; $6) of the triangular track, cruising down the back straight and around the steeply banked turns—in a bus, at a modest 20 mph.

On the speedway grounds, the racing experience is brought to life at the very enjoyable **Daytona USA**, part museum and part amusement park, where you can learn the history of stock car racing, take part in a simulated pit stop, play video games, and watch a loud and totally thrilling big screen movie that lets you experience the pace and power of Daytona—without having to wear seat belts. (After a visit, you may want to spend some time practicing your skills at the go-cart track across the street.)

On the other side of I-95 from Daytona Speedway, the best collection of classic Corvettes anywhere can be enjoyed at the **Klassix Auto Museum**, 2909 W. International Speedway Boulevard (daily 9 AM-6 PM; $8), where each model year is displayed in a setting that evokes the year of its creation. Besides the classic 'Vettes, there are hundreds of other machines filling over 50,000 square feet of display space, including 1970s muscle cars, hot rods, rare Harleys and other motorcycles—everything a speed freak or classic car fan could want.

You can still drive on the beach at Daytona during the day, but there's a $5 fee and the maximum speed is a strictly enforced 10 mph.

Daytona Beach Practicalities

Daytona Beach is party central during March and April, when thousands of college kids escape from northern climes to defrost and unwind with a vengeance. There has been a concerted effort to keep a lid on things recently, but if you're after peace and quiet you should head somewhere else. The same is true of the springtime "Bike Week" before the Daytona 200, and fall's "Biketoberfest," when thousands of motorcycling enthusiasts descend upon Daytona for a week or more of partying in between races at Daytona Speedway. The Daytona 500 is held around Valentine's Day, but getting one of the 110,000 tickets is all but impossible for casual fans.

A world apart from the Spring Break and biker scenes, but just a block from the beach, the modern retro **Starlight Diner** at 401 N. Atlantic Avenue has better-than-average cafe food—and the hugest mug of coffee you'll find anywhere. There's an unusual place to stay just up the street: the **Traveler's Inn**, 735 N. Atlantic Avenue (904/253-3501), where the inexpensive motel rooms are all decorated with murals of movie stars (from Marilyn Monroe to John Wayne) and biker chicks. There are also thousands of rooms in the hotel towers along beachfront Atlantic Avenue, many advertising off-season or midweek deals.

For further information, contact the Daytona Beach **visitors bureau**, 126 E. Orange Avenue (904/255-0415 or 800/854-1234).

Detour: Orlando and Walt Disney World

Entire guidebooks are devoted to covering the mind-boggling array of tourist attractions in and around Orlando, but three words would probably suffice: Walt Disney World. Over 100,000 people come here every day to experience the magic of the Magic Kingdom, which is divided into four main areas—the Magic Kingdom amusement park, a new "Animal Kingdom" animal park, the futuristic EPCOT Center, and the Disney-MGM studio tours. A day at each of these will set you back around $40; to see all of them, get a "park-hopper" pass, which is valid for four days and costs about $150. An annual pass goes for around $275; for further information, call 407/ 824-4321.

At time of writing, there's still no law that says you have to go to Disney World just because you've come to Florida, but it is a cultural phenomenon and more than a little fun. While you're here, you may want to visit other Orlando attractions, which include a branch of most major amusement parks—Sea World and Universal Studios are both here. Orlando also has some funky, pre-Disney-era tourist traps, with ad budgets small enough that you won't have to fight the crowds. Best of the bunch is probably **GatorLand** (800/393-5297), where thousands of alligators, crocodiles, snakes and other reptiles are gathered together in a cypress swamp between Hwy-417, US-17/441 and the Florida Turnpike. You enter through a gator's gaping jaws, and inside can see such sights as live chickens being dangled over a pond, taunting the hungry carnivorous gators just of out reach below. Continuing south along US-441, past the world headquarters of Tupperware, another sight of offbeat interest is the 100-year-old historic district at the heart of **Kissimmee** (pop. 30,100), where a 50-foot stone and concrete pyramid, constructed in 1943 with rocks from most states, as well as 21 countries, stands in Lake Front park.

Disney World and the other Orlando attractions can put a gaping hole in your travel budget, but you can save considerable cash by staying at the handy **HI Kissimmee Hostel**, 4840 W. Hwy 192 ($15 per person; 407/396-8282) on the grounds of a former lakefront resort (with free use of pedal boats for guests!). Disney has a whole range of accommodations, and there are also dozens and dozens of roadside motels lining US-192, the main route between Orlando and Kissimmee. For additional information, contact the Kissimmee **visitors bureau** (800/333-KISS or 800/333-5177).

The Space Coast: Cape Canaveral

It's ironic that one of the most extensive sections of natural coastal wetlands left in Florida is home to the launch pads of the nation's space program. Though the natural aspects—thousands of seabirds and wide open

---

Adding to Daytona's already broad mix of pop culture icons is the **Hamburger Hall of Fame.** This wacky collection of burger-related memorabilia is displayed in a private home, but is open for tours by appointment (904/254-8753).

For a Disneyfied view of the ideal American town, visit the Walt Disney Company's retro-Victorian planned community of **Celebration** (pop. 700 and growing), south of US-192 at the I-4 junction. Contrary to popular belief, this is not the town seen in the Jim Carrey movie *The Truman Show* (that was Seaside, in the Florida Panhandle), but it could have been. For details, or to make reservations for a tour, phone 407/566-2200.

Between Orlando and the Space Coast, the **Beeline Expressway** (Hwy-528) is a fast, flat toll road, with only three exits in the 30 miles between I-95 and greater Orlando.

One of the best places to eat in this part of Florida is west of the Space Center, in the town of Titusville: **Dixie Crossroads**, 1475 Garden Street (407/268-5000), an immense (and immensely popular) place to eat seafood, especially massive plates of shrimp. All-you-can-eat piles of small shrimp cost $20, while jumbo shrimp cost around $1 apiece; the Crossroads is away from the water, two miles west of I-95 exit 80, and is open daily 11 AM-10 PM.

stretches of sandy beaches—are attractive enough in their own right to merit a visit, most people are drawn here because the undeveloped landscape allows clear and generally unobstructed views of missile launches, and Space Shuttle take-offs and landings, at Cape Canaveral's Kennedy Space Center. All the big milestones in the history of the U.S. space program—the Mercury, Gemini and Apollo launches—happened here, and if names like Alan Shepard, John Glenn or Neil Armstrong mean anything to you, set aside time for a visit.

The Kennedy Space Center itself, eight miles west of US-1 via the "NASA Parkway" (Hwy-405), is open to the public, but only on guided tours. The tours all leave from the large **visitor complex** (daily 9 AM-dusk; free; 407/452-2121) where a pair of IMAX theaters ($5) show films of outer space to get you in the mood. There are also some small museums, a simulated Space Shuttle mission control center, a half-dozen missiles in the Rocket Garden, and an actual Space Shuttle, which you can walk through. The visitor center also has a couple of fast-food restaurants and a kennel for pets.

To see the Kennedy Space Center up close, join one of two tours: the Blue Tour, which visits the Canaveral Air Force station and the sites of many early "Space Race" adventures, and the Red Tour, which visits the Apollo and Space Shuttle launch pads and other sites. Each tour takes about two hours, and costs $8.

At the entrance to the Kennedy Space Center visitor center, the **Astronaut Memorial** is a huge black granite block backed by high-tech mirrors that reflect sunlight on to the surface of the stone, illuminating the names of the men and women who have given their lives exploring space.

To watch a Space Shuttle or other launch at Kennedy Space Center, you can get passes from the visitor center, or simply watch from the many good vantage points: Playalinda Beach, in the Canaveral National Seashore at the west end of Hwy-402 from Titusville; across the Indian River, along US-1 in Titusville; or the beaches west of Hwy-A1A in Cocoa Beach.

Cocoa Beach

The town of Cocoa Beach, familiar to anyone who ever watched the 1960s Space Age sitcom *I Dream of Jeannie*, sits south of the Kennedy Space Center, and the town pier that juts out into the Atlantic Ocean at the north end of town is a prime spot for viewing Space Shuttle launches. Cocoa Beach is also the gateway to a less-hyped half of the NASA experience, the **Air Force Space and Missile Museum** (Mon.-Fri. 10 AM-2 PM; free; 407/853-3245), on the grounds of Cape Canaveral Air Station, the launch site for the unmanned space probes of the late 1950s, including the first U.S. satellite (Explorer 1), and the famous "astro chimps" (Gordo, Able, and Miss Baker, who were launched into orbit to test the effects of weightlessness). Along with historical exhibits and dozens of missiles, from today's Patriots back to German V2s (which were fired at England during WW II, and provided the engineering basis for the American rockets of a decade later), the museum includes early computers and other equipment, housed inside the blockhouse from which the first launches were controlled.

Though travel to outer space is clearly on the minds of many residents, especially personnel stationed at Patrick Air Force Base here, the real focus here is catching the perfect wave: Cocoa Beach is surf center of the Space Coast. Along with a clean,

10-mile-long beach, the town also holds a batch of good-value motels, located within a short walk of the waves. Choose from chains (including a Motel 6), or check out the garish **Fawlty Towers**,100 E. Cocoa Beach Causeway (407/784-3870), which is sadly devoid of John Cleese or put-upon Juan. It is, however, next door to Cocoa Beach's main event, the massive **Ron Jon Surf Shop**, open 24 hours every day at 4151 Atlantic Avenue (407/799-8888), *the* place to buy or rent surfboards, body boards or bicycles.

The least expensive accommodations in the Space Coast area are at the **Melbourne Beach HI Hostel**, 1135 N. Hwy-A1A (407/951-0004) right on the beach, 15 miles south of Cocoa Beach or a half-mile north of US-192, with dorm beds and a few private rooms available for around $15 per person.

> East from Hwy-A1A on the south side of Cocoa Beach, "I Dream of Jeannie Lane" leads down to a nice beachfront park.

Vero Beach

As a boy growing up in sunny Los Angeles, I could never understand why the Dodgers felt they had to disappear to distant Florida to get in shape during Spring Training. I knew the weather couldn't be so much better there (after all, didn't L.A. have the heavenly climate?), and I never quite figured out what the big attraction of Vero Beach, the Dodgers' off-season home, could be. But when I discovered that the Dodgers had started playing here way back in 1948—back when they still called Brooklyn home —it all began to make sense. And it still does, once you see the spacious grounds of **Dodgertown**, their Florida training complex, which spreads amidst the grapefruit orchards on the west side of town at 3901 26th Street. The Dodgers train here in

---

SPRING TRAINING: GRAPEFRUIT LEAGUE BASEBALL

Every February and March hundreds of baseball players at all levels of expertise head to Florida to earn or keep their places on some 20 different Major League teams and their minor league farm club affiliates. The informality and ease of access during this spring training, which is known as the **Grapefruit League**, attracts thousands of baseball fans as well. Though they're not necessarily played to win, Grapefruit League games are played in modern 10,000-seat stadia that approach the major leagues in quality, and the smaller sizes allows an up-close feel you'd have to pay much more for during the regular season. (And your chances of snagging balls during batting practice are infinitely better, too.)

Most of the teams make their springtime homes on the Gulf Coast, but many others locate in cities and towns along Florida's Atlantic coast, as the **Los Angeles Dodgers** do in Vero Beach. Three teams are in the Orlando area, including the **Atlanta Braves**, who train in Walt Disney World's "ABC Wide World of Sports' Complex"; the **Houston Astros** play in nearby Kissimmee, and the Kansas City Royals in Davenport. Back on the coast, the **New York Mets** train in Port St. Lucie, the **Montreal Expos** and **St. Louis Cardinals** play in Jupiter, and the **Baltimore Orioles** can be found in Fort Lauderdale.

February and March, when the place is packed with thousands of baseball fans from all over the country, and their Class A farm team, the **Vero Beach Dodgers**, play here all summer, drawing fans to sunny Holman Stadium ($4; 561/ 569-6858).

Besides baseball, Vero Beach also has a really nice beach, in South Beach Park at the end of the Palmetto Causeway. This South Beach is family-friendly and about as far as you can get from Miami's South Beach and still be in Florida: the sands here are clean, grainy and golden, the waves are good-sized, and there are showers and free parking.

Vero Beach also has a nice place to stay and eat: the **Driftwood Resort**, 3150 Ocean Drive (561/231-7091), which has funky 1950s-style motel rooms and the fun and good-value **Waldo's**, a poolside cafe and bar overlooking the ocean.

Fort Pierce

South of Vero Beach, Hwy-A1A continues along North Hutchinson Island past the **UDT Navy Seals Museum** (daily 10 AM-4 PM; $3.50) which describes the various roles played by underwater divers in demolishing enemy property during wartime. Among the displays of wet suits and explosives is an Apollo capsule—it's Navy SEALS who rescued returning astronauts after they "splashed down" in the ocean. On the either side of the museum, undeveloped stretches of the coast have been preserved in a pair of parks, where you can enjoy uncrowded beaches or wander along boardwalks through thickly forested mangrove swamps.

South of Fort Pierce, Port St. Lucie is the Spring Training home of the New York Mets (561/871-2100), who play at 525 Peacock Boulevard, off I-95 exit 63C.

Bending inland across the North Bridge, Hwy-A1A links up briefly with US-1, the Old Dixie Highway, through the town of Fort Pierce (pop. 36,800), a market center of the famous "Indian River" produce-growing district. After this half-mile detour, Hwy-A1A returns to the shore, passing along the way by the very good **St. Lucie County Historical Museum** (Tues-Sun. 10 AM-4 PM; $3), at the east end of the South Bridge, where broad-ranging displays tell the history of the region, showing off a hand-carved canoe and explaining the "fort" in Fort Pierce (it was built in 1835, during the Seminole Wars).

On the coast north of Palm Beach, the town of Jupiter has long been home to movie star Burt Reynolds; the park surrounding the town's excellent **Florida History Center** (Tues.-Fri. 10 AM-5 PM; Saturday and Sunday 1-5 PM; $4) off Hwy-A1A at 805 N. US-1, is named in Burt's honor, though he himself is conspicuously absent from the museum's displays.

South of Fort Pierce, Hwy-A1A embarks on a nearly 30-mile run along Hutchinson Island, where dense stands of pines block the views of largely undeveloped beachfront.

The Kennedy family compound in Palm Beach is on North Ocean Boulevard, on the coast about two miles north of The Breakers resort.

Palm Beach

A South Florida sibling to the conspicuous consumption that once defined Newport, Rhode Island, Palm Beach (pop. 9,800) has been a winter refuge for the rich and famous since Henry Flager started work on his fashionable (but long-vanished) resort hotel, the 1,150-room Royal Poinciana; this was the world's largest wood building when completed in 1894, but the site is now an upscale shopping district at the center of town. Away from here, most of Palm Beach is well-guarded private property, off-limits to most mere mortals. The best way for anyone not named Kennedy or Pierpont to get a look at Palm Beach life is to spend some time at the Hearst Castle of the East Coast, the **Henry Morrison Flagler Museum** (Tues.-Sat. 10 AM-5 PM, Sunday 1-5 PM; $7), on the inland side of downtown Palm Beach, at the north end of Cocoanut Row. Officially known as Whitehall, this opulent 60,000-square-foot mansion was Flagler's private home, and the 50-plus rooms (many of which were taken from European buildings and re-installed here) contain historical exhibits tracing the life of Flagler, the Standard Oil baron (John D. Rockefeller's right-hand man) who made a fortune while making Florida into an immensely popular vacation destination. (For more on Henry Flagler, see page 421.)

Even bigger and better than Whitehall is **The Breakers**, a stately resort hotel that faces the ocean at the east end of Palm Beach, and retains much of its 1920s mock-Mediterranean style and grace. Rooms will set you back anywhere from $150 to $350 a night (much more for suites), but you can enjoy the lobby and have a drink or afternoon tea, or take a tour (Wednesday at 3 PM only; free; 561/655-6611).

At the south end of Cocoanut Row, on Worth Avenue a mile from the Flagler Museum, another ultra-exclusive haunt is the Everglades Club, whose home is credited with being the building that turned wealthy Floridians towards postmodern pan-Mediterranean architecture.

Not surprisingly, there are some very good and very expensive restaurants in and around Palm Beach, but happily there's also a very nice, normal, all-American coffee shop right at the center of town: **Green's Pharmacy**, at 151 N. County Road, serving very good diner-style meals on the main route down Palm Beach Island.

For more information on the Palm Beach area, contact the Palm County **visitors bureau**, 1555 Palm Beach Lakes Drive (561/471-3995), in working-class West Palm Beach.

Inland from Palm Beach, you can wave at rhinos, lions and wildebeest in a 500-acre, drive-through simulation of African ecosystems at **Lion Country Safari,** 18 miles west of I-95 via US-98 (561/793-1084). No convertibles allowed!

The town of Lantana, on the coast between Palm Beach and Boca Raton, is the home of the **National Enquirer** tabloid.

Boca Raton

Whoever named Boca Raton (pop. 61,500), which translates literally as the "Rat's Mouth," clearly didn't have an ear for future promotional bonanza, but despite the awkward name the town has become one of the more chichi spots in the state. As in Palm Beach, Coral Gables and Miami's South Beach, the best of Boca dates from the 1920s, when architect and real estate promoter Addison Mizner, flush from his success building Mediterranean-style manors in Palm Beach, created a mini-Venice of resorts and canals, which survives mainly in the shocking pink palazzo of the **Boca Raton Resort**, on the southeast side of town at 501 El Camino Royal (561/395-6766).

Downtown Boca has been turned into a massive stucco shopping mall, but it's worth braving for a look inside the ornate Mizner-designed Town Hall, on US-1 (Old Dixie Highway) in Palmetto Park downtown, which now houses the local historical museum (Tues.-Fri 10 AM-4 PM; free). The main Boca Raton shopping mall, misleadingly called "Mizner Park," is the unlikely home of the **International Museum of Cartoon Art** at 201 Plaza Real, formerly of New York City but now in the center of town (Tues.-Sat. 11 AM-6 PM, Sunday noon-6 PM; $6; 561/391-2200), which displays over 200 years worth of comic strips, editorial caricatures, storyboards, and animation cels from the Roadrunner (and other) cartoons!

US-1, the main route through town, also holds the **Boca Diner,** serving above-average coffee shop fare at 2801 N. Federal Highway, and one of Florida's better BBQ joints, **Tom's Place** at 7251 N. Federal Highway (US-1), two good places to eat in this quiet, mostly residential community.

Hwy-A1A misses most of Boca Raton, cruising past along the densely pine-forested coast. The beaches are accessible but hard to find; one well-marked stop along the way is the **Gumbo Limbo Nature Center** (Mon.-Sat. 9 AM-4 PM, Sunday noon-4 PM; free) on the inland side of the highway, a mile north of Mizner Park. A variety of native Floridian landscapes have been re-created here, letting you wander at will past coastal dunes, mangrove wetlands, and rare sabal palm hammocks. Across Hwy-A1A, Red Reef Park is a popular surfing beach.

Fort Lauderdale

Famed for the annual "Spring Break" that sees tens of thousands of college kids descending here for an orgy of drunken round-the-clock partying, Fort Lauderdale (pop. 162,800) is a surprisingly residential city, brought to a more human scale by the many waterways that cut through it. One of the largest cargo ports in the state, Fort Lauderdale also boasts more boats per capita than just about anywhere else in the U.S., and over 165 miles of canals, inlets, and other waterways flowing through the city.

Fort Lauderdale is said to be one of the points that form the "Bermuda Triangle," so of course there's a beachside bar where college kids try to simulate its supernatural effects by imbibing too many margaritas.

Water is also the medium of the city's main tourist attraction: the **International Swimming Hall of Fame** (daily 9 AM-7 PM; $5), which, along with the expected gold medals and aquatic artifacts also has a very nice swimming pool ($3). The hall is across from the beach, on Hwy-A1A a block south of Las Olas Avenue.

Downtown Fort Lauderdale has a few big dull office towers, but along the New River there are some well-preserved historic buildings, dating back to 1905 when the city first emerged from the swamps. Find out more by visiting the **Historical Museum,** west of US-1 at 219 S.W. 2nd Avenue (Tues.-Fri. 10 AM-4 PM; $2), which has lots of old photos and walking-tour maps, or the nifty **Stranahan House,** off US-1 on Las Olas Boulevard at S.E. 6th Avenue (Wed.-Sun. 10 AM-4 PM; $5), a circa 1901 trading post and house, with broad verandahs and a high ceiling to help cool down in pre-a/c days. Still owned by the same family that built it, the Stranahan House is one of the most evocative historic places in the state.

Fort Lauderdale's main beachfront bar and nightclub district is along Atlantic Avenue and Las Olas Boulevard, where you'll find some nice sidewalk cafes and fast-food restaurants. For breakfast, or a big cup of coffee, head south of town to **Lester's Diner,** near the airport at 250 S.W. 34th Street (Hwy-84). For good fried seafood, cold beer, and live blues, head south down US-1 to **Ernie's BBQ Lounge,** 1843 S. Federal Highway, famous for its conch fritters, calamari rings and rooftop deck. In Lighthouse Point, on Hwy-A1A about 10 miles north of Fort Lauderdale, a great old Florida hangout is **Cap's Place** a casual seafood-and-steak place that's been in business since 1929—FDR and Winston Churchill both ate here. It's hard to find, so call for directions (954/941-0418).

Miles of inexpensive motels line Hwy-A1A north of Fort Lauderdale, and unless there's something big going on you shouldn't have trouble finding a room for under $80—half that in summer. For complete listings of restaurants and accommodations, contact the **visitors bureau,** 1850 Eller Drive (954/765-4466 or 800/356-1662).

North of Fort Lauderdale, Hwy-A1A winds in along the coast through a series of funky, friendly beachside communities. South of Fort Lauderdale, Hwy-A1A heads inland and merges into US-1, returning to the coast for the run south to Miami Beach.

North Miami Beach

Between Fort Lauderdale and Miami Beach, Hwy-A1A runs along the shore, first as Ocean Drive and later as Collins Avenue, while US-1 runs inland parallel to the old Dixie Highway. There's nothing here to compare with the attractions farther south, but the town of North Miami Beach does have one oddity: the **Ancient Spanish Monastery**, at 16711 W. Dixie Highway (daily 10 AM-4 PM; $5), a 12th-century monastery bought in the 1920s by William Randolph Hearst, who had it dismantled and shipped to the U.S. for his "Hearst Castle." However, it was confiscated by U.S. Customs, and finally rebuilt here as an Episcopal church.

On the coast, Hwy-A1A runs past a number of indistinct beach towns before hitting **Bal Harbour**, home to one of Miami's biggest and best shopping malls, and one of its biggest beaches, Haulover Beach. From here south to Miami Beach, the road is lined by towering concrete condos and hotels.

At the far north end of Miami Beach, one place you'll want to stop, especially if you're hungry, is **Wolfie Cohen's Rascal House**, 17190 Collins Avenue (Hwy-A1A), a super-sized NYC deli done up in Miami's favorite colors: shocking pink walls and turquoise green booths. The sandwiches here are good and huge—big enough to feed two or more.

The stately Mediterranean Revival manor where fashion designer Gianni Versace lived and was murdered sits at the heart of South Beach, on Ocean Drive just north of 11th Street.

Miami Beach

Covering a broad island separating downtown Miami from the open Atlantic Ocean, Miami Beach (pop. 92,639) has long been a mecca for fans of 1930s Art Deco architecture and design. More recently, it's also become one of the world's most fashionable and bacchanalian beach resorts, with deluxe hotels and high-style nightclubs and restaurants lining the broad white sands of South Beach, the relatively small corner of Miami Beach that gets 99% of the press and tourist attention. Here, along beachfront Ocean Drive and busier Collins Avenue (Hwy-A1A) a block inland, you'll find dozens of glorious Art Deco hotels, many lighted with elegant neon signs. Guided walking tours ($10) of the district leave every Saturday at 10 AM from the **Art Deco Welcome Center**, 1001 Ocean Drive (daily 9 AM-5 PM or later; 305/531-3484), which also sells guidebooks, posters, postcards and anything else you can think of that has to do with the Art Deco era.

No matter how intoxicating the architecture, beach life and nightlife along South Beach are, while you're here be sure to set aside an hour or two to explore the fascinating collection of pop culture artifacts on display a block inland at **The Wolfsonian**, 1001 Washington Avenue (Tues.-Sat. 11 AM-6 PM, Sunday noon-5 PM; $5; 305/531-1001). One of the odder high-brow museums you'll find, the Wolfsonian (officially the "Mitchell Wolfson Jr. Collection of Decorative and Propaganda Arts") fills a retrofitted 1920s warehouse with four floors of furniture, sculpture, architectural models, posters and much more; two areas of excellence are drawings and murals created under the New Deal auspices of the WPA, and similar agitprop arti-

---

CARL FISHER: FATHER OF MIAMI BEACH

Fisher Park, on the bay side of Miami Beach on Alton Road at 51st Street, holds a small monument to the fascinating Carl Fisher, the man most responsible for turning Miami Beach from a mangrove swamp into America's favorite resort. Before building up Lincoln Avenue into Miami Beach's first commercial district, Carl Fisher had played an important role in America's early automotive history. Called the "P.T. Barnum of the Automobile Age," Fisher made millions through the Prest-O-Lite company, which in the early 1900s developed the first functioning car headlight. Around 1910, he invested this fortune in building and promoting the Indianapolis Motor Speedway, then went on to plan and publicize both the Lincoln Highway, America's first transcontinental road, and the Dixie Highway, the first main north-south route in the eastern U.S. He invested heavily in Miami Beach property, but was ruined by the Great Depression and the sudden drop in land values. He died here, nearly penniless, in 1939, just as the economy was rebounding and the Art Deco hotels of South Beach were bringing new life to Miami Beach.

---

facts created in Weimar Germany. Only a small portion of the extensive collection is on display at any one time, and most of the floor space is given over to changing exhibitions—on anything from World's Fairs to Florida tourism to William Morris chairs—but it's a thought-provoking place. With an unexpressed but overriding theme of how art can counterbalance, or at least respond to, the demands of industrial society, the Wolfsonian is a much-appreciated antidote to the hedonistic consumerism of the rest of Miami Beach.

Speaking of hedonistic consumerism, for the complete South Beach experience check into one of the great old Art Deco hotels, especially one that's been updated with modern conveniences, like the **Delano**, 1685 Collins Avenue (305/672-2000 or 800/555-5001), a high-style symphony in white, or the **Raleigh**, 1775 Collins Avenue (305/534-6300 or 800/848-1775), with the coolest pool in South Beach. Both of these, with peak season rooms in the $150-250 range, are at the mid-to-upper range of South Beach rates. The wonderful architecture of the South Beach hotels, alas, doesn't always manage to mask the 24-hour hubbub that surrounds them, so be wary of staying at ones in the Ocean Drive nightclub district—at least if you want to sleep at night. Ocean Drive, by the way, is undriveable on weekend nights, since so many cars cruise up and down it, stereos blasting.

There's also the large **HI Miami Beach Hostel**, 1438 Washington Avenue (305/534-2988), with $13 dorm beds and a few private rooms in the heart of South Beach.

There are scores of cafes and restaurants in and around South Beach, and a couple in particular are worth searching out. Two blocks west of the beach, the **11th Street Diner** on 11th and Washington is a 1948 Paramount pre-fab diner, plunked down in 1992 and open 24 hours ever since. Back on the beach, filling a patio in front of a great newsstand and postcard shop, the upscale **News Cafe** is open 24 hours every day at 800 Ocean Drive; this was Gianni Versace's favorite breakfast spot.

MIAMI SURVIVAL GUIDE

EQUAL PARTS JET-SET GLITZ AND MULTI-CULTURAL grit, Miami (pop. 358,500), more than elsewhere in the country, really embodies the state of the nation at the tail end of the 20th century. Having sprung up from swampland in the 1920s, Miami has weathered hurricanes, race riots—not to mention *Miami Vice* and the dismantling of the World Series champion Florida Marlins—and is now an energetic, bustling city. For some visitors, the best parts of Miami are the independent cities that surround it, especially Art Deco Miami Beach, which we've covered separately, but there are a couple of diverting stops in Miami proper.

Approaching from Miami Beach past the cruise ship docks along the MacArthur Causeway, or the older and more leisurely Venetian Causeway, you experience the view of Miami made famous by *Miami Vice*—downtown towers rising above Biscayne Bay. The ziggurat-shaped Dade County Courthouse, built in 1926, is still the Miami skyline's most prominent feature (especially when it's lit up at night); across the street, the Phillip Johnson-designed **Metro-Dade Cultural Center** is a collection of museums including the excellent **Historical Museum of Southern Florida** (daily 10 AM-5 PM; $4), which traces regional history from Native Americans to Cuban Americans.

The Latin American influence on Miami is evident everywhere you go, but for proof of just how deep the connections run, consider the fact that two of Cuba's deposed presidents, Gerardo Machado and Carlos Prio, are buried in Miami's Woodlawn Park Cemetery, a mile west of Little Havana. Former Nicaraguan dictator Anastasio Somoza is buried there, too.

West of downtown, Miami's most engaging district is **Little Havana**, which focuses along S.W. 8th Street (aka the Tamiami Trail, "Calle Ocho," and US-41) between 12th and 16th Avenues. Since the 1950s and '60s, when the first refugees fleeing Castro's regime fetched up here, this neighborhood has been the heart of Cuban-American Miami. Like

Away from South Beach, comfortable and reasonably priced accommodation options in the rest of Miami Beach include the friendly **Abbey Hotel**, a newly restored Art Deco hotel, three blocks from a nice broad beach at 300 21st Street (305/531-0031, 888/61-ABBEY or 888/612-2239), with rooms from $120 a night, including breakfast.

Stylish though it is, South Beach is not frequented by many locals, who tend to spend time on Lincoln Road, a half-mile north of South Beach. The Mediterranean Revival-style commercial district along Lincoln Road, developed in the 1920s by Carl Fisher, was the original main drag of Miami Beach; it has been pedestrianized

many ethnic neighborhoods that get hyped by the tourism industry, Little Havana can be a disappointment, but if you hang out for a while with the old men who congregate in the Domino Park on 8th Street and 14th Avenue, or visit the Martyrs of Giron (aka "Bay of Pigs") Monument along 8th Street between 12th and 13th Streets, you'll definitely get a feel for it, especially if your trip happens to coincide with the April 17th anniversary of the ill-fated 1961 anti-Castro invasion. Better yet, stop for something to eat or drink at one of Little Havana's many great Cuban cafes.

Practicalities

A main reason for visiting Miami is Miami International Airport, which is one of Florida's busiest points-of-entry. The primary connection between North America and Central and South America, the airport has a chaotic ambience that may well make you feel you've landed in a foreign country, but the usual shuttle and car rental services are all here, and it's a quick six miles to downtown via the I-195 Airport Expressway.

What's left of the 1997 World Champion **Florida Marlins** baseball team plays at Pro Player Stadium, 2269 199th Street (305/626-7400), 15 miles north of downtown Miami.

In downtown Miami, a fun place to stay is the characterful and historic **Miami River Inn**, 118 S.W. South River Drive (305/325-0045), a well-preserved circa 1908 hotel with B&B rooms in the $90-150 range. The major chains, including **Best Western, Holiday Inn** and **Hampton Inn**, all have locations on the downtown waterfront; at these and all other Miami area accommodations, room rates tend to increase considerably during the peak season (Jan.-April). For good food, again South Beach is the place to go, though to get a feel for the "real" Miami, sample some of Little Havana's many great Cuban cafes, such as **El Exquisito**, 1510 S.W. 8th Street, **La Esquina de Tejas**, 101 SW 12th Avenue (where former U.S. Presidents Reagan and Bush wined and dined anti-Castro Cubans), or **Casa Panza**, 1620 S.W. 8th Street, which turns into a flamenco dance club on Tuesday and Thursday nights.

The best source of information on greater Miami, including Miami Beach, is the Greater Miami **visitors bureau**, south of downtown at 701 Brickell Avenue (305/539-3063 or 800/283-2707). The *Miami Herald* is the main daily newspaper; the free weekly *New Times* is a better bet for listings of events and nightlife.

and nicely landscaped and is now packed with pleasant sidewalk cafes like **Tiramesu**, 721 Lincoln Road, and **Pacific Time Cafe**, 927 Lincoln Road, next to the very good **Books and Books** store. For people-watching and pizza alfresco, go to **Pizza da Leo**, 826 Lincoln Road.

In 1983, Bulgarian artist Christo wrapped 11 Biscayne Bay islands in bright pink plastic as part of his photogenic "Surrounded Islands" installation.

Across Miami

In her 1987 book *Miami*, Joan Didion describes the city as a place where it's possible "to pass from walled enclaves to utter desolation while changing stations on the

One of Florida's largest national parks, **Biscayne National Park,** stretches from near Miami to the top of the Florida Keys, but is almost completely underwater. Snorkeling and diving tours (around $30-35) leave every morning (9 AM) from the main Convoy Point visitor center (305/230-7275), near the Homestead Motorsports Complex (and a nuclear power plant), nine miles east of US-1 at the end of 328th Street.

Hurricane Andrew leveled most of the Homestead area in 1992, and the damage is still visible in the many stunted palms and other trees all over South Florida.

car radio." Because the borders between ultra-wealthy and utterly deprived (aka "safe" and "unsafe") areas are painfully sharp, until you know your way around it's best to take care when driving in Miami. The I-95 freeway, and the old main route, US-1, both enter Miami in the very rough "Little Haiti" neighborhood north of downtown, while the infinitely more scenic Hwy-A1A coastal route crosses Biscayne Bay from Miami Beach. Around downtown, Biscayne Boulevard winds along the waterfront, merging into historic Brickell Avenue, now lined by flashy post-modern bank and condo towers. From here, detour west through the one-way system along 7th and 8th Streets through Little Havana, then south along Granada Boulevard through Coral Gables, joining the old Dixie Highway (US-1) for the drive south through Homestead to the Florida Keys.

Coral Gables

South of Miami's Little Havana neighborhood, accessible through grand gates off the Tamiami Trail (8th Street), the stately community of Coral Gables is one of the few Florida resort towns that survives fairly unchanged since the boom years of the 1920s. Developed beginning in 1921 by George Merrick, Coral Gables boasts many grand boulevards, fine fountains and plazas, lush gardens and carefully detailed Mediterranean Revival-style buildings, all lovingly cared for by residents and businesses that clearly take pride in preserving the original vision. Once you've entered Coral Gables, preferably via the impressive gates (from 8th Street, the two main ones are along Granada Boulevard and Country Club Prado), the landmark to look for is the 26-story **Westin Biltmore Hotel**, 1200 Anastasia Avenue off Granada Boulevard (305/445-1926 or 800/727-1926). This opulent hotel, which opened in 1926 and boasted the world's largest swimming pool (and Johnny Weismuller as celebrity lifeguard!), was recently restored to its original glory.

The southern edge of Coral Gables is occupied by the drab campus of the University of Miami, which is bounded by US-1, the old Dixie Highway.

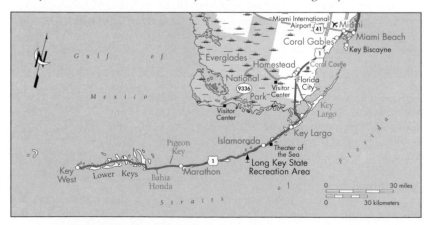

Homestead: Coral Castle
One of the most diverting stops between Miami and the Florida Keys has to be the Coral Castle (daily 9 AM-5 PM; $8), an amazing house hand-carved out of blocks of oolitic coral by the enigmatic Ed Leedskalnin in the 1930s. Located right along the highway, two miles north of Homestead, the house is filled with furniture also carved from stone—a 3,000-pound sofa and a 500-pound rocking chair—and no one has figured how Ed did it all, without help or using any heavy machinery.

Homestead, along with neighboring Florida City farther south, forms the main gateway to Everglades National Park, and there are tons of reasonably-priced motels hereabouts—all the usual suspects lining up here along US-1, including the very nice Best Western **Gateway to the Keys** (305/246-5100). For good, down-home food—great BBQ, shrimp, and ultra-fresh local Redlands veggies—stop into the **Potlikker,** 591 Washington Avenue (305/248-0835).

Detour: Everglades National Park
Covering over 1.5 million acres at the far southwestern tip of mainland Florida, the Everglades National Park protects the largest subtropical wilderness in the United  States. A fair portion of the park is actually underwater, and the entire Everglades ecosystem is basically a giant, slow-flowing river that is 50 miles wide but averaging only a few inches deep; the whole system is fed by Lake Okechobee. Much altered by irrigation in-flows and out-flows—and by the redirection of water to Miami and other cities—the Everglades are under constant threat, yet seem to vibrate with life. Some 300 species of birds breed here, as do 600 different kinds of fish and animals, ranging from rare manatees to abundant alligators.

The backcountry parts of the Everglades can be visited by boat, but by road there are only two main routes. In the north, the Tamiami Trail (the "Tampa to Miami Trail," aka US-41) heads west from Miami to misnamed **Shark Valley,** where you can rent bikes ($4/hour) or take a tram tour ($8) on a 15-mile loop through the "sawgrass" swamps that make up the heart of the Everglades. Gazing at the gators, eagles and hawks here, it's hard to believe you're just a half-hour from South Beach.

The main access to the Everglades is from the east, via Hwy-9336 from the Florida Turnpike or US-1. This route takes you past the main visitor center, where interpretive displays and a pair of nature trails give an appetizing taste of the Everglades (and almost guaranteed sightings of alligators). The road continues nearly 40 miles west to the former town of Flamingo, where both the residents and the namesake birds have all moved on, leaving a few sportfishermen, tour boat operators and hardy canoeists, as well as the Everglades' only eating and accommodation option, the **Flamingo Lodge** (941/695-3101).

In the Everglades, and anywhere in Florida, **mosquitoes** are intensely annoying pests, so if you're here at any time but the dry middle of winter, bring strong repellent—and lots of it. In parts of the Everglades, the bugs are so bad that full-body cover is recommended, in addition to the most potent sprays and lotions you can lay your hands on.

Along the Tamiami Trail (US-41), just west of Shark Valley, the **Miccosukee Indian Village** (daily 9 AM-5 PM; $5) is a reminder of the Everglades native peoples, the Seminoles, some of whom now wrestle alligators, run souvenir shops, and give airboat tours of their ancestral lands.

Key Largo is home to the **Key Lime Products** store at MM 95 (305/853-0378), selling all manner of Key Lime pies, juice, cakes, cookies, suntan lotions—even Key Lime trees, though commercial Key Lime orchards are a thing of the past.

THE OVERSEAS HIGHWAY

Imagine a narrow ribbon of asphalt and concrete hovering between emerald seas and azure blue skies, and lined by swaying palm trees and gorgeous, white sand beaches. Add a generous taste of exotic wildlife, including alligators and dolphins, the country's only tropical coral reefs, and a romantic history rich with tales of buccaneering pirates and buried treasure. Hang it off the far southern tip of Florida, and you have the Overseas Highway, one of the country's most fascinating scenic drives.

Running for over 125 miles, from the Everglades to the edge of Caribbean, the Overseas Highway is the southernmost section of US-1, the historic route that winds for over 2,400 miles along the full length of the East Coast. From its very inception, the Overseas Highway has been unique. It was built on top of the legendary Florida and East Coast Railroad, which at the turn of the century linked the great resort hotels of St. Augustine and Palm Beach with Key West and Cuba. An engineering masterpiece, the railroad cost $50 million and hundreds of lives to complete in 1912, but lasted only two decades before the century's most powerful hurricane destroyed the tracks in 1935. The state of Florida bought the remnants of the railroad for $650,000, and proceeded to convert it into a two-lane highway, the Overseas Highway, which opened to traffic in 1938. Most of the old road has since been superseded by a more modern highway, but many old bridges and causeways still stand as evocative remnants of an earlier era.

As in much of Florida, ramshackle roadside development has uglified much of the route—in the larger Keys towns, like Key Largo, Islamorada and Marathon, signs hawking restaurants, motels and snorkel tours are more common than pelicans—but you can't help but be hypnotized by the scenic beauty of what pockets of "nature" still remain. Many of the best views are from the road itself, and specifically from the bridges, such as the Long Key Bridge and soaring Seven Mile Bridge, which run north and south of Marathon. Two state parks, John Pennecamp on Key Largo, and Bahia Honda in the Lower Keys, offer a respite from the commercialism, and all along the Overseas Highways, unmarked roads and driveways lead across the narrow keys down to the waterside, where all manner of sport-fishing marinas and Margaritaville-type bars give you another outlook on the true "Key" experience.

All the way along the Overseas Highway (US-1), the roadside is lined by marker posts counting down the miles from Florida City to Key West: starting at MM 127 and ending up at MM 0; addresses usually make reference to these numbers. Though it's only about 160 miles, be sure to allow at least four hours for the drive between Miami and Key West—plus however many hours you manage to spend out of the car, of course.

The main Everglades National Park **visitor center** (305/242-7700) is west of Florida City, just inside the park boundary. The park entrance fee is $10 per car, or $5 per person. Camping is available at many backcountry sites; for cars and RVs at Long Pine Key, four miles west of the main visitor center, and on the Gulf Coast at Flamingo.

Key Largo

The Overseas Highway (US-1) officially starts in Florida City, near the Everglades some 50 miles south of Miami, but doesn't really come alive until it leaves the mainland and lands at Key Largo, the first and largest of the dozens of "keys" (from the Spanish word *cayos*, meaning small islands) the highway links together. The Overseas Highway reaches Key Largo at the very popular John Pennecamp Coral Reef State Park (daily 8 AM-dusk; $4; 305/451-1202), at MM 102.5. The first place where you can really get a feel for life on the Keys, the park is the starting point for a variety of **guided tours** (scuba diving, snorkeling, or in glass-bottomed boats, costing around $40, $30 or $20, respectively) that offer up-close looks at the only tropical coral reef in the continental U.S., and all but guarantee that you'll see enough sealife to fill an album or two. Along with the adjacent Key Largo Coral Reef National Marine Sanctuary, the park gives access to more than 175 square miles of diving spots, including reefs, shipwrecks and a nine-foot-high bronze statue called "Christ of the Deep." The visitors center has a replica reef in a 30,000-gallon aquarium full of colorful fish, allowing a quick look at the fascinating underwater world without getting your feet wet; the park also has other on-land attractions, like a boardwalk over a mangrove swamp and a pleasant campground.

Across from Pennecamp park, the **Maritime Museum of the Florida Keys** (daily 10 AM-5 PM, closed Thursday; $5) displays real treasures recovered from sunken shipwrecks offshore; display cases show off lots of pieces of pottery, and if you're feeling strong, you can pick up an 80-pound solid silver bar that dates back to 1620.

The rest of Key Largo (which was the title and setting of a 1948 film noir movie starring Bogie, Bacall and Edward G. Robinson) is a rather tawdry four-mile stretch of seashell stands, dive shops, boat shops and margarita bars. There are many good restaurants, including **Mrs. Mac's Kitchen** at MM 99.4, a small and friendly place with inexpensive food all day, and more beers to drink than seats to sit on. Key Largo also has two characterful places to stay: the funky old **Sunset Cove Motel** at MM 99.5 (305/451-0705), and the unique **Jules' Undersea Lodge**, a two-room motel that's 22 feet beneath the sea—a quick scuba dive down from 51 Shoreland Drive, off MM 103.2 (305/451-2353).

Islamorada

Continuing south on US-1, Key Largo blends into Islamorada (EYE-la-mo-RA-da), the self-proclaimed "Sportfishing Capital of the World," where anglers from all

Between MM 106 and MM 86, a hiking and bicycling path parallels US-1— sometimes very closely— but it's a rare long-distance route on these tiny islands.

There are three places in the Florida Keys where you can pay to **swim with dolphins**: Dolphins Plus in Key Largo (305/451-1993); Theatre of the Sea in Islamorada (305/664-2431); and the Dolphin Research Center in Marathon (305/289-1121). Each costs around $100 for a short but memorable swim.

Entering Islamorada from the north, you are welcomed to town by the "World's Largest Lobster," standing at MM 87 in front of the Treasure Village gift shop. He hasn't yet been boiled or grilled, so he's a naturally greeny-brown color, not bright red.

over the world come to try their hands at catching the illusive, hard-fighting bonefish that dwell in the shallow saltwater "flats," and the deep-sea tarpon, marlin and sailfish. Though now famous for its fishing and fun-in-the-sun, Islamorada (which means "purple island") used to be synonymous with death and destruction: on September 2, 1935, a huge tsunami, whipped up by 200-mile-per-hour hurricane winds, drowned over 400 refugees trying to escape on what turned out to be the last train ever to travel along the old Florida and East Coast railroad. Most of the dead were WW I veterans, members of the "Bonus Army" who had marched on Washington, D.C. in 1934 and had been given jobs working to build the Overseas Highway. A stone pillar at the south end of Islamorada, along US-1 at MM 81.6, was erected by the WPA to remember the event.

From Islamorada, you can take a boat trip to **Indian Key State Historic Site,** which was inhabited during the early 1800s before being destroyed by a Seminole Indian attack in 1840. Indian Key is just offshore from MM 78; on the opposite (Gulf) side, you can see Lignumvitae Key, named for the tropical tree whose wood is so hard it sinks in water. Both islands can be visited; for details, call Long Key Campground (305/664-4815).

At the center of Islamorada sits one of the older tourist traps in south Florida: the **Theatre of the Sea,** at MM 84.5 (daily 9 AM-4:30 PM; $15), a funky, friendly place where you can watch performing sea animals or even swim with live dolphins, one of three places you can do this in the Florida Keys.

Islamorada is home to two of the plushest accommodation options in the Keys: the large and prominent **Checca Lodge** (305/664-4651 or 800/327-2888), offering over 200 spacious $200-a-night rooms, two pools, a pier, a palm-lined beach and a golf course at MM 82.5; and the delightful but harder-to-find **The Moorings,** on the ocean side of MM 81.5 at 123 Beach Road (305/664-4242). The Moorings is an idyllic retreat, with 18 self-sufficient wooden cottages ($150-200 a night) on 18 acres, alongside a beautiful 1,100-foot white sand beach.

The Moorings also has a nice restaurant, **Morada Bay,** serving urbane renditions of traditional Key favorites on US-1 at MM 81.6. For a more down-to-earth taste of the Keys, try the nearby **Green Turtle Inn,** or the waterfront dive known as **Papa's Joe's,** a popular bar and fish restaurant at the southern tip of Islamorada (MM 79.7) that has good food, cold beers, and incredible sunset views.

South of Islamorada, up and over the high "Channel 5" bridge, the roadside scene gets pretty again very fast, especially at the Long Key State Recreation Area at MM 67.5, where boardwalks wind through coastal "hammocks"—dense stands of mahogany and dogwood trees that bunch together on the small humps of land that lie above the tide line. There's a campground (305/664-4815) in the park, with showers, and some nice but narrow beaches; there's another campground at MM 70 on Fiesta Key, where there's a full-service **KOA Kampground.**

For more information on Islamorada, stop by the little red caboose (at MM 82.5) that holds the visitors bureau (305/664-4503 or 800/322-5397). Outside, in the parking lot, informational plaques tell the story of the ill-fated railroad that became the Overseas Highway.

Marathon and Pigeon Key
The second-longest of the many bridges that make up US-1, the elegant multi-arched Long Key Bridge supports a long flat causeway where the road finally earns its other name, the Overseas Highway. Unobstructed views of the distant horizon are yours in all directions, with the narrow ribbon of highway seemingly suspend-

ed between the sky and the sea. Fortunately, turnouts at both ends of the causeway let you take in the vista without worrying about oncoming traffic.

The Long Key Bridge marks the northern end of Marathon, a sprawling community that's second-largest in the keys, stretching between MM 65 and MM 47, over a series of islands. One of the visitor highlights of Marathon is at MM 59, on Grassy Key, where the **Dolphin Research Center**, a rest home for dolphins who've been kept in captivity for too long, is marked by a 30-foot-tall statue of a leaping dolphin

Accessible by tram from a visitor center in Marathon at MM 48, Pigeon Key (daily 9 AM-4 PM; $7.50; 305/743-5999) is one of the least famous but perhaps most fascinating spots along the Overseas Highway. A National Historic District, preserving substantial remnants of the clapboard construction camp that housed some 400 workers employed on the original Seven Mile Bridge from 1912 to 1935, Pigeon Key offers a glimpse of blue-collar Keys history the likes of which you'll find nowhere else.

On Bahia Honda Key, near MM 37, you can see a double-decker remnant of the original Keys railroad, with the 1938 Overseas Highway supported atop the trestle. Widening the rail bed to accommodate cars was impossible, so a new deck was added to the top of the bridge.

The Lower Keys: Bahia Honda

The old Seven Mile Bridge, which carried first the railroad and later US-1 over Pigeon Key between Marathon and Big Pine Key, was replaced in the early 1980s by a soaring new bridge that gives another batch of breathtaking ocean-to-Gulf views. (The old bridge, which was seen in Arnold Schwarzenegger/Jamie Lee Curtis movie *True Lies*, still stands below the new one, but is now used as a very long fishing pier.)

The south end of the Seven Mile Bridge, near MM 40, marks the start of the "Lower Keys," which are considerably less commercial than the others, and boast some of the best beaches in all of south Florida. The best of the Lower Keys is yours to enjoy at MM 36.5, where the entrance to **Bahia Honda State Park** (daily 8 AM-sundown; $4 per car plus 50¢ per person; 305/872-2353) leaves the highway and brings you back to the way the Keys used to be: covered in palms and coastal hardwood hammocks, and lined by broad, white sand beaches. Facilities are limited to a few cabins and a general store, but it's a great place to spend some time fishing, beachcombing, sunbathing or swimming in the deep, warm waters of the Atlantic Ocean or Gulf of Mexico.

From Bahia Honda, US-1 bends along to Big Pine Key, second-largest of the keys and suffering from a bout of suburban mini-mall sprawl. Though it looks about as far from natural as can be, Big Pine Key happens to be part of the **National Key Deer Refuge**, set up to protect the increasingly rare Key Deer, the "world's smallest deer" at around three feet tall. Some 250 Key deer now live on the island.

The last big key before Key West is Sugarloaf Key, formerly full of pineapple plantations but now known for its **Perky Bat Tower**, a National Historic Landmark alongside US-1 at MM 17. Built by a man named Perky in 1929, the 35-foot tower was designed to house a colony of bats, who were supposed to feast on the plentiful mosquitoes here; however, the bats stayed away, and the mosquitoes stayed put. Sugarloaf Key is also home to the wild **Mangrove Mama's**, an anarchic roadhouse tucked away south of the bridge at MM 20. The food is very good, the Key Lime pie as good as it gets, and there's often live music in the evenings.

Next stop, Key West.

Though Key West is the southwestern end of the Overseas Highway, the name is thought to derive from a corruption of the Spanish *Cayo Hueso*, or "Island of Bones." When the first explorers set foot here, they found piles of human bones.

Just so you know, the seashell that's been adopted as a Key West emblem, the conch, is pronounced "konk."

At sunset over the Gulf of Mexico, keep your eyes open for the visual effect known as the "green flash."

Key West

Closer to Cuba than to the U.S. mainland, and still proudly preserving the anarchic spirit of a place that was founded by pirates, Key West is definitely a world unto itself. The main drag, Duval Street, has been overrun by tacky souvenir shops, but the rest of Key West is still a great place for aimless wandering.

Just a block from the official "Mile Zero" end of US-1, one of Key West's most popular stops is the **Hemingway House**, an overgrown mansion on Hwy-A1A at 907 Whitehead Street (daily 9 AM-5 PM; $6), where the burly writer produced some of his most popular works, including *To Have and Have Not* and *For Whom the Bell Tolls*. Writing in a small cabin connected to the main house by a rope bridge, and spending his nights in the roughneck bar (originally called "Sloppy Joe's," now known as "Captain Tiny's") that still survives at 428 Greene Street, "Papa" Hemingway lived in Key West for around 10 years until his divorce in 1940, when he moved to Havana.

A half-mile away, at Whitehead and South Streets, a brightly painted buoy marks the "Southernmost Point in the USA"; next to this is the "Southernmost House." (There's also a "Southernmost Motel.")

At the other end of Duval Street, one place you ought to go—especially if you can time it to be there around sunset—is Mallory Square, which faces west across the Gulf of Mexico and the open Caribbean Sea. Street performers juggle and play music on the broad, brick-paved plaza all day and much of the night. This historic waterfront area is lined by old warehouses and some fascinating museums, includ-

ing **Mel Fisher's Treasure Exhibit**, at 200 Greene Street (daily 9:30 AM-5 PM; $6), which displays many millions of dollars worth of jewels, silver and gold recovered from a pair of 17th-century Spanish shipwrecks.

Key West Practicalities

Amid the tourist clutter, Duval Street and Mallory Square hold many very good restaurants, enough to suit all tastes and budgets. For breakfast or lunch, fight your way into **Camille's**, 703 Duval Street, where crisp waffles, the usual variety of egg dishes, lox and bagels, and sandwiches are served up. A block away at 615 Duval, but at the other end of the price and style spectrum, swanky **Antonia's** has great fresh pastas and grilled meats. But for a real taste of Key West, you can't beat **B.O.'s**, a ramshackle fish stand, a block from the water and three blocks north of Duval at 801 Caroline Street—softshell crab and oyster po' boys, fresh mahi fish 'n'chips, cold beer and frequent live blues bands make this a great place to soak up Key West's party-hardy-at-the-end-of-the-world ambience.

The cheapest beds in Key West are at the **HI Key West Hostel**, 718 South Street (305/296-5719), which is just two blocks from the water, open 24 hours, and offers bike rentals and scuba lessons. The aforementioned **Southernmost Motel in the USA**, 1319 Duval Street (305/296-6577), has a poolside bar and AAA-rated rooms from $69 in summer, $120 in peak season. A surprisingly desirable option is the **Holiday Inn**, 430 Duval Street (305/296-2991), which plastered its name on the facade of the La Concha Hotel, one of Key West's oldest and largest hotels, but otherwise kept the historic 1920s character intact. Rooms start at $130 a night, and you can't get more central than this. Gay male travelers (and there are many in Key West) flock to the **Atlantic Shores**, 510 South Street (305/296-2491), a lavender-painted motel with a lively poolside scene and an on-site, all-night cafe called Diner Shores (geddit?). There are also many nice old B&Bs around Key West, like the landmark **Eaton Lodge**, 511 Eaton Street (305/292-2170), an 1880s Greek Revival mansion with a gorgeous garden.

For more information on Key West, contact the **visitors bureau**, 3840 N. Roosevelt Boulevard (305/296-4444), at the north edge of town near MM 4, where the Overseas Highway lands on Key West island.

Key West is the end of the Overseas Highway, but it's not the end of the sightseeing opportunities, so if you don't want to turn around and head home just yet, you don't have to. You can board a sunset cruise, or take a seaplane tour of historic **Fort Jefferson,** a 150-year-old fortress and prison located on an island in Dry Tortugas National Park, 68 miles west of Key West. Prisoners held here included the hapless doctor, Samuel Mudd, who set the broken leg of Lincoln assassin John Wilkes Booth.

The official end of US-1 is marked by a zero milepost sign in front of the Key West post office, on Truman Avenue.

US-2:
THE GREAT
NORTHERN

US-2: THE GREAT NORTHERN

Though many come close, no other cross-country route takes in the variety and extremity of landscape that US-2 does.  Dubbed the Great Northern in memory of the pioneer railroad that parallels the western half of the route, US-2 is truly the most stunning and unforgettable, not to mention longest, of all the great transcontinental road trips.

Starting in the west at the beautiful Pacific port city of Seattle, US-2 runs steeply up and over the volcanic Cascade Range, climbing from sea level to alpine splendor in around an hour. From the crest the road drops down onto the otherworldly Columbia Plateau, a naturally arid region reclaimed from sagebrush into fertile farmland by New Deal public works projects like the great Grand Coulee Dam, one of the largest pieces of civil engineering on the planet. From Washington, US-2 bends north toward the Canadian border, clipping across the top of the Idaho Panhandle before climbing up into the Rocky Mountain majesty of western Montana, a land of forests, rivers, and wildlife that culminates in the bold granite spectacle of Glacier National Park.

On the eastern flank of the Rockies the route drops suddenly to the windswept prairies of the northern Great Plains. Though empty to look at—especially when you're midway along the 1,000-mile beeline across Montana and North Dakota, wondering how long it will be until you see the next tree or peak—this is a land rich in history, where the buffalo once roamed freely, where Plains tribes like the Shoshone, Blackfeet, Sioux, and Cheyenne reigned supreme, and where the Lewis and Clark expedition followed the Missouri River upstream in search of a way west to the Pacific.

Midway across the continent, the Great Plains give way to the Great North Woods country of Minnesota—birthplace both of Paul Bunyan and Judy Garland—and then to the Great Lakes lumber and mining country of northern Wisconsin and Michigan's Upper Peninsula. Continuing due east, the route crosses the border into Ontario, Canada, through the capital city of Ottawa, and the francophile environs of Montreal before returning to the U.S. near lovely Lake Champlain in upstate New York.

From there US-2 passes through yet another mountainous landscape, the hardwood forests of Vermont's Green Mountains and the rugged granite peaks of New Hampshire's White Mountains, two very different ranges though only 50 miles apart. The route winds down to the coast of Maine, reaching the Atlantic Ocean at Bar Harbor and Acadia National Park.

Landscapes, rather than cities and towns, play the starring roles on this route. Between Seattle and Montreal, the biggest cities along the route are Spokane and Duluth. Still, after a few days spent following US-2 through small towns and wide-open spaces, you'll probably consider Duluth bustling and fast-paced; driving even a short stretch of the Great Northern highway is guaranteed to bring new meaning to the expression "getting away from it all."

ACROSS WASHINGTON

The 350 miles of US-2 across Washington state contain enough contrasting landscapes to fill many states. West to east, the route begins at the industrial fringes of Seattle and the Puget Sound, passing through a couple of Victorian-era towns before climbing steeply up toward the towering peaks, dense forests, and pristine lakes of the Cascade Mountains. East of the Cascade crest, the rugged volcanic landscape suddenly becomes drier and much more sparse, the dense forests fading first into lush farmlands and orchards reclaimed from the natural desert, then continuing across increasingly barren sagebrush plains into Idaho.

Though traffic can be heavy on long summer weekends, and also in winter in the Cascades section, along US-2 it is usually light, since most of the 18-wheelers and other heavy vehicles follow the parallel I-90 freeway, which runs 25 miles to the south.

Midway between Seattle and Everett, the town of Edmonds has frequent Washington State Ferry service (206/464-6400 or 800/843-3779) across Puget Sound to the Olympic Peninsula, start of our Coastal West Coast road trip, which begins on page 24.

Everett

Thirty-odd miles north of downtown Seattle via the I-5 freeway or the older, funkier Hwy-99, at the west end of transcontinental US-2, busy Everett (pop. 69,961) is a thoroughly blue-collar place that feels a lot farther from Seattle's high-tech flash than the mere half-hour it is. A heavy industry center economically dependent upon two of the largest livelihoods in the Pacific Northwest—wood products and

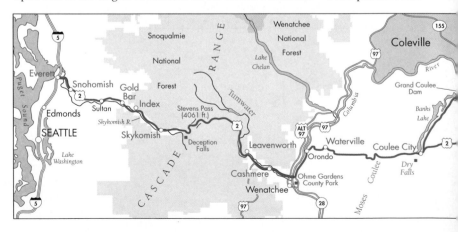

aircraft manufacturing—Everett has a few large turn-of-the-century mansions overlooking the all-business waterfront, where a Kimberly-Clark paper mill shares space with a big U.S. Navy base that's home port to the carrier USS *Abraham Lincoln*. The old-fashioned downtown, a half-mile west of I-5 around Hewitt and Colby avenues, has some neat antique and junk shops, a dozen or so roughneck bars and taverns, and a very nice brew-pub restaurant, the **Flying Pig**, next to the historic Everett Theatre at 2929 Colby Avenue (425/339-1393). For milk shakes or great fish 'n' chips, stop by **Ray's Drive-In**, 1401 Broadway.

Everett's one big tourist draw is the huge **Boeing assembly plant** on the southwest edge of town, well marked from I-5 exit 189, at the west end of Hwy-526. The factory, where they make 747s and 757s, is worth a look if only for the 11-story-high, quarter-mile-long building, which is said to be the largest in the world; first-come, first-served 90-minute tours (Mon.-Fri. 9 AM-3 PM; free; 425/342-4801) leave on the hour, but these fill up quickly, so try to get there early in the day.

If a Boeing tour doesn't get your blood flowing, maybe a baseball game will: the always-entertaining **Everett Aquasox** (425/258-3673), Class A affiliate of the Seattle Mariners, play at 39th and Broadway, off I-5, exit 192. Games are broadcast on commercial-free KSER 90.7 FM.

US-2 leaves Everett on Hewitt Avenue, which crosses I-5 then takes a historic old drawbridge over the Snohomish River before winding across low-lying fields toward the town of Snohomish.

Snohomish

Though they're spreading fast, Seattle's suburbs haven't yet reached the tidy Victorian town of Snohomish (pop. 6,499), a 100-year-old former logging center that lines the north bank of the Snohomish River, 25 miles upstream from Puget Sound. Six blocks of well-preserved warehouses and commercial buildings stand along First Street, across the river from a whining old sawmill, while the blocks above hold dozens of charming homes and quite a few impressively steepled churches. One of these old homes has been restored and now houses the **Blackman Museum** (daily

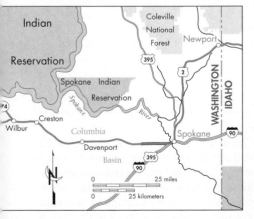

noon-4 PM in summer, weekends only in winter; $1). Located at 118 Avenue B, the museum features period-style furnishings and displays on the town's early history. The range of antique shops, taverns, and cafes in the historic center has made Snohomish a popular day-trip from Seattle, but the town has maintained an admirable balance of history and commerce, and is well worth a short stop if you're passing by.

Around Snohomish, the old US-2 road has been replaced by a four-lane freeway that loops around to the north, so follow signs for the "historic center."

SEATTLE SURVIVAL GUIDE

AN ENGAGING AND ENERGETIC COMBINATION OF scenic beauty, blue-collar grit and high-tech panache has made Seattle one of the most popular cities in the U.S., to visit or to live. A young city, historically and demographically, Seattle has managed to preserve much of its heavy industrial heritage, as parks and museums if not as economic engines, while cultivating a strong, high-wage economy: two of America's hugest companies, Boeing and Microsoft, are based here, and eco-conscious, civic-minded Seattle has also given birth to such diverse phenomena as grunge music, Starbuck's McCoffee chain, and mountain bike-mounted police patrols. Spreading over

a series of hills, surrounded by the waters of Puget Sound (be sure to ride a ferry or two!), with a backdrop of the snow-capped Cascade and Olympic Mountains, evergreen Seattle can be an entrancing city—at least when the sun comes out, which no matter what people say is likely to happen at least once during your stay.

The heart of downtown Seattle, Pike Place Market is a raucous farmers', fish, and crafts market with some 250 different stalls and stores filling a municipal-feeling building that steps down along the waterfront. For a respite from the hubbub, head two blocks south to the postmodern **Seattle Art Museum**, 100 University Street (Tues.-Sun. 10 AM-5 PM; $6), and enjoy the amazing collection of regional Native American art and artifacts on display.

At the south edge of downtown, a half-mile from the Pike Place Market, the 30-block **Pioneer Square** historic district preserves the original core of the city, which boomed in the late 1890s with the Klondike Gold Rush. A small museum (daily 9 AM-5 PM; free) at 117 S. Main Street recounts the Klondike era, and the endlessly browsable **Elliott Bay Book Company**, next door at 101 S. Main Street, has a good cafe in its basement and a wonderful free evening reading series. In a small park a block away at Second Avenue and Main Street there's a waterfall crashing onto large rocks, and a plaque marking the birthplace of United Parcel Service.

East of Monroe, just west of the town of Sultan, a dollhouse-sized church stands along US-2 as a roadside rest stop and mini-shrine. Sultan is also home to an annual "Summer Shindig and Logging Show" every July.

Gold Bar and Index

Surprisingly little of the route traversed by US-2 on its way between the flatlands and Stevens Pass high up in the Cascades is given over to ski shops, bike shops, and espresso stands—except for the section around Munroe, where a mile-long gauntlet of mega-malls and fast-food franchises catering to Seattleites racing to and from the slopes comes as a shock to the system.

*downtown
Seattle*

Pending completion of a nice new ballpark, the **Seattle Mariners** (206/346-4001) are stuck at the Kingdome, south of Pioneer Square.

One last Seattle place-to-go is the **Seattle Center**, Broad Street and 5th Avenue North (206/684-8582). Built for the 1962 World's Fair, this 75-acre park is a little bit of Disneyland on the north side of downtown Seattle. Take the elevator to the top of the landmark **Space Needle** ($8.50), learn something at the **Pacific Science Center** ($7.50), or, best of all, ride the Windstorm roller coaster, bumper cars, or dozen other funfair attractions at the summer-only **Fun Forest** (noon-midnight; pay-per-ride). Seattle Center is also home to the city's opera, symphony and ballet, and a don't-miss photo opportunity: a statue of Chief Seattle with the Space Needle rising behind him.

Practicalities

Seattle's main airport is Seattle-Tacoma International ("Sea-Tac"), midway between the two cities, a half-hour drive south of downtown Seattle via the I-5 freeway. The usual array of rental car companies can be found there (though tax and surcharges add around 30% to quoted rates), and the usual shuttles to serve downtown. By road, the main route from the north and south is the I-5 freeway, from the east, I-90 and US-2 cross the Cascades,

(continues on next pages)

East of Munroe, the one-time mining, logging, and railroad camp of Gold Bar stretches along US-2, halfway between Stevens Pass and Puget Sound. Besides all the gas stations and cafes you could want, Gold Bar also holds the well-posted trailhead (follow First Street north from the center of town) for the 3.5-mile hike to 250-foot **Wallace Falls**, one of the tallest in the northern Cascades, tantalizingly visible from US-2.

while ferry boats run across Puget Sound from the Olympic Peninsula and western Washington. Seattle's freeways are often filled to capacity most of the day, but the best drive-through tour of Seattle follows old US-99 along the Alaska Way Viaduct, a concrete freeway that cuts along the downtown waterfront, runs through a tunnel, then follows Aurora Avenue on a soaring bridge over the Lake Union Canal. (By the way, under the Aurora Bridge sits one of Seattle's biggest pieces of auto-art: the Aurora Troll, caught in the act of eating an old VW bug.)

Fortunately, most everything of visitor interest is within the walkably compact downtown, where an extensive bus system runs in a fare-free zone; there's also a silly little mile-long monorail ($1), linking 5th and Pine Streets downtown with the Seattle Center and landmark Space Needle.

The cheapest and most convenient place to stay has to be the **HI Seattle Hostel**, 84 Union Street (206/622-5443), which offers clean and comfortable dorm beds for around $18, right along the waterfront next to Pike Place Market. The **YMCA**, near Pioneer Square at 909 Fourth Avenue (206/382-5000), has the cheapest private rooms in downtown, with doubles going for around $40 a night; men, women, and children are all welcomed. The similarly central **Pacific Plaza Hotel** at 400 Spring Street (206/623-3900) is a step up in comfort, but still well under $100; away from downtown, near the University of Washington (aka "You Dub") the **College Inn**, 4000 University Way (206/633-4441) is a moderately priced B&B, popular with youthful and budget-conscious travelers. Doubles $75-90.

Seafood, not surprisingly, is the thing Seattle restaurants do best, and the best place to eat fish is the **Flying Fish**, 2234 1st Avenue (206/728-8595), a fashionable, boisterous but not all-that expensive restaurant that serves some of the West Coast's freshest sea creatures in a variety of inventive ways—Alaskan King salmon in a subtle Thai ginger sauce, anyone? Make reservations, though. For fish 'n' chips, or cheap fresh oysters (and Washington produces more oysters than anywhere else in the U.S.), head down to **Emmett Watson's Oyster Bar**, at the north end of Pike Place Market; more down-home fare is served up for breakfast, lunch, and dinner at the **5 Spot**, 1502 Queen Anne Avenue in the residential Queen Anne district, a mile northwest of downtown high above Lake Union.

The best source of advance information on visiting Seattle is the **Seattle-King County Convention and Visitors Bureau**, 666 Stewart Street (206/461-5840). The best source of entertainment and events listings is the *Seattle Weekly*, available free at book and record shops and from newsracks on the street.

Farther east, Index, on a side road a mile north of US-2, sits at the western foot of the Cascade Mountains at the point where the scenery changes suddenly from pastoral to alpine. Besides a riverfront tavern, a general store/post office, a neat little historical museum featuring Great Northern Railroad photographs, and constant trains rumbling over the swimmably deep (but often freezing cold) Skykomish River, Index offers good food and comfortable lodging at the 100-year-old **Bush House Inn** (360/793-2312), where rooms cost $60-85.

In a park at the center of Index, a giant saw blade is a reminder of the town's early industry: a granite quarry that cut the steps used in the state capitol. High above here, another reminder of the town's rocky past is the so-called "Index Town Wall," a 400-foot sheer granite cliff that attracts Seattle rock climbers and features many first ascents by Tor Archer, a sculptor and climber who earned at least 15 minutes of fame for climbing the Federal Building in Seattle—while wearing a "Human Fly" costume.

Skykomish and Deception Falls
Lining the busy Burlington Northern Santa Fe railroad tracks, a block south of US-2, Skykomish is a quirky and engaging place that seems to belong somewhere else, some long time ago. The two-block town revolves around the rustic, circa 1905 **Hotel Skykomish**, which has huge sunny balconies, basic rooms for around $35, and **Flynn's Cafe** on the ground floor, where you can still get a good breakfast—so long as you're not in any hurry.

Around eight miles east of Skykomish, a well-marked turnout along US-2 gives access to one of the region's prettiest and most historically significant sites. On the north side of the highway, the parking area's interpretive exhibits tell the story of the Great Northern Railroad, the transcontinental railroad which was completed on this spot in 1893. A plaque displays a photograph showing the driving of the traditional golden spike, while other exhibits discuss the construction and importance of the railroad in the growth of Puget Sound.

If you're not interested in railroad lore, head along the 100-yard-long paved trail that loops back under the highway to the powerful cascade of Deception Falls. If you can stand the usually bone-chilling snowmelt, you'll be pleased to find a number of deep and clean swimming holes in the area.

Stevens Pass
At the crest of the Cascades, US-2 climbs over 4,061-foot Stevens Pass, the highest and northernmost Cascade pass that's kept open year-round.

Stevens Pass was named in honor of John F. Stevens, the Great Northern Railroad engineer who also plotted the Panama Canal.

Stevens Pass was also a historically vital railroad crossing, though Amtrak and other trains now avoid the pass, detouring instead through an eight-mile-long tunnel cut through the mountains in 1929. In 1910, before the completion of the tunnel, which is the longest still in use in the western hemisphere, the pass was the site of the worst avalanche disaster in U.S. history: 96 passengers and railroad workers were killed by a mile-long snow slide.

Besides providing grand views of the nearby peaks and more distant valleys, Stevens Pass is also a popular **ski area**, with 10 chair lifts and a 1,800-foot vertical drop; for prices, ski conditions, and other information, call 360/973-2441.

Tumwater Canyon
Heading east through the Cascades from Stevens Pass, US-2 runs through the forests of Tumwater Canyon, a breathtaking place when fall color sweeps through it, and quite scenic any other time of year. Much of the surrounding wilderness was badly burned in the "Rat Creek Fire" of 1994, but much of the area along US-2 survived unscathed, though here and there entire hillsides are still charred, five years or more afterwards.

All along this stretch, US-2 winds along the raging Wenatchee River through evergreen conifer forests highlighted by occasional aspens. The roadside is pretty much undeveloped, with one exception: at Coles Corner, 15 miles west of Leavenworth, the '59er Diner is a popular roadfood restaurant. Farther east, where US-2 crosses the Wenatchee River, there's the very nice USFS-run **Tumwater Campground**, with shady riverside sites for around $8 a night (509/763-3103).

Leavenworth

Leavenworth's faux-European reconstruction was inspired in part by Danish-flavored Solvang, California (see page 91).

Sitting in the eastern foothills of the Cascades, 125 miles from Seattle, Leavenworth (pop. 1,692) has successfully transformed itself from an economically depressed railroad town into one of the most popular day-trip destinations in the Pacific Northwest. After the local lumber mills closed down in the mid-1960s, the town took advantage of its spectacular location and re-created itself as an ersatz Bavarian village and has been drawing huge crowds of tourists ever since—over a million visitors annually. Check out the old photographs on the walls of **Der Markt Platz** shopping center, on the corner of Eighth and Commercial Streets, for the whole story.

Over a dozen blocks of half-timbered pseudo-chalets and Tyrolean shopping malls house a range of low-budget craft galleries and T-shirt stores, which you can escape by walking two blocks south to an attractively landscaped park along the Wenatchee River. Eat and drink at the **Heidel Burger Drive-In**, or **Gustav's** sausage-beer-and-burger garden, both on US-2 at the west end of town, or at the elaborate mock-Bavarian McDonald's, on US-2 farther east. The pleasant and moderately priced **Evergreen Inn** (509/548-5515), a block south of US-2 at 1117 Front Street, has quiet rooms and bike rentals. For more complete listings, contact the **visitor center** (509/548-5807).

Cashmere

At the heart of the Wenatchee Valley, surrounded by apple orchards and bare brown eastern Cascade foothills, Cashmere (pop. 2,500) has an attractive downtown district, its unusual red-and-white striped metal awnings both shading the sidewalks and giving the town some visual identity. The main sight here is the large **Chelan County Historical Museum** (Mon.-Sat. 10 AM-4:30 PM, Sunday 1-4:30 PM; $3), off US-2 at the east end of town, with an excellent collection of Native American arti-

*Two miles northwest of Cashmere, right along US-2, the sandstone slabs and spires of **Peshastin Pinnacles State Park** provide a popular rock-climbing spot—but no camping.*

facts and a free outdoor Pioneer Village made up of 18 different historic structures from around the county.

Cashmere is also the home of **Aplets and Cotlets** fruit-and-nut candy, started here in the 1920s by two Turkish brothers. These sweet treats are so dominant in the local scheme of things that the main route into town has been renamed Aplets Street. The factory, across from the railroad depot, is open daily for free tours and samples.

For road food, stop by **Rusty's Drive-In**, at the east edge of town near the big Tree Top apple juicery, or head to the block-long downtown district, where you'll find a handful of cafes and taverns, and the quiet **Village Inn,** 229 Cottage Avenue (509/782-3522), which has rooms from $40 a night.

Ohme Gardens County Park

Overlooking the confluence of the Wenatchee and Columbia Rivers on a bluff above the US-2/US-97 junction, Ohme Gardens County Park (daily 9 AM-5 PM, April 15-Oct. 15; $5; 509/662-5785) maintains nine acres of immaculate greenery that offers a cool contrast to eastern Washington's arid terrain. Created beginning in 1929 by the Ohme family, the lush plantings of ferns and evergreens have transformed an otherwise rugged Cascade crest. Stone pathways wind past waterfalls and rocky pools, culminating in a rustic lookout that gives sweeping views of Wenatchee and the surrounding Columbia River valley.

Wenatchee

Just south of US-2, Wenatchee (pop. 21,756) is the commercial center of the Wenatchee Valley, one of the world's most productive apple and pear-growing regions—it's responsible for about half the nation's annual crop. The **Washington Apple Commission Visitor Center** (Mon.-Fri. 8 AM-5 PM, plus Sat.-Sun. 10 AM-4 PM in summer; free), a block north of US-2 below the Ohme Gardens, is the place to go to find out all about the state's apple industry, and to enjoy free apples and apple juice (not to mention potent air-conditioning).

From Wenatchee, US-97 runs north along the west bank of the Columbia River to beautiful **Lake Chelan,** at the southern edge of the North Cascades National Park. For visitor information, call 800/4-CHELAN (800/424-3526). US-2, which briefly shares the riverfront route with US-97, veers east at Orondo, some 15 miles north of Wenatchee.

Wenatchee stretches south from US-2, with three miles of shopping malls, car dealerships, and anonymous highway sprawl before you reach the downtown business district. Many large fruit warehouses, and a nice park, line the railroad tracks along the riverfront; one place worth stopping at is the excellent **North Central Washington Museum** (Mon.-Fri. 10 AM-4 PM, Sat.-Sun. 1-4 PM; $2), at 127 S. Mission Street, which contains extensive displays tracing the region's prehistoric and pioneer past, from native rock art to a working model of the railroad route over the Cascades. An adjacent building houses a large exhibit on Washington's apple industry, including an antique but fully functioning apple sorting and packing line.

Along with every fast-food franchise known to humankind, Wenatchee also has some great local haunts, including **Dusty's,** famous for burgers and shakes (and words of wisdom on their sign) since 1949, one block north is the **Windmill,** a classic western steakhouse at 1501 Wenatchee Avenue. There are also lots of motels, ranging from the low-budget **Travelodge,** 1004 N. Wenatchee (509/662-8165), to the business-oriented **West Coast Wenatchee Center Hotel,** 201 N. Wenatchee Avenue (509/662-1234).

Waterville

Standing at the center of fertile wheat fields 10 miles east of the Columbia River, the compact farming town of Waterville (pop. 995) was laid out in 1886 around the stately, whitewashed brick **Douglas County Courthouse,** which still stands at Birch and Rainier Streets. Most of downtown Waterville has been declared a

National Historic District, and the four blocks of attractive brick buildings still house franchise-free banks, cafes, and grocery stores—making it a very nice place to stop on a journey across the state. There's a photogenic, sign-painted barn at the west end of town, and midway along US-2's zig-zag through town, across from the historic (and recently reopened) **Hotel Waterville**, the **Douglas County Historical Museum** (Wed.-Sun. 11 AM-5 PM in summer; donations), at 124 W. Walnut Street, has an intriguing display of objects tracing regional history, including Native American artifacts and a perfectly preserved pioneer post office.

Moses Coulee

One of the last vestiges of eastern Washington's unirrigated landscape, Moses Coulee is an 800-foot-deep gorge bounded by vertical walls of ruddy brown volcanic basalt, brightened by splashes of green and orange lichen. From the rolling plains above, US-2 cuts down into the coulee, then back up the other side, passing through some of the Columbia River Basin's sole surviving sagebrush and giving a strong sense of how profoundly irrigation has changed the region.

Coulee City and Dry Falls

A shipping center for the wheat farms of eastern Washington, Coulee City (pop. 600) calls itself the "Friendliest Town in the West." Despite this claim, there's no more reason to stop now than there was during the pioneer days of the 1860s, when it was said that transfer times on stagecoaches and trains were arranged so that travelers were forced to spend the night in Coulee City, like it or not. If you find yourself here, you can choose from a pair of motels and three gas stations.

Northwest of Coulee City, the large Dry Falls dam impounds Columbia River water to form Banks Lake. Highway 155 runs along its sluggish shores on the way to the Grand Coulee Dam. Though you can see the coulee's towering basalt walls from this road, to get a sense of what the Grand Coulee looked like before the dams were built, follow Hwy-17 four miles south from Coulee City to where the Dry Falls escarpment stands out as the most impressive reminder of the region's tumultuous geology. Interpretive exhibits along the highway explain that during the last Ice Age, when the Columbia River flowed over the falls, this was the most powerful waterfall on the planet: twice as high as Niagara, and over three miles across.

Grand Coulee Dam

The centerpiece of the massive project of dams and canals that have "reclaimed" the Columbia Basin, the Grand Coulee Dam is one of the civil engineering wonders of the world. Built from 1933 to 1942 under the auspices of FDR's New Deal, at a cost of many millions of dollars and 77 lives, the dam is the largest concrete structure in the world: 550 feet high, 450 feet thick at its base, and nearly a mile across. Exhibits on the construction and impact of the dam fill the large, modern **Visitor Arrival Center** (daily 8:30 AM-10 PM in summer, 9 AM-5 PM rest of the year; free) just downstream, where you can listen to Woody Guthrie and Bonnie Raitt singing a continuous loop of "Roll On, Columbia." On summer evenings a very cheesy, half-hour laser light show (Memorial Day to September 30 nightly at 8 PM; free) is projected onto the spillway of the dam. Take an elevator down into the powerhouses and inspect the massive turbines, which have a combined generating capacity of over six

million kilowatts—half of which comes from
the Third Powerplant, added in 1975.

There are three small towns—Coulee Dam,
Grand Coulee, and Electric respectively, east
to west from the dam—all of which service
the needs of boaters, anglers and other visitors. You can see the Grand Coulee Dam light
show from your room at the **Ponderosa Motel**
(509/633-2100) or the **Coulee House** (509/
633-1101) in the town of **Coulee Dam.**

In Electric City, along Hwy-
155 a mile southwest of
Coulee Dam, take a look at
the **Gehrke Windmill
Garden,** a whimsical
collection of whirligigs and
windmills made by folk
artist Emil Gehrke, who
lived here until his death
in 1979.

The Columbia Basin

The 150 miles of rolling farmland that lie to the east of the Cascades are a natural desert, receiving an average of 10 inches of
annual rainfall. Though small-scale farming limped along here
for over a century, the region underwent a wholesale change
after WW II, when irrigation water from reclamation projects
along the Columbia River and its many tributaries turned the
sagebrush plains into the proverbial amber waves of grain,
spreading toward the horizon against an (almost) always clear blue sky.

US-2 runs directly across the heart of this sparsely populated, nearly treeless region, passing through a few very small towns. In **Wilbur,** at the turnoff to Coulee
Dam, an old service station has been brought back to life as a drive-by espresso
stand; eight miles east, the blink-and-you'll-miss-it community of **Creston** ("Home
of 1982 and 1984 Girls State B Champions") is worth a stop for a bite to eat at cow-
boy-themed **Deb's Cafe,** right on US-2 in the center of town, serving good food for
breakfast, lunch, and dinner and hosting country-western bands in the dance hall
next door.

Twenty miles east of Creston, **Davenport,** one of the oldest towns in eastern
Washington, has a handful of quaint old houses as well as the small **Lincoln County Historical Museum,** located a block south of US-2 at Park and 7th Streets, with a
circa 1879 log cabin schoolhouse preserved across the street. There's a nifty old
courthouse on a hill just north of US-2, and **Edna's Drive-In,** on US-2 at the east
end of town, is the place for burgers and shakes.

Spokane

The only real city in eastern Washington, Spokane
(pop. 188,000) feels even bigger than it is, thanks to its
location amidst the prosperous agricultural hinterlands of the Columbia River
Basin. First established as a fur-trading outpost around 1810, Spokane began to
grow when railroads arrived in the 1870s, and has boomed since the advent of irrigation in the 1940s. The second largest city in Washington, and the biggest between Seattle and Minneapolis, Spokane is economically dependent on
warehousing and transportation, taking advantage of its busy railroads as well as its
location at the junction of US-2, US-395, and the I-90 freeway.

Though downtown Spokane boasts a number of grand buildings—one recent
guidebook called Riverside Street between Jefferson and Lincoln "the loveliest

The agricultural flatlands around Spokane were the seat of power for Democratic Party leader and former Speaker of the House of Representatives **Tom Foley,** who was voted out of office in the Republican landslides of 1994.

Some people in Spokane insist that, rather than dying in a shootout in South America, Wild West legend Butch Cassidy actually lived here, under an assumed name, until his death in 1937.

three blocks in the Pacific Northwest"—Spokane really came of age when it hosted the 1974 World's Fair, for which much of the riverfront was cleared and converted to the attractive, 100-acre **Riverfront Park.** Designed, but never implemented, by Frederick Law Olmsted a mere century earlier, the park gives good views of tumbling Spokane Falls, which form a deep canyon at the center of downtown. Besides an opera house and a convention center, other remnants of the fair include numerous kiddie rides, a summer-only **gondola** sky ride (daily 11 AM-dusk; $3) which drops down to the base of the falls, a 1909 **Looff carousel** ($1) complete with hand-carved wooden horses, and a landmark sandstone clock tower that's the sole reminder of the Great Northern rail yards which lined the riverfront for most of the previous century.

Riverfront Park is right at the heart of downtown, and a quick walking tour can take in dozens of well-preserved, creatively reused architectural treats like the Spokane **City Hall,** which faces the southwest corner of Riverfront Park at 808 Spokane Falls Boulevard—the only government I know of that's housed in a converted Montgomery Ward department store, a terra-cotta gem dating from 1929. Another worthwhile stop is **Auntie's Bookstore,** a full service independent bookstore with a popular cafe at 404 W. Main Avenue.

Northeast of downtown, across the Spokane River via Division Street (US-2), the best known dropout of **Gonzaga University,** Bing Crosby, is fondly remembered in a small museum in the Crosby Library at the heart of the small campus. Spokane's other center of visitor interest is **Browne's Addition,** a turn-of-the-century residential district a mile or so west of downtown where, among many stately homes, the **Cheney Cowles Memorial Museum** (Tues.-Sat. 10 AM-5 PM, Sunday 1-5 PM; $3), at 2316 W. 1st Avenue, has an above-average range of exhibits tracing Native American and recent regional history.

One of Spokane's most popular roadside attractions is the giant-sized Radio Flyer wagon, 12 feet tall with a slide down the "handle," near the clock tower in Riverfront Park.

There's no shortage of good places to eat in Spokane, ranging from hearty and homespun to eclectic and expensive. One of the former is **Frank's Diner**, near downtown at 1516 W. 2nd Avenue, where very good, inexpensive meals are served in an elegant old 1906 railroad car, moved here from Seattle in 1991. An example of the latter is **Patsy Clark's**, one of Washington's finest restaurants, housed in an opulent old Browne's Addition mansion at 2208 W. 2nd Avenue. In between are brew pubs aplenty, and many reliably good places downtown like **Fugazzi**, a bakery and sandwich spot near Riverfront Park at 1 N. Post Street, and the local favorite **Someplace Else**, 518 W. Sprague Avenue. In Browne's Addition, another good bet is the **Elk Cafe**, 1931 W. Pacific Avenue, with bistro-style food (and a soda fountain).

Spokane's most characterful place to stay, the **Fotheringham House B&B** at 2128 W. 2nd Avenue (509/838-1891), is a lovely Queen Anne Victorian (with flower garden, porch swing, and a turret!) across the street from Patsy Clark's. Motels line the main highways in and out of Spokane, especially along I-90 west of downtown.

For further information on visiting Spokane, contact the **visitor center**, 201 Main Avenue (509/624-1341 or 800/248-3230) at the east edge of downtown.

In summer, enjoy a Spokane Indians baseball game at Seafirst stadium. For details, call 509/535-2922.

Heading northeast from Spokane, US-2 crosses a few miles of suburban sprawl before winding through 35 miles of beautiful forested uplands and occasional crossroads communities on the way to Newport, on the Idaho border.

To get a feel for local life in Newport, tune in to **KMJY 700 AM,** which broadcasts country music, CNN news, and an hour long "Swap and Shop" on-air flea market, daily 11 AM-noon.

Newport

Straddling the Idaho/Washington border, Newport (pop. 1,700) began as a small trading post on the Idaho side in 1889, then moved to Washington when the Great Northern Railroad arrived in 1892. The original town site, overlooking the Pend Oreille (pronounced PON-doo-ray) River, holds most of the modern shopping malls, while the railroad legacy still defines much of the main part of town. Two depots face each other along US-2 at the south end of the three-block main street, Washington Avenue, one holding the offices of a lumber company, the other housing the small but enjoyable **Pend Oreille County Historical Museum** (daily 10 AM-4 PM; $1 donation), which has farming and mining artifacts—plus a pencil collection. Overlooking the river on the northeast edge of town, technically in Old Town, Idaho, **Fay's Lounge Steak House** has reliable American food.

ACROSS IDAHO

Even though the route zigzags for some 75 miles along the
Kootenai and Pend Oreille Rivers, it doesn't take long for US-2
to cross the narrow neck, known as the Panhandle, of northern
Idaho. Following the Pend Oreille River east from Washington, the
route passes through the resort community of **Sandpoint** before threading the deep
gorge of the Kootenai River upstream toward Montana.

Priest River

Roughly five miles east of the Washington border, and taking its name from the
renowned trout-fishing stream that flows into the Pend Oreille River nearby, Priest
River (pop. 1,560) is a supply center for hunters, anglers, and river-runners, as well
as a busy lumber town, with two huge Louisiana Pacific mills dominating the local
economy.

Priest River may not look like much from the highway, but the three blocks
of Main Street running south from US-2 hold an interesting mix of hardware and
antique stores, taverns, and the popular **River Pigs** restaurant, at 114 Main Street.

Sandpoint

Located at the junction of US-2 and US-95 at the northern end of Idaho's largest
lake, Pend Oreille, Sandpoint (pop. 5,500) is a resort community with a relaxed,
welcoming feel. The highly regarded **Schweitzer Mountain Resort** (208/263-9555

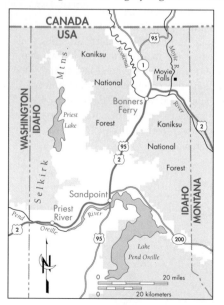

or 800/831-8810) north of Sandpoint
attracts skiers in winter and mountain
bikers in summer. The mix of Rocky
Mountain scenery and abundant recreation has made Sandpoint a popular
place to visit and live in; despite the
dozens of real estate agents and other
signs of potential despoliation, it still
feels like a small town.

As you might guess from the name,
Sandpoint boasts a fine, quarter-mile-
long beach: **City Beach,** just a few
blocks' walk from downtown at the east
end of Bridge Street, complete with volleyball courts and a dock where you can
board tour boats ($14) and cruise the
lake.

The main business district, around
1st Avenue (US-2/95), fills a half-
dozen blocks around the landmark

Panida Theater (208/263-9191), where big-names and locals still perform. You'll find a number of good cafes here, like the **Whistle Stop** at 312 N. 1st Avenue, and **Eichardt's**, a beer-drinker's delight with great food (burgers, sandwiches, fish 'n' chips) at 212 Cedar Street. Two blocks east, the **Cedar Street Bridge** was rebuilt as a shopping mall in the mid 1970s and now houses the HQ and showcase store of Coldwater Creek, an outdoorsy clothing company. Besides the rooms and condos at Sandpoint's resorts, there are many motels, including national names like **Super 8**, **Quality Inn**, and **Best Western**.

For more information, or for details of Sandpoint's festivals, contact the chamber of commerce (208/263-2161 or 800/800-2106).

Naples and Bonners Ferry

North from Sandpoint, US-2 and US-95 run together through broad flat valleys dotted with small timber towns. The largest of these, Naples, draws travelers to its friendly, $10-a-night **HI Hostel** (208/267-2947), housed above the general store. Next door, the Northwoods Tavern is a great place to meet locals over a beer and a game of pool (or three).

Ten miles north of Naples, named after a ferry service across the Kootenai River that started here in 1864, Bonners Ferry (pop. 2,193) is a busy blue-collar town with a natural resource-based (read: logging and farming) economy—and the **Kootenai River Inn**, an Indian-run casino and Best Western. One sight to see is the **Barber Ship**, on US-2 at center of town, a land-locked houseboat now housing a barber shop. There's an equally unusual accommodation option, too: the **Shorty Peak Fire Lookout**, way up in the wild Selkirk Mountains, where two people can spend the night and take in the panoramic views for a bargain $25 a night. For reservations, and information on hiking in the surrounding wilderness, contact the USFS **ranger station** on US-2/95 at south edge of town (208/267-5561).

Between Bonners Ferry and the Montana state line, US-2 crosses the once wild, now dammed Moyie River on a 450-foot-high bridge.

Though it's a pretty languid place, Sandpoint has gained unwanted notoriety as the home of former Los Angeles Police Department detective Mark Fuhrman, whose presence compounded the infamy focused upon the neo-Nazi compound at Hayden Lake, 30 miles south of town. Ruby Ridge, another notorious northern Idaho place name, refers to a spot just outside of Naples, 20 miles to the north.

The Idaho/Montana line marks the boundary between the Pacific and mountain time zones, so adjust your clocks and watches accordingly.

ACROSS MONTANA

Crossing northern Montana roughly 30 miles south of the Canadian border, US-2 gives an up-close look at two very different parts of this huge state. The western quarter, on the slopes of the Rocky Mountains, offers incredible scenic beauty and innumerable options for outdoor recreation, not least in magnificent Glacier National Park. East of Glacier, it's like a completely other world as two-lane US-2 (popularly known as the "Hi-Line") races across glaciated Great Plains range lands along the many tributaries of the broad Missouri River. A few low buttes and cylindrical grain silos rise up in sharp silhouettes, but

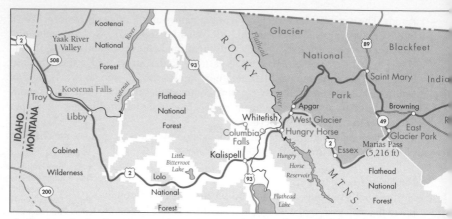

the horizon is the dominant aspect, stretching for what feels like hundreds of miles in all directions. Apart from dozens of one-side-of-the-road blink-stops, the towns along US-2 in the eastern stretches of Montana—**Culbertson, Wolf Point, Glasgow, Malta**, and **Havre**—are few and far between. It's here you realize what the "Big Sky Country" is all about: cruising along at 70 mph, pacing a freight train and waving at the engineer, and never, repeat, *never,* passing a gas station with the tank less than a quarter full.

How big is Montana? It stretches for over 650 miles east to west, covering an area larger than New England and New York put together, but has a total population smaller than that of Hartford, Connecticut.

The many roadside crosses you'll see while driving through Montana each mark a traffic fatality. They have been placed along the roads over the past 35 years by the American Legion; many are now elaborate shrines to lost loved ones.

Writer and resident **Rick Bass** has documented the isolated Yaak River Valley, north of US-2 via the scenic Hwy-508, in a trio of compelling books: the nonfiction titles *Winter: Notes from Montana* and *The Book of Yaak,* and a 1998 novel, *Where the Sea Used to Be.*

Troy: Kootenai Falls

On the banks of the broad Kootenai (pronounced KOOT-nee) River, 14 miles east of the Idaho border, the mining and lumber-milling town of Troy (pop. 1,000) is at very nearly the state's lowest elevation—1,892 feet above sea level. There's not a lot to the place, apart from a short stretch of motels, gas stations, taverns, churches, and cafes—the best of which is the family-friendly **Silver Spur**, right on US-2—plus a small **historical museum** at the east end of town. Some seven miles west of Troy, there's a nice USFS campground at the confluence of the Yaak and Kootenai Rivers.

Though the only sign says simply "Historic Point," the nicest spot to stop is nine miles west of Libby, two miles east of Troy, where the thundering cascade of Kootenai Falls drops down a half-mile-long series of terraces. A pair of hiking trails leave from the well-marked roadside parking area, one leading 400 yards upstream to the main falls, the other heading downstream to a rickety old swinging bridge that sways from cables suspended 50 feet above the green water.

Libby

The lumber town of Libby (pop. 2,750) was first founded as a gold-mining camp but grew into its present, elongated form after the Great Northern railroad came through in 1892. On the south bank of the Kootenai River, Libby is just downstream

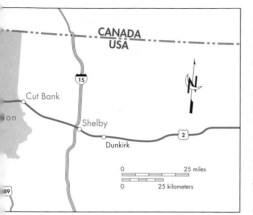

from the Libby Dam, which was built in 1972 and forms the Lake Koocanusa Reservoir, stretching north into Canada. Parallel to the railroad tracks, Libby is strung out for a few miles along US-2 frontage, where you can find casinos and gas stations galore (the Conoco station offers **hot showers**) and a half dozen motels, including the **Sandman** (406/293-8831), which has a hot tub and doubles from $30, and a pricey **Super 8** (406/293-2771). Places to eat include Beck's Montana Cafe, 2425 W. US-2 at the west end of town; the old center of town, along Mineral Drive north of US-2 toward Libby Dam, holds the **Pasttime Saloon**, serving beer since 1916.

A number of pleasant **campgrounds** operate in and around Libby, including excellent spots in the nearby Cabinet Wilderness; for details contact the USFS ranger station (406/293-8861), which also handles reservations for Libby's most interesting accommodation option: spending a night or two in the **Baldy Mountain Fire Lookout Tower**, 20 miles north of town; it sleeps up to six people and costs around $25 a night.

Between Libby and the busy mini-metropolis of the Columbia Falls/Whitefish/Kalispell area, US-2 traverses 70 miles of Kootenai National Forest, an all but uninhabited area, much of which was badly charred by the 1994 Houghton Creek forest fires. A small display at milepost 63 explains the role of fire in the natural scheme of things.

West of Glacier National Park, US-2 crosses US-93, which runs through the towns of Whitefish and Kalispell. We've described both of these places on pages 127-129.

For most of the way between Troy and Libby, US-2 is bordered by marked turnouts where trails lead to the narrow twisting **old highway,** preserved as a hiking and cross-country skiing trail through the dense forest.

Libby is the hometown of Montana Governor Mark Racicot.

Columbia Falls and Hungry Horse

Two intriguingly named towns line US-2 between Kalispell and Glacier National Park. A roadside collection of gas stations and industrial plants, including a massive Plum Creek lumber mill, make up the much larger town of Columbia Falls (pop. 3,200) where, despite the name, there are no falls. There are, however, a ton of entertaining roadside attractions, ranging from Grizzly Go-Karts to the Dino-Land Mini-Golf, which overstates the scale of its "World's Largest Jackalope." (It's big, but not as big as the one in Douglas, Wyoming, which appears on pages 557-558.)

If you like this sort of thing, you're in for an even bigger treat as you head east along US-2. The town of Hungry Horse, a service center for the large reservoir to the southeast, proclaims itself "The Friendliest Dam Town in the Whole World," and boasts ever bigger roadside attractions, starting with the **House of Mystery,** "Montana's Only Vortex," on the north side of US-2 (Apr.-Oct. only, daily 9 AM-9 PM; $3). Located along the Flathead River at the mouth of Bad Rock Canyon (which Native Americans thought was haunted), this is among the more credible of these places where, to quote from the brochure, "the laws of physics are bent, if not broken altogether . . . where birds won't fly and tress grow at odd angles. Could it be a bearing point for extraterrestrial visits centuries ago? . . . Nobody knows!" It's as fun as these places get (which is to say very, if you get into the "spirit" of the place), and well worth the minimal admission fee; there's a good gift shop, too.

If you're a fan of local newspapers, do what you have to do to get a copy of the *Hungry Horse News* (50 cents), organ of record for stories of mountain lion maulings and other events in the Glacier National Park region.

The stretch of US-2 between here and the turnoff to Glacier National Park holds one after another of other "attractions," including a Drive-Thru Bear Park and a wildlife museum marked by a pair of neon polar bears.

Even if you're appalled by the brashness of the above, you'll want to stop in Hungry Horse for a piece of pie or a milk shake at the **Huckleberry Patch**, on US-2 at the center of town. It's a full-service restaurant, boasting over 25 different fresh berry and cherry concoctions.

West Glacier

Like many tourist towns on the edges of our national parks, West Glacier has its share of tackiness, but here it's on a tolerably small scale, and limited to the approach along US-2 from the west. After all the billboards advertising scenic helicopter rides, taxidermy museums, and "The World's Greatest Maze," the actual town of West Glacier seems serenely quiet and peaceful, with little more than a couple of restaurants and comfortable motels, including the **River Bend** (406/888-5662), right on the Flathead River, and the **Vista** (406/888-5311 or 800/831-7101), which is open all year.

There's also a large **visitor center** for Glacier National Park (406/888-7800).

Essex: The Izaak Walton Inn

Avoiding the most extreme alpine scenery and the heavy winter snows, US-2 winds around the southern edge of Glacier National Park, climbing over the Continental Divide at 5,216-foot **Marias Pass**, the lowest of the Rocky Mountain passes. Though the road and the railroad are kept open year-round, there's very little visible development. Numerous trailheads access the southern reaches of the Glacier National Park backcountry.

One place that's well worth a stop, or better yet an extended stay, is the **Izaak Walton Inn** (406/888-5700), midway between East and West Glacier, a half-mile south of US-2 in the railroad village of Essex. Especially in winter, when the inn overlooks miles of cross-country ski trails, this is one of the best (and least known) stops in the state. A more humble (and less expensive) version of the Glacier Park lodges, the inn was built to house railroad workers (which it still does) and is now a popular, year-round alternative to the often overbooked accommodations

At Marias Pass, a roadside rest area holds an obelisk marking the old Roosevelt Highway and a statue of a Great Northern Railroad engineer.

within the park. Rooms start at $75 a night. The inn also serves very good food for breakfast, lunch, and dinner.

Another place worth a stop in early summer is the so-called **Goat Lick** on US-2, near milepost 182 about five miles east of the Essex turnoff, where dozens of shaggy white mountain goats regularly congregate around a mineral-rich spring.

East Glacier Park

Situated along US-2 at the southwest edge of the Blackfeet Indian Reservation, the town of East Glacier Park is, as the name suggests, the eastern gateway to Glacier National Park. It's a tiny place, barely more than a wide spot in the road, with a couple of general stores and gas stations, **Serrano's**, a good Mexican restaurant, and **Blondie's**, a bar, grill and pizza place.

With the main park entrance over 30 miles to the northeast at St. Mary, East Glacier Park is not an especially convenient base, though it does have one compelling attraction: the **Glacier Park Lodge** (406-226-9311), the grandest of all the historic park lodges. Built by the Great Northern Railroad to attract visitors to the park (and to their trains), the lodge centers on a four-story lobby built of huge Douglas fir logs—each of which runs floor to ceiling, with the bark still on it. It's an impressively rustic space, and well worth a look, though the individual rooms are somewhat disappointing, especially at standard rates of over $100 a night.

North of the lodge, about a half-mile north of US-2 via Hwy-49, there's a pair of restaurants and the very basic **HI East Glacier Hostel** (406-226-4426), with dorm beds above Brownie's Grocery Store for $12 a night. Continuing north, Hwy-49 runs into US-89 for the 30-mile run to the east entrance to Glacier National Park at the town of St. Mary.

St. Mary

Located on the Blackfeet Indian Reservation at the east entrance to Glacier National Park, the town of St. Mary makes a great alternative to the in-park lodges. At the east end of the historic Going-to-the-Sun Road, St. Mary has a large visitor center, a pair of clean modern motels—**St. Mary's Lodge** (406/732-4431) and the **Rising Sun** (406/732-5523)—and a great little cafe, the **Park Cafe and Grocery** (406/732-4482) serving mega-breakfasts and great berry pies a half-mile north of the park entrance.

St. Mary makes an especially handy base for visiting the comparatively quiet Many Glacier section, and for seeing the sights of adjacent Waterton National Park, across the border in Canada.

The Blackfeet Indian Reservation

The 1.5-million-acre Blackfeet Indian Reservation, stretching north to the Canadian border along the eastern border of Glacier National Park, is a weather-beaten land home to 7,500 members of what was once the most powerful tribe on the

(continues on page 468)

GLACIER NATIONAL PARK

The wildest and most rugged of all the Rocky Mountain national parks, Glacier National Park protects some 1,500 square miles of high-altitude scenery, including the glaciers for which the park is named, more than 200 lakes, and countless rivers and streams. Knifelike ridges of colorful sedimentary rock rise to over 10,000 feet, looming high above elongated glacier-carved valleys. Grizzly bears, black bears, bighorn sheep, mountain lions, and wolves roam the park's wild backcountry, which is criss-crossed by some 700 miles of hiking and riding trails.

The park's main features are reached via 50-mile-long **Going-to-the-Sun Road**, a magnificent serpentine highway that is arguably the most scenic route on this planet. Climbing up from dense forests to the west and prairie grasslands to the east, this narrow road is the only route across the park's million acres. Note that the road's middle section—everything east of Lake McDonald, basically—is usually closed by snow from late October until early June. No vehicles or combinations over 21 feet are allowed on the Going-to-the-Sun Road.

On the west side of the park, lovely **Lake McDonald** is Glacier's largest lake, and also the most developed area, with an attractive lodge, two restaurants, a gas station, and a nice campground. A boat offers hour-long narrated cruises ($6) throughout the summer. Between the lake and Logan Pass, five miles east of the Lake McDonald Lodge, **Avalanche Creek** is the most beautiful short hike in the park, winding through dense groves of cedar and fir alongside a creek that cascades noisily down a sharp cleft in the deep red rock. The two-mile trail ends up at Avalanche Lake, hemmed in by 1,500-foot-high cliffs.

The heart of the park is **Logan Pass**, a 6,680-foot saddle straddling the Continental Divide, which comes alive when the snow melts to reveal a rainbow of brightly colored wildflowers. Two very popular trails run from the large visitor center: the shorter but more strenuous one heads south on a wooden boardwalk across an

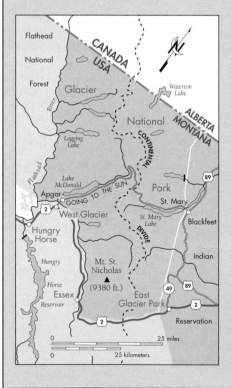

alpine meadow to a viewpoint overlooking **Hidden Lake**, while the fairly flat **High Line Trail** runs north, high above the Going-to-the-Sun Road, to the backcountry Granite Park Chalet (see below for details).

Along with the extensive facilities along US-2 at West Glacier, East Glacier, and St. Mary, you'll find a couple of rustic lodges and motels within the park. The nicest of these is the intimate, comfortable—and inexpensive, with doubles starting around $80 a night—**Lake McDonald Lodge** (406/888-5431), with a lovely lobby filled with comfy chairs arrayed around a fireplace, and lots of bearskin and buffalo rugs; it also serves the park's best food. In the park's northeast corner, the **Many Glacier Lodge** (406/732-441) is a circa 1917 pseudo-Swiss chalet on the shores of Swiftcurrent Lake, looking up at Grinnell Glacier. Besides the grand lodges, a few other relics of Glacier Park's early days as a "Grand Tour" destination still survive: bright red, open-top vintage touring cars run along the Going-to-the-Sun Road, providing guided tours as well as a shuttle service. There are over a dozen **campgrounds** in Glacier but they fill up fast; none has RV hookups, and only two take reservations (406/888-7800). Another option is the backcountry **Granite Park Chalet** ($60 per person per night; 406/387-5555), built in 1914 and recently renovated, which lets visitors overnight in the wilds without the hassles of hauling along tents and stoves.

Admission to the park is $10 per car for a seven-day pass, and the required backcountry camping permits are an additional $4 per person per night. For a more complete overview of the park, stop in at one of three main **visitor centers** in Glacier National Park, located in **West Glacier**, at **Logan Pass** (summer only), and at the eastern entrance in the town of **St. Mary**. For information in advance, call the park **headquarters** (406/888-7800).

Northern Plains. The Blackfeet, whose nomadic lives took them all over the plains in pursuit of buffalo, were feared and respected for their fighting and hunting abilities, though contact with white traders brought smallpox, alcoholism, and other diseases that devastated the tribe. Their strength in battle won the Blackfeet concessions from the encroaching U.S. government, including a huge swath of land that in 1855 included everything north of the Yellowstone River between the Dakotas and the Continental Divide. Much of this land, including what's now the eastern half of Glacier National Park, was later bought back or simply taken away; the tribe now earns most of its income from ranching, and from oil and natural gas leases.

The Blackfeet's tribal headquarters and main commercial center is **Browning** (pop. 1,170), located on US-2 near the eastern entrance to Glacier National Park. Like many reservation towns, Browning has a desolate and depressing feel to it, but there are a couple of places worth stopping at, including the **Museum of the Plains Indian** (daily 9 AM-5 PM June-Sept., Mon.-Fri. 10 AM-4:30 PM rest of the year; free), near the west end of town at the junction of US-2 and US-89. Operated by the U.S. government's Bureau of Indian Affairs, the bland building contains a small collection of Plains Indian arts and crafts, mostly blankets and jewelry. Also in Browning: the stuffed menagerie of the **Montana Wildlife Museum**, plus a couple of cafes and a pair of concrete teepees. More interesting, though harder to find, is the **Blackfoot Indian Writing Company**—maker of the finest Number 2s in the country, as well as Lindy pens —which you can tour informally (Mon.-Fri. 8 AM-2 PM; free; 406/ 338-2535 or 800/392-7326). The factory lies a mile off US-2 on the southeast edge of town, on the road to Heart Butte.

Blackfoot Indian Writing Company

The two-week-long **North American Indian Days** celebration, held in mid-July on the Blackfeet Tribal Fairgrounds next to the Museum of the Plains Indian, attracts native peoples from all over the U.S.A. and Canada. Call for information (406/338-7276).

Thirteen miles east of Browning, or 22 miles west of Cut Bank, a much-abused monument along US-2 points out the most northerly point reached by **Lewis and Clark** on their cross-country expedition. On July 23, 1806, Meriwether Lewis, searching for the headwaters of the Marias River, made it to a spot four miles north of US-2, which he called Camp Disappointment, before turning back because of bad weather.

Cut Bank

It's hard for travelers heading west along US-2 to believe that, despite having covered over 1,000 miles of undulating Great Plains, they have yet to reach the mountains. It isn't until Cut Bank (pop. 3,329) that the see-forever glaciation looks like it might be waning. You crest a hill and suddenly there they are: the rugged Rocky Mountains. Popularly known as the coldest city in the U.S., thanks to the presence of a U.S. weather-service monitoring station, Cut Bank is a friendly and pretty enough place, bisected neatly by US-2 and the railroad tracks.

Downtown, on US-2, the **Golden Harvest Cafe** is great for rubbing shoulders with the locals at breakfast, lunch, or dinner, but the best spots are a little east: the **Point Drive-In** is a classic roadster drive-up, while across the highway a 27-foot-tall penguin stands next to the **Glacier Gateway Inn**, 1121 E. Railroad Avenue (406/873-5544 or 800/851-5541), the town's nicest motel.

For great shotgun-seat reading along the way, William Least Heat Moon's *Blue Highways* contains an honest, lyrical account of the highs, lows, and endless in-betweens along this stretch, including a brief account of a day in Shelby.

Shelby

Despite what a quick map-read would indicate, or local tourist boosters would proclaim, the fact that Shelby is bustling is due solely to the busy I-15 interstate freeway, which crosses US-2 here, 25 miles south of the Canadian border. Even so, Shelby's activity—typical truck-jockey, blue-smoke activity—is relegated to the area immediately around the I-15 exit, and to the busy "multi-modal" depot along the Burlington Northern tracks. Otherwise, it's an oversized version of all the other Great Northern Railroad towns, one that extends farther than most along the tracks, with wide streets and a much-appreciated hill flaring up to the south of downtown.

Around Cut Bank and Shelby, tune to **96.3 FM** for country ballads and local news.

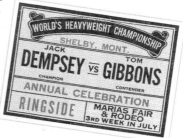

Shelby is not rowdy, but neither does it roll up its sidewalks by 8 PM. Shelby has an impressive line-up of bars along Main Street (The Mint, the Mountain Club, the Alibi Lounge, the Tap Room . . .), but the town's major claim to fame is that it hosted the 1923 world heavyweight fight between Jack Dempsey and Tommy Gibbons, a 15-round decision for Dempsey that was closer than it should have been. The match was produced as a publicity stunt to lure people to the oil boomtown, and Shelby built a 40,000-seat arena, but after Dempsey's managers hemmed and hawed about canceling the bout, only 7,000 showed up.

If you're here in the middle of July, try to check out the Marias County Fair in Shelby, which has rodeos, horse racing, amusement park rides, and lots of live music.

A replica arena and a room full of artifacts from the fight are among the many intriguing items on display at the **Marias Museum of History and Art** (Mon.-Fri. 1-5 PM and 7-9 PM, Saturday 1-4 PM in summer; free), in a former residence at the corner of 12th Avenue and 1st Street North. It feels much more like a home than a museum, which adds a welcome amount of weirdness to the usual battery of dusty old stuff. Best of all, the museum is across the street from the local **swimming pool** ($4), an essential rest stop on a hot mid-summer afternoon.

Great food is standard at **Kathy's Kitchen**, 156 Main Street, while an absolutely huge "Motel" sign down the street marks the entrance to **O'Haire Manor** (406/434-5555) at 204 S. 2nd Street, one of Shelby's better half-dozen motels, with doubles from $35.

Shelby boasts the last good range of services for the next 100-plus miles from here to Havre, so be sure to fill up the tank before setting off. Heading east, US-2 crosses bare plains broken by cattle ranges, Cold War-era missile silos, and occasional wheat farms but is otherwise pretty short on interest. It's a thumb-on-wheel, greased-lightning, straight-shot road from here, miles and miles of your own thoughts.

Havre

The largest town along eastern US-2, Havre (pop. 10,200, pronounced "HAV-ver") was founded by the Great Northern Railroad and named, for no good reason, after the French port Le Havre, though you'd never tell by the pronunciation. Havre retains more than a little of its Wild West feel and has enough unusual attractions to merit an extended stop. North of town is a large area of eroded **badlands**, and just west of town behind the Holiday Village Shopping Center is **Wahkpa**

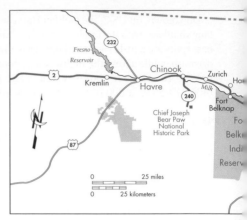

Chu'gn Archaeological Site. Dating back to prehistoric times, the area has been used by many cultures, including Plains Indian tribes, to drive bison to their deaths. It's open late May-Sept. only and costs $3.50. Many of the artifacts recovered from the area are displayed inside nearby **H. Earl Clack Memorial Museum** (daily 9 AM-9 PM May-Sept.; donations), which manages the site. The museum also offers scheduled tours ($2) of the archaeological site as well as of **Fort Assiniboine**, eight miles southwest off US-87, the largest fort ever built in Montana—over 100 buildings, though only a couple remain. The fort was under the command of John J. Pershing.

The town itself is engaging and rowdy. Numerous poker clubs (everything has "casino" tacked onto it) and cowboy bars line the compact downtown area, underneath which is a defunct underground world of illicit bordellos and opium dens—all part of the whiskey trail that flourished a century ago and again during

---

MONTANA: BIG SKY, NO SPEED LIMIT?

Up until the oil crisis of 1974, when lawmakers enacted a national speed limit of 55 mph, Montana law stipulated only that drivers should travel at a reasonable and prudent speed, with no legal maximum, though speeds of over 100 mph were generally considered ticket-worthy. The national speed limit was later raised to 65 in 1987, and in 1996 federal legislation returned speed-limit control to the states. In the case of Montana, this meant you could drive as fast as you wanted during daylight hours. In December of 1998, the U.S. Supreme Court declared Montana's "reasonable and prudent" speed limit unconstitutional. To avoid fines, don't drive faster than 75 mph on major interstates, 65 on the state highways. Besides, US-2 is a fairly narrow road, and is a popular long-distance cycling route, which makes it unsafe for full-throttle driving.

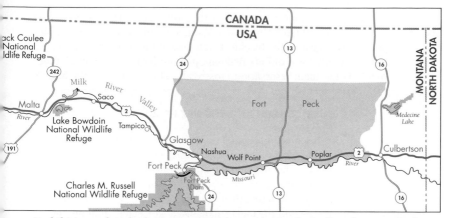

Prohibition, when bathtub gin—copious quantities from Canada a stone's throw north—was run through. Tours ($5) are available through **Havre Beneath The Streets** (406/265-8888) at 104 3rd Avenue.

Along First Street (US-2) you'll find all the usual fast-food suspects, and good Italian food at **Navlikis**, or Chinese at **Canton Chinese**, at 439 W. 1st Street. There's also the smaller, fresher **Lunch Box** deli/cafe at 213 3rd Avenue. For a place to stay, the plush **Duck Inn** (406/265-9615) has a silly name but good rooms and a surprisingly nice restaurant. There are strings of others along US-2; for listings, contact the **chamber of commerce** (406/265-4383) right downtown at 518 1st Street.

Chinook and Chief Joseph

Chinook (pop. 1,500), which takes its name from the Northwest intertribal patois for the warm southerly winds that rip through the area in January and February, raising temperatures some 60-70° F in a matter of hours, melting the winter snow, and allowing cattle to forage. Now a small cattle ranching town, Chinook is best known for its proximity to the surrender site of Nez Percé Chief Joseph to the U.S. Army in 1877—which effectively marked the end of the Indian Wars of the Plains. The very good **Blaine County Museum** (Tues.-Sat. 8 AM-5 PM, Sunday 1-5 PM in summer, Mon.-Fri. 1-5 PM rest of the year; free), four blocks south of US-2 at 501 Indiana Street, includes an impressive collection of fossils and local pioneer artifacts, as well as an informative multimedia presentation on the events leading up to the final surrender of Chief Joseph.

Far more compelling, if the weather's fine and you can spare half a day, is the actual site where the Nez Percé were captured, now preserved (with an interpretive trail and a few plaques, but otherwise unchanged) as **Chief Joseph Bear Paw Battlefield National Historic Park**, 16 miles south of Chinook via Hwy-240.

Fort Belknap Indian Reservation

Between Chinook and Malta, US-2 runs along the northern border of the Fort Belknap Indian Reservation, which covers some 650,000 acres stretching south to near the Missouri Breaks, a rock-and-sagebrush landscape that provided perfect hiding spots for outlaws like Kid Curry, Butch Cassidy, and the Hole-in-the-Wall Gang.

The Fort Belknap reservation was established in 1887 to contain the surviving members of the once-feared Gros Ventre and Assiniboine Indians, who before siding with the U.S. Army against the Blackfeet were one of the major powers on the northern Plains. The tiny town of **Fort Belknap**, just south of US-2 about 25 miles east of Chinook, is the main reservation crossroads. The town hosts the annual

---

CHIEF JOSEPH AND THE NEZ PERCÉ

The odyssey of Chief Joseph and his 600 followers is perhaps the most familiar tale of the final days of freedom of the North American Indians. Having led his band over 1,600 miles throughout the summer from their lands in Idaho, from which they were forcibly removed by the U.S. government (which had "re-negotiated" an initial treaty, in effect reducing the Nez Percé's holdings by 90%), Joseph and the ragtag, exhausted Nez Percé, thinking the cavalry farther south and Canada closer north than either really were, chose to camp and rest here near Chinook in 1877.

The U.S. Army, in hot pursuit, sent ahead a 400-man contingent, which reconnoitered the tribe and camped 12 miles to the southeast on September 28. The Nez Percé awoke to attack on September 30. The Army, expecting to prevail on the basis of surprise, instead met fierce resistance and a five-day siege ensued. After losing their herd of horses, 30 warriors, and three chiefs, and suffering high casualties among the women and children, the Nez Percé gave up. Chief Joseph's words upon surrendering were an eloquent and tragic encapsulation of the Native American experience:

Our chiefs are dead; the little children are freezing to death. My people have no blankets, no food . . . I want to have time to look for my children and see how many I can find . . . Hear me, my chiefs. I am tired. My heart is sick and sad.

Chief Joseph

From where the sun now stands, I will fight no more forever.

After receiving promises from the US commanders that the Nez Percé would be allowed to return to Idaho, Chief Joseph instead suffered the government's forked-tongue duplicity. Most of the Nez Percé were dispersed to several reservations, eventually winding up in Oklahoma. In 1885, through the Herculean efforts of Chief Joseph and with help from his old nemesis Colonel Miles, some 120 Nez Percé were allowed to return to Idaho. Chief Joseph, however, was never allowed to see his homeland again, finishing out his days in exile on the Colville Reservation in Washington, where he is buried.

Milk River Indian Days at the end of July, which features athletic contests as well as dances and country-fair festivities.

The larger town of **Harlem**, west of Fort Belknap and two miles north of US-2, is off the reservation but holds the tribal headquarters (406/353-2205); the 1939 WPA *Guide to Montana* described Harlem as "enlivened by the presence of Indians in bright and complicated mixtures of native and white dress. . . ."

As you approach Malta, the Milk River gives sly hints of lushness in the dust, showing a mirage-like ribbon of green south of the road, which itself is still rather bleak.

Butch Cassidy

Malta

Twenty miles east of the Fort Belknap reservation is Malta, named for the Mediterranean island but otherwise just another ranching town that grew up along the Great Northern Railway. Besides the above-average **Philips County Historical Museum** (Tues.-Sat. 10 AM-noon and 1-5 PM, June-Sept. only; donation) in the old Carnegie Library at 133 S. 1st Street W, Malta holds the region's best place to eat, drink, and sleep: the landmark **GN Hotel** (406/654-2100) at 2 S. 1st Avenue E, which has a bar-cum-steak house, a cafe with good breakfast specials, and double rooms from $40 a night.

Malta, where the eastbound and westbound trains of Amtrak's Empire Builder pass each other, is just one of dozens of flyspeck US-2 Montana towns with names borrowed at random by Great Northern Railway promoters from all over the globe. Heading along the highway, you pass near or through Dunkirk, Kremlin, Havre, Zurich, Harlem, and Tampico, all of which were founded by the railroad and settled in the main by Northern and Eastern European immigrants enticed here around the turn of the century by the railroad's offers of farmlands and homesteads.

Roughly 20 miles north of US-2, the 15,500-acre **Black Coulee National Wildlife Reserve** (daily 8 AM-4:30 PM; free) shelters one of the few nesting areas of the white pelican in the northwestern U.S.

At the tiny farming town of **Saco,** 28 miles east of Malta, pride of place is given to the one-room schoolhouse where TV journalist Chet Huntley received his education.

Milk River Valley

East of Malta, the road and the railroad cross and recross the banks of the sluggish and narrow Milk River. Highway signs proclaim your entrance to "Beef Country"; just check out the menu options in the cafes and you'll know you've arrived. US-2 continues its jaunts over the Milk River tributaries, winding along the swampy **Lake Bowdoin National Wildlife Refuge,** once the state's best duck-hunting grounds and now warm-weather home to pheasants, grouse, and sage hens as well as pelicans, ibises, and herons.

Unless you're a keen birdwatcher, the only place worth stopping at along this stretch is 10 miles west of Saco, and four miles north of US-2. Here the large and enticing **Sleeping Buffalo Hot Springs** resort (406/654-2100) offers a huge (60 by

80 feet) naturally heated swimming pool as well as hot tubs (as hot as 106° F) and cabins from $30 a night.

Glasgow

Glasgow (pop. 3,600), on the north banks of the Milk River 50 miles west of Wolf Point, is one of the few Hi-Line towns that's more than a collection of grain elevators, though its own dominant visual aspects are spreads of combines and threshers. Founded as a railroad town by the Great Northern Railroad in 1889, Glasgow is now the largest town in northeastern Montana. Stop in for a look at the tremendously cluttered, diorama-filled **Valley County Historical Museum** (Mon.-Sat. 9 AM-9 PM, Sunday 1-9 PM, summer only; free) on US-2 at 8th Avenue, worth a look for its barroom exhibit.

Johnnie's Cafe at 433 1st Avenue S serves great roadfood; the **Country Cafe** on the west side of town on US-2 features a Sunday buffet and 25-cent coffee, as well as the largest "EAT" sign this side of Texas.

Fort Peck and Fort Peck Dam

Fifteen miles south of Glasgow and US-2 via Hwy-24, the enormous Fort Peck

In the premier issue of *Life* magazine (Nov. 23, 1936), documentary photographer Margaret Bourke-White profiled the town of Fort Peck as well as the other 18 boomtowns that sprang up in the surrounding area during construction of Fort Peck Dam.

Lake collects the waters of the Missouri River behind massive Fort Peck Dam, one of the largest construction projects of the New Deal era and still the world's second-largest earthen dam. From 1933 until 1940, a friendly invasion of ultimately 10,000 civilian workers, earning between 50 cents and $1.20 per hour, hacked, dug, poured, sweated, and wrested a sea out of High Plains desolation. As a result, 20-million acrefeet of water is impounded behind the nearly fourmile-long dam, corralled to a maximum depth of 220 feet and with a serpentine shoreline longer than California's—1,600 miles! Surrounding the whole sprawling lake are countless recreation areas, campsites, and other diversions; the reservoir is home to a huge array of wildlife, including elk, bighorn sheep, pronghorn, and migrating waterfowl, all protected within the **Charles M. Russell National Wildlife Refuge.** Free tours of the old **powerhouse**, with a museum inside, are given hourly daily 9 AM-5 PM in summer.

The lake is most easiest approached via Hwy-117, 15 miles south from US-2 at the town of Nashua; you can also reach it from Glasgow via Hwy-24, along which there's an **information center** (406/526-3431 or 406/538-8706) whose chatty staff willingly supplies details on hiking, cycling, and camping in and around the refuge or other recreation areas.

Besides the dam and lake, the area's best surviving example of New Deal spirit is the snug town of Fort Peck (pop. 300), built from scratch to house the construction workers, though its current population is but a small fraction of the number that once

Fort Peck Theater

called it home. A few of the old buildings still stand, including the landmark **Fort Peck Theater** (406/ 228-9219) on Hwy-24, a huge draw in the area with its summertime plays and musicals. The **Fort Peck Cafe** has basic but good food, while one of the greatest places to stay near US-2 in Montana is the original **Fort Peck Hotel** (406/526-3266), long dormant but recently taken over and touchingly (with nary an ounce of avarice) brought back into a semblance of its classic old self. Rates start under $30 a night for a single or double with shared bath; the restaurant is by far the best in the area, as well.

Fort Peck Indian Reservation

The sprawling Fort Peck Indian Reservation, Montana's second-largest, stretches for nearly 100 miles along US-2, and for 50 miles north. Home to 6,800 Assiniboine and Yanktonai Sioux, but co-owned by non-Indians as a result of unscrupulous land dealings encouraged by the 1887 Dawes Act, the reservation offers few sights or services to outsiders. Travelers interested in tribal life have to make do with occasional events like the annual **Red Bottom Day** celebrations (held every June in Frazer, west of Wolf Point), the **Wadopana Pow Wow** (early August), or the **Wild Horse Stampede** rodeo in Wolf Point, the oldest rodeo in Montana.

The largest town, **Wolf Point**, is halfway across the reservation, 55 miles west of Culbertson. Wolf Point is certainly not frenetic with activity on a daily basis, and strewn corpses of some great antique vehicles rust on the outer fringes of town. Also in Wolf Point, on the lower level of the county library at 220 2nd Avenue, is the **Wolf Point Area Historical Society Museum** (Mon.-Fri. 10 AM-5 PM in summer only; donations), worth a look as much for the local artists' work as for exhibits detailing the region's fur-trapping and cattle ranching past, including a nice rifle collection. Also in Wolf Point you'll find some of the best cafes and motels for miles. The **Stockman's Cafe** at 220 Main Street has low prices and down-home comfort food, while the **Sherman Motor Inn** (406/653-3600) at 200 Main Street includes a decent restaurant; room rates average $30 for a double. For more information on local draws, especially the prestigious rodeo, contact the **chamber of commerce** (406/653-2012) at 201 4th Street S.

Near the eastern edge of the reservation, **Poplar** is quickly crossed and forgotten, though its **Assiniboine/Sioux Tribal Museum** (Mon.-Fri. 8 AM-4:30 PM; free) exhibits some excellent relics from Custer's defeat at Wounded Knee, as well as artifacts relocated from the Chicago Historical Society.

Fort Peck Indian Reservation holds Native American celebrations an average of every other weekend. And the granddaddy of 'em all in Montana, July's **Wild Horse Stampede** in Wolf Point, is the oldest in the state; contact the tribe for more information (406/768-5155).

In winter, northeastern Montana suffers some of the worst weather in the lower 48 states, as arctic winds racing across the plains lower temperatures to average winter highs of 10° F.

Because trees are scarce on the eastern Montana plains, early settlers built homes by impaling slabs of sod over thin poles. A few of the museums in towns along US-2 display mock-ups of these **sod houses.**

Immediately west of Culbertson, keep your eyes peeled for a herd of **bison** in a tiny valley, grazing peacefully alongside their calves.

Though it's hardly worth the 120-mile drive south along the Yellowstone River, the tiny town of Ismay (pop. 19) unofficially changed its name to **Joe, Montana,** in honor of the retired '49ers football superstar.

Culbertson

Culbertson (pop. 796) is a quiet town with a disproportionate number of farm implement and feed dealers—the tourist brochures brag about the "ever-expanding SVO Oilseed processing plant." Located a mile east of town, the **Montana Visitor Center** (8 AM-8 PM in summer, 8 AM-5 PM May and Sept.; free) houses the outstanding **Culbertson Museum**, a huge, well-designed place. The guides can give you a lickety-split tour if necessary.

There are a couple cafes in town, including the classic breakfast-lunch-dinner **Wild West Diner** right on US-2 at 20 E. 6th Street, immediately next to **M&Ms Place**, which is more of a lunch/dinner option. The **King's Inn**, 408 E. 6th Street (406/787-6277), is a clean, modern, $35-a-night motel.

ACROSS NORTH DAKOTA

Apart from the likeable small city of **Grand Forks**, at the state's eastern border, much of North Dakota's landscape lives up to those nondescript clichés from childhood family trips: it hems and rolls and yawns *forever*. Montana may be Big Sky Country, but North Dakota sure seems to be High Sky Country, the land where, if you tire of watching dancing golden wheat mirages, you can exercise your finger channel-surfing on the radio. It's a long, flat (and, dare we say it?: dull) drive across the state, with little here but plains or pseudo-prairie, and even the most epic side trip offers minimal relief. The state has done what it can to help out bored travelers by eliminating roadside mowing for most of the trip across, opting for native prairie and a potential refuge for wildlife —and road kill.

That said, the 300 miles across the state do hold a few points of interest, including

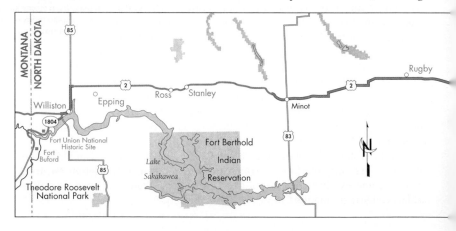

Fort Union, an evocative outpost of the early frontier; popular Devil's Lake recreational areas; the agricultural centers of Minot and Williston; and the geographical center of North America, marked by a stone monument in the town of Rugby.

Crossing between North Dakota and Montana, you switch between central and mountain time zones, so set your clocks and watches accordingly.

For an alternative to US-2 between the Montana border and Minot, if you have some time and the inclination to explore, swing south about 15 miles east of Culbertson, Montana, and join up with Hwy-1804, which follows the well-signed **Lewis and Clark Trail** along the Missouri River and sluggish Lake Sakakawea.

Fort Union National Historic Site

Astride the Montana/North Dakota border, standing proud atop the banks at the confluence of the Yellowstone and Missouri Rivers, the Fort Union Trading Post National Historic Site was once the largest and busiest outpost on the upper Missouri River. Despite the "fort" in its name, it was never a part of the U.S. military; it was, however, the most successful and longest-lived of all the frontier trading posts. In 1804, Lewis and Clark visited the site, which they called "a judicious position for the purpose of trade." Twenty-five years later, John Jacob Astor's American Fur Company proved them right, establishing an outpost here

Kenneth McKenzie, founder of Fort Union.

in a successful attempt to end the Hudson Bay company's monopoly on northwest trade. Linked by steamboat with St. Louis some 1,800 miles away, Fort Union reigned over the northern plains. Its bon vivant overseer, Kenneth McKenzie, the "King of the Missouri," kept the fine china polished and the wines cool in the cellar, offering a taste of displaced civilization to such luminary explorers as George Catlin, Prince Maximilian, and James Audubon.

The fort was abandoned as the fur trade declined in the 1850s, and portions of original buildings and walls were taken down by the U.S. Army in 1867 to construct Fort Buford, a mile to the east. In the late 1980s, the park service reconstructed the buildings atop the original foundations, giving a palpable if somewhat overly polished idea of how the old fort looked. McKenzie's old home and office, Bourgeois House, is now a **visitor center** (daily 8 AM-8 PM in summer, 9 AM-5:30 PM rest of the year; donations; 701/572-9083) with some surprising artifacts. The fort hosts occasional reenactments of boisterous frontier life: mid-June, for example, brings the annual **Fort Union Rendezvous,** a rollicking re-creation of fur-trapper gatherings to trade, talk, and compete in wilderness skills.

Fort Buford

Built in 1866 and now a state historic site, Fort Buford is eerily quiet, with only the stone powder magazine and a museum in an original soldiers' quarters open for viewing. Home to a company of "Buffalo Soldiers," as the Sioux called the black cavalrymen, the fort is best known for its sad contribution to the U.S. extermination campaign of Native Americans: it was here that Chief Sitting Bull surrendered to the U.S. Army in 1881, and here that Chief Joseph of the Nez Percé was brought after his "I will fight no more forever" surrender in Montana (see the special topic on page 472).

Williston's Sod Busters' Memorial

In the past, the historic sites of Fort Buford and neighboring Fort Union used to be more easily reached from Montana, though recent roadwork has made them accessible from either side of the border. Signs point the way south from US-2.

Across western North Dakota, tune to **KMHA 91.3 FM** for commercial-free country music and community news and features from the Fort Berthold Indian Reservation, home to descendants of the Native American Mandan, Arikara, and Hidatsa tribes.

Roughly 65 miles southeast of Williston via US-85, the north unit of **Theodore Roosevelt National Park** preserves one of the largest contiguous areas of semi-natural Great Plains landscape.

Williston

The first settlement east of the Montana line, Williston (pop. 13,100) is a classic, just-big-enough, one-movie-theater town. Always a boom or bust kind of place, "Champion City" (no apparent reason for the self-proclamation) today has shed its turn-of-the-century roughshod image, turning away from wheat-growing and oil-pumping industries and staking a tenuous claim instead on tourism. Refineries and other heavy industry are still sorely prevalent in some areas of town, but the downtown area is basically overgrown, *Our Town* placid.

Apart from filling the tank before a trip to Fort Union or farther afield, there's not a lot to do in Williston except in May, when the **Roughrider Art Show** brings in a strong regional art collection. Responding to an impromptu breakfast poll, locals will likely recommend **Gramma Sharon's** as the eatery of choice; it's located right on US-2 on the east edge of town—attached to a Conoco station, as most good cafes in the northern Great Plains seem to be. At the junction of US-2 and Hwy-85 is a **Super 8** motel (701/572-8371), the best of many highway motels offering decent rooms from under $30 a night.

Epping

Like many other North Dakota rural communities, the old Great Northern railway town of Epping (pop. 55) has all but disappeared thanks to changes in farming practices, the railway's move to diesel instead of steam, and sundry other common complaints. Here, however, the rapidly vanishing Great Plains lifeways have been partially preserved, thanks to the lifelong efforts of a local preacher who single-handedly preserved the abandoned buildings and artifacts as the **Buffalo Trails Museum** (Mon.-Sat. 9 AM-5 PM, Sunday 1-5 PM; $2; 701/859-4361), which grew to encompass almost the entire town. Main Street is still dusty dirt, lined by a general store, a hardware store, a pool hall, and other essential services. Most of these old buildings have been converted to house an amazing array of animated dioramas (papier-mâché dummies dressed up like dentists and patients) and the usual old tools and other junk, but the best reason to stop may be the **Buffalo Inn Cafe** across from the museum entrance, serving good food daily but especially popular on Sunday, when farming families come from near and far to enjoy the $8 buffet lunch.

Ross and Stanley

East of Epping toward Minot, US-2 twists up and through a hundred miles of gentle chocolate-drop hillocks, residuals of the great Ice Age glaciers, with some beautiful, almost ski-slope rises and plateaus capped by an occasional abandoned squad of dwellings. Along the way, podunk villages whiz by: Ross (pop. 61), for example, is a typically funky old town with some dilapidated, boarded-up buildings and huge grain elevators that look more like spacecraft engines.

The one sizeable place, Stanley (pop. 1,371), resting along the horizon-straight railroad tracks seven miles east of Ross and 47 miles west of Minot, is worth a stop for a whirl-a-whip at the old-fashioned soda fountain, inside the Rexall Drug Store on Main Street, north of US-2. There's also a free municipal campground at the north end of town.

Many places along the Missouri River are named for the intrepid and enigmatic Shoshone woman who guided explorers Lewis and Clark across the Plains in 1804. **Sacagawea** is alternately rendered as "Sakakawea" or "Sacajawea" and translated either as "Bird-Woman" or "Boat-Launcher."

Minot marks the junction of US-2 and US-83, "The Road to Nowhere," which runs from Canada to Mexico. Minot is covered on pages 173-174.

Just west of Minot, US-2 offers surprisingly fine views of the city and of a giant old railroad bridge spanning valley bluffs on the south side of the highway.

Rugby

Midway between Devil's Lake and Minot, Rugby (pop. 2,909) is an important agricultural hamlet, known to road wanderers as the town nearest to the **geographical center of North America**. The exact spot is marked with a two-story stone cairn along the south side of US-2, in front of the Conoco station. Nearby is the **Pioneer Village Geographical Center Museum** (Mon.-Sat. 8 AM-7 PM, Sunday 1-7 PM in summer only; $3), featuring 27 restored buildings—train depot, schoolhouse, even a hobo jungle—relocated here from around the county, as well as an exhibit on the life of a 8-foot-plus-tall local man, Clifford Thompson. The **Cornerstone Cafe**, inside the Conoco station, and the **Hub Motel** (701/776-5833) across US-2, complete the list of reasons to stop.

Midway between Minot and Rugby, the tiny town of Denbigh is the burial site of **Sondre Norheim,** a Norwegian national hero who invented the telemark turn in cross-country skiing. Royalty have paid their respects to her; you can too.

The landscape along this stretch of US-2 consists of immense stretches of hay fields typical of the Great Plains, and only occasional morasses of miniature cattails, goldenrod, and sunflower. The toponymy here is decidedly Anglocentric, with towns named Rugby or Leeds or York after the hometowns of English investors who, during the 1880s, pumped the fledgling towns full of cash. The general population, however, has always been decidedly Scandinavian.

marking the geographic center of North America

Devil's Lake and Fort Totten

The waters and wetlands south of the eponymous town of Devil's Lake (pop. 7,782) are one of the biggest natural draws in the state, with birdwatching, hunting, and fishing opportunities aplenty. The town itself, situated on the largest body of water in North Dakota, 58 miles east of Rugby and 85 miles west of Grand Forks, has clearly tried to remake itself into an upscale tourist trap, boasting lots of sandblasted "historic" buildings hung with spanking new signs. The whole community, cheery to a fault, seems done up in Sunday best, especially during the annual summer-long **North Dakota Chautauqua**, a reminder of the days when Devil's Lake was a major stop on the educational, recreational, and religious chautauquas that traveled across the country until the 1920s. The local **visitor center** (701/662-4903), on US-2 at the south edge of town, can provide information on the area's history and recreation.

Historic Fort Totten (daily 7:30 AM-dusk; free), 14 miles south of town on Hwy-57, is one of the country's best-preserved 19th-century military forts, with numer-

---

ROADSIDE GIANTS OF NORTH DAKOTA

It may be the long cold winters, the endless flat landscape, or the incredible solitude of life on the northern Great Plains, but there's something about North Dakota that makes people do strange things. The most obvious signs of this odd behavior are the many giant sculptures that stand along the roadside all over the state. Bigger and better than their cousins elsewhere in the U.S., the Roadside Giants of North Dakota quite simply have to be seen to be believed.

The following are a few of the biggest and best:

World's Largest Turtle
Nicknamed "Wee'l," this giant turtle was made out of old tractor wheels, and stands along Hwy-5 near Bottineau, 45 miles northwest of Rugby.

World's Largest Buffalo
This 60-ton giant looms over I-94 in Jamestown, 100 miles south of Devil's Lake.

World's Largest Cow
"Salem Sue" stands along I-94 in New Salem, 30 miles west of Bismarck.

ous restored buildings set around a spacious central square, as well as a museum and a theater (productions Thursday, Saturday, and Sunday in July and August). A rodeo and powwow, featuring highly competitive Native American dances, are held during **Fort Totten Days** the last weekend in July. Next to the fort is **Sully's Hill National Game Preserve**, a 1,600-acre refuge for bison, elk, deer, and other wildlife, which you may spot while hiking the nature trail.

Both the fort and the nature preserve are located on the 137,000-acre **Fort Totten Sioux Indian Reservation** (701/766-4221), centering around the mission village of **St. Michael's**, four miles east of the fort. The main attraction to visitors is the **Dakotah Sioux Casino** (800/WIN-UBET or 800/946-8238), one of North Dakota's largest, standing outside Tokio 18 miles southeast of downtown Devil's Lake.

Grand Forks

The oldest and second-largest community in North Dakota, and frequently rated one of the "Top Ten Most Livable Places" in the country, Grand Forks (pop. 52,500) gained a place in the national headlines during the terrible floods which devastated the city in April 1997. Following one of the worst winters on record, during which blizzard after blizzard dumped over eight feet of snow and ice on the surrounding plains, Grand Forks prepared for the worst floods the Northern Plains had ever seen. The Red River of the North, which forms the state border between North Dakota and Minnesota, was expected to crest at more than twice its usual peak. In the aftermath of a hurricane-force rain and snow storm on April 7, the river rose an inch every hour, two feet a day, day after day, while volunteers and relief workers struggled to protect the town.

Under the watchful eyes of the national news media, the river continued to rise, finally breaching its sand-bagged banks on April 15 and inundating the town. The entire population was evacuated, and over 75% of the homes and buildings were flooded; many were partially submerged for more than a month until the waters finally receded and clean-up could begin. The worst destruction occurred in the downtown core, where electrical short-circuits set off fires that raged for days and turned historic landmarks into scorched empty shells. Total damage reached over $1 billion, but, miraculously, not a single death was attributed to the floods.

Signs of flood and fire are still visible everywhere in Grand Forks, but what is most remarkable is how quickly and energetically the community set about rebuilding itself. While many of the downtown businesses have remained closed or have fled to new premises on the outskirts of town, there are plenty of signs that Grand Forks will regain its role as the cultural capital of the region.

One of Grand Forks' liveliest institutions is the 11,000-student University of North Dakota, whose campus lines Grand Forks' massive railroad yards north of De Mers Avenue (old US-2). A former campus gym is now home to the **North Dakota Museum of Art**, (Mon.-Fri. 9 AM-5 PM, Sat.-Sun. 1-5 PM; donations; 701/777-4159), which survived the flood unscathed and has since been home to theatre and dance performances along with the state's only contemporary art collection. Also on campus you'll find the acoustically exquisite (Tony Bennett raved about it) **Chester Fritz Auditorium,** the local venue for touring national and international acts, as well as the aeronautically-minded **Center for Aerospace Studies,** which trains pilots.

EAST GRAND FORKS, MINN.

For weary road trippers, the saddest loss caused by the floods has to be the legendary **Whitey's Bar & Cafe**. Though legally in Minnesota, this was a true Grand Forks institution, a genuine speakeasy dominated by the fabulous art deco-styled "Wonder-bar"—a horseshoe-shaped, stainless steel sculpture, surrounded by comfy booths with individual jukeboxes. Good news: Late in 1998, Whitey's reopened, with almost all of its original fixtures and furnishings intact, just east of the Red River bridge at 121 De Mers Avenue (218/773-1831). Otherwise, the best bet for food and drink is **Bonzer's**, a popular sandwich and beer bar that's open 11 AM-1 AM at 420 De Mers Avenue, across from the landmark Empire movie theater.

Long the commercial center of northern Great Plains agriculture, in 1893 Grand Forks was the birthplace of Cream of Wheat cereal.

Accommodation options include the usual range of national chain motels out around the junction of US-2 and I-29, plus close to downtown there's the very attractive **Best Western Town House**, 710 1st Avenue North (701/746-5411 or 800/867-9797), with an indoor pool and on-site miniature golf course—all for around $50 a night.

For the latest information, contact the Grand Forks **visitors bureau** (701/746-0444 or 800/866-4566).

ACROSS MINNESOTA

In its trek across northern Minnesota, US-2 offers nearly 250 miles of open road before winding up in the busy but surprisingly attractive lakefront city of **Duluth**. Midway across the state, after the endless wheat fields of the west, the scenery turns slightly turbid with the remnants of old iron mines and a series of still-busy lumber and paper mills. Opportunistic little cells of roadside community crop up to serve the beer-and-bait needs of those bound for the myriad "recreational opportunities" of Minnesota's "Lake Country" along the headwaters of the mighty Mississippi River. At either edge of this summertime playground, two largish towns, **Grand Rapids** and **Bemidji**, serve as gateways to the gaping spreads of Chippewa National Forest and many of Minnesota's 10,000 lakes.

The **Minnesota Welcome Center**, 11 miles east of the North Dakota border on US-2, has a full range of maps and information on both states.

Fisher

The first town east of the North Dakota state line, tiny Fisher (pop. 413) doesn't look like much, but was once a bustling frontier port, thanks to its location at the navigational headwaters of the Red River of the North. River traffic has all but disappeared, but the local sugar beet industry pulls in a billion dollars a year, which may explain the town's prosperous air. For good food, stop at the **Fisher Cafe**, across the street from the spindly water tower, three blocks south of US-2.

Near Fisher stretches the **Malmberg Prairie**, one of the few extant virgin prairies left, here protected by the Nature Conservancy.

Crookston

Crookston (pop. 8,119), 25 miles east of the North Dakota border, has a series of bridges over the meandering and tree-lined Red Lake River, which winds along the south side of the compact downtown business district. There's a statue of pioneer Joe Roulette in front of the community center on US-2, and a small **Polk County Museum** (daily noon-5 PM late-May-Sept; donations), containing the usual slew of 19th-century stuff with the addition of the world's largest ox-cart, but that's about it as far as sights go.

There are also two rather big festivals in Crookston: August's Ox-Cart Days, and Red River Valley Winter Shows and Rodeo, the latter drawing up to 40,000 visitors from the U.S. and Canada. Call 800/809-5997 for tourist info.

Erskine and Bagley

In the 100 miles east of the North Dakota border, US-2 spreads into a divided four-lane, climbing out of the fecund Red River Valley of the North (not to be confused with the *real* Red River Valley, down in Texas) onto the flat glaciated plains, while the roadside colors alternate between the dark reds and greens of sugar beets and the buff and leafy tones of the wheat, soy beans, and potatoes for which the area is known.

Continuing east, US-2 passes occasional isolated pockets of trees, planted as windbreaks amidst the furrowed fields. In the tiny village of Erskine (pop. 422), a classic one-horse Midwest town, you'll find **Joe DiMaggio's Bar**, neither a misprint nor the genuine article. (The owner, Mr. D., is a Bronx native who used to get oodles of wrong numbers for the legendary Yankee Clipper. Not surprisingly, his bar is full of baseball memorabilia.) Erskine also has a municipal swimming beach on Lake Cameron, and takes civic pride in being the home of the "World's Largest Northern Pike."

Thirty miles east of Erskine, at the western turnoff to Lake Itasca, Bagley (pop. 1,388) features a large wildlife museum packed with stuffed polar and Kodiak bears, among 750-odd creatures, right on US-2 at the western edge of town.

> The tiny town of **Fosston**, midway between Erskine and Bagley, holds one of two stoplights on this 100-mile stretch of US-2. Fosston also marks the sudden switch between the Great Plains and the Great North Woods; the town motto is unusually appropriate: "Fosston, Where the Plains Meet the Pines."

> On Hwy-33, 11 miles south of US-2 and 15 miles west of Duluth on the edge of the Fond Du Lac Indian Reservation, the town of **Cloquet** boasts the only gas station ever designed by famed architect Frank Lloyd Wright. Cloquet also has a large, Fond du Lac Indian-owned casino (800/321-0005).

Between Bemidji and Grand Rapids, US-2 runs parallel to the slower but more scenic Great River Road, which winds along the Mississippi River, from Lake Itasca all the way south to New Orleans. The entire GRR route, including the towns of Bemidji and Grand Rapids, is detailed beginning on page 220.

Skyline Parkway and Hwy-61

One of the greatest loop trips in the country, Skyline Parkway is a 25-mile (over 30 with side trips) bucolic wind along the bluffs above Duluth. Accessed from West Duluth off I-35, the parkway takes in numerous historical sites, but it's mostly just jaw-drop scenery, especially **Hawk Ridge**, which offers perfect wind conditions for viewing up to 30,000 hawks, eagles, and falcons daily in fall; also along the ridge is a fantastic network of trails, boarding stations, and observation posts. The parkway,

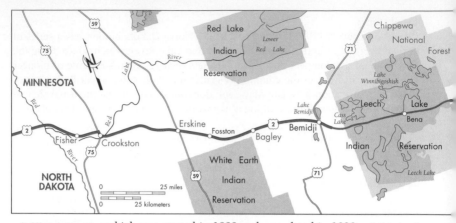

In Minnesota and Wisconsin, the "On and Off" and "Off Sale" signs on many bars and roadhouse restaurants designate whether they can sell beer and wine for consumption on or off the premises.

which was started in 1889 and completed in 1929, connects at its north end with famed Hwy-61, which, if you've got the time to spend, is an even more beautiful jaunt along Lake Superior's granite cliffs to Grand Portage and Canada, 150 miles to the northeast. Along the way are some of the region's best places to eat: numerous **smokehouses** touting their smoked fish, plucked from the frigid waters of the great lake.

Hwy-61 north of Duluth is the road that inspired the title of Bob Dylan's album *Highway 61 Revisited*. Dylan himself was born in Duluth and grew up in the nearby iron-mining town of **Hibbing,** which is also where Greyhound Bus Lines got its start, shuttling between the mines and the town. Home run-hitter Roger Maris was another Hibbing product.

Duluth

Though it doesn't get a lot of positive press, Duluth (pop. 85,493) has to be one of the most beautiful and underappreciated travel destinations in the Midwest, "a Lilliputian village in a mammoth rock garden," the old WPA *Guide to Minnesota* aptly noted. Gracefully etched into the side of tough, 800-foot granite slopes and gazing over the dark harbor hues, Duluth, from the attractively redone red-brick paving of gentrified Superior and Michigan Streets downtown to the grittier heights atop the bluff, quietly goes about its business, usually with foghorns belching in the background. It is a city of maritime and timber history, but it is a city of stunning, pervasive, pristine, *healthy* wilderness as well.

Tracts of forest, harbor preserves, shoreline, and parks flourish in the city, and there are dozens of interesting Great Lake or historical museums, mansions, lakefront walks, boat or foot tours, and festivals—from Native American powwows (mid-August) to midwinter dogsled races. Many visitors start with the **Canal Park Maritime Museum** (daily 10 AM-9 PM in summer, 10 AM-4:30 PM rest of the year; free) on Canal Park Drive next to the Aerial Lift Bridge.

Another good stop is **The Depot** (daily 10 a.m. -5 p.m. in summer, Sunday 1-5 p.m. in winter; $5), across I-35 but walkably close to the waterfront at 506 W. Michigan Avenue, an enormous, magnificently restored example of early city architecture as well as home to many of the city's artistic and cultural centers. Around it are the historic locomotives of the Lake Superior Museum of Transportation, and two dozen shops re-creating turn-of-the-century Duluth, right down to the old ice cream parlor.

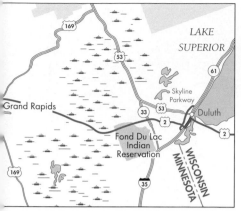

Crossing the St. Louis River delta on the Bong Memorial Bridge (named after a famous WW II flying ace) between Superior, Wisconsin, and downtown Duluth travelers on US-2 are afforded a resplendent view of the harbor and Duluth's landmark, the **Aerial Lift Bridge**, a 385-foot-tall monster connecting the mainland to the mouth of the harbor.

A fun and filling place to eat, **Grandma's Saloon**, serves up heaps of Italian-American food at the foot of the Aerial Lift Bridge, at 522 S. Lake Avenue. For more information on Duluth, contact the main **visitor center** (218/722-4011 or 800/4-DULUTH or 800/438-5884) near the bridge at 100 Lake Place Drive. There's also a **ship watcher's hotline** (218/722-6489) if you want to head down to the harbor and check out the ore-boat traffic.

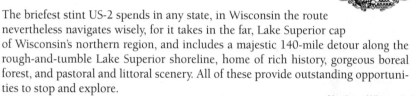

The Aerial Lift Bridge over Duluth's harbor can be raised 138 feet in under a minute, to let ships pass underneath.

ACROSS WISCONSIN

The briefest stint US-2 spends in any state, in Wisconsin the route nevertheless navigates wisely, for it takes in the far, Lake Superior cap of Wisconsin's northern region, and includes a majestic 140-mile detour along the rough-and-tumble Lake Superior shoreline, home of rich history, gorgeous boreal forest, and pastoral and littoral scenery. All of these provide outstanding opportunities to stop and explore.

Superior

Both rival and best friend of bigger Duluth across the harbor, Superior (pop. 27,100) is sometimes the butt of jokes, usually regarding its comparatively lower geography (which means Superior catches all of Duluth's flotsam), its hardy, blue-collar mentality and mountains of coal, and an apparent lack of trees. It is also proud, along with Duluth, of being one of the busiest harbors in the nation, shipping millions of tons of ore a year from the nation's most inland port.

Northern Wisconsin is in the heart of big snow country, a promontory jutting into the maw of bad-tempered **Gitcheegumee,** where 35 inches of snow a month during the winter don't begin to crease a frown on a native Wisconsinite's face. So play it safe if you're traveling along Lake Superior then.

Superior's lack of pretense is perhaps its biggest attraction. The route on US-2 through the city is decidedly industrialized, featuring a seemingly endless amount —almost 30 miles—of bay shore crowded with trains, tracks, elevators, and spindly working piers jutting out into the lake almost to the horizon. The city itself is sedate but offers a few things of historical or Great Lake interest, including its biggest draw, **Fairlawn Mansion** (daily 9 AM-5 PM; $5), the sprawling 42-room ex-residence of a lumber and mining baron, now the main local history museum.

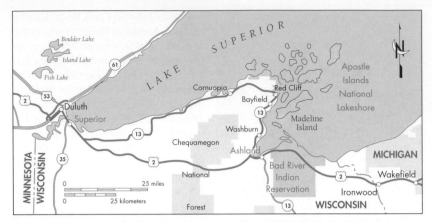

If you're here on a Friday evening, be sure to head 20 miles west of Bayfield to the Lake Superior hamlet of Cornucopia for the traditional Scandinavian Fish Boil, held at the Village Inn Restaurant (715/742-3941), which also has rooms. Tip a beer or two at Fish Lipp's (715/742-3378), and enjoy the incredible Lake Superior sunsets.

There are plenty of places to stay along the main strip through town, including a nice **Days Inn** (715/392-4783), a couple of blocks north of the junction of US-2 and Hwy-53, which has rooms for around $50. For food, try the **Town Crier,** a full service, family-oriented cafe at 4927 E. 2nd Street; for more information, contact the **visitor center** (715/392-2773 or 800/942-5313), on US-2 at the west end of town, giving superior views both of the lake and town.

Hwy-13 Loop to the Apostle Islands

One of the best alternative routes on the Upper Midwest stretch of US-2 is Hwy-13's 100-mile loop along Lake Superior's western shores. The 45 miles, and at least four hours, that this loop adds to your journey across the state are without question worth it, taking in the superlative Apostle Islands, charming peninsula communities, and unbeatable road views.

Starting in the west at the blue-collar harbor town of Superior, Hwy-13 zigzags northeast to the lakeshore and follows it to picturesque Cornucopia. Each little hill you climb reveals a new view of mosaics of farmland, dispersed boats, and archaic farming equipment. East of Cornucopia, the road veers inland, emerging again onto the lakefront at the peninsula's main Ojibwa town, **Red Cliff,** which has a marina and boat slip, a lakeside campground within view of Basswood and Madeline Islands, a casino, and an annual 4th of July **powwow.** The outskirts of Red Cliff include some lake views and some great views of open pastureland meshed with dense evergreen forests on what appears to be slight tableland. Boats and canoes are ever-present, scattered among rural jetsam, decades-old Chevys and Ford pickups, their classic rondure rusting mutely in the cattails. You whiz by tottering, one-eyed cabins hardly larger than hunting shacks, their grainy, weather-beaten shingled siding obscured by weeds.

The nerve center of the Apostle Islands region is the diminutive, laid-back resort village of **Bayfield** (pop. 775), the most touristy place in the area, though you'll hardly notice. Bayfield itself dates from 1856 and looks at first glance about as Lilliputian as you can get, with a curvy (10 mph on the corners) narrow road winding beside impeccably tailored cottages and modest local brownstone mansions. Virtu-

---

APOSTLE ISLANDS NATIONAL LAKESHORE

A composite of glacial debris and pre-Cambrian bedrock, the 22 micro- to mini-sized islands that represent the Apostle Islands National Lakeshore are among the best gems of the Great Lakes. These pristine, windswept sandstone islands, surrounded by the deep blue waters of Lake Superior, contain a fantastic array of bluffs, sea caves, beaches, rookeries, and forests, and offer memorable primitive camping, hiking, and unique kayaking. Information on courses and rentals is available in the town of Bayfield. One of the largest and most famous, historic **Madeline Island**, which technically isn't in the park since it's inhabited, has long been a popular Wisconsin escape spot, more for long-term vacationers than casual visitors, since services are limited.

The main National Park Service **visitor center** (715/779-3397) for the Apostle Islands is headquartered in the old county courthouse building on Washington Avenue in the center of Bayfield; a few contact stations are also scattered along the north shoreline and on the islands themselves.

The route to the Apostle Islands from US-2, looping along Hwy-13 between Ashland and Superior, is described above.

---

ally every hairpin turn offers an outstanding glimpse of the Apostle Islands and the boats plying the waters, especially on the far northern edge of town.

There are plenty of classy or quaint places to stay in Bayfield, from cottages and motels to the ritzy **Old Rittenhouse Inn**, 301 Rittenhouse Avenue (715/779-5111), which is famed for its comfy rooms and multi-course gastronomic feasts. Hearty meals for the common man and woman have been served up since the Civil War at **Greunke's**, across from the marina at 17 Rittenhouse Avenue, which is famous throughout the state for its whitefish livers, weekend fish boils and generally funky feel. From the marina, there are also plenty of **ferries** (windsleds over the ice in winter) to Madeline Island or certain parts of the Apostle Islands. The Bayfield **visitors bureau** (715/779-3335) has more complete listings of things to do and places to stay.

A unique draw is **Bayfield's Big Top Chautauqua** (715/373-5552), a revival of old traveling tent shows that offers great summertime concerts, plays, and musical revues; listen for it on public radio on Big Top Radio Network.

South of Bayfield, Washburn is a pleasant enough little community; it's also close to two **ski slopes**. Downtown parks offer great lake vistas and even a lakeshore walking trail. Approaching Ashland and US-2, Hwy-13 heads through classic Wisconsin agrarian stretches hacked from the wilderness, with occasional lake views, quick rises in wind, or foreboding dark thunderheads.

Ashland

As you enter Ashland on US-2, some 40 miles west of the Michigan border, Lake Superior finally pokes its great nose at you. Ashland (pop. 8,700), a big fish in sparsely populated north-woods Wisconsin, likes to call itself the "Garland City of the Inland Seas" but what it is really is a town full of trestles, all the roads dipping and drooping under the mud-brown wood framework or plain faded steel of Soo Line bridges. Built up on an ever-so-slight rise above the lake, the town has an attractive Main Street with many well-preserved old buildings—where else does Romanesque revival compete with neoclassical and art deco?—and a lakeshore lined with great parks, frigid-looking beaches, especially on the west side of town, and gritty pull-offs where you can gaze at the gargantuan **Ashland Soo Line Ore dock**, the largest of its kind in the world. At 618 Beaser Avenue, there's the very good **Northern Wisconsin Interpretive Center** (Thurs.-Mon. 10 AM-4:30 PM; $3; 715/682-6600) with displays on local history, especially railroads.

Listed on the National Register of Historic Places, **The Depot** at 400 W. 3rd Avenue (715/682-4200) is a luxurious restaurant inside a restored Soo Line depot, with great—but pricey—regional fare, and a downstairs brew-pub. The nicest hotel in town—with a fine restaurant to boot—is the grand **Hotel Chequamegon** (pronounced shuh-WAH-muh-gun; 715/682-9095), on the lakeshore at the junction of US-2 and Hwy-13. This was a century-old Victorian until a 1955 conflagration destroyed the original structure, but the reconstruction has sacrificed none of the decorative charm or taste; rates start at $75 in summer. There are plenty of other cheaper **motels** scattered throughout town; for listings contact the local **visitor center** (715/682-2500 or 800/284-9484), at 320 W. 4th Avenue.

In Northern Wisconsin, tune your radio to **WOJB 88.9 FM,** run by the Lac Court Oreille Ojibwa Nation and featuring excellent, eclectic music as well as National Native and NPR news.

Along the border with Michigan, the first greeting Wisconsin proffers to westbound travelers is a giant liquor store's **corkscrew** statue, beckoning you to imbibe.

Bad River Indian Reservation

Home to one of Wisconsin's six Ojibwa communities, the Bad River Indian Reservation encompasses 56,697 acres owned by approximately 1,800 descendants of the original Ojibwa Loon Clan who settled near the delta confluence of the Bad and White Rivers; the reservation serves as the tribal **headquarters** (715/682-7111). The tribe holds its annual **Manonin powwow** in late August, and their local wood-products factory builds log-home kits.

From the eastern edge of the reservation, it's another 20 uneventful miles to the Michigan border.

ACROSS MICHIGAN'S UPPER PENINSULA

There are two alternatives across Michigan's Upper Peninsula (the "U. P."), which stretches for nearly 300 miles from Canada to Wisconsin between Lake Superior and Lake Michigan. Between Ironwood in the west, and Sault Ste. Marie on the Canadian border in the east, you can choose between **US-2** along the north shore of Lake Michigan, or the more direct option, **Hwy-28**, which runs near the south shore of Lake Superior near Pictured Rocks National Lakeshore; either way takes a full day, and this is not a place to try and make up time.

In either case, you're privy to one of the greater finds of the Midwest, the sparsely populated and thoroughly underappreciated (especially by the "trolls" of southern Michigan) land of the "Yoopers," as the proud residents have christened themselves, many still ensconced in the logging and mining enclaves their forebears founded. The U.P. boasts a surprisingly mountainous and larger-than-it-looks stretch of land dotted with boom-to-bust towns relying on summer tourism and one or more of the industrial triumvirate up here: timber, mining, and fishing.

All over the U.P. you'll see signs advertising **pasties.** The quintessential miner food, Cornish pasties (which rhymes with nasty, not tasty—hang onto the vowel a bit, like a true Yooper) were introduced to Copper Country 100-odd years ago by immigrant Cornish miners. These dense baked crust-pockets, stuffed with minced meat and vegetables, are ubiquitous in U.P. cafes and restaurants.

East of Ironwood, at the town of Wakefield, our route divides: US-2 runs south along Lake Michigan, while Hwy-28 veers north along Lake Superior.

Ironwood

In the first 75 miles east of the Wisconsin border, you never really leave the forest, though you do pass dozens of decaying old mining towns built back when the U.P. made Michigan the country's biggest iron-ore producer. Approaching Ironwood, US-2 crests a rise that marks the edge of the roller-coaster hills of the Gogebic Range, which give great sunset views over the Wisconsin forests and distant Lake Superior.

The first U.P. town east of Wisconsin is Ironwood, the lead town of the Gogebic Range. This mountain town has grown into a big-time winter sports arena. The **Copper Peak Sky Flying Hill** (daily June-Sept.; weekends Sept.-Oct.) is North America's only ski-flying facility, and even sponsors international competitions; for a great view of much of three states and Canada, take a chair lift up.

Ironwood is worth a look for its absolutely huge, 52-foot-high fiberglass statue of **Hiawatha,** the fictional hero of Henry Wadsworth Longfellow's famous poem.

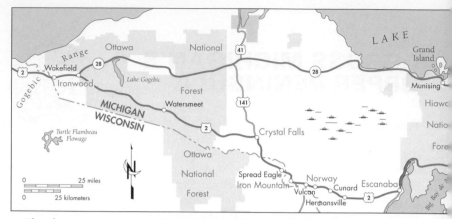

The place to eat in Ironwood is **Joe's Pasty Shop,** two blocks off US-2 at 116 Aurora Street, serving pasties since 1946. Ironwood's also the only town along US-2 to keep the U.P. Finnish tradition of sauna alive; many of the $35-a-night motels strung along US-2, including the **Sandpiper Motel** (906/932-2000) right on the highway on the east side of town, boast real cedar saunas like the old country—alas without the birch twigs for self-flagellation in the snow banks.

US-2: Ottawa National Forest

Just a dozen miles east of Ironwood, the immense verdant spread of the Ottawa National Forest begins. At 1.7 million acres, including subsumed state and county land, Michigan's largest national forest covers a vast amount of the western U.P. and contains some of the region's most diverse geology, flora and fauna, and simple isolated wilderness, including 35 waterfalls accessible from woodland trails. The road passes through epic tracts of trees obviously older and denser than anywhere else along the route. (North in the Porcupine Mountains stands one of the last remaining true wilderness areas in the Midwest.)

For information, the little town of **Watersmeet** has a U.S. Forest Service **ranger station** (906/358-4724) at the junction of US-2 and Hwy-45, and it serves as the access town to the grand **Cisco Chain of Lakes/Sylvania Wilderness,** a spattering of over 300 lakes offering fantastic recreation.

Crystal Falls

The first real town east of the Ottawa National Forest, Crystal Falls (pop. 1,950) is a charming, postcard kind of place built into a bluff near a rivulet waterfall on the Paint River. Time seems to stand still here, the town sporting original (read: *old*) street signs still pointing the way, and huge trees overhanging US-2 as it slowly hairpins through town. The only "sights" here are the local courthouse, won in a poker game in the 1880s, and a water-filled old pit mine outside of town.

Southeast from Crystal Falls, US-2 passes something the western U.P. specializes in: numerous rock and ore formations jutting out of the hillsides, usually covered with graffiti. The road, still wide and black and smooth as glass, sweeps into the **Copper Country State Forest** which gives every appearance of symmetrical reforestation, then flits through 15 miles of northern Wisconsin, zig-zagging along a

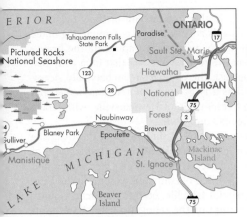

nice lake before passing through the oddly named town of **Spread Eagle**, just west of Iron Mountain.

Iron Mountain and Norway
Though separated by six blacktopped miles, the sister towns of Norway and Iron Mountain both grew up with the lumbering and iron-mining industry, producing over 300,000 tons annually from three big mines. Both are slightly somnolent but by no means decaying.

The larger of the two, Iron Mountain (pop. 8,525), backs up against the easy grade of its eponymous mountain, and seems casually strewn about in parts: east side is mini-mall sprawl, while the west is older, traditional "downtown." The must-see here, everyone will tell you, is the local **Cornish Pump and Mining Museum** two blocks off US-2 on Kent Street (Mon.-Sat. 9 AM-5 PM, Sunday noon-4 PM May-Oct.; $4), and it is great, with the most enormous steam-driven pump engine you could imagine—54-feet tall, and weighing in at many tons. But the *real* must-see is the freebie, the **Majestic Pine/Roosevelt Mountain Ski Jump** (800/236-2447), most easily accessed west of town off US-2 onto Pine Mountain Road. This 90-meter jump hosts annual international competitions in February and is the site of the current U.S. distance record. The local gendarmes have given up trying to stop you from crab walking up it and getting the best view in the U.P., but it sure is creaky and intimidating.

San Francisco '49ers coach Steve Mariucci grew up in Iron Mountain.

There aren't many cafes to speak of in Iron Mountain—it specializes in supper clubs—but there is one unique lunch spot: **Bimbo's**, a bar at 314 E. Main Street next to the Citgo gas station, north of US-2. On weekdays the place features lunches of its own "porketta" sandwiches, cut from a roast pig. They also have homemade Italian sausages.

The mines at Norway (pop. 2,910) were so close together and active that the village once caved in and they had to rebuild it down the hill. Gritty Norway—which once produced more shingles than anywhere else, as shown by the numerous houses still coated with gritty shingles—also boasts the area's best cafe, the **Country House Restaurant**, right downtown off US-2, where you can rub shoulders with virtually every local. For enormous burgers, stop at the **Thirsty Whale Bar**, right on US-2.

Another true find in Norway is **Piers Gorge**, a couple of miles south off US-8, where the raging waters of the Menominee River scraped out this fascinating gorge on the border between Michigan and Wisconsin.

Escanaba
Between Norway and Escanaba, US-2 provides 45 miles of open, occasionally dipping, road with only sporadic breaks in the sameness of the birch or pine backdrops. In fact, it's so monotonous that you may not be at all miffed by the shamelessness

Fifteen miles west of Escanaba, at the eastern edge of the tiny Potawatomi Indian Reservation, you pass between the central and eastern time zones. Adjust your clocks and watches accordingly. that the powers that be in the town of **Vulcan** show by snow-balling enormous billboards advertising—nay, hammering home —the **Iron Mine**, an obnoxious tourist trap where the heavy-handed self-promotion overwhelms the fact that it's a truly historic site. Continuing east, the hamlets are archetypally sleepy, like **Cunard**, which has a large aqua-colored warehouse that looks like a standing freezer-pack, or **Hermansville**, with sedate and spartan little dwellings up and off the road on a bluff.

Escanaba (pop. 13,659), with perfect geography at the mouth of the Escanaba River at the Little Bay de Noc, was born in typical Lake Michigan fashion, out of the country's insatiable need for timber and ore. At one time its three timber and ore docks contributed to the largest ore-shipping operation of its kind in the U.S., shipping that continues today. To get a feel for lake life, head to the **Delta County Museum** (daily 11 AM-7 PM June-Sept.; free) or the renovated 1867 **Sandpoint Lighthouse** (same hours; $1) along the lushly landscaped waterfront. The annual **U.P. State Fair**, held here in August, is great, and Escanaba also has a Hiawatha National Forest **ranger station** (906/786-4062) at 2727 N. Lincoln Road, if you want to explore a little off-road.

Hiawatha National Forest

Heading northeast from Escanaba, US-2 broadens into a fast four-lane along the Big and Little Bay de Noc, and you'll pass through a slew of little "resorts," some with their own beaches. As you head east toward Manistique, the landscape reverts to trees and more trees; you're in the chevroned conifers of the Hiawatha National Forest. There are two separate sections of this immense 879,000-acre forest, which has shoreline on three of the Great Lakes—Huron, Michigan, and Superior. The fly-speck communities here haven't changed much—ubiquitous flashing yellow lights, matchbox dwellings attached to bulbous propane gas tanks, and, in a few communities, forlorn old Soo Line railcars aging gracelessly on the tracks right off the highway. There might be a smoked-fish house or two, but more than likely it'll be a forgettable roadhouse offering greasy pasty at best.

The best turnoff comes in **Garden Corners**—don't blink—which spins you down Hwy-183 to the excellent **Fayette State Park** (May-Oct.; $3.50), an extant ghost community, original, not renovated. It's an impressive, perhaps eerie place, situated on a sheer limestone cliff peninsula.

Manistique

The only sizeable town between St. Ignace and Escanaba, Manistique (pop. 3,456) tends to underwhelm, apart from its Lake Michigan frontage. Mountains of gravel and mini-smokestacks line the road into town on the east side, and the sweetly pungent smell of paper permeates the air. Despite that, Manistique does have a sleepy tourist draw, with the lake right there and the bizarre **Kitch-Iti-Kipi** up the road in **Palms Book State Park**, where 16,000 gallons of water a minute bubble up, propelling tourists on rafts. Downtown is the **Imogene Herbert Museum** (daily 10 AM-4 PM in summer) with a nice century-old cabin and majestic brick water tower. Nearby, off US-2 at 223 S. Cedar Street, **Jax Bar & Restaurant** is a classic cafe with a single-sheet plastic menu and lots of newsprint scuffed into the original smoky Formica counter.

US-2: Along Lake Michigan

The route that US-2 follows along Lake Michigan between Escanaba and St. Ignace is one of the U.P.'s best autumn scenic drives. The true heart of U.P. lies here, with patches of pine or birch woodland followed by brief lakeshore, then a dormant ore-mine, a trailer park, or a long-abandoned fishing camp.

The first hint of anything special comes in tiny **Blaney Park,** 22-odd miles east of Manistique, which boasts two grand B&Bs—the **Celibeth House B&B** (906/283-3409), an 1895 mansion with eight rooms from $50, and the posher **Blaney Lodge B&B** (906/283-3883), which June-Oct. maintains one of the best dining rooms in the U.P.—and even a private airstrip. The whole area was once a 22,000-acre company playground for the Wisconsin Land and Lumber Company and nowadays offers relief from the pervasive local architectural hybrid of ranch-style mashed with trailer home.

East of here, as you approach St. Ignace, the scenery becomes increasingly gorgeous: bay views give way only occasionally to pesky pockets of trees; then in one grand stretch, the lake breaks through fully, and you're literally skimming a beachside causeway. Bordering the road are huge dunes, real sand dunes with green tufts of mixed grass sprouting amidst the golden grains, and you hardly notice the little towns born as fishing villages—**Naubinway,** **Epoufette,** and **Brevort**—that line the highway.

In Manistique, old US-2 (Hwy-94) crosses the **Siphon Bridge**—featured in Ripley's *Believe It or Not!* for being partially supported by water and having a roadway four feet below the water level.

From the flyspeck town of **Gulliver,** 13 miles east of Manistique, a road leads southeast to Michigan's most picturesque lighthouse, at **Seul Choix Pointe.**

For concentrated kitsch, don't miss **Paul Bunyan Pasties** on US-2, eight miles west of the Mackinac Bridge; they're in the *Guinness Book of World Records* for having baked a 223-pound monster.

St. Ignace

Coming into St. Ignace along US-2, travelers are tempted by a number of "scenic overlooks" west of town, all proffering a chance to stretch and view the often fog-shrouded Mackinac Bridge over blue Lake Michigan—not the deep steely blue of Lake Superior, which you'll see later; this is a gentler, more somber blue.

Picturesque St. Ignace (pop. 2,600) lies east of, and down a hill from, the concrete river of the I-75 freeway. This little town, at one time 70% French-Canadian, is more important than its obviously tourism-contrived loveliness would indicate, situated as it is at the crossroads of the upper and lower regions of Michigan, with Mackinac Island just across the bay. The town is busy and cheerful, in places gentrified and meticulously maintained; downtown you can stroll along a bright lake promenade lined with gift shops, restaurants (try **Lehto's,** at the west end of the main drag, for the freshest pasties), and dozens of $45-a-night motels.

Straits State Park ($3 admission) west of St. Ignace off US-2, a mile from the junction with I-75 (turn south at the Howard Johnson's), includes the **Father Jacques Marquette Memorial and Museum,** where "living history" enthusiasts recreate a 17th-century French Catholic mission. Downtown, next to the Chamber of Commerce, **Marquette Mission Park and Museum of Ojibwa Culture** (daily 10 AM-8 PM May-Oct.; $2) traces over three centuries of life along the Straits of Mackinac, detailing the Ojibwa, Huron, and French missionary history and cultures.

The main attraction around St. Ignace, besides the landmark Mackinac Bridge, is anachronistic **Mackinac Island,** one of the top draws in the Midwest. Pronounced "Mackinaw," this flyspeck island has never had motor vehicles on it and is now

---

HWY 28: PICTURED ROCKS NATIONAL LAKESHORE
AND TAHQUAMENON FALLS

There are two excellent reasons to bypass US-2 across the Upper Peninsula and to follow Hwy-28 instead. Pictured Rocks National Lakeshore, a lovely, undisturbed stretch of sand dunes, beaches, and colorful bluffs, lines Lake Superior in the middle of the U.P. It's best visited by boat, since there are no roads through it; in summer three-hour **cruises** ($21) leave about every two hours from the pier in **Munising**, right on Hwy-28 at the west edge of the park. In winter Pictured Rocks is a popular place to cross-country ski. For more information, contact the Pictured Rocks **visitor center** (906/387-2607).

East of the Pictured Rocks, you come to a real gem, Hwy-123, a must-do loop road (particularly during autumnal color sweeps) which heads north from US-2 past the outstanding—and popular—Tahquamenon Falls State Park ($4 per car). The 50-foot-high, 200-foot-wide Upper Falls here were mentioned in Longfellow's *Song of Hiawatha*. Hwy-123 also passes through the lakefront vacation village of **Paradise**, from where another road runs north up to Whitefish Point for some of the best isolated beaches in the U.P.; the oldest lighthouse (circa 1849) on the Great Lakes; and the **Great Lakes Shipwreck Historical Museum** (daily 10 AM-6 PM, May-Oct.; $6; 906/635-1742), to learn about the wreck of the *Edmund Fitzgerald*. This legendary graveyard point is where the ship actually went down, with 29 crew members on board, in November 1975.

---

billed as a sort of bygone-days living museum, actually a first-class tourist trap that's not *too* embarrassing. Room rates start well above $100 at most of the island's hotels and B&Bs—for details, call the **visitor's bureau** (906/847-3783 or 800/454-5227)—but it's a great place to rent a bike and cruise around, and day-trips aboard ferries from St. Ignace cost around $13.

Running north to Sault Ste. Marie, US-2 is buried beneath I-75, which passes through 50 miles of desiccated earth tones, broken by wide swaths of ersatz prairie and miniature stands of trees.

Goggle-eyed travelers come to St. Ignace just to stare at what locals like to call the "Eighth Wonder of the World," the **Mackinac Bridge**, one of the longest suspension bridges in the world at 7,400 feet (with approaches, the total length is over five miles). Lots of scenic views are found throughout St. Ignace and from Straits State Park, west of town.

Sault Ste. Marie

Michigan's oldest community, and perhaps the third oldest in the U.S., Sault Ste. Marie (pop. 14,700, pronounced soo saint ma-REE) is known historically for the tussles over the area between the French and British, and as the only land link between the U.S. and Canada for hundreds of miles. It is also the most populous, but certainly not the most touristed, of the Upper Peninsula towns—that title goes to St. Ignace—passed through on this route.

Beneath the steel-span International Bridge that links this Michigan town with Ontario's twin "Soo," the raging torrents that impelled French Fr. Jacques Marquette to dub the newly established mission *Le Sault de Sainte Marie*, literally "falling waters of Saint Mary," are no longer readily apparent. The U.S. Army Corps of Engineers long ago corralled and tamed the rapids between 20-foot-higher Lake

Superior and Lake Huron with four enormous locks, the largest and busiest in the world. During mining heydays the locks conveyed many times the tonnage of the Panama and Suez Canals combined—with no tolls paid. The locks area are worthy of at least an hour's siesta; lush parks and a walkway line the locks, with observation points, Soo Lock boat **tours** ($14), the great but expensive **Museum Freighter Valley Camp** (daily June-Sept. 9 AM-9 PM; $6), and the landmark 21-story **Tower of History** at 326 E. Portage (daily 10 AM-6 PM May-Oct.; $3).

South of the water at 532 Ashmun Street is what may be the oldest operating restaurant in the U.P.: since 1902, the **American Cafe** has served up homey breakfasts, lunches, and Friday-night dinners (4-7 PM) in a warm atmosphere with just enough elbow room. If the American has character, then rollicking **Antler's**, on the waterfront at 804 E. Portage, has attitude: voted the U.P.'s best restaurant by a couple of newspapers, it's always packed, usually with a waiting list.

The best place to stay, the **Water Street Inn B&B** (906/632-1900 or 800/236-1904), is near the locks at 140 E. Water Street. There are also dozens of motels. For more information, the local **visitor center** (906/632-3301, 800/MI-SAULT or 800/647-2858) is at 2581 Ashmun Street (Business I-75).

ACROSS CANADA

Between Sault Ste. Marie and the Canadian capital, Ottawa, Hwy-17 is the continuation of the Trans-Canada Highway; it is also part of the "Voyageurs Trail," roughly retracing the route taken by the early fur traders between their winter trapping grounds—the wilderness of forests, lakes, and streams to the northwest—and Montreal, the summer fur market. The scenery varies from rivers and forests to paper mills and coal mines, and most of the way Hwy-17 is a two-lane road with a 90 kph (55 mph) maximum and occasional passing lanes to help you get around the timber trucks.

East of Ottawa, it's a short run to French-speaking Montreal, Canada's second-largest city and one of the most European places in North America. The change between bi-lingual Ontario, and French-speaking Quebec, is sudden and extreme, as if England and France were divided by a river, not the Channel. Though the landscape *looks* oddly familiar, the differences are striking. Just to be different, our route follows the Quebec side, taking a scenic two-lane journey along the Ottawa River. If you're in a hurry, freeways link Ottawa and Montreal, and Montreal with the U.S., so you can race across. Either way, we re-join US-2 near Vermont's Lake Champlain.

The double suspension bridge (toll US$1.50) linking the Canadian and American Sault Ste. Maries gives memorable views of the Algoma Steel Mill, the second largest in Canada, and the St. Mary's River rapids below. The Canadian and American locks here are among the busiest on the St. Lawrence Seaway system. Flags in the middle mark the boundary between the two nations.

Sault Ste. Marie—The Soo

Crossing over the busy harbor from Michigan, the road enters Canadian Sault Ste. Marie (pop. 81,000), also known as The Soo, "Home of Canada's First Female Astronaut." Graffiti on a railway bridge proclaims: "This is Indian Land." Sault Ste. Marie

Unless otherwise noted, prices in the Canadian sections of this book are given in Canadian dollars, which at time of writing were worth roughly 65 U.S. cents—giving Americans a significant discount on everything. The Canadian colloquial equivalent of "buck" (for a dollar) is "Loonie," for the picture of a bird that adorns the dollar coin.

was founded at the rapids—"sault" means "falls"—in St. Mary's River. Its original name was Bawating, "place of the rapids," where local tribes caught whitefish and tapped maple trees. French explorers arrived in 1622, and the Jesuits established a mission here later that century. Permanent settlement came with the fur trade in the 18th century; later, lumber and transportation helped build the local economy. The Canadian locks were completed in 1895, allowing deep draft boats to pass from one lake to another. Today The Soo, and its sister city across the river in Michigan, are mildly depressed industrial towns (though there is a *big* steel mill here). However, tourism is increasingly important to the local economy, and it may turn out to be the engine that leads to some revitalization.

To see downtown's sights, turn onto Bruce Street and drive two blocks to Bay Street, which runs west to east along the water. Here you'll find the Station Mall, the Art Gallery of Algoma (10 East Street), and an excellent view of the river and the International Bridge. A path near the bridge takes you down to **Roberta Bondar Park** (summer only), built around the original 1895 locks, which are no longer in operation; you'll also find an observation deck over the locks.

At 129 Bay Street stands the Algoma Central Railway Terminal from which depart the **Agawa Canyon Wilderness Tours**, the area's main tourist attraction (705/946-7300 or 800/242-9287). Throughout the summer, you can take day-long train trips (daily at 8 AM; $55) north through a roadless wilderness featuring narrow river canyons, spectacular views, and a two-hour stop midway, so you can get out and stretch your legs or have a picnic. From January through March there is also a "Snow Train" for the hardy, and there's also an "End of the Line" tour, which takes two days (and does return, despite the name).

Bay Street ends at Pim Street to the east; a left will take you by the **Ermatinger Old Stone House**, the oldest stone house in Canada west of Toronto (open daily in summer; Mon.-Fri. rest of the year). Built in 1814 by an early local fur magnate, the house has been restored with period furnishings. Demonstrations on preparing pioneer cuisine are given in the cookhouse.

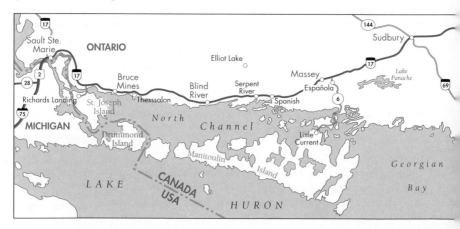

DRIVING IN CANADA

Between the US and Canada, the rules of the road don't really change, but the measurements do. Both countries drive on the right, and the speed limits are similar: in Canada it's generally 90 kilometers (55 miles) per hour on two-lane roads, 100 kph (63 mph) on freeways. All cars are required to have their headlights illuminated night and day; to the unaccustomed, a daytime traffic jam can look like a massive funeral procession. Other rules: all passengers must wear seat belts, and turning right on red is illegal in the Province of Quebec; in the rest of Canada, it is legal after stopping first. Another important difference is that proof of insurance is mandatory in Canada. Deciphering parking zones, especially in French-speaking Quebec, can really test your interpretive abilities.

Gas in Canada tends to be more expensive than in the States, and it's priced by the liter (3.785 liters equals 1 US gallon). Some gas stations accept U.S. currency (and almost all accept credit cards) but give you a less-than-favorable rate of exchange.

Crossing the border, there are brief checkpoints (and sundry duty-free shops) on both sides. Customs officers usually do a cursory check, asking your address, reason for travel, when you last visited the country, and whether you are carrying firearms, tobacco, or alcohol. For U.S. or Canadian citizens a passport is not necessary, but having proof of citizenship and identity is never a bad idea. Other nationalities should confirm their visa status well before attempting to cross the border; it may be difficult (or impossible) to return, and border officials are not known for their hospitality to people they suspect are trying to enter illegally.

Sault Ste. Marie lodgings include a couple of motels right on the river, such as the **Holiday Inn**, 208 St. Mary's River Drive (705/949-0611), and the **Bay Front-Quality Inn**, 108 Bay Street (705/945-9264). The cheaper motels are all found north of town on Hwy-17 (also known as the Great Northern Road) heading to Thunder Bay, and there's a nice **youth hostel** in the old Algonquin Hotel, 865 E. Queen Street (705/253-2311). The Soo is something of a culinary wasteland, but there are a surprising number of American-style diners lined up along blue-collar Queen Street: choose from **Ernie's**, 13 E. Queen Street; **Mike's**, 518 E. Queen Street; and **Mary's**, 66 E. Queen Street.

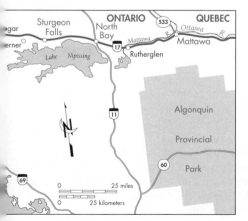

St. Joseph Island
East of Sault Ste. Marie, Hwy-17 winds along Lake Huron's North Channel waterfront for most the way to Sudbury. Roughly 30 miles (50 km) east, a turnoff heads south to St. Joseph's

Island, part of the Manitoulin Island chain. The main sight here lies at the island's south end: **Fort St. Joseph National Historic Park.** When the fort was built by the British in 1796, it was the westernmost outpost of their Canadian empire. At first the fort protected the fur trade; it then served as a base for attacking the Americans during the War of 1812. The Americans burned the fort in 1814, and the park is built around its scenic remains.

At the island's north end is the tiny town of **Richards Landing**; the general store at the dock serves good burgers and soft ice cream.

Bruce Mines to Blind River

Twelve miles (20 km) east of the St. Joseph Island turnoff lies the town of Bruce Mines, founded in 1846 around some copper mines. The earliest settlers were miners from Cornwall in England. An old church south of Hwy-17 has been transformed into the **Bruce Mines Museum** relating the local history (summer only).

The road then runs slightly inland, returning to lakeside a dozen miles later at **Thessalon**, a lumber town just south of the road. Aside from a mini-mall and a supermarket, the main downtown attraction is Lakeside Park and its excellent beach. You can also find a beach at **Carolyn's Motel** (705/842-3330) just west of town. Carolyn's restaurant always has fresh fish on the menu. The island visible on the southern horizon, Drummond Island, belongs to the United States.

The next town is Blind River, so called because the mouth of the river of the same name is all but invisible from the lake. Blind River was originally a lumber town, but today it is home to a major uranium processing center, working ore from Elliot Lake a few miles to the north. The downtown **Village Museum**, besides its gift shop, art gallery, tourist information center, and great view of the lake, offers exhibits on local history, which is mainly logging and mining. The **Old Mill Motel** (705/356-2274) features a small beach.

Hwy-17 east toward Massey continues through flat land with occasional rocky outcrops. Just west of the settlements of Spanish and Serpent River, you have a great view across the North Channel, an arm of Lake Huron, to Manitoulin Island in the distance.

Massey and Manitoulin Island

As you continue east along Hwy-17, the next town, 45 miles (70 km) east of Blind River, is Massey, "The Home of Chutes Provincial Park and Lots of Friendly People," at the confluence of the Sable and Spanish Rivers. The sole downtown tourist sight is the Massey Area Pioneer Museum, and the place to stay is the **Mohawk Motel** (705/865-2722), with "kozy rooms." East of town, just north of Hwy-17, Chutes Provincial Park offers swimming, camping, picknicking, and several scenic waterfalls along the Sable River.

Manitoulin Island is one of the largest freshwater islands in the world, and it still has a substantial aboriginal "First Nation" population.

Twenty miles (32 km) east of Massey, 40 miles (64 km) west of Sudbury, Hwy-17 intersects with Hwy-6, which heads south to **Española**, home to the massive E.B. Eddy pulp paper mill, and then continues on to Manitoulin Island, the world's largest freshwater island, set in the northern end of Lake Huron. Manitoulin is a popular vacation spot, ringed with picturesque bays and excellent beaches; try Meldrum Bay, Providence Bay, and South Baymouth.

Approaching Sudbury, Hwy-17 continues over 30 miles (50 km) of rolling hills dotted with a few forests and many small dairy farms.

Sudbury

The clearest sign that you are nearing Sudbury (pop. 93,000) is that the pines disappear and the birches shrink into stunted dwarfs clinging to black rock outcroppings. Sudbury lies in the middle of a geological basin that contains one of the world's largest concentrations of nickel as well as numerous other precious metals. Originally an Ojibwa tribal settlement, the town began to develop after the 1883 arrival of the railway and boomed when nickel and copper were discovered here three years later. Uncontrolled development followed, and mines and processing plants sprang up all over the landscape.

Soon the area was a classic industrial-era ecological disaster. No trees grew for miles around, and a haze of toxic smoke choked the inhabitants, who lived in narrow valleys below the mine heads. In 1950, Sudbury undertook a massive urban renewal and land reclamation project to return at least a vestige of the original beauty and unpolluted air to the area. For older residents, the city has changed dramatically for the better; the air is cleaner, and the city is dotted with trees. First-time visitors still may be shocked by the lack of vegetation and the huge industrial plants that circle the town. Today, Sudbury is Canada's most important mining community, producing as much as 85% of the world's nickel and operating the country's largest copper mine, INCO, along Hwy-17 west of town.

If you're planning to spend some time in Sudbury, consider buying a combination ticket, which gives admission to Science North and the INCO-Big Nickel mine complex for a discounted price.

INCO AND THE "BIG NICKEL"

To get an up-close look at the root of Sudbury's economy and ecology, follow Hwy-17 at the western edge of town. Along the busy highway rises the huge smokestack, one of the tallest in the world, that belongs to INCO, one of the world's largest nickel producers. A turn takes you up a denuded hilltop to the famous Big Nickel—exactly what it sounds like, a 30-foot-tall replica of a Canadian nickel—and the entrance to the mine of the same name, which has been turned into a museum (daily 9 AM-5 PM in summer only; $8). Here you can don a hard hat and descend 65 feet into this non-working exploratory mine. You can also arrange guided tours of the INCO refinery here.

As it passes through Sudbury, Hwy-17 turns into a crowded two-lane road with frequent traffic lights and a number of cheap motels. Turn south onto Paris Street (Hwy-80) to reach the heart of town, where you'll find the Downtown Mall and the Civic Square surrounded by government buildings, including the Sudbury visitor center. If you continue south on Paris Street, Hwy-80 becomes an expressway heading to Science North.

South of downtown Sudbury, along Lake Ramsey, the region's biggest draw is **Science North**, a fairly new science and technology museum featuring many hands-on displays for kids and adults (daily 9 AM-5 PM; $10; 705/522-37000 or 800/461-4898). Inside the snowflake-shaped structure, you can experience a simulated hurricane, watch flying squirrels fly, talk to HAM radio operators around the world, enjoy a show in the IMAX theater ($12), or take a "virtual reality" voyage to Mars ($7).

Science North also has one of Sudbury's better places to eat—the "Snowflake Restaurant"—which says a lot about the town's culinary offerings. Among the better Sudbury hotels are the downtown **Best Western Peter Piper Inn**, 151 Larch Street (705/673-7801), and the **Travelodge Hotel Sudbury**, 1401 Paris Street (705/522-1100) south of town.

For more complete information, contact the Sudbury **visitor center**, downtown at 200 Brady Street (705/674-3141).

Sturgeon Falls

East of Sudbury, Hwy-17 enters the narrow Vueve River Valley lined with scraggly pines and picturesque rock outcroppings. Apart from a couple of very small towns —such as **Hagar**, with the **Manor** restaurant and a general store—it's mostly dairy farming country for the 80 miles (130 km) of Hwy-17 between Sudbury and North Bay. The sole sizeable town between Sudbury and North Bay, Sturgeon Falls, 24 miles (38 km) west of North Bay boasts a few cheap motels, restaurants offering "Canadian and Chinese food," and the **Sturgeon River House Museum** for local history.

Approaching North Bay from Sturgeon Falls, 24 miles (38 km) to the west, Hwy-17 runs for a few miles along the north shore of Lake Nipissing, giving you a scenic view over the waters.

North Bay

The hills flatten out and birch trees replace pines as you enter the outskirts of North Bay ("Gateway to Opportunity"), its population of 55,000 making it the largest community between Sudbury and Ottawa. North Bay was originally a fur-trading post that boomed after the 1882 arrival of the railway. Today North Bay is a trade and transportation center, and its fur auctions are among the largest in the world. Many tourists use it as a jumping-off point for wilderness expeditions.

In 1934, North Bay achieved worldwide fame with the birth of the **Dionne Quintuplets,** the world's only identical quints, an event that kept the tabloid mills churning for decades.

Just southeast of town, Hwy-17 joins Hwy-11, which runs south to Toronto. Near the junction there's a **visitor center** and the **Dionne Quintuplets Museum** (daily 9 AM-5 PM in summer only; $3) housed in the cabin that was their 1934 birthplace. (The house was moved from its original site in nearby Corbeil.) Inside are toys, dresses, baby carriages and photographs, but little that gives a sense of what a phenomenon the girls were: the Ontario government took the infants away from their destitute family and raised them in public, in a zoo-like environment, until they were nine years old—effectively doing everything possible to keep them from having a "normal" childhood. At age five (of course) they were introduced to the King and Queen of England, and later appeared in movies and "wrote" their own autobiography, *We Were Five*. The quints also did product endorsements, promoting soap, toothpaste, cereal, and Carnation milk. Three of the girls are still alive, and have been trying to win remuneration from the provincial Ontario government; early in 1998, Ontario offered to raise the women's old-age pensions from under $200 to over $1400 a month, but at time of writing things were still in litigation. (Continuing the quintuplets' lifelong exploitation, there's a nifty gift shop on the museum premises. . . .)

Apart from the Dionne Quintuplets, the main attractions of downtown North Bay are the *Chief Commanda II* cruises that leave from the Waterfront Park and follow the old voyageurs' route across Lake Nipissing (reservations required, 705/494-8167). Many of the motels are found on Lakeshore Drive, such as a **Comfort Inn** (705/494-8461) and the moderate **Lincoln Motel** (705/472-3231). The fancy restaurant in town is **Churchill's Prime Rib House** (705/476-7777) at 631 Lakeshore Drive.

The stretch of Hwy-17 between North Bay and Mattawa unreels a nondescript view of scrubby forests broken by the small community of Rutherglen.

Mattawa and the Ottawa River

Approaching Mattawa, Hwy-17 runs through scenic country largely empty of human habitation; the road hugs the river while rolling over steeper hills, through birch and pine forests and by many lakes and ponds. For the next 95 miles (150 km), the road is served by a couple of very small towns and a handful of gas stations and small motels and restaurants that are worth stopping at only from necessity.

The Ottawa River marks the border between Ontario and Quebec, whose bluffs may be seen across the water.

The relatively large town of Mattawa ("There Is A Story Here Where Rivers Meet") lies at the confluence of the Ottawa and Mattawa Rivers. The town is home to two passable restaurants, **Draper's Bakery and Cafe** and **Mr. T's Family Restaurant**, as well as the **Mattawa District Museum** housed in a log cabin. Hwy-17 here hits the river downtown at a traffic light, then turns right; a left will take you to the museum, and beyond that the boondocks via Hwy-533. The Mattawa River is the focus of the Samuel de Champlain Provincial Park which offers campgrounds, canoeing, and hiking trails.

Algonquin Provincial Park

Between Mattawa and Deep River, Hwy-17 runs along the northern boundaries of the enormous **Algonquin Provincial Park**, which stretches for many miles to the south. Ontario's oldest and most popular, the park protects 3,000 square miles (7,600 square km) of almost untouched wilderness, offering a wide variety of wildlife (including moose, bears, beavers, and timber wolves), dozens of lakes, and hundreds of miles of backcountry hiking and canoeing trails. The main **visitor**

(continues on page 504)

OTTAWA SURVIVAL GUIDE

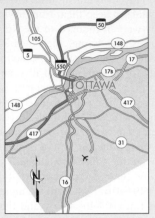

CANADA'S CAPITAL, OTTAWA (POP. 307,000) WAS originally an Algonquin settlement that traders converted into a fur and lumber outpost around 1800. In the mid-19th century, there was a bitter rivalry among Canadian cities such as Montreal and Toronto, as to which would become the nation's capital. As a compromise of sorts, on December 31, 1857 Queen Victoria declared Ottawa the capital, and construction of the Parliament buildings began the following year. However, government only became the largest employer after World War II, when the lumber mills began to decline. Today the train tracks and factories have been replaced with miles of parks and green belts, making Ottawa one of the most peaceable and pleasant of the world's capitals. Even though winters are freezing cold, tourism is now the city's number two industry, and there are enough excellent museums, parks and other sights to comfortably fill a couple of days or more.

Orientation within Ottawa is easy: Parliament Hill, which holds the most prominent buildings, is on the north edge of town, with its back turned on the Ottawa River and the French-speaking province of Quebec. Getting around is easy, since most of the sights are gathered together around Parliament Hill and the adjacent Byward Market. To see Ottawa, you should park the car, get out, and walk (or bike, or rollerblade, etc.) around the town.

Parliament Hill is home to the three buildings that comprise Canada's Parliament, the seat of the federal government. The architecture is reminiscent of England's Houses of Parliament as redesigned by the cartoonist Charles Addams: elegant, Gothic-style carved stone walls rise to copper mansard roofs topped with fantastically filigreed wrought iron. The East Block (circa 1865) is the oldest of the three. The Centre Block, with its imposing Peace Tower in the middle, contains the chambers of the Senate and the House of Commons, which you can see in session, as well as the beautiful **Library of Parliament**, which survived the 1916 fire that destroyed the rest of the building.

On the lawns of the Parliament Buildings, the **Changing of the Guard Ceremony** (daily at 10 AM, late June-late Aug.; free) is extremely popular with tourists, as is the firing of the **Noonday Gun** (daily at noon, May-Aug.), which you can watch from the bluffs above the Ottawa River.

East of Parliament Hill stands the **National Gallery of Canada**, 380

Sussex Drive (daily 10 AM-6 PM, May-Oct.; Wed.-Sun. 10 AM-5 PM, Oct.-April; free). Disregard the unnecessary "of Canada" in the museum's name—which may well confirm your suspicions of Canadian national lack of self-esteem—and plan to spend some time at this imposing, glass-walled museum, which contains large European (Rembrandt to the post-Impressionists) and American collections, as well as the world's most extensive display of Canadian art—enough high quality work to prove that there really *is* such a thing. Along with many floors of fine paintings from colonial times up through Pop Art, including George Segal's automobilia assembly *The Gas Station,* there's also a large collection of Asian and Inuit art.

Alongside the National Gallery, you can also check out a **Ski Museum** and a **War Museum,** which bought Hermann Göring's Mercedes but displays it as **Hitler's Car,** apparently thinking that will draw more tourists.

Practicalities

Ottawa's airport is 20 minutes south of the city, but handles very few flights; shuttles from there into town cost $10, $15 roundtrip. The major east-west access is via Hwy-17, the Trans-Canada Highway; within town, this becomes the Hwy-417 freeway. From the south, Hwy-31 links up with Hwy-401, the interstate freeway along the north shore of Lake Ontario.

Places to stay in Ottawa are centrally located and not all that expensive—the capital of Canada is not really a major tourist destination. **Chateau Laurier,** 1 Rideau Street (613/241-1414), situated in an opulent tower directly across from Parliament Hill, is luxurious but not all that expensive; doubles start at $125, with discount rates worth asking about. **Albert House,** 478 Albert Street (613/236-4479), is a large mansion converted into one of Ottawa's nicest bed-and-breakfast inns; doubles from $85. One of the most interesting budget options anywhere has to be the **Ottawa HI Hostel,** 75 Nicholas Street (613/235-2595), a 10-minute walk from Parliament Hill, which occupies the old jail; guests sleep in cell bunks for $20. (Solitary confinement is now the laundry room.)

Byward Market, east of Parliament Hill across the Rideau Canal, is the place to go for food. The market stalls offer a variety of fresh produce, cafes are abundant (try **Cafe Wim** at 537 Sussex Drive), and the restaurants and bars lively and pretty good. **Blue Cactus Bar & Grill,** 2 Byward Market, is one of many good restaurants here, featuring Tex-Mex food in a cheery ambience. There's a popular ersatz American diner, **Zak's,** at 16 Byward Market, and a very nice East Indian place, **Cafe Shafali,** at 308 Dalhousie Street.

An overwhelming quantity of visitor information on Ottawa is available from the **Capital Infocentre,** 90 Wellington Street (613/239-5000 or 800/465-1867), which publishes all sorts of handy free guides to the city. Daily **newspapers** include the *Citizen* and the *Sun,* and the Francophone *Le Droit.*

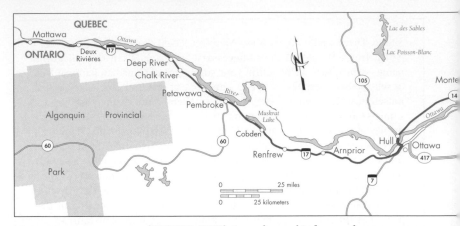

center (705/633-5572) is at the park's far southwest corner, south of North Bay or west of Pembroke and Renfrew via Hwy-60, the "Parkway Corridor," the only road through the park. Here you can get details on the park's abundant camping and cabins, and pick up all the necessary permits.

Deep River and Chalk River

The first real town east of Mattawa is Deep River, Canada's first "Atomic Town," a planned community built for employees of the Chalk River labs. The **Diplomat Motor Hotel** (613/584-1234) here dates to the Cold War era and would be equally at home in the former Soviet Union. The real attraction is the **Laurentian View Dairy Bar** a few blocks west, featuring downhome cooking and homemade ice cream.

Nine miles (14 km) farther east, you enter Chalk River. In 1945, this tiny logging center became the home of the first atomic reactor outside of the United States. Seven years later, Atomic Energy of Canada Ltd., a nuclear research organization, was founded here. At the **Chalk River Laboratories**, you can "tour the atomic age" and clamber around a research reactor (Mon.-Fri., summer only; 613/584-3311, ext. 4428).

Petawawa and Pembroke

Southeast of Chalk River, Hwy-17 crosses the namesake river of the town of Petawawa, home since 1905 to a Canadian Forces base. You can visit two small military museums on the base, but otherwise the area is strictly off limits, as the numerous signs along the road warn.

Wrapping around the eastern edge of Algonquin Provincial Park, Hwy-17 nears Pembroke, another timber town along the Ottawa River, north of the highway. The main sights here are a towering totem pole, along the river, and the **Champlain Trail Museum**, with exhibits on local history, at the corner of Angus Campbell and Pembroke Streets. **Casey's Restaurant** at 100 Pembroke Street is the most popular place to eat.

Renfrew and Arnprior

Midway between Pembroke and Renfrew, you can see the Ottawa River loop north around Cobden, a little town on Muskrat Lake. Renfrew, another of Ontario's many

Scots-founded towns, is now a center of high-tech industry.

Twenty seven miles (42 km) east of Renfrew, Hwy-17 approaches the banks of the Ottawa near Arnprior, another town on the route that began as a lumber center. Arnprior was founded in 1823 by Archibald McNab, a despotic Scottish lord who imported dozens of his country people to the settlement and ruthlessly exploited them. This reign of terror ended when the townsfolk banded together and drove him away. Aside from the **museum** in the old stone post office building, downtown boasts some moderately priced motels.

East of Arnprior, Hwy-17 continues its two-lane trek toward Ottawa with a 90 kph (55 mph) maximum speed posted; occasional passing lanes help you get around the timber trucks. The highway curves gradually southward, away from the Ottawa River, through mostly flat woodlands and a few farms, then converts to freeway for the run into Ottawa.

Hull

Offering the best views of Ottawa's dramatic riverside setting, the francophone town of Hull (pop. 58,800) is a nice change-of-pace from the Canadian capital. Older than Ottawa, French-speaking, despite having been founded in 1800 by an American Loyalist (Philemon Wright) fleeing the Revolution, and named after an English port, despite being miles from any ocean, Hull has managed to retain its traditional identity in the face of the multi-cultural federalizing of its cross-river neighbor.

The best thing about Hull, apart from the chance to walk across the bridges and wander the riverside parks that link it to Ottawa, is the **Canadian Museum of Civilizations** (daily 9 AM-5 PM, closed Monday Oct-April; $5; 819/776-7000), a huge and fascinating institution, housed in a sinuously curving 35,000-square-foot (3,200-square-meter) complex on the banks of the Ottawa River at 100 Rue Laurier, directly across the water from the Parliament Buildings at the foot of the Alexandria Bridge. The main lobby is filled with historic totem poles and canoes made by Canada's diverse native peoples, and

A quick Quebecois sampler for travelers:
"Arrêt" = "Stop";
"Cul de Sac" = "Dead End";
"Bar Latière" = "Ice Cream Stand"; and *"Poutine"* = "Chili Cheese Fries"

Six miles (10 km) northwest of Renfrew, Hwy-17 passes **Storyland,** a summer-only amusement park that brings to life 40 different fairy tales.

Just west of the truck-stop town of Antrim, Hwy-17 crosses the Mississippi River, an ambitious stream that is not the "Father of the Waters" but a tributary of the Ottawa River.

Hwy-17 is fairly boring between Ottawa and Montreal, and you're better off taking the much faster Hwy-417, called the **Queensway,** or following our two-lane route across Quebec, along the north bank of the Ottawa River.

galleries elsewhere in the building highlight everything from whaling communities in Labrador to life on the vast western prairies. It's a fun and educational place, well worth half a day at least.

Across the street from the museum is one of Hull's, and Ottawa's, most enjoyable French restaurants, **Cafe Henry Burger**, at 69 Rue Laurier (819/777-5646).

Montebello and Carillon

East from Hull, Hwy-50 runs as a fast freeway along the north bank of the Ottawa River before calming down into a two-lane sojourn along Hwy-148. About an hour east of Ottawa, 80 miles (130 km) west of Montreal, the town of Montebello holds one of the region's most famous landmarks: **Chateau Montebello** (819/423-6341), an enormous octagonal palace, built of red cedar logs, that has evolved into one of Canada's most exclusive hotels, frequently hosting international conferences by the likes of NATO, G7 and similar power brokers. The grounds of the hotel hold an even more historic landmark, Papineau Manor, a manor house built in 1850 by a notable French-Canadian politician.

Farther east, 45 miles (72 km) west of Montreal via sinuous Hwy-344, the roaring rapids at **Carillon** (pop. 193) have been harnessed by a massive hydropower facility, and a lock system that provides the largest single lift of any in Canada—65 feet (20 meters). East of Carillon, Hwy-344 winds through sleepy farming country along the Ottawa River, before ending up at the edge of the Montreal metropolis.

Driving across Montreal

Montreal is as scythed by freeways as any American city, and it helps to be prepared to deal with the sudden shift from quiet countryside to confusing urban madness. If you've followed the rural route across Quebec from Ottawa, you enter the city from the northwest, on the Hwy-640 Autoroute; the freeway route from Ottawa brings you in on the Hwy-40 Autoroute, straight into downtown.

Any east-west freeway you find yourself on will cross the Hwy-15 Autoroute, the main route between Montreal and the U.S. border.

A quiet town and provincial park along the Ottawa River, 20 miles (32 km) west of Montreal, **Oka** gained international prominence in 1990, when native Mohawk Indians, protesting plans to turn a burial ground into a golf course, blocked the main highway to and from Montreal.

Travelers bound for Canada from the U.S. should be aware of the rules of the road north of the border. See "Driving in Canada" on page 497 for more.

South to Vermont

The region south of Montreal was among the hardest hit by the ice storm of 1998, and the damage (misshapen trees, mainly) is still readily apparent as you pass through. Even before the storm, there wasn't a lot to see, to be honest, and taking the Hwy-15 freeway for the 30-mile (48 km) ride south to New York and Vermont won't make you miss much at all. After crossing the U.S. border, take the second exit off the I-87 freeway, and head east along US-11/US-2 to Rouses Point NY, at the north end of Lake Champlain, to re-join our two-lane road trip route.

MONTREAL SURVIVAL GUIDE

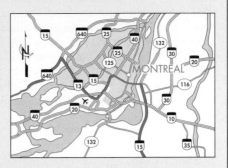

LOCATED ON AN ISLAND IN THE ST. Lawrence River, and first settled as a frontier outpost by fur-trapping French *voyageurs,* Montreal has grown into Canada's second-largest city, and today is easily the most European city in North America, with the largest French-speaking population outside La France. Hotbed of the separatist movement, Montreal tolerates the polyglot federalism of Canada, but the accent here is most definitely on the "French" in French-Canadian; in a wide variety of gourmet restaurants, stylish boutiques, nightclubs, museums, and theaters—you can half-close your eyes and pretend you're in Paris. While the issue of cultural identity remains volatile, and resentment of "American Cultural Imperialism" is as high here as it is everywhere in Canada, pragmatism rules Quebec politics: during all the debates and conflicts, Quebeçois have never lost sight of the importance of tourism to the local economy. Rest assured that you, and your money, will be welcomed everywhere. (Note: all prices listed below are in Canadian dollars.)

The city takes its name from a 700-foot-high hill, now a very pleasant tree-covered **Mount Royal Park** (daily, sunrise-sunset; 514/872-1415), just north of downtown. Planned by Frederick Law Olmsted and opened in 1876, roads, stairs and paths lead up to a belvedere, from which you have a sweeping view of the city, the St. Lawrence River, the southern suburbs and, on the eastern slope, a huge steel cross that's lit up at night.

At the foot of Mount Royal Park runs Sherbrooke Street, Montreal's most prestigious and majestic street, lined with grand 1920s buildings as impressive as any on Park Avenue. Among the many posh boutiques (Chanel, Armani, et al.) and luxury hotels (like the Ritz-Carlton, where Richard Burton married Elizabeth Taylor), you'll find the **Montreal Museum of Fine Arts**, 1380 Sherbrooke Street (Tues.-Sun. 11 AM-6 PM; free, special exhibits $10; 514/285-1600). The oldest museum in Canada, the Museum of Fine Arts has a large permanent collection of European, Canadian and American art, as well as an extensive display of Eskimo artifacts. A half-mile east, the **McCord Museum** at 690 Sherbrooke Street (Tues.-Fri. 10 AM-6 PM; $7; 514/398-7100) has a wonderful collection of art and artifacts related to Montreal, Quebec, and Canada—everything from Victorian evening gowns to "First Nation" masks and carvings. South of the Museum of Fine Arts, the elegantly modern **Canadian Center for Architecture** (Tues.-Sun. 10 AM-6 PM; $5; 514/939-7026) has mounted a fascinating series of shows devoted to the built environment.

(continues on next page)

About a mile southeast of Mount Royal, just off the riverfront, the two-block-long, cobblestoned square of **Place Jacques Cartier** is the heart of Old Montreal, a picturesque neighborhood that was the site of the earliest European settlement. The surrounding buildings are mainly 19th century—the mansard-roofed Hotel de Ville (circa 1878) at the top of the hill is Montreal's city hall—but a number of earlier structures are found nearby. In the summer the square is transformed into an open-air market, and all year round you can sample the area's excellent cafes and restaurants.

The **Montreal Expos** (514/253-3434) play at Astroturf-ed Olympic Stadium.

Practicalities

Two international airports serve Montreal. The closer, known as **Dorval**, lies 22 km (13 miles) west of downtown and is used for almost all domestic Canadian, U.S. and other international flights. Charter flights land at **Mirabel**, 55 km (33 miles) north of downtown. Rentals cars are surprisingly cheap (and you can drive back and forth across the U.S. border, making Montreal a handy base for exploring northern New England), but taxes add 20% or more to quoted rates.

Numerous freeways criss-cross Montreal, and driving around is pretty easy (though all signs, including the complicated parking rules, are in French), but if you want to escape from your car for a day or two, the city is eminently walkable. Montreal also has excellent **public transportation.** The **Metro** ($1.85) is world-class; its orange and green lines connect downtown with the majority of tourist destinations. Taxis are moderately-priced compared to major U.S. cities.

The best budget place to stay is the large **Montreal Youth Hostel**, 1030 Mackey Street ($18; 514/843-3317), a five-minute walk south of Mount Royal Park. For something a bit more special, **Chateau Versailles**, 1659 Sherbrooke Street (514/933-3611) is composed of four Victorian townhouses converted into one charming, antique-filled hotel; doubles from $120. The **Four Seasons**, 1050 Sherbrooke Street (514/284-1100) is about as fancy as it gets in Montreal, and that is pretty fancy: whirlpools in the rooms and a gourmet "spa cuisine" restaurant; doubles from $300.

For food, Montreal has something for everyone, thanks to the city's truly international population—sizeable immigrant communities make Montreal a dining adventure. For a taste of Canadian food, try **Ben's**, a cavernous deli at 1475 Metcalfe Street that serves a classic version of Montreal's beloved "smoked meat," aka corned beef: the Big Ben Sandwich, best washed down with a Ben's Ice Cold Drink; Ben's is open early until late, from 6 AM daily till 3 or 4 in the morning. Another great old deli is **Schwartz's**, 3895 St. Laurent Street. At lunchtime workers from the Montreal financial district cram into **Chez Delmo**, 211 Notre Dame Street, a very traditional Old Montreal seafood restaurant where dishes are always fresh, simple, and reasonably priced. Nice oyster bar, too. You really must eat French at least once while in Montreal, and French restaurants do not come more traditional than **Le Paris**, 1812 St. Catherine Street. Another reliable (but fairly expensive) bet is **L'Express**, 3927 St-Denis Street.

For tourist information, contact the **Greater Montreal Convention and Tourism Bureau**, 1555 Peel Street (514/873-2015 or 800/363-7777). If you are already in the city, there's a very handy, English-speaking **Centre Infotouriste** off the Place Jacques-Cartier, at 174 Notre Dame Street. The English language daily is the *Montreal Gazette,* and there are also two good free weeklies (including the alternative-minded *Mirror*) featuring entertainment listings and current events.

ACROSS VERMONT

Starting at the state's northwestern corner, US-2 crosses the heart of verdant Vermont. From the shores of Lake Champlain, our route winds south to the university town of Burlington, then east past Montpelier, the state capital, all the way to New Hampshire, some 150 miles in all. Paralleled for much of the way by the modern I-89 freeway, US-2 makes a slower but much more diverting alternative to the fast lane, passing through some of the state's most attractive small towns and giving an up-close look at its rural charms, not to mention Vermont's untrammelled mountains, forests, lakes, and rivers.

Between Vermont and the Canadian border, US-2 nips briefly and uneventfully across the northeast corner of New York State, crossing the international border on the I-87 freeway between the U.S. and Quebec.

Lake Champlain Islands

After its brief jaunt across New York from the Canadian border, US-2 winds across the sleepy Lake Champlain Islands. Pancake flat and covered with cows, orchards, and pick-your-own fruit farms, this trio of islands themselves are very pretty to drive across, with the Adirondacks rising up to the west and the Green Mountains to the south and east, but there's not a lot to do; far more farm animals than people populate the route, and tractors clog the road, flinging clods of mud and manure (here pronounced man-OO-ah) with abandon.

Vermont has completely banned roadside advertising, replacing billboards with a standardized series of signs symbolizing lodging, food, recreation, and other services available nearby.

From the middle of the Alburg Peninsula, where US-2 crosses from New York into Vermont, a turn west onto Route 129 leads to Isle La Motte, home of the first French settlement in Vermont, established in 1666. The site is now occupied by **Saint Ann's Shrine**, a popular pilgrimage destination featuring daily outdoor

A mile north of the town of Grand Isle, along US-2 next to a school, stands the **Hyde Log Cabin,** considered by many to be the country's oldest log cabin, dating from 1783. The interior (Wed.-Sun. 11 AM-5 PM in July and Aug.; $1) contains period furnishings and exhibits on frontier life.

The roaring waterfalls that powered the Champlain Mill have been adapted with a fish lift; in spring and fall you can watch trout and salmon make their way upstream.

masses in summer and a granite statue of the explorer Samuel de Champlain, for whom the lake is named.

Continuing south on US-2, the town of **North Hero** (pop. 502) has a gas station, a stone courthouse, a number of quietly luxurious vacation homes dating from the early decades of the 20th century, and the very handy **Hero's Welcome,** a cafe-cum-gift shop at the center of the two-block-long town. A mile south along US-2, **Shore Acres Resort** (802/372-8722) offers tennis courts, boating and swimming, moderately priced lakeside rooms, and a restaurant famed for its chocolate pie—served at dinner only.

Seven miles and another bridge to the south, the town of **Grand Isle** (pop. 1,642) ambitiously claims to be "The Beauty Spot of Vermont." A well-marked turn leads to tiny **Grand Isle State Park,** on the shores of the lake, where there's a nice campground. At the other end of the island, connected by a causeway to the mainland, South Hero is another quaint little place; it and North Hero were named after those famous Vermont Revolutionary War heroes, the Green Mountain Boys, Ira and Ethan Allen.

From South Hero, US-2 rejoins the mainland at the entrance to **Sand Bar State Park,** set in a forest with picnic tables and bathing beaches, surrounded by sprawling, wildfowl-rich marshes on either side. From here US-2 heads east through rolling hills, linking up with the I-89 freeway for the fast route into Burlington, 10 miles to the south.

Winooski

If you have time, or an abiding interest in America's industrial heritage, consider making the detour just north of Burlington to Winooski, an old mill town now focusing on the totally restored Champlain Mill, downtown at 1 Main Street. This former woolen mill now houses over 20 cafes and specialty shops, including the very pleasant **Book Rack,** and the rest of town provides a blue-collar balance to Burlington's upscale airs. The town green is marred by a bank and large parking lot, but the surrounding buildings hold some interesting spots, including **Sneakers**

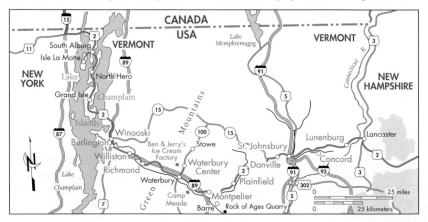

Bistro, 36 Main Street, which serves great breakfasts and lunches; for burgers, beers and Red Sox memorabilia, stop by **Champlains**, next door. Another popular spot for road food is **Libby's Blue Line Diner**, on Main Street at I-89 exit 16.

Main Street in Winooski is a section of the old Roosevelt Highway (US-2/US-7), which you can follow southwest into central Burlington.

Winooski's historic Centennial Field is home to the Class A **Vermont Expos** (802/655-4200).

Burlington

After the original French settlers were ejected from the Lake Champlain region in 1760 at the end of the French and Indian Wars, English settlers soon arrived, and Burlington (pop. 39,150) was chartered in 1763. The area was abandoned during the Revolutionary War; afterward Ethan Allen, leader of the famous "Green Mountain Boys" band of guerrillas, and his brothers were granted huge tracts of land along the eastern shore of Lake Champlain.

The Allen brothers were ambitious: not only did they encourage settlement and industry in Burlington, but in 1791 they founded the University of Vermont here. The town boomed, aided by its strategic position on Lake Champlain, the quickest route between New York's Hudson River and Montreal. Burlington quickly became the center of Vermont industry, finance, education, and culture—a position it has held ever since.

US-2 passes right through the center of Burlington, following Winooski Avenue in the north, then along Main Street, lined by motels and restaurants on the outskirts but eventually crossing the lively, sprawling campus of the **University of Vermont**. Downtown Burlington offers all the delights of a typical college town: bookstores, bars, ethnic food, and trendy but inexpensive shopping. At the center of town is **Church Street Marketplace**, a four-block pedestrian mall with good bookstores, numerous cafes, and restaurants usually crammed with students. For food, the Chinese **Five Spice Cafe** (175 Church Street) and the **Daily Planet** (15 Center Street, between the Marketplace and US-2), featuring pastas and Latin American dishes, are two local favorites.

Another reason to visit Winooski is to tour the restored farm of Vermont patriot Ethan Allen, preserved as the **Ethan Allen Homestead** (Mon.-Sat. 10 AM-5 PM, Sunday 1-5 PM in summer; $3.50) along Route 127 two miles northeast of Winooski.

Burlington was the home of **Dr. Nelson Jackson**, who in 1902 (along with his chauffeur and a stray dog they picked up along the way) became the first to cross the country by automobile.

In 1981, the people of Burlington elected one of America's few socialist mayors, **Bernie Sanders.** He was reelected three times and has since served as U.S. Congressman from the "People's Republic" of Vermont.

Main Street continues four blocks west to Lake Champlain, where the **Burlington Waterfront Park** has a strollable boardwalk linking up with **Battery Park**, home to a collection of cannons pointing menacingly across the lake. In 1812, these cannons were used against British warships that bombarded the town.

On the University of Vermont campus, which stands on a shallow hill on the east side of town, the **Robert Hull Fleming Museum** (Tues.-Fri. 9 AM-4 PM, Saturday and Sunday 1-5 PM; donations) on Colchester Avenue on the north side of campus is the main visitor attraction, with a small but wide-ranging collection of fine

THE SHELBURNE MUSEUM

Downtown Burlington's attractions are mainly mercantile and culinary; for more enlightening fare, head south on Union Street (US-7) five miles to the town of Shelburne. This is the home of the Shelburne Museum (daily 10 AM-5 PM, mid-May to mid-Oct. only; $17.50; 802/985-3346), an overwhelming agglomeration of historic buildings and artifacts hauled here from all over New England. Besides the 40-odd immaculately presented historic structures, the collection includes an original Lake Champlain paddle wheeler, a train, a full-sized model circus, gardens, and an enormous collection of European and American paintings and decorative arts. The core of the Shelburne collection was amassed by a rich and indefatigable collector, Electra Havemeyer Webb. Tax troubles have forced the sell-off of some of the collection, but it's still an amazing assembly, well worth setting aside most of a day to enjoy.

and applied arts from ancient Egypt to the present. A less rarefied campus sight is the anarchic **W.H.A.M.K.A.**—the Williams Hall Art Museum of Kitsch Art—which covers the main hallways of the art school. It's free, and open whenever the buildings are (usually 7 AM-11 PM).

For additional information on the Burlington area, contact the **visitors bureau,** 60 Main street (802/863-3489).

Williston and Richmond

Between Burlington and Montpelier, US-2 follows the Winooski River valley, lined with dairy farms. For most of this journey, the road parallels the less-than-attractive concrete expanse of I-89. However, a few sights make the two-lane route preferable.

The first of these, Williston (pop. 4,887), sits roughly 10 miles east of Burlington, and less than a mile north of the freeway. Though on the large size by local standards, Williston is a classic northern New England town, its streets lined by towering maple trees and white clapboard houses.

A mile southeast of Williston, on the other side of the I-89 freeway, the country town of Richmond is home of the unique **Old Round Church.** Turn at the town's only stoplight and drive a half-mile south, where this 16-sided, two-story, white clapboard structure stands just east of the road. The church was built in 1813, the communal effort of five different Protestant denominations. They eventually feuded, of course, and the structure lapsed into civic use, becoming the town hall. Today it is used as a meeting house, and on summer weekends the local historical society gives guided tours.

Waterbury Center: Ben & Jerry's

Though it's known for beautiful mountains and the brilliant fall color of its hardwood forests, Vermont's number one tourist attraction is none other than **Ben &**

Jerry's Ice Cream Factory, a kind of hippie Disneyland in Waterbury Center, on the hillside above Route 100, a mile or so north of I-89. The grounds of the brightly painted factory includes a number of large cartoonish artifacts strewn outside to play on—weird vehicles, whimsical picnic tables, and the like. Ben & Jerry began making its ultra-rich ice cream in 1978; today the company sells its products across the country and abroad. The company is also famous for its activism, donating a percentage of its profits to philanthropies supporting "progressive social change."

You can tour the factory (daily 9 AM-5 PM; $2; 802/244-TOUR or 800/244-8687 for information), although production is halted on Sunday, holidays, and company celebration days—when you get a video presentation. The premises also feature a gift shop and the "Scoop Shop," featuring all of Ben & Jerry's ice cream, frozen yogurt and sorbet flavors. Outside are many picnic tables where you can enjoy the ice cream and a view over the valley.

Camp Meade

On US-2 just west of Middlesex stands Camp Meade, a Depression-era Civilian Conservation Corps camp that once housed workers building dams and flood control projects and since has been turned into a popular restaurant and motel ($45; 802/223-5537). It is also a shrine to America in the 1930s and 1940s, from the New Deal to D-Day, mostly the latter: a fighter plane, a tank, and military trucks adorn the grounds, a gift store sells army surplus, and the cabins are named after luminaries such as General Patton and Colonel Oliver North. The restaurant sports camouflage tablecloths and a bomb suspended from the rafters.

Montpelier

The smallest capital in the country, Vermont's Montpelier (pop. 8,200) was settled in 1787 and designated the state capital in 1805. Today Montpelier's economy is based around government, insurance, and tourism.

Your arrival in Montpelier is foretold by the gold dome of the capitol building hovering in the valley ahead. Constrained by the Winooski River on one side and the narrow valley on the other, Montpelier is so compact that you can park your car and find all the sights within a 10-minute walking distance. (Thankfully, the I-89 freeway is south of the river.) A quick poll of shops along State and Main Streets reveals the cosmopolitan nature of the town: bookstores, coffee bars, and wine merchants, as well as multiple combinations of the same.

The north side of State Street opens up into a broad lawn fronting the **State Capitol,** the focal point of the Republic of Vermont (like Texas, the state takes some pride in the fact that it was an independent "country" before joining the rest

North of Waterbury Junction on Route 100, the ski resort of **Stowe** was built by the musical von Trapp family, whose escape from the Nazis inspired *The Sound of Music.*

Don't confuse Waterbury Center, birthplace of Ben & Jerry's, with Waterbury, a satellite community of Montpelier with some lovely colonial-era homes, located just *south* of the I-89 freeway. Waterbury Center is about two miles north of Waterbury.

Running south from Waterbury, **Route 100** travels through the heart of the Green Mountains all the way south to Massachusetts, and is one of the state's most popular "leaf-peeping" routes. Just north of Ben & Jerry's on Route 100, the Green Mountain Club (802/244-7037) is the best resource for hiking in Vermont.

Rising up a hill off State Street (US-2) a few blocks west of the capitol, the **Green Mountain Cemetery** is filled with impressive granite monuments. Many of these were carved by the immigrant stonecutters of nearby Barre for their own family plots.

Near Montpelier, watch sap being turned into delicious maple syrup at the **Morse Farm and Sugarhouse,** three miles northeast from the capitol dome along Main Street.

Montpelier thrived off the granite quarries of the nearby town of Barre. The **Rock of Ages quarry** (daily 8:30 AM-5 PM in summer; free; 802/476-3119), four miles southeast of Barre, is one of the world's largest.

of the United States). The original building was opened in 1808; it burned in 1859, whereupon the current, more heroic structure was erected from local granite. The statue on the dome represents Ceres, the goddess of agriculture; Doric columns hide a Revolutionary War cannon and a statue of Ethan Allen. The state legislature is only in session from January to April—being a Vermont politician is a part-time job; the rest of the year they go back to being farmers, businesswomen, and so on—but you can tour the building year-round (Mon.-Fri. 8 AM-4 PM; guided tours available). Atop the hill behind the capitol lies **Hubbard State Park,** a favorite rest and recreation spot for locals.

Just west of the capitol is the **Vermont Historical Society Museum** (Tues.-Sat. 9 AM-4:30 PM, Sunday noon-4 PM; $3), where permanent and temporary displays illustrate different aspects of Vermont's history, and you also find lots of 19th-century furniture and a small bookstore and gift shop.

Montpelier residents take their eating seriously. Very good and very inexpensive food is readily available, thanks to the presence in town of the New England Culinary Institute, a cooking school that operates the **Main Street Bar and Grill** and **Chef's Table,** both at 118 Main Street. Montpelier fast food means bagels, Ben & Jerry's ice cream, and breads from **Manghis' Bread** at 28 School Street, just east of Main Street. An atmospheric breakfast place is the **Coffee Corner,** on the corner of State and Main Streets. For upscale lodgings in period surroundings, the place to go is **The Inn at Montpelier** (802/223-2727), two renovated 19th-century homes that have been joined into one hotel. The best moderate choice is the **Econo Lodge** (802/223-5258) on Route 12 south of the river.

At Montpelier, US-2 diverges northeast from the I-89 freeway, taking a rolling ride over the mountains to New Hampshire.

Plainfield

Plainfield is where the 1960s live. This tiny town boasts a bookstore, a pair of huge barns, a fly-fishing shop, and the **Maple Valley Country Store,** a combo deli-cafe-pizzeria that's the local hangout (tie-dye welcome). The store's parking area is built on a foundation of recycled granite, leftovers from the nearby quarries and stonecutters. Plainfield also has a great place to eat breakfast: the **River Run,** at 3 Main Street, where you can get a great heap of pancakes studded with fresh blueberries for around $5.

Just west of Plainfield is the campus of **Goddard College,** one of the nation's most renowned countercultural institutes of higher learning, where you can sometimes get a cheap room in summer (802/454-8311). Hitchhikers are common on US-2 between Montpelier and Plainfield.

Danville: Joe's Pond

Ten miles east of Plainfield, US-2 finally turns north away from the **Winooski River,** a prime trout fishery, which it follows all the way from Lake Champlain. Leaving the Winooski River valley, US-2 hits **West Danville,** a summer community on the edge of Joe's Pond, which is ringed by vacation cabins, some of them seeming to date back 100 years or more. The pond, which at sunset in summer is one of the more idyllic spots imaginable, was originally called "Indian Joe's Pond," which explains the presence of "Indian Joe's Court," a set of roadside cabins dating from the pre-politically correct era. At the center of town, at the junction of US-2 and Route 15, you'll see a micro-sized covered bridge and Hastings Store, the local "if we ain't got it you don't need it" emporium, selling cheddar cheese, maple syrup, fishing supplies and other Vermont essentials.

All along US-2, and all over New England for that matter, the old roads are lined by 1940s-style knotty pine cabins and motor courts, like the photogenic Wallinda Cabins east of Plainfield.

Heading east, the next place you'll pass is Danville, yet another picture-postcard Vermont town, set on a hill surrounded by farmland. The center of Danville is a classic New England village green, with a general store and the customary churches. Just off the green you'll find the headquarters of the **American Society of Dowsers** (Mon.-Fri. 9 AM-4:30 PM), whose members have refined their talents for finding water or mineral deposits using a dowsing rod. The building houses a small exhibit on the history and practice of the art and a shop where you can buy dowsing books and rods.

St. Johnsbury

In the early 19th century, the economy of St. Johnsbury (pop. 7,600) was based on maple products and the manufacture of platform scales—Fairbanks Scales, founded by the inventor of platform scales, still operates a plant here. Today it is the commercial center of Vermont's "Northeast Kingdom," at the junction of the US-2 and US-5 highways, the I-91 and I-93 freeways, and the Maine Central and Canadian Pacific railroad tracks. The contemporary economy is somewhat

depressed, meaning the town's extensive stock of historic landmark architecture has been preserved almost totally unchanged: elegant four- and five-story brick buildings line the riverfront and railroad line along US-2 and US-5; on the hill above, a more genteel commercial district, surrounded by massive trees and dozens of grand Victorian homes, is highlighted by two of the most fascinating institutions in the state, both funded by the largess of the Fairbanks family.

At the center of town, at 30 Main Street, stands the **St. Johnsbury Athenaeum, Art Gallery and Public Library** (Mon.-Fri. 10 AM-5:30 PM; free) in a red-brick 1871 building. The building houses a surprisingly good collection of 19th-century paintings, the jewel of which is Albert Bierstadt's monumental *Domes of Yosemite*.

A block east down Main Street, you'll find my very favorite museum in all New England: the **Fairbanks Museum** (Mon.-Sat. 10 AM-6 PM, Sunday 1-5 PM; $5), a charmingly quirky, Victorian-era center of knowledge, established by Franklin Fairbanks in 1889. A pair of menacing stuffed bears greet visitors inside the entrance, and these are followed by a seemingly endless display of taxidermied wildlife—a veritable Noah's Ark of North American fauna. Climb the spiral stairs to the mezzanine of the main gallery, a grand Richardsonian Romanesque space topped by a coffered barrel vault and furnished with fireplaces and other homey touches, and you'll find more fascinating oddities: arrowheads and other anthropological artifacts, rocks and fossils, art made out of bugs (including a portrait of General Pershing made out of flies and moths!), exhibits on local history, a set of doll's house furniture made by author Mark Twain, and a very funny letter written by Robert Louis Stevenson in which he wills his birthday (which he said he was to old to need anymore) to Fairbanks' daughter, whose own birth fell on Christmas, meaning she effectively missed out.

St. Johnsbury's eating options include **Hilltopper Restaurant**, 45 Main Street, across the street from the Athenaeum. For motels, try the **Fairbanks Motor Inn**, on US-2 at 32 Western Avenue (802/748-5666), or creekside **Aime's Motel** (802/748-3194), on US-2 about five miles east of town, a half-mile north of I-93 exit 1.

Taking a scenic alternative to the I-93 freeway east from St. Johnsbury, US-2 passes over the Memorial Bridge (1943) spanning the Passumpsic River. One mile east of the bridge you'll find the **Maple Grove Farms** complex based around an old mill building. Highlights include the maple museum and the "world's largest maple candy factory" (tours Mon.-Fri. 8 AM-4:30 PM, May-Oct.); the factory store is open year-round. Vermont is in the heart of maple sugaring territory, which runs all the way from Maine to Michigan, and up into Canada.

Concord and Lunenburg

Approaching the New Hampshire border, US-2 heads across rolling rocky hills covered with forests, largely pine and birch, with a few scattered farms. This corner of the state, a recreational paradise of hills and lakes and few year-round residents, is known as the "Northeast Kingdom." The road drops down into the narrow, pastoral valley of the Moose River before reaching Concord, which features a country store and a small historical society. Concord was the home of the **First Normal School**, America's first teachers' academy, founded in 1823.

Fifteen miles east of Concord, along the banks of the broad Connecticut River, Lunenburg is a perfect New England village of white clapboard houses clustered around a church—Vermont specializes in this species of quaintness.

From Lunenburg, you can follow US-2 to the northeast, or take a highly recommended detour across the Connecticut River on a covered bridge, then proceed north along Route 135, rejoining US-2 at Lancaster.

ACROSS NEW HAMPSHIRE

Crossing the broad Connecticut River, which forms Vermont's 200-mile-long border with New Hampshire, US-2 makes a short but scenic run across the state. From the historic commercial center of Lancaster, just east of the state border, US-2 winds along the wide valley of the Israel River before reaching Jefferson, home to two of the state's biggest tourist traps. Continuing east, US-2 curves around the northern flank of towering Mount Washington and the rugged White Mountains, an area rich in outdoor recreation and scenic splendor. At Gorham, US-2 reaches the valley of the Androscoggin River, which it follows east into Maine.

Lancaster

Crossing over the Connecticut River from Vermont, you enter the outskirts of Lancaster (pop. 3,550), a market town that was first settled in 1764. US-2 becomes Main Street through Lancaster, lined with dozens of attractive old homes and churches, a cemetery on a knoll to the north and, on the south side, a heroic red-brick courthouse that dates from 1887. At the junction of US-2 and US-3 at the west side of town stands the **Lancaster Historical Society.**

Two miles south of Lancaster via US-3, the mountaintop estate of the man who saved New Hampshire's forests from the lumber industry has been preserved as **John Wingate Weeks Historic Site** (Wed.-Sun. 10 AM-6 PM in summer only; $2.50), complete with a tourable mansion and an observation tower giving grand views of Mount Washington and Vermont's Green Mountains.

Your welcome to New Hampshire is a sign—"Brake for Moose." Apparently moose are hard to see at night and are involved in many serious collisions because headlights shine through the legs of this towering beast, rather than reflect off its body.

Just west of Lancaster, the broad **Connecticut River** flows south all the way to Long Island Sound. To the north of Lancaster it is a well-known trout stream; smallmouth bass and brown trout are abundant. If you weren't thrilled by the modern bridge that carries US-2 just upstream from Lancaster, head south of downtown on Route 135 five miles to an impressive old **covered bridge** that spans the Connecticut River and meets US-2 in the Vermont town of Lunenburg.

There are at least three pizza places in Lancaster, and the **S&S Lancaster Diner**, 60 Main Street, has American and Chinese food, cold beers, and pool tables upstairs. For a place to stay, downtown you'll find the **Lancaster Motor Inn**, 112 Main Street (603/788-4921), and other moderately priced motels line US-2 east of town.

Jefferson

High above the Israel River on the flanks of the White Mountains, the small resort town of Jefferson (pop. 965) is home to two big tourist draws. For the truly masochistic parent, about a mile west of Jefferson is **Santa's Village** (daily 9:30 AM-7 PM, summer only; $15, under age 4 free), with candy canes looming threateningly at the entrance, a Ferris wheel, a roller coaster, the Yule Log Flume and, of course, Santa himself. Just east of town is **Six Gun City** (daily 9 AM-6 PM, summer only; $11.95), an ersatz Wild West town featuring cowboy skits ("Come on out, you varmints!"), frontier shows, a carriage museum, and a pair of water slides.

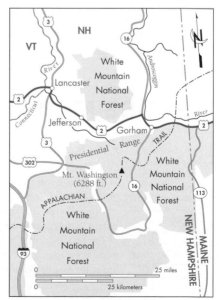

Two accommodations in town deserve mention. The friendly **Applebrook B&B** (800/545-6504; $45-60 for a double or $20 per person in the seven-bed dorm) offers full Victorian splendor gilded with summer raspberries and a hot tub under the stars. **Jefferson Inn** (800/729-7908; $44-70 for a double, suites from $65) has a Dutch- and German-speaking innkeeper, panoramic views, and a swimming pond.

> *A roadside marker along US-2 just west of Jefferson commemorates the birth nearby of inventor **Thaddeus Lowe,** who pioneered balloon aviation during the Civil War.*

East of Jefferson the road ascends, the valley narrows, and the scenery becomes more spectacular with every mile, as the Presidential Range looms larger and larger to the south.

Eight miles south of Gorham, towering Mount Washington marks the start of our Appalachian Trail route, which follows along these landmark mountains all the way south to Atlanta. See page 298 for more.

Gorham

Gorham (pop. 3,173), incorporated in 1836, was another early tourist town; its boom began after the railroad came through in 1851. Tourism is still the main industry, from the summer tourists to the autumn "leaf-peepers" to the winter skiers. (Nobody visits much during the early spring mud season.) There is a **visitor center** on Main Street (US-2), and the **Gorham Historical Society** (Monday, Wednesday and Friday 1-5 PM; donations) stands in an old depot at 25 Railroad Street, a half-block off Main Street.

For lunch and dinner try **Wilfred's**, 117 Main Street, specializing in bounteous and inexpensive turkey dinners; **Welch's Restaurant** serves the most popular breakfast. The **Royalty Inn** (603/466-3312), 130 Main Street, is a good full-service motel with a large health club next door.

Just east of Gorham, the road passes through a famous grove of birch trees. Here you find the pleasant **Town & Country Motor Inn** (603/466-3315) with some spa and resort facilities, such as saunas and a golf course. This is also where the **Appalachian Trail**, which runs from Maine's Mount Katahdin to northern Georgia, crosses US-2.

ACROSS MAINE

> *Just east of the Maine border, 10 miles west of Bethel, a sign marks a turn south from US-2 onto Route 113 toward **Evans Notch**. This narrow, mostly gravel road, which is posted Not Maintained For Winter Travel, runs along the Wild and Cold Rivers up to a stunningly scenic mountain pass.*

Following the Androscoggin River across the New Hampshire border, US-2 enters Maine at the forested eastern flank of the White Mountains. Winding east along the river, the route passes through alternating mountain resorts and mill towns, starting at sedate Bethel and ending up 135 miles later at Bangor, once one of the wildest lumber towns in the country. From Bangor the route veers south toward the coast, hitting the Atlantic Ocean at beautiful Acadia National Park.

Bethel

At the far west end of its run across Maine, US-2 winds along the south bank of the Androscoggin River, through dense pine and birch forests of the White Mountain National Forest. Ten miles east of the border, along a placid stretch of the Androscoggin, Bethel (pop. 2,329) was first settled in 1774, and at the tail end of the Revolutionary War the town, then named Sudbury, suffered the last

the Shaker Museum at Sabbathday Lake

Indian raid inflicted on New England. In 1836, Gould Academy, one of Maine's oldest prep schools, was established at the west end of town, near the "historic" Main Street. Information on Bethel's many other well-preserved old buildings can be had from the circa 1813 **Moses Mason House**, 15 Broad Street, which doubles as a small museum (Mon.-Fri. 10 AM-4 PM; $2).

After the railroads came through, Bethel quickly became a center for White Mountain area tourism. The **Bethel Inn and Country Club** (207/824-2175 or 800/654-0125), founded in 1913, was one of New England's early health and fitness resorts and, surrounded by an 18-hole golf course, continues that tradition today. For upscale lodging and dining, this is the place to go. The **Red Top Restaurant** right downtown on US-2 is the polar opposite; try the hash. The **River View Motel** (207/824-2808), on the east side of Bethel at the junction of US-2 and Route 26, is the moderate lodging choice.

For outdoor enthusiasts, the **Sunday River Ski Area** (800/543-2SKI), six miles east of town, draws thousands of visitors to the area for skiing in winter and hiking and mountain biking in summer. There's a nice picnic area with a covered bridge, along the US-2 and the Androscoggin River, about 10 miles east of Bethel.

From US-2 at Bethel, Route 26 runs southeast toward Portland and the coast, passing through the spa town of Poland Spring and the world's last remaining intact Shaker community at **Sabbathday Lake,** where a small museum gives tours (Mon.-Sat. 10 AM-4 PM in summer; $5; 207/926-4597).

Rumford's main claim to fame is as the birthplace of **Edmund Muskie,** governor, U.S. Senator and Secretary of State, and vice-presidential and presidential candidate in 1968 and 1972 respectively.

Rumford

US-2 continues along the north bank of the Androscoggin River for 20 miles before reaching Rumford (pop. 7,078), a grungy mill town with low brick buildings and a downscale downtown along the river. Just upstream from all the heavy industry lie the Androscoggin Falls, which provided the hydropower that led to the original settlement of the town. Now, enormous steam-puffing smokestacks loom in the valley around the Mead Publishing Paper Division—New England's largest paper mill— surrounded by huge piles of logs, chips and wood residue. You may wish to leave town as quickly as possible, but the road winds around the valley as the Androscoggin makes an oxbow. If you want an up-close view of the goings on in Rumford, walk across to the mill on the narrow footbridge suspended above the river.

Five miles east of Rumford, in the heart of the broad valley of the Androscoggin River, Dixfield (pop. 2,574) is a small town with a mild aura of the 1960s; at least, there is inside the **Village Restaurant and Bakery**, at the west edge of town. East of Dixfield toward Farmington, US-2 passes through increasingly wild country, with

At a junction in Dixfield, a single sign points the way toward Peru and Mexico. Paris, Leeds, Canton, Madrid, Belgrade, and Rome are also within 30 miles—only in America!

In the town of Rangeley, an hour northwest of Farmington via Route 4, the **Wilhelm Reich Museum** (Tues.-Sun. 1-5 PM in July and August; $5; 207/864-3443) preserves the flat-roofed final home and tomb of the iconoclastic psychoanalyst, who died in 1957.

In 1976, the Kennebec River at Skowhegan was the site of the last log drive in Maine.

The Skowhegan Art Colony outside of town is one of the nation's most renowned summer art schools.

excellent views of the tree-covered White Mountains rising to the west. Midway between the two, the town of Wilton is home to famous shoemaker **G. H. Bass Company**. On a hill above US-2, a large windmill marks the **Dutch Treat Drive-in**, where you can enjoy fish 'n' chips or an ice cream while watching the world go by.

Farmington

Like many other northern Maine towns, Farmington (pop. 4,200) was first settled by soldiers who fought in the Revolutionary War. The rolling hills that surround it still hold a few farms and orchards, but as elsewhere the economy revolves around trees—both as tourist fodder during the fall color sweeps, and as pulp for paper mills. There's not a lot worth stopping for, though the University of Maine at Farmington has an **art gallery** (Sun.-Thurs. noon-4 PM; free) at 102 Main Street downtown, showing local artists.

East of Farmington, US-2 runs through almost 20 miles of forests and farms alongside the Sandy River. At **Norridgewock**, first settled by French Jesuits in 1688, you reach the broad Kennebec River, which US-2 follows five miles east into Skowhegan.

Skowhegan

First settled in 1771 on an island in the Kennebec River, the mid-sized mill town of Skowhegan (pop. 8,725) was also the birthplace of the late Margaret Chase Smith, one of Maine's most renowned politicians and a 36-year veteran of the U.S. House and Senate. Her home is now the **Margaret Chase Smith Library Center** (Mon.-Fri. 10 AM-4 PM; donations) and includes a museum of her life and a conference center. The **Skowhegan History House** (Tues.-Fri. 1-5 PM in summer only; donations), 40 Elm Street, is a brick Greek Revival structure with exhibits on town history., and off US-201, just north of US-2, the **Skowhegan Indian**, a 62-foot statue sometimes billed as the "Largest Wooden Indian in the World," stands unloved and unmarked in the parking lot behind a gas station.

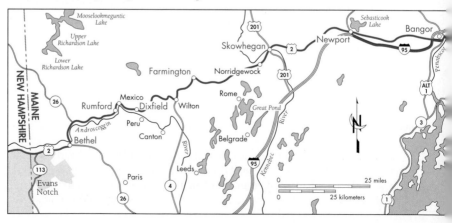

East of Skowhegan, US-2 veers away from the river across low, rolling hills covered with pine and birch forests, the only signs of habitation a few trailers and scraggly farms.

In August, Skowhegan is home to the **Maine State Fair.** Celebrated annually since 1818, it is one of the oldest state fairs in the country.

Newport

Midway across the state, at the point where two-lane US-2 joins the high-speed I-95 freeway, Newport (pop. 3,036) is known as "The Hub of Maine." Like most other towns that play up their connections to the rest of the world, Newport is not really a place to linger, but it does have the **Log Cabin Restaurant** on US-2 three miles east of town, as well as a Wal-Mart and the usual array of fast food and cheap motels.

Between Newport and Bangor, 20 miles to the east, there's no good reason to follow badly pot-holed old US-2; you may as well race across on I-95.

Bangor

Built on the banks of the Penobscot River, Bangor (pop. 33,200, pronounced BANG-gor) is the largest town in northern Maine. This site was an important rendezvous for local tribes, who called it Kendusbeag, or "eel-catching place." In 1604 Samuel de Champlain sailed up the Penobscot River as far as Treats Falls here, but long-term settlement did not begin until 1769. Throughout the next century, Bangor was the most important lumber town of the eastern U.S.; it also developed into a ship-building center, and Bangor's lumber circled the globe. A large sector of the population was devoted to providing amusement for the loggers and sailors who would arrive in town with free time and fat wallets. In a riverside neighborhood called the Devil's Half Acre, dozens of bars, bordellos, and gambling dens competed to empty the men's pockets, but now the only sign of life is the **Sea Dog Brewery**, one of Bangor's most popular bars and restaurants.

Nineteenth-century Bangor was as wide open as any town in the Wild West, but traces of rougher days have all but disappeared, though modern Bangor is still a

center for the lumber industry: coming into town across the Penobscot River, you'll turn right onto Main Street and see a Day-Glo statue of **Paul Bunyan**, erected in 1959. The compact business center, mostly red-brick 19th-century buildings interspersed with church spires, lies a few blocks to the east of Paul Bunyan. Here you'll find some impressive 100-year-old buildings, now housing a little of everything: an Internet cafe, two comic shops, and at least four good bookstores.

The **Bangor Historical Society** (Mon.-Fri. noon-4 PM; $2), housed in a circa 1836 Greek Revival mansion at 159 Union Street, has the usual range of exhibits, furnishings, and paintings reflecting 19th-century life. Another place worth checking out is the **Cole Land Transportation Museum** (daily 9 AM-5 PM, May-Nov.; $3), off I-95 at 405 Perry Road, which displays over 200 historic vehicles, from wooden wagons to modern 18-wheelers.

For a good quick bite to eat, try the **Bagel Shop**, a kosher restaurant in the heart of downtown Bangor at 1 Main Street, or the more trendy **New Moon**, next door. There are also a couple of inexpensive Indian places nearby, and the **Whig and Courier Pub**, which serves good food and very good beers. The pick of area lodgings is the **Phenix Inn** (207/947-0411), a restored 1873 hotel at 20 Broad Street downtown. The national chains (**Motel 6, Rodeway, Super 8**) have their motels out on US-2 near the airport west of town, which is where the fast food is, too.

> Bangor is home to best-selling horror writer **Stephen King,** who lives in a suitably Gothic and surprisingly visible mansion at 47 W. Broadway.

For more information on Bangor, contact the **visitors bureau**, next to Paul Bunyan at 519 Main Street (207/947-0307).

> From Bangor, US-2 winds northeast along the Penobscot River, ending up near the Canadian border at Houlton. We've opted to head "Down East," ending our cross-country odyssey at Acadia National Park.

Ellsworth

Ellsworth, chartered in 1763, began as a lumber town with its own opera house, but now is a thriving commercial center, located southeast of Bangor at the junction of Route 3 and busy old US-1, the main highway along coastal Maine. Downtown Ellsworth is lots of red brick and little excitement—all the action is out by the malls—but worth a visit if only to eat at **The Riverside Cafe**, a great breakfast and lunch place at 42 Main Street.

South of Ellsworth, Route 3 is the mainland's main connection to Mount Desert Island and Acadia National Park, Maine's top tourist draw. North of the bridge to the island, around **Trenton**, the land is flat and the roadside along Route 3 is heavily commercialized, with a Wal-Mart, numerous service stations, motels, and fast-food outlets sprinkled amongst some tired roadside attractions, including go-carts, a

---

MOUNT DESERT ISLAND

Mount Desert Island is an idyllic 11- by 14-mile chunk of forest-covered mountains and rocky inlets just off the coast of Maine. The island was first settled by the Penobscot people and was not explored by Europeans until 1609, when Samuel de Champlain named it Isle de Monts Déserts and claimed it for France; the English razed the French settlement in 1613. In 1844, the Hudson River School artist Thomas Cole painted a stunning series of scenes of Mount Desert, and the island soon became a summer playground for elite Eastern families. Many of the 19th-century elite built elegant "cottages" here, largely around Bar Harbor. In 1916, the Mount Desert summer colony, led by the Pulitzer and Rockefeller families, donated most of the island's land to the federal government, to establish Acadia National Park. The Great Depression and World War II effectively put an end to the Bar Harbor high life, subsequently a huge fire in 1947 destroyed most of Bar Harbor's mansions.

miniature golf course, and the private Acadia Zoo. Just before the bridge stands the brochure-packed, business-oriented **Acadia Information Center** (800/248-9250), and midway across the bridge, on Thompson Island, the more thorough **Mount Desert Island Regional Information Center** (207/ 288-3411) is the best single source of maps and info on Mount Desert and the Acadia area. Across the bridge, you quickly come to a junction: Route 102 and Route 198 head straight to Southwest and Northeast Harbors, respectively, while Route 3 veers east toward Bar Harbor.

At 1,532 feet, **Cadillac Mountain** on Mount Desert Island is the highest point on the Eastern Seaboard of North America. It also shares a namesake with the classy automobile marque.

Bar Harbor is the terminus for the **ferry** to Yarmouth, Nova Scotia, a six-hour each-way cruise ($45 roundtrip per passenger, plus $55 for a car; 888/249-7245) that will save you hours of driving time if you are continuing east. The boats also turn into casinos when crossing international waters.

Bar Harbor

Approaching Bar Harbor from the mainland, Route 3 runs along Frenchman Bay, which borders the northeast corner of the island. The big attraction here is the Bar Harbor branch of the **Mount Desert Oceanarium** (daily 9 AM-5 PM, May-Oct. only; $5.95; 207/288-5005), which has harbor seals and other marine animals on display, a nature trail along the waterfront, and the Maine Lobster Museum, where working lobstermen explain the ups and downs and tricks of the lobstering trade. (There's another jointly operated Oceanarium in Southwest Harbor.) Many of the national motel chains, including Holiday Inn and Marriott, have outposts nearby. About midway between the turnoff and Bar Harbor proper, at Hulls Cove, Route 3 passes the main entrance to Acadia National Park (see callout **Mount Desert Island**), where a large and informative visitor center provides an excellent introduction to the park and to Bar Harbor, detailing the history of the exclusive summer playground Mount Desert was up until the 1920s, when the park was established.

A half-mile out of Bar Harbor, you pass the College of the Atlantic, on the grounds of which you'll find the **Natural History Museum** (daily 9 AM-5 PM June-August; $2). Housed in a granite summer "cottage," the museum offers exhibits and lectures on the region's flora, fauna, and geology.

Finally, traffic willing, you'll reach the town of Bar Harbor (pop. 4,400). The largest center on Mount Desert Island, and once the summertime haunt of Rockefellers, DuPonts, Pulitzers and other East Coast elites, Bar Harbor has turned to catering to the less well-heeled visitor as the "Old Money" has retreated to more discreet settlements to the west, such as Northeast Harbor—aka "Philadelphia on the Rocks." The town's principal thoroughfares, lined with gift shops, hotels, restaurants, and outfitters, are Cottage Street, Main Street, and Mount Desert Street, the latter two intersecting at the lively and pleasant Village Green, in the heart of town. On West Street, which runs along the waterfront, the West Street Pier is home to the **Lobster Hatchery** (daily 9 AM-5 PM in summer only), where you can see exhibits on the popular crustacean's life cycle.

Since most of Bar Harbor's mansions have been destroyed, there aren't all that many sights to search out, though the Tiffany windows of **St. Saviour's Church**, on the west side of the Village Green, gives some sense of the wealth that once lingered here. (As a sign of how times have changed times, the church hall is now a summer-only HI **youth hostel**; 207/288-5587). Otherwise, visitors tend to spend time exploring Acadia National Park, and come to Bar Harbor to eat and drink, and maybe watch a movie at the Art Deco **Criterion Theater**, a National Historic Landmark at 35 Cottage Street (207/288-3441).

Lobsters, not surprisingly, occupy the center of the town's culinary life, and two of many places to sample them are **Fisherman's Landing** at 35 West Street on the West Street Pier, and the **Island Chowder House** at 38 Cottage Street. There are dozens of good restaurants and pub-like places crammed together around Bar Harbor's few short blocks, so wander around and take your pick. Many of these are aimed directly at the tremendous tourist trade, like the amiable **Freddie's Route 66 Restaurant**, 21 Cottage Street, a pseudo-1950s diner that's absolutely packed with high-quality nostalgic memorabilia—juke boxes, gas pumps, neon signs, soap box racers, and a whizzing Lionel train. It's got nothing to do with "Down East Maine," or Route 66 for that matter, but it's fun and the food (everything from Turkey Dinners to veggie lasagnas) is plenty good.

If you are visiting during the summer high season, reserve your lodging well in advance; despite the dozens of motels and B&Bs here, the town is often booked solid. Rates vary widely depending on the season; lodgings in July and August may cost almost twice as much as in winter. The nicest and most central place to stay has to be the **Bar Harbor Inn** (207/288-3351), right on the downtown waterfront; more reasonable accommodations can be found at the **Aurora Motel** (207/288-3771) on Mount Desert Street (Route 3) a quarter-mile northwest of town.

Acadia National Park

Mount Desert Island's natural glories have been preserved by the establishment of Acadia National Park, occupying 41,634 acres of the island's most scenic areas. In the summer, thousands flock to the park's hiking trails, which wind among the beautiful inland lakes and mountains. The 20-mile-long **Park Loop Road** (large campers and trailers prohibited) circles the park, passing Sand Beach, one of the few sandy beaches in Maine (but with *very* chilly water), and the Thunder Hole tidal cavern, just south of Sand Beach.

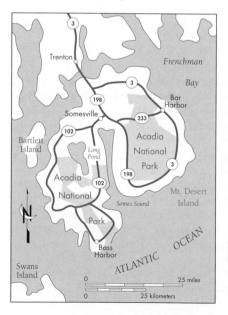

The Park Loop also gives access to the road up Cadillac Mountain—for a clear-day panorama over what seems like the entire coast of Down East Maine or to get a feel for how the Rockefellers and their friends saw Mount Desert and Acadia, take the time to ride a bike (or horse, or horse-drawn carriage) along the network of car-free carriage roads that wind through the park.

Three miles north of Bar Harbor, along Route 3 on the edge of Hulls Cove, you'll pass the main **Acadia National Park Visitors Center** (daily 8 AM-4:30 PM April-Oct., till 6 PM July-Aug.; 207/288-3338), the best place to start a tour.

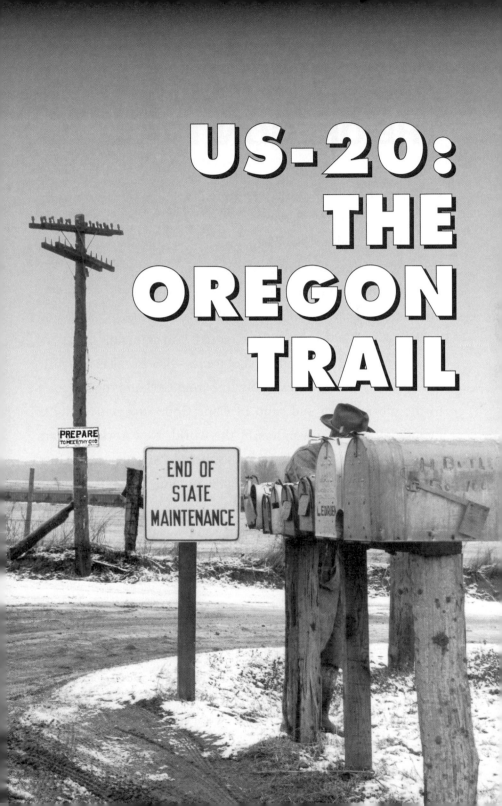

US-20:
THE OREGON TRAIL

From the wide-open spaces of the West to the dense urban jungles of the East, this route offers the longest and most involved road trip in the book. Connecting an exceedingly diverse range of places and totaling over 3,200 miles—many more if you count all the potential detours, side trips, and parallel routes—US-20 takes in a little of everything during its two-lane trek from Oregon's rugged coast to the glorious sea and sand of Cape Cod. Superlative sights include at least two wonders of the world, New York's Niagara Falls and Wyoming's Yellowstone National Park; the great cities of Boston and Chicago; and two halls of fame, one in Cleveland celebrating rock 'n' roll, the other in Cooperstown idolizing the national pastime, baseball. Odd museums, classic diners, idyllic towns, and post-industrial decay—you'll find it all along this great cross-country highway.

This route also offers unprecedented opportunities for following in the footsteps of pilgrims and pioneers. Starting in the West, the route parallels, and in places runs right on top of, the broad path that formed the Oregon Trail. The landscape across Oregon, Idaho, and Wyoming, along US-20 and parallel to US-26, is still as lonesome as it was 150 years ago when pioneer families followed this one-way route west to the promised lands of the Pacific coast. Midway across the country you can visit two notable monuments, Mount Rushmore and Carhenge; you also can test the wisdom of Walt Whitman, who wrote, "While I know the standard claim is that Yosemite, Niagara Falls, the upper Yellowstone and the like afford the greatest natural shows, I am not so sure but the Prairies and Plains last longer, fill the aesthetic sense fuller, precede all the rest and make North America's characteristic landscape."

Drive across the Sand Hills of northern Nebraska on your way past Iowa's "Field of Dreams," and see for yourself what's so great about the Great Plains.

Crossing the Mississippi River at Dubuque, which along with Galena on the Illinois side are two of the oldest settlements on what was once the nation's western frontier, US-20 stops off for a look at Chicago before winding east through the newly resurgent, former "Rust Belt" along the Great Lakes. Though scythed by freeways and malled very nearly to death, this densely populated region also holds some perfectly preserved historic sites, including Amish farmlands, the automobile plants responsible for the country's classiest cars, even the sleepy little town that inspired Sherwood Anderson's great book, *Winesburg, Ohio*.

In the East, there is so much to see that we've split the route into two alternates, both of which bypass the freeways and tourist traps in favor of more fascinating places, many you may never have heard about. The more traveled route follows US-20 along a historical middle ground between the slow boats of the Erie Canal and the high-speed toll road of the I-90/New York Thruway, winding along the north edge of the lovely Finger Lakes and detouring to the intriguing smaller cities of upstate New York before crossing the Hudson River into the Berkshires of western Massachusetts. The historic Mohawk Trail carries us past Lexington and Concord and into Boston, retracing Paul Revere's historic ride—in reverse.

A southerly alternative is provided by little-known US-6, which twists across Allegheny hill country. Here "Pennsylvania Crude" oil was first discovered and coal mines fed the iron furnaces of Scranton. Here, too, Stephen Foster wrote folk songs, Zane Grey wrote his Wild West tales of the Riders of the Purple Sage, and Jack Kerouac first set off *On the Road*. Slipping around the backside of New York City's upper-crust suburbs, US-6 curves east across Connecticut and Rhode Island, among the picturesque villages and Industrial Revolution-era relics you just can't see from I-95, before winding up at the lively Cape Cod resort of Provincetown—the place where the Pilgrims *really* arrived in America, way back in 1620—weeks before setting foot on Plymouth Rock.

ACROSS OREGON

Starting at one of the state's most enjoyable small towns, the arts-and-craftsy Pacific Ocean resort community of Cannon Beach, this route traverses the heart of Oregon. From the salty cow pastures along the Pacific Ocean, over the evergreen mantle of the Coast Range to culturally vibrant Portland and the lush Willamette Valley, the route starts where history says we should end up—amid the bountiful land at the west end of the Oregon Trail. From Portland, the state's largest city, you'll climb into the Cascade Mountains, through the amazing Columbia Gorge alongside its signature peak, Mount Hood. East of the Cascades the route drops down into the suddenly dry and desert-like landscape of the otherworldly Columbia Plateau, across which the highway rolls and rocks for 300 miles through old mining camps, fossil beds, and wide open rolling ranch lands before crossing the Snake River into Idaho.

*Cannon Beach marks the farthest point reached by the **Lewis and Clark** expedition to the West Coast. From here, they retreated back to their outpost at Fort Clatsop, near the mouth of the Columbia River, where they spent the winter of 1805-06.*

Scenic US-101's winding route along the Oregon coast is covered more fully on the Coastal West Coast route; for more, see page 26.

Cannon Beach

Unlike most Oregon coast towns, Cannon Beach (pop. 1,221) is hidden from the highway, but it's one place you won't want to miss. Though it has long been known as an artist's colony, and has grown considerably in recent years thanks to its popularity as a weekend escape from Portland, Cannon Beach retains a rustic quality, a walkably small size, and a coastline that rates second to no other in the state.

For further information on Cannon Beach and the Oregon coast, see pages 39-52.

Klootchy Creek and Saddle Mountain State Park

Climbing the edge of the coastal plain, our first stop is the old-growth spruce and fir forest preserved in Klootchy Creek Park, two miles east of US-101. Among the many huge firs and spruce trees is the "World's Largest Sitka Spruce." More than 215 feet high, almost 16 feet in diameter, and thought to be over 700 years old, the tree is pointed out by a sign along the north side of the highway.

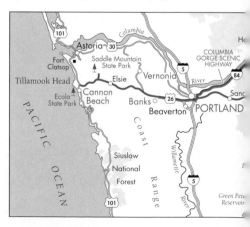

About 10 miles east of US-101, an eight-mile sidetrip to the northeast, along well-signed (but unpaved) Saddle Mountain Road, will lift you quickly above the frequent coastal clouds and fog. Named for a geographical saddle that sits high above the surrounding forests, Saddle Mountain State Park (800/551-6949) has a very steep 2.5-mile hiking trail to the summit, with opportunities to view bleeding heart, Indian paintbrush, monkey flowers, and other rare plants and wildflowers. From the 3,283-foot top of the trail, you can often see the mouth of the Columbia River and the spine of the Coast Range; on a clear day, the panorama may include 50 miles of Pacific coastline and Mounts Hood, St. Helens, and Rainier (with more than a few ugly acres of clear cuts in between). Primitive campsites are open mid-April to October; RVs and other wide bodies should avoid this narrow road.

North of Cannon Beach and Ecola State Park, at the junction where US-26 cuts inland from US-101, the **Crab Broiler** roadside diner (503/738-5313) serves crab and cheese dishes.

Running over the coastal mountains between Cannon Beach and Portland, US-26 is known as the **Sunset Highway.**

Camp 18

Continuing east on US-26, about 20 miles from the coast and a mile west of the hamlet of Elsie, the remarkable **Camp 18 Restaurant** (Sun.-Thurs. 7 AM-9 PM, Friday and Saturday till 10 PM; 503/755-1818 or 800/874-1810) draws travelers for a variety of reasons. Some people come for the absolutely massive portions of very good food, from the gigantic fresh-baked cinnamon rolls and liter jugs of coffee at breakfast, to the steaks, chicken and seafood served up at lunch and dinner. Others are drawn by the playful, Paul Bunyanesque scale of the place: the front door handle is a hefty old ax, the spacious dining room roof is held up by a single log—85-feet-long and probably 8-feet-thick—and many of the tables are made from foot-thick planks of planed and polished wood.

The whole room is packed with an amazing collection of old logging gear, but best of all is the setting, overlooking a babbling brook, with dozens of birdfeeders attracting flocks of finches and other colorful songbirds. Outside, an extensive museum in the parking lot lets visitors examine more old logging equipment to get a feel for a bygone era of misery whips, 20-foot handsaws, and steam donkeys. (Surprise, surprise: there's also a good gift shop.)

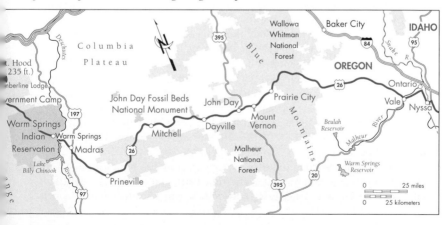

By state law, there is no self-service gasoline in Oregon; all stations have attendants who pump the gas for you. There's no sales tax, either.

Banks-Vernonia Linear State Park

Midway between the coast and Portland, US-26 reaches the 1,635-foot crest of Sunset Summit, then winds east through the verdant delights of the leeward Coast Range, zipping through tunnels and sliding down slopes to the farm country of north-west Willamette Valley. At the western edges of Portland's burgeoning suburbia, one more recreational opportunity is worth a gander: the Banks-Vernonia Linear State Park (503/633-8170), a 21-mile stretch of abandoned railroad that roughly parallels Hwy-47, from the town of Banks, on US-26 20 miles from downtown Portland, to the tucked-away timbertown of Vernonia. Six well-marked trailheads along Hwy-47 provide access to the fairly level gravel trail, Oregon's first rail-to-trail park.

PORTLAND SURVIVAL GUIDE

PORTLAND, OREGON'S LARGEST CITY WITH 450,000 residents (1.5 million in the metro area), is located inland from the coast near the confluence of the Willamette and Columbia Rivers. Due to its strategic location, the pioneer municipality grew so fast it was nicknamed Stumptown for the hundreds of fir stumps left by early loggers, and while railroad tracks and other heavy industrial remnants are still highly visible around town, Portland's riverfront park and numerous winding greenways show that this mini-metropolis is not a smokestack town but a community that values art and nature as highly as commerce. Along with the largest (5,000-acre Forest Park) and the smallest (24-inches in diameter Mill Ends

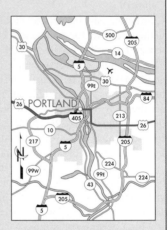

Park) urban parks in the nation, and one of the coolest urban skate parks anywhere (under the Burnside Bridge) Portland also has more movie theaters, restaurants, microbreweries, and bookstores per capita than any other U.S. city.

The oldest part of Portland, along the Willamette River north and south of the Burnside Bridge, has over the past few years been renovated into a lively **Old Town** district. The centerpiece of the neighborhood is the Skidmore Fountain at First and Ankeny Streets, placed there in 1888 to provide refreshment for "horses, men and dogs." The cast-iron facades of surrounding buildings hold some of the city's most popular bars, clubs, and cafes, and intriguing pop culture hotspots like the **American Advertising Museum** at 2nd Avenue and Ash Street, inside the New Market Theater, and the see-it-to-believe-it **24-hour Church of Elvis,** 750 S.W. Ankeny Street.

South of Burnside along the river, an ugly freeway has been torn down to form the mile-long Tom McCall Waterfront Park, and a free light rail train takes you the half-mile southwest to downtown, which centers upon Pioneer

Across Portland

Coming in from the west on the Sunset Highway (US-26), our route enters Portland next to sylvan Washington Park, then crosses the downtown area along Jefferson and Columbia Streets. Crossing the Willamette River, US-26 follows Powell Boulevard across East Portland.

South of US-26 on the western fringes of Portland, the mega-suburb of **Beaverton** is base camp for the high-tech companies of Silicon Forest and, most famously, corporate headquarters for Nike, the international sports apparel giant.

The Mount Hood Highway

Starting out along Powell Boulevard east from Portland, US-26 —now dubbed the Mount Hood Highway—follows, albeit in reverse, the final leg of the historic Oregon Trail. Passing first through the comically named photo-stop town of Boring, the road some 20 miles east of Portland reaches Sandy, a boisterous

Courthouse Square at 6th Avenue and Yamhill Street. South of the square, the **South Park Blocks** between Park and Ninth Avenues were set aside as parklands in the original city plan and are now bounded by two of Portland's prime museums: the Oregon Art Museum, 1219 S.W. Park Avenue, which offers both European paintings and Northwest Indian artifacts, and the Oregon Historical Center, 1200 S.W. Park Avenue, where exhibits tell the story of the state from ancient epochs to the golden days of the Bill Walton-lead Portland Trailblazers.

One more essentially Portland place is **Powell's Books**, 1005 W. Burnside Street (across from the Blitz-Weinhard Brewery); reportedly the largest (and certainly among the best) new-and-used bookshop in the world. The **Portland Rockies** (503/223-2837) play at circa 1926 Civic Stadium, downtown off Burnside at 1844 S.W. Morrison, one of the largest and oldest ballparks in the minor leagues. Another grand old place, **Oaks Park** (503/233-577), is a wonderful circa 1905 amusement park, with ancient and modern thrill rides all packed together in a sylvan, oak-tree dotted park, eight miles south of town.

Practicalities

Air travelers can land at **Portland International Airport** (PDX), but most long-distance flights here come and go via Seattle's Sea-Tac, which is only about two hour's drive to the north, via the I-5 freeway. Getting around public-spirited Portland is a breeze thanks to the combination of an efficient bus system and a light rail train (called MAX), which focus on the downtown area around Pioneer Courthouse Square; for further information, call 503/238-RIDE or 503/238-7433.

There are all sorts of places to stay in Portland, starting with a pair of popular $15 a night **youth hostels**, one east of downtown at 3031 Hawthorne Boulevard (503/236-3380) and a new one in the Northwest District, 1818 N.W. Glisan (503/241-2783). The comfortable, close-to-downtown, and moderately priced **Mallory Motor Hotel**, 729 S.W. 15th Avenue (doubles $75 a night; 503/223-6311 or 800/228-8657), offers moderately priced rooms and

(continues on next page)

Every summer, fans flock to historic 1920s-era Civic Stadium to watch Class A baseball played by the **Portland Rockies** (503/223-2837). Games are broadcast on KKSN 910 AM.

gateway to the mountains. Nestled in berry-farm country, Sandy is full of ski shops, pizza parlors, and other enterprises geared for outdoor enthusiasts, who fuel up at places like the **Kaffee Klatch**, a converted gas station serving decent java at 38871 Proctor Boulevard, or the **Elusive Trout** at 39333 Proctor Boulevard, a pub/restaurant serving gourmet hamburgers and homemade soup. After Sandy's lively commerce, the road ambles through pastureland and into the foothills of the Cascades.

East of Sandy, oddly named towns along US-26 hold good places to eat and drink before or after a day out in the mountains. The **Inn Between** (503/622-5400) in **Wemme**, one of the little wide spots clustered at the base of Mount Hood, has affordable eats varying from teriyaki chicken to macho nachos. Wemme merges into

---

free parking, and there are some nice B&Bs, too, like the **Clinkerbrick House**, 2311 N.E. Schuyler Street (503/281-2533), a turn-of-the-century house in residential East Portland, offering rooms for around $95 a night.

If you feel like splurging after a few too many anonymous boxes on the road, try the impeccably restored downtown landmark, the **Heathman Hotel** at 1009 S.W. Broadway (503/241-4100 or 800/551-0011), the poshest of Portland's posh, with an elegant lobby and sumptuously appointed rooms. Doubles will set you back around $200, though weekend discount rates may be available.

Though it doesn't have a trendy reputation, Portland does have some great restaurants in all stripes and sizes. **Esparza's Tex-Mex**, 2725 S.E. Ankeny Street (503234-7909), is hidden away behind a hole-in-the-wall facade a block south of E. Burnside Street; it's worth searching out for its cornmeal pancakes with chicken and cactus sauce, smoked pork tacos, and other truly authentic Tex-Mex dishes. To complete the sensory overload, the jukebox features Tejano, *norteño*, and Marty Robbins hits. For a more traditional Portland fare, head to **Jake's Famous Crawfish**, 401 S.W. 12th Street, which for over a century has been the place to go for the finest, freshest seafood. Warm woodsy decor, a marvelous wine list and great desserts—not to mention prices that are lower than they could be—make this a real standout. And for meat, nothing beats the **Ringside**, near Civic Stadium at 2165 W. Burnside Street, long famous for its great beef, fine fried chicken, monster Walla Walla Sweet onion rings, and Hemingwayesque ambience—hunting trophies and boxing photos adorn the walls, and many diners choose to eat in the glaring red bar. If your taste happens to run more to Marilyn Manson than to Marilyn Monroe, you'll probably prefer to eat across town at **Dots Cafe**, 2521 S.E. Clinton Street, a late-night hangout that has comfy dark booths, great black bean burritos, microbrewed beers, and pool tables.

The best source of visitor information on Portland is the **Portland Visitors Association**, 25 S.W. Salmon Street (503/222-2223 or 800/962-3700). The daily newspaper is *The Oregonian*, and the free *Willamette Week* has the best take on entertainment and local issues.

another "W" town—**Welches Junction,** where the **Chalet Swiss** (503/622-3600) is famous for both Northwest seafood and continental cuisine by chef Kurt Mezger.

The other suggested stop is the **Mount Hood Visitor Center** (daily 8 AM-4:30 PM; 503/622-4822), in Welches at 65000 E. US-26, operated by the U.S. Forest Service and loaded with maps, brochures, and other information on the mountain and surrounding recreational hotspots.

East of the Mount Hood hamlet of **Zigzag,** US-26 drops to an old-fashioned, undivided two-lane road. Summer-only **Lolo Pass Loop** (Hwy-18) cuts off north from here on a scenic half-circle around the base of Mount Hood to Hood River, on the Columbia River and I-84.

Government Camp

Just off US-26 at the southern foot of Mount Hood, Government Camp is but another wide spot in the road with a range of food and drink options. For espresso, microbrews, sandwiches, pizzas, and pastas, stop at the **Mount Hood Brewing Company** (503/272-3724), at the west end of town. Another good stop is the **Huckleberry Inn** (503/272-3325), open 24 hours a day, seven days a week, and famous for its wild huckleberry pies, huckleberry pancakes, and huckleberry shakes. If you're unable to move after a berry feast, the inn also offers low-priced rooms, and dorm beds from $15 a night per person.

Government Camp's main attraction is the **Mount Hood Ski Bowl** (503/222-2695), a year-round recreation center with skiing and snowboarding in winter and mountain biking in summer, plus guided horseback trips, go-carts, paintball games, and a 100-foot bungee jump.

Timberline Lodge

East of Government Camp, near the junction of US-26 and Hwy-35, which comes from Hood River and the Columbia Gorge, be sure to turnoff north toward Mount Hood to visit **Timberline Lodge** (503/231-5400 or 800/547-1406), an elegantly rustic national landmark built in 1937 by the Depression-era artisans of the Works Progress Administration. The actual hotel seen (from the outside, not the inside) in Stanley Kubrick's creepy 1983 film, *The Shining,* Timberline Lodge is an unforgettable place, with a humongous fireplace in the three-story main lobby, grand dining rooms, cozy guest rooms decorated in characterful Pacific Northwest motifs, not to mention an unbeatable setting high atop the Cascade Mountains. Rooms run $70-170 a night, but even if you don't stay, check out the Cascade Dining Room's award-winning cuisine, the more casual pizza and sandwiches at the Blue Ox, and the Ram's Head Bar, which has locally brewed beers and ales.

Detour: Columbia Gorge

Though our route across Oregon generally follows scenic US-26, the fastest route east from Portland is I-84, which races along the Columbia River, rejoining US-26 at the Idaho border. Freeway the whole way, I-84 is worth considering for its one incredible feature: the Columbia Gorge, the deep, verdant basalt canyon

Columbia Gorge

through which the mighty river, the freeway, not to mention a busy railroad, all run. The heart of the Columbia Gorge is between the small towns of Sandy and Cascade Locks, some 15 and 35 miles east of Portland respectively, and is best experienced by driving the historic Columbia Gorge Scenic Highway—the oldest scenic route in the country, built beginning in 1913, and still retaining all its old road character.

The highlight (and approximate midpoint) of this historic highway is the aptly named **Vista House**, built in 1917 to mark the completion of the road, which here rises over 700 feet above the Columbia River. East of Vista House, a series of tremendous waterfalls drop down along the road: first comes **LaTourell Falls**, then the 242-foot cascades of **Wahkeenah Falls**, then, saving the best for last, famous **Multnomah Falls**, which drops 620 feet into a densely forested canyon, bridged by a delicate

Enticing though it is, snowcapped **Mount Hood** is also a difficult and dangerous peak to climb—there is no trail to the 11,239-foot summit, and all routes require a high degree of technical ability and specialized equipment. There are lots of fine hikes around its base, however, and the year-round white stuff on Palmer Snowfield makes it the only ski and snowboard area (503/272-2311) in the lower 48 states that's open in summer.

END OF THE OREGON TRAIL

After long months of hardship and danger, pioneers nearing the end of the Oregon Trail had two choices when they reached the narrow gorge of the Columbia River: they could float their wagons down the perilous river to Fort Vancouver, or climb over the Cascades to the Willamette Valley via the Barlow Road, a route that parallels today's US-26. While much safer than the river route, the Barlow Road had its own precarious moments—emigrants struggled down muddy declines, hanging onto ropes hitched around trees to keep wagons from runaway destruction. Such moments assuredly gave the pioneers second thoughts about their choice of passage. At $5 per wagon and 10 cents a head for cattle, horses, and mules, following the privately owned Barlow Road was also expensive. Nonetheless, in 1845, the first year of operation, records report that 1,000 pioneers in 145 wagons traveled the route.

Heading east, you're going backwards along the Barlow Road, so bear that in mind as you take a few historical sites that record the struggles of pioneers on the last stretch of their 2,000-mile overland journey. The steepest section of the road was the **Laurel Hill "Chute,"** where wagons skidded down a treacherous grade; a sign and pull-out five miles east of Rhododendron mark the start of a short, steep hike up to the chute. Just west of Laurel Hill, at Tollgate Campground, you'll find a reproduction of the **Barlow Road Tollgate**, where the road's owner, Sam Barlow, stood with his hand out.

Look for other markers depicting Barlow Road history on Hwy-35, the loop road that traverses the eastern slope of Mount Hood down to Hood River. The first, **Pioneer Woman's Grave**, is a quarter-mile north of the junction with US-26; a sign marks a right turn onto Forest Road 3530, and points toward a grave site with a brass plaque commemorating the women who traveled the Oregon Trail. Two miles north of the junction is 4,161-foot **Barlow Pass**, where ruts grooved in the Barlow Road lead downhill from a parking area, mute testament to the perseverance of westward-driven settlers.

concrete arch. Each of these waterfalls is within a short walk from parking areas along the scenic highway, and many smaller falls can be seen cascading from canyon walls.

The Columbia Gorge Scenic Highway rejoins I-84 a few miles east of Multnomah Falls, at the town of Cascade Locks. Another 20 miles east, at the east end of the Columbia Gorge, the lively town of Hood River has everything the outdoorsy traveler could want: the historic Columbia Gorge Hotel (503/386-5566) preserves its Jazz Age elegance, while the rest of the town is packed with brew-pubs, espresso bars, bookshops, and good restaurants.

From Hood River, the very scenic (and very steep!) Hwy-35 climbs up along the historic Barlow Road, the next-to-last leg of the Oregon Trail, linking up with US-26 near Timberline Lodge. See above for more.

Warm Springs Indian Reservation

East of the Cascades crest, US-26 becomes the Warm Springs Highway as it angles down out of the mountains across the sage and juniper country of eastern Oregon. Most of the land between here and Madras is part of the 600,000-acre Warm Springs Reservation, home to the Confederated Tribes of Warm Springs (Wasco, Paiute, and Warm Springs).

From US-26, follow signs to **Kah-Nee-Tah** (pronounced ca-NEE-da, all run together despite the odd spelling), a resort complex that cheerfully blends modern and ancient lifestyles. You can soak in the famously soothing hot springs, camp in a teepee, play golf along the banks of the Warm Springs River, and savor salmon fillet cooked over an alderwood fire. Lodging rates at Kah-Nee-Tah, which also includes the large "Indian Head" casino, vary tremendously, but are in the $100-a-night range. For further information, phone 541/553-1112, 800/554-4SUN or 800/554-4786.

Back on US-26, the real attraction of the reservation is the modern, 27,000-square foot **Museum at Warm Springs** (daily 10 AM-5 PM; $6; 541/553-3331). Check out exhibits of more than 20,000 artifacts, replicas of a Paiute mat lodge and a Wasco plank house, recordings of tribal languages, and a pushbutton-activated Wasco wedding scene. Across the highway, a stylized mini-mall holds a gift shop and the very good **Indian Trail Restaurant**.

A mile east, at the edge of the reservation where US-26 bridges the deep canyon of the Deschutes River, the **Deschutes Crossing Cafe** offers good food including Indian fry bread, best followed by a slice of fresh huckleberry pie.

Madras

After crossing the Deschutes River from the Warm Springs reservation, US-26 climbs up a deep canyon then plateaus at Madras, birthplace of the late actor River Phoenix. Contrary to what you might expect from its East Indian name, few in this hardworking town wear plaid, and the beatific followers of a certain Indian guru are red-clad memories: it's been nearly 20 years since Bhagwan Shree Rajneesh and

The Columbia Gorge Scenic Highway was built by millionaire lawyer Sam Hill, who built the road to link Portland with the pacifist agricultural colony he planned at his 7,000-acre estate at Maryhill, Washington. **Maryhill** is now a fascinatingly eclectic museum (509/773-3733), near the I-84/US-97 junction; three miles east of Maryhill, Hill also constructed a concrete replica of **Stonehenge,** in memory of local men killed in WW I.

The Columbia Gorge west of Hood River is one of the world's best windsurfing spots, and throughout the summer dozens of brightly colored sails can be seen racing along the river.

Around the Warm Springs Reservation, tune to **KWSO 91.9 FM** for an intriguing array of music (from The Eagles to talking drums) and National Native News.

One of eastern Oregon's landmarks, and a celebrated challenge to rock-climbers, **Smith Rock State Park** stands 17 miles south of Madras along US-97.

In every U.S. presidential election since Oregon became a state (in 1859), the people of **Crook County** around Prineville voted for the winner; until, that is, they voted for George Bush in 1992, putting an end to their reputation as the national bellwether.

his disciples lived on their 175,000-acre commune, 30 miles to the northeast at the village of Antelope.

There's not a lot to see or do in Madras, which stands at the junction of US-26 and busy US-97, but there are stores and gas stations and at least one good place to stay: **Sonny's Motel**, 1539 S.W. US-26/97 (541/475-7217), which has clean rooms and a pool for around $50 a night, plus an adjacent restaurant famed for its steaks.

Prineville

From Madras, US-26 veers farther away from the Cascades, crossing the Crooked River National Grasslands, which mark the geographical center of Oregon. Strolling the streets of Prineville (pop. 6,295), a town with a vivid heritage of cattle and sheep ranching, you'll notice plenty of cowboy hats (or "gimme" caps, emblazoned with the logos of the wearer's favorite fertilizer or tractor company) atop the heads of dusty citizens piloting dusty pickup trucks. It's been a ripsnorter of a town since Barny Prine built his blacksmith and saloon here in 1868 following the discovery of gold in nearby hills. People of Prineville these days are ranchers, loggers, miners, and employees of the Les Schwab tire company, which has its HQ here, though tourism is slowly but surely taking its place as an economic force.

You can learn more about the region's history at the **A.R. Bowman Museum**, two blocks north of the landmark Crook County Courthouse at 246 N. Main Street (Mon.-Fri. 10 AM-5 PM, Saturday noon-5 PM; 541/447-3715).

Towns in eastern Oregon have taken to decorating their buildings with large and colorful murals, usually with historical or outdoorsy themes.

Two floors of exhibits include a campfire setup, a moonshine still, and a country store with a pound of Bull Durham tobacco. If you hanker after a sit-down meal, check out the **Ochoco Inn and Cinnabar Restaurant**, 123 E. 3rd Street, known for its generous and eclectic menu; **Barr's Cafe**, 887 N. Main Street, serves coffee-shop food 24 hours a day. Lodging choices include the **City Center Motel**, 509 E. 3rd Street (541/447-5522), in the middle of the city in the middle of the state, and eminently affordable.

The drive along US-26 east of Prineville takes you up into the Ochocos, a low-slung gem of a mountain range once the heartland of the Paiutes. Seven miles from Prineville, US-26 skirts **Ochoco Lake**, a popular recreational reservoir with fishing, boating, hiking, camping, and a picnic bench or two for travelers—but not a lot of shade. The rest of the Ochoco Range, which reaches heights of nearly 7,000 feet, holds acres and acres of lovely meadows, clear streams, pristine pine forests, and views of the jagged Cascade Range, rising on the western horizon.

Mitchell

The only concentration of human habitation near the John Day Fossil Beds National Monument is Mitchell, a semi-ghost town 50 miles east of Prineville and two miles east of the turnoff for the Painted Hills section of the fossil beds. The main "town" of Mitchell lines up along the short stretch of old road signed as the "Business Loop," just south of US-26, where the old-fashioned general store **Wheeler County Mercantile** captures the flavor of the 1870s. If you need sustenance more than gossip over the cracker barrel, stop by the **Sidewalk Cafe** on the main drag, or

the **Blueberry Muffin Restaurant**, back on the main highway.
Mitchell also holds one of the more atmospheric old places to
stay in this part of eastern Oregon, the **Oregon Hotel**, 104 Main
Street (541/462-3027), with a comfy front porch, a resident
border collie for company, and B&B rooms starting around $30
a night.

ammonite fossil

John Day Fossil Beds National Monument

East of the Ochocos, midway across Oregon, the John Day Fossil Beds National Monument documents many millions of years
of prehistoric life, from thundering dinosaurs to delicate plants.
Discovered in the 1860s by a frontier preacher and amateur geologist named Thomas Condon, the beds contain one of the
world's richest and most diverse concentrations of mammalian and dinosaur fossils. Offering a complete and easily accessible record of life on earth, spanning
some 50 million years, the monument is made up of three distinct units, totaling
some 14,000 acres.

The eerie, empty moonscape can be easily toured from US-26. Start in the west
with the **Painted Hills Unit**, just west of Mitchell, then six miles north of US-26,
where trails and overlooks offer views of striated hills and bluffs formed by fallen
ash and brilliantly colored in bands of red, pink, black, and bronze. A life-sized
Georgia O'Keeffe landscape, Painted Hills is a popular spot with photographers and
painters, especially the short Painted Cove trail, which winds through the most
intensely colored section.

About 30 miles east of Mitchell, six miles west of Dayville
along US-26, then three miles north on Hwy-19, the **Sheep
Rock Unit** is the best place to see fossils in their natural state;
the monument headquarters and a small museum are also here,
housed inside the **Cant Ranch Visitor Center** (541/987-2333).
East of the turnoff to the Sheep Rock fossil beds, US-26 runs
right along the John Day River through the 500-foot-deep
basalt canyon of Picture Gorge, so named because of the abundance of Native American pictographs.

There's also a more distant
section of the fossil beds at
the Clarno Unit, along the
John Day River some 50
miles northwest of Painted
Hills, between the towns of
Antelope and Fossil. This
area includes the most
ancient rocks—ranging from
37 to 54 million years old.

Dayville and Mount Vernon

After gazing at striped hillsides and fossilized remains, regain
some perspective by strolling through any of the towns that line
the John Day River along this part of US-26—Dayville, Mount
Vernon, John Day, Canyon City, or Prairie City. Founded as
miners' camps after gold was discovered here in 1862, many
now cater mostly to local ranchers—but offer a warm welcome
to the few visitors who brave a trip through this uninviting but
unforgettable part of the world.

The namesake of the fossil
beds, **John Day** was a fur
trapper hunting along the
Columbia River in 1810
when he was attacked by
Indians. He turned up two
years later at Astoria on the
coast, but never again went
anywhere near the river, the
town, or the region that now
bear his name.

Starting in the west, the **Dayville Diggins** in Dayville will take care of your dust-
choked palate; Dayville (pop. 185) also has a great roadside "antiques" store, and
what has to be among the world's smallest city halls—a one-room shack at the east
edge of town. The **Fish House**, 110 Franklin (541/987-2124), a 1908 bungalow
turned antique-bedecked B&B, will cater to both your appetite and road-weariness,

for a bargain $40-65 per night. Farther east, at the junction of US-26 and US-395, Mount Vernon is home to **The Wounded Buffalo**, a local landmark known for its Buffalo Bill Burger and juicy rib-eye steaks.

John Day

The town of John Day (pop. 1,836), the metropolis in this chain of gold towns, holds the area's one not-to-be-missed attraction: **Kam Wah Chung Museum**, 250 N.W. Canton (May 1 to Oct. 31 only, Mon.-Thurs. 9 AM-noon and 1-5 PM, Saturday and Sunday 1-5 PM; $2), run by the city and located in a nice park just north of US-26 at the center of John Day. Built as a trading post in 1866-67, in the late 1880s it became a general store and medical center for the Chinese workers who toiled in the mines, and for 60 years it continued to be the center of the almost exclusively male Chinese community of eastern Oregon, which at times made up a majority of the regional population. Most of the building is preserved intact, displaying a fascinating collection of items ranging from herbal remedies and ornate red Taoist shrines to gambling paraphernalia and ancient canned goods. There's also a bedroom, with bunks and a wood stove left as they were by the last residents, Ing Hay and Lung On, the herbalist and storekeeper who lived and worked here until the 1940s.

John Day's one and only radio station, **KJDY 1400 AM**, broadcasts country-tinged Top 40 music and local news across eastern Oregon. For truly twangy C&W—à la Waylon, Hank and Merle—tune to **KFXD 580 AM**.

Right next to the museum is the John Day **swimming pool** ($2.50); for more on the area's fascinating history, take a two-minute side trip south along US-395 to Canyon City, where the **Grant County Historical Museum** (Mon.-Sat. 9 AM-4:30 PM, Sunday 1-5 PM in summer only) stands at the center of this evocative, unrestored old mining town.

Back in John Day, the **Grubsteak Mining Company**, 149 E. Main Street (541/575-1970), has a sumptuous menu of rib eyes and other beef entrees. **The Dreamers Lodge Motel**, 144 N. Canyon Boulevard (541/575-0526), and a **Best Western**, 315 W. Main Street (541/575-1700), both have reasonable rates. Last but not least, you may want to avail yourself of the honestly named **Weary Traveler Laundromat**, 755 S. Canyon Boulevard (US-395).

Prairie City

Back on US-26, the first town east of John Day is tidy little Prairie City (pop. 1,120), an old-fashioned ranching community that is fast becoming a western false-front photo-opportunity. A surprisingly hip hangout here is **Ferdinand's**, right on US-26 at 128 Front Street (Wed.-Sat. 5-9 PM; 541/820-9359). Once a butcher shop established in 1902, this restaurant/saloon has an impressive menu and a bounty of antiques. The most memorable are a pair of beauties called "The Twin Virgins" surmounting a long bar that is an architectural marvel itself. The two sculptures were carved in Milan in 1879 and shipped around Cape Horn, up the Columbia by sternwheeler, and into the mining country via wagon. There are also a pair of pleasant B&Bs, perfect for a weekend getaway or a taste of local life: the 100-year-old **Riverside Schoolhouse** (541/820-4731), located on a working cattle ranch, and the **Strawberry Mountain Inn**, in the foothills south of town.

Leaving the John Day River watershed, US-26 heads east, climbing over mile-high Dixie Pass (which is exactly one mile high—5,280 feet above sea level) while rambling through the Malheur and Wallowa-Whitman National Forests, where campgrounds, cool mountain lakes, natural hot springs and dense forests abound. There's a **ranger station** in John Day (541/575-3000), which can provide maps and current information.

East of the crest, dropping down from the mountains across the Snake River plain, US-26 crosses another 75 miles of rolling sagebrush, with little more than an occasional cattle ranch, or a golden eagle sitting atop a telephone pole, to attract your attention. Tiny little tavern-and-post-office towns like Unity, Ironside, Brogan, and Willow Creek will make you slow to 45mph (or risk a ticket), while on a hot summer's day the smell of juniper and sage is so potent it perfumes the dry desert air, unmistakable even if you cruise through at 70 mph with the a/c blasting away.

Halfway between Prairie City and Vale is the dividing line between Pacific and mountain time zones. Adjust clocks accordingly as you head over Eldorado Pass.

Vale

The seat of Malheur ("Bad Smell") County, Vale (pop. 1,701), sits on the banks of the Malheur River at the junction of US-20 and US-26. The comparatively easy river crossing and the presence of a natural hot spring made it a prime stopping place on the Oregon Trail. Murals and markers around town explain something of the history, and point out sights like the **Malheur Crossing**, next to the bridge on the eastern edge of the town, where pioneers dunked their aching bods in the still-hot Malheur River springs, and **Keeney Pass**, just south of downtown Vale on Enterprise Avenue, where 150-year-old wagon ruts can still be seen along the roadside.

Taking a breather at Vale is an honored tradition—it was here that pioneers rested before climbing out of the Snake River Valley into the Blue Mountains—but if you're feeling tired and hungry after your own long treks through the dry gulches and sagebrush flats, these days there's not a lot to choose from. One entertaining option is a night at the **Bates Motel**, on US-20 at 1101 A Street W (541/473-3234); it has nothing to do with Hitchcock's *Psycho,* but has been run by the Bates family (no Normans among them) for over 30 years, offering clean showers, a pizza restaurant, and a good night's sleep. Another unusual option is the **1900 Sears & Roebuck Home**, 484 N. 10th Street (541/473-9636), a B&B originally ordered from the Sears catalog back around the turn of the twentieth century.

For more information on Vale and the Oregon Trail, stop by the helpful **visitor center**, 275 N. Main Street (541/473-3800).

Toward Idaho: Ontario & Nyssa

Approaching the Idaho border, you have two choices: to follow I-84, head east via Ontario (pop. 9,392), the largest of many mid-sized farming and ranching communities in the surrounding area; or continue along the more atmospheric older roads. The official Oregon Trail Auto Route, US-20/26, bends to the south along the Snake River, passing one last Oregon town, Nyssa, before crossing into the Land of Famous Potatoes. Nyssa calls itself the "Thunderegg Capital of the World," because

*Oregon's biggest and most developed Oregon Trail historic site is at Flagstaff Hill, off I-84 near Baker City, where a set of well-preserved wagon ruts provide a focus for the extensive **National Historic Oregon Trail Interpretive Center** (daily 9 AM-4 PM, till 6 PM in summer; free; 541/523-1843).*

of the many geodes found there, but it's primarily a shipping point for the tons of spuds, onions, and sugar beets grown nearby—the different crops are even labeled along the highway for your edification. While Nyssa doesn't have a lot else to offer, it does have a very large riverfront sugar beet refinery, and the more enjoyable Sugar Bowl, a bowling alley off US-20/26 on the north edge of town.

ACROSS IDAHO

US-20's route across Southern Idaho cuts through one of the most magnificently empty American spaces, an arid, volcanic region cut by life-giving rivers and isolating mountain ranges, with strange geological outcrops that encourage travelers to stop and explore the inhospitable terrain. Irrigation has altered the look of the land considerably, so much so that vineyards and lush fields now thrive in the otherwise barren gray-green sagebrush plains, but little else has changed since this region provided the greatest challenge to pioneers crossing the country along the Oregon Trail. The provision of visitor services may have improved considerably in the intervening 150 years, but southern Idaho is still a wild and demanding land. Like much of the West, it's also addictively satisfying.

The quickest route across Idaho is the I-84 freeway, though the historic Oregon Trail route, marked by large highway signs, follows a much more scenic route along the Snake River.

Parma and Fort Boise

Just as US-20/26 does today, the historic Oregon Trail crosses between Idaho and Oregon at the confluence of the Boise and Snake Rivers, southwest of I-84 at the town of Parma. Sugar beets and onions fill the fields around the tiny town, which takes pride in its replica of Fort Boise, one of the first European outposts in the Pacific Northwest. Originally established in 1834 by the Hudson's Bay Company, Fort Boise was famous for its frontier hospitality, entertaining and supplying travelers and traders until the mid-1850s, when it was closed because of declines in demand and an increase in Indian hostilities.

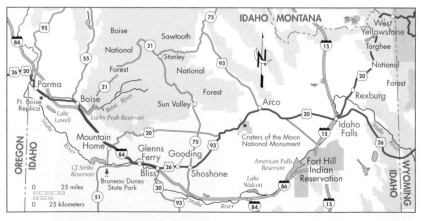

The less than authentic steel-and-stucco reconstruction of the old fort that stands along US-20 near the center of town is the site of the annual "Old Fort Boise Days" in early May.

East of Parma, US-20/26 runs along the north bank of the Boise River for a dozen miles before crossing I-84 at the city of Caldwell—home of the mid-August **Caldwell Night Rodeo**. From here, you can follow the freeway into Boise, but it's more interesting, and depending on traffic, possibly even quicker as well, to stay on US-20/26 (aka Chinden Boulevard), which runs right atop the old Oregon Trail into downtown, past corn and wheat fields that have been rapidly sprouting golf course estates, a Hewlett-Packard factory, car parts stores, and the usual Asphalt Nation sprawl. One fun spot out here is the Western Idaho Fairgrounds, home to year-round events and the Class A baseball games of the **Boise Hawks** (208/322-5000).

The original Fort Boise stood along the banks of the river and was washed away long ago. The site is marked today by an odd, horse-headed stone obelisk festooned with the Hudson Bay Company flag, which stands along the Snake River at the end of Old Fort Boise Road, two miles west of US-20/26.

Boise

Capital of Idaho and perennial contender for the title of "most liveable" city in the U.S., Boise is a very pleasant medium-sized city of over 125,000 people. A lush green oasis in the middle of the barren lava lands of the Snake River plain, Boise was so named by fur-trappers for its dense groves of cottonwood trees ("bois" is French for "wood"), which made the area an especially welcome respite before irrigation turned the brown desert much greener than it naturally would be. The presence of the state government and the 12,000 students at Boise State University lend a degree of sophistication and vitality mixed in with the more usual Idaho trappings—more than anywhere else for miles, roller blades and mountain bikes compete with pickup trucks as the main method of transportation here, and bookshops and espresso bars line the downtown streets.

Downtown Boise focuses on the **state capitol** (Mon.-Fri. 8 AM-6 PM, Saturday 9 AM-5 PM; free), three blocks north of Main Street between 6th and 8th Streets, a typically grand, neoclassical structure, built of local sandstone with a giant eagle atop its landmark dome. The usual exhibits of the state's produce fill display cases, and free guided tours are given upon request.

South of the capitol, restaurants and cafes have reclaimed the blocks of 100-year-old brick buildings around 6th and Main streets, historic center of Boise. In the heart of this lively, pedestrian-friendly neighborhood, a block south of Main at 611 Grove Street, the small but intriguing **Basque Museum** (Tues.-Fri. 10 AM-3 PM, Saturday 11 AM-2 PM; donations), documents the culture of the Basque people who work in Idaho's ranching industries. A block west stands **The Grove**, Boise's convention center and main shopping complex featuring a large fountain through which daredevils like to skate and cycle. Don't miss **Taters**, which sells all manner of Idaho souvenirs, from postcards and fridge magnets to cookbooks describing 100 things you can do with potatoes.

Farther east, where Main Street turns into Warm Springs Road, the **Old Idaho Penitentiary** (daily noon-5 PM daily in summer, noon-4 PM rest of the year; $3; 208/368-6080) served as the main state prison for over 100 years from its construction in 1872. High sandstone walls, cut by prisoners, surround the complex, and the old cell blocks are now filled with displays on prison life—from collections of tattoos to the gallows where many prisoners met their end.

Boise Practicalities

By Idaho standards, Boise has a truly exciting range of restaurants, with many good places around 6th and Main Streets and elsewhere in the compact downtown area. One favorite stop is the **Bar Gernika**, near the Basque Museum on the corner of Grove and Capitol avenues (208/344-2175), which serves up delicious tastes of Basque-inspired food (lamb sandwiches, chorizo *tapas,* and out of this world shoe-string fries), plus wines and beers, in a friendly, unpretentious room—with a sidewalk seating area in summer. And if this doesn't hit the spot, within a few blocks are the excellent **Guido's Pizzeria**, 235 N. 5th Street; the upscale **Grape Escape** wine and *tapas* bar at 800 W. Idaho Street, and maybe a million coffeehouses and juice-and-smoothie bars.

For a huge breakfast, or an out-of-this-world milk shake, stop by **Moon's Cafe**, in the back room of a gift shop that used to be a gun shop at 815 W. Bannock Street. (NB: They close at 3 PM.)

Boise's downtown restaurant district doubles as its nightlife zone as well, so after a meal you can stagger between old fashioned, carved-wood bars like **Pengilly's**, 513 Main Street, and nightclubs like the excellent **Blues Bouquet**, 1010 Main Street, and alt-rock **Neurolux**, around the corner at 111 N. 11th Street.

There are all the usual places to stay along the I-84 freeway, but downtown holds one great place, the wonderful old **Idanha**, 928 Main Street (208/342-3611), built in 1901 and featuring ornate corner turrets, opulent public spaces, and Idaho's oldest elevator. Rooms are good value at about $70 a night, but the public areas are worth a look even if you're just passing through. For a cheap but still restful sleep, head to the **Cabana Inn**, on the west side of downtown at 1600 Main Street (208/343-6000).

For more complete listings or other information, contact the Boise **visitors bureau** (208/344-7777 or 800/635-5240), or stop by its office next to the fountain in The Grove, downtown.

Mountain Home and Bruneau Dunes

Across southern Idaho, the I-84 freeway has effectively replaced the older highways, especially in the area southeast of Boise. The huge Mountain Home Air Force Base, 35 miles southeast of Boise, is the only thing for miles, which is no doubt by design: the base is a testing ground for the latest high-tech weapons systems and aircraft. One of the more contentious side effects of Mountain Home's presence is that the powers-that-be have decreed that much of the surrounding wilderness, including the wild Owyhee Mountains and almost the entire southwest corner of the state, should be closed to the public and turned into a bombing range—so pilots can gain experience firing missiles and dropping live munitions.

the Idanha Hotel

Eighteen miles south of Mountain Home and the I-84 freeway via Hwy-51, **Bruneau Dunes State Park** protects the highest free-standing sand dune in North America—rising over 400 feet above the Snake River plain. Since the temperatures can hit 100° throughout the summer months, mornings or sunsets are the best times to exercise your legs by climbing up and careening back down the white sands.

Although it's on the interstate, the town of Mountain Home has little more than the average, sparse services, including all the usual pizza places plus a few motels. **Best Western Foothills Motor Inn** is off I-84 exit 95 at 1080 US-20 (208/587-8477).

Glenns Ferry

The tiny town of Glenns Ferry, 28 miles southeast of Mountain Home on the Snake River and I-84, would hardly rate a mention were it not the site of one of the most important crossings on the old Oregon Trail. This site, now preserved as **Three Island Crossing State Park**, a mile southwest of town, gives one of the strongest impressions of the tough going for Oregon-bound pioneers. A very good **visitor center** (daily 9 AM-5 PM), with a Conestoga wagon out front, has displays of trail lore and history, and every August enthusiasts get together to reenact the river crossing. Go for a swim to cool off, and feel the powerful currents—more placid here than most anywhere else, which is why it was considered the best place to ford the river. This is also a fine place to camp; the usually clear night sky makes for excellent star-gazing and there's even a very docile herd of buffalo.

Northeast from Boise, Hwy-21 makes a very scenic trip through the Sawtooth Mountains to Stanley, which is described more fully on page 137.

At Mountain Home, US-20 cuts off northeast from I-84, following a branch of the Oregon Trail known as **Goodale's Cut-off** *across the harsh volcanic plains.*

Bliss: Thousand Springs Scenic Byway

Along with the chance to add to your collection of city limits signs, or to send a postcard saying you're in Bliss, this idyllically named town (pop. 186) is worth a stop to see the deep canyon of **Malad Gorge State Park** (daily dawn-dusk; free; 208/837-4505), well-signed southeast of town, off I-84 exit 147. It doesn't look like much until you get out of the car and walk 100 feet down the trail, where you suddenly come upon a truly awesome sight: a 250-foot-deep gorge with a crashing waterfall. The freeway passes overhead, oblivious to the natural wonder directly below.

From Bliss, US-26 cuts due east from the I-84 freeway, running across hard-edged lava beds. Bliss also marks the turnoff onto US-30, which follows the old Oregon Trail along the south bank of the Snake River through the lovely, waterfall-rich region known as **Thousand Springs**, rejoining I-84 at Twin Falls.

US-26: Gooding and Shoshone

In the midst of inhospitable volcanic badlands, a pair of small towns that grew up along the railroad tracks have somehow survived intact to the present day. Coming from the west along US-26 from Bliss, the first one you reach is Gooding (pop. 2,820), named for local sheep rancher Frank Gooding, who went from being mayor to Idaho governor to ending his days in 1928 as U.S. Senator. The best thing about Gooding is the surprising presence of a very pleasant **HI Hostel**, in the historic Gooding Hotel at 112 Main Street (208/934-4374), which has $10/person dorm beds and B&B rooms for $40.

A straight shot east along the tracks brings you to Shoshone (pop. 1,249), another ranching and railroad center—with Amtrak service! Some of its buildings have been constructed from

Across the Snake River from Malad Gorge, **Hagerman Fossil Beds National Monument** *contains what's been called "the richest known deposit of Pliocene Age terrestrial fossils," mainly horses (Equus simplicidens) that roamed the area some three million years ago. The undeveloped monument also preserves one of the longest sections of visible wagon ruts in the entire length of the Oregon Trail. The visitor center is across the river in Hagerman (208/837-4793).*

THE OREGON TRAIL

In 1993, the 150th anniversary of the opening of the Oregon Trail renewed interest in this best known of emigrant trails across the Wild West. History buffs got together for summer-long reenactments of the arduous crossing, building authentic wagons and eating, dressing, and sleeping as the pioneers did—with the inestimable comfort of knowing that they, unlike their predecessors, could easily return home at any point.

From 1843 until the 1860s, some 400,000 men, women, and children followed this 2,000-mile trail, averaging four months to make the cross-country journey. Long followed by fur trappers and traders, and first charted by a series of U.S. Army expeditions led by Kit Carson and John C. Fremont in the early 1840s, the Oregon Trail followed the path of least resistance across the western half of the continent. Beginning at various points along the Missouri River, the trail followed the valley of the Platte River across the Great Plains, crossed the Rockies at Wyoming's gentle South Pass, then set off across the desert of southern Idaho. The most difficult parts were saved for the end, when emigrants had a choice of floating downstream on the turbulent Columbia River or struggling over the rugged Cascades to reach the Willamette Valley. Nearly half of the travelers who set off along the Oregon Trail from Missouri actually had other destinations in mind: more than 100,000 turned off south toward the California gold mines, and some 30,000 Mormons followed the route west to their new colony at Salt Lake City.

The Oregon Trail had many variants and shortcuts and was never a sharply defined track, but clear traces survive in a number of places along the route. Many evocative sites survive, often as reconstructions of pioneer forts, trading posts, and river crossings. There are also many fine museums along the way, not to mention the many good books on the subject, the best of which we've included in Road Trip Resources on page 852.

THE OREGON TRAIL

Many Oregon Trail sites are covered in more detail under our Road Trip routes. As shown on the map, some of the most interesting Oregon Trail sites are:

Oregon City: Western end of the Oregon Trail, 10 miles south of downtown Portland along the Willamette River.

The Barlow Road: To avoid the treacherous falls of the Columbia Gorge, many emigrants opted to follow this difficult toll road that cuts inland around Mount Hood. See page 534.

The National Oregon Trail Interpretive Center: A well-preserved set of wagon ruts and an array of historical artifacts are displayed here. See page 539.

Fort Boise: This fortress, a reconstruction of a fur trapping post built nearby in 1834, stands along the banks of the Snake River. See pages 540-541.

Three Island Crossing State Park: One of the best places to get a feel for life as an Oregon Trail pioneer: Camp where they camped and swim where they swam, at one of the most important crossings of the Snake River. See page 543.

Fort Caspar: A credible reconstruction of a frontier fort houses a good museum and the remains of an early ferry and bridge over the Platte River. See page 556.

Fort Laramie: Located 40 miles southeast of Douglas, Wyoming, this restored fort is among the best stops on the contemporary trail. The most impressive set of preserved wagon ruts survive in an evocative state park outside Guernsey, upstream from the fort.

Santa Fe Trail Junction: For the first few miles, the Santa Fe and Oregon Trails coincided, and a sign here pointed the way: right to Oregon, left to Santa Fe.

Independence, Missouri: Where most travelers on the Oregon Trail began, this is also the site of one of the best museums on the subject of the westward migrations. See page 702.

local volcanic rock. Though it's a fairly timeworn place, Shoshone looks great at sunset, when its steel water tower glows and places like the **Frosty Isle Drive-In** on the north side of town and the neon-signed **Manhattan Cafe** along the railroad tracks look especially appealing. One of Shoshone's most notable old buildings is the stately McFall Hotel, on the north side of the tracks, which dates from 1896 and is being lovingly restored to its original glory. At the very least stop in for a look at the bar or inquire about a room (208/886-7016).

If you're hungry, thirsty, or low on gas, be sure to fill up here, as services are rare between Shoshone and Arco, 75 miles to the east.

Shoshone sits at the junction where US-20 crosses Hwy-75, which runs
north to Sun Valley, and US-93, which runs south to Twin Falls. For more,
see our "Border to Border" Route, pages 114-167.

Craters of the Moon National Monument

Described by writer Washington Irving as a place "where nothing meets the eye but
a desolate and awful waste, where no grass grows nor water runs, and where nothing is to be seen but lava," the vast tracts of volcanic fields known as Craters of the
Moon National Monument aren't totally devoid of life—they just look that way.
Covering some 60,000 acres at an average altitude of 6,000 feet, the lava fields are
but a small part of the extensive Snake River volcanic plain, which forms a 100-
mile-wide swath across southern Idaho. The rounded cinder cones and acres of
glassy black stone were formed between 2,000 and 15,000 years ago, and, despite
first impressions, they do shelter a wide variety of plant and animal life, from pines
and prickly pears to various raptors and a population of mule deer. May and June
see abundant wildflowers, and temperatures stay cool, so it's altogether an ideal
time to visit.

Easily accessible from a seven-mile loop road that runs south from US-20/26, the
most striking remnants of the region's volcanic activity are the huge cones that rise
above the generally flat plain. These huge knolls of lightweight cinder give great
views of the overall area, but they're not volcanoes, and there's no crater to look
down into. The closest Craters of the Moon comes to real craters are the **spatter
cones** midway along the loop, where the deep openings are often filled with snow
late into summer. The most interesting section of the monument is at the end of
the loop, where—provided you have a flashlight—you can wander through sub-
surface **lava tubes** called Boy Scout Cave, Beauty Cave, and Indian Tunnel, which
at 830 feet is the longest in the park.

For further information or to pick up the useful park brochures, stop by the
small **visitor center** (daily 8 AM-6 PM in summer, 8 AM-4:30 PM rest of the year;
208/527-3257), where you ought to pay the entry fee. A basic, 52-site **campground**
offers water and restrooms but no showers, hookups, or dump station.

Northwest of Arco, the
highest peak in Idaho,
12,662-foot **Mount Borah,**
was epicenter of a powerful
1983 earthquake that
registered 7.3 on the
Richter scale.

Arco

"The first city in the free world to be powered by nuclear-gen-
erated electricity," Arco (pop. 1,230) sits on the banks of the
Big Lost River, so-called because it disappears a few miles
downstream, vanishing into the volcanic labyrinth of the Snake
River plain. Arco itself, a crossroads town straddling the junc-
tion of US-20 and US-93, is a handy stop for food (try **Pickles Cafe**, on the east
side of town), gas or supplies; signs and historic plaques point out its connections
with the early days of nuclear power.

If you have more than a passing interest in nuclear fission, you'll want to check
out the anonymous-looking red brick structure 18 miles southeast of Arco on the
south side of US-20, which holds the inoperative remains of **Experimental Breeder
Reactor Number One.** Sitting at the edge of the massive Idaho National Engineering Lab (INEL), the deactivated reactor is open for self-guided **tours** (daily 8 AM-4
PM in summer only; free; 208/526-0050), on which you can get an up-close glimpse

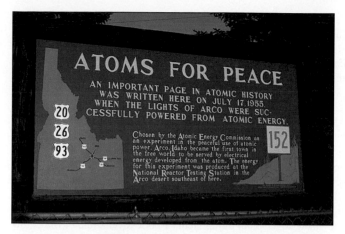

Atoms for Peace, Arco

of the turbines and control room, even the fuel rods that first produced nuclear power on December 20, 1951. Among other things, INEL is now the nation's primary repository for nuclear waste.

Idaho Falls

Taking its name from the wide but short waterfall completely tamed to form a pleasant green lake at the center of town, Idaho Falls (pop. 43, 929), at the junction of US-20 and I-15, is a busy big city with a very attractive, Middle American downtown set along the banks of the Snake River. Grain elevators and stockyards stand along the railroad tracks, train whistles blow throughout the night, and all manner of neon signs line the highways, offering a concentrated dose of rural Americana, while its hotels, supermarkets, and restaurants make Idaho Falls a handy last stop before heading on to the diverse wilderness areas that rise to the north, east, and west. Apart from the chance to wander around a business district that's hardly changed since 1956 —if you have the time, nose around the Royal Shoe Shop at 321 Park Avenue, which reeks of leather and polish—you can stroll along the waterfront park, feeding the geese or just watching the waters tumble over the weirs.

Though it's rich in small town Americana, Idaho Falls also has a few pockets of big city sophistication, no doubt thanks to the well-paid engineers employed at INEL west of town, and the skiers bound for Grand Targhee in the mountains to the east. Cafes and bakeries crowd together around Park Avenue and A Street downtown, serving a wide enough range of pastries, coffees and sandwiches to suit any palate. For a place to stay, try the well-placed **Holiday Inn**, overlooking the falls at 475 River Parkway (208/523-800 or 800/432-1005).

Summer fun in Idaho Falls: drive-in movies at either (or both) the **Motor Vue** or **Sky Vue** theatres, on US-20 north and south of town, respectively, or an **Idaho Falls Braves** Pioneer League baseball game (208/522-8363)

West of US-20, 15 miles north of Idaho Falls, the sleepy town of Rigby played a hugely important role in the development of contemporary culture: it was here that young **Philo T. Farnsworth,** the inventor of the cathode-ray television, grew up and went to school.

Rising to the east of Idaho Falls, the serrated crest of the **Grand Tetons** stands out along the Idaho/ Wyoming border. Though the US-20 route through Yellowstone National Park is closed in winter, you can get across the Rockies by detouring via US-26 through Jackson Hole, Wyoming—a beautiful route that's described more fully on pages 554-555.

Rexburg

First settled in the 1880s, the town of Rexburg (pop. 14,302) is best known for the near-disaster of 1976, when the huge Teton Dam collapsed and unleashed eight billion gallons of floodwater onto the valley below. Fortunately, engineers noticed the warning signs and were able to evacuate the area beforehand; though damage was extensive, fatalities were few. Rexburg was initially established by Mormon homesteaders, and still has a pronounced Mormon feel; the **Teton Dam Museum**, 51 W. Center Street in the basement of the Mormon church across from city hall, has the usual displays of quilts and cattle brands tracing the history of the region, plus a large section devoted to the great flood of 1976. A short film shows the actual collapse of the dam. There's also an exhibit on the terrible forest fires that burned much of Yellowstone National Park in 1988.

Rexburg's radio station **KRXK 98.1 FM,** *plays oldies by request. Call in your favorite at 800/833-8211.*

From Rexburg, US-20 runs northeast through the Targhee National Forest, climbing from the Snake River plain along Henry's Fork River—one of the country's top fishing streams, loaded with cutthroat trout as big as 10 pounds—into the heart of the Rocky Mountains. On the Idaho/Montana border, 7,072-foot Targhee Pass marks the **Continental Divide**.

West Yellowstone, Montana

Western gateway to Yellowstone National Park, the Montana town of West Yellowstone (pop. 913) sits just over the Idaho border, offering all the motels, gas stations, and cafes you could ever want, plus a lot more. The primary access point for early tourists visiting Yellowstone on the Union Pacific Railroad, West Yellowstone preserves a great deal of old-style tourist facilities—the old terminal is now the engaging if small **Museum of the Yellowstone** ($4), and the town's many roadside motels (there are more motel rooms than residents!) display a mouthwatering assembly of nifty neon signs while still serving the food-and-fuel needs of today's travelers. There's also a huge IMAX theater, 105 S. Canyon Street (daily 9 AM-9 PM; $6), in case you prefer the Memorex version to real-life Yellowstone; the theater is part of a contentious wildlife theme park that intends to collect "problem" bears and wolves and put them on display—rather than kill them as is currently done.

West Yellowstone's main drag, Canyon Street (US-20), is lined by cafes and Wild West souvenir shops. The excellent **Book Peddler**, 106 Canyon Street, boasts an espresso and sandwich bar along with a wide array of fiction and nonfiction titles. The **Silver Spur** cafe, across the street at 111 Canyon, serves a fine bowl of chili along with fluffy omelets. Motels abound on the backstreets, so drive around and take your pick, or contact the **visitors bureau** at 100 Yellowstone Avenue (406/646-7701).

ACROSS WYOMING

Most visitors to Wyoming have one thing in mind: Yellowstone National Park. This amazing spectacle, which our route takes us right through, is deservedly the state's premier visitor attraction, but the rest of Wyoming holds a surprising variety of interesting places, from Wild West cow towns to the wide open spaces of the Great Plains. The least populated of the 50 states, Wyoming has more wide open space than just about anywhere else. If you like the idea of traveling for miles and miles without seeing anyone before coming upon a crossroads outpost where the post office shares space with the general store and gas station, you'll want to take the time to explore Wyoming.

Yellowstone National Park

Sitting astride the Continental Divide, high up in the northern Rockies at the northwest corner of Wyoming, Yellowstone National Park is one of the true wonders of the natural world. A veritable greatest hits of Mother Nature, the park is packed full of burbling geysers, magnificent canyons, raging waterfalls, and still-wild wildlife. The country's (and the world's) oldest national park, established in 1872, Yellowstone was first explored by frontiersman John Colter, who passed through in 1808; it's also one of the largest parts of the Lower 48 states never to be farmed or fenced.

You probably already know something about what Yellowstone has in store for you: the one essential Yellowstone sight is **Old Faithful Geyser**, in the southwest quarter of the park. One of the world's most famous natural features, Old Faithful is known for its clockwork eruptions, in which some 5,000 gallons of boiling water are sent 150 feet into the air, forming a solid, steamy column. Hundreds of people line up around the

In 1808, when fur trapper **John Colter** described the scenes he saw in what's now Yellowstone—gurgling, spouting steam vents, prismatic pools of sulfurous boiling water—nobody believed him, and many thought he was mad, calling the fantastic land "Colter's Hell."

Though the forests of Yellowstone are recovering, damage from the terrible fires of 1988 is still readily apparent around the western half of the park.

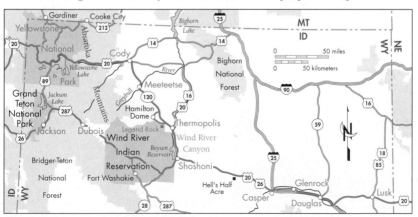

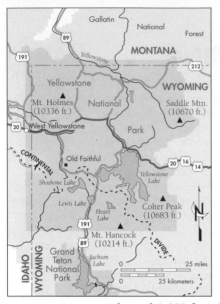

geyser waiting for it to blow, and rangers are able to predict it with good deal of accuracy—the visitor center will list the expected times of the day's eruptions, which occur roughly every 75 minutes and last for another two to five minutes. In between eruptions, take the chance to wander around to the dozens of other features in the Old Faithful basin, including a number of other geysers (the Old Faithful area has the greatest concentration in the world) as well as colorful pools and other geothermal features, all linked by well-marked boardwalks and trails along the Firehole River.

The other main sight is the **Grand Canyon of the Yellowstone River**, where a pair of powerful waterfalls cascade into a 20-mile-long, half-mile-wide, and 1,000-foot-deep canyon of eroding yellow stone. Parking areas line the north and south rims of the canyon, allowing access to trails along the edge of the gorge. A personal favorite is **Uncle Tom's Trail**, leaving from the south side of the falls. More a staircase than a trail, this route zigzags steeply down the walls of the canyon, bringing you face to face with the falls. Farther along the south rim is **Artist's Point**, which gives the classic view of the canyon. Also, two "**Brink of the Falls**" routes lead from the north side down to where the waters plunge.

One rarely mentioned aspect of life in Yellowstone is the profusion of bison (aka buffalo) droppings: everywhere you look—all around the geysers, hot springs, etc.—they've made their mark. And though they may seem placid, bison can be dangerous, so keep your distance.

Along with these two main attractions, there are many more sights to see, so take the time to visit the visitor centers, talk to the rangers, and find out what other wonders await. Covering a roughly 100-by-100-mile square, Yellowstone is a big place, plenty big enough to absorb the many tourists who come here during the peak summer season. Whatever you do, don't try to see it all in a day or two; if time is tight, choose one or two places and spend all your time there. Get out of the car, hike a few trails, and enjoy.

the first car at Yellowstone

Yellowstone Practicalities

Yellowstone's visitor facilities book up well in advance (sometimes up to a year), so if you want the complete experience it's best to plan ahead as much as possible. **Accommodations** are the main thing you ought to sort out as soon as you can, as bed space is at a premium. The first choice is the wonderful **Old Faithful Inn**, next to the famous geyser. Built of split logs and huge boulders and exuding rough-hewn elegance, this delightful inn was completed in 1904 and maintains its original appearance. Rooms in the old lodge, without baths, start at about $45; a newer wing has larger rooms and modern conveniences for $100-250 a night—some of these rooms have Old Faithful views. Another historic lodge, at Yellowstone Lake, is plusher but architecturally less distinctive; a half-dozen other inns, cabins, and motels are scattered around the park. All rooms are handled through a central service (307/344-7311), which also handles reservations for the park's campgrounds, most of which operate on a first-come, first-served basis and fill up by noon daily. **Backcountry camping** is another option, though be careful of bears and be sure to get an overnight permit from the park rangers.

Places to eat include the usual cafeteria-type restaurants at all of the park's hotels and lodges, plus a truly remarkable restaurant at the classic Old Faithful Inn, with a three-story log-cabin dining room and food that's as good as its gets in the national parks.

You'll find gas stations, gift shops, and general stores at just about every road junction in the park. There are **ranger stations** at most main features, and large **visitor centers** at Mammoth Hot Springs, Old Faithful, and the Canyon. For further information, contact **park headquarters** (307/344-7381).

Though Buffalo Bill gets most of the publicists' ink, another famous Cody figure is the abstract impressionist "action painter" **Jackson Pollock,** who was born here.

Note that the Yellowstone visitor season is very short—roads are usually blocked by snow from November until April, May, or even June. To find out current road conditions, phone 307/344-7381. A year-round alternative, US-26 through the Grand Tetons and Jackson Hole, is described below.

Cody

Eastern gateway to Yellowstone National Park, and an enjoyable overnight stop in its own right, Cody is a self-conscious frontier town and a busy center

for local ranching and wood products industries. The outskirts are lined by Wal-Marts, Kmarts, and all the fast-food franchises you could name, but the town center along Sheridan Avenue (US-20) still looks like the Wild West town Cody was built to be.

Sitting on the Bighorn Basin plains at the foot of the mountains, Cody was founded in the late 1890s by Wild West showman "Buffalo Bill" Cody, whose name graces most everything in town, including the **Buffalo Bill Historical Center** (daily 7 AM-10 PM in summer, Tues.-Sun. 8 AM-5 PM rest of the year, closed December, January, and February; $8; 307/587-4771). One of the country's great

MISS ANNIE OAKLEY,
THE PEERLESS LADY WING-SHOT.

museums, and certainly the best in the Wild West, this place tells all you could want to know about the American frontier. The center is divided into four main collections. First stop should be Buffalo Bill's home, which was moved here from LeClair, Iowa in 1933, then move on to the Buffalo Bill Museum, which includes a battery of movies and artifacts from his famous "Wild West Show," a circus-like extravaganza that toured the world. The curatorial heart of the Buffalo Bill center is the Whitney Gallery of American Art, one of the country's most extensive collections of western art, which displays important works by George Catlin, Thomas Moran, Albert Bierstadt, and Frederic Remington. Gun freaks will enjoy the Cody Firearms Museum, which displays more than 5,000 historic weapons. Saving the biggest and best for last, the Plains Indian Museum has an amazing collection of art and artifacts created by the diverse Plains Indian peoples, from beadwork dresses to a reconstructed Sioux village complete with full-sized teepees. An array of leather moccasins adorn an entire wall, and pride of place is given to the extraordinary buffalo robe painted with scenes of the legendary Battle of Little Big Horn.

At the west edge of Cody is **Trail Town** (daily 8 AM-8 PM mid-May to mid-September; $3), a low-key but engaging collection of old buildings moved here from northwestern Wyoming and southern Montana. Wagons, buffalo robes, and other relics are on display. A memorial cemetery holds the remains of Wild West figures, including Jeremiah Johnson, whom Robert Redford played in the movie named for the man.

You'll find most of Cody's good places to eat on Sheridan Avenue. **Silver Dollar Bar and Grill**, 1313 Sheridan Avenue, serves great burgers and bottles of beer. A block away, the **Proud Cut Saloon**, 1227 Sheridan Avenue, has an interesting array of sandwiches at lunch and great steaks at dinner.

The historic **Irma Hotel** at 1192 Sheridan Avenue (307/587-4221; $50 in winter, $75 in summer), built by Buffalo Bill and named for his daughter, features a lovely cherrywood bar given by Queen Victoria, and an evening gunfight on the front porch.

For historic B&B rooms, try **Cody Guest Houses**, 1401 Rumsey Avenue (307/587-6000 or 800/587-6560), and there are also lots of $40-a-night motels elsewhere along US-20. For complete listings, contact the **visitor center**, 836 Sheridan Avenue (307/587-2297).

At the Norris Geyser Basin, the small **Museum of the National Park Ranger** describes the evolution of the national parks; for instance, from 1886 to 1916 Yellowstone was under the protection of the U.S. Army!

Between Yellowstone and Cody, US-20 drops steeply through lovely **Wapiti Valley.** Teddy Roosevelt supposedly called this area "the most scenic 50 miles in America." Another scenic route, the Beartooth Highway (US-212), runs northeast to Red Lodge, Montana, and was rated by Charles Kuralt as "the most beautiful roadway in America."

The **Cody Nite Rodeo** (nightly at 8:30 PM; $9; 307/587-5155) at the huge rodeo grounds at the west end of town has been held June-Sept. since 1938, making it the nation's longest-running rodeo.

Meeteetse

East of Cody, Hwy-120, a prettier alternative to US-20, angles south over the rugged foothill badlands of the Absaroka (pronounced ab-SOR-ka) Mountains, historic homeland of the Crow Indians but now equal parts cattle ranches and oil wells. Thirty miles along this lonely highway brings you to Meeteetse (pop. 375), one of the oldest settlements in central Wyoming and still much the same for the past 125 years. The broad Greybull River—and an occasional cattle drive—runs right through town, which still retains wooden boardwalks and hitching posts for cowboys' horses.

Besides being wonderfully evocative of an earlier era, Meeteetse also has a pair of good museums documenting diverse aspects of the region's past. Most unusual is the **Charles J. Belden Museum** (daily 9 AM-5 PM; free), which holds an extraordinary collection of cowboy photography that includes the first "Marlboro Man" ads, shot on the nearby Pitchfork Ranch by the eponymous rancher and photographer. Also worth a look is the **Meeteetse Archive**, in a turn-of-the-century bank building a block south along Main Street.

Along with an old but fully stocked general store, Meeteetse has a few restaurants (try **Lucille's** cafe or the **Broken Spoke** steakhouse) and the $30-a-night **Oasis Motel**, 1702 State Street (307/868-2551), with camping and a Conestoga wagon.

Legend Rock

One of Wyoming's most significant collections of petroglyphs, Legend Rock contains over 250 images dating back some 2,000 years, carved into sandstone cliffs in the oil-rich foothills of the Owl Creek Mountains. To get there, follow US-120 for 21 miles from Thermopolis, or 33 miles from Meeteetse, then turn south at the Hamilton Dome turnoff and follow the dirt road for eight miles to a locked gate. The petroglyphs are a quarter-mile beyond the gate. The Thermopolis **visitor center** has detailed information.

Aviator **Amelia Earhart** was having a ranch home built for her near Meeteetse along the Greybull River in 1934, but construction stopped after she disappeared on her round-the-world flight.

Thermopolis

Despite the highfalutin' resonance of its classical-sounding name, Thermopolis (pop. 3,300) is a sleepy little retirement town, surrounded by red rock canyons and centered among a remarkable set of natural hot springs. The land was bought in 1896 from local Shoshone chief Washakie on the understanding that the spring waters be kept open to the public, white and Indian alike. This spring, which flows at a rate of 20 million gallons of 135° F water daily, was the basis of Wyoming's first state park, which still covers the east bank of the Bighorn River. A state-run **bathhouse** (Mon.-Sat. 8 AM-5 PM, Sunday noon-6 PM; free) has showers and changing rooms—you can rent towels and bathing suits for a nominal charge. There are also a pair of commercial enterprises in the park—the **Hot Springs Water Park**, and **Star Plunge**—with water slides, saunas, and so on, charging $7 admission.

Across the river in the center of town, the enjoyable **Hot Springs Historical Museum** (daily 8 AM-5 PM; $2), at 700 Broadway, has a wide-ranging collection of historic photos, farming and oil-drilling implements, and even the cherrywood bar from the Hole-in-the-Wall Saloon where Butch and Sundance supposedly bellied up for a drink or two. The final big draw in Thermopolis—and I mean BIG—is the **Wyoming Dinosaur Center**, on the east side of town at 100 Carter Ranch Road (daily 8 AM-8 PM in summer, shorter hours rest of year; $6; 307/864-2997, 800/455-DINO or 800/455-3466). Follow the green dinosaur footprints from the center of town to this fairly new museum, which is basically a paleontology dig that's open to the public.

The friendly Thermopolis **visitor center** (307/864-3192 or 800/786-6772), in the same building as the Hot Springs Historical Museum, has listings of motels and campgrounds and other information on the area.

Wind River Canyon

South of Thermopolis, US-20 winds through Wind River Canyon, one of the most memorable drives in a state of memorable drives. The 2,500-foot-deep canyon, with the highway on one side of the broad river and the railroad on the other, reveals millions of years of sedimentary rock. As you drive along heading south, you reach deeper and deeper into the earth; each layer is labeled with signs explaining its geological age and significance, with the oldest layers dating back to the Precambrian era, some 2.5 billion years ago.

Due in part to the visual effect of the uplifted sedimentary layers, the river at times gives the illusion of flowing uphill; this may explain why Indians and early explorers thought there were two distinct rivers, and called the canyon itself the **"Wedding of the Waters."** The river still has two distinct names: upstream from Wind River Canyon, it is called the Wind River; downstream from the canyon, it's called the Bighorn River.

Driving along US-20 between the Wind River Canyon and Shoshoni, keep an eye out for the many pronghorn antelope that play on the rolling rangeland.

At the south end of the river, Boysen Reservoir, a popular place for fishing and water-skiing, backs up behind Boysen Dam, which was completed in 1961. The land west of the reservoir forms the two-million acre Wind River Indian Reservation, home to descendants of the Eastern Shoshone and Northern Arapahoe tribes; a woman thought by some to be Sacagawea (the Shoshone guide of Lewis and Clark fame) is buried on the reservation, along the Wind River near Fort Washakie.

*Jackson Hole is one of the country's most exclusive winter resorts, with world-class ski areas including **Grand Targhee** (800/827-4433), powder-hound heaven on the Idaho border, and **Jackson Hole Ski Resort** (800/450-0477), which boasts the longest vertical drop in the USA: an astounding 4,139 feet!*

Jackson Hole and Grand Teton National Park

In winter, the only road kept open through Yellowstone is US-212 between Gardiner and Cooke City, Montana, at the northern edge of the park. But if you're here anytime but summer, don't despair: US-26, a very different but still unforgettable route is open year-round, running south of Yellowstone between Idaho Falls and Casper, through the spectacular scenery of Grand Tetons National Park, and the Wild West town of Jackson Hole.

Climbing up from Idaho Falls along the banks of the Snake River, US-26 crosses into Wyoming on a sinuously scenic route, past cottonwood trees and whitewater-running kayakers, before linking up with north-south US-89. The tourist mecca of Jackson Hole, one of the country's most popular "wilderness" destinations, takes its name from the main town, **Jackson** (pop. 6,500) which sits at the center of a broad, mountain-ringed valley. Drawing upwards of 35,000 visitors on a summer day, Jackson isn't exactly an idyllic spot, but it has managed to retain its Wild West character, especially in the few blocks around the lively Town Square. Here, false-fronted buildings linked by a raised wooden sidewalk hold upscale boutiques and the wonderfully kitsch likes of the **Million Dollar Cowboy Bar**, on the west side of the square, a huge and always lively hangout with silver dollars implanted in the bar top and real leather saddles instead of bar stools.

Jackson has many very good (and very expensive) restaurants, like the art deco-style **Cadillac Grill**, which has grilled ahi tuna and similarly sophisticated fare on the Town Square at 55 N. Cache (307/733-3279). The Cadillac Grill shares space with Jackson's best burger spot, **Billy's Giant Burgers**, which burger-loving President Bill Clinton rated as the best he'd ever tasted. Another handy, good food place is the lunch counter inside the historic **Jackson Drug**, on the north side of Town Square at 15 E. Deloney Avenue, where you can get a soup and sandwich for under $5, or a great milk shake. Jackson caters to so many visitors that accommodations, however plentiful, can be booked solid in summer. There's something for everyone here: campgrounds and RV parks, B&Bs, $60-a-night highway motels—including a Motel 6 and the nifty log cabins of **Wagon Wheel Village** (307/733-2357)—and $4,000-a-week guest ranches.

For listings, or any other information on the Jackson Hole area, contact the **visitors center**, on US-26/89 at 532 N. Cache Street (307/733-3316).

From Grand Teton National Park, US-89 runs north to the heart of Yellowstone National Park.

North of Jackson, the silver peaks of Grand Teton National Park cut into the sky, their slopes offering some of the best hiking and mountaineering in the lower 48 states. US-26/89 runs right along the base of the mountains, giving grand views and tempting travelers to stop and explore. West of the main highway, Teton Park Road winds past Jenny Lake, where you can board a boat ($5) and ride across to a short trail that leads up past Hidden Falls to **Inspiration Point**, at the foot of 13,770-foot Grand Teton.

On US-26, 18 miles west of Dubois, a roadside monument remembers the work of the "tie hacks" who, from the 1870s until WW II, cut down lodgepole pines to form railroad ties.

Details on the abundant hiking, skiing, fishing, and other recreational activities, as well as camping and lodging options, are available by contacting the main Grand Teton National Park **visitor center**, a mile west of US-26 on Teton Park Road (307/739-3600).

Dubois

Between Casper and the Grand Tetons, US-26 is a mostly scenic highway, crossing the Continental Divide at 9,644-foot Togwotee Pass before winding along the Wind River through the multi-colored badlands that surround the town of Dubois (pop. 1,100, pronounced "Dew-Boys"). A low-key ranching and logging center that's still in the infancy as a tourist destination, Dubois does have one unique attraction: the **National Bighorn Sheep Center** (daily 9 AM-4 PM in summer, shorter hours in winter; $2; 307/455-3429), right on US-26 at the west edge of town, documenting the life and times of the thousands of bighorn sheep that congregate in the winter months around Whisky Mountain, south of Dubois. At the center of Dubois, another unique sight is inside historic **Welty's General Store**, 113 W. Ramshorn (US-26),

Midway between Dubois and Shoshoni, north of US-26, the tiny town of **Pavillion** has a great little cafe, packed with 1950s memorabilia and serving great hamburgers and homemade pies.

where you can see a Colt .44 revolver with the name "Butch Cassidy" carved in the handle; Butch lived and rustled horses here back in the 1880s.

There are a few saloons, steak houses and fly-fishing shops, and one great place to stay in Dubois: the log cabin **Twin Pines Lodge**, 218 Ramshorn (307/455-2600).

Shoshoni

Named for the Shoshone Indians who once held sway over this part of the Great Plains, the forlorn town of Shoshoni (pop. 497) sits at the junction of US-20 and US-26, at the southeast edge of the Boysen Reservoir. Since the oil boom went bust, most of the motels and cafes look like they're on the verge of drying up and blowing away, though recent plans for a massive toxic waste repository have brought a surge of new money.

There is, however, one excellent reason to stop: the **Yellowstone Drug Store**, at the center of Shoshoni's block-long business district. It sells the state's best milk shakes and ice cream floats at the ancient-looking soda fountain.

Between Shoshoni and Casper, the only attraction worth mentioning is the odd geology of **Hell's Half Acre**, a 300-acre concentration of grotesquely eroded stone south of US-20 amid the arid badlands landscape. Scenes from the movie *Starship Troopers* were filmed here in 1996.

Casper

Casper was the heart of the oil fields that led to the notorious Teapot Dome scandal of the 1920s, in which Secretary of Interior Albert Fall went to prison for accepting a $100,000 bribe.

Like other towns in southern Wyoming, Casper began as a way station on the many frontier trails that followed the North Platte River, first as a ferry crossing (log rafts were run by Salt Lake City-bound Mormons from 1847 to 1852; non-Mormons were charged $1.50) and later toll bridges, culminating with an elaborate plank bridge built by Louis Guinard in 1859. The second-largest city in Wyoming, only slightly smaller than capital city Cheyenne, Casper (pop. 46,742) is still dependent upon passing trade; its key location along the I-25 corridor has enabled Casper to survive the downturns in its other main industry, oil.

Most of the places of interest in Casper (which was originally spelled Caspar) have to do with the westward migration. **Fort Caspar** (Mon.-Sat. 8 AM-7 PM, Sunday noon-4 PM; free), west of downtown off Hwy-220, is a New Deal-era replica of the original rough log fort and Pony Express station. There's also a reconstruction of the Mormon-operated ferry, and displays of pioneer artifacts in the small museum.

While the rest of the city has a definite roughneck feel, downtown Casper is also rich in 1920s Americana, with a pair of great old movie theater marquees (tickets cost just $2), rusty neon signs, and art deco storefronts, plus an above-par range of junk stores and secondhand bookshops. One of the country's largest cowboy clothing stores, **Lou Taubert's**, has over 10,000 pairs of boots and three floors of blue jeans, rhinestones, and other essential range-riding gear at 125 E. 2nd Street.

East of downtown, the one place you really ought to visit is the **Nicolaysen Art Museum** (Tues.-Sat. 10 AM-5 PM; $2; 307/235-5247), housed in an imaginatively converted old power plant at 400 E. Collins Street, along the railroad tracks. The finest contemporary art museum in Wyoming, with frequent shows of regional artists, the Nicolaysen also has a permanent collection of Plains Indian arts and crafts, plus a hands-on art center for children.

The **Red and White Cafe**, 1620 E. Yellowstone Highway (US-20/26), is a classic roadside greasy spoon, one of a handful along the old highway frontage. On the west side of downtown, **First Street Bakers**, at 260 W. 1st Street, has good coffees, teas, and baked goods in the mornings, and fresh pasta dishes in the evenings. Casper's accommodation prices are very low, with room rates at the many motels along Yellowstone Avenue (US-20) starting under $25 a night. More modern (i.e., cleaner and more expensive) places along the I-25 frontage include most of the national chains.

For detailed listings or other local information, including detailed maps of Oregon Trail and Pony Express sites in the area, contact the Casper **visitor center** (307/234-5311 or 800/852-1889) at 500 N. Center Street, south of I-25.

Glenrock

Midway between Casper and Douglas along the south bank of the North Platte River, Glenrock (pop. 2,153) was a vital rest stop and supply station on the Oregon and other emigrant trails. Several downtown buildings have endured since its heyday, when Glenrock was known as Deer Creek Station and some 20,000 migrants came through each year, many of them camping overnight at the "rock in the glen" on the west side of town, where a sandstone boulder still holds the names of passing pioneers. Nowadays Glenrock is known for its massive coal-fired power plant, one of the largest in the country.

Between Casper and Glenrock, US-26 winds along the river, but between Glenrock and Douglas the old road has been replaced by the I-25 freeway.

A dozen miles west of Douglas, five miles south of I-25 via Natural Bridge Road, **Ayers Natural Bridge** arches 30 feet above La Prele Creek.

Douglas

Situated far enough off I-25 to retain its Wild West cowboy character, the enjoyable town of Douglas (pop. 5,076) was founded in 1886 across the river from Fort Fetterman, which for the previous 25 years had protected traffic on the old Oregon and Bozeman trails along the North Platte River. The location of Owen Wister's genre-inventing Western novel *The Virginian,* and more recently birthplace of that other Wild West icon, the **jackalope** (see sidebar), Douglas is a quietly picturesque small town with a wild history, and a great place to break your long-distance road trip.

The Wyoming State Fairgrounds, along the river at the west end of Center Street, hosts a livestock-frenzied fair at the end of August, and also features the year-round **Pioneer Museum** (Mon.-Fri. 8 AM-5 PM, shorter hours in winter; free; 307/358-9288), packed full of artifacts from the late 1800s—everything from rifles and a roulette table to fossils and farm implements. It also houses a Sioux-style hide teepee made for the movie *Dances with Wolves.* The wilder side of Douglas history is perhaps most vividly apparent in tombstones in the **cemetery** on the east edge of town at the end of Pine Street, where legendary cattle rustler George Pike is interred beneath a marker that reads in part

> *Underneath this stone in eternal rest,*
> *Sleeps the wildest one of the wayward west.*

JACKALOPES 'R' US

Traveling around the Great Plains, you're bound to come across all sorts of oversized wildlife—giant fish, giant cows, giant bison—plus some more that defy anatomical description. Most of the latter—fur-bearing trout, in particular—are seen primarily on postcards, but at least one species can usually be found mounted on the wall of any self-respecting saloon or taxidermist's shop: the jackalope. So rare that one has never been seen in the wild, the jackalope has the body of a jackrabbit and the horns of an antelope; dozens of examples are displayed around town, with the "world's largest" standing over eight feet head-to-tail in Jackalope Square at 3rd and Center Streets downtown. The enigmatic creature is also celebrated during Jackalope Days every June.

The best one-stop option for eating, drinking, and sleeping, in Douglas or most anywhere else for that matter, is the **Labonte Inn and Lounge**, 206 Walnut Street (307/358-9856), which offers a little of everything: bacon-and-eggs breakfasts, late-night beers, weekend country bands, and $35-a-night rooms. Another place to consider, **Through the Grapevine**, across the street from the giant jackalope, serves good coffee and lunchtime sandwiches. Other possibilities line the old US-20 alignment, Richards Street in the east and the Yellowstone Highway in the west, which forms a loop between exits off I-25.

Douglas's own **KKTY 99.3 FM (1470 AM)** plays local news, country hits, and Colorado Rockies baseball games.

For further information, contact the Douglas **visitor center**, in an old train depot, around the corner from the giant jackalope at 121 Brownfield Road (307/358-2950).

A marker on the south side of US-20, a mile east of Lusk, stands where US-20 intersects the **Texas Trail**—in the 1870s over 500,000 head of cattle were driven each year between Fort Worth and the open range of Wyoming and Montana along this route.

Lusk

A cattle-ranching and farming center, Lusk (pop. 1,500) is the largest town in the least populated county in the country's least populated state. It also boasts the only traffic light on US-20 between Douglas, Wyoming, and Chadron, Nebraska. And if those claims to fame don't make you want to stop, the **Stagecoach Museum** at 322 S. Main Street (daily 1-5 PM and 7-9 PM in summer, shorter hours rest of the year; $2) definitely will, if only to see the sole authentic 1880s Cheyenne-Deadwood Stagecoach—the one Doris Day sang about in *Calamity Jane*. (The only other stagecoach from this legendary route is now in the Smithsonian.) Behind the museum building is another frontier icon—a one-room schoolhouse—and along US-20 at the east edge of town a plaque points out a redwood water tower dating from 1886, when steam locomotives still chugged across the plains.

Lusk also has a good range of motels, including the good value **Covered Wagon Motel**, 730 S. Main Street (307/334-2530 or 800/341-8000). For food, try either of two diners: the **Coffee Cup** or **The Diner**, both on Main Street within a block of the stoplight. The Diner is more popular; the Coffee Cup has a better sign.

Guernsey: Oregon Trail

A worthwhile detour from Douglas or Lusk via I-15 and US-26 takes you 40-plus miles south to the town of Guernsey on the North Platte River, where you can visit two of the most evocative Oregon Trail historic sites. The Oregon Trail passed through along the south bank of the river, and a well-signed but otherwise undeveloped park, a mile south of town via Wyoming Avenue, holds the best surviving set of Oregon Trail **wagon ruts**, cut shoulder deep in the soft sandstone. Nearby is a small obelisk marking the grave of an unfortunate pioneer, and three miles to the southeast along the same road, **Register Cliff** is carved with the names of over a thousand pioneers and explorers, many dating back to 1840-60, the heyday of the trail.

Both of these sites are being developed into state parks, but are pretty much unchanged from pioneer days. For maps and more details, contact the Guernsey **visitors center** (307/836-2715), on Wyoming Avenue a block south of US-26. Fort Laramie National Historic Site, another frontier landmark, is a dozen miles east of Guernsey via US-26.

ACROSS NEBRASKA

In its 454-mile trek across Nebraska, US-20 passes through a surprising variety of landscapes. In the west, the highway skirts the edge of the huge and desolate Sand Hills, where North America's largest system of sand dunes underlies a grassy pastoral scene. Across the midsection the road runs parallel to the broad Niobrara River, one of the few rivers in the Great Plains not blocked behind a dam, before reaching the bluffs above the Missouri River.

One of the last reaches of the country to be settled and domesticated, northern Nebraska is still sparsely populated, and looks like the Great Plains are *supposed* to look. Towns are few and far between, and come and go in the proverbial blink of an eye; the rolling ranch lands are marked every mile or so by spinning Aermotor windmills pumping up water for wandering cattle herds, while historical plaques point out the sites where, barely a century ago, cowboys rode and Indians did battle with the U.S. Cavalry. Besides being rich in Wild West history—and in prehistoric fossil beds—the region has a strong literary tradition, thanks to writers such as Mari Sandoz and John G. Neihardt. All in all, few corners of the country pay back time spent with as much interest as does northern Nebraska; hard to believe, perhaps, but true.

Nebraska publishes a handy free booklet about US-20's route across the state. Copies are available at most visitor centers, or through the Nebraska US-20 Association, R.R. 1, Box 218, Plainview, NE 68769 (402/582-3798).

Harrison and Agate Fossil Beds National Monument

Just over the Wyoming border, the tiny town of Harrison is an attractive wide-spot-in-the-road, worth a stop to sample the huge (up to 28-oz!) burgers and silky milk shakes at **Sioux Sundries**, corner of Main and 2nd Streets. Twenty-three miles south

The US-20 highway through Harrison was unpaved as recently as 1941.

of Harrison, on the banks of the Niobrara River, Agate Fossil Beds National Monument (daily 8:30 AM-5:30 PM; free; 308/436-4340) contains the 20-million-year-old remains of bison-sized pigs, twin-horned proto-rhinos, and other vanished creatures.

Fort Robinson

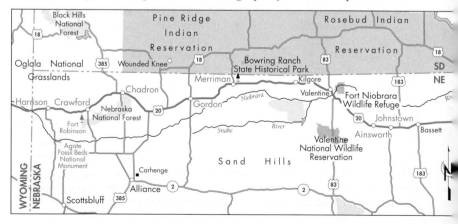

Thirty miles from the Wyoming border, Fort Robinson was established in 1874 to control the 15,000 restless natives of the Red Cloud and Pine Ridge Sioux Indian agencies. Now a state park, and planted with groves of mature trees where 100 years ago all was grassland prairie, Fort Robinson has perhaps the most tragic and uncomfortable history of all the many old forts on the Wild West frontier: this is where the unarmed Sioux chief Crazy Horse was stabbed to death with bayonets while in the custody of the U.S. Army; it's where the controversial Red Cloud Treaty, in which the Sioux gave up the Black Hills, was signed; and it's where the last of the Cheyenne under Chief Dull Knife were killed in battle rather than transported south to a reservation in Oklahoma.

Knowing this history, it can be hard to take Fort Robinson as the enjoyable respite it is today. The hundreds of hardwood trees make it an oasis on the generally treeless plains, and the whitewashed wooden barracks, many now converted to cultural centers and museums, give it the air of a college campus—especially on summer weekends, when the park turns into a living history museum complete with cookouts and evening melodramas.

The only part of the park open year-round is the **Fort Robinson Museum** (Mon.-Fri. 8 AM-5 PM, longer hours in summer; $1) in the old headquarters building, with full displays on the fort's history, plus walking-tour maps of the entire post. Accommodations are offered in the officers' quarters, and there are many good camping spots; phone 308/665-2660 for details.

Crawford

Three miles east of Fort Robinson, Crawford has settled into a sedate life as a ranching and farming center. Pines and cottonwoods line the White River which foot the weirdly eroded Legend Buttes, making a pretty scene. Even prettier are the

Oglala National Grasslands, 17 miles north of Crawford via Hwy-2, which occupy nearly 100,000 acres along the Nebraska/Wyoming/South Dakota borders, highlighted by the eerie landscape of **Toadstool Geological Park**, where ancient fossils can be found amongst weirdly eroded figures. An archaeological site known as the **Hudson-Meng Bison Bone Bed** is a shallow arroyo holding the enigmatic remains of over 600 bison, plus stone tools and arrowheads, dating from approximately 10,000 years ago. For details on either place, contact the USFS ranger station (308/432-4475).

In 1893, Chadron's early boosters found a perfect way to get their town in the news: they sponsored a 1,000-mile horse race from Chadron to Chicago, which made front pages across the country. A plaque in front of the black-and-white Blaine Hotel, a block east of Main Street, marks the start of the race.

Chadron: Museum of the Fur Trade

The largest town in northwest Nebraska, Chadron (pop. 5,588) sits at the northern edge of the Sand Hills region, bounded by pine forests to the south and the Pine Ridge Sioux Reservation to the north, across the South Dakota border. The highway frontage along US-20 isn't especially inviting, but the two-block town center preserves its turn-of-the-century character with sandstone and brick-fronted buildings along the south side of the still-used railroad tracks.

There's not a lot to do in Chadron, but it does make a handy base for trips north to the Pine Ridge lands and the Black Hills, or south to the marvelous Carhenge. Besides a couple of motels, including a Best Western and a Super 8, you can stay the night in the **Old Main Street Inn**, 115 Main Street (308/432-3380). Part old railroad hotel, part cozy B&B, the inn has rooms for $45-70 a night, a popular restaurant and saloon downstairs, and Chadron's only espresso machine. (In 1890, General Miles stayed at this hotel before heading north to massacre Sioux women and children at Wounded Knee.)

If you're anywhere nearby, don't miss the excellent **Museum of the Fur Trade** (8 AM-5 PM June-Sept., by appointment rest of the year; $2.50; 308/432-3843), on US-20 three miles east of downtown Chadron. One of the great small museums in the U.S., this privately run collection focuses on the material culture of the North American frontier. Its extensive displays bring to life the few first centuries of interaction between Native Americans and Europeans. Besides giving the overall historical context of the fur trade and its many related enterprises, the collection emphasizes the day-to-day realities of life on the Great Plains in the 18th and 19th centuries. Walls decked with weapons and bottles of whiskey (from the Americans), rum (from the English), and brandy (from the French) document the better-known aspects, but what captures your attention are the little things: packs of playing cards, a checkerboard—even a waterproof parka made out of seal intestines by the Inuit.

Behind the museum building is an in situ reconstruction of the fur trading

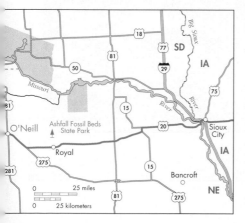

MOUNT RUSHMORE, CRAZY HORSE, AND CARHENGE

Three of the nation's most distinctive outdoor sculptures stand along US-385 within a manageable drive from US-20. One is perhaps the best-known artwork in the U.S.: the giant presidential memorial at Mount Rushmore. Roughly 100 miles north from Chadron, at the far eastern side of the beautiful Black Hills, Mount Rushmore is graced by the 60-foot heads of four U.S. Presidents—Washington, Jefferson, Lincoln, and Teddy Roosevelt —carved into a granite peak. It's equal parts impressive monument and kitschy Americana, and one of those places you really have to see to believe.

On the way to Mount Rushmore, be sure to stop and see the ambitious **Crazy Horse Memorial**, a work-in-progress along US-385 four miles north of Custer, South Dakota which, when completed, will be over 500 feet tall and 600 feet long—10 times the size of Mount Rushmore.

Another newer, less famous monument to America sits in a flat field along US-385 outside the town of Alliance, 62 miles south of Chadron. Built in 1987 as part of a local family reunion, **Carhenge** is a giant-sized replica of the famous Druid ruin, Stonehenge; this one, however, is built entirely out of three dozen late-model American cars, stacked on top of one another to form a semi-circular temple.

For more information on Mount Rushmore, contact the Rapid City visitor center (800/ 487-3223). For more information on the Crazy Horse Memorial, contact the Custer visitor center (800/992-9818). For more on Carhenge, call the Alliance Chamber of Commerce (308/762-1520).

post built in 1833 by the American Fur Company and home in the mid-1840s to French fur trapper James Bordeaux, who hosted such luminary "explorers" as John C. Fremont and Francis Parkman on their travels around the western U.S.

Museum membership is a good deal; for $6 a year, you get unlimited free admission and a subscription to the museum's quarterly journal.

In north-central Nebraska, an interesting radio alternative is the commercial-free music and news broadcast from the Pine Ridge reservation on **KILI 90.1 FM**—"*The Voice of the Lakota Nation.*"

Gordon: Mari Sandoz Country

The tiny town of Gordon, midway between Merriman and Chadron, is a typical northwestern Nebraska ranching town with a strong connection to the "Storycatcher of the Plains," Mari Sandoz, whose many books document the lives and times of the surrounding Sand Hills region. Sandoz, who wrote about growing up on a nearby ranch in her first book, the haunting classic *Old Jules,* captured the spirit and history of the Great Plains in her many works of fiction and nonfiction, all of which are available in the **Mari Sandoz Room** (Mon.-Fri. 9 AM-5 PM, Saturday 9 AM-noon; free; 308/282-9972), 117 Main Street, north of US-20 beyond the grain elevators and railroad tracks at the center of town. The Sandoz museum, which shares space with the Ad-Pad stationery store, has extensive displays of her personal effects, and free pamphlets describing a driving tour of Sandoz-related sites in the area. For aficionados of her work, a local woman, Sybil Berndt, offers guided **tours** (308/282-2133), and Mari Sandoz's sister, Caroline Sandoz Pifer, has a small museum and bookshop at her home, 20 miles south of Gordon via Hwy-27, then six miles east on a gravel road; for details and hours, phone 308/282-1687.

Gas stations line the US-20 frontage in Gordon, and the one-stop **Hacienda Motel** (308/282-1400), on the west side of town, has rooms and a popular restaurant and bar.

In Merriman, a block south of US-20, a roadside display shows the many different cattle brands used by Sand Hills ranches.

Merriman

East of Gordon, US-20 winds along the northern edge of the Sand Hills, coming within a few miles of the South Dakota border. The town of Merriman (pop. 151) may not look like much, but it does mark the turnoff north to the nearby **Arthur Bowring Sand Hills Ranch State Historical Park** (daily 9 AM-5 PM in summer; $2 per car), a working cattle ranch preserved pretty much as it was at the turn of the century. The site is lovely, with a sod house surrounded (in springtime, at least) by rolling green hills. A modern visitor center has displays on windmills and other facts of Sand Hills life, plus biographical displays on the politically powerful Bowring family, who lived and worked here from 1895 until 1985. To get there, head 1.3 miles north of town on Hwy-61, then two miles northeast following good signs.

Kilgore marks the dividing line between central and mountain time zones; adjust your clocks and watches accordingly.

Between Merriman and Valentine, US-20 passes through flyspeck former railroad towns including Kilgore (pop. 71), Crookston (pop. 99), and Cody (pop. 177).

Valentine marks the junction with US-83, "The Road to Nowhere." The town and surroundings are fully described on pages 188-189.

Johnstown

In the village of Johnstown, 40 miles southeast of Valentine and eight miles west of Ainsworth, a block of wooden storefronts and boardwalks were gussied up as a backdrop for a TV production of Willa Cather's *O Pioneers!* Behind the contrived facades you'll find a dusty old general store, and a beer bar and pool hall complete with backyard privy.

On Norden Road, 16 miles north of Johnstown, the Nature Conservancy protects the 50,000-acre Niobrara Valley Preserve, which has both Sand Hills and riparian ecosystems. Self-guided trails wind through the preserve past a small but expanding herd of bison.

Ainsworth

Roughly the midway point of US-20's long cruise across Nebraska, Ainsworth (pop. 1,800) calls itself the state's "country music capital" and hosts a popular concert and festival in early August. Ainsworth also hosts a Middle of Nowhere Festival in June, celebrated with a Wild-West-style trail ride and a black powder rendezvous. For details on either of these events, contact the visitor center (402/387-2740).

Eat big burgers at **Big Jo's**, on US-20 on the east side of town, and stay the night at the **Remington Arms Motel** (402/387-2220).

O'Neill

East of Ainsworth, US-20 runs through an especially scenic section of the Sand Hills around the artsy hamlet of **Bassett** (home to what may be Nebraska's only operating **drive-in movie theater**, the Pineview, right on US-20 west of town) before following the Elkhorn River to the town of O'Neill, 66 miles downstream. Nebraska's official "Irish Capital," O'Neill hosts a very popular St. Patrick's Day parade and celebration, but also has a fascinating history: the town was founded in 1874 by Irish settlers led by John O'Neill, who commanded a brigade of black infantrymen during the Civil War and afterwards became involved in the Fenian invasions of still-British Canada.

Another of O'Neill's many distinctions is that it has the only McDonald's along US-20 in Nebraska; this outlet is said to make O'Neill the "smallest town not on an interstate to have a McDonald's"—or something like that. O'Neill's half-dozen motels include a Super 8, plus the historic **Golden Hotel**, 406 E. Douglas Street (402/336-4436), which has well-restored rooms at the center of town from $30 a night. Free camping, a large swimming pool, and a championship-class set of horseshoe-tossing courts are available in Carney Park.

Ashfall Fossil Beds State Park

Six miles north of US-20 via Hwy-59, from a well-signed junction two miles west of the tiny village of Royal, you can watch paleontologists at work uncovering giant fossils at Ashfall Fossil Beds State Park (Mon.-Sat. 9 AM-5 PM, Sunday 11 AM-5 PM, shorter hours in winter; $2.50 per car; 402/893-2000). Unusual for a fossil bed, the skeletons here are preserved completely intact because the original residents—including prehistoric herds of rhinoceros, camels, and saber-toothed deer—got caught in a volcanic eruption some 10 million years ago. Since the bones haven't been disturbed, you can get a clear sense of the creatures' size and the sheer numbers of their populations around a prehistoric watering hole.

Eastern Nebraska

Because it's a fascinating part of the country, fairly detailed coverage has been directed at the places along US-20 across most of northern Nebraska. The same, however, cannot be said of Nebraska's far northeast quarter. To be honest, there's not a lot worth stopping for in the 90-odd miles west of the Missouri River (which marks the beginning of Iowa, where there's not a lot either). All of which is to say, if you're doing a long-distance haul along US-20, and time is tight, you can drive all night through northeast Nebraska and no one will ever point out anything you missed.

If you want to learn more about the fascinating histories and cultures of the Great Plains, head south of US-20 to the tiny town of Bancroft, where the **John G. Neihardt Center** (Mon.-Sat. 9 AM-5 PM, Sunday 1:30-5 PM; free; 402/648-3388) exhibits the personal collection of Nebraska's poet laureate and writer of the Native American classic *Black Elk Speaks.*

ACROSS IOWA

US-20 cuts straight across the midsection of Iowa between the Missouri and the Mississippi Rivers, running along the invisible border that divides the flat, agricultural tableland that distinguishes the northern half of the state from the more heavily industrialized south. The first industry here was lead mining in the 1840s, but the predominant activity these days is livestock raising. Cows and pigs feed on the abundant corn that grows in fields all along the highway. Popcorn is also a major crop.

Over 95% of Iowa is cultivated farmland—the highest percentage of any U.S. state.

Sioux City

The honey-producing and hog-butchering center of Sioux City (pop. 80,505) is not most people's idea of a vacation treat, but it does offer a few diversions to the road-tripping traveler. Grain elevators and huge brick warehouses fill the riverfront district, and some interesting Victorian-era rooming houses stand on the surrounding hills, but otherwise the main attraction is the **Sioux City Public Museum**, a mile north of downtown at 2901 Jackson Street (Mon.-Sat. 9 AM-5 PM, Sunday 2-5 PM; free; 712/279-6174), with all the usual displays tracing the Native American, pioneer, and agricultural histories of the area. There's another small museum, focusing on river history, in a dry-docked riverboat that doubles as the Sioux City **visitor center** (712/279-4840 or 800/593-2228), along the river near the Argosy riverboat casino.

Sioux City's favorite daughters are the sisters and fellow advice columnists **Ann Landers** and **Abigail "Dear Abby" Van Buren.**

Sioux City's unaffiliated Northern League baseball team, the **Explorers,** play throughout the summer in modern Lewis & Clark Park, where you can sometimes get standing room tickets ($3; 712/277-9467) and linger on the grass along the foul lines.

Lewis and Clark buffs will also want to stop south of Sioux City at the **Floyd Monument,** where a 100-foot stone obelisk marks the place where expedition member Sgt. Charles Floyd—the Corps of Discovery's only fatality—died of appendicitis in August 1804, two months after they had set off from St. Louis. Besides the historical homage, the site offers a great panorama of the Missouri River.

Sioux City doesn't offer a terribly enticing range of eating or accommodation options, though one long-standing local favorite, **Green Gables Restaurant,** a half-

mile north of downtown at 1800 Pierce
Street (712/258-4246), has bountiful,
cheap food and very good desserts.
Back across the Missouri River in
South Sioux City, Nebraska, the **Main
Event** on the one and only main street
is painted like a pink and white circus
tent and serves up slabs of prime rib.

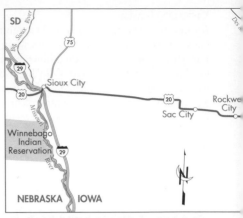

Sac City and Rockwell City

East of Sioux City, US-20 alternates between four-lane freeway and rapidly
disappearing two-lane highway, passing acres of farmland and occasional
towns. Sac City (pop. 2,492) is one of the few places along this stretch of road that
tries to preserve its past intact, with a log cabin along US-20 and a small historical
museum on Main Street. Twenty miles farther east, in Rockwell City (pop. 1,981),
the **Leist Oil Company** has an incredible collection of old neon and enamelled
metal roadside signs advertising cars, car parts, soda pop, and sundry other things.

Fort Dodge

Founded in the 1850s to protect settlers from roving bands of Sauk and Black
Hawk Indians, Fort Dodge is today a sleepy Midwestern town, economically dependent upon local farms, gypsum wallboard plants, and a huge Friskies cat food
factory. Amid many stately homes on the south side of downtown, one place really
worth a look is the **Blanden Memorial Art Museum**, 920 3rd Avenue South (Tues.-
Fri. 10 AM-5 PM, Saturday and Sunday 1-5 PM; free). Housed inside a grand neoclassical 1930s building, the collections include examples of pre-Columbian pottery,
Renaissance sculpture, and Japanese prints. Modern paintings include works by
people you wouldn't expect to find in the middle of Iowa—Max Beckmann, Marc
Chagall, and Rufino Tamayo, to name three—along with works by Grant Wood
and other Iowa artists.

The famous **Cardiff Giant**, a seven-foot tall skeleton supposedly unearthed in
New York in 1868, was thought by experts to be the bones of a prehistoric man.
However, the skeleton, which was kept on prominent display by showman P.T. Barnum for the next 35 years, was later proven to be a hoax, carved
from a slab of gypsum quarried at Fort Dodge. A replica is on
display at the Fort Museum and Frontier Village ($4) on US-20.

*Waterloo is worth a look if
you can be here on
Memorial Day, when
vintage car enthusiasts
from around the Midwest
participate in the Fourth
Street Cruise.*

Cedar Falls and Waterloo

US-20 turns to fast, four-lane freeway around Cedar Falls, a historic industrial town founded in the 1850s along
the Cedar River. Now home to the University of
Northern Iowa, Cedar Falls preserves the remnants of its manufacturing heritage with a half-
dozen historical museums; for details, contact the
visitor center, 10 Main Street (319/266-3593).

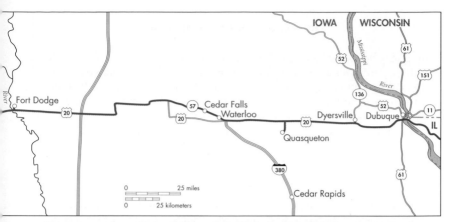

Downstream from Cedar Falls, and similarly bypassed by the modern US-20 freeway, Waterloo (pop. 66,467) is a bigger and busier city, with an almost urban feel and yet more good museums, including the **Grout Museum** (which, despite the name, is a general science and history museum—not a collection of great tile-setting materials!). Waterloo is also home to the massive **John Deere Tractor** assembly plant on the outskirts of town at 3500 E. McDonald Street. The general tour (Mon.-Fri. at 9 AM and 1 PM; free) takes you through the main plant; upon request, they may arrange tours of the foundry and engine works. There's also a small shop where you can stock up on their trademark caps and souvenirs.

Waterloo was the hometown of the Sullivan Brothers, five young men who were all killed at the battle of Guadalcanal. The US Navy has named ships after them.

The Waterloo **visitor center**, 215 E. 4th Street (319/233-8350 or 800/728-8431), can help with practical information.

Quasqueton: Cedar Rock

Midway between Waterloo and Dyersville, the tiny town of Quasqueton (pop. 579) holds Cedar Rock, a wonderful riverside house completed in 1950 by architect Frank Lloyd Wright for local-boy-done-good businessman Lowell Walter, who got rich by developing and patenting a method of sealing highway surfaces. One of seven houses Wright built in Iowa, and one of only 17 of the 1000-plus house Wright built that he "signed" with a signature tile, Cedar Rock is an excellent and complete example of his "Usonian" ideals, and everything in the house—from the soaring roof, the smooth flow of interior space, and the signature hearth, right down to designs of the carpets and cutlery—embodies Wright's idealized vision of middle-class American houses, designed for simple if stylish living in close accord with nature.

Carved into a limestone ridge overlooking a bend in the Wapsipinicon River, Cedar Rock is two miles northwest of Quasqueton, seven miles south of US-20, and surrounded by acres of rolling woodland. The house and grounds are now owned and managed by the state of Iowa and are open in summer only for guided **tours** (Tues.-Sun. 11 AM-5 PM; free; 319/934-3572).

You've kept up with the Joneses — You've been in Jones County!

THE LINCOLN HIGHWAY IN IOWA

Iowa may not be everybody's idea of a vacation destination, but fans of old highways are in for a treat here: the state has some of the best-preserved remnants of the nation's first cross-country route, the Lincoln Highway. Running between New York and San Francisco, the Lincoln Highway was the main transcontinental road from its opening in 1915 until 1927, when it was converted to the less-inspiring US-30, which, improvements notwithstanding, it still is today. Much of the original alignment survives, especially in small towns, and the old road makes a fascinating alternative across the state.

Thanks to its many dedicated devotees, the old route is well marked all across Iowa—just keep an eye out for the red, white and blue blazes, and the giant "L." Two of the many evocative sites on the Lincoln Highway in Iowa are in the midsection, between Ames and Cedar Rapids. The city of **Belle Plaine**, for example, has hardly changed since its 1915 heyday, and in the town of **Tama** a historic bridge, with the words "Lincoln Highway" spelled out in the concrete guardrails, has been preserved as a riverside park, on 5th Street a block west of the US-30 bypass.

Though Iowa's first white explorers were French, the earliest settlements in eastern Iowa were established by the English, which explains place-names like Epworth, Nottingham, and Manchester.

Quasqueton itself is a great little place, worth a stop for a cup of coffee at the quaint **Big Q Cafe**, or dinner and a drink at the **Friendly Tavern**. The two face each other across Water Street at the center of the block-long town.

Dyersville: The Field of Dreams

"If you build it, they will come. . . ." Ever since the movie *Field of Dreams* came out in 1989, some 60,000 people have flocked each year to Dyersville (27 miles west of Dubuque) to reenact the fairy tale baseball movie, major scenes from which were filmed just outside of town. Acres of cornfield surround the rather municipal-looking diamond, where people can play for free. Though privately owned, the attraction is "open" daily 10 AM-6 PM April-Nov.; to get there, take Hwy-136 north from US-20, then follow signs northeast along 3rd Avenue and Field of Dreams Road for about 3.5 miles from US-20. Alongside the playing field, there are two rival souvenir stands: one along the right field line, one along the left.

Considering it's such a small town, Dyersville has a lot in store. Besides the Field of Dreams, the town boasts one of only 36 Catholic basilicas in the U.S. (St. Francis Xavier, that can't-miss gothic pile in the center of town). The **National Farm Toy Museum**, right off US-20 at 1110 16th Avenue (daily 8 AM-7 PM; $3), has over 30,000 miniature tractors and plows showcasing 100 years of toys—from horse-drawn wooden ones to die-cast modern ones—many of them made by Dyersville's three model toy companies. One of these, the **Ertl Toy Company**, offers free hour-long tours of the die-cast manufacturing process; for reservations, call 319/875-5699.

For details on any of the above attractions, or for suggested restaurants and accommodations, contact the Dyersville **visitor center**, just north of US-20 at 1424 9th Street (319/875-2311).

Between Dyersville and Dubuque, the old Chicago Great Western Railroad right-of-way has been converted into a very pleasant, 30-mile hiking and cycling trail.

Dubuque marks the junction with our road trip along the Mississippi. The town and surroundings are fully described in the Great River Road chapter on pages 240-241.

ACROSS ILLINOIS

US-20 angles across northern Illinois from the Mississippi River to Lake Michigan, bringing you from the unglaciated scenery of the "Driftless Region" to the towering city of Chicago in less than 200 miles. The western stretches pass through hill-and-valley regions where water power and mineral deposits were harnessed by early industry. The old two-lane road is still in use, climbing onto stony ridges, then dropping into hardwood-forested valleys across the undulating region that stretches east from the Iowa border. This stretch of old road has as great a variety of barns and grain bins as anywhere in the country; however, there's considerable pressure to widen and "improve" it, so enjoy it while you can. In contrast, the rolling flatlands of the northeastern half is mostly Chicagoland suburbs mixed with occasional pastures and woodlands. Approaching Chicago, old US-20 all but disappears as a useful alternative, replaced by the busy I-90 North West Tollway.

Northwestern Illinois was the site of many skirmishes between settlers and Indians during the Black Hawk War of the early 1830s.

Galena
Spawned by Wisconsin's mid-19th-century lead mining rush, Galena (pop. 3,647) became the social and cultural capital of the Upper Mississippi basin. In the 1840s, while Chicago was still a mean collection of tents in a swamp around Fort Dearborn, and the Twin Cities were but a trading post in the woods around Fort Snelling, Galena was producing upwards of 75% of the world's lead, and the town was filled with bankers, merchants, and speculators who built mansions, hotels, and emporiums stuffed with fine goods and furnishings from around the world. This part of the Driftless Region saw some of the greatest wealth and commerce of the upper Mississippi, with Galena alone higher in population—some 15,000 lived here during the Civil War—than the entire Minnesota Territory.

But the California gold rush, played-out lead mines, a river silting up from miner-induced erosion, and a national economic panic all drove Galena to become a handsome ghost town that nobody bothered to tear down. For 100 years it slumbered, but beginning in the 1960s Galena was resurrected as a quaint tourist town. The brick warehouses were converted into shops and galleries, and anything but the most subtle, hand-carved signage was banned: in Galena, preserving the historical complexion of the streetscape isn't just a good idea, it's the law. The outskirts, especially along the US-20 frontage, are fairly typical franchised sprawl, and there are still a few everyday businesses in the historic core (including a funeral parlor and a large and busy metal foundry), but the overall result is so complete that passing through the downtown levee floodgates is like entering Brigadoon. Even the innumerable galleries and shops selling T-shirts and "collectibles" can't spoil the remarkable effect of the place. One essential: park the car and *stroll*.

Besides the integrity of its mid-19th century buildings, Galena was the town that saw a local store clerk win both the Civil War and the presidency. The modest **Ulysses S. Grant Home** (daily 9 AM-5 PM except major holidays; $2 donation; 815/777-0248), given to the general by a grateful group of local Republicans, sits up Bouthillier Street across the river from downtown. It is now a state historic site restored to the period immediately preceding Grant's move to the White House. A small museum behind the house traces Grant's life, from the Civil War to the presidency to his burial in Grant's Tomb.

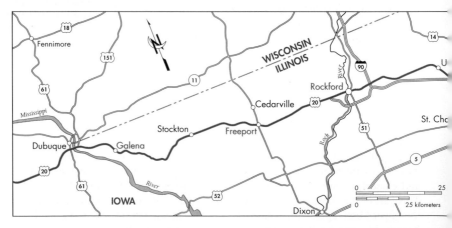

Even if you're blind to Galena's manifold aesthetic and historical delights, you'll probably enjoy its culinary variety. Starting at 5:30 AM daily, the **Steakburger Diner**, on Main Street below the "Fresh Pies Daily" clock, dishes up your basic omelets and meatloaf at rock-bottom prices for a local clientele that drops in for a cuppa joe, smoke, and small talk. Only breakfast and lunch are served, until 2 PM. One of a handful of good local bakeries, **Jakel's Bäckerie** at 200 S. Main Street offers white-flour-and-sugar salvation to all faithful dessert worshippers, and light lunch items, too. Heartier, less-refined baked goods, along with decent vegetarian fare, are found in the **Lost Art Cafe**, at 317 N. Main near Franklin.

For a good, cheap dinner in a comfortable ambience, try the **Log Cabin**, 201 N. Main, Galena's oldest restaurant, with a great big green-and-red sign that predates the town's anti-neon ordinance; it's served industrial-strength Italian food, plus steaks and seafood, since 1937 and is well frequented by locals. Despite the supposed gentrification of the community and apparent sophistication of its residents, Galena restaurants serve up a lot of "continental" (aka dull) cuisine. One of the best top-dollar exceptions is **Eldorado Grill**, 219 N. Main, with a standout Southwestern-influenced menu and vegetarian choices way beyond the lettuce-and-tomato fare found elsewhere.

There are some 60-odd hotels, guest homes, and B&B inns here in "the B&B capital of the Midwest." The central **DeSoto House**, 230 S. Main Street (815/777-0090), was U.S. Grant's headquarters during his 1868 presidential campaign; rooms start around $100 a night. You'll find many other places to stay within walking distance of the historic area. The spacious and comfortable **Belle Aire Mansion** (815/777-0893) stands along US-20 west of town. If you're just passing through, the cheapest decent sleep in town is at the **Grant Hills Motel** (815/777-2116) along US-20 east of town, next to a small antique car museum.

The Galena/Jo Daviess County Convention and Visitors Bureau operates an excellent **visitor center** (815/777-0203 or 800/747-9377), across the river via a pedestrian-only bridge, in the old Illinois Central Railroad depot at the base of Bouthillier Street. Stacks of brochures cover everything from accommodations to bike tours. This is also the best place to **park** the car, as spaces are at a premium in the often crowded downtown area.

Mrs. Grant didn't like the fact that her late husband's statue in Galena's Grant Park showed the general with his hand in his pocket. Not that she wanted it changed. "Oh, no!" she told the sculptor, "Leave it as it is, but dear me, I've told that man 20 times a day to take his hand out of his pocket."

Thanks to the three large cheese plants along US-20 in the northwest corner of the state, Illinois is the top-ranked Swiss cheese producer in the U.S.

Along US-20, 12 miles east of Galena, a 75-foot-tall lookout tower gives tourists a "Tri-State View" over the Driftless Area.

The multinational Kraft Foods got its start in **Stockton**, Illinois.

Freeport

Midway between Galena and Rockford, the oddly named town of Freeport (pop. 25,840) is neither a port nor even near any body of water. According to the WPA *Guide to Illinois,* the name was bestowed by the wife of an early settler to satirize his fondness for providing free room and board to passersby.

There's no free lunch here today, but Freeport does offer at least one good reason to stop: the **Union Dairy Ice Cream Parlour**, on Douglas Street two blocks north of the US-20 Business Loop. Enjoy a creamy, cool milk shake

Jane Addams, founder of Chicago's reform-minded Hull House, was born in 1860 and is buried near the town of Cedarville, six miles north of Freeport.

The Class A farm club of the Chicago Cubs, the **Rockford Cubbies** (815/962-2827) play at Marinelli Field, north of US-20 at Main and 15th Streets. Home games are broadcast on WQFL 101 FM.

If you have the time, Hwy-2 follows a lovely route from Rockford along the Rock River southwest to the quaint old town of Dixon, where the **Ronald Reagan Boyhood Home,** 816 S. Hennepin Avenue (815/288-3404) preserves the house where the Great Communicator spent his teenage years.

The small town of Woodstock, 10 miles northeast of Union, stood in for the Pennsylvania town of Punxsutawney in the Bill Murray movie *Groundhog Day.*

or sundae, then step next door to the small park, where an oddly distorted statue marks the site of the second **Lincoln-Douglas debate,** held here on August 27, 1858. A plaque quotes both men equally, with Lincoln's "This government cannot endure permanently half-slave and half-free" opposing Douglas saying, "I am not for the dissolution of the Union under any circumstance."

Rockford

Spreading haphazardly along the leafy banks of the Rock River, Rockford (pop. 139,426) is a big, somewhat sprawling industrial city at the west end of the I-90 toll road from Chicago. US-20 bypasses the down-at-heel downtown area which, if the residents wore more hats, would look like a film set on "Main Street" of industrial America circa 1949. After exploring Rockford's nooks and crannies, including many nice parks and the 1,500-plus clocks collected inside the amazing **Time Museum** (Tues.-Sun. 10 AM-5 PM; $3) in the Clock Tower complex at 7801 E. State Street off the US-20/I-90 junction, reward yourself with lunch or dinner at one of Illinois's great roadfood haunts, **The Rathskeller,** 1132 Auburn Street (815/963-2922), off Main Street a mile north of downtown Rockford. Since 1931, this Teutonic institution has been serving up skillets of sausage and potatoes, corned beef sandwiches, and very good desserts.

For more information, contact the Rockford **visitor center,** 211 N. Main Street (815/963-8111 or 800/521-0849).

Union: Illinois Railway Museum

Between Rockford and Chicago, US-20 is a slow, winding, and poorly signposted alternative to the high-speed I-90 toll road. It's a leisurely route, with few identifiable attractions except for the road itself, which cruises through small towns surrounded by farmlands and lined by fruit-and-vegetable stands. The one real draw here is a mile east of the tiny town of Union, where the Illinois Railway Museum (daily 11 AM-4 PM, longer hours in summer; $7; 815/923-4000) displays a great range of track-based transportation: streetcars, trolleys, and railroad cars, with a working steam train running weekends throughout the year.

US-20 across Chicago

Running parallel and south of the I-90 Northwest Tollway, old US-20 approaches Chicago from the northwest along Lake Street, past Schaumberg and O'Hare Airport before bending south near Oak Park, Chicago's most interesting suburb. (For Frank Lloyd Wright fans, at least—see below.) After crossing the Des Plaines River and the "Sanitary Canal," US-20—which somehow has managed not to be diverted onto one of Chicago's many Interstate freeways—bends east again onto 95th Street, following that road all the way to the Lake Michigan waterfront, into Hammond, Indiana and the industrial districts along the Calumet River.

CHICAGO SURVIVAL GUIDE

NEW YORK MAY HAVE BIGGER AND BETTER MUSEUMS, shops, and restaurants, and even Los Angeles has more people, but Chicago is still the most all-American city, and one of the most exciting and enjoyable places to visit in the world. Commerce capital of Middle America, where something like 80% of the nation's agricultural produce is bought and sold, Chicago's location at the crossroads between the settled East and the wide-open West has helped it to give birth to many new things we now take for granted: the skyscraper, the blues, and the atomic bomb.

Apart from **The Loop**, the skyscraper-spiked lakefront business district that holds the world's tallest and most impressive collection of modern architecture in its oblong square mile, much of Chicago is surprisingly low-rise and residential. Also surprising, considering its inland location, is that Chicago has the highest percentage of immigrants of any American city—300,000 Poles form the largest community outside Warsaw, and Hispanics constitute 20% of Chicago's three million population—with a multi-ethnic character readily apparent in numerous enclaves all over the city. Whatever their origin, however, residents take a particular pride in identifying themselves as Chicagoans, and despite the city's rusting infrastructure, their good-natured enthusiasm for the place can be contagious.

For an unbeatable introduction to Chicago, hop aboard **Chicago River by Boat,** departing North Pier, 455 E. Illinois Street (daily May-Oct. only; $15; 312/922-3432). Operated by the Chicago Architecture Foundation, these informative and enjoyable tours offer an unusual look up at the city's magnificent towers from a boat cruising the Chicago River. Guides give the city's general historical background as well as pointed architectural history, making an ideal introduction. North from North Pier, the "Magnificent Mile" of Michigan Avenue is a bustling shopping strip that holds yet more distinctive towers, along with many of the city's top shops, restaurants, and hotels. Starting with the gothic-style **Tribune Tower**—decorated with bits of famous buildings stolen by *Tribune* staffers from around the globe—and running past the circa 1869 **Historic Water Tower** at its midpoint, the "Mag Mile" ends in the north with the 95-story **John Hancock Center.**

Along the lakefront at the heart of downtown, the **Art Institute of Chicago,** 111 S. Michigan Avenue (Mon.-Sat. 10 AM-5 PM, Sunday noon-5 PM; $6.50, free Tuesday; 312/443-3600), boasts one of the world's great collections of 19th- and 20th-century French painting, and a broad survey of fine art from all over the

(continues on next page)

world. Among the many fine paintings the Institute also demonstrates a pride of place with Grant Wood's *American Gothic,* which he painted as a student and sold to the Institute for $300.

West of Chicago proper, in the suburb of Oak Park, visit the **Frank Lloyd Wright Home and Studio**, 951 Chicago Avenue, Oak Park (daily 11 AM-4 PM; $8; 708/848-1976), for a fascinating look into the life and work of the great architect. Take a guided tour of the house he designed, and lived and worked in from 1890 to 1910, remodeling almost constantly as his practice, and his family, grew. He also completed many other buildings in this turn-of-the-century suburb. This area was also the boyhood home of Ernest Hemingway, just 10 miles west of the Loop at the end of the Lake-Dan Ryan CTA "El" line.

Last but not least, there is **Wrigley Field**, 1060 W. Addison Street (773/404-2827). More than just another baseball game, watching the Cubs play at Wrigley Field is a rite of passage into the deepest meanings of the national pastime. It's also a hugely pretty scene, with ivy covering the red-brick outfield walls, and Chicagoans of all stripes rooting on the perennial not-quite winners. For American League baseball, you can watch the White Sox at the much-newer Comiskey Park, 33 W. 35th St. (312/674-1000).

Practicalities
Chicago is home to America's busiest and most infuriating airport, **O'Hare** (ORD), 17 miles northwest of the Loop and well served by Chicago Transit Authority (CTA) subway trains, shuttle services, and taxis. There are also all the usual rental car firms. Chicago's other airport, Midway, is closer to the center but served mainly by Midwestern commuter flights. Chicago is also the hub of the national Amtrak system, with **trains** pulling in to Union Station from all over the country. Chicago's roads and highways have been undergoing seemingly continuous reconstruction since they were built, making traffic horrendous, so you'll really be better off leaving the car behind and riding the CTA elevated train (the "El"), subway, or bus system (312/736-8000), which serves the entire city around the clock.

Places to stay in Chicago range from the budget likes of the **Arlington House International Hostel**, near Wrigley Field at 616 W. Arlington Place (708/929-5380), where dorm beds offer central Chicago's only real cheap accommodation. A few steps up, and just steps away from the Loop, the **Best Western River North**, 125 W. Ohio Street (312/467-0800), offers easy access to the trendy River North gallery district, within a quick walk of the "Magnificent Mile" along Michigan Avenue; doubles start at around $100. A more characterful place, the **Blackstone Hotel**, near the Art Institute at 636 S. Michigan Avenue (312/427-4300 or 800/622-6330), is a graciously updated older hotel offering all modern conveniences plus that certain extra something that only comes from experience; doubles from $125. Top of the line is the **Drake Hotel**,

140 E. Walton Place (312/787-2200), Chicago's classiest hotel, with elegant public areas and gracious staff. Doubles here start around $200.

Chicago has all sorts of top-quality, cutting-edge-cuisine restaurants, but to get a feel for the city you'll be better off stopping at the many older places that have catered to Chicagoans forever. **The Berghoff**, 17 W. Adams Street (312/427-3170), is one of these, a picture perfect turn-of-the-century saloon and steakhouse, serving up excellent food (sandwiches at lunch, hearty roast beef at dinner); cash only, often crowded. **Little Al's Italian Beef BBQ**, 1079 W. Taylor Street (312/226-4017). Step up to the counter and chow down on a juicy mess of shredded beef soaked with garlicky gravy. Truly good food. On old Route 66, **Lou Mitchell's**, 625 W. Jackson Street, is one of the greatest breakfast places on the planet, open Mon.-Sat. 5:30 AM-3 PM, Sunday 7:00 AM-3 PM.

The best source of information in advance is the **Chicago Office of Tourism**, 78 E. Washington Street (312/744-2400), which has maps and all the usual ad-packed promotional brochures. The two daily papers are the *Sun-Times* and the *Tribune;* one of the nation's best free weeklies is the Chicago *Reader,* available all over town after noon on Thursday.

ACROSS INDIANA

So close and yet so far away from the excitement of Chicago, northern Indiana can't help but seem somewhat boring. In the northwest, the state is bounded by Lake Michigan, along whose shores Rust Belt hulks of derelict heavy industry stand side by side with the pristine sands of the fascinating and beautiful Indiana Dunes National Lakeshore. The northeastern corner, even in the estimation of the state tourist office, offers little more than a few lakes and the so-called "muck lands" around the Fighting Irish homeland of South Bend. In between stretch endless acres of rolling farmland, Amish homes, and other tourist-attractive agricultural communities, as well as some of the most important sites in early American (meaning, pre-Detroit "Big Three") automotive history: the homes of Studebaker, Cord, Duesenberg, and other now-defunct car companies.

Though its etymology sparks heated debates, the nickname "Hoosier" has come to connote all that is Middle American about Indianans—their independence, their practicality, and their thrift (or is it their cussedness, conservatism, and cheapness?).

Unless you have a particular interest in documenting Rust Belt decay, there's no real reason to turn off the I-90 or I-94 freeways in the heavily industrialized first 25 miles southeast of Chicago.

Gary

If you ever watched and enjoyed the Hollywood musical *The Music Man*—in which the song "Gary, Indiana" paints a picture of idyllic homespun Americana—you'll be surprised by the reality of the place. In contrast to the rural rest of the state, this far northwest corner of Indiana is among the most heavily industrialized and impoverished areas of the country. Massive factories and oil refineries are surrounded by decaying communities,

and the streets are lined by strip malls, strip clubs, stripped-down cars—and signs for the big new casinos. During the region's heyday around the turn of the 20th century, the steel mills, foundries, and factories along the Calumet River pumped out millions of dollars' worth of products every day; nowadays, economic times are so hard that local authorities have had to call in the National Guard to police the streets.

Indiana Dunes National Lakeshore

Covering 15,000 acres along 15 miles of Lake Michigan shoreline, 25 miles east of Chicago, Indiana Dunes National Lakeshore is a striking and surprising collection of golden sand dunes, freshwater beaches, and dense forests. Chicago poet Carl Sandburg said the dunes "are to the Midwest what the Grand Canyon is to Arizona." Formally established in 1972, the park includes a huge variety of plant life —groves of maples and red oaks, pine tree and prickly pear cactus, grasslands and berry bushes—linked by many miles of hiking trails and highlighted by 125-foot Mount Baldy at the far northeast corner of the park.

Three huge steel mills and a number of small vacation home communities share space among the dunes. Also here, two miles northeast of the main visitor center, is the unusual **Beverly Shores**, a model community constructed for the "Century of Progress" World's Fair in Chicago in 1933 and reassembled here soon after in an attempt to attract buyers to a new resort community. Six of these then-futuristic structures survive along Lakefront Drive, including three steel-framed, enamel-paneled "Lustron" houses, designed to provide low-cost housing during the Great Depression. Next door is the "House of Tomorrow," an ordinary-looking house designed with an additional garage to hold the private plane every future family was sure to have.

Pick up maps, guides, and other information at the **visitor center** (daily 8 AM-5 PM, till 6 PM in summer; free; 219/926-7561) on Kemil Road between US-20 and US-12.

South Bend

With the great exception of the Indiana Dunes, there's not a lot worth stopping for east of Chicago until you reach South Bend. The largest city in Indiana's northern tier, South Bend (pop. 105,511) is best known as the home of the "Fighting Irish" of Notre Dame University, and home of the car- and carriage-making Studebaker Company. The Notre Dame campus is most visitors' destination, whether or not it's a Saturday during football season; the 1,250-acre campus, along Michigan Street a mile north of downtown, is worth a stroll to see its many Catholic icons, including a replica of the grotto

of Lourdes and the famous "Touchdown Jesus." For more information, call the campus **visitor center** (219/631-5726).

On the south side of downtown, the **Studebaker National Museum**, 525 S. Main Street (Mon.-Sat. 9 AM-5 PM, Sunday noon-5 PM; $4.50; 219/235-9714), displays a comprehensive survey of carriages and motor vehicles produced by the South Bend-based company before it closed in 1963. Behind the museum, the 5,000-seat Coveleski Stadium hosts Midwest League baseball games of the **South Bend Silver Hawks**; tickets costs $3-6 (219/235-9988).

One of South Bend's best restaurants, **Tippecanoe Place**, 620 W. Washington Street, is housed in the old Studebaker Mansion. Across the street is the **Book Inn**, a secondhand bookstore and B&B. For further information, contact the South Bend **visitor center**, 401 E. Colfax Avenue (219/234-0051 or 800/828-7881).

The small town of Peru, on US-31 midway between South Bend and Indianapolis, was the home base of many traveling circuses during the mid-19th century, an era remembered in the **Circus City Museum** (317/472-3918) at 154 N. Broadway downtown. Peru was also the birthplace of songwriter **Cole Porter,** who is buried in the town's Mount Hope Cemetery.

Trickle-down improvements to passenger cars from Indy racing have included inflatable "balloon" tires, rear-view mirrors, and high octane gasoline.

Detour: Indianapolis

Before Detroit came to dominate the world, Indianapolis was an early center the nascent American automobile industry, home to such classy marques as Stutz, Marmon, and Duesenberg, and of course the Indianapolis 500, perhaps the most famous car race in the world. Held the Sunday before Memorial Day almost every year since 1911, the Indianapolis 500 is still the biggest thing in town, drawing upwards of a half-million spectators to "The Brickyard," the oldest race track in the country. The rest of the year, the speedway is open for tours, on a bus

The first Indy 500 in 1911

that cruises around the legendary oval; tours ($2) leave from the excellent **museum** (daily 9 AM-5 PM; $2; 317/484-6747), which displays some 75 racing cars, from the

Marmon "Wasp" which won the inaugural Indy 500 race to the latest Indy champions. The museum is located on the speedway grounds at 4790 W. 16th Street in the city of Speedway (pop. 13,092), in the northwest quarter of Indianapolis's pancake-flat sprawl.

For more information on visiting Indianapolis, contact the **visitors bureau**, 201 S. Capitol Avenue (317/237-5200, 800/824-INDY or 800/824-4639), next to the landmark RCA Dome football stadium downtown.

Elkhart

A light industrial center, once famous for producing over half the brass band instruments made in America, Elkhart now makes RVs and pharmaceutical products: drug giant Miles Laboratories was founded here in 1884 and still has a major presence. In many ways it's a sleepy little Midwest town, home to both the energetic little **Midwest Museum of American Art** (Tues.-Fri. 11 AM-5 PM, Sat.-Sun. 1-4 PM; $1; 219/293-6660), downtown at 429 S. Main Street in a restored bank building; and to the **S. Ray Miller Antique Car Collection** (Mon.-Fri. 1-4 PM; $3), 2130 Middlebury Street off US-20 on the east side of town, which has the 1930 Duesenberg convertible once owned by Al Capone's lawyer among the 40 classic cars and automobile ephemera (including the world's largest collection of radiator emblems and hood ornaments) on display.

Elkhart was the boyhood home of writer **Ambrose Bierce,** whose family home stood five blocks west of downtown at 518 W. Franklin Street.

Also in Elkhart: the **RV Hall of Fame**, 801 Benham Avenue (Mon.-Fri. 9 AM-4 PM; free; 800/378-8694), which tells the industry side of the travel trailer-RV-mobile home-manufactured housing story.

Indiana's Amish Country: Middlebury and Shipshewana

East of South Bend, US-20 again becomes a road worth traveling, especially through the quiet agricultural expanses around the towns of Middlebury and Shipshewana, heartland of Indiana's sizeable Amish populations. As in other Amish areas, it's the general look of the land, rather than specific attractions, that make it enjoyable to visit; as elsewhere, the few attractions that offer an "authentic Amish experience" leave a lot to be desired. One of the largest tourist traps, **Das Dutchman Essenhaus**, sits along US-20 at the west edge of Middlebury. Rather than fight your way through the bus-tour hordes, turn north here into the quiet town center, and stop by the **Village Inn**, 104 S. Main Street (219/825-2043). The country cafe is run by, and popular with, local Amish and Mennonites, who along with everyone else enjoy the hearty coffee-shop food—not to mention great homemade pies for around $1 a slice.

Back on US-20, seven miles east of Middlebury, Hwy-5 runs north just short of a mile to the intriguing **Menno-Hof Mennonite-Amish Visitor Center** (Mon.-Sat. 10 AM-5 PM; $4 donation; 219/768-4117), outside the hamlet of Shipshewana. Operated by the local Amish and Mennonite communities, who built the large barn that houses the center during a six-day "barn-raising," the center gives an overall introduction to the Amish and Mennonite beliefs and lifeways. Surprisingly high-tech multimedia exhibits also tell of their resistance to modern technology, their long struggle for religious freedom, and their love of peace, which has helped them through centuries of torture and abuse—often at the hands of other Christians.

Ten miles south of Shipshewana via Hwy-5, the tiny town of Topeka holds the **Yoder Popcorn Shop** (800/537-1194), one of many popcorn sellers whose signs you'll see all around this part of Indiana.

Auburn: Auburn-Cord-Duesenberg Museum

Though it's a bit out of the way (20 miles south of US-20 via the I-69 freeway), lovers of vintage American cars will want to make the effort to visit the elegant **Auburn-Cord-Duesenberg Museum** (daily 9 AM-5 PM; $6; 219/925-1444), in a lovely art deco showroom at 1600 S. Wayne Street in the town of Auburn. Considered by most aficionados the finest, most innovative, and most all-around gorgeous automobiles ever produced in America, these instant classics were the brainchild of Auburn industrialist Errett Cord. During the 1920s and 1930s, Cord's company designed and produced the covetable cruisers right here in Indiana—Auburns and the front-wheel-drive Cords were produced in Auburn, while the "Dusies" were made in Indianapolis—and they're now on display inside the original showroom, built in 1930 and immaculately preserved.

The collection includes beautifully restored examples of all these classic makes, plus representatives of other classic roadsters—Packards, Cadillacs, even a Rolls-Royce or two—numbering around 150 altogether, and making this one of the top auto museums in the world. It also hosts an annual classic car festival every Labor Day weekend, attended by as many as 200,000 people.

Errett Lobban Cord

ACROSS OHIO

The many routes across Ohio along the Lake Erie shore have long been major thoroughfares. Traders and war parties of Iroquois and other Native American tribes regularly passed this way hundreds of years before European and American pioneers started coming through in Conestoga wagons. Nowadays, historical survivors, including a number of colonial-era taverns and other early roadside Americana, and a rapidly decreasing number of vegetable farms and greenhouses fill the flatlands, threatened by ever-expanding suburbia. All over northern Ohio you'll also see Rust Belt remnants of massive industrial activity that took place here from the 1880s to the 1950s, when the Great Lakes were the "Anvil of America," producing the bulk of the nation's—and the world's—iron, steel, and petroleum products.

Rather than try to follow one or another of the many old roads that crisscross the state, it's best to alternate between a variety of routes to either side of the part-toll-

way, part-freeway known as I-90. In the western half of the state, we follow US-20 from Toledo through a rural landscape of gambrel-roofed, red-painted barns, daubed with "Chew Mail Pouch" signs and made immortal by Sherwood Anderson's classic portrait *Winesburg, Ohio*. In the middle, we detour north to the lakeshore along US-6, which passes through idyllic summer home communities, gritty old ports, and one of the country's great old amusement parks, Cedar Point. East of the metropolitan Cleveland area, US-20 veers north along the Lake Erie shore, while US-6 zigzags south through the fertile farming country of northeastern Ohio—a region accurately described by the 1939 WPA *Guide to Ohio* as an "enchanting country of tumbling hills, valleys and forests."

Toledo

One of Ohio's most important industrial centers, Toledo (pop. 332,900) is the third busiest Great Lakes port, with many miles of docks, bridges, warehouses, factories, refineries, and power plants lining the mouth of the Maumee River. That may not sound like a good reason to visit, but Toledo is a fascinating place, big enough to be impressive but small enough to get around and get a feel for. Downtown Toledo is a rather anonymous place that empties after 5 PM (that world renowned-expert on tedium, John Denver, went so far as to write a song saying, "Saturday night in Toledo, Ohio, is like being nowhere at all"), but the streets just south hold dozens of unrestored cast-iron warehouses and commercial buildings just waiting for the gentrifiers to arrive.

A mile west of the waterfront, Toledo's pride and joy is the very good **Museum of Art** (Tues.-Sat. 10 AM-4 PM, Sunday 1-5 PM; free), 2445 Monroe Street, where works by El Greco (who

One place worth a stop in the 50 miles of sandy scrub-oak country east of the Indiana border is the **Sauder Farm and Craft Village** ($9; 800/590-9755), a living history museum on Hwy-2 outside the town of Archbold.

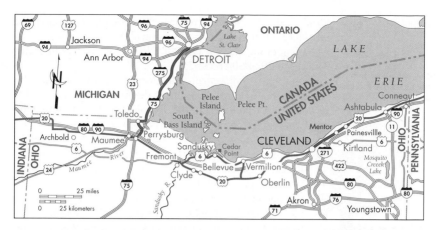

lived and worked in Toledo, Spain) highlight a survey of European painting. The real strength of the collection is its glassware, with dozens of beautiful goblets and vases dating back to Roman times.

Toledo's blue-collar multiethnicity has given rise to some good places to eat, starting with **Ansara's Board Room**, 233 N. Huron Street downtown, an only-in-Toledo combination of chop house and Middle Eastern restaurant housed in a dark, wood-panelled room. The one truly not-to-be-missed Toledo eatery is **Tony Packo's Cafe**, across the river at 1902 Front Street (419/691-6054); Packo's addictive chili dogs were made famous by Corporal Klinger (played by real-life Toledo native Jamie Farr) on the long-running TV series *M.A.S.H.,* and still pack the crowds into this East Toledo haunt—despite its location near a huge Toledo Edison coal-fired power plant.

Accommodation rates at the many motels around Toledo are lower than elsewhere, making it an even better place to break a journey. For more information, or for details on the lively **Rock, Rhythm and Blues Festival** held every Memorial Day, contact the Toledo **visitor center**, 218 Huron Street (419/243-8191 or 800/243-4667).

For the full Toledo experience, chow down on Tony Packo's chili dogs before, during, or after a Class AAA baseball game at the Toledo Mud Hens stadium in nearby Maumee, off the I-90/I-75 junction. For tickets and schedules, call 419/893-9483.

Detour to Detroit

Though Detroit (45 miles north of Toledo via I-75) is a ways off our route across Ohio, no guidebook as car-focused as this could feel complete without covering the "Motor City," heart of America's automotive industry. In nearby Dearborn you can pay homage to the man who made your car affordable at the **Henry Ford Museum** and **Greenfield Village**. The Henry Ford Museum, not surprisingly, has an incredible collection of cars and car-related objects that illustrate the massive impact the car has had on American life. The adjacent, open-air complex of Deerfield Village is a virtual microcosm of American history, holding everything from Abe Lincoln's law office to Thomas Edison's workshop, arranged by Henry Ford and his heirs to form an

In Monroe, Michigan (between Toledo and Detroit) you can kick back in a selection of easy chairs past and present at the **La-Z-Boy Museum,** in the company headquarters! It's free, but by reservation only (734/242-1444).

inside the Ford Museum

ideal village of American creativity. The complex is located just off US-12, 10 miles west of downtown Detroit, at 20900 Oakwood Boulevard (daily 9 AM-5 PM; $12.50 each or $22 for both; 313/271-1620 or 800/835-5237).

Along with its massive collection of art from around the world, the huge **Detroit Institute of the Arts,** is worth a look for its powerful Diego Rivera mural, *Detroit Industry,* celebrating the workers who built Detroit's wheels. The museum is located at 5200 Woodward Avenue (Wed.-Sun. 11 AM-4 PM; $4) in Detroit proper. Also in Detroit proper is the **Motown Historical Museum,** contained in the very house where Berry Gordy, Jr. produced the great hits of the 1960s. This museum documents the making of the Motown Sound by the likes of Smokey Robinson, Martha Reeves, Marvin Gaye, Stevie Wonder, the Temptations, and Diana Ross and the Supremes. It can be found in the heart of Detroit at 2468 W. Grand Boulevard open daily 10 AM-5 PM; ($6).

Finally, Detroit remembers Joe Louis, the "Brown Bomber," with **The Big Fist,** a 25-foot-high fist looming over Detroit's main thoroughfare, in the middle of Woodward Avenue at Jefferson Avenue, across from the landmark Renaissance Center in downtown Detroit. For detailed Detroit information, contact the **visitors bureau** (800/DETROIT or 800/338-7648).

Maumee and Perrysburg

South of Toledo along the Maumee River, a pair of towns preserve important parts of western Ohio's early history. On the west bank of the river, Maumee (pop. 15,561; pronounced Mommy) was founded in 1817 at the western edge of settled territory, and holds remnants of the Miami and Erie Canal. In summer, it's home to the Toledo Mud Hens, the Detroit Tigers' International League farm club.

Across the river, Perrysburg (pop. 12,251) is a pretty little town of white colonial-style houses, with a nice waterfront park and a short strip of restaurants and bars running east along Louisiana Street (US-20). A mile upstream from town, past the cemetery and a set of expensive-looking tract houses, **Fort Meigs** (Wed.- Sun. 9:30 AM-5 PM in summer; $4) is a full-scale 1950s reconstruction of the wooden fortress that played a key role in defending the frontier against British and Indian attack during the War of 1812.

Fremont

In Fremont (pop. 17,600), where in the 1700s native Wyandot Indians established a village along the main trail between Pittsburgh and Detroit, a small JCPenney and a movie theater provide a focus for the old-fashioned downtown along the Sandusky River, while strip malls and fast-food chains line the US-20 bypass and the access roads to and from the I-90 freeway.

Fremont's main attraction is the **Rutherford B. Hayes Presidential Center** (Mon.-Sat. 9 AM-5 PM, Sunday noon-5 PM; $4; 419/332-2081), south of US-20 at

1337 Hayes Avenue, which encompasses the 25-acre estate of Civil War general and former U.S. president Rutherford B. Hayes, who lived here 1873-93 and served as president 1877-81. The nation's first presidential library, the Hayes center includes the rather plain, red-brick family house and a large museum displaying his public and private papers, sundry mementos, and his daughter Fanny's doll house collection. Hayes is buried on a wooded knoll on the grounds, alongside his wife and their favorite horses.

Clyde: Winesburg, Ohio

Five miles east of Fremont, the town of Clyde (pop. 5,776) is a perfect little place, still very much the typical farm town that the New Deal-era WPA *Guide to Ohio* said might well have served as a model for one of Thomas Hart Benton's murals of rural America: "Old Indian paths and sand ridges are now angular streets; cheek by jowl with an odd assortment of business houses is the railroad cutting across Main Street, gyved with station, elevator, and spur track; around the decorous houses are gardens, flower beds, and shrubbery tended by friendly and loquacious folk."

*In Clyde, the McPherson Cemetery along US-20 holds the remains of **Brigadier Gen. James "Birdseye" McPherson,** the highest-ranking Union officer killed in the Civil War.*

Clyde's brick-paved streets are still quiet, lined by mature trees and most of the same houses as when writer **Sherwood Anderson,** who was born in southern Ohio in 1876, grew up here in the 1880s and 1890s. Because the people of Clyde took offense at Anderson's sharply drawn and only slightly disguised portraits of them in his groundbreaking book *Winesburg, Ohio*—which was published in 1919, 20 years after Anderson left Clyde for Chicago—the town doesn't celebrate him in any obvious way. The only real sign of him is in the local library, 222 W. Buckeye Street, a block west of the town center, where visitors can check out a collection of his books and a short documentary video of his life and times. The library is also the best place to pick up the pamphlet that points out Anderson's home and the sites of many scenes from *Winesburg.*

Beside the Winesburg legacy, Clyde also offers a couple of very good road food stops: **Bogey's Diner** at 222 W. McPherson Highway, and nearby, the photogenic **Twistee Treat,** shaped like an ice-cream cone and serving great shakes. To complete the Sherwood Anderson tour, stay at the AAA-recommended **Winesburg Motel,** 214 E. McPherson Highway (419/547-0531).

Bellevue

The railroad and factory town of Bellevue, on US-20 seven miles east of Clyde, was the place where the psychopathic killer in the movie *Silence of the Lambs* held his victims hostage. As late as the 1940s, the town used the cavelike limestone sinkholes seen in the film for disposing of its wastewater; during heavy rains, underground pressure turned these into bubbling geysers spouting sewage all over town.

Needless to say, there's not a lot to tempt you to stop.

Sandusky: Cedar Point

Midway between Toledo and Cleveland, a fine natural harbor has enabled Sandusky to remain a busy port, albeit now more for recreational ferries to the offshore islands than for the coal and iron ore it once handled. The waterfront is good for a short stroll, and the town is rich in elaborate mid-1800s houses like the **Follett**

House Museum (daily 1-4 PM; free), 404 Wayne Street, a well-preserved 1827 Greek Revival house filled with period artifacts and a few displays on the area's history.

Another sort of history can be experienced at the wonderful old-time amusement park of Cedar Point (hours vary, usually daily 10 AM-10 or 11 PM June-Sept.; $31.95 adults, $6.95 for children under four feet tall; 419/627-2350), which has a dozen great roller coasters ranging from fragile-looking old wooden ones to high-speed modern monsters like the **Magnum,** a 15-story colossus that sends riders racing along at more than 70 mph, and the even more terrifying **Raptor,** in which riders swing on benches hanging upside down from the track—a complete inversion of the usual roller-coaster experience. Cedar Point is one of the most popular amusement parks in the country, so expect crowds if you come on summer weekends. The 360-acre park sits on a peninsula across the water from downtown Sandusky, and has animal shows, a Lake Erie beach, and a water park called Soak City ($12.95), as well as restaurants and on-site camping and hotel accommodations.

Back in downtown Sandusky, stop for a bite to eat at **Markley's,** a classic little 1950s diner on the corner of Market and Wayne Streets, a block east of Columbus. For more information on the Sandusky area, including Put-in-Bay and the offshore islands, contact the **visitor center,** 231 W. Washington Row (419/625-2984, 800/255-ERIE or 800/255-3743).

On South Bass Island in Lake Erie, 15 miles by boat from Sandusky, a stone column commemorates the victory of **Adm. Oliver Perry,** who defeated a British fleet here on September 10, 1813, announcing his success with the laconic words, "We have met the enemy, and they are ours." The islands are popular summer resorts; contact the Sandusky visitor center for details.

The tiny town of Milan, two miles south of I-90 via US-250, was the birthplace in 1847 of the great inventor **Thomas Edison.** His childhood home at 9 Edison Drive is preserved as a museum.

Much of Oberlin's endowment comes from the bequest of Oberlin graduate **Charles Hall,** who in 1886, a year after graduating, discovered a viable process for refining aluminum and later founded Alcoa Corporation.

Vermilion

One of the more attractive resorts on Ohio's Lake Erie frontage, Vermilion took its name from the rich red clay that colors the soil. Along with a fine beach backed by dozens of attractive summer homes, the town also holds the **Inland Seas Maritime Museum** (daily 10 AM-5 PM; $4), along the waterfront at 480 Main Street. The museum's usual array of scale models and paintings of ships is augmented with preserved timbers from Perry's ship *Niagara,* and a 62-foot-tall replica of a Lake Erie lighthouse.

A great old-fashioned ice cream and sandwich parlor, **Edna Mae's,** stands at 5598 Liberty Avenue at the center of town; for a more complete meal, try the comfortable **Old Prague Restaurant** next door. A reliable place to stay is the **Motel Plaza,** 4645 Liberty Avenue (440/967-3191).

Oberlin

Away from the lakeshore, 25 miles west of Cleveland between I-90 and US-20, the attractive college town of Oberlin (pop. 8,191) serves up an idyllic slice of Middle Americana. Founded along with the surrounding town in 1833, Oberlin College has a history of being at the leading edge of American education, despite (or perhaps because of) its location far from the madding crowds. In 1837 Oberlin became the country's first co-educational college. It was also the first to embrace the education of

African-Americans: in the nineteenth century, Oberlin awarded more degrees to black students than all other mainstream American colleges combined.

The Oberlin College campus spreads west of the town's green main square, which is also graced on the east side by the neo-classical facade of the **Allen Art Museum** (Tues.-Sat. 10 AM-5 PM, Sunday 1-5 PM; free), which displays an overall survey of world art—Japanese prints, Islamic carpets, and modern painting by the likes of Cezanne and Diebenkorn. Architecture fans should take note: the old gallery was designed by Cass Gilbert, who also planned a handful of Romanesque buildings on campus; a new wing was added in 1977 by Robert Venturi. The museum also offers guided **tours** ($5) of a nearby house designed in 1947 by Frank Lloyd Wright.

The town of Oberlin seems preserved in a time warp, totally devoid of the trend-swapping cafe culture of many college towns. Its few blocks are lined by an old five-and-dime, an Army surplus store, and a hardware store, and there's also a classic **Dairy Twist** ice-cream and burger stand, on US-20 just east of the Hwy-58 turnoff from Oberlin.

In the past 30 years much of Ohio has been turned from farmland to suburbia, a development that inspired Pretenders singer and Ohio native Chrissie Hynde to write "My City is Gone"—which coincidentally is the theme song for Rush Limbaugh's radio program.

I went back to Ohio / but my
* pretty countryside*
Had been paved down the
* middle / by a government*
* that had no pride*
The farms of Ohio / had been
* replaced by shopping*
* malls*
And Muzak filled the air /
* from Seneca to Cuyahoga*
* Falls*

US-20 across Cleveland

The nicest old road route into Cleveland from the west is US-6, which winds along Lake Erie as Sandusky Road, Lake Avenue and Clifton Boulevard. Running right through downtown, past "The Flats" along Shoreway, then east along Superior Avenue, US-6 gives a great taste of the city.

US-20, on the other hand, diverges slightly east of downtown Cleveland, following Euclid Avenue past the Museum of Art, then crosses to the north of US-6, following the lakeshore all the way into Pennsylvania.

North of I-90 along US-20, a half-mile from the center of Mentor, a large white house is preserved much as it was when **James Garfield** lived here before assuming the presidency. Ten miles northeast, at 792 Mentor Avenue in Painesville, the **Rider Tavern** was built in 1818 along the stagecoach route between Buffalo and Cleveland.

Kirtland

The rolling farmlands of northeastern Ohio around Kirtland were, from 1831 to 1837, the center of the Mormon religion. Joseph Smith, Jr., along with 1,000 of his followers, settled here and built a large temple—the first Mormon temple anywhere—and developed industries and a bank (known as the "Kirtland anti-BANK-ing Company"). The bank failed in 1838 and Smith fled, first to Liberty, Missouri, and later to Nauvoo, Illinois, where in 1844 he was killed by a mob.

The **Kirtland Temple** at 9020 Chillicothe Road (Hwy-306) is surrounded by pleasant gardens and open to the general public on guided **tours** (Mon.-Sat. 9 PM-5 PM, Sunday 1-5 PM; free; 440/256-3318). The stately Greek Revival structure has a gleaming white interior built in part by Brigham Young, with elaborately crafted woodwork pulpits (one at each end) and an upstairs classroom with more of the unusual double pulpits. The temple and most of the town have been preserved under the auspices of the Reorganized Church of Jesus Christ of Latter Day Saints (RLDS), which was set up in 1852 by Joseph Smith, Jr.'s oldest son and those followers who didn't go west to Salt Lake City with Brigham Young.

A newer temple across the street is used for most services; adjacent to it is **Kokomo's**, a very good burger and milk shake stand.

Ashtabula and Conneaut

On the shores of Lake Erie, 18 miles from the Pennsylvania border, Ashtabula (pop. 21,633) is a large and busy pleasure-boating port, first dredged at the mouth of the Ashtabula River in 1826 and later home to some of the biggest shipyards on the

CLEVELAND SURVIVAL GUIDE

POOR CLEVELAND. JUST WHEN IT seemed on the verge of recovering some semblance of civic pride, thanks to the success of the Rock and Roll Hall of Fame, and the Cleveland Indians making it to the World Series, everything went black when pro football's much-loved Browns abandoned the city for pastures new—in Baltimore, as if to add insult to injury. Home

base of John D. Rockefeller's Standard Oil, for decades to either side of the turn of the twentieth century Cleveland was one of the biggest and heaviest of all the Great Lakes heavy industrial giants. Despite spending much of the past 50 years reeling from Rust Belt decay, the city does seem to be coming back to life, energized out of all proportion by Jacob's Field, the fan-friendly (and always sold-out) downtown baseball stadium that opened in 1994.

The Rock and Roll Hall of Fame, North Coast Harbor (daily 10 AM-5:30 PM; $12.50; 216/781-ROCK, 216/781-7625 or 800/493-ROLL, 800/493-7655), opened with a splash at the end of 1995. Q: Why Cleveland? A: The Hall of Fame was located here because it was a Cleveland DJ, Alan Freed, who is credited with naming the music "rock and roll," way back in 1951. Housed in a striking modern building designed by I.M. Pei, 50,000 square feet of galleries fill a 165-foot tower with a barrage of "Entertainment Industry"-centered multimedia exhibits tracing the roots and branches of the rock family tree. West of the Rock and Roll Hall of Fame along the Cuyahoga River waterfront, "**The Flats**" district is a test case in post-industrial redevelopment.

Cleveland's old heavyweight industrial district of "The Flats" has undergone a successful face-lift, with water taxis running back and forth across the river, linking the bars and restaurants that now fill gigantic old mills, factories, and warehouses. The whole district is overlaid by a network of bridges (drawbridges, lift bridges, swing bridges, all kinds of bridges) that form a feast for the eyes of any post-industrial amateur archaeologist.

A half-mile to the southeast, at the heart of downtown, **Jacobs Field**, Carnegie Avenue at Ontario Avenue, is the place that made Cleveland a winner —inspiring not just the **Cleveland Indians** baseball team (tickets 216/420-

Great Lakes. Now primarily recreation-oriented, Ashtabula still has a few signs of its industrial past, including the lakefront coal conveyor that forms an archway over the river, next to a squat lighthouse and a small local history **museum** (Fri.-Sun. 1-6 PM; donations) housed in the old lighthouse keeper's quarters.

A block south of the lakefront, pride of place goes to a burly bascule drawbridge and to the many turn-of-the-century industrial and business premises along Bridge Street that form a three-block parade of gift shops, bars, and restaurants, including

---

4200), who won the American League championship for the first time in two generations the year the stadium opened, but a general renaissance of civic pride. Jacobs Field is packed full with 42,000 fans every game, so buy tickets as far in advance as possible.

Practicalities
The Cleveland airport, **Hopkins International**, a major hub for Continental Airlines, is 12 miles southwest of downtown, linked by I-71 freeway and RTA subway (216/621-9500) to central Cleveland. To get a feel for the place, a car is hard to beat, especially since the city tends to sprawl sideways rather than concentrate vertically. In the downtown area, finding your way around the Cuyahoga River waterfront takes patience, as many roads dead-end and some of the old bridges are closed to traffic; on foot, the Ohio City RTA stop is a good place to start exploring.

For a place to stay, the **Holiday Inn—Lakeside**, 1111 Lakeside Avenue (216/241-5100), is hard to beat. It offers the usual Holiday Inn comforts and is very near the Rock and Roll museum; doubles cost around $95. Right downtown, across from Claes Oldenberg's "World's Largest Rubber Stamp" statue, the **Stouffer Renaissance Cleveland Hotel**, 24 Public Square (216/696-5600), has been immaculately updated into the city's nicest place to stay. Formerly known as the Tower City Plaza, this beautiful old hotel has good-value weekend specials; doubles run $100-200.

For food, the **Great Lakes Brewing Company**, 2516 Market Avenue in Ohio City (216/771-4404), west of the Cuyahoga River, in an artsy low-rent district, has good food, great beer, and a generally convivial crowd.

While here, check out the West Side Farmer's Market, and Allstate Barber College, across the street on 26th and Lorain Avenue—20 chairs, no waiting! In a light industrial and warehousing district east of I-90, a half-mile from downtown, **Slyman's**, at 3106 St. Clair Avenue (216/621-3760), has the best corned beef in Cleveland, bar none. For real good road food, **Ruthie & Moe's Diner**, 4002 Prospect Avenue (216/431-8063), is a pair of vintage diners joined together, now serving road food classics like meatloaf, macaroni and cheese, and milk shakes, plus unusual specials: Hungarian goulash, Louisiana gumbo, matzo ball soup. Open Mon.-Fri., for breakfast and lunch only.

For more complete visitor information, contact the **Cleveland Convention and Visitors Bureau**, 3100 Terminal Tower, 50 Public Square (216/621-4110 or 800/321-1004). The morning *Cleveland Plain Dealer* is the main daily **newspaper**.

the **Doxsie Deli and Ice Cream Parlour**, 1001 Bridge Street, open daily for sandwiches and sundaes.

A dozen miles east of Ashtabula, right on the Pennsylvania border, the historic port town of Conneaut (pop. 13,200, pronounced KAH-nee-ut) has another great road food restaurant, the **White Turkey Drive-Inn**, 388 E. Main Road (US-20), a summer-only place that's famous for two things: turkey sandwiches and frosty mugs of root beer.

ACROSS PENNSYLVANIA

US-20 takes little more than the proverbial blink of an eye to cross the 45 miles of northwestern Pennsylvania, which is part of Pennsylvania only because the country's founding fathers thought it was unfair to deny the Keystone State a share of the Lake Erie shoreline. I-90 is most travelers' route of choice, but US-20 does have a couple of worthwhile stops. Twelve miles east of the Ohio border, the town of **Girard** (pop. 4,722) has the nifty little **Hazel Kibler Museum**, 522 E. Main Street, documenting local history and local circus clown Dan Rice, who posed as Uncle Sam in the famous "I Want You" posters. In **Erie**, the big city in these parts, a replica of Commodore Perry's flagship *Niagara* is moored along the waterfront at 164 E Front Street. The art deco Union Pacific depot at 123 W. 14th Street is now home to a stylish brew pub and restaurant, **Hoppers,** or for more old-fashioned fare try **George's,** near the US-19/20, junction at 2614 Glenwood Park Avenue, serving classic diner fare since 1926.

Beginning in the summer of 1999, Erie will also have a Class AA baseball team, the Pittsburgh Pirates-affiliated **Erie Seawolves** (814/456-1300).

This part of Pennsylvania also marks the spot where our routes diverge: one branch continues along US-20 across upstate New York and on to Boston, while the other follows US-6 from Meadville ("Birthplace of the Zipper") east across Pennsylvania, Connecticut, and Rhode Island, ending eventually at the tip of Cape Cod. The US-6 route is described beginning on page 628.

ACROSS NEW YORK

From inauspicious beginnings in the marshlands and vineyards
of the Lake Erie "grape belt" at the state's far western tip, the
portion of US-20 that runs across upstate New York cuts a wide,
scenic swath through a diverse terrain of flatlands, rippling hills, and spring-fed
lakes. This well-maintained, mostly four-lane road glides surreptitiously through
four centuries of history, slicing through vast Dutch patroonships, serene Shaker
colonies, blood-soaked Revolutionary War battlefields, Native American hunting
grounds, the birthplace of the women's movement, Underground Railroad hide-
outs, and the long-calmed waters of the once-mighty Erie Canal. Sparkling baseball
diamonds, dairy bars by the dozens, petrified creatures, stately longhouses, abandoned motor courts, prancing wooden horses, off-key nose whistles, and succulent,
grill-toughened hot dogs are just a few of the countless other reasons to slow down
and pull over early and often as you cross the Empire State.

The "Romance Road," as labeled by a 1940s travel writer, follows several old Iroquois Indian trails as it nudges its way through the western Niagara Frontier, then
traces the 19th-century Great Western Turnpike through the Finger Lakes region
before easing down into the historically rich Hudson Valley near Albany, where it
begins a gradual ascent of the Taconic Mountains and Berkshire foothills that hug
the Massachusetts border. All the way across the state, US-20 roughly parallels the
crowded, rumbling I-90 New York Thruway toll road—a necessary evil that lures
most of the diesel-spewing, view-obscuring 18-wheel traffic away from placid US-
20 with a 65 mph speed limit and the promise of uneventful, predictable fast-food
rest-stop dining experiences and fluorescent-lit motels.

**While US-20 runs across the heart of New York State, a parallel route, US-6,
runs across the wilds of Northern Pennsylvania. This alternate route, which
continues east across Connecticut and Rhode Island to the tip of Cape Cod,
is described beginning on page 628.**

Westfield: New York's Wine Country

The salt-whitened, snowplow-scraped roadway and endless, slightly hilly expanse
of shaggy, kudzu-like vineyards on the south side of the road continue for a dozen
monotonous miles between the state line and proud, hardworking Westfield (pop.
3,500), known locally as Vine City because of its large Italian-American grape-
growing community and its proximity to some of Chautauqua County's finest wineries.
The **Johnson Estate Winery** (716/326-2191, 800/DRINK-NY or 800/374-6569)
and **Vetter Vineyards** (716/326-3100) are within a goblet's throw of Main Street
(US-20), as are the waterfalls and hiking trails of nearby Chautauqua Gorge, seven
sylvan miles long and 100 feet deep.

The tangy Concord grape was introduced to the region in 1859, but it wasn't
until 1897 that Dr. Charles Welch and his father moved to Westfield and founded

the factory that led to Westfield's long-standing nickname, "The Grape Juice Capital of the World." Though many of the canneries have since vanished, **Welch Foods** still maintains a large plant and its corporate offices on N. Portage Street, on the western edge of Westfield's compact downtown.

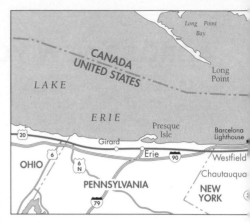

Across I-90 on waterfront Hwy-5, Lake Erie's Barcelona Harbor is home to the landmark **Barcelona Lighthouse**, which was the first lighthouse in the world to be lit by natural gas when constructed in 1830. Drop by **Jack's Barcelona Drive-In** for fast food or the **Barcelona Harbor House** for finer, sit-down fare with a lakeside view. The no-frills **Main Diner** back in downtown Westfield is a pleasant place to grab a cup of coffee and sandwich while watching the pickup trucks cruise up and down the several-block Main Street.

The **Sleepy Hollow Motel** at 7254 E. US-20 (716/326-3266) and the **Candlelight Lodge** at 143 E. Main Street (716/326-2830) are two low-priced lodging options. The what-you-see-is-what-you-get **Theater Motel and Restaurant** on the eastern edge of town lets you stare at an abandoned drive-in movie theater, grab a greasy bite to eat, and flop in a budget ranch motel room with a vineyard view without having to move your car.

Detour: Chautauqua

Comedian **Lucille Ball** grew up in Jamestown, at the southeast end of Chautauqua Lake. A glass case in the lobby of the Civic Center Theater, 116 E. 3rd Street, displays lots of "I Love Lucy" memorabilia.

Chautauqua was founded in 1874 by Lewis Miller, inventor Thomas Edison's father-in-law. More recently, Bill Clinton came here during the 1996 presidential campaign to prepare for his debates with Bob Dole.

One of the few utopian-minded nineteenth-century communities to survive to the present day, Chautauqua (pop. 4,554) is an idyllic Victorian village of quaint pastel cottages, tidy flower gardens and pedestrian-friendly streets—a genteel model of

idyllic Chautauqua

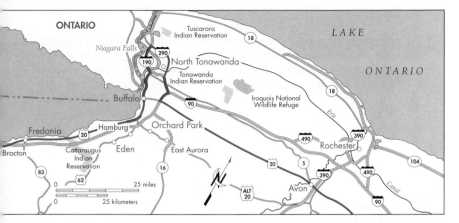

middle-class, small-town civilization. Established as a summer training ground for Methodist Sunday school teachers, and now preserved as a nonprofit foundation, in the first decades of the twentieth century Chautauqua had an immeasurable effect on American culture, sponsoring correspondence courses and cross-country lecture tours that brought liberal arts education to the masses, especially in the rural Midwest.

Chautauqua, which is located along Hwy-394 about 20 miles south of Westfield on US-20 (off I-90 exit 60), has hardly changed since its heyday, and still welcomes all comers to its summer-long series of lectures and concerts, which are held in a delightful old open-air amphitheater. Though the emphasis is on education, Chautauqua is not entirely academic: in between broadening their minds, visitors can relax on the white sand beaches that line the lakeshore. Day visitors to Chautauqua have to pay admission (about $10, free on Sunday) and pass through a set of ancient turnstiles, as if entering a mind-improving amusement park; others come for a week or two, renting a cottage or staying at the wonderful old **Athenaeum Hotel**, built in 1881.

For further information, or to request a schedule of classes, lectures and events, call 716/357-6200 or 800/836-ARTS (800/836-2787).

Fredonia
US-20 trucks through the cherry orchards and vineyards of Portland and Brocton before ebbing into the center of neatly maintained Fredonia (pop. 10,400), the namesake of the Marx Brothers' beloved *Duck Soup* homeland. Site of the first natural gas well in the U.S. (1825), Fredonia was also the birthplace of the agricultural Grange (1868) and—ironically, for a town in the heart of the western New York Wine Belt—the Women's Christian Temperance Union (1873).

Downtown Fredonia boasts the gracefully shaded, New England-style Barker Commons town square, bordered by a restored opera house and a host of Greek Revival, Italianate, Victorian, and gothic 19th-century commercial buildings. A stroll down tree-lined Central Avenue to the north of Main Street (US-20) reveals an equally diverse array of turn-of-the-century homes, which stand in marked contrast to the sterile modernity you encounter up the road in the several I.M. Pei-designed buildings that define the State University of New York (SUNY) Fredonia campus, site of the Buffalo Bills' summer training camp.

A **Days Inn** near I-90 and the restored, veranda-fronted **White Inn** at 52 E. Main Street near Barker Commons (716/672-2103) are two distinctly different answers to the proverbial lodging question. The White Inn's stately dining room may tempt you, as may the **Barker Brew Co.** at 34 W. Main Street, which offers slab-like deli sandwiches and an alehouse full of great microbrews in a restored 1860 building fronting the commons. Nearby, the **Park Pub**, 26 W. Main Street, is a homey, old-fashioned diner that packs in a mostly local crowd.

East of Fredonia, the vineyards suddenly vanish, replaced by the thick stands of scruffy pine trees and cigarette vendor stands that crowd the roadside along US-20's two-mile passage through the northeastern corner of the Cattaraugus Indian Reservation.

Eden: Original American Kazoo Company

US-20 bumps up north along the lakeshore through several miles of scraggly forest, and you won't miss a thing by taking the I-90/NY Thruway to exit 57A, which lands you on a two-lane back road bound right for sleepy downtown Eden (pop. 3,088). Eden, a make-your-own-music lover's paradise that lays claim to an annual summer Corn Days festival, is home to the one-and-only Original American Kazoo Company museum, gift shop, and factory at 8703 S. Main Street. Established in 1916, the company boasts the world's only still-operating metal kazoo factory (most of the plastic ones are stamped out these days in China and Hong Kong). A restored, two-story clapboard house contains an all-too-country-store-cute gift shop and a tiny free museum offering an up-close-and-personal view of the factory's belt-and-pulley metal kazoo production line and the opportunity to sign a petition aimed at getting the kazoo declared America's national instrument.

After viewing a short, jumpy video extolling the virtues of one of the few musical instruments invented in the U.S., visitors can gaze at a cramped display of antique kazoos, ranging from an original wooden model to the bottle-shaped kazoos churned out to celebrate the repeal of Prohibition. A large sign chimes in with some fascinating kazoo-related trivia, finally putting to rest those long-vexing questions concerning the most requested tune played on the kazoo ("Far, Far Away"), the most popular kazoo (the slide trombone), the largest kazoo ever made (the 43-pound Kazoophony, replete with four mouth pieces, resonator, and cymbal), and the number of kazoo bands registered in the U.S. (15,000 and still counting). You can pick up an adenoid-popping nose flute, a trombone kazoo, and a variety of noisemakers in the gift shop on your way out, or grab some wax paper, rubber bands, and an empty toilet paper or paper towel roll and invent your own kazoo.

Orchard Park

A thick slice of suburban sprawl in the shadow of Rich Stadium (home of the Buffalo Bills football team), Orchard Park offers the culinary pleasures of the **Donuts and Cream** doughnut stand, 6494 E. Lake Avenue. In the heart of Orchard Park, dive into a salty, crusty sandwich full of a Buffalo specialty, beef on weck, or down a plate of fiery chicken wings (another local delicacy) at **Eckl's**, 4936 Ellicott Road, an area supper club institution since 1934; it's only open in the evening, so plan your route accordingly.

Detour: Buffalo

Founded as a Niagara frontier outpost in the early 1800s, Buffalo (pop. 328,100) exploded into a bustling shipping, manufacturing, and railroad center after the 1825 opening of the Erie Canal made the city the linchpin of trade between the Great Lakes, Canada, and the eastern seaboard. The departure of many factories and corporate headquarters to warmer, cheap-labor climes, has dented Buffaloans' self-confidence over the past several decades. Added to this are the legendary snowy winters, which leave their mark in the many potholes and bumps pockmarking the city's concrete street grid; not to mention the Bills' seeming inability to win a Super Bowl. But the optimistic made-in-Buffalo spirit captured so eloquently in Verlyn Klinkenborg's 1990 magical portrait of Polish-American bartender Eddie Wenzek, *The Last Fine Time,* lives on in the city's burly, passionate sports fans, spunky local music scene, spicy local eateries, and ample cultural resources.

The south Buffalo suburb of Hamburg, "The Town That Friendship Built" and one of many supposed birthplaces of the hamburger, holds the retro **Uncle Joe's Diner,** open daily 6 AM-11 PM at 4869 S.W. Boulevard (US-20).

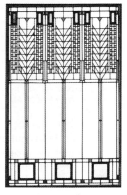

Art Glass Window Pane, *by Frank Lloyd Wright*

A 15-minute drive from downtown up tree-lined Elmwood Avenue takes you to Buffalo's premier attraction, the extensive collection of Picassos, de Koonings, and Pollocks and other important modern masterpiece's inside the **Albright-Knox Art Gallery** (Tues.-Sat. 11 AM-5 PM, Sunday noon-5 PM; $4; 716/ 882-8700). This world-class museum stands amidst the grassy expanses and ponds of **Delaware Park**, designed by Frederick Law Olmsted, the landscape architect for New York City's Central Park and Brooklyn's Prospect Park. Across the road you'll see the marble neoclassical structure that has housed the Buffalo and Erie County Historical Society **museum** (Tues.-Sat. 10 AM-5 PM, Sunday noon-5 PM; $3.50) since its construction in 1901 for the historic Pan-American Exposition. The non-air-conditioned gallery can be a bit stifling on hot summer afternoons, but the wonderful "Made in Buffalo" and "Dividing the Land" local manufacturing and immigration exhibits should satisfy most of your local history thirsts.

Another Buffalo suburb, East Aurora, was the home of **Roycroft Campus** (716/652-0571), a turn-of-the-century arts-and-crafts community whose furniture shops and studios still stand at the center of town.

Bookhounds will want to brave the leaning towers of tattered, bargain-priced old hardbacks leering from the dusty, grease-streaked windows of the dense, rewarding **Circular One Bookstore**, 799 Elmwood Avenue in the casually bohemian Elmwood Village neighborhood. A few blocks north, you can enjoy a breakfast, burger, milk shake, or piece of pie at the **Elmwood Soda Bar**, 929 Elmwood Avenue, or get the lowdown on the hottest local band or live music club at the venerable **Home of the Hits** record store at 1105 Elmwood Avenue—the place to pick up the city's biweekly *Arts Voice* for a listing of local clubs, films, and offbeat attractions, most of which are found in the funky, historic "Allentown" neighborhood around the junction of Elmwood Avenue and Allen Street, just north of downtown.

The infamous **Anchor Bar**, "Birthplace of Buffalo Wings," is a short walk away at 1047 Main Street. Skip the bland Italian entrees in favor of the bar's much-hyped specialty—the saucy, fiery, deep-fried chicken wings, now a great American fern bar cliché. Combine this required road trip activity with the more subtle pleasures of a baseball game at the Buffalo Bisons' beautiful 21,000-seat **North AmeriCare Park** (716/846-2000), a.k.a. Pilot Field, tucked away downtown at the corner of Swan and Washington Streets.

Most of the national chain motels are clustered east of town around I-90 and the Buffalo airport. The in-town **Best Western**, 510 Delaware Avenue (716/886-8333), is a bit higher-priced at around $75 a night, but its central Allentown location saves you hours of driving time and grounds you smack in the middle of the city's Allentown bar, restaurant, and club district. Even better value is the immaculate **HI Buffalo Hostel**, 667 Main Street (716/852-5222), with $17 dorm beds in a historic downtown building.

Home and away games of the Buffalo Bisons, the Cleveland Indians top farm team, are broadcast play-by-play on WWKB 1520 AM.

For additional information, and maps of Buffalo's wealth of significant architecture (Louis Sullivan, H.H. Richardson, Eliel Saarinen and Frank Lloyd Wright all completed major buildings here), contact the Buffalo/Niagara County **visitors center** (800/BUFFALO or 800/283-3256).

Niagara Falls

If you have time for a quick upriver side trip, head up I-190 to that archetypal tourist trap, Niagara Falls. There's plenty to see (and pay for) on the U.S. side of the foaming falls—the famous *Maid of the Mist* boat ride costs $8.95, walking through the **Cave of the Winds** costs $5, climbing the observation tower costs 50 cents, even the National Park Service charges $4 just for parking at Prospect Point, the best place to see the falls—but the very tackiest tourist attractions (Tussaud's Waxworks, Movieland Wax Museum, IMAX, the Skylon Tower, Ripley's Believe It or Not!, etc.) are on the Canadian side. It also costs 50 cents to walk back across Rainbow Bridge, so take quarters, and your passport, if you go.

*The power of Niagara Falls was first used to generate electricity by the remarkable inventor **Nikola Tesla** in 1896. A monument to him stands near the falls in Prospect Park.*

Once you've seen the powerful falls, you might want to zoom four miles north on the Robert Moses freeway to the **Niagara Power Project Visitor Center** (716/285-3211) for a free view, a Thomas Hart Benton mural, and technical lessons about how the surging Niagara River waters have been harnessed to produce some 2,000 megawatts of power.

All the major chain have hotels on the American side of the falls, averaging around $75 a night in summer, but you'll probably have more fun if you shuffle back to Buffalo for the night.

North Tonawanda

Between Buffalo and Niagara Falls, North Tonawanda is a tough-looking factory town concealing one of the Buffalo area's best-kept secrets, the **Herschell Carousel Factory Museum** (daily 11 AM-5 PM in summer, Wed.-Sun. 1-5 PM rest of the year; $3; 716/693-1885) at 180 Thompson Street a half-mile to the east of Hwy-265. The old, barn-like 1915 factory-shed houses a restored 1916 pulley-driven carousel and a stable of immaculately painted wooden steeds, zebras, roosters, ostriches, frogs, bears, and bulls hand-carved by the factory's immigrant artisans for the countless carousels and kiddie rides turned out by the factory in its 1920s, 1930s, and 1940s heyday for amusement parks from the Jersey Shore to Santa Monica. Check the factory log at the front desk or chat with one of the veteran carvers during one of the sporadic demonstrations to find out if your favorite hometown carousel was built at the Herschell factory. Chances are, it was.

Before this Coney Island state of mind has a chance to wear off, head back south along the Niagara River to two Tonawanda fast-food jewels, both specializing in foot-long red hots with "all that jazz" (sauerkraut, chili, onions, Cheez Whiz, peppers, relish, and mustard), long-cut cheese fries, and cold, sweet loganberry juice. The cleaner, brightly lit **Mississippi Mudd's**, 313 Niagara Street, also serves up some great butter-topped Louisiana sweet fries. **Ol' Man River**, 375 Niagara Street, makes up for this one-up-manship with its trademark Buffalo burgers, beef on weck sandwiches, and badly chipped plaster whale mascot, which flops over this grease joint's sagging roof like a bloated, roadfood-stuffed kidney bean.

Avon

East of Buffalo, US-20 widens to four lanes, making a rigidly straight run through the flat corn and hay fields that climb the gradually rising plateau toward the Finger Lakes district. This 40-mile stretch is virtually devoid of traffic, thanks to the faster-moving NY Thruway and serpentine Hwy-5, which links up with US-20 at Avon. Splash some cold homemade root beer down your throat to wake up and address the burning sensation left by the grilled, vinegar-doused, chili-drenched Texas Hot and Pork Hot Zweigle brand hot dogs that are family staples at **Tom Wahl's**, at the US-20/Hwy-5 junction. This rambling, log-beamed Avon institution has been a required tour-bus stopover since 1955 thanks to its soft ice cream, frosty mugs, and gut-busting Wahlburgers (ground steak on a six-inch bun, topped with a slice of grilled Virginia ham and Tom's special, mayonnaise-based sauce).

A 30-foot wooden Indian and white horse stand guard over opposite corners of the US-20/Hwy-5 and Hwy-15 intersection in nearby East Avon, where US-20 crosses I-390.

Detour: Rochester

There's plenty of culture in the sprawling Genesee River manufacturing center of Rochester (pop. 231,600), and the best of it is of the vernacular variety, making the 25-mile detour well worth your time and effort. Start your visit with the vast holdings of the Americana-rich **Strong Museum** (daily 10 AM-5 PM; $5), clearly marked off I-490 downtown. This 500,000-item collection of toys, appliances, dolls, perfume bottles, marbles, salt-and-pepper shakers, and classic board games is a must-visit for closet pack rats and pop culture fanatics.

The **George Eastman House**, 900 East Avenue (daily 10 AM-4:30 PM; $6.50), is a 10-minute drive along Rochester's fashionable mansion-lined main boulevard. In addition to relaying the Horatio Alger-like story of workaholic Eastman's incredible success and philanthropy as the founder of the city's still-thriving Eastman Kodak Company, the 50-room Georgian mansion in which he lived be-

The Rochester Red Wings Class AAA baseball team (716/454-1001) play at Frontier Field downtown, having left behind the oldest continually used stadium in the minors in 1996. Games are broadcast on WHTK 1280 AM.

South of Rochester, the I-390 freeway runs alongside a still-intact section of the original Erie Canal waterway.

fore shooting himself in the head in 1932 also houses a fascinating exhibit ("Enhancing the Illusion") on the history of photography.

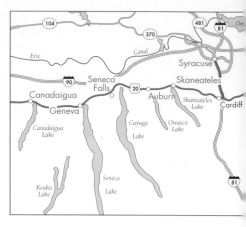

Canandaigua
East of the I-390 interchange, US-20 continues on its gentle, barely rolling course, gradually rising out of the flatlands to lap at the rim of the westernmost Finger Lake town, Canandaigua (pop. 10,700), an unassumingly pretty town that sits on a small hill to the north of the highway, overlooking the placid, 17-mile Canandaigua Lake. Iroquois legend has it that the 11 narrow Finger Lakes (five of which—Cayuga, Onondaga, Oneida, Seneca, Tuscarora—bear the names of the Six Nations of the Iroquois Confederacy) were created by the handprint of God.

East of Canandaigua, **Calhoun's Books** at 1510 US-20 (315/789-8599) is a low-key but seemingly limitless treasure trove of dusty period postcards, old maps, prints, and books in various stages of neglect, collectibility, and historical importance. The information-hungry road-tripper will thrill to the store's casually organized storehouse of 1930s WPA/Federal Writers' Project state guidebooks, as well as the boxes upon boxes of early 20th-century "Greetings From . . . " hand-tinted postcard folios.

Geneva
Geneva (pop. 14,100) sits at the head of Seneca Lake, the largest of the Finger Lakes, but is cut off from this sailboat-flecked jewel by a sadly unimproved section of lakefront to the south of the US-20/Hwy-5 roadbed. A worthwhile detour off the busy four-lane highway is a quick pass through the busy downtown on Main Street, grabbing lunch or a cup of coffee at Leo's Diner before parking near Hobart and William Smith Colleges to take in a relaxing view of the lake.

Save your roadfood appetite for **Waterloo**, 10 miles east, where the sagging, peel-

Picturesque, flag-draped downtown Waterloo has an all-American feel, befitting its contentious claim of holding the nation's first observance in 1866 of now-popular Flag Day.

ing **Mac's Drive-In Curb Service Restaurant**, 1166 Waterloo-Geneva Road, dishes out creamy Richardson's root beer floats ($1.60), frosty 16-ounce mugs of Pabst Blue Ribbon ($1.45), butter-dipped sweet corn (50 cents), and burgers-in-a-basket ($3, with french fries and cabbage salad) at an awning-covered counter or right at your car window.

Seneca Falls: Women's Rights National Historical Park
You'd never know it from the signs for "Peaches Sports Bar" and "Filthy McNasty's Saloon" that greet you as you roll through the diminutive red-brick town of Seneca Falls, but the American women's movement was born here when the first women's rights convention was spearheaded by Lucretia Mott and Elizabeth Cady Stanton in July 1848.

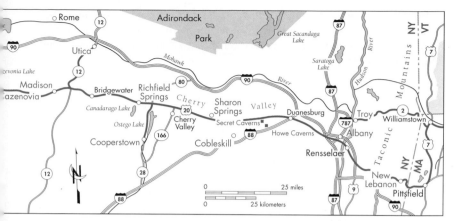

The remains of the Wesleyan Chapel where the convention was held can still be viewed at the center of town, on a guided tour staffed by the well-informed National Park Service rangers who run the highly interactive visitor center of the **Women's Rights National Historical Park** (daily 9 AM-5 PM; free; 315/568-2991) at 136 Fall Street. A brief exhibit on the scandalous pants-like "bloomers" popularized in 1851 by local feminist Amelia Bloomer combines with displays on transcendentalism, abolitionism, and phrenology to place the rise of this revolutionary movement in historical context. A block away, the **National Women's Hall of Fame**, 76 Fall Street, is a reading-intensive monument to the likes of Georgia O'Keeffe, Harriet Tubman, Emily Dickenson, Billie Jean King, and Jane Addams. You can listen to a saucy blues selection from Bessie Smith while dodging an endless stream of group tours.

Red's Place at 57 Fall Street, and the aforementioned **Filthy McNasty's** at 41 Fall Street, are dark, beer-soaked dens where you can scarf up chicken wings or sandwiches with a cold Genesee before wandering out back to gaze at the abandoned Seneca Knitting Mill. The falls in Seneca Falls disappeared in 1918 when the Cayuga and Seneca Canal flooded to form Van Cleef Lake. A five-minute drive east out of town along E. Bayard Street lands you at **Cayuga Lake State Park**, a shaded beach where you can sit by the lake, pitch some horseshoes or a tent, and ponder your rising cholesterol level.

Along US-20 on the western outskirts of Auburn, keep your eyes peeled and your camera at the ready as you pass the **Finger Lakes Drive-In Theater.**

Auburn

Auburn (pop. 31,300) is a proud industrial city with a solid, hilly downtown and a rich stock of historical homes, including that of William H. Seward, the anti-slavery Whig governor of New York, founder of the Republican Party, and secretary of state under presidents Abraham Lincoln and Andrew Johnson, who single-handedly negotiated the purchase of Alaska from Russia in 1867. The **Seward House**, on Hwy-34 a block south of US-20 at 33 South Street (Tues.-Sat. 1-4 PM; $4), contains all the original furniture and many fascinating historic exhibits. Down the street from the Seward home, you can also tour the home of escaped slave and underground railroad heroine **Harriet Tubman**, who, after the Civil War, settled into the tidy white house at 180 South Street (Tues.-Fri. 10 PM-4 PM; donations). Seward and Tubman are both buried in the town's Fort Hill cemetery, west of South Street between the two homes.

Right downtown at 18 Genesee Street, the sparkling, streamlined **Hunter's Dinerant** offers 24-hour-a-day slices of thick lemon meringue pie and a panoramic view of the aging Genesee Beer sign that watches over the wide streets of the hill-hugging downtown.

Skaneateles

Roughly midway across New York State, Skaneateles (pop. 2,700) is a pristine, sun-dappled resort nestled on the crest of shimmering Skaneateles Lake. This popular summer family escape houses arts, crafts, and antique stores along its immaculate Genesee Street (US-20), which fronts the lakeside **Cliff and Thayer Parks**. A stroll up the main downtown north-south drag of Jordan Street leads you past the delightfully unadorned **Skaneateles Bakery** to the Skaneateles Historical Society's petite **Creamery Museum** and elm-lined side streets full of well-maintained Greek Revival homes.

Along US-20 just west of the I-81 interchange, the tiny crossroads of Cardiff is where the 10-foot, 2,700-pound "fossil" of the P.T. Barnum-hyped Cardiff Giant was "unearthed" in 1869.

If you're hungry, the stuffy colonial **Kreb's Inn**, across from the lakefront at 53 W. Genesee Street, will empty your wallet with its pricey-but-hearty lobster, roast beef, and chicken specialties. Greasemonger roadfood-seekers will feel more at home at the high-quality but self-effacing **Doug's Fish Fry**, 8 Jordan Street, "not famous since 1962" for its beer, fried haddock, clams, and Coney Island hot dogs. West of downtown, the **Hilltop Restaurant** at 813 W. Genesee Street offers one-stop family dining—and bowling in the adjoining **Cedar House Bowling Center.**

A number of $50-a-night motels like the **Hi-Way Host**, 834 W. Genesee Street (315/685-7633), line US-20 east and west of Skaneateles.

Detour: Syracuse

A short, 25-minute side trip from US-20 north to Syracuse (pop. 163,900) via I-81 yields an informative tour of the fascinating **Erie Canal Museum** (daily 10 AM-5 PM; free) at 318 E. Erie Boulevard in the shadow of I-690. Housed in an 1850 weighlock building straddling the paved-over canal bed, the museum has a 65-foot restored 1850s canal boat, and offers guided walking tours (free) of the city that gave birth to the electric typewriter, the loafer, and the turn-of-the-century, arts-and-crafts-style furniture of Gustave Stickley. A short film describes the staggering impact of the canal's 1825 opening on the city, an impact also visible in the cast-iron commercial districts of the historic downtown, south and west from the museum around Clinton and Armory Squares.

Just three blocks north of Clinton Square, nearly under the I-81 freeway, the best thing about Syracuse is the exciting new **Museum of Automobile History**, 321 North Clinton Street (Wed.-Sun. 10 AM-5 PM; $5 ; 315/478-CARS or 315/478-2277), which shows off the largest private collection of automobilia in the world. Covered in an eye-popping set of original 1940s billboards, the 12,000-square-foot, purpose-built museum is packed with rare advertising (including a set of legendary Burma-Shave roadside rhyming signs), gas pumps, road signs, folk-art models, pedal cars and toys galore. Everything you can imagine related to cars and car culture—but no cars.

Cazenovia and Madison

East of I-81, US-20 follows the route blazed by the old Great Western Turnpike over gradually steepening roller-coaster hills, past sweet-corn stands, dairy bars, and cabbage fields, and into the western reaches of picture-perfect Cherry Valley. After passing through the Syracuse suburb of Cazenovia, which offers a refreshing breeze from whitecapped Cazenovia Lake, US-20 rolls east for another 15 miles to Madison, where the roadhouse-like **Quack's Diner**, 7239 US-20, harbors no delusions of grandeur, just a huge faded duck-adorned sign and a sprawling dining room where area families, Colgate University students, and antique hunters fresh from a weekend run gorge themselves on chicken dinners, milk shakes, and cling peaches in whipped cream. You can even buy T-shirts and coffee cups with the diner's trademark yellow duck mascot uttering such pun-ishing lines as, "It quacks me up to cook here."

Detour: Utica

Hilly downtown Utica (pop. 68,637) lies on I-90 about 30 minutes north of US-20 along the Mohawk River and New York state's Barge Canal, the seabound industrial water route that follows part of the pathway of the Erie Canal. Beer fans will want to make the trip to the **F.X. Matt Brewing Co.** at Court and Varick Streets west of downtown, where the old West End Brewery still pumps out barrels of Matt's trademark Utica Club and Matt's Premium regional beers alongside its more heavily promoted Saranac line of premium microbrews. In-depth **tours** ($3; 315/732-0022; $3) of the compact, family-owned facilities take you through the entire production process—where you are apt to spy some contract-brewed Brooklyn Lager, New Amsterdam, Dock Street Ale, or Olde Heurich slipping out the door—and drop you off in a velvet-lined Victorian tavern for your complimentary glasses of Saranac or frothy root beer.

Shake off your post-lager drowsiness with a thick, delicious cheeseburger, coffee, and slice of lemon meringue pie at the timeless **Triangle Coffee Shop**, 244 Genesee Street at Bank Place, which manages to cram four sit-down tables, seven counter stools, and a hungry crowd of professionals into its tiny, bright, triangular space. In the midst of even the most hectic lunch rush, the friendly waitresses still find the time to call every customer "Hon" and whip out a clean knife at a moment's notice to unjam a clogged ketchup bottle.

Northwest of Utica, the decidedly nonclassical city of **Rome** was the site of Fort Stanwix, which played a decisive role in the struggle for control of upstate New York during the Revolutionary War.

A step or three up the culinary scale, **Cafe Ca Nole** at 900 Culver Avenue is one of Utica's many great Italian places; many others line Bleecker Street, a few blocks to the north.

The Utica Blue Sox, a New York-Penn League Class A baseball team, holds court June-Aug. a few miles south at cozy, 4,000-seat Donovan Park (315/738-0999 for information), which serves up cold Matt's beers and stunning views of the summer sunset from the tiny stands running along the first-base line.

Richfield Springs: Petrified Creatures Museum

Back on US-20 east, refuel for the rolling road ahead at the ramshackle **Gatesdale Dairy Bar** in Bridgewater, which sports a cooler full of creamy, rich ice cream and a sagging neon sign featuring a dripping milk bottle under the portrait of a satisfied heifer in a floppy chef's hat. Continuing east, the road slows down and becomes a rural two-laner at Richfield Springs (pop. 1,565), a peaceful crossroads with a gazebo in the center of its grassy town square.

On the south side of US-20, at the crest of a large hill several miles east of Richfield Springs, sits the terminally tacky **Petrified Creatures Museum of Natural History** (Thurs.-Mon. 10 AM-5 PM; $7). The steep admission buys you an information-intensive (but entertainment-lacking) tour of outdoor chicken-wire Devonian fossil displays, narrated by a tape-recorded, nasal-voiced announcer. You also get a self-guided tour of the tiny wooded backyard site's collection of several garishly painted, life-sized dinosaur sculptures, and the option of using the proprietor's crusty old pickax to hack out a few fossilized keepsakes from the totally picked-over slate pit—where most of the "petrified creatures" came from.

Farther east, your time and money are probably better spent at Burger World, at the US-20/Hwy-80 junction, a cabin-styled family fast-food restaurant that lives up to its "We're more than just burgers" slogan with filling chicken cutlet, pork chop, and meat loaf dinner plates and tottering, five-scoop ice-cream cones. The takeout menu includes a 1927 map of the Cherry Valley Turnpike route now occupied by US-20.

The combination admission ticket (around $25) to the Baseball Hall of Fame also gains you entrance to the other two Cooperstown museums.

Detour: Cooperstown

A dozen miles south of US-20 along Hwy-80, quietly bustling Cooperstown (pop. 2,200) has been known since 1939 as the home of the **National Baseball Hall of Fame** (daily 9 AM-5 PM, till 9 PM in summer; $9.50), where a beautifully organized timeline of dioramas and display cases walks you through the sport's greatest—and most embarrassing—moments. You'll see a pair of cracked black leather shoes worn by the ill-fated and latterly famous 1919 "Black Sox" player Shoeless Joe Jackson; the first plaster-covered batting helmet; and special exhibits on home run king Henry Aaron, amid a voluminous collection of uniforms, periodicals, programs, player records, scrapbooks, and film and audio holdings.

The neat, prosperous village of Cooperstown, founded in 1786 by the father of *Last of the Mohicans* novelist James Fenimore Cooper, has been transformed into a family tourist mecca, with the always-thronged Hall of Fame augmented by the subtler delights of the **Fenimore House Museum** (daily 10 AM-4 PM in summer, weekends only in winter; $9), which along with memorabilia of the writer has a massive new Native American artifacts collection and the equally engaging folk art and Hudson River School galleries. The Fenimore House is on Lake Street a mile north of town along the shores of Otsego Lake—the source of the Susquehanna River known locally as "Glimmerglass" for its spectacular, sparkling appearance.

Near the Fenimore House, the **Farmer's Museum** (daily 10 AM-4 PM in summer, weekends only in winter; $9) has illuminating exhibits on 19th-century rural life.

Amid the dignified agricultural and local history exhibits that occupy most of the sturdy stone structures speckling this 1918 farm, the "remains" of the previously encountered Cardiff Giant lie in stony silence.

Avoid the in-town parking hassles and stash your car in one of the free lots near the Fenimore House. Then catch a city-operated trolley ($1.50 for an unlimited day pass) down Hwy-80 toward downtown.

The several-block central business district, where every other bookstore, restaurant, and variety store seems to be cashing in on their tourist customers' insatiable appetite for baseball-related camp and nostalgia, also holds **Black Bart's BBQ**, 64 Main Street, which serves up good grub without a hint of major league interference. There are literally dozens of motels from which to choose in the Cooperstown area, but remember to make your reservations far in advance to beat the summer rush. The **Bay Side Motor Inn** (607/547-2371) is one of the countless motels crowding Hwy-80 between Cooperstown and US-20, while in-town accommodation options include the circa 1874 **Inn at Cooperstown**, 16 Chestnut Street (607/547-5756), which has nice rooms from under $100.

For more complete information, including details on the summertime Glimmerglass Opera Festival, contact the **visitors bureau**, 31 Chestnut Street (607/547-9983).

Three miles south of Cooperstown, on Hwy-28 in the hamlet of Hartwick Seminary, the **Corvette Americana Hall of Fame** (daily 10 AM-8 PM; $9.50) is a must-see display of every Corvette model since the car's introduction in 1953, accompanied by the popular music of the times and every sort of 'Vette-related memorabilia imaginable.

Cherry Valley

East of the Cooperstown area, US-20 begins its roller-coaster ride through the patchwork of hillside cornfields and dairy farms that drape the bubbling landscape through the fertile Cherry Valley region. On the south side of US-20 near the crossroads of East Springfield, wander through a 1930s motor court and grab a filling stack of pancakes or slice of homemade pie at the **Otsego Diner and Motel**. Just south of the highway, attractive little Cherry Valley (pop. 600) contains a small local history museum that recalls this tiny crossroads' early 19th-century boom period as a rowdy turnpike stagecoach stop. A small obelisk in the village cemetery on S. Main Street pays homage to the residents killed in 1779 in the Cherry Valley Massacre, a British-backed Iroquois raid during the Revolutionary War.

The **Tryon Inn** (607/264-3790), at 124 Main Street (Hwy-166), serves up large, delicately prepared portions of pasta, seafood, steak, and poultry in an elegant 1927 dining room. The guest house out back has a handful of rooms for rent at incredibly cheap rates that vary by season; you'll have to share a bathroom down the hall, but the peaceful, wooded setting and antique washbasins in each room make this a pleasant sleeping alternative.

Sharon Springs

The 19th-century spa and resort community of Sharon Springs (pop. 543) was once on a par with Saratoga Springs, but those days are long gone, and the silent streets are lined by the slowly crumbling remains of once-grand wooden Victorian-era hotels. It's not totally dead; in fact, Sharon Springs has seen something of a resurgence of its fortunes, thanks to its unlikely role as a seasonal escape for Hasidic Jews fleeing the heat of New York City summers.

East of Sharon Springs off US-20, **The TePee** is a 50-foot-tall, silvery, teepee-shaped attraction, which has lured souvenir-starved travelers since 1950 with its array of Native American trinkets, famous "TePee Taffy," and "Grand Panoramic View" telescope.

The health-giving waters still flow in Sharon Springs, bubbling up into a small fountain in a gazebo in the small park at the center of town.

Cobleskill: Iroquois Indian Museum

Southeast of Sharon Springs, the road from tidy Cobleskill (pop. 5,268) to Howe's Cave bypasses the threatening new Wal-Mart and follows the brightly colored Howe Caverns and sly, psychedelic Secret Caverns signs up the hill to the Iroquois Indian Museum (daily 10 AM-5 PM; $5). The imposing, longhouse-shaped structure contains artifacts, arrowheads, and more recent works of art associated with the Native Americans descended from the Six Nations of the Iroquois Confederacy, as well as an interactive, hands-on children's museum. The museum's collection of contemporary Native American painting and sculpture also asks tough, probing questions about the one-dimensional casino culture that has recently come to dominate reservation life across the U.S.

Howe Caverns vs. Secret Caverns

All over this part of New York, massive roadside billboards blare out the competitive presence of Howe Caverns (marked by simple, yellow-and-black "Howe Caverns" directional signs) and Secret Caverns (on which a Deadhead-ish wizard beckons you onward with pesky lines like "If you haven't seen the underground waterfall, you ain't seen guano!"). Though located within two miles of each other, these two tourist attractions are about as far apart as Pat Boone and Jimi Hendrix.

The sanitized-for-your-protection **Howe Caverns** (daily 9 AM-6 PM; $11) boasts a well-lit, guided elevator and flat-bottomed boat tour of a 156-foot-deep underground cave. But you know you're in for something completely different the moment you enter the dark, foreboding **Secret Caverns** (daily 9 AM-6 PM; $8)—through the mouth of a giant, leering bat. Don't let the "Abandon hope all ye who enter here" sign scare you off from taking the twisting (and twisted) one-and-a-half hour guided trek down into the clammy 180-foot-deep innards along a narrow, randomly lit footpath, which terminates at a steaming, 100-foot waterfall. Sarcastic guides point out Frozen Niagara Falls, Grand Canyon, and Liberty Bell slices of stalactite/stalagmite Americana along the way, and the gift shop sells tie-dyed T-shirts, psychedelic bumper stickers, and coffee cups emblazoned with swirling designs and countless cavern-related barbs in the mold of "good to the last drop," "most of it's over your head," "the cavity dentists prefer," and "whole lotta hole."

Schoharie Valley

A nearly deserted US-20 climbs in and out of rippling extensions of the Cherry Valley and Susquehanna River watershed before cutting a dramatic path through the gorgeous Schoharie Valley around Esperance. An abandoned, sun-darkened set of Depression-era motor court cabins still stands in neat formation on the north side of the road, awaiting the waves of long-departed turnpike travelers whose unimaginative, fearful descendants now troll the lonesome, sterile NY Thruway. Dairy bars, hay bales, and yard sales proliferate nonetheless, as the wide, smooth four-lane road bestows limitless views of distant, farm-draped hills and hollows upon the patient traveler willing to pull off every now and then to take it in.

Outside of Duanesburg, the neat, geometric farmlands give way to a shaggier, flatter landscape, with creosote-soaked telephone poles and thick stands of weeping willows crowding the narrow two-lane roadway.

Albany

The New York state capital, Albany (pop. 101,100) was founded in 1609 when Dutch traders traveling up the Hudson River from New Amsterdam on Henry Hudson's ship *Half Moon* went ashore and established a fur trading post. As the gateway between upstate New York and the increasingly powerful New York City port, Albany remained a powerful trading center through the 1820s and 1830s, extending its reach with the opening of the Erie Canal and the city's growth as a central railroad terminus and manufacturing center. Nowadays, the legendary canal has long since vanished, and the glamorous New York Central railroad's French renaissance-style, turn-of-the century Union Station, at Broadway and Clinton Street, has been transformed into the sleepy corporate headquarters of the Fleet banking group—Amtrak passenger trains now stop at a lonely platform on the opposite side of the Hudson River.

As the seat of the New York state government, however, Albany still wields obvious political power. Its rich array of museums, parks, and tree-lined boulevards—plus a few barely preserved historical neighborhoods that survived the wrecker's balls in the early 1960s—confirm the fact that the Capital City is still very much alive and well. The towering granite slabs and flying-saucer-like structures that stick out at the heart of the 100-acre Empire State Plaza government center hold exhibition halls, theaters, a 44-story observation tower, and the excellent **New York State Museum** (daily 10 AM-5 PM; donations), which includes a sensitively organized exhibit on the state's Iroquois and Mohawk Native American cultures, replete with a reconstructed longhouse. A huge section devoted to the history of the metropolitan New York City area blows away anything in "The City That Never Sleeps," with a re-created Upper West Side Hispanic barber shop, a Horn and Hardart Automat food dispenser, and a restored 1940s car from the A-train IND subway line.

For a lengthier foray into Albany's local history, trek over to the **Albany Institute of History and Art**, 125 Washington Avenue (Tues.-Fri. 10 AM-5 PM, Sat.-Sun. noon-5 PM; $3), a 200-year-old gallery that houses an Albany oral history exhibit, a group of locally made cast-iron stoves, several rooms full of Hudson River School paintings from the likes of Thomas Cole and Asher Durand, and a crowded little Egyptian room with two minor league mummies.

A mile northeast of downtown, the rolling hills and meadows of the Olmsted-inspired **Washington Park** have a beautiful, art deco lake house that hosts outdoor concerts and theatrical productions in the summer months. In between downtown and the park, the blue-collar bohemian Lark Street neighborhood is Albany's answer to Greenwich Village, sporting several tattoo parlors and some good restaurants. The roadhouse-style **Lark Tavern**, 453 Madison Avenue at Lark Street, serves big mugs of cheap beer in a cavernous, dark setting thronged with an eclectic mix of yuppies, old-timers, and artsy types; for late-night coffee and/or poetry, pop into **Lulu's**, 288 Lark Street, which doles out a potpourri of poetry readings, art exhibits, and open mike nights.

Back downtown, if all the high culture and power politics leave you hungry for a back-to-basics roadfood experience, head to **Jack's Diner**, 547 Central Avenue. This New Jersey-built 1930s chrome-plated diner car attracts a diverse batch of families, local crazies, and travelers with its hearty meat loaf and burgers, bottomless cups of coffee, and friendly, loquacious staff; it's open Mon.-Fri. 6 AM-7:30 PM, Saturday till 2:30 PM.

Your motel options are legion in the Albany area, but the **Motel 6** and **Quality Inn** off the I-90 Everett Road exit offer the best combination of value and central location. (They're also right next door to the **Albany Bowling Center** if you want to take out your pent-up car-bound frustrations on any of your fellow travelers.) One very nice, centrally located place to stay is the **Mansion Hill Inn**, near the Governor's Mansion at 115 Philip Street (518/465-2038), which offers B&B rooms for around $100 and doubles as a fine restaurant.

For more detailed information, or to pick up walking-tour maps of Albany, contact the **visitor center**, 52 S. Pearl Street (518/434-1217 or 800/258-3582).

Troy

Downtown Troy's cast-iron buildings are popular with set designers, who transform them into backdrops for films like Martin Scorsese's 1992 adaptation of Edith Wharton's *The Age of Innocence.*

The grave of Uncle Sam and the birthplace of the detachable shirt collar are both across the river in Troy (pop. 54,300), 10 minutes north via the I-787 freeway. A world removed from downtown Albany, this narrow riverfront city was strategically situated at the point where the Erie Canal headed west from the Hudson River. It rose to national prominence as a manufacturing center in the 19th century, when its foundries and factories cranked out iron for stoves, stagecoaches, bells, and battleships.

TROY'S UNCLE SAM

Troy's prominent Uncle Sam monument, along the waterfront at River and Front Streets, memorializes bearded local meat-packer Samuel Wilson, who supplied beef to the soldiers quartered at the local Watervliet Arsenal during the War of 1812. Wilson's donations were quickly dubbed "Uncle Sam's beef," and the nickname and character have become the finger-pointing stuff of legend. Wilson himself is buried in the macabre, gothic hillside Oakwood Cemetery, at the head of 101st Street north of Troy via Oakwood Avenue. A vegan restaurant around the corner from the monument, Uncle Sam's Natural Foods at 77 4th Street, admonishes passersby with an "I want you . . . to enjoy good health" window poster.

Troy's factories have given way to a quietly picturesque college town, with Rens-selaer Polytechnic rising on the steep hill to the east above the cast-iron business district downtown. In addition to its many impressive buildings, Troy's dense downtown has two great roadfood finds: **Manory's Restaurant**, 99 Congress Street, doles out stuffed combo sandwiches, home-cooked pasta, meat and seafood din-ners, and really, really big breakfasts; **The Famous Lunch**, 111 Congress Street, is a delightfully worn-down greasy spoon with hand-lettered signs, tall wooden booths, and an eye-opening clientele of cops, winos, RPI students, and local business peo-ple—nearly all of whom from noon to midnight every day but Sunday chow down on multiple four-inch-long, chili-doused hot dogs served on Styrofoam plates with cold RC Colas on the side.

The quickest route east from Troy is Hwy-2, a rural back road across the Taconic Mountains to Williamstown, Massachusetts. Alternately, you can follow old US-20 east through New Lebanon to Pittsfield, Massachusetts, then follow a short stretch of the Appalachian Trail route along US-7 north to Williamstown. For details on Pittsfield, Williamstown, and the rest of the Appalachian Trail route, see pages 316-374.

New Lebanon

Heading east from Albany across the Hudson River toward the Massachusetts state line, US-20 follows Columbia Avenue through the warehouse and factory town of Rensselaer, then climbs a long, retail-lined hill past innumerable liquor stores, mini-marts, gas stations, and motels into the Taconic Mountains. After this 25-mile barrage of contemporary consumer culture, the tranquil hillside remains of **Mount Lebanon Shaker Village**, on the south side of US-20 a few hundred yards west of the Massachusetts border, come as a welcome relief.

Of the 20 Shaker communities once scattered over the eastern U.S., practicing a passionate but celibate form of Christianity, Mount Lebanon was the head ministry, founded here in 1785. The community endured until 1947, and some two dozen historic buildings still stand, including a 192-foot stone barn—the largest stone barn in the world when constructed in 1859—and a no-frills, but cleverly con-structed, 1854 washhouse boasting hidden wall drawers and perfectly fitted floor-boards. All of which is testimony to the Shaker edict, "Hands to work, hearts to God."

A small museum (daily 9:30 AM-5 PM in summer only; $4) gives background on the Shakers, sells some Shaker-style crafts, and has walking-tour maps of the former colony.

Across the Massachusetts border, **Hancock Shaker Village** is a more visitor-oriented place to get a feel for the Shaker way of life. See page 320 for more.

ROUTE 2: ACROSS MASSACHUSETTS

The leafy amble from New York State, up and over the ridge of the Taconics, brings you through a beautiful region dense with visitor appeal, including the Shaker communities along US-20 and the industrial and literary sites of the Berkshires, not to mention Williamstown, a New England poster town if ever there was one. This region is covered in detail in our Appalachian Trail chapter; for the full scoop on what to do in and around these broad green quads and red brick facades, see pages 316-326.

Across Massachusetts, we follow the very scenic Route 2, also known as the "Mohawk Trail," across the state's northern tier, rather than US-20, which runs more or less underneath the Massachusetts Turnpike, I-90. Passing across some of the least populous and most deeply forested acres in the whole Commonwealth of Massachusetts, you can easily imagine you're in Vermont rather than the so-called Bay State. Picking its way over the flattened summits of the Hoosac Range foothills to the Green Mountains in the north, Route 2 follows rock-strewn trout streams flecked with whitewater and shaded by boreal forests of hemlock, yellow birch, and red spruce—including some of the state's only remaining stands of old growth. Midway across Massachusetts, Route 2 bridges the Connecticut River above Turners Falls, lopes through the trees, and emerges at historic Lexington and Concord, at Boston's back door.

In Massachusetts and the rest of New England, we have adopted the use of "Route" instead of "Hwy-," in keeping with regional practice.

North Adams

Next-door neighbors could hardly be more dissimilar than Williamstown and North Adams, the working-class, former company town of North Adams faltering just a few miles upstream of all that collegiate gentility. Nearly from its inception North Adams tied its fortunes to major manufacturing plants, churning out printed cotton until textiles went south, then rolling out capacitors for everything from the first atomic bomb to the television sets of the 1950s and 1960s. When electronics went solid-state and overseas, North Adams nearly died clinging to the belief that some new assembly line would come fill its sprawling 28-building 19th-century mill complex on the Hoosic River next to downtown. The long-awaited reprieve from welfare and unemployment finally seems to be taking shape, but

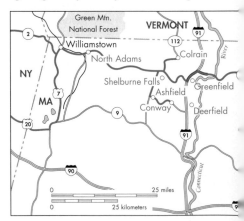

folks who remember days of industrial wages on a union scale have a hard time envisioning their city being salvaged by . . . *art*. Conceived over a decade ago and then nearly aborted by the recession of the early 1990s, the first 200,000 square feet of the Massachusetts Museum of Contemporary Art—**Mass MoCA**—have finally started to fill parts of the old Sprague Mill, on Marshall Street just north of Route 2. If the master plan is ever fully implemented, the 13-acre "multidisciplinary cultural center" will become one of the world's largest art museums. To check on this work-in-progress, call 413/664-4481.

In the meantime, the region's historic gravy train is faithfully recollected in the galleries of the **Western Gateway Heritage State Park** (daily 10 AM-5 PM late May to early November, closed Tues.-Wed. rest of the year; donations; 413/663-8059) on Route 8 just south of the Route 2 overpass. Occupying the renovated freight-yard buildings of the Boston and Maine Railroad, the park's visitor center highlights the landmark construction of the five-mile-long Hoosac Tunnel and North Adams's front-row seat on the Boston-to-Great Lakes rail connection it made possible.

Affluence gives neighboring Williamstown a decided edge over North Adams when it comes to good eating, but for local color detour down Route 8 about five miles to the spiffy little town of **Adams**, birthplace to suffragette Susan B. Anthony and present home to the incomparable **Miss Adams Diner** (breakfast and lunch daily). Sitting opposite the Congregational church on downtown Park Street, this handsome Worcester lunch car has all the steak and eggs, Blue Plate Specials, and tapioca pudding you'd expect from a place with a 1949 pedigree, but you'll also find good vegetarian specials, superb homemade pies (try the banana cream), and locally made Squeeze sodas. For a pleasant digestive, feed the meter with your extra pennies—yes, 12 minutes' parking costs but one cent—and stroll around the beautifully restored commercial district before returning to Route 2.

It was during the blasting of the Hoosac Tunnel that nitroglycerin was first used as a construction explosive. Just so you know, the river is the Hoosic, the mountain range is the Hoosac.

Adams profited mightily from the protectionist trade policies of **Pres. William McKinley,** which is why his statue—by Augustus Lukeman, who also carved Atlanta's "Stone Mountain"—stands at the north end of Park Street. The work was commissioned by a local mill-owning friend after McKinley's 1901 assassination.

an admonition from the menu at Miss Adams Diner

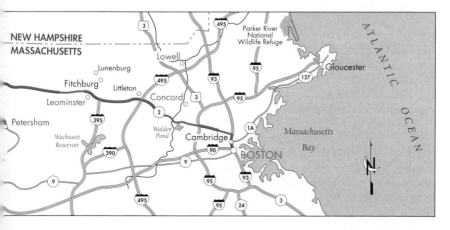

Should the Miss Adams run out of **walking-tour** brochures from the local Historical Commission, the town hall just a couple doors down has a ready supply, accompanied by friendly suggestions.

The Mohawk Trail

Taking its name from the warpath used for raids against Algonquian settlements along the upper Connecticut River Valley, the modern Mohawk Trail was one of the nation's first scenic highways, improved and paved as early as 1914 as part of a massive state effort to lure tourists into the cash-deprived farm belt of New England. If you're driving an overloaded or underpowered vehicle, you'll appreciate the thrill and radiator-popping risks that once attended the slow switchback grind up out of North Adams, around the attention-getting Hairpin Turn, and over the edge of the Western Summit, where tidy **Wigwam Cottages** (413/663-3205), one of many photogenic old $50-a-night motor courts along the route, have been taking in guests since Calvin Coolidge was still an unknown Northampton lawyer. Don't

be fooled by the short stretch of gentle ups and downs east of the summit over the glacier-flattened mountain peaks of the Hoosac peneplain: the route along the tortuous Cold River ravine quickens the pulse even in these days of power steering and anti-lock brakes, especially if you get sandwiched between a pair of 18-wheelers, whose burning brakepads sometimes scent the air all the way down the valley.

The Long View Gift Shop, eastern summit of the Mohawk Trail

Scenic Route 116: Ashfield and Conway

Come fall, the sugar maples in the surrounding mixed hardwood forest add a blaze of brilliant orange to the landscape, making Route 2 a favorite of leaf-peepers between the end of September and Columbus Day weekend. If sharing the two-lane road with thousands of rubbernecking drivers becomes wearisome, consider taking a road less traveled. Almost any road will do, but a loop along Route 116 through Ashfield and Conway to the south of Route 2 passes over several historic covered bridges and offers enough pastoral beauty to more than compensate for the detours.

Shunning the main highway doesn't require skipping meals, either. For instance, there are thin-crust whole pizzas and slices at the **Countrypie Pizza Company** (open daily till 9 PM), 343 Main Street across from Ashfield's rock-solid public library; given the fresh fancy toppings available, the prices are a real steal. Or coast down Route 116 to **Baker's Country Store**, just east of Conway's old water tower, and sit down to a simple soup or sandwich amid the fishing tackle and canned goods. (If you like your pastry crusts short and white, be sure to sample the fresh pies, particularly in summer during berry season.)

For a place to stay, **The Farm at Ashfield** (413/628-4067) is a warm, hospitable, and reasonably priced retreat, far from just about anything you might want to leave behind.

Shelburne Falls

Travelers along the Mohawk Trail, Route 2, should take a turn at the signs for the lively, artsy little town of Shelburne Falls, which is actually two towns, Shelburne and Buckland, facing one another across the Deerfield River. The two are linked by the **Bridge of Flowers**, a former electric trolley bridge converted to a linear display garden. Another oft-touted wonder is the sculptured riverbed below Salmon Falls, just east of Bridge Street: here, beside the spillway of diminutive Deerfield Dam and Powerhouse #3, the **Glacial Potholes** are popular for picnics, geological ruminations, hanging out with schoolmates, and boulder-hopping. Just don't fall asleep with your hearing aid turned down; the dam makes frequent releases of water, especially during the summer whitewater rafting season.

Nearby food and beverage options include: espresso concoctions from Bridge Street's **Shelburne Falls Coffee Roasters**; vegetarian-friendly deli selections at the rear of **McCusker's Market**, facing the south end of the iron bridge; and richly sauced, red-meat-free entrees and salads at the **Copper Angel Cafe**, on the Buckland side of the bridge.

A short six miles north of Shelburne Falls along scenic Route 112, the town of **Colrain** holds another great place: the charming and whimsical **Green Emporium** (413/624-5122), where you can enjoy creative dinners (Thurs.-Sun.) and a nice Sunday brunch—in a former Methodist church. To contemplate the pastoral landscape with the eye and tempo of a true country rambler it would be best to make a local **farm stay** or B&B the base for your perambulations. Friendly **Penfrydd Farm** in Colrain (413/624-5516) is a fine example, with unpretentious $65-a-night rooms in an attractively renovated 19th-century farmhouse, a small herd of llamas, wonderful hilltop views across pastures and forest, and night skies thick with stars no city-dwellers will ever see from their roof decks.

You'll find excellent wooded streamside campsites in **Mohawk Trail State Forest** just above where the Cold River empties into the Deerfield. There are five year-round rustic cabins, too, but make reservations at least six months in advance (413/339-5504) if you have your heart set on staying in one.

Although early spring is aptly known as Mud Season throughout New England's back country, it's also when the sugar maple sap starts to flow. Boil away nearly 98% of the sap and you have genuine maple syrup delicious enough to make muddy, frost-heaved farm roads positively inviting. Call the Sugar Season Hotline (413/628-3912) to obtain a list of maple producers you can visit.

Greenfield

As Route 2 speeds down into the Connecticut River valley, it veers along I-91 just long enough to skirt the county seat of Greenfield, a place once known for its cutlery, tap-and-die, and other metals-related manufacturing. The proximity of the interstate has endowed Greenfield with some of the only **chain motels** in western Massachusetts; if you prefer a Howard Johnson's or Super 8 to a B&B or campground, you'll find them beside the rotary at the junction of Route 2 and I-91. For one of the least expensive rooms in the state, take the interstate south two exits to the **Motel 6** on I-91 at Route 5, outside Deerfield.

Historic Deerfield

A world away from the modern interstate aesthetic, but just three miles south of Greenfield along Route 5, Historic Deerfield (daily 9:30 AM-4:30 PM; $12; 413/774-5581) is an immaculately preserved architectural ensemble dating from the early 1700s to around 1850. Over a dozen clapboard buildings, shaded by a canopy of stately old elm trees, form a mile-long reminder of the time when this part of Massachusetts formed the frontier of western "civilization," and English settlers waged bloody war against the native Pocumtuck Indians. The surrounding town of Deerfield, and the famous Deerfield Academy prep school, hardly intrude, leaving the Historic Deerfield to stand as it was—fanlight windows, wrought iron, well-worn stones and all. Inside each house, guides discuss the lives, belongings, and historical contexts of the former inhabitants, often with such parental intimacy that you half-expect these long-dead Ebenezers, Jonathans, and Marys to be napping upstairs. One of the finest surviving colonial townscapes in America, Historic Deerfield is well worth a visit, no matter how brief, especially since there's no admission charge if you just want to stop and walk around.

A new addition to Historic Deerfield is the **Flynt Center of Early New England Life** (daily 9:30 AM-4:30 PM; adults $6, students $3; 413/774-5581), which opened late in 1998 at the edge of a field, behind Main Street. The 27,000-square-foot museum, designed to look like a colonial tobacco barn, displays thousands of "fancy goods" and other consumer treasures—pewter teapots, silk waistcoats, and the like—that were keys to civilized life here on the edge of wilderness.

Northeast of Deerfield, near the Vermont border, the town of Northfield had the first **youth hostel** in the U.S. in 1934. Now, you can sleep cheap and meet fellow travelers at the **HI Northfield Hostel,** in a Victorian house at 91 Highland Avenue (413/498-3505).

Across much of central Massachusetts, the older two-lane alignment of the Mohawk Trail (Route 2) is still in use as Route 2A, running through a series of small towns like Orange, Athol, Templeton, and Gardner, which was once one of the busiest chair-making centers in the US.

Petersham

About 10 miles east of I-91, Route 2 crosses high over the Connecticut River atop the huge, art deco French King Bridge, giving grand views over the surrounding landscape. From here east the route becomes a mini-freeway as it launches into a 40-mile stretch of almost nothing but forest; though nearly unimaginable today, some two-thirds of the landscape you see out your windows was totally deforested in the early 1800s. After some 150 years, that statistic has been reversed, although much of the forest along this stretch is relatively young, having grown up since a devastating hurricane in 1938 blew down nearly every pine tree in its path. An extraordinarily detailed set of handmade dioramas in the **Fisher Museum at Harvard Forest** (Mon.-Fri. 9 AM-5 PM, plus weekends May-Oct.; free), about a half-dozen miles south of Route 2, on Route 32 north of Petersham, explain the history of modern human settlement in this part of the state, and plainly illustrate both natural forest succession and active forest management. After this introduction to silviculture, be sure to check out Petersham's classic village green with its ring of pristine white civic buildings, including the stately **Country Store,** whose homemade fruit pies deserve as much attention as the Greek Revival architecture.

Leominster and Vicinity

As you approach the Tri-Town area of Leominster (pronounced LUH-minster), Fitchburg, and Lunenburg, rooftops begin to supplant treetops and Boston radio stations crowd the dial. Although "the Hub" is still some 30 miles away, its gravitational attraction seems to compel a majority of cars to exceed the speed limit. If you already know that you would rather walk barefoot over hot coals than be caught driving in Boston, you can start looking for accommodations now, as you

LOWELL: JACK KEROUAC

At "five o'clock of a red-all-over suppertime" on March 12, 1922, Jack Kerouac—baptized John L. (Jean-Louis) Kirouac by his French Canadian parents—was born in Lowell, a city sincerely regarded as one of the wonders of the world back when the Industrial Revolution was as fascinating as the Internet is now. Although this original Dharma Bum is more widely remembered for hanging out with Ferlinghetti in San Francisco or with Ginsberg in New York, or for pasting the Beat Generation firmly across the map of American culture, Kerouac also wrote five novels based on friends and familiar places in his native city, and his fictional work, from *On the Road* on, is that much more interesting when read in the context of his real life, here, along the Merrimack River.

Reciprocating Kerouac's lifelong love for Lowell, the National Park Service and the **Lowell National Historical Park**, keepers of the massive red-brick remains of America's first planned industrial city, publish a walking-tour brochure on Jack and his life in Lowell; they also help sponsor the annual **Lowell Celebrates Kerouac!** festival the first full weekend in October. Maps and guides to the man and the town are available from the **visitor center**, 246 Market Street (daily 8:30 AM-5 PM; free; 978/970-5000).

If you want to pay your respects to Kerouac, who died in Florida in 1969, he is buried in Edsom Cemetery, two miles south of downtown Lowell via Gorham Street. Fans by the hundreds beat a path to his grave, which is on Lincoln Avenue between 7th and 8th Streets, marked by a pile of beer cans and other ritual offerings.

Leominster was the birthplace in 1774 of one John Chapman, a man better known as Johnny Appleseed.

are within the sphere of the **MBTA Commuter Rail** service to downtown (617/722-3200 or 800/392-6100). Purely by way of an example, the hour-long journey from end-of-the-line Fitchburg to Boston's North Station, made 10 times daily on weekdays, five times daily on weekends, costs under $10 roundtrip —equivalent to a few hours' parking in most Boston lots.

Accommodations here, along I-495 on the 20-mile perimeter of the metropolitan area, are largely geared toward business travelers, though the aptly named **Friendly Crossways HI Hostel** (978/456-3649), in Littleton just north of the Route 2/I-495 junction, has dorms beds for $12 and a few private rooms, too.

Even without the Kerouac connection, Lowell—with its working water-powered looms, canal tours, and engaging interpretive tours—would deserve attention. Befitting its blue-collar past, Lowell is home to several classic diners— best of which is the excellent **Four Sisters' Owl Diner,** open every day at 244 Appleton Street near the Commuter Rail station.

Concord

Fairly flying into the thick of metropolitan Boston, Route 2 runs along the outskirts of lovely little Concord, the destination of British Redcoats that fabled day in April 1775, when the war for American independence began. A reconstructed **Old North Bridge,** site of the "shot heard round the world," still arches o'er the placid Concord River next to open fields, drystone walls, and **The Old Manse** (daily 10 AM-5 PM, April-Oct.; $5.50; 978/369-3909), whose study window views are not so very different from when Ralph Waldo Emerson and Nathaniel Hawthorne lived here. The **Minute Man National Historical Park** maintains a free year-round visitor center on the hillside overlooking the famous battlefield; stop in and pick up a guide to the rest of the park's holdings along the "Battle Road" (Route 2A) between Concord and Lexington.

Although it often seems as if you can't toss a stick anywhere in eastern Massachusetts without hitting something of historic significance, this is especially true in Concord, where some of the most influential American writers either lived and worked. Visit a few of these literary lions—Ralph Waldo Emerson, Nathaniel Hawthorne, Henry David Thoreau, Louisa May Alcott, to name the most famous four—along "Author's Ridge" in **Sleepy Hollow Cemetery,** off Bedford Street northeast of the town center. Visitors may be struck by the quantity of No Parking signs lining the streets of Concord, but the reason for this barrage of apparent inhospitality may be seen on any sun-drenched summer weekend, when long columns of cars bound for the beach at nearby **Walden Pond** jam the streets. Serious fans of Henry David Thoreau's little experiment in simple living may be able to overlook its overstressed condition, but more than likely you'll be taken aback by the erosion, the illegal kamikaze mountain bikers, the crowds, and the racket of passing commuter trains. Of course, there is still some magic to the place, although it usually takes a near-dawn in late spring or near-dusk in late fall to find any hint of transcendence along the pond's well-worn circumferential path.

standing guard at Minute Man National Historical Park

A slightly different philosophy of simplicity may be found in the design of the nearby **Gropius House**, on Baker Bridge Road in Lincoln. Built in 1937-38 by and for Bauhaus founder Walter Gropius at the start of his tenure at Harvard University, this small showcase blends Bauhaus form-is-function precepts with traditional New England simplicity. Extremely knowledgeable guides give hourly **tours** (Fri.-Sun. noon-4 PM in summer; $5; 781/259-8098). For information about the Concord area, contact the historic Wright Tavern **visitor center**, 2 Lexington Road (978/369-3120), by the town common.

Perhaps you haven't got a week like Thoreau to row down the Concord River, but you can make your own abridged journey with a summer or fall canoe rental from South Bridge Boat House, 496-502 Main Street in Concord (978/369-9438).

On to Boston

The remaining dozen miles to Boston are most quickly devoured along Route 2, although you can take slower Route 2A if you wish to follow the footsteps of those retreating British redcoats; either way will bring you to the same gateway for the metro area, Route 16 in North Cambridge. Whether or not you're staying outside the city, you would be well advised to leave your car in the Alewife "T" Station commuter parking garage (about $5 a day) at the Route 2/Route 16 junction, and use the **MBTA subway** to get around the city.

Coming into Boston from the west, old US-20 approaches by way of Waltham and Watertown, where it follows Main Street. Twice crossing the Charles River, US-20 finally comes in to Boston proper along Commonwealth Avenue, ending up at Boston Common.

BOSTON SURVIVAL GUIDE

THREE AND A HALF CENTURIES OF HEADLINE-making have given Boston a superabundance of historical significance, all within a city that's surprisingly compact. The youthful energy of the city's many college students helps cloak the inbred parochialism, but the ghosts of Puritan moralists haven't entirely lost their grip on the city. So, while the club scene is vibrant, the coffee shops legion, and bookstores nearly outnumber video stores, don't expect to shop for wine on Sunday or find many places open for dinner after 10 PM.

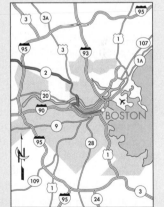

There are lots of places to start a Boston tour, but my favorite is the **Old North Church**, 193 Salem Street (daily 9 AM-5 PM, services Sunday at 9 AM, 11 AM, and 4 PM; free; 617/523-6676), a Boston landmark since colonial times, when Paul Revere set off from here on his midnight ride. The steeple has been rebuilt, but most everything

(continues on next page)

else is original; Paul's house, the oldest in Boston, is a block away at 19 North Square. Best of all, the surrounding neighborhood is the city's oldest and most wanderably interesting quarter, the now predominantly Italian North End.

The other must-see Boston place is Fenway Park, southwest of the center off Boylston Street at 4 Yawley Way, home of the **Red Sox** (tickets 617/267-1700), the smallest and perhaps the most characterful old stadium in the U.S. Before a game, you can improve your mind by whiling away a few

hours at the nearby **Isabella Stuart Gardner Museum**, 280 The Fenway (Tues.-Sun. 11 AM-5 PM; $7; 617/566-1401). In the late 19th century "Mrs. Jack" Gardner built her home as a Venetian palazzo, stuffed it with exquisite art, and then opened it as a museum. Her idiosyncratic taste is partially the charm of this place, along with the breathtaking interior courtyard.

Atop the tallest building in New England, **John Hancock Observatory**, 200 Clarendon Street at Copley Square (daily 9 AM-10 PM; $5; 617/247-1977), is simply the best place to get an overview of Boston. The I.M. Pei-designed monolith made headlines early on, when its windows developed a tendency to pop out and shatter all over the sidewalks below. To contrast Boston landmarks new and old, step across the square to **Trinity Church**, designed by H.H. Richardson in his trademark Romanesque style.

Practicalities

Boston sits spider-like at the center of a web of major arterial highways and interstates, including I-90, I-93, and I-95. Conveniently for air travelers **Logan International Airport** is just a seven-minute ride across Boston Harbor from downtown—if you take the **Water Shuttle** to or from Rowes Wharf, that is (every 15 minutes weekdays, 30 minutes on weekends; $10 one way, $17 roundtrip). Logan is also connected to the city by the Blue Line subway ($.85); scheduled vans such as **Back Bay Coach**, which makes hourly rounds to a dozen downtown hotels (617/698-6188; $7.50); on-demand vans like **U.S. Shuttle** (800/449-4240; $7-13 depending on destination); and of course, taxis.

Boston's 20th-century traffic and 17th-century streets are not for the faint-hearted. Narrow, frequently unidentified, poorly maintained, and laid out in irregular patterns conforming to long-buried topography, the city's avenues are also home to some of the most aggressive give-no-quarter bumper-riding red-light-runners you'll ever meet. Since such conditions create a fundamental nightmare for out-of-town drivers, the best bet is to leave your car as far out of the city as you can (see page 613 for some suggestions), and either take public transit like nearly everyone else, or use your feet. All the hotels, restaurants, and attractions you might want are within walking distance of "**The T,**" the generic name for the Massachusetts Bay Transportation Authority's network of subways, buses, trolleys, ferries, and commuter trains.

Places to stay start with the budget **HI Boston Hostel**, 12 Hemenway Street, near the Green Line's Hynes/ICA station (617/536-9455), a standard urban hostel—which is to say that if the person in the next bunk snores, good luck catching a good night's rest. Book private rooms ($54 for two) a month in advance; dorm beds cost $19 for members, $22 for nonmembers. Many steps up the comfort scale, the **Boston Park Plaza Hotel**, 64 Arlington Street, near the Green Line's Arlington station (617/426-2000 or 800/225-2008), is grand and enormous (966 rooms) yet not impersonal; doubles cost $109-149, parking $18/day. For a B&B at the foot of historic Beacon Hill, try **John Jeffries House**, 14 Embankment Road, near the Red Line's Charles station (617/367-1866). Across from the Charles River Esplanade—where the Boston Pops Orchestra performs their July 4th concert—this Victorian inn proves comfort and convenience don't have to be sacrificed for savings. Doubles go for around $100, parking is $15/day.

Thanks no doubt to Boston's Puritan past, the city has never had much of a reputation for its food—hearty sustenance has always had priority over delighting the senses. That said, there are some fun places like **The Daily Catch**, 323 Hanover Street, walking distance from the Orange Line's Haymarket station (617/523-8567). This North End joint is so tiny, the cook could shake hands with half his customers without leaving his stove. Calamari (squid) is the house specialty, but the menu's mainstay is Sicilian seafood-over-linguine ("red or white"), served in saute pans instead of on plates. Cash only and no reservations, so expect a wait after 6 PM. **Mucho Gusto Cafe and Collectibles**, 1124 Boylston Street (617/236-1020), not far from Fenway Park at the edge of the Back Bay, has meaty Cuban food for breakfast, lunch, and dinner, amidst a wild barrage of *I Love Lucy* (and Desi!) memorabilia. A yuppie-free zone in the heart of the Back Bay, **The Other Side Cosmic Cafe**, 407 Newbury Street (617/536-9477), cater-corner from the Green Line's Hynes/ICA station, is a popular place for people who want fruit and vegetable smoothies, wheat grass shots, and veggie lasagna to accompany that late-night espresso and cigarette.

And if you really have to have one "authentic Boston" meal, go to **Durgin Park**, in Faneuil Hall at 340 N. Market Street, for beef, seafood, and baked beans served up at shared tables to a mix of tourists and masochistic locals.

For further information, drop by the **Boston Common Visitor Center** on Tremont Street near the Park Street T station for all your little fan-folded flyer needs. Lists of attractions and accommodations are also available in advance from the **Greater Boston Convention and Visitors Bureau** (617/267-6466 or 800/888-5515).

US-6 ACROSS PENNSYLVANIA

Winding between the parallel I-90 and I-80 turnpikes, US-6 takes its time crossing the Keystone State, following the course of several ancient Indian trails and meandering rivers as the road wanders its way past a dizzying array of industrial wonders, hardscrabble factory towns, drive-in movie theaters, spit-polished diners, and farm-studded mountain valleys. In the west, the well-maintained two-lane roadway is clearly marked from the moment it crosses the Ohio border, with bright green signs labeling it the "Grand Army of the Republic Highway," a sobriquet US-6 has quietly borne since 1948.

Long before Pennsylvanians got turnpike and motor-touring fever, Native Americans carved twisting footpaths through the shady forests and narrow Allegheny Mountain valleys now navigated by US-6. In the western quarter of the state, the roadbed follows portions of the old Venango Trail, which provided a gateway to Lake Erie for the nomadic Senecas. Centuries before, Uncle Billy Smith and Colonel Drake struck oil along the petroleum-rich beds of Titusville's Oil Creek, igniting a mad frenzy of speculation and boom-and-bust development that left its mark in the smoky refineries and gray, soot-stained towns that dot the craggy western Pennsylvania landscape.

As the rugged Allegheny landscape gives way to the tiny mountain farms and abandoned logging camps of the north-central portion of the state, the two-lane road winds through the bustling Allegheny River towns of Warren and Coudersport, and the New England tidiness of Wellsboro—the gateway to the deep Pine Creek Gorge region known as the Grand Canyon of Pennsylvania. Continuing east, US-6 suddenly transforms itself into a limited-access, concrete four-laner cutting a wide swath through the tough anthracite coal mining northeastern corner of the state. Here, the post-industrial and home-cooked charms of Scranton provide a

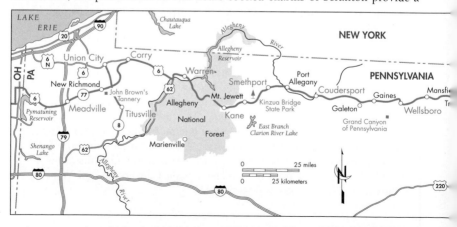

welcome excuse for an extended stopover before tackling the
monotonous stretch of dank, fetid swamps and wetlands that
slope down to the damp, thickly forested Delaware Gap lowlands at the tri-state border of Pennsylvania, New York, and
New Jersey.

When it was designated the "Grand Army of the Republic Highway" after WW II, US-6 begrudgingly parted with the Roosevelt Highway signposts it had proudly displayed since its construction as one of the state's original highways in 1923.

Meadville

The rigidly straight course cut by US-6 across Ohio's farm-dot-
ted "Western Reserve" immediately gives way to a more casual,
winding approach as you enter Pennsylvania, where you are greeted by a large blue
sign bearing the state's geographically challenged tourism slogan, "Pennsylvania—
America Starts Here," and a more discreet, rectangular, forest-green Grand Army of
the Republic Highway marker. The narrow two-lane road, whitened by the ravages
of winter storms and de-icing salts, is spattered with syrupy black tar drippings as
it descends rolling, shaded hills studded with John Birch Society and gun show
billboards near the campgrounds, and bait and tackle shops that service the vast
Pymatuning Reservoir recreational area.

Gently twisting past a random mix of roadside hay bales, sweet corn vendors,
ranch houses, deer crossing signs, and rusty trailer parks, US-6 becomes a four-lane
divided highway with limited-access exit ramps before joining forces with US-322
and dumping you onto a featureless strip where Wal-Mart reigns supreme. This intense dose of highway sprawl marks the western edge of Meadville (pop. 14,300),
the birthplace of actress Sharon Stone, and of the **zipper**. (Though invented as early
as 1893, hookless slide fasteners did not become a big commercial success until the
Goodrich Company installed ones made in Meadville in its popular rubber galosh-
es in 1923). To get to the carefully hidden downtown, take Park Avenue past the
motels (Super 8, Day's Inn, Holiday Inn) and minimarts that line US-6/322 outside
of town.

The Talon zipper plant, which put this shady, peaceful college town on the map,
has long since fled for cheap-labor climes. Rather than dwell on this departure,
Meadville quietly goes about the business of maintaining its elm-shaded streets,
parks, and ample stock of well-preserved 19th-century homes, and feeding off the

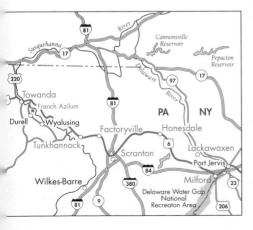

profitable influx of college students
who wander down the hill from Allegheny College's stately grounds to
quench their collective thirst at the
dark, smoky, working-class bars—like
Otter's Pub, 378 North Street, and Two's
Company, 414 North Street—and
restaurants that line North Street on
the top edge of the small but active
downtown. Try the Deerhead Inn, 412
North Street, open 24 hours for cheap
but filling spaghetti dinners in a cramped, windowless, and woodsy setting.
Those with a ceaseless longing for
reassuring dim lights, thick smoke,

Founded in 1815, **Allegheny College** is one of the oldest universities west of the Appalachians, and boasts a collection of beautiful historic Greek Revival, Georgian, and federal-style buildings on its spacious campus on the north side of Meadville, at the crest of Park and Main Streets.

and loud, loud music will also want to head south of downtown to **Theodore's**, 964 Park Avenue, affectionately known locally as Teddy's, where a long, well-worn bar, a cooler full of Genesee beers, and a mixed bag of blue-collar locals and slumming collegians are the order of the night.

For a more salubrious educational experience, relax by the gazebo and grassy lawn of Diamond Park along shady Main and Chestnut Streets and take in the 1835 Greek Revival architecture of the Unitarian church, before strolling over to view the Market House (continuously occupied since its construction in 1870 and now housing the Meadville Council on the Arts) on Market Street in the heart of the several-block downtown.

John Brown's Tannery

From Meadville, Hwy-77 runs northeast through a 10-mile, two-lane stretch of hardwood forest and rippling cornfields to the tiny crossroads of **New Richmond**, where Hwy-1033, a well-signed but bumpy dirt road, leads east past several modest homes and truck farms into a wooded clearing where the stone foundations of John Brown's Tannery rise from the grassy meadow floor.

The future abolitionist operated a tannery here from 1825 to 1835—his longest period of continuous residence in one place as an adult—after helping found the town of New Richmond with a band of settlers from Ohio's Western Reserve. Brown started the town's first post office and personally carried the mail to and from Meadville, where his outspoken nature almost got him lynched one night by an angry mob of Freemasons. The quick temper and passionate anti-slavery zeal that fired Brown's 1850s raids on Pottawatomie, Kansas, and Harper's Ferry, West Virginia (see page 346), seem like thunder from a distant storm in this quiet glen, where the graves of Brown's first wife and two of his infant sons attest to the hardships of the simple pioneer life he tried to forge from the rugged Pennsylvania wilderness.

Titusville: Birthplace of the Oil Industry

One place that road-tripping travelers through the wilds of western Pennsylvania really shouldn't miss is Titusville (pop. 6,400), the self-proclaimed "Birthplace of

Titusville celebrates its heritage with an annual "Drake Day" oil festival each August.

Save your ticket stub from the Drake's Well Museum—it will earn you discounted admission to two dozen other historical sites operated throughout the state by the Pennsylvania Historical and Museum Commission. A free guide and map is available at the museum gift shop.

the Oil Industry." The fascinating **Drake Well Museum** (Tues.-Sat. 9 AM-5 PM, Sunday noon-5 PM; $4), a half-mile south of town off Hwy-8, relates the story of Col. Edwin Drake and driller Uncle Billy Smith's 1859 oil strike and the subsequent "black gold" rush it set off in the surrounding hills and creekbeds. A re-created model of the original well still pumps slippery, pure paraffin-based Pennsylvania crude, which you are encouraged to touch and smell by enthusiastic guides with an encyclopedic knowledge of local history and all things related to oil.

The museum also screens a humorously dated, but still entertaining, 1954 documentary film, *Born in Freedom*, starring a young, tentative Vincent Price as the pensive Drake (who, ironically, never reaped any financial rewards from his efforts and died in poverty in 1880 in Bethlehem, Pennsylvania) and tow-headed Alan Hale, Jr. (the Skipper in TV's *Gilligan's Island*) as a beefy, back-slapping drill hand.

The museum also boasts a rich library of oil-related and regional historical documents and early photographs detailing the incredible boom-and-bust cycle that gave birth to the nearby Oil Creek Valley town of Pithole, which saw its population shoot to 15,000 as speculators, con men, and prospectors poured into town to occupy the town's 57 hotels soon after another oil strike in 1865. Having the third-busiest post office in the state in its 1866 heyday, Pithole was virtually abandoned as soon as the oil ran dry in 1867. A free map and tour guide available at the museum direct you through Oil Creek State Park to the original town site, now an empty meadow of grasses and wildflowers.

Back in Titusville, stop at **Papa Carone's Restaurant**, 317 S. Franklin Street across the Oil Creek bridge (open daily from 11 AM), for a quick pizza slice, meatball sub, or soda.

No matter how tempting its name may be, skip the 20-mile detour south to grimy Oil City (pop. 12,000), where mammoth Pennzoil refinery smokestacks blacken the skyline over the narrow, traffic-choked streets of this grimy, hardworking city still coming to grips with the recent flight of its lifeblood, the Quaker State corporation, to Texas.

Warren

Perched above the banks of a wide bend in the southward-flowing Allegheny River, downtown Warren (pop. 11,100) is a bustling jewel of Depression-era luncheonettes, dry goods stores, and a well-preserved commercial district in which sun-faded early 20th-century advertisements still adorn the dusty brick facades of many of the town's three- and four-story office buildings and warehouses. Park in the thriving central business district and wander along one of the shady side streets down to the river, taking in the old Liberty Theatre (on 3rd Avenue, now housing community arts productions), the neoclassical public library (on Market Street), and the tin-ceilinged, turn-of-the-century G.C. Murphy five-and-dime store on the corner of Liberty and Pennsylvania Streets.

Take a break with a meal or a cup of coffee at the timeless **Busy Bee Restaurant and Lounge,** open since 1936 for lunch and again for dinner at 229½ Pennsylvania Avenue. Across the street, **Roy's Texas Lunch** serves up a hearty, cholesterol-rich fare of red hots (hot dogs grilled in the tough western New York tradition), goulash, and macaroni and cheese in a more pedestrian, no-nonsense setting. A **Holiday Inn,** a **Super 8,** and the locally owned and operated **Penn Laurel Inn** (814/ 723-8300), 706 W. Pennsylvania Street, offer reasonably priced lodging options along US-6 on the western edge of town.

Kane

Approaching Kane (pop. 4,590) from the west, the road rolls unassumingly through a series of farm-laden hills before zipping through a monotonous 20-mile slice of the pine-shaded Allegheny State Forest preserve. Sitting atop a high ridge, Kane's busy turn-of-the-century downtown sports the old **Temple Theatre** (now doing some prime business with the pre-pubescent crowd as Shirley Temple's Rollerskating Rink), an old **McCrory's** five-and-dime store, and the wonderful

Texas Hot Lunch at 24 Field Street, an early-opening, late-closing bar and restaurant where chili-doused dogs are served hot off the grill with sweet relish, onions, and hot mustard at a price (95 cents each) bound to encourage multiple purchases. The **Kane Motel** (814/837-6161) and **Kane View Motel** (814/837-8600) are both on the eastern edge of town.

Kane is proud of its favorite recent son, **Chuck Daly,** coach of the two-time NBA champion Detroit Pistons and the 1992 U.S. Olympic "Dream Team."

Kinzua Bridge State Park

At the lonesome, nondescript crossroads of Mount Jewett (pop. 1,000), follow signs along a bumpy, narrow roller coaster of a road to Kinzua Bridge State Park, four miles north of US-6 amid dark pine *Deer Hunter*-like forest. The park straddles the steep Kinzua Creek Gorge, which was finally spanned in 1882 by the 301-foot-high, 2,053-foot-long Kinzua Viaduct, constructed by the Erie Railroad to extend its economic reach southward into the fertile McKean County coal, timber, and oil fields. At the time, it was the highest railroad bridge ever built, earning the structure its proudly worn badge as the "**Eighth Wonder of the World**."

A short walk over the rough, tar-soaked railroad-tie crosswalk to the center of the bridge leads to an exhilarating view of the dense tree cover leading down the steep slopes to the narrow creekbed. Alternately, the **Knox and Kane excursion railroad** (814/837-8621 or 717/334-6932) offers a roundtrip package tour from nearby Kane or more distant Marienville for those who want to test the structural soundness of the steel-reinforced viaduct under the weight of a period passenger steam train.

Smethport

Back on US-6, leafy trees and stately Victorian homes line the route through downtown Smethport (pop. 1,734), home of **America's First Christmas Store** (800/841-2721), housed in an old brick building on the eastern edge of town. If you lose out to your better judgment and find yourself overcome with that holly-jolly feeling, you might want to recuperate with a piece of homemade pie at the **Smethport Diner**, 423 W. Main Street, a 1930s diner clad in 1960s Perma Stone that draws weary road-trippers with the promise of half-pound "Hubber Burgers," healthy stir-fries, and yummy desserts, including a gorgeous apple crisp.

East of Smethport, which marks the approximate boundary of western Pennsylvania's once-potent oil industry, an endless sea of junked cars, dense forests, and swampy lowland truck farms laps at the roadbed as US-6 passes the historic Allegheny River crossing at Port Allegany.

Coudersport: The Pennsylvania Lumber Museum

In tidy downtown Coudersport (pop. 2,800), a gazebo graces the pretty courthouse square across from the **Crittenden Hotel,** 133 N. Main Street (814/274-8320), where you can dine, drink, and crash for the night without ever setting foot outside. East of Coudersport, US-6 descends into thickly forested piney woods at the northern lip of the Susquehannock State Forest. A 10-mile-long, virtually retail-free stretch of road leads to the **Pennsylvania Lumber Museum** (daily 9 AM-4:30 PM; $4), which pays homage to the region's prosperous mid-19th-century lumber boom. A period logging camp, a two-story mill with circular saw upstairs and steam-powered engines below, and a chestnut log cabin from the Depression-era Civilian Conservation Corps (CCC) reforestation program are among the 3,000 lumber-related objects on display at this refreshingly self-effacing museum.

The **Nine Mile Lakeside Cottage and Motel** (814/435-2394), on the north side of US-6 just east of the museum, features a set of redwood-stained motor court cabins for those who plan to make a weekend out of it.

*Every July, the Lumber Museum hosts the **Bark Peelers' Convention,** when wanna-be Paul Bunyans can try their hand at felling a tree or two amid bluegrass bands and country picnics.*

Continuing east from the museum, US-6 wanders along the wooded Pine Creek Valley through **Galeton** (pop. 1,370) and the minuscule village of **Gaines**, approaching the western rim of the grandly named "Grand Canyon of Pennsylvania." A six-mile-long, pothole-strewn concrete road leads south from US-6 outside of Gaines to **Colton Point State Park,** built during the New Deal by the CCC to provide a dramatic alternate view of the gorge's shimmering waterfalls and craggy, tree-covered slopes. Check the weather before making this tough, bumpy detour, however, as even the slightest hint of fog will obscure the expansive vistas.

Wellsboro

The most popular jumping-off point for tourists who flock to the Grand Canyon of Pennsylvania for a weekend getaway, Wellsboro (pop. 3,400) has a gorgeous Main Street business district with a warm, comfortable feel created by the authentic gas-lit streetlights that line the lush, grassy median strip, and by the red neon glow of the flickering sign that fronts the historic, well-worn **Penn Wells Hotel,** 62 Main Street (717/724-2111), built in 1869 and seemingly not remodeled since 1969.

A free walking-tour guide, available at the visitor center and most of the town's businesses, points the way to Wellsboro's main historic sight, the **Lincoln Door House** at 140 Main Street, which bears a red door donated in 1858 by then-Illinois governor Abraham Lincoln, whom the house's occupants had known before relocating to Wellsboro from Springfield, Illinois. A casual stroll along the shaded side streets to view some of Wellsboro's historic 19th-century homes is the town's main entertainment option, which otherwise consists of a movie at the one-screen **Arcadia Theatre** or a drink and a game of pool at the friendly **North Star Bar**, both on Main Street.

For food, the Penn-Wells Hotel's shabbily elegant **Mary Wells Dining Room**—which, sadly, bears no relation to the "My Guy" chanteuse—has hearty breakfasts and pricier pasta dinners, but the place to eat is the low-slung, green-roofed, porcelain-plated **Wellsboro Diner,** 19 Main Street (717/724-3992), an immaculately restored Sterling diner manufactured in 1939 by the J.B. Judkins Co. of Merrimac, Massachusetts. The diner closes its doors early, so make a point of grabbing an early dinner, or even earlier lunch or breakfast; if you are going to hang around town for a few hours, they will even custom-bake a pie of your choosing to tide you over for the rest of your trip.

The peeling yellow wallpaper, orange shag carpet, and grease-streaked curtains lining the hallways and rooms of the once-grand Penn-Wells Hotel arouse suspicions that the next wave of renovations are long overdue, and your overnight dollars are better spent at the adjacent **Penn Wells Lodge,** 4 Main Street (717/724-3463 or 800/545-2446), which has full facilities and rates from under $50 a night. The **Canyon Motel**, two blocks east at 18 East Avenue (717/724-1681 or 800/255-2718), has bargain-priced rooms from under $30. For something a bit more special, settle in at the cozy, Victorian-style **Four Winds Bed and Breakfast** (717/724-6141) at 58 West Avenue.

For more information, contact the Wellsboro **visitor center**, 114 Main Street (717/724-1926).

The Grand Canyon of Pennsylvania

The thickly forested mountain ravine known as the "Grand Canyon of Pennsylvania" bears little resemblance to the red rocks and more dramatic dropoffs associated with the eponymous Arizona landmark. That said, it's still an impressive sight—especially at sunset—with clouds hovering above its 1,000 feet of pine-covered walls.

To reach the Grand Canyon's eastern rim, take Main Street (Hwy-660) west out of Wellsboro, past beautiful Victorian homes and through a lush dairy farming district marked by cud-chewing cows and freshly painted barns and silos. The main "entrance" to the canyon is at Leonard Harrison State Park, which provides an easily accessed view of the gorge and a well-maintained trail dropping down to the river. The former Penn Central railroad right-of-way in the base of the canyon is being converted into a cycling and cross-country skiing trail. You can also see the canyon from Colton Point State Park on the west rim (see page 621 for more).

Towanda

US-6 rolls lazily through a 40-mile stretch of rich dairy farmland and gentle hills east of Wellsboro, through Mansfield and Troy and into Towanda (pop. 3,200), an odd mix of nicely maintained Victorian homes and a no-nonsense, telephone-pole-crowded downtown. Historical markers recite the achievements of Towanda's two most famous residents—19th-century politician David Wilmot, who authored the 1846 anti-slavery document known as the Wilmot Proviso; and composer Stephen Foster, who penned the now-ubiquitous "Camptown Races" many years after wandering the banks of the Susquehanna River as a student at the Towanda Academy in 1840-41.

You can get *just about* anything you want—in the way of breakfast or lunch—at **Alice's Restaurant**, 318 Main Street (6 AM-8 PM, Sunday 8 AM-1 PM). Or check out a movie at the still-operating **Keystone Theatre.**

French Azilum

From Towanda on down to Tunkhannock, US-6 runs a high ridge above the steep Susquehanna River bed, along the course of an ancient Seneca Indian trail. En route, the road passes within sight of the French Azilum, a short-lived agricultural colony of French aristocrats who fled here after the French Revolution in 1793 in the hope of providing safe harbor for Marie Antoinette and her son, the heir to the French throne. The colony more or less disintegrated in 1803 when most of the nobles were lured back to France by Napoleon's pardoning decree. The **Marie Antoinette Overlook**, on the south side of US-6 about six miles southeast of the Masonite mill town of Wysox, provides a sweeping view of the patchwork quilt of fertile flatlands on the south shore of the Susquehanna where the remains of Azilum still stand. The five log cabins and a model of the original village, which adjoin a large working dairy farm that extends to the river bank, are being restored by the Pennsylvania Historical and Museum Commission.

Though it's just across the river from US-6, extensive detours and road repairs make getting to the actual site a patience-trying endeavor that will eat up at least an hour of roundtrip driving time. The easiest way to get there from US-6 is to take Hwy-187 across the river from Wyalusing, continue for eight miles to Durell, then head west on Hwy-204, following the clearly marked signs to the site.

Tunkhannock and Factoryville

After passing through the false-fronted late-1890s banks and businesses lining the road through Wyalusing, US-6 continues its rapid downhill run to Scranton along a narrow ridge above the Susquehanna, pulling into the pleasant, flag-lined business district of aging lumber center Tunkhannock (pop. 2,251), where a Pampers disposable diaper factory now reigns supreme as the town's largest employer. The **Prince Hotel** (717/836-2292) in the center of town has a few old rooms upstairs at about $25 a night, within stumbling distance of the lively Red Lion Inn bar that occupies the first floor.

The dense evergreen groves crowding the two-lane road down the sharp, fast descent into the Scranton/Wilkes-Barre area are broken by a sign at the outskirts of little Factoryville (pop. 1,310), advertising itself as the birthplace of turn-of-the-century New York Giants baseball hurler, Hall of Famer **Christy Mathewson**, who played for northern Pennsylvania factory and mill teams before establishing himself as the king of Upper Manhattan's Polo Grounds in the early 1900s.

A few miles south of Factoryville, along an abandoned Delaware, Lackawanna and Western Railroad right-of-way, US-6 suddenly widens into a four-lane, limited-access highway split by a steel guardrail median strip, whizzing past a crowded stretch of old motels, supermarkets, liquor stores, and mini-marts along the steep Moosic Mountain grade down into Scranton.

Scranton

The tough, sprawling coal town of Scranton (pop. 81,800) is in the midst of a remarkable revitalization that revolves largely around the successful, sensitively conceived promotion of its mighty industrial past as a regional tourist attraction. Aside from the diverse, engaging museums that celebrate Scranton's historical importance as a mining, manufacturing, and railroad hub, the city lays claim to a Class AAA minor league baseball team (the Philadelphia Phillies' affiliate, Scranton/Wilkes-Barre Red Barons), an architecturally rich downtown, and a savory set of greasy spoons, streamlined diners, dairy bars, and pizza joints.

Scranton is an easy place to get lost; from US-6, which skirts the northern lip of the city, take the Scranton Expressway (US-11) south into the downtown area.

The town was founded in the 1840s when brothers George and Seldon Scranton and their cousin, Joseph Scranton, started the Lackawanna Iron and Coal Company and built the Scranton Iron Furnaces located at Lackawanna Avenue and Moosic Street, to produce iron rails for the construction of the Erie Railroad line. The brothers' need for a local rail spur led to the founding of the Delaware part of the Lackawanna and Western (DL&W) line in 1853, and firmly established the city as a major rail producer and railroad hub, a position that grew in importance in the

1890s when Scranton emerged as the center of the country's anthracite coal production.

The old 40-acre DL&W railroad yard and locomotive roundhouse on the west side of downtown Scranton have been exquisitely restored by the National Park Services as part of the **Steamtown National Historic Site** (daily 9 AM-5 PM; $6; 717/340-5200), which opened its doors in July 1995. The sprawling rail yards contain over 100 completely restored steam-era locomotives, dining cars, and Pullman sleepers, while a steam-powered passenger train ($8) makes short tourist excursions over to the nearby Iron Furnaces. The brightly lit roundhouse is full of fascinating historical and technological exhibits that trace the development of steam railroading and the growth of the DL&W over its century-long reign as the mighty "Road of Anthracite" that, along with the Erie line, linked the key Atlantic and Great Lakes ports of New York and New Jersey to the lumber camps, coal mines, and oil fields of Pennsylvania. No details are spared, down to a glossary of colorful slang expressions from every walk of railroad life that explain why the caboose was known both as a "monkey house" and "brainboat," while "the pig's in the pen" was a downhome way of saying that a locomotive had just entered the roundhouse.

The **Anthracite Heritage Museum**, northwest of downtown in McDade Park via Scranton Expressway/US 11 to Keyser Street (daily 9 AM-5 PM; $3.50), celebrates the social and cultural history of the Welsh, Polish, Italian, Ukranian, and Lithuanian immigrant miners whose backbreaking labors allowed Scranton's mine owners and railroad barons to reap immense personal fortunes and build grand public buildings and private homes. In addition to detailing the dangerous working conditions and tragic history of the miners' labor movement, the museum tells the painful story of the breaker boys, child laborers who picked out nonburnable slate from raw anthracite in massive, poorly ventilated coal breaker structures that dotted the Scranton skyline well into the mid-1900s.

Next door to Anthracite Heritage Museum, the **Lackawanna Coal Mine Tour** (daily 11 AM-4:30 PM; $5) lets you experience the claustrophobia and terror of the miners' daily life firsthand with a railcar trip 300 feet deep into the bowels of a once-active anthracite mine.

Scranton Practicalities

All this history and museum-going is bound to make you mighty hungry—a condition Scranton can amply remedy. The Old Forge neighborhood extending southwest along Main Street, about four miles from downtown Scranton, is home to a bevy of Italian family restaurants and bars that dish out the area's locally famous "Old Forge" white pizza—gobs of mozzarella and onions, no tomato sauce. This cheesy concoction cannot be ordered by the slice (the lack of sauce makes it dry out too quickly), and most of the neighborhood restaurants serve it—including **Talarico's**, 103 S. Main Street, and **Arcaro and Genell**, 443 S. Main Street—both of which are open only in the evening. Downtown, **Coney Island Lunch** at 515 Lackawanna Avenue is the home of the Texas Wiener hot dog, while a five-minute drive on Moosic

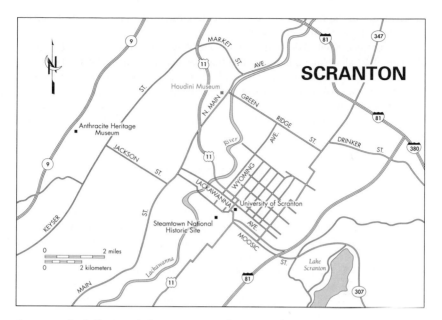

Street up the hill toward the University of Scranton lands you at the foot of red-trimmed, stainless-steel **Chick's Diner**, 1032 Moosic Street at Meadow Avenue (717/344-4156), a classic all-night eatery with a loud, gregarious local clientele.

A place to appreciate even if you don't stay the night is the restored neoclassical 1908 train station, now the 145-room **Lackawanna Station** luxury hotel, 700 Lackawanna Avenue (800/347-6888). It summons the grandeur of the steam era with a revitalized Grand Lobby flanked by a set of rare Siena marble walls and mosaic murals. Most of the moderate motel chains (Best Western, Hampton Inn, Days Inn, Red Roof Inn, Econo Lodge, etc.) cluster around Wilkes-Barre's I-81 exit 47, while smaller, locally owned motels line US-6 to the north of Scranton.

Along US-6 north of Scranton, the majestic **Circle Drive-In** movie theatre (717/489-5731) still shows first-run films high on a hilltop overlooking the Scranton Valley. A prime source of local nightlife and entertainment options is *The Weekender,* a free weekly newspaper published out of nearby Wilkes-Barre that can be picked up at bookstores, clubs, restaurants, and bars in the Scranton/Wilkes-Barre vicinity.

For more information, contact the Greater Scranton **visitor center**, 222 Mulberry Street (717/342-7711).

The Scranton/Wilkes-Barre Red Barons Class AAA baseball team (717/963-6556) play their home games at the 10,800-seat **Lackawanna County Stadium,** an AstroTurf arena cut into a hillside off I-81 at Davis Street, exit 51. Games are broadcast on WICK 1400 AM.

Honesdale

In case you're wondering, the name of Scranton's neighbor, Wilkes-Barre, is pronounced "Wilkes Barry."

East of Scranton, US-6 veers away from the high-speed I-84 freeway, following a slow, twisting two-lane course through rugged anthracite fields and the fading remnants of the once-prosperous coal towns of Jermyn, Carbondale, and Steen. East of Steen, old road markers for US-6's original designation, The Roosevelt Highway, are still visible on the right side of the road, amid the damp undergrowth scuttling up from the creek coursing to the south of the roadway.

In downtown Honesdale (pop. 5,000), the **Wayne County Historical Society Museum**, 810 Main Street, houses a full-sized replica of the **Stourbridge Lion**, the locomotive that made the first commercial steam-engine run in the U.S. in 1829 in an effort to tow coal from the nearby mines to the Delaware and Hudson Canal. The **Maple City Restaurant**, nearby at 734 Main Street, is a timeworn coffee shop where you can rest and fill your gills with coffee, a burger, and a slice of cherry pie before making the final run through the swampy, nondescript deer hunting area

---

THE FAMOUS HOUDINI MUSEUM

Long hours and hard-earned pay meant that Scranton's factory workers, railroad hands, and miners had to be selective when spending their minimal extra funds on family-minded social diversions like a traveling variety show, circus, or county fair. The Famous Houdini Museum, 1433 N. Main Avenue (717/342-5555), commemorates the amazing showmanship of the Hungarian-born magician, Harry Houdini, one of countless traveling acts that passed through the area in the early 1900s. Scranton was then considered a proving ground for New York-based vaudeville performers eager to get the promotional backing needed to take their city-honed act on the road. The expression, "If you can make it in Scranton, you can make it anywhere," was coined by promoters who viewed the demanding working-class immigrant audience as a litmus test that would gauge a particular act's ability to "play in Peoria" long before advertisers and film studios made focus groups and test markets a key part of all their market research efforts.

Owned and operated by two professional magicians—Dorothy Dietrich and Jerry Bravo, who managed New York's Magic Towne House performance/dinner theater for 15 years—the cramped storefront Houdini Museum celebrates the mysterious life and achievements of Erich Weiss, who took the stage name of Harry Houdini when he decided to pursue a career as a magician after his family relocated from his boyhood home of Appleton, Wisconsin, to New York in the 1890s. Houdini's bewildering escapes from sausage skins, jail cells, coffins, and countless locks and straitjackets are recalled in a short video presentation, followed by a tour of the museum's vast collection of Houdini's favorite tricks, mechanisms, and scrapbooks. There's even a delightful live magic show.

bordering the Delaware State Forest en route to Milford, Matamoras, Port Jervis, and the Delaware Water Gap National Recreation Area.

Lackawaxen

The tiny town of Lackawaxen (pop. 2,832), along the Delaware River seven scenic miles north of US-6 via Hwy-590, holds two fascinating attractions: the preserved home of writer Zane Grey, and a unique suspension bridge built by Brooklyn Bridge designer John Roebling. It comes as something of a surprise to find out that Zane Grey, author of the classic Western novel *Riders of the Purple Sage,* was in fact a fly-fishing Pennsylvania dentist, but he was. His home was preserved by his family, and as the **Zane Grey Museum** (Fri.-Sun. noon-5 PM; free; 717/685-4871) now offers an intimate look into his life and works. The Roebling Bridge is about 100 yards upstream from Zane Grey's home and has been preserved by the National Park Service—though it's now used by cars instead of canal boats as it was originally.

Zane Grey

Milford was the longtime home of forestry pioneer and two-term Pennsylvania Governor Gifford Pinchot, whose Grey Towers estate off US-6 is often open for tours (717/296-9630).

Milford

Just off I-84 at the northern end of Delaware Water Gap National Recreation Area, Milford (pop. 1,400) is a cutesy tourist town cashing in on the hordes of rafters, campers, and B&Bers who make the two-hour weekend journey here from New York or Philadelphia. Drive slowly when passing through Milford's deceptively peaceful central business district, because the local police maintain carefully concealed **speed traps** that result in heavy fines for even the most minor speed limit violation.

The **Blue Spruce Motel** motor court (717/491-4969) and **Milford Motel** (717/296-6411) on the northern outskirts of town off US-6 are the low-priced alternatives to the higher-brow **Tom Quick Inn,** 411 Broad Street (717/296-6514), a B&B in the heart of downtown Milford.

Milford marks the western junction of US-6 and our Appalachian Trail route, described beginning on page 296, which runs south from here through Delaware Water Gap National Recreation Area.

US-6 ACROSS NEW YORK

According to the map, US-6's corner-cutting path across the southern edge of the state seems well outside New York City's sprawl, but there is no escape from the greater reality of the urban northeast: this part of the Atlantic seaboard is the original megalopolis. The map may not make it obvious that some tens of millions of people live within an hour's drive of this route, but the volume of traffic will. Despite a pleasant foray onto curvaceous and scenic parkways through Harriman and Bear Mountain State Parks, and a dramatic crossing of the Hudson River, US-6 is often immersed in long stretches of commercial roadside development, particularly east of the Hudson. Putnam County's seemingly endless strip malls will help anesthetize you against the urban landscape found all along the remainder of your journey. If you weary of studying the subtle regional differences in architectural and typographic vernacular, there are several chances to switch over to the bland but expeditious interstate.

Port Jervis

A curious mixture of small-town dereliction and commercial bustle, Port Jervis wears its empty storefronts like an elderly professor wears a fraying tweed jacket. Transportation has clearly been a major historical force here, with the influence of successive eras—the river, the railroad, and the federal highway—inscribed in the very layout of the town. For a glimpse of the long reign of the iron horse, check out the intriguing artifacts and photos in the restored waiting room of the old **Erie Lackawanna Depot** on Front Street. The arrival of the interstate provided the last major makeover, with the placement of I-84 on the outskirts of this everlasting pit stop sparing its center from the aluminum implants of modern prefabricators. Signs of the next shift—back to the sturdy brick commercial blocks beside the old depot—are visible in the "shoppe" signs sprouting among the old mom 'n' pop stores downtown.

The wary traveler seeking either the comfort and safety of a brand-name burger or the excitement of roast duck with plum-balsamic vinaigrette will have to hit the road, Jack, for Port Jervis still believes in the virtues of home cooking. **Homer's Coffee Shop**, unmissable at the corner of Orange and Main, is a prime example, with its democratic social club of elderly regulars, young tie-wearing businessmen, and tradespeople with company names stitched on their shirt pockets, all drawn to the bargain meals. Despite the acoustic tile and too-new counter and seating, it's a welcoming spot, with the added attraction of a soda fountain in case you need to wash down that turkey club or beef stroganoff with a Tin Roof Sundae. With "soda bars" and confectionaries so plentiful in these parts, you may wonder if some local zoning law requires the vintage counters found in general merchandise stores, so residents can perpetually relive their collective youth.

Minisink Valley

Leaving Port Jervis and the Delaware River, the route gradually rises over a scenic dozen miles along the low flanks of the Shawangunk Mountains. Bright red leaves of late summer's sumac stand out amid the thick deciduous woods like the ripening apples in the many orchards whose roadside stands are always worth a stop as soon as autumn's crop is heralded by these hand-lettered declarations: "fresh-baked pies" and "fresh-pressed cider."

Shaking the country air off its shoulders, US-6 joins four-lane Route 17M, chock full of fast drivers intent on cutting the corner between northward-tending I-84 and the big-city-bound New York Thruway, I-87. After a headlong dash eastward from one interstate to the next, US-6 peels itself from the rush and enters **Harriman State Park**. In utter contrast to the get-out-of-my-way style of later highway construction, the few parkway miles you'll sample here were intentionally designed to encourage the Sunday afternoon family outing in the motor car, the lazy meandering roadbed calculated to lengthen the journey and maximize exposure to the surrounding forests. Even the rustic Romanesque stone arch bridges attempt to harmonize with local rock outcroppings.

Hudson Valley: Hyde Park

Since the narrow toll bridge over the **Hudson River** affords only a quick glance for whomever is behind the wheel, pull into the parking lot on the west end before crossing to get a good vista of the spindly iron span between the steep palisades. If you want to walk across, you can, since the Georgia-to-Maine **Appalachian Trail** comes down out of the hills to cross this very bridge. Several nearby state parks help preserve this pretty stretch of the river: besides Harriman and the contiguous **Bear Mountain**, there's the fabulous 400-acre sculpture park at **Storm King Art Center** (daily 11 AM-5:30 PM; $7; 914/534-3115) off Hwy-32 on the north side of the expansive U.S. Military Academy at West Point.

While there's no camping at Harriman State Park, there are hiking trails and even a swimming beach and a bathhouse at **Lake Welch;** take the Palisades Interstate Parkway south from the US-6 (Long Mount Parkway) rotary.

At the beginning of Jack Kerouac's *On the Road,* the main character, Sal Paradise, sets off on an ill-fated attempt to follow US-6 coast to coast. Hoping to hitch a ride along the "one red line called Route 6 that led from the tip of Cape Cod clear to Ely, Nevada, and there dipped down to Los Angeles," Sal set off for Bear Mountain but got caught in a rain storm and had to head home, giving up on the "stupid hearthside idea that it would be wonderful to follow one great line across America instead of trying various roads and routes."

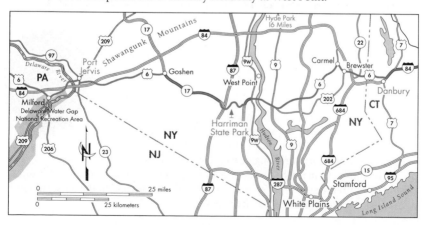

West Point, the Army's famous military academy, is a few miles north of US-6—on the west bank of the Hudson, naturally.

If you prefer a dash of history and decorative arts to a jog through the woods, cross to the east bank of the Hudson and detour upstream on Route 9 about 35 miles to the town of Hyde Park, just north of Poughkeepsie, for a peek into a pair of famous homes now preserved as National Historic Sites: the **home of Franklin D. Roosevelt** and the **Vanderbilt Mansion** (both houses Wed.-Sun. 9 AM-5 PM, grounds daily 7 AM-sunset; $5 for FDR and $2 for Vanderbilt; 914/229-9115). Also on the grounds of FDR's home is the **National Archives' library and museum** (daily 9 AM-5 PM; admission free with Park Service fee; 800/337-8474).

In the nearby village of Haviland, on parallel Route 9G about two miles north of the presidential home, the **Eleanor Roosevelt Historic Site** (same hours; free) will complete your ramble back to the era of the New Deal. Eleanor built this home, Val-Kill, as a weekend escape from her life as First Lady, and lived here after 1945, entertaining world leaders and working on drafts of the United Nations Declaration of Human Rights.

Westchester County

Soak up as much of that scenic Hudson valley as you can—it's the last commercial-free panorama you'll get until well into neighboring Connecticut. Once US-6 leaves the river it becomes a heavily developed corridor of suburban malls, muffler shops, quick-lube garages, office parks, and Park 'n' Ride lots for Manhattan commuters. Not that businesses don't try to sprinkle a dash of foliage around their parking lots—in fact, nearly everybody cultivates more than just token landscaping—but compared to the apple orchards you passed an hour ago and the quaint New England villages an hour ahead, these few dozen miles are hardly a sight for sore eyes.

If you want to make them go a little faster, the town of Brewster provides the first of three chances to hop onto I-84; if you stay on US-6—now a fast four lanes itself—you'll end up crossing the unmarked state line about 40 miles east of the Hudson.

US-6 ACROSS CONNECTICUT

In nighttime satellite photos from space, Connecticut is that bright swath of light splayed between the major metropolitan hotspots of New York City and Boston. It may often seem to contain nothing more than suburbs and office parks, but in fact this third smallest state has some very pleasantly rural landscape tucked away in its northern corners. Expansive colonial farms and elegant frame houses are glimpsed briefly as you skirt their edges, but alas, the bulk of this route plainly parallels the dense mega-urban corridor along coastal I-95, 25 miles south. If the flux of traffic and strip malls becomes too overwhelming, escape north for a more circuitous but relaxing ride, or give up and join the jet stream on the adjacent (and occasionally contiguous) I-84/395 freeways.

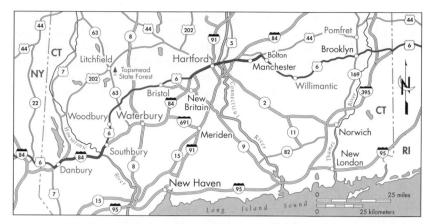

Danbury marks the eastern junction of US-6 and the Appalachian Trail route, which winds north to Mount Washington and south all the way to Atlanta. For details, see pages 296-374.

In New England, locals call their highways "routes," and we've followed suit, using Route as a generic term (Route 100 for example, rather than Hwy-100). The Interstates (I-93) and federal highways (US-3) are abbreviated as usual.

Danbury

Since US-6 joins I-84 within a few miles of crossing the state line, it hardly matters which route you choose—and given the abutters vying for your business along every inch of the old road, you may actually find the interstate more scenic. US-6 skips off on its own for a few miles for a glimpse of upscale residential Newtown, only to merge again with the interstate on the far side of the town's huge flagpole.

Unless you can't hold out for the gourmet shops of Litchfield County, you may as well skip the diversion and stay aboard I-84 until exit 15, when the route gets out of its four-lane rut and gives you a good reason to slow down. For easy-to-find accommodations around Danbury, try the **Super 8** at the first I-84/US-6 junction in the state (exit 4), or the **Best Western** on US-6 at I-84 exit 9.

Woodbury

Take some horse farms with lush green fields outlined by neat stone walls or zigzagging knit-pole fences, mix in big old clapboard colonials with wide lawns and wood split-shingle roofs, add a couple needle-spired churches and historic burial grounds beneath the tall maples and oaks, and you have all the trappings of a place that should live by the gentle stroke of a tall grandfather clock rather than the nervous second-splitting tick of a stopwatch. Alas, all of the Woodbury residents who keep time by the old Seth Thomas wind-ups must be at home taking naps, while all the sprinters caught up in lives like 100-meter dashes are out taking turns trying to read the fine print on your rear license plate.

Since the rush of traffic on US-6 makes architectural appreciation impossible without suffering whiplash, stop by Woodbury's town office building on Main Street and pick up a free brochure detailing two local **walking tours** around the former sheep-raising capital of the American colonies, liberally endowed with fine

18th-and 19th-century structures. One colonial home open to the public is the restored **Glebe House** (Wed.-Sun. 1-4 PM, April-Nov.; $4; 203/263-2855), on Hollow Road (Route 317) in southern Woodbury. The first Episcopalian bishop was elected by a secret meeting of clergy at this minister's farm in 1783 and consecrated by Scottish Anglicans a year later—an extraordinarily radical act in that age, because it required accepting two unorthodoxies: religious freedom (the Anglicans, after all, were the official church of the defeated enemy) and the separation of church and state. These liberties weren't enshrined in the Constitution, by the way, until three years later.

Besides ecclesiastical history and colonial crafts, the Glebe House also possesses the only remaining garden in the U.S. designed by **Gertrude Jekyll**, the horticulturist who perfected what's known as the English country garden.

Long before bishops and the Bill of Rights, the land around here was farmed and hunted by Algonquian tribes like the Pootatucks, who finally sold it in 1659. **The Institute for American Indian Studies** (IAIS) (daily to 5 PM, closed Mon.-Tues. Jan.-March; $4; 860/868-0518) off Route 199 in nearby Washington has extensive exhibits on exactly who these people were, what they did around here in the centuries prior to the "discovery" of their homeland, and how anthropology and archaeology have brought some of this information to light. The IAIS also reminds visitors that not all Indians are casino owners, and that traditional Native Americans continue to live and work here; crafts and technology demonstrations, performances, and workshops are offered. From Southbury take Route 67 north to Route 199, or from Woodbury take Route 47 to Route 199; the IAIS sign is about halfway between the Washington-Roxbury town line and the Route 47 junction.

> Signs of Litchfield County: even the local IGA in Woodbury is called Le Bonne's Epicure Market. But don't let the name fool you—it's still an IGA at heart.

Waterbury: Holy Land

About 10 miles due east of Woodbury, the large old manufacturing town of Waterbury is home to Holy Land, above I-84 on the hill—look for the giant illuminated cross. Plaster, carpet remnants, reflective mailbox-style adhesive lettering, plastic dolls, and Biblical scripture are some of the basic ingredients in this folk art extravaganza built over a couple postwar decades by a very, very dedicated Christian. The fact that vandals had their way with the place for at least another decade or two doesn't deter devout pilgrims, and the utter ruin should certainly appeal to anyone with a dark, well-honed sense of irony and metaphor.

As long as you're in town, be sure to visit **Noujaim Middle Eastern Bakery and Grocery**, a plain-looking convenience store at 1650 E. Main Street near Route 69 (I-84 exit 23), for excellent Lebanese sweets and savories; if at a loss as to what to choose, start with the *kadaif* squares (shredded phyllo with pistachio paste).

Litchfield County

From Woodbury to just past Plymouth, this route skirts the edge of Litchfield County, bucolic home to Manhattan-accented money, manners, and food (but mostly money), conspicuously framed by the white clapboard facades of some of New England's signature towns. Detour up Route 63, for example, and get an eyeful of the county seat of Litchfield, whose tidy green, stately old residences and photogenic churches epitomize the area's attractions.

Some exceptional meals are to be had in this place, but don't expect any early bird specials around here: local restaurateurs can and do charge exactly what they think the meals are worth, and given that their regulars include a fair number of big names from the mastheads of major Manhattan publishers to the credits of major Hollywood movies, you can bet self-esteem is not in danger of any downswing in *these* kitchens.

West Street Grill, on the Litchfield Green, is widely considered one of the best restaurants in the state. If triple digits won't make you flinch at the end of your dinner, then lucky you won't have to worry whether to skip the appetizers or skimp on the wine simply to afford that fine crackly creme brulee or those tropical fruit sorbets for dessert. If you aren't so well-heeled, drop by for lunch and sample haute bistro cuisine and service as impeccable as the town is pretty, and maybe, just maybe, walk out with change for that $20. If you still want to be able to afford one of those lobsters by the time you reach Cape Cod, West Street's owners have a more *rustique* wood-fired brick-oven kind of place called **Grappa**, in the Litchfield Commons shops just west of the town center on Route 202; no one will question your expense report if you enjoy yourself here instead.

> Litchfield must have something to recommend it: **Eugene Fodor,** well-traveled founder of the guidebook line that bears his name, calls it home.

Topsmead

Just east of Litchfield off of Route 118 lies Topsmead, the former summer estate of Edith Morton Chase, daughter of a Waterbury brass magnate. Miss Chase bequeathed her hilltop Tudor mansion to the people of Connecticut after her death, along with over 500 acres of wooded and landscaped grounds; now **Topsmead State Forest** is one of the crown jewels of the state park system, ideal for rambles down to the bird blind in the woods, picnics upon the expansive lawns, or—if you packed your horse—afternoon canters along tree-lined farm lanes. Its status as a hidden treasure is due in no small part to the absence of good signage, but head east on Route 118 from Litchfield, take a right on East Litchfield Road, another right at Buell Road, and you won't miss the stone-gate entrance. Topsmead is open year-round until sunset, with house tours noon-5 PM on alternate weekends, June-Oct. (860/567-5694). By the way, that white residence opposite the parking lot is private property unrelated to the state forest; please don't confuse its inhabitants with park rangers.

> Topsmead doesn't permit camping, but two nearby state parks do: **Black Rock** on US-6 east of Watertown, and **Burr Pond** just off Route 8 north of Torrington. For current fees and site reservations, call the State Parks Division at 860/566-2304.

Bristol

The influence of Litchfield County on US-6 may be seen in the dearth of billboards, the subdued signage, and the fact that national chain stores don't blanket the highway like ticker tape at a parade. But even Litchfield's refinement and taste can't restrain the welter of "Petro Pantries" and other caterers to the convenience of the populous Connecticut River valley. For the 15 miles between busy Route 8 in Thomaston and the interstate on-ramp in Farmington, this route becomes the playground of paving contractors and outdoor lighting salespeople, and unless you're out shopping for mufflers, videos, hardware, sub sandwiches, or discount clothing, driving it becomes an act of penance.

You'll find the nation's largest collection of locks, keys, and Victorian hardware behind the plain brick facade of the **Lock Museum of America** (Tues.-Sun. 1:30-4:30 PM, May-Oct.; $3; 860/589-6359) in Terryville, opposite the Congregational church on Main Street (US-6).

Press on toward Hartford if you have a budget rather than a blank check for accommodations; otherwise, consider a stop at the all-suites **Centennial Inn**, on US-6 and Route 177 in Farmington (800/852-2052; $89-115 with full kitchen); or the friendly **Chimney Crest Manor B&B** on Federal Hill in Bristol (860/582-4219; $100-115, some suites with kitchens).

Mark Twain

Of course, behind the highway clutter are several attractions worthy of the name—two alone in the heart of Bristol, for example. A few blocks off US-6, the **American Clock and Watch Museum**, 100 Maple Street (daily 10 AM-5 PM March-Nov.; $4; 860/583-6070), has exactly what you'd expect—room after room of timepieces, over 3,000 in all—but expectation can't begin to detract from the ingenuity and craftsmanship on display. And yes, most of the collection keeps the correct time, as you'll find out at the top of the hour; stand in the newer wing of the building to catch the best cacophony of striking, chiming, and ringing. Not very far away, **The New England Carousel Museum**, 95 Riverside Avenue (Route 72), will charm any kid alive, even if the kid in question is old enough to remember Joni Mitchell's refrain about painted ponies going up and down. The beautiful collection of colorful antique jumpers and prancers is augmented by artisans doing restoration work or carving new carousel animals at one end of the long gallery (Mon.-Sat. 10 AM-5 PM, Sunday noon-5 PM; $4; 860/585-5411).

Hartford

If you're able to temper your first impressions of a city with an appreciation for its salad days—if you don't let generic modern covers obliterate the handsomely lettered pages from the past—then perhaps you'll be able to cultivate an instant liking for the state's capital, Hartford. A century ago it could have been said that this town was a pillar of the nation's civilizing forces: books and guns. Epitomizing the shift to a service economy, *Tom Sawyer* and Colt .45s have been superseded by actuarial tables and death benefits: Hartford is an insurance company town now, which may explain why the downtown sensibly rolls up its sidewalks and turns out the lights after the office towers empty out at 5 PM.

While mergers, downsizing, recession, defense conversion, and other euphemisms for bad times at the home office have bruised modern Hartford repeatedly in recent years, local history offers several excellent distractions, most famously in the form of the **Mark Twain House** (daily 9:30 AM-4 PM; $9; 860/493-6411) at 351 Farmington Avenue, two right turns and under a mile from I-84 exit 46. Samuel Clemens (the pseudonymous Twain) built this elaborately picturesque Victorian mansion with Tiffany interiors and a shipload of fine furnishings in order to be close to his publisher. After 17 years of a lavish lifestyle—and the completion of some of his most famous novels—Clemens and his family gave up their Hartford life and moved to Europe to escape financial hardship. Besides guided tours, this restored National Historic Landmark hosts regular lectures, readings, "Conversations with American Humorists," and a summer "Twain at Twilight" concert series, which always includes some great gospel music—the author's favorite.

The distinction of being the oldest public art museum in the U.S. belongs to the **Wadsworth Atheneum**, an institution that hasn't rested on its 150-year-old laurels behind its prodigious stone facade at 600 Main Street in downtown Hartford (Tues.-Sun. 11 AM-5 PM; $7, free first Thursday of each month; 860/278-2670). Permanent collections ranging around the globe and across the ages are leavened with major traveling exhibitions, films, and gallery programs. The state's premiere showcase for contemporary artists is another of Hartford's crown jewels: **Real Art Ways** (Wed.-Sat. till 5 PM; galleries free; 860/232-1006), across from Pope Park in the former Underwood Typewriter factory at 56 Arbor Street. Its recently expanded galleries and auditoriums host an eclectic Sept.-May film, video, music, and performance series (various admission fees), along with such annual special events as the January Gender Bender Ball, October Halloween party, and summer jazz festival.

Trinity College, on Summit Street near the center of Hartford, offers free Wednesday-evening concerts in June and August. Call 860/297-2139 for more info.

The best source of arts and entertainment listings in the region is the free weekly *Hartford Advocate,* available in newspaper boxes around town.

If you ever wondered where **Katharine Hepburn** acquired her accent, look no further than the affluent, liberal, old Connecticut Yankee enclave of west Hartford.

Hartford Practicalities

Dining in downtown Hartford is a choice between your average convention hotel restaurant and the sort of watering hole that draws tie-loosening office workers more concerned with rinsing the taste of the office out of their mouths than with the complexity and freshness of the soup du jour. More interesting than either is a trip to the **Oasis Diner**, on Farmington Avenue walking distance east of the Twain House and open daily until midnight except Sunday, when it shuts earlier. It's an unusual double-wide stainless-sided 1949 Paramount diner, its excellent condition complemented by the retro-American menu, with new upscale touches like ricotta-stuffed French toast, veggie selections, Southwestern stylings, and local microbrews on draft. While the Oasis fits the streamlined stereotype of the neon-reflecting jukebox-and-soda haven, neighboring West Hartford's **Quaker Diner**, 319 Park Road (off I-84 exit 43, then right), sheathed in boxy red brick, captures dinerdom's pre-Raymond Loewy roots right down to the Moxie soda and other staples as familiar to its first customers as Herbert Hoover's campaign promises. Prices are anachronisms, too, even on items like oat bran pancakes and spinach omelets; open for breakfast and lunch only.

If you plan upon spending the night around Hartford, you'll find a handful of familiar names in both Hartford proper (Days Inn, Sheraton, Holiday Inn, Super 8, Susse Chalet) and on I-84 in adjacent East Hartford (Ramada, Holiday Inn), as well as a dozen miles north of the city near Bradley International Airport (Motel 6, Fairfield Inn, Holiday Inn).

Near the Mark Twain House, there's the handy **HI Hartford Hostel**, 131 Tremont Street (860/523-7255), with $15 dorm beds and a few private rooms.

For more information, contact the Hartford **visitors bureau** (860/728-6789), or the state-run **Connecticut Vacation Center** (800/CT-BOUND or 800/282-6863).

Willimantic

US-6 separates from the interstate in East Hartford, following surface streets through a very nondescript urban landscape of housing from the 1940s and convenience stores from the 1980s. If idling at red lights staring at cigarette and liquor billboards fits your vacation plans, go ahead and keep tracking US-6; otherwise, we recommend picking up US-6 in Bolton after following I-84 and I-384 east out of the capital.

From Bolton it's a rapid 16 miles through the tree-lined Hop River valley, along a stretch of highway notorious for its high accident rate. The 19th-century mill town of Willimantic (pop. 14,746) has been bypassed by a four-lane freeway, but if you have an abiding interest in the lives and labors of the people who worked in early American industry, stop by the small **Windham Textile and History Museum** (Thurs.-Sun. noon-5 PM; $3), 157 Union Street opposite the giant American Thread mill, which closed down in 1984 after doing business for 120 years.

East of Willimantic, US-6 quickly becomes more rural as it enters the state's most secluded quarter, picturesque Windham County.

Windham County: Pomfret and Vicinity

Although the major interstate I-395 cuts its way across eastern Connecticut from the coast, motorists rarely leave the passing lane long enough to take a peek behind the brow of the hills that border both the highway and the Quinebaug River, which are roughly parallel. If they did, they would find small valley towns raised around historic 19th-century milling operations and railroad depots, and rural hill towns with farmland cultivated with corn since before the arrival of the *Mayflower.*

Before crossing into Rhode Island, consider a detour through this historic landscape, either along Route 12, the mill town route, or Route 169, the old Norwich-Woodstock Turnpike. One of the most scenic highways in the northeast, if not the nation, Route 169 intersects US-6 in **Brooklyn,** hometown to Gen. Israel "Battle of Bunker Hill" Putnam, just five miles west of the I-395 freeway.

A century ago, wealthy New Yorkers spent their summers in the northeast corner of Connecticut, particularly in and around tiny Pomfret; now they own second homes here and send their kids to one of the two prep schools in town. Besides contributing to the community's graceful architectural treasury, the schools help support the year-round existence of the fine **Vanilla Bean Café** at the center of town, open till at least 8 PM most days, till 3 PM on Monday and Tuesday. If you aren't ashamed to park your rusting Pinto next to new Jaguars and BMWs owned by 17-year-olds, this casual counter-service eatery inside a restored old barn is worth a stop for excellent sandwiches, soups, and bakery goods, or for that eye-opening hit of espresso in the morning.

Predictably for such a lovely rural setting, there are plenty of **B&Bs** tucked into the Windham hills, as well as **camping** at the Wolf Den Campgrounds in **Mashamoquet Brook State Park** off Route 169/US-44.

For a complete up-to-date list of available lodgings here in what the tourism authorities call "The Quiet Corner," contact the **Northeast Connecticut Visitors District** (860/928-1228).

US-6 ACROSS RHODE ISLAND

In the half-hour it takes to cross Rhode Island, US-6 runs along the foot of the low hills that fill this coastal state's northern corners. It's a quiet, mostly rural region, and there's little to stop for until you reach the I-95 corridor at lively Providence, an entertaining, small city rich in history and college-town character.

Providence

Sitting at the north end of Naragansett Bay, Providence (pop. 160,728) was established in 1636 by Roger Williams, founder of the Baptist faith who had been exiled from neighboring Massachusetts for his religious views. A compact city climbing hills from the busy, partly industrial and partly recreational waterfront, Providence preserves its historic quarters intact, and boasts more colonial-era houses per square foot than any

The plush resort community of **Newport,** with its incredible collection of mansions, is 20 miles south of Providence. For information, contact the Newport visitor center, 23 America's Cup Avenue (401/849-8098 or 800/326-6030).

other American city. Along with the government bureaucracy of the nation's smallest state, Providence is also home to Rhode Island's two premier colleges, Ivy League Brown University and the Rhode Island School of Design.

From the west, US-6 drops you at the center of town, where a confusing ganglia of roads, canals, and freeways intertwine at the base of the landmark **state capitol**, 82 Smith Street (daily 8:30 AM-4:30 PM; free), which was completed by McKim, Mead and White in 1904 and features a marble dome capped by a 12-foot-tall gilded bronze statue of the "Independent Man." Two hundred yards east of the capitol, across the railroad tracks and the narrow Moshassuck River, the **Roger Williams National Memorial**, 282 N. Main Street (daily 8 AM-4:30 PM; free), recounts his life in a three-minute slide show. The memorial stands at the heart of historic Providence, and the surrounding streets, especially Benefit Street a block farther east, contain some of the finest intact colonial and early federal-era houses in the country. Walking tours are offered by the Providence Preservation Society (401/831-7440).

At the south end of the historic center, the small **Museum of Art of the Rhode Island School of Design**, 224 Benefit Street (Wed.-Sat. noon-5 PM, Sunday 2-5 PM; $2), has an excellent survey of painting and sculpture from around the world. The marvelous **Providence Athenaeum**, 251 Benefit Street (Mon.-Fri. 8:30 AM-5 PM; free) exhibits selected items from its extensive collection of early American prints, maps, and books. Yet more culture is concentrated on College Hill above, where the grounds of Brown University mix with a leafy neighborhood of stately 200-year-old homes.

Walter Scott created history and inspired a new industry in 1872, when he started selling hot food from a converted horse-drawn freight wagon in Providence, thereby giving birth to the diner. The diner legacy will be explored in a new museum, to be housed in the former Narragansett Electric Co. building at 360 Eddy Street. Opening day is slated for 2001; for current information, contact museum director and diner expert Daniel Zilka (401/461-7932).

Driving across Providence, keep an eye out for "Nibbles Woodaway," the giant blue termite sitting atop the New England Pest Control building, along I-95 at exit 19.

For the complete lowdown on who and what's playing in Providence's nightclubs and theaters, call the club report (401/455-8278) compiled by Brown University's alternative radio station, WBRU-FM.

In summer, complete your Pawtucket tour with a AAA-International League baseball game at McCoy Stadium, home of the Pawtucket Red Sox (401/724-7300).

There are good restaurants in and around the historic center, but some of the best places to eat are in the predominantly Italian Federal Hill neighborhood, a half-mile west of the waterfront on the other side of the I-95 freeway. Try the very good **Grotta Azurra**, 210 Atwells Avenue, or any of a dozen other places packed along these few short blocks. For less expensive food, look to the cafes along Thayer Street, at the east edge of the Brown University campus.

Places to stay in Providence include the usual interstate hotels and motels, plus a few pleasant B&Bs in and around the historic core, like the **Old Court**, 144 Benefit Street (401/751-2002). For more complete listings and other information, contact the Providence **visitor center**, 30 Exchange Terrace (401/274-1636 or 800/233-1636).

Pawtucket

North and east of Providence, under a mile via the I-95 freeway or Main Street (old US-1), the blue-collar city of Pawtucket (pop. 72,644) has played a vital role in American history. Though it looks tiny compared to the massive factories of 19th-century New England, the plank walls of **Slater's Mill** (Tues.-Sat. 10 AM-5 PM, Sunday 1-5 PM in summer, weekends only March-May; $4; 401/725-8638), sitting in a pleasant waterfront park at the center of town, saw the start of America's Industrial Revolution.

Despite the export bans placed by England after the Revolutionary War, Derbyshire-born Samuel Slater succeeded in introducing the latest mechanized cotton spinning technology, which he had gleaned from an apprenticeship in Richard Arkwright's mills. Slater also brought with him significant management skills, and in partnership with others transformed American manufacturing from handicrafts to mass production.

Numerous exhibits trace the historical context of Slater's efforts, but the real reason to visit is to watch and listen as the eight-ton water wheel creaks and groans around and around, powering the many belts and pulleys that still turn the machines, much as they did in Slater's day.

Pawtucket's other significant historic site is also well worth a visit, though it can be more difficult to find: the **Modern Diner**, 364 East Avenue just east of I-95. A classic streamlined Sterling diner, the Modern was the first diner to be registered as an official historic landmark, but it's still open every day from 7 AM (8 AM on Sunday) for breakfast and lunch, with dinner available Tues.-Fri. until 8 PM. Check it out.

Old Slater's Mill

US-6 ACROSS MASSACHUSETTS

You won't find a pretty red carpet rolled out for US-6 in southeastern Massachusetts, where some of the Bay State's most economically depressed cities have paved over the coastal lowlands. The ivy-covered brick of Harvard Yard and the long weathered tobacco barns of the Pioneer Valley might as well belong to another state —or so it would seem as this route rolls by the gunmetal gray of retired naval vessels, acres of outlet malls, and hillsides carpeted with Victorian-era triple-decked, triple-family houses built for workers drawn to the great textile mills of the Industrial Revolution.

While there are comely seaside towns just to the south (along what the tourist brochures call the "Heritage Farm Coast"), the 30 miles of US-6 east of the Connecticut border are strictly for those with a romantic eye for commercial tack, or for anthropologists of urban decline; others are advised to stay on I-195 and make haste. Although US-6 is worth picking up again in Captain Ahab's home port of New Bedford, postcard views don't return in spades until after the Cape Cod Canal. Even here, you'll miss them if you stay on double-barreled US-6, so we recommend taking a spin along slow-but-scenic US-6A to catch the Cape's best face. The route finally comes to its conclusion in the lee of Cape Cod National Seashore's shifting dunes, on the narrow, cottage-lined streets of outermost Provincetown.

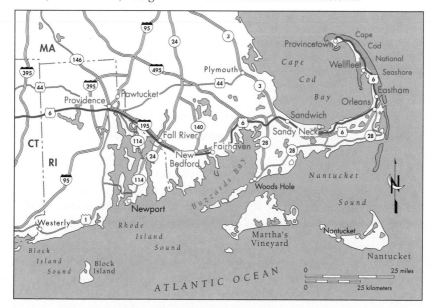

Fall River

Cotton mills put this town on the map, and their demise nearly wiped it off again. One of the nation's leading industrial cities at the turn of the century, Fall River (pop. 92,703) swiftly became one of the leading casualties of the Depression, propelled into a decade of bankruptcy by the triple whammy of mill flight to cheaper Southern labor, a devastating downtown fire, and the Wall Street Crash of 1929. Although receivership ended with WW II, the giant brick mills have only recently awakened from their decades of boarded-up slumber, reanimated by the factory stores that contribute to Fall River's new stature as southern New England's discount retailing center.

If 30% off assorted clothing and housewares doesn't lure you down the exit ramps, perhaps a fascination with warships will. A small armada awaits your exploration in **Battleship Cove** (daily 9 AM-sunset; $9), plainly visible from the interstate bridge over the broad, brackish Taunton River: the battleship *Massachusetts,* destroyer *Joseph P. Kennedy, Jr.,* submarine *Lionfish,* and a pair of P.T. boats from WW II.

Along the waterfront, adjacent to the anchored ships, the galleries of **Fall River Heritage State Park** (daily 10 AM-6 PM in summer, till 4 PM otherwise; free) tell the city's story with excellent archival photos and period artifacts, one of nine such innovative parks dedicated to the state's industrial, labor, and immigration history.

While numerous eateries in this city subscribe to the four major food groups—salt, grease, sugar, and carbonation—decent dining does exist if you're willing to hunt around for it. Try hearty Eastern European stick-to-your-ribs soups and meats at the **Ukrainian Home** on Globe Street off South Main Street (Route 138), about eight miles south of I-195. The latest immigration trends are reflected in the tasty, inexpensive Southeast Asian cuisine found at the **New Phnom Penh Restaurant** in the Angor Plaza (closed Monday; 508/324-4909) on Quequechan Street, next to the huge Wampanoag Mill factory outlet mall.

This being Massachusetts, there's also a fine 1950s diner, **Al Mac's**, at the base of President Hill on US-6 at the junction with the Route 79/138 elevated highway. In great shape inside and out, this place not only serves coffee in pint-sized mugs, it stays open late: Sun.-Tues. till midnight (till 10 PM in winter), Wed.-Thurs. till 3 AM, and Fri.-Sat. till 4 AM (508/679-5851).

LIZZIE BORDEN

"Lizzie Borden took an ax/And gave her mother 40 whacks . . ." If you've heard this couplet before, you're already acquainted with Fall River's most notorious citizen, a wealthy financier's daughter (and Sunday school teacher) accused of double murder in 1892. Lest children's rhymes prejudice your opinion of Ms. Borden, know that a jury of her peers returned a verdict of *not guilty.*

The **Fall River Historical Society** (Tues.-Fri. 9 AM-4:30 PM, weekends in summer only; $3.50) has a complete exhibit on the subject—including trial evidence and the alleged weapon—in its mansion headquarters at 451 Rock Street in the Highlands historic district.

A small rash of chain names among local accommodations include a Howard Johnson, a Hampton Inn, a Holiday Inn, a Super 8, an Econo Lodge, and a Comfort Inn.

New Bedford

Predominantly Portuguese New Bedford is remembered as a capital of the whaling industry back in the days when spermaceti candles and whale oil lamps were necessities, not antiques. The city's harbor at the mile-wide mouth of the Acushnet River was home port for the East Coast's largest commercial fishing fleet until nearly two decades of flagrant overfishing brought the industry to collapse, but the immutable charm of the downtown historic district, with its cobblestone streets and brick façades, remains virtually unaltered since Herman Melville shipped out of here in 1847 aboard a whaler bound for the Pacific. For a good orientation to the area, drop by the New Bedford National Historic Park **visitor center**, at the corner of William Street and N. 2nd Street (508/996-4469).

That tall ship sometimes anchored in summer near the mothball navy is the **HMS *Bounty*** (Fri.-Sun. 10 AM-6 PM, May-Oct.; $4; 508/673-3886)—or, rather, the movie version, built from the original naval blueprint for MGM's 1962 production starring Marlon Brando and Trevor Howard. A fully functioning sailing vessel used for education and training, the replica makes frequent appearances at harbor and maritime festivals around New England and Canada, so call ahead for the port schedule if you don't want to miss her.

Before or after a stroll around town, head to the top of Johnny Cake Hill and visit the excellent **Whaling Museum** (daily 9 AM-5 PM; $4.50). Scrimshaw (carved whale ivory), tools of the whaling trade, historic photos, special maritime exhibits, and an 89-foot ship model are a few of the artifacts found in the not-to-be-missed museum collection maintained by the Old Dartmouth Historical Society. Across the street from the museum, the gorgeous little **Seamen's Bethel**, built in 1832 and featuring a pulpit shaped like a ship's bow, was featured in a chapter of Herman Melville's classic *Moby Dick*.

New Bedford Practicalities

If the sounds of the seagulls' *scree*-ing around downtown whets your appetite for seafood, then drive down to **Davy's Locker**, way out on E. Rodney French Street at Billy Woods Wharf, where the ferry for Martha's Vineyard departs. There outside the rocky sea wall you can watch the gulls wheel over the harbor as you dig into some of the freshest seafood in town. Given that you're in a city that's 60% Portuguese, you might consider acquainting yourself with this local cuisine, although if you're a light eater, bring along a pair of friends to finish your meal. For maximum quality at a minimal (cash only) price, **Antonio's**, on Coggeshalle and N. Front Streets, slightly northeast of the I-195/Route 18 interchange (exit 15), is a good choice, as is **Vasco da Gama**, on the opposite end of town on Dartmouth at Washington, a block south of Metro Pizza (look for the 7UP sign over a plain brick-fronted, bar-like place). Kale soup, rabbit or shellfish swimming in spicy tomato-based sauces, and of course *bacalhau* (salt cod) are typical menu items, in portions designed to thoroughly satisfy a boat crew's most mutinous rumblings.

Diner fans will appreciate New Bedford's offerings, too. The easiest diner to find is **Angelo's Orchid Diner**, a 1951 O'Mahony stainless-steel-sided model right on

New Bedford isn't immune to the espresso craze, as proven by **Java Bean** on Water Street a block south of the Whaling Museum. Good biscotti, too.

For a good example of the kind of downhome folk music performance found in church and grange halls throughout New England, check out the **Tryworks Coffeehouse** (Saturday 8 PM, mid-Sept. to early May) in the First Unitarian Church on 8th and Union Streets.

New Bedford's Acushnet Avenue has a significant place in the world of late 19th-century American art: **Albert Pinkham Ryder,** visionary "painter of dreams," was born here, across from the childhood home of **Albert Bierstadt,** Romantic painter of the American West.

The first Japanese resident of the U.S., **Manjiro Nakahama,** lived in Fairhaven in the 1840s after returning with the whalers who rescued him from shipwreck in the Pacific. Displays about "John" Manjiro and the town's sister city of Tosashimizu, Japan, are found in the Millicent Library.

Perhaps H.H. Rogers's financial support for his hometown was compensation for the fact that his company's profits came at the expense of New Bedford's and Fairhaven's: the 1859 discovery of eastern Pennsylvania's oil fields dropped the bottom out of the market for whale oil and "coal oil" (coal-derived kerosene, a Fairhaven product).

US-6 at Rockdale; its menu is solid short-order cookery enlivened by, you guessed it, a Portuguese influence. For a traditional Greek hand over the grill, check out the pristine **Shawmut Diner**, another 1950s O'Mahony on Shawmut Avenue at Hathaway, near Route 140 (daily 5 AM-7 PM); the neon Indian alone makes it worth a visit.

Choices of accommodations are limited. The warmest welcome and greatest convenience to downtown attractions and restaurants is **1875 House B&B**, on 7th Street in the historic district (cash only; 508/997-6433), where rooms with private baths go for $55-65. There's also a **Days Inn** on Hathaway Road by the airport, at I-195 exit 13B.

Fairhaven

There was a time when families could signal their improving lot by moving out of New Bedford's hurly-burly mills and wharves and across the harbor to aptly named Fairhaven (stress the second syllable), which straddles US-6 within spyglass view of Johnny Cake Hill. Turn south on Main Street, at the intersection dominated by the palatial Italianate high school, and you'll discover a surprising amount of monumental gothic-spired civic architecture, most of it generously donated at the start of this century by Henry Huttleston Rogers, a native son and robber baron who made a mint as a director of John D. Rockefeller's Standard Oil Company. Stop by the marvelous Renaissance-style library on Center Street—described as "a heaven of light and grace and harmonious color and sumptuous comfort" by Rogers's friend Mark Twain—for a **walking tour** brochure.

Besides Portuguese and Cape Verdeans, the local maritime trades have attracted a fair number of Norwegians—the Isaksen family, for example, whose waterfront restaurant down on Main Street, **Margaret's,** is one of the hands-down best places for seafood in the area. If deep-sea scallops are on the menu—probably fresh off the family's own boats—don't pass them by; as anyone around here will tell you, the tiny bay scallops from Mexico and China can't compare to the more flavorful and meaty Atlantic deep-sea variety.

Approaching Cape Cod: Buzzards Bay

Skirting the glacially formed coastline of Buzzards Bay—whose major shipping lane is especially visible at night, as vessels bound to and from the Cape Cod Canal blink like fireflies offshore—US-6 passes through residential **Mattapoisett** and **Marion,** communities whose modest appearances belie both property values and average incomes, just as the sandy soil and brittle-looking trees belie the original swampy conditions that made this coast so ecologically rich for its native inhabitants,

Cape Cod lodgings boarded up during the off-season

the Wampanoag Indians. A half-dozen small rivers still drain these coastal low-lands, but despite the occasional stands of tall reeds, it goes almost without saying that here, as in far too many places along the Atlantic seaboard, wetlands have been drastically reduced. Modern developers aren't exclusively to blame, however: settlers have been accelerating nature's designs ever since 17th- and 18th-century colonists stripped the land of its rot-resistant Atlantic white cedars—old-growth giants found here near the northern extent of their range—and thus contributed to the silting-up of fertile fish-feeding marshes and ponds.

This stretch of US-6 is still fertile territory for the fruits of the sea, especially if it's fried, broiled, or served up in creamy chowder. The **Mattapoisett Chowder House** and **Oxford Creamery** are two particularly good examples, the best you'll find between here and the Outer Cape. The Creamery—which, as the name implies, also specializes in ice cream—is the more low-key of the two, downright fast-food-like; it also is only open in summer, daily until 10 PM. If you prefer ham and brown gravy or spaghetti and meatballs to anything with shells or fins, the **Mattapoisett Diner** on US-6 is your dream come true.

US-6 becomes a sprawl mart as it joins Route 25 and Route 28 in **Wareham**, fast food and tire dealers greasing the approach to the WPA-era Sagamore Bridge over the Cape Cod Canal. (US-6 eastbound crosses via the nearly identical Bourne Bridge, which feeds into I-195/495 if you aren't careful. Westbound travelers: stay awake in this stretch, or you could find yourself halfway to Boston.)

If you're looking for a place to park the ol' RV for the night before hitting the Cape, you might choose **Scusset Beach State Reservation** (508/888-0859) in Sagamore, on Cape Cod Bay; $8 gets you a full hookup near the beach, across the canal from the blinking hulk of a gas-fired electric generating station. More tent-friendly sites are found in Shawme-Crowell State Forest ($6; 508/888-0351), just over the bridge on Route 130 in Sandwich.

A **clam-eater's key:** Steamers are usually soft-shell (longneck) clams, preferably caught on a muddy rather than sandy bottom (unless you like grit in your teeth), steamed and served with their salty "liquor" and drawn butter for dipping. Fuller-flavored hard-shell quahogs (pronounced KO-hogs or K'WOGS) are a chef's favorite chowder clam, although some folks will bake and stuff them, too. Cherrystones and littlenecks are small quahogs served raw on the half shell or sometimes steamed. Bon appetit!

"Mattapoisett" means "place of rest" in Algonquian—a name originally applied to a small neck of land about 25 miles west on Mount Hope Bay, in what's now the town of Swansea.

Although not as attractive to mansion-building plutocrats as nearby Newport, 19th-century **Marion** was still among New England's most prominent seaside resorts, attracting such visitors as Pres. Grover Cleveland and novelist Henry James.

Bayside Cape Cod: Sandwich

Although it rides the ridge of the terminal glacial moraine that is body and backbone to the entire Cape, the forest-clad Mid-Cape Highway (US-6) affords few good vistas. Traffic willing, you'll sail clear ahead to the Outer Cape in about 30 minutes, surrounded by more green than blue. One preferred route is parallel US-6A: never more than a mile or two away, swimming steadily through towns otherwise invisible behind that protective march of pitch pine, this slower road is a good introduction to that part of the Cape that does its utmost to stay quaint without being too cute. Generally, it succeeds.

Take Sandwich, for example: its center, on Route 130 just south of US-6A, is composed of a small irregular green bordered by a tall white Christopher Wren-inspired church, a stately carriage-stop inn, and the Historical Society's **Sandwich Glass Museum** (daily 9:30 AM-4:30 PM April-Oct., Wed.-Sun. only Nov.-

---

A CAPE COD PRIMER

To avoid frustration visiting Cape Cod, it's best to understand its basic directions and seasons. The compass isn't your friend here, as you will discover when faced with highway signs stubbornly directing you *south* to Province-town, when south would sooner bring you to Venezuela than to the Cape's northernmost town. Instead, the principal directions are up and down: *up-Cape* means westward, toward the rest of North America, while *down-Cape* is eastward, toward the Outer Cape, Provincetown, and the briny deep. Further distinctions are made between the three sides of the Cape's bended arm: *bay-side* is the entire convexity facing Cape Cod Bay; the *south shore* faces Nantucket Sound, between Buzzard's Bay and the Cape's "elbow" at Chatham; and the *backside* braves the open Atlantic from Chatham's elbow to Provincetown's "fist."

As it so happens, development of the Cape has also segregated itself fairly neatly between bayside US-6A, with its demure white-clapboard, gray-shingled neo-colonial villages, and the south shore's Route 28, a helter-skelter shock corridor of shopping plazas, motel courts, saltwater taffy shoppes, and eat-in-the-rough shacks that seem to consume more plastic dinnerware and frying oil than fresh fish.

But the most important aspect to Cape travel is timing: Between Memorial Day weekend in late May and Labor Day weekend in early September, several million tourists and "summer people" (seasonal residents) converge on this sandy spit, which is why traffic jams get measured in miles on good days, hours on bad. On the worst weekends—4th of July, for example—you could drive to Montreal in less time than it would take to cross the canal, drive 16 miles to Wood's Hole, find parking, and catch the next available ferry to Martha's Vineyard! Needless to say, pack your car as if you might have to live in it for a day or two.

March; $3.50). Although the town's various glassworks could and did produce consummate artistic pieces, the bulk of their output was inexpensive mass-market stuff—such as 10-cent oil lamp chimneys—for household, rather than decorative, use. In other words, a collector's interest helps with the appreciation of the Glass Museum's rooms of lacy glass saucers, pressed plates, and molded jars, the vast majority of which are unmarked products of the Boston and Sandwich Glass Co., earliest and most famous of the region's 19th-century glass factories. Nearby on Pine

To learn more than you ever thought possible about thermometers, pay a visit to the world's largest thermometer collection proudly on display in the basement of Dick "Thermometer Man" Porter's home in Onset; call 508/295-5504 for directions.

and Grove Streets (follow signs from Route 130) is an even more diverse collection of Americana, the **Heritage Plantation of Sandwich** (daily 10 AM-5 PM mid-May to mid-October; $8), where nearly 80 landscaped acres surround collections of Currier & Ives prints, military miniatures, antique autos, cigar store figures, American primitive portraiture—more unflattering likenesses of children have never been conceived —and even a working 1912 carousel.

If you *are* island-bound, know that a major turnover of cottage rentals occurs every fortnight, which is why the ferry landings are twice as hectic, with tickets and parking twice as scarce, on alternate Fridays. Factories in southern New England shut down for two weeks in July, flooding the Cape's south shore with workers and their families; August brings flocks of psychiatrists, lawyers, doctors, and other professionals to bayside towns, as well as to Chatham, at the Outer Cape's southern extremity. Meanwhile, campgrounds are often surprisingly full even midweek and in bad weather, in part because quadrupling and quintupling of rents during high season forces some of the Cape's more marginal residents to take summer sabbaticals in tents.

While high season may have its disadvantages, it's also when everybody is open for business, seven days a week, 16 hours a day. Out of season, businesses close up like flowers after a frost, not necessarily because the visitors have disappeared—fall and spring are quite popular with a discerning few hundred thousand people—but because the employees have. In high season, the Cape is in fact wholly operated by teenagers, students, and Irish on temporary work visas; after schools start in September, only the Irish remain as a skeleton crew —until their classes begin in October. (This employment phenomenon also explains why some places may be shuttered even as high season kicks in: they haven't lined up any help yet.) Sufficient workers or not, businesses that do stay open into the off season don't significantly lower prices until the dead of winter.

A final note: It is possible to escape the crowds, even in the height of summer. Parks and sanctuaries are notably free of ringing cash registers and sizzling deep-fryers, and even popular beaches can yield a mote of solitude if you keep in mind that about 90% of the Cape's visitors don't walk more than 20 minutes from their car.

Those low-lying square plots of land filled with short, dark-leaved shrubs and divided by narrow irrigation channels are some of Plymouth County's famous cranberry bogs. The cheeky red fruit is best seen during the October harvest, when it carpets the flooded fields.

If you're willing to pay a small price ($10-15) for the aid of a B&B reservation service, put yourself in the competent hands of either House Guests Cape Cod and the Islands (800/666-HOST or 800/666-4678) or Orleans Bed and Breakfast Associates (800/541-6226).

Massachusetts is one of two states that recognizes private property ownership down to the low tide line, which is why you should respect the No Trespassing signs you may encounter on some beaches. Fortunately, plenty are amended with "Walkers Welcome."

Sandy Neck

Continuing east on US-6A from Sandwich, keep an eye out for Sandy Neck Road (next to the Sandy Neck Motel), the turnoff to Sandy Neck and its namesake barrier beach ($10 summer parking fee). Here, six miles of windswept dunes provide a picturesque backdrop for contemplating the changing light upon the relatively calm waters of Cape Cod Bay. Depending on season and time of day, you may catch sight of passing white-tailed deer or such endangered shorebirds as the least tern and piping plover.

Between Sandy Neck and our reunion with US-6 in **Orleans**, there are some 18 beaches, most of which are found simply by turning north on whatever small residential or unimproved roads intersect the route. If you don't live here, expect to fork over a parking fee of at least $7 or $8 in season. Temporary residents and guests may obtain weekly or monthly permits; ask your hosts or the beach attendant to explain how. One way to skirt the parking fees for beach use is to spend the night locally and *walk* to the water.

Bayside Practicalities

Restaurants and motels tend to gravitate toward Cape Cod's south shore, and the few bayside establishments seem determined to make up in total billings what is lacking in total volume. If, on the other hand, you subscribe to the belief that a good meal is worth at least as much as a night's pampering at a little seaside inn, than treat yourself to sophisticated Italian cuisine at **Abbicci**, on US-6A in Dennis (reservations advised, 508/362-3501). Don't be fooled by the downhome yellow-clapboard exterior; the interior is as contemporary and artfully designed as the food.

You can always balance your budget the next day with a visit to **Jack's Out Back**, behind 161 Main (US-6A) in Yarmouth Port. The undisputed king of the Cape's white-bread cookery, Jack whips up basic breakfasts and lunches at rock-bottom prices—made possible in part by requiring that customers do everything but stand over the grill. Copious hand-lettered, phonetically spelled construction-paper signs combine menu items, warnings about selling unattended children into slavery, and instructions for writing up your own ticket and busing your own dirty dishes; follow these last to the letter or irascible ol' Jack will amuse his audience of regulars at your expense.

Between these two extremes, geographically and economically, is **Mattakeese Wharf** on Barnstable Harbor (turn at the traffic light east of Barnstable Village), a casual you-want-french-fries-with-that kind of place (open May-Oct. only) elevated from the pack by its quality seafood and great location. Enjoying bouillabaisse on the deck while looking out over the marina in that golden light of a late summer evening is the sort of experience liable to have you planning ahead to your next Cape vacation.

One of many historic B&Bs along this stretch of the Cape is the **Isaiah Hall B&B Inn**, 152 Whig Street in Dennis (508/385-9928 or 800/736-0160), within walking distance of the beach and costing less than a meal at Abbicci's; doubles go from $60 a night.

For a full list of accommodation options, stop by a Cape Cod Chamber of Commerce **information booth**—either at the Sagamore rotary just before crossing the canal, or mid-Cape at the junction of Route 132 and US-6—to pick up an extensive directory to both south shore and bayside accommodations. Or call the Massachusetts Office of Travel and Tourism's **info line** (617 /727-3201) and request a free copy of the latest *Massachusetts Getaway Guide*.

Orleans and Eastham

The classic Cape Cod dwelling, a porchless, rectangular, peak-roofed shed not unlike an oversized shingle or clapboard Monopoly piece, should be a familiar feature of the landscape by the time you arrive at the Outer Cape towns of Brewster, Orleans, and Eastham, given the number of such houses along this part of route. US-6, 6A, and the south shore Route 28 all come together here, just before the Cape narrows to its slender forearm.

Here, too, the **Cape Cod Rail Trail** (see below) mingles with this route, which is why in summer the streets crawl with cyclists in search of refreshment. If that's your goal, too, look no further than **The Brown Bag Restaurant and Bakery** (daily till 3 PM), on the corner of West Road and Old Colony Way, for decent omelets, soups, sandwiches, and quiche. For something to fill the cup-holder on your dash, stop in at the **Orleans Whole Food Store** on Main Street a block south of the Rail Trail and 6A. For a taste of some of the best fried clams on the Cape, detour south about 10 miles to the **Kream 'n' Kone** (March-Nov.), opposite the A&P supermarket on Route 28 between Chatham and Harwich.

Another of Cape Cod's many exquisite B&Bs is the **Whalewalk Inn**, 220 Bridge Road in Eastham (508/225-0617), where free bicycle rentals and delicious breakfasts make for an idyllic respite from the "real" world. Budget travelers will be pleased to find the well-situated **HI Mid-Cape Hostel** right next door (mid-May to mid-September; $17, members $14; 508/255-2785).

Cape Cod National Seashore

The remaining two dozen miles to Provincetown parallel Cape Cod National Seashore, a 40-mile-long National Park Service property encompassing the whole of the outermost coast: squat lighthouses, shrub-covered dunes, freshwater ponds, tidal flats, cedar swamps, and spectacular, often austere beaches whose boundaries are in constant flux. Pick up information detailing the various nature trails and interpretive programs at either the **Salt Pond Visitor Center** (daily 9 AM-4:30 PM,

Take in excellent Cape Cod views from atop **Scargo Tower** in **Dennis,** on Scargo Hill Road; turn toward South Dennis at the Mobil station, then follow signs.

Not all the Cape's glass furnaces have been extinguished: the glass blowers of the **Pairpoint Crystal Company,** on US-6A in Sagamore (behind the Christmas Tree Shop), can be observed at work on weekdays.

Dennis is the setting for the nation's oldest professional summer stock theater, the **Cape Playhouse** (box office 508/385-3911) on 6A just east of the Mobil station. If you prefer film over stage, the **Cape Cinema,** on the grounds behind the Playhouse, specializes in movies you won't find at the mall. If you arrive late, stick around until the lights go up after the credits or you'll miss one of the Cape's best public artworks, the mural of Prometheus on the cinema's ceiling.

CYCLING ON CAPE COD

After broiling yourself on the beach in a light marinade of SPF 45, enjoy one of the best Cape escapes astride a bike. The **Cape Cod Rail Trail**, a 25-mile, fully paved pedestrian and bicycle path between Dennis and South Wellfleet, is the foremost attraction for casual cyclists.

If you're driving to the trail, you'll find parking at either end or in Nickerson State Park, adjacent to where the trail crosses under US-6A in Brewster. Convenient bike rentals are available from **Rail Trail Bike Shop** on Underpass Road in Brewster; **Idle Times** on US-6A beside the trail at the main entrance to Nickerson State Park; **Orleans Cycle** in Orleans at the junction of the trail and Main Street, one block north of US-6A; and **Black Duck Bike Shop** in South Wellfleet, next to the tourist info booth. Rentals are also available in Provincetown and all over the Cape.

Three other paved bike paths are found in Cape Cod National Seashore, ranging from a one and a half-mile trail starting from the Salt Pond Visitor Center to the seven mile-plus, headwind-bucking meander through the dunes and kettlehole ponds behind Provincetown.

---

weekends only Jan.-Feb.; 508/255-3421), prominently signposted beside US-6 in **Eastham**, or the **Province Lands Visitor Center** on Race Point Road in Provincetown (see below).

Miles and miles of gorgeous beaches fill the seashore's Atlantic coast, but one of the park's highlights is a visit to **Sunset Hill** in Wellfleet, on Chequesset Neck Road heading toward Duck Harbor Beach. The late-afternoon views over Cape Cod Bay will reward the sedentary, while walkers will find a fine scenic escape along the Great Island Trail that begins from the hill's parking lot. Mind the tide tables if you do take a hike out to Jeremy Point, or you'll be wading on your return.

Campers will want to check out **Nickerson State Park** on US-6A at the Brewster-Orleans line, one of the largest and most popular campgrounds in the state (year-round for RVs only, otherwise April 15 to Oct. 15; $6; reservations taken at 508/896-3491).

Wellfleet

The town of Wellfleet (pop. 2,493) is one of the Cape's most picturesque communities, favored for some reason by writers, psychiatrists, and oysters. Although home to a cluster of fine art galleries, crafts and clothing shops, and pricey restaurants, the place succeeds handsomely in finding a niche between self-conscious quaintness and residential seclusion. It's also blessed by two additional rarities: a public beach with year-round free parking (**Mayo Beach**, just west of the town pier) and a New American fusion-cuisine restaurant worth every dollar (**Painter's**, on Main Street beside the Duck Creeke Inn; dinner and Sunday brunch only; reservations 508/349-3003).

Alas, there are drawbacks: most of the town beaches are strictly for residents or local guests between late June and early September. Those that aren't off-limits charge $10. Painter's restaurant is only seasonal—winter food mavens seeking curried lamb with raita and arugula or snapping fresh tuna with gin-soaked juniper berries and lime tomato chutney will have to go elsewhere. If it is summer and you didn't intend to hang around till 5 PM to catch a bite to eat, drop in on the local sandwich-eaters at **Uncle Frank's** (a.k.a. Scallywag's), a friendly, inexpensive hangout next to Mayo Beach, in the same building as the Wellfleet Harbor Actors Theatre (W.H.A.T. box office, 508/349-6835).

While the Outer Cape has but one chain motel outside of Provincetown (a Sheraton on US-6 in Eastham), you'll still find plenty of characterful locally owned **accommodations**, from classic little prewar dune shacks sitting cheek-to-cheek along the beach, to B&Bs nestled among the pines. Save dinner money by staying at the **HI Truro Hostel**, beautifully situated between cranberry bogs and ocean beach in a former Coast Guard station on N. Pamet Road in nearby Truro (late June to early Sept. only; $17, members $14; 508/349-3889). It fills almost daily, so reservations are advised.

The Wellfleet Chamber of Commerce (508/349-2510) has an exceptionally comprehensive directory of lodgings, available by mail or from its **information booth** on US-6.

Provincetown

The end of your journey was almost the end of the line for another band of travelers, babes in the woods who came expecting warm weather—in November 1620. Had the *Mayflower* Pilgrims and their fortune-seeking shipmates been able to find sufficient fresh water, the cornerstone of American myth and clock-start of Anglo-American civilization might have been enshrined here in Provincetown rather than across the bay at Plymouth Rock. But no: The first landfall was eclipsed by the first Thanksgiving, and P-town (as natives and in-the-know locals call it) has had to butter its bread with something other than the national creation myth.

Where once the sea sustained P-town—as trading spot, whaling village, and fishing port—now the summer fun does. In 1901 Charles Hawthorne opened up an art school, christening the town with the art colony status that persists to this day. Bohemians followed, including the likes of John Reed, Eugene O'Neill, Susan Glaspell, and George Cram Cook, whose Provincetown Players made theater history. And on the heels of Greenwich Village's fashionable flock came the car-borne tourists, who have proven themselves as faithful as Capistrano swallows.

The summer trade prompts P'town to do its beach-boardwalk strut, as boatloads of day-trippers from Boston mob aptly named Commercial Street each afternoon, tanned couples mingle among the restaurants and outdoor cafes each evening, and fun-seeking Danceteria types fill up the bars and clubs each night. Out of season, however, the beach shuttle goes back to being a school bus, the wait for a table is negligible, and there's actually an off-chance that you'll find a place to park. Meanwhile, the sunsets are still worth a visit to **Herring Cove Beach**, even if they come at an earlier hour and require extra layers of clothing.

To at least vaguely disguise your off-Cape origins, you should know that Chatham is pronounced "CHAT-em," but Eastham is "EAST-HAM."

If you've never watched a movie in the comfort of your own car, it's time you caught up with lost pleasures at the **Wellfleet Drive-In** on US-6, a genuine throwback to the era of car-hops on roller skates and Mustang convertibles.

While portions of several Outer Cape beaches are traditional gathering spots for "naturists"—Herring Cove in P-town is probably the most well-known, drawing a largely gay, lesbian, and bisexual crowd—the national seashore beaches have a specific prohibition against nudity. If you see a park ranger, you should cover up to avoid a potential ticket.

The fury of the Atlantic constantly reworks Cape topography, borrowing up to 10 feet from the Outer Cape's cliffs each year for loan to Provincetown and Monomoy Island beaches, and stealing over 30 acres annually through erosion and rising sea levels.

Pilgrim Monument

That 252-foot tower jutting up over the town is the **Pilgrim Monument and Museum** (9 AM-5 PM, mid-March to Nov.; $5), with the best panorama on the Cape: in clear weather the entire peninsula can be seen, as well as the Massachusetts coast at Plymouth.

Sixteenth-century Europeans who regularly crossed the Atlantic to fish for cod along these shores saw a peninsula covered in beech and white oak, juniper and holly—mature forests consumed by the English colonial appetite for construction, firewood, turpentine, potash, and grazing land. Within a century after the *Mayflower* landing, tree and topsoil loss on the outer Cape was so severe, homes had to be built on stilts to avoid being buried by blowing sand. Today's beech forests around Provincetown are the product of a major campaign begun in 1893 to save the town from a sandy grave.

Whalewatching cruises aren't confined to the high-season crush, since the finback, minke, humpback, and right whales that feed offshore arrive in April and stay through October. Dolphin Fleet (800/826-9300), Provincetown Whale Watch (800/992-9333), and Portuguese Princess (800/442-3188) all offer daily trips out to the whales' feeding grounds in the Stellwagen Bank National Marine Sanctuary just offshore.

Provincetown Practicalities

After a day spent cycling amid dunes speckled with wild rose and beach plum, or admiring the handiwork of windowbox gardeners in P-town's cottage-lined lanes, you'll probably have an appetite for more than sugar-coated *trutas* (sweet potato fritters) from the **Portuguese Bakery** at 299 Commercial Street. If a harborside table is required, consider the moderately priced **Lobster Pot** at 321 Commercial just east of MacMillan Wharf (enter through the kitchen) for heaping portions of time-tested local favorites such as cioppino or *sopa do mar,* veggie pastas, and of course lobster every which way you want it. Open year-round, too—an exception in these parts. **Pucci's**, 539 Commercial Street (closed Thursday), commands such a first-row harborside seat that at high tide you're as good as in a boat. You don't need to compete for a table at sunset to savor the changing light on the harbor—it can also be enjoyed at the bar, or over lunch and breakfast.

For food, check out the multicultural menu—one of the few to please vegetarians—at **Napi's**, tucked away on Freeman Street at Standish; south-of-the-border spices heat up the top-notch Mexican-New American menu at **Lorraine's**, 229R Commercial Street (down the alley near the Pennsylvania Co. store), where you'll find some of P-town's best meals for the money. A burrito from **Big Daddy's** in the Olde Aquarium Mall in the 200 block of Commercial Street will also leave your travel allowance intact. **Spiritus**, across the street at 190 Commercial, is another good low-cost savior, dishing up pizza, foccacia sandwiches, ice cream, and latte to a steady clientele of tattooed young smokers and slackers.

If you're more in the mood for a linen and crystal celebration, look no further than the **Martin House**, 157 Commercial Street (508/487-1327). Fine fireside dining in cozy 18th-century parlors won't come cheap, but if you have reason to splurge, this is the place to do it.

Planning to spend the night? If it's a summer weekend, make reservations or you may spend your time searching for a bed rather than basking on the beach. Friendly, efficient, and free, the **Provincetown Reservations System** (800/648-0364) can help find accommodations to match your budget and taste, or you can make the calls yourself with the aid of the chamber of commerce directory, available from its **information booth** (508/487-3424) at Lopes Square on MacMillan Wharf. The list of apartments, cottages, guest houses, inns, motels, and B&Bs is extensive enough to invite speculation as to whether there is any house in all of town unavailable to visitors.

If you don't mind the occasional bout of late-night laughter from Commercial Street carousers, the **Somerset House**, 378 Commercial Street (508/487-0383), has comfortable rooms and a very central location in a bracketed old Cape Cod manse. Rounding out the lodging options are the national chains (two Best Westerns and a Holiday Inn); a pair of private campgrounds (Coastal Acres Camping Court, 508/487-1700; Dunes Edge Camp Ground, 508/487-9815); and the bargain-priced shared little cottages of the **Outermost Hostel** (May-Oct.; $14; 508/487-4378) on Winslow Street past the Pilgrim Monument parking lot.

Somerset House

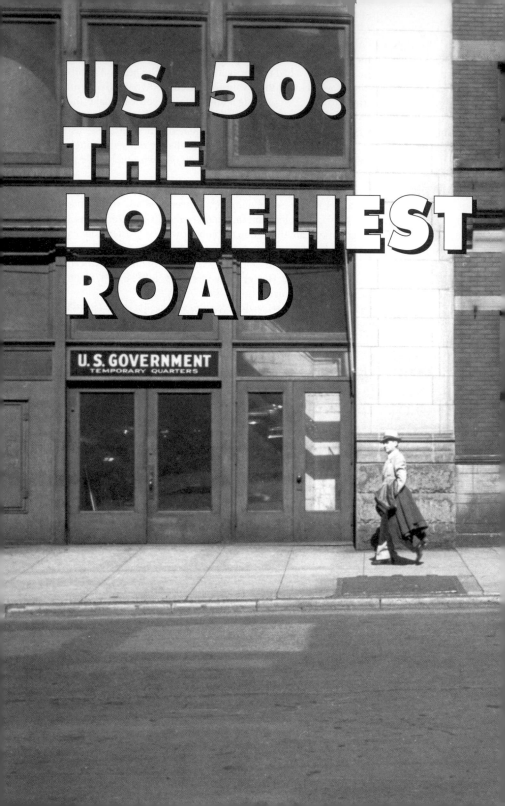

US-50: THE LONELIEST ROAD

US-50: THE LONELIEST ROAD

R unning coast-to-coast through the heart of America on a 3,200-mile odyssey from sea to shining sea, US-50 passes through

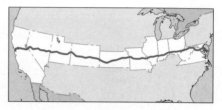

a dozen different states and four state capitals, as well as the nation's capital, Washington, D.C. Along the route are some of the country's most magnificent landscapes: the Appalachian, Rocky, and Sierra Nevada Mountains, the endless farmlands of the Great Plains, and the desiccated deserts of Utah and Nevada. It follows the footsteps of pioneers along the Santa Fe Trail and the route of the Pony Express, and gives an uncannily consistent timeline of national development. Heading west to east, you can travel back in history from the cutting-edge high tech of contemporary Silicon Valley, across the Wild West frontier of the mid-1800s, through lands the likes of Daniel Boone and countless others pioneered in the 1700s, before arriving at the Atlantic Ocean near some of the oldest and best-preserved colonial-era landscapes in the USA.

All the way across the country, US-50 passes through literally hundreds of time-worn small towns, the great majority of which have survived untouched by the modern onslaught of Wal-Marts and fast-food franchises. Writing about US-50, *Blue Highways* author William Least Heat Moon says that "for the unhurried, this little-known highway is the best national road across the middle of the United States." The route offers such a compelling cross-section of the nation that *Time* magazine devoted nearly an entire issue (July 7, 1997) to telling the story of the road it called the "Backbone of America."

From its start at San Francisco, the route cuts across California's midsection, passing the state capital at Sacramento before following the route of the old Pony Express up into the Sierra Nevada to the shores of Lake Tahoe and into Nevada. The Nevada portion of the route, dubbed "The Loneliest Road in America" by travel writers and tourist boards, is one of the most compelling long-distance drives in the country—provided you find miles and miles of little more than mountains, sagebrush, and blue sky compelling. The Great Basin desert continues across half of Utah, but then the route climbs over the Wasatch Front and onto the national park-packed red-rock country of the Colorado Plateau.

Continuing east, you cross the Continental Divide atop the Rockies, then follow the Arkansas River along the historic Santa Fe Trail, passing many of the most significant sites of the Wild West frontier. For fans of vanishing Americana, the route really comes into its own here across the Great Plains, with its hypnotically repetitive landscape of water towers, windmills, railroad tracks, and grain elevators, and one small town after another, each featuring its variations on the archetypal lineup of cafe, post office, tavern, and general store.

After bisecting Missouri from Kansas City to St. Louis, US-50 crosses the Mississippi River into a much older and more settled landscape, through the agricultural heartlands of Illinois, Indiana, and Ohio. After climbing into the Appalachian backwoods of West Virginia, US-50 emerges suddenly into the wealth and power of downtown Washington, D.C., before passing through the still perfectly picturesque fishing and farming communities of Maryland's Eastern Shore.

ACROSS CALIFORNIA

If you're interested in following the real route of old US-50, which formed the original Lincoln Highway in the days before highways were numbered, from the foot of the Bay Bridge the old road wound southeast along the approximate route of today's I-580 freeway, up and over Altamont Pass (site of a huge wind farm and the Rolling Stones' notorious 1969 "Gimme Shelter" concert). From Tracy, old US-50 ran north to Sacramento, where the old road rejoins the current route.

Heading east from San Francisco across the heavy-duty Oakland Bay Bridge, the route across California starts off along the busy I-80 freeway through the urbanized San Francisco Bay Area. Passing diverse bayfront towns, including blue-collar Oakland and collegiate Berkeley, the busy and often congested eight-lane highway heads northeast across the historically important but increasingly suburbanized flatlands of the Sacramento Delta. Beyond Sacramento, the state capital of California, US-50 finally emerges, first as a freeway but later as a two-lane mountain road climbing through the heart of the Sierra Nevada foothills, where many of the small towns slumber in a gold rush dream of the 1850s. Continuing east, US-50 winds through endless tracts of pine forest before cresting the Sierra to reach alpine Lake Tahoe, a year-round resort lying astride the California-Nevada border.

For particulars on what to see and do in the City by the Bay, consult the San Francisco Survival Guide in the Coastal West Coast chapter on pages 71-73.

Oakland's native son Jack London worked in factories and along the waterfront near present-day Jack London Square before becoming the first writer to earn $1 million with his pen.

Oakland

Though many dismiss it as the West Coast equivalent of Newark, New Jersey, the hardworking and long-suffering city of Oakland (pop. 365,000) is actually a lively and intriguing place. The main attraction for visitors is its waterfront **Jack London Square** honoring the city's favorite prodigal son. Covering a few blocks at the foot of Broadway, the modern outdoor shopping complex contains a large bookstore, a couple of restaurants, an ancient log cabin supposedly lived in by Jack London in the Yukon Territory, and last but not least, the truly funky **Heinold's First and Last Chance**, a rickety old saloon that's the only survivor from the waterfront's wild past, right on the water at 56 Jack London Square.

Oakland's other main draw is the excellent **Oakland Museum** (Wed.-Sat. 10 AM-5 PM, Sunday; noon-7 PM $4), housed in a landmark modernist ziggurat on the east edge of downtown, at 1000 Oak Street. Inside, exhibits cover everything from California's natural history to the photography of Dorothea Lange. An in-depth look at the state's popular culture is highlighted by a lively display of Hollywood movie posters, neon signs, jukeboxes, and classic cars and motorcycles.

Berkeley

The intellectual, literary, and political nexus of the San Francisco Bay Area, left-leaning Berkeley (pop. 120,000) enjoys an international reputation that overshadows its suburban character. The town grew up around the attractively landscaped University of California campus, which during the 1960s and early 1970s was the scene of ongoing battles between "The Establishment" and unwashed hordes of anti-war, sex-and-drugs-and-rock-and-roll-crazed youth. Today Berkeley maintains a typical college town mix of cafes and CD stores. Its site is superb, looking out across the bay to the Golden Gate and San Francisco.

The square-mile **University of California** Berkeley campus sits at the foot of eucalyptus-covered hills a mile east of the University Avenue exit off the I-80 freeway. Wander along Strawberry Creek, admiring the mix of neoclassical and postmodern buildings. Berkeley's cacophonous main drag, Telegraph Avenue, runs south from the heart of campus in a crazy array of tie-dye and tarot, lined by a half-dozen good cafes and some of the country's best bookstores.

There are dozens of good-value places to eat and drink in Berkeley, including one of the best breakfast joints on the planet, **Bette's Ocean View Diner**, 1807 4th Street, two blocks from the I-80 University Avenue exit, at the center of a boutique shopping district. Berkeley also has many top-rated restaurants, including world-renowned **Chez Panisse**, birthplace of California cuisine, located in the heart of Berkeley's gourmet ghetto at 1517 Shattuck Avenue (reservations essential; 510/548-5525).

Vallejo

On the north side of the Carquinez Straits, through which the Sacramento and San Joaquin Rivers flow into San Francisco Bay, Vallejo is a blue-collar maritime town still reeling from the closure of its huge and historic Mare Island naval shipyard, which from 1854 to 1994 built and maintained many of the country's fighting ships and submarines. An early state capital of California, Vallejo's bona fide attraction these days is the **Marine World/Africa USA** theme park (Wed.-Sun. 9:30 AM-5:30 PM, daily till 6:30 PM in summer; $26.95), on the north side of town just west of I-80, with 160 acres of elephants, tigers, sea lions, and killer whales, all trained to perform tricks on cue. There's also an adjacent amusement park with the usual array of thrill rides.

The big "C" above the University of California campus is over 100 years old. It was the first of these giant letters, which have since been repeated on hillsides all over the country.

In the past decade Oakland has suffered one disaster after another. The 1989 earthquake did far more damage (and killed twice as many people) in Oakland than it did across the bay in San Francisco, and in 1991 a terrible fire destroyed 3,000 hillside homes, killing 27 people. In 1995, the Raiders football team returned, robbing city and county coffers of millions of dollars, then in 1998, eccentric former California Governor Jerry Brown was elected mayor.

San Francisco is easily accessible from both Berkeley and Oakland via the high-speed, trans-bay **BART trains,** which run under the Bay between a half-dozen East Bay stations and downtown San Francisco.

While Berkeley students were rioting in the streets in 1968, a Berkeley plumber was putting the finishing touches on the air-bubbling bath device that bears his name—**Jacuzzi.**

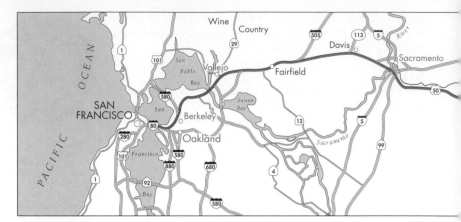

The town of Vallejo served as state capital of California on two different occasions in the gold rush years of the early 1850s.

Vallejo also marks the turnoff for Hwy-12, which runs west through the Wine Country of the Napa and Sonoma valleys.

Three of the biggest roadside attractions along I-80 are no more. The Nut Tree, the giant restaurant and souvenir stand in Vacaville, has closed; the Milk Farm restaurant, with its giant signs of a cow jumping over the Moon, is shuttered; and Dixie the Dixon Dinosaur has been relocated to I-680 in Benicia—where she's now a he, re-named Benny.

Sacramento also marks the official western end of US-50, as marked by the sign along the freeway in West Sacramento, where I-80 and US-50 diverge. It reads: US-50 Ocean City, Maryland—3,073 miles.

Vallejo effectively marks the edge of the San Francisco Bay Area. Once you cross over the hills east of here, the landscape turns suddenly flat and agricultural, with a few pockets of suburbia, and the roadside alternates from farmland to mini-mall sprawl.

I-80 Towns

Between the San Francisco Bay Area and Sacramento, I-80 passes through an ever more suburbanized corridor of towns like **Fairfield** (pop. 78,000), home of Travis Air Force Base, the Herman Goelitz jelly bean factory that makes Ronald Reagan's favorite candies (800/522-3627), and a large Anheuser-Busch beer refinery (open Tues.-Sat. for free tours). The other biggish city here is **Vacaville** (pop. 71,500), home to the state's largest psychiatric prison, and a ton of factory outlet stores. Approaching Sacramento, I-80 races past **Davis**, a quiet former farm town that's now home to a University of California campus renowned around the world for its wine-making school.

The route I-80 follows parallels old US-40, which, beginning in 1927 when the Carquinez Straits were first bridged, was part of the Lincoln Highway, one of the earliest transcontinental roads. Many portions are still there, including an untouched section east of Davis, on the north side of I-80, that's now a billboard-lined bike path.

Sacramento

Spreading for miles at the heart of California's 500-mile-long, agriculturally rich Central Valley, Sacramento (pop. 369,400) is not what most would expect of the capital of the Golden State. Green and suburban, with only the state capitol and a few modern towers rising over fine Victorian houses that line the leafy downtown streets, Sacramento is a relatively quiet backwater that effectively embodies California's bi-polar politics, forming a sort of neutral ground between the liberal urban centers, which contain 90% of the state's

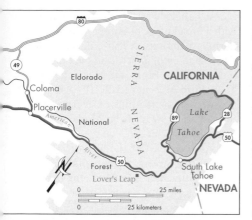

population, and the conservative, rural rest, which covers 90% of the land.

Now scythed by freeways, and stretching for miles along the banks of the Sacramento and American Rivers, the city was chosen as the state capital during the Gold Rush era, when Sacramento was the main jumping-off point for the Sierra Nevada mines. Dozens of buildings dating from that era have been restored to form **Old Sacramento**, a diverting shopping complex and tourist trap along the riverfront, where ersatz paddle-wheel steamboats offer sightseeing cruises, and the excellent **California State Railroad Museum** (daily 10 AM-5 PM; $5) documents the history of western railroads. Along with the wealth of Gold Rush architecture, there are memorials to the Pony Express and the Transcontinental Railroad, both of which had stations here. During Memorial Day weekend, Old Sacramento hosts the **Sacramento Jazz Jubilee** (916/372-5277), which draws an enormous crowd intent on hearing the 100 or so mostly Dixieland bands.

Away from the riverfront, and under the unforgiveably ugly I-5 freeway, "Old Sac" connects up with the wanderable Downtown Plaza shopping mall, which has all the fast-food and upscale boutiques you could want, plus a branch of the Hard Rock Cafe chain. Two blocks south, standing at the west end of a pleasantly landscaped park, the impressive **California State Capitol** (daily 9 AM-5 PM; free) has publicly accessible legislative chambers of the state's Senate and Assembly, a small museum, and hallways full of exhibits on the Golden State's diverse counties. A block south of the Capitol, the brand-new **Golden State Museum** (Wed.-Sat. 10 AM-5 PM; $6.50; 916/653-7524), at 1020 "O" Street, is a marvelous multimedia extravaganza that recounts the many diverse stories of California's past, present, and possible future. Paid for by the state, but run by an independent non-profit group, the 3,500-square-foot museum opened late in 1998, and touches on everything from natural resources to the impact of roads on the landscape, involving the visitor through a variety of interactive displays: a sit-down diner has a jukebox on which you can call up conversations between deal-making politicos, and a 1960s vintage bus tells the tales of California's many immigrants, from Dust Bowl refugees to migrant farmworkers.

Two other museums are worth a look, too. The **Crocker Art Museum**, two blocks from the riverfront at 216 O Street (Tues.-Sun. 10 AM-5 PM; $4.50), is the

California's capitol as it appeared in the early 1900s. A 40-acre park surrounds the building; guided tours of both are offered in spring, summer, and fall. Call (916) 324-0333 for details.

In 1849, quiet Sutter's Mill in Coloma became the focus of worldwide attention after gold was discovered there.

oldest gallery west of the Mississippi, with a broad range of European and Californian paintings. A half-mile south of Old Sacramento, underneath the I-80/I-5 interchange at Front and V Streets, the **Towe Ford Museum** (daily 10 AM-6 PM; $5) displays examples of every Ford made before 1952, from Model T's to massive Ford V-8s.

Two miles east of the waterfront, at 27th and L Streets, Sacramento's main historic attraction is **Sutter's Fort** (daily 10 AM-5 PM; $2), a reconstruction of the frontier outpost established here in 1839 by Swiss settler Johannes Sutter. The first commercial, as opposed to religious, settlement in Alta California, Sutter's Fort played a vital role in early West Coast history—this is where the Donner Party was headed, and where the Gold Rush really began, when Sutter's employee James Marshall discovered flakes of gold at Sutter's Mill (see next page), in the Sierra Nevada foothills above Sacramento. The grounds of Sutter's Fort also hold the small but interesting **California State Indian Museum**, which has displays of baskets and other California Native American handicrafts.

Finding your way around Sacramento is pretty easy: north-south streets are numbered starting from the riverfront, while east-west ones are in alphabetical order. Capitol Avenue, at the center, takes the place of M Street, and Broadway should have been Y Street.

Sacramento Practicalities

The Old Sacramento area, along the downtown waterfront, has some good but touristy restaurants and bars, but the Midtown neighborhood south of Sutter's Fort holds Sacramento's best range of restaurants, including the tasty but inexpensive **Cafe Bernardo** at 2726 Capitol Avenue, with fresh salads, pizza and pasta dishes, and great fruit smoothies; cocktails are available from the Monkey Bar next door. On the opposite corner stands **Biba**, perhaps the city's best (and most expensive) restaurant, and other good bets nearby include **Paragary's** and the **Capitol Grill**, facing each across 28th and N streets. Another group of good places is a half-mile west: **Paesano's** has great cheap pizzas at 1806 Capitol, **Greta's** does a bohemian range of salads and sandwiches on the corner of Capitol and 19th Street, and all sorts of coffee drinks can be had at **New Helvetia**, 1215 19th Street, or **Weatherstone's**, 812 21st Street.

Another lively spot is the **Tower Cafe**, attached to the landmark 1920s Tower Theater (which plays art-house hits) at 1518 Broadway, and serving healthy, multi-ethnic food with a world-beat attitude. (The cafe is where the Sacramento-based

Tower Records CD and bookstore company got its start; both have stores across the street, open till midnight every night.)

Though Sacramento can't compete with San Francisco for cutting-edge cuisine, it does excel in one culinary niche: hamburgers. There are some truly great old burger places in and around downtown Sacramento, like **Ford's Real Hamburgers**, at 1948 Sutterville on the south side of expansive

Land Park, **Nationwide Meats,** 1015 24th Street in Midtown, and funky little **Jim Denny's,** a 1930s burger stand at 816 12th Street, downtown between H & I.

Places to stay include the wonderful **HI Sacramento International Hostel,** in a fabulous Victorian mansion right downtown at 900 H Street (916/443-1691) with beds from $13/night for members, $16/night non-members, plus a **Motel 6** along the river near Old Sacramento at 227 Jibboom Street (916/441-0733). For a more unusual experience, how about staying the night in a 1920s paddlewheel riverboat? The *Delta King* (916/444-KING or 916/444-5464) is permanently moored off Old Sacramento, and has rooms in the $100-150 range. There are many B&Bs in the historic Midtown residential district, including the **Hartley House,** 700 22nd Street (916/448-5417) and **Abigail's,** 2120 G Street (916/441-5007).

For further information, contact the Sacramento **visitors bureau,** 1421 K Street (916/264-7777).

Between Sacramento and Placerville, US-50 is an eight lane freeway—and one of the California Highway Patrol's most lucrative speed traps, especially for westbound (downhill) travelers.

Placerville and Coloma: Gold Country

The main US-50 stop in the Sierra Nevada foothills, Placerville (pop. 8,400; elev. 1,860 feet) takes its name from the placer gold deposits recovered from the South Fork of the American River, which flows just north of town. The historic core of Placerville is well preserved, with a few cafes (like **Sarah's Cafe,** at 301 Main Street) and bars paying homage to its rough-and-tumble past. A reminder of the town's gold-rush heritage is the **Gold Bug Mine** (daily 10 AM-4 PM in summer, weekends only rest of the year; $1), a mile north of US-50 off the Bedford Avenue exit. A stamp mill and other mining equipment stand outside the entrance to the mine tunnel, which you can explore on a self-guided tour.

If you want to explore the region's many evocative gold rush-era remnants, Placerville makes a good base, with its handful of motels (including a Best Western and a Days Inn) fronting the highway.

The original site of the discovery of gold, Sutter's Mill, has been reconstructed as part of **Gold Discovery State Historic Park** in Coloma, now an idyllic place along the banks of the American River, nine miles north of Placerville along Hwy-49. The park is also a prime spot for whitewater rafting and kayaking, especially on weekends, so don't be surprised to find the place thronged with wet-suited and Teva-shod hordes.

North and south of Placerville, Hwy-49 runs along the Sierra Nevada foothills through the heart of the Gold Country. Starting in the north beyond beautiful Nevada City, Hwy-49 winds through one historic town after another, all the way to the gates of Yosemite National Park, 150 miles to the south.

One great old Gold Country haunt can be reached within a short drive of US-50 from Placerville. The ancient and very popular **Poor Red's Barbecue** (530/622-2901), housed in a Gold Rush-era stagecoach station in the hamlet of El Dorado, five miles south of Placerville on Hwy-49, has full lunches and dinners (and great margaritas) for very little money.

Throughout the gold-rush era, Placerville was known as Hangtown, with a reputation for stringing up petty thieves and other law-breakers. An effigy still hangs at the center of town, in front of a bar.

The American River and Lover's Leap

Some 20 miles east of Placerville, US-50 changes suddenly from a four-lane freeway into a twisting, narrow, two-lane road over the crest of the Sierra Nevada mountains. The usually busy highway, which every year is battered and frequently closed by winter storms, runs right alongside the steep banks of the American River. The lushness of the western Sierra Nevada is immediately apparent as the road passes luxuriant groves of pine, fir, and cedar, with numerous old resorts and vacation cabins lining the highway.

About six miles west of the summit, the towering granite cliff of Lover's Leap stands out to the south of the highway, its 1,300-foot face attracting rock-climbers, while to the north the delicate cascade of **Horsetail Falls** offers a more serene pit stop. Climbing east up US-50's steepest set of hairpin turns, you'll reach 7,365-foot Echo Summit, which gives great views of the Lake Tahoe basin—the shining blue waters beckoning you along another steep stretch of US-50, downhill this time, if you're heading east, to the lakeshore itself.

South Lake Tahoe

One of the biggest (12 miles wide, 22 miles long, and 72 miles of coastline) and deepest (over 1,000 feet in places) lakes in the country, straddling the Nevada/California border at 6,220 feet above sea level, Lake Tahoe is a beautiful sight from any angle—from the crest of the alpine peaks surrounding it, from a car or bicycle as you cruise along the shoreline roads, or from a boat out on the lake itself.

Sitting, as the name suggests, at the southern end of Lake Tahoe, the ungainly resort community of South Lake Tahoe is a place of multiple personalities. On the California side, low-rise motels line the US-50 frontage, and the atmosphere is that of a family-oriented summer resort, with bike-rental stands and T-shirt shops clogging the roadside. Across the Nevada border, glitzy 20-story casinos rise up in a sudden wall of concrete and glass, ignoring the surrounding beauty in favor of round-the-clock "adult fun"—gambling, racy nightclub revues, and more gambling. (For more on the attractions of Nevada's half of Lake Tahoe, see below.) A few strategically placed pine trees work hard to retain a semblance of the natural splendor, but in peak summer season it's basically a *very* busy stretch of road, on both sides of the state line.

To get away from it all, head along Hwy-89 around the west side of the lake to the magnificent state parks around Emerald Bay, where acres of shoreline forest and numerous mansions built as summer resorts back around the turn of the 20th century have been preserved and are open for tours. Start at **Tallac Historic Site** (530/573-2600), three miles west of US-50, or stop by the **ranger station** at 870 Emerald Bay Road, near the US-50/Hwy-89 junction. In winter, the Tahoe area turns into an extremely popular ski resort—Heavenly (530/541-7544) on the south shore and Squaw Valley (530/583-6985) in the north are among the largest and busiest ski areas in the U.S.; both have sightseeing chair lifts in summer.

Despite the lake's great popularity, year-round prices for Tahoe accommodations are surprisingly low; with three **Travelodges**, a **Motel 6**, and dozens of others to choose from, you shouldn't have trouble finding something suitable for around $50 a night. Food, however, is not really a Tahoe strength, though for a carbo-loading breakfast head to the **Red Hut Waffle Shop** at 2749 Lake Tahoe Boulevard (US-50), or for burgers and shakes, stop by the **50's Drive-In**, farther east on Lake Tahoe Boulevard. For a well-prepared and not overly pricey dinner, try **Nephele's**, at 1169 Ski Run Boulevard at the foot of Heavenly ski area.

ACROSS NEVADA

Between Lake Tahoe in the west and Great Basin National Park on the Utah border, US-50 crosses more than 400 miles of corrugated country, climbing up and over a dozen distinct mountain ranges while passing through four classic mining towns and the state capital, Carson City. Early explorers mapped this region, Pony Express riders raced across it, and the long-distance Lincoln Highway finally tamed it, but the US-50 byway has always played second fiddle to I-80, the more popular northern route across the state. Besides being a more scenic alternative to the mind-numbing, and therefore accident-prone, I-80 freeway, US-50 across Nevada has gained a measure of notoriety in its own right—it's known as the "Loneliest Road in America." As you travel along it you'll see road signs, T-shirts, bumper stickers, and even state-sponsored travel passports proclaiming it as such.

Stateline

Right where US-50 crosses from California into Nevada, the casino complex at Stateline forms, for a few short blocks, a mini-Las Vegas, with four 20-story resort hotels towering over the lakeshore. **Harvey's** (800/648-3361) started it all in the 1940s, with six nickel slot machines, still in use in a corner of the casino; it's now the largest, with over 650 lakeside rooms. **Harrah's** (800/648-3773), across US-50, is the most opulent, its luxurious 500-square-foot suites yours to enjoy for a mere $200 a night. Altogether, over 2,000 rooms are available, combined with at least that many more across the California border. The multitudes of game-hungry visitors that converge here create a definite charge in the rarefied atmosphere when the casino tables are turning at full speed, and it's also a great place to catch your favorite performers, or a Vegas-style floor show.

Nevada Beach and Zephyr Cove

From the casino district at Stateline, US-50 winds along Lake Tahoe's southeastern shore for over 20 miles, passing by a pair of waterfront parks at Nevada Beach and Zephyr Cove (where you can ride the faux paddle wheeler MS *Dixie* on a two-hour cruise across the lake). Otherwise, lakeshore access is severely limited, since most of the waterfront is privately owned, though numerous roadside turnouts (most easily accessible to westbound, lakeside travelers) offer ample opportunities to take in unforgettable views.

Midway along the lake's eastern shore, US-50 turns sharply and begins climbing up and over the 7,140-foot crest of Spooner Summit, all the way giving great views of the tantalizing blue gleam below. At the summit, stretch your legs by taking a quick hike on the Tahoe Ridge Trail, a work-in-progress which will eventually circumnavigate the entire Lake Tahoe basin. Dropping down swiftly from Spooner Summit into the Great Basin desert, US-50 links up with US-395 for the final few miles into Carson City.

Detour: Genoa

Between Stateline and Carson City, a delightful little back-door route takes you through Genoa, the oldest city in Nevada. Founded by Mormon farmers way back in 1851, Genoa still retains its rural frontier feel, especially since most of the twentieth-century development has been focused elsewhere, leaving Genoa pleasantly far behind the times—for the time being, at least, though new houses for Carson City commuters have been springing up on the outskirts of the historic downtown.

At the center of town is **Mormon Station State Park** (daily 10 AM-5 PM; 775/782-2590), which has a small museum and a stockade dating back to the 1850s. Across the way, at Main and 5th streets, the **Genoa Courthouse Museum** (daily 10 AM-4:30 PM; donations; 775/782-4325) has more comprehensive displays of historical items—everything from Native American baskets to the keys of the old jail, with an especially interesting exhibition on Wild West legend John A. "Snowshoe" Thompson, who carried the mail over the mountains between Genoa and Sacramento.

> The **Genoa Bar,** near Walley's Hot Springs at 2282 Foothill Road, is the oldest licensed premises in the state, in operation since 1863.

There's also a little tidbit on mining engineer and native son George Ferris, who designed and built the first of his namesake Ferris wheels for the 1893 World's Fair in Chicago.

A mile south of town via Foothill Road, Genoa's other great attraction is **Walley's Hot Springs** (775/782-8155) a resort hotel complex built around natural 160-degree hot springs. Another nice place to stay is the **Genoa House Inn**, 180 Nixon Street (775/782-7075), a quaint historical B&B. Thriving on the tourism Genoa's charm generates, there are also some good shops and restaurants around town, including **Casentini's**, an Italian lunch and dinner place near the courthouse.

To get to Genoa from Stateline and Lake Tahoe, go east on Hwy-207, down the very steep Kingsbury Grade, then turn north on Hwy-206. From Carson City, turn off US-395 south of the US-50 junction onto Jack's Valley Road (Hwy-206), and follow that for 12 miles.

Carson City

Nevada's state capital and third largest city, Carson City (pop. 40,443) was named in honor of Wild West explorer Kit Carson. Nestled at the base of the sheer eastern scarp of the Sierra Nevada, the city was founded in 1858—just a year before the discovery of the Comstock Lode riches, and six years before Nevada became a state.

Carson City is a hard place to characterize. Considering it's the capital, life is rather slow, with the main buzz

being the few casinos like the **Carson Nugget** at 507 N. Carson Street (775/882-1626) on the main US-50/395 route through town, which has a million-dollar collection of raw, unprocessed gold on display, along with roulette, craps, and blackjack tables and the usual army of old ladies feeding banks of slot machines.

Gambling aside, the one place to stop in Carson City is the excellent **Nevada State Museum** (daily 9 AM-5:30 PM; $3), which stands across the street from the stately capitol—and catercorner from the Nugget—at 600 N. Carson Street. Housed inside the solid old U.S. Mint, built in 1870 to make coins from Comstock silver, are displays on mining (including a large, full-scale mock-up of a working mine), as well as on Nevada and Great Basin natural history. Also worth a look are the **Stewart Indian Museum** (daily 9 AM-5:30 PM; donations; 775/882-1808), which has Native American artifacts, and a great collection of Edward Curtis's anthropological photography, on the former campus of a Bureau of Indian Affairs school, off US-395 south of town at 5366 Snyder Avenue, and the old Virginia & Truckee steam engines at **Nevada State Railroad Museum**, farther south along US-50/395.

Good Mexican meals are the order of the day at **El Charro Avitia**, south of town at 4389 S. Carson Street, and the specials at the **Carson Nugget** can be incredibly cheap ($2 steak sandwiches). However, the best and most expensive fare is served at **Adele's**, where power brokers broker their power at 1112 N. Carson Street (775/882-3353). Motels line Carson Street north and south of the capitol; try the classic 1950s-style **Frontier** at 1718 N. Carson (775/882-1377), the **Motel Orleans** at 2731 S. Carson (775/882-2007), or **Motel 6** at 2749 S. Carson (775/885-7710). Finally, if you're looking for something to do after dark besides gamble, Carson City also has what's possibly the country's cheapest movie theater, the **Cinema 50** on US-50 a mile east of Carson Street: four screens show recent releases, and all seats cost $1.50-3, all the time.

For more complete visitor information, contact the **Carson City Convention and Visitors Bureau**, 1900 S. Carson Street (800/NEVADA1 or 800/638-2321).

In 1861, Orion Clemens was appointed secretary to the governor of Nevada Territory, and his younger brother Sam came with him to Nevada. Sam submitted dispatches of his mining and travel adventures around the territory to Virginia City's largest daily newspaper, the *Territorial Enterprise.* Sam eventually accepted a reporter's position on the newspaper and began perfecting his unique brand of Western frontier humor under the pen name **Mark Twain.**

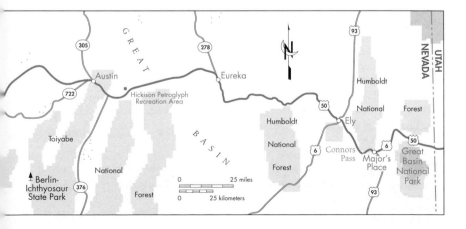

Virginia City

In 1859, prospectors following the gold deposits up the slopes of Mount Davidson discovered one of the richest strikes in world history: the **Comstock Lode**. Almost overnight, the bustling camp of Virginia City grew into the largest settlement between Chicago and San Francisco, and over the next 20 years nearly a billion dollars in gold and silver (in 19th-century money!) was grubbed from deep underground. Afterward the town very nearly dried up and blew away, but thanks in part to the 1960s TV show *Bonanza,* in which Hoss and company were always heading over to Virginia City for supplies or to fetch the sheriff, tourists discovered the town and gave it a new lease on life.

The Castle, Virginia City's elegant 1868 mansion, was built by the superintendent of the Empire Mine.

These days Virginia City is both a tacky tourist trap and one of the most satisfying destinations in the state. Reachable via a very steep (grades in excess of 15%!) eight-mile drive up Hwy-341 from US-50, dozens of hokey but enjoyable attractions—like the amiable **Bucket of Blood Saloon**, which offers a panoramic view down the mountain—line the five-block-long main drag, C Street. The streets above and below—and I do mean above and below: the town clings to such a steep slope that C Street is a good three stories higher than neighboring D Street—hold some of the most authentic sites. B Street, for example, has the elegant **Castle**, Nevada's premier mansion, with all the original furnishings and fittings, a block south of the ornate Victorian **Storey County Courthouse** and the landmark **Piper's Opera House**. Down the hill on D Street was once a more raucous quarter, where brothels and opium dens shared space with railroad tracks, cemeteries, and the mines themselves: the Gold & Curry, the Ophir, and the Consolidated Virginia.

Before or after a wander around town, be sure to stop in to the excellent museum on the ground floor of the **Fourth Ward School** (daily 10 AM-5 PM May-Nov.; $2), the Victorian gothic landmark at the south end of C Street. Exhibits inside recount the lively history of Virginia City, from mining technology to Mark Twain, who made his start as a journalist with Virginia City's *Territorial Enterprise.* An intact classroom is preserved as it was in 1936 when the last class graduated. Another not-to-be-missed spot is the **Red Light Museum** (daily 11 AM- 5 PM; $1), in the basement of the Julia C. Bulette Saloon on C and Union Streets, which displays an amazing barrage of antique condoms, pornographic postcards, opium pipes, and other sexually explicit oddities, impossible to describe.

Unless you're tempted by the many places to eat hot dogs and drink sarsaparilla along C Street, food options in Virginia City are very limited, though the **Brass Rail** and the **Delta Saloon** are both above par. For complete listings, contact the Virginia City **chamber of commerce** (775/847-0311).

Reno's famous arch, which spans Virginia Street at 3rd Street downtown, was first erected in 1926 to mark the Lincoln Highway route through town. The current arch, the fourth to stand on the site, was built in 1987.

Detour: Reno

Nothing helps heighten the contrast between the rest of the world and life along the "Loneliest Road" than making a stop, before or after a US-50 tour, in Reno, "The Biggest Little City in the World," as the bold archway over Virginia Street downtown proclaims. An ancient city by Nevada standards, dating back to pioneer days (the Donner Party camped here on their ill-fated way west), Reno first came to national prominence in the 1930s as a center for quickie divorces, and now has all the gambling of its larger sibling, Las Vegas, with a pleasantly homey, settled-down feel.

THE PONY EXPRESS

Of all the larger-than-life legends that animate the annals of the Wild West, none looms larger than that of the Pony Express. As is typical of frontier adventures, accounts of the Pony Express are often laced with considerable exaggeration, but in this case the facts are unusually impressive. Beginning in April 1860, running twice a week between St. Joseph, Missouri, and Sacramento, California, where it was linked with San Francisco by steamship, the Pony Express halved the time it took to carry news to and from the West Coast, making the 1,966-mile trek in just 10 days. Eighty riders (including 14-year-old William "Buffalo Bill" Cody, who made the record single run of 322 miles) were employed to race between the 190 stations en route, switching horses every 10-15 miles and averaging 75 miles per run—day or night, in all kinds of weather, across 120° F deserts or snowbound Sierra passes.

Covering nearly 2,000 miles of the wildest and ruggedest land on the frontier, the Pony Express established the first high-speed link between the two coasts. At a time when the nation was divided against itself, with the Civil War looming on the horizon, the Pony Express connection played a key role in keeping the valuable mines of California and Nevada in Union hands. A private enterprise that lasted just 18 months and lost considerable amounts of money before being put of out business for good, the Pony Express proved that overground connections across the still-wild western U.S. were both necessary and possible.

The completion on October 28, 1861 of the transcontinental telegraph made the Pony Express obsolete overnight, and not so much as a saddle survives from this legendary endeavor. Apart from a few postmarked letters, and various statues and plaques marking the Pony Express route, there are very few tangible signs of it today. The most evocative sites survive in the dry Nevada desert, within easy access of the US-50 highway. East of Fallon, for example, the highway runs right on top of the old Pony Express route, and the remains of two relay stations can still be seen. One is at **Sand Springs**, at the foot of Sand Mountain. More substantial remains survive at **Cold Springs**, 32 miles east, where plaques recount the history and a short trail brings you to what was once among the most isolated and dangerous of the Pony Express stations.

1860 1861

PONY EXPRESS TRAIL

Besides taking advantage of Reno's cheap hotel rooms and 24-hour fun, car culture fans will want to visit the $10 million, 100,000-square foot **National Automobile Museum**, south of the Truckee River at 10 S. Lake Street (Mon.-Sat. 9:30 AM-5:30 PM, Sunday 10 AM-4 PM; $7.50; 775/333-9300), perhaps the best and probably the most extensive car collection in the country. (Great gift shop, too.) Reno's other national attraction: the **National Bowling Stadium**, a state-of-the-art 80-lane extravaganza, at Center and 4th streets.

Reno is located at the eastern foot of the Sierra Nevada mountains, on I-80 about 30 miles north of Carson City, 25 miles from Virginia City. For more information, or for details of midweek accommodation deals at the dozen or more casinos, contact the Reno **visitors bureau**, 4590 S. Virginia Street (775/827-RENO, 775/827-7366 or 800/367-RENO, 800/367-7366).

Dayton

On the north side of US-50, just east of the turnoff for Virginia City, Dayton is one of the oldest settlements in Nevada. Gold was first discovered here in 1849, and later the town's massive stamp mills pounded the ore carried through the massive Sutro Tunnel from the fabulous Comstock Lode in the mountains above. The historic town center is little more than the two blocks of Main Street north from the traffic light on US-50, where you can choose from a couple of combination cafes-and-saloons, including the **Old Corner Bar** at 30 Pike Street, a favorite hangout of John Huston, Arthur Miller, Marilyn Monroe, and company when they were in Dayton in 1960 to film *The Misfits*.

East of Dayton, around Lahontan Dam, irrigated fields of alfalfa quickly give way to 50 miles of sandy desert, tumbleweed, and scruffy grasses.

Fallon

Coming into Fallon, especially after crossing the Great Basin deserts of Utah and Nevada that stretch to the east, can be a shock to the system. First, relative to Nevada's other US-50 towns, Fallon is big: upwards of 7,000 residents, with all the attendant shopping malls, traffic lights, and fast-food franchises. Second, but perhaps more striking, Fallon is green: alfalfa, onions, garlic, and cantaloupe as far as the eye can see. Otherwise, Fallon offers the ATMs, gas stations, and motels lining along US-50, as well as the usual Pizza Huts and Subways, and a handy 24-hour Safeway.

About the only radio station along this stretch of US-50 is Fallon's **KBLB 980 AM**, which plays a standard array of country hits.

Though it had long existed as a crossroads for the surrounding mining camps, and was first laid out as a town around the turn of the century, Fallon didn't really begin to grow until the completion of Lahontan Dam west of town in 1915 brought irrigation water from the Carson River. Besides agriculture, Fallon's other main employer is the U.S. Navy, whose air base and target range is an important training center for carrier-based fighters and bombers—the "Top Guns" of Tom Cruise fame.

While it's not a particularly attractive place, Fallon does have what they accurately call "The Best Little Museum on the Loneliest Road in America," the eclectic and engaging **Churchill County Museum** (Mon.-Sat. 10 AM-5 PM, Sunday noon-5 PM; free) at 1050 S. Maine Street, less than a mile south of US-50. Filling an old Safeway supermarket, the exhibits contain native Paiute basketry, clothing and hunting gear, the usual array of pioneer quilts and clothing—plus a player piano, and the gift shop sells a wide range of books and historical postcards.

Grimes Point and Sand Mountain

The 110 miles of US-50 between Fallon and Austin, the next town to the east, look pretty empty on most maps, but there's more to see than you might think. In the midst of a U.S. Navy target range, where supersonic fighters play electronic war games across the alkali flats, there are historical plaques marking Pony Express and Butterfield Stage way stations, a solitary brothel, and two unique attractions—a singing sand dune and an extensive petroglyph site.

Ten miles east of Fallon, the extraordinary grouping of petroglyphs at Grimes Point is not to be missed. Just 100 yards north of US-50, a self-guided trail leads past hundreds of images etched into the lichen-covered, espresso-brown basalt boulders. Some 8,000 years ago, when the carvings were made, Grimes Point was on the shores of now-vanished Lake Lahontan, a prime hunting and fishing ground for prehistoric Great Basin peoples. These days fast and fierce lizards, and the occasional antelope, share the arid setting with the shiny rocks, into which a huge array of abstract and figurative images have been pecked and chiseled. If you're intrigued and want to know more, stop by the excellent Churchill County Museum in Fallon (see above) or join a BLM-run guided tour (775/885-6000) of nearby **Hidden Cave** where significant archaeological remains have been uncovered.

Sand Mountain, 15 miles east of Grimes Point, 84 miles west of Austin, and just a half-mile north of US-50, is a giant sword-edged sand dune that makes a deep booming sound when the cascading crystals oscillate at the proper frequency—somewhere between 50 and 100 hertz. On weekends you're more likely to hear the sound of unmuffled dirt bikes and dune buggies, but at other times the half-hour trudge to the top is well worth making, to watch the swirls of sand dance along the ridges.

Forty-five miles east of Fallon, Hwy-361 heads south to the magnesium-mining company town of Gabbs. East of Gabbs lies fascinating **Berlin-Ichthyosaur State Park** (775/964-2440), which holds an only-in-Nevada combination: the 100-year-old ghost town of Berlin and a 225-million-year-old marine fossil quarry. Camping is available year-round, and guided tours of the town and the fossil beds are given weekends in summer.

At the turn-off to Sand Mountain, a battered sign marks the official (solar-powered!) **"Loneliest Phone on the Loneliest Road in America."**

Austin

Some 110 miles east of Fallon and 70 miles west of Eureka, tiny Austin (pop. 300) huddles well above 6,000 feet on the north slope of the mighty Toiyabe Mountains. The steep incline of Main Street (US-50) as it passes through town attests to the precariousness with which Austin has clung to life since its 10-year mining boom ended—in 1873. Unlike Fallon or Eureka, which wear their prosperity on their sleeves, Austin hangs on to the rustic, steadfastly un-whitewashed nature that was once—and in some places, remains—central to Nevada's character. Austin takes its central assignment seriously, since the state's exact geographical center is a mere 12 miles to the south.

According to local legend, a Pony Express rider accidentally discovered silver ore here in 1862, and the rush was on. Prospectors fanned out from Austin, which was named after the Texas hometown of one of its founders, to establish Belmont, Berlin, Grantsville, Ione, and dozens of other boomtowns-turned-ghost towns; roughly $50 million in gold and silver was shipped out over the next 10 years. Since then Austin has experienced a long, melancholy decline, though recent efforts to mine the abundant turquoise and barium in the region have met with some success.

A two-minute drive (at 10 mph) along Main Street takes you past all there is to see in Austin today. The impressive steeples of the Catholic, Methodist, and Baptist churches dominate the townscape, while at the west (downhill) end of town you can glimpse **Stoke's Castle**, a three-story stone sentinel built in 1897 and lived in for all of a month. It looks best from a distance, looming over the cemeteries at the west end of town, but if you want to get closer, follow Castle Road for about a half-mile south from US-50.

For its 300 residents, Austin has three gas stations (it's a very long way to the next town, so fill up here), three motels, and three cafes: the ancient **International**, moved here board by board from Virginia City in 1863, opens first at around 6 AM, followed by **Carol's Country Kitchen** at 7 AM, then the **Toiyabe Cafe**. All three are right on Main Street and close around 9 PM.

Hickison Petroglyph Recreation Area

Bookended by 7,000-foot mountain ranges at either end, the route between Austin and Eureka is perhaps the longest, flattest, straightest stretch of the entire trans-Nevada length of US-50, over 70 miles of Great Basin nothingness. Cattle ranches fill the plains, which were crisscrossed by early explorers like John C. Fremont, who passed through in 1845, as well as by the Pony Express and the Butterfield Stage. Such recent history, however, pales in comparison to the relics from the region's pre-historic past, particularly the fine petroglyphs carved into the rocks on the eastern side of 6,594-foot Hickison Summit, 28 miles east of Austin and 46 miles west of Eureka.

Across Nevada, US-50 follows the route of the Lincoln Highway, the nation's first trans-continental route.

Now protected as part of the BLM-operated Hickison Petroglyph Recreation Area, the petroglyphs stand in a shallow sandstone draw on the north side of the highway. A half-mile trail loops through sagebrush, junipers, and piñon pines from the parking area-cum-campground past dozens of these enigmatic figures, some of which are thought to date back as far as 10,000 B.C. Somewhat surprisingly, so far they are graffiti-free.

Eureka

Right in the middle of a 100-mile stretch of spectacular Great Basin scenery, Eureka is one of the most engaging and enjoyable stops in the state. Unlike a lot of places along the Loneliest Road, Eureka is fairly thriving, thanks to numerous gold mines still in operation in Eureka County, including the largest and most productive in the U.S., the Newmont Mine near Carlin.

The four blocks of 100-year-old buildings lining the steeply sloping, franchise-free Main Street (US-50) are a mix of well-restored brick and wood storefronts alongside less fortunate ruins, some merely sets of cast-iron pilasters holding up false fronts. The focal point is the grand 1879 **Eureka County Courthouse**, still in use. Behind it stands the **Eureka Sentinel Museum** (Mon.-Fri. 11 AM-5 PM, shorter hours weekends), with displays tracing the lively local history as well as typesetting equipment and printing presses of the newspaper published here from 1870 to 1960.

Besides an intriguing place to stroll around (walking-tour booklets are available from the Sentinel Museum and many local shops), Eureka is also a good place to break a journey. The most comfortable place to stay is the historic **Jackson House** hotel (775/237-5577) on Main Street, which also has a bar and restaurant. More good food is served at the **Owl Club** cafe and casino, down Main Street.

Ely marks the junction of US-50 and our US-93 route, which is covered beginning on page 114.

Ely

Ely (pop. 4,756; pronounced E-lee, as in Robert) is a sprawling crossroads community where US-6, US-50, and US-93 all intersect. For nearly 100 years Ely was a boomtown flush with the wealth from the massive Kennecott-owned Liberty Pit copper mines, Nevada's largest and longest-lived mining venture, which produced over a billion dollars' worth of ore while employing nearly 10,000 people at its peak during the 1950s.

The state-run Nevada Commission on Tourism sponsors a tongue-in-cheek promotion in which travelers along US-50 can earn themselves a certificate saying **"I Survived the Loneliest Road in America"** by getting their official US-50 travel passports stamped at locations along the highway. For details, contact the commission at Capitol Complex, Carson City, NV 89710 (800/237-0774).

Mountains of mine tailings tower over US-50 west of Ely, and five miles west of town there's a turn marked Historic Mining Viewpoint that leads south along a part-paved, part-dirt road for just over a mile to a viewpoint high above the huge crater where hundreds of tons of ore were dug. The Magma mining company is currently leaching the metal out of the previously discarded ore, and has encircled the viewing area with historical photographs of the old mining operations, alongside chunks of rock— all of which are labeled to explain their geologic makeup.

After the mines closed down in 1982, the railway that had shuttled pay dirt from the mines to the smelter was abandoned—track, stock, and depot. The entire operation was turned into **Nevada Northern Railway Museum** (Wed.-Sun. 9 AM-4 PM; $3; 775/289-2085) in 1985, and now you can take a 90-minute, 14-mile loop tour of the rail yards aboard the Ghost Train, a 1910 Baldwin Steamer. The train leaves from the depot at the north end of East 11th Street and uses a ton of coal and 1,000 gallons of water; trips are offered weekends only, and tickets cost around $15.

Ely's other main stop is the **White Pine Public Museum**, 2000 Aultman Street (US-50), which has a wide-ranging collection of minerals, mining implements, and Pony Express memorabilia on display.

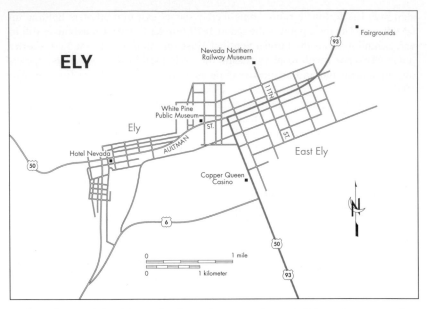

Apart from mining history (and motels, gas stations, and the only supermarket for the next 250 miles!) there's not a whole lot to Ely. The heart of town is a neon-rich few blocks of Aultman Street (US-50) west of the US-93 junction, centering upon the landmark **Hotel Nevada** (775/289-6665), with its giant cowboy and neon-lit slot machines. Inside there are real (as opposed to video) slot machines, pool tables, a cafe, and a bar with nightly live music. Rooms upstairs start at a bargain $25. Another place worth stopping at is the **Copper Queen Casino** (775/289-4883), on the south side of Ely, where pricey motel rooms open directly onto a lobby shared by banks of slot machines and a small swimming pool. Also nice is the quiet **Four Sevens Motel**, a block north of Aultman at 500 High Street (775/289-4747); chains have arrived more recently, in the form of a Holiday Inn and a Motel 6.

For food, Ely has three coffee shop-style restaurants, plus franchised fast food, including a newish McDonald's. A better bet: down a milk shake at the soda fountain inside **Economy Drug**, Aultman and 7th Streets.

The route east toward Great Basin National Park is an official "scenic route," rolling across sagebrush plains and climbing over the Schell Creek and Snake mountain ranges through dense groves of pine and juniper.

The world's oldest known bristlecone pine, dubbed **Prometheus,** was cut down on Wheeler Peak by the U.S. Forest Service in 1964, which discovered too late that, at 4,900 years old, the tree had been the oldest living thing on earth. A cross-section of the trunk is displayed at the Bristlecone Convention Center, 150 6th Street in Ely.

Ely's lively **KELY 1230 AM** plays "the best of everything": oldies from the 1950s and 1960s, plus Rush Limbaugh all morning long.

Connors Pass and Major's Place

East of Ely, US-50, spliced together with US-6 and US-93 into a single two-lane highway, continues for 25 miles before crossing the narrow waist of the Schell Creek Range at 7,722-foot Connors Pass. As you ascend toward the pass, the air cools and freshens, the single-leaf piñon and Utah juniper appear and increase and, cresting the summit, the mighty Snake Range, including 13,061-foot Wheeler Peak, comes into view.

East of the pass, at Major's Place (where there's a roadhouse), US-93 cuts due south, heading 80 long, solitary miles to the next contact with humans at Pioche, while US-50 heads east toward Great Basin National Park.

Great Basin National Park

Approaching Nevada from the east, travelers are greeted by the towering silhouette of **Wheeler Peak**, at 13,063 feet the second highest and most impressive mountain in the state; from the west, similarly sheer escarpments tower over lush green open range for miles and miles along US-50. In 1987 the 77,000 acres around Wheeler Peak

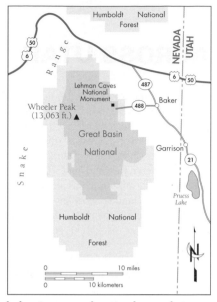

were designated Great Basin National Park, but its remote location has made it one of the least-visited national parks in the United States. Hikers and campers will have no trouble finding solitude amidst the alpine forests, ancient bristlecone pines, glacial lakes, and small ice field.

Thanks to the well-maintained road climbing to over 10,000 feet, the wilderness areas are easily accessible to people willing to take a short hike, though many visitors go no farther than the park's centerpiece, **Lehman Caves**. Geological forces have been sculpting Lehman Caves for roughly 70 million years, but they weren't noticed until homesteader Absalom Lehman stumbled upon the small entrance to the caves in 1885. They were declared a national monument in 1922, and since then only minor improvements have been made, leaving the mind-bending limestone formations alone—no flashy light-and-sound show, just hundreds of delicate stalagmites, stalactites, helictites, aragonites, and the like. Hour-long guided tours ($4) are conducted at intervals throughout the day; on summer evenings at 6 PM there's a memorable candlelight tour. Tours leave from the small **visitor center** (daily 8 AM-5 PM, longer in summer; 775/234-7331), which has details of hiking and camping as well as exhibits on Great Basin wildlife—from birds and bats to mountain lions. There's even a small summer-only cafe.

If you're not camping and self-relying, or if you are and want a break, the nearest food and drink are at the foot of the park in tiny **Baker** (pop. 55), which boasts one gas station, the seven-room **Silverjack Motel** (775/234-7323), and the friendly, homey **Outlaw Cafe and Bar**, which serves breakfast, burritos, and beer from early till late.

Back on US-50, just west of the Utah/Nevada border stands the **Border Inn** cafe/gas station/motel, open 24 hours a day (775/234-7300). Apart from Baker, the only other reliable services are in Ely, 70 miles west, or in Delta, 85 miles to the east, so pass by at your peril.

ACROSS UTAH

For most of the way across Utah, the high-speed I-70 freeway has replaced US-50, but if you have time to take a couple of detours you'll be rewarded with some of the most incredible scenery in the world. Most of this is concentrated in the southeastern corner of the state, where a number of national parks, including Canyonlands and Arches, preserve the sandstone "Canyon Country" of the Colorado Plateau. In the west a few old mining towns stand amidst the arid desert of the Great Basin. Distances are huge and services few and far between, but if you have the time and plan ahead, this is one of the most satisfying and memorable corners of the country.

Delta

About 85 miles east of the Nevada border, the landscape changes suddenly from barren desert to lush pastures around the town of Delta, which is irrigated by the green Sevier River. Delta bills itself the "Gateway to Great Basin National Park," and it does have a **Best Western** and other motels, gas stations, and a large supermarket —but very little else to attract visitors. One place worth a stop is the small **Great Basin Museum** (Tues.-Sat. 10 AM-4 PM; free), a block north of Main Street at 328 W. 100 North Street. The museum features mineral, arrowheads and local history exhibits, including a small display of artifacts relating to **Topaz Camp,** an internment camp set up in the desert west of Delta by the U.S. government to imprison Americans of Japanese descent during WW II.

From Delta, US-50 officially cuts southeast across I-15, linking up with I-70 at Salina for the trip east to Grand Junction. Our route, however, follows US-6 (old US-50) toward the Great Salt Lake area, then east over the Wasatch Front, rejoining official US-50 (now I-70) at Green River.

Little Sahara Recreation Area

From Delta, the route follows the Sevier River northwest, racing across the featureless desert for 32 miles before reaching the well-posted turnoff north to the Little Sahara Recreation Area.

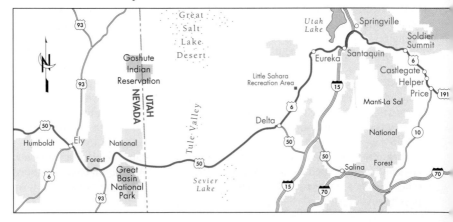

Visible from the highway four miles north of US-6, the Little Sahara Recreation Area holds 60,000 acres of sand dunes and sagebrush flats, the prettiest parts of which are preserved for hikers and campers, though motorcyclists and ATVers can overwhelm any sense of peace and tranquillity, turning it into a campground from hell.

Eureka

Fifty miles east of Delta, 20 miles west of the I-15 freeway, the weather-beaten town of Eureka (pop. 750) climbs steeply up surrounding mountainsides at the heart of the once-thriving Tintic Mining District, where as recently as the 1930s thousands of miners dug millions of dollars' worth of gold, silver, copper, and lead out of the ground every year. Now the massive wooden head frames of long-closed mine shafts stand high above the houses and prefab trailers that cling to the slopes, while fading signs advertise abandoned businesses along Main Street. The one place you can get a bite to eat is **Joe's Diner**, 546 E. Main Street.

Though diehard residents still speak of plans to reopen one or more of the mines, prosperity seems a distant dream in Eureka, and while it's not quite a ghost town, it is well on its way there. The glory days are recounted in the small **Tintic Mining Museum**, next to city hall on Main Street, and at the west edge of town a historical plaque stands alongside the heavy timber head frame of the Bullion-Beck Mine, one of the area's most productive.

Santaquin and Springville

Heading east from Eureka, our route bends across rock-strewn sagebrush hills around the southern shore of Utah Lake toward the I-15 freeway. Utah Lake, which is freshwater in contrast to the briny expanse of the Great Salt Lake to the north, used to be much larger than it is now, before so much of it was diverted to water the apple, peach, and cherry orchards that line US-6 around Santaquin—whose three gas stations are the last reliable source of fuel for westbound travelers until Delta, 70 miles to the southwest.

From Santaquin, follow the I-15 freeway north to Springville, where you'll find one of the cleanest and most comfortable truck stops in the U.S., the **Mountain Springs Travel Center** (801/489-3641), which, besides good food, cheap gas, and $40-a-night rooms, offers free showers with every fill-up.

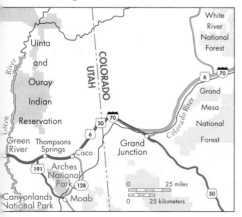

From Springville, the Salt Lake City megalopolis stretches north along I-15 for nearly 100 miles, from Provo to Ogden.

Detour: Salt Lake City

With no other city for some 500 miles in any direction, Salt Lake City (pop. 160,000), an hour north of Springville via the I-15 freeway, seems like the oasis it naturally is. Taking its name from the undrinkable alkaline Great Salt Lake, the city is actually blessed with abundant fresh water, thanks to

Salt Lake City isn't exactly a gourmet paradise, but it does have one great road food stop: **Bill and Nada's Cafe,** 479 S. 600 Street East, an all-night diner with a truly great jukebox and greasy-spoon food that ranges from incredible to indigestible.

The mountains above Salt Lake City hold some of the country's best ski resorts (Park City, Alta, and Snowbird), which together will host the Winter Olympics in 2002.

the rain- and snow-making properties of the Wasatch Range, which rises knife-like to the east. Founded by Mormons in 1847, and effectively controlled by Mormon elders ever since, Salt Lake City is not exactly a thrilling place, but it's clean and pleasant enough to merit a detour. Most of what there is to see has to do with the Mormons, better known as the Church of Latter-day Saints, which has its worldwide HQ at **Temple Square** downtown. (Street numbers and addresses are measured from here, not the nearby State Capitol, which goes to show just how predominant the LDS church is in local life.) On the west side of Temple Square are the amazing genealogical libraries the Mormons maintain; a block east of Temple Square is the **Beehive House,** preserved as it was in the 1850s, when Brigham Young lived here. In the basement of the Capitol, a history museum displays the amazing **Mormon Meteor,** the 18-cylinder, 750-horsepower machine in which Ab Jenkins set the land speed record at Bonneville Salt Flats in 1931.

For more information on Salt Lake City, contact the **visitors bureau,**180 S. Temple Street (801/521-2868).

victims of the 1900 Scofield mine disaster

Soldier Summit

Heading east from Springville, the drive along US-6 (old US-50) up and over 7,477-foot Soldier Summit is truly beautiful, as the two-lane highway passes through bright red sandstone canyons along the stark eastern side of the towering Wasatch Range, then twists alongside pines and cottonwoods to the crest. The summit itself, where there's a handy gas station-cum-general store (their motto: "Radiators Filled, Bladders Emptied"), marks the boundary between the Colorado River drainage and the Great Basin.

Castlegate and Helper

Dropping down from Soldier Summit, US-6/191 winds along the Price River through Castlegate, a steeply walled sandstone canyon lined with working coal mines, many of which you see from the highway. While most now rely on heavy machinery to do the dirty work of digging out the coal, the Castlegate area has been the site of the two worst mining disasters in Utah history: 173 men and boys killed in a 1924 explosion, and another 200 killed at nearby Scofield on May Day, 1900.

Tiny Helper (pop. 2,148), at the downstream edge of Castlegate, six miles northwest of Price, is a classic railroad town preserved almost unchanged for nearly a century. The six-block downtown area, fronting onto the tracks, includes so many turn-of-the-century brick- and stone-fronted buildings that it's been declared a National Historic District—though the sad truth is that most of these have stood abandoned since the railroad switched to diesel power in the 1950s. Before that,

BUTCH CASSIDY AND THE HOLE-IN-THE-WALL GANG

Long before Paul Newman played him alongside Robert Redford's Sundance Kid, Butch Cassidy was one of the great outlaw legends of the Wild West. Thanks to his habit of sharing the proceeds from his crimes with the widows and children of men killed or ruined by bankers and cattle barons, Butch Cassidy earned a reputation as the "Robin Hood of the Wild West." That, plus the fact he never killed anyone while committing his crimes, gained him popular admiration from the cowboys, miners, and homesteading pioneers among whom he worked his trade.

Born Robert Leroy Parker to a family of Mormon farmers in Beaver, Utah, on Friday the 13th of April, 1866, the man who came to be known as Butch Cassidy spent his youth as a ranch hand in Utah, Colorado, and southern Wyoming. The first major crime attributed to Butch Cassidy is the robbery of a bank in Telluride in 1889, which netted him and his three accomplices some $20,000. From 1894 to 1896 he was imprisoned in Wyoming for cattle theft, and following this he joined up with Harry Longabaugh (a.k.a "The Sundance Kid") and the rest of the gang. Together they robbed over a dozen banks, trains, and stagecoaches throughout the West, netting an estimated $350,000 in five years. One of their many daring heists was the daylight robbery of a coal-mining company in Castlegate, Utah, in April 1897; while the payroll was being taken from a train, Butch simply grabbed the satchel and rode off in a cloud of dust, $9,000 richer.

According to the movie and many others, Butch and Sundance died in 1909, in a shoot-out in South America. But some people (including his sister, who lived until the 1970s) say that Butch survived to a ripe old age, living in Spokane, Washington under the name William T. Phillips until his death in 1937.

Helper was a buzzing boomtown; it earned its name in 1892 when the Denver and Rio Grande Railroad built a depot and roundhouse here to hold the "helper" engines that were added to trains to help push them over Soldier Summit, 25 miles to the west.

Though the line of boarded-up hotels, bars, and pool halls along Main Street may not encourage you to linger, the excellent **Western Mining and Railroad Museum** (Mon.-Sat. 9 AM-5 PM in summer; donations) at 296 S. Main Street contains enough raw material on railroading and coal mining, not to mention the region's diverse immigrant cultures, to keep you occupied for an hour or more. There's also a brief display recounting the exploits of Butch Cassidy and his gang, who raided banks and rustled cattle throughout the region in the late 1890s, hiding out in surrounding hills. Behind the museum, an outdoor lot displays some of the giant machines used in the coal mines, which unlike the railroad still employ a large number of local people.

The one Main Street business showing any sign of life last time I passed through was the **Sunshine Video and Tanning Salon**, at the middle of town. Along with the double-barreled services suggested by its name, it also has a soda fountain serving up milk shakes ($1.50) and a pool table. Other Helper storefronts seem to serve as "phantom galleries," displaying some surprisingly lively art works in the windows of otherwise dead spaces.

Price

The largest city in eastern Utah, Price (pop. 8,712) is located roughly midway between the I-15 and I-70 freeways, 65 miles northwest of Green River. Coal is so prevalent in the area that roadcuts reveal solid black seams, but the town itself is lush and green, thanks to irrigation provided by the Price River, which flows south from town into the Green and Colorado Rivers.

Coal mining, and to a lesser extent agriculture, still power Price, and you won't miss much by following the bypass around the town center. That said, the small **Prehistoric Museum** at 155 E. Main Street (daily 9 AM-6 PM in summer; donations) is worth a look for its extensive displays on the Native American cultures of the region, and for its range of full-sized dinosaur skeletons, including a stegosaurus and a mammoth. Many of these were reassembled from fossils collected from the **Cleveland-Lloyd Dinosaur Quarry**, 30 miles south of town.

Price also has all the highway services travelers might need: numerous gas stations, places to eat, and six motels, including a **Days Inn.**

Southwest from Price, bound for Green River and the I-70 freeway, US-6/191 runs alongside the busy Denver and Rio Grande mainline railroad through a region of arid plateaus highlighted every few miles by brilliantly colorful, weirdly sculpted sandstone mesas. Though barren and empty at first glance, the region is particularly rich in two things: coal mines and, more unusually, dinosaur bones. (Why do you think they call them fossil fuels?)

Green River

Straddling the eponymous river on the north side of the I-70 freeway, Green River (pop. 744) makes a handy base for exploring southeastern Utah, but it offers very little in and of itself. The town holds numerous 24-hour gas stations, a couple of good places to eat (try the **Tamarisk**, overlooking the Green River at 870 E. Main Street), and a handful of motels, including a nice **Best Western**, a **Motel 6**, and the small **Mancos Rose Motel** at 20 W. Main Street (435/564-9660), which has the cheapest rooms.

Even if you don't need fuel, food, or a place to sleep, Green River offers one very compelling reason to stop: the spacious modern **John Wesley Powell River History Museum** (daily 8 AM 8 PM in summer; 9 AM-5 PM rest of the year; $2). In 1869 Powell and his crew were the first to travel the length of the Colorado River through the Grand Canyon; though the legendary explorers started their epic adventure in Green River, Wyoming, not here in Utah, the spacious modern museum, on old US-50 along the east bank of the Green River, is the best single repository of artifacts relating to their feat. The collection concentrates on Powell in particular and on waterborne transport in general, but there are also displays chronicling the adventures of other early explorers (including Juan de Oñate in 1605 and the Dominguez and Escalante expedition of 1776), and of fur-trappers, miners, and Mormons—all of whom contributed to the exploration and mapping of the American West.

To get some sense of what Powell and crew experienced, take a raft, canoe, or kayak trip down the Green or Colorado Rivers. Dozens of outfitters offer equipment rentals, shuttles, and guided trips, from all-day to week-long tours. For details, contact the Grand County visitors bureau (435/564-3526), which has an office in the Powell museum.

Canyonlands National Park

The largest and least-visited park in the Southwest, Canyonlands National Park is both breathtakingly beautiful and totally inhospitable, an arid wilderness of high plateaus and deep canyon carved by the mighty Green and Colorado Rivers. The park is divided into three very different areas, each of which is at least a 100-mile drive from the others, so it pays to plan ahead. The most popular section, the Island-in-the-Sky, stands high above the confluence of the rivers and gives the most sweeping panoramas—100 miles in every direction from over 6,000 feet above sea level. South of the rivers, **The Needles** district holds 50 square miles of spires, arches, and canyons and is the best place to undertake lengthy hikes. One trail leads from the end of the road, where there's a primitive campground, down to the mouth of Cataract Canyon on the Colorado River. The third and final area of Canyonlands, **The Maze**, is west of the rivers and virtually inaccessible.

Uranium mined from Temple Mountain, west of Canyonlands, was used to make the first atomic bombs.

There's a **visitor center** near the entrances to Island-in-the-Sky and The Needles. The Canyonlands headquarters in Moab, 125 W. 200 S (435/259-7164), also has extensive information. Adjacent to Canyonlands are two state parks, **Dead Horse Point** in the north and **Newspaper Rock** in the south, both of which are well worth a look.

Arches National Park

Taking its name from the hundreds of naturally formed sandstone arches scattered here, Arches National Park is the most feature-packed of southeast Utah's national parks. Ranging in size from around three feet to nearly 300 feet in span, the arches are the result of erosion over millions of years, the same agent that formed the thousands of brilliantly colored spires, pinnacles, and canyons that cover southeast Utah. Piñon pines and junipers add a splash of green to the red and brown backdrop, but mostly what you see are red stone and blue sky—lots and lots of both.

A word of warning: Even if you're not planning to venture from your car, it's a good idea to carry at least a gallon of water per person when traveling in the desert.

The park's highlights can be easily reached from the 20-mile paved road that runs through the center of the park. A **visitor center** (daily 9 AM-5 PM; 435/259-8161) at the entrance, east of US-191 and five miles north of Moab, has maps, pamphlets, and displays on the geology and natural history of Arches.

From the entrance, the road switchbacks uphill past the sandstone skyline of **Park Avenue** before reaching a turnoff east to **The Windows**, whose dense concen-

JOHN WESLEY POWELL AND THE CANYONS OF THE COLORADO RIVER

Of the many chronicles of the exploration of America's western frontier, few have stood the test of time better than those written by John Wesley Powell, who led the first expedition down the Colorado River through the canyons of Utah and Arizona. Until Powell's journey, the entire Colorado Plateau region, roughly 200 miles wide and some 500 miles long, was a large blank space on the map, simply labeled "Unexplored."

Powell's life story reads like something out of Horatio Alger. Born in upstate New York in 1834, "Wes" Powell grew up in the Midwest and attended various frontier colleges where he taught himself the fundamentals of geography, geology, and other natural sciences. Volunteering for service in the Civil War, he rose to the rank of major despite losing the lower part of his right arm at the Battle of Shilo. After the war he took up a position as professor of geology in Illinois and led summer research trips to the Rocky Mountains in search of fossils.

In 1869, thanks to his wartime friendship with then-President Grant, he secured a small measure of federal funding for an ambitious survey of the Colorado River and its as-yet unexplored canyons. Powell organized a party of 10 men, who set off in four boats from the newly completed Union Pacific railroad at Green River, Wyoming, on May 24, 1869. Three months, 900 miles, one mutiny, and many near-disasters later, Powell and party emerged at the mouth of the Grand Canyon, the first people to pass through the canyon by river. To this day, Powell's enthusiastic and painstakingly accurate accounts of these magnificent red-rock canyons are the most readable and evocative descriptions of the region—required reading for any interested traveler.

Delicate Arch at Arches National Park

tration of arches and spires is required viewing, no matter how little time you have. Four miles beyond The Windows, a dirt road leads east to **Wolfe Ranch**, trailhead for **Delicate Arch**, the park's most postcard-worthy feature, a three-mile roundtrip hike. Three miles farther along the main road, **Fiery Furnace** is an otherwordly collection of narrow canyons, which despite the name is quite cool and shady; park rangers give guided walks here throughout the summer. At the far end of the road there's a first-come, first-served **Devil's Garden campground** and a two-mile trail leading to **Devil's Garden**, where you can see **Landscape Arch**, the park's largest (and second largest in the world)—291 feet across and 105 feet high.

The annual **Fat Tire Festival,** held the week before Halloween, brings mountain bikers from all over the world to Moab.

Moab

Driving across southern Utah, you have two main options: race along I-70 and get somewhere else in a hurry, or slow down and search out the truly unforgettable scenery the state has to offer. One of the best places to base yourself for an exploration of the region is Moab (pop. 3,971), an old uranium mining town that's located 30 miles south of the freeway, surrounded by two national parks (Arches and Canyonlands) and hundreds of thousands of acres of desert wilderness.

Thanks to *Outside* magazine and the recent mania for outdoor athleticism, in the past five years Moab has experienced a massive tourist boom—Edward Abbey, cantankerous poet of the Southwest who wrote his first book, *Desert Solitaire,* about a season he spent at nearby Arches National Park, would probably turn in

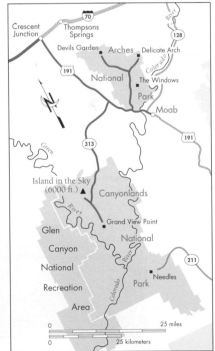

his grave if he saw the gangs of Lycra-clad mountain bikers milling around Moab's Main Street T-shirt stores and brew pubs. But despite the addition of fast-food franchises and hundreds of new motel rooms, Moab is still a dusty little back-of-beyond hamlet, albeit one that gives easy access to the wilds nearby.

If you're not prepared to camp out in the backcountry (if you are, see Arches and Canyonlands for details), Moab has the usual franchised motels, including a **Days Inn**, a **Travelodge**, a **Ramada**, and a **Super 8**, plus local ones like the **Apache**, 166 South 400 E (435/259-5727 or 800/228-6882), where John Wayne slept while filming *Rio Bravo* here in 1950. Budget travelers will appreciate the **Lazy Lizard Hostel**, 1213 S. Hwy-191 (435/259-6057), which costs $7 for a bed but lacks air conditioning; showers for non-guests cost just $2.

Eat healthy veggie fare on the patio of **Honest Ozzie's**, open daily 7 AM-10 PM in summer at 60 N. 100 West Street, or enjoy a gourmet dinner at the upscale **Center Cafe** at 92 E. Center Street. Meat-eaters will love the **Fat City Smoke House**, serving up sausages and BBQ at 36 S. 100 West Street, or the **Cattleman's Restaurant**, a 24-hour coffee shop a mile south of town at 1991 S. Main Street (US-191).

For more information on visiting the Moab area, contact the **Grand County Travel Council**, 125 E. Center Street (435/259-1370 or 800/635-6622), or stop by the very helpful **Moab Information Center** (daily 8 AM-9 PM; 435/259-8825) at Main and Center in the middle of town. There you can pick up a free copy of *Moab Happenings*, which lists accommodations, restaurants, local events, and recreation opportunities—from mountain-bike trails to river-rafting expeditions.

The prettiest route east from Moab, Hwy-128, winds along the broad and brown Colorado River past 25 miles of swimming, kayaking, and camping spots. Hwy-128 links up with I-70 23 miles west of the Colorado border at junction 212, near the former sheep-ranching center of **Cisco**, a ghostly old US-50 crossroads abandoned after completion of the interstate, where old gas station buildings are slowly evolving into a post-apocalyptic art installation.

Fifteen miles south of Moab along US-191, one of Utah's oddest attractions is the **Hole 'n The Rock** *(daily 9 AM-6 PM; $2.50; 435/686-2250) a 5,000-square-foot home carved out of a sandstone cliff over a 20-year period, beginning in the 1940s, by Albert and Gladys Christensen. Now open to tourists, the site also includes a large carving of FDR's face.*

For westbound travelers, there's a helpful Utah state **Welcome Center** *on I-70 at Thompsons Springs, 39 miles west of the Colorado border.*

ACROSS COLORADO

Driving across southern Colorado on US-50 takes you through almost every landscape landlocked North America has to offer. From the geological wonderland of the Colorado River plateau, which stretches west into Utah, the route climbs up and over the 13,000-foot Rocky Mountains, which form a formidable wall down the center of the state. Continuing east, the alpine meadows, deeply etched river canyons, and snow-covered peaks of the southern Rockies fade away into the flat, agricultural prairies that stretch east across the middle of the country. While there is considerable ranching and farming, outdoor recreation—fishing, hiking, skiing, and mountain biking—is the basis for the economy, and the region is well provided with tourist facilities, especially in the mountainous middle.

Grand Junction

Thirty miles east of the Utah border, US-50 diverges from the high-speed I-70 freeway at the city of Grand Junction (pop. 29,034) on the Colorado River. After all the desert that surrounds it, Grand Junction feels much bigger than you'd expect, with its thriving old downtown, complete with cobblestoned streets, odd bits of outdoor sculpture, great antique shops—and tons of free parking. Catering to passing traffic, Grand Junction's I-70 frontage has all the motels and places to eat you could want, but downtown holds one really nice older place, the **Hotel Melrose** at 337 Colorado Avenue (970/242-9636), which has clean and comfortable rooms from $20, $25 with private bathroom—just look for the red neon sign.

More complete listings are available from the **visitor center** off I-70 at exit 31 (970/244-1480).

Like the rest of western Colorado and eastern Utah, the Grand Junction area is rich in two things: the scenic splendor of rivers and red-rock canyons, and fossilized dinosaurs, a fine array of which are on display in the **Museum of Western Colorado** (Tues.-Sat. 10 AM-5 PM; $2), downtown at 248 S. 4th Street and in their "Dinosaur Valley" faux fossil beds, two blocks away at 362 Main Street.

Colorado National Monument

Rising nearly 2,000 feet above the Colorado River, southwest of Grand Junction, the brilliantly colored cliffs of Colorado National Monument are simply impossible to miss. Deep canyons, alive with piñon pines and cottonwood trees, nestle at the foot of sheer rock walls, at the top of which you get panoramic views over miles and miles of the Colorado Plateau. The 23-mile-long **Rim Rock Drive** winds along the tops of the cliffs, giving quick access to numerous trails for up-close looks at the various layers and hues of sandstone and shale, which have eroded over the eons into masses of sculpted stone.

To reach the monument from US-50 in downtown Grand Junction, follow Grand Avenue west to Broadway (Hwy-340) across the river; the monument's main entrance is four miles southeast of town, and there's another, off I-70 exit 19, at the northern end of the park. Both are very well signed, and an entry fee of $5 per car is charged, though cyclists brave enough to tackle the steep climb are usually waved through for free.

There's a large **visitor center** (daily 9 AM-5 PM; 970/858-3617) at the main entrance, and a basic **campground** four miles from the northern entrance to the monument, near the top of the Book Cliffs.

Delta

From Grand Junction, US-50 briefly becomes a four-lane freeway, then reverts to two lanes following the Gunnison River as far as Delta (pop. 3,789). The half-dozen building-sized murals of elk and local agricultural products support Delta's claim that it is "The City of Murals," but the biggest attraction to travelers is the reconstructed **Fort Uncompaghre** (10 AM-4 PM Wed.-Sun.; $3), at the confluence of the Gunnison and Uncompaghre Rivers on the northwest side of town. One of the best and most authentic "living history" museums in the country, the city-sponsored fort re-creates the lifestyles of trappers and traders who first settled in the western Rocky Mountains in the early 1820s. Ed Maddox, the fort's well-versed live-in guide, takes you around the small palisaded compound, discussing the historical context of the fur trade while demonstrating (and encouraging visitors to take part in) the arts and crafts necessary for frontier life: metalworking, tanning, and tomahawk-throwing, not to mention hunting, shooting, and fishing.

The New Deal-era documentary photography project, which included Walker Evans and Dorothea Lange and which provides most of the frontispieces to the chapters in this book, was directed by **Roy Stryker,** who spent his youth on a ranch outside Montrose.

Delta has its fair share of motels (including a **Best Western**) and fast-food places. It's also home to a classic piece of roadside Americana: the log-and-stone cabins of the **Westways Court Motel,** 1030 Main Street (970/874-4415) on US-50 in the center of town.

Southeast of Delta, US-50 runs along the banks of the Uncompaghre River, passing lots of farms and one very large Louisiana-Pacific lumber mill at Olathe, midway to Montrose.

Montrose

With the San Juan Mountains standing out to the south, and Black Canyon just up the road, Montrose, a farming community of some 9,000 souls that spreads from the heart of the fertile Uncompaghre (pronounced un-com-PA-gray) Valley, makes a good base for exploring the region. Though the town itself is less charming than many others in the region (it's roughly twice as big but only half as interesting as Delta, for example), it does have plenty of motels and places to eat, especially along US-50 east of downtown.

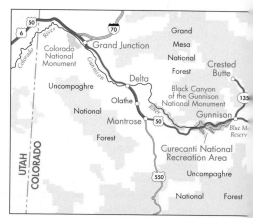

Eight miles east of Montrose, Hwy-347 turns off north toward the Black Canyon of the Gunnison National Monument.

Montrose

Black Canyon of the Gunnison National Monument

Some of the hardest and oldest rocks on earth form the sheer walls of 2,000-foot-deep Black Canyon of the Gunnison, the deepest and most impressive gorge in the state. The river cutting through the canyon falls faster than any other in North America—dropping 2,150 feet in under 50 miles—and the canyon bottom is so rugged that there are no trails along it. Unless you're a serious mountaineer, you'll have to content yourself with looking down into it from the rim, which is accessible on the north side via Hwy-92, and from US-50 on the south via Hwy-347. The **visitor center** (daily 9 AM-6 PM in summer; 970/249-7036) on the south rim provides details on hiking trails and camping, and can tell you more than you ever wanted to know about the canyon's unique geology: for instance, unlike the Grand Canyon with its layers of exposed rock, the Black Canyon is basically one solid hunk of stone.

Curecanti National Recreation Area

Upstream from the Black Canyon turnoff, US-50 parallels the Gunnison River, renowned for its excellent trout and landlocked salmon fishing, though sadly the once-raging waters have been backed up behind dams to form a series of reservoirs, jointly managed as the Curecanti National Recreation Area (970/641-3128). Midway along, the highway crosses Blue Mesa Dam, from where a scenic detour, Hwy-92, cuts off north around the Black Canyon of the Gunnison National Monument.

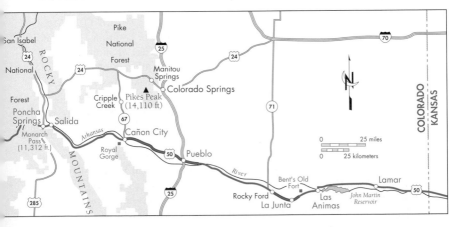

Gunnison and Crested Butte

A crossroads cattle town with a rapidly-growing recreational aspect and the only airport for miles, Gunnison (pop. 4,636) is made livelier than many Colorado towns by the presence of Western State College, whose students were responsible for the huge "W" that fills a mountainside north of town. To get a feel for Gunnison, stop by the lively **Steaming Bean** coffeehouse, downtown off US-50 at the Hwy-135 junction. Motels, including a **Days Inn**, a **Super 8**, and an **Econolodge**, line up along US-50, making Gunnison a handy base for exploring the region.

If you're taken with the scenery around Gunnison and want to see more, head north along Hwy-135 and the Gunnison River to the area's skiing and mountain-biking center, Crested Butte (pop. 898), 25 miles away. As in Telluride and Aspen, this 100-year-old gold-mining camp won a second lease on life thanks to tourism, though compared to other Colorado places Crested Butte is low-key and somewhat off the beaten path. Skiers in search of solitude flock here in winter to cruise the 1,100-plus acres of Mount Crested Butte (970/349-2222 or 800/544-8448), while in summer Crested Butte is a mountain bike mecca, with miles and miles of mining roads and single-track trails winding through the mountains. The town also has some of the best restaurants in the state, according to *The Denver Post* and others. Start the day at the **Bakery Cafe**, at 3rd and Elk Streets downtown, and recharge your batteries with a burger and a beer or two at the **Wooden Nickel**, nearby at 222 Elk Street. A whole range of places can be found within a block or two, including the **Idlespur Brewpub**, 226 Elk Avenue, and the inventive (and expensive) French country cuisine of **Le Bosquet**, on Elk and 2nd.

Three blocks north of Elk Avenue, the **HI Crested Butte International Hostel**, 615 Teocalli Avenue (970/349-0588), has dorms beds for $14 in summer, $21 in winter.

For further information, contact the **chamber of commerce** (970/349-6438 or 800/545-4505), on the south side of Crested Butte. For details on the plentiful **camping**, riding and hiking in the surrounding Gunnison National Forest, check in at the USFS **ranger station** in Gunnison (970/641-0471).

The first European explorers to pass through this part of the Rockies were the Spanish missionaries **Domínguez and Escalante,** in 1776.

Some 75 miles southwest of Poncha Springs, the potato-farming town of Monte Vista is home to the **Movie Manor,** a drive-in movie theater, restaurant, and Best Western motel at 2860 W. US-160 (719/852-5921).

Monarch Pass and Poncha Springs

East of Gunnison, the landscape changes swiftly as US-50, and a few masochistic cyclists, climb steeply through a gorgeous alpine landscape of meadows and cattle ranches toward 11,312-foot Monarch Pass. The pass marks the highest point on US-50 and straddles the Continental Divide: the 30 feet of annual snowfall on the east side of the pass end up in the Atlantic, while (in theory, at least) moisture falling farther west makes its way to the Pacific. There's a ski and snowboarding area here in winter, and in summer you can ride a **tram** (daily 8 AM-6 PM; $5) or hike to a nearby summit for a 360-degree view over the Rocky and Sangre de Cristo Mountains.

At the eastern foot of Monarch Pass, the tiny town of Poncha Springs has a pair of places perfect for weary travelers: a truck stop featuring great Mexican food, and the historic **Jackson Hotel**, 6340 US-285 (719/539-4861), an 1870s stage stop that has hosted (or at least, claims to have hosted) every Wild West figure from Billy the Kid to Teddy Roosevelt. Rooms are a bargain, at around $40 a night.

Salida

Sitting alongside the Arkansas River east of Monarch Pass, Salida (pop. 4,737; elev. 7038) is a riverfront railroad town gradually switching over to the tourist trade. Close your eyes to the sprawl of Wal-Mart and McDonald's along US-50, and head a few blocks north to the historic downtown. Here, a half-dozen brick buildings along 1st Street house a slightly hippyish cafes—the **Laughing Ladies** and the **First Street Cafe** are both good bets—and outdoor supply shops, including **Headwaters,** 228 N. F Street (719/539-4506) right along the river, which rents and sells mountain bikes and kayaks and is the best source of information on the area's wealth of recreational opportunities. The comfortable **Manhattan Hotel** (719/539-3138), a B&B, shares the historic building. A new **Days Inn** and a slew of other places to sleep line US-50.

Every December, Salida lights up a tree on Christmas Mountain with 10,000 bulbs.

Salida Hot Springs, next to the visitors bureau on US-50 at Rainbow Avenue, is the largest in the state. The WPA-built indoor pool and baths are open year-round; call 719/539-6738 for times and prices.

East of Salida, river rafters can be seen riding the rapids of the Arkansas River for most of the next 45 miles. Steeply walled sandstone gorges alternate with broad meadows and sagebrush plains all the way to Royal Gorge and Cañon City.

Royal Gorge

It would be easy to object to the rampant commercialism of Royal Gorge (daily 7 AM-6 PM; $12), but if you don't mind seeing impressive works of humankind amidst a stupendous show of nature's prowess, I heartily recommend a visit. The gorge itself is unforgettable, its sheer red granite cliffs dropping over 1,000 feet straight down to the Arkansas River, and the experience is enhanced by a barrage of civil engineering feats, includ-

ing aerial trams, incline railways, and an impossibly delicate suspension bridge, all enabling visitors to experience the area in diverse ways. You can look down from the rim, dangle from a gondola across to the other side, and from there follow a short nature trail that offers good views of Pike's Peak. Walk back across the wooden planks of the bridge—which is the highest in the world, but feels like a rickety old seaside pier—then drop down on a funicular to the gorge's bottom, where you can stand alongside the raging river, listening to the roar or admiring the famous Denver and Rio Grande Railroad line that passes through the gorge, in places suspended out over the river from the solid rock walls.

The main problem with Royal Gorge, apart from the steep admission fee, is that to get there you have to run a gauntlet of some of the tackiest tourist traps in creation, worst of which is the self-proclaimed "Real Historic Buckskin Joe—Gunfights and Hangings Daily." Similarly hyped outfits line the well-marked, two mile-long road to Royal Gorge, which cuts south from US-50 eight miles west of Cañon City.

Cañon City

One of the last remaining Wild West towns in the lower 48 states, Cañon City (pop. 12,687) is carved out of the eastern flank of the Rocky Mountains. Over a mile high and surrounded by a ring of 14,000-foot peaks, Cañon City's short Main Street, a block north of US-50, is lined by workaday saddle shops, gun shops,

Cripple Creek's first newspaper office, 1892

From US-50, one of the West's most scenic (unpaved but easily passable) drives, Phantom Canyon Road, 25 miles west of Pueblo and seven miles east of Cañon City, winds north to the old mining camp, now prosperous gambling town, of **Cripple Creek.**

convicted cannibal Alferd Packer

According to the WPA *Guide to Colorado,* the poet **Joaquin Miller,** who served as mayor, judge, and minister in Cañon City's early days, wanted to change its name to Oreodelphia, to highlight the region's many gold mines. Local miners, however, protested, insisting that "the place is a canyon, and it's goin' to be ·called Cañon City."

All along US-50 west of Cañon City, you can see rafters racing along the wild Arkansas River. Many companies offer guided trips, including Arkansas River Tours (800/321-4352).

bookshops, and saloons (eight in four blocks!). But the local economy prospers not so much from tourism as from prisons: 14 in all, including Colorado's newest maximum-security penitentiary, nicknamed "Supermax," and its oldest, the **Territorial Prison** (daily 9 AM-5 PM; $3) at the west end of Main Street, in which 32 cells have been preserved as a somewhat gruesome but compelling museum. The $60 million Supermax prison holds the nation's most notorious inmates, including Oklahoma City bomber Timothy McVeigh, Ramzi Yousef, mastermind of the World Trade Center bombing, Unabomber Ted Kaczynski, and actor Woody Harrelson's alleged hit-man dad Charles; the Territorial Prison's most famous guest was Alferd Packer, a miner and Wild West gunslinger convicted of cannibalism and other crimes.

Despite the notoriety of its many prisons, Cañon City's main attraction is the surrounding scenery, particularly the views along **Skyline Drive**, accessible from just west of town. It's a three-mile, one-way drive across the top of an 800-foot hill, as close to riding a roller coaster as you're ever likely to get while inside a passenger car. Royal Gorge to the west (which the city owns and operates; see above) is another major draw, and Cañon City makes a good base for explorations, with a few moderately priced motels like the **Pioneer**, 201 Main Street (719/269-1745) next to the old prison, plus a **Days Inn**, and a **Best Western**. Best place for cheap food and drink is **The Owl**, 626 Main Street, a combo cigar store, soda fountain, diner, and pool hall at the heart of the lively Main Street business district north of US-50.

For further information, contact the **chamber of commerce** (719/275-2331 or 800/876-7922), at 403 Royal Gorge Boulevard, on US-50 at the center of town.

PIKE'S PEAK

The highest point you can drive to in the continental USA, Pike's Peak has been a road trip destination since 1901 when the first car (a two-cylinder Locomobile Steamer) made its way to the 14,110-foot summit. Opened as a toll road in 1915, the Pike's Peak Highway now winds its way to the top—climbing nearly 7,000 feet in under 20 miles, with no guardrails to comfort you or block the amazing 360-degree Rocky Mountain panorama. The road is now owned and operated by the city of Colorado Springs, which charges a $5 per person toll (daily 7 AM-6 PM, summer only); go early, before the clouds and haze build up, for the best long-distance views.

And if the views aren't enough, another good reason to climb Pike's Peak is that to get there you pass through the delightful old resort town of **Manitou Springs.** A National Historic District, Manitou Springs has all the grand hotels, hot springs, tourist traps, and cave tours you could want, plus my very favorite pinball arcade in the entire world—dozens of ancient machines in perfect working order, and still charging the same nickel or dime they did in the 1920s, 30s, and 40s.

North of Manitou Springs, the 1,350-acre **Garden of the Gods** (daily 5 AM-11 PM; free) is a photogenic geological outcrop of red sandstone spires, some rising to heights of 300 feet.

Pike's Peak and Manitou Springs are along US-24, just west of Colorado Springs. For more information, contact the **visitors bureau,** 354 Manitou Avenue (719/685-5089 or 800/642-2567).

Pueblo

At the foot of the mountains, 38 miles east of Cañon City and 150 miles west of the Kansas border, the heavily industrialized city of Pueblo (pop. 98,640) spreads to both sides of the Arkansas River. Colorado's third-largest city, Pueblo was founded by legendary black fur-trapper **Jim Beckwourth** in 1842, but the town really grew in the 1870s following the arrival of the railroad and the discovery nearby of vast amounts of coal. Steel mills, including some of the largest west of the Mississippi, still stand around the fringes of the pleasant, tree-lined downtown area, but Pueblo is increasingly more bucolic than brawny, and the historic areas are slowly filling up with artsy cafes, bookshops, and antique stores, especially along Union Avenue on the south side.

US-50, however, bypasses the town, crossing the I-25 freeway with its usual phalanx of motels, including a **Motel 6,** a **Holiday Inn** and a **Super 8,** and fast-food franchises. Don't be too put off by all this—stop at the **visitors bureau** (719/543-1742) on US-50 just west of I-25 and pick up listings and walking-tour maps of Pueblo's historic districts.

After a visit to the top of Pike's Peak in 1893, Katharine Lee Bates wrote the words to "America the Beautiful." Purple mountains majesty above the fruited plain, etc.

The **Pike's Peak Hill Climb** has been held around the 4th of July almost every year since 1916. Top Indy Car, NASCAR, and Formula One racers like Bobby Unser sometimes compete, hitting speeds of up to 100 mph on the twisting mountain road.

SANTA FE TRAIL

For over half a century, beginning in the 1820s and lasting until the railroads were completed in the 1880s, the Santa Fe Trail was the primary link between the U.S. and the Spanish and Mexican Southwest. Running from the Missouri River ports around present-day Kansas City, the trail angled along the banks of the Arkansas River, splitting west of what's now Dodge City into two routes: the Mountain Branch, which US-50 follows, and the quicker but more dangerous Cimarron Cut-off, across the arid plains of the Jornado del Muerto. The two branches rejoined before climbing the Sangre de Cristo Mountains into what was then, as it is now, the capital of the Southwest, Santa Fe.

Unlike many of the routes across the Wild West frontier, the Santa Fe Trail was established by commercial traders rather than emigrant pioneers, and travel along it was active in both directions: merchants from the U.S. brought manufactured goods by the wagon load, which they exchanged for Mexican silver. First blazed by trader William Becknell in 1821, the year the newly independent Republic of Mexico opened the border (which Spain had kept closed), the 750-mile-long trail was surveyed by the U.S. government in 1826, and traffic increased slowly until the Mexican-American War brought Santa Fe, and all the land in between, under U.S. control. Military forts were established to protect traders from the marauding Comanche and other native tribes; at the time of the Civil War commerce along the trail reached at peak, with over 5,000 wagons making the trek to Santa Fe, carrying over $50 million worth of trade goods. The extension of the railroads across the Great Plains in the 1870s diminished the importance of the trail, and by 1880, when the Santa Fe railroad reached Santa Fe itself, the trail became a part of history.

THE SANTA FE TRAIL

Though US-50 follows the Santa Fe Trail almost exactly, from Las Animas east to Kansas City, very little remains, apart from outposts like Bent's Fort and Fort Larned and a few all-but-invisible stretches of old wagon ruts. Numerous plaques mark historic sites, and it's still possible to get a powerful sense of what the trail might have been like—provided you take the time to park the car and walk even a few hundred yards in the footsteps that crossed here a century ago.

The following are some of the most evocative sites along the Santa Fe Trail, west to east.

Santa Fe, NM: The second-oldest city in North America, preserving a vivid taste of its Spanish, Mexican, and American past.

Bent's Old Fort, CO: A reconstructed adobe trading post along the banks of the Arkansas River in the Rocky Mountain foothills. See below for more.

Dodge City, KS: One of the best-preserved remnants of the original Santa Fe Trail wagon ruts stretches across the rolling farmlands just west of this Wild West landmark town.

Fort Larned, KS: A well-preserved U.S. Army fortress, intact since the 1850s and protecting a fine set of wagon ruts. See pages 695-696.

Council Grove, KS: The last American town on the trail west, hardly changed since the heyday of the trail. See page 690 for more.

Westport, MO: Now surrounded by suburban Kansas City, this was the real start of the trail from the 1840s on.

Independence, MO: The original start of the Santa Fe and the Oregon Trails, with a fine museum detailing the westward frontier movements. See page 702 for more.

Detour: Denver

Though it's 100 miles north of Pueblo via the I-25 freeway, Denver (pop. 281,000) has the biggest, newest, and coolest airport in the Rockies, which may make it a handy starting or stopping point. (The airport, which opened in 1996 and operated for a year without a fully functioning baggage system, is in the middle of nowhere, 25 miles northeast of town, at the end of its own freeway.)

On the west side of the Colorado State Capitol, a benchmark at the unlucky 13th step lets you stand exactly 5,280 feet above sea level—a mile high.

Other reasons to visit Denver include: the **U.S. Mint**, right downtown at 320 W. Colfax Avenue, where you can watch and hear coins being pressed into shape; **Coors Field**, lively home of the Colorado Rockies baseball team (303/ROCKIES or 303/762-5437); and **Lakeside Park**, off I-70 at 4601 Sheridan Boulevard (303/477-1621), a nifty old, summer-only amusement park with art deco architecture, a wooden Cyclone roller coaster, and other rides dating back to 1908.

A dozen miles west of La Junta, **Rocky Ford** is a small and quiet farming community that comes alive every August during a celebration of its nationally known cash crop, cantaloupes.

For details on these or anything else to do with Denver, contact the **visitors bureau**, 225 W. Colfax Avenue (303/892-1112 or 800/645-3446).

La Junta

For eastbound travelers La Junta (pop. 7,637), a busy railroad town on the banks of the Arkansas River, is where we begin tracing the historic Santa Fe Trail. The name La Junta, which means "the junction," is apt, since the town has long been a key crossroads, first on the Santa Fe Trail and now as the division between the main line and the Denver branch of the Santa Fe Railroad, and as the junction of US-50 and US-350. Besides gas stations and a good range of places to eat (Mexican restaurants are a particular strength, and **Christina's** on Colorado Avenue, a half-block south of US-50, is very popular), a two-screen movie theater, and an ancient-looking barber shop, La Junta also offers the excellent **Koshare Indian Museum** (Tues.-Sun. 9 AM-5 PM; $2), on the campus of Otero Junior College on the south side of town. Sleep cheap at the **Mid-Town Motel**, 215 E. 3rd Street (719/384-7741).

La Junta also marks the spot where the "Mountain Branch" of the Santa Fe Trail finally cuts away to the south, following what's now US-350 through the Comanche National Grassland and continuing over Raton Pass into New Mexico and on to Santa Fe. Eastbound travelers are in luck, as we follow this historic route all the way to the other side of Kansas City.

Bent's Old Fort

William Bent ran Bent's Fort on the Arkansas River from 1833 to 1848. Besides minding the store, Bent served as an unofficial ambassador to area tribes.

From La Junta, an interesting quick detour off US-50, Hwy-194 runs along the north bank of the Arkansas River to one of Colorado's most evocative historic sites, Bent's Old Fort (daily 8 AM-6 PM in summer, 9 AM-4 PM in winter; $2). It lies eight miles east of La Junta, or 15 miles west of Las Animas. From 1833, when it was built by the fur traders William and Charles Bent, until 1848, when war with Mexico and increasing unrest among the local Arapahoe, Apache, and Cheyenne tribes put an end to their business, Bent's Fort was the Southwest's most important outpost of white civilization and a stopping place for travelers, trappers, and explorers, including John C. Fremont, Francis Parkman, and just about every other Wild West luminary.

Though it was abandoned and left to decay for over 100 years, the large adobe fort has been authentically rebuilt by the National Park Service, and now stands as a palpable reminder of the early years of the frontier era. Thick adobe walls, 15 feet tall with circular bastions at the corners, protect a roughly 100-square-foot compound. Rangers dressed in period clothing work as wheelsmiths, coopers, and carpenters, or process the many buffalo robes and beaver pelts piled up in storerooms.

Las Animas

The farming community of Las Animas (pop. 2,481) takes its name from the Arkansas River tributary originally known as Río de las Animas Perdidas en Purgatorio—the River of Lost Souls. Las Animas is also the place where, on November 15, 1806, Lt. Zebulon Pike first laid eyes on the Rocky Mountains peak that now bears his name—Pike's Peak, 120 miles to the northwest.

Beyond Las Animas, US-50 continues its gradual descent across the Rocky Mountains foothills. The area was first known as Big Timbers for the tall cotton-woods that grew here along the Arkansas River, though most of these trees were cut down soon after the arrival of white settlers. In the 1840s and 1850s, local Cheyenne, Arapaho, Kiowa, and Apache tribes bartered bison hides at William Bent's trading post, and Wild West explorer **Kit Carson** died here on May 23, 1868, in his family home at what was then the U.S. Army's Fort Lyon, south of present-day US-50. Carson's remains were later moved to Taos, New Mexico, and his lands were flooded after the Arkansas River was dammed to form the large John Martin Reservoir, which stretches most of the way downstream to Lamar.

Lamar

Following the Arkansas River downstream toward the Kansas border, US-50 runs along what was known as the "Mountain Branch" of the Santa Fe Trail, a longer but safer alternative to the main route along the Cimarron Cut-off. There's little to see here apart from acres and acres of irrigated farmlands, though the region's main town, Lamar (pop. 8,343), is worth a quick stop. Very good Mexican-American food is available all day long at the **Main Street Cafe**, 114 S. Main Street in the center of town. A block away, the handy state-run **Welcome Center** (719/336-3483) in the old Santa Fe depot on the east side of Main Street (US-50) has reams of information on the area and the rest of Colorado.

> Lamar's **KCC 93.3 FM** plays good country music and broadcasts Colorado Rockies and Broncos games.

ACROSS KANSAS

In its nearly 500 miles across Kansas, US-50 and its selected variants pass across the agricultural heartland of America, winding through dozens of small farming towns that dot the generally level landscape. (Locals definitely seem to prefer the word "level" to the equally accurate "flat," if only because it sounds less boring.) This is the heart of the "Wheat Belt," where most of the country's grain is grown—as much as half the bread baked in America is made from Kansas wheat—and it's also prime cattle country, with towns like Dodge City and many less famous ones maintaining their historic dependence on cows and cowboys.

All the way across Kansas, we follow almost exactly in the footsteps of the trappers and traders who braved the Santa Fe Trail along the western frontier, stopping at preserved old outposts like Fort Larned and Council Grove while tracking the few more evocative remnants of this pioneer Wild West corridor.

Holcomb

Apart from numerous feedlots fattening cattle for slaughter, and a few wheat, corn, and beet farms fed by water diverted from the Arkansas River, there's not much to see in the

120 miles of barren plains that stretch east from the Colorado border. On the western outskirts of Garden City, the region's biggest town, US-50 runs through the meat-packing town of Holcomb, notorious as the site of the *In Cold Blood* murders documented by Truman Capote. In 1959, Perry Smith and Richard Hickock ruthlessly and without provocation killed the entire Clutter family during a robbery attempt. Both killers were eventually captured, convicted, and executed.

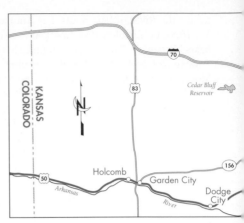

At Garden City, 50 miles west of Dodge City, US-50 crosses US-83, the "Road to Nowhere," which follows the 100th Meridian from Canada to Mexico. Garden City is described on pages 196-197.

The dividing line between central and mountain time zones is 15 miles west of Garden City. Set your clocks accordingly.

Santa Fe Trail Ruts

One of the best-preserved sections of Santa Fe Trail **wagon ruts** is along this stretch of US-50, nine miles west of Dodge City. Marked by a large sign, just west of the Howell grain elevator, the ruts lie in a rolling field 100 yards north of the parking area and are basically a broad depression in the soil, approximately 800 yards wide and two miles long. Farther west, at Cimarron, 32 miles east of Garden City and 16 miles west of Dodge City, the main track of the Santa Fe Trail crossed the Arkansas River and headed southwest across the waterless plain of the Jornada del Muerto on what was known as the **Cimarron Cut-off.** This desolate region is also where, in 1831 during the earliest days of the trail, legendary mountain man **Jedediah Strong Smith** was killed by a band of Comanche warriors.

Dodge City

One of the most notorious places on the Wild West frontier, Dodge City (pop. 21,129) can be something of a disappointment if you come here looking for a rip-roaring frontier town. In its heyday, which lasted roughly from 1872, when the railroad arrived, to 1884, when the cattle drives were effectively banned, Dodge City was the undisputed capital of the buffalo-hunting, cattle-driving Wild West, with as many as 100 million bison hides and seven million head of cattle shipped out from here in that decade alone. At the same time, Dodge City was known as "Hell on the Plains," famous for its gunfights and general lawlessness, despite marshals like **Bat Masterson** and **Wyatt Earp** keeping order and planting bad guys in the Boot Hill cemetery above town.

However, almost nothing in Dodge City survives from that era. Boot Hill, for example, was bought by the city and is now the site of a small office building. Most of what you see dates from the 1920s at the earliest. Dodge City is still a busy farming and cattle-ranching community, with extensive stockyards and slaughterhouses surrounding the small downtown area, but for travelers there's little here apart

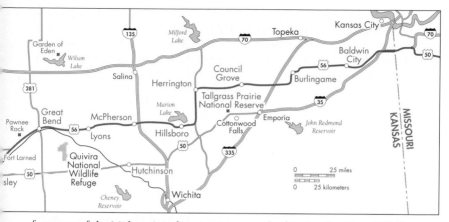

from one of the Midwest's tackier tourist traps, the fake but fun **Boot Hill Museum** (daily 8 AM-8 PM in summer, shorter hours rest of the year; $6) and its re-created Front Street, where actors stage gunfights and "medicine shows" throughout the day; there's also an evening burlesque show, featuring "Miss Kitty and her Can Can Girls." Not surprisingly, Boot Hill is hard to miss, well marked on the west side of town, just north of the railroad tracks off Wyatt Earp Boulevard (US-50/56), the main route through town.

Across the street from Boot Hill stands the **Kansas Teachers' Hall of Fame** (Sunday 11 AM-3 PM; free), with plaques and a wax museum remembering contributions to education in the state.

Wyatt Earp Boulevard (US-50) holds most of Dodge City's eating options, like the **Hitch'n Post** truck stop, at the east end of town. There are also large and popular **Econo Lodge** and **Super 8** motels.

Kinsley: Midway USA

Paralleling the mainline Santa Fe Railroad across the flattest, emptiest 50 miles of Kansas cornfields, east of Dodge City we follow US-50 as far as Kinsley, where we switch onto US-56 (which used to be known as "US-50 North") to follow the Santa Fe Trail. Kinsley, which calls itself "Midway USA," lies equidistant from New York and San Francisco, 1,561 miles from either place. This geographical fact is pointed out by a large sign outside the entertaining (and free!) **Edwards County Historical Museum**, at the US-50/56 junction on the west side of town, surrounded by an old locomotive and a variety of old farming and ranching equipment.

If you prefer to follow US-50 all the way, rather than detour north along the Santa Fe Trail and US-56, one place you'll want to stop is Cottonwood Falls, heart of the country described in the book *PrairyErth,* and the nearest town to the new Tall Grass Prairie National Park (see pages 699-700 for more).

Fort Larned

One of the best-preserved vestiges of the Santa Fe Trail, Fort Larned (daily 9 AM-5 PM; $1; 316/285-6911), now six miles

west of US-56 via Hwy-156, was established in 1859, and for the next 20 years troops stationed here protected travelers on the Santa Fe Trail from the threat of attack by local Arapahoe and Cheyenne tribes. The fort also served a vital role in the many Indian Wars of 1860s, but by 1878, when the trail was no longer in active use, the fort was deactivated. It was sold and used as a ranch until 1960, but has survived the intervening years in excellent condition. Careful restoration by the National Park Service has made Fort Larned an excellent place to experience what the frontier really looked like, albeit from the military perspective.

Sandstone buildings, which replaced the original adobe after the end of the Civil War, surround a 400-square-foot parade ground, and interior rooms have been filled with accurate reproductions of original fixtures and fittings, ranging from barracks to blacksmith's shops to a large storehouse. A nearby farm preserves a set of ruts surviving from the Santa Fe Trail days, though you really need to have an active imagination to get much from them.

In between Fort Larned and US-56, the **Santa Fe Trail Museum and Cultural Center** (daily 9 AM-5 PM; $3; 316/285-2054) is a private, nonprofit museum focusing on the overall history of the Santa Fe Trail region. Diorama-like exhibits feature full-scale mock-ups of wagons and frontier trading posts, and behind the main building are a sod house and a one-room schoolhouse.

Back on US-56, the town of **Larned** has a typical crossroads collection of motels and McDonald's. There's also the unique **Central States Scout Museum**, 815 Broadway (Saturday and Sunday 9 AM-5 PM; $1), full of exhibits telling the story of Midwestern Boy Scouts through the years.

Pawnee Rock

Just eight miles northeast of Larned, a half-mile north of US-56 and the Arkansas River, Pawnee Rock was once one of the most important landmarks on the Santa Fe Trail. However, so much of the original 60-foot-high tower of Dakota sandstone has been quarried—to build houses as well as the roadbed of the Santa Fe railroad—that it's little more than a stubby hump. But you can still get a grand view of the surrounding countryside from the easy trail that leads to the rock's much-diminished summit.

Great Bend

Spreading along the northern bank of the Arkansas River at the northernmost point on its sweep across central Kansas, Great Bend (pop. 15,427) was originally established as a fort along the Santa Fe Trail, but really began to grow after the railroad came through. As with Dodge City to the southwest, the arrival of the railroad in 1872 attracted cattle drovers from the Chisholm Trail, who turned Great Bend into a raucous Wild West town. It's now a quiet rural city, earning its livelihood from wheat farms and, since the 1930s, oil.

There's not a lot to see or do in Great Bend, though the outskirts of town are more promising, starting with the engaging **Barton County Historical Society Museum** (Tues.-Sun. 1-4 PM; $1; 316/793-5125), just south of the railroad tracks and the river along US-281. Farther afield, the Great Bend area holds two of the largest wildlife refuges in Kansas, **Cheyenne Bottoms** to the northeast and **Quivira** to the southeast, both of which offer excellent bird watching (and hunting . . .) opportunities.

Great Bend does have a fairly good range of places to eat, with franchise fast food supplemented by a handful of local restaurants like **La Mexicana, Pancho's**, and the **Golden Corral**, all along 10th Street (US-56). Along with a **Holiday Inn**, a **Best Western**, and a **Super 8**, another reliable place to stay in Great Bend is the **Traveler's Budget Inn**, 4200 W. 10th Street (316/793-5448), with double rooms for around $30.

Detour: The Garden of Eden

If you're one of those bi-coastal types who thinks that the Midwest is full of conventional-minded folks leading ordinary lives as contented consumers, you owe it to yourself to visit the Garden of Eden, one of the country's oldest and oddest folk art environments. Located in the tiny town of Lucas, Kansas (pop. 459), the Garden of Eden is the sort of place that puts the gothic back in American Gothic, a front yard forest of Biblical scenes and Populist political allegories—Adam and Eve, Cain and Abel, and the Crucifixion of Labor at the Hands of Preachers, Bankers, and Lawyers—created out of concrete from around 1910 to 1930 by one Samuel Dinsmoor. An Ohio native and Civil War veteran, Dinsmoor actively promoted his Garden as a tourist attraction, managing to draw many hundreds of visitors to this distant and fairly inaccessible corner of the Kansas. Dinsmoor died at age 89 in 1932 and is buried in a glass-covered tomb on the property, yet carried on his hucksterism even after death, insisting in his will that no one be allowed "to go in and see me for less than $1."

The Garden of Eden (daily 10 AM-5 PM; $4; 913/525-6395) is at the corner of 2nd and Kansas in Lucas, which is on Hwy-18, north of Great Bend and 15 miles north of I-70.

The next town east of Great Bend along US-50 is Ellinwood, where a couple of antique shops mark the historic downtown area. **Ellinwood** sits atop a series of tunnels, used as tornado shelters and occasionally as storerooms for contraband. They are occasionally open for guided tours as part of "Underground Ellinwood" ($2; 316/564-2218).

From Great Bend, Hwy-96 and US-183 run 35 miles northwest to the town of Lacrosse, home to the **Kansas Barbed Wire Museum** at 202 W. 1st Street (913/222-2607).

Lyons

The farming, oil-drilling, and salt-mining town of Lyons (pop. 3,688), 30 miles due east of Great Bend, doesn't look much different from most other Kansas towns, but it has an unusually impressive history—and a very nice courthouse square downtown. There's a 150-foot-long intaglio serpent carved into the prairie eight miles northeast of town, and some Santa Fe Trail ruts, but the most compelling remains are those left behind by Coronado's expedition through the region in 1541, in search of the fabled golden city of Quivira. Exhibits on all of these, as well as Indian and pioneer American cultures, are displayed inside the modern, purpose-built **Rice County Historical Museum** (Mon.-Sat. 9 AM-5 PM, Sunday 1-5 PM; $1.50) at 105 W. Lyon Street, two blocks south of the landmark county courthouse off US-56.

Two miles west of Lyons along US-56, a large cross marks the site where Father Padilla, who accompanied Coronado on his expedition and returned the following year to convert the natives, was killed by unreceptive Indians, thereby becoming the first "Christian martyr" in the present-day USA.

If you happen upon one, check out a public **auction,** held irregularly in towns across the rural Midwest. Fast-talking auctioneers take bids on various lots, ranging from real antiques to boxes of junk and cast-off clothes.

For a place to stay, try the **Lyons Inn**, on US-56 at 817 W. Main Street (316/257-5185).

US-50: Hutchinson

If you've opted to follow US-50 rather than the Santa Fe Trail tour along US-56, be sure to check out Hutchinson (pop. 40,000), a large and lively city that's home to the world's longest grain elevator (over a half-mile long) and old salt mines, some 600 feet below ground, that are now used for storage of important archives, including the original negatives of many classic Hollywood films. The mines, not surprisingly, aren't open to visitors, but Hutchinson does have another surprising attraction: the **Kansas Cosmosphere and Space Center**, at 1100 N. Plum Street (Mon.-Sat. 9 AM-9 PM, Sunday noon-9 PM; $2; 316/662-2305 or 800/397-0330). This boasts a great collection of historic air- and spacecraft, including Mercury, Gemini and Apollo capsules, a Lockheed SR-71A "Blackbird" spy plane, and a pair of German V-1 and V-2 rockets, plus a planetarium ($3) and an IMAX theater ($5).

McPherson

From a distance across the flat plains, the towering grain elevators make McPherson (pop. 12,422) look more impressive than it really is. Thirty-five miles east of Lyons, it marks the junction of US-56 and the I-135 freeway between Salina and Wichita. You can fill the gas tank or get a bite to eat (all the usual franchise food places and gas stations are here) or just stretch your legs wandering around the four-block Main Street business district.

The small **McPherson Museum**, well-marked in a residential district at 1130 Euclid Street (Tues.-Sun. 1-5 PM; donations; 316/241-5977), displays rooms furnished in typical turn-of-the-century Kansas style. It also holds the world's first man-made

The gold medal-winning 1936 U.S. Olympic basketball team was formed by the company team from a McPherson oil refinery.

diamond, produced by Willard Hershey, a local chemistry teacher.

Herrington and Hillsboro: Mennonite Country

The central Kansas farmlands around **Goessel** are home to one of the largest Mennonite communities in the United States.

One of the centers of the sizeable local Mennonite community, Hillsboro (pop. 2,704), 13 miles west of US-77, serves as market center for the area's highly productive farmlands. Tabor College, on the east side of town, is the most visible sign of the Mennonite presence; although it's a coed nondenominational college, about half the students are local Mennonites.

The tidy town of Goessel (population 506), 15 miles southwest of Hillsboro, was also founded by Mennonite farmers, and now holds the worthwhile **Mennonite Heritage Center**, 200 N. Poplar Street (Tues.-Sat. 10 AM-5 PM, Sunday 1-5 PM; $3; 316/367-8200), where numerous buildings, including two schools, a barn, and a bank, have been moved for preservation. The flat black earth around Goessel is among the world's greatest producers of wheat, in particular the hearty hybrids able to withstand the Midwest winter. The original seed, known as "Turkey Red," was brought to Kansas in the early 1870s by Russian Mennonites who immigrated here after their 100-year exclusion from military service was rescinded.

Zigzagging east from Hillsboro and then north along US-77/US-56, after another 37 "level" miles US-56 reaches the town of Herrington, whose central square holds a monument to Father Padilla, who passed through southern Kansas in search of the mythical Golden City of Gran Quivira as part of Coronado's expedition.

Council Grove

Just 75 miles southwest of the suburban sprawl of Kansas City, 25 miles west of the I-335 Kansas Turnpike, Council Grove (pop. 2,228) still looks much as it did over a century ago when, from the 1830s to the 1860s, it was the most important of all way stations on the Santa Fe Trail. Council Grove's lush maples and oaks were the last hardwoods available on the long route west across the treeless plain, which meant traders and travelers could make final repairs and stock up on spare axles and other essentials. It was also the western extent of "safe territory"; beyond here travelers were subject to frequent attacks by hostile Indians.

Nowadays the town proudly preserves its many historic sites, and in many ways serves as the most not-to-be-missed stop for modern travelers heading along the Santa Fe Trail. The sites of two of the most important trail icons, the **Council Oak** under which in 1825 the native Kansa and Osage Indians agreed to allow Americans to cross their territory, and the **Post Office Oak** that served as a natural message center for early travelers, are marked along Main Street (US-56), east of the bridge over the small Neosho River. Four blocks west, the **Last Chance Store** at Main and Chautauqua Streets has served as a bank and a post office in the years since it was built in 1857.

The **Kaw Mission State Historic Site**, in Council Grove five blocks north of Main on Mission Street, was built by Methodist missionaries in 1851 as a school for local Indian children. Students included Charles Curtis, who served as U.S. vice president from 1929 to 1933.

In between, the banks, cafes, and stores along Main Street, which the Santa Fe Trail followed through town, make little obvious effort to cater to tourists, and the town basically goes about its day-to-day business without forgetting its extraordinary past. The **Hays House,** in the center of town at 112 W. Main Street (316/767-5911), lays fair claim to being the oldest restaurant west of the Mississippi; originally built as a frontier home, and later serving as a saloon, supply post,

The Cottage House

courthouse, and hotel, it has stood on this site since 1847. Now modernized, it is still the focus of the town's social and political life and is open all day—with excellent fried chicken. Across Main, the soda fountain inside the **Aldrich Apothecary** has good milk shakes. The best place to stay is the comfortable **Cottage House Hotel** at 25 N. Neosho (316/767-6828 or 800/727-7903).

Further information is available from the Council Grove **visitor center**, 313 W. Main Street (316/767-5882 or 800/732-9211).

US-50: Tallgrass Prairie National Preserve

The delights of the Flint Hills landscape are pastoral in the extreme, with few roaring waterfalls or towering cliffs to take your breath away or make you pull out the camera, but the unique ecosystem has enough admirers that a section of it was recently set aside as the Tallgrass Prairie National Preserve. Located along Hwy-177 about 17 miles south of Council Grove, or two miles north of Strong City and US-50, the 11,000-acre preserve protects the largest remaining portion of the extensive tallgrass prairie which once covered over 400,000 square miles of the Great Plains —most of the present-day Midwest. Interpretive facilities are housed in an old stone barn, on a hill above the highway, which has a **visitor center** (daily 9 AM-5 PM, $2 donation; 316/273-8494) with exhibits and videos on the natural flora, fauna and geography of the area. A 1.5 mile nature trail starts here, winding along to the historic one-room Fox Creek Schoolhouse while giving an up-close look at the head-high (or taller) flowering grasses that give the tallgrass prairie its name.

The best base for a visit to the Tallgrass Prairie National Preserve is **Cottonwood Falls**, two miles south of Strong City and US-50 via Hwy-177. The town boasts the beautiful Chase County Courthouse, the oldest still in use in the state, standing

like a French chateau at the south end of a sleepy Main Street business district, where you'll also find a couple of cafes and crafts shops, and the elegant 10-room **Grand Central Hotel**, 215 Broadway (316/273-6763), which has a fine, subtly Western-themed restaurant. For a night out in the country, consider the **1874 Stonehouse on Mulberry Hill** (316/273-8481), located on 60 rolling acres just outside town, on the banks of the Cottonwood River.

the oldest operating courthouse in Kansas

Writing about US-50, *Blue Highways* author **William Least Heat Moon** has said that "for the unhurried, this little-known highway is the best national road across the middle of the United States."

Burlingame and Baldwin City

Between Council Grove and Kansas City, US-56 passes through the lovely cattle-ranching grasslands of the northern Flint Hills, zigzagging at 90-degree angles through one-time coal-mining towns like Worden, Overbrook, and Scranton. Burlingame (pop. 2,735), the largest of this bunch, is noteworthy for its very broad, brick-paved 20-mph Main Street (US-56), lined by diverse 100-year-old buildings painted with a barrage of signs advertising player pianos as well as the usual liquor, food, and auto parts.

At the northeast edge of the Flint Hills, 13 miles west of the I-35 freeway from Kansas City, US-56 skirts the leafy, brick-paved streets of Baldwin City (pop. 2,961), a small town that was once a main rest-and-repair stop on the Santa Fe Trail—four days' travel west of Independence. In 1858, the first college on the western frontier was founded here in a three-story sandstone building now preserved as "The Castle," alongside a combination general store and post office on the east side of the pleasant campus of Methodist-run **Baker University**. The library (Mon.-Fri. 8 AM-5 PM; free) three blocks west displays the **Quayle Collection** of rare religious texts, including clay tablets dating from Old Testament times, and a range of hand-bound bibles, arranged to trace the development of printing techniques and typography styles.

For the rest of the way east to Kansas City, US-56 parallels the I-35 freeway across lush rolling grassland pastures and farms, marked in places by signs reading

---

BLUE HIGHWAYS TO PRAIRYERTH

After traveling 13,000 miles of back road through the nooks and crannies of 38 states to write his first book, the author of road trip classic *Blue Highways,* William Least Heat Moon, began work on a very different study. Straying no farther than the 744 square miles of Chase County, Kansas, Moon embarked upon what he termed a "deep map" of the area that sits atop the lush rolling Flint Hills, the nation's last remaining grand expanse of tallgrass prairie, split by US-50 and the Santa Fe Railroad.

The result was the 1991 book *PrairyErth,* a 600-plus-page evocation of history and contemporary life in this otherwise unremarkable corner of the country, which Moon describes as being "five hours by Interstates from home, eight hours if I follow a route of good cafe food." Combining folk history and contemporary anecdotes with captivating quotes from sundry novels, Native American legends, travel guides, essays, and old newspaper clippings, this unique project—which has been described as the nonfiction equivalent of the Great American Novel—manages to capture the rhythms of ranching life here in the middle of the great American nowhere.

"Old US-50." Along this route, two miles west of Gardner, a historical marker stands on the site where the Santa Fe and Oregon Trails once divided. For many years, a crude wooden sign pointed westbound travelers in the proper direction: left to Santa Fe, right to Oregon.

ACROSS MISSOURI

From Kansas City, and its noteworthy neighboring towns of Independence and Liberty, US-50 makes a lazy trek across Missouri's rolling prairie farmlands, stopping at the historic railroad town of Sedalia before reaching the state capital, Jefferson City, roughly midway across. Continuing east, climbing through second-growth hardwood forests of the Ozark uplands, US-50 is a slow and not particularly scenic road; we suggest following a similarly slow but more interesting detour, Hwy-100, which winds through a number of historic towns along the banks of the Missouri River before approaching St. Louis via the I-44 freeway.

More than almost anywhere else on this cross-country trek, to be honest if you're in any sort of a hurry you won't miss much by taking the 70-mph I-70 freeway straight across Missouri from Kansas City to St. Louis, 250 miles away.

US-50 across Kansas City

US-50 is now submerged beneath the Interstates and runs west-east around Kansas City via I-35, I-435, and I-470. The older, pre-Interstate route also avoided downtown, but did pass through the south side of the city, following what's now signed

Harry S. Truman

as US-169 along Park Avenue and 47th Street, past the Country Club Plaza and the Nelson-Atkins Museum of Art, before dipping south again on the Swope Parkway to Lee's Summit, where the old alignment rejoins the current US-50 routing.

To reach the downtown area from US-50, you can follow any of many north-south streets, like Troost Avenue, the down-at-heel old main drag, or the parkway-like El Paseo.

Independence

A quiet suburb lying on the eastern fringe of greater Kansas City, Independence (pop. 112,301) doesn't look like a special place, but it is. One of the country's most history-rich small cities, Independence came to life during the early years of the westward expansion, serving as the jumping-off point for the Santa Fe and later Oregon and California Trails. A century later, Independence again gained prominence as the hometown of U.S. President Harry Truman, who lived here from boyhood until his death in 1972.

The city-run **National Frontier Trails Center** (Mon.-Sat. 9 AM-4:30 PM, Sunday 12:30-4:30 PM; $3), four blocks south of the town square at 318 W. Pacific Street, is one of the best museums dedicated to America's pioneers. Beginning with a brief account of Lewis and Clark, the exhibits explore the heyday of the Santa Fe Trail, which throughout the 1820s and 1830s made Independence the leading town on the western frontier. The later Oregon Trail, on which some 300,000 people left Independence for the West Coast, is recounted through an engagingly displayed series of diary entries and drawings made by pioneers.

While very little remains from the pioneer days, Independence has hardly changed since Harry Truman grew up here around the turn of the 20th century. The soda fountain where he held his first job, and the courtroom where he presided as judge, still stand in the town square. His home, northwest of the square at 219 N. Delaware Street, is open for **tours** (daily 9 AM-4 PM; $2), and the large **Harry S Truman Library** (daily 9 AM-5 PM; $5) four blocks north contains his presidential papers, a replica of his White House office, and the gravesites of Truman and his wife Bess.

Clinton's Soda Fountain, at 100 W. Maple Street ("Where Harry Had His First Job"), still serves milk shakes and sandwiches. For chicken dinners and apple fritters, head 10 miles south of Independence to **Stephenson's Apple Farm Restaurant**, 16401 E. US-40 at Lee's Summit Road. For a place to stay, try the historic **Serendipity B&B**, 116 S. Pleasant Street (816/833-4719), within a short walk of all the Independence attractions.

For more information, contact the Independence **visitors bureau**, 111 E. Maple Street (816/325-7111).

Liberty

Another ideally named small town on the fringes of Kansas City, Liberty (pop. 20,459) is worth a visit for rather different reasons. This is where, on February 13, 1866, **Jesse James** and his brother Frank staged the first-ever daylight bank holdup,

(continues on page 705)

KANSAS CITY SURVIVAL GUIDE

THOUGH IT COVERS A HUGE AREA, STRETCHING FOR some 20 miles on both sides of the Missouri/Kansas border, and nearly 30 miles north to south, Kansas City (pop. 450,000) never really feels like a big city. It's more like a conglomeration of small towns, once separate from each other but now joined together by tract house sprawl and surrounded by the 100-mile-long I-435 Beltway. The historic center of Kansas City lines the south bank of the Missouri River, where 30-story skyscrapers stand above hefty brick warehouses, huge stockyards, railroad tracks, and banks of grain elevators all testifying to Kansas City's role as the main distribution point for Midwestern farm products.

All of this isn't meant to imply the city is ugly, just that it sometimes seems to go on forever, and that places of interest can be hard to find. Besides the ones described below, another place definitely worth a visit is the historic town of **Independence**, on US-50 on the northwest outskirts of Kansas City (see previous page).

Southwest of the city center, Westport is the birthplace of Kansas City. Before the Kansas River switched course and left it high and dry, Westport was the westernmost steamboat landing in the U.S., and quickly grew into a prime supply point on the Santa Fe and Oregon Trails. Now a mile south of downtown, just west of Main and 40th Streets, Westport is home to many lively cafes and nightspots, with perhaps the liveliest being **Kelly's Westport Inn** at 500 Westport Road. The oldest building in Kansas City, the inn dates from 1837 and is now a popular tavern.

Located on the south side of Westport, the remarkable **Nelson Atkins Museum of Art**, Main and 47th Streets (Tues.-Sat. 10 AM-5 PM, Sunday 1-5 PM; $4; 816/751-1278), would do any city proud, with strong surveys of both Asian and American art, including in-depth coverage of K.C.-based Thomas Hart Benton. Two blocks west, **Country Club Plaza** was one of the country's first shopping malls, and its opulent Spanish Revival styling still attracts the upscale likes of Gucci, Saks, and the Body Shop.

Right downtown, the **Hallmark Visitors Center** (Mon.-Fri. 9 AM-5 PM, Saturday 9:30 AM-4:30 PM; free; 816/274-5672) is at Main and 25th Streets, on the top floor of the Crown Center Mall. It is much better, or at least much less nauseatingly saccharine, than you might expect: 14 galleries trace the history of the Hallmark company, which started here in 1910, and explain the design and production processes behind the 50,000 different types of greeting cards ($3.8 billion worth!) they sell each year. *(continues on next page)*

A mile east of downtown K.C., in the revitalized 18th and Vine neighborhood, the heartland of Kansas City's post-war jazz scene, is the marvelous **Negro Baseball Leagues Museum**, 1616 E. 18th Street (Mon.-Sat. 10 AM-4:30 PM, Sunday noon-4:30 PM; $6; 816/221-1920). The newly renovated building houses an outstanding new museum dedicated to documenting the various professional baseball leagues that existed side-by-side with the majors before the color barriers began to be broken down in the late 1940s, as well as the excellent, highly interactive Jazz Museum documenting KC's prolific jazz heritage. The city's big band golden age (1930s-'40s) spawned jazz greats Charlie Parker, Lester Young, Count Basie, and Jo Jones, whom are all honored, alongside national jazz greats like Louis Armstrong and Duke Ellington, in a series of listener-friendly exhibits. For those wanting to hear a slice of the real thing, the adjacent Blue Room jazz club hosts nightly jazz combos and jam sessions in a funky, comfortable new space.

Even further east of town, the **Kansas City Royals** (816/921-8000) play at 40,000-seat Kauffman Stadium.

Practicalities

Kansas City spreads for miles at the junction of the I-29, I-35 and I-70 interstate freeways. Small but efficient **Kansas City International Airport** (KCI), 15 miles northwest of downtown, has the usual car rental outlets and is also served by **KCI Shuttles** ($15; 800/243-6383).

To get around Kansas City, drive. As in Los Angeles, which Kansas City resembles more than residents of either city are likely to admit, cars rule the roads. Distances are huge and public transportation is basically nonexistent.

All the usual chain motels line up along the I-435 beltway, and there's a good-value **Red Roof Inn** at 6800 W. 108th Street (913/341-0100) on I-435/US-50 in Overland Park (exit 79) and another near Independence at 13712 East 42nd Terrace (816/373-2800). In downtown Kansas City, the anonymously named **Historic Suites of America**, two blocks from the City Market at 612 Central Avenue (816/842-6544), offers spacious accommodations in a nicely converted 100-year-old warehouse. Budget-conscious travelers can also stay a bit closer to Midtown, Westport, and the Plaza area at the Rodeway Inn Center City, 3240 Broadway (816/531-9250).

For food, there's no better introduction to the delights of K.C. cuisine than **Arthur Bryant's**, east of downtown at 1727 Brooklyn Avenue (816/231-1123). Meat-eaters drive for miles to eat at this classic no-frills rib shack, located near the Negro Leagues Baseball Museum, where heavenly BBQ sauces come in plain plastic bottles. Way away from downtown, but not far from old US-50 in a photogenic roadhouse on the south side of the city (take the Holmes Road exit off I-435), **Stroud's**, at 1015 E. 85th Street (816/333-2132), serves simply perfect fried chicken, rated by *Roadfood* writers and *Gourmet* magazine critics Jane and Michael Stern as the very best in the country. With huge portions of mashed potatoes, peppery gravy, and sweet cinnamon buns, it's certainly hard to beat.

Kansas City's once-vaunted nightlife is nothing like it was during the jazz and R&B heyday of the 1940s and 1950s, though a few good places remain. The best bet for blues is the **Grand Emporium**, near Westport at 3832 Main Street (816/531-1504), while the **Phoenix**, at 302 W. 8th Street (816/472-0001) in the downtown loft district, features jazz. The historic **Kelly's Westport Inn** at 500 Westport Road (see above) is a great place to enjoy a budget-priced beer while soaking up some old K.C. ambience.

For more complete information, contact the Kansas City **visitor center** (816/221-5242 or 800/767-7700) at 1100 Main Street, or stop by the state-run **Missouri Information Center** (daily 9 AM-5 PM; 816/861-8800), near I-435 east of downtown on I-70 at exit 9. The main daily newspaper is the *Kansas City Star.*

getting away with over $60,000. The bank building itself, at 103 N. Water Street on the northwest corner of the preserved-in-amber town square, is pretty much as it was, complete with the vault, safe, and banknotes; it's now a small **museum** (Mon.-Sat. 9 AM-4 PM, Sunday noon-4 PM; $2).

A block north of the square stands another historic site, the oxymoronic **Liberty Jail** (daily 9 AM-9 PM; free) at 216 N. Main Street, where Mormon prophet Joseph Smith and his followers were imprisoned during the winter of 1838-39. It's a significant site for Mormons, and has been faithfully reconstructed.

Liberty also has a good place to eat: the **Fork and Spoon Cafe**, west of the square at 12 W. Kansas Street.

Sedalia

East of Kansas City the roadside along fast, four-lane US-50 is endless open, rolling prairie, most of it planted in wheat and corn. As with most of the West, early development here occurred along the railroad lines, which were constructed beginning in the 1850s; the region wasn't substantially settled until the Civil War years. Towns boomed when the trains arrived, but most went bust as the tracks were extended westward to Kansas City and beyond.

Sedalia (pop. 19,808), 75 miles east of Kansas City, was one of the few that survived, growing into a small city thanks to its position straddling the main line between St. Louis and Kansas City. Sedalia reached its peak of prosperity around 1900, when both the Missouri-Pacific and the Missouri-Texas railroads had their maintenance shops here. The empty storefronts downtown are misleading, since the town is generally thriving, and for travelers it offers many great places to stop and eat. **Eddie's**, on US-50 at

Outlaw Jesse James grew up near Liberty.

In 1867, the militant prohibitionist **Carry Nation** moved to the village of Holden, nine miles south of US-50 via Hwy-131, with her alcoholic first husband Dr. William Gloyd, who died the following year.

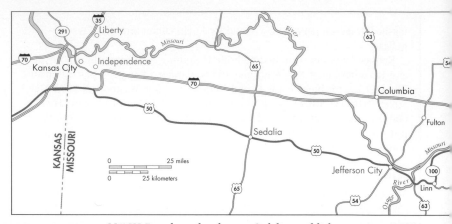

Sedalia hosts a **Scott Joplin Ragtime Festival** every June, and the annual **Missouri State Fair** attracts thousands of people here every August. For details, call the Sedalia visitor center (660/826-2222).

115 W. Broadway, has been a Sedalia establishment since 1937, serving steak burgers—with meat ground fresh each day. The best homemade pie in Sedalia is at the **tea room** (open 11 AM-1:30 PM approximately, or until they run out of food) at the Maple Leaf Antique Mall. Go early for the best pie selection. **Le Maire's Cajun Seafood**, 3312 S. US-65, has great fried catfish, boiled shrimp, crab legs, frog legs, crayfish, and other swamp, creek, and seafood fare; for a taste of Cajun Country, it saves the 600-mile drive down US-65 to the Louisiana bayous. Last but not least is the **Wheel Inn Drive In**, at the US-50/US-65 junction, which since 1947 has been serving the unique specialty "Gooberburgers"—hamburgers slathered with peanut butter.

SCOTT JOPLIN: THE KING OF RAGTIME

Music is among the most mobile of the arts, equally affecting anywhere and anytime, but many forms are strongly identified with a given place and era. New Orleans means jazz, the Delta has the blues, Detroit will always be equated with the Motown sound, and if credit were given where credit is due, Sedalia, Missouri, would join the above places as the source of another classic African-American music—ragtime. The first ragtime tunes, so-called because of their ragged, syncopated rhythms, were played in the early 1890s, but later came into full flower out of the musical mind of Scott Joplin, the universally acclaimed king of ragtime.

Born in 1868 near Texarkana, Texas, to a former slave and freeborn mother, Scott Joplin was one of six children in a musical family. After moving around the Midwest throughout his youth, in the late 1890s Joplin settled in Sedalia, which was then a raucous railroad town, where he studied music theory at Sedalia's small black college. To pay his way, Joplin played piano at many of the clubs that lined Main Street in Sedalia, which had a reputation both for multiracial harmony and as an adult playground of bars and brothels catering to the many itinerant men passing through; as late as 1940, *Life* magazine said

Jefferson City

Roughly at the center of the state, 130 miles west of St. Louis and 140 miles east of Kansas City on the south bank of the Missouri River, Jefferson City (pop. 35,481) is a strangely small and somnolent place. The handsome neo-classical **state capitol** (daily 8 AM-5 PM; free), modeled on the U.S. Capitol and completed in 1918, is the central landmark, rising from the river at the heart of town. Inside, the rotunda and ground floor area is packed with informative exhibits tracing the state's political and natural history, while hourly **guided tours** take in the entire building, including a famous mural by Thomas Hart Benton on the walls of the third-floor House Lounge.

Below the capitol, along the river and the railroad tracks, a trio of brick buildings from the mid-1800s, including one that still serves as the city's Amtrak station, are preserved in a park-like setting. On a knoll just east of here stands the Governor's Mansion, but otherwise there's precious little to see or do.

It was at Westminster College in the town of Fulton, 20 miles northeast of Jefferson City, that Winston Churchill made his famous "Iron Curtain" speech in 1946.

If you find yourself in Jefferson City, good salads, soups, and pasta dishes are available at **Madison's**, 216 Madison Street. The **Big Dipper** on High Street has ice cream and sandwiches. Both places are within a block of the capitol.

Sedalia still had one of the "most notorious red-light districts" in the Midwest.

One of these nightclubs gave its name to the "Maple Leaf Rag," the composition that made Joplin's reputation and which, at a penny-per-sheet royalty, earned around $500 a year—enough to support him, but far from a fortune. Joplin later lived in St. Louis, where the home in which he wrote "The Entertainer" (the piece used as theme song in the movie *The Sting*) is preserved as a museum. Eventually Joplin ended up in New York, where he sought but failed to find support for his increasingly complex orchestral and operatic compositions. Scott Joplin died, poor and all-but-forgotten, on April 1, 1917.

The great frontiersman **Daniel Boone** settled along the northern banks of the Missouri River in 1799, and lived near what's now the town of Defiance for the next 20 years until his death in 1820. His home, five well-signed miles outside town, is now owned by his descendants and open for tours (daily 9 AM-5 PM; $5; 314/987-2221).

Hwy-100: Hermann and Washington

Turning off US-50 at Linn, 20 miles east of Jefferson City, Hwy-100 offers a more interesting and not much longer alternative to the uneventful US-50 route east to St. Louis. Following the Missouri River downstream, you eventually fetch up at the town of Hermann (pop. 2,754), founded by German immigrants in 1837. Surrounded by small wineries and standing right on the riverfront, Hermann reminds some visitors of a Rhine Valley village, its German heritage kept alive at the **Historic Hermann Museum** (daily 10 AM-5 PM; $1), housed in the old Deutsche Schule at 4th and Schiller Streets downtown.

Another 30 miles downstream, or roughly 50 miles from the Gateway Arch at downtown St. Louis, the timeless town of Washington (pop. 10,704) rises on narrow streets above the broad Missouri River. Now full of upscale restaurants and B&B inns—the **visitor center**, 323 W. Main Street (314/239-2715), has extensive listings—many of the town's balconied brick buildings date from the mid-1800s, when large numbers of Germans settled the region.

The small **Washington Historical Society Museum**, 314 W. Main Street (Saturday and Sunday 10 AM-5 PM; free), has exhibits on early settlers and the town's current main industry (after tourism, that is): manufacturing **corn-cob pipes**.

West of St. Louis, Hwy-100, US-50 and the I-44 freeway all run together, roughly on top of historic Route 66. For more on Route 66, see the chapter beginning on page 794.

Driving St. Louis

West of St. Louis, Hwy-100 and US-50 merge into the high-speed I-44 freeway in Eureka, very near the massive Six Flags amusement park ($30; 314/938-4800), which has great roller coasters and various "theme" areas evoking aspects of Missouri's past.

For most of the way across St. Louis, old US-50 followed Route 66, which is covered on pages 794-849. The two diverged in East St. Louis, and the old US-50 alignment followed St. Clair Avenue, just south of present-day I-64.

St. Louis is the only city where three of our Road Trip USA routes coincide—US-50, the Great River Road, and Route 66. For details on visiting St. Louis, see the Survival Guide in the Great River Road chapter, on pages 258-259.

ACROSS ILLINOIS

US-50 runs straight across over 150 miles of Southern Illinois's pancake-flat farmlands—acres of corn and soybeans as far as the eye can see, with small towns dotting the roadside every 10 or so miles. For much of the way, US-50 follows the "Trace Road," a slightly raised causeway originally traced across the swampy marshlands by the same prehistoric people who built the enigmatic mounds at Cahokia, which still stand in the eastern suburbs of St. Louis. Midway across Illinois, US-50 passes through the quirkily historic town of Salem (birthplace of two American icons: William Jennings Bryan and Miracle Whip), then crosses over the Wabash River into Indiana.

Cahokia Mounds, a massive prehistoric ruin, are marooned in the Illinois suburbs east of St. Louis. Also nearby: the **World's Largest Catsup Bottle,** in Collinsville. Both are described more fully in the Route 66 chapter, on page 843.

Lebanon

From the dangerous and decrepit industrial districts of East St. Louis, US-50 follows the I-64 freeway east from St. Louis across the flat prairie, whose fertile alluvial soil has earned it the nickname "Little Egypt." The highway parallels the Illinois Central Railroad through a dozen small towns, the most significant of which is Lebanon (pop. 3,688), 20 miles east of the Mississippi River. An attractive town, with a number of stately mansard-roofed Victorian-era commercial buildings now housing antique shops along Main Street and St. Louis Street (US-50), Lebanon grew up around the bucolic campus of McKendree College, founded here in 1828 and one of the oldest in Illinois.

The best reason to stop, however, is the small **Mermaid House Hotel,** on US-50 at 114 E. St. Louis Street. Charles Dickens, who visited the area to see the rich but muddy prairie east of town, stayed here for a night in 1842, and described it in *American Notes* as comparing "favorably with any village ale house of a homely kind in England." After spending most of the past 150 years as a private home, the building is now undergoing restoration, but is open for tours (Saturday and Sunday10 AM-4 PM; donations).

Salem

Halfway across Illinois, just east of the busy I-57 freeway, US-50 cuts through the center of Salem (pop. 7,470), a historically fascinating if visually less-than-thrilling city best known as the birthplace and boyhood home of William Jennings Bryan. The turn-of-the-century politician and orator, who served as leader of the Democratic Party for 15 years, prosecuted the so-called "Monkey Trial" of 1925 and led the successful attack on Tennessee schoolteacher John Scopes (who, coincidentally, was also born and raised in Salem) for breaking a local ban on teaching evolution. Bryan was born in 1860 in the small frame house at 408 S. Broadway, four blocks south of Main Street (US-50). It has been preserved as a small **museum** (daily except Thursday 1-5 PM; free). There's a statue of Bryan, crafted by Mount Rushmore

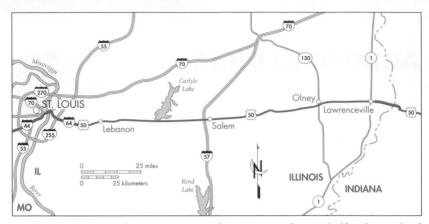

The birthplace of Miracle Whip, Max Crossett's Cafe, is now a parking lot at the center of Salem.

Bible-packing 18th-century settlers of the uplands opposite St. Louis referred to their chosen homesteads as "Goshen" and the flood-prone flats to the south as "Egypt." Comparisons between the Mississippi and Nile rivers were deliberately reinforced with place-names like Karnak, Joppa, Thebes, and Cairo; for generations now, all of Southern Illinois has borne the nickname "Little Egypt."

On the east side of Carlyle, 22 miles west of Salem, a very delicate suspension bridge built in 1860 has been preserved in a riverside park, on the northeast side of where US-50 crosses the Kaskaskia River.

sculptor Gutzon Borglum, on Broadway a half-mile north of Main Street, in front of the Roller Palace skating rink.

Besides William Jennings Bryan, Salem has given America two very important things. The **G.I. Bill of Rights**, also known as the G.I. Bill, which entitled military veterans to subsidized education and other services, was first proposed by the local American Legion branch before being signed into law in 1944. **Miracle Whip** was created at Max Crosset's Cafe on Main Street before being sold to Kraft Foods (for $300!) in 1931.

Salem has a good place to eat, **Austin's Restaurant** at 1479 W. US-50, and two good inexpensive motels, the **Lakewood** (618/548-2785) and the **Continental** (618/548-3090), next to each other on US-50 just east of town.

Olney and Lawrenceville

The flat farmlands of southeast Illinois are dotted with occasional oil wells and signs painted on barn sides encouraging travelers to "Chew Mail Pouch Tobacco" or "See Rock City," but towns are few and far between. The first of these is the attractive town of Olney (pop. 8,664). Besides boasting a large number of grand old mansions set behind broad green lawns along quiet, leafy streets, Olney has the singular attraction of **albino squirrels**, which were set loose in town around the turn of the century. By 1940, the WPA *Guide to Illinois* noted that "thousands of the little animals now scamper about the parks and courthouse square, and frisk over lawns, trees, and rooftops," though these days you're most likely to see them if you head to the **city park** north of the courthouse square.

WILLIAM JENNINGS

BRYAN

1860 1925

"YOU SHALL NOT PRESS DOWN UPON THE BROW OF LABOR THIS CROWN OF THORNS. YOU SHALL NOT CRUCIFY MANKIND UPON A CROSS OF GOLD"

Olney is famous for its large population of albino squirrels.

Perhaps the best reason to detour through Olney is to sample the incredibly good, inexpensive burgers and milk shakes at **Hovey's**, on old US-50 at 412 E. Main Street—look for the Mike's Ice Cream sign.

East of Olney, US-50 reverts to two-lane highway, running for 23 miles before passing by Lawrenceville (pop. 4,897), which stakes its claims to fame on two very different fronts. It was named for U.S. Navy Capt. James Lawrence, best remembered for his dying words, "Don't give up the ship," during the War of 1812. Later, in 1845, Lawrenceville gained notoriety as the first place in Illinois to execute a woman by hanging.

In Odin, five miles west of Salem, **Vernon's Reproductions** (618/775-6545) along US-50 has an incredible array of weather vanes and lawn ornaments: ducks, geese, cowboys, Indians, Statues of Liberty—you name it, they'll have it.

East of Lawrenceville, follow the old road south of the modern freeway, crossing the Wabash River into Indiana at historic Vincennes.

ACROSS INDIANA

From the Wabash River at its western end, to the Ohio River in the east, the 170 miles of southern Indiana that lie in between presents an immensely varied landscape. The hilly eastern sections are surprisingly rugged, though the central and western reaches are comparatively flat and largely agricultural. Besides numerous well-preserved historic Ohio River towns like Madison and Aurora, there are a number of unlovely industrial sections, especially around Bedford and the famous limestone quarries in the central parts of the state.

Vincennes

First settled by the French in 1732, and intensely fought over during the Revolutionary War, Vincennes (pop. 19,859) remained a lawless frontier until 1803, when it was named the territorial capital. A handful of early buildings, including a bank, a church, and a newspaper office, have been restored as the **Indiana Territory State Historic Site** (Wed.-Sat. 9 AM-5 PM, Sunday 1-5 PM; free) at 1st and Harrison Streets in the historic downtown area. Nearby, overlooking the Wabash River, the **George Rogers Clark National Historical Park** ($2) is a classical dome honoring Revolutionary War general George Rogers Clark, who led local militiamen in the capture of Vincennes from the British in 1779. (George Rogers Clark was the older brother of William Clark, of Lewis and Clark fame.)

The Wabash River between Indiana and Illinois marks the boundary between the central and eastern time zones. Subtract an hour heading east, add an hour heading west. At the west end of the bridge over the river, a roadside memorial recounts the westward migration of young Abraham Lincoln and his family.

The monument, built as a WPA project during the Great Depression, wouldn't look out of place in D.C., but the rest of Vincennes is decidedly down-to-earth, with grain elevators along railroad tracks, and dime stores and cafes like **Oink!**, a BBQ place on Main Street near 10th Street.

The area around Vincennes is very flat farming country, notable for its large Amish communities (and numerous roadside "Amish Kountry Korner" stores and cafes), especially around **Loogootee**, 30 miles east of Vincennes.

French Lick and Mitchell

Between Vincennes and Bedford, US-50 winds its way through the hilly groves of the Hoosier National Forest, but a worthwhile detour heads south through the hometowns of two of Indiana's best-known sons. The first of these, on Hwy-56 just south of US-150, is French Lick (pop. 2,087), where Boston Celtics star (and Indiana Pacers head coach) Larry Bird, "The Hick from French Lick," learned his game. The town itself is little more than a two-block-long business district—pick up souvenirs at the **French Lick Five and Dime** at 111 Maple Street.

The surrounding area was a popular vacation resort, and thousands of Midwesterners (including Al Capone and other Chicago mobsters) came here to stay at the monumental **West Baden Springs Hotel** and take the mineral-rich waters that still flow from local artesian springs. The hotel, a 1902 National Landmark, has been undergoing restoration for years, but is open for tours (Saturday and Sunday 10 AM-3 PM; 812/639-4534).

The other famous hometown, Mitchell, is about six miles south of Bedford, and was the boyhood home of astronaut Virgil "Gus" Grissom, who captained Mercury and Gemini space flights before dying in the Apollo 1 disaster. There's an impressive memorial—a 30-foot-high limestone statue of a Titan rocket—to Grissom south of Main Street on 6th Street, next to the police station.

Bedford

Nicknamed "Stone City" because it holds some of the largest and most famous limestone quarries in the country, Bedford (pop. 13,817) is a busy, industrial-looking city, the largest on the Indiana stretch of US-50. The quarries that earned Bedford's reputation are still in use, producing the durable stone that has clad many high-profile structures, including the Empire State Building. Though you can see the limestone in situ at many road cuts along US-50, perhaps the most prominent examples in Bedford are the monuments and gravestones in the cemeteries lining the highway through town.

Bedford's main hard-rock attraction is **Bluesprings Caverns** (daily 9 AM-5 PM May-Oct.; $7), five miles west of downtown on US-50, where you can descend into a cave and take an hour-long boat tour along the largest underground river in the U.S.

Brownstown, Seymour, and North Vernon

Roughly 27 miles east of Bedford and 10 miles west of the I-65 freeway, Brownstown (pop. 2,872) is an unusually pretty Indiana town set around a large central square shaded by 100-year-old maple trees—and a war surplus tank. An old-fashioned general store and a couple of downhome restaurants make it worth a brief stop, particularly during the annual Watermelon Festival in late August.

East of Brownstown, it's a scenic 10 miles to Seymour (pop. 15,576), with its many motels (including a Holiday Inn and an Econolodge), fast-food franchises, 24-hour gas stations and an absolutely HUGE Wal-Mart distribution center marking the junction with the I-65 freeway. Blue-collar Seymour is the birthplace of rock star **John** "Don't Call Me Cougar" **Mellencamp**, and you can get a good feel for the place by stopping for a meal at the **Townhouse Cafe**, 206 E. 4th Street. Alternately, there's the ersatz but enjoyable **Heartbeat Cafe**, a "Fabulous 1950s Diner" on US-50 two miles west of downtown.

Twelve miles east of Seymour, turn south from US-50 at neat little **North Vernon** onto Hwy-7, which runs toward the Ohio River town of Madison across miles of rolling farmland, closely paralleling the route of Morgan's Raid, when Gen. John Morgan and 2,000 Confederate soldiers invaded Indiana during the Civil War.

Madison and the Ohio River Towns

The route east along US-50 is uneventful, so if you have some time, loop to the south along **Hwy-56**, which curves along the north bank of the broad Ohio River. The riverside here is rich in history, and the 60-mile drive passes by modest tobacco farms and timeless small towns, the pastoral scene marred only by occasional power plants, most of them across the water on the Kentucky side.

*One thing to see along US-50 is 10 miles east of North Vernon, in Butlerville, where a roadside plaque marks the 1885 birthplace of **Hannah Milhous Nixon,** Richard's mother.*

Though the drive is nice enough in itself, it's most worthwhile because it brings you to **Madison** (pop. 12,006), one of the best-preserved historic Ohio River towns. Now a popular vacation destination, especially during the **Chautauqua Arts Festival** in late September and the rowdier **Madison Regatta** during the 4th of July, when 200-mph hydroplanes race along the river, Madison has managed to stay alive economically without sacrificing its small-town charms. Wandering around a few blocks of the franchise-free Main Street, you can enjoy a milk shake at the soda fountain in the back of **Rogers Drug Store**, listen to the town gossip while getting a haircut at the chrome and red-leather barber shop, or tour the many **historic homes**. The best of these is the impressive Greek Revival mansion of Civil War financier James Lanier, now a state **museum** (Tues.-Sat. 9 AM-5 PM, Sunday 1-5 PM; free) near the river at 511 W. 1st Street. Also worth a look is the perfectly preserved **doctor's office** at 120 W. 3rd Street, which served as the only hospital between Cincinnati and Louisville from 1882 to 1903, when it was closed and preserved intact; it's now open for tours (Mon.-Sat. 10 AM-4:30 PM, Sunday 1-4:30 PM; $2).

The town of Vevay, 20 miles east of Madison, was the birthplace of Edward Eggleston, author of The Hoosier Schoolmaster. Another important area native was engineer Elwood Mead, the man for whom Lake Mead is named.

Madison

Louisville is world headquarters for the fast-food chain formerly known as Kentucky Fried Chicken (now called KFC); in the corporate HQ, a small museum (502/456-8353) tells the story of Colonel Sanders and his 11 herbs and spices.

Louisville is also home to one of the better BBQ places you'll find anywhere: **Vince Staten's,** northeast of downtown at 9219 US-42 (502/228-7427). Owner Vince is also a noted historian of hardware, having written *Did Monkeys Invent the Monkey Wrench?* (Simon and Schuster, 1997). Stop by and say hi.

Besides the wealth of Americana, Madison has a number of good places to eat along Main Street, including **Our Place, Lacey's,** and **Hinckle's**; the latter is open 24 hours (except Sunday) for great greasy spoon burgers. Places to stay range from the 1847 federal-style **Schusser House B&B** at 514 Jefferson Street (812/273-2068 or 800/392-1931) to the motel-type rooms at the **Clifty Inn** (812/265-4135) in wooded Clifty Falls State Park, a mile west of town.

For complete information on Madison, contact the **visitor center** at 301 E. Main Street (812/265-2956 or 800/559-2956), across from the landmark Jefferson County Courthouse.

Detour: Louisville

Home of the world's greatest horse race (the Kentucky Derby), the world's biggest baseball bat (a 120-foot-tall Louisville Slugger), and the man who was and is simply "The Greatest" (boxer Muhammed Ali, for whom the city is proposing to build a major museum), Louisville is a characterful mid-sized city on the south bank of the Ohio River. During Kentucky Derby week, the mint julep-fueled party leading up to the first Saturday in May, the whole city comes alive, but any time of year Louisville is an enjoyable place to explore. Along with some well-above average art museums and high culture institutions, Louisville also has some top pop culture destinations, best of

which is the **Louisville Slugger Museum**, 800 W. Main Street (Mon.-Sat. 9 AM-5 PM; $5), marked by that giant baseball bat, and full of memorabilia on big hitters from Babe Ruth to Hank Aaron. Along the waterfront, which has undergone some successful resuscitation after the I-71 freeway was cut through, take a look at the **Louisville Falls Fountain,** which spurts water 375 feet into the air every 15 minutes. Outside Louisville, along US-31 30 miles to the southwest, you can cruise past **Fort Knox** and dream about the 150 million ounces of gold locked inside. At current prices, it's worth *almost* as much as Bill Gates.

Louisville is an hour's drive south on I-65 from US-50, or along the Ohio River from Madison. For more information, contact the **visitors bureau,** 400 S. 1st Street (502/584-2121 or 800/626-5646).

Rising Sun

Farther along Hwy-56, nine miles south of Aurora and US-50, the village of Rising Sun holds a handful of frontier-era structures as well as one of the state's biggest riverboat casinos, the **Hyatt Grand Victoria** (800/GRAND-11 or 800/472-6311), which opened in 1996 and actually cruises out onto the river so you can play its 1,300 slot machines. The historic

parts of town have managed to stay quaint despite the influx of gamblers, and the old-fashioned (but newly repaved . . .) downtown area has the very good **Ohio County Historical Museum** at 212 S. Walnut Street.

Aurora and Lawrenceburg

Our Ohio River detour along Hwy-56 rejoins US-50 at Aurora (pop. 9,192), a small riverside town that's well worth at least a brief stop. The highlight here is the handsome **Hillforest Mansion** (Tues.-Sun. 1-5 PM; $4), an exuberant survivor from the steamboat era whose colonnaded facade is topped by a circular lookout tower from which residents could gaze out at river traffic up and down the Ohio. Built in 1852 and preserved in fine condition, the hillside mansion gives a strong sense of how comfortable and sophisticated life was for the wealthy, even on the so-called frontier.

East from Aurora, approaching the Ohio state line, US-50 forms a seedy gauntlet of roadside motels, diners, cut-rate liquor stores, and fireworks stands, all competing with giant billboards for the tri-state trade. Lawrenceburg (pop. 4,375), along the I-275 freeway three miles west of the Indiana/Ohio/Kentucky border, seems to revolve around the sale of cheap booze, perhaps because the main employer is the massive red-brick **Seagram's** distillery at the north end of Main Street—one of the oldest and largest in the USA.

Aurora, Indiana, is home to Aurora Casket Company, a leading producer of caskets in the USA.

Apart from a wonderfully photogenic collection of old auto-related advertising signs in a used car lot on the west side of town, near the Wal-Mart, the view of Lawrenceburg from US-50 is unpromising with railroad tracks and a huge levee cutting off the town from the waterfront. However, the historic town center, south of the highway along Walnut Street, holds a number of interesting old buildings dating from the steamboat era of the early 1800s, when Lawrenceburg was a favorite Ohio River port of call. Among the many church spires competing for preeminence is that of the Presbyterian church, where in 1837 orator Henry Ward Beecher (father of Harriet Beecher Stowe, she of *Uncle Tom's Cabin* fame) held his first pastorate.

Places to eat in old-town Lawrenceburg emphasize the 80-proof aspects of local life: **Whisky's** serves steaks in an old button factory on Front Street, and **Whisky Island** has more unusual fare (try the coconut shrimp!) on Walnut Street.

ACROSS OHIO

Winding along the Ohio River from Indiana, US-50 cuts east
from Cincinnati across the hill-and-valley country of southern
Ohio before finally crossing the Ohio River into West Virginia. The
220 miles US-50 takes to cross the state are a fairly constant mix of upland forest
and bottomland farms, with a single industrial district in the middle, around Chillicothe, and a refreshing small college town, Athens, farther east.

North Bend

East from the Indiana line, US-50 winds along the partly industrial, partly rural
Ohio River waterfront, without much to detain you before Cincinnati. The one
place really worth a stop is the hamlet of North Bend (pop. 541), five miles east of
the state border. A tall sandstone obelisk, overlooking the river and US-50 amidst a
14-acre park, marks the final resting place of William Henry Harrison (1773-1841),
the ninth president of the United States, who lived here for many years when North
Bend was a thriving frontier port. Born in Virginia, Harrison came to fame fighting
Shawnee tribes in and around the Ohio Valley, and served in Congress for many
years before he was elected president; he died of pneumonia after only a month in
office. His grandson Benjamin Harrison, who became president in 1889, was born
in the nearby family home in 1833.

Continuing along US-50, five miles west of downtown Cincinnati, the tiny **Anderson Ferry** ($2.50 per car, 25 cents for foot passengers) has been chugging back
and forth since 1817, though the broad river is nothing like the busy river it was
back then. But as recently as 1940, the WPA *Guide to Ohio* wrote that "fleets of
barges pushed by snub-nosed towboats crawl along the motionless water; and now
and then appears one of the Greene Line packets, all white and triple-decked."

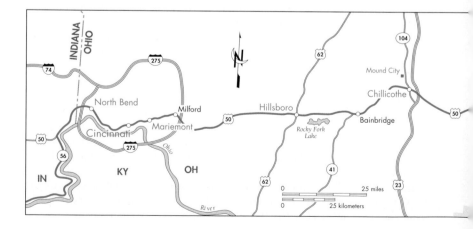

US-50 across Cincinnati

US-50 survives pretty much intact across Cincinnati, though most of its former traffic now follows the freeways that loop around and cut through the city. West of downtown, US-50 follows the Ohio River along River Road, but the old alignment veers away from the freeway-sliced waterfront along State Avenue, running through downtown along 7th, 8th and 9th Streets. East of downtown, old US-50 rejoins the riverfront around Mount Adams, then follows the Columbia Parkway east to the garden city of Mariemont, where we rejoin it.

Mariemont

From Cincinnati, US-50 follows surface streets through the warehouse and residential districts along the Ohio River, before becoming a freeway for the quick drive east to Mariemont (pop. 3,118). Built in the mid-1920s as one of the nation's first planned communities, Mariemont's mock-Tudor downtown centers around the historic and very comfortable **Best Western Mariemont Inn**, right on US-50 at 6880 Wooster Pike (513/271-2100). Across the street there's a branch of the excellent local ice-cream chain, **Graeter's**, and the sole surviving neighborhood of Mariemont's original 1920s half-timbered Arts-and-Crafts homes is an easily walkable block to the southeast.

East of Mariemont, US-50 crosses the Little Miami River at the scenic, 25-mph town of **Milford** (where there's a great old "Big Boy" sign, straight out of *American Graffiti*) before racing east across 40 miles of flat and sparsely settled farming country to Hillsboro.

Hillsboro

Hillsboro (pop. 6,235), 60 miles east of Cincinnati and 40 miles west of Chillicothe, is the biggest and busiest town along the way. Besides the gas stations and good cafes like **Maggie's Snack Shop**, Hillsboro has a unique, alcohol-related history. During Christmas 1873, the town's 13 saloons were closed down by one of the country's earliest temperance movements, and more recently, country singer **Johnny** "Take This Job and Shove It" **Paycheck** did time in prison for shooting a man in Hillsboro's North High Saloon. (Even more recently, that saloon was torn down to make way for a new city office building.)

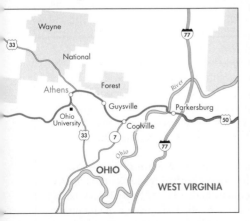

East from Hillsboro toward Chillicothe, US-50 winds past whitewashed farmhouses and broad cornfields flanked by low hills. The region also holds two remnants of the "mound builder" people who once lived here. Just west of the sleepy village of Bainbridge, turning south onto Hwy-41 brings you to the **Serpent Mound**, which stretches alongside a creek for almost 1,500 feet. The **Seip Mound**, 16 miles west of Chillicothe, is another of the region's many ancient archaeological sites.

CINCINNATI SURVIVAL GUIDE

SPREADING ALONG THE NORTH BANK of the Ohio River, Cincinnati, whose nicknames range from "Queen City" to "Porkopolis," was once the largest and busiest city on the western frontier. During the heyday of steamboat travel in the first half of the 19th century, the city's riverside location made it a prime transportation center, but as the railroad networks converged on Chicago, Cincinnati was eclipsed as the prime gateway to the western U.S. Procter & Gamble, the world's largest consumer products company, started here in the 1830s, making soap out of the abundant animal fat from the city's hundreds of slaughterhouses. Cincinnati has also won accolades from a broad range of notables, including Winston Churchill, who called it "the most beautiful of America's inland cities." Cincinnati's current population of some 400,000 ranks it just ahead of Toledo as Ohio's third largest city, which from a traveler's point of view makes it an easily manageable and usually stress-free place to visit. Even if you're racing through, no road-tripper in his or her right mind should pass through Cincinnati without sampling its excellent road food—mounds of chili and/or stacks of melt-in-your-mouth ribs, finished off with a scoop or two of Graeter's ice cream, available at their own parlors all over the city and at most good restaurants.

The best first stop in Cincy is the **Museum Center**, in the former Union Terminal on Ezzard Charles Drive, off I-75 exit 1 (Mon.-Sat. 9 AM-5 PM, Sunday 11 AM-6 PM; 513/287-7000 or 800/733-2077). This 1930s Art Deco railroad station has been converted into one of the best museum complexes in the country. Besides the soaring architecture, the highlight here is the collection of the **Cincinnati Historical Society** ($5), where expansive and engaging displays trace the city's evolution from riverboat days—including a full-scale mock-up of a paddlewheel steamer—to the present. There's also a **Museum of Natural History** ($5), complete with live-in bats.

The city's most interesting neighborhood, **Mount Adams**, is east of downtown, high above the Ohio River. Once connected to downtown by an incline railway but now somewhat cut off by the I-71 freeway, this 300-foot-high hilltop neighborhood has emerged from years of neglect as an artsy district of crafts shops and cafes. Nearby **Eden Park** holds the respected **Cincinnati Art Museum** (Tues.-Sun. 10 AM-5 PM; $5), as well as a planetarium and conservatory amidst acres of greenery.

Unfortunately, most of Cincinnati's once vibrant waterfront area known as "The Basin" has been torn down in the name of urban renewal—the concrete of Riverfront Stadium, where the **Cincinnati Reds** (513/421-4510) play, taking the place of what the 1940 WPA *Guide to Ohio* called "a museum of city history and the building styles of the past century." The sole survivors of old Cincinnati are found across the river in Covington, Kentucky, which you can get to by walking across the **Roebling Bridge**, built in 1865 as a precursor to the more famous Brooklyn Bridge. East of the bridge, a line of well-preserved 1820s houses, many of which served as way stations on the anti-slavery Underground Railroad, overlook the point where the Licking River flows into the Ohio River.

Practicalities

Cincinnati lies along the north bank of the Ohio River, very near Indiana and the Kentucky border just across the river. Most major airlines fly into the **Greater Cincinnati International Airport**, which actually lies southwest of downtown in Kentucky. Getting around town is best done by car, if only so you can drive back and forth across the Ohio River on the Roebling Bridge—being careful not to end up in the bus station at its northern end.

There are hundreds of rooms available in national chain motels along the I-71 and I-75 freeways, plus the handy and spacious **Embassy Suites** (606/261-8400) overlooking the Ohio River from the Kentucky side of the Roebling Bridge. The nicest place to stay is the classic art deco **Omni Netherland Plaza** at 35 W. 5th Street (513/421-9100 or 800/843-6665), one of the country's grandest old hotels, its lovely lobby clogged with ad execs courting Procter & Gamble business.

For food, try **Camp Washington Chili**, corner of Hopple and Colerain, three miles north of downtown, right off I-75 exit 3. Along with ribs, Cincy is also known for its chili, poured over spaghetti and served either "3-Way" (spaghetti, chili, and grated cheese); "4-Way" (add onions); or "5-Way" (add beans). Over 100 places around town serve this subtly spiced local specialty (there's even a 3-Way Pentecostal Church!), with some of the best coming out of the kitchens of Camp Washington, which is open around-the-clock (except Sunday). Downtown, **Arnold's**, at 210 E. 8th Street (513/421-6234), is a fine old place, a cozy circa 1860 tavern and deli that also features good live music. Along the river east of downtown, **Montgomery Inn at the Boathouse**, 925 Eastern Avenue (513/721-7427), serves what, according to Bob Hope and the late Billy Carter, are the best BBQ ribs in America. In tandem with the original **Montgomery Inn**, about 12 miles northeast of downtown, off I-71 at 9440 Montgomery Road (513/791-3482), these two restaurants manage to serve over 200 tons of ribs annually, more than anywhere else in the country. For a real push-the-boat-out celebration, **Maisonette**, 114 E. 6th Street (513/721-2260), is elegant (jacket required for men at dinner), expensive, and one of best French restaurants between the coasts—Mobil 5-Star rated for the past thirty-something years.

The main source for visitor information is the **Greater Cincinnati Visitors Bureau**, 300 W. 6th Street (513/621-2142 or 800/344-3445), which also operates a branch on the main concourse of the Museum Center (see above). Both offer free information and maps of Cincinnati. Daily newspapers are the morning *Enquirer* and the afternoon *Post*.

Midway between Chillicothe and Hillsboro, the nice little town of Bainbridge was the site of the first dental school in the U.S., now a **dental museum** at 208 W. Main Street (US-50).

Chillicothe and Mound City

In the middle of the state, Chillicothe (pop. 21,923; pronounced chill-a-COTH-ee) comes as a sudden surprise after the pastoral landscape that surrounds it. It is one of the state's oldest industrial centers; since 1812 Chillicothe's economy has revolved around the massive Mead Paper mill on the south side of town, whose red-and-white striped smokestack belches a pungent white cloud around the clock.

Heavy industry aside, Chillicothe has done an admirable job of preserving its history, most notably in the recently spruced-up "First Capital" district along Main Street (US-50) downtown. Dozens of elaborate late Victorian commercial buildings and Greek Revival-style mansions, mostly dating from the mid-1850s, surround the overwrought Ross County Courthouse, which has a different entrance for each government department.

While the downtown area is worth a quick stroll, specific sites are few, and the area's real attraction is three miles north of town via Hwy-104. Officially known as the Hopewell Culture National Historical Park, but usually called **Mound City**, this complex of prehistoric burial sites sits on the west bank of the Scioto River, just beyond a huge prison complex. Two dozen distinct, grass-covered mounds, the largest of which is about 15 feet high, are reachable on a mile-long trail that starts at the **visitor center** (daily 8 AM-5 PM; $2), where films and exhibits explore aspects of this 2,000-year-old culture.

Chillicothe makes a good place to break a journey. **Johnny's Famous Fried Chicken**, on US-50 next to McDonald's a mile west of downtown, serves very

---

THE MOUND BUILDERS

The broad area between the Mississippi River and the Appalachian crest is rich in early American history, but the human story here goes back way beyond Daniel Boone and Abraham Lincoln to an era not often discussed in textbooks. From around 800 B.C. until A.D. 1500, this region was home to two successive prehistoric cultures which were roughly simultaneous with the legendary Mayans and Aztecs of Mexico, but are now all but forgotten, remembered solely for the massive earthen mounds they left behind.

The older of these two prehistoric peoples is known as the **Hopewell** culture, since the first scientific studies were conducted in 1891 at a farm owned by a man named Hopewell. Some 50 years earlier, the mounds had already become famous, as stories spread tracing their construction back to a "lost race" of mysterious origin, not unlike the Anasazi of the desert Southwest. As the Hopewell culture began to decline, around A.D. 500 another culture, called the **Mississippian**, came into being. Similarities between these two hunter-gatherer cultures, with their far-flung trading networks and hierarchical societies, are much greater than their differences, but archaeologists consider them to be completely distinct from one another. A key difference: almost all of the Hopewell mounds were rounded or conical, and built as burial sites, while Mississippian sites tended to be more rectilinear, with the mounds serving not

good food but closes at 8 PM. The $30-a-night **Chillicothe Inn** lies a half-block north of US-50 at 24 N. Bridge Street (740/774-2512); there's also a Holiday Inn and a Travelodge.

Chillicothe is known throughout Ohio as the site of **Tecumseh**, an outdoor pageant dramatizing the life of the Shawnee Indian warrior. Shows are at 8 PM nightly in summer ($13; 740/775-0700). More fun, and cheaper, are the baseball games played by the Frontier League **Chillicothe Paints** (bleacher seats $2; 740/ 773-TEAM or 740/773-8326), who play from June through August near Mound City.

Athens

East of Chillicothe, US-50 passes through Vinton County, one of the state's poorest and least developed regions. Hidden amidst forested hills, the remains of coal mines and overgrown, rail-fenced cornfields line the next 50 miles, and little has changed (for the better, at least) since the WPA *Guide* described the scene in 1939: "Abruptly the road sweeps into a rock-bound gorge dotted with the rickety houses of hill-folk . . . who make a living by seasonal mining, moonshining, trapping, or on Government relief projects."

Chillicothe served as capital of the Northwest Territory from 1800 to 1802, and later as the first capital of Ohio.

After all this rural poverty, US-50 finally arrives at Athens (pop. 21,265), one of the most attractive small towns in Ohio. Set, like its classical namesake, on a series of hills, Athens is an idyllic little town that has grown up around the leafy campus of Ohio University, which opened here in 1809. Brick-paved streets lined by bookstores, copy shops, and clothing stores, mostly catering

---

as interments but as bases for long-vanished wooden structures built atop them. In Hopewell sites, buried along with the usually cremated human remains, archeologists and treasure hunters have recovered a compelling array of artifacts—obsidian tools (from the Pacific Northwest), shell beads (from the Gulf of Mexico), and silver and copper objects (from the Great Lakes)—which give some hint of the quality of ancient Native American life.

Ohio is particularly well provided with these enigmatic earthworks; at the Hopewell Culture National Historic site near Chillicothe (see previous page), over two dozen burial mounds have been preserved by the National Park Service. West of Chillicothe, the low-lying Serpent Mound (see page 717 stretches for a quarter-mile along a river, and over 100 other sites have been identified across the state.

Further west on US-50, along the Mississippi at Cahokia Mounds State Historic Site (see page 843 the remnants of the largest prehistoric city in North America now sit across the river from St. Louis. North along the river, the Effigy Mounds National Monument in Iowa across from Prairie du Chien (see page 239) preserves yet more burial mounds, while down south, the Natchez Trace Parkway features the prehistoric Emerald Mound (see page 283); Macon, Georgia has the major mounds of Ocmulgee National Monument (see page 789); and in Louisiana, perhaps the most extensive site of all is being excavated at Poverty Point, north of Monroe (see page 770).

to the college's 18,000 well-groomed twenty-somethings, fill the eight-block "Uptown" neighborhood along College and Court Streets on the north side of the neoclassical College Green, a National Historic Landmark dating from 1816.

US-50 follows the Hocking River and bypasses the heart of town, so follow Stimson Avenue or State Street from the highway, past the cafes and shops that fill the few blocks around the Ohio University campus. **The Pub**, 39 N. Court Street, has Athens's best burgers (and Happy Hour specials), though the best food by most accounts is four miles east of town at the **Big Chimney Baking Company**, in the historic Canaan Coal Company building just off US-50 (740/592-4147). Accommodations in Athens include a **Days Inn** and other motels along Columbus Road (US-33) on the north side of town. Further information is available from the **visitor center** (740/592-1819 or 800/878-9767) in the city park on US-50 east of town.

East of the Athens area, US-50 passes through 40 miles of scrubby second-growth forests and the abandoned but enticingly named coal-mining towns of Guysville and Coolville, before reaching the West Virginia border at the Ohio River and Parkersburg.

ACROSS WEST VIRGINIA

The slowest part of US-50's transcontinental crossing is the 150-mile section across West Virginia, which twists and turns its way over the rugged Allegheny Mountains. Starting along the Ohio River in the western, more developed half of the state, US-50 runs briefly as a fairly fast freeway before beginning its climb into the rugged hill country. Though there are many fine hardwood forests and whitewater rivers, including some of the most extensive semi-wilderness areas left in the eastern states, this part of West Virginia is mostly rural, with more than few corners where things seem straight out of a De-

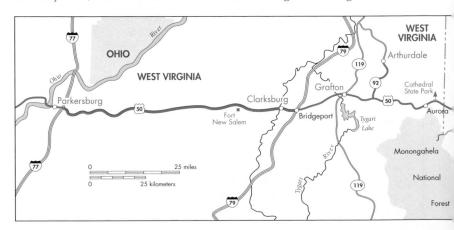

pression-era Walker Evans photograph. Rusting appliances and broken-down cars fill the front and back yards of the shanties, shacks, and trailer parks alongside the highway, but around the next corner you may come across a lovely old covered bridge, or a waterfall that takes your breath away. The few towns along the route, formerly bustling thanks to the railroads or coal mines towns, are still dominated by the empty remnants of industries that have vanished, never to return, and most places are populated by people who seem to have lived there forever. The self-reliant, "Mountaineer" ethos still runs strong, and Montana-style militia types may lurk in the hills and hollows, but the lingering impression West Virginia leaves behind is of taking a step back in time to a world where men work hard in mines and mills, women raise the kids, and everybody goes to church on Sunday.

Parkersburg

Northern West Virginia's largest and most heavily industrialized city, Parkersburg (pop. 33,862) is located strategically at the junction of the Ohio and Little Kanawha Rivers. The town's economy is based around an unusual pair of employers: the federal Bureau of the Public Debt, which redeems U.S. Savings Bonds, and a massive DuPont Teflon factory.

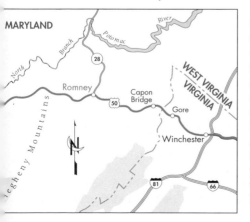

Though the first impression can be fairly bleak, Parkersburg does merit a closer look. The **Blennerhasset Museum** (Tues.-Sun. 9:30 AM-5 PM; $1), housed in a turn-of-the-century brick warehouse at 2nd and Juliana Streets, traces regional history, with a focus on the escapades of the Irish aristocrat Harman Blennerhasset, who in 1806 conspired with Aaron Burr to establish an independent fiefdom in Texas and the Southwest. If you're interested, you can ride a paddle wheeler to and from the Ohio River island on which Blennerhasset built the palatial home where the plot was hatched. The house has been restored as a state park ($2), and **boats** ($4) leave hourly from Point Park, which is two blocks west of the museum, under the railroad bridges and on the far side of the 25-foot concrete flood walls at the confluence of the rivers.

There are a couple of coffee shops along 7th Street (US-50), like the **Travelers Restaurant** and the 24-hour **Mountaineer Family Restaurant**, near I-77 on the east side of town. Parkersburg also has a good range of motels, including most of the chains and the unique **Stables Motor Lodge**, 3604 E. 7th Street (304/424-5100), marked by a pair of white horses.

For more information, contact the Parkersburg **visitors bureau**, 350 7th Street (304/428-1130 or 800/752-4982).

Fort New Salem

Between Parkersburg and Clarksburg, US-50 winds along as a fast, four-lane freeway through a mountainous one-time oil- and gas-producing region dotted with tiny, all-but-forgotten towns. The small farms are cultivated by descendants of Scotch-Irish immigrants who settled here in the late 18th century. One place that's well worth a stop is Fort New Salem (Wed.-Fri. 10 AM-5 PM, Saturday and Sunday 1-5 PM; $4), 14 miles west of Clarksburg. Just south of US-50, on the campus of half-Japanese Salem-Teikyo University, the fort is a credible reconstruction of the frontier outpost of palisaded log cabins, erected near here in 1795.

Clarksburg

The house where "Stonewall" Jackson was born is marked by a plaque at 326 Main Street in Clarksburg.

Birthplace of Confederate Civil War hero Thomas "Stonewall" Jackson, Clarksburg (pop. 18,059) is a tidy railroad town sitting on a branch of the Monongahela River. The downtown area is a sampler of turn-of-the-century commercial buildings, great for taking pictures of old signs and brick walls, but with no particular sights to see. The town's large Italian population, estimated at around 40%, supports numerous good restaurants like **Minard's Spaghetti Inn**, 813 E. Pike Street on old US-50, at the Joyce Street exit off the US-50 freeway.

On the east side of Clarksburg, US-50 climbs a steep hill before becoming suddenly urban and ugly at **Bridgeport**, which straddles the I-79 freeway, around which the highway is lined by a two-mile sprawl of Wal-Marts, Kmarts, franchised fast-food chains, and **motels**, including a Holiday Inn, a Comfort Inn, and a Days Inn.

The Grafton area saw the first fatality of the Civil War, when Union soldier Bailey Brown was killed by Confederate forces during the battle of Philippi.

Grafton: Mother's Day Shrine

Grafton (pop. 5,524), the first large town west of Winchester, Virginia, grew up as a bustling B&O railroad town beginning in the 1850s but is now among the most economically and socially depressed places in the state. Dozens of architecturally interesting but run-down houses and churches drop on brick-paved streets down the steep hills to the Tygart River and the railroad tracks, where a monumental station and a grand but boarded-up hotel are grim reminders of Grafton's formerly busy self.

Besides its impressive physical setting, Grafton's main claim to fame is as the birthplace of Mother's Day, first celebrated here in 1908 in a Methodist church that's been converted into the **International Mother's Day Shrine** (Mon.-Fri. 9:30 AM-3:30 PM; donations), on Main Street across from the old train station.

East of Grafton, the landscape becomes more mountainous, and isolated villages replace the small towns that line the western half of the route.

South of Grafton, US-119 passes through the town of **Philippi,** where the largest covered bridge in West Virginia spans the Tygart River. Originally constructed in 1852, the 285-foot-long red-and-white bridge was badly burned in 1989 but has been totally restored.

Arthurdale

Northeast of Grafton, a half-hour north of US-50 via Hwy-92, the homestead community of Arthurdale was the first and perhaps the most important of the many anti-poverty rural resettlement projects initiated during the Depression-era New Deal. Though not the largest, Arthurdale was prominent because of the personal involvement of then-First Lady Eleanor Roosevelt, who not only helped plan the project but also visited many times, handing out diplomas at school graduations.

Beginning in 1934 with the construction of some 165 homes, plus schools and factories, a cooperative farm, a health center, and a small hotel, Arthurdale was an ideal community set up to relieve the dire living conditions of unemployed Morgantown coal miners. Most of the houses are still intact and still inhabited by the original homesteaders or their descendants. The old community center is being restored and now holds a small **museum** (daily by appointment; $2; 304/864-3959) that chronicles the whole story.

Cathedral State Park

Four miles west of the Maryland border, US-50 runs right through Cathedral State Park, where over 130 acres of stately maples and hemlocks constitute one of the few first-growth stands left in this lumber-hungry state. Beyond here, US-50 makes a quick seven-mile jaunt across a corner of Maryland before crossing the north branch of the Potomac River back into West Virginia.

From the bridge, US-50 climbs steeply up the densely wooded Alleghenies, twisting over 3,000-foot-high ridges with turns so tight the posted speed limit is 15 mph—the going is very slow, and not much fun if you're prone to car sickness.

Romney and the Eastern Gateway

The oddly shaped arm of eastern West Virginia, which juts between Maryland and Virginia at the headwaters of the Potomac River, is promoted as the "Eastern Gateway" and offers quick access to the mountainous wilderness of Monongahela National Forest that stretches south of US-50, and to the raging whitewater of the Cheat and Gauley Rivers. Originally inhabited by Shawnee Indians, the region was settled during colonial times as part of the six million-acre Virginia estate of Lord Fairfax. The B&O railroad came through in the 1850s, which made the region strategically important during the Civil War, nowhere more so than around Romney (pop. 1,966), the Eastern Gateway's largest town, which changed hands over 50 times in four years of fighting.

Midway across western Maryland's short stretch of US-50, around a mile east of Redhouse next to an immaculate "Chew Mail Pouch Tobacco" barn, the **Route 50 Quilt House** has hundreds of high-quality handmade quilts.

Across West Virginia, US-50 follows the approximate route of the colonial-era Northwest Turnpike, which was surveyed in 1748 by a 16-year-old George Washington.

Heading east toward Winchester, US-50 passes through mountain hamlets like Capon Bridge (on the West Virginia side) and Gore (on the Virginia side), which consist of little more than a gas station, a tavern, and a post office, plus one or two antique stores selling everything from colonial-era furniture to old highway signs. It's hard to help feeling light years from the modern world, even though Washington, D.C. is only 90 miles away.

ACROSS VIRGINIA

Dropping from the Allegheny and Appalachian Mountains of West Virginia, US-50 enters Virginia at the northern tip of the Shenandoah Valley, passing through the center of the quietly attractive small city of Winchester. Continuing east, in short order the road climbs the foothills of the Blue Ridge Mountains and crosses the Shenandoah River, delighting John Denver fans and carrying travelers through the heart of the ultra-wealthy "Hunt Country" of northern Virginia, a rural and unspoiled landscape of small towns, horse farms, and vineyards that's home to more well-connected millionaires than just about anywhere in the USA.

Approaching the outer suburbs of the nation's capital, however, US-50 swiftly loses its luster, and while you *can* follow it through miles of suburban sprawl on both sides of the I-495 Beltway, you might prefer to follow the misleadingly numbered I-66 freeway—which has nothing at all to do with the *real* Route 66—into the city. In any event there's little worth stopping for in the 22 miles between Dulles Airport and D.C. itself, though US-50's final approach takes you past the startling Iwo Jima Memorial statue, arriving in D.C. at the Lincoln Memorial.

Winchester

Northern Virginia's largest city, Winchester (pop. 21,947) is a surprisingly quiet and very pleasant small city, best known for the extensive apple orchards that fill

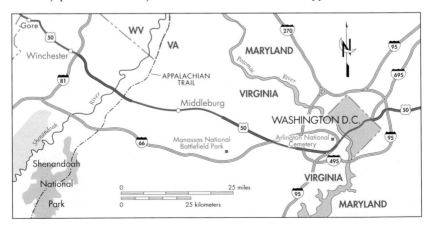

the surrounding countryside, producing some 250 million pounds each year. The I-81 freeway, complete with the usual sprawl of shopping malls and fast-food franchises, cuts across US-50 along the east side of Winchester, but the downtown district is eminently strollable, especially the pedestrianized Old Town area around Loudon Street, between Piccadilly (US-50) and Cork Street, where you can visit George Washington's office or Stonewall Jackson's Civil War headquarters.

Patsy Cline, September 8, 1932–March 5, 1963

After apples and American history, Winchester is probably most famous as the hometown of **Patsy Cline**, the inimitable country singer who died in a plane crash on March 5, 1963, at age 30. Patsy Cline, whose greatest hits include "Crazy," "Sweet Dreams," and "Walking After Midnight," lived in Winchester from age 3 to age 16 in a small house at 608 S. Kent Street near downtown, and dropped out of high school to earn money making milk shakes at **Gaunt's Drug Store**, south of downtown at Loudon Street and Valley Avenue. She's buried in **Shenandoah Memorial Park**, a mile southeast of town.

Other sites associated with Patsy Cline are included in the handy brochure "Celebrating Patsy," available free at the **Kurtz Cultural Center**, in Old Town Winchester at 2 N. Cameron Street (Mon.-Sat. 10 AM-5 PM, Sunday noon-5 PM; free; (540/722-6367), which also has extensive displays on local and Civil War-era history and culture. For complete listings of eating and accommodation options, contact the Winchester **visitor center**, 1360 S. Pleasant Valley Road (540/662-6550 or 800/662-1360).

US-50 crosses our Appalachian Trail route near 1,100 foot-high Ashby Gap, 15 miles east of Winchester. The magnificently preserved town of Harpers Ferry, West Virginia, 26 miles north of US-50 via US-340, and scenic Shenandoah National Park, just south of US-50, are covered in detail on pages 346 and 349, respectively.

Middleburg

Located at the heart of northern Virginia's "Hunt Country," where senators, ambassadors, and aristocrats mix at multi-million-dollar country estates, Middleburg (pop. 549) is a small but immaculate town with a four-block business district packed with antique shops, art galleries, real estate agencies—and a lone Safeway supermarket, just west of the only traffic light.

Many of Middleburg's brick- and stone-fronted buildings date from colonial times, including the **Red Fox Inn**, 2 E. Washington Street (540/687-6301 or 800/ 223-1728), on US-50 at the center of town. Originally built in 1728 as a coach inn and tavern, it's now a comfortable and upscale B&B and restaurant. There's a couple of other places to eat, including the **Back Street Cafe**, at 4 E. Federal Street, and the eminently affordable **Huckleberry's** ice cream and sandwich shop, at 3 W. Washington Street.

East of Middleburg, US-50 winds through gently rolling farmlands for a dozen miles before hitting the outlying suburbs of Washington, D.C.

John Brown 1800-1859

Confederate hero Thomas "Stonewall" Jackson earned his nickname at the first battle of Manassas, where his steadfastness under fire helped rally rebel troops.

As much as half of all Internet traffic is routed through Fairfax County in D.C.'s western suburbs, home to America Online and other major cyberspace companies.

Manassas National Battlefield Park

Site of the first major land battle of the Civil War, Manassas National Battlefield Park has been preserved intact despite the suburbanizing pressures of the surrounding towns, and despite the aborted efforts of the Walt Disney Company to build a massive American history-themed amusement park nearby. The prospect of battle-view tract houses still looms in the future, but for now Manassas (which in the North was also known as Bull Run) is among the most evocative of all the Civil War sites, its five square miles of rolling hills and woodlands kept as they were, with few intrusions of modern life.

Manassas, which controlled transportation links between Washington, D.C. and the Shenandoah Valley, was the site of two major battles. The first battle, fought here on July 21, 1861, was strategically inconclusive, though the fact that the Confederate "rebels" forced the overconfident Union army into a panicked retreat surprised the many onlookers who had traveled out from Washington to watch the fighting, and foreshadowed the next four years of war. The second battle, fought August 28-30, 1862, followed the instatement of Robert E. Lee as commander of the Confederate forces. That conflict marked the beginning of the bloodiest year of fighting, culminating in the battle of Gettysburg the following July.

Hundreds of monuments and memorials, along with rows of artillery set up along battle lines, dot the grassy hills and point out the many key moments of the battles. A loosely structured 1.4-mile walking tour begins at the small **visitor center** (703/361-1339) where audiovisual displays and collections of military artifacts give a sense of what the war was like.

To reach Manassas Battlefield, follow the I-66 freeway from Washington, D.C., or the Lee Highway (US-29) west from Fairfax. From US-50, follow US-15 or the smaller Hwy-659 south.

Arlington National Cemetery

Across the Potomac River from Washington, D.C., one of the most compelling and thought-provoking places in the capital region is Arlington National Cemetery (daily 9 AM-5 PM, till 7 PM in summer; free), a 600-acre hillside that contains the mortal remains of over 250,000 U.S. soldiers, sailors and public servants. Row after row of nearly identical, unadorned white tablets cover most of the cemetery, but special plots are dedicated to the most prominent people, such as John F. and Jacqueline Kennedy, who are buried together beneath an eternal flame, 200 yards straight beyond the main gate. Bobby Kennedy's grave is adjacent.

Located high on a ridge at the top of Arlington Cemetery, the neoclassical mansion of Arlington House was the antebellum home of Confederate General Robert E. Lee. Besides providing great views of the Mall and the heart of monumental Washington, the house serves as a vivid reminder of the deep rift caused by the Civil War. During the war, the grounds of the house were made into a cemetery for war dead, which formed the basis for Arlington National Cemetery. Washington, D.C.'s French-born designer, Pierre L'Enfant, lies in front of the mansion, in a tomb marked by his plan for the city. The somber Tomb of the Unknowns is a quarter-mile south of Arlington House, where a US Army honor guard is formally "changed" every half-hour during hot summer days, every two hours on cold winter nights.

One place worth stopping at in the D.C. suburbs is the **Tastee 29 Diner,** 10536 Lee Highway (US-50) in Fairfax, a National Landmark chrome and blue enamel diner that's open 24 hours every day.

WASHINGTON, D.C., SURVIVAL GUIDE

EVEN IF YOU SLEPT THROUGH HIGH school civics and have less than zero interest in national politics, visiting Washington, D.C., is still an unforgettable experience. The monuments and monoliths that line the city's many grand avenues embody nearly two centuries of American political history, and museums show off everything from ancient art to the first flying ma-

chines. Best of all, almost everything is free, though there are a few caveats every would-be tourist should know about: substantial parts of D.C. are definitely dangerous, so take care, especially after dark. Also the weather varies tremendously, from freezing cold in winter to swelteringly hot and humid in summer, though both spring and fall can be lovely. Assuming that most visitors will be able to find their way to the White House, and to the presidential memorials and Smithsonian museums along the Mall, this guide focuses on pointing out the lesser-known sights—ones you won't have to wait in line to see—to give a more complete picture of the engaging metropolis that lies beneath D.C.'s high-powered political sheen.

Sometime during your visit to D.C., you ought to spend a few hours at the **National Museum of American History,** on Constitution Avenue between 12th and 14th Streets (daily, 10 AM-5:30 PM; free; 202/357-2700). Part of the huge Smithsonian Institution, and the best example of its role as the "Nation's Attic," this huge and endearingly quirky museum displays a little of everything: the giant flag that inspired Francis Scott Key to write the "Star-Spangled Banner," the ruby slippers Judy Garland wore in the *Wizard of Oz*, even Archie Bunker's overstuffed chair from *All in the Family.*

Northwest of downtown D.C., the extensive gardens around **Dumbarton Oaks,** 1703 32nd Street NW (Tues.-Sun. 2-5 PM; donations), cover 16 acres at the heart of historic Georgetown. The main house, now owned and maintained by Harvard University, was built circa 1800, and contains significant collections of Byzantine and pre-Columbian art.   *(continues on next page)*

The best reason to brave the scruffy southeast corner of D.C. is to visit the **Frederick Douglass National Historic Site**, 1441 W Street SE (daily 9 AM-5 PM; free; 202/426-5961). On a hill above the predominantly black neighborhood of Anacostia, this simple Victorian house, Cedar Hill, was where the former slave and pioneer civil rights activist Frederick Douglass lived from 1877 until his death in 1895. Behind the house is a small stone shed, which Douglass called the "Growlery," where he did much of his writing.

If you're not the most serious student of historical globalpolitik, your favorite memory of visiting Washington may turn out to be the same as mine: watching workers pushing wheelbarrows full of money across the floors of the **Bureau of Engraving and Printing**, 14th and C Streets SW (Mon.-Fri. 9 AM-2 PM; free; 202/622-2000), the high-security printing plant where all your hard-earned cash is born. Postage stamps, too.

Practicalities

Washington's **Ronald Reagan National Airport** (DCA) is D.C.'s main airport, very near downtown and easily accessible on the Metro subway system. The other two D.C. airports are Dulles (IAD), way out in the western suburbs, which handles most international flights, and Baltimore/Washington International (BWI), midway between D.C. and Baltimore to the northeast. All three airports offer the standard car rental chains and good ground transportation into the city center. D.C. lies on the busy north-south I-95 corridor, encircled by the I-495 Beltway. US-50, redubbed "I-595" east of D.C., and supplemented in the west by the I-66 freeway, is the main east-west artery.

Because of D.C.'s baroque street-plan, and the extensive one-way systems, driving can be very confusing. The basic layout is fairly simple, as the entire diamond-shaped city is divided into four quadrants (NE, NW, SE, and SW) with the Capitol at the center. East-west streets begin alphabetically (E, F, G, etc.) from the Mall, north-south running streets are numbered (1st, 2nd, 3rd, etc) from the Capitol, and diagonal avenues are named for states. Parking is difficult, and the few on-street spaces around the Mall are the only alternative to expensive lots downtown. To get around, you'll do well to avail yourself of the handy "Metro" subway which serves most of the places you'll want to go. Cab fares are not metered, but instead are charged at a set rate ($3.70 and up) based on a system of designated zones within the city.

D.C. is not an especially difficult city to drive (or park!) in, but you may find it easiest to leave your car at a Metro station, such as the one at Arlington National Cemetery, and ride the subway around town.

To explore the cemetery more completely, stop first at the **visitors center** (703/557-0613) near the cemetery entrance for a gridded map of the grounds that identifies the grave sites of many other famous people interred here, including boxer Joe Louis, explorer Robert Peary, civil rights martyr Medgar Evers, and writer Dashiell Hammett. Arlington is ideal for wandering around, but if it's hot and humid (as it often is in D.C.'s swampy summers) you might want to hop on a Tourmobile tram ($4; free for those over 65) and take a guided ride up the hill.

The cheapest and most convenient place to sleep is the modern **HI Washington, D.C. Hostel**, 1009 11th Street NW (202/737-2333), which has $18 dorm beds within walking distance of the White House. Directly across Lafayette Square from the White House, and at the plushest end of the price and comfort spectrum, the **Hay Adams Hotel**, 1 Lafayette Square NW (202/ 638-6600), is a lushly appointed old hotel, with a grand lobby full of expense-account lobbyists; doubles start around $300 a night. Mid-range places tend to be located on the outskirts, like the **Days Inn—Richmond Highway**, 6100 Richmond Highway, in Alexandria, Virginia (703/329-0500), which has a pool and free parking, across from Metro station in historic Alexandria; doubles cost $55. The best-value in-town hotel may well be the high-rise **Howard Johnson**, 2601 Virginia Avenue NW (202/965-2700), a good value, family-oriented hotel across from the notorious Watergate complex; it has a rooftop pool, free parking, and rooms from $109.

There are also some nice B&Bs in D.C. proper, like the **Kalorama Guest House**, 1854 Mintwood Place (202/667-6369), which has clean, nicely furnished rooms in a number of historic houses near the National Zoo and trendy Adams-Morgan neighborhood.

After watching your elected representatives in action (or inaction), eat cheap at the unique **Senate Dining Room**, in the basement of the U.S. Capitol; be sure to sample the famous bean soup. It's open to the public Mon.-Fri. 8 AM-4 PM. North of the White House, tucked away inside the Esplanade Mall at 1990 K Street NW, **Sholl's Colonial Cafeteria**, is a godsend for poor, hungry travelers: huge portions of good fresh all-American food (fried chicken, meat loaf, stews . . .) at low, low prices. The desserts, especially the pies, are as good as you'll find anywhere. A small step up in price, and a giant leap back to a time when polished wood bars and brass spittoons were the order of the day, the **Old Ebbitt Grill**, east of the White House at 675 15th Street NW, serves everything from burgers to filet mignon to a well-heeled media-savvy crowd.

Washington D.C. is a hugely popular destination, and tourist information is easy to come by; the **Committee to Promote D.C.**, at 1212 New York Avenue NW (202/347-2873 or 800/422-8644), has tons of brochures and extensive listings of discount accommodation offers. D.C.'s daily newspapers are the *Washington Post* and the *Washington Times,* while the *CityPaper,* a free weekly, has listings of entertainment and current events.

Driving D.C.

Following US-50 across Washington, D.C. takes you through the heart of the nation's capital. Starting in the west, alongside Arlington National Cemetery at the Iwo Jima Memorial (which sits in the middle of a traffic circle and is all-but-impossible to reach), US-50 crosses the Potomac River, entering "The District" on the Theodore Roosevelt Bridge—making a beeline toward the State Department. US-50 then follows Constitution Avenue along the north side of The Mall, running past the Lincoln and Vietnam Veteran's memorials and between the White House and the Washington Monument, before zigzagging to the northeast along 7th Street and New York Avenue, which turns into a freeway and runs east to Annapolis and the Chesapeake Bay.

ACROSS MARYLAND

Racing out of Washington, D.C., on a high-speed multi-lane freeway, US-50 accesses one of the state's most popular destinations, the colonial Chesapeake Bay port town of Annapolis. From Annapolis, heading toward the Atlantic coast and the massively popular beach resort of Ocean City, the final leg of US-50's 3,200-mile transcontinental trek is a mad dash across 100 miles of Maryland's Eastern Shore. This is one of the more captivating areas in the northeastern U.S., but the four-lane US-50 freeway doesn't encourage sightseeing, so if you want to get a feel for the *real* Eastern Shore of piney woods, cornfields, and fishing fleets, you'll have to follow the many back roads and search out the many historic towns and villages—many of which we point out as worthwhile detours, including some that are among the oldest and most carefully preserved in the nation.

Between D.C. and Annapolis, the town of Bowie is home to the Orioles' Class AA farm team, the **Bowie Baysox** (301/805-6000).

Annapolis

State capital of Maryland, and one of the most attractive and well-preserved historic cities in the U.S., Annapolis (pop. 33,187) is one place you won't want to miss. First settled in 1649 and chartered in 1708, Annapolis makes fair claim to being the oldest city in the country. Its historic importance was as the nation's first capital, though it's now best known for its maritime heritage, both as a yachting center and as home of the U.S. Naval Academy, which stands guard along the Chesapeake Bay waterfront.

The historic center of Annapolis is just south of US-50 via Hwy-70, which leads straight to the **State House** (daily 9 AM-5 PM; free), where the U.S. Congress met in 1783-84 and ratified the Treaty of Paris, thus ending the Revolutionary War. From the State House, Main Street drops downhill to the City Dock waterfront, where a **visitor center** has walking-tour maps and guides to the wealth of historic build-

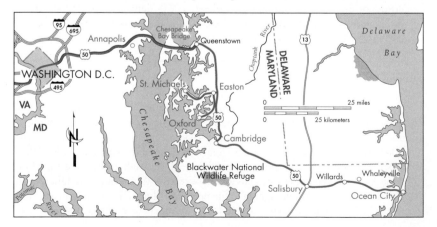

ings, including the beautiful colonial-era **Hammond Harwood House** (Mon.-Sat. 10 AM-4 PM; $4) at 19 Maryland Avenue, two blocks north.

Annapolis has a number of good places to eat, including the venerable **Chick & Ruth's Delly**, open 24 hours at 165 Main Street, and the waterfront **Middleton Tavern**, 2 Market Space, with fine fish and chips. Apart from the historic **Maryland Inn**, 16 Church Circle (410/263-2641), most of the places to stay are anodyne motels along US-50 west of town; the visitor center (410/280-0445) has complete lists of options.

In Annapolis, **WRNR 103.1 FM** is an anarchic modern rock station, playing everything from The Animals to Frank Zappa.

Baltimore has more than its fair share of wacky museums, on everything from incandescent light bulbs (717 Washington Place; 410/752-8586) to Baltimore's favorite son, Babe Ruth (216 Emory Street; 410/727-1539).

Detour: Baltimore

From Annapolis, it's just a quick 20 minute drive north along Hwy-2, or I-97 past BWI airport, to downtown Baltimore. The best description I've ever heard of Baltimore's quirky charms came from film director John Waters, who has drawn considerable inspiration from his offbeat hometown. In his book *Shock Value,* Waters wrote: "I would never want to live anywhere but Baltimore. You can look far and wide, but you'll never discover a stranger city with such extreme style. It's as if every eccentric in the South decided to move north, ran out of gas in Baltimore, and decided to stay." Best known recently for Cal Ripken and the **Baltimore Orioles**, the only baseball team Hoagie Carmichael ever wrote a song about, who play at always packed Camden Yards (410/685-9800) right downtown, Baltimore is also home to the wild new **American Visionary Art Museum**, 800 Key Boulevard (410/244-1900) near the popular Inner Harbor waterfront redevelopment, which displays an array of works by "outsider" and "self-taught" artists in every medium imaginable—painted packing crates, "art cars," and so on.

For food (crab cakes galore!) and drink, head to historic Fell's Point, a mile east of the flashy Inner Harbor. For more information, contact the Baltimore **visitors bureau** at the Inner Harbor (410/837-4636 or 800/282-6632).

Chesapeake Bay Bridge

Before the four-mile long Chesapeake Bay Bridge was completed in the early 1950s, Maryland's Eastern Shore was physically and spiritually an island, protected by the broad Chesapeake

Maryland's Eastern Shore is excellent bicycling country, with generally flat, quiet roads winding through farmlands, forests, and waterfront fishing villages.

Bay from the sprawling modern cities of Washington and Baltimore, and cut off at its neck by the Chesapeake and Delaware Canal. Now thousands of travelers cross the bridge each summer, many of whom race right through on US-50, headed for the coastal resorts like Rehoboth Beach ("The Beltway by the Bay") and Ocean City. The bridge itself has a toll of $2.50, charged to eastbound travelers only.

At the west end of the bridge, US-50 lands at **Sandy Point State Park,** where you can swim, hike, or launch a boat. At the eastern end, US-50 is joined by US-301, and together the two roads race along as a six-lane freeway as far as **Queenstown,** a busy port in the early 1800s but now little more than an upscale suburb of the greater Baltimore/Washington urban area.

*skipjacks on
Chesapeake Bay*

Easton

Midway across Maryland, 20 miles southeast of the Chesapeake Bay Bridge, turn off the freeway and head a half-mile west to explore the well-preserved heart of Easton (pop. 9,372), where the stately Talbot County Courthouse overlooks a compact business district that could easily pass as an English country High Street. Besides the many 18th-century structures, including a federal-style townhouse at 25 S. Washington Street that's been converted into the Talbot County historical society **museum** (Tues.-Sat. 10 AM-4 PM, Sunday 1-4 PM; $2), the most interesting place to stop is the white wood-frame **Third Haven Meeting House,** on the edge of town on South Washington Street, built in 1684 and still in use by a Quaker congregation.

The most impressive place to stay in Easton is the stately **Tidewater Inn,** a recently restored landmark in the center of town at 101 E. Dover Street (410/822-1300 or 800/237-8775), which offers guests free carriage rides around town and the option of a 4:30 AM breakfast—designed for early-rising duck-hunters. Easton also holds the comfortable **Bishop's House** B&B, at 214 Goldsborough Street (301/820-7290), and the usual range of motels and fast-food places along the US-50 frontage.

West of St. Michaels, at the far end of Hwy-33, **Tilghman Island** is home port for Chesapeake Bay's sole surviving fleet of skipjacks, the unique sail-powered vessels used to harvest oysters from the bay.

St. Michaels and Oxford

The pride and joy of the Eastern Shore is the Chesapeake Bay village of St. Michaels, a colonial-era shipbuilding center turned yachting haven that's home to the excellent **Chesapeake Bay Maritime Museum** (daily 10 AM-4 PM, longer hours in summer; $6). Located right on the waterfront at the center of town, the museum has extensive displays of skipjacks and other historic sailing vessels—which you can watch being restored in the museum workshops. There are also diverse pieces of fishing and hunting gear, plus a working lighthouse, all displayed to conjure up traditional Eastern Shore maritime life.

Though full of lovingly maintained old houses and commercial buildings as well as working wharves, chandlers, and sail lofts, St. Michaels, it has to be said, is definitely a major tourist trap, with the usual array of souvenir shops, overpriced restaurants, and overquaint B&Bs.

After seeing the museum and wandering around the town, if you want to get a feel for the unspoiled Chesapeake follow the signs southeast from St. Michaels to the **Tred Avon Ferry** (daily 7 AM-sunset; $4.50 a car, 75 cents pedestrian each way), which shuttles across the Tred Avon River every half-hour or so to Oxford (pop. 700), a sleepy little village that has hardly changed since the 1760s, when it was one of two authorized ports-of-entry into colonial-era Maryland. Wander along the waterfront or south along Morris Street to the village center, through what may be the best-preserved colonial town left in America. There are no museums or displays proclaiming Oxford a special place, though no less an authority than James Michener (who lived in St. Michaels for many years) did go so far as to say that the crab cakes served inside the circa 1710 **Robert Morris Inn** (410/226-5111) opposite the ferry dock were among the best he'd ever tasted; at $20 a plate they're a bit rich, but the inn is an evocative old place, with rooms at $70-220 a night.

From Oxford, you can ride the ferry back by way of St. Michaels, or return directly to US-50 via Hwy-333.

US-50 through Cambridge is the "Harriet Tubman Highway." Her birthplace is eight miles west of town.

Cambridge

Founded in 1684 on the south bank of the broad Choptank River, unlike sleepy Oxford, busy Cambridge (pop. 11,514) is a market town for the surrounding farmlands. Still somewhat industrial in feel, thanks to its now-closed canning and packing plants, Cambridge does have some attractive corners, though its one apt but unique sight is the decaying old **Cape Charles ferry**, which once sailed south to Norfolk but is now moored on the northwest side of the US-50 bridge over the Choptank River, housing a funky junk shop.

Throughout the summer, Salisbury is home to the popular **Delmarva Shorebirds,** the Baltimore Orioles' Class A farm team, who play at the modern Perdue Stadium off US-50 on Hobbs Road. For tickets or schedules, call 410/219-3112. Games are broadcast on WICO 1320 AM.

Cambridge is also home to the Eastern Shore's most bizarre range of annual festivals, from the winter National Muskrat Skinning Championship to powerboat and antique airplane fairs held throughout the summer; for details, contact the **visitor center** (410/228-3575).

Salisbury

Though largely modern and commercial, Salisbury (pop. 20,059) has preserved part of its older townscape in a pedestrianized downtown shopping district and in the Newton Historic District, a collection of dainty Victorian-era houses along Elizabeth Street. The one place to stop is the **Ward Museum of Wildfowl Art** (daily 10 AM-5 PM; $4), 900 S. Schumaker Drive, which has a comprehensive collection of carved decoys and other hunting-related arts and crafts.

Crossing the coastal wetlands and estuaries, US-50 races east from Salisbury, bypassing a few small towns like Willards and Whaleyville, which are best seen by following the Hwy-346 frontage road. The two routes run parallel, joining each other 30 miles east in the old-time beach resort of Ocean City.

Ocean City, and the rest of the Atlantic Coast, is covered in the Coastal East Coast chapter, which begins on page 376.

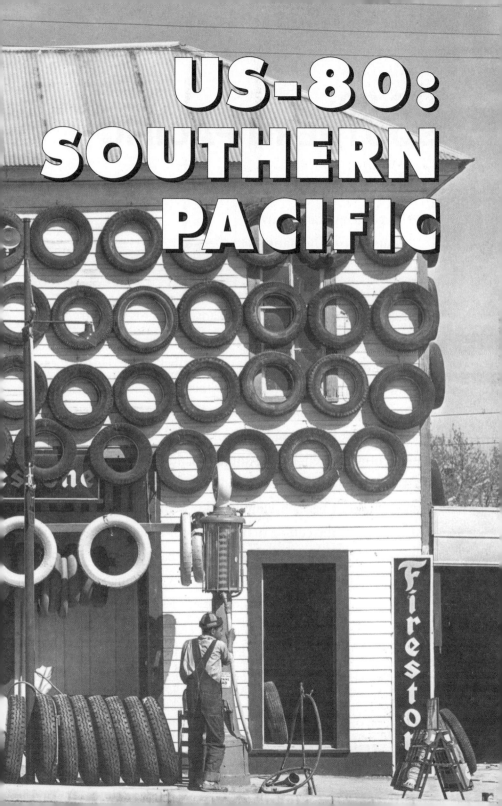

US-80: SOUTHERN PACIFIC

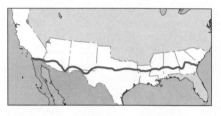

Following old US-80 and its contemporary equivalents across the nation's southern tier takes you through more varied cultural and physical landscapes than you'll find along any other cross-country route. Throughout this 3,000-mile journey you can shift from one world to another in the time it takes to watch a football game. Heading east from the golden sands of San Diego, within a few hours you reach the harshly beautiful Southwest deserts, their trademark saguaro cacti creating a backdrop straight out of a Roadrunner cartoon. The route's central segment crosses the thousand-mile, "you can see for two days" plains of New Mexico and Texas, where pumpjacks jig for oil and cattle graze beneath a limitless sky. To the east spreads another land, starting at the cotton-rich Mississippi Delta and continuing along the foot of the Appalachians to the bayous and sea islands surrounding the country's grandest little city, Savannah.

Especially memorable is the diversity of people and of prevailing customs along the route, all highlighted by a range of accents and lingos. For travelers, this cultural diversity is perhaps most accessible in the food. Many regional American cuisines —Tex-Mex, Cajun, Creole, BBQ, to name a few—were originally developed somewhere along this route, and roadside restaurants continue to serve up local specialties that lend new meaning to the word "authentic." Along the open borders between Texas and New and old Mexico, in unselfconscious adobe sheds with corrugated metal roofs, chile-powered salsa accompanies roast steak fajitas; in Louisiana, entrees featuring catfish fillets or bright red boiled shrimp grace most menus; and everywhere you turn, roadside stands dish out reputedly the best BBQ in the universe. We've noted favorite places along the route, but all you really need do is follow your nose, or look for a line of pickup trucks, and you'll find yourself in culinary heaven.

On an equal footing with the fine food is the incredible variety of music you'll hear, whether it's in a Texas honky-tonk or in the juke joints and gospel-spreading churches of Mississippi and Alabama. Along the Mexican border, from San Diego well past El Paso, radio stations blast out an anarchic mix of multilingual music, part country-western, part traditional Mexican, with accordions and guitars and lyrics flowing seamlessly from one language to the other and back—often in a single line of a song. Along the way, you can visit the hometowns of Buddy Holly, Little Richard, and Otis Redding, or pay your respects at the final resting places of Hank Williams, Jimmie Rodgers, and Duane Allman. After dark, listen to the current and next generation making music in roadside bars and clubs.

A wealth of distinctive literature has grown out of these regions, and you can visit dozens of characteristic literary scenes, live and in the flesh: Carson McCullers's "Ballad of the Sad Cafe" and other tales, which capture 1920s life in Columbus, Georgia; Cormac McCarthy's wide-open tales of the Texas frontier; the diner from *Fried Green Tomatoes;* and the original God's Little Acre and Tobacco Road. But there's also sober history, from Wild West Tombstone and Bonnie and Clyde's death site, to the Dallas intersection where JFK was assassinated, to the streets of Selma, where the Civil Rights Movement burst forth onto the nation's front pages. Best of all, many of the most fascinating places along the way remain refreshingly free of the slick promotion that greets you in more established tourist destinations. The relatively low profile of tourism here, and the fact that only a few big cities lie in wait to swallow your vacation dollars, help make this particular trip a relatively inexpensive one—but even at twice the price, it would be well worth experiencing.

ACROSS CALIFORNIA

From the Pacific bays and golden beaches of San Diego, you can choose between two routes as you head east across Southern California: the high-speed I-8 freeway up and over pine-forested mountains, or a winding drive along the Mexican border. We've covered the slower, more southerly route that follows the remnants of old US-80 through sleepy border towns and past a pair of unique roadside attractions—the funky old Desert View Tower, and the oddly endearing "Official Center of the World" at tiny Felicity. Also included is a quick side trip south of the border to beer-making Tecate. But no matter which way you choose, eventually you'll have to cross many monotonous miles of the Mojave Desert, a barren, dry, and inhospitable land.

Point Loma: Cabrillo National Monument
The sturdy headland that protects San Diego's extensive harbor from the open Pacific Ocean, Point Loma has long been occupied by the military, whose many fences, radio towers, and gun emplacements all seem to disappear at the very tip, where the Cabrillo National Monument (daily 9 AM-5 PM; $4 per car; 760/557-5450) protects a breathtaking 150 acres of cliffs and tidepools. Set aside in 1913 to remember the efforts of Portuguese sailor Juan Cabrillo, who explored the California coast in 1542, there's also an old lighthouse, some nice trails, and a visitor center describing the whole shebang.

San Diego is the southern end of our Coastal West Coast road trip, which is described on pages 24-111. For details on visiting San Diego, see the "Survival Guide" on pages 109-111.

Across San Diego: Old US-80
From Point Loma and the Pacific Ocean, old US-80 bends south past the airport (named for Charles Lindbergh, and featuring one of the most hair-raising landing patterns of any big American airport) and through downtown along 12th Avenue and Market Street, then veers north again along the Cabrillo Freeway (one of the oldest in the country) through historic Balboa Park, home to the San Diego Zoo, a replica of London's old Globe Theater, and many grand Spanish Colonial-style buildings that have been standing here since the 1915 Panama International Exposition.

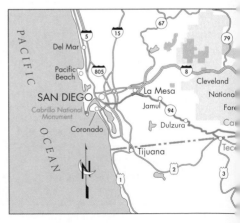

East of San Diego, old US-80 follows El Cajon Boulevard, past San Diego State University and a dozen miles of unsightly but surviving motels, cafes, and gas stations, before it reaches the foothill town of La Mesa, where you can leave old US-80 (which runs alongside the high-speed I-8 freeway), and turn onto the two-lane blacktop of Hwy-94. Twisting to the southeast around the 4,000-foot peaks of the Cleveland National Forest, Hwy-94 traverses classic Southern California landscape: rolling, chaparral-covered hillsides rising above grassy ranch lands and stately valley oaks.

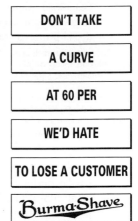

DON'T TAKE

A CURVE

AT 60 PER

WE'D HATE

TO LOSE A CUSTOMER

Burma-Shave

Detour: Tecate

After passing through **Jamul** and **Dulzura**, two quiet ranching towns that appear on the verge of extinction as San Diego rapidly approaches, some 40 miles east of downtown San Diego along Hwy-94 you'll spot a sign marking the turnoff south to the Mexican border town of Tecate (pop. 45,000). Known around the world as the source of tangy Tecate beer—by most accounts, the brew that started people drinking beer with a squeeze of fresh lime—Tecate is in the top tier of enjoyable border towns, if only by virtue of being cleaner, quieter and much less "touristy" than Tijuana. Potential stops include the usual restaurants, cantinas, and souvenir shops; the main stop is the **Tecate Brewery** itself, the biggest building in town, located on Avenida Hidalgo a half-dozen blocks from the border. Free **tours** (Saturday 10 AM-4 PM) include samples.

Because of insurance concerns, it's a good idea to leave your car on the U.S. side of the border and cross into Mexico on foot. East of Tecate, Hwy-94 runs along the U.S. side of the border for 41 miles before joining the I-8 freeway.

Campo

Set in a broad valley midway between Tecate and the I-8 freeway, tiny Campo (pop. 1,102) has one main attraction, the **San Diego Railroad Museum** (Saturday, Sunday, and holidays 9 AM-5 PM; free), well-posted at the west end of town on Forest

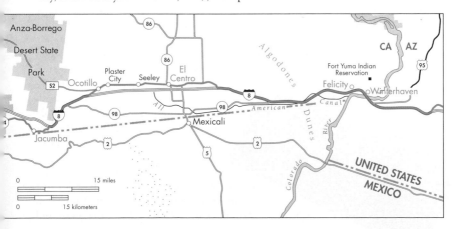

Gate Road. Along with an extensive outdoor collection of old locomotives and carriages, the museum offers rides (noon and 2:30 PM; $10) on restored steam- and diesel-powered trains, including a 16-mile round trip through the surrounding countryside. Occasionally, the museum also offers all-day trips south to Tecate, Mexico.

For more on traveling in Mexico, by car or other means, see page 213.

Campo marks the southern end of the **Pacific Crest Trail,** which winds for 2,638 miles between Canada and Mexico.

Jacumba

South of the I-8 freeway on a surviving stretch of the old US-80 highway, Jacumba is a former spa and resort town where Clark Gable, Marlene Dietrich, and countless others soaked themselves silly in the free-flowing natural hot springs. Established in 1852 as a station on the stagecoach mail route across the desert, Jacumba had its heyday during the 1920s, and while little remains apart from the water, it makes a great offbeat place to stop. The mineral-rich hot springs still flow into outdoor pools and private jacuzzis at **Jacumba Hot Springs Spa,** 44500 Old US-80 (760/766-4333), which includes motel rooms for around $40, and a good on-site restaurant and bar.

For more information on visiting **Anza-Borrego State Park,** contact the ranger station in Borrego Springs (760/767-4205).

From atop the Desert View Tower, you can see places where the excavations for I-8 have left sections of the old US-80 roadway stranded on man-made mesas, 50 feet or more higher than the modern freeway.

From 1858 to 1861 the original Butterfield Stage, which carried mail and passengers from St. Louis to San Francisco, followed the approximate route of I-8 across Southern California. The route was originally blazed by Spanish explorer Juan de Anza, on his way to found San Francisco in 1775.

Ocotillo: The Desert View Tower

Southern gateway to the splendid, 600,000-acre Anza-Borrego State Park, the largest and wildest desert park in the country, Ocotillo lies north of the I-8 freeway on the old US-80 highway (designated S2 on maps). Ocotillo itself is little more than a gas station-cum-grocery store, bar, and volunteer fire station, but five miles west of town the **Desert View Tower** (daily 9 AM-5 PM; $3; 760/766-4612) is well worth searching out. The four-story, cut-stone structure was built in 1922 by Burt Vaughn (who owned much of neighboring Jacumba) to commemorate the pioneers who struggled across the arid desert. Inside the tower, a small but interesting museum displays a haphazard collection of desert Americana such as Navajo blankets and Native American artifacts, with similar items on sale in the gift shop. At the top of the tower, an observation platform offers views across 100 miles of desert landscape, sliced by the I-8 freeway.

Across the parking lot from the tower, a hillside of quartz granite boulders has been carved with dozens of three-dimensional figures. Most of the figures are of skulls, snakes, and lizards—with real lizards sometimes racing each other across the rocks—and the whole ensemble was created during the Depression by an out-of-work engineer named W.T. Ratliffe.

The Desert View Tower stands at a cool 3,000 feet above sea level, six miles east of the Jacumba turnoff from I-8, at the In-Ko-Pah Road exit; billboards point the way. East of the tower, old

US-80 is designated as S80 and runs parallel to I-8 all the way east to El Centro, passing through ghostly old industrial towns like Seeley and Plaster City, where a section of original US-80 roadbed survives along the south side of the current highway).

El Centro

Located some 50 feet below sea level, midway across California at the heart of the agricultural Coachella Valley, El Centro (pop. 31, 384) was founded in 1905 and has since bloomed into a bustling small city, thanks to irrigation water diverted from the Colorado River. Melons, grapefruit, and dates are the region's prime agricultural products, along with alfalfa grown to feed the many dairy cows. There's not a lot here that doesn't depend upon farming.

Though not much of a destination, El Centro is still the best place to break a journey between San Diego and the Arizona border, so fill your gas tank if nothing else. Places to eat include **Millie's Restaurant**, a popular truck-stop cafe on 4th Street south of I-8, and the usual franchise fast-food places. All the national motel chains are here as well, along with neon-signed local ones along the I-8 Business Loop, advertising rooms for as little as $18 a night.

El Centro is the winter home of the aerial acrobats of the U.S. Navy's **Blue Angels,** who can sometimes be spotted practicing their loops and rolls in the skies around the city. It is also the birthplace of **Cher.**

From El Centro, it's a quick 10 miles south across the Mexican border to **Mexicali,** capital of Baja California and a busy big city focused more on commerce than on catering to tourists.

When driving in the desert, always keep the gas tank as full as possible, and always carry at least one gallon of drinking water per person. In case of trouble, stay with your car. Don't walk off in search of help; let it find you.

The Algodones Dunes

In the middle of the southern Mojave Desert, 42 miles east of El Centro, a rest area south of the I-8 freeway at the Grays Well Road exit gives access to the enticing sands of the Algodones Dunes, which stretch to both sides of the freeway for over 50 miles. The slender dunes, which measure at most 10 miles across and reach heights of 200 feet, often cover the highway in blowing sandstorms. Though you can amble around on foot, be aware that the dunes themselves are under constant abuse from hordes of motorcycles and dune buggies.

If you're really really interested in old highways, you won't want to miss the re-constructed remnants of a **wooden plank road,** built across the sands in 1914 and later used as part of the original US-80 highway. Preserved by the dry desert air, and arranged to form a 100-foot section across the dunes, this fenced-off museum piece is along the south side of the I-8 freeway, two miles west of the Grey's Well Road exit. The All-American Canal, which waters the Coachella Valley, runs along the north side of the I-8 freeway.

Felicity: "The Center of the World Pyramid"

One of the odder sites in the Southwestern deserts—and competition for this title is pretty fierce—sits just north of the I-8 freeway in the tiny but happily named town of Felicity (pop. four). Local resident Jacques-Andres Istel—author of a children's fairy tale concerning a scholarly, fire-breathing dragon named Coe who lives at the center of the world reading fireproof books and eating the nearby Chocolate Mountains—convinced France, China, and Imperial County that Felicity is, legally and officially, the center of the world.

A 25-foot-high pink terrazzo pyramid stands above the exact spot, which you can visit on regular guided **tours** (daily 10 AM-5 PM, late November to mid-April only; $1; 760/572-5000); the fee also buys a certificate saying you've stood at "The Official Center of the World." You can climb a set of stairs that used to belong to the Eiffel Tower and sift through sundry souvenirs in the gift shop.

Winterhaven

The last California town before the Colorado River, Winterhaven is the modest center of the Quechan community on 44,000-acre Fort Yuma Indian Reservation. A few reminders of its pre- and post-colonial past are displayed inside the small **Fort Yuma Indian Museum** (Mon.-Fri. 7 AM-noon, 1-4 PM; $1) alongside the white-walled St. Thomas missionary church. Both structures overlook the Colorado River from atop Indian Hill off the end of 1st Street.

The **Colorado River** forms the border between California and Arizona, and marks the line between the Pacific and mountain time zones.

ACROSS ARIZONA

Between the Colorado River, which divides Arizona from California, and the Phoenix-Tucson megalopolis in the middle of the state, there is not very much to attract the traveler off the freeway. However, the rather complete absence of interesting places in southwestern Arizona is more than made up for by the wealth of fascinating things to see in the state's southeast corner. Here you'll find such legendary sites as Tombstone—home of the OK Corral—and other finely presented reminders of the state's Wild West heritage, along with some of Arizona's most beautiful natural scenery.

Along with dozens of Spanish-language stations north and south of the Mexican border, Yuma's **KBLU 560 AM** plays oldies and local news.

Yuma

Among the hottest and driest towns in the country, Yuma (pop. 54,900) was first settled in 1779 at the site of one of the few good crossings along the Colorado River. Dozens of decaying old adobe buildings around town testify to Yuma's lengthy history, and a select few places are preserved as historic parks. The **Yuma Crossing** (daily 10 AM-5 PM; $2), along the river and I-8 at the north end of 4th Avenue, has been restored to its appearance prior to the arrival of the railroad in 1876, when supplies for U.S. troops throughout the Southwest arrived here by steamboat from the Gulf of California.

Around the time the railroad arrived, a full century after its founding by Spanish missionaries, Yuma was the site of Arizona Territory's main prison. Built out of stone and adobe by convicts struggling in the 120° heat, over the next 33 years until it was closed in 1909, the prison earned a reputation as the "Hellhole of Arizona," due in large part to the summer heat and the brutality of its regime, though park rangers emphasize the fact that prisoners had access to a library and other facilities unusual at the time. Now preserved as the state-run **Yuma Territorial Prison** (daily 8 AM-5 PM; $3), well-posted along the north side of I-8 at the 4th Ave-

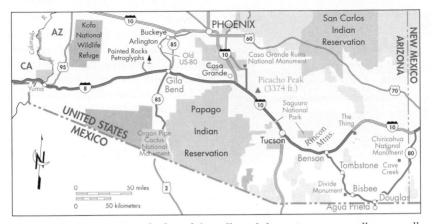

nue exit, the site consists of a few of the cells and the main gate, as well as a small museum.

From the prison, a rickety pedestrians-only steel bridge leads across the Colorado River to California and the **St. Thomas mission church** on the Quechan Indian Fort Yuma Reservation. The entire riverfront area, much of it under the I-8 bridge, is being restored as the Yuma Crossing Park.

Along with the usual national franchises, Yuma has a number of decent places to eat, ranging from the big breakfasts and afternoon BBQ at **Brownie's Cafe,** open daily 6 AM-9 PM at 1145 S. 4th Avenue (old US-80), to the pool tables, burgers, and sandwiches at ancient **Lutes Casino** 221 S. Main Street (520/782-2192) in the historic old downtown area. Voted the "Best Place to Stop in Yuma" by the *Arizona Republic* newspaper, Lutes is a barn-like hall full of old photos, political posters, street signs, and all manner of junk, well worth a look at least for its passionately played domino games.

Along with the national chains (two **Motel 6's** and a **Travelodge**), places to sleep in Yuma include the pleasant **Yuma Cabana,** 2151 S. 4th Avenue (520/783-8311 or 800/874-0811), with palm trees and a nice pool.

Yuma to Gila Bend: I-8

Spanning 110 miles of barren desert east of Yuma, between the U.S. Air Force's 14 million-acre Barry M. Goldwater Bombing Range and a U.S. Army Proving Ground, the I-8 freeway follows the route of early Spanish explorers and settlers on the flat but forbidding Camino del Diablo, along the banks of the usually dry Gila River.

East of 767-foot-high Telegraph Pass, 20 miles outside Yuma, the old US-80 highway reappears along the north side of the freeway, running through old-time desert outposts. If you're hungry, the flyspeck ranching community of **Tacna** has a great place to eat: **Basque Etchea.** Take I-8 exit 42, then head north across the railroad tracks. It's open every day but Monday 11 AM-10 PM for burgers and lamb chops and a full menu of other Mexican and American dishes. **Dateland,** 25 miles farther east along I-8, has a cafe and gift shop selling dates in all possible forms, including milk shakes, but otherwise there is really nothing to stop for between Yuma and Gila Bend.

Twenty-two miles west of Gila Bend, off I-8 at exit 102, Painted Rocks Road leads 11 miles north to a BLM-managed site where an array of petroglyphs, carved into the boulders by the Hohokam people around A.D. 1400, cover the rocks.

From Gila Bend, Hwy-85 runs south to the beautiful and totally deserted **Organ Pipe Cactus National Monument,** before linking up with Hwy-86 to loop east to Tucson.

Gila Bend

The only place approaching a town between Yuma and Phoenix or Tucson, Gila Bend (pop. 1,747) is regularly the "Hottest Spot in the Country"—a title of which it is so proud that, more than once, it's been caught inflating the numbers. First settled as a main stop on the Butterfield Stage route, Gila Bend doesn't offer much relief for the senses, though it does have some photogenic old motels and all the gas stations, rest rooms and restaurants you could reasonably expect to find in the middle of the Arizona desert.

One unique place to eat is the **Outer Limits Coffee Shop,** open 24 hours at 401 E. Pima Avenue, downtown off exit 115. Marked by a flying-saucer-shaped sign, it's part of the **Best Western Space Age Lodge** motel (520/683-2273 or 800/528-1234). Both are essential stops for any Jetsons-aged traveler.

Old US-80 to Phoenix

I-8 is by far the fastest way east from Gila Bend to Tucson and beyond, but if you have the time and inclination to follow the old road, it took the long way around: from Gila Bend US-80 veered north across the usually dry Gila River along what's now an unmarked county road, then east through the towns of Arlington, Palo Verde, and **Buckeye,** where a 40-odd-foot statue of "Hobo Joe" stands along Baldy Street downtown. US-80 ran through downtown Phoenix on Van Buren Street (which was also US-60 and US-70), before heading south to Tucson.

Casa Grande Ruins National Monument

Just as there is almost nothing to see in the 110-mile stretch of I-8 between Yuma and Gila Bend, there is precious little to stop for in the 120-odd miles of superslab freeway between Gila Bend and Phoenix or Tucson. From the I-8/I-10 junction, a worthwhile detour runs east to the well-posted Casa Grande Ruins National Monument, which preserves some of the state's largest and most perplexing prehistoric remains. A small **visitor center** (daily 8 AM-5 PM; $4 per car) at the entrance gives some background on the Hohokam people who, approximately six centuries ago, built the four-story Big House and the surrounding village, but no one knows for sure what Casa Grande was used for, or why it was abandoned.

larger-than-life "Hobo Joe"

Between Phoenix and Tucson, north and south of the Casa Grande area, the I-10 freeway parallels our US-93 road trip route, which runs about 20 miles to the east, along Hwy-79. From Phoenix, the route passes such enticing desert oddities as the famous Biosphere II earthbound space station, and a memorial to cowboy actor Tom Mix. Phoenix and Tucson, and the alternate route between them, are covered on pages 158-165.

Picacho Peak

Looming like a giant battleship alongside the I-10 freeway, 75 miles southeast of Phoenix and 45 miles northwest of Tucson, 3,374-foot Picacho Peak has served as a Sonora Desert landmark for as long as there have been people here. Native Americans, Spanish explorers, American pioneers, you name it, they've used the volcanic peak to keep them on track. Now a state park, Picacho Peak also played a role in the Civil War, as the official westernmost battlefield of the War Between the States was fought here on April 15, 1862, when a dozen Union soldiers skirmished with 17 Confederate cavalrymen. These days people come here to enjoy the Saguaro cactus and the desert wildflowers (in spring mainly, when they're at their most colorful), or to hike to the summit (two miles each way, with roughly 1,500-feet elevation gain) for a desert panorama. The park (520/466-3183) is open for day use ($4 per car) and camping ($10).

> If you're interested in following the route of old US-80 across California and western Arizona, pick up a copy of the entertaining and informative *Old US-80 Highway Traveler's Guide*, by Eric J. Finley. Nicely illustrated, with many helpful maps, the 144-page book is available for $13.95 postpaid from Narrow Road Communications, PO Box 42852, Phoenix, AZ 85080 (602/996-4595).

Along the freeway at the foot of Picacho Peak, a sprawling ostrich farm lets you feed the ungainly beasts or purchase a variety of ostrich-made products.

Saguaro National Park: Tucson Mountain

Northwest of Tucson, the more popular (and free!) half of Saguaro National Monument protects extensive stands of saguaro cactus as well as ancient petroglyphs, spring wildflowers, and generally gorgeous desert scenery.

> The saguaro cactus, whose creamy white blossoms are the Arizona state flower, blooms in May.

From I-10 at Cortaro (exit 246), a loop road runs southwest, then back east through rugged, mountainous terrain, which though popular, is a great place to get a feel for the Sonora Desert landscape. A newish **visitor center** (daily 8 AM-5 PM; free; 520/733-5158) has details of the many hikes here, the longest of which winds its way to the 4,687-foot summit of Wasson Peak. There's more hiking, and camping, in the adjacent **Tucson Mountain Park** (520/883-4200), where **Old Tucson Studios** (daily 9 AM-7 PM; $14.95) has the old movie sets used to film more than 300 movies and TV shows; these days, the "action" is mostly staged gunfights and dance hall revues.

Tucson Mountain Park is also home to the excellent **Arizona Sonora Desert Museum** (daily 8:30 AM-5 PM, longer hours in summer; $9; 520/883-2702). Apart from spending a lifetime in the desert itself, there's really no better place to get a sense of the abundant flora and fauna of the Sonora Desert than this creatively presented zoological park.

From Tucson Mountain Park, Gates Pass Road drops down into Tucson's main east-west road, Speedway Boulevard.

Across Tucson: Old US-80

From the north and west, the best old road introduction to Tucson is the so-called **Miracle Mile**, a wonderful few blocks of neon-signed old motels, right off the I-10 freeway, exit 255. From here, old US-80 follows a series of one-way surface streets into compact downtown Tucson, first following 5th Avenue, then 6th Avenue, the pre-interstate main highway. South of town, 6th Avenue becomes the Old Nogales Highway, the old road south to Mexico, which crosses the freeway and hits **Benson Highway** (I-10 Business), another old road now serving as a freeway frontage. This is a pretty scruffy part of town, with old motels renting rooms by the month (or by the hour), and you don't miss much by jumping on the I-10 freeway for the ride east.

Tucson, which marks the junction with our road trip along US-93, is covered in the Survival Guide on pages 163-165.

Saguaro National Park: Rincon Mountains

A dozen miles east of Tucson, on the slopes of the Tanque Verde and Rincon Mountains, the eastern half of the fabulous Saguaro National Park covers 57,000 acres of rolling desert landscape. Named in honor of the anthropomorphic saguaro (SWA-row) cactus, which here reach heights upwards of 40 feet and live as long as 200 years, the monument is best seen by following eight-mile Cactus Forest Drive, along which numerous trails give close-up looks at the multi-limbed succulents. For more information and details of hiking opportunities, stop at the **visitor center** (daily 8 AM-5 PM; 520/296-8576), where the $5-per-car entry fee is collected.

On the road to the Rincon Mountains, **Colossal Cave** (daily 9 AM-5 PM, longer hours in summer; $6.50) is a huge old limestone cavern which offers, if nothing else, a cool escape from the sweltering summer heat. One of the state's most enduring tourist attractions, Colossal Cave was used in Wild West times by train robbers who escaped here with $62,000; the money bags were recovered, but not the money.

Benson's radio station **KAVV 97.7 FM** plays lots of good Waylon-and-Willie-type country hits, plus captivating accounts of local news and activities.

Benson and the Amerind Foundation

On the banks of the San Pedro River, Benson (pop. 3,824), already home to a large and stable population, was founded as a Santa Fe railroad connection to booming Tombstone and the Mexican harbor town of Guaymas. Trains still rumble through town, but there's not much to see apart from fading roadside signs. The **Horse Shoe Cafe**, 154 E. 4th Street across from the railroad tracks, is where locals go to eat.

From Benson, our route cuts south on old US-80 (now Hwy-80), while I-10 races east over the mountains that 100-plus years ago were a stronghold of Apache warriors under Geronimo and

Cochise. If you're following the interstate, a couple of sights are worth looking for. The more satisfying of these, the Amerind Foundation Museum (daily 10 AM-4 PM; closed Monday and Tuesday in summer; $3; 520/586-3666), lies 12 miles east of Benson, off Dragoon Road a mile southeast of I-10 exit 318. Started in 1937, the private, nonprofit museum is devoted to the study of local Native American cultures, with everything from ancient arrowheads to contemporary Pueblo pottery on display in the spacious mission-style buildings. Not surprisingly, the best collections are of Hopi, Navajo, and Apache artifacts, with well-presented exhibits of ceremonial and domestic objects—kachina dolls, rugs, and ritual costumes.

I-10: The Thing!

Advertised by signs all along the freeway, one of the country's odder roadside attractions stands atop 4,975-foot Texas Summit, along I-10 at exit 322: **The Thing** (hours vary; 75 cents admission). A gas station, a gift shop, and a Dairy Queen stand in front of a prefab shed full of stuff ranging from a Rolls Royce once used by Adolf Hitler to The Thing itself, a mummified corpse whose "secret identity" has yet to be revealed. "What is it?" the signs ask . . . .

Tombstone

While I-10 races east over the mountains, our more scenic route, promoted by tourism authorities as the "Cochise Trail," winds south on old US-80 through the Wild West town of Tombstone, "The Town too Tough to Die." The route loops along the Mexican border before rejoining I-10 across the New Mexico border.

Though it's just 22 miles south of the freeway, and regularly inundated by bikers, RVers and busloads of tourists, the rough-and-ready mining town of Tombstone (pop. 1,220) has kept itself looking pretty much as it did back in the 1880s, when 10,000 miners called it home, and one of the more mythic events of the Wild West took place here: the shoot-out at the OK Corral.

Historians, and everyone in Tombstone, still debate the chain of events of October 26, 1881. Was Wyatt Earp a sharp-shooting savior, out to make Tombstone safe for decent society?  Or was he really a grandstanding cowboy whom history has romanticized? Decide for yourself after hearing all sides of the story. The **OK Corral** (daily 8 AM-5 PM; $2.50) is still there, a block south of Fremont Street (old US-80), on Allen Street between 3rd and 4th Streets, with life-sized, black-leather-clad figures taking the places of Virgil and Wyatt Earp facing down the Clanton brothers. Next door to the OK Corral, the entertaining **Historama** (daily 9 AM-4 PM; $2.50) re-creates the events at the OK Corral through movies and animatronic figures.

The dead men, and many hundreds of others, ended up at **Boot Hill Cemetery** (daily 8 AM-6 PM; free), along the highway at the northern edge of town, where you can wander among the wooden grave markers inscribed with all manner of rhyming epitaphs. The Boot Hill Cemetery is the real thing, and the souvenirs in the large gift shop at the entrance are as wonderfully tacky as they come.

Every summer, daily and every hour on the hour, historic gunfights are reenacted all around Tombstone, at places like "Six Gun City" just south of the historic area, and in October, the whole town comes alive with a weekend of shoot-outs and parades during Helldorado Days. For details, contact the **visitor center,** 4th and Allen Streets (520/457-2211).

Bisbee offers what has to be the most unusual accommodations in Arizona: the **Shady Dell RV Park,** on US-80 a mile east of Bisbee at 1 Douglas Road (520/432-3567), where you can stay the night—or longer—in one of seven well-restored 1940s Airstream, Silver Streak, and Spartanette trailers, all filled with period furnishings. Rates are a bargain $30-45 per night, and include use of a VCR stocked with classic B-movies; you can also pitch a tent or pull up your own RV.

Though the OK Corral and Boot Hill are both fun, the best place to learn about Tombstone's real, as opposed to mythic, history is at the **Tombstone Courthouse State Historic Park,** at 3rd and Toughnut streets. Built in 1882, this old courthouse building holds 12,000 square feet of artifacts documenting and describing the *real* Wild West.

Considering the huge numbers of people who descend upon Tombstone every day, and the gauntlet of T-shirt shops catering to them, the town is still a very appealing place to visit. Eat breakfast, lunch, or dinner at **Nellie Cashman's,** 5th and Toughnut Streets, Tombstone's oldest eatery. Enjoy a cool drink at the **Crystal Palace Saloon,** 420 E. Allen Streets, or at the local biker hangout **Legends of the West,** two doors down at 414 E. Allen Street. Places to stay are not extensive, nor very expensive: try the centrally located, $40-a-night **Tombstone Motel,** on the main road at 502 E. Fremont Street (520/457-3478).

Divide Monument

About 20 miles southeast of Tombstone, three miles west of Bisbee at the 6,030-foot Mule Pass summit of old US-80, the much-abused stone obelisk of the Divide Monument commemorates the convict-laborers who first constructed the road in 1913. The monument stands in a somewhat scruffy parking area directly above the modern tunnel, and from it you get a great panorama view of the surrounding Mule Mountains.

Bisbee

A classic boom-and-bust mining town, Bisbee (pop. 6,288) is one of the most satisfying off-beat destinations in Arizona, combining scenic beauty, palpable history and a good range of places to eat, drink, and enjoy yourself. Climbing up winding streets lined by 100-year-old structures—Victorian cottages, board shacks, and stately brick churches—Bisbee has attracted a diverse population of desert rats, bikers, working artists, and New Age apostles, all of whom mix amiably in the town's cafes and bars.

The heart of Bisbee lies north of old US-80 along Main Street, stretching west from the **Bisbee Mining and Historical Museum** (daily 10 AM-4 PM; $3), which displays dioramas, old photos, and sundry artifacts inside the old Phelps Dodge company headquarters. Main Street has many cafes, antique shops, art galleries, and restaurants.

The main event in Bisbee is the **Queen Mine.** Put on a hard hat and a miner's lamp, and take a train ride down into the mine shafts and tunnels, which were in operation until WW II. Hour-long **tours** (daily 9 AM-3:30 PM; $8) leave every 90 minutes from the Queen Mine building, just south of downtown along old US-80.

FLY'S PHOTOS

Wild West photographer Camilius S. Fly, whose work forms one of the primary records of life in frontier Arizona, had his main studio in Tombstone, now restored as part of the OK Corral. His images, displayed in the small gallery, include some of the earliest photos taken of Chiricahua Apache warrior Geronimo, as well as shots of Wyatt Earp, "Doc" Holliday, and many others. What Matthew Brady was to the Civil War, Fly was to Tombstone in its 1880s heyday.

One of Arizona's most unforgettable sights, the massive **Lavender Open Pit** forms a gigantic polychrome crater along Hwy-80, just south of the Queen Mine. Named not for its color—which is more rusty red than purple—but for a mine superintendent, Harry Lavender, this was a true glory hole with ore deposits that provided the bulk of Bisbee's eight billion pounds of copper before they were shut down in 1974. The Queen Mine also offers hour-long tours ($7) of the mile-wide, 1,000-foot-deep pit.

At the center of Bisbee, the **Copper Queen Hotel**, looming over downtown along Howell Street (520/432-2216), has been the best place to stay since it opened in 1902. Most of the rooms have been upgraded to include modern conveniences without losing their old-fashioned charm, and rates start at around $75. Another nice place to stay is the **Bisbee Inn**, 450 K Street (520/432-5131), overlooking Brewery Gulch and offering B&B rooms (shared bathrooms) from about $45 for two.

La Vuelta de Bisbee, a highly competitive professional cycling race held every April, sees hundreds of world-class riders racing up and down Bisbee's steep streets. There's also a 4th of July Soap Box Derby.

One of the famous events in Bisbee's busy history occurred in July 1917, when over 1,000 miners on strike for better pay and conditions were forcibly deported—literally railroaded out of town and dumped in the desert outside Columbus, New Mexico.

The Copper Queen Hotel has a good restaurant and popular bar; other good bets include breakfast or lunch at the **Quarter Moon Cafe** or **Renaissance Cafe**, both at the "bottom" of town, and dinner at the gourmet **Cafe Roka**, at 35 Main Street. Brewery Gulch, which runs north from Main Street at the east side of downtown Bisbee, once held over 50 different saloons and gambling parlors; it's considerably quieter now, but still home to such fun haunts as the **Stock Exchange** bar, inside the old Bisbee Stock Exchange, and **St. Elmo's**, which has live music most nights.

For further information, walking-tour maps, or details of special events, contact the Bisbee **visitor center**, 7 Main Street (520/432-5421).

Travel along the Mexican border is enlivened immeasurably by the many radio stations, varying from the country twang of Douglas's **KDAP 96.5 FM** to the many south-of-the-border stations, like "Radio Sonora" **101.3 FM,** that play a part-English, part-Spanish Tejano mélange typified by songs like "Mama, No Deje Que Sus Hijos Grow Up To Be Vaqueros."

Agua Prieta was the site of skirmishes between revolutionary **Pancho Villa** and the Mexican army.

A monument along old US-80, a half-mile east of the tiny town of Apache, points out the nearby site of Skeleton Canyon, where Apache warrior **Geronimo** finally surrendered to the U.S. Army in 1886, effectively ending the "Indian Wars."

Much of southeastern Arizona is still open range, so keep an eye out for livestock on the highway.

The Border: Douglas and Agua Prieta

Like Bisbee, the border town of Douglas (pop. 12,822) grew up on copper mining, which here lasted until fairly recently: the huge smokestack of the Phelps-Dodge smelter a mile west of town was in operation until 1987, processing ores from mines in Mexico. Now most of the economy revolves around cross-border trade with *maquiladora* plants in its much larger Mexican neighbor, Agua Prieta (pop. 80,000), which in the past decades has quadrupled in size.

There's not a lot to see in either Douglas or Agua Prieta, though Douglas does boast one fabulous attraction: the landmark **Gadsden Hotel**, 1046 G Avenue (520/364-4481). Rebuilt in 1928 after a fire destroyed the 1907 original, the spacious gold-leafed lobby—one of the grandest public spaces in the state —has a pretty Tiffany-style stained-glass mural decorating its mezzanine. The small and basic rooms start at a bargain $35, and there's also a good Mexican-American restaurant and a very popular bar, the Saddle and Spur, its walls decorated with over 200 cattle brands from area ranches.

Across the street from the Gadsden Hotel, a few doors down from the ornate facade of the Grand Theater, the **Grand Cafe**, 1119 G Street, is another great place to sample some very good and very cheap border town Mexican food.

Cave Creek and Chiricahua National Monument

For the 50-odd miles between Douglas and the New Mexico state line, old US-80 cuts diagonally across the southeast corner of Arizona, a rugged country of mountains, canyons, and volcanic outcrops rising above sagebrush plains. There's not much to see along the highway, but to the northwest rise the enticing Pendregosa Mountains, whose forested peaks, now protected as part of the Coronado National Forest, long served as sanctuary to Chiricahua Apaches and sundry outlaws and wanted men.

While you can also reach them from the north off I-10, the best access to the mountains from the south is via the aptly named hamlet of **Portal**, west of old US-80 from the New Mexico border, where the **Portal Peak Lodge, Store and Cafe** (520/558-2223) is a welcoming oasis, offering fresh food and comfortable rooms.

Above Portal rise the sheer cliffs of Cave Creek Canyon, which writer William Least Heat Moon described in *Blue Highways* as "one of the strangest pieces of topography I've ever seen," its pale sandstone walls looking like a sun-bleached twin of Utah's Zion National Park. A narrow but passable (except in winter) 20-mile dirt road from Cave Creek climbs over the mountains' pine-covered, 7,600-foot-high crest, ending up in the west at the foot of intriguing **Chiricahua National Monument**, a veritable "Wonderland of Rocks" whose contorted shapes were formed out of soft volcanic stone by eons of erosion.

The **visitor center** (daily 8 AM-5 PM; 520/824-3560) near the monument entrance has information on hiking, camping, and wildlife-watching opportunities in the Chiricahuas. Be aware that there are no services—gas, food, or lodging—near the park.

ACROSS NEW MEXICO

Between Arizona and Texas, the I-10 freeway crosses the part of New Mexico known as the Bootheel, for the way it steps down toward Old Mexico. Until the Gadsden Purchase of 1853, all this was part of Mexico, and the Hispanic influence still dominates the Anglo-American. The few towns here, like Lordsburg and Deming, were founded and remain primarily based on the railroad, and offer little for the passing traveler. However, at least one place is definitely worth a stop: the historic village of Mesilla, set around a dusty plaza just south of the region's one big city, Las Cruces.

Lordsburg and Shakespeare

Coming in from southeastern Arizona, old US-80 rejoins the I-10 freeway at a crossroads community aptly called Road Forks, and 15 miles farther east the freeway swerves south to bypass the town of Lordsburg (pop. 2,951). Named not from any religious conviction but in honor of the Southern Pacific railroad engineer who plotted it in 1880, Lordsburg has little to offer other than its 17 gas stations, 11 cafes (try **El Charro** along the train tracks at the center of town), and 10 motels, which line "Motel Drive," the three-mile-long I-10 Business Route (old US-80).

After delving into Texas at El Paso, you'll enter New Mexico again near Carlsbad Caverns National Park, which is described below on page 760.

Across New Mexico, towns along the interstate post road signs that total up their tourist services. Deming, for example, has 27 gas stations, 21 restaurants, and 13 motels.

Like something out of *The Andromeda Strain,* Lordsburg feels oddly abandoned, as if everyone has just packed up and left town. In fact, the one good reason to stop is New Mexico's best preserved ghost town, Shakespeare, three miles south of Lordsburg on a well-marked dirt road. Briefly home to some 3,000 silver miners during the early 1870s, Shakespeare was abandoned when the mines dried up, only to be reborn during another brief mining boom in the 1880s. By the 1930s it was

turned into a ranch by the Hill family, whose descendants still live here, care for the buildings and conduct irregularly scheduled guided **tours** (weekends 10 AM and 2 PM; $3; 505/542-9034) of the Grant House saloon, the general store (where you can buy books and postcards), and the Stratford Hotel, where Billy the Kid washed dishes as a young boy.

Deming

Some 60 miles east of Lordsburg, halfway to Las Cruces, the dusty ranching and farming community of Deming (pop. 10,970) advertises itself as "Deming—Home of Pure Water and Fast Ducks." This motto, which is repeated on billboard after billboard along I-10, makes more sense than it may at first: Deming's water comes from the underground Mimbres River, and every year at the end of August the town hosts duck races (for living ones, not the rubber kind) with prizes of some $10,000 going to the winners.

All this is little more than a cheap ploy to get hapless (or bored stiff, or both) travelers to turn off tedious I-10 and visit their city. Fortunately, it's not a bad place, boasting the excellent **Deming-Luna-Mimbres Museum**, 301 S. Silver Street (Mon.-Sat. 9 AM-4 PM, Sunday 1-4 PM; donations), three blocks south of Pine Street (old US-80), Deming's main drag. Besides the usual range of old pottery, sparkling rocks, and pioneer artifacts, the museum displays an endearing collection of old toys, dolls, quilts, and dental equipment—well worth a quick look at the very least.

Rooms range from local places like the neon-signed **Butterfield Stage Motel**, at 309 W. Pine Street (505/544-0011) to a **Best Western**, a **Holiday Inn**, and a **Motel 6** (off I-10 at exit 85). Best place to camp is southeast of town in **Rockhound State Park** ($8; 505/546-1212), where besides finding nice sites with hot showers you can collect up to 15 pounds of geodes, agates, or quartz crystals—something the rangers urge you to do.

Las Cruces

Spreading along the eastern banks of the Rio Grande, at the foot of the angular Organ Mountains, Las Cruces (pop. 62,126) is the commercial center of a prosperous agricultural and recreational region. Named for a concentration of pioneer grave markers, Las Cruces was first settled by Spanish missionaries but is now a thoroughly modern, American-looking place, with all the motels you could want (from a **Motel 6** to an upscale **Hilton**), but only a couple of places really worth searching out, such as **Nellie's**, a Mexican restaurant famed for spicy salsas and delicious chile cheeseburgers, housed in a little brown box at 1226 W. Hadley Street, off Valley Boulevard on the northwest edge of downtown.

Silver City, an evocative old mining town high in the mountains 45 miles northeast of Lordsburg, was another early stomping ground of Wild West outlaw **Billy the Kid** and makes an excellent sidetrip between Lordsburg and Deming.

Midway between Lordsburg and Deming, where I-10 imperceptibly crosses the 4,585-foot **Continental Divide,** Bowlin's Trading Post sells fireworks, rattlesnake eggs, and sundry other road trip essentials, as advertised by dozens of billboards along the highway.

Deming's own **KNFT 102.9 FM** plays Top 40 country hits of the past 25 years.

In southwestern New Mexico, the I-10 freeway roughly parallels the route followed in the 1850s by the Butterfield Stage, the 2,800-mile-long main overland link between St. Louis and San Francisco.

Along US-70 some 50 miles northeast of Las Cruces, **White Sands National Monument** protects over 60,000 acres of gleaming white gypsum dunes.

Mesilla

The best thing about Las Cruces is its nearness to a truly neat little place, the historic village of Mesilla, three miles southwest of Las Cruces via Hwy-28. Low-slung adobe buildings set around a shady central plaza hold a couple of historic sites—including an old jail from which Billy the Kid escaped in 1880—and a pair of excellent cantina-type restaurants, including very popular **La Posta** and less pricey but equally good **El Patio**.

Another, place to eat is on the main road south of the historic center: the **Old Mesilla Pastry Cafe**, which has great pastries all day (Wed.-Sun.) and a full range of Mexican-American breakfasts; it's not historic, but it is delicious.

Also in Mesilla, on Barker Road across Hwy-28 from the plaza, the **Gadsden Museum** (daily 9-11 AM, 1-5 PM; $2) traces local history from pre-conquest to current times.

Mesilla was founded across the Rio Grande on the Mexican side of the border in 1848, after the agreement of the Mexican-American War gave everything to the north to the Americans. Six years later, Mesilla became (legally at least) American again, after the Gadsden Purchase bought the entire, 30,000-square-mile "Bootheel" region for $10 million.

Hwy-28: Juan de Onate Trail

Southeast from Las Cruces and Mesilla, our route dips south across the Texas border to El Paso, then continues on US-180 for some 60 miles east before re-entering New Mexico at Carlsbad Caverns National Park. For the run to El Paso you have your choice between I-10 or slower and more scenic Hwy-28, the "Juan de Onate Trail," which avoids the freeway and runs through the pecan groves, pepper fields and dusty small towns that spread along the west bank of the Rio Grande.

This part of New Mexico is chili country, and there's no better place to sample the great variety of spicy peppers than at **Chope's** (505/233-9976), an unpretentious cinder block cafe along Hwy-28 in La Mesa, roughly midway between Mesilla and El Paso. House specialty here is *chiles rellenos*—whole chiles stuffed with cheese and deep-fried.

One of my all-time favorite roadside finds is right behind Chope's, in the front yard of an unforgettable old man named Francisco Alaniz. A former boxer who fought under the name "Kid Chimuri," the 88-year-old Alaniz has created a remarakble sculpture garden using cast-off industrial and consumer goods, aka "junk." Old trophies, advertising signs, mass-produced statues —they're all combined into visually delightful little scenes, featuring everything from Don Quixote to a replica of the "Little Boy" A-Bomb ("Built by Lazy Ignorant People—Tested in Japan"). Stop by for a guided tour.

the colorful outdoor sculpture garden of Francisco Alaniz

ACROSS TEXAS AND SOUTHEAST NEW MEXICO

Mileage-wise the haul across Texas is the longest part of this coast-to-coast route, but as far as things to see, the state doesn't offer a very high quotient per gallon. In the far-western stretches near El Paso, to maximize scenic interest, follow the slower but significantly more attractive route along US-180 past the beautiful Guadalupe Mountains, and veer across a corner of New Mexico to see the remarkable Carlsbad Caverns.

Q. Why do they call it Texas?
A. Because it "Texas" so long to drive across.

From Carlsbad it's a straight shot across the painfully flat Llano Estacado, which stretches to both sides of the New Mexico/Texas border; this section of the route is one of the least action-packed in the country—there's literally nothing for miles, apart from oil derricks, cattle ranches, and cotton plantations. Only a few of the sporadic towns here have any historic claim or aesthetic interest; it's basically a long day's drive across the open plains. If you're in a hurry, you won't miss much by following the route of old US-80, alongside the I-20 freeway between El Paso and the Dallas/Fort Worth metropolitan area, through roughneck oil towns like Odessa and Midland.

In eastern Texas, the landscape gradually evolves into that of the Deep South, the dense pine woods doing their best to disguise the historic dependence on the oil industry—with profits far more apparent in the towers of Dallas than here at the often poverty-stricken source. Again, the Interstates offer a faster way across, and you can turn off where you want to visit the few sites of interest, like tiny **Kilgore**, home of the "World's Richest Acre" and the captivating East Texas Oil Museum.

El Paso

Part of the largest international community in North America, El Paso (pop. 515,342) was originally settled because of its site at one of the safest crossings of the Rio Grande. It later grew into a vital way-station on the transcontinental Butterfield Stage and Southern Pacific Railroad. As its name suggests, for most people El Paso is a place to pass through, but there are many things here for visitors to enjoy.

One of the most interesting aspects of El Paso is the border itself, which for years followed the Rio Grande (known as the Río Bravo in Mexico), whose frequent changes in course caused innumerable problems for the two governments. Finally, in 1963, the river was run through a concrete channel so it could not change course. The border is now the location of the **Chamizal National Memorial**, on San Marical Street off Paisano Drive, where a small museum (daily 8 AM-5 PM; free) tells the border story and is surrounded by a pleasant green park. The Bridge of the Americas leads across to Ciudad Juárez (pop. 1.2 million) on the Mexican side.

Another unique attraction hidden away amidst El Paso's horizontal sprawl is the Spanish colonial missions that still stand southeast of downtown. The oldest missions in what is now the United States, this trio of churches—Ysleta, Socorro, and

A TORTILLA BY ANY OTHER NAME

Carne adovada, calabacitas, posole, sopapillas .... Menu items like these put you squarely in the lower left-hand quadrant of any U.S. map. But how do you know whether you're eating traditional New Mexican cooking, Southwestern Cuisine, or the popular hybrid known as Tex-Mex? Truth is, they're all hybrids, launched nearly five centuries ago when the Spanish brought European spices and domestic animals to combine with indigenous ingredients. As Spanish and Mexican settlers followed El Camino Real north from Chihuahua to Santa Fe, culinary distinctions grew out of regional variations in locally grown products along the way.

What's new is the categories: a generation ago, folks just helped themselves to "Mexican food." Still, certain characteristics distinguish each cuisine. In New Mexico, the chiles set the dishes apart—and set your taste buds afire. New Mexico's Mesilla Valley is to chiles what California's Napa Valley is to wine production. When you order a local specialty, the server may ask, "Red or green?"—referring to red or green chile. You can ask which is hotter and order accordingly, or try a little of each one.

Tex-Mex, as its name implies, draws from both sides of the international border, from grazing lands where *vaqueros* roast meat over mesquite fires. Hearty foods like *carne asada* (grilled meat) are accompanied by refried beans, guacamole, flour tortillas, and *pico de gallo*—an essential tomato and chile salsa. Fajitas, too, once signaled Tex-Mex territory, but that was before the rest of the country discovered the tasty strips of skirt steak.

When the food fusion goes farther afield than Mexico and the American Southwest, as in, say, Southwestern roasted chile bruschetta or spring rolls with green chile, you know you've entered the nebulous realm of contemporary Southwestern Cuisine, and all bets are off. The world-class chefs of Santa Fe recognize no limits, creative or otherwise. The world is their blue-corn fried oyster.

A tip for tender palates: if the chile's heat has you reaching for your Dos Equis, don't. Like water on gasoline, beer, soda pop, and even ice water only spread the fire. Try milk or, failing that, chew on a tortilla.

(And speaking of oysters—just because you're in the desert doesn't mean you have to do without seafood. The Sea of Cortez is a quick hop over the border and supplies the region's restaurants with oxymoronic jumbo shrimp and delicious sea bass.)

San Elizario—stand along the well-signed "Mission Trail," between the Rio Grande and I-10, roughly 15 miles from the center of town.

Along with the missions, all of which are still in use, El Paso holds a number of small special-interest museums, including ones dedicated to such diverse subjects as the U.S. Border Patrol, Napoléon Bonaparte, and frontier medicine. Four more—the U.S. Army Air Defense Artillery Museum, the Third Cavalry Museum, the Museum of the Non-Commissioned Officer, and the Fort Bliss Museum—are located at Fort Bliss, tracing El Paso's significant military history. All four are free and open daily 9 AM-4:30 PM.

Socorro Mission

El Paso has at least three unique claims to fame: it's the home of **Tony Lama** boots, which are available at significant discounts at four showrooms around town; the "World's Largest Harley-Davidson Dealership," Barnett's, is along I-10 at Lee Trevino Drive; and the **UTEP** campus, along I-10 west of town, which has the only buildings in North America designed to look like Tibetan monasteries.

Places to eat in and around El Paso tend, not surprisingly, to specialize in Tex-Mex food. Peruse the menus at **JJ's Drive-In**, 5320 Doniphan Avenue, off I-10 exit 11; at classic old **Forti's Mexican Elder**, 321 Chelsea Street east of downtown near the Paisano Avenue exit off I-10; and at **Grigg's**, east of town near Fort Bliss at 9007 Montana Avenue (US-180), which has been serving classic New Mexican food since 1939. One unique option: breakfast (and a car wash!) at the **H&H Coffee Shop**, 701 E. Yandell Avenue.

El Paso's finest place to stay is the grand old **Camino Real Paso Del Norte Hotel**, 101 S. El Paso Street (915/534-3000), one of the classiest hotels anywhere, with a beautiful bar off the lobby and rates (starting around $100) lower than you might think. All the usual mid-range chains are here too, plus a handy HI-approved youth hostel at the historic **Gardner Hotel**, 311 E. Franklin Street (915/532-3661).

For maps or more information on El Paso or neighboring Juárez, contact the **visitors bureau** downtown at 1 Civic Center Plaza (915/534-0696 or 800/351-6024).

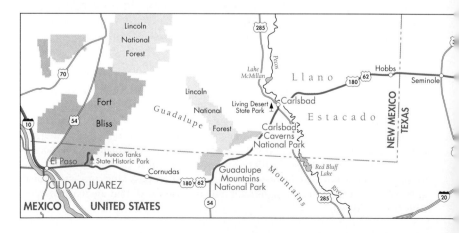

Detour: Ciudad Juárez

Largest by far of the Mexican border cities, Ciudad Juárez (pop. 1.2 million, and growing fast) is a compelling, disturbing, exciting and very worthwhile place to visit. Though the city sprawls through miles and miles of some of the worst pollution and direst poverty in Mexico—thanks in part to abuses of the *maquiladora* system—the downtown areas offer a quick taste of the country, and a half-hour walk can take you very far away from the USA. From the El Paso side, don't drive; park and walk down Santa Fe Street from downtown and cross the bridge on foot. This crossing drops you at the head of Avenida Juárez, the main drag, lined by cantinas and nightclubs and stalls and stores selling everything from mass-produced "crafts" to knock-off designer goods and Cuban cigars. (The latter items will be confiscated if you try to bring them back into the U.S.)

About a half-mile south of the border, at the junction with Avenida 16 de Septiembre, Avenida Juárez brings you to the heart of Juárez, where the very good historical museum (Tues.-Sun. 10 AM-6 PM; free), housed in the old customs building, and a large, often packed cathedral give glimpses into the city's history and culture. Among the many restaurants and bars along Avenida Juárez, a couple to check out are the **Kentucky Club,** 629 Avenida Juárez, a 1930s-looking bar that could be used as a set for some Raymond Chandler underworld adventure. Legend has it that Marilyn Monroe got drunk here, celebrating her Juárez divorce from playwright Arthur Miller. Next door, **Martino's** is a very popular Mexican restaurant. Be warned, however, that many Juárez bars double as brothels—these tend to have giveaway names like "The Pink Lady."

Food and drink aside, the best thing about a trip south is the chance to enjoy some **Lucha Libre**, professional wrestling, Mexican style. Dramatic and impassioned bouts (US$5 for a ringside seat) are held Sunday nights in the large municipal auditorium near the cathedral.

While in Texas, why not catch a Texas League baseball game? The **El Paso Diablos** (915/755-2000) play April-Aug. at Cohen Stadium, north of I-10 via the "North-South Freeway." Games are broadcast on KROD 600 AM.

El Paso's hard-to-find Concordia Cemetery (it's just northwest of the I-10/US-54 junction) is the final resting place of **John Wesley Hardin,** the "Fastest Gun in the West" before he got killed in 1895.

For the first 35 miles east of El Paso, US-180 runs along the southern edge of gigantic **Fort Bliss,** which stretches north for 50 miles into New Mexico and is home to about 20,000 U.S. troops.

The 70-mph section of US-180 east of El Paso is also signed as "Camino Buena Suerte," the "Good Luck Highway."

Hueco Tanks State Historic Park

In the 100 miles of arid West Texas desert between El Paso and the Guadalupe Mountains, look forward to precious little but the tiny Hueco Tanks State Historic Park (daily 8 AM-dusk; $2; 915/857-1135) on the fringes of Fort Bliss, some 30 miles east of El Paso, then eight miles north on Hwy-2775. Established to preserve the approximately 3,000 pictographs painted

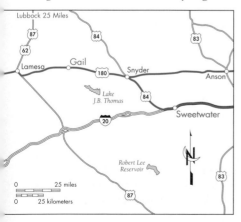

on the syenite basalt boulders, the 850-acre park also protects the remains of a stagecoach station and an old ranch house. The "tanks" of the title are naturally formed rock basins, which collect rainwater and have made the site a natural stop for passing travelers, from prehistoric natives to the Butterfield stagecoach. Unfortunately sometimes the "historic" graffiti is overwhelmed by more contemporary spray-paint versions, but the site is pleasant enough, with a popular campground and good opportunities for birdwatching and rock-climbing.

Some 35 miles east of the Hueco Tanks turnoff, the tiny highway town of **Cornudas** has a nice cafe—"Home of the World Famous Cornudas Burger"—and a row of false-fronted Wild West buildings.

From 1859 to 1861 the legendary Butterfield Overland Mail ran between St. Louis and San Francisco by way of El Paso, carrying mail and passengers across the country in 24 days. Running twice a week in both directions, the Butterfield line had some 140 relay stations along the route, each supplied with a Concord stagecoach and a fresh team of horses.

Along with New Mexico, El Paso and the Guadalupe Mountains area are in the mountain time zone. The rest of Texas is on central time.

Guadalupe Mountains National Park

One of the few un-hyped wonders of Texas, Guadalupe Mountains National Park covers the rugged peaks that rise along the New Mexico border, 110 miles east of El Paso. Formed as part of the same Capitan Reef of 250 million-year-old limestone as the great caverns of Carlsbad, the Guadalupe Mountains, a cool contrast to the surrounding desert, rise in sheer faces about 2,000 feet above the desert floor and offer the chance to experience many different and contrasting ecosystems side by side, within easy reach of the highway.

Even if you're not prepared to do any serious hiking—which is really the best way to experience the grandeur of the park or to see signs of the abundant wildlife (including mountain lions)—the quickest way to get a feel for the Guadalupes is to walk the half-mile **nature trail** that runs between the main **visitor center** (daily 8 AM-4:30 PM; free; 915/828-3251) and the remains of a Butterfield stagecoach station, passing well-signed specimens of all the major desert flora. If you have more time, head to **McKittrick Canyon**, off US-62/180 in the northeast corner of the park. From the small **visitor center** (daily 8 AM-4:30 PM; free; 915/828-3251) at the end of the road, a well-marked, well-maintained, and generally flat 3.5-mile trail winds along a stream, through a green landscape that changes gradually from the cactus of the Chihuahuan Desert to the oaks, walnuts, and maples of the inner canyon. It's best in spring, when the desert wildflowers bloom, or in autumn, when the hardwoods turn color.

Camping is available on a first-come, first-served basis at Pine Springs Campground near the main visitor center, and at numerous sites in the backcountry.

Carlsbad Caverns National Park

Carved out of the solid limestone of Capitan Reef by eons of dripping water, the Carlsbad Caverns contain over 30 miles of underground caves, some over 1,000 feet across. A two-mile trail (daily 8 AM-3:30 PM in summer, last entry at 2 PM rest of year) drops steeply from the large visitor center; or you can board an elevator (daily 8 AM-3 PM; $6 adults, $3 children; 505/785-2232) and ride 750 feet straight down to the "Big Room," where after wandering among the countless stalactites, stalagmites, and other formations, you can chow down on cheeseburgers at a classic 1950s-style cafeteria. Everyone has to ride the elevator back to the surface.

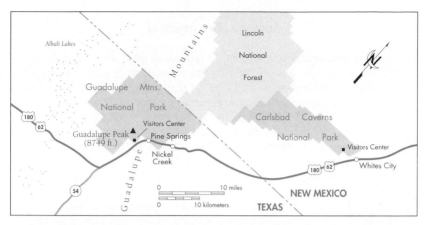

The trail down to the caverns closes early in the afternoon so that visitors don't interrupt the increasingly popular spectacle of the "**Bat Flight**," in which hundreds of thousands of Mexican freetail bats swirl out of the caverns at sunset. Every evening (usually around 7 PM, except in winter when the bats have migrated to Mexico), rangers give a brief free talk about bats—proselytizing about how really great and harmless they are—waiting for them to set off into the night.

The nearest places to stay and eat are in **Whites City**, a giant complex of motels, restaurants, pinball arcades and souvenir shops along Hwy-180 at the turnoff to the park. Rooms at the two **Best Westerns** (505/785-2291, 800/CAVERNS or 800/228-3767) there cost about $60 a night.

The one highlight of Whites City's tourist clutter is the **Million Dollar Museum** ($3), a bizarre but captivating collection.

Carlsbad

Twenty miles northeast of the Carlsbad Caverns, the town of Carlsbad (pop. 25,000) makes its living from the 750,000 tourists who visit the caves every year and has the motels to prove it: lining Canal Street (aka US-180, the "National Parks Highway"), the main road through town, you'll find national chains like Best Western, Holiday Inn, Motel 6, and Travelodge, and funkier local counterparts like the **Stagecoach Inn**, 1819 S. Canal Street (505/887-1148). There's also one very good Mexican restaurant, the **Casa de Cortez** at 506 S. Canal Street, a plain brown-brick building where locals come for heaping helpings of *frijoles refritos* and *chiles rellenos;* no booze, no credit cards, but great fresh sopaipillas.

North of Carlsbad Caverns, state-run radio station 530 AM broadcasts Ricardo Montalban continuously recounting the story of the famous **Goodnight-Loving cattle trail,** which ran along the nearby Pecos River.

As part of a federal program known as WIPP—the Waste Isolation Pilot Plant—the underground potash mines east of Carlsbad are in the process of being adapted into a contentious disposal site for the nation's **nuclear waste.**

Apart from the caverns, the one other thing to see in the Carlsbad area is the **Living Desert State Park** (8 AM-sunset; $3), four miles northwest off US-285, which shows off the plant and animal life of the arid Chihuahuan Desert region.

ROSWELL: UFO CENTRAL

If you can remember anything about the summer of 1997, this word will probably ring a few bells: Roswell. Seventy-five miles north of Carlsbad, Roswell (pop. 44,650) has become a catch-word for flying saucers, UFOs, extraterrestrials, and a complicated U.S. government cover-up of all the above. The cover-up is the one thing that's pretty much a given, since the Air Force has gone so far as to deny officially that anything ever happened in Roswell—which is equivalent to a confession, in the minds of UFO believers. Everything else about Roswell is, so to speak, up in the air.

The Roswell story goes something like this: in 1947, at the start of Cold War hysteria, something strange and metallic crashed into a field outside town, and the Army Air Corps (teams of tight-lipped operatives wearing special suits and dark glasses, no doubt) came and recovered it. Reports to the effect that a flying saucer had landed in Roswell appeared in the local paper, and quickly spread around the globe, only to be denied by the government, which claimed the "flying saucers" were actually weather balloons. Thirty-one years later, a retired military intelligence officer from the Roswell base sold a story to the *National Enquirer,* repeating details of the 1947 "flying saucer" crash, and telling of his subsequent capture of extraterrestrial beings. This in turn spawned countless other stories, books and videos, and spurred the growth of a battery of tourist attractions and events in and around Roswell, including at least two "museums": the **UFO Enigma Museum** at 6108 S. Main Street (505/825-2389), four miles south of Roswell near the Roswell Air Force Base, and the **International UFO Museum and Research Center**, in downtown Roswell at 400 N. Main Street (505/625-9495).

US-180: The Llano Estacado

From Carlsbad, US-180 crosses the Pecos River, then snakes across the barren Llano Estacado, the "Staked Plain," which covers most of eastern New Mexico and the Texas Panhandle. Supposedly named by early explorers who drove wooden stakes into the ground to mark their way, the Llano Estacado area is pretty much the same on both sides of the border—flat, dry, and mostly devoid of settlement. For eastbound travelers, this is the place where oil first becomes noticeably important—pumpjacks can be seen pumping away from here all the way to Alabama.

This is also cowboy country, thanks to the extensive pastures irrigated by water pumped up from aquifers deep underground. For travelers, however, the dominant image is of land stretching

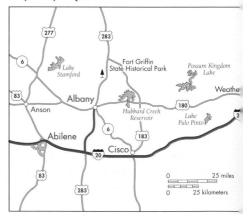

out far and wide: mile after mile after mile of endless flat cotton fields, interrupted every now and then by brilliant green alfalfa fields and a few surprisingly large towns like **Hobbs,** New Mexico (pop. 29,115), right on the border, its main street lined by various "Drilling Supply" companies and huge piles of old pipe. The Texas side is dotted with towns like **Seminole** (pop. 6,342), **Lamesa** (pop. 10,809, pronounced la-MEE-sa), which has an intact old Dairy Queen Drive-in along US-180, and **Gail,** which has the friendly Caprock Cafe and hosts an annual Fiddler's Festival. These towns seem like bustling hives of activity after the open, red-earth prairie in between them, but compared to other parts of the route Texas has fewer than usual places to stop; to be honest, there's not all that much in the 325-odd miles between the New Mexico-Texas border and the fringes of Fort Worth. A highlight of the drive is **Snyder** (pop. 12,195), which has a life-sized statue of an albino buffalo on its courthouse square, a great old Sinclair filling station, and a very good country music station, 101.5 FM.

Gail

Midway between Lamesa and Snyder, the tiny town of Gail (pop. 189)—which the *Texas State Travel Guide* describes as a "cow town without bank, theater, railroad, hotel, doctor, or lawyer"—was the site of violent feuds during the land rush of 1902, the history of which is recounted in the tiny **Borden County Museum** (Thurs.-Sun. noon-4 PM; $1). The town, and the county, are named in memory of pioneer surveyor and newspaper editor **Gail Borden,** who is perhaps best known as the inventor of condensed milk and founder of Borden Foods.

At the town of Anson, US-180 crosses US-83, the original "Road to Nowhere." Anson is described on pages 204-205.

Albany

Albany, one of the more interesting towns in this part of Texas, was first settled as a stage stop on the route of the Butterfield Overland Mail in 1854. It's still a tiny place, with no more than 2,000 residents, but it has a lively feel and, more surprisingly, a small but intriguing **art museum** (Tues.-Sat. 9 AM-5 PM, Sunday 2-5 PM; free;

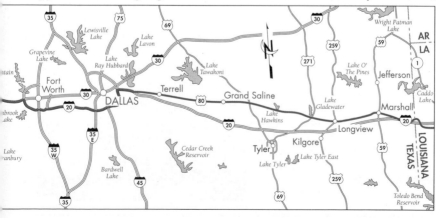

915/762-2269) in the Old City Jail at 211 S. 2nd Street. A big surprise in the middle of the ranch lands, the museum contains an outstanding permanent collection of art by Modigliani, Picasso, and others, and also displays Chinese ceramics from the Tang and Ming dynasties.

The nearby courthouse is the oldest in Texas, in use since 1883. Fifteen miles north of Albany on US-283, **Fort Griffin State Historical Park** (daily 8 AM-10 PM; $3 per car) preserves the remains of the main base of U.S. Cavalry sorties against Comanche raiders during the late 1860s.

I-20: Sweetwater and Cisco

If you've decided to take the high-speed route along I-20, midway across Texas you'll pass Sweetwater, where every March, during the **Rattlesnake Round-Up,** townspeople get together and collect hundreds of rattlers from the surrounding ranch lands, winning prizes for the biggest, shortest, and most snakes handed in. The town, 25 miles west of Abilene, also has shops selling all manner of rattlesnake-related souvenirs, and any time of year, Sweetwater—which was first settled in the 1850s and now earns its livelihood mining gypsum for use in wallboard—is worth a stop for a meal at one of the best restaurants in West Texas, **Allen's Family-Style Meals,** 1301 E. Broadway (915/235-2060), along old US-80.

The I-20 town of **Cisco,** 45 miles east of Abilene, is where **Conrad Hilton** bought and ran his first hotel, the Mobley, in 1919. East of Cisco the town of **Eastland** has two world-class oddities. The middle entrance to the county courthouse displays the embalmed body of "Old Rip" the Toad, who survived 29 years embedded in the cornerstone of the old courthouse before being discovered, alive, when

---

LUBBOCK: PANHANDLE MUSIC MECCA

The largest city in northwest Texas, Lubbock (pop. 186,206) is a busy and unattractive agricultural center, best known for having given the world Buddy Holly, whose songs ("Peggy Sue," "That'll Be The Day," "Rave On") paved the way for rock 'n' roll. For music fans, the trip downtown to pay homage at the statue of Buddy at the corner of 8th Street and Avenue Q is worthwhile. He's surrounded by plaques honoring other Lubbock boys and girls made good, including Roy Orbison, Waylon Jennings, Tanya Tucker, and Joe Ely. Buddy, who died in a 1959 plane crash at age 22, is buried near the entrance of Lubbock Cemetery, at the east end of 31st Street.

Another main attraction of Lubbock is Prairie Dog Town, in Mackenzie State Park at the northeast edge of downtown, somewhat hard to find off Avenue A.

For more information, contact the tourist office at Avenue K and 14th Street (806/763-4666 or 800/692-4035).

it was being torn down. A few blocks away at 411 W. Main Street, the post office contains a huge stamp-themed mural made entirely of 11,217 postage stamps, created over a seven-year period by former postmistress Marene Johnson (a postcard of the mural is available).

Old US-80 across Dallas/Fort Worth

Coming from the west, US-80/180 enters Fort Worth on Camp Bowie Boulevard (US-377), then passes through the historic heart of the city before heading east on a bee-line across to Dallas. The old road between Fort Worth and Dallas, now signed as Hwy-180, approaches downtown Dallas on Commerce Street and heads down Main Street before leaving town past the Cotton Bowl.

DALLAS/FORT WORTH SURVIVAL GUIDE

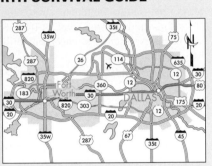

LIKE WARRING BRANCHES OF AN EX-tended family, Dallas and Fort Worth are inseparable arch-rivals. Both towns lay fair claim to being capitals of their respective industries: Fort Worth calls itself "Cowtown" but has a surprisingly sophisticated range of cultural centers, and feels like an altogether more "Texan" place; it was founded during the heyday of the Chisholm Trail and still retains much of its Wild West past. Upstart Dallas, which boomed after the discovery of oil in east Texas during the 1930s, plays the role of nouveau riche to the nth degree, home to Neiman Marcus and TV's eponymous soap opera.

In terms of things to see and do, Fort Worth holds the winning hand. The wonderful **Kimbell Art Museum**, 3333 Camp Bowie Boulevard (Tues.-Sat. 10 AM-5 PM, Sunday noon-5 PM; free; 817/332-8451), is one of the most perfectly beautiful modern buildings on the planet, designed as a series of vaulted galleries by Louis Kahn. This small museum, which has an impressive collection of pre-Columbian art and some notable Post-Impressionist paintings, stands at the heart of the Fort Worth Cultural District. Across the street, the **Amon Carter Museum** (817/738-1933) displays one of the country's finest collections of Wild West and other American art.

In downtown Fort Worth, the **Caravan of Dreams**, 312 Houston Street, (817/877-3000) is funded by the same Texas billionaire who brought you Biosphere II, Fort Worth "ecopreneur" Ed Bass. This fascinating multipurpose art center and nightclub is all but indescribable; see it to believe it. The Caravan is located right downtown on Sundance Square, whose four blocks of red-brick streets preserve the flavor of old Fort Worth. Two miles north of downtown Fort Worth, head to the **Stockyards**, on Main and Exchange Streets. For a taste

(continues on next page)

Terrell

East of Dallas, US-80 is, except during rush hour, a fast four-lane freeway across the suburbs. A dozen miles east of downtown, a huge number of antique shops fill pre-fab industrial sheds along the highway, just before the freeway merges into I-20.

The old road parallels the freeway through Terrell (pop. 12,490), the birthplace of the U.S. Department of Agriculture Cooperative Extension Service program, which first brought modern science and technology to traditional family farms in the 1930s. Terrell's small airport is home to the unique **Silent Wings Museum** (Tues.-Sat. 10 AM-5 PM, Sunday noon-5 PM; free), which has one of the only fully re-stored CG-4A gliders in existence, along with lots of exhibits recounting the ex-ploits of glider planes during WW II.

of how Texas used to be, spend some time wandering these two short blocks of turn-of-the-century buildings, stretching west from the still-busy Fort Worth Stockyards, and housing some of the city's most popular places to eat, drink, and be merry; after dark, check out **Billy Bob's** (817/624-7177), the "World's Largest Honky Tonk."

In Dallas, sightseers head to the **Texas School Book Depository—"The Sixth Floor,"** 411 Elm Street (daily 10 AM-6 PM; $7; 214/747-6660). Besides the gruesome novelty value of looking out from the very same place where Lee Harvey Oswald shot (or didn't shoot . . .) President John F. Kennedy on No-vember 22, 1963, this extensive museum describes the historical context and discusses the myriad of conspiracy theories. Oddly, the entire museum is copyrighted, so No Photography signs abound. On the south side of down-town, outside the Dallas Convention Center, the **"Longhorns on the Trail"** sculpture on Young Street is easy to miss, but worth searching out—a life-sized herd of bronze Longhorn cattle seemingly frozen mid-stride, gathered around a watering hole.

In between the two cities, off I-30 at the Ballpark Way exit in Arlington, the **Texas Rangers** (817/273-5100) play at the fabulous new Ballpark. (Yes, that's the full name—no corporate sponsors. Yet.)

Practicalities

Linked (or is it divided?) by a trio of fast freeways (I-20, I-30 and Hwy-183), Dallas and Fort Worth lie some 25 miles apart from each other across the plains of northeast Texas. Each city is circled by its own ring road, and two north-south freeways (I-35W through Fort Worth and I-35E through downtown Dallas) complete the high-speed network. **Dallas/Fort Worth International Airport** (DFW), midway between the two cities, is the main airport for the region and home base of American Airlines. **SuperShuttle** vans (817/329-2000) will carry you to either city from the air-port for around $10. Dallas also has a second airport, Love Field, eight miles northwest of the city, which is used mainly by **Southwest Airlines**. All the usual car rental firms have branches at both airports.

Grand Saline

East of Terrell, US-80 winds over rolling hills, where small farms grow fruits and berries in the sandy loam. Halfway between Dallas and Longview spreads Grand Saline, so named because of the massive mines of salt used as a seasoning and preservative since at least the early 1800s, when displaced Cherokee Indians discovered the deposits here. At first the salt was reclaimed from the broad salt flats that spread out from the town, but mine shafts were later dug to reach the hard-rock salt hundreds of feet beneath the ground. Morton Salt now owns and operates the mines. Hot water is pumped underground, the resulting brine is evaporated and crystallized, and the salt is packaged for home and industrial uses.

For a place to stay in Fort Worth, the **Ramada Hotel**, 1701 Commerce Street (817/335-7000 or 800/272-6232), is centrally located, just across from the convention center and the modern Fort Worth Water Gardens, last seen in the movie *Logan's Run*. Doubles from $60. Bonnie & Clyde (both of whom are buried in Dallas) stayed in the **Stockyards Hotel**, 109 E. Exchange Avenue, Fort Worth (817/625-6427), a turn-of-the-century hotel that has been restored and re-decorated according to various themes, including the aforementioned bank robbers. Doubles cost $75, and the downstairs bar has saddles instead of bar stools.

In Dallas, the **Adolphus Hotel**, 1321 Commerce Street (214/742-8200), is a historic four-star downtown hotel, built in 1912 by beer magnate Adolphus Busch and worth a look for the plush interior even if you can't afford the $200-a-night rates.

Food in Fort Worth, not surprisingly, tends to the beefy. **Angelo's BBQ**, 2533 White Settlement, Fort Worth (817/332-0357), is located in a banal industrial area between the "Cultural District" and the Stockyards, and doesn't look like much from the outside, but it serves up some of the juiciest BBQ brisket in Texas. **Cattlemen's Steak House**, 2458 N. Main Street (817/624-3945), has steaks of all cuts and sizes, plus BBQ and some seafood. **Joe T. Garcia's**, 2201 N. Commerce Street (817/626-4356), may or may not be the World's Biggest Tex-Mex restaurant, but it sure can feel like it. Finally, the very friendly **Paris Coffee Shop**, 704 W. Magnolia (817/335-2041), has great fried chicken and delicious fresh fruit pies.

In Dallas, east of the I-35E Central Expressway from downtown, the **Deep Ellum Cafe**, 2706 Elm Street (214/741-9012), is a popular and stylish "New American" restaurant located in the heart of "Deep Ellum," a scruffy-looking, post-industrial district of boutiques, bars, restaurants, and nightclubs. A northwest Dallas institution, the **Prince of Hamburgers** drive-in at 5200 Lemmon Avenue (214/526-9081) has been serving burgers, fries, and milk shakes since 1927.

For maps and more extensive information, contact the Dallas **visitors bureau**, 1201 Elm Street (daily 9 AM-5 PM; 214/746-6677). Fort Worth has three visitor centers, including one in the Stockyards at 130 E. Exchange Avenue (817/624-4741).

Northwest of Fort Worth, 22 miles south of Wichita Falls, writer Larry McMurtry has been turning his hometown of Archer City into the world's largest used book store. Housed in a number of downtown buildings, many of which are featured in McMurtry's *The Last Picture Show* and other works, his **Booked Up** bookstore has over 300,000 volumes, mostly rare and out-of-print editions.

The salt deposits under Grand Saline are estimated to be over 16,000 feet thick and nearly 10,000 feet across, enough to supply the world's needs for the next 20,000 years.

South of I-20, the town of **Tyler** grows thousands and thousands of roses, including the famous yellow ones, the "National Rose of Texas." For road-trippers, Tyler is also worth a stop for the fine food at **Bodacious Bar-B-Q,** hard to miss on the north side of I-20 at the Hwy-14 exit and open daily 10 AM-9 PM.

Kilgore: Oil!

The pine-covered, red earth hills of East Texas are covered with creaking old pumpjacks, still pumping up the crude oil that has kept the region economically afloat since the 1930s. The oil business here has gone through numerous booms and busts since it gushed into existence in December 1930 at a well outside Kilgore (pop. 11,100), on the south side of I-20. Ten miles southwest of Longview via US-259, this smaller and quieter oil town is a much more satisfying place to visit, with street lamps disguised as oil rigs and a set of 100-foot-tall derricks standing along the railroad tracks in memory of the "**World's Richest Acre**," a plot of downtown land that produced over 2.5 million barrels of oil through the 1960s. The site was so productive and so valuable that one of the wells was drilled through the terrazzo floor of a local bank, and over a thousand derricks once loomed over the downtown area.

The history of the local petroleum industry is recounted in entertaining detail at the **East Texas Oil Museum,** (Tues.-Sat. 9 AM-5 PM, Sunday 2-5 PM; $4) on the campus of Kilgore College, on Ross Street off US-259. The museum includes displays of drilling equipment and old gas stations, plus a simulated "elevator ride" a mile deep into the earth to show off the oil-bearing geology. Also on the Kilgore College campus is a small free museum devoted to the **Kilgore Rangerettes,** a college-trained precision drill and dance team that performs at college and professional football games.

Kilgore is decidedly not a typical tourist destination, with only minimal motels and restaurants available, though there is at least one good place to eat: **Lupe's**, serving up traditional Tex-Mex food at 2607 N. US-259 (903/983-1457), north of downtown. Back on US-80, another good place to eat is Creole-spiced **Johnny Cace's Seafood**, east of downtown Longview at 1501 E. Marshall Road.

Marshall and Jefferson

North of I-20 some 25 miles west of the Louisiana state line, Marshall (pop. 23,682) is one of the older, and once among the wealthiest, towns in Texas. Now a fairly quiet place, in its early years Marshall was the commercial capital of the East Texas cotton country, and during the Civil War two local residences served as the Confederate capital—of Missouri. This anomaly, along with general regional history, is chronicled in the **Harrison County Historical Society Museum** (Tues.-Sat. 9 AM-5 PM; $2), housed in the supremely ornate, yellow brick courthouse on the town square.

If you have the time and inclination to get a more palpable sense of the varied culture and history of East Texas, take US-59 15 miles north of Marshall to Jefferson (pop. 2,199), an almost perfectly preserved bayou town that looks much as it did during the 1870s when, with a population of nearly 30,000, it was the busiest inland port west of the Mississippi. Among the most prominent of the hundreds of historic structures here is the 1858 **Excelsior House**, 211 W. Austin Street; across the street, you can tour Jay Gould's private railroad car, the *Atalanta*, or simply explore the many good antique shops, cafes, and restaurants, like the Creole-flavored **Black Swan**, 210 Austin Street. For more information, contact the Jefferson **tourist office** at 116 W. Austin Street (903/665-2672).

ACROSS LOUISIANA

Northern Louisiana, which covers some 200 miles of forested, rolling hills between Texas and Mississippi, is a far cry from the Cajun fun of the southern half of the state. A Baptist-dominated "Bible Belt" heartland, it's also a very diverse place, part heavily industrial, part poor rural backwater, with a mix of people and products that encapsulates its transitional position between the agricultural Deep South and the petrochemical plants of Texas.

The main city here is the oil town of Shreveport, which has recently become a prime place for gamblers, with flashy casinos lining the riverfront. However, you'll mostly find small towns ranging from Gibsland (where Bonnie and Clyde met their doom) to the college town of Ruston (home to Louisiana Tech and Grambling Universities).

North of Shreveport on Hwy-1, **Oil City** has one of the region's better history museums, housed inside the old railroad depot and displaying a wonderful collection of old postcards.

Shreveport

GIBSLAND, LOUISIANA

"AUTHENTIC BONNIE & CLYDE FESTIVAL"

See Where The Outlaws Were Killed 59 Years Ago

FESTIVAL
may 22, 1993

A King Cotton town that thrived in the antebellum years and survived the war physically, though not economically, unscathed, Shreveport (pop. 198,525) is now a busy industrial city rising on the west bank of the Red River. Along with its industrialized ugly stepbrother, Bossier City (pronounced BO-zyur) across the river, Shreveport is a center of the Louisiana oil business—which is small only when compared to that of Texas, and still hugely important despite slumps in supplies and prices. Also, the cities emerged in recent years as two of the hotspots of Louisiana's nascent gambling industry, with four major casinos—including the lively **Horseshoe**, a four-story faux riverboat floating in a shallow pond on the Bossier City side—along the riverfront attracting people from all over the tri-state "Ark-La-Tex" region.

Shreveport is named in honor of **Capt. Henry Shreve,** who in the 1830s cleared the Red River of a 165-mile-long logjam that had blocked navigation. He then "bought" the land from native Caddo Indians.

The Class AA **Shreveport Captains** (318/636-5555) play Texas League baseball at the Louisiana State Fairgrounds. Games are broadcast on KWKH 1130 AM.

Shreveport and Bossier City have long hosted the Louisiana Hayride, a country-western radio program in which Hank Williams and Elvis Presley both started their careers. The same sort of music can still be heard on **KWKH 94.5 FM,** your best bet for late-night bluegrass in northwest Louisiana.

Downtown Shreveport is the usual mix of turn-of-the-century brick buildings and boarded-up shopfronts, loomed over by a solitary 10-story glass office tower, with a handful of interesting structures surviving near the riverfront; walking-tour maps of the area are available from the **visitor center**, a block west of the river at 629 Spring Street (318/222-9391 or 800/551-8682). One place car culture fans will want to check out is the **Ark-La-Tex Car Museum**, 601 Spring Street (daily 10 AM-5 PM; $5), which has a futuristic 1948 Tucker on display alongside old fire engines.

One of the most significant concentrations of archaeological remains in North America is known as **Poverty Point,** 18 miles north of I-20 off Hwy-17, where 3,000-year-old burial mounds have been protected within a 400-acre state park.

The nicest part of town is the leafy Highland district, stretching south from the end of Market Street, south of I-20 between the river and the new I-49 freeway. This is where you'll find the grand old houses of the landed gentry, many of which look like they belong in *Gone With The Wind,* despite the fact that almost all of them date from the 20th century. The Highland district also holds one of Shreveport's better places to eat: **Don's Seafood House**, 3100 Highland Avenue, serving moderately priced Cajun-spiced specialties. All the usual hotel and motel chains line I-20.

Gibsland: Bonnie and Clyde

East of Shreveport, the old US-80 highway winds through dozens of somnolent little towns, following the rolling land while crisscross-

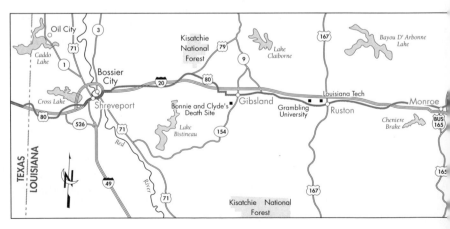

Clyde Barrow

ing back and forth under the high-speed I-20 freeway. After passing the pawn shops and girlie bars outside Barksdale Air Force Base, the route parallels railroad tracks along the remains of a historic log turnpike, built in the 1870s to provide all-weather passage across the muddy bogs and bayous.

Apart from the usual barrage of roadside businesses, there's not a lot to stop for until you reach the tiny town of Gibsland (pop. 1,224), just south of I-20, 45 miles east of Shreveport. This pleasantly unremarkable little hamlet has one unique claim to fame: it was here, in 1934, that the notorious Depression-era gangsters Clyde Barrow and Bonnie Parker (a.k.a. **Bonnie and Clyde**) were ambushed and killed. A small, town-run museum tells their story, and sells gruesome postcards of their bullet-riddled bodies, while every May locals dress up and stage gun battles and car chases—more for cops-and-robbers fun than out of any real dedication to historical accuracy.

A battered stone marker, eight miles south of Gibsland along Hwy-154, stands on the site where the desperate duo—who in "real life" were nasty cold-blooded murderers, nothing like the romantic pair played by Warren Beatty and Faye Dunaway in the Hollywood movie—were shot by state troopers.

Ruston

Roughly halfway across the state, Ruston (pop. 20,027) calls itself the "Peach Capital" but is best known for its two major colleges: Louisiana Tech, which is right in town but lacks the expected collegiate ambience; and smaller Grambling University, one of the nation's top African-American schools, three miles west of town, just south of I-20.

stone marker where Bonnie and Clyde were killed

There's not a lot to look out for, but a number of local and franchised fast-food places line California Street (US-80) on the south side of town.

At Grambling University's **KGRM 91.5 FM,** student DJs play a wide range of classic soul, reggae, and R&B, plus contemporary rap and hip-hop.

Monroe

Considering that it is one of the largest towns in northern Louisiana, Monroe (pop. 54,909) feels strangely abandoned, even though the downtown area has a number of classic commercial buildings dating from the period between the two World Wars, and even though Victorian-era warehouses and hundreds of ancient-looking "shotgun" shacks line the railroad tracks and US-80.

Apart from its photogenic architecture and fading roadside signs, Monroe doesn't really offer much reason to stop, though the gorgeous greenery of the **Louisiana Purchase Gardens and Zoo** (daily 10 AM-5 PM; $3.50), south of I-20 off US-165, makes it a great place to stretch your legs (or take a steam train or boat ride) among the moss-draped oaks and cypress trees.

East of Monroe, it's an hour's drive across the bayous before you reach the fascinating city of Vicksburg, across the Mississippi River.

ACROSS MISSISSIPPI

US-80, which for much of the way has been replaced by the I-20 freeway, cuts across the middle of Mississippi, passing through its three largest cities—Meridian, Jackson, and Vicksburg—whose small sizes show how rural and diffuse the state still is. Only Jackson, the capital and by far the biggest city in the state, is anything like an urban center, with a couple of "skyscrapers" and nearly 200,000 people. Mostly what you see along this stretch is small farms and Civil War battlefields, the most extensive and important of which rises above the Mississippi River in Vicksburg.

The Mississippi River town of Vicksburg marks the junction of US-80 with our Great River Road route, and its antebellum homes, Civil War sites, and great food are all covered in full detail on pages 277-280.

Bovina: Earl's Art Gallery

If you've ever been to a House of Blues, you've probably seen some of the rough-hewn folk art of Mississippi artist Earl Simmons, who for the past 20 years has lived and worked in a ramshackle studio near Bovina, 10 miles east of the Mississippi River. It's hard to pin down a "style" to these works, because most of them are made from materials Earl finds lying around (or in the local garbage dump), but there is definitely something special in the things he makes—and sells—at his workshop. To visit, turn off I-20 at Bovina, then head south across old US-80 and the railroad tracks, veering left at the "Y" and continuing south for about a half-mile. Tours (by appointment or good timing; 601/636-5264) cost $2, and the artworks range anywhere from a few dollars to a couple of hundred—or more.

Clinton and the Natchez Trace

The one-time Choctaw Indian agency of Clinton, north of I-20 10 miles west of

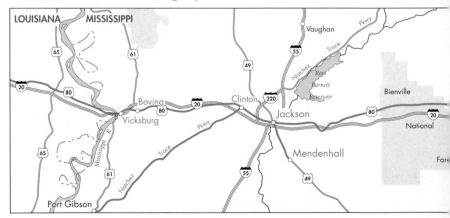

Jackson, was renamed in 1828 in honor of New York Gov. De-Witt Clinton, who oversaw construction of the Erie Canal. Now a small cotton-growing and shipping center, with a few blocks of "olde towne" around the Baptist-run Mississippi College, along Leake and Jefferson Streets, in its early years Clinton sat on the notorious Natchez Trace, now followed by the blissfully pleasant Natchez Trace Parkway, which runs southwest to Port Gibson (see p. 283 for more), and northeast all the way to Nashville.

Though it survived the Civil War relatively unscathed, Clinton later saw some of the worst Reconstruction-era race riots in the state, with an estimated 50 unarmed blacks killed during a single rampage in 1875.

Jackson

Spreading west from the banks of the Pearl River, Jackson (pop. 196,637) was established as state capital in 1822. Named for Andrew Jackson, hero of the Battle of New Orleans during the War of 1812 and later president of the U.S., it was destroyed during the Civil War but is now a prosperous city, Mississippi's political and commercial heart and biggest city—though you wouldn't know it by the somnolent look of the place.

The very attractive Greek Revival **Old State Capitol**, built in 1838 and used until 1903, rises at the center of town at State and Capitol Streets, and is open for free self-guided **tours** (Mon.-Fri. 8 AM-5 PM, Saturday 9:30 AM-4:30 PM, Sunday noon-4:30 PM) of the building and the well-presented historical exhibits that fill it. Substantial floor space is given over to the 20th century, including a thoughtful (and thought-provoking) examination of the Civil Rights Movement. The few other fine old antebellum buildings—under a dozen altogether—that survive around Jackson were used by Union forces and were thus spared destruction. These include the art-filled **Governor's Mansion,** a short walk east of the old capitol, at 300 E. Capitol Street (Mon.-Fri. 9:30-11 AM; free), and **The Oaks**, 823 N. Jefferson Street (Tues.-Sat. 10 AM-3 PM; $3), in which General Sherman lived. Restored to prewar splendor,

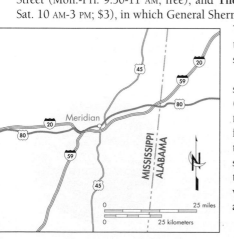

The Oaks is furnished with period antiques and, surprisingly for the South, a sofa from Abraham Lincoln's law office.

On the south side of downtown Jackson, the **Mississippi Museum of Art** (Mon.-Sat. 10 AM-5 PM, Sunday noon-5 PM; $3; 601/960-1515) gained national fame when it was the only U.S. museum to host the touring "Treasures of Versailles" exhibition in 1998. Year-round, the spacious modern galleries display works by local and international painters and sculptors.

All across Mississippi, you'll see highway signs emblazoned with the insipid slogan "Only Positive Mississippi Spoken Here."

The tiny town of **Vaughn,** 30 miles north of Jackson via the I-55 freeway, was the site of the crash that killed legendary train engineer **Luther "Casey" Jones.** A small museum, a mile east of I-55 exit 133, has exhibits on Casey and the history of railroading in the South.

After burning Jackson to the ground during the Civil War, Gen. Ulysses S. Grant is said to have coined the expression "War is Hell."

How times change, Mississippi style: Jackson's main streets have been renamed to honor Civil Rights Movement martyrs Martin Luther King, Jr. and Medgar Evers.

Away from downtown, the main attraction is the **Mississippi Agriculture and Forestry Museum** (Mon.-Sat. 9 AM-5 PM, Sunday 1-5 PM; $4; 601/354-6113), a 40-acre complex on Lakeland Drive northeast of downtown, off I-55 exit 98B. Despite the dull name, it's a hugely engaging and entertaining place, with a composite "Crossroads Town" made up of authentic buildings, including a general store, filling station, and sawmill brought here from all over Mississippi. Nearby is a fully restored working farm, and museum exhibits trace state history with an emphasis on transportation and agriculture. Especially if you have kids along, the whole complex is well worth a look—if only so you can say you've visited the **National Agricultural Aviation Hall of Fame**, which displays historical and contemporary crop-dusting equipment along with sundry devices used in the days before pesticides to catch cotton-eating boll weevils.

The museum complex stands next to the very popular **Jackson Generals** Texas League baseball stadium (tickets $3-5; 601/981-4664), though the franchise has been slated to move to New Orleans.

Jackson Practicalities

Downtown, the best bet is upscale **Ironhorse Grill**, 320 W. Pearl Street, serving "New American" food for lunch and dinner in a building that's on the "wrong side of the tracks," but also on the National Register of Historic Places. Also great: for

---

DEEP SOUTH ROADSIDE SHRINES

Among the many pleasures of traveling around the southern states is the likelihood of coming upon a striking monument in the middle of nowhere. Rural back roads that for miles and miles have run quietly through woodlands or along cotton fields will be suddenly marked by giant crosses or a pylon of hand-lettered signs. In the Midwest, you'll often see a fiberglass dinosaur or other giant creature constructed by some well-intentioned civic organization and intended to draw highway traffic to local businesses. In the South, however, what you see are intensely personal creations, built by eccentric and often outcast individuals (99% of them men), and instead of acting as an advertising gimmick they usually spout chapter and verse of Scripture, warning about the impending Apocalypse or the inevitable coming of Judgment Day.

Among the Deep South roadside shrines, don't miss the one that stands outside Margaret's Grocery (see page 279), along Business US-61 on the north side of Vicksburg, Mississippi, at 4535 N. Washington Street (601/638-1163). At a glance, the assemblage of huge hand-lettered signs atop various red-and-white constructions resembles a fanatical Lego-Land. The Biblically-inspired injunctions are worth at least a pause, but caveat visitor: the friendly owners will talk your ears off if you aren't careful.

There's another fascinating folk art environment at Earl's Art Gallery, in Bovina, east of Vicksburg (see above). Further east, within a short drive of US-80 in Prattville, northwest of

more local flavor, try **Franks' Biscuits**, open from 6 AM at 219 N. President Street; the **Elite Restaurant**, 141 E. Capitol near the Mississippi Museum of Art; or the other old-timey cafes dotted around downtown Jackson, many featuring great old neon signs.

Places to stay in Jackson tend to be either rough but cheap highway motels lining old US-80, or anodyne chains along the I-20 and I-55 interstate frontages. Among the nicest of the latter is the **Best Western Metro Inn**, 1520 Ellis Avenue off I-20 exit 42B (601/355-7483 or 800/528-1234).

For a more complete list or for any other information, contact the Jackson **visitors bureau**, 921 N. President Street (601/960-1891 or 800/354-7695).

Detour: Mendenhall

For a one-of-a-kind, down-home Mississippi eating experience, take a trip 20 miles southeast of Jackson via US-49 to the hamlet of Mendenhall (pop. 2,463), where the **Mendenhall Hotel Revolving Tables**, right on Main Street (601/847-3113), serves all-you-can-eat, family-style portions of absolutely great chicken, juicy ham steaks, barbecued beef, and at least a half-dozen vegetables, all to be washed down with pitchers of sweet iced tea—in the dining room of a very comfortable old railroad hotel. Lunch (and only lunch) is served 11 AM-2 PM every day; worth planning your trip around—don't miss it!

Montgomery, Alabama, W.C. Rice has constructed an intense garden of white crosses that resembles a military cemetery. Rice himself, who lives on-site, always wears a large wooden cross around his neck and is said to be friendly to visitors.

The best known of these "Gardens of Revelation," as scholar John Beardsley has called them in his excellent book of the same name, is Howard Finster's Paradise Garden, near Summerville in the Appalachian foothills of northwest Georgia. Recently famous for his primitivist paintings, which have appeared on album covers by REM and Talking Heads, Finster has created a series of Gaudi-esque shrines, embedding seashells, bits of tile and old car parts into concrete forms. Pictures of Henry Ford, Hubert Humphrey, and Hank Williams are arrayed alongside dozens of signs quoting Scripture, but the spirit of the place is best summed up by Finster's own verse: "I built this park of broken pieces to try to mend a broken world of people who are traveling their last road."

Only two hours from Atlanta, the Paradise Garden is now one of the more popular attractions in the area, and is open daily 10 AM-6 PM, with a $3 admission fee ($5 on Sundays, when Howard Finster is on-site in the afternoon). To get there, make your way to Summerville, then head north on US-27 for three miles to Pennville, and turn right at Jim's Auto Supply. For details, or more explicit driving directions, call 800/FINSTER or 800/346-7837.

These roadside shrines are by no means limited to states south of the 35th Parallel; northern states have their share as well, including two of the most intense: the Garden of Eden in Lucas, Kansas (see page 697), and Holy Land outside Waterbury, Connecticut (see page 632).

FATHER OF COUNTRY MUSIC

The collision of Mississippi's rural past with the early stages of industrial development was embodied in the life and work of Meridian's favorite son, Jimmie Rodgers, whose original mixing of black Delta blues and white Appalachian folk songs earned him the title "Father of Country Music." What Elvis Presley was to the 1950s, Rodgers was to the previous generation. Born in Meridian on September 8, 1897, Rodgers worked briefly on the railroad, lost his job after coming down with tuberculosis, then became the original overnight success. After he was discovered by an RCA talent scout in 1927, Rodgers' first record, "Sleep, Baby, Sleep," sold over a million copies. For the next five years he called himself the "Singing Brakeman" and was the world's best-selling recording artist. Rodgers's life and legend are honored in the small **Jimmie Rodgers Museum** (Mon.-Sat. 10 AM-4 PM, Sunday 1-5 PM; $2; 601/485-1808) at 41st Avenue and 19th Street in Highland Park, well-signed two miles northwest of downtown. It contains all manner of odd Rodgers-related memorabilia, plus his boots and his custom Martin guitar. Jimmie Rodgers died of tuberculosis in May 1933 and is buried alongside his wife in Oak Grove Cemetery, two miles south of Meridian.

Between Jackson and Meridian, US-80 runs parallel to I-20 across the pine forests of **Bienville National Forest,** replanted in the 1930s after lumber companies clearcut the original pine groves. The town of Forest is just one of a series of quirkily named communities along this route; others include Hickory and Chunky, 13 miles west of Meridian.

The incidents recounted in the film *Mississippi Burning* (the murders of civil rights activists by Ku Klux Klan members in June 1964), took place in the small town of Philadelphia, 30 miles northwest of Meridian.

Meridian

At the junction of US-80, I-20 and I-59, the main route to and from New Orleans, modern Meridian (pop. 41,036) is a medium-sized industrial center that started from rubble in the aftermath of the Civil War, and owes its existence to strategic geography: after the native Choctaw Indians were removed in 1831, Meridian became a railroad junction and served as a Confederate stronghold until Sherman destroyed it in February 1864, saying afterwards, "Meridian no longer exists." Despite this, the town recovered with a vengeance, and from the 1890s until the 1930s Meridian was the largest and most prosperous city in this very poor state, as shown by the many fine Edwardian and art deco buildings that still stand (in varying stages of repair) around the leafy and clean downtown area.

Two of Meridian's most intriguing stops are two miles northwest of downtown, in Highland Park on 41st Avenue at State Boulevard. First is the **Dentzel Carousel** (daily 1-5 PM; 25 cents), a cheerful and historic wooden merry-go-round dating from the 1890s preserved in its original condition. Nearby is the Jimmie Rodgers Museum, described more fully in the "Father of Country Music" callout. Another offbeat but interesting Meridian "attraction" is the gravesite of the "**King and Queen of the Gypsies**," Emil and Kelly Mitchell, whose circa 1914 plot in Rosehill Cemetery (west of downtown on 40th Avenue between 7th and 8th Streets) is a place of pilgrimage for Gypsies from all over America. Marked by a set of wrought-iron patio furniture and traditional headstones, the grave is often piled high with strands of beads, fruit, and other offerings.

Continuing its musical traditions, Meridian is also the birthplace and corporate headquarters of the **Peavey Electronics** company, amplifier and instrument makers to Eddie Van Halen and others at $500 million per year. The original Peavey music shop is still in business downtown.

Meridian has one classic place to eat: **Weidman's Restaurant**, downtown at 208 22nd Avenue (601/693-1751), a half-mile north of I-20. Choose from the greatly varied menu of traditional Southern dishes—and great pies—in a wood-paneled, brass-railed dining room that's packed with moose heads, mounted fish, and photos of everyone famous who's ever eaten there. Family-owned and -operated for 125 years, Weidman's is open 6 AM-9 PM every day; pass by at your peril. Two blocks north of Weidman's, Meridian's most (only?) upscale bistro, **Caffe Latte**, has real salads (no iceberg lettuce!) and grilled meat and fish dishes.

Places to stay in Meridian lie along the I-20 and I-59 junction; for listings or other information contact the **visitor center**, 721 Front Street (601/693-1306 or 800/748-9970).

ACROSS ALABAMA

Our route across the midsection of Alabama cuts through the rural Black Belt—a name that comes from the richly fertile but often swampy lowland soil, but which also reflects its predominantly African-American population. Prime cotton-growing country, central Alabama was feverishly supportive of slavery and secession—Montgomery, the state capital, was also the first capital of the Confederacy—and later became a crucible in the civil rights battles of the 1950s and 1960s.

Events of both of these historical moments provide most of what there is to see and do in the state, but the intimate scale of things—even the biggest city, Montgomery, feels like a sleepy, small town—makes for an enjoyable tour, as does the fact that for most of its 230-odd miles, US-80 alternates between old-style two-laner and newer style four-lane freeway, far away from the anodyne Interstates and passing through some of the South's most interesting places.

For soothing soul or Sunday gospel in west-central Alabama, tune to **WNPT 102.9 FM.**

Demopolis

Standing just north of US-80 on a bluff above the east bank of the Tombigbee River, Demopolis (pop. 7,512) has an interesting history to explain its unusual name—which means "City of the People" in Greek. In 1817, a band of French aristocrats in exile for their allegiance to Napoleon arrived here after the U.S. Congress granted them the land to found a colony based on growing grapes and olives. Not surprisingly, the colonists, a group of soldiers and courtiers whom the WPA *Guide to Alabama* described as "cultured people . . . from the glittering drawing rooms of the French aristocracy . . . none of whom had ever set foot in a plowed field," failed miserably, and survived thanks only to the local Choctaw Indians, who gave them food and taught them to grow viable crops.

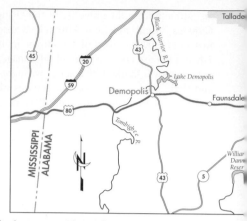

By the 1820s the last of the French had quit, and the lands were swiftly taken over by slave-owning American cotton planters, whose mansions still stand in and around town. Though it's not overly imposing from the outside, the biggest and best of these is **Gaineswood**, 805 Whitfield Street E (Mon.-Sat. 9 AM-5 PM, Sunday noon-5 PM; $3), just north of US-80 off Cedar Street next to the high school. The finest antebellum mansion in Alabama, and one of the top three in the country according to the *Smithsonian Guide to Historic America,* Gaineswood began as a rough cabin in 1821 and over the next 40 years grew into a classic Greek Revival manor, built by slaves according to pattern-book designs. Most unusually, it is still decorated with the original furniture, fixtures, and fittings.

The **Tombigbee River** at Demopolis comes to life the first weekend of December for Christmas on the River, when lighted, animated "floats that really float" parade downstream.

The other well-maintained plantation home still standing in Demopolis is **Bluff Hall**, 405 Commissioners Avenue (Tues.-Sat. 10 AM-5 PM, Sunday 2-5 PM; $3), overlooking the river at the west edge of town. Smaller than Gaineswood, but more attractively situated, Bluff Hall contains a wider array of furniture, with pieces dating from throughout the 19th century; the kitchen in particular is packed with Victorian-era gadgets.

Though little more than a speck on the map, tiny **Faunsdale** (pop. 175), on the south side of US-80 about 15 miles east of Demopolis, is worth a stop to enjoy the gorgeous home-cooked food and live music at the **Faunsdale Bar and Grill** (Wed.-Sun. 5-9 PM only) in the block-long center of town.

Demopolis's franchise-free downtown fills four blocks of Washington Street east from Bluff Hall and the river. It's centered upon one of the South's oldest public squares, with a cast-iron fountain and many comfy benches.

Apart from the family-oriented **Riverview Landing** north of town on US-43, the standard places to eat (**Hardee's, McDon-ald's,** and a 24-hour **Mr. Waffle**) line US-80, as do a **Best Western** and a **Days Inn,** the main accommodation options.

Alabama's original state capital, **Cahawba** was founded along the Alabama River in 1820 but was totally abandoned by the 1860s. Its few buildings and other remains are preserved as a state historic park (daily 8 AM-5 PM; free), 13 miles southwest of Selma via Hwy-22 and Hwy-9.

Selma

A full century before it played a seminal role in the Civil Rights Movement of the 1960s, Selma (pop. 23,755) was second only to Richmond as an industrial arsenal for Confederate forces—Selma's foundries and forges produced weapons, ammunition, and ironclad warships, including the legendary CSS *Tennessee*—and altogether accounted for nearly half of Confederate-made munitions. As in Richmond, the factories were destroyed by Union forces toward the end of the war in April 1865, but a few

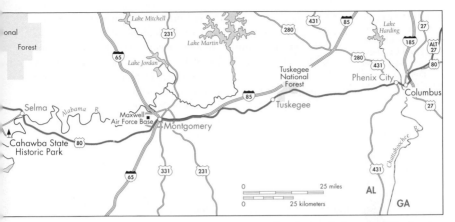

blocks of downtown's Water Avenue were spared and now form one of the few intact antebellum business districts left in the South. Hundreds of Civil War-era houses line Selma's streets, marked by blue shields and forming one of the largest collections of historic houses in the country.

Along the north bank of the broad Alabama River, Water Avenue's five blocks of well-maintained commercial structures, many now housing antique shops, include the former St. James Hotel, 1200 Water Avenue, the oldest hotel still standing in the South, built in 1837 and recently restored to its original grand stature. At the west end of Water Avenue, the humpbacked landmark **Edmund Pettus Bridge** still carries old US-80 over the river, and at the north foot of the bridge the small but significant **National Voting Rights Museum**, 1012 Water Avenue (Tues.-Sat. 1-5 PM; $4) uses photographs and handbills to tell the story of the civil rights struggles of the 1950s and 1960s. While most accounts focus on the high-profile political leaders, the story here is of the local grass-roots activists who struggled for years to win the right to vote. The big names, particularly Rev. Martin Luther King, Jr., clearly played key roles, but the sense you get from visiting the Voting Rights Museum is that it was the many brave but uncelebrated heroes who really made the Civil Rights Movement happen.

Five blocks east, at the other end of the Water Avenue historic district, on the site of Selma's largest Civil War foundry, the **Old Depot Museum** (Mon.-Sat. 10 AM-4 PM, Sunday 2-5 PM; $4) traces regional history from before the Civil War up through the Civil Rights Movement, and features a large selection of Confederate currency, much of which was printed in Selma. The depot also marks the juncture of Selma's Civil War history with the more recent battles for civil rights: north along Martin Luther King (formerly Sylvan) Street, markers point out the unchanged sites of key moments in the Civil Rights Movement up to the 1965 March to Montgomery fronted by Dr. King. Twenty different displays explain the significance of Selma and point out the historic importance of such sites as the Brown Chapel AME church, where marchers set off toward Montgomery before being violently turned back at the Edmund Pettus Bridge; and the simple brick public housing of the George Washington Carver Homes, where most of the original activists lived.

Responding to the civil rights marches of 1965, Pres. Lyndon Johnson said, "At times, history and fate meet at a single time, in a single place to shape a turning point in man's unending search for freedom. So it was at Lexington and Concord. So it was a century ago at Appomattox. So it was last week in Selma, Alabama."

Dozens of sites in Selma and Montgomery, and the entire length of US-80 between them, are being documented, preserved and protected as part of the **Civil Rights Movement National Historic Trail.** One of these sites is the place where Viola Liuzzo, a white housewife from Detroit who volunteered to help shuttle marchers between Montgomery and Selma, was murdered by the KKK. A small memorial stands on the site, on the south side of US-80 between Petronia and Lowndesboro.

Fans of roadside giants will want to keep an eye out for the Big Loaf of Bread, which stands in front of a bakery along US-80 in Montgomery, a mile west of I-65.

Along more vivid history per square foot than just about anywhere else in the South, Selma has a couple of good places to eat: **Ed's Pancake House**, 1617 Broad Street (US-80), and **Major Grumbles**, off Water Avenue at 1 Grumbles Alley, which serves up fried chicken and steaks in a converted cotton warehouse overlooking the river. Stay the night at the historic and very central **St. James Hotel**, 1200 Water Avenue (334/872-3234), or at **Grace Hall**, 506 Lauderdale Street (334/875-5744), a green-shuttered circa 1857 Italianate cottage converted into a nice $75-a-night B&B. Motels along US-80 include a **Best Western**, 1915 W. Highland Avenue (334/872-1900), and a **Holiday Inn**.

For further information, including details of the Alabama Tale Tellin' Festival held in Selma each October, contact the **visitors bureau**, 513 Lauderdale Street (334/875-7241, 800/45-SELMA or 800/457-3562).

Montgomery

Original capital of the Confederate States of America, and now the state capital of Alabama, Montgomery (pop. 187,106) is among the more engaging destinations in the Deep South. Not surprisingly, much of what there is to see has to do with the Civil War, which officially started here when Jefferson Davis gave the order to fire on Fort Sumter. Montgomery survived the war more or less unscathed and is now a very pleasant little city with lovely houses lining leafy streets and an above-average range of restaurants, thanks to the presence of politicos and the 6,000 students at Alabama State College.

Montgomery's landmark is the circa 1851 **state capitol** (Mon.-Sat. 9 AM-4 PM, Sunday noon-4 PM; free), which served as the Confederate capitol for four months in 1861 and is still in use. A bronze star on the west portico marks the spot where Jefferson Davis took the oath of office as President of the Confederate States of America on February 18, 1861, and a spiral staircase surrounded by historical murals climbs the three-story domed rotunda. Moved to a site across the street from the capitol in 1921, the **White House of the Confederacy** is where Jeff Davis and family lived before moving from Montgomery to Richmond. Yet more Confederate memorabilia is on display next door at the **State Archives and History Museum** (Mon.-Sat. 9 AM-5 PM; free), which has displays tracing Alabama history from Creek Indian and pioneer times up through today.

A single block west of the state capitol complex—mind-bogglingly close, considering the historic gulf between whites and blacks in Alabama—stands the **Dexter Avenue Baptist Church**, a simple brick building where Martin Luther King, Jr. served as pastor from 1954 to 1960. One of the key landmarks of the Civil Rights Movement, it was here that supporters rallied around Rosa Parks in the Montgomery bus boycott of 1955-56, which led to an end to official segregation. (A historical plaque in front of the Eureka Theater marks the bus stop where Mrs.

Parks refused to give up her seat for a white passenger, sparking off the struggle.) Downstairs from the church a large mural depicts Dr. King's leading role in the civil rights struggles.

Around the corner from the Dexter Avenue Church, Montgomery's most powerful site is the **Civil Rights Memorial**, two blocks west of the state capitol at the entrance to the Southern Poverty Law Center, 400 Washington Avenue. Designed by Vietnam Memorial architect Maya Lin, the monument consists of a circular black granite table inscribed with the names of 40 people killed in the struggle for civil rights, with a brief description of how and when they died radiating like the hands of a clock from a central water source, which flows gently over the edges of the stone. Behind the table, a waterfall tumbles over a marble wall inscribed with Martin Luther King's favorite Biblical passage, which says that we will not be satisfied "until Justice rolls down like water, and righteousness like a mighty stream."

Montgomery also has sites to see that have nothing at all to do with the Civil War or the Civil Rights Movement. The first of these is the **Hank Williams Memorial**, marking his final resting place on the northeast side of downtown in Oakwood Cemetery, 1304 Upper Wetumptka Road. Hank Williams was an Alabama native and singer and writer of such enduring classics as "Your Cheating Heart," "Jambalaya," "Hey, Good Lookin'," "I'm So Lonesome I Could Cry," and "Lost Highway." Williams's last concert in Montgomery took place on December 28, 1952, three days before his death; he died in the back of his Cadillac while en route from Knoxville, Tennessee, to a scheduled New Year's Day concert in Canton, Ohio. His song, "I'll Never Get Out of This World Alive," was rising up the charts at the time of his demise. His grave is on the east side of the central circle, with a marker alongside it on which his son Hank, Jr. asks people not to vandalize the place. A life-sized statue of Hank (Sr.) stands downtown on Perry Street, across from City Hall.

Hank Williams, Sr.

Another notable local was **Zelda Fitzgerald**, who was born and raised in Montgomery and later lived here with her husband F. Scott while he wrote *Tender is the Night* during the winter of 1931-32. The house, south of downtown at 919 Felder Avenue, has been converted into apartments, one of which (Apt. B, on the ground floor) is now a small museum (Wed.-Fri. 10 AM-2 PM, Saturday and Sunday 1-5 PM; donations; 334/264-4222) that details their lives and works through videos and memorabilia—press clippings, first editions, photographs, and more. It's the only museum dedicated to either of them, anywhere.

Montgomery Practicalities

There's a clutch of very good "Authentic Southern" restaurants within a short walk of the visitors center and State Capitol. Across the street is the popular lunch spot **Amy's Young House**, 231 N. Hull Street, where a half-dozen rather dainty dining rooms fill a historic home. The next block west holds the cacophonously huge (and hugely popular) cafeteria-style **Farmers Market Cafe and Pit BBQ**, at 315 N. McDonough Street. One more block, and you can enjoy the smaller and more relaxed **Moses and Crawford**, 322 N. Lawrence Street, which soothes the heart and soul with its extensive buffet of freshly prepared soul food.

Places to stay in Montgomery include the usual national chains, plus the pleasant **Riverfront Inn** at 200 Coosa Street (334/834-4300), in the historic riverfront district west of downtown; and the very comfortable, turn-of-the-century **Lattis Inn B&B**, 1414 S. Hull Street (334/832-9931), in a residential neighborhood a half-mile south of I-85.

Montgomery's **Maxwell Air Force Base,** established by the Wright Brothers in 1910, is now home to the Air University and War College, national finishing school for fighter pilots and military tacticians. Tuskegee, just east, was the training base of the Tuskegee Airmen, black pilots who fought in WW II.

For more information, contact the **Montgomery Visitor Center**, 401 Madison Avenue (334/240-9455), on the corner of Hull Street northwest of the capitol, near the restored buildings of Old Alabama Town.

Tuskegee

Midway between Montgomery and the Georgia border, Tuskegee (pop. 12,257) is a medium-sized town that has grown up around the **Tuskegee Institute**, founded in 1881 by the industrious former slave, Booker T. Washington, in order to help black Americans rise up the economic ladder. Now a National Historic Site, many of the early buildings built by student laborers still stand around the 1,500-acre campus, but the main points of interest are close to the entrance off Old Montgomery Road. Here you'll find the **Carver Museum** (daily 9 AM-5 PM; free), which traces the career of Tuskegee teacher George Washington Carver, with displays of the various products Carver developed during his life-long tenure at Tuskegee.

Facing the Carver Museum across the lawn is the strikingly modern Tuskegee Chapel, designed by noted architect Paul Rudolph in 1969 but unfortunately rarely open to visitors because of budgetary concerns. The graves of both Booker T. Washington and George Washington Carver are next to the chapel.

East of the college, the center of Tuskegee is a broad square dominated by the large Macon County Courthouse. At the Rexall Drug Store on the west side of the square, the store windows are filled with lessons in African-American history, as illustrated by a "Tuskegee Airman" edition of GI Joe.

East of Tuskegee, the I-85 freeway races up to Atlanta (which is described in the Appalachian Trail chapter on pages 372-374) while US-80 rolls its way east to the engaging old industrial city of Columbus, across the Georgia border.

Phenix City

Across the Chattahoochee River from Georgia, Phenix City, apart from being oddly spelled, is interesting only for being the site of Fort Mitchell National Cemetery—the "Arlington of the South," holding the graves of soldiers from the Civil War to Operation Desert Storm. Before the cemetery was established, this is where thousands of native Creek Indians were rounded up in 1836 before being sent west on the notorious Trail of Tears to Indian Territory in Oklahoma.

ACROSS GEORGIA

Running across the middle of Georgia, US-80 follows the "fall line," a geological divide where rivers drop in a series of rapids from the higher Piedmont Plateau to the lower coastal plain. Because the fall line marked the limits of navigation in from the sea, settlements naturally sprung up along it: **Columbus** was founded on the banks of the falling Chattahoochee, while in the middle of the state **Macon** was built along the Ocmulgee River.

These, the second- and third-biggest cities, respectively, in this still-rural state, are the only real cities our route passes through, and both are fascinating places in very different ways. Apart from these exceptions, however, in its trip across Georgia US-80 takes in more than 300 miles of rolling countryside covered with dozens of dozens of small towns; runs along ancient-looking two-lane blacktop winding through thick hardwood-and-pine forests; and passes stately white columned farmhouses with wide lawns and run-down tin-roofed shacks with yards full of rusting refrigerators and old bangers-on-blocks.

In the west, you can detour to explore the surprisingly simple homes of two U.S. presidents, Franklin Delano Roosevelt at **Warm Springs**, and Jimmy Carter at **Plains**. At the heart of Georgia, Macon is home to the engaging Georgia Music Hall of Fame, and a prehistoric Mound City. Continuing east toward Savannah and the Atlantic Coast, US-80 has been replaced by the much faster I-16 freeway, bypassing numerous small towns across an agricultural region that was devastated during General Sherman's Civil War "March to the Sea." Fortunately, Sherman spared the colonial capital **Savannah**, a lushly verdant gem generally considered to be among the most beautiful cities in North America.

The Chattahoochee River between Alabama and Georgia officially marks the line between the central and eastern standard time zones, though Phenix City, Alabama, also observes Georgia time.

Especially in the western half of the state, US-80 runs across rolling Piedmont countryside past extensive orchards at the heart of "Georgia Peach" country. Follow You-Pick-'Em signs in early summer for a field-fresh selection or stop at roadside stands along the route selling this Georgia specialty along with other local fruits and vegetables, including, of course, peanuts.

Columbus

Crossing the Chattahoochee River from Alabama to Georgia, look north to see the rushing waterfalls around which the city of Columbus (pop. 179,278) grew. Built on the site of a Creek Indian village, Columbus is now Georgia's second largest city, home of the brutal Army Ranger training school at Fort Benning and also host of the 1996 Olympic Games softball competitions. During the Civil War, its iron foundries and water-powered factories converted to munitions production, but Columbus was untouched until Union Gen. James H. Wilson stormed across the Chattahoochee in 1865; unaware that the treaty of Appomattox had already ended the war, "Wilson's Raiders" destroyed much of the city. The huge brick textile mills now lining the river's eastern bank date from the post-Reconstruction years up through the turn of the century, when

Columbus emerged as an industrial giant, an era captured in the stories of Columbus author Carson McCullers, and in the recordings of blues singer Gertrude "Ma" Rainey, whose home still stands downtown at 805 5th Avenue.

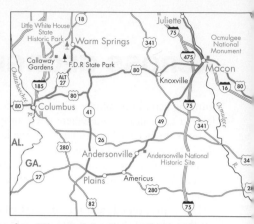

Most city sights are conveniently located in a compact riverside district. Stroll along the Riverwalk promenade for a close-up look at the river, or rumble down the cobblestone lanes of Broadway and Front Street past block after block of graceful old homes and fountain-studded parks. Stop by the Italianate mansion that houses the **Columbus Historical Society** at 700 Broadway (Mon.-Fri. 9 AM-5 PM) for maps and guided tours ($2) of several neighborhood homes, including the former residence of J.S. Pemberton, the inventor of **Coca-Cola**. The elegant little Springer Opera House, 103 10th Street, is the highlight of the adjacent commercial district, where beautifully renovated buildings mix with funky shops selling wigs and voodoo trinkets.

On a hill east of downtown, a half-mile from the river, the **Columbus Museum**, 1251 Wynnton Road (Tues.-Sat. 10 AM-5 PM, Sunday 1-5 PM; free; 706/649-0713), is the major cultural center for the region, with engaging displays tracing the history of the river valley from the time of the Creek Indians—don't miss the 20-minute movie "Chattahoochee Legacy," which screens frequently throughout the day. A wide-ranging collection of fine and folk art is on display in the spacious galleries. Overall, this is one of the state's more captivating small museums, well worth an hour at least.

South of downtown at the foot of 4th Street, the modest **Woodruff Confederate Naval Museum** (Tues.-Fri. 10 AM-5 PM, weekends 1-5 PM; free), next to the stadium constructed for the 1996 Olympic women's softball competition, contains the charred remnants of two ironclads and other naval memorabilia. Southeast from the museum, Victory Road winds toward Fort Benning, holding most of Columbus's budget accommodations amidst a gauntlet of strip clubs and pawn shops catering to the young soldiers.

The nicest place to stay is the **Hilton Hotel**, 800 Front Avenue (706/324-1800, 800/HILTONS or 800/445-8667), impressively carved out of a foundry started here in 1853. The Ironworks next door has been converted into a convention center and performance space and is the site of the city's major festival, the RiverFest, in April.

At either end of historic downtown, restaurants span the range from downhome to upper-crust. **Country's on Broad**, 1329 Broadway, serves up classic country cookin' and barbecue in a spruced-up 1940s bus depot. Historic **Goetchius House** (pronounced GET-chezz), overlooking the river at 405 Broadway, serves upscale dinners Monday through Saturday—if the chateaubriand is too rich for your blood, stop for a mint julep at their speakeasy downstairs. The adventurous might try the lunch counter of the **Dinglewood Pharmacy**, out past the museum at 1939 Wynnton Road, for an unusual local specialty, the Scrambled Dog, a hot dog buried under chili, onions, and oysterette crackers.

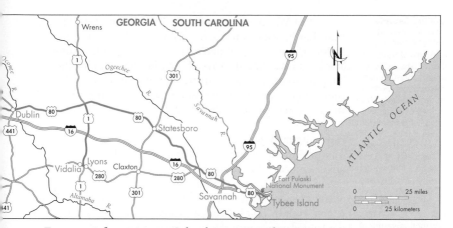

For more information on Columbus, contact the **visitor center**, 1000 Bay Avenue (706/322-1613 or 800/999-1613).

The Class A **Columbus Redstixx** (706/571-8866) play all summer long at the 1950s-era Golden Park, off Victory Drive south of town.

Warm Springs: FDR's "Little White House"

About 15 miles north of Columbus, the rising, forested flanks of Pine Mountain attract flatlanders in search of cooler temperatures and an overlook of the surrounding countryside. In 1924, the therapeutic natural hot springs here also drew the future president Franklin Delano Roosevelt who, in between losing in the election for vice-president in 1920 and winning the governorship of New York in 1928, was struck with polio and left unable to walk. FDR loved the area so much he built a wooded, three-bedroom retreat called the "Little White House" (daily 9 AM-4 PM; $4) and established a treatment center nearby for himself and fellow polio sufferers, funded by a charity that grew into today's March of Dimes. He returned

FDR's characteristic pose

regularly over the next two decades and as president formulated much of the "New Deal" and managed the conduct of WW II while staying here. On the afternoon of April 12, 1945, FDR died, leaving an unfinished portrait propped on an easel.

The house and grounds are very much like they were when Roosevelt died, with a small museum displaying various artifacts, including a wall of crafts items made under the auspices of various WPA programs. Also here are the heavy leg braces FDR wore during public appearances, and the dark blue Ford V-8 convertible (with hand controls) that he drove around the Warm Springs countryside.

At nearby **FDR State Park** (on land donated by Roosevelt) you can take in the terrific views, swim at the pool, hike a portion of the 26-mile Pine Mountain Trail, or stay the night in one of the many state park cabins (706/663-4858 for reservations). In the small town of Warm Springs (pop. 400), a half-mile north of the "Little White House" park, **Mac's Bar-B-Q**, a block east of US-41, has hickory-smoked ribs and chicken; and the historic **Hotel Warm Springs**, 17 Broad Street (706/655-2114), offers B&B accommodations. There's also plenty of craft, gift, and antique stores to browse through.

Knoxville, Georgia, 25 miles west of Macon and just north of US-80, is built around a typical Southern courthouse square, which holds a unique monument to the local girl, Joanna Troutman, who designed the Lone Star flag of Texas. She gave the flag, which featured a blue star on a white background but which was otherwise identical to the current one, to a battalion of Macon volunteers heading west to fight for the Texas Republic.

In 1975, then-governor of Georgia **Jimmy Carter** announced his bid for the presidency at FDR's Warm Springs cottage.

the 39th president in his hometown

West of Warm Springs off US-27, **Callaway Gardens** has 14,000 lushly landscaped acres (daily 7 AM-7 PM; $10 adults, $5 children) covered in topiary gardens, a lakeside swimming beach, and dazzling displays of colorful flowers, plus the Day Butterfly Center, a 7,000-square-foot atrium with exotic varieties of free-flying butterflies. Resort accommodations are available (706/663-2281 or 800/225-5292).

Plains: Jimmy Carter

Another stop along central Georgia's "Presidential Trail," 45 miles southeast of Columbus via US-285, Plains (pop. 116), the home of former president Jimmy Carter, stands as a living monument to small-town America. Here, in a town that's small and remote even by South Georgia standards, the 39th president of the United States was raised, mounted his presidential campaign, and now officiates on matters of international diplomacy —that is, when he isn't teaching Sunday School at the Maranatha Baptist Church. Though the Carter family compound is off-limits, visitors can see Carter's high school, stop by Brother Billy's old gas station (the only one in town), and buy signature peanuts at the general store.

Much of Plains has been proclaimed the "Jimmy Carter National Historic Site," and self-guided touring maps are available at the **visitor center** (daily 9 AM-5 PM; 912/824-3413) in the old train depot, which served as Carter's campaign headquarters in 1976 and again in 1980.

Ten miles northeast of Plains, in the market town of Americus (pop. 16,512), the wealth generated by the region's cotton plantations is embodied in the towering brick **Windsor Hotel,** 125 W. Lamar Street (912/924-1555 or 800/678-8946). A truly elegant Victorian-era hotel with a three-story atrium lobby, one of the grandest interior spaces in the state, the Windsor is worth a look, and makes a great base for exploring central Georgia.

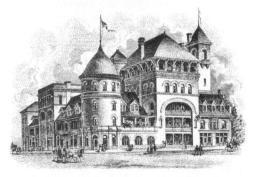

The elegant Windsor Hotel is north of Plains in Americus, Georgia.

Andersonville Prison

Ten miles north of Americus, the Andersonville National Historic Site (daily 8 AM-5 PM; free) stands on the site of the largest and most notorious Confederate military prison. During the final 18 months of the Civil War, as many as 30,000 Union soldiers were imprisoned here in overcrowded conditions, and 13,000 died as a result of disease, poor sanitation, and exposure. Once this was uncovered after the war, public outrage was so great that the camp's commandant, Capt. Henry Wirz, was convicted of murder and hanged in Washington, D.C., though historians generally agree that there was little he could have done to alleviate the suffering.

Only a few parts of the prison have been reconstructed, but the prisoners' harrowing stories are told in a small museum (which also recounts the stories of American POWs during wars up through Vietnam) and most affectingly through the thousands of gravestones in the Andersonville National Cemetery, a half-mile north of the prison site.

In early spring, Macon's 200,000 cherry trees come into bloom. In late Spring, from May until September, the Class A **Macon Braves** take to historic Luther Williams Field, just south of downtown, where "The Best Seats in the House" are raffled off each game—allowing the lucky winners to kick back in a pair of La-Z-Boy recliners along the first base line. For tickets and other information, call 912/745-8943.

Macon

Near the geographic center of the state, the city of Macon (pop. 106,612) was founded along the Ocmulgee (pronounced "oak-MUL-gee") River in 1825, and flourished with the cotton trade. The downtown area holds the modern Georgia Music Hall of Fame (see sidebar above) alongside dozens of well-preserved, historically significant public buildings, including a 110-year-old **Opera House** at 639 Mulberry Street and the turn-of-the-century **Douglass Theater** on Broadway west of Mulberry Street, where such Macon-born music legends as Lena Horne, Otis Redding, and Little Richard got their start. The best place to get a sense for Macon's vibrant black heritage is the small but eye-opening **Harriet Tubman African-American Museum** (Mon.-Fri. 10 AM-5 PM, weekends 2-6 PM; $3; 912/743-8544), a block to the east at 340 Walnut Street, which features a mural of the city's famous sons and daughters along with displays of African-oriented arts and crafts.

Another aspect of Macon heritage, the city's collection of well-preserved antebellum mansions, stands on a low hill at the north end of downtown, having survived the Civil War unscathed apart from one brief battle: while most of Sherman's troops skirted by to the north, a band of Union soldiers engaged young Confederate soldiers at the city limits and fired a cannonball that landed in the foyer of a stately residence, now known as the **Cannonball House**, 856 Mulberry Street. A small museum (Tues.-Fri. 10 AM-4 PM, weekends 2-4 PM; $3) behind the house displays the usual barrage of Confederate memorabilia, and inside the house you can see the dented floor and original cannonball. A block away, the stunning **Hay House**, 934 Georgia Avenue (Mon.-Sat. 10:30 AM-4:30 PM, Sunday 2-4 PM; $6), is among the most beautiful antebellum houses in the state. You can see these two and other restorations on a meandering walk led by a tour guide posing as Sidney Lanier, the city's famous 19th-century poet; call Sidney's Old South Tours ($9 adults, $4.50 children; 912/743-3401).

Little Richard, among others, got his start in Macon.

Macon Practicalities

Along with music and architecture, Macon also has a number of good places to eat. Among the very best, and a Macon institution, is **Len Berg's**, downtown off Broadway and Walnut in Old Post Office Alley. Since 1908 the restaurant has been serving up heaping helpings of fried chicken and other Southern treats, plus platefuls of sweet Vidalia onion rings and fresh-baked pies for dessert (lunch only, every day but Sunday 11 AM-2:30 PM). Also downtown, try the bare-bones **H&H Restaurant**, across from a large hospital at 807 Forsyth Street, where the huge portions of down-home fare are still prepared by "Mama" Louise Hudson, who cooked for the Allman Brothers on their road trips.

MACON MUSIC

Many people dismissed the creation of Macon's new Georgia Music Hall of Fame as simply another symptom of the state's desperate urge to create tourist attractions to complement Atlanta's hosting of the Olympic Games in the summer of 1996. While Olympic enthusiasm was clearly a key to raising $6.5 million in seed money from the state, the end result is one of the most engaging and enjoyable music museums in the entire country: 12,000 square feet of guitars, amps, albums, posters, costumes, jukeboxes, sunglasses, and blue suede shoes, with just enough curatorial explanation to let you piece together the whole crazy story of Georgia music. The displays are anything but dry, using all manner of artifacts to memorialize their subjects. Best of all the Hall of Fame is free from the "music industry" bias that says sales equals success—not all of the artists honored here were by any means world famous or commercial superstars.

Macon may not have the legendary status in music circles as say, Memphis or Detroit, but its claim to fame goes beyond its location at the center of the state. The city's music scene had its heyday in the 1950s and 1960s, when it gave birth to such diverse artists as Little Richard, Otis Redding, and the Allman Brothers, all of whom are enshrined here. Display cases are packed with instruments and memorabilia donated in many cases by the artists themselves, which lends an air of personality to the place that's missing from many other museums.

Besides telling the musical life and times of Georgia musicians from Thomas Dorsey to TLC, the museum does an admirable job of evoking the social, racial, and economic contexts in which the different forms of music were created. It also gives overdue credit to the many people working behind the scenes, casting the spotlight on songwriters, producers, and engineers, not to mention diverse promoters, hucksters, and hangers-on. Documenting the contributions of everyone from Ma Rainey to the B-52s, and genres from jazz to rap, the museum makes a strong case for Georgia being the true musical crossroads of America.

The Georgia Music Hall of Fame is located at the center of downtown Macon, across from the visitor center at 5th and Mulberry Streets. It is open Mon.-Sat. 9 AM-5 PM, Sunday 1-5 PM, and admission is $7.50. For further information, call 912/750-8555, 888/GA-ROCKS! or 888/427-6257.

Places to stay are more limited: choose from the many motels lining Riverside Drive north of town along the I-75 frontage, like the **Comfort Inn**, 2690 Riverside (912/746-8855). Or, splurge a little on the very comfortable **1842 Inn**, 353 College Street (912/741-1842), a white-columned antebellum mansion converted into a bed-and-breakfast with tons of historical ambience for around $100 a night.

For more information on visiting Macon, contact the **visitors bureau**, 200 Cherry Street (912/743-3401 or 800/768-3401) inside the massive old Terminal Station, across from the Georgia Music Hall of Fame.

The **Allman Brothers'** "Ramblin' Man" was "born in the back seat of a Greyhound Bus, rolling down Highway 41," but most of today's traffic follows its modern replacement, I-75. Band members Duane Allman and Berry Oakley are both buried in Rose Hill Cemetery, off Riverside Drive; Oakley's epitaph reads ". . . and the road goes on forever . . ."

Ocmulgee National Monument

Across the Ocmulgee River, well-signed from I-16 exit 4, two miles east of Macon along the Emory Highway (US-80), the settlement now preserved as the Ocmulgee National Monument was a center of pre-conquest Native American culture. By the time the first colonists arrived, it had been inhabited for over 800 years, with remains dating from A.D. 900.

Macon police officer Dominick Andrews has written a book, called **What's Your Excuse?** which documents the best excuses he's heard from people he stops for speeding. If yours is funny enough, he may let you go.

From the small, WPA-era **visitor center** (daily 9 AM-5 PM; free; 912/752-8257), where you can watch a short film and admire pieces of elaborate pottery found on the site, a short trail leads you to a restored earth lodge (complete with thinly disguised air-conditioning ducts!), where you walk through a narrow tunnel to the center of the circular, kiva-like interior. The trail continues past the excavated remains of a Creek Indian trading post, then crosses a set of railroad tracks before climbing a 45-foot-high "Great Temple Mound," where you can see downtown Macon across the rumbling I-16 freeway—two thousand years of "culture" in one very pleasant half-mile walk.

Juliette: Fried Green Tomatoes at the Whistle Stop Cafe

Tucked away upriver on the Ocmulgee, in the heart of the Piedmont forests of middle Georgia, sits the town of Juliette, recently somewhat revived after a long slumber because of its Whistle Stop Cafe. The cafe, town, and river were the backdrop for the 1991 film *Fried Green Tomatoes,* based on Fannie Flagg's novel.

You can get its famous barbecue, along with a plate of fried green tomatoes, Mon.-Sat. 8 AM-2 PM, Sunday noon-7 PM. Juliette lies due north of Macon along US-23, or 10 miles east of the I-75 town of Forsyth via Juliette Road.

All across the Deep South, but across Georgia in particular, US-80 is still lined by old filling stations, many with accommodations on the upper floor—above the gas pumps.

A landmark pit stop for locals and savvy travelers since 1966, the misnamed **Surf 'n' Turf** serves up killer barbecue in a concrete-block restaurant, a quarter-mile south of I-16 at the Hwy-29/Soperton exit.

Off I-16: Dublin, Vidalia, and Lyons

Named by its Irish founders in 1812, Dublin (pop. 16,312) continues to celebrate its Irish heritage with shamrocks painted on the center dividers, and an all-out St. Patrick's Day festival that lasts most of two weeks. The historic district is centered along Bellevue Avenue, where you can glimpse the town's graceful old homes and look inside the local historical museum (Tues.-Fri. 1-4:30 PM; free) at Bellevue and Academy Streets. Eat at **Ma Hawkins Cafe**, 124 W. Jackson Street near the down-

Around Dublin you can tune to one of the greatest old-time country stations I've found anywhere: **WXLI 1230 AM,** broadcasting Hank Williams, Hank Snow, Johnny Cash, and other country pioneers "from a little building just off the Interstate . . ."

town courthouse, which has grits and greens and other Southern specialties.

East of Dublin, around 15 miles south of I-16, Vidalia (pop. 11,078) is known to food lovers around the world as the home of the delectable Vidalia onion, so sweet it can be eaten raw, like an apple. To the locals, this single crop represents a $30-million industry. In late April and early May, follow the scent to the Vidalia Onion Festival for taste treats. The **Vidalia Welcome Center,** 2805 Lyons Highway, can hook you up with tours of local onion farms and processing plants in spring; they also offer cotton and tobacco tours in the fall.

Five miles east of Vidalia on US-280, find the **Robert Toombs Inn** at 101 S. State Street (912/526-4489) in downtown Lyons (pop. 4,502) to enjoy a meal at its refined restaurant, a drink at its full bar (a rare find in South Georgia), and an overnight stay in its period-furnished B&B rooms.

Between Macon and Savannah, Swainsboro's **KISS 98.1 FM** airs CCR, REM, and all the latest NASCAR news.

North of US-80 via US-1, the town of Wrens (pop. 2,414) was the boyhood home of **Erskine Caldwell,** author of the classic stories *Tobacco Road* and *God's Little Acre,* both of which were set in this part of rural Georgia.

Ten miles south of I-16 at the intersection of US-280 and US-301, the town of Claxton bills itself as the **Fruitcake Capital of the World.** In the fall fruitcake-making season, the Claxton Bakery in the center of town offers free samples of the 3,000 tons of fruitcake they pound out each year.

Statesboro

Directly on old US-80, 12 miles north of I-16, Statesboro (pop. 15,854) was also one of Sherman's stops. Here in 1864 his troops torched the courthouse; today's historic courthouse dates from the late 19th century. Georgia Southern University, with an enrollment of 10,000, dominates the town and has a small museum on campus displaying a 26-foot Monasaur skeleton.

If you're feeling hungry, generous Southern buffets are served boardinghouse-style (bring your plate to the kitchen when you're through) at the **Beaver House Restaurant,** in a large white-columned mansion at 121 S. Main Street. For one reasonable price, you receive serving dishes full of meats, vegetables, cornbread, and biscuits.

The beautiful city of Savannah, which marks the junction of our US-80 route with our Coastal East Coast road trip, is covered on pages 411-414.

US-80 across Savannah

Old US-80 comes into Savannah on Louisville Road, past the swanky new Savannah International Airport on the northwest edge of town. This turns into Bay Street for the final approach, then runs south across the historic downtown area before turning east onto Victory Drive, which runs along the southern foot of Savannah, then across to the barrier islands.

Fort Pulaski

The drive east from Savannah to the Atlantic Ocean passes through picturesque fishing villages standing out from serene marshlands, where a maze of riverlets and creeks weaves through the tall green reeds, and fishing boats bob along the tidal waters as they head off to harvest shrimp and oysters.

Amid the calm stands Fort Pulaski National Monument (daily 8:30 AM-sunset; $1; 912/786-5787), 15 miles east of Savannah on US-80, a well-preserved stone-and-brick fortress completed in 1848 at a commanding site at the mouth of the Savannah River. Its prominent island site originally held colonial-era Fort Greene, which was demolished by a hurricane in 1804 and replaced by the architecturally impressive, pentagon-shaped bulwark that survives in its battered and breached state today, surrounded by a moat and many acres of grassy lawn.

Beginning in 1829, construction of Fort Pulaski, proclaimed "as strong as the Rocky Mountains," took 18 years, used 25 million bricks, and cost just over a million dollars. During the Civil War, its seven-foot-thick walls withstood bombardment by the Union forces' new rifled cannon for only 30 hours, which prompted the fort's surrender in April 1862.

Near Fort Pulaski, just west of the Bull River Bridge along US-80, **Williams Sea Food Restaurant** is a popular place to sample local cuisine. Harder to find, but worth the effort to reach, is the waterfront **Crab Shack**, just across the bridge to Tybee Island on Estill Hammock Road (912/786-9857), where "The Elite Dine in Their Bare Feet" on plates of shrimp-and-sausage, "Low Country Boil," and Key Lime Pie raved about by such dignified aficionados as the *New York Times*.

Tybee Island

You made it! The Atlantic Ocean at last! The easternmost of many islands filling the delta at the mouth of the Savannah River, the town of Tybee Island (pop. 2,842) is a funky old family-oriented resort, with four blocks of burger-and-corn-dog stands, taverns, amusement arcades, thrill rides and miniature golf courses at the eastern end of US-80, just 18 miles east of central Savannah. Locally famous for the annual Beach Bum's Parade in the middle of June, Tybee Island's main attraction is its endless and usually uncrowded powdery white sand beaches, which spread to either side of the new pier and pavilion at the end of 16th Avenue. Another draw here is the wacky, slightly ersatz, diner-style **Breakfast Club**, right at the center of things at 1500 Butler Avenue, open daily 6 AM-1 PM.

Tybee Island's stretch of US-80 also holds the world's first **Days Inn** motel, upgraded and still in business at 1402 Butler Avenue (912/786-4576); rooms go for $50-100 depending on season.

At the north end of Tybee Island, whence the Union forces bombarded Fort Pulaski during the Civil War, a centuries-old lighthouse stands next to the WW II-era concrete bunkers that house the **Tybee Museum** (daily 10 AM-6 PM in summer, shorter hours rest of the year; $2; 912/786-5801), which includes the old lighthouse keeper's cottage among its collections tracing the island's history.

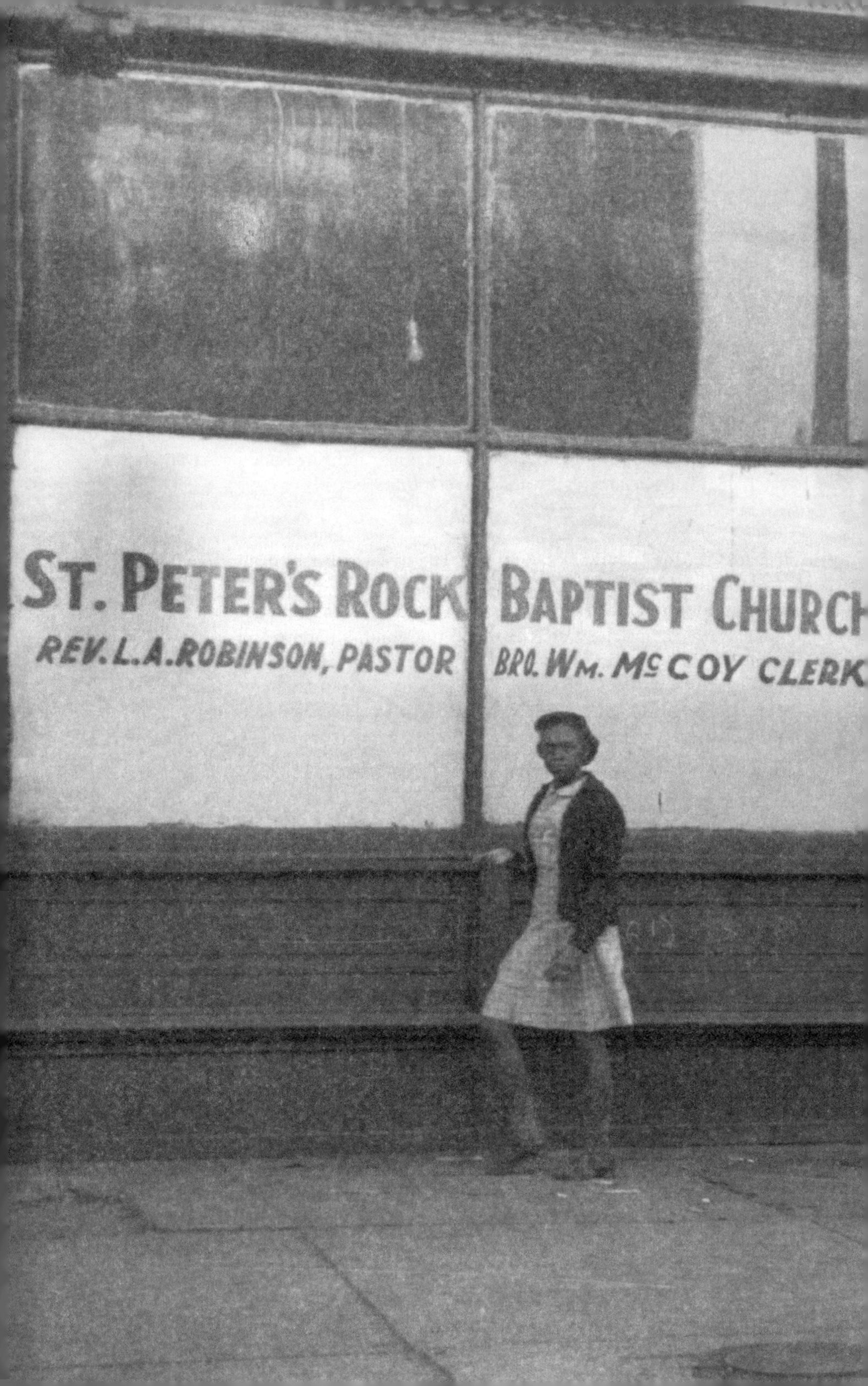
ST. PETER'S ROCK BAPTIST CHURCH
REV. L. A. ROBINSON, PASTOR
BRO. WM. MC COY CLERK

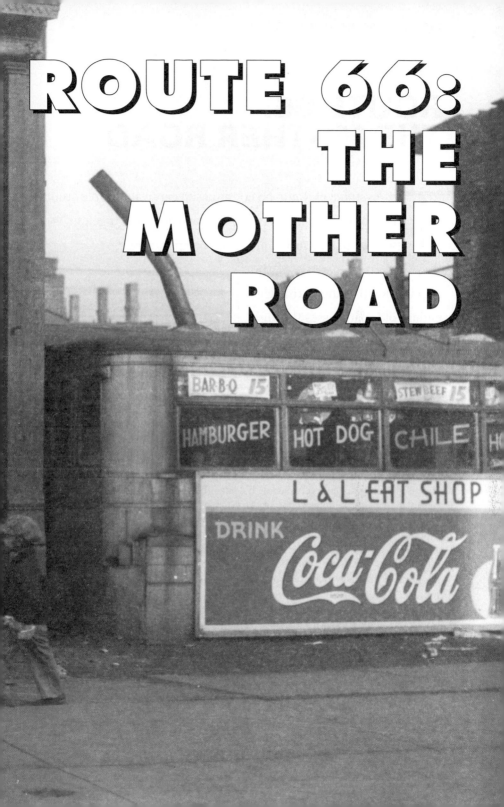

ROUTE 66: THE MOTHER ROAD

The mystique of Route 66 continues to captivate people around the world. Running between Chicago and Los Angeles, "over two thousand miles all the way" in the words of the popular R&B anthem, this legendary old road passes through the heart of the U.S. on a diagonal trip that takes in some of the country's most archetypal roadside scenes. If you're looking for great displays of neon signs, rusty middle-of-nowhere truck stops, or kitschy Americana, do as the song says and "get your kicks on Route 66."

But perhaps the most compelling reason to follow Route 66 is to experience the road's ingrained timeline of contemporary America. Before it was called Route 66, and long before it was even paved in 1926, this corridor was traversed by the National Old Trails Highway, one of the country's first transcontinental roads. For three decades before and after WW II, Route 66 earned the title "Main Street of America" because it wound through small towns across the Midwest and Southwest, lined by hundreds of cafes, motels, gas stations, and tourist attractions. During the Great Depression, hundreds of thousands of farm families, displaced from the Dust Bowl, made their way west along Route 66 to California, following what John Steinbeck called "The Mother Road" in his vivid portrait, *The Grapes of Wrath*. After WW II, many thousands more expressed their upward mobility by leaving the industrial East bound for good jobs in the suburban idyll of Southern California—again, following Route 66, which came to embody the demographic shift from the Rust Belt to the Sun Belt.

Beginning in the late 1950s and continuing gradually over the next 25 years, old Route 66 was bypassed section by section as the high-speed interstate highways were completed. Finally, in 1984, when the last stretch of freeway was finished, Route 66 was officially decommissioned; the old route is now designated "Historic Route 66."

Though it is no longer a main route across the country, Route 66 has retained its mystique in part due to the very same effective hype, hucksterism, and boosterism that animated it through its half-century heyday. It was a Route 66 sight, the marvelous Meramec Caverns, that gave the world the bumper sticker, and it was here that the American art of vacation as driving tour first flourished. Billboards and giant statues along the highway still hawk a baffling array of roadside attractions, tempting passing travelers to swim alongside giant blue whales, to see live rattlesnakes, mountain lions, and other creatures on display in roadside menageries, or to stay at "Tucumcari Tonight—2,000 Rooms."

The same commercial know-how and shameless self-promotion has helped the towns along the old route stay alive. Diners and motels play up their Route 66 connections, however tenuous they may be, and thanks to the numerous guidebooks and magazine articles that proclaim the charms of the old road, many bona fide Route 66 landmarks are kept in business by nostalgic travelers intent on experiencing a taste of this endangered American experience. That said, along many stretches of Route 66, the contrast between characterful old-road landscape and contemporary franchised freeway culture is painfully sharp. Many quirky old motels and cafes hang on by a thread of hope, sit vacant, or survive in memory only—all for want of an interstate exit. In fact, of all the routes covered in this book, Route 66 is the closest to the freeways; for many stretches you'll be forced to leave the old two-lane and follow the super slabs that have been built right on top of the old road.

Route 66 passes through a marvelous cross-section of American scenes, from the golden sands and sunshine of Los Angeles, past the Grand Canyon and the Native American communities of the desert Southwest, to the gritty streets of St. Louis and Chicago. Whether you are motivated by an interest in its history, feel a nostalgic yearning for the good old days the route has come to represent, or simply want to experience firsthand the amazing diversity of people and landscapes that line its path, Route 66 offers an unforgettable journey into America, then and now.

ACROSS CALIFORNIA

From the beautiful beaches of Santa Monica, through the cit-
rus-rich inland valleys, over mountains and across the demanding Mojave Desert, Route 66 passes through every type of
Southern California landscape. The old road, which survives intact
almost all the way across the state, is marked for most of its 315 miles by signs
declaring it "Historic Route 66"; in the Mojave desert the route is also marked as
"National Old Trails Highway," its title before the national numbering system was
put into effect in the late 1920s.

Santa Monica

Old Route 66 had its western terminus at the edge of the Pacific Ocean in Santa
Monica, on a palm-lined bluff a few blocks north of the city's landmark pier. South
of the pier is Venice Beach, heart of bohemian L.A., but near where Santa Monica
Boulevard dead-ends at Ocean Boulevard, a brass plaque marks the official end of
Route 66, the "Main Street of America," also remembered as the "Will Rogers
Highway," one of many names the old road earned in its half-century of existence;
the plaque remembers Rogers as a "Humorist, World Traveler, Good Neighbor"—
not bad for an Okie from the middle of nowhere. (For more on Will Rogers, see
page 835.)

Two blocks east of the ocean, stretch your legs at Santa Monica Place, an in-
door/outdoor shopping mall and icon of contemporary Southern California urban
culture. Across the street from the mall, the **Santa Monica HI Hostel**, 1436 2nd
Street (310/393-9913) has 200 dorm beds for under $20 a night—an ideal budget
base for seeing Los Angeles—and the surrounding streets are among the liveliest in
Southern California; people actually walk, enjoying street performers, trendy cafes,
bookshops, and movie theaters.

Route 66 across Los Angeles

Diehard old roads fans will be pleasantly surprised to know that Route 66 across
Los Angeles still exists, almost completely intact. Heading east from Santa Monica
—and now marked by prominent beige road signs as "Historic Route 66 1935-
1964"—old Route 66 follows Santa Monica Boulevard through the hearts of Beverly Hills (where Will Rogers once was mayor) and West Hollywood. In Hollywood
itself, Santa Monica Boulevard runs past **Hollywood Memorial Cemetery** (daily 9
AM-5 PM; free; 323/469-1181) where such luminaries as Rudolf Valentino and Mel
Blanc are entombed, overlooked by the water tower of legendary Paramount Studios. Route 66 then merges into Sunset Boulevard for the long winding drive to
downtown L.A., ending up at the historic core of the city: Olvera Street and the
Plaza de Los Angeles State Historic Park.

East of downtown L.A., you have your choice of Route 66 routings. You can hop
onto the Pasadena Freeway for a trip back to freeways past: opened in 1939, when
it was called the Arroyo Seco Parkway, this was California's first freeway and fea-

tured such novel (and never repeated) concepts as 15 mph exit ramps and stop signs at the entrances. Or, you can follow Figueroa, which in L.A. lingo is known as a "surface street," running parallel to the freeway past some fascinating pieces of Los Angeles, new and old, including the concrete-lined Los Angeles River, hilltop Dodger Stadium, and the nifty **Southwest Museum** (Tues.- Sun. 10 AM- 5 PM; $5; 323/221-2164), an extensive and unusual collection of Native American art and artifacts from all over western North America, Arizona to Alaska.

The sights and sounds of Los Angeles are covered in a Survival Guide in the Coastal West Coast route, on pages 99-101.

Pasadena

The Pasadena Freeway drops you off unceremoniously short of Pasadena, but following Figueroa Street brings you in with a bang, on the soaring **Colorado Boulevard Bridge**, an elegantly arching concrete bridge at the western edge of Pasadena, which long marked the symbolic entrance to Los Angeles from the east. Recently restored, the bridge spans Arroyo Seco along the south side of the Ventura Freeway (Hwy-134). Arroyo Seco itself is full of significant sights, including college football's Rose Bowl and some of the most important arts and crafts-era architecture in Southern California. Above the arroyo, on old Route 66 at 411 W. Colorado Boulevard, the **Norton Simon Museum** (Thurs.-Sun. noon-6 PM; $4; 626/449-6840), which has a medium-sized but impeccably chosen collection of western and southeast Asian art, ranging from Hindu sculpture to one the world's foremost collections of Degas paintings, drawings, and sculptures.

Colorado Boulevard Bridge

Colorado Boulevard in Pasadena holds the annual **Tournament of Roses Parade,** every New Year's Day before the famous Rose Bowl football game.

For more information on Pasadena, contact the visitors bureau (626/795-3355).

The San Gabriel Valley

East of Pasadena, though effectively swallowed up in Southern California's never-ending sprawl, the San Gabriel Valley used to be the west-bound traveler's first taste of Southern California. After crossing the Mojave Desert and the high mountains, Route 66 dropped down into what might have seemed like paradise: orange groves as far as the eye could see, a few tidy towns linked by streetcars, and houses draped in climbing roses and bougainvillea. The San Gabriel Valley embodied this suburban ideal until the mid-1950s, when Route 66 gave way to high-speed freeways, and the orange groves were replaced by endless grids of tract houses.

In the 1950s, San Bernardino was where **Maurice and Richard McDonald** perfected the burger-making restaurant chain that bears their name. In 1961, the McDonald brothers sold their company to Ray Kroc, and the rest is fast-food history.

If you're willing to search and to close your eyes to mini-mall sprawl, Route 66 still offers a window onto this golden age.

At the western edge of San Bernardino, a remnant of old Route 66 road culture still survives: the 19 concrete teepees that form the **Wigwam Motel,** at 2728 W. Foothill Boulevard. It's every bit as seedy as the "Do It In A TeePee" sign outside suggests.

WIGWAM MOTEL, RIALTO, CALIFORNIA —
A CLASSIC "PROTO-MOTEL" DESIGN, THE WIGWAM VILLAGES WERE THE BRAINSTORM OF FRANK REDFORD, WHO WAS INSPIRED BY A TEE-PEE-SHAPED DRIVE-IN RESTAURANT IN LONG BEACH, CAL., IN THE 1930's. REDFORD PATENTED HIS WIGWAM MOTIF, & BUILT SEVEN OF THEM. THE FIRST, IN HORSE CAVE, KENTUCKY, WAS DESTROYED RECENTLY. #2 IS IN NEARBY CAVE CITY, KENT. ONE OF THE ORIGINAL 7, IS STILL OPERATING IN HOLBROOK, ARIZONA. #7 WAS IN RIALTO (ABOVE), ON THE FAMOUS FOOTHILL BOULEVARD — OLD RT. 66... THESE 14 UNITS CURVE AROUND THE FRONT OFFICE, WHICH ADJOINS A TEE-PEE. IN THE CENTER OF THE COMPLEX IS A COURTYARD & TINY, KIDNEY-SHAPED SWIMMING POOL.
OLD ROUTE 66 Scenes! by R. Waldmire [23]

Winding between Pasadena and San Bernardino, along the foothills of the sometimes snowcapped San Gabriel Mountains, the old road links a number of once distinct communities.

From Pasadena, old Route 66 runs along Colorado Boulevard and then Huntington Drive, turning into Foothill Boulevard around the landmark racetrack at **Santa Anita.** (The Marx Brothers filmed *A Day at the Races* here.) Foothill Boulevard, which is signed as "Historic Route 66," jogs along the foothills through **Azusa,** home of the classic Foothill Drive-In and one of the country's oldest McDonald's restaurants—complete with red-tiled arches. In **Upland,** the old road features a grass median strip, and runs right past a statue of the pioneer "Madonna of the Trail," which officially marked the western end of the National Old Trails Highway, the immediate precursor to Route 66.

At **Rancho Cucamonga,** Foothill Boulevard crosses the I-15 freeway, which is the quickest route over Cajon Pass. Rancho Cucamonga is now best known as the home of the Epicenter, where the very popular **Cucamonga Quakes** (909/481-5000) play Class A baseball, and a statue of Jack Benny welcomes you through the turnstiles. (If you ever heard his radio show, you'll know why he's there. . . .)

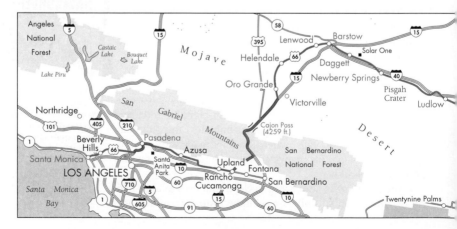

The old Route 66 alignment continued east for another 15 miles, passing through Fontana, birthplace of the Hell's Angels' Motorcycle Club (and L.A. culture critic Mike Davis), before bending north at San Bernardino to join I-15 at the summit.

Cajon Pass

Very picturesque stretches of the old road go over Cajon Pass, though it is not a through route; the main road is now I-15. At the top, turn off the freeway at the "Oak Hills" exit and stop for a burger and fries at the **Summit Inn**, one of the few survivors of the old road businesses along this stretch of highway. You can follow a section of the old road east a few miles to the east, rejoining I-15 at Cleghorn Road.

Victorville: Roy Rogers

It takes about two hours to get here from the west end of Route 66, but it's not until you reach Victorville, the distant extent of Los Angeles's sprawl, that old Route 66 begins to seem real—as real as Hollywood cowboys, anyway. Victorville, a rapidly growing desert community of over 50,000 residents, is home to the **Roy Rogers and Dale Evans Museum** (daily 9 AM-5 PM; $6; 760/243-4547), a living memorial to America's favorite cowboy and cowgirl, west of I-15 at the Roy Rogers Drive exit. Along with an encyclopedic collection of old movie stills and posters

stand the taxidermied remains of Roy and Dale's favorite animals: Roy's horse Trigger (a larger-than-life concrete copy of Trigger stands in front of the museum as well); Dale's horse Buttermilk; their dog Bullet; plus hundreds of trophy heads of other less-loved creatures. Nearly up until the day he died in 1998, Roy himself was on hand to welcome visitors, and the homespun charm of the museum he and Dale created here perfectly suits the characters they created, onscreen and off. However much the name "Roy Rogers" makes you think of anodyne suburban restaurants,

the real Roy Rogers was comic book hero come to life, and he really did embody all those Boy Scout virtues that are so easy and fun to sneer at.

That said, the Roy Rogers Museum really does reveal a lot about a certain generation—the rural-born, Depression- and World War II-surviving people who are now our "seasoned citizens"—who came of age in and set the tone for the all-American 1950s. In their museum, Roy and Dale really opened their hearts, displaying so many family photo albums and worldly knickknacks that you feel

---

Hula Ville, formerly California State Landmark No. 939, bordered old Route 66 on the west side of Victorville. It's gone through hard times since the 100-year-old creator and caretaker, "Fry Pan" Miles Mahan, passed away in 1996, but the hundreds of beer bottles and hand-lettered memorials to sundry bums, hobos, and other travelers he called his friends have been moved to the California Route 66 museum in town.

San Bernardino County is the largest in the United States.

you're nosing around their living room. Whatever you may think about the politics —or about killing wild animals, which Roy did with glee—you simply have to admire his taste in cars—check out the 1960s Pontiac Bonneville, with a Texas Longhorn hood ornament, saddle leather upholstery, and—best of all—a gear shift lever in the shape of a six-shooter!

Now is that cool, or what?

Victorville is also home to a small new **California Route 66 Museum**, on the old road at 16849 D Street (Thurs.-Sun. 10 AM-4 PM; donations; 760/261-US66), with a small but growing collection of road signs, photographs and reminiscences, plus the remnants of Hula Ville.

The **Mojave Desert** is one of the driest places on the planet; parts of it receive less than three inches of rainfall in an average year, sometimes going for more than two years without getting a drop.

Old Route 66 follows 7th Street through town, past a few neon-signed old motels like the **New Corral**, 14643 7th Street (760/245-9378) with its animated bucking bronco, and the large **Best Western Green Tree Inn**, with its 24-hour restaurant, just off the freeway at 14173 Green Tree Boulevard.

For more information, contact the **Victorville Chamber of Commerce** (760/245-6506).

EXOTIC WORLD

Victorville is about as far as one could get from the bright lights and bump-and-grind of a big city, but the sprawling desert east of town is the unlikely home of the world's only museum dedicated to the art and craft of striptease dancing—Exotic World. Exotic World fills many rooms in the ranch house of Dixie Lee Evans, a former burlesque dancer who, during the early 1960s, was semi-famous for her striptease impersonations of Marilyn Monroe. Dixie gives each visitor a personally guided tour of the extensive collection, which includes dozens of elaborate costumes as well as posters, photos, props (including one of fan-dancer Sally Rand's famous fans), and rare movies. Most of the items on display were assembled by another burlesque dancer, Jennie Lee, who ran a strip club in San Pedro, California and who started the collection in order to document the forbidden story of striptease. Jennie Lee's effort to preserve the history of burlesque, and the dancers who made the "hubba-hubba" happen, is carried on by Exotic World's Burlesque Hall of Fame, a wall of 8x10 glossies remembering the shimmying efforts of such striptease luminaries as Lily St. Cyr, Tempest Storm, Blaze Starr, Sally Rand, and Gypsy Rose Lee.

Despite the XXX-rated connotations of striptease, Exotic World is a fun place, not at all seedy or licentious, and Dixie's energetic and illuminating presentation makes it well worth the detour. Located on a former goat ranch, behind a set of elaborate wrought iron gates at 29053 Wild Road, just north of old Route 66 in Helendale, Exotic World (Tues.-Sun. 10 AM-4 PM; donations; 760/243-5261) is about 17 miles east of D Street from Victorville—call Dixie for directions and reservations.

Old Route 66 Loop: Oro Grande, Helendale, and Lenwood

Between Victorville and Barstow, old Route 66 survives as an "old roads" trek across the Mojave Desert. The 36-mile route, called the Old National Trail Highway, parallels the railroad tracks and the usually parched Mojave River, passing through odd little towns like Oro Grande, which is still home to a huge cement plant and lots of roadside junk shops. Outside Barstow at the west end of Main Street, keep an eye out for the Christian Motorcycle club sign welcoming you to Lenwood, a crossroads near where the old road reconnects with I-15.

Midway between Victorville and Barstow is Helendale, where you can find the nearly famous stripper's "museum," Exotic World, (see the special topic, **Exotic World**) a mile west of old Route 66—call 760/243-5261 for directions, because it's hard to find.

Barstow

Though by population it's under half the size of Victorville, the burly railroad and transportation center of Barstow (pop. 21, 495) seems a much bigger place. Located midway between Los Angeles and Las Vegas, at the point where I-15 veers north and I-40 takes the place of old east-west Route 66, Barstow was the first large watering hole west of the Arizona border, a role it still plays judging by the numerous truck depots arrayed around town. It's scruffy and a little scary in the way railroad towns can be, and along Main Street, the old Route 66 corridor, many of the old cafes and motels are now closed and boarded up, including the landmark old **El Rancho Motel** at 112 E. Main Street—the one whose 100-foot neon sign is supported by a pair of massive pylons visible from all over town.

At the center of town, just north of old Route 66, the old Harvey House "Casa del Desierto" hotel next to the train station looks like the Doge's Palace in Venice, its gothic-style arcades a substantial reminder of a time when travel meant more than just getting somewhere.

> Northeast of Barstow, **Calico Ghost Town** (daily 9 AM-5 PM; $6; 800/TO-CALICO or 800/862-2542) is an enjoyably silly resurrection of the silver mining camp that boomed here during the 1890s.

Daggett and Newberry Springs: *The Bagdad Cafe*

East of Barstow all the way to the Arizona border, old Route 66 survives in a series of different stretches alongside the I-40 freeway. The first place of interest, Daggett, is a rusty old mining and railroad town six miles east of Barstow along the north side of the freeway. A couple of abandoned old hotels keep company with one still-functioning restaurant, the **Daggett Restaurant**, serving bowls of chili and ice-cold beers along the south side of the tracks. Old Route 66 runs due east from Daggett, past the region's current claim to fame: the acres of shiny mirrors of the **Solar One power plant**, an experimental electricity generating station three miles from Daggett and north of the old road.

Almost 1.5 million acres between I-40 and I-15 have been set aside as the **Mojave National Preserve,** but left in limbo by a lack of federal funds. One of many places here worth the trip is Mitchell Caverns at the center of Providence Mountains State Park, 25 miles north of I-40 at the end of Essex Road.

Amboy Crater has been the focus of a contentious plan which would turn the entire area into a massive trash dump, eventually forming a mountain 400 feet high, a mile wide, and three miles long, growing by up to 21,000 tons a day.

According to Route 66 historian Tom Teague, author of the book *Searching for 66,* Santa Fe Railroad supply points across the Mojave Desert were named in alphabetical order: Amboy, Bristol, Cadiz, Danby, Essex, Fenner, Goffs, Home, Ibex, Java, and Klinefelter.

Fifteen miles east of Daggett comes the next I-40 junction and the next small town, Newberry Springs, where the popular Percy Adlon movie *Bagdad Cafe* was shot at the town's one and only cafe, the newly re-named **Bagdad Cafe.** It's open daily 6 AM-8 PM for the best food on this stretch of old Route 66. The old road continues along the south side of I-40 for another 25 miles, passing the lava flows of Pisgah Crater before crossing over to the north of the freeway for the final 10 miles into Ludlow, where old Route 66 rejoins the freeway.

Old Route 66 Loop: Ludlow, Amboy, and Chambless

If you want a quick and convincing taste of what traveling across the Mojave Desert was like in the days before air-conditioning and cellular phones, turn south off I-40 at Ludlow, 50 miles east of Barstow, and follow the well-signed "National Old Trails Highway," one of the many monikers Route 66 has carried over the years, on a 75-mile loop along the old road. At Ludlow, where two gas stations, a coffee shop, and a motel represent civilization between Barstow and Needles, the old road wends slightly southeast, passing first through Bagdad, a turn-of-the-century gold mining town now defunct. Continuing east, old Route 66 cuts across another lava flow, this one part of the Amboy Crater, beyond which another road heads south to Twentynine Palms and Joshua Tree National Monument.

Midway along the old road loop, Amboy (pop. 2) is a museum-worthy assembly of roadside architecture that has survived solely due to the willpower of its lord, master, and owner since 1938, Buster Burris. Since traffic dropped with the building of I-40, the whole town—complete with a classic late-1940s roadside cafe called Roy's, a disused motel, and a set of gas pumps—was for sale for decades, until Buster finally upped sticks in 1996. Still photogenic, Amboy is well worth a stop, but the new owners haven't made many friends with their high prices and lack of hospitality—charging $1 for a glass of water, for example.

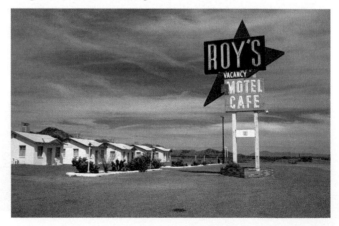

heading West

Huge chunks of the Mojave Desert have been used as military training grounds since WW II, when **Gen. George Patton** used this area to prepare his tank battalions for battle in the North African desert. As many as 90,000 soldiers were based here during the war years; the remains of the camp can still be seen in the desert along Crucero Road, just north of the I-40 Ludlow exit.

The Amtrak station in Needles stands next to what was formerly El Garces Hotel, one of many palatial railroad hotels run by **Fred Harvey.**

From Amboy, it's another 48 miles back to I-40 at the town of Fenner. If you're keen on traveling as much of the old road as possible, another stretch of Route 66 runs east from Fenner on a roller coaster of undulating two-lane blacktop, parallel to the railroad track through the desert hamlet of **Goffs,** near the spot where comedian Sam Kinison was killed in a car wreck. Fifteen miles east of Goffs, old Route 66 joins up with US-95, which continues north to Las Vegas, 90-odd miles away, and south to I-40, linking up with the freeway 10 miles west of Needles.

Needles was the boyhood home of Snoopy and Charlie Brown cartoonist **Charles Schulz,** and is featured in the comic strips as the desert home of Snoopy's raffish sibling, Spike.

From Needles, it's a quick 25-mile drive north along the Colorado River into Nevada to visit the gambling center of **Laughlin.** Since the mid-1980s Laughlin has boomed into a sparkling city with huge casinos and over 10,000 cheap rooms. See pages 154-155 for details.

Needles

Founded soon after the Santa Fe Railroad came through in 1883, and named for the group of sharp stone spires that stand near where I-40 crosses the Colorado River from Arizona, Needles (pop. 5,191) is one of the hottest places in the country, with summertime highs hovering between 100° and 120°F for months on end. Though unbearable in summer, Needles is a popular place with winter snowbirds escaping colder climes; it also has a very rich Route 66 heritage. Besides magnificent El Garces Hotel, which is undergoing long-term renovation into a historical museum, the stretch of old Route 66 through Needles—along Broadway, alternating along both sides of the freeway—holds the Route 66 Motel, with its great arrow-shaped sign. Across the street from the "Welcome to Needles" wagon, the motor court at 304 Broadway was known as the "Palm Motel" during its Route 66 heyday and later on was briefly brought back to life by Hank Wilde as a nostalgic B&B in the early 1990s, but it's since closed again. Stop by and see if its fortunes have improved, and hope for a sense of the *real* old Route 66.

Despite the unforgiving summer weather, Needles is a friendly town and well worth getting to know. Drive around a while to get your bearings, and stop by the **chamber of commerce** office (760/326-2050), at Front and G Streets across from El Garces, for a free map or other useful information.

ACROSS ARIZONA

If you're not a die-hard Route 66 fan when you get there, traveling the old route across Arizona is bound to convert you. The high-speed I-40 freeway gives quick access to some of the best surviving stretches of the old road, and these are some of the most captivating parts of Route 66 anywhere. Starting at the Colorado River, the route runs from the arid Mojave Desert past dozens of remarkable old highway towns along some of the oldest and longest still-driveable stretches of the Mother Road.

Crossing the Colorado River between Arizona and California, look downstream from the I-40 freeway to see the arching silver steel bridge that carried Route 66 up until 1966. It's still in use, supporting a natural gas pipeline; beyond it, the red-rock spires for which Needles is named rise sharply out of the desert plains.

Midway across the state, the route climbs onto the forested (and often snowy) Kaibab Plateau for a look at the mighty Grand Canyon. East of Flagstaff, the old road is effectively submerged beneath the freeway, which drops down to cross desolate desert, passing through desiccated towns and the Petrified Forest National Park. Remnants of numerous old roadside attractions—Indian trading posts, wild animal menageries, and Holbrook's famous "Sleep in a Teepee" Wigwam Village—all survive in varying degrees of preservation along Arizona's section of Route 66.

Lake Havasu City and London Bridge

The crossing over the Colorado River at the California/Arizona border was the site of illegal but effective roadblocks during the Dust Bowl, when vigilante mobs turned back migrant Okies if they didn't have much money.

The first stop east of the Colorado River, nine miles from the border and 23 miles south of I-40, Lake Havasu City is a thoroughly modern vacation town built around a thoroughly odd centerpiece: London Bridge, brought here stone by stone between 1967 and 1971. Terribly tacky souvenir shops and faux London pubs congregate around the foot of the bridge, which spans a man-made channel to a large island, but the bridge itself is an impressive sight.

Unless you plan to retire here—or simply relax on a boat on the river—there's not a lot to do at Lake Havasu. Have an English muffin and a cup of tea, pay your respects and take a photograph or two, then hit the road again.

Old Route 66: Oatman

One of the most demanding, desolate, and awesomely satisfying stretches of the old road climbs from I-40 along the Colorado River, beginning just east of the California border and rejoining the freeway at Kingman. Following at first along the wildlife refuge that lines the Colorado River, the old road then cuts across a stretch of desert that brings new meaning to the word "harsh." The narrow, roughly surfaced roadway passes few signs of life on this 50-mile loop, so be sure you and your car are prepared for the rigors of desert driving.

LONDON BRIDGE

It may not have stood out as the finest of engineering art when it spanned the Thames, but London Bridge is a marvelous sight in the middle of the Arizona desert. A replacement for a series of bridges that date back to medieval times, inspiring the children's rhyme, "London Bridge Is Falling Down," this version of London Bridge was constructed in the 1830s. When it was no longer able to handle the demands of London traffic, the old bridge was replaced by a modern concrete span and its stones were put up for sale in 1967.

Bought by property developer Robert McCulloch for $2.4 million, the 10,246 blocks of stone were shipped here and reassembled at a cost of another $3 million. After a channel was cut under the bridge to bring water from the Colorado River, the Lord Mayor of London flew in to attend the rededication ceremonies in October 1971; the bridge now stands as the centerpiece of a retirement and resort community that's home to some 25,000 residents. There's no admission charge to see this oddly compelling sight, its finely carved stonework standing in permanent rebuke to the tacky stucco, mock Tudor souvenir shops lining the base of the bridge.

From I-40 and the California border, take the Park Moabi exit and follow Hwy-95, then Hwy-66, due north; you can also reach Hwy-95 directly from Needles or from Laughlin, Nevada. (Westbound drivers have it the easiest—simply follow the well-signed "Historic Route 66" west from Kingman, exit 44 off I-40.) Whichever way you go, you can't avoid the steep hills that bring you to Oatman (elev. 2,700 feet), an odd mix of ghost town and tourist draw that's one of the top stops along Route 66. A gold mining town whose glory days had long faded by the time I-40 passed it by way back in 1952, Oatman looks like a Wild West stage set, but it's the real thing—awnings over the plank sidewalks, bearded roughnecks (and a few burros) wandering the streets, lots of rust, and slumping old buildings. The gold mines here produced some two million ounces from their start in 1904 until they panned out in the mid-1930s; at its peak, Oatman had a population of over 10,000, with 20 saloons and a half-dozen hotels lining the three-block Main Street. One of these, the old **Oatman Hotel** (520/768-4408), was where Clark Gable and Carole Lombard spent their first night after getting married in Kingman in 1939; you can sample Oatman's highly recommended Navajo tacos, have a beer in the downstairs bar, peer through a Plexiglas door at the room where Clark and Carole slept, or spend the night in one of the other $35-50 rooms, hardly changed for half a century.

Saloons and rock shops line the rest of Main Street, where on weekends and holidays Wild West enthusiasts act out the shoot-outs that took place here only in the movies. Oatman does get a considerable tourist trade, but after dark and out of the peak summer tourist season the town reverts to its rough-and-tumble ways, and the conservative, libertarian bent of most of the local population ensures that nothing is likely to change Oatman's crusty charms.

For more information, contact the small but helpful **chamber of commerce** (520/768-8070).

East from Oatman the road passes the recently reactivated gold workings at **Goldroad** before climbing up and over the angular Black Mountains. Steep switchbacks and 15 mph hairpin turns make the 2,100-foot change in elevation over a very short eight miles of blacktop; the route then continues for another 20 miles into Kingman, which seems like a bustling metropolis after this hour-plus roller coaster of a drive.

Kingman

At **Yucca,** Arizona, just south of I-40 exit 26, and 18 miles west of Kingman, the Ford Motor Company maintains an automobile "proving ground" where it runs cars for countless miles around an oval track in the hottest summer heat.

The only town for miles in any direction since its founding as a railroad center in 1880, Kingman (pop. 12,750) has always depended upon passing travelers for its livelihood. Long a main stopping place on Route 66, and still providing the only all-night services on US-93 between Las Vegas and Phoenix, and along I-40 between Flagstaff and Needles, the town remains more a way station than a destination despite the increasing number of people who have relocated here in recent years, attracted by the open space, high desert air, and low cost of living.

Everything that's ever happened in and around Kingman is documented to some degree at the **Mojave Museum**, 400 W. Beale Street (Mon.-Fri. 10 AM-5 PM, Saturday and Sunday 1-5 PM; $1), right on US-93 a block south of I-40. Besides the usual dioramas and displays on regional history, there's an extensive section devoted to local Hualapai culture and crafts, as well as samples of turquoise mined nearby. There's also a display on the life of local boy Andy Devine and a photograph of Clark Gable and Carole Lombard, who fled Hollywood to get married in Kingman's Methodist church.

Quite a few of the old Route 66 cafes and motels still flourish alongside the old road, now called Andy

Andy Devine

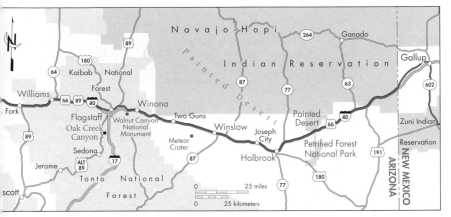

Devine Avenue through town; modern development borders the I-40 freeway. Among many places to eat are the very good **Mr. D's Route 66 Diner**, right downtown and impossible to miss thanks to its bank of neon; and the **House of Chan**, 960 W. Beale Street, on US-93 a block north of I-40, which serves a full menu of American food as well as Cantonese specialties. Besides the usual chain motels—two nice Best Westerns, two Days Inns, a Holiday Inn, and a Travelodge—accommodation options include the pleasant **Hill Top Motel**, 1901 E. Andy Devine Avenue (520/753-2198), forever infamous as the place where Timothy McVeigh stayed for a week before blowing up the federal building in Oklahoma City.

For more information, or to pick up a copy of the town's very good Route 66 brochure, contact the Kingman **visitor center**, 333 W. Andy Devine Avenue (520/753-6106).

For the hits of the 1960s, tune to "Radio Crazy," **KRCY 105.9 FM.**

The stretch of Route 66 through Kingman has been renamed in memory of favorite son **Andy Devine,** who was born in Flagstaff in 1905 but grew up here, where his parents ran the Beale Hotel. One of the best-known character actors of Hollywood's classic era, the raspy-voiced Devine usually played a devoted sidekick, the sort of role taken by Gabby Hayes, whom Devine replaced in the later Roy Rogers movies. Devine's most famous role was as the wagon driver in the classic 1939 John Ford western *Stagecoach*. He remained active in films and TV until his death in 1977.

Hualapai Mountain Park

To escape the summer heat, Kingmanites head south along a well-marked 14-mile road to Hualapai Mountain Park, where pines and firs cover the slopes of the 8,417-foot peak. Hiking trails wind through the wilderness, where there's a campground ($6) and a few rustic cabins ($25) built by the Civilian Conservation Corps during the New Deal 1930s. Contact the ranger station (520/757-3859) near the park entrance for detailed information or to make reservations.

Old Route 66 Loop: Hackberry, Valentine, and the Hualapai Reservation

Probably the most evocative stretch of old Route 66 runs northeast from Kingman through the high desert Hualapai Valley, along the Santa Fe Railroad tracks through all-but-abandoned towns bypassed by the "modern" interstate world. Leaving Kingman on a 20-mile-long straightaway, the road (now named Hwy-66) bends back south around the Peacock Mountains through the old railroad town of Hackberry, home to the ever-evolving **International Bioregional Old Route 66 Visitor Center and Preservation Foundation**. A marvelous establishment, created by

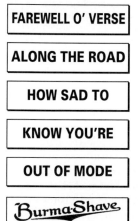

Old Hackberry Store, HACKBERRY, ARIZONA (ALT. 3,500 FT.)
IN THIS VIEW FACING NORTH, ACROSS 66, THE RUGGED FOOT-HILLS OF THE GRAND WASH CLIFFS FORM A DRAMATIC BACKDROP. THE CLIFFS—WHICH FORM PART OF THE COLORADO PLATEAU'S EDGE—STRETCH AWAY TO THE NORTHWEST, CLEAR TO THE GRAND CANYON. THE STORE, WITH ITS OUTBUILDINGS & OLD HOUSE, WAS A TYPICAL ROADSIDE OASIS, SERVING TRAVELLERS SINCE THE 1930's UNTIL THIS STRETCH OF 66 WAS LEFT HIGH & DRY WHEN THE INTERSTATE BYPASSED IT IN 1978. THE TINY VILLAGE OF HACKBERRY—NAMED FOR TREES AT THE NEARBY HACK-BERRY MINE (EST. 1870's) IS TO THE SOUTH (OUT OF VIEW). JUST BEYOND THE SANTA FE'S DOUBLE TRACKS. BEFORE RT. 66 WAS CONSTRUCTED, TRAFFIC WENT RIGHT THROUGH THE TOWN, ON THE OLD NATIONAL TRAILS ROAD. THE STORE & ADJACENT PROPERTY WAS PURCHASED IN 1993 BY THE WALDMIRE FAMILY OF ILLINOIS, & PLANS ARE TO ESTABLISH AN "INTERNATIONAL BIOREGIONAL OLD ROUTE 66 VISITOR CENTER." by R. Waldmire ©1992

renowned Route 66 artist Bob Waldmire, the center serves multiple purposes: the 22-acre site includes everything from cactus gardens to a solar oven, while the main building, built in 1934 as the Hackberry General Store, now houses a museum and gift shop, and a library with books on Route 66 and the complete works of Thomas Paine, Thomas Jefferson, and other free thinkers. Future plans include the development of a hostel and B&B, but for now, whenever Bob's around—and rumor has it that he's threatening to move to the Chiricahua Mountains in southeastern Arizona —you can be assured of a warm welcome and a hot cup of coffee. For more information, call or write: P.O. Box 46, Hackberry AZ 86411 (520/769-2605).

Downhill from the Route 66 center, the old town of Hackberry grew up along the original alignment of Route 66, which continues east across a small section of the Hualapai Indian Reservation, centered around the village of Valentine. Another 10 miles east brings you to the town of Truxton, where the **Frontier Cafe** on the south side of the highway is the one reliable place to eat in this sparsely populated region—good pie and great chat, open weekdays 7 AM-7 PM, weekends 9 AM-5 PM. **Grandma's Bar** across the highway gives you another chance to sample local lore and lifeways.

FAREWELL O' VERSE

ALONG THE ROAD

HOW SAD TO

KNOW YOU'RE

OUT OF MODE

Burma-Shave

Another mile east is the boundary of the main Hualapai (pronounced WALL-ah-pie) reservation lands. The 700-strong tribe has its community center at the town of **Peach Springs** which marks the halfway point of this 90-mile, old-roads loop and offers at least one reason to stop: the comfortable and well-placed new **Hualapai Lodge** (520/769-2230) hotel and "River Runners'" restaurant, right on Route 66. Apart from this, Peach Springs is mostly a prefab Bureau of Indian Affiars housing project with few services, though there is a photogenic old Route 66 filling station at the center of town.

Grand Canyon Caverns

A dozen miles east of Peach Springs, 26 miles from I-40, a large green sign marks the entrance to Grand Canyon Caverns (daily 10 AM-5 PM, 8 AM-6 PM in summer; $7.50; 520/422-3223), which has somehow managed to survive despite being bypassed by the

I-40 superslab. Once one of the prime tourist draws on the Arizona stretch of Route 66, the Grand Canyon Caverns were discovered and developed in the late 1920s and still have the feel of an old-time roadside attraction. Start your tour at the gift shop, buy a ticket, and hop on the elevator, which drops you 300 feet to underground chambers, including the 18,000-square-foot Chapel of the Ages. Tours last around 45 minutes. There's also a motel (doubles $22 in winter, $45 in summer) and a restaurant on the site.

Seligman

At the east end of the long loop of old Route 66, the sleepy little town of Seligman (pop. 510; pronounced SLIG-man) is a perfect place to take a break before or after rejoining the interstate hordes. The town retains a lot of its historic character—old sidewalk awnings and even a few hitching rails—and offers lots of reasons to stop, but two of the biggest are the brothers Angel and Juan Delgadillo, ringleaders of local Route 66 preservation efforts. Angel is the town barber, and his shop is a pilgrimage point for old roads fans; Juan, the practical joker of the pair, runs the wacky **Snow Cap Drive-In** a block to the east. The burgers, fries, and milk shakes are plenty good, but Juan's sense of humor is more than a little strange: he has handles on doors that don't open, a sign that says "Sorry, We're Open," and a menu advertising "Hamburgers without Ham." Behind the restaurant, in snow, rain, or shine, sits a roofless old Chevy decorated with fake flowers and an artificial Christmas tree. Go ahead, ask him why.

Apart from the Delgadillo brothers, Seligman also has a very good cafe, the **Copper Cart**, at the center of town; a neat old mock-Tudor railroad station that once doubled as a Harvey House hotel and restaurant; a half-dozen motels including "Unique Motel" (which is now a sign only) and the **Historic Route 66 Motel**, 500 W. Route 66 (520/422-3204). After dark, head to the **Black Cat** saloon, where actor Nicholas Cage has been known to stop in for a drink or two.

Midway between Peach Springs and the Grand Canyon Caverns, Hwy-18 cuts off 65 miles to the northeast toward the Havasupai Indian Reservation, which includes one of the most beautiful and untrammelled corners of the Grand Canyon. For further details, contact the tribally owned and operated **Havasupai Lodge** (520/448-2111).

Between Seligman and Ash Fork, a nice section of the old Route 66 two-lane runs just north of, and parallel to, the I-40 freeway.

Between Ash Fork and Flagstaff, a long but beautiful scenic loop winds along US-89 and US-89A through Prescott, Jerome, Sedona, and wonderful Oak Creek Canyon.

Delgadillo's Snow Car

Williams

The last Route 66 town to be bypassed by the I-40 freeway, Williams (pop. 2,532; elev. 6,780 feet) held out until the bitter end, waging court battle after court battle before finally surrendering on October 13, 1984. Despite the town's long opposition, in the end Williams gave in gracefully, going so far as to hold a celebration-cum-wake for the old road, highlighted by a performance atop the new freeway overpass by none other than Mr. Route 66 himself, Bobby "Get Your Kicks" Troup.

Williams today is primarily a gateway to the Grand Canyon, but it also takes full tourist advantage of its Route 66 heritage. The downtown streets sport old-fashioned street lamps, and every other store (including the friendly and well-stocked World HQ of **Route 66 Magazine**, at 326 W. Route 66; 520/635-4322) sells a variety of Route 66 souvenirs, but the town is still a charming place, much more than a bedroom community for Grand Canyon-bound travelers.

Apart from the Route 66 connections, Williams's pride and joy is the vintage **Grand Canyon Railway**, which whistles and steams its way north to the canyon every morning March-Dec., taking roughly two hours each way and allowing a three-hour layover—or longer, if you go up on one train and come back another day. Call for current schedules and fares (roundtrip tickets cost $50; 800/THE-TRAIN or 800/843-8724), or stop by the historic depot, a former Harvey House hotel restored in 1990.

As any good road trip destination must, Williams has at least one decent place to eat breakfast, **Old Smokey's Pancake House**, 624 W. Bill Williams Avenue at the west end of town. The town is also home to a landmark old Route 66 restaurant, **Rod's Steak House**, 301 E. Bill Williams Avenue, in business since 1946.

For a place to stay, try any of the town's many motels, such as the **Westerner Motel**, 530 W. Bill Williams Avenue (520/635-4312 or 800/385-9313); or the British-run **Norris Motel** (520/635-2202), at the far west end of town, offering clean rooms from under $30 a night, rising to $55 a night in summer.

For more information, contact the **chamber of commerce**, 200 W. Railroad Avenue (520/635-4061).

Rod's STEAK HOUSE
WILLIAMS, ARIZONA

Gateway to the Grand Canyon

Detour: Grand Canyon National Park

From the east end of Williams, Hwy-64 continues 60 miles due north to one of the wonders of the natural world, the Grand Canyon of the Colorado River. Two hundred miles long, a mile deep, and anywhere from five to 15 miles across, the Grand Canyon defies description, and if you're anywhere nearby you owe it to yourself to stop for a look. This book can do little more than hint at all there is to see and do there, but if you have time for nothing else, hike down into the canyon to get a real sense of its awesome scale.

Most of what you need to know to enjoy a visit is contained in the brochure you're given at the entrance, where you pay the $10-per-car fee, or can be found out at the very good **visitor center** (daily 8 AM-5 PM; 520/638-7888). Here you can

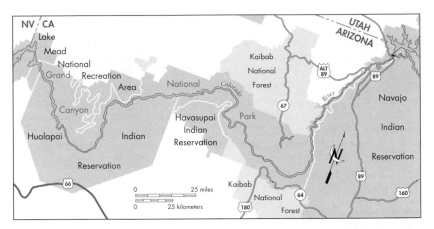

pick up information about the park's many hiking trails, the canyon's geology, the burro rides that take you down and back up again, and splendid Phantom Ranch, a rustic complex of cabins and dormitories halfway down the canyon.

To make advance reservations for accommodations, a good idea at any time of year but essential in the peak summer months, phone the park concessionaire (303/ 297-2757). The most characterful and best-value place to stay is the **Bright Angel Lodge**, which overlooks the canyon; there are also many other motels and swanky **El Tovar Hotel**, where rooms cost from $200 a night.

If all the in-park accommodations are full, more rooms are available outside the park's southern boundary at **Tusayan**, including a Best Western and a Quality Inn. Tusayan is where the park service plans to concentrate all future development at the Grand Canyon, if and when cars are finally banned and replaced by the proposed light rail train.

Flagstaff

An old railroad and lumber-mill town given a new lease on life by an influx of students at Northern Arizona University, and by the usual array of ski-bums and mountain bikers attracted by the surrounding high mountain wilderness, Flagstaff (pop. 45,857) is an enjoyable, energetic town high up on the Coconino Plateau. The natural beauty of its forested location has meant that, compared to other Route 66 towns, Flagstaff was less affected by the demise of the old road. That said, it still takes pride in the past, notably in the form of the **Museum Club**, 3404 E. Route 66 (520/526-9434), an old road-house brought back to life as a country-western nightclub and ad-hoc nostalgia museum. There are also dozens of vintage neon signs along the old Route 66 alignment: check out the Western Hills Motel and the Grand Canyon Cafe downtown, and the Flamingo Motel five blocks west.

In his 1945 *Guide Book to Highway 66,* Jack Rittenhouse wrote, "Cowboys and Indians can be seen in their picturesque dress on Flagstaff streets year 'round. . . ."

Flagstaff also has a pair of non-Route 66 related attractions. First and foremost of these stands on a hill at the west end of Flagstaff, reachable from the west end of Santa Fe Avenue (old Route 66): the **Lowell Observatory**, established in 1894 by Percival Lowell and best known as the place where, in 1930, the planet Pluto was discovered. A visitor center (daily 9 AM-5 PM in summer, shorter hours rest of the year; $3) has descriptions of the science behind what goes on here—spectroscopy, red shifts, and expanding universes, for example—and the old telescope, a 24-inch refractor, is open for viewings 8-10 PM most nights in summer. For more detailed information, call the observatory at 520/774-2096. The other main draw, the **Museum of Northern Arizona** (daily 9 AM-5 PM; $4), perches at the edge of a pine-forested canyon three miles northwest of downtown via US-180, the main road to the Grand Canyon; extensive exhibits detail the vibrant cultures of northern Arizona, from prehistoric Anasazi to contemporary Hopi, Navajo, and Zuni.

Downtown Flagstaff has more than enough espresso bars— probably a dozen within a two-block radius of the train station —to satisfy its many multiply pierced, twentysomething residents. There are also ethnic restaurants specializing in Greek, Thai, German, or Indian, so finding suitable places to eat and drink will not be a problem. For breakfast and lunch, it's hard to beat **Kathie's**, a cozy cafe at 7 N. San Francisco Street.

Accommodations, too, are plentiful, and you can pick either the motel with the most appealing sign or step back into an earlier time and stay at the classy old **Hotel Monte Vista**, right on old Route 66 at 100 N. San Francisco Street (520/779-6971 or 800/545-3068). It was good enough for Gary Cooper and has been restored to its Roaring Twenties splendor.

For more complete listings or other information, contact the **visitor center**, right downtown at 101 W. Route 66 (520/774-9541 or 800/842-7293).

Flagstaff's San Francisco Street was named not for the California city but for the nearby volcanic peaks, so called by early Spanish missionaries and still held sacred by the native Hopi Indians.

Flagstaff very nearly became an early movie center, when young **Cecil B. DeMille** *stopped here briefly while scouting locations to shoot the world's first feature-length film, a Western called* The Squaw Man. *It was snowing in Flagstaff that day, so he moved on to L.A.*

Walnut Canyon National Monument

The most easily accessible of the hundreds of different prehistoric settlements all over the southwestern U.S., Walnut Canyon National Monument (daily 8 AM-4 PM, 7 AM-5 PM in summer; $4; 520/526-3367) is also one of the prettiest places imaginable, with piñon pines and junipers clinging to the canyon walls, and walnut trees filling the canyon floor. On the edge of the canyon, a small visitor center gives the historical background, but the real interest lies below, on a short but very steep path that winds through cliff dwellings tucked into overhangs and ledges 400 feet above the canyon floor.

The entrance to the monument, which contains some 300 identified archaeological sites, lies seven miles east of Flagstaff, accessible from I-40 exit 204.

Don't Forget: Winona

East of Flagstaff, following old Route 66 can be a frustrating task, since much of the roadway is blocked or torn up or both. Unlike the long stretches found in the western half of the state, here the old road exists only as short segments running through towns, and most of the way you're forced to follow the freeway, stopping at exit after exit to get on and off the old road. Among the places worth considering is the one town mentioned out of sequence in the Route 66 song: "Flagstaff, Arizona, don't forget Winona," which, alas, is now little more than a name on the sign at I-40 exit 211.

East of Winona, the route drops swiftly from the cool pines onto the hot red desert, but old-road fanatics will want to take the time to explore what remains of two old-time tourist traps lining the next 20 miles of highway.

First of these is **Twin Arrows**, where if you're lucky, a pair of red arrows will point you toward a small but thriving cafe, right off the freeway at exit 219. Continuing east, approaching exit 230, the freeway crosses deep Diablo Canyon, where an old Route 66 bridge still spans the dry wash, and the walls of a half-dozen bleached buildings are all that's left of the **Two Guns Trading Post**, just south of exit 230. A roadside attraction par excellence, Two Guns had a zoo full of roadrunners, gila monsters, and coyotes, and one building still has a sign saying Mountain Lions—all for the entertainment of passing travelers. According to various reports down the Route 66 grapevine, Two Guns has been on the verge of reopening in recent years, but most of the time the old road is blocked by a sign reading No Trespassing by Order of Two Guns Sheriff Department. Probably a good thing, since the old buildings are all dangerously close to collapse. It's an evocative site, nonetheless, and photogenic in the right light.

Meteor Crater

Three miles east of Two Guns, and six miles south of I-40 exit 233, sits Meteor Crater (daily 8 AM-5 PM, longer hours in summer; $8), Arizona's second most distinctive hole in the ground. Formed by a meteorite some 50,000 years ago, and measuring 570 feet deep and nearly a mile across, the crater is a privately owned tourist attraction, offering an "Astronauts Hall of Fame" as well as a chance to look down into the huge hole; you can't climb down into it, however.

Winslow

Winslow, Arizona, didn't make it into Bobby Troup's original Route 66 hit list, but the town more than made it a generation later with the Eagles tune "Take It Easy," which begins, "Standin' on a corner in Winslow, Arizona," a line that has caused more people to turn off in search of the place than anything else. What you may find in Winslow is not a lot, actually. Chain motels and fast-food franchises stand at either end of town around the I-40 exits, and in between, a couple of cafes and cheap motels are the only signs of life along the old Route 66 frontage, which followed 2nd Street eastbound and 3rd Street westbound.

In between the I-40 and Route 66 is the funky **Old Trails Museum**, 212 Kinsley Street (Tues.-Sat. 1-5 PM; 520/289-5861),

At the west end of Joseph City, right off I-40 exit 274, stop at the **Jackrabbit Trading Post,** the one whose signs you've probably noticed over the past hundred miles, and take a picture or buy a postcard of the giant jackrabbit, one of a long line of creatures who have stood here since 1949.

Winslow and Holbrook are the nearest towns to the Navajo Nation Indian Reservation, home of radio station **KTNN 660 AM,** which broadcasts a fascinating mélange of Navajo chants and Jimi Hendrix riffs. It's also the only station in the U.S. that broadcasts Dallas Cowboys football games—in Navajo.

which sells a range of "Standin' on the Corner" T-shirts, and displays a few reminders of Winslow in its heyday. Down the block, on 2nd and Kinsley, a little sign stakes a claim to being *the* corner the Eagles sang about; in 1994, Eagles songwriter Don Henley donated $2,500 to help beautify the spot with an appropriate monument.

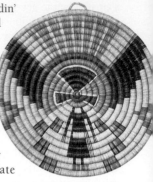

Hopi coiled basket, circa 1920s

snow kachina doll

Holbrook

Holding a concentrated dose of old Route 66 character, Holbrook (pop. 4,686) is definitely worth a quick detour off the I-40 freeway. More than the other Route 66 towns in the eastern half of Arizona, it still feels like a real place, with lively cafes and some endearing roadside attractions. Be sure to stop at **Joe and Aggie's Cafe** at the center of town, or **Romo's** across the street; and be sure to check out the dinosaur collection outside the **Rainbow Rock Shop** a block south on Navajo Boulevard near the railroad tracks. Best of all, stop for the night at the marvelous **Wigwam Village**, 811 W. Hopi Drive (520/524-3048) at the western edge of town, and sleep in a concrete teepee. One of around a dozen built across the country, this one opened in 1950 and was fully modernized in 1988. Rooms cost around $35 a night, so you really should stay here at least once in your life.

Kiowa beaded cradle board, circa 1890-1907

Another worthwhile place to stop is the **Navajo County Museum** (Mon.-Fri. 8 AM-5 PM, plus Saturday in summer; free) in the old Navajo County Courthouse, four blocks south of I-40 at the corner of Navajo Boulevard (old Route 66) and Arizona Street. The collections are wide-ranging and include a walk downstairs to the old county jail, in use from 1899 until 1976. The museum is next door to the **Holbrook Chamber of Commerce** (520/524-6558), which has walking and driving tour maps and general information on the town.

Navajo jewelry

SONGS OF ROUTE 66

GET YOUR KICKS ON ROUTE 66

If you ever plan to motor west,
Travel my way, that's the highway that's the best,
Get your kicks on Route 66.

It winds from Chicago to L.A.,
More than 2,000 miles all the way
Get your kicks on Route 66.

Now you go through St. Looey, Joplin, Missouri
And Oklahoma City is mighty pretty.
You'll see Amarillo, Gallup, New Mexico,
Flagstaff, Arizona, don't forget Winona,
Kingman, Barstow, San Bernardino.

Won't you get hip to this timely tip:
When you make that California trip
Get your kicks on Route 66.
Get your kicks on Route 66.

—Bobby Troup

One of the most popular road songs ever written, and a prime force behind the international popularity of Route 66, "Get Your Kicks on Route 66" was penned by jazz musician Bobby Troup in 1946 while he was driving west to seek fame and fortune in Los Angeles. Troup consistently credited his former wife Cynthia, with whom he was traveling, for the half-dozen words of the title and refrain. The rest of the song simply rattled off the rhyming place-names along the way, but despite its apparent simplicity, it caught the ear of Nat King Cole, who made it into a hit record and also established the pronunciation as "root" rather than "rout," as repeated in later renditions by everyone from Bob Willis to the Rolling Stones.

If you haven't heard the song for a while, there's a jazzy version by Bobby Troup along with some lively Route 66-related songs, including a world-weary "What's Left of 66" by traveling troubadour Jason Ecklund, on the 1995 compilation tape and CD, *The Songs of the Route 66—Music from the All American Highway,* available at souvenir stores en route and from Lazy SOB Records, P.O. Box 49884, Austin, TX 78765.

Painted Desert and Petrified Forest National Park

The easternmost 60 miles of I-40 across Arizona are little more than one long speedway, since any sign of the old road has been lost beneath the four-lane interstate. One place that's worth a stop here is Petrified Forest National Park (daily dawn-dusk; $10 per car). The polished petrified wood on display in the visitor center is gorgeous to look at, but seeing the stuff in its raw natural state is not particu-

Thirty-eight miles north of I-40 from exit 333, a mile west of the town of Ganado, the **Hubbell Trading Post National Historic Site** is a frontier store preserved as it was in the 1870s, when trader John Hubbell began buying the beautiful rugs made by local Navajo weavers.

larly thrilling. The story of how the wood got petrified is interesting, though: about 225 million years ago, a forest was buried in volcanic ash, then slowly embalmed with silica and effectively turned to stone. You can take a look at 93,000 acres of the stuff outside the visitor center.

While the park contains a vast array of prehistoric fossils and pictographs as well as the petrified wood, one of the more interesting sights is the old **Painted Desert Inn**, a Route 66 landmark during the 1920s and 1930s that was converted into a museum and bookstore after the park service took it over in the 1960s. There are no services here, but there's a handy Fred Harvey restaurant and gas station at the visitor center, and the desert views, especially at sunrise or sunset, are worth waiting around to see.

East of the park, along the New Mexico border, Arizona welcomes westbound travelers with an overwhelming display of trading-post tackiness—huge concrete teepees stand at the foot of brilliant red-rock mesas, while gift shops styled after everything from TV's "F Troop" to *Dances With Wolves* hawk their souvenirs to passing travelers.

ACROSS NEW MEXICO

Following old Route 66 across New Mexico gives you a great taste of the Land of Enchantment, as the state calls itself on its license plates. There is less of the actual "old road" here than in other places, but the many towns and ghost towns along I-40, built more or less on top of Route 66, still stand. In Albuquerque, Route 66 runs through the center of this sprawling Sun Belt city, while in other places finding the old road and bypassed towns can take some time, though the effort is usually well rewarded.

Western New Mexico has the most to see and the most interesting topography, with sandstone mesas looming in the foreground and high, pine-forested peaks

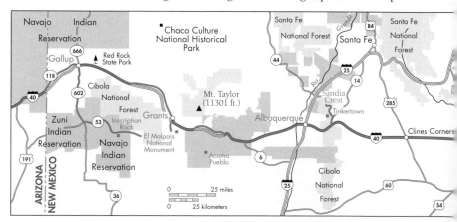

rising in the distance. Paralleling the Santa Fe Railroad, the route passes through the heart of this region, and numerous detours—to Inscription Rock and Chaco Canyon, among others—make unforgettable stops along the way. In the east, the land is flatter and the landscape drier as the road approaches the Great Plains.

Gallup

Despite the obvious poverty and other signs of genuine despair, Gallup (pop. 19,154) is a fascinating town. Founded in 1881 when the Santa Fe Railroad first rumbled through, and calling itself "The Gateway to Indian Country" because it's the largest town near the huge Navajo and other Native American reservations, Gallup has some of the Southwest's largest trading posts offering great deals, and one of the best strips of neon signs you'll see anywhere on old 66.

Stretching for over a dozen miles across the border between the two states, Hwy-118 runs north of the I-40 freeway, following old Route 66 between exit 357 in Arizona and exit 8 in New Mexico.

Gallup also hosts the annual "Inter Tribal Ceremonial," perhaps the largest Native American gathering in the country, held every August in Red Rock State Park eight miles east of Gallup, and culminating in a Sunday parade that brings 30,000 people out to line old Route 66 through town.

For travelers intent on experiencing a little of the charms of old Route 66, Gallup also has **El Rancho**, 1000 E. Route 66 (505/863-9311), a delightful old hotel lovingly restored to its 1930s glory. Built by a brother of movie director D.W. Griffiths, El Rancho feels like a national park lodge, with a large but welcoming lobby dominated a huge stone fireplace. All the rooms in the old wing are named for the movie stars who have stayed here over the years —the W.C. Fields Room, the John Wayne Room, the Marx Brothers Room (which sleeps six), even the Ronald Reagan Room—and signed glossies of these and many more actors and actresses adorn the halls. Rooms cost $40-75 a night for two people, depending upon the individual room and the time of year. El Rancho also has a good restaurant serving regional food daily 6 AM-10 PM, and a gift shop selling souvenirs and fine jewelry, pottery, and rugs made by Native American crafts people. The shop's owner, Armand Ortega, is one of Gallup's most respected crafts dealers.

For further listings or more information, contact the Gallup **visitors bureau** on the north side of I-40 exit 22, at 701 Montoya Boulevard (505/863-3841 or 800/242-4282), which will no doubt try to direct you away from the many classic motels lining Route 66, like the **Log Cabin Inn** in the middle of town, offering rooms for as little as $15-20 a night, $85 a week. Many of these are scary-looking enough to give your mother sleepless nights; for peace of mind there are all the usual chains as well—nearly 2,000 rooms altogether—if El Rancho is fully booked.

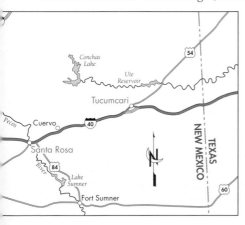

Detour: Inscription Rock and El Malpais

Western New Mexico is among the most beautiful places on the planet. One of the best drives through it, Hwy-53, loops south of I-40 between Gallup and Grants across the Zuni and Navajo Nation Indian Reservations. Skirting

the southern foothills of the 9,000-foot Zuni Mountains, the route follows ancient Indian trails that Coronado used on his ill-fated 1540 explorations, winding past piñon-covered hills, open grasslands, and the fascinating graffiti collection of El Morro National Monument. Better known as Inscription Rock, the 200-foot-high sandstone cliffs of El Morro have been inscribed by travelers like Juan de Oñate, who wrote his name with a flourish in 1605, after he discovered the Gulf of California.

Atop the cliffs are the partially excavated remains of a small Anasazi pueblo dating from around A.D. 1200. A two-mile loop trail to the inscriptions and the ruins starts from a small **visitor center** (daily 8 AM-5 PM; till 7 PM in summer; $4 per car; 505/783-4226), where exhibits outline the history of the site. The trails are closed an hour before sunset, so get here early enough in the day to enjoy the beautiful scenery. There is also a small campground (no showers, pit toilets) amidst the junipers.

Every bit as impressive and memorable as the cliff dwelling of Mesa Verde, the extensive archaeological remains protected inside **Chaco Culture National Historical Park** are well worth your time. Though it's an hour's drive from I-40 via unpaved roads, the park is one of the wonders of the Southwest desert; for details, call 505/786-7014.

East of Inscription Rock, after crossing the Continental Divide where there's a roadside rest stop, Hwy-53 winds along the edge of the massive El Malpais lava flow—thousands of acres of pitch-black, concrete-hard, glassy sharp rock—before rejoining I-40 and old Route 66 at Grants.

Midway between Grants and Gallup, I-40 crosses the 7,250-foot Continental Divide, where the "Top O' the World" dance hall used to tempt travelers off old Route 66. From here (exit 47), it's possible to follow the old road for 30 miles, running east along I-40 as far as Grants.

Grants

Along with the usual Route 66 range of funky motels and rusty neon signs, the former mining boomtown of Grants has the unique attraction of the **New Mexico Museum of Mining** (Mon.-Sat. 9 AM-6 PM, Sunday noon-6 PM; $3), right downtown on old Route 66 (Santa Fe Avenue) at the corner of Iron Avenue. Most of the exhibits trace the short history of local uranium mining, which began in 1950 when a local Navajo rancher, Paddy Martinez, discovered an odd yellow rock that turned out to be high-grade uranium ore. Mines here once produced half the ore mined in the U.S., but production has now ceased. From the main gallery, ride the elevator down to the highlight of the mining museum: a credible re-creation of a uranium mine, complete with an underground lunch room emblazoned with all manner of warning signs.

Across the street from the Mining Museum, the **Uranium Cafe** is still in business (we hope), serving up breakfast and lunch every day and dinner on Friday and Saturday. Just look for the atomic neon sign, a Route 66 landmark.

Acoma Pueblo: Sky City and Enchanted Mesa

A dozen miles east of Grants and 50 miles west of Albuquerque, one of the Southwest's most intriguing sites, Acoma Pueblo, stands atop a 357-foot-high sandstone mesa. Long known as "Sky City," Acoma is one of the very oldest communities in North America, inhabited since A.D. 1150. The views out across the plains are unforgettable, especially the Enchanted Mesa on the horizon to the northeast.

Few people live on the mesa today, though the many adobe houses are used by Pueblo crafts people, who live down below but come up to the mesa-top to sell their pottery to tourists. To visit, stop at the visitor center at the base of the mesa, and join a guided tour (daily 8 AM-4 PM, till 7 PM in summer; $6; 505/470-4966 or 800/747-0181). Tours begin with a bus ride to the mesa-top and end with a visit to **San Esteban del Rey Mission**, the largest Spanish colonial church in the state. Built in 1629, the church features a roof constructed of huge timbers that were carried from the top of Mount Taylor on the backs of neophyte Indians—a distance of more than 30 miles.

Acoma Pueblo is 15 miles south of I-40, from exit 96 (eastbound) or exit 108 (westbound). Between these two exits, another stretch of old Route 66 survives, passing crumbling tourist courts and service stations across the Laguna and Acoma Indian Reservations.

Broadcasting on **530 AM** around the Acoma area, actor Ricardo Montalban narrates the story of the pueblo's conquest by the Spanish, and the story of the building of San Esteban church high atop the mesa.

If you're here in summer, check out a home game of the L.A. Dodgers Class AAA farm club, the **Albuquerque Dukes.** For schedules and prices, call 505/243-1791.

Albuquerque was also the home of the great travel writer and war correspondent **Ernie Pyle.** His old house, at 900 Girard Avenue a half-mile south of Central Avenue, later became the city's first public library, which includes his collected works and a few personal items on display.

Albuquerque

Roughly located at the center of New Mexico, the sprawling city of Albuquerque (pop. 463,300) spreads north and south along the banks of the Rio Grande and east to the foothills of 10,000-foot Sandia Crest. By far the state's biggest city, Albuquerque is a young, energetic, and vibrantly multicultural community, which among many features boasts a great stretch of old Route 66 along Central Avenue through the heart of the city —eighteen miles of diners, motels, and sparkling neon signs.

Apart from the Route 66 legacy, one of the best parts of town is **Old Town**, the historic heart of Albuquerque. Located a block north of Central Avenue, at the west end of the route's cruise through the city, Old Town offers a quick taste of New Mexico's Spanish colonial past, with a lovely old church, the circa 1706 San Felipe de Neri, as well as shops and restaurants set around a leafy green park. An information booth in the park has walking-tour maps of Old Town and other information about the city. Another Old Town attraction, one that carries on the Route 66 tradition of reptile farms and private zoos, is the **Rattlesnake Museum** (daily 10 AM-6 PM; $2), 202 San Felipe Street, where you can see a range of rattlers from tiny babies to full-sized diamondbacks, about 50 altogether.

A very different look into New Mexico's varied cultural makeup is offered at the **Indian Pueblo Cultural Center** (daily 9 AM-5:30 PM; $3; 505/843-7270 or 800/766-4405), a block north of I-40, exit 158 at 2401 12th Street. The center is owned and operated by the state's 19 different Pueblo communities; its highlight is a fine museum tracing the history of the region's Native American cultures, from Anasazi times up to the Pueblo Revolt of 1680, with the contemporary era illustrated by video presentations and a mock-up of a typical tourist—camera, shorts, and all. There's also a small cafeteria where you can sample food like fry bread and Navajo tacos. On most weekends ceremonial dances are held in the central courtyard, free, and open to the general public.

The best range of places to eat lies within walking distance of Old Town. It includes the very good Mexican food at **La Hacienda**, 302 San Felipe Street, with a front porch overlooking the park; and the mix of Mexican and American diner food at **Garcia's**, 1736 W. Central Avenue beneath a glorious neon sign. The excellent **Route 66 Diner**, housed in an old Phillips 66 station at 1405 E. Central Avenue near the University of New Mexico campus, burned down in 1995 and reopened in February 1996, serving top-quality burgers, malts, and shakes, and regional specialties like blue corn pancakes, 8 AM-midnight, Sunday till 10 PM. Another old Route 66 landmark, **Mac's La Sierra**, serves up "Steak in the Rough" and other beefy specialties in a cozy, dark wood dining room west of town at 6217 W. Central Avenue.

Though most people associate computer giant Microsoft with Seattle, the company actually began here in Albuquerque in 1975, in a series of dingy Route 66 motels.

Albuquerque's "Coyote Radio," **KIOT 102.5 FM,** plays a lively range of alternative popular music, from Hank Williams and John Lee Hooker to Talking Heads and the Grateful Dead.

Like most of New Mexico, Albuquerque has a ton of inexpensive accommodations, with all the usual chain motels represented along the interstate frontage roads. For the total Route 66 experience, stay the night at lovely **El Vado**, 2500 W. Central Avenue (505/243-4594), a well-maintained 1930s motel between Old Town and the Rio Grande. The nicest old hotel has got to be the grand **La Posada**, a block off old Route 66 at 125 2nd Street (505/242-9090 or 800/777-5732), one of the first inns built by New Mexico-born hotel magnate Conrad Hilton; doubles here start at $85 a night.

For more information, contact the Albuquerque **visitor center**, 121 Tijeras Road (505/842-9918 or 800/733-9918).

True completists of the Route 66 tour, and anyone interested in the art and architecture (and food!) of the American Southwest, will want to make the detour to the state capital, Santa Fe. The original Route 66 alignment ran north from Albuquerque along the I-25 corridor, then curved back south from Santa Fe, along what's now US-84, to rejoin I-40 west of Santa Rosa. For further information on the city, contact the **Santa Fe visitor center** (505/984-6760 or 800/777-2489).

Tinkertown and the Sandia Crest

Not that there's any shortage of wacky roadside Americana along what's left of Route 66, but one of the most endearing of them all, Tinkertown (daily 9 AM-6 PM April-Oct.; $3; 505/281-5233), is a quick 10-minute drive north of the old road. Like an old-fashioned penny arcade run riot, Tinkertown is a marvelous assembly of over a thousand delicately carved miniature wooden figures, arranged in tiny stage sets to act out animated scenes —a circus Big Top complete with side show, a Wild West town with dance hall girls and a squawking vulture—all housed in a ramshackle building made in part out of glass bottles and bicycle wheels, created over the past 45 years by Ross and Carla Ward and family. It's impossible to describe the many odds and ends on show here—one display case holds over 100 plastic figures taken from the tops of wedding cakes, for example—especially since the whole thing is always being improved and "tinkered" with, but the spirit of the place is aptly summed up in the Tinkertown motto: "We Did All This While You Were Watching TV." The Dalai Lama loved it, and so will you.

To get to Tinkertown, turn off I-40 at exit 175, six miles east of Albuquerque, and follow Hwy-14 for six miles, toward Sandia Crest. Tinkertown is on Hwy-536, 1.5 miles west of the Hwy-14 junction, hidden off the highway among the juniper trees.

Sandia Crest itself is another 12 miles uphill at the end of Hwy-536 National Scenic Byway; the ridge offers a phenomenal panorama from an elevation of 10,678 feet. Some 80 miles of hiking trails wind through the surrounding Cibola National Forest. Back on Hwy-14, four miles north of I-40, the **Sandia Mountain Hostel** (12234 N. Hwy-14 in Tijeras; 505/281-4117) offers clean bunks in a bike-friendly environment.

Clines Corners, midway between Albuquerque and Santa Rosa off I-40 exit 218, is a truck stop cafe that dates back to 1934 and is, as the signs say, Worth Waiting For—for the huge gift shop if not for the unexciting food.

Santa Rosa

The I-40 freeway has bisected the town of Santa Rosa (pop. 2,263) and cut its old Route 66 frontage in two, but for over 65 years, travelers crossing New Mexico along Route 66 and I-40 made a point of stopping here for a meal at **Club Cafe**, "The Original Route 66 Restaurant Since 1935." Thanks to signs lining the road for miles in both directions, emblazoned with the smiling face of the "Fat Man," the Club Cafe became nationally famous for its always-fresh food. Despite its "EZ-OFF, EZ ON" location right along the interstate, the restaurant closed in 1992 but has been on the verge of reopening many times since. If you're lucky, it will be open when you pass through. If not, try **Joseph's**, on old Route 66 a half-mile southwest of I-40 exit 275, which has very good food at reasonable prices.

Santa Rosa's other main attraction is unique: the **Blue Hole**, a 60-foot wide, 80-foot-deep artesian well filled with water so crystal-clear that it draws scuba-divers from all over the western states to practice their underwater techniques here. The water of the Blue Hole, at around 61°, is too cold for casual swimming, but in the summer heat it's a great place to cool your heels. The Blue Hole is well signed at the end of Blue Hole Road, a half-mile south of old Route 66.

East of Santa Rosa, along the south side of I-40 as far as Cuervo, you can trace one of the older stretches of Route 66, only partly paved, and best done in a 4WD or on a mountain bike. Here you get an indelible sense of what travel was like in the very early days, when less than half the route's 2,400-odd miles were paved. Another stretch of old Route 66 now serves as the runway for Santa Rosa's small airport.

Along I-40 near Cuervo, Ricardo Montalban broadcasts a brief, State of New Mexico-sponsored history of Route 66 on **530 AM.**

Along the Pecos River via US-84, some 50 miles southwest of Santa Rosa, the grave site of Wild West legend **Billy the Kid** is outside the town of Fort Sumner. The grave is part of a private museum (daily 9 AM-5 PM; $2) adjacent to Fort Sumner, where 7,000 Navajo people were imprisoned from 1864 to 1869.

Tucumcari

Subject of one of the most successful advertising campaigns in Route 66's long history of roadside hype, Tucumcari (pop. 6,831) looks and sounds like a much bigger place than it is. Also known as "the town that's two blocks wide and two miles long" (though Tucumcari Boulevard, which follows the route blazed by old Route 66 through town, stretches for closer to

seven miles between interstate exits), Tucumcari does have a little of everything, including a great range of neon, but it can be hard to explain the attraction of the town that hundreds of signs along the highways once trumpeted as Tucumcari Tonight—2,000 Motel Rooms. (A new ad campaign plays on this legacy, but signs now say Tucumcari Tonight— 1,500 Motel Rooms.)

Hype or no hype, Tucumcari is a handy place to break a journey, and even if you think you can make it to the next town east or west, you will never regret stopping here for a night. The famous **Blue Swallow Motel**, 815 E. Tucumcari Boulevard (505/461-9849), which no less an authority than *Smithsonian* magazine called "the last, best, and friendliest of the old-time motels," is under new ownership; but thanks to the warm hospitality of former owner Lillian Redman, few who stayed there during her long reign would disagree.

Across Route 66 from the Blue Swallow stands another survivor, the old **Tee Pee Trading Post**, worth a look to add to your collection of Southwest or Route 66 souvenirs. For a place to eat, try the Mexican food at **La Cita**, under the turquoise and pink sombrero on the corner of 1st Street and old 66.

ACROSS TEXAS

Known as the Panhandle because of the way it juts north from the rest of Texas, this part of the route is a nearly 200-mile stretch of pancake-flat plains. Almost devoid of trees or other features, the western half, stretching into New Mexico, is also known as the Llano Estacado or "Staked Plains," possibly because early travelers marked their route by driving stakes into the earth. The Texas Panhandle was the southern extent of the buffalo-rich grasslands of the Great Plains, populated by roving bands of Kiowa and Comanche Indians as recently as 100 years ago. Now oil, gas, and helium production, as well as trucking and Route 66 tourism, have joined ranching as the region's economic basis.

The line between Texas and New Mexico marks the boundary between central and mountain time zones. Set your clocks and watches accordingly.

Even more so than in New Mexico or Oklahoma, old Route 66 has been replaced by I-40 most of the way across Texas, though in many of the ghostly towns like McLean, Shamrock, or Vega, and the sole city, Amarillo, old US-66 survives as the

main business strip, lined by the remains of roadside businesses. A select few are still open for a cup of coffee and a sharp
taste of the living past.

In Glenrio, just over the
border from New Mexico, a
rapidly decaying sign
advertises the "First/Last
Motel in Texas"

Vega and Old Tascosa

Between Amarillo and the New Mexico border, the landscape is identical to what
lies east of the city: endless flat plains dotted with occasional oil derricks and Aermotor windmills. Vega, midway between the border and Amarillo, is a sprawling
cow-town that marks the turnoff onto US-385, which heads north to the remains

---

CADILLAC RANCH

No, you're not seeing things—
there really *are* nearly a dozen
Cadillacs upended in the Texas
plain west of Amarillo, roughly
midway between Chicago and
L.A. Two hundred yards south
of I-40 between the Hope Road
and Arnot Road exits (62 and
60, respectively), some six miles
west of Amarillo, where old US-
66 rejoins the interstate, the rusting hulks of 10 classic Caddies are buried
nose-down in the dirt, their upended tail fins tracing design changes from
1949 to 1964.

A popular shrine to America's love of the open road, Cadillac Ranch was
created by the San Francisco-based Ant Farm artists' and architects' collective
in May 1974, under the patronage of the eccentric Amarillo helium millionaire
Stanley Marsh III. The cars were all bought, some running, some not, from
local junkyards and used car lots at an average cost of $200 each. Before the
Cadillacs were planted, all the hubcaps and wheels were welded on, a good
idea since most of the time the cars are in a badly vandalized state. Every once
in a while advertising agencies and rock bands tidy them up for use as backdrops during photo shoots. In August 1997 the Cadillacs got another 15 minutes of fame when Marsh decided to dig them up and move them a mile west
from where they'd been—to escape the ever-expanding Amarillo sprawl and
preserve the natural horizon.

There's a well-worn path from the frontage road if you want a closer look,
and visitors are allowed any time, day or night.

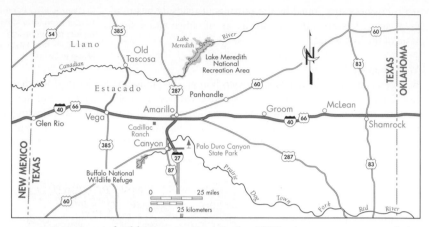

Most of the Texas Panhandle's 20 inches of annual rain falls during summer thunderstorms that sweep across the plains between May and August.

In Amarillo, radio station **KIXE 940 AM**—"Kicks," as in Get Your—plays a lively variety of 1940s swing and earlier jazz, as well as crooners like Bing and Perry, to help get you in the Route 66 mood. The best alternative is on the other dial, where the local Amarillo College station, **89.9 FM,** prides itself on playing "less music from dead guys."

of Old Tascosa. During the 1870s the town was one of the wildest on the Texas frontier. Twenty-two miles north of I-40, just east of US-385 on the north bank of the Canadian River, a few buildings, a barbed-wire museum, and the old Boot Hill cemetery have been preserved; the entire townsite is part of **Cal Farley's Boys Ranch** (daily 8 AM-5 PM; free; 806/372-2341), a working 10,000-acre cattle ranch that doubles as a foster home for some 400 troubled teenagers.

Amarillo

At the heart of the Llano Estacado, midway across the Texas Panhandle, Amarillo (pop. 157,615—and yes, you pronounce the "l"s) is a busy big city that retains its cowboy roots. Center of the local ranching industry that raises some two million head of cattle each year, Amarillo is also one of the few places on earth where helium is produced; an estimated 90% of the world's supply comes from here.

Old Route 66 followed 6th Street through Amarillo, past the brick-paved streets of the Old San Jacinto district around Western Avenue, where you can wander amongst ancient-looking gun and saddle shops and numerous Wild West-themed clothing shops. East of downtown, follow East Amarillo Boulevard past a line of authentic honky-tonks around the 20-acre **Western Stockyards**, at Grand Avenue and 3rd Street. Livestock auctions are held here most weekday mornings; Tuesday is the biggest day. Visitors are welcome and there's no entry fee. Phone for details (806/373-7464).

Along with the one and only health-food place, the **OHMS Cafe**, downtown at 619 S. Tyler Street, Amarillo is known for its many good steakhouses, including the **Iron Horse Cafe**, 401 S. Grant Street, housed in the old train depot near the stockyards. The most famous has to be the **Big Texan Steak Ranch**, which started along Route 66 and now stands on the east side of Amarillo off I-40 exit 74, marked by a false-front Wild West town and a giant cowboy atop a billboard. This is the place where they offer free 72-ounce steaks, provided you eat it all—plus a table full of salad, baked potato, and dessert—in under an hour. If you don't make it, the cost is around $50; regular meals and very good steaks are available as well.

There's a $35-a-night motel featuring a Texas-shaped swimming pool at the **Big Texan** (806/372-5000), and dozens of inexpensive chain motels (two Travelodges, two Comfort Inns) stand along the I-40 and I-27 frontages, so rooms shouldn't be hard to find. For more complete listings or other information, contact the **visitor center** (806/373-7800 or 800/692-1330).

Palo Duro Canyon State Park

Lovely Palo Duro Canyon, one of the most beautiful places in all Texas, is just 25 miles southeast of Amarillo, east of the town of Canyon via the I-27 freeway. Cut into the Texas plain by the Prairie Dog Fork of the Red River, Palo Duro stretches for over 100 miles, with canyon walls climbing to over 1,200 feet. Coronado and company were the first Europeans to lay eyes on the area, and numerous Plains tribes, including Apache, Kiowa, and Comanche, later took refuge here.

On US-60 west of the town of Panhandle, 11 miles northeast of Amarillo, a wire fence on the south side of the road protects the **First Tree in Texas,** planted here on the desolate plains in 1888 by settler Thomas Cree. The trees growing here today are seedlings taken from the original "Bois D'Arc" tree, which was killed by pesticides in 1969.

From the end of Hwy-217, a well-paved road winds past the park **visitor center**, from where a short trail leads to a canyon overlook. Beyond here the road drops down into the canyon and follows the river on a 15-mile loop trip through the Canyon's heart. It's prettiest in spring and fall, and fairly popular year-round; for more information, or for camping reservations, contact the **visitor center** (daily 8 AM-5 PM; 806/488-2227).

Canyon: Tex the Giant Cowboy

On your way to or from Palo Duro Canyon, be sure to stop by the Cowboy Cafe, on US-60 west of Canyon, marked by the towering statue of Tex, the giant (47 feet and 7 tons!) cowboy. Not that you need one, but another great reason to visit Canyon is the excellent **Panhandle-Plains Historical Museum** (Mon.-Sat. 9 AM-5 PM, Sunday 1-5 PM; donations), one of the state's great museums, with extensive exhibits on the cultural and economic life of the Panhandle region and its relations with Mexico, the Texas Republic, and the United States. The museum, which is housed in a WPA-era building on the campus of West Texas A&M University, has a special section on rancher Charles Goodnight, who once owned a half-million acres here and was also an early advocate of saving the bison from extinction. His cabin is preserved in the Pioneer Town behind the museum.

Groom

The town of Groom, 40 miles east of Amarillo on the north side of I-40 at exit 113, holds two of the more eye-catching sights along old Route 66. One of these is a water tower that leans like the Tower of Pisa, causing drivers to stop and rub their eyes, then pull out the camera to take some snapshots to show the folks back home. The other landmark is even harder to miss, a gigantic stainless steel cross, erected by a religious group in 1995 and easily 150 feet tall.

Both of these sights are along the I-40 freeway, but if you head south into town, another photo opportunity awaits: the ruins of the "66 Courts" motel court, highlighted by a rusty old Edsel in the driveway.

McLean

Founded around the turn of 20th century by an English rancher, Alfred Rowe, who later lost his life on the *Titanic* in 1912, McLean is now perhaps the most evocative town along the Texas stretch of Route 66. Bypassed only in the early 1980s, the old main drag is eerily silent, with a few businesses—a barber shop, a boot shop, and some motels, including one with a fine Texas-shaped neon sign—holding on despite the drop in passing trade.

McLean is now headquarters of the state's "Historic Route 66 Association," and

efforts are being made to preserve the town in prime condition, which explains the lovingly restored Phillips 66 station at 1st and Gray streets, and the many other odds and ends on display around town. The center of activity here is the wonderful **Devil's Rope Museum** (Tues.-Sat. 10 AM-4 PM; free ; 806/779-2225), 100 S. Kingsley Street at the east end of downtown, which has a huge room full of barbed wire—the "Devil's Rope"

—and some of the most entertaining and educational collections of Route 66 memorabilia you'll find anywhere. No hype, just lots of good stuff and friendly people telling you all about it.

East of McLean along the old Route 66 frontage, north of the freeway near exit 148, a skeletal sign still spells out the command: Rattlesnakes Exit Here.

Midway between McLean and the Oklahoma border, the town of Shamrock marks the junction of Route 66 and US-83, our "Road to Nowhere" route along the 100th Meridian. Shamrock is covered on page 202.

ACROSS OKLAHOMA

Apart from occasional college football teams, Oklahoma doesn't often get to crow about being the best in the country, but as far as Route 66 is concerned, the state is definitely number one. Containing more miles of the old highway than any other state, and in far better condition, this is definitely Mecca for old roads fans.

Underneath the promotional hoopla that Route 66 generates everywhere it ever went, all over Oklahoma, signs declare that barely a century ago this was Indian Territory, last refuge of Kiowa, Apache, Comanche, and other tribes before the U.S. government took even this land away from them during "land rushes" in the 1890s. A few years later oil was discovered and the state started on one of a series of boom-and-

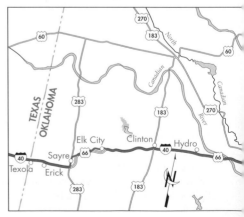

bust cycles. The Dust Bowl exodus of the 1930s was the greatest downturn, as thousands of Oklahoman families headed west on Route 66. Many of the towns along the road take bittersweet pride in *The Grapes of Wrath* connections.

Texola and Erick

The first town over the Texas border, Texola has dried up and all but blown away since it was bypassed by I-40, but a few remnants still stand, awaiting nostalgic photographers. The only signs of life hereabouts are the shouts and swears emanating from the combination pool hall and beer bar housed in the large metal shed on the south side of the old highway, where you're welcome to watch the most passionate domino games this side of Yuma, Arizona.

East from this borderline ghost town, a mile south of the I-40 freeway, a nice stretch of late-model Route 66 continues as a four-lane divided highway, passing through the great little town of Erick (pop. 1,083), six miles east of Texola. Route 66 through town has been renamed Roger Miller Boulevard in memory of the late favorite son. Erick has another unique draw, the **100th Meridian Museum** (Friday and Saturday 9 AM-4 PM, except during severe weather; donations), on Route 66 at the only stoplight in town. Displays inside trace life on what used to be considered the edge of the habitable world—everything west of the 100th Meridian was officially thought to be the "Great American Desert"—and also explain that Erick used to be on the Texas border, until the border was realigned.

The museum, and the other three buildings at the crossroads, all have chamfered corners and form an oblong X-shaped intersection rather than the usual 90-degree square. A mile north of Route 66, next to

In Jack D. Rittenhouse's original *Guide Book to Highway 66;* published in 1946 and now widely available in reprinted versions, he described Erick as "the first town you encounter, going west, which has any of the true 'western' look, with its wide, sun-baked street, frequent horsemen, occasional sidewalk awnings, and similar touches."

Erick was the hometown of singer and songwriter **Roger Miller,** the original "King of the Road."

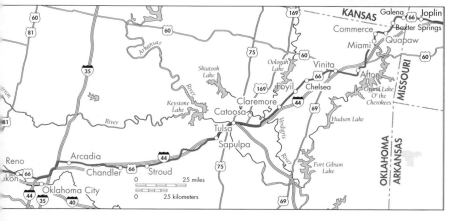

BOOKS ON ROUTE 66

Considering the old road's great fame, it's hardly surprising that over a dozen different books in print deal with the Route 66 experience. Some are travel guides, some folk histories, others nostalgic rambles down what was and what's left along the Mother Road. Photographic essays document the rapidly disappearing architecture and signage, and at least one cookbook catalogs recipes of dishes served in cafes along the route. The following is a sampling of favorite titles, most of which can be found in stores along the route if not in your local bookstore.

The Grapes of Wrath, John Steinbeck (Viking, 1937). The first and foremost Route 66-related story, this compelling tale traces the traumatic travels of the Joad family from Dust Bowl Oklahoma to the illusive Promised Land of California. Brutally vivid, *The Grapes of Wrath* was an instant bestseller at the tail end of the Depression and was the source of Route 66's appellation, "The Mother Road."

A Guide Book to Highway 66, Jack Rittenhouse (University of New Mexico, 1989). A facsimile reprinting of the self-published 1946 book that the late author sold door-to-door at truck stops, motor courts, and cafes along the route.

Route 66: The Illustrated Guidebook to the Mother Road, Bob Moore and Patrick Grauwels (RoadBook International). The most detailed driver's guide to old Route 66, packed with mile-by-mile instructions and information as well as photographs and illustrations. Spiral bound for on-the-road ease of use.

Route 66: The Mother Road, Michael Wallis (St. Martin's Press, 1987). A richly illustrated and thoroughly researched guide to the old road. This is more armchair companion than practical aid, but the book captures the spirit of Route 66, and the writer has been a key promotional force behind its preservation and rediscovery.

Route 66 Traveler's Guide, Tom Snyder (St. Martin's Press, 1990). State-by-state description of Route 66, with an emphasis on the stories behind the sights you see. Illustrated with 1930s-era auto club maps adapted to show the path of modern freeways but still evoking the spirit of the old road.

Searching for 66, Tom Teague (Samizdat House, 1996). More personal than other titles on Route 66, this book of vignettes describes the author's interactions with the many people along Route 66 who have made it what it is. As a bonus, the book is illustrated with the fine pen-and-ink drawings of Route 66 artist Bob Waldmire, some of which are reproduced in this book as well.

the Texaco station along the I-40 frontage at exit 7, make time and save room in your stomach for a stop at **Cal's Diner**, a timeworn place with fresh-baked bread, short-order home-style food, and a generous dose of Midwest hospitality from the hosts, former navy cook Cal Rogers and his family, who've run it for 50-plus years. The diner is open all day, every day, 6 AM-9 PM, till 10 PM in summer. As the sign says, You'll Be Glad You Did.

Sayre

If you want a quick flashback to the dark days of Steinbeck's *The Grapes of Wrath*, turn north off the I-40 freeway into sleepy Sayre (pop. 2,881). The landmark Beckham County Courthouse, which looms over the east end of Main Street, was prominently featured in the movie version as Henry Fonda and the rest of the Joads rattled down Route 66 toward California. While on Main Street, stop in for a milk shake at the friendly fountain in the **Owl Drug Store** on the corner of 4th Street. Take a look in the ever-expanding **Shortgrass Country Museum** (hours vary; free), housed in the old Rock Island Line railroad depot at 106 E. Poplar Street, with changing displays documenting regional history from Cheyenne times to the arrival of homesteading settlers during the great Land Rush of 1892. East of the museum stands a giant grain elevator that has rusted into a gorgeous orange glow.

Elk City

The first—or last, depending on your direction—sizeable town east of the Texas border, Elk City (pop. 10,450) was a popular stopover on Route 66, as evidenced by the many old motels along the various alignments of the old highway through town. Unfortunately, the mom-and-pop operations along 3rd Street (Business I-40) and brick-paved Broadway have closed and been replaced by national chains, all of which are here.

Long before Elk City had its Route 66 heyday, it was a wild frontier town along the cattle trails from Texas to Dodge City, Kansas. The area's cowboy and pioneer history is recounted in the **Old Town Museum** (Mon.-Sat. 9 AM-5 PM, Sunday 2-5 PM; $5; 580/225-2207), on the far west side of town, where there's a re-created Wild West town complete with doctor's office, schoolhouse, "Indian TeePee," and rodeo museum. A new addition to Old Town Elk City is the official "National Route 66 Museum," which has an old pickup truck decorated to look like the one from *Grapes of Wrath*, and lots of other old road-related memorabilia.

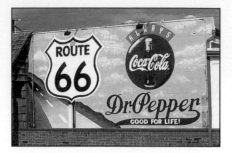

During the 1940s oil was discovered underground, and the town experienced another short boom; this aspect of Elk City's past is the focus of the small **Anadarko Basin Museum**, housed in the lobby of the old Casa Grande Hotel at 107 E. 3rd Street. Most impressive is towering Rig 114, a record-breaking, 180-foot-tall drilling rig installed in the park next to the museum in 1990.

Clinton

Named for Judge Clinton Irwin and not for President Bill, Clinton (pop. 9,268) started life as a trading post for local Cheyenne Arapahoe people, and is now in the spotlight as home of the official **Oklahoma Route 66 Museum**, near the west end of town at 2229 Gary Boulevard (Mon.-Sat. 9 AM-5 PM, Sunday 1-5 PM; $3; 580/323-RT66 or 580/323-7866). Unlike many other "museums" along the route, this one is a true showcase and not just another souvenir stand. Funded by a variety of state and local sources, the museum reopened in late 1995 after undergoing a massive, million-dollar expansion and improvement, and is one of the better museums of the old road along the old road. Collectors from all over the country, including Clinton's own Gladys Cuthbert, whose husband Jack Cuthbert was the primary promoter of Route 66 throughout its glory years, donated signs, artifacts, and memorabilia which have been organized into a comprehensive exhibition of Mother Road history and culture not to be missed by any Route 66 aficionado. It's not as much fun as it should be, and the audio tour has a very self-important narration, but in terms of sketching the outlines of the Route 66 story, it's an excellent introduction. (There's a good gift shop, too.)

Clinton also has the very nice McLain Rogers public park, with a swimming pool and water slides, at the center of town along 10th Street (old Route 66), next to the Route 66 Miniature Golf Course.

For food, the **Tradewinds** restaurant across from the Route 66 museum is reliable and good value, but the best place to eat in Clinton is **Pop Hick's Restaurant**, on the east side of town at 223 Gary Boulevard, a traditional Route 66 rest stop that's been open 24 hours a day since 1936, featuring good food and low prices. West of town along the I-40 frontage, just north of exit 62, **Jiggs Smoke House** is a tiny cabin selling BBQ sandwiches but specializing in travel-friendly beef jerky.

Elvis himself stayed four times at the **Tradewinds Best Western**, across from the Route 66 museum at 2128 Gary Boulevard (580/323-2610), where doubles go for around $50 a night. Elvis's room has been "preserved" as a mini-shrine, and you can stay in it and experience a time warp back to the mid-1960s. If the Tradewinds is full, there are at least 10 other motels from which to choose.

For more on Clinton's Route 66 connections, contact the helpful **visitor center**, 400 Gary Boulevard (580/323-2222 or 800/759-1397).

Hydro: Lucille's

There's no clearer contrast between the charms of the old road and the anonymity of the interstate than tiny Hydro, midway between Clinton and Oklahoma City on

the west bank of the Canadian River. A wonderful length of old Route 66 runs along the
north side of I-40 exit 89, right past the ancient service station and souvenir stand operated by Lucille Hammons since 1941. Though
it's just 50 yards from the fast-lane of the freeway, visiting Lucille's place to buy a soda or
a postcard and have a quick hello with the
energetic proprietor is a Route 66 rite of passage, and offers a rare chance to sit and talk

with someone who has lived the history of the road. Unfortunately, environmental
restrictions mean Lucille can no longer sell you a tank of gas, but otherwise her little outpost is unchanged since the glory days of the road. (She may insist you buy a
copy of her book, *Mother of the Mother Road*, though. . . .)

West of Lucille's, a surviving, six-mile stretch of old Route 66 follows the lay of the
land up and down, offering a better sense of the landscape than does the new road,
completed in 1966, which has cut and filled and bridged the route to death. East of
Lucille's, the old road turns north briefly through the somnolent center of Hydro.

El Reno and Yukon

For westbound travelers, El
Reno marks the first
appearance of one of the
longest-running ad
campaigns along Route 66:
dozens of billboards
advertising "Tucumcari
Tonight," 350 miles from its
New Mexican subject.

Established as Fort El Reno in 1874, as part of U.S. Army efforts
to subdue the Cheyenne, El Reno (pop. 15,414) later saw duty
as a P.O.W. camp during WW II; more recently it earned a measure of fame as the site of a motel seen in the off-beat road
movie *Rain Man*. In the movie, the motel was in Amarillo, but
the "real" one, called the Big Eight, still sits along old Route 66
at the east edge of town; just look for the sign, a leftover from the movie, which
says "Amarillo's Finest" and continues to baffle passersby. For hungry road-trippers, another place not to pass by is **Robert's Grill**, 101 W. Wade Street, open daily
6 AM-9 PM, Sunday 11 AM-6 PM, and famed since 1926 for its Fried Onion Burger.
Every Memorial Day, Robert's cooks up the "World's Largest Hamburger," a 500-
pound behemoth.

East of El Reno, all the way into Oklahoma City (OKC), old Route 66 runs along
the north side of the I-40 freeway; in places it's a three-lane road, with a dangerous
passing lane in the center. The last real town beyond the OKC suburbs is Yukon,
hometown of country crooner Garth Brooks and of a giant "Yukon's Best Flour"
grain mill, whose huge sign lights up the night sky and draws shutterbugs off the
highway. Also worth a stop in Yukon are the Chisholm Trail mural, the town's huge
roller rink, and **Johnnie's Cafe**, all on old Route 66 along Yukon's short Main Street.

Oklahoma City

It's hard to go about your nostalgic Route 66 tour in the aftermath of the 1995
bombing of the federal building, but Oklahoma City was one of the primary stops
along the Mother Road. In the Bobby Troup song, it was the only place along the
route singled out for praise, no doubt more for the easy rhyme ("Oklahoma City is
mighty pretty") than for its special charms. The city was the biggest boomtown of
the 1889 Land Rush, when Oklahoma was opened for white settlement after being

set aside "for eternity" as Indian Territory. Between noon and sundown on April 22, over 10,000 people flocked here to claim the new lands—many of them having illegally camped out beforehand, earning the nickname "Sooner," which is still applied to the state's college football team. A second boom took place during the Depression years, when oil was struck; there are still producing wells in the center of the city, including some on the grounds of the state capitol, which is one of the few in the country without a dome, and the only one right on Route 66.

Across from the capitol along a stretch of old Route 66 at 2100 Lincoln Boulevard, the **Oklahoma State Museum of History** (Mon.-Sat. 8 AM-5 PM; free) has exhibits tracing the state's history, with special collections on the Native American presence, on pioneers, and on the oil industry. There's also a sizeable oral history of the Mother Road.

Oklahoma City boasts a number of non-Route 66 related attractions, best of which is the **National Cowboy Hall of Fame** (daily 9 AM-5 PM; $6), a huge complex at 1700 N.E. 63rd Street, a half-mile west of I-44 off I-35. Spacious modern galleries, and a comprehensive display of everything from Charley Russell paintings to John Wayne's kachina dolls, make this one of the nation's top Western art collections—after the Gilcrease in Tulsa (see page 834), the Buffalo Bill Center in Cody (see pages 551-552), and the Amon Carter Museum in Fort Worth (see page 765).

On the western outskirts of Oklahoma City, commonly abbreviated "OKC," Bethany is the home of the **Route 66 Trading Post,** 6229 39th Expressway, which sells a great selection of memorabilia and just about every Route 66 guide ever published.

Following old Route 66 across Oklahoma City can be confusing, but if you're heading west to east, keep an eye peeled for the Route 66 Bowl on 39th Street; a bottle-shaped building on Classen Boulevard; and a retro McDonald's featuring a "Speedie" sign and carhop service, on the corner of 23rd Street and Pennsylvania Avenue.

Ten miles north of the Cowboy Hall of Fame, on the campus of Oklahoma Christian University at 2501 E. Memorial Road, at the far edge of OKC's nearly endless sprawl, **Enterprise Square** (Tues.-Sat. 9 AM-4 PM, Sunday 1-4 PM; $5) is a very odd place, a high-tech Horatio Alger story designed to instruct busloads of schoolkids about how America was built by hard work and free enterprise. Oklahoma City is also the home of the **National Softball Hall of Fame** (Mon.-Fri. 9 AM-4:30 PM; $1, teams in uniform free), off I-35 at 2801 N.E. 50th Street, which includes a quirky museum and souvenir shop; it also hosts the national championships on a complex of diamonds.

Oklahoma City Practicalities

Oklahoma City has more BBQ stands and steak houses than just about anywhere else in the country, and the overall range of restaurants is very good. One old Route 66 landmark, the Kentucky Club speakeasy and roadhouse once frequented by Pretty Boy Floyd, still survives in a new guise, gussied up as the **Oklahoma County Line**, an upscale BBQ restaurant on the northeast edge of town, near the Cowboy Hall of Fame at 1226 N.E. 63rd Street. For great BBQ right on old Route 66, go to **Jack's**, a hole-in-the-wall joint at 4418 N.W. 39th Street Expressway. Other places to check out are the friendly and cholesterol-conscious **Classen Grill**, off old Route 66, next to the I-44 freeway at 5124 Classen Boulevard; and popular **Ann's Chicken Fry House**, near Jack's BBQ along the 39th Street Expressway (old Route 66) west of downtown—look for the police cars in the parking lot. For a quiet respite from the highway life, stop by **Sleepy Hollow**, 1101 N.E. 50th Street near the Softball Hall of Fame, for a family-style dinner of steaks or fried chicken accompanied by fresh veggies and great desserts.

The usual interstate chain motels include a **Super 8**, 1117 N.E. 17th Street (405/232-0404) across from the capitol; and a handy **Comfort Inn**, 4445 N. Lincoln Boulevard (405/528-2741 or 800/221-2222), in a modern building on old Route 66 north of downtown.

For more complete information on visiting Oklahoma City, contact the **visitor center**, 123 Park Avenue (405/297-8912 or 800/225-5652).

The Class AAA **Oklahoma Redhawks** (405/218-1000) play at brand-new Southwestern Bell Park, near the junction of I-35 and I-40. Games are broadcast on **WKY 930 AM.**

Old Route 66: Arcadia, Chandler, and Stroud

Between OKC and Tulsa, the I-44 Turnpike carries 99% of the traffic, but the old road is still here, paralleling the freeway all the way but hard to reach because there are so few access points —exits are spaced 15 to 30 miles apart. Lots of towns along here vanished after being bypassed, but the fortunate few that were given freeway exits have stayed alive and now thrive on nostalgic Route 66 trade.

North of OKC, Route 66 continued through the town of **Edmond,** the place where aviator Wiley Post is buried (he was the pilot killed in the same crash as Will Rogers); the town is also notorious for the fact that a disgruntled postal employee killed 14 of his co-workers here in 1986.

Northeast of Oklahoma City, one of the state's best surviving stretches of Route 66, known locally as the "Free Road," runs for over 30 miles along the north side of the turnpike, accessible at the east end from I-35 at exit 141. East of the interstate, the first stop is the old highway town of Arcadia (pop. 320), which holds a recently restored red round barn built in 1898. The ground floor of the much-loved landmark is now a mini-museum and gift shop selling some highly collectible original Route 66 memorabilia.

The old road runs east from Arcadia along the north side of I-44, crossing under the freeway, but with no legal access to it, west of Chandler. Four miles west of Chandler stands a metal barn emblazoned with a photogenic "Meramec Caverns— Stanton MO" sign, and Chandler (pop. 2,596) itself is one of the most idyllic old Route 66 towns in Oklahoma. The town stands out for a number of good reasons, not least of which is the restored filling station at the center of town. For a place to stay, the classic **Lincoln Motel**, 740 E. 1st Street (405/258-0200), along old Route 66 at the east edge of town is still as neat and tidy as it was the day it opened in 1939—two dozen cabins, each with an American flag and a pair of yellow lawn chairs for watching the world whizz by. For food, choose from a handful of good cafes in town, like **Martha's.**

Continuing east, old-roads fanatics will probably want to follow the winding alignment of Route 66, which continues along the south side of the turnpike for over 40 miles. On the west side of Stroud (pop. 2,666), at the next I-44 exit, check out the **Rock Cafe**, a Route 66 relic built in 1939 out of paving stones from the original highway, but (at time of writing) no longer churning out its better-than-average roadside fare.

East of Stroud, old Route 66 runs past the tidy little town of **Depew** before crossing I-44 again at exit 196. From here east, it zigzags back and forth along the freeway for the next 25 miles, through Sapulpa and into Tulsa.

Sapulpa

Best known as the home of Frankhoma Pottery (tours weekdays 9:30 AM-2 PM; free; 918/224-5511), Sapulpa (like everywhere else in Oklahoma) started as an Indian trading post back in 1850 and is now a light industrial center with a significant amount of Route 66 history. Along with a Route 66 roller skating rink and a Meramec Caverns sign, Sapulpa draws Route 66 aficionados because of **Norma's Diamond Cafe**, on Route 66 at 408 N. Mission Street, next to a glass factory at the center of town. Two other good stops are nearby: the lively **Hickory House BBQ**, 626 N. Mission Street, where an all-you-can-eat barbecue buffet costs under $10, open every day but Sunday, and **Marge's**, 826 N. 9th Street, which has some of the state's best cherry cream pie, at $2 a slice.

Between Sapulpa and Tulsa, old Route 66 followed Southwest Boulevard, which runs along the south side of the I-44 turnpike.

Tulsa is also the home of **Oral Roberts University,** marked by a futuristic, 15-story tower and an 80-foot-high pair of praying hands along Lewis Avenue, six miles south of downtown.

Tulsa was the home of **Cyrus Avery,** the gas-station owner whose grassroots organizing and lobbying efforts eventually resulted in Route 66 acquiring its official designation during the 1920s.

The Texas League **Tulsa Drillers** (918/744-5998), a Texas Rangers farm club, play at Drillers Stadium at 15th Street and Yale Avenue, three miles north of I-44. Games are broadcast on **KQLL 1430 AM.**

One of the country's grand old country-western radio stations, **KVOO 1170 AM,** "The Voice of Oklahoma," can be heard for miles around Tulsa.

Tulsa

Though it has some fine art deco buildings built during the boom years of the Oklahoma oil industry, and boasts the Thomas Gilcrease Institute, one of the country's top art museums, Tulsa is not many people's idea of a good time. Route 66 used to wind into town along Southwest Boulevard, then cut across the city along 11th Street, but now high-speed freeways scythe through the city and very little remains of the old roadside landscape. As Michael Wallis writes in his Route 66 bible, *The Mother Road,* Tulsa has "turned its back on the old road and the businesses that made a living from the highway traffic . . . and sold out for the fast lanes of the Interstate."

That said, and if your time is limited, spend it at the **Thomas Gilcrease Institute** (Mon.-Fri. 9 AM-5 PM, Sunday 1-5 PM; donations), on the northwest edge of Tulsa. Bought with the fortune Gilcrease made when oil was discovered on his land, the collection includes some of the most important works of Western American art and sculpture, with major works by Thomas Moran, George Catlin, and others, plus Native American artifacts and early maps that put the frontier region into its historical contexts. Also on the grounds is Gilcrease's old house, now home to the Tulsa Historical Society and displaying photographs and objects related to the evolution of the city.

For dinner or a drink, the liveliest part of Tulsa is the Brookside district, south of downtown around 34th Street and Peoria Avenue, where there's a handful of trendy cafes, nightclubs, and restaurants. For a taste of old Route 66, stop at the retro **Metro Diner**, 3001 E. 11th Street, which isn't a *real* diner but still serves decent diner food.

The usual chain hotels and motels line all the freeways, and there's a reasonably inexpensive **Howard Johnson's** downtown at 17 W. 7th Street (918/585-5898), with doubles from under $40 a night.

For more complete information, contact the Tulsa **visitor center,** 616 S. Boston Street (918/585-1201).

Catoosa: The Blue Whale
One of Tulsa's premier Route 66 attractions
was the giant Blue Whale, in the suburb of
Catoosa, northeast of Tulsa along the stretch
of the old road that runs from I-44 exit 240.

In its heyday, traveling families would stop
here to play in the pool, slide down the
slides, and have a picnic on the grass, but
the park closed down long ago and was left
to crumble. As with so many other long-suffering Route 66 landmarks, the Blue Whale
now benefits from fund-raising efforts toward restoration, but at time of writing
was not yet open again. Here's to hoping.

Catoosa, surprisingly, is also a major port, linked, by way of impressively engi-
neered improvements to the Arkansas River system, to the Gulf of Mexico.

Claremore
Twenty miles northeast of Tulsa, Claremore (pop. 13,300) is a bigger-than-average
Route 66 town, one that will be forever connected with its favorite son, Will
Rogers. Rogers was born nearby in a rough log cabin "half-way between Claremore
and Oologah before there was a town at either place," on November 4, 1879. He
rose from a vaudeville career as a side-show rope-tricks artist to become one of the
most popular figures in America, thanks to his folksy humor.

Before he could retire back home to Claremore, Rogers was killed in a plane
crash in 1935; his land was later turned into the **Will Rogers Memorial** (daily 8
AM-5 PM; donations), a mile west of downtown Claremore on a hill overlooking the
town. A statue of Rogers greets visitors at the front door, and
his tomb is here, along with a small archive and museum that
recounts his life story, showing off his collections of saddles,
lariats, and other cowboy gear.

Another popular Claremore stop is the **J.M. Davis Arms and
Historical Museum**, right off Route 66 at 333 N Lynn Riggs Boulevard (Mon.-Sat. 8:30 AM-5 PM; donations). Besides one of the
largest and most comprehensive gun collections anywhere in the
world (over 20,000!), the museum has antique musical instruments and hundreds of posters dating back to World War I.

The Route 66 roadside in Claremore is lined by some fine old
neon signs, like the buckin' bronco on the **Round-Up Motel**,   *the young Will Rogers*
860 S. Route 66 (918/341-5322). For great food, and out-of-
this-world pies, stop by the **Hammett House**, 1616 W. Will Rogers (918/341-7333).

Foyil
Between Claremore and Vinita, old Route 66 survives in regular use, alternating between two-lane and divided four-lane highway. The most interesting wide spot
along this stretch of hallowed road is Foyil, where in the 1940s and 1950s folk
artist Ed Galloway sculpted an outdoor garden of giant totem poles—the tallest is
over 90 feet—and other Native American-inspired objects out of concrete. After

Foyil was the hometown of **Andy Payne,** the Cherokee youth who in 1928 won the "Bunion Derby," a coast-to-coast foot race that followed Route 66 from Los Angeles to Chicago, then headed east to New York City—equivalent to running a marathon and a half every day for the 86 days it took him to finish.

fading and weathering for many years, the poles, four miles east of town via Hwy-28, were restored in 1993-94, and now are a fascinating place to stop for a picnic or to simply admire the effort that went into these "Watts Towers of the Plains."

Vinita and Afton

Old Route 66 crosses the Interstate again at Vinita, where the region's Native American heritage is brought into focus at the **Eastern Trails Museum** (Mon.-Sat. 1-4 PM; free), next to the public library at 215 W. Illinois Street. The exhibits center on the Cherokee "Trail of Tears," which brought the tribe here after a forced march from North Carolina in the 1830s, but the museum also covers the general history of the surrounding area.

The "Largest McDonald's in the Free World," as it used to be called, bridges the I-44 freeway at Vinita. It doesn't serve all that much food, but counting cubic feet it's one of the biggest outside Bejing.

Vinita is home to the Will Rogers Memorial Rodeo, held here each August since 1935, the year he died; Rogers attended secondary school in Vinita after growing up near Claremore.

Vinita also has a great old Route 66 restaurant, **Clanton's Cafe,** right at the center of town at 319 E. Illinois Street. Another old road landmark, the friendly and popular **Route 66 Cafe,** is 15 miles up the road in Afton, at 5 NE 1st Avenue.

Miami, Commerce, and Quapaw

In the far northeastern corner of Oklahoma, a fine stretch of old Route 66 leaves I-44 exit 313 from the town of Miami, zigzagging to the Kansas border. Passing through a former mining region, this stretch of old Route 66 is fascinating but more than a little disturbing. Because of the obvious poverty of this leftover region; the corner of Kansas it crosses is also not among the highlights of a Route 66 tour.

Between Afton and Miami, some of the oldest paved stretches of Route 66 were constructed only one lane wide, because in 1926 the state did not have enough money to build a full-width version. Not surprisingly, these lengths of the road became known as the "Sidewalk Highway," and can still be driven. Look for the "66" shields painted on the pavement.

However, the town of Miami holds the magnificent Spanish revival-style Coleman Theater, built in 1929 and luxuriating in the riches that came out of the surrounding lead and zinc mines. The mines shut long ago, leaving huge piles of tailings to mar the roadside. The next town along, Commerce (pop. 2,426), was another old mining town, noteworthy as the boyhood home of the late great Yankee player Mickey Mantle, in whose honor the old Route 66 alignment down Main Street has been renamed.

Quapaw, the first or last Oklahoma town you visit, depending upon your direction, is another fading old mining town, worth a look for the many murals painted on the walls of downtown businesses. The Kansas border is another three miles farther along.

ACROSS KANSAS

The shortest but perhaps best-signed stretch of Route 66's eight-state run is its 14-mile slice across the southeast corner of Kansas. Be careful not to blink your eyes, or you'll be saying, as Dorothy did in *The Wizard of Oz*: "I don't think we're in Kansas anymore."

If you're coming from Oklahoma, **Baxter Springs** is the first town you reach. **Murphey's Restaurant**, on the corner of 11th Street, is open daily 6 AM-2 PM, serving great pies. In a previous incarnation, the same building housed a bank robbed by Jesse James in 1876. East of Baxter Springs are a couple of old rainbow-arched concrete bridges and a few other Route 66 relics. In **Riverton**, the next town along, the **Old Riverton Store**, aka "Eisler Bros.," is headquarters of the small but active Kansas Route 66 Association (316/848-3330) and an essential stop for fans of the old road—and of the old-fashioned milk shakes whipped up there. Also popular: the **Spring River Inn**, a restaurant open since 1905, on old Route 66 opposite an ugly brick power plant.

During the Civil War, Baxter Springs saw one of the worst massacres in the country's history, when 87 Union soldiers, held prisoner by William Quantrill's rebel Confederate forces, were killed by gunshots to the back of the head. A monument to the soldiers stands in **Baxter Springs National Cemetery,** the second oldest military cemetery in the nation, off US-166 two miles west of town.

The last town in Kansas is **Galena**, a rough-looking place where Main Street gives off an air of less-than-benign neglect. The funky **Galena Mining and Historical Museum,** just off the main drag and marked by a big "Old 66" sign at 319 W. 7th Street, is stuffed with old newspaper clippings and other items that give a glimpse of town life during its 1920s-era mining heyday, and various rusting tools and machines testify to the work that once went on here.

ACROSS MISSOURI

The Ozark Highlands of southern Missouri, which Route 66 crosses in its 300-odd-mile journey between Illinois and Kansas, are about the only significant hills the road crosses east of Arizona. This plateau region, though not by any means alpine or breathtaking, is visually dynamic in a way the broad flatlands of Illinois and the Great Plains rarely are. Though the I-44 freeway has replaced the old road all the way across the state, many signs of the old highway line the surviving stretches of the original route, and every exit drops you within a moment's drive of the Mother Road. Missouri also holds one of the greatest of the old Route 66 tourist attractions—Meramec Caverns, an extensive set of limestone caves offering the most over-the-top underground tour you can take.

On the Kansas/Missouri border, tune to **KRPS 89.9 FM** for classical music and NPR news.

Joplin

If you travel the old Route 66 alignment across Kansas, you'll also pass through Joplin (pop. 40,961), a Missouri border town that's the industrial center of the tri-state region. Formerly a lead- and zinc-mining town, Joplin is not an especially pretty place, better known for its high-quality limestone than for its cultural offerings. Though many of its businesses have fled to the fringes, Joplin's downtown area does hold one unlikely attraction, a vibrant mural by artist Thomas Hart Benton depicting life in Joplin at the turn of the century. The mural, which turned out to be the artist's final complete work, is in the lobby of the banal 1960s-era Municipal Building, east of Main Street at 303 E. 3rd Street.

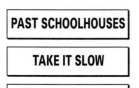

PAST SCHOOLHOUSES

TAKE IT SLOW

LET THE LITTLE

SHAVERS GROW

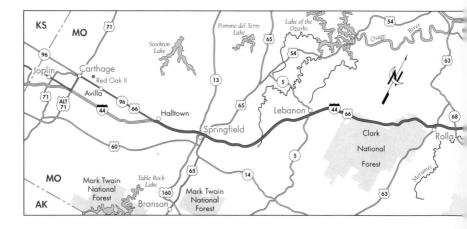

Carthage

Six miles north of the I-44 freeway, right on old Route 66, Carthage (pop. 10,747) is a perfect little town, looking for all the world like the model for the idyllic though fictional town of Hill Valley from the *Back to the Future* movies. The center of Carthage is dominated by the outrageously ornate limestone Jasper County Courthouse, which features a local history mural and an open-cage elevator in the lobby. The rest of the town is fairly franchise-free, away from the interstate at least, and the residential areas hold well-maintained Victorian houses. The downtown area also holds at least one good cafe, **Our Place** on Main Street, and within a short walk is an elegant B&B, the **Leggett House**, 1106 Grand Avenue (417/358-0683).

Carthage also holds two old Route 66 landmarks. On the west side of downtown, look for the glowing red-and-green neon sign of the **Boots Motel**, still open for business at 107 S. Garrison Street (417/358-9453); a mile or so west on Old Route 66, just south of the US-71 highway, enjoy Hollywood blockbusters in the comfort of your car at the reopened **66 Drive-In.**

Carthage was the boyhood home of naturalist Marlin Perkins, host of Mutual of Omaha's *Wild Kingdom* TV show. A life-sized statue of him stands in Central Park, three blocks southwest of the courthouse square. Carthage was also the girlhood home of Wild West outlaw **Belle Starr.**

If you have a soft spot for hyperbolic sentimentality, one not-to-be-missed monument is the **Precious Moments Chapel** (daily 9 AM-7 PM in summer, 10 AM-7 PM rest of the year; $1), featuring the wide-eyed characters from the greeting card series. The chapel is well signed, west of US-71 on the southwest edge of Carthage.

Red Oak II

On the northeast edge of Carthage, off Hwy-96 three miles from the town center, an entire pioneer Missouri town has been moved from its original site 25 miles away and reassembled as Red Oak II (daily 10 AM-6 PM, closed January and February; free; 417/358-9018). Heralded by roadside Burma-Shave signs, the buildings here have been preserved as a credible replica of a crossroads town, circa 1929, and include an antique Phillips 66 gas station, a fully functioning general store, a blacksmith's shop incongruously filled with penny arcade games, and a small cafe. A small museum tells the life story of Belle Starr, the Carthage woman who became a Confederate spy and Wild West gunslinger.

Though it's off the main road, Red Oak isn't hard to find: look for the propane gas tank along Hwy-96 (old Route 66), and drive north for a mile from there.

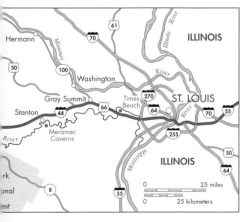

Springfield

The largest city in southern Missouri, Springfield (pop. 140,000) doesn't feel nearly as big as it is, though it does sprawl for many miles in all directions. It was here in 1926 that plans for Route 66 were made, and the city preserves much of the old highway frontage along St. Louis Street east of downtown, as well as the grandly named "Chestnut Expressway" west of downtown. The 20-mph speed limit on downtown streets—and tons of free parking—enable Route 66 pilgrims to pay homage to the town's

A great stretch of old Route 66, renumbered Hwy-96, runs for 50 miles along the north side of I-44 between Carthage and Springfield, passing rolling pastures and little towns like Avilla and Halltown, with antique shops and abandoned cafes lining the old highway frontage.

Arabesque landmark Shrine Theater, 601 E. 1st Street.

Springfield is also celebrated as the place where "Wild" Bill Hickok killed fellow gambler Dave Tutt, apparently because Tutt wore the watch he'd won from Hickok playing cards. A plaque in the central square tells one of many variations on the tale.

One place you have to see to believe—though the bass angler in your family will already know about it, for sure—is "The World's Greatest Sporting Goods Store," **BASS Pro Shops Outdoor World**, 1935 S. Campbell Street. Along with acres of floor space, the store has a 140,000-gallon fish tank, a 40-foot waterfall, and even its own McDonald's.

Springfield has a couple of the earliest and most stylish models of the Steak and Shake burger chain, and all the franchise restaurants and motels you could want, lined up around the I-44 exits.

For more detailed information, contact the **visitor center**, 3315 E. Battlefield Road (417/881-5300 or 800/678-8767).

Detour: Branson

A Middle-American Las Vegas with all the tackiness and none of the style, Branson is a century-old Ozark resort that hit the big time in the 1980s through clever promotion and cunning repackaging of country-and-western music and god-fearing recreation. There are over 30 major performance venues in Branson, and looking down the list of people who make a living playing here all summer—the Osmond Brothers, Tony Orlando, Andy Williams, and Jim "I Don't Like Spiders and Snakes" Stafford—you'd think that anyone who had a hit record or a TV show, or who can sing in a twang and impersonate a country-western star, can have their own showcase theater. Most offer two shows a day plus optional breakfast shows at 10 AM—imagine Hank Williams doing one of those—for the hordes of bus tours transported here every summer.

However cruel this assessment sounds, once you visit you'll see it is, if anything, not biting enough. Branson simply embodies everything that's annoying and disappointing about mass-merchandising of "culture"—a Disney version of American music without the slightest sense of humor or moment of sincere feeling.

But go see it and judge for yourself. Branson is south of Springfield on US-65. The Ozark Mountain area around Branson is still a lovely place to explore. For visitor information, contact the Branson **visitor center** (417/334-4136).

The best thing about Branson is **Silver Dollar City** (daily 9 AM- 6 PM, May-Nov. only; $29; 417/338-2611), nine miles west of Branson via Hwy-76, a turn-of-the-century theme park devoted to Ozark arts, crafts, and music—and roller coasters.

Lebanon and Rolla

Between Springfield and St. Louis, the I-44 freeway has been built right on top of the old Route 66 corridor, and dozens of ruins of old motels, motor courts, gas stations, and other highway-dependent businesses line the remains of the old road, which serves as a frontage road for most of the way. There are plenty of antique shops and cafes to make the journey interesting, but unless you have all the time in the world you may want to stick to the interstate, which offers a scenic drive through the upland forests of the Ozark plateau.

The two biggest towns along the way, Lebanon and Rolla, grew up along the railroad in the late 1850s, and both now boast essential stops for old-roads fans. In Lebanon, the stretch of old Route 66 running along the north side of I-44 holds the marvelous **Munger Moss Motel**, a landmark since 1949, with clean rooms and a swimming pool for a bargain $25 (or less!) a night; call for reservations (417/532-3111).

In Rolla (RAW-la, pop. 14,100), right along old Route 66 on the campus of the University of Missouri at Rolla, there's a working replica of that ancient Druidical observatory, Stonehenge. If you have trouble finding it, this mini-Wonder of the World stands across from the Great Wall of China on Route 66 —a Chinese restaurant. Talk about "small world . . . ."

Along I-44 east of Rolla, the old Route 66 roadside is lined by ramshackle wooden stands which, at the end of summer, sell Concord grapes from local vineyards. The stands are located along the frontage roads (which in many cases are the remnants of the original Route 66), but people park along the freeway and walk to them.

Midway between Lebanon and Rolla, off I-44 exit 169, old Route 66 passed the **"Devil's Elbow,"** a section of the Big Piney River that turns so acutely it caused repeated logjams. Until 1981, Route 66 followed what's now the very hilly Hwy-Z, which preserves the last sections of the old road to be bypassed by I-44. The Devil's Elbow also inspired the title of a great little travel 'zine, *Devil's Elbow: The Magazine for People Who Don't Care Where They're Going*, available at Tower bookstores and for $2 an issue from 2623 E. 2nd Street, Box 12, Bloomington, IN 47401.

Among its many other claims to fame, Meramec Caverns is known as the "Birthplace of the Bumper Sticker."

Meramec Caverns

The best stop along old Route 66's trek across Missouri, and one of the most enjoyable and charming roadside attractions along the entire Mother Road, Meramec Caverns (daily 10 AM-4 PM, longer hours in summer; $9.50; 314/468-CAVE or 314/468-2283) is a set of limestone caves advertised by signs on barns and buildings all along the route, and all over the Midwest. First developed during the Civil War, when the natural saltpeter was mined for use in manufacturing gunpowder, the caves were later popularized as a place for local farmers to get together for dances; the largest room in the caves is still used for Easter Sunrise services and occasional crafts shows and chamber of commerce meetings. Meramec Caverns opened as a tourist attraction in 1935 by Lester Dill, who guided visitors through the elaborate chambers.

Jesse James used these caverns as a hideout, and at least once took advantage of the underground river to escape through the secret "back door." The natural formations are among the most sculptural and delicate of any cave you can visit, and the man-made additions are all low-tech enough to be charming: the hand-operated light show ends with a grand finale of Kate Smith singing "God Bless America" while Old Glory is projected onto a limestone curtain.

Meramec Caverns is near the town of **Stanton**, 55 miles west of St. Louis, three miles south of I-44 exit 230. There's a small cafe and a motel on the grounds, which spread along the banks of the Meramec River. At the I-44 exit, the odd little **Jesse James Museum** (daily 9 AM-5 PM; $3) insists despite all evidence to the contrary that a 100-year-old man who turned up in Stanton in 1948 was in fact Jesse James.

From Gray Summit at I-44 exit 251, Hwy-100 runs northwest along the Missouri River to the historic towns of Washington and Hermann, which are covered in our US-50 trip. See page 708 for more.

The best of many Route 66 survivors along the I-44 frontage roads is the **Red Cedar Inn,** on the south side of the freeway along the banks of the Meramec River, between I-44 exits 253 and 264, a mile east of the town of Pacific. Open since 1934, the Red Cedar Inn (314/257-5681) serves dinner every day but Tuesday.

Times Beach

There's no plaque or notice marking the spot, but the story of Times Beach (pop. 0) deserves mention. Founded in the 1920s as a mountain getaway along the Meramec River, thanks to Route 66 the town grew into a working-class commuter suburb, with no paved streets except for the highway, which passed through the center of town. Times Beach remained a quiet hamlet until 1982, when the federal government discovered that the industrial oil sprayed on streets to keep down dust had in fact been contaminated with toxic dioxins. The toxic waste, combined with a flood that buried the town for over a week, made Times Beach uninhabitable, and in 1984 the government paid $33 million to buy Times Beach and tear it down.

You can see what's left of Times Beach from the freeway—large fences surround the site, which looks like it was hit by a bomb blast—but the closest you can get to it is the old Route 66 bridge over the river, where 24-hour guards will turn you back to the freeway. Work is still in progress to remove the last traces of dioxin, and once that's done there are plans to re-open Times Beach as a state park, with river access.

Route 66 across St. Louis

It can be maddening to follow old Route 66 across St. Louis, but its many great spots—Ted Drewe's Frozen Custard Stand, in particular—make it well worth the effort. From the southwest, the old road followed Watson Road and Chippewa Street, which led into Gravois Avenue for the main ride across town. From downtown, the main route crossed the Mississippi River into Collinsville, Illinois (which is covered below), while another "City 66" route headed north along Florissant Avenue and Riverview Drive, crossing the Mississippi on the historic Chain of Rocks Bridge, which has long been undergoing renovation for use as a bike and hiking trail, just south of the modern I-270 freeway.

St. Louis, the only place where three of our Road Trip routes coincide, marks the junction of old Route 66, cross-country US-50, and the Great River Road along the Mississippi. St. Louis itself is covered as a Survival Guide on pages 258-259.

ACROSS ILLINOIS

Heading diagonally across the state between St. Louis and Chicago, what remains of Route 66 is a surprisingly rural cruise through endless fields of corn. Despite the urban conglomerations at both ends, for most of its nearly 300-mile trek here, Route 66 and its modern usurper, I-55, pass along flat prairies with nary a smokestack or skyscraper as far as the eye can see.

The heavy industrial and poverty-stricken suburbs of East St. Louis aren't terribly rewarding for travelers in search of the Mother Road, but a couple of intriguing attractions—one a prehistoric city, the other a water tower shaped like a catsup bottle—are worth searching out. The only real city along the route and the state capital, Springfield, has preserved its sections of Route 66, as have most of the small towns en route. All of them play up their Route 66 connections, and most boast at least one true old-road landmark.

> Old Route 66 used to cross the Mississippi River on the **Chain of Rocks Bridge,** which still stands, complete with its unique 45-degree bend at the midway point.

Collinsville: Cahokia Mounds State Historic and World Heritage Site

Old Route 66 followed today's I-270 from the north side of St. Louis, but one of southern Illinois's biggest attractions sits directly east of the Gateway Arch, off the I-55/70 freeway at exit 6. Clearly visible to the south side of the interstate, the enigmatic humps of Cahokia Mounds State Historic and World Heritage Site (daily 8 AM-9 PM) are the remains of the largest prehistoric Indian city north of Mexico. Over 100 earthen mounds of various sizes were built here by the indigenous Mississippian culture while Europe was in the Dark Ages; the largest covers 14 acres—more ground than the Great Pyramid of Cheops.

But don't expect the works of the pharaohs: symmetrical, grass-covered hills sitting in flat, lightly wooded bottomlands are what you'll find here. The view of the Gateway Arch in distant St. Louis from the 100-foot-top of Monks' Mound (open daily 9 AM-dusk) lends an odd sense of grandeur to the site, and a sophisticated Interpretive Center (daily 9 AM-5 PM, closed on major U.S. holidays; $2 suggested donation) is a recommended first stop for its exhibits, award-winning multimedia orientation show, and guided and self-guiding tours.

The nearest town to the Cahokia Mounds is **Collinsville**, a pleasant little place that's famous for its 170-foot-high **World's Largest Catsup Bottle**, which rises high above 800 S. Morrison Avenue (Hwy-159), a half-mile south of town, on the grounds of what used to be the Brooks Catsup Company. This decorated water tower was constructed in 1949, and

Cahokia Mounds sit in the middle of the American Bottom, a floodplain whose gunpowder-black alluvial soils have long been considered among the richest and most productive in the world—for example, about 80% of the world's horseradish supply comes from right here, making the region the official "Horseradish Capital of the World." However, Charles Dickens called it an "ill-favored Black Hollow" after enduring its mud, which had "no variety but in depth."

On the stretch of old Route 66 that forms the frontage road at I-55 exit 63, near the town of **Raymond,** a marble statue of the Virgin Mary forms a shrine that has become known as "Our Lady of the Highways."

restored in 1993. Downtown Collinsville also has a well-preserved old **Bull Durham** tobacco sign, painted in 1908 on a wall at 111 E. Main Street but only recently re-exposed, making the town doubly worth the trip for lovers of oddball Americana.

For details on visiting Cahokia Mounds, or the World's Largest Catsup Bottle, contact the downtown Collinsville **visitors bureau,** 216 E. Main Street (618/345-5598).

Mount Olive and Litchfield

East of the Cahokia Mounds and Collinsville, the first really interesting stretch of old Route 66 begins at I-55 exit 41, and runs along the east side of the freeway for over a dozen miles. First stop is the hamlet of Mount Olive (pop. 2,126), which in the early 20th century was a bustling coal-mining center. It's now a sleepy little community where the only signs of its mining past are in the cemetery, along old Route 66 at the northwest edge of town. Near the entrance is a granite shaft rising from an elaborate pedestal, which serves as a memorial to "Mother" Jones, the celebrated union activist who died in 1930 at age 100. Her grave is nearby, marked by a simple headstone.

North of Mount Olive, the old road continues for seven miles to Litchfield, another old mining center that is home to one of the best of the many good Route 66 restaurants, the **Ariston Cafe**, right in the heart of town. The food is a step or two up from the usual roadside fare, and the white linen and refined decor have earned it a spot in the Route 66 Hall of Fame; it's open daily 11 AM-11 PM (217/324-2023). The rest of Litchfield reeks of the old road, with cafes, motor courts, and old billboards aplenty.

Parts of the old road survive between Litchfield and Springfield, but the route is incomplete and confusing; I-55 makes much shorter work of the 25-mile drive.

Springfield

As the Illinois state capital, Springfield (pop. 105,277) embodies the rural small-town character of most the state and feels much farther away from Chicago than the three-plus-hour drive it actually is, traffic willing. Springfield also takes the "Land of Lincoln" state's obsession with Abraham Lincoln to its height, for it was here that Honest Abe worked and lived from 1837 to 1861. He left Springfield after being elected president and was buried here after his assassination at the end of the Civil War.

The only home Lincoln ever owned, now a National Historic Site at 8th and Jackson Streets (daily 8:30 AM-5 PM in winter, 8 AM-8 PM in summer; free), is the focus of Springfield's extensive memorial to him. Other nearby sites include the law offices where he practiced, at 209 S. 6th Street; the train depot at 10th and Monroe Streets where he left Springfield for Washington, D.C.; even the family pew in the First Presbyterian Church, 321 S. 7th Street. Lincoln's Tomb, an impressive monument that includes the remains of his wife and three of his four children, is two miles north in Oak Ridge Cemetery.

Though quite sincere and understated, the Lincoln homage can overwhelm. Even the tried-and-truest Lincoln admirers may pass on the chance to look at his bank account book, on display in the Bank One branch at 6th and Washington Streets. One place that lets you escape from Lincoln Land is the beautiful **Dana-Thomas House** (Wed.-Sun. 9 AM-4 PM; $3; 217/782-6776) at 301 E. Lawrence Avenue, a half-mile south of the state capitol. Designed by Frank Lloyd Wright in 1902, it is the most luxurious, best preserved and most fully furnished of his houses—and is open for hour-long guided tours. Actually a complete remodel of a house that already stood on the site, the Dana-Thomas house was built for socialite Susan Dana, who lived here until the late 1920s, when it was sold to a publishing company and used as offices until the state of Illinois purchased it in 1981.

Another worthwhile place is the **Oliver Parks Telephone Museum**, near the Lincoln Home at 529 S. 7th Street (Mon.-Fri. 8 AM-5 PM; free), where you can see a fascinating collection of antique telephones—over 100 on display—assembled by a longtime Ma Bell employee.

Springfield also has a favorite Route 66 watering hole, the **Cozy Dog Drive-In**, on the old road south of downtown at 2929 S. 6th Street. The birthplace of the corn dog, which here goes by the nicer name "Cozy," this Hall of Fame haunt was founded in 1949 by Ed Waldmire and has been run since his death by son Buzz, the self-declared

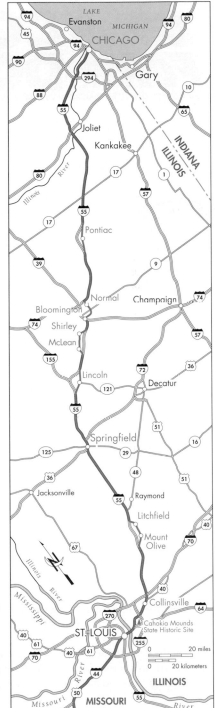

GO FOR COZY DOGS

LOCATED ON HISTORIC ROUTE 66 SINCE 1949, SPRINGFIELD, ILLINOIS

"smarter and better-looking brother" of Route 66 artist Bob Waldmire, who runs the Route 66 center in Hackberry, Arizona (see pages 807-808). Check out the small Route 66 museum; pick up a few postcards or your favorite libertarian, gun-loving, and nose-thumbing bumper stickers; or simply sit and chow down on a Cozy Dog or two—four dogs, a drink, and a big basket of french fries cost around $5.

Frank Lloyd Wright~Architect

Almost all the national chain hotel and motels have operations in Springfield, so you shouldn't have trouble finding a room. For more information, contact the Springfield **visitor center**, 109 N. 7th Street (217/789-2360 or 800/545-7300).

Lincoln

The only town named for Abe in his lifetime, Lincoln (pop. 15,418) took his name before he became a famous figure. As a young lawyer, Abraham Lincoln drew up the legal documents for founding the town but warned developers that he "never knew of anything named Lincoln that amounted to much." At the dedication ceremonies, Lincoln supposedly "baptized" the place by spitting out a mouthful of watermelon seeds—hence the plaster watermelon and historical plaque remembering the great event, next to the train station at Broadway and Chicago Streets in the center of town.

On the south side of Lincoln, along a section of Route 66 that's now the frontage road of I-55 exit 123, the landmark Pig Hip restaurant stood from 1937 until 1991, when it closed down. The Pig Hip, and the motel next door, are vivid ghosts of the good life along the old road.

McLean and Shirley

Westbound drivers will encounter this pair of places in the more sonorous order of Shirley and McLean, but wordplay aside, the stretch of Illinois farmland between Bloomington and Springfield is rich in Route 66-related heritage. In McLean, 47 miles from Springfield and 15 miles from Bloomington, old Route 66 emerges from the shadow of I-55 at the **Dixie Truckers Home**, the oldest and best truck stop in Illinois and home of the Route 66 Hall of Fame. Besides getting a very good burger and fries, you can have a look at the plaques and artifacts that line the corridors and tell the stories of the many people along Route 66 who made it such a special place to get your kicks.

From the Dixie, follow old Route 66 along the west side of I-55 for just over four miles north to another stop, **Funks Grove**, where the friendly Funk family has been tapping trees and making delicious maple sirup (that's how they spell it) since

1891. If you're here in the spring you can watch them tap the trees and hammer in the spouts; each tree can produce four gallons of sap a day, but it takes 50 gallons for each gallon of the final product. Free tastings are available, and a full range of bottles is on sale.

From Funks Grove, the old road continues north, rejoining I-55 after four miles near the town of Shirley, for the run into (or through) Bloomington-Normal.

Bloomington-Normal

Hometown of Adlai Stevenson (and Col. Henry Blake of TV's *M*A*S*H*), Bloomington sits at the junction of five different interstate freeways surrounded by miles of cornfields. Its one claim to fame is that it shares a main street, Franklin Avenue, with neighboring Normal; it's also the only place in the world where that classic bar snack, Beer Nuts, is made. For tours and tastings, stop by the Shirk Products factory at 103 N. Robinson Street (309/827-8580).

For more hearty sustenance you can visit the **Steak and Shake** at 1219 Main Street, the first of many for this Midwest-based chain of quality fast-food restaurants.

Pontiac

Some 90 miles southeast of Lake Michigan, the former coal-mining town of Pontiac (pop. 11,428) surrounds the stately circa 1875 Livingston County Courthouse. The courthouse's green lawns hold the usual battery of monuments, including one to the namesake Ottawa chief whose visage also graces the General Motors marquee. According to the WPA *Guide to Illinois*, another of these monuments, the Soldier and Sailors Monument, received the shortest presidential dedication in history when, in 1902, it was "dedicated with a few hasty words by President Theodore Roosevelt, before an audience of less than a dozen people, who congregated briefly under a terrific downpour."

Pontiac is also home to a long-lived Route 66 landmark, the **Old Log Cabin Inn** (815/842-2908) on Pontiac Road on the north edge of town. When the road was rerouted behind the original location, the inn was jacked up and flipped around; the old road, which dates from 1918, is still there, behind the cafe along the railroad tracks.

From the Log Cabin, you can follow old Route 66 northeast through small towns, though the route is obscure and not all that rich in history or aesthetic delights. The final alignment of the old road is now Hwy-53, which runs along the southeast side of I-55 through Odell, Dwight, and Wilmington, where the famous "Rocketman" statue stands outside the **Launching Pad Drive-In**, 810 E. Baltimore Street (815/476-6535).

Route 66 across Chicagoland

Following the first or last leg of Route 66 across Chicago and its hinterlands is really not worth the effort for anyone except the most die-hard end-to-ender—even Jack Rittenhouse, in his original 1946 *Guide Book to Highway 66,* didn't bother to describe the route until it reached Plainfield, 35 miles southwest of the Loop. For a symbolic end point, you can use the grand old Art Institute of Chicago in Grant Park along the lakeshore, since the last US-66 shield used to hang from a streetlight just south of the gallery. If Chicago is your "end of the road," you'll probably prefer to avoid the final few miles of surface streets and make your way to town as quickly as possible via I-55; starting from Chicago, as the song says you should, you may be more willing to take the time to see what's left of the Mother Road.

From Lake Michigan, the old road ran west via Adams Street (take Jackson Boulevard eastbound; both are one-way) before angling southwest along Ogden Avenue—a long, diagonal exception to the city's main grid of streets. Near **Cicero**, which prides itself on having been a haven to Al Capone and other mobsters during the Prohibition era, one oddity worth checking out is "**The Spindle**," a tower of ruined cars impaled on a 50-foot steel spike standing in the parking lot of a shopping mall at the corner of Cermak Road and Harlem Avenue, two miles north of old Route 66.

Farther southeast, you have to follow the I-55 freeway, which was built right on top of old Route 66 through suburban **Plainfield**, where Route 66 crossed the old Lincoln Highway (US-30). The old road then follows the Des Plaines River and the Chicago Ship and Sanitary Canal as far as **Joliet**, where Route 66 resurfaces again, here as Chicago Street (Hwy-53). The route then continues as a four-lane frontage road along the southeast side of I-55 through Pontiac, a good place to join it.

Chicago, which marks the junction of Route 66 and our cross-country route along US-20, is covered in a Survival Guide on pages 573-575.

ROAD TRIP
RESOURCES

RECOMMENDED READING

ROADSIDE AMERICA

American Diner: Then and Now, by Richard J.S. Gutman (HarperPerennial, 1993). Lushly illustrated, encyclopedic history of that great American roadside institution, from its humble beginnings in the lunch wagons of the late 1880s to the streamlined stainless-steel models so beloved of art directors everywhere.

American Quest, by Jack Barth (Fireside Books, 1990). The subtitle, "He went looking for America and found it all over the country" sums up what this book is about. An anarchic tour of roadside culture, in which the author takes a job in the "Largest McDonald's in the Free World," visits Babe Ruth's grave, and traces the route of *Easy Rider* in a rented Cadillac.

American Space, by J. B. Jackson (Norton, 1972). Written by the late godfather of contemporary interpreters of the American landscape, this engaging volume studies the development of the rural and urban scene around the country in the crucial decade immediately after the Civil War. In the title essay of another thought-provoking book, *The Necessity for Ruins* (University of Massachusetts Press, 1980), Jackson explores such topics as Americans' love of "living history" environments and the impact of the garage on the evolution of house design.

Americans on the Road: From Autocamp to Motel, 1910-1945, by Warren James Belasco (M.I.T. Press, 1979). The best book there is about the early evolution of automobile-based tourism. Engagingly written, with clever analysis and an eye for the telling detail.

Asphalt Nation: How the Automobile Took Over America and How We Can Take It Back, by Jane Holtz Kay (Crown Publishers, 1997). An enthusiastic

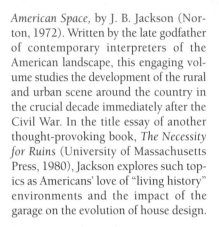

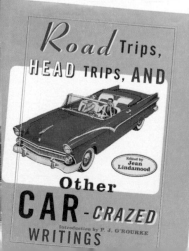

and informative account of how cars, and the commuter culture they've spawned, has sapped the strength of the nation's communities. Not as histrionic as the title might make you think (though it does treat General Motors as the Evil Empire), this is an engaging and insightful book that aims to help us cut down on the eight billion annual hours Americans spend stuck in traffic.

Autoamerica: A Trip Down U.S. Highways from World War II to the Future, by Ant Farm (E.P. Dutton, 1976). An anarchic, cheerful look at America's love/hate relationship with the automobile, by the boys who brought you the Cadillac Ranch.

Divided Highways: Building the Interstate Highways, Transforming American Life, by Tom Lewis (Viking, 1997). Companion to a PBS television series, *Divided Highways* tells the story of the nation's turnpikes and freeways through the eyes of Thomas MacDonald, chief of the U.S. Government's Bureau of Public Roads, and architect of the highway network.

Documenting America 1935-1943, edited by Carl Fleishauer and Beverly W. Brannan (University of California Press, 1988). The most complete collection of New Deal photography yet published, this book traces the work of Dorothea Lange, Walker Evans, Marion Post Wolcott and the many others who documented the facts of life in Depression-era America. Large format, with many revealing essays and over 300 images.

Flattened Fauna: A Field Guide to Common Animals of Roads, Street and Highways, by Roger M. Knutson (Ten Speed Press, 1987). Lighthearted look at that under-studied ecosystem, the highway. Besides being a helpful guide to identifying the sundry dead objects along the roadside, the book also details the nat-ural life and habitats of the unfortunate road-killed creatures.

Gardens of Revelation: Environments by Visionary Artists, by John Beardsley (Abbeville Press, 1995). Lushly illustrated, intelligently written guidebook celebrating the "idiosyncratic genius, tenacious faith and unalienated labor" that has gone into the creation of hundreds of different sculptural environments across the country, from L.A.'s Watts Towers to Georgia's Paradise Garden.

The Highway as Habitat, by Ulrich Keller (UCSB Art Museum, 1986). Vivid photography of the American roadside, c. 1943-55, produced under the auspices of the Standard Oil Company by Roy Stryker, who led the New Deal documentary programs of the Farm Security Administration.

100 Years on the Road : The Travelling Salesman in American Culture, by Timothy B. Spears (Yale University Press, 1995). An oddly compelling little book, captivating and entertaining despite the academic tone.

The Lincoln Highway: Main Street Across America, by Drake Hokansen (University of Iowa Press, 1987). The bible of Lincoln Highway history, tracing America's first transcontinental highway from its beginnings in 1915 to its gradual fade-out in the post-interstate world.

Main Street to Miracle Mile: American Roadside Architecture, by Chester H. Liebs (Ney York Graphic Society, 1985). This lushly illustrated historical survey of roadside design is the best single introduction to the familar yet fascinating environment that lines the nation's highways.

Open Road: A Celebration of the American Highway, by Phil Patton (Simon and Schuster, 1986). An energetic account of how the American roadside landscape came to look the way it does today, masterfully blending a discussion of the economic and political forces behind the nation's highway network with a contagious enthusiasm for the inherent democracy the automobile embodies.

Orange Roofs, Golden Arches: The Architecture of American Chain Restaurants, by Philip Langdon (Knopf, 1986). Fascinating study of the story behind the look of franchised restaurants, from Fred Harvey's turn-of-the-century railroad whistlestops, through the rise and demise of drive-ins in the postwar era, to today's mass-market fast-food emporia.

Pump and Circumstance: Glory Days of the Gas Station, by John Margolies (Little, Brown, 1993). Profusely illustrated coffee-table book that uses photographs, advertising, enamel signs, road maps, and brief but revealing text to track the development of the essential feature of the American highway landscape, the gas station. The same author/photographer has produced many other great books, including *The End of the Road: Vanishing Highway Architecture in America* (Penguin Books, 1981).

Roadside America, by Jack Barth et al. (Fireside Books, 1993). The best guidebook to the wackiest and weirdest attractions along the Great American Roadside. Organized by theme rather than by location, but still an entertaining and agreeable travel companion.

Roadside America: The Automobile in Design and Culture, edited by Jan Jennings (Iowa State University Press, 1990). Produced by the Society for Commercial Archeology, these fully illustrated essays document the changes, for better and for worse, that the automobile has brought to the American landscape.

Roadside Empires: How the Chains Franchised America, by Stan Luxemburg (Viking Books, 1985). Business-oriented history of franchised fast-food industry, treating the major chains as financial successes without diminishing their usually negative impact on local businesses —and palates. No illustrations, unfortunately.

Where the Road and the Sky Collide: America Through the Eyes of its Drivers, by K.T. Berger (Henry Holt, 1993). A folk history of America's automotive obsession, this is the second of a pair of informal studies of cars and their drivers, written by two brothers, Kevin and Todd Berger, a psychologist and a journalist. Their earlier book is *Zen Driving: Be A Buddha Behind the Wheel of Your Automobile.*

TRAVEL GUIDEBOOKS

American Guide Series: Federal Writers Project Guides to the States. Invaluable documents of the state of the nation during the 1930s and 1940s, these state-by-state, road-by-road, somewhat socialist-minded guidebooks were compiled during the Depression and later by teams of writers put to work under the auspices of the New Deal Works Project Administration (W.P.A.). Many great writers, including Saul Bellow, Richard Wright, Studs Terkel, Ralph Ellison, Kenneth Patchen, Nelson Algren and Jim Thompson, contributed to the series, selected volumes of which have been brought back into print by small presses.

The Amusement Park Guide, by Tim O'Brien (Globe Pequot, 1997). The subtitle says it all: Coast to Coast Thrills, containing full descriptions and practical information for 275 small, medium, and large amusement parks all over the U.S. and Canada.

Ballpark Vacations, by Bruce Adams and Margaret Engel (Fodor's, 1997). Enjoyable and informative travel guide detailing the best minor and major league baseball parks in the country, with details on the teams and well-chosen suggestions of places to eat and sleep in 75 different cities and towns; professional teams are included. Baseball fanatics should also pick up a copy of the annual *Baseball America Directory* (Baseball America, 1999), which gives details of every professional and semi-pro team in the U.S. and Canada.

Eat Your Way Across the USA, by Jane and Michael Stern (Broadway Books, 1997). The latest version of the cross-country compendium of All-American diners, drive-ins, lobster shacks and BBQ stands, put together by road food experts and *Gourmet* magazine correspondents.

Little Museums, by Lynne Arany and Archie Hobson (Henry Holt, 1998). Perfect for anyone who thinks they've been there done that, this little book is packed full of fascinating little places you've never heard of but will never forget. Two other books mining this same rich vein are *America's Strangest Museums,* by Sandra Gurvis (Citadel Press, 1996) and *Offbeat Museums: The Collections and Curators of America's Most Unusual Museums,* by Saul Rubin (Santa Monica Press, 1997).

Next Exit, (Next Exit, 1998). "The Most Complete Interstate Highway Guide Ever Printed," this newsprint compendium contains telegraphic listings of all there is within a half-mle of every one of the over 10,000-plus exits along America's Interstate Highway System—so you know for sure whether there that "gas-food-lodging" sign means Pizza Hut or McDonalds, Exxon or BP, Motel 6 or Best Western.

Watch It Made In the USA, by Bruce Brumberg and Karen Axelrod (John Muir Publications, 1998). A travel guide that takes you to watch the manufacture of such All-American products as Crayola crayons, Louisville Slugger baseball bats, Hershey's chocolates and Harley-Davidson motorcycles.

TRAVELOGUES

Blue Highways: A Journey Into America, by William Least Heat Moon (Little, Brown and Company, 1982). One of the best-selling travel books ever written, this intensely personal yet openhearted tale traces the path of a part-Indian, part-time English teacher who travels the back roads "in search of places where change did not mean ruin and where time and men and deeds connected."

Drive, They Said: Poems About Americans and Their Cars, edited by Kurt Brown (Milkweed Editions, 1994). If you like to drive, and like to read or write poetry, you'll love this thick volume of contemporary verse, which samples the work of over 100 poets. See Stephen Dunn's offering in these pages.

Driving to Detroit: An Automotive Odyssey, by Lesley Hazleton (The Free Press, 1998). A British auto industry journalist takes a five-month, 13,000-mile journey all over America, visiting hollowed ground of car culture (Bonneville Salt Flats, Cadillac Ranch, etc.) while contemplating her own need for speed.

Elvis Presley Boulevard: From Sea to Shining Sea, Almost, by Mark Winegardner (Atlantic Monthly Press, 1987). An energetic mix of road trip journal and coming-of-age autobiography, this short book recounts a summer-long tour around the southern and central United States. The Elvis obsession hinted at by the title is only a small part of the book, which looks at many of the odder corners of America.

Fear and Loathing in Las Vegas, by Hunter S. Thompson (Random House, 1972). Subtitled "A Savage Journey to the Heart of the American Dream," this riotus blast of a book starts with the words "We were somewhere around Barstow on the edge of the desert when the drugs began to take hold," and goes on to tell the story of a long lost weekend in Sin City, and much much more.

Great Plains, by Ian Frazier (Farrar, Straus and Giroux, 1989). In-depth, top-to-bottom study of the wide-open land where the buffalo roamed, tracing historical themes like water, cowboys, and Indians, while capturing the contemporary scene.

Highway 50: Ain't That America, by Jim Lilliefors (Fulcrum Publishing, 1994). A cranky journalist heads west from Ocean City, Maryland, following the longest and loneliest road across the continent to California. Working his way along, and spending more time in dingy bars than in the great outdoors, the writer has packed the book with vivid portraits of the downside of rural America.

Let Us Now Praise Famous Men, by James Agee, photographs by Walker Evans (Houghton Mifflin, 1941). The talented collaborators spent the summer of 1936 living with three families of poor white cotton sharecroppers in the Appalachian foothills of northwest Alabama, and together created a vivid and compassionate portrait of rural America during the depths of the Great Depression.

The Lost Continent: Travels in Small Town America, by Bill Bryson (Secker and Warburg, 1989). Iowa-born British transplant returns to America in search of material for his sarcastic commentary on con-temporary life. Hilariously funny in parts, mean-spirited in others, and packed with trivial truths about life in the land of liberty.

Mad Monks on the Road, by Michael Lane and Jim Crotty (Simon & Schuster, 1993). Two left-of-center, postmodern pilgrims set off from Paradise and spend the next eight years on the road, graduating from a 1972 Econoline van to a queen-sized Fleetwood Bounder mobile home and generally getting up to no good while putting the camp back into camping and producing their notorious mobile magazine, *Monk.*

Making Hay, by Verlyn Klinkenborg (Vintage Departures, 1986). The enigmatic title is truer than you might think, for this is a book about alfalfa, about farming, and about the patterns of life in two very different places: the plains of Iowa, where the writer grew up on farms now worked by high-tech machines; and the mountain valleys of Montana, where hay is still made the old-fashioned way.

On the Road, by Jack Kerouac (Viking, 1957). What the Beatles were to music, the Beats were to literature, and this wild ramble of a road story was Kerouac's first Number One hit, inspiring a generation or two to hightail it along America's highways in the tracks of Sal Paradise and Dean Moriarty.

Out West: American Journey Along the Lewis and Clark Trail, by Dayton Duncan (Viking Penguin, 1987). The best travel book since *Blue Highways,* this marvelous tale retraces the route blazed by the Corps of Discovery on their epic adventure. With a combination of concise history lessons, captivating storytelling, and wry humor, Duncan vividly points out what has and hasn't changed in the 200-odd years since the captains first trekked across the country and back.

Road Scholar: Coast to Coast Late in the Century, by Andrei Codrescu (Hyperion, 1993). Taken from a PBS TV series, this series of vignettes tracks the progress of the Romanian-born poet and commentator as he travels from New Orleans to San Francisco via New York, Las Vegas, and a hundred other places along the way.

Road Trips, Head Trips and Other Car-Crazed Writings, edited by Jean Lindamood (Atlantic Monthly Press, 1996). An introduction and description of a road trip along the Mexican border by P. J. O'Rourke sets the tone for this compilation of car and driver tales, which also features pieces by Kerouac, Steinbeck and Hunter S. Thompson.

Spirit of Place: The Making of an American Literary Landscape, by Frederick Turner (Sierra Club Books, 1989). A multilayered tapestry of biography, travel writing, and literary criticism, this wonderful book explores how different locales have inspired and defined many of America's greatest writers.

Travels with Charley: In Search of America, by John Steinbeck (Viking, 1962). Rambling around "this monster of a land" in his camper Rocinante, accompanied only by his eponymous French poodle, Steinbeck returns to his California haunts from self-imposed exile in New York to find that, even if you can't go home again, there are many intriguing things along the way.

Zen and the Art of Motorcycle Maintenance: An Inquiry into Values, by Robert M. Pirsig (William Morrow and Company, 1974). The subtitle points out this big book's more ponderous aspects, but at its best this is a captivating, full-throttle ride down America's back roads in search of meaning in the modern age.

PERIODICALS

Out West: The Newspaper That Roams. For over 10 years, writer Chuck Woodbury has been traveling the back roads of the western U.S., documenting in a quarterly newsprint tabloid the many wild and wonderful things he finds there. Chuck, wife Rodica, daughter Emily, and a team of contributors cover the people they meet and the places they eat, photograph funny signs and roadside dinosaurs, and generally bring the open road alive, straight to your mailbox. They also run a very good mail-order bookstore.

Out West
9792 Edmonds Way Suite 265
Edmonds, WA 98020
800/274-9378

Roadside Magazine. Doing for the northeastern U.S. what *Out West* does out west, *Roadside* covers the back roads and small-town Main Streets, with a particular focus on diners, those uniquely American institutions that are a traveler's best friend. Along with articles aimed at "getting America out of the franchises, the malls, the Interstates," and back into the real things that foster community and make this country interesting, each issue includes a "Diner Finder," which lists, locates, and describes the make and models of all the surviving diners in a certain area. For more information, contact:

Coffee Cup Productions
P.O. Box 652
West Side Station
Worcester, MA 01602
508/791-1838

Route 66 Magazine. An impressive full-color quarterly, entirely dedicated to the Mother Road and to the people and places, past and present, that have made it such an icon of restless America. Strong graphics, lively writing, and not *too* many ads make it a great resource for armchair or front-seat readers. For subscription information, contact:

Route 66 Magazine
326 W. Route 66
Williams, AZ 86046
520/635-4322

Yesterday's Highways: Exploring the U.S. Off the Interstates. This homespun newsletter has the expressed aim of inspiring "persons of all ages, whether by armchair or actual experience, to travel and explore the back roads and history of America." *Yesterday's Highways* comes out every two months and features a very handy, mile-by-mile guide to various old roads, describing their histories and characters as well as listing practical information for travelers. For subscription information, contact:

Yesterday's Highways
49 Church Street
Weaverville, NC 28787
704/645-9045

Devil's Elbow: The Magazine for People Who Don't Care Where They're Going. For a generally laconic, frequently ironic, and always entertaining guide to the back-roads of the Midwest and Deep South, pick up a copy of this intensely illustrated, engagingly written little 'zine, which is available at Tower Bookstores and by subscription for around $2 an issue.

Devil's Elbow
2623 E. 2nd Street
Box 12
Bloomington, IN 47401

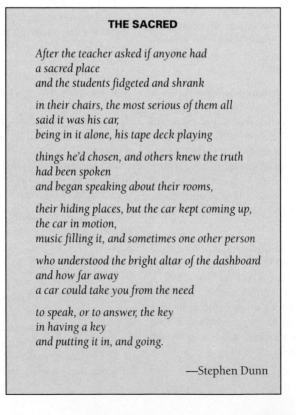

THE SACRED

*After the teacher asked if anyone had
a sacred place
and the students fidgeted and shrank*

*in their chairs, the most serious of them all
said it was his car,
being in it alone, his tape deck playing*

*things he'd chosen, and others knew the truth
had been spoken
and began speaking about their rooms,*

*their hiding places, but the car kept coming up,
the car in motion,
music filling it, and sometimes one other person*

*who understood the bright altar of the dashboard
and how far away
a car could take you from the need*

*to speak, or to answer, the key
in having a key
and putting it in, and going.*

—Stephen Dunn

ORGANIZATIONS

American Automobile Association is an indispensable resource, and no traveler in his or her right mind should hit the road without a membership card. Besides the free roadside assistance, 24 hours a day across the country, they also offer free maps, useful guidebooks, and tons of related information. Look in the Yellow Pages for a local office, or contact the national headquarters.

Lincoln Highway Association is a group of old-roads aficionados who work to preserve remnants of the nation's first coast-to-coast highway and to promote its memory. They also get together for annual meetings to retrace the route.

National Route 66 Federation is the only nationwide, nonprofit organization committed to revitalizing Route 66, and to promoting awareness of its historic role as the Main Street of America. Members receive a high-quality quarterly magazine, and all dues go directly toward lobbying governments to preserve what's left of Route 66.

American Automobile Association
1000 AAA Drive
Heathrow, FL 32746
800/922-8228

Lincoln Highway Association
111 S. Elm Street
PO Box 308
Franklin Grove, IL 61031
815/456-3030

National Route 66 Federation
PO Box 423
Tujunga, CA 91043-0423
818/352-7232

Anyone interested in the cultural landscape lining America's highways and byways will want to join the **Society for Commercial Archaeology**, an all-volunteer organization working to preserve and interpret roadside culture. Studies cover everything from diners to giant roadside dinosaurs, and the enterprise is geared toward appreciation and enjoyment of quirks and crannies of the highway environment. Dues are $25 a year, and members receive a full-color magazine and a quarterly newsletter, which details preservation efforts as well as get-togethers for annual tours of different regions.

Society for Commercial Archaeology
PO Box 2423
Atlanta, GA 30301-2423
202/882-5424

ROAD TRIP TIME LINE

c. 3800-3600 B.C. . . . . The wheel is invented.

30,000 B.C.-A.D. 1800 . . Native American trails criss-cross North America.

600 B.C. . . . . Babylonians use tar to pave streets.

A.D. 500 . . . . Mississippian culture builds great mound city at Cahokia, opposite St. Louis.

A.D. 1150 . . . . Pueblo villages of Acoma and Moenkopi established.

1539-42 . . . . Hernándo de Soto explores southeastern United States. On June 18, 1541, his party crosses the Mississippi River, and he dies a year later near present-day Vicksburg.

1540-42 . . . . Arriving overland from Mexico, Coronado explores southwestern deserts in search of the fabled Seven Cities of Cíbola.

1542 . . . . Juan Cabrillo explores the coast of California.

1565 . . . . Spanish establish St. Augustine, Florida.

1579 . . . . Sailing from the Hawaiian Islands, Sir Francis Drake explores the coasts of Oregon, Washington, and northern California.

1585 . . . . Sir Walter Raleigh establishes ill-fated colony at Roanoke, North Carolina.

1607 . . . . First successful British colony established at Jamestown, Virginia.

1609 . . . . Spanish colony at Santa Fe, New Mexico established.

Nov.-Dec. 1620 . . . . Pilgrims arrive in Massachusetts on the *Mayflower.*

1682 . . . . Starting from near Lake Michigan, La Salle descends the Illinois and Mississippi Rivers to the Gulf of Mexico.

1742-43 . . . . Coming from French Canada, the de la Verendrye brothers explore North and South Dakota, leaving behind a lead plate to claim the land for France.

1770 . . . . Spain establishes first Franciscan missions in California.

1781 . . . . Cornwallis surrenders at Yorktown at end of the Revolutionary War.

1791 . . . . Bill of Rights ratified as first 10 amendments to the Constitution.

1803 . . . . Louisiana Purchase.

1804-06 . . . . Lewis and Clark lead Corps of Discovery across continent, from St. Louis to mouth of the Columbia River and back.

1805-06 . . . . Zebulon Pike explores southern Great Plains and Rockies.

1808 . . . . Importation of slaves into the U.S. prohibited by Congress.

1821 . . . . Santa Fe Trail opened by businessman William Becknell.

1825 . . . . Erie Canal opens, between Albany and Buffalo, New York.

1826 . . . . Jedediah Strong Smith becomes first white man to cross from the Rockies to southern California overland. He repeats the feat the following year.

1838 . . . . Cherokee Indians forced west along "Trail of Tears."

1843 . . . . Oregon Trail opened.

1848 . . . . California gold rush, and migration of Mormons from Nauvoo, Illinois, to Utah.

1853 . . . . Gadsden Purchase completes present-day outline of lower 48 United States.

1858-61 . . . . Butterfield Overland Mail links St. Louis and Los Angeles via El Paso.

1859 . . . . Nation's first successful oil well drilled in Pennsylvania.

1860-61 . . . . Pony Express links Missouri and California.

April 12, 1861 . . . . Confederate forces fire on Fort Sumter, South Carolina.

April 9, 1865 . . . . Lee surrenders at Appomattox.

May 10, 1869 . . . . Transcontinental railroad completed at Promontory, Utah.

1870 . . . . Boardwalk resorts open at Atlantic City, New Jersey.

June 25, 1876 . . . . Battle of Little Big Horn—"Custer's Last Stand."

1877 . . . . Amzi Lorenzo Barber establishes Trinidad Asphalt Company, and gives Washington, D.C., the nation's first asphalt-paved streets.

1884 . . . . Santa Fe Railroad links Los Angeles, Santa Fe, and Kansas City.

1886 . . . . Karl Benz creates the first car by adding a motor to a tricycle. Coca-Cola invented by Atlanta pharmacist John Pemberton. Geronimo surrenders to General Miles.

1893 . . . . Southern Pacific Railroad links Los Angeles and New Orleans; Great Northern links Seattle and St. Paul. "Rural Free Delivery" of mail introduced. Frank and Charles Duryea build first American motor car in Springfield, Massachusetts, on September 21, 1893.

1895 . . . . First gasoline-powered cars sold in U.S., made by Duryea Motor Wagon Company of Springfield, Massachusetts. Duryeas also win first automobile race in U.S., covering a 50-mile course around Chicago at an average speed of five mph.

1896 . . . . Buffalo, New York, becomes first major city to pave all its streets.

1898 . . . . "Stanley Steamers" introduced. Pepsi-Cola invented.

1899 . . . . A "Stanley Steamer" climbs Mount Washington, New Hampshire.

1900 . . . . Electric cars outnumber gasoline-powered cars 2 to 1. Steering wheel replaces the tiller for first time, on a Packard "Ohio."

1901 . . . . Oil discovered at Spindletop field in eastern Texas. Speedometers introduced by Oldsmobile.

1903 . . . . Henry Ford founds Ford Motor Company. Wright Brothers make first powered flight. To win a $50 bet, Dr. Horatio Jackson, along with his chauffeur and dog, becomes first person to drive across the country, taking 65 days.

1904 . . . . Only 40,000 out of a total of over two million miles of U.S. roads are fully paved. Bicyclist organizations lead charge for better public roads. Henry Ford sets world land speed record of 91 mph, at Daytona Beach.

1905 . . . . Total number of cars on roads: 75,000.

1907 . . . . Nation's first "gas station" opens in St. Louis.

1908 . . . . General Motors incorporates. Ford Motor Company introduces the Model T.

1909 . . . . Nation's first mile of rural highway is paved. Alice Ramsey becomes first woman to drive across the country—the trip took 41 days.

1910 . . . . Union Oil Company of California gives out the first free gas station road maps, starting a tradition that continued until the 1970s.

1911 . . . . First Indianapolis 500-mile race held.

1912 . . . . Nation's first lane markings are painted onto the streets of Redlands, California.

1915 . . . . Total number of cars on roads: 2.3 million. The Lincoln Highway, the country's first coast-to-coast route, is marked from New York to San Francisco.

1916 . . . . General Pershing leads U.S. Army into Mexico in pursuit of Pancho Villa. Federal Aid Road Act establishes first federal funding for road-building.

1918 . . . . First three-color traffic signal is installed, in Detroit. Wisconsin introduces the concept of numbering roads and highways.

1919 . . . . First A&W Root Beer stand opens, in Lodi, California. Dwight Eisenhower leads a military convoy across the country, which takes two months and points out the need for well-paved transcontinental roads.

1920 . . . . Beginning of Prohibition. Total number of cars on roads: 6.5 million.

1921 . . . . Original White Castle hamburger stand built in Wichita, Kansas, foreshadowing the arrival of fast food.

1922 . . . . Balloon tires and gas gauges introduced. Ford Motor Company produces nearly half of nation's four million new cars and trucks.

1925 . . . . System of numbering federal highways is introduced, to replace route names. The "shield" symbol is designed by Michigan engineer Frank Rogers. First "Burma-Shave" signs installed along Minnesota highways. World's first motel opens, in San Luis Obispo, California.

1926 . . . . Route 66 established, winding between Chicago and Los Angeles.

1927 . . . . Ford ceases production of Model T, having sold 27 million of them. Lincoln Highway, the first coast-to-coast highway, is paved all the way from New York to California.

1933 . . . . End of Prohibition.

1934 . . . . First Steak and Shake opens, in Normal, Illinois.

1935 . . . . Howard Johnson pioneers franchising restaurants. First parking meters installed

1939 . . . . Norman Bel Geddes popularizes freeways with the Futurama display at the New York World's Fair.

1940 . . . . Total number of cars on roads: 20 million. Pennsylvania Turnpike opens. Arroyo Seco Parkway, now the Pasadena Freeway, opens. First Dairy Queen opens.

1941 . . . . Mount Rushmore dedicated.

1944 . . . . National System of Interstate and Defense Highways authorized by Congress. Basic wartime gasoline ration is two gallons per week. National speed limit is 35 mph.

1946 . . . . Bobby Troup composes "Get Your Kicks on Route 66," which becomes a hit record for Nat King Cole.

1947 . . . . Henry Ford dies.

1949 . . . . VW Beetle introduced in the United States. Tastee-Freez founded in Chicago. Richard and Maurice McDonald perfect cheap fast food: 15-cent hamburgers, 10-cent French fries.

1952 . . . . First Holiday Inn opens, in Memphis, Tennessee. The New Jersey Turnpike opens.

1953 . . . . McDonald's opens first restaurant featuring the "Golden Arches" in Phoenix, Arizona, followed soon after by one in Downey, California, that still stands.

1954 . . . . Dwight Eisenhower adds phrase "under God" to the Pledge of Allegiance.

1955-56 . . . . Boycott ends racial segregation on public buses in Montgomery, Alabama.

1956 . . . . Interstate Highway system inaugurated, planning 42,500 miles of freeways with federal funds paying 90% of the estimated $27 billion. (The cost so far has been over $125 billion.)

1957 . . . . Ford launches the Edsel—the first car designed by market research polls. Jack Kerouac's *On the Road* published.

1958 . . . . First Pizza Hut opens, in Wichita, Kansas.

1959 . . . . Ford cancels the Edsel—after losing $350 million.

1960 . . . . First Hardee's established, in Greenville, North Carolina.

1961 . . . . Ray Kroc buys McDonald's for $2.7 million.

1962 . . . . First Chart House opens, in Aspen, Colorado.

1963 . . . . Last set of Burma-Shave signs taken down. California becomes first state to require emission controls on cars.

1964 . . . . Pontiac's GTO, with its triple-carbed, 350 horsepower V-8 engine, ushers in the era of the "muscle car." First Arby's opens, in Youngstown, Ohio.

1965 . . . . First T.G.I. Friday's opens, in midtown Manhattan.

1969 . . . . Community activism forces cancellation of proposed freeway through the French Quarter in New Orleans, and the Inner Beltway in Boston. First Wendy's opens, in Columbus, Ohio.

1974 . . . . "Arab oil crisis" causes federal government to set a national speed limit of 55 mph. Cadillac Ranch is constructed outside Amarillo.

1975 . . . . Bruce Springsteen releases *Born to Run.*

1983 . . . . Stephen King publishes the novel *Christine,* about a 1958 Plymouth Fury that's possessed by demonic spirits.

1984 .... Chrysler introduces the original minivan. Last stretch of old Route 66 still in use, at Williams, Arizona, is bypassed by the I-40 freeway.

1992 .... Lyn St. James becomes first woman to complete the Indy 500, finishing 11th.

1995 .... U.S. government abolishes national speed limit.

1996 .... American automobile industry celebrates its 100th anniversary. Interstate Highway System celebrates its 40th.

1997 .... "On the Road" journalist Charles Kuralt dies on the 4th of July, aged 62. British team lead by Richard Noble sets new land speed record of 763 mph in the Black Rock Desert of northern Nevada.

1998 .... Congress and President Bill Clinton approve a new transportation bill, setting aside $203 billion for infrastructure improvements, including $167 billion for highways and $36 billion for mass transit.

At present, there are over 175 million licensed drivers in the U.S., driving 200 million registered vehicles an estimated 2.5 trillion (2,500,000,000,000!) annual miles along four million miles of paved roads and highways.

LIST OF MAPS

INDEX

ACCOMMODATIONS	
Best Western	800/528-1234
Budgetel Inns	800/428-3438
Comfort Inns	800/228-5150
Courtyard by Marriott	800/321-2211
Days Inn	800/325-2525
Econo Lodge	800/553-2666
Embassy Suites Hotels	800/362-2779
Fairfield Inns	800/228-2800
Friendship Inns	800/453-4511
HI Hostels	202/783-6161
Hampton Inns	800/426-7866
Hilton Hotels	800/445-8667
Holiday Inns	800/465-4329
Howard Johnson Lodges	800/654-2000
Hyatt Hotels	800/233-1234
ITT Sheraton Hotels	800/325-3535
La Quinta Inns	800/531-5900
Marriott Hotels	800/228-9290
Motel 6	800/466-8356
Quality Inns	800/228-5151
Ramada Inns	800/228-2828
Red Lion Inns	800/547-8010
Red Roof Inns	800/843-7663
Rodeway Inns	800/228-2000
Super 8 Motels	800/800-8000
TraveLodge Hotels	800/578-7878

AFRICAN-AMERICAN HISTORY AND HERITAGE

AMUSEMENT AND THEME PARKS

BASEBALL

Baseball Hall of Fame: 600
Cactus League baseball: 157
National Softball Hall of Fame: 832
Negro Baseball Leagues Museum: 704
Spring Training—Arizona: 157
Spring Training—Florida: 428-429

The Majors
Anaheim Angels: 99, 157
Arizona Diamondbacks: 157-158
Atlanta Braves: 373, 428
Baltimore Orioles: 428, 733
Boston Red Sox: 614
Chicago Cubs: 157, 574
Chicago White Sox: 157, 574
Cincinnati Reds: 718-719
Cleveland Indians: 586-587
Colorado Rockies: 157
Florida Marlins: 434-435
Houston Astros: 428
Kansas City Royals: 704
Los Angeles Dodgers: 99, 428-429
Milwaukee Brewers: 157
Minnesota Twins: 230
Montreal Expos: 428, 508
New York Mets: 331, 429
New York Yankees: 331
Oakland Athletics: 72, 157, 657
San Diego Padres: 110, 157
San Francisco Giants: 72, 157
Seattle Mariners: 157, 451
St. Louis Cardinals: 259, 428
Texas Rangers: 766

The Minors
Albuquerque Dukes: 819
Asheville Tourists: 363
Boise Hawks: 541
Bowie Baysox: 732

Buffalo Bisons: 594
Charleston Riverdogs: 409
Chillicothe Paints: 721
Colorado Rockies: 691
Columbus Redstixx: 785
Cucamonga Quakes: 798
Delmarva Shorebirds: 735
El Paso Diablos: 759
Erie Seawolves: 588
Everett Aquasox: 449
Frederick Keys: 345
Idaho Falls Braves: 547
Jackson Generals: 774
Las Vegas Stars: 152
Macon Braves: 787
Memphis Redbirds: 267
Norfolk Tides: 391
Oklahoma Redhawks: 833
Pawtucket Red Sox: 638
Pittsfield Mets: 319
Portland Rockies: 532
Quad City River Bandits: 245
Rochester Red Wings: 595
Rockford Cubbies: 572
Savannah Sand Gnats: 411
Scranton/Wilkes-Barre Red
    Barons: 623, 625
Shreveport Captains: 769
Sioux City Explorers: 565
South Bend Silver Hawks: 577
Spokane Indians: 459
St. Paul Saints: 230
Toledo Mud Hens: 581
Tucson Sidewinders: 164
Tulsa Drillers: 834
Utica Blue Sox: 599
Vermont Expos: 511
Vero Beach Dodgers: 429

CAMPING INFORMATION

National Park Service: 202/208-4747 or 800/365-2267
U.S. Forest Service: 202/205-1706 or 800/280-2267
Bureau of Land Management: 202/452-5125

COOL COLLEGE TOWNS

GREAT ROADS AND SCENIC DRIVES

LIGHTHOUSES

MUSICIANS AND SINGERS

NATIONAL PARKS, MONUMENTS, AND HISTORICAL SITES

NATIVE AMERICA

NEW DEAL PROJECTS

PRESIDENTS

RV AND CAMPER RENTAL INFORMATION

Cruise America-Motorhome Rentals: 800/327-7799
Recreational Vehicle Rental Association: 800/336-0355

ROADSIDE ART AND CURIOSITIES

(continues on next page)

ROADSIDE ART AND CURIOSITIES (continued)

Peace by Beniamo Bufano—Timber Cove, CA: 67
Popeye—Crystal City, TX: 211
Prairie Dog Town—Oakley, KS: 194
Radium Wood Carvers—Radium Hot Springs, Canada: 125
Roadside America—Shartlesvile, PA: 337
Robert Pershing Wadlow, the world's tallest human—Alton, IL: 257
"Rocketman" statue—Wilmington, IL: 848
Santa Claus Lane—Summerland, CA: 95
720-stone monuments—border of North and South Dakota: 183
Skowhegan Indian—Skohegan, ME: 520
Smallest Church in America—Savannah, GA: 414
Southernmost Point in the USA—Key West, FL: 442
South of the Border: 403
"The Spindle" tower of ruined cars—Cicero, IL: 848-849
stainless steel cross—Ballinger, TX: 208
The TePee—Sharon Springs, NY: 602
The Thing, AZ: 749
Tinkertown, NM: 820-821

Titan rocket—Warren, NH: 306
24-hour Church of Elvis—Portland, OR: 530
Vernon's Reproductions—Odin, IL: 711
Wally-the-26-Foot-Walleye—Garrison, ND: 174
Wendover Will—Wendover, NV: 144
Wigwam Motel—Pasadena, CA: 798
William Jennings Bryan—Salem, IL: 710
World's Largest Bat—Louisville, KY: 714
World's Largest Buffalo—Jamestown, ND: 480
World's Largest Catsup Bottle—Collinsville, IL: 709, 843-844
World's Largest Cow—New Salem, ND: 179, 480
World's Largest Jackalope—Columbia Falls, MT: 463
World's Largest Jackalope—Douglas, WY: 558
World's Largest Lobster—Islamorada, FL: 439
World's Largest Sitka Spruce—Klootchy Creek Park, OR: 528
World's Largest Turtle—Bottineau, ND: 172, 480

Road conditions: 206/368-4499
Tourism info: 360/586-2088 or 800/544-1800

WATERFALLS

The wonderful black-and-white images used as frontispieces to the various chapters in this book were created in the 1930s and 1940s by some of the country's finest photographers, working under the direction of Roy Stryker. From 1935 to 1943, Roy Stryker headed the federally funded, New Deal-era documentary projects known as the Resettlement Administration and the Farm Security Administration. After the war, he hired many of the same artists when he worked in the advertising department of Standard Oil of New Jersey. The photographs made under federal auspices are collected at the Library of Congress; the Standard Oil photographs are collected at the Ekstrom Library at the University of Louisville.

Half-title page: Early motorist at the Grand Canyon. Photographer unknown. (Library of Congress number 607262, 262-7119)

Coastal West Coast: Marion Post Wolcott (Library of Congress number LC-USF-34-56924-E)

US-93: Edwin Rosskam (Standard Oil of New Jersey)

US-83: John Vachon (Standard Oil of New Jersey)

Great River Road: (Cairo, IL 1940) John Vachon (Library of Congress number LC-USF-33-1883-M3)

The Appalachian Trail: Walker Evans (Library of Congress number LC-USF-342-8274A)

Coastal West Coast: Russell Lee (Library of Congress number 11392-M4)

US-2: Edwin Rosskam (Standard Oil of New Jersey)

US-20: Arthur Rothstein (Library of Congress number LC-USF-34-26922-D)

US-50: John Vachon (Library of Congress number 1631-M4)

US-80: Russell Lee (Library of Congress number LC-USF-34-35601)

Route 66: Russell Lee (Library of Congress number LC-USF-33-5184-M4)

Road Trip Resources: Marion Post Wolcott (Library of Congress number LC-USF-34-56932-E)

PHOTO AND ILLUSTRATION CREDITS

Albert-Knox Art Gallery 593; Andrew Hempstead 122, 123; Arizona Office of Tourism 163, 750; Mike Booher 392; Karl Bremer 282; Buffalo Bill Historical Center, Cody WY 551, 677; California Department of Parks and Recreation 67, 70, 74, 75, 82, 83, 87 (2), 656, 659, 660, 803; City of Tucumcari 822; Colorado Historical Society 688, 692; Commonwealth of Massachusetts 612; Crazy Horse Memorial Archives 562; Desert Book Company 143; Drive-Thru Tree Park 61; Elvis Presley Enterprises 265; Festival of Arts of Laguna Beach 104 (2); Eric J. Finley 746; Louise Foote 678; Mike Gassmann 843; Shelle Graham 813, 835, 836, 848; Philip Greenspun 409, 467, 643, 681; Hannibal Convention and Visitor's Center 252; The Heard Museum 814 (4); Henry Ford Museum 582; Houdini Museum 626; Tom Huhti 171, 489, 499; Illinois State Tourism 844; International Speedway Corporation 424; Courtesy of IMS Properties 577; Jamie Jensen 33, 44, 55, 60, 76, 89, 90, 95, 105, 125, 135, 140, 146, 153, 161, 166, 172, 175, 181, 182, 199, 209, 211, 223, 235, 236, 280, 356, 380, 391, 403, 457, 464, 465, 468, 479, 505, 517, 555, 562, 568, 571, 574, 580, 590, 611, 660, 667, 669, 695, 700, 710, 714, 715, 746, 748, 749, 749, 755, 764, 771, 781, 787, 791, 801, 802, 804, 809, 818, 819, 822-823, 827, 834, 840, 841, 841, 848, 849, 443, 443; Marjorie Jensen 396; Jimmie Rodgers Museum 776; Las Vegas News Bureau 149-151; Lazy SOB Records 815; Mike LeMasters 197, 697; Library of Congress 198; Maryland Office of Tourism 734; Mayberry Motor Inn 357; Menno-Hof Amish Visitors Center 578; Metropolis Convention and Visitor's Bureau 262; Mississippi State Division of Tourism 280; Missouri Division of Tourism 253; Montana Historical Society, Helena 129, 474, 477; Michael Murphy 215; National Archives 336, 472, 679, 751 (2); North Carolina Travel and Tourism 401; North Dakota Tourism Department/Dawn Charging 478, 480 (3); Oklahoma Tourism and Recreation Department/Fred Marvel 831; Oklahoma Tourism and Travel/Fred Marvel 830; Oregon Tourism Department/Rick Schafer 41; Oregon Tourism Department/Steve Terrill 50; *Out West Newspaper* 805; Doug Pappas 225, 271, 311, 381, 533, 558, 650; Pasadena Convention and Visitor's Bureau 797; Pennsylvania Dutch Convention and Visitor's Bureau 341; The Pony Express Historical Association 705; Bob Race 666, 745; Kevin Roe 95, 566, 567, 602; Ronald Reagan Boyhood Home 572; Santa Cruz Parks and Recreation Department 75; South Dakota Tourism186, 562; State Historical Society of North Dakota 181, 173; State of Washington Tourism Division 26, 38, 451, 458; Sterling and Francine Clark Art Institute 318; Sun Valley Co. 138; Bill Swislow 279; Texas Department of Commerce/Elizabeth Grivas 208; Texas Department of Commerce/Richard Reynolds 758; Texas Tourism Agency/R. Reynolds 214; Craig Thom 711; Ben Thompson 328, 685, 714; Turner Entertainment 227; Utah State Historical Society 676; Virginia Division of Tourism 388; Bob Waldmire 202, 788, 808, 829, 846, 846; Bill Weir 167; Mildred Wheeler 156, 806; Whyte Museum of the Canadian Rockies 120; Wyoming Division of Cultural Resources 191, 553; Wyoming State Museum 473

ACKNOWLEDGMENTS

A proverbial cast of thousands—in ranger stations, visitor centers, libraries, B&Bs, and cafes across the country—has helped shape this book, providing directions, suggestions, story ideas, and endless cups of coffee, and I can't thank you all enough for your kindness and hospitality. And to all the readers who've written in with helpful tips, snapshots, comments, corrections, and compliments—keep those pictures and postcards a'coming!

For making this book happen in the first place, I am grateful for the support and enthusiasm of the entire team at Avalon Travel Publishing, especially my editor Emily Kendrick, for fine-tuning my caffeinated prose and never flinching in the face of yet more last minute changes; publisher Bill Newlin, without whom I never would have spent half my recent life on the road; and my guidebook-writing, road-tripping colleagues, particularly Kap Stann, Julian Smith, Tom Huhti, Deke Castleman, and Andrew Hempstead. Sincere thanks are also due Kevin "Roots" Roe (and Debbie, and Big, Little and Hank!) for neverending encouragement, musical accompaniment, and insight into the inner life of the Great Plains; to Doug Pappas for sharing his love and knowledge of the old roads, his library of photos and postcards, and his complete set of WPA travel guides; and to Richard Weingroff at the Federal Highway Adminstration, a one-man archive of everything to do with old roads. I'd also like to acknowledge my debt to William Least Heat Moon, Ian Frazier, J.B. Jackson, Jack Kerouac, Chester Leibs, Brett Leveridge, John Margolies, Chuck Woodbury, Dayton Duncan, Phil Patton, John Steinbeck, Tom Teague, Frederick Turner, and all the other writers and travelers on whom I have relied for insight, information, and inspiration. And to all (well, most . . .) of the people who live, work, and play in the places I've passed through and written about—thanks for being there.

So much has happened in the years since this book first came out that I don't know where to begin. I do know I owe my friends and extended family—Mom, Dad and Bobbie, Sherry Sirotnik, Jim Gibson, Jeff, Johanna, Simon and Sophie Gunter, Danny, Maayan, Liore and Nadav Klein, Cheri, Chris and Mackenzie Larsen Hoeckley, Joe Gordon and Mark Bauer, Jane Leek, Jim, Lauren and Rudi Brandt, and last but definitely not least, my big brother Bob Jensen—more kindness and hospitality than I could ever hope to repay, so here's a heartfelt "thank you" for welcoming me when I've dropped in out of the blue, in need of care and feeding. I'd also like to offer my sincere gratitude to the wonderful doctors and nurses of the Special Care Nurseries at the UC Davis Medical Center for looking after my newest traveling companions, Tom and Alex Jensen, and once again to express my love and devotion to my wife Catherine Robson, for a dozen years (and counting) of seeing the bright side and making everything turn out right.

—Jamie Jensen

AVALON
TRAVEL
publishing

BECAUSE TRAVEL MATTERS.

AVALON TRAVEL PUBLISHING knows that travel is more than coming and going—travel is taking part in new experiences, new ideas, and a new outlook. Our goal is to bring you complete and up-to-date information to help you make informed travel decisions.

AVALON TRAVEL GUIDES feature a combination of practicality and spirit, offering a unique traveler-to-traveler perspective perfect for an afternoon hike, around-the-world journey, or anything in between.

WWW.TRAVELMATTERS.COM

Avalon Travel Publishing guides are available at your favorite book or travel store.

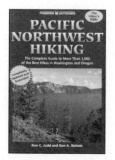

FOR TRAVELERS WITH
SPECIAL INTERESTS

GUIDES

The 100 Best Small Art Towns in America • Asia in New York City
The Big Book of Adventure Travel • Cities to Go
Cross-Country Ski Vacations • Gene Kilgore's Ranch Vacations
Great American Motorcycle Tours • Healing Centers and Retreats
Indian America • Into the Heart of Jerusalem
The People's Guide to Mexico • The Practical Nomad
Saddle Up! • Staying Healthy in Asia, Africa, and Latin America
Steppin' Out • Travel Unlimited • Understanding Europeans
Watch It Made in the U.S.A. • The Way of the Traveler
Work Worldwide • The World Awaits
The Top Retirement Havens • Yoga Vacations

SERIES

Adventures in Nature
The Dog Lover's Companion
Kidding Around
Live Well

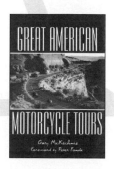

MOON HANDBOOKS

provide comprehensive coverage of a region's arts, history, land, people, and social issues in addition to detailed practical listings for accommodations, food, outdoor recreation, and entertainment. Moon Handbooks allow complete immersion in a region's culture—ideal for travelers who want to combine sightseeing with insight for an extraordinary travel experience.

USA

Alaska-Yukon • Arizona • Big Island of Hawaii • Boston
Coastal California • Colorado • Connecticut • Georgia
Grand Canyon • Hawaii • Honolulu-Waikiki • Idaho • Kauai
Los Angeles • Maine • Massachusetts • Maui • Michigan
Montana • Nevada • New Hampshire • New Mexico
New York City • New York State • North Carolina
Northern California • Ohio • Oregon • Pennsylvania
San Francisco • Santa Fe-Taos • Silicon Valley
South Carolina • Southern California • Tahoe • Tennessee
Texas • Utah • Virginia • Washington • Wisconsin
Wyoming • Yellowstone-Grand Teton

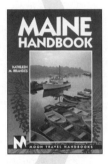

INTERNATIONAL

Alberta and the Northwest Territories • Archaeological Mexico
Atlantic Canada • Australia • Baja • Bangkok • Bali • Belize
British Columbia • Cabo • Canadian Rockies • Cancún
Caribbean Vacations • Colonial Mexico • Costa Rica • Cuba
Dominican Republic • Ecuador • Fiji • Havana • Honduras
Hong Kong • Indonesia • Jamaica • Mexico City • Mexico
Micronesia • The Moon • Nepal • New Zealand • Northern Mexico
Oaxaca • Pacific Mexico • Pakistan • Philippines • Puerto Vallarta
Singapore • South Korea • South Pacific • Southeast Asia • Tahiti
Thailand • Tonga-Samoa • Vancouver • Vietnam, Cambodia and Laos
Virgin Islands • Yucatán Peninsula

www.moon.com

www.travelmatters.com

User-friendly, informative, and fun: Because travel *matters*.

Visit our newly launched web site and explore the variety of titles and travel information available online, featuring an interactive *Road Trip USA* exhibit.

also check out:

www.ricksteves.com

The Rick Steves web site is bursting with information to boost your travel I.Q. and liven up your European adventure.

www.foghorn.com

Visit the Foghorn Outdoors web site for more information on the premier source of U.S. outdoor recreation guides.

www.moon.com

The Moon Handbooks web site offers interesting information and practical advice that ensure an extraordinary travel experience.

U.S.~METRIC CONVERSION

1 inch = 2.54 centimeters (cm)
1 foot = .3048 meters (m)
1 yard = 0.914 meters
1 mile = 1.6093 kilometers (km)
1 km = .6214 miles
1 fathom = 1.8288 m
1 chain = 20.1168 m
1 furlong = 201.168 m
1 acre = .4047 hectares
1 sq km = 100 hectares
1 sq mile = 2.59 square km
1 ounce = 28.35 grams
1 pound = .4536 kilograms
1 short ton = .90718 metric ton
1 short ton = 2000 pounds
1 long ton = 1.016 metric tons
1 long ton = 2240 pounds
1 metric ton = 1000 kilograms
1 quart = .94635 liters
1 US gallon = 3.7854 liters
1 Imperial gallon = 4.5459 liters
1 nautical mile = 1.852 km

To compute celsius temperatures, subtract 32 from Fahrenheit and divide by 1.8. To go the other way, multiply celsius by 1.8 and add 32.

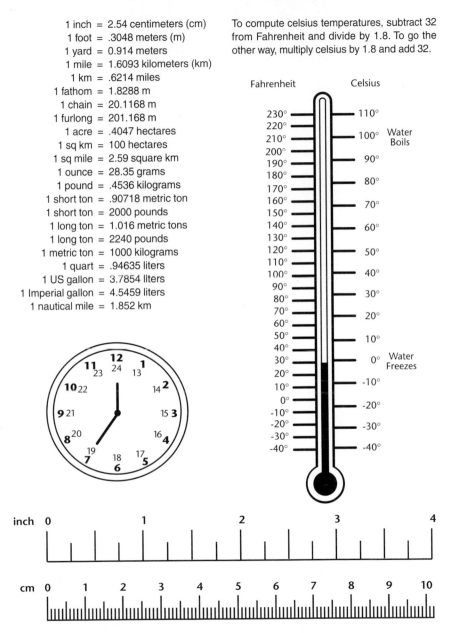